T0180503

More information about this series at http://www.springer.com/series/1244

Ngoc Thanh Nguyen · Bao Hung Hoang ·
Cong Phap Huynh · Dosam Hwang ·
Bogdan Trawiński · Gottfried Vossen (Eds.)

Computational Collective Intelligence

12th International Conference, ICCCI 2020
Da Nang, Vietnam, November 30 – December 3, 2020
Proceedings

 Springer

Editors
Ngoc Thanh Nguyen (iD)
Department of Applied Informatics
Wrocław University of Science
and Technology
Wroclaw, Poland

Faculty of Information Technology
Nguyen Tat Thanh University
Ho Chi Minh, Vietnam

Cong Phap Huynh
Vietnam - Korea University of Information
and Communication Technology
University of Da Nang
Da Nang, Vietnam

Bogdan Trawiński (iD)
Department of Applied Informatics
Wrocław University of Science
and Technology
Wroclaw, Poland

Bao Hung Hoang
Thua Thien Hue Center of Information
Technology
Hue, Vietnam

Dosam Hwang (iD)
Department of Computer Engineering
Yeungnam University
Gyeungsan, Korea (Republic of)

Gottfried Vossen
Department of Information Systems
University of Münster
Münster, Germany

ISSN 0302-9743   ISSN 1611-3349 (electronic)
Lecture Notes in Artificial Intelligence
ISBN 978-3-030-63006-5   ISBN 978-3-030-63007-2 (eBook)
https://doi.org/10.1007/978-3-030-63007-2

LNCS Sublibrary: SL7 – Artificial Intelligence

This Springer imprint is published by the registered company Springer Nature Switzerland AG
The registered company address is: Gewerbestrasse 11, 6330 Cham, Switzerland

Preface

This volume contains the proceedings of the 12th International Conference on Computational Collective Intelligence (ICCCI 2020), which was at first planned to be held in Danang, Vietnam. However, due to the COVID-19 pandemic the conference date was first postponed to November 30 – December 3, 2020, and then moved to virtual space.

The conference was co-organized jointly by The University of Danang, Vietnam, Korea University of Information and Communication Technology, Vietnam, Wrocław University of Science and Technology, Poland, International University - VNU-HCM, Vietnam, and the Wrocław University of Economics and Business, Poland, in cooperation with the IEEE Systems, Man, and Cybernetics Society (SMC) Technical Committee on Computational Collective Intelligence, European Research Center for Information Systems (ERCIS), and Nguyen Tat Thanh University, Vietnam.

Following the successes of the first ICCCI (2009) held in Wrocław, Poland, the second ICCCI (2010) in Kaohsiung, Taiwan, the third ICCCI (2011) in Gdynia, Poland, the 4th ICCCI (2012) in Ho Chi Minh City, Vietnam, the 5th ICCCI (2013) in Craiova, Romania, the 6th ICCCI (2014) in Seoul, South Korea, the 7th ICCCI (2015) in Madrid, Spain, the 8th ICCCI (2016) in Halkidiki, Greece, the 9th ICCCI (2017) in Nicosia, Cyprus, the 10th ICCCI (2018) in Bristol, UK, and the 11th ICCCI (2019) in Hendaye, France, this conference continued to provide an internationally respected forum for scientific research in the computer-based methods of collective intelligence and their applications.

Computational collective intelligence (CCI) is most often understood as a subfield of artificial intelligence (AI) dealing with soft computing methods that facilitate group decisions or processing knowledge among autonomous units acting in distributed environments. Methodological, theoretical, and practical aspects of CCI are considered as the form of intelligence that emerges from the collaboration and competition of many individuals (artificial and/or natural). The application of multiple computational intelligence technologies such as fuzzy systems, evolutionary computation, neural systems, consensus theory, etc., can support human and other collective intelligence, and create new forms of CCI in natural and/or artificial systems. Three subfields of the application of computational intelligence technologies to support various forms of collective intelligence are of special interest but are not exclusive: the Semantic Web (as an advanced tool for increasing collective intelligence), social network analysis (as the field targeted at the emergence of new forms of CCI), and multi-agent systems (as a computational and modeling paradigm especially tailored to capture the nature of CCI emergence in populations of autonomous individuals).

The ICCCI 2020 conference featured a number of keynote talks and oral presentations, closely aligned to the theme of the conference. The conference attracted a substantial number of researchers and practitioners from all over the world, who submitted their papers for the main track and four special sessions.

The main track, covering the methodology and applications of CCI, included: knowledge engineering and Semantic Web, social networks and recommender systems, collective decision making, applications of collective intelligence, data mining methods and applications, machine learning methods, computer vision techniques, biosensors and biometric techniques, natural language processing, as well as innovations in intelligent systems. The special sessions, covering some specific topics of particular interest, included: applications of collective intelligence, deep learning and applications for Industry 4.0, experience enhanced intelligence to IoT, intelligent management information systems, intelligent modeling and simulation approaches for games and real-world systems, low resource languages processing, computational collective intelligence and natural language processing, computational intelligence for multimedia understanding, and intelligent processing of multimedia in Web systems.

We received more than 310 submissions from 47 countries all over the world. Each paper was reviewed by two to four members of the International Program Committee (PC) of either the main track or one of the special sessions. Finally, we selected 70 best papers for oral presentation and publication in one volume of the *Lecture Notes in Artificial Intelligence* series and 68 papers for oral presentation and publication in one volume of the *Communications in Computer and Information Science* series.

We would like to express our thanks to the keynote speakers: Richard Chbeir from Université de Pau et des Pays de l'Adour (UPPA), France, Thanh Thuy Nguyen from VNU University of Engineering and Technology, Vietnam, Klaus Solberg Söilen from Halmstad University, Sweden, and Takako Hashimoto from Chiba University of Commerce, Japan, for their world-class plenary speeches.

Many people contributed toward the success of the conference. First, we would like to recognize the work of the PC co-chairs and special sessions organizers for taking good care of the organization of the reviewing process, an essential stage in ensuring the high quality of the accepted papers. The workshop and special session chairs deserve a special mention for the evaluation of the proposals and the organization and coordination of the work of seven special sessions. In addition, we would like to thank the PC members, of the main track and of the special sessions, for performing their reviewing work with diligence. We thank the Local Organizing Committee chairs, publicity chair, Web chair, and technical support chair for their fantastic work before and during the conference. Finally, we cordially thank all the authors, presenters, and delegates for their valuable contribution to this successful event. The conference would not have been possible without their support.

Our special thanks are also due to Springer for publishing the proceedings and sponsoring awards, and to all the other sponsors for their kind support.

It is our pleasure to announce that the ICCCI conference series continues to have a close cooperation with the Springer journal *Transactions on Computational Collective Intelligence*, and the IEEE SMC Technical Committee on Transactions on Computational Collective Intelligence.

Finally, we hope that ICCCI 2020 contributed significantly to the academic excellence of the field and will lead to the even greater success of ICCCI events in the future.

December 2020

Ngoc Thanh Nguyen
Bao Hung Hoang
Cong Phap Huynh
Dosam Hwang
Bogdan Trawiński
Gottfried Vossen

Organization

Organizing Committee

Honorary Chairs

Pierre Lévy	University of Ottawa, Canada
Cezary Madryas	Wrocław University of Science and Technology, Poland

General Chairs

Ngoc Thanh Nguyen	Wrocław University of Science and Technology, Poland
Bao-Hung Hoang	Thua Thien Hue, Center of Information Technology, Vietnam
Cong-Phap Huynh	University of Danang, Vietnam - Korea University of Information and Communication Technology, Vietnam

Program Chairs

Costin Bădică	University of Craiova, Romania
Dosam Hwang	Yeungnam University, South Korea
Edward Szczerbicki	The University of Newcastle, Australia
The-Son Tran	University of Danang, Vietnam - Korea University of Information and Communication Technology, Vietnam
Gottfried Vossen	University of Münster, Germany

Steering Committee

Ngoc Thanh Nguyen	Wrocław University of Science and Technology, Poland
Shyi-Ming Chen	National Taiwan University of Science and Technology, Taiwan
Dosam Hwang	Yeungnam University, South Korea
Lakhmi C. Jain	University of South Australia, Australia
Piotr Jędrzejowicz	Gdynia Maritime University, Poland
Geun-Sik Jo	Inha University, South Korea
Janusz Kacprzyk	Polish Academy of Sciences, Poland
Ryszard Kowalczyk	Swinburne University of Technology, Australia
Toyoaki Nishida	Kyoto University, Japan
Manuel Núñez	Universidad Complutense de Madrid, Spain

| Klaus Solberg Söilen | Halmstad University, Sweden |
| Khoa Tien Tran | International University - VNU-HCM, Vietnam |

Special Session Chairs

Bogdan Trawiński	Wrocław University of Science and Technology, Poland
Marcin Hernes	Wrocław University of Economics and Business, Poland
Sinh Van Nguyen	International University - VNU-HCM, Vietnam
Thanh-Binh Nguyen	University of Danang, Vietnam - Korea University of Information and Communication Technology, Vietnam

Organizing Chairs

| Quang-Vu Nguyen | University of Danang, Vietnam - Korea University of Information and Communication Technology, Vietnam |
| Krystian Wojtkiewicz | Wrocław University of Science and Technology, Poland |

Publicity Chairs

| My-Hanh Le-Thi | University of Danang, Vietnam - Korea University of Information and Communication Technology, Vietnam |
| Marek Krótkiewicz | Wrocław University of Science and Technology, Poland |

Webmaster

| Marek Kopel | Wrocław University of Science and Technology, Poland |

Local Organizing Committee

Hai Nguyen	University of Danang, Vietnam - Korea University of Information and Communication Technology, Vietnam
Van Tan Nguyen	University of Danang, Vietnam - Korea University of Information and Communication Technology, Vietnam
My-Hanh Le-Thi	University of Danang, Vietnam - Korea University of Information and Communication Technology, Vietnam
Marcin Jodłowiec	Wrocław University of Science and Technology, Poland

Bernadetta Maleszka   Wrocław University of Science and Technology,
                                        Poland
Marcin Maleszka   Wrocław University of Science and Technology,
                                        Poland
Artur Rot   Wrocław University of Economics and Business,
                                        Poland
Anna   Wrocław University of Economics and Business,
    Chojnacka-Komorowska   Poland

Keynote Speakers

Richard Chbeir   Université de Pau et des Pays de l'Adour (UPPA),
                                        France
Thanh Thuy Nguyen   VNU University of Engineering and Technology,
                                        Vietnam
Klaus Solberg Söilen   Halmstad University, Sweden
Takako Hashimoto   Chiba University of Commerce, Japan

Special Session Organizers

ACI 2020 – Special Session on Applications of Collective Intelligence

Quang-Vu Nguyen   University of Danang, Vietnam - Korea University
                                        of Information and Communication Technology,
                                        Vietnam
Van Du Nguyen   Nong Lam University, Vietnam
Van Cuong Tran   Quang Binh University, Vietnam

CCINLP 2020 – Special Session on Computational Collective Intelligence
and Natural Language Processing

Ismaïl Biskri   L'Université du Québec à Trois-Rivières, Canada
Thang Le Dinh   L'Université du Québec à Trois-Rivières, Canada

DDISS 2020 – Special Session on Data Driven IoT for Smart Society

P. W. C. Prasad   Charles Sturt University, Australia
S. M. N Arosha Senanayake   University of Brunei, Brunei

DLAI 2020 – Special Session on Deep Learning and Applications for Industry 4.0

Anh Duc Le   Center for Open Data in the Humanities, Japan
Tho Quan Thanh   Ho Chi Minh City University of Technology, Vietnam
Tien Minh Nguyen   Hung Yen University of Technology and Education,
                                        Vietnam
Anh Viet Nguyen   Le Quy Don Technical University, Vietnam

EEIIOT 2020 – Experience Enhanced Intelligence to IoT

Edward Szczerbicki	The University of Newcastle, Australia
Haoxi Zhang	Chengdu University of Information Technology, China

IMIS 2020 – Special Session on Intelligent Management Information Systems

Marcin Hernes	Wrocław University of Economics and Business, Poland
Artur Rot	Wrocław University of Economics and Business, Poland

IMSAGRWS 2020 – Special Session on Intelligent Modeling and Simulation Approaches for Games and Real World Systems

Doina Logofătu	Frankfurt University of Applied Sciences, Germany
Costin Bădică	University of Craiova, Romania
Florin Leon	Gheorghe Asachi Technical University of Iaşi, Romania

IWCIM 2020 – International Workshop on Computational Intelligence for Multimedia Understanding

Behçet Uğur Töreyin	Istanbul Technical University, Turkey
Maria Trocan	Institut supérieur d'électronique de Paris, France
Davide Moroni	Institute of Information Science and Technologies, Italy

LRLP 2020 – Special Session on Low Resource Languages Processing

Ualsher Tukeyev	Al-Farabi Kazakh National University, Kazakhstan
Madina Mansurova	Al-Farabi Kazakh National University, Kazakhstan

WEBSYS 2020– Intelligent Processing of Multimedia in Web Systems

Kazimierz Choroś	Wrocław University of Science and Technology, Poland
Maria Trocan	Institut supérieur d'électronique de Paris, France

Program Committee

Muhammad Abulaish	South Asian University, India
Sharat Akhoury	University of Cape Town, South Africa
Stuart Allen	Cardiff University, UK
Ana Almeida	GECAD-ISEP-IPP, Portugal
Bashar Al-Shboul	University of Jordan, Jordan
Adel Alti	University of Setif, Algeria
Taha Arbaoui	University of Technology of Troyes, France
Mehmet Emin Aydin	University of the West of England, UK
Thierry Badard	Laval University, Canada

Daniela Gifu	Alexandru Ioan Cuza University, Romania
Daniela Godoy	ISISTAN Research Institute, Argentina
Antonio Gonzalez-Pardo	Universidad Autonoma de Madrid, Spain
Manuel Grana	University of the Basque Country, Spain
Foteini Grivokostopoulou	University of Patras, Greece
William Grosky	University of Michigan, USA
Kenji Hatano	Doshisha University, Japan
Marcin Hernes	Wrocław University of Economics, Poland
Huu Hanh Hoang	Hue University, Vietnam
Bonghee Hong	Pusan National University, South Korea
Tzung-Pei Hong	National University of Kaohsiung, Taiwan
Frédéric Hubert	Laval University, Canada
Maciej Huk	Wrocław University of Science and Technology, Poland
Dosam Hwang	Yeungnam University, South Korea
Lazaros Iliadis	Democritus University of Thrace, Greece
Agnieszka Indyka-Piasecka	Wrocław University of Science and Technology, Poland
Dan Istrate	Universite de Technologie de Compiegne, France
Mirjana Ivanovic	University of Novi Sad, Serbia
Jaroslaw Jankowski	West Pomeranian University of Technology, Poland
Joanna Jedrzejowicz	University of Gdansk, Poland
Piotr Jedrzejowicz	Gdynia Maritime University, Poland
Gordan Jezic	University of Zagreb, Croatia
Geun Sik Jo	Inha University, South Korea
Kang-Hyun Jo	University of Ulsan, South Korea
Christophe Jouis	Université Sorbonne Nouvelle Paris 3, France
Przemysław Juszczuk	University of Economics in Katowice, Poland
Petros Kefalas	University of Sheffield, UK
Marek Kisiel-Dorohinicki	AGH University of Science and Technology, Poland
Attila Kiss	Eötvös Loránd University, Hungary
Marek Kopel	Wrocław University of Science and Technology, Poland
Leszek Koszalka	Wrocław University of Science and Technology, Poland
Ivan Koychev	Sofia University St. Kliment Ohridski, Bulgaria
Jan Kozak	University of Economics in Katowice, Poland
Adrianna Kozierkiewicz	Wrocław University of Science and Technology, Poland
Ondrej Krejcar	University of Hradec Králové, Czech Republic
Dariusz Krol	Wrocław University of Science and Technology, Poland
Marek Krotkiewicz	Wrocław University of Science and Technology, Poland
Jan Kubicek	VSB -Technical University of Ostrava, Czech Republic

Elzbieta Kukla	Wrocław University of Science and Technology, Poland
Marek Kulbacki	Polish-Japanese Academy of Information Technology, Poland
Piotr Kulczycki	Polish Academy of Science, Systems Research Institute, Poland
Kazuhiro Kuwabara	Ritsumeikan University, Japan
Halina Kwasnicka	Wrocław University of Science and Technology, Poland
Hoai An Le Thi	University of Lorraine, France
Sylvain Lefebvre	Toyota ITC, France
Philippe Lemoisson	French Agricultural Research Centre for International Development (CIRAD), France
Florin Leon	Gheorghe Asachi Technical University of Iasi, Romania
Doina Logofatu	Frankfurt University of Applied Sciences, Germany
Edwin Lughofer	Johannes Kepler University Linz, Austria
Juraj Machaj	University of Zilina, Slovakia
Bernadetta Maleszka	Wrocław University of Science and Technology, Poland
Marcin Maleszka	Wrocław University of Science and Technology, Poland
Adam Meissner	Poznan University of Technology, Poland
Héctor Menéndez	University College London, UK
Mercedes Merayo	Universidad Complutense de Madrid, Spain
Jacek Mercik	WSB University in Wrocław, Poland
Radosław Michalski	Wrocław University of Science and Technology, Poland
Peter Mikulecky	University of Hradec Kralove, Czech Republic
Miroslava Mikusova	University of Zilina, Slovakia
Javier Montero	Universidad Complutense de Madrid, Spain
Manuel Munier	Université de Pau et des Pays de l'Adour, France
Grzegorz J. Nalepa	AGH University of Science and Technology, Poland
Laurent Nana	Université de Bretagne Occidentale, France
Anand Nayyar	Duy Tan University, Vietnam
Filippo Neri	University of Napoli Federico II, Italy
Linh Anh Nguyen	University of Warsaw, Poland
Loan T. T. Nguyen	International University - VNU-HCM, Vietnam
Sinh Van Nguyen	International University - VNU-HCM, Vietnam
Adam Niewiadomski	Lodz University of Technology, Poland
Adel Noureddine	Université de Pau et des Pays de l'Adour, France
Agnieszka Nowak-Brzezinska	University of Silesia, Poland
Alberto Núñez	Universidad Complutense de Madrid, Spain
Manuel Núñez	Universidad Complutense de Madrid, Spain
Tarkko Oksala	Aalto University, Finland

Mieczyslaw Owoc	Wrocław University of Economics, Poland
Marcin Paprzycki	Systems Research Institute, Polish Academy of Sciences, Poland
Isidoros Perikos	University of Patras, Greece
Marcin Pietranik	Wrocław University of Science and Technology, Poland
Elias Pimenidis	University of the West of England, Bristol, UK
Nikolaos Polatidis	University of Brighton, UK
Hiram Ponce Espinosa	Universidad Panamericana, Brazil
Piotr Porwik	University of Silesia, Poland
Radu-Emil Precup	Politehnica University of Timisoara, Romania
Ales Prochazka	University of Chemistry and Technology, Czech Republic
Paulo Quaresma	Universidade de Évora, Portugal
Mohammad Rashedur Rahman	North South University, Bangladesh
Ewa Ratajczak-Ropel	Gdynia Maritime University, Poland
Tomasz M. Rutkowski	University of Tokyo, Japan
Virgilijus Sakalauskas	Vilnius University, Lithuania
Khouloud Salameh	Université de Pau et des Pays de l'Adour, France
Imad Saleh	Université Paris 8, France
Ali Selamat	Universiti Teknologi Malaysia, Malaysia
Andrzej Sieminski	Wrocław University of Science and Technology, Poland
Paweł Sitek	Kielce University of Technology, Poland
Vladimir Sobeslav	University of Hradec Kralove, Czech Republic
Klaus Söilen	Halmstad University, Sweeden
Stanimir Stoyanov	University of Plovdiv "Paisii Hilendarski", Bulgaria
Libuse Svobodova	University of Hradec Kralove, Czech Republic
Martin Tabakov	Wroclaw University of Science and Technology, Poland
Muhammad Atif Tahir	National University of Computer and Emerging Sciences, Pakistan
Yasufumi Takama	Tokyo Metropolitan University, Japan
Trong Hieu Tran	VNU-University of Engineering and Technology, Vietnam
Diana Trandabat	Alexandru Ioan Cuza University, Romania
Bogdan Trawinski	Wrocław University of Science and Technology, Poland
Jan Treur	Vrije Universiteit Amsterdam, The Netherlands
Chrisa Tsinaraki	European Commission - Joint Research Center (EC - JRC), Europe
Ualsher Tukeyev	Al-Farabi Kazakh National University, Kazakhstan
Olgierd Unold	Wrocław University of Science and Technology, Poland
Natalie Van Der Wal	Vrije Universiteit Amsterdam, The Netherlands

Bay Vo	Ho Chi Minh City University of Technology, Vietnam
Thi Luu Phuong Vo	International University - VNU-HCM, Vietnam
Lipo Wang	Nanyang Technological University, Singapore
Roger M. Whitaker	Cardiff University, UK
Adam Wojciechowski	Lodz University of Technology, Poland
Krystian Wojtkiewicz	Wrocław University of Science and Technology, Poland
Farouk Yalaoui	University of Technology of Troyes, France
Slawomir Zadrozny	Systems Research Institute, Polish Academy of Sciences, Poland
Drago Zagar	University of Osijek, Croatia
Danuta Zakrzewska	Lodz University of Technology, Poland
Constantin-Bala Zamfirescu	Lucian Blaga University of Sibiu, Romania
Katerina Zdravkova	Ss. Cyril and Methodius University, Macedonia
Aleksander Zgrzywa	Wrocław University of Science and Technology, Poland
Haoxi Zhang	Chengdu University of Information Technology, China
Jianlei Zhang	Nankai University, China
Adam Ziebinski	Silesian University of Technology, Poland

Special Session Program Committees

ACI 2020 – Special Session on Applications of Collective Intelligence

Quang-Vu Nguyen	University of Danang, Vietnam - Korea University of Information and Communication Technology, Vietnam
Van-Du Nguyen	Nong Lam University, Vietnam
Van-Cuong Tran	Quang Binh University, Vietnam
Adrianna Kozierkiewicz	Wrocław University of Science and Technology, Poland
Marcin Pietranik	Wrocław University of Science and Technology, Poland
Chando Lee	Daejeon University, South Korea
Cong-Phap Huynh	University of Danang, Vietnam - Korea University of Information and Communication Technology, Vietnam
Thanh-Binh Nguyen	University of Danang, Vietnam - Korea University of Information and Communication Technology, Vietnam
Tan-Khoi Nguyen	University of Danang, University of Science and Technology, Vietnam
Tuong-Tri Nguyen	Hue University, Vietnam

Minh-Nhut Pham-Nguyen   University of Danang, Vietnam - Korea University
                                            of Information and Communication Technology,
                                            Vietnam
Xuan-Hau Pham   Quang Binh University, Vietnam

CCINLP 2020 – Special Session on Computational Collective Intelligence and Natural Language Processing

Ismaïl Biskri   Université du Québec à Trois-Rivières, Canada
Mounir Zrigui   Université de Monastir, Tunisia
Anca Pascu   Université de Bretagne Occidentale, France
Éric Poirier   Université du Québec à Trois-Rivières, Canada
Adel Jebali   Concordia University, Canada
Khaled Shaalan   The British University in Dubai, UAE
Vladislav Kubon   Charles University, Czech Republic
Louis Rompré   Cascades Papier Kingsey Falls, Canada
Thang Le Dinh   Université du Québec à Trois-Rivières, Canada
Usef Faghihi   Université du Québec à Trois-Rivières, Canada
Nguyen Cuong Pham   VNU-HCM - University of Science, Vietnam
Thuong Cang Phan   Can Tho University, Vietnam

DDISS 2020 – Special Session on Data Driven IoT for Smart Society

Minoru Sasaki   Gifu University, Japan
Michael Yu Wang   Hong Kong University, Hong Kong
William C. Rose   University of Delaware, USA
Le Hoang Son   Vietnam National University, Vietnam
Darwin Gouwanda   Monash University, Malaysia
Owais A. Malik   University of Brunei, Brunei
Ashutosh Kumar Singh   National Institute of Technology, India
Lau Siong Hoe   Multimedia University, Malaysia
Amr Elchouemi   Forbes School of Business and Technology, USA
Abeer Alsadoon   Charles Sturt University, Australia
Sabih Rehman   Charles Sturt University, Australia
Nectar Costadopoulos   Charles Sturt University, Australia
K. S. Senthilkumar   St. George's University, Grenada
Yuexian Zou   Peking University, China

DLAI 2020 – Special Session on Deep Learning and Applications for Industry 4.0

Anh Le Duc   Center for Open Data in the Humanities, Japan
Minh-Tien Nguyen   Hung Yen University of Technology and Education,
                                            Vietnam
Hai-Long Trieu   National Institute of Advanced Industrial Science
                                            and Technology, Japan

Shogo Okada	Japan Advanced Institute of Science and Technology, Japan
Nguyen Van-Hau	Hung Yen University of Technology and Education, Vietnam
Vu-Huy The	Hung Yen University of Technology and Education, Vietnam
Thanh-Huy Nguyen	Saigon University, Vietnam
Van Loi Cao	Le Quy Don Technical University, Vietnam
Kenny Davila	University at Buffalo, USA
Nam Ly	Tokyo University of Agriculture and Technology, Japan
Tien-Dung Cao	Tan Tao University, Vietnam
Danilo Carvalho	Japan Advanced Institute of Science and Technology, Japan
Thuong Nguyen	Sungkyunkwan University, South Korea
Huy Ung	Tokyo University of Agriculture and Technology, Japan
Truong-Son Nguyen	VNU University of Science, Vietnam
Hung Tuan Nguyen	Tokyo University of Agriculture and Technology, Japan
Truong Thanh-Nghia	Tokyo University of Agriculture and Technology, Japan
Thi Oanh Tran	International School, VNU, Vietnam
Anh Viet Nguyen	Le Quy Don Technical University, Vietnam
Ngan Nguyen	University of Information Technology, Vietnam
Quan Thanh Tho	Ho Chi Minh City University of Technology, Vietnam
Ha Nguyen	Ambyint, Canada

EEIIOT 2020 – Experience Enhanced Intelligence to IoT

Fei Li	Chengdu University of Information Technology, China
Zhu Li	University of Missouri, Kansas City, USA
Juan Wang	Chengdu University of Information Technology, China
Lingyu Duan	Peking University, China
Cesar Sanin	University of Newcastle, Australia
Yan Chang	Chengdu University of Information Technology, China
Kui Wu	University of Victoria, Canada
Luqiao Zhang	Chengdu University of Information Technology, China
Syed Imran Shafiq	Aligarh Muslim University, India
Ming Zhu	Chengdu University of Information Technology, China
Dave Chatterjee	University of Georgia, USA

IMIS 2020 – Special Session on Intelligent Management Information Systems

Eunika Mercier-Laurent	Université Jean Moulin Lyon 3, France
Małgorzata Pankowska	University of Economics in Katowice, Poland

Mieczysław Owoc	Wrocław University of Economics and Business, Poland
Bogdan Franczyk	University of Leipzig, Germany
Kazimierz Perechuda	Wrocław University of Economics and Business, Poland
Jan Stępniewski	Université Paris 13, France
Helena Dudycz	Wrocław University of Economics and Business, Poland
Jerzy Korczak	International University of Logistics and Transport in Wrocław, Poland
Andrzej Bytniewski	Wrocław University of Economics and Business, Poland
Marcin Fojcik	Western Norway University of Applied Sciences, Norway
Monika Eisenbardt	University of Economics in Katowice, Poland
Dorota Jelonek	Częstochowa University of Technology, Poland
Paweł Weichbroth	WSB University in Gdansk, Poland
Jadwiga Sobieska-Karpinska	Witelon State University of Applied Sciences in Legnica, Poland
Marek Krótkiewicz	Wrocław University of Science and Technology, Poland
Paweł Siarka	Wrocław University of Economics and Business, Poland
Łukasz Łysik	Wrocław University of Economics and Business, Poland
Adrianna Kozierkiewicz	Wrocław University of Science and Technology, Poland
Karol Łopaciński	Wrocław University of Economics and Business, Poland
Marcin Maleszka	Wrocław University of Science and Technology, Poland
Ingolf Römer	Leipzig University, Germany
Martin Schieck	Leipzig University, Germany
Anna Chojnacka-Komorowska	Wrocław University of Economics and Business, Poland
Krystian Wojtkiewicz	Wrocław University of Science and Technology, Poland
Jacek Winiarski	University of Gdansk, Poland
Wiesława Gryncewicz	Wrocław University of Economics and Business, Poland
Tomasz Turek	Częstochowa University of Technology, Poland
Marcin Jodłowiec	Wrocław University of Science and Technology, Poland
Anna Sołtysik-Piorunkiewicz	University of Economics in Katowice, Poland
Paula Bajdor	Częstochowa University of Technology, Poland

Dorota Jelonek	Częstochowa University of Technology, Poland
Ilona Pawełoszek	Częstochowa University of Technology, Poland
Ewa Walaszczyk	Wrocław University of Economics and Business, Poland
Krzysztof Hauke	Wrocław University of Economics and Business, Poland
Piotr Tutak	Wrocław University of Economics and Business, Poland
Andrzej Kozina	Cracow University of Economics, Poland

IMSAGRWS 2020 – Special Session on Intelligent Modeling and Simulation Approaches for Games and Real World Systems

Alabbas Alhaj Ali	Frankfurt University of Applied Sciences, Germany
Costin Bădică	University of Craiova, Romania
Petru Cașcaval	Gheorghe Asachi Technical University of Iași, Romania
Gia Thuan Lam	Vietnamese-German University, Vietnam
Florin Leon	Gheorghe Asachi Technical University of Iași, Romania
Doina Logofătu	Frankfurt University of Applied Sciences, Germany
Fitore Muharemi	Frankfurt University of Applied Sciences, Germany
Julian Szymański	Gdańsk University of Technology, Poland
Pawel Sitek	Kielce University of Technology, Poland
Daniel Stamate	Goldsmiths, University of London, UK

IWCIM 2020 – International Workshop on Computational Intelligence for Multimedia Understanding

Enis Cetin	Bilkent University, Turkey, and UIC, USA
Michal Haindl	Institute of Information Theory and Automation of the CAS, Czech Republic
Andras L. Majdik	Hungarian Academy of Sciences, Hungary
Cristina Ribeiro	University of Porto, Portugal
Emanuele Salerno	National Research Council of Italy (CNR), Italy
Ales Prochazka	University of Chemistry and Technology, Czech Republic
Anna Tonazzini	National Research Council of Italy (CNR), Italy
Gabriele Pieri	National Research Council of Italy (CNR), Italy
Gerasimos Potamianos	University of Thessaly, Greece
Gorkem Saygili	Ankara University, Turkey
Josiane Zerubia	Inria, France
Maria Antonietta Pascali	National Research Council of Italy (CNR), Italy
Marie-Colette Vanlieshout	CWI, Amsterdam, The Netherlands

Marco Reggiannini	National Research Council of Italy (CNR), Italy
Nahum Kiryati	Tel Aviv University, Israel
Rozenn Dahyot	Trinity College Dublin, Ireland
Sara Colantonio	National Research Council of Italy (CNR), Italy
Shohreh Ahvar	Institut supérieur d'electronique de Paris (ISEP), France
Tamás Szirányi	SZTAKI - Institute for Computer Science and Control, Hungary

LRLP 2020 – Special Session on Low Resource Languages Processing

Miguel A. Alonso	Universidade da Coruña, Spain
Pablo Gamallo	University of Santiago de Compostela, Spain
Nella Israilova	Kyrgyz State Technical University, Kyrgyzstan
Marek Kubis	Adam Mickiewicz University, Poland
Belinda Maia	University of Porto, Portugal
Madina Mansurova	Al-Farabi Kazakh National University, Kazakhstan
Gayrat Matlatipov	Urgench State University, Uzbekistan
Marek Miłosz	Lublin University of Technology, Poland
Diana Rakhimova	Al-Farabi Kazakh National University, Kazakhstan
Altynbek Sharipbay	L. N. Gumilyov Eurasian National University, Kazakhstan
Ualsher Tukeyev	Al-Farabi Kazakh National University, Kazakhstan

WEBSYS 2020 – Intelligent Processing of Multimedia in Web Systems

Shohreh Ahvar	Association ISEP, Paris, France
Frédéric Amiel	Association ISEP, Paris, France
František Čapkovič	Slovak Academy of Sciences, Slovakia
Kazimierz Choroś	Wrocław University of Science and Technology, Poland
Patricia Conde-Cespedes	Association ISEP, Paris, France
Marek Kopel	Wrocław University of Science and Technology, Poland
Mikołaj Leszczuk	AGH University of Science and Technology, Poland
Bożena Kostek	Gdańsk University of Technology, Poland
Alin Moldoveanu	Politehnica University of Bucharest, Romania
Tarkko Oksala	Helsinki University of Technology, Finland
Andrzej Siemiński	Wrocław University of Science and Technology, Poland
Maria Trocan	Association ISEP, Paris, France
Aleksander Zgrzywa	Wrocław University of Science and Technology, Poland

Contents

Applications of Collective Intelligence

Data Mining Methods and Applications

Machine Learning Methods

Biosensors and Biometric Techniques

Innovations in Intelligent Systems

Natural Language Processing

Low Resource Languages Processing

**Computational Collective Intelligence and Natural
Language Processing**

Computational Intelligence for Multimedia Understanding

Intelligent Processing of Multimedia in Web Systems

Knowledge Engineering and Semantic Web

Towards a Holistic Schema Matching Approach Designed for Large-Scale Schemas

Aola Yousfi$^{(\boxtimes)}$, Moulay Hafid El Yazidi, and Ahmed Zellou

ENSIAS, Mohammed V University, Rabat, Morocco
aola.yousfi@gmail.com, {my-hafid.elyazidi,ahmed.zellou}@um5.ac.ma

Abstract. Holistic schema matching is a fundamental challenge in the big data integration domain. Ideally, clusters of semantically corresponding elements are created and are updated as more schemas are matched. Developing a high-quality holistic schema matching approach is critical for two main reasons. First, identifying as many accurate and holistic semantic correspondences as possible right from the beginning. Second, reducing considerably the search space. Nevertheless, this problem is challenging since overlapping schema elements are not available. Identifying schema overlaps is further complicated for two main reasons: (1) there is a large number of schemas; and (2) overlaps vary for different schemas. In this paper we present **HMO**, a **H**olistic schema **M**atching approach based on schema **O**verlaps and designed for large-scale schemas. **HMO** can balance the search space and the quality of the holistic semantic correspondences. To narrow down the search space, **HMO** matches schemas based on their overlaps. To obtain high-accuracy, **HMO** uses an existing high-quality semantic similarity measure. Experimental results on four real-world domains show effectiveness and scalability of our matching approach.

Keywords: Holistic Schema Matching · Large-scale schemas · Search space · Big data integration

1 Introduction

Holistic schema matching or collective schema matching [10] is of a great importance in the big data integration domain. It helps identify semantic correspondences also called matches [17] between multiple, autonomous, distributed, heterogeneous, and scalable large-scale schemas. However, matching large-scale schemas results in the greatest increase of the search space (huge search space) which refers to the total number of element comparisons (see Definition 2.1) necessary to match schemas; thus, causes the matching approach to take longer to find out the matches.

The abundance of schema matching approaches offer a very wide range of matching choices. Pairwise matching approaches (e.g. COMA++ [1], QOM [4],

© Springer Nature Switzerland AG 2020
N. T. Nguyen et al. (Eds.): ICCCI 2020, LNAI 12496, pp. 3–15, 2020.
https://doi.org/10.1007/978-3-030-63007-2_1

and CUPID [9]) have been developed to take as input two schemas at a time, and are sufficiently fast for small inputs plus they were proved to provide superior quality matches. But because of their quadratic time complexity, they are not suited to match multiple schemas at once. Hence, a considerable amount of research work is increasingly focused on holistic schema matching [7,10]. Since in P2P systems there is no initial integrated schema or intermediate schema that represents all peers, schemas are typically matched incrementally in a series of two-way matching steps and the clusters of semantically corresponding elements are updated as more schemas are matched. A state of the art example of this is PORSCHE [12] which first matches and integrates two schemas, then matches a new schema at a time to the integrated schema. Incremental schema matching has two main disadvantages. First, it depends on the order in which schemas are matched and integrated [10]. Second, it matches only two schemas at a time.

To deal with the missing information about the intermediate schema and to generate as many holistic semantic correspondences (see Definition 2.2) as possible right from the start, we use overlapping schema elements (because in general schemas in the same domain have many elements in common), which enable multiple schemas to be matched simultaneously and reduce significantly the total number of element comparisons. If all schemas include the same exact elements, matching is straightforward: schemas all elements inclusive are matched simultaneously to schema overlaps and the number of element comparisons per schema is reduced to the number of elements in the schema squared. Nevertheless, different schemas in the same domain may contain some distinct elements, and such distinctions added to the missing information about schema overlaps make holistic schema matching much more challenging.

In this paper, we propose **HMO** which is a **H**olistic schema **M**atching approach based on schema **O**verlaps and designed for large-scale schemas. The key idea of **HMO** is to first match multiple schemas simultaneously based on their overlaps; and then for their distinct elements, **HMO** matches two schemas at a time. This way schemas are matched semi-simultaneously which result in the greatest reduction of element comparisons. The use of the similarity measure introduced in [14–16] in both phases maximizes the accuracy of the final matches. **HMO** solves the problem of unavailable information about schema overlaps as follows: it uses pre-defined matches identified by means of the similarity measure in [15] to infer schema overlaps. We have developed **HMO** carefully such that (1) it provides high-quality matches; and (2) it is scalable.

In this paper, we study how to match multiple schemas holistically. In summary, we make the contributions below:

1. We present an algorithm that uses the matches identified by means of the semantic similarity measure described in [15] to generate overlapping schema elements.

2. We propose a holistic schema matching approach that matches multiple schemas semi-simultaneously using their overlaps.

3. We evaluate **HMO** over real-world domains and show that it significantly reduces the total number of element comparisons and achieves high-quality matches.

The rest of this paper is organized as follows. Section 2 discusses related work. Section 3 defines the problem of holistic schema matching. Section 4 describes the architecture of **HMO**. Section 5 presents experimental results. Section 6 concludes this paper and discusses future work.

2   Related Work

To our knowledge, there has been very little work on holistic schema matching (PORSCHE [12] and HSM [13]) compared to the huge amount of work on pairwise schema matching (we refer the reader to [2] for surveys). Also, some state of the art holistic schema matching approaches are not able to match all schemas at once but instead they match schemas incrementally through a series of two-way matching steps (PORSCHE [12]).

Moreover, since pairwise schema matching approaches are typically limited to a small number of schemas and in general require human assistance (COMA++ [1], QOM [4], CUPID [9], FMAMS [5], and S-Match [6]), they are not recommended when we have to match multiple schemas in order to avoid quadratic time complexity [10]. Furthermore, most holistic schema matching approaches consider matching accuracy without considering techniques to cut down element comparisons (PORSCHE [12] and HSM [13]).

PORSCHE (Performance Oriented SCHEma mediation) [12] is an automatic schema matching system designed for XML schemas. It uses tree mining techniques and exploits string-based and language-based information along with external thesauri. PORSCHE first depicts XML schemas as rooted ordered labeled trees. It then combines all schemas into an integrated schema. Finally, it defines the mappings between the integrated schema and the input schema trees.

HSM (Holistic Schema Matching) [13] is an approach to holistically identify semantic correspondences between different Web query interfaces. It proceeds in three main steps. First, it searches for synonym attributes by computing their matching scores. Second, it identifies grouping attributes by calculating their grouping scores. Finally, it uses a greedy algorithm based on both scores to generate the matches.

Although there are plenty of schema matching approaches, none of them studied holistic schema matching with the consideration of both narrowing down the total number of element comparisons and generating high-quality holistic semantic correspondences. Therefore, we proposed in this paper an approach to holistic schema matching based on schema overlaps and designed for large-scale schemas and then showed that (1) it requires much less element comparisons than PORSCHE and HSM; and (2) it outperforms PORSCHE and HSM in terms of matching accuracy.

3   Problem Statement

In this section, we provide definitions related to the problem we are studying.

Definition 2.1. (Element Comparison). *Let $\varphi_1 = \{e_{1,1}, e_{1,2}, ..., e_{1,|\varphi_1|}\}$ and $\varphi_2 = \{e_{2,1}, e_{2,2}, ..., e_{2,|\varphi_2|}\}$ be two schemas. An element comparison is the process of comparing semantically $e_{1,i}$ and $e_{2,j}$, where $(i,j) \in [\![1, |\varphi_1|]\!] \times [\![1, |\varphi_2|]\!]$, typically by means of a similarity measure to see whether they are similar.*

Definition 2.2. (Holistic Semantic Correspondence). *Let $\varphi_1 = \{e_{1,1}, e_{1,2}, ..., e_{1,|\varphi_1|}\}$, $\varphi_2 = \{e_{2,1}, e_{2,2}, ..., e_{2,|\varphi_2|}\}$, ..., $\varphi_n = \{e_{n,1}, e_{n,2}, ..., e_{n,|\varphi_n|}\}$ be n schemas. A holistic semantic correspondence is a tuple $\theta = (e_{1,i}, e_{2,j}, ..., e_{n,k})$ where $e_{1,i} \in \varphi_1$, $e_{2,j} \in \varphi_2$, $e_{n,k} \in \varphi_n$ with up to n semantically similar elements identified through a series of element comparisons and which satisfy that no element appears in more than one holistic correspondence. The holistic semantic correspondences are a set of tuples $\Theta = \{\theta_1, \theta_2, ..., \theta_{|\Theta|}\}$.*

Remark: The non-matched elements in φ_1, φ_2, ..., and φ_n are defined as a set of schemas $\overline{\Theta} = \{\overline{\theta_1}, \overline{\theta_2}, ..., \overline{\theta_n}\}$, where $\overline{\theta_1}, \overline{\theta_2}, ...,$ and $\overline{\theta_n}$ contain only the non-matched elements in $\varphi_1, \varphi_2, ...,$ and φ_n respectively.

Definition 2.3. (Overlapping Schema Elements). *Let φ_1, φ_2, ..., φ_n be n schemas. Schema overlaps between φ_1, φ_2, ..., and φ_n is a set $\Gamma_{overlaps} = \{e_1, e_2, ..., e_{|\Gamma_{overlaps}|}\}$ of distinct elements which satisfy that each element has semantic correspondences in at least two schemas from φ_1, φ_2, ..., φ_n. Note that elements in $\Gamma_{overlaps}$ are not semantically similar.*

Definition 2.4. (Distinct Schema Elements). *Let φ_1, φ_2, ..., φ_n be n schemas. Distinct schema elements between φ_1, φ_2, ..., and φ_n is a set $\Gamma_{distinctions} = \{e_1, e_2, ..., e_{|\Gamma_{distinctions}|}\}$ of elements from $\overline{\theta_1}$, $\overline{\theta_2}$, ..., and $\overline{\theta_n}$.*

Definition 2.5. (Problem Statement). *Given a set of schemas $\Phi = \{\varphi_1, \varphi_2, ..., \varphi_{|\Phi|}\}$, let schema overlaps $\Gamma_{overlaps}$ be generated by a schema matching tool and $\Gamma_{distinctions}$ determined accordingly. Our goal is to match multiple schemas holistically in few element comparisons and obtain high quality matches.*

Table 1 lists the notations used throughout this paper.

Table 1. Summary of symbol notations

Notation	Description
φ, e	schema, schema element
$\Phi, \|\Phi\|$	set of schemas, cardinality of Φ
$\Theta, \overline{\Theta}$	holistic semantic correspondences, non-matched elements
$\Gamma_{overlaps}, \|\Gamma_{overlaps}\|$	schema overlaps, cardinality of $\Gamma_{overlaps}$
$\Gamma_{distinctions}, \|\Gamma_{distinctions}\|$	distinct schema elements, cardinality of $\Gamma_{distinctions}$

In the next section, we describe the **HMO** solution to the problem presented in Definition 2.5.

4 The HMO Approach

The **HMO** architecture (see Fig. 1) consists of three main modules: Overlaps & Distinctions Generator, Schema Overlaps Matcher, and Distinct Elements Matcher. Given a set of schemas $\Phi = \{\varphi_1, \varphi_2, ..., \varphi_{|\Phi|}\}$. Let $\Phi_{\alpha\%}$ (α is a tuning parameter that controls the number of schemas to be matched in order to generate the initial set of schema overlaps $\Gamma_{overlaps}$) be a subset of $\lfloor \alpha\% \times |\Phi| \rfloor$ schemas from Φ. The *Overlaps & Distinctions Generator* applies an existing semantic similarity measure to $\Phi_{\alpha\%}$ in order to generate the initial sets of $\Gamma_{overlaps}$ and $\Gamma_{distinctions}$. Then, **HMO** operates in two phases: *parallel* and *sequential*. In the parallel matching phase, the *Schema Overlaps Matcher* applies the same similarity measure to match simultaneously schemas in $\Phi \setminus \Phi_{\alpha\%}$ or new schema(s), which we both denote by Φ^*, to $\Gamma_{overlaps}$. While in the sequential matching phase, the *Distinct Elements Matcher* applies the same similarity measure to match sequentially schemas from $\overline{\Theta}_{\Phi^*}$ to $\Gamma_{distinctions}$. It is important to note that Overlaps & Distinctions Generator is executed only once at the beginning of the matching process then $\Gamma_{overlaps}$ and $\Gamma_{distinctions}$ are updated by the Schema Overlaps Matcher and Distinct Elements Matcher.

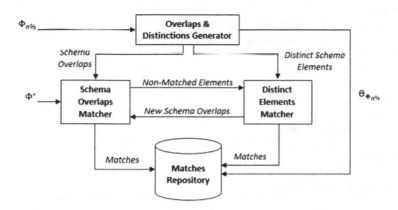

Fig. 1. The **HMO** architecture

Prior to calculating the similarity between different schema elements, **HMO** first uses the pre-matching strategy described in [15] to generate, for each simple type element, a set of words that clarifies its meaning. We use then the semantic similarity measure in [15] to calculate the similarity between sets of words. The use of that measure is justified by the fact that it provides better results when compared to some state of the art similarity measures and distances.

The rest of this section describes Overlaps & Distinctions Generator (see Subsect. 4.1), Schema Overlaps Matcher (see Subsect. 4.2), and Distinct Elements Matcher (see Subsect. 4.3).

4.1 Overlaps and Distinctions Generator

Given a set of schemas $\Phi = \{\varphi_1, \varphi_2, ..., \varphi_{|\Phi|}\}$, the Overlaps & Distinctions Generator operates in three main steps to generate both the initial sets of schema overlaps $\Gamma_{overlaps}$ and distinct schema elements $\Gamma_{distinctions}$ (see Algorithm 1). First, for every two schemas $\varphi_i, \varphi_j \in \Phi_{\alpha\%}$, the Overlaps & Distinctions Generator calculates the semantic similarity between every two elements $(e_i, e_j) \in \varphi_i \times \varphi_j$ to

---

Algorithm 1. OverlapsAndDistinctionsGenerator($\Phi_{\alpha\%}$)

Input:
    $\Phi_{\alpha\%}$
Output:
    $< \Gamma_{overlaps}, \Gamma_{distinctions} >$

1: $\Theta_{\Phi_{\alpha\%}} \leftarrow \emptyset$
2: $\Gamma_{overlaps} \leftarrow \emptyset$
3: $\Gamma_{distinctions} \leftarrow \emptyset$
4: **for** each $(e_1 \in \varphi_i$ and $e_2 \in \varphi_j)$ in $\Phi_{\alpha\%}$ **do**
5:     Calculate the semantic similarity between e_1 and e_2 according to the similarity measure described in [15]
6:     **if** e_1 and e_2 are semantically similar according to the matching approach in [15] **then**
7:         **if** $\exists\, \theta \in \Theta_{\Phi_{\alpha\%}}$ such that $e_1 \in \theta$ **then**
8:             $\theta \leftarrow \theta \cup e_2$ /* *Similarly, we compare to e_2* */
9:         **else**
10:             $\Theta_{\Phi_{\alpha\%}} \leftarrow (e_1, e_2)$
11:         **end if**
12:     **end if**
13: **end for**
14: **for** each θ in $\Theta_{\Phi_{\alpha\%}}$ **do**
15:     $\Gamma_{overlaps} \leftarrow \Gamma_{overlaps} \cup e$ /**e is an element from θ* */
16: **end for**
17: $\Gamma_{distinctions} \leftarrow \overline{\Theta}_{\Phi_{\alpha\%}}$
18: **return** $< \Gamma_{overlaps}, \Gamma_{distinctions} >$

identify the semantically corresponding elements $\Theta_{\Phi_{\alpha\%}}$ in $\Phi_{\alpha\%}$. Second, it adds one element per holistic semantic correspondence (tuple) to the schema overlaps. Third, it adds the non-matched elements in $\Phi_{\alpha\%}$ to the distinct schema elements.

Next, we identify simultaneously the holistic semantic correspondences between Φ^*.

4.2 Schema Overlaps Matcher

The Schema Overlaps Matcher (see Algorithm 2) first matches simultaneously schemas in Φ^* to $\Gamma_{overlaps}$. It then stores the new matches in the *Matches Repository* and sends the non-matched elements in Φ^* to the Distinct Elements Matcher.

Algorithm 2. SchemaOverlapsMatcher(Φ^*, $\Gamma_{overlaps}$)

Input:
  Φ^*

  $\Gamma_{overlaps}$
Output:
  $< \Theta, \overline{\Theta}_{\Phi^*} >$ /* Θ denotes the new and previously $\Theta_{\Phi_{\alpha\%}}$ identified semantic correspondences $(\Theta = \Theta_{\Phi_{\alpha\%}} \cup \Theta_{\Phi^*})$*/
  1: **for each** $e \in \varphi$ in Φ^* **do**
  2:   **for each** o in $\Gamma_{overlaps}$ **do**
  3:     Calculate the semantic similarity between e and o according to the similarity measure described in [15]
  4:     **if** e and o are semantically similar according to the matching approach in [15] **then**
  5:       $\theta \leftarrow \theta \cup e$ /* $o \in \theta$ */
  6:     **end if**
  7:   **end for**
  8: **end for**
  9: Send $\overline{\Theta}_{\Phi^*}$ to DistinctElementsMatcher
10: **return** $< \Theta, \overline{\Theta}_{\Phi^*} >$

Having generated the distinct schema elements $\Gamma_{distinctions}$, next we use them to match $\overline{\Theta}_{\Phi^*}$.

4.3 Distinct Elements Matcher

The Distinct Elements Matcher (see Algorithm 3) uses the similarity measure in [15] to identify semantically similar elements between schemas in $\overline{\Theta}_{\Phi^*}$ and $\Gamma_{distinctions}$ (from line 1 to line 17). It then stores the new matches in the Matches Repository, adds the new schema overlaps in $\Gamma_{overlaps}$, and removes the matched schema elements from $\Gamma_{distinctions}$. It is important to note that the Distinct Elements Matcher compares a schema at a time to $\Gamma_{distinctions}$.

Algorithm 3. DistinctElementsMatcher($\overline{\Theta}_{\Phi^*}$, $\Gamma_{distinctions}$)

Input:

$\overline{\Theta}_{\Phi^*}$

$\Gamma_{distinctions}$

Output:

$< \Theta, \Gamma_{overlaps}, \Gamma_{distinctions} >$

1: $\Gamma \leftarrow \emptyset$ /*New schema overlaps*/
2: **for** each $\overline{\theta}$ in $\overline{\Theta}_{\Phi^*}$ **do**
3:    **for** each e in $\overline{\theta}$ **do**
4:       **if** $\exists f \in \Gamma_{distinctions}$ semantically similar to e **then**
5:          **if** $\nexists \theta = (e_1, e_2, \ldots, e_i) \in \Theta$ such that $f \in \theta$ **then**
6:             $\Theta \leftarrow \Theta \cup (f, e)$
7:          **else**
8:             $\theta \leftarrow (e_1, e_2, \ldots, e_i, e)$
9:          **end if**
10:         **if** Γ does not contain any semantically similar element to e **then**
11:            $\Gamma \leftarrow \Gamma \cup f$
12:         **end if**
13:       **else**
14:          $\Gamma_{distinctions} \leftarrow \Gamma_{distinctions} \cup e$
15:       **end if**
16:    **end for**
17: **end for**
18: $\Gamma_{overlaps} \leftarrow \Gamma_{overlaps} \cup \Gamma$
19: $\Gamma_{distinctions} \leftarrow \Gamma_{distinctions} \setminus \Gamma$
20: **return** $< \Theta, \Gamma_{overlaps}, \Gamma_{distinctions} >$

---

5   Experimental Results

We conducted extensive experiments to evaluate **HMO** based on a real implementation. We focused on evaluating two main issues. First, we examined the capability of **HMO** to produce holistic semantic correspondences in few element comparisons. Second, we verified the effectiveness of **HMO** in obtaining high-quality holistic semantic correspondences.

5.1   Experimental Settings

Datasets: We evaluated **HMO** on four real-world domains (see Table 2). *Books* provides information about books on diverse areas. *Car Rentals* contains information about cars available for rent. *Airfare* lists the prices of journeys by plane. *Job* posts jobs on different sectors. The schemas are extracted from Web forms available publicly on the TEL-8 dataset of the UIUC Web Integration Repository[1].

---

[1] http://metaquerier.cs.uiuc.edu/repository.

Table 2. Evaluation datasets

Domain	# of schemas	$|\Gamma_{overlaps}|$	$|\Gamma_{distinctions}|$
Books	53	12	21
Car rentals	58	7	14
Airfare	48	11	14
Job	42	14	17

Implementation: We compare **HMO** to both PORSCHE [12] and Holistic Schema Matching (HSM) [13] in terms of both the total number of element comparisons needed to generate the matches and the quality of the holistic correspondences. To this end, we implemented **HMO** using the similarity measure described in [15] and a test version of PORSCHE called tPORSCHE since we did not have access to its implementation. For HSM, we used the results published in [13].

Measures: We use the metrics below [3,8] to evaluate the quality of the matches.

$$Precision = \frac{True\ Matches}{True\ Matches + False\ Matches} \qquad (1)$$

(1) measures the percentage of true matches among all matches returned by the matching system.

$$Recall = \frac{True\ Matches}{Missed\ Matches + True\ Matches} \qquad (2)$$

(2) measures the percentage of true matches returned by the matching system among all reference matches (matches defined by a human expert).

$$F - Measure = \frac{2 \times Precision \times Recall}{Precision + Recall} \qquad (3)$$

(3) is the harmonic mean of *Precision* and *Recall*.

$$Overall = Recall \times (2 - \frac{1}{Precision}) \qquad (4)$$

(4) measures the amount of human effort necessary to remove false matches and add missed matches. In contrast to *Precision* and *Recall*, *Overall* can have negative values if *Precision* < 0.5. It is important to note that if *Overall* < 0 then most matching will be done manually. The best case scenario is when *Precision* = *Recall* = *F* − *Measure* = *Overall* = 1.

5.2 Results and Discussion

Number of Element Comparisons: We first calculated $|\Gamma_{overlaps}|$ for 2%, 4%, 6%, 8%, 10% and 12% schemas (see Table 3). For *Books*, we obtained 2, 6,

12, 12, 12 and 12 overlapping schema elements after matching 2%, 4%, 6%, 8%, 10% and 12% schemas; respectively. For *Car Rentals*, we obtained 2, 4, 7, 7, 7 and 8 overlapping schema elements after matching 2%, 4%, 6%, 8%, 10% and 12% schemas; respectively. For *Airfare*, we obtained 5, 7, 11, 11, 12 and 12 overlapping schema elements after matching 2%, 4%, 6%, 8%, 10% and 12% schemas; respectively. For *Job*, we obtained 4, 7, 14, 14, 14 and 14 overlapping schema elements after matching 2%, 4%, 6%, 8%, 10% and 12% schemas; respectively. In other words, we obtain the initial set of schema overlaps after matching only 6% schemas, the rest of the schemas do not really bring any new overlaps. Thus, we used 6% schemas per domain to generate the initial sets of schema overlaps $\Gamma_{overlaps}$ and distinct schema elements $\Gamma_{distinctions}$ (see Table 2).

Table 3. $|\Gamma_{overlaps}|$ for 2%, 4%, 6%, 8%, 10%, and 12% Schemas

Domain	$\alpha = 2\%$	$\alpha = 4\%$	$\alpha = 6\%$	$\alpha = 8\%$	$\alpha = 10\%$	$\alpha = 12\%$
	$|\Gamma_{overlaps}|$	$|\Gamma_{overlaps}|$	$|\Gamma_{overlaps}|$	$|\Gamma_{overlaps}|$	$|\Gamma_{overlaps}|$	$|\Gamma_{overlaps}|$
Books	2	6	12	12	12	12
Car rentals	2	4	7	7	7	8
Airfare	5	7	11	11	12	12
Job	4	7	14	14	14	14

Figure 2 shows the results for **HMO**, tPORSCHE, and HSM. The results are quite similar for all domains. **HMO** uses less element comparisons than both tPORSCHE and HSM. The total number of element comparisons required to match the first 6% schemas is the same for both **HMO** and tPORSCHE (the line graphs are overlapping). However, there is a visible difference between the number of element comparisons used by tPORSCHE and **HMO** to match the remaining schemas. The former requires much more element comparisons than the latter (the line graph of tPORSCHE is above **HMO**'s). HSM uses much more element comparisons than both **HMO** and tPORSCHE. This is due to the fact that HSM compares twice every element from the first schema to every element from the second: it calculates both the matching score and the grouping score. While, tPORSCHE matches schemas incrementally in a series of two-way matching steps, which implies that the new schema elements are compared against the union of the previously integrated elements. And finally **HMO** matches schemas based on their overlaps which considerably narrows down the total number of element comparisons. Based on these observations, scalability to multiple schemas is much more easier with **HMO**.

Accuracy of the Holistic Correspondences: We calculated *Precision*, *Recall*, *F-Measure* and *Overall* for **HMO** and tPORSCHE; and compared those to HSM. The new and previously published results are presented in Fig. 3. The findings indicate that **HMO** and HSM achieve better matching quality than

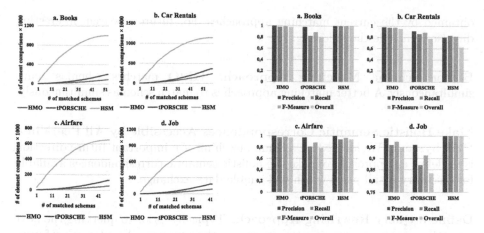

Fig. 2. Number of matched schemas versus the total number of comparisons

Fig. 3. Quality of the matches generated by **HMO**, tPORSCHE and HSM

tPORSCHE. This is due to the fact that the semantic similarity approaches used by either HSM (see Sect. 2) or **HMO** achieve better accuracy than tPORSCHE. **HMO** utilizes an existing semantic similarity measure that considers the context of schema elements, uses explicit sets of words to represent elements instead of confusing element labels, and combines reliable information from WordNet. Moreover, the measure has proved to achieve high accuracy when applied on Miller & Charles benchmark dataset [11]. The findings also indicate that **HMO** and HSM achieve almost the same matching quality, this is due to the fact that they both use semantic similarity scores-based matching approaches. Overall, all three systems achieve good quality, which leaves minimum post-matching work to the user (*Overall* > 0).

6   Conclusion and Future Work

We have shown that holistic schema matching is important for identifying as many holistic semantic correspondences as possible right from the beginning. Current state of the art holistic schema matching approaches often operate in a series of two-way matching steps. Therefore, we have developed **HMO**, a **H**olistic schema **M**atching approach based on schema **O**verlaps.

Given a set of schemas $\Phi = \{\varphi_1, \varphi_2, ..., \varphi_{|\Phi|}\}$. Let $\Gamma_{overlaps}$ be the initial set of schema overlaps generated from Φ and $\Gamma_{distinctions}$ be the initial set of distinct schema elements found in Φ. Our key idea is to match schemas in two main phases. First, match schemas in Φ simultaneously to $\Gamma_{overlaps}$. Second, match a schema from $\overline{\Theta}_\Phi$ to $\Gamma_{distinctions}$ at a time. This way, schema matching is semi-simultaneous. We evaluated **HMO** over four real-world domains. The results show that the holistic correspondences obtained by **HMO** achieve a higher matching accuracy in less element comparisons compared to the matches obtained by the current matching approaches. For future research, interesting directions include the following:

Better Schema Matching Approach. **HMO** matches schemas semi-simultaneously. A better matching approach is to match schemas simultaneously.

Make Holistic Semantic Correspondences Accessible by All Peers in a P2P System. We focused on schema matching. An important future direction is to define an approach to make the holistic semantic correspondences available for discovery by all peers which will enable data exchange.

Define a Query Rewriting Approach. Typically, prior to querying the next peer, the current peer rewrites the query over the next peer. An interesting future direction is to optimize the query rewriting process.

References

1. Aumueller, D., Do, H.-H., Massmann, S., Rahm, E.: Schema and ontology matching with coma++. In: Proceedings of the 2005 ACM SIGMOD International Conference on Management of Data, pp. 906–908. ACM (2005)
2. Bernstein, P.A., Madhavan, J., Rahm, E.: Generic schema matching, ten years later. In: Proceedings of the VLDB Endowment, vol. 4, no. 11, pp. 695–701 (2011)
3. Do, H.-H., Rahm, E.: Coma: a system for flexible combination of schema matching approaches. In: Proceedings of the 28th International Conference on Very Large Data Bases, pp. 610–621. VLDB Endowment (2002)
4. Ehrig, M., Staab, S.: QOM – quick ontology mapping. In: McIlraith, S.A., Plexousakis, D., van Harmelen, F. (eds.) ISWC 2004. LNCS, vol. 3298, pp. 683–697. Springer, Heidelberg (2004). https://doi.org/10.1007/978-3-540-30475-3_47
5. El Yazidi, M.H., Zellou, A., Idri, A.: Fmams: fuzzy mapping approach for mediation systems. Int. J. Appl. Evol. Comput. (IJAEC) 4(3), 34–46 (2013)
6. Giunchiglia, F., Autayeu, A., Pane, J.: S-match: an open source framework for matching lightweight ontologies. Semant. Web 3(3), 307–317 (2012)
7. Gruetze, T., Böhm, C., Naumann, F.: Holistic and scalable ontology alignment for linked open data. LDOW 937, 1–10 (2012)
8. Kastner, I., Adriaans, F.: Linguistic constraints on statistical word segmentation: the role of consonants in Arabic and English. Cogn. Sci. 42, 494–518 (2018)
9. Madhavan, J., Bernstein, P.A., Rahm, E.: Generic schema matching with cupid. vldb 1, 49–58 (2001)
10. Rahm, E., Peukert, E.: Holistic schema matching (2019)
11. Resnik, P.: Using information content to evaluate semantic similarity in a taxonomy. arXiv preprint cmp-lg/9511007 (1995)
12. Saleem, K., Bellahsene, Z., Hunt, E.: Porsche: performance oriented schema mediation. Inf. Syst. 33(7–8), 637–657 (2008)
13. Su, W., Wang, J., Lochovsky, F.: Holistic Schema Matching for Web Query Interfaces. In: Ioannidis, Y., et al. (eds.) EDBT 2006. LNCS, vol. 3896, pp. 77–94. Springer, Heidelberg (2006). https://doi.org/10.1007/11687238_8

14. Yousfi, A., El Yazidi, M.H., Zellou, A.: hmatcher: matching schemas holistically. Int. J. Intell. Eng. Syst. **13**(5), 490–501 (2020)
15. Yousfi, A., Elyazidi, M.H., Zellou, A.: Assessing the performance of a new semantic similarity measure designed for schema matching for mediation systems. In: Nguyen, N.T., Pimenidis, E., Khan, Z., Trawiński, B. (eds.) ICCCI 2018. LNCS (LNAI), vol. 11055, pp. 64–74. Springer, Cham (2018). https://doi.org/10.1007/978-3-319-98443-8_7
16. Yousfi, A., Yazidi, M.H.E., Zellou, A.: xmatcher: Matching extensible markup language schemas using semantic-based techniques. Int. J. Adv. Comput. Sci. Appl. **11**(8) (2020)
17. Zhang, C., Chen, L., Jagadish, H., Zhang, M., Tong, Y.: Reducing uncertainty of schema matching via crowdsourcing with accuracy rates. IEEE Trans. Knowl. Data Eng. **32**, 135–151 (2018)

Overcoming Local Optima for Determining 2-Optimality Consensus for Collectives

Dai Tho Dang[1] ⓘ, Zygmunt Mazur[2] ⓘ, and Dosam Hwang[1](✉) ⓘ

[1] Department of Computer Engineering, Yeungnam University, Gyeongsan, Republic of Korea
daithodang@ynu.ac.kr, dosamhwang@gmail.com
[2] Wroclaw University of Science and Technology, Wrocław, Poland
zygmunt.mazur@pwr.edu.pl

Abstract. Collective knowledge or consensus is used widely in our life. Determining the collective knowledge of a collective depends on the knowledge states of collective members. However, in a collective, each member has its knowledge, and knowledge states are often contradictory. Determining consensus satisfying postulate 2-Optimality of a collective is an NP-hard problem, and heuristic algorithms have been suggested. The basic algorithm is the most popular for this task. However, this algorithm can get stuck in local optima, which limits its consensus quality. To obtain consensus with high quality, in this study, we propose two approaches to avoid getting stuck in local optima. The experimental results show that the consensus quality generated by these approaches is at least 2.05% higher than that of the basic algorithm.

Keywords: Collective intelligence · Collective knowledge · Consensus · Overcoming local optima · Postulate 2-Optimality

1 Introduction

A collective is ordinarily regarded as a set of intelligent units, for example, experts or agent systems, and each member independently give the resolution of a problem [1]. Knowledge of collectives is widely applied in many fields. One example is multi-agent systems [2, 3], including social networks, sensor networks, robot systems, etc., consists of a set of autonomous entities known as agents operating in a network environment. This system bases on the set of agents, or collective members, to make decisions [1, 2].

A representative of members is called collective knowledge or consensus. In a collective, collective knowledge is determined based on knowledge states of collective members. Each member has its knowledge, and knowledge states of collective members are often contradictory [4]. For example, in the United States, before a presidential election happens, people often predict the outcome. However, the predictions of people are often inconsistent. Interestingly, the inconsistency of the collective states creates the strength of a collective [1], but it also causes the elaborate in the consensus determination.

Nguyen [5] build a formal model for collectives and use Consensus theory to determine collective knowledge, and Consensus theory has proved to be a useful tool for this

© Springer Nature Switzerland AG 2020
N. T. Nguyen et al. (Eds.): ICCCI 2020, LNAI 12496, pp. 16–26, 2020.
https://doi.org/10.1007/978-3-030-63007-2_2

task [6]. This theory proposes many postulates, in which 2-Optimality is an essential one for the consensus determination. A consensus satisfying the postulate 2-Optimality is the best representative, and the distances from it to collective members are uniform.

One useful structure for representing the knowledge states is binary vector, and it appears in many applications in economics [7], robotic network [8], transportations [9], bioinformatics [10], etc. Determining the 2-Optimality consensus of a collective consisting of binary vectors is an NP-hard problem, and heuristic algorithms are suggested for this task. In practical algorithms, the basic algorithm [11] is the best one, and it is widely used for this task.

The basic algorithm is a local search algorithm [11, 12]. In step initialization, this algorithm randomly generates an initial consensus, called the current solution. In step 1, the algorithm transforms the current solution by changing the 1st component of the current solution. If a new solution is better than the current solution, the new solution is chosen, and it is considered the current solution. Otherwise, the new solution is discarded. This task repeats until l^{th} component is considered, where l is the length of collective members [11]. The consensus found by the basic algorithm depends on the initial consensus, and it can get stuck in local optima [12, 13]. This issue limits the consensus quality of this algorithm and other previous algorithms.

In this study, we focus on overcoming local optima [14, 15]. In OLS1 algorithm, firstly the basic algorithm is used to determine one consensus that is considered the current solution. Then it repeats a preset number of following tasks: (1) transforming the current solution to a new solution by randomly changing values of some components of the current solution, (2) choosing the better solution, and considering it as the current solution. OLS2 algorithm keeps track of k initial consensuses instead of one initial consensus in the first approach. The consensus of the collective is the best solution from consensuses of k initial consensuses. Experimental results show that the consensus quality generated by these two algorithms is at least 2.05% higher than that by the basic algorithm, and their running time is acceptable.

The remainder of this work is constructed as follows. Section 2 introduces the related work, followed by the discussion of basic notions in Sect. 3. The proposed approaches are introduced in Sect. 4. Experimental outcomes and evaluation are presented in Sect. 5, before finally presenting overall conclusions in Sect. 6.

2 Related Work

Consensus problem is studied in various areas, such as computer sciences [16], economics [17], bioinformatics [18]. In computer sciences, this problem and its applications have been studied for a long time [19, 20], and it has received increasing attention from computer scientists nowadays because of the development of Internet of Things [21], and blockchain that is considered a novel distributed consensus scheme [22]. Three main methods are proposed to solve this problem in the literature: axiomatic, constructive, and optimization.

The axiomatic method, initiated by Arrow, uses axioms to specify the conditions for consensus or consensus choice functions. Arrow presents seven conditions to determine consensus functions [23]. In [5], Nguyen proposes ten postulates for consensus choice functions: Unanimity (Un), Reliability (Re), Consistency (Co), Simplification (Si), General consistency (Gc), Quasi-unanimity (Qu), Proportion (Pr), Condorcet consistency (Cc), 1-Optimality, and 2-Optimality. It does not exist any consensus choice function meets all postulates contemporarily. In these postulates, postulates 1-Optimality and 2-Optimality are very important because fulfilling one of these two postulates means fulfilling major postulates. In general, no consensus choice function simultaneously fulfills both postulates 1-Optimality and 2-Optimality. A consensus function satisfying the postulate 2satisfies postulates Si, Re, Qu, Co, Pr and Cc, and a consensus function satisfying the postulate 2-Optimality meets postulates Si, Re, Qu, Co, Pr and Cc [5].

In the constructive method, to resolve the consensus problem, we need to define macrostructure and microstructure of a universe U of objects. Macrostructure is a relation between elements, such as distance function, preference relation. The microstructure is the structure of elements [5, 24].

The optimization method solves the consensus problem basing on optimality rules. They are Condorcet's optimality, maximal similarity rules, and global optimality [5].

Heuristic algorithms have proposed to find the 2-Optimality consensus of a collective containing binary vectors. The basic algorithm, termed algorithm H1, is first introduced. Next, based on the algorithm H1, algorithms H2 and H3 are suggested for this task [11]. The time complexity of these three algorithms is $O(nl^2)$. Experimental results show that H1 is quicker than H2 and H3 by 3.8% and 3.71%, respectively. Besides, the difference between the consensus quality of these three algorithms is not statistically significant. A heuristic algorithm basing on the vertical partition and the basic algorithm is introduced in [25]. Its time complexity is also $O(nl^2)$. The difference between the consensus quality of this algorithm and the basic algorithm is not statistically meaningful.

Gen 1 and Gen 2 are genetic algorithms [11]. The algorithm Gen 1 applies a roulette wheel selection and a fitness function $f(x) = \frac{1}{\delta(x,X)+1}$. The algorithm Gen 1 applies a tournament selection and the fitness function $f(x) = \delta(x, X)$. From the analysis of experimental results, the consensus quality of the algorithm Gen 1 is lower than that of the algorithms Gen 2 and basic by 1.43% and 1.34%, respectively. The consensus quality of the algorithm Gen 2 is 0.1% higher than that of the basic algorithm. The basic algorithm is quicker than the algorithms Gen 1 and Gen 2 by 99.47%, 99.56%, respectively. Algorithms Gen 1 and Gen 2 are not feasible because of their time performances. Only consensus quality of the algorithm Gen 2 is 0.1% higher than that of the basic algorithm, but the algorithm Gen 2 is not feasible [11].

3   Basic Notions

By symbol U we denote a finite set of objects describing all possible knowledge states for a given problem. Symbol 2^U denotes the set of all subsets of U. Let $\prod_p (U)$ denote the set of all p-element subsets with repetitions of set U for $p \in \mathbb{N}$, ($\mathbb{N}$ is the set of natural numbers), and let

$$\prod(U) = \bigcup_{p \in \mathbb{N}} \prod_p (U)$$

Thus, $\prod(U)$ is the finite set of all nonempty subsets with repetitions of set U. Each set $X \in \prod(U)$ is reckoned as a collective, and each element $x \in X$ describes the knowledge state of a collective member [1] [5].

The members of set U have two structures. The microstructure represents the structure of the members of U, for example, n-tree, binary vector, and linear order [5]. The macrostructure of the set U is a distance function $\delta : U \times U \rightarrow [0, 1]$, which meets the following conditions: nonnegative, reflexive, and symmetrical. A consensus choice function in space (U, δ) indicates a function

$$C : \prod(U) \rightarrow 2^U$$

For a collective $X \in \prod(U)$, the set $C(X)$ is termed the representation of X, and $c \in C(X)$ is termed a consensus of collective X [5].

Let Con(U) denote the set of all consensus choice functions in space (U, δ).

Definition 1. *For a given collective* $X \in \Pi(U)$, *a consensus choice function* $C \in Con(U)$ *satisfies the postulate of 2-Optimality iff*

$$\left(c \in C(X) \Rightarrow \delta^2(c, X) = \min_{y \in U} \delta^2(y, X) \right)$$

The postulate 2-Optimality requires the sum of the squared distances from a consensus to the collective elements to be minimal.

If U is a finite set of binary vectors with length l, set U has 2^l elements.

Definition 2. *A collective containing binary vectors* $X \in \Pi(U)$ *is defined as*

$$X = \{x_1, x_2, \ldots, x_n\}$$

where each x_i $(i = 1, 2, \ldots, n)$ is a binary vector with a length of m.

Each element x_i is represented as

$$x_i = \left(x_i^1, x_i^2, \ldots, x_i^l \right), x_i^k = \{0, 1\}, k = 1, 2, \ldots, l.$$

4 Proposed Approach

Determining consensus satisfying the postulate 2-Optimality of a collective X containing binary vectors is an NP-hard problem. The search space [12, 13] includes 2^l elements. The computational complexity of the brute-force algorithm to determine the optimal consensus is $O(n2^l)$; thus, this algorithm is not practical. Heuristic algorithms are proposed to solve this problem.

The sum of squared distances between a candidate solution cs_t to members of the collective X is described as

$$\delta^2(cs_t, X) = \sum_{i=1}^{n} \left(\sum_{k=1}^{l} \left| cs_t^k - x_i^k \right| \right)^2$$

Candidate solution cs_t is better than candidate solution cs_e if $\delta^2(cs_t, X) < \delta^2(cs_e, X)$. We try to find a solution to minimize the value of $\delta^2(cs_t, X)$.

The basic algorithm is a local search algorithm [12]. It starts from one solution and evolves that solution into a mostly better and better solution. In step initialization, the basic algorithm generates randomly one initial solution, called the current solution $cs_{current}$. In step 1, a new solution cs_{new} is created by changing the 1st component of the current solution. If $\delta^2(cs_{new}, X) < \delta^2(cs_{current}, X)$, the new solution is chosen, and it is considered the current solution. Otherwise, the new solution is discarded.... Similarity, in step l, a new solution cs_{new} is created by changing the lth component of the current solution. If $\delta^2(cs_{new}, X) < \delta^2(cs_{current}, X)$, the new solution is chosen, and it is considered the current solution. Otherwise, the new solution cs_{new} is discarded.

After step l, the current solution $cs_{current}$ is the consensus of the collective X.

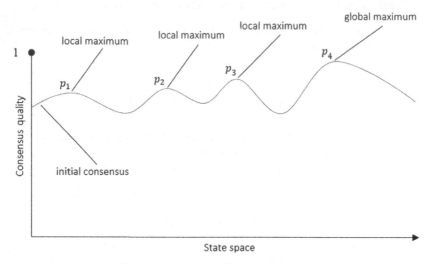

Fig. 1. State space and consensus quality

The consensus determined by the basic algorithm can be the best solution in a bad region. For example, in Fig. 1, p_1, p_2 and p_3 are local maximums, and p_4 is the global maximum of the consensus quality. Note that value the global maximum of the consensus quality is equal to 1. Suppose that $p_1 < p_2 < p_3 < p_4 = 1$. The basic algorithm can obtain a local maximum value which depends on the initial consensus. For example, with an initial consensus in Fig. 1, the basic algorithm can generate a consensus quality of p_1. In other words, this algorithm can stop at the first local optima. Thus, overcoming local maxima is essential to increase consensus quality.

In the OLS1 algorithm, the basic algorithm is first used to find a consensus that is called the current consensus $cs_{current}$. This consensus is often a local maximum, and even it can be the best solution in a bad region. In order to overcome local optima, this algorithm repeats a preset number t following tasks:

It creates a new consensus cs_{new} by changing randomly values of some components of the current consensus $cs_{current}$.

- If $\delta^2(cs_{new}, X) < \delta^2(cs_{current}, X)$, the new consensus is chosen, and it is considered the current consensus: $cs_{current} = cs_{new}$.
- If $\delta^2(cs_{new}, X) \geq \delta^2(cs_{current}, X)$, it discards the change.

The algorithm is presented as follows:

Algorithm. OLS1

  Input: $X = \{x_1, x_2, ... x_n\}$
  Output: 2-Optimality consensus
BEGIN
 1. Randomly generating $cs_{current}$ //initial consensus
 2. For $i = 1$ to l do
 3. Begin
 4. $cs_{new} = cs_{current}$
 5. $cs_{new}^i = cs_{current}^i \oplus 1$
 6.   If $\delta^2(cs_{new}, X) < \delta^2(cs_{current}, X)$ then
 7. $cs_{current} = cs_{new}$
 8. End
  //repeating t times
 9. For $j = 1$ to t do
 10. Begin
 11. cs_{new} is generated by randomly changing values
     of some components of $cs_{current}$
 12.   If $\delta^2(cs_{new}, X) < \delta^2(cs_{current}, X)$ then
 13. $cs_{current} = cs_{new}$
 14. End
 15. Return $cs_{current}$
END

The computational complexity of lines $\{1\}$, $\{4\}$, $\{5\}$, $\{6\}$, $\{7\}$, $\{12\}$, $\{13\}$, and $\{15\}$ are $O(l)$, $O(l)$, $O(l)$, $O(nl^2)$, $O(l)$, $O(mnl^2)$, $O(m)$, and $O(1)$, respectively. We have $max\ \{O(l),\ O(l),\ O(l),\ O(nl^2),\ O(l),\ (tnl^2),\ O(t),\ O(1)\}$ is $O(tnl^2)$. Thus, the computational complexity of the algorithm OLS1 is $O(tnl^2)$. In which, t is the number times of randomly changing the current consensus and users can choose the value of t.

OLS2 algorithm keeps track of many initial consensuses to avoid local optima. It generates k initial consensuses randomly. For each initial consensus, the algorithm generates one consensus of the collective X. A set of k consensuses generated from k initial consensus is created. The consensus of the collective generated by OLS2 is the best solution from this set.

The algorithm is presented as follows:

Algorithm. OLS2

Input: $X = \{x_1, x_2, \ldots x_n\}$
            m: number of initial consensuses
Output: 2-Optimality consensus
BEGIN
1. $CT = \{\}$
2. For $p = 1$ to m do
3.   Begin
4.   Randomly generating $cs_{current}$ //initial consensus
5.   For $i = 1$ to l do
6.   Begin
7. $cs_{new} = cs_{current}$
8. $cs_{new}^i = cs_{current}^i \oplus 1$
10.   If $\delta^2(cs_{new}, X) < \delta^2(cs_{current}, X)$ then
11. $cs_{current} = cs_{new}$
12.   End
13. $CT = CT \cup \{cs_{current}\}$
14.   End
15. Choosing $cs_* \in CT$ satisfying: $\delta^2(cs_*, X) = \min_{y \in CT} \delta^2(y, X)$
16. Return cs_*
END

It is similar to the analysis of the previous algorithm, the computational complexity of the algorithm OLS2 is $O(mnl^2)$, in which m is the number of initial consensuses, and we can choose the value of m.

5   Experiments and Evaluation

In this section, the two proposed approaches are evaluated through experiments. These two approaches are evaluated in two aspects: consensus quality and time performance. The basic algorithm is the most common algorithm to determine the consensus of a collective containing binary vectors; thus, the two approaches are compared to the basic algorithm. Besides, we need to compare the efficiency of two proposed approaches. This work uses a value of 0.05 as the desired significant level.

The quality of the consensus generated by a heuristic algorithm is calculated as the following:

$$Q_u(c, X) = 1 - \frac{\left| \delta^2(c, X) - \delta^2(c_*, X) \right|}{\delta^2(c_*, X)}$$

where $\delta^2(c_*, X)$ is the sum of squared distances from optimal consensus c_* to collective members, and $\delta^2(c, X)$ is the sum of squared distances from the consensus c of the heuristic algorithm to collective members.

5.1 Consensus Quality

Dataset was randomly generated. It comprises 15 collectives, sizes of collectives are shown in Table 1, and the length of collective members is 20. The basic algorithm, OLS1 algorithm, and OLS2 algorithm run on this dataset. The number for iteration in the OLS1 algorithm and the number of initial consensuses in the OLS2 algorithm is 50. Their consensus quality is presented in Table 1. The Shapiro-Wilk test is utilized to ascertain the distribution of three samples. The results indicated that these samples are not normal distributions.

Table 1. Consensus quality of the algorithms basic, OLS1, and OLS2.

Collective size	Quality of consensus		
	Basic algorithm	OLS1 algorithm	OLS2 algorithm
300	0.97622	1.00000	1.00000
350	0.98122	0.99760	0.99877
400	0.97988	0.99905	1.00000
450	0.97945	0.99903	1.00000
500	0.98266	0.99884	1.00000
550	0.97897	0.99848	1.00000
600	0.97928	0.99891	1.00000
650	0.97056	0.99888	0.99997
700	0.97969	0.99923	1.00000
750	0.97973	0.99877	1.00000
800	0.97850	0.99891	0.99998
850	0.97021	0.99922	1.00000
900	0.97562	0.99890	1.00000
950	0.98313	0.99905	1.00000
1,000	0.98028	0.99856	0.99972

The hypothesis to compare consensus quality of three algorithms is stated as the following:

- H_0: Consensus quality of the three algorithms is equal.
- H_1: Consensus quality of the three algorithms is not equal.

Because the samples are not a normal distribution, we use the Kruskal-Wallis test for this task. The *p-value* is smaller than the significant level, it indicates strong evidence against the null hypothesis. Therefore, the null hypothesis H_0 is rejected, and the alternative hypothesis H_1 is accepted. In other words, consensus quality of the three algorithms is not equal. Medians of samples are compared in pairs. The consensus quality of the OLS1 algorithm is 2.05% higher than the consensus quality of the basic algorithm. The consensus quality of the OLS2 algorithm is higher than that of the OLS1 algorithm and the basic algorithm 0.1% and 2.15%, respectively.

5.2 Running Time

This experiment aims to analyze and compare the running times of these fourth algorithms. Dataset was randomly created. It contains 15 collectives, and their sizes are detailed in Table 2. The length of the collective member is 20. The algorithms OLS1, OLS2, basic, and brute-force execute with this dataset. Running time of these algorithms is described in Table 2.

The Shapiro-Wilk test is utilized to ascertain the distribution of four samples. Because their $p - value > \alpha$, we can conclude that the samples follow a normal distribution. In order to compare the time performance of these algorithms, hypotheses are stated as the following:

- H_0: Running time of the four algorithms is equal.
- H_1: Running time of the four algorithms is not equal.

Table 2. Consensus quality of the algorithms brute-force, basic, OLS1, and OLS2.

Collective size	Running time			
	Brute-force	Basic	OLS1	OLS2
300	86.858	0.0102	0.0181	0.092
350	99.989	0.0118	0.0203	0.107
400	115.746	0.0120	0.0232	0.122
450	130.226	0.0140	0.0260	0.137
500	148.178	0.0151	0.0290	0.155
550	157.463	0.0160	0.0318	0.167
600	169.945	0.0180	0.0346	0.182
650	183.088	0.0190	0.0365	0.198
700	196.214	0.0200	0.0390	0.214
750	210.520	0.0210	0.0435	0.234
800	224.199	0.0230	0.0457	0.241
850	239.242	0.0240	0.0471	0.257
900	257.820	0.0250	0.0514	0.275
950	267.640	0.0261	0.0515	0.286
1,000	315.668	0.0275	0.0546	0.292

Because samples follow a normal distribution, we used the one-way ANOVA for this test. The *p-value* is smaller than the significant level, it means that the null hypothesis H_0 is rejected. In other words, the running time of the four algorithms is not equal. The variances are unequal, the Tamhane's T2 post hoc test was utilized.

The result shows that the basic algorithm, OLS1 algorithm, and OLS2 algorithm are 99.99%, 99.98%, and 99.89% faster than the brute-force algorithm, respectively. The basic algorithm is 81.33% and 90.45% more quickly than the OLS1 algorithm and OLS2 algorithm, respectively. The OLS1 algorithm is 48.81% faster than the OLS2 algorithm. Algorithms OLS1 and OLS2 are practical because their running times are acceptable.

6   Conclusions

In this study, we propose two approaches to overcome local optima for determining the 2-Optimality consensus of collectives containing binary vectors. The first algorithm keeps track of one initial consensus, and the second algorithm keeps track of many initial consensuses. The experimental results show that the consensus quality of these approaches is at least 2.05% higher than that of the basic algorithm. Besides, the two algorithms are practical because their running times are acceptable.

In the future, we will investigate to improve the consensus quality of other structures, such as n-tree, incomplete ordered partitions, non-ordered partitions.

Acknowledgment. This research was supported by the National Research Foundation of Korea (NRF) grant funded by the BK21PLUS Program (22A20130012009).

References

1. Nguyen, N.T.: Processing inconsistency of knowledge in determining knowledge of a collective. Cybern. Syst. **40**, 670–688 (2009)
2. Knorn, S., Chen, Z., Member, S., Middleton, R.H.: Overview: collective control of multiagent systems. IEEE Trans. Control Netw. Syst. **3**(4), 334–347 (2016)
3. Juszczyszyn, K., et al.: Agent-based approach for distributed intrusion detection system design. In: Alexandrov, V.N., van Albada, G.D., Sloot, P.M.A., Dongarra, J. (eds.) ICCS 2006. LNCS, vol. 3993, pp. 224–231. Springer, Heidelberg (2006). https://doi.org/10.1007/11758532_31
4. Wu, T., Liu, X., Qin, J., Herrera, F.: Consensus evolution networks: a consensus reaching tool for managing consensus thresholds in group decision making. Inf. Fus. **52**, 375–388 (2019)
5. Nguyen, N.T.: Advanced Methods for Inconsistent Knowledge Management. Springer, London (2008). https://doi.org/10.1007/978-1-84628-889-0
6. Nguyen, N.T.: Inconsistency of knowledge and collective intelligence. Cybern. Syst. **39**(6), 542–562 (2008)
7. Griva, A., Bardaki, C., Pramatari, K., Papakiriakopoulos, D.: Retail business analytics: customer visit segmentation using market basket data. Expert Syst. Appl. **100**, 1–16 (2018)
8. Fagiolini, A., Bicchi, A.: On the robust synthesis of logical consensus algorithms for distributed intrusion detection. Automatica **49**(8), 2339–2350 (2013)

9. Pira, M.L., Inturri, G., Ignaccolo, M., Pluchino, A.: Analysis of AHP methods and the pairwise majority rule (PMR) for collective preference rankings of sustainable mobility solutions. Transp. Res. Procedia **10**, 777–787 (2015)
10. Lezzhov, A.A., Atabekova, A.K., Tolstyko, E.A., Lazareva, E.A.: RNA phloem transport mediated by pre-miRNA and viral tRNA-like structures. Plant Sci. **284**, 99–107 (2019)
11. Kozierkiewicz, A., Sitarczyk, M.: Heuristic algorithms for 2-optimality consensus determination. In: Nguyen, N.T., Hoang, D.H., Hong, T.-P., Pham, H., Trawiński, B. (eds.) ACIIDS 2018. LNCS (LNAI), vol. 10751, pp. 48–58. Springer, Cham (2018). https://doi.org/10.1007/978-3-319-75417-8_5
12. Michiels, W., Aarts, E., Jan, K.: Theoretical Aspects of Local Search. Springer, Berlin (2007). https://doi.org/10.1007/978-3-540-35854-1
13. Rossi, F., Beek, P.V., Walsh, T.: Handbook of Constraint Programming. Elsevier, Amsterdam (2006)
14. Michalewicz, Z., Fogel, D.B.: How to Solve it: Modern Heuristics. Springer, Berlin (2004). https://doi.org/10.1007/978-3-662-07807-5
15. Oliveto, P.S., et al.: How to escape local optima in black box optimisation: When non-elitism outperforms elitism. Algorithmica **80**(5), 1604–1633 (2018)
16. Dang, D.T., Nguyen, N.T., Hwang, D.: Multi-step consensus: an effective approach for determining consensus in large collectives. Cybern. Syst. **50**(2), 208–229 (2019)
17. Zhang, Y., et al.: Consensus-based ranking of multivalued objects: a generalized Borda count approach. IEEE Trans. Knowl. Data Eng. **26**(1), 83–96 (2014)
18. Tsai, M., Blelloch, G., Ravi, R., Schwartz, R.: A Consensus tree approach for reconstructing human evolutionary history and detecting population substructure. IEEE/ACM Trans. Comput. Biol. Bioinf. **8**(8), 918–928 (2011)
19. Olfati-saber, B.R., Fax, J.A., Murray, R.M.: Consensus and cooperation in networked multi-agent systems. Proc. IEEE **95**(1), 215–233 (2007)
20. Uddin, M.N., Duong, T.H., Nguyen, N.T., Qi, X.M., Jo, G.S.: Semantic similarity measures for enhancing information retrieval in folksonomies. Expert Syst. Appl. **40**(5), 1645–1653 (2013)
21. Alaslani, M., Nawab, F., Shihada, B.: Blockchain in IoT systems: End-to-end delay evaluation. IEEE Internet Things J. **6**(5), 8332–8344 (2019)
22. Zhang, R., Xue, R., Liu, L.: Security and privacy on blockchain. ACM Comput. Surv. **51**(3), 1–34 (2019)
23. Arrow, K.J.: Social Choice and Individual Values. Wiley, New York (1963)
24. Nguyen, N.T.: Using consensus methods for solving conflicts of data in distributed systems. In: Hlaváč, V., Jeffery, K.G., Wiedermann, J. (eds.) SOFSEM 2000. LNCS, vol. 1963, pp. 411–419. Springer, Heidelberg (2000). https://doi.org/10.1007/3-540-44411-4_30
25. Dang, D.T., Nguyen, N.T., Hwang, D.: A new heuristic algorithm for 2-Optimality consensus determination. In: 2019 IEEE International Conference on Systems, Man and Cybernetics (SMC), pp. 70–75 (2019)

Fundamentals of Generalized and Extended Graph-Based Structural Modeling

Marcin Jodłowiec$^{(\boxtimes)}$ ⓘ, Marek Krótkiewicz ⓘ, and Piotr Zabawa ⓘ

Department of Applied Informatics, Wrocław University of Science and Technology,
Wybrzeże Stanisława Wyspiańskiego 27, 50-370 Wrocław, Poland
{marcin.jodlowiec,marek.krotkiewicz,piotr.zabawa}@pwr.edu.pl

Abstract. The subject of the paper is connected to defining data structures, which are or can be used in metamodeling and modeling disciplines. A new and general notion of Extended Graph Generalization has been introduced. This notion enables to represent arbitrarily complex such the structures. A way of introducing constraints, which allows to reduce this general form to any well known structure has been introduced as well. As the result of the extension and generalization mechanisms applied to the original graph definition any form of graph generalization exceeding well-known structures can be defined. Moreover, the way of associating any form of data to each such structure has been defined. Notions introduced in the paper are intended to be used while defining novel family of metamodels.

Keywords: Graph · Hypergraph · Multigraph · Data modeling · Graph generalization · Graph extension · Metamodeling

1 Introduction

The paper is dedicated to the subject of defining abstract structures in the context of data modeling. These structures are or may be apllied in the disciplines of data modeling, knowledge representation as well as defining modeling languages and models in these languages. The last area is applied in software engineering and can be used for the model-driven automated generating of software systems [9]. In the software engineering domain there are some commonly known standards, which are continuously developed by the Object Management Group (OMG), like the Meta-Object Facility (MOF), Unified Modeling Language (UML) and the remaining standards, which support the approach to the software development processes contained in the concept of the Model-Driven Architecture (MDA) [11]. The approaches and standards mentioned above are based on the graph notion in its basic version, which limits the full use of the complete potential of the modeling as long as the basic data structures are used.

A graph is composed of the two fundamental semantic categories: Vertex – a connected element and Edge – a connecting element. The Vertex type elements

ⓒ Springer Nature Switzerland AG 2020
N. T. Nguyen et al. (Eds.): ICCCI 2020, LNAI 12496, pp. 27–41, 2020.
https://doi.org/10.1007/978-3-030-63007-2_3

have the only ability to be connected, while the Edge type elements have the only ability to connect the Vertex type elements. In the case of the classical, primal graph an Edge may connect exactly two Vertex type elements. This concept has been developed and reached many solutions. There are many concepts of structural world representations, which are known from the scientific literature like graphs and hypergraphs [3,13] and scientific research dedicated to the more general structures, like ubergraphs [6] is carried out. These structures are needed for modeling phenomena not only in the field of information systems but also in many different areas (see e.g. [10]). This research forms a deep groundwork for elaborating tools and standards used for data modeling [4]. The structures, which are more general than graphs are also applicable for the problems connected to data modeling like e.g. constructing intermediate models used for the transformations of data models expressed in different metamodels [2].

In contrast to the approaches, which just adapt existing formalisms or extend them, in this work it was decided to make a systematization of the extensions and generalizations needed at modeling through the proposing a new approach to the graph-based modeling. As the result of observations made when defining own metamodels the authors came into conclusion that the graph notion is too simple (in the semantic sense) and it should be generalized to reduce some important limitations as well as extend to some extra elements, which allow for enriching the graph semantics. The graph notion is however a very good starting point for developing generalizations and extensions mentioned above. An extended and generalized structure, which is common for many concepts cited above is presented in the paper. It may form a basis for constructing arbitrary data structures applicable in the computer science. A decomposition of the identified features of the proposed structure into generalizations and extensions is also introduced in the paper. The introduced concept assumes a far-reaching flexibiliy with regard to configuring meta-structures through the flexible choice of particular generalizations and extensions. With this approach it is possible to create the whole family of meta-structures adapted to the specific needs. The defined solution covers also the known concepts like *graph, mutligraph, hypergraph, ubergraph* reducing them to the one, coherent, complementary, universal form, which in turn has important additional features.

The required general graph structure named *Extended Graph Generalization* (EGG) is introduced and defined in the paper, first with the help of a set theory based formal definition contrasted with analogical graph definition and then - with the abstract syntax expressed in the UML together with the constraints specified in both natural language and in the Object Constraint Language (OCL). The semantics of abstract syntax elements is also specified in natural language. Moreover, the concrete syntax is introduced to allow defining EGG in a graphical form. The EGG application is presented on the example of interrelationships in a social network.

2   Formal Definitions

The following section shows formal definition of a graph and extended and generalized *Extended Graph Generalization* structure proposed hereby. A graph has been defined in a standard way, focusing on its two fundamental sets: Vertex, Edge.

Definition 1. *A graph G is an ordered pair of a set V of vertices and a set E of edges. It is written as:*

$$G = (V, E), \tag{1}$$

where

$$|V| = n, \ n \in \mathbb{N}^+, \ |E| = m, \ m \in \mathbb{N}. \tag{2}$$

Each edge $e \in \mathbb{N}$

$$e = \{v_a, v_b\}, \ |e| = 2 \tag{3}$$

is such the multiset of vertices

$$v_a, v_b \in V, \ 1 \le a, b \le n. \tag{4}$$

Analogously to *graph*, a *multi-graph* is defined as an ordered pair of a set V of vertices and a *multiset* E of edges.

The EGG structure comprise all the extensions and generalizations proposed for a Graph. The EGG definition has been supplemented by a unique identifier *id*. It is essential for distinguishing Vertex, Edge and EGG instances.

Definition 2. *An Extended Graph Generalization EGG is an id, tuple of a set V of vertices, a set E of edges, set of nested Extended Graph Generalizations EGG^N, and set D of data. It is written as:*

$$EGG = (id, V, E, EGG^N, D), \tag{5}$$

where id is a unique identifier,

$$|V| = n_V, \ n_V \in \mathbb{N}, \tag{6}$$

$$|E| = n_E, \ n_E \in \mathbb{N}, \tag{7}$$

$$|EGG^N| = n_{EGG}, \ n_{EGG} \in \mathbb{N}, \tag{8}$$

$$n_V + n_E + n_{EGG} \ge 0. \tag{9}$$

Each vertex $v \in V$ is a tuple of an id, and a set of data D_v:

$$v = (id, D_v). \tag{10}$$

Each edge $e \in E$ is a tuple of an id, a multiset C_e of connection tuples, and a set of data D_e:

$$e = (id, C_e, D_e), \tag{11}$$

where

$$C_e = \{(\mu_a, \theta_a), (\mu_b, \theta_b), (\mu_c, \theta_c), \ldots\}, \; |C_e| \geq 0, \tag{12}$$

where

$$\mu_a, \mu_b, \mu_c, \ldots \in V \cup E \cup EGG^N, \tag{13}$$

$$\theta_a, \theta_b, \theta_c, \ldots \in \{EdgeToElement, ElementToEdge, Bidirectional\}. \tag{14}$$

EdgeToElement, ElementToEdge, Bidirectional represent direction of naviga-tion i.e. possibility of traversing from one EGG element to another. $\mu_a, \mu_b, \mu_c, \ldots$ represent elements of EGG i.e. vertices, edges and nested Extended Graph Gen-eralizations. For the sake of brevity, it was assumed that: $EdgeToElement \equiv \rightarrow$, $ElementToEdge \equiv \leftarrow$ and $Bidirectional \equiv \leftrightarrow$.
      Set D of data:

$$D = \{d_x, d_y, d_z, \ldots\}, \; |D| \geq 0. \tag{15}$$

   Each of $d_x, d_y, d_z, \ldots$ is an abstract concept which represents data with any internal structure.

3 *Extended Graph Generalization* Abstract Syntax

The abstract syntax of *Extended Graph Generalization* expressed in UML 2.5.1 and OCL 2.4 is presented on Fig. 1. The fact that *Extended Graph Generalization* is the set of entities of **Element** abstract type belongs to its most important features. According to the polymorphism concept each **Element** type entity is of exactly one type: **Vertex**, **Edge** or **EGG**. Moreover, each **Element** type entity may contain a set of an arbitrary number of abstract **Data** type entities.
   Generalization-related constraints:

- NOT HYPER **[nH]** – the connection arity limit, which must be = 2; the multi-plicity constraint 2 for the connection property belonging to **Edge**
  `context Edge inv: self.connection -> size() = 2`
- NOT ULTRA **[nU]** – connecting other connections excluded; no generalization between **Edge** and abstract category **Element**
- NOT MULTI **[nM]** – the elements cannot be multiply connected by the same connecting element; the uniqueness of **connection** property elements in the **Edge**
  `context Edge inv: self.connection -> isUnique(e : Element | e.id)`
- NOT SHARED AGGREGATION **[nS]** – **Element** type entities may belong to exactly one **EGG**; the shared aggregation end in the association between **Graph** and **Element** has the multiplicity constraint equal to 1
             `context Element inv: self.graph -> size() = 1`

   The EGG is presented formally in Sect. 2, while in Sect. 3 the *Extended Graph Generalizations* abstract syntax is shown. In both cases a convention based on the complete EGG form that is the one having all generalizations and exten-sions is assumed. As the result, both approaches are possible: adding particular generalizations and extensions to the fundamental **Graph** structure like SHARED

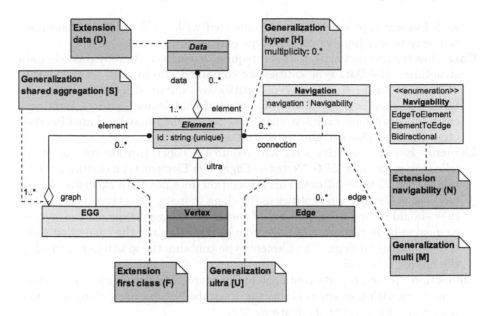

Fig. 1. *Extended Graph Generalization* abstract syntax expressed in UML 2.5.1 and OCL 2.4

AGGREGATION or adding their negations marking the exclusions of a particular generalization or extension from the complete EGG like NOT SHARED AGGREGATION.

EGG   constitutes a set of the Element abstract type entities. The set may be empty, which means that an EGG having no elements may exist. It is also important that each Element entity must belong to at least one EGG entity and it may belong to many EGG entities as well. It guaranties realization of the SHARED AGGREGATION feature. The EGG itself is an Element specialization, which provides the possibility of nesting the Graph type entities. In the consequence, the EGG constitutes the FIRST CLASS semantic category (first class citizen) [12] in the EGG, which in turn means that EGG as well as Vertex and Edge can be connected using Edge.

Vertex   is the Element abstract type specialization. Vertex is a first class category in EGG and Vertex, EGG, and Edge can be connected using Edge.

Edge   is the Element abstract type specialization, which guaranties realization of the ULTRA feature. According to [1] the Edge is of the same importance in representing data structures as the Vertex is. It has the connection property, which joins Element abstract type entities. Edge may contain any number of elements, which provides the realization of HYPER feature. The case in which Edge does not join any Element type entity is also allowed. There is no limit for joining the same elements many times by the connection property, which in turn corresponds to the fature specified as MULTI. In other words, each Element type entity may be connected with the help of the connection property by any number of Edge type entities.

Data   has the abstract type, that is it requires a concretization by concrete data structures. The Data type entities are contained also in abstract type entity Element. It means that Data type entities are contained in such entities like EGG, Vertex or Edge. It should be remarked that being a part of Data type entity does not have exclusive character, that is thay may be shared between other entities. This category provides DATA feature.

Element   has abstract character and requires a concretization by one of the following structures: EGG, Vertex or Edge. The Element type entities are contained in EGG type entities. This association does not have exclusive character, that is Element type entities may belong to many EGG type entities while they should belong to at least one of them. The Element type entities may be connected by any number of Edge type entities through the connection property belonging to Edge. The Element type contains the id attribute, which is the unique text chain.

connection   is the property contained in Edge type. The association class, which joins Edge with Element contains the Navigability type *navigation* attribute. It provides the NAVIGABLE feature.

4   *Extended Graph Generalization* Features

The basic, classical *graph* (1) has connected element and connecting element and for the purpose of discussion in the paper it constitutes the basic structure, the basis and fundament for other generalizations and extensions. A set of generalizations and extensions being the essence of the *Extended Graph Generalization* is presented below.

Generalization is a removal of constrains existing in Graph while *extension* is an addition of new elements to the Graph, i.e. the EGG as a new semantic category, Data and Navigability.

Generalizations:

- HYPER (**H**): the lack of the limit on the connection arity, which may be ≥ 0. Realized by the 0..∗ multiplicity constraint for the connection property belonging to the Edge.
- ULTRA (**U**): the possibility of joining different connections. Realized by the generalization between the Edge and the Element abstract category. It is related to the 12, 13 i 14 expressions in the formal definition.
- MULTI (**M**): the elements may be connected multiple times by the same connecting element. Realized by the lack of the constraint to the uniqueness of the connection property elements in the Edge. It is related to the statement that E is a multiset.
- SHARED AGGREGATION (**S**): the Element entities may belong to more than one EGG. This feature is represented by the shared aggregation end of the association between the EGG and the Element having the multiplicity constraint defined as 1..∗.

Extensions:

- FIRST CLASS (**F**): EGG becomes the first-class semantic category that is it exists as an independent entity and it may be a connected element anologically to the Vertex and Edge type elements.
- DATA (**D**): the EGG type elements, Vertex and Edge may contain data sets represented by the Data abstract semantic category. In the formal definition the *Extended Graph Generalization* is related to the (5, 10, 11, 15) expressions.
- NAVIGABLE (**N**): the connecting elements have the navigability property, which makes it possible to add extra constraints in the scope of the possibility of traversing from one EGG element to another. This feature is realized by the association class between the Edge and the Element. In the formal definition of EGG it is related to the (11) and (12) expressions.

Constraints:

- *acycled* (**A**): acyclic – the constraint, which makes the structure acyclic,
- *planar* (**P**): planar – the constraint, which makes the structure planar.

Many constrains may be defined, but they do not constitute the basis for modifying the basic EGG structure, as they only put additional constraints on the chosen form of the EGG.

5   *Extended Graph Generalization* Semantics

Element it is the abstract structure, which represents one of the following elements: EGG, Vertex, Edge. It has the *id* attribute, which is responsible for the uniqueness of the identifiers of the mentioned above semantic categories. Moreover, the Data element is associated to this category, which means that each element inheriting from the Element category may have a set of data.

EGG it is a recursive structure, i.e. the EGG may be composed of other EGG type structures. This is a first-class element, i.e. it may exist as an independent entity, including the possibility of containing other elements and it may be joined by the Edge on a pair with the Vertex and the Edge. The EGG itself does not have any defined semantics, because it is a universal structure dedicated to constructing the data models.

Vertex it is an element, which may be independent, but always in an EGG as well as in the connection realized by the Edge. From the semantic point of view the Vertex is a connected element and it is its only responsibility.

Edge is a connecting element and it is its main responsibility. But it may also have the responsibility of the connected element.

Data is an abstract element responsible for representing data. Data may have a simple form, e.g labels or simple values or a more complicated form. Data has abstract character and the definition of the data structure inside Data is out of the scope of the *Extended Graph Generalization* definition. Data is not independent entity, i.e. it has supplementary role for EGG, Vertex and Edge. Data may be shared between different elements.

connection constitutes a property of the association between the Edge and the abstract Element entity. It groups the Element type entities within a concrete Edge type entity. From the semantic point of view it joins elements, which are in an association represented by the Edge.

6   *Extended Graph Generalization* Concrete Syntax

Vertex is represented by a circle with the *id* placed inside or close to it (Fig. 2). The $\bigcirc id$ lub $id : Vertex$ symbols are introduced to unify formal notation.

Fig. 2. Graphical representation of Vertex

Edge is represented by a diamond with the *id* placed inside or close to it (Fig. 3). The $\Diamond id$ lub $id : Edge$ symbols are introduced to unify formal notation.

Fig. 3. Graphical representation of Edge

connection of diagram elements, that is a particular Edge with other element or with itself is represented by a solid line joining a particular Edge with a joined element. The small filled dot is placed at the end which is at Edge side. In the case of navigability its direction is determined by an arrow or arrows (Fig. 4). The $\bullet\!\!-$ symbol and symbols taking into account navigability $\bullet\!\!\rightarrow$, $\bullet\!\!\leftarrow$, $\bullet\!\!\leftrightarrow$ are introduced to unify formal notation.

Fig. 4. Graphical representation of connection

Figure 5 illustrates three EGG elements, namely Edge, connection and Vertex and it shows the following examples of joining Edge with Vertex: $\Diamond edge \bullet\!\!\rightarrow \bigcirc vertex$ as well as two Edge type elements: $\Diamond edge \bullet\!\!\rightarrow \Diamond edge$.

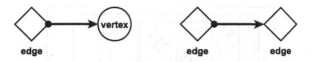

Fig. 5. Graphical representation of Edge, connection and Vertex

EGG   is represented by a rectangle with the corners rounded. An EGG g_0 and three nested EGGs: g_1, g_2, g_3 are depicted on Fig. 6. EGGs are independent each of other. EGG g_1 i g_2 share with g_3 some area. As the result, the situation where some Edge and Vertex are shared by these EGGs can be illustrated.

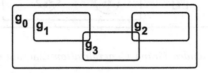

Fig. 6. Graphical representation of EGGs

Data   is represented by a rectangle. The Data d_1 is shown on Fig. 7.

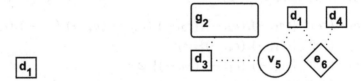

Fig. 7. Graphical representation of Data   **Fig. 8.** Graphical representation of connected Data

Data is associated to to EGG, Edge or Vertex with the help of a dotted line (Fig. 8).

Both color and character format do not have any meaning for the grammar.

6.1   *Extended Graph Generalization* Diagram Example

An example EGG$_{\text{FDN}}^{\text{HUMS}}$ symbolized by g_0 and expressed in the graphical concrete syntax is presented on Fig. 9.

The diagram from Fig. 9 is also presented in the form of formal symbolic notation.

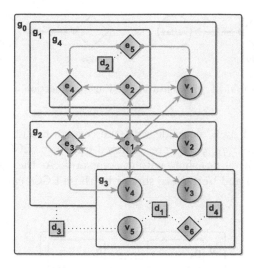

Fig. 9. *Extended Graph Generalization* diagram example

$g_0 = (\text{``}g0\text{''}, \varnothing, \varnothing, \{g_1, g_2, g_3\}, \varnothing);$    $v_1 = (\text{``}v1\text{''}, \varnothing);$

$g_1 = (\text{``}g1\text{''}, \{v_1\}, \varnothing, \{g_4\}, \varnothing);$    $v_2 = (\text{``}v2\text{''}, \varnothing);$

$g_2 = (\text{``}g2\text{''}, \{v_2, v_3, v_4\}, \{e_1, e_3\}, \varnothing, \{d_3\});$    $v_3 = (\text{``}v3\text{''}, \varnothing);$

$g_3 = (\text{``}g3\text{''}, \{v_3, v_4, v_5\}, \{e_6\}, \varnothing, \varnothing);$    $v_4 = (\text{``}v4\text{''}, \{d_1\});$

$g_4 = (\text{``}g4\text{''}, \varnothing, \{e_2, e_4, e_5\}, \varnothing, \varnothing).$    $v_5 = (\text{``}v5\text{''}, \{d_1, d_3\}).$

$e_1 = (\text{``}e1\text{''}, \{(v_1, \rightarrow), (v_2, \rightarrow), (v_2, \rightarrow), (v_3, \rightarrow), (v_4, \rightarrow), (e_2, \rightarrow), (e_3, \leftrightarrow)\}, \varnothing);$

$e_2 = (\text{``}e2\text{''}, \{(v_1, \rightarrow), (e_4, \rightarrow)\}, \varnothing);$

$c_3 = (\text{``}c3\text{''}, \{(v_4, \rightarrow), (c_1, \leftarrow), (c_3, \rightarrow)\}, \varnothing);$

$e_4 = (\text{``}e4\text{''}, \{(g_2, \rightarrow)\}, \varnothing);$

$e_5 = (\text{``}e5\text{''}, \{(v_1, \rightarrow), (e_4, \rightarrow)\}, \{d2\}).$

7 A Social Network Model Example Expressed in the EGG Categories

A domain example of the EGG structures usage for representing social networks is shown in order to present the concept introduced in the paper. The way the examples are presented illustrates how the addition of subsequent features (generalizations and extensions) allows to represent the subsequent relationship kinds. The role of vertices is played in the examples by persons, while the role of edges – the connections between them. Figure 10 shows EGG, which is semantically equivalent to the graph structure. A structure, which represents mutual bi-directed inter-personal relationships *is friend of* is shown on the diagram.

The *chats with* relationship between persons, which talk between each other is shown on Fig. 11. The EGG^H structure was applied to express this information.

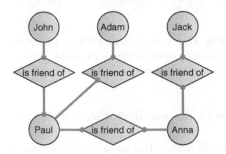

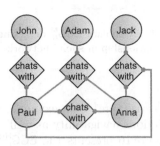

Fig. 10. Exemplary EGG depicting *is friend of* relationship in social network

Fig. 11. Exemplary EGG^H depicting *chats with* relationship in social network

Figure 12 shows a social network, which takes into account the persons grouping aspect. The subgroups can be identified inside the groups as well. In order to realize this kind of relationships the connections between connections (group – subgroup) must be applied. The EGG^{HU} structure is used for this purpose. In order to enrich this structure by data annotations, the EGG$_D^{HU}$ structure with both verticeas and edges annotations is used in the way shown on Fig. 13.

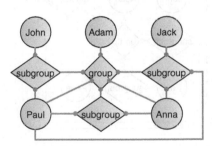

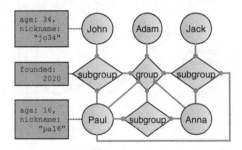

Fig. 12. Exemplary EGG^{HU} depicting *group* and *subgroup* relationship in social network

Fig. 13. Exemplary EGG$_D^{HU}$ depicting *group* and *subgroup* relationship in social network and data annotation of nodes and vertices

Some connections require the ability of connecting the same element multiple times. The *follows* relationship is an example of such the case. It is used to express that a person is interested in the events initiated by other person. However, there is no need to forbid the option of following updates to own events. Figure 14 shows how this requirement is achieved with the application of the

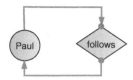

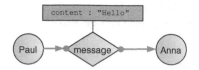

Fig. 14. Exemplary EGG_N^M depicting *follows* relationship in social network

Fig. 15. Exemplary EGG_{DN} depicting *message* relationship with data annotation in social network

EGG_N^M structure. This example, together with the one from Fig. 15 illustrates connections navigability as well.

Figure 16 presents the EGG_F^{HU} structure. It shows the relationship between a person named *Jack* in the *follows updates of* connection with EGG, which represents the network of relations followed by *Jack*. The example is extended according to the Fig. 17 to involve the EGG_F^{HUS} structure. It models the sharing some elements by persons named *Sally* and *Jack* within their followed networks.

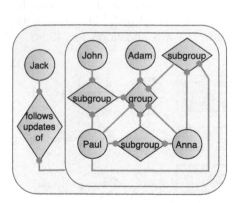

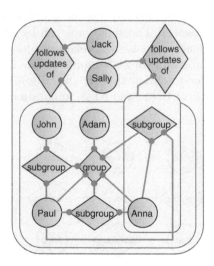

Fig. 16. Exemplary EGG_F^{HU} depicting *follows updates of* relationship between node and EGG in social network

Fig. 17. Exemplary EGG_F^{HUS} depicting *follows updates of* relationship between node and EGG in social network with shared sub-EGG

8   Conclusions

The concept, which constitutes the basis for defining contemporary known data structures has been revisited in the paper. As the analysis result, the connected element (Vertex) and the connecting element (Edge) as well as data representation element (Data) have been identified. Then, the set theory based definition (Definition 2) being a generalization of the fundamental set theory based graph definition (Definition 1) has been introduced. This generalization has been named *Extended Graph Generalization* (EGG). The notion is compliant to all known data structures. As the result of introduction of the general EGG definition all possible data structures definitions have been caught in one place. A kind of standardization has been proposed this way, which is expected to be helpful for future research work in the metamodeling and modeling domains.

Then, the abstract syntax of EGG (Definition 2) has been introduced and it has been enriched by syntactical elements semantics description. The abstract syntax and the Definition 2 are equally general. The EGG abstract syntax enables defining features like Generalizations, Extensions and Constraints. It is worth noticing that two kinds of constraints may be introduced to the abstract syntax. The first group of constraints constitutes negation of Generalizations and Extensions features and introduces structural changes to the EGG, while the second one (Constraints) has the form, which does not modify the EGG structure.

The EGG structure constitutes both generalization and extension of classical graphs and it is not possible to express it in the form of the graph without a modification of graph elements semantics. For example the ULTRA feature consisting in that the *edge* may also play the role of a connected element can be expressed with the help of a classical graph only if the Vertex semantics is changed - it should take the edge functions. Analogically, in the case of HYPER feature, where the Edge arity is greater than 2 the Edge element should be represented by nodes, which again would change the original semantics of classical graph elements. That is why the EGG is actual generalization and extension of the graph concept and not just a typical construction of more complex structures based on the graph definition. As the result, the new general EGG structure has been defined, which, together with the mentioned features, constitutes a form convenient for defining more expressive and semantically rich metamodels and models than the graph ones. The examples of such metamodels are the Association-Oriented Metamodel (AOM) [5,7] and the Context-Driven Meta-Modeling (CDMM) language [8,14,15]. Their definitions based on the EGG structure will be presented in succeeding publications.

The introduced EGG abstract syntax with semantics constitutes the basis for defining EGG concrete syntax. The semantics of its syntactical elements is identical to the semantics of their counterparts from the EGG abstract syntax. The EGG concrete syntax is general enough to apply it for representing arbitraly complex EGG structures as well as their any constraints in the uniform way. It is also universal enough for constructing EGG graphs or their particular special forms in any metamodel, including AOM and CDMM.

The need for defining own symbolic language has been shown in the paper. The graphical language introduced in the paper as a concrete syntax corresponds to the symbolic language. As the result of the possible introducing concrete syntaxes based on common abstract syntax the languages application fields can be differentiated.

A very important element of the paper is that both in the Definition 2 and in the EGG abstract syntax the clear separation between data and the structure has been introduced. Since now, the structure can be named the data carrier while data can be told to be spread on the structure. The data (Data) itself may have any form. Particularly, Data may have the EGG structure as one possible form. It is, at the same time the most general data form. This fact was not shown in the EGG abstract syntax due to the need of underlying the arbitrariness of Data and the possibility of the use of Data for representing Constraints in the EGG. As the result, Data can play two roles in the EGG. It could represent domain-specific data and/or represent information about the EGG itself, which are in turn used in Constraints. The arbitrariness of the forms and roles that could be associated to Data in the EGG abstract syntax has been underlined by making this syntactical element abstract.

References

1. Bildhauer, D.: Associations as first-class elements. In: Proceedings of the 2011 Conference on Databases and Information Systems VI: Selected Papers from the Ninth International Baltic Conference, DB&IS 2010, pp. 108–121. IOS Press, NLD (2011)
2. Boyd, M., McBrien, P.: Comparing and transforming between data models via an intermediate hypergraph data model. In: Spaccapietra, S. (ed.) Journal on Data Semantics IV. LNCS, vol. 3730, pp. 69–109. Springer, Heidelberg (2005). https://doi.org/10.1007/11603412_3
3. Bretto, A.: Hypergraph Theory: An Introduction. Mathematical Engineering. Springer, Cham (2013). https://doi.org/10.1007/978-3-319-00080-0
4. Ebert, J., Winter, A., Dahm, P., Franzke, A., Süttenbach, R.: Graph based modeling and implementation with EER/GRAL. In: Thalheim, B. (ed.) ER 1996. LNCS, vol. 1157, pp. 163–178. Springer, Heidelberg (1996). https://doi.org/10.1007/BFb0019922
5. Jodłowiec, M.: Complex relationships modeling in association-oriented database metamodel. In: Nguyen, N.T., Hoang, D.H., Hong, T.-P., Pham, H., Trawiński, B. (eds.) ACIIDS 2018. LNCS (LNAI), vol. 10752, pp. 46–56. Springer, Cham (2018). https://doi.org/10.1007/978-3-319-75420-8_5
6. Joslyn, C., Nowak, K.: Ubergraphs: A definition of a recursive hypergraph structure. arXiv preprint arXiv:1704.05547 (2017)
7. Krótkiewicz, M.: A novel inheritance mechanism for modeling knowledge representation systems. Comput. Sci. Inf. Syst. 15(1), 51–78 (2018)
8. Krótkiewicz, M., Zabawa, P.: AODB and CDMM modeling – comparative case-study. In: Nguyen, N.T., Hoang, D.H., Hong, T.-P., Pham, H., Trawiński, B. (eds.) ACIIDS 2018. LNCS (LNAI), vol. 10752, pp. 57–68. Springer, Cham (2018). https://doi.org/10.1007/978-3-319-75420-8_6

9. Luoma, J., Kelly, S., Tolvanen, J.P.: Defining domain-specific modeling languages: collected experiences. In: 4th Workshop on Domain-Specific Modeling (2004)
10. McQuade, S.T., Merrill, N.J., Piccoli, B.: Metabolic graphs, life method and the modeling of drug action on mycobacterium tuberculosis. arXiv preprint arXiv:2003.12400 (2020)
11. Mellor, S.J., Scott, K., Uhl, A., Weise, D.: MDA Distilled: Principles of Model-Driven Architecture. Addison-Wesley Professional, Boston (2004)
12. Strachey, C.: Fundamental concepts in programming languages. Higher-Order Symb. Comput. **13**(1–2), 11–49 (2000)
13. Voloshin, V.I.: Introduction to Graph and Hypergraph Theory. Nova Science Publisher, New York (2009)
14. Zabawa, P.: Meta-modeling. In: Nguyen, N.T., Hoang, D.H., Hong, T.-P., Pham, H., Trawiński, B. (eds.) ACIIDS 2018. LNCS (LNAI), vol. 10752, pp. 91–101. Springer, Cham (2018). https://doi.org/10.1007/978-3-319-75420-8_9
15. Zabawa, P., Hnatkowska, B.: CDMM-F – domain languages framework. In: Świątek, J., Borzemski, L., Wilimowska, Z. (eds.) ISAT 2017. AISC, vol. 656, pp. 263–273. Springer, Cham (2018). https://doi.org/10.1007/978-3-319-67229-8_24

Social Networks and Recommender Systems

Topic Diffusion Prediction on Bibliographic Network: New Approach with Combination Between External and Intrinsic Factors

Quang Vu Bui[1], Thi Kim Thoa Ho[2,3(✉)], and Marc Bui[3]

[1] University of Sciences, Hue University, Hue, Vietnam
buiquangvu@hueuni.edu.vn
[2] University of Education, Hue University, Hue, Vietnam
thi-kim-thoa.ho@etu.ephe.psl.eu
[3] EPHE, CHArt Laboratory, PSL Research University, EA 4004 Paris, France

Abstract. In this research, we propose a novel approach for the topic's propagation prediction on a bibliographic network with a combination of external factors and intrinsic factors. We utilize a supervised method to predict the propagation of a specific topic where combining dissimilar features with the dissimilar measuring coefficient. Firstly, we propose a new method to calculate activation probability from an active node to an inactive node based on both meta-path and textual information. This activation probability is considered as an external factor. Moreover, we exploit the author's interest in the topic, which is propagated as an intrinsic factor. Finally, we amalgamate the activation probability feature and the author's preference feature in the topic's spreading prediction. We conducted experiments on dissimilar topics of the bibliographic network dataset and have attained satisfactory results.

Keywords: Social network · Bibliographic network · Multi-relation network · Information diffusion · Activation prediction

1 Introduction

Information diffusion has been widely researched in networks, with the objective is to simulate and predict the information propagation process among objects when they connect. The information diffusion process can be described as nodes are considered *active* if they have already taken the action related to information, for instance, an author is called *active* with topic *"machine learning"* since he researched and published papers on that topic or in an iPhone marketing scenario, a customer is tagged as *active* if he purchased the product. Majority existing researches have been studied on homogeneous networks where only one type of object and one type of link exist in the network, for instance, co-author network with object author and co-author link or object user and link follow

© Springer Nature Switzerland AG 2020
N. T. Nguyen et al. (Eds.): ICCCI 2020, LNAI 12496, pp. 45–57, 2020.
https://doi.org/10.1007/978-3-030-63007-2_4

on Twitter. Nevertheless, in the real world, majority networks are heterogeneous where there are various object types and multiple relations in network, for instance, bibliographic network is a heterogeneous network where contain multiple objects, including authors, papers, venues, affiliation and so on, concurrently exist numerous relationships among authors such as co-author relation, relation with common co-author and so on. In this research, we concentrate on research information spreading in the heterogeneous network.

There are several approaches for modeling and predicting information spreading on a heterogeneous network. Firstly, diffusion process have been modeled through models including linear threshold model (LT) [5,10], independent cascade model (IC) [4], decreasing cascade model [8], general threshold model [9], heat diffusion-based model [17] and so on. With this approach, some *active* nodes will influence their *inactive* neighbors in the network and turn them into active nodes. For instance, in IC, an active node can infect an inactive node with a certain probability. In LT, an inactive node will be activated if and only if the total weight of its active neighbors is at least a threshold. There are various expanded models from IC such as Homophily Independent Cascade Diffusion (Textual-Homo-IC) [7] with infected probability is estimated based on textual information or Heterogeneous Probability Model - IC (HPM-IC) [11] where infected probability is calculated by a conditional probability based on meta-paths information. Besides, there are several expanded models of LT including Multi-Relational Linear Threshold Model - Relation Level Aggregation (MLTM-R) [6] or Probability Model-LT (HPM-LT) [11]. All the above models proposed methods to calculate the activation probability of an inactive node based on meta-paths information or textual information separately. Furthermore, they just considered influence factors from active neighbors, haven't taken into account the intrinsic factors of inactive nodes or other features, for instance, the interest level of the nodes to the topic or each node's influence and so on. Therefore, the second approach appears with the amalgamation of dissimilar features.

The second approach for predicting information propagation on a heterogeneous network is to utilize supervised learning and deep learning where exploit various features. Spreading of a tweet on Twitter has been studied with a supervised learning method [16] where utilized user's interests and content similarity between the active user and inactive user using latent topic information. Besides, information diffusion on Github has researched using supervised learning [1]. Moreover, deep learning has been used to predict information propagation on a heterogeneous network [12]. Topic diffusion on the bibliographic network has been studied with the first approach under dissimilar spreading models. Besides, that problem has been researched with the second approach under deep learning method [12], but supervised learning method has not been utilized. Therefore, in this study, we will focus on predicting topic diffusion on the bibliographic network using a supervised learning method.

In this research, we propose a new approach that amalgamates external factor and intrinsic factor in predicting topics spreading on a bibliographic network. Firstly, we consider the influence factor from active neighbors by proposing a new method for calculating infected probability from active nodes to inactive nodes based on both meta-path information and textual information. Moreover, we take into account the intrinsic factor of inactive nodes that is their interest level on a specific topic be propagated. We utilize a supervised learning framework to learn the best weights associated with extracted features. Experimental results demonstrate that new activation probability using both meta-path and textual information contributes to enhancing the performance of the topic's diffusion prediction compare with old activation probability only based on meta-path information or textual information separately. Moreover, the combination of external factor and intrinsic factor can bring higher accuracy in comparison with using one of them independently. Particularly, the amalgamation between the external factor under the new activation probability method and the intrinsic factor can obtain the highest accuracy.

Our research has the following contributions:

- Propose a new method to estimate the probability of infection as an external factor from active neighbors using both meta-path information and textual information. This new activation probability contributes to the performance enhancement of the topic's diffusion prediction.
- Exploit intrinsic factor is the author's interest level on the propagated topic.
- Apply supervised learning methods in predicting topic diffusion on the bibliographic network by combining external factor and intrinsic factor. We conducted experiments and obtained satisfying results.

2   Preliminaries

2.1   Meta-Path

A meta-path P is a path defined over the general schema of the network $T_G = (A, R)$, where A and R denote the nodes and their relations, respectively [6,11, 15]. The meta-path is denoted by $A_1 \xrightarrow{R_1} A_2 \xrightarrow{R_2} ... \xrightarrow{R_l} A_{l+1}$, where l is an index indicating the corresponding meta-path. The aggregated relationship is obtained as $R = R_1 o R_2 o ... R_l$ between A_1 and A_{l+1}, where o is the composition operator.

The length of P is the number of relations in P. Furthermore, we say a meta path is symmetric if the relation R defined by it is symmetric. For example, in the bibliographic network, the co-author relation can be described using the length-2 meta path $A \xrightarrow{\text{writing}} P \xrightarrow{\text{written-by}} A$.

A path $p = (a_1 a_2 ... a_{l+1})$ between a_1 and a_{l+1} in network G follows the meta path P, if $\forall i$, $\phi(a_i) = A_i$ and each link $e_i = \langle a_i a_{i+1} \rangle$ belongs to each relation R_i in P. We call these paths as path instances of P, which are denoted as $p \in P$.

3   Proposed Approach

In this section, we describe the details of our approach to tackling the problem of predicting active nodes for a specific topic diffusion in a bibliographic network.

This includes the description of supervised learning method for topic diffusion prediction and feature extraction.

3.1 Supervised Learning for Topic Diffusion on Bibliographic Network

We will utilize supervised learning methods for predicting topic propagation on the bibliographic network. For a topic's spreading, we predict whether an inactive author will activate with that topic in future time T_2 based on available factors of the author in the past time T_1. All nodes with published papers on our particular topic of interest are tagged as active and vice versa.

In the training stage, we firstly will sample an author's set that they haven't been active in the past period T_1, then extracting features. After that, the machine learning method will be utilized to build a training model to learn the best coefficients associated with features by maximizing the likelihood of relationship formation. In the test stage, we will apply the trained model for the test set and compare predicted accuracy with ground truth.

3.2 Activation Probability Feature

Firstly, we consider the external influential factor which is one of the reasons for infection. An inactive node can be infected from its active neighbors with a certain probability. This probability is called *activation probability, infected probability* or *propagation probability*. The activation probability from an active neighbor u to inactive node v can be identified under dissimilar methods: based on meta-path information or textual information. In this subsection, we overview methods of activation probability estimation based on meta-path information and textual information separately from previous works, then propose a new method for estimating this probability by combining that information.

Activation Probability Based on Meta-Path Information. On the one hand, the activation probability has been estimated based on similarity about meta-path information under the following methods:

PathSim: A meta-path-based similarity measure [6,15]. Given a symmetric meta path E_k corresponding relation type k, PathSim between two objects can be defined at Eq. 1:

$$s^{E_k}(u,v) = \frac{2|P^{E_k}_{(u,v)}|}{|P^{E_k}_{(u,u)}| + |P^{E_k}_{(v,v)}|} \tag{1}$$

where $P^{E_k}_{(u,u)}$ is the set of meta-paths of relation type k, starting from node u and ending at node v, and $|.|$ donates the size of the set.

Activation probability based on meta-paths and using Bayesian framework [11]:

$$P^k(u|v) = \frac{P^k_{(u,v)}}{P^k_v} = \frac{n^k_{v->u}}{\sum_{r\in nei_v} n^k_{v->r}} \tag{2}$$

$$P(u|v) = \frac{\sum_{k=1}^m \alpha_k n^k_{v->u}}{\sum_{k=1}^m \alpha_k \sum_{r\in nei_v} n^k_{v->r}} \tag{3}$$

$$P(u|\{v\}) = max_{M=1:n}(P(u|v)) \tag{4}$$

Equation (2) presents activation probability from active node v to inactive node u in meta-path k. $n^k_{v->u}$ illustrate the path instances between nodes in meta-path k. The activation probability from node v to u is demonstrated at Eq. (3) with aggregation all types of meta-paths k. Finally, we define the activation probability of an inactive node u by maximizing activation probabilities from its active neighbors v.

Activation Probability Based on Textual Information. On the other hand, the activation probability also has been estimated based on textual information [7] since it contains significant information about authors. In the bibliography network, textual information in scientific publications plays a significant role in illustrating the specific domain of researchers' works. In fact, there is a higher infected probability from the author to another in research on a particular topic if they are in narrow fields compared with the dissimilar fields. Therefore, textual information can contribute significantly in predicting topic diffusion between scientists. The textual content can be extracted from keywords of papers, titles, abstracts or full text of the papers.

Firstly, we can estimate author's information based on textual information by text mining technologies including Term Frequency – Inverse Document Frequency [14] (TFIDF) or Topic Modeling [2,13]. TF-IDF is usually utilized for text mining with a small corpus such as text is extracted from keywords or titles of papers since two drawbacks are the high dimensionality as a result of the high number of unique terms in text corpora and insufficient to capture all semantics. Therefore, topic modeling was proposed to solve these issues. Corpus is extracted from abstracts or the whole papers can be dealt with topic modeling. Recently, there are dissimilar methods of topic modeling, including Latent Dirichlet Allocation (LDA) [2], Author-Topic Model (ATM) [13], etc.

After text mining, we can use distance measures to estimate interest similarity between two nodes. For text mining with TF-IDF, we usually use cosine distance to measure similarity (see Eq. 5). For text mining with topic modeling, the output of topic modeling is probability distribution vectors. We can choose some distance measures related to the vector distance, such as Euclidean distance, Cosine Similarity, Jaccard Coefficient, etc. However, experimental results in our previous work [3] illustrated that it is better if we choose distance measures related to the probability distribution such as KullbackLeibler Divergence (see Eq. 6), Jensen-Shannon divergence (see Eq. 7), Hellinger distance (see Eq. 8), etc.

Cosine distance:

$$IS(u,v) = Cos(T_u, T_v) = \frac{T_u.T_v}{||T_u||.||T_v||} \tag{5}$$

KullbackLeibler Divergence:

$$IS(u,v) = d_{KL}(P||Q) = \sum_{x \in X} P(x)\frac{P(x)}{Q(x)} \tag{6}$$

Jensen-Shannon distance:

$$IS(u,v) = d_{JS}(P,Q) = \frac{1}{2}\sum_{i=1}^{k} p_i ln\frac{2p_i}{p_i + q_i} + \frac{1}{2}\sum_{i=1}^{k} q_i ln\frac{2q_i}{p_i + q_i} \tag{7}$$

Hellinger distance:

$$IS(u,v) = d_H(P,Q) = \frac{1}{\sqrt{2}}\sqrt{\sum_{i=1}^{k}(\sqrt{p_i} - \sqrt{q_i})^2} \tag{8}$$

where T_u, T_v are TFIDF vectors of u and v corresponding; P, Q illustrate for topic's distribution probability of two nodes u and v respectively.

Aggregated Activation Probability Based on Meta-Path and Textual Information. Meta-path and textual information were utilized for estimating activation probability, but they were used sporadically. Therefore, in this study, we propose a new method to estimate activation probability of inactive node with amalgamation meta-path information and textual information, namely aggregated activation probability (AAP):

$$AAP(u,v) = (1 - \sigma) * P(u|v) + \sigma * IS(u,v) \tag{9}$$

$$AAP(u,\{v\}) = max_{M=1:n}(AAP(u,v)) \tag{10}$$

Equation (9) illustrates for aggregated activation probability from active node v to inactive node u based on meta-path information and textual information. $P(u|v)$ is the activation probability be estimated based on meta-path information at Eq. (3) and $IS(u,v)$ present for interest similarity based on textual information, can be calculated by Eq. (5), (6), (7) or (8). σ is a parameter which controls the rates of the influence of active probability based on meta-path and interest similarity on aggregated activation probability. $\sigma \in [0,1]$, if the larger σ means that we focus on text information and vice versa.

Finally, we can define the aggregated activation probability of an inactive node u by maximizing aggregated activation probabilities from its active neighbors v (see Eq. 10).

Table 1. Feature's combination

No.	Features
1	Activation probability based on meta-path (AP(MP))
2	Activation probability based on textual information (AP(IS))
3	Aggregated activation probability (AAP(MP + IS))
4	Author's interest on topic (AI)
5	AP(MP) + AI
6	AP(IS) + AI
7	AAP(MP+IS) + AI

3.3 Author's Interest Feature

Besides external influence from neighbors, we consider the intrinsic factors of authors in predicting a topic propagation on a bibliographic network. Intrinsic factors can be the author's influence, the author's preference and so on. In this study, we concentrate on the author's preference for the topic to be propagated. Besides external influence of active neighbors, an author can activate with a topic depend on their interest on that topic. The author's preference for a topic can be formed from the different approaches through friends, articles, papers, conferences and so on. Conferences are where providing an academic forum for researchers to share their latest research findings in major areas, for instance, NIPS is a conference specializing in neural information processing systems with specific topics such as artificial intelligence, machine learning and so on. Participating conferences are opportunities to meet, discuss, cooperate, and start to research a new topic. Therefore, to estimate the interest level of a user on these topics, we propose to calculate number conferences related to the propagated topic that the author participated in.

4 Experiments and Results

4.1 Experiments

Dataset. We utilized dataset "DBLP-SIGWEB.zip" which is derived from September 17, 2015 snapshot of the dblp bibliography database. It contains all publications and authors records of 7 ACM SIGWEB conferences. The dataset also contains the authors, chairs, affiliations and additional metadata information of conferences that are published in ACM digital library.

Experimental Setting. We will consider the propagation of a specific topic T. We experiment with three topics: *Data Mining*, *Machine Learning* and *Social Network*. Firstly, we find all authors that they activate with topic T and use these authors as positive training nodes. We also sample an equal-sized of negative nodes corresponding to inactive authors. Therefore, in the training dataset, the size of the positive nodes is balanced with negative nodes.

For our experiments, we utilize classification methods as the prediction model. In training dataset, active author X activate with topic T in year y_{XT}, we extract features of X in past time period $T_1 = [1995, y_{XT} - 1]$. Besides, inactive author Y, we extract features of Y in past time period $T_1 = [1995, 2015]$. We perform experiments with different sets of features and evaluate the incremental performance improvement. These feature's combinations are shown in Table 1.

We implemented seven experiments with combination activation probability and the author's interest on the topic. The experiments (1) and (2) reveal for the old methods in calculating activation probability based on meta-path information and textual information correspondingly while (3) is the method that we propose. The experiment (4) illustrates for author's preference for the considered topic. The experiments (5), (6) and (7) demonstrate amalgamation activation probability in dissimilar calculated methods and the author's interest feature. We utilized the results of the experiment (1, 2) as baselines to compare with experiment (3), from that point on the effectiveness of the new activation probability method. Besides, the experimental results of (1, 4) (2, 4) and (3, 4) are baselines for experiments (5) (6) and (7) respectively, from that to see the significance of the author's interest feature and also the effectiveness of combination between active probability feature and the author's interest feature.

For calculating AP(MP), we utilized two meta-paths, including APA (Author-Paper-Author) and APAPA (Author-Paper-Author-Paper-Author). To calculate AP(IS), we firstly collected textual information from keywords of the author's papers in the interval T_1 and then used the Eq. (5) to estimate interest's similarity. Finally, AAP(MP+IS) is computed with parameter σ equals 0.5.

In this research, we experimented with three different classification algorithms, including Support Vector Machine (SVM, Linear Kernel), Decision Tree (DT) and Random Forest (RF). To evaluate the accuracy of the topic's diffusion prediction under the supervised learning framework, there are several common metrics, including Accuracy, ROC-AUC, Precision-Recall and so on. We chose two metrics Accuracy and ROC-AUC to evaluate the performance in which the former is the classification accuracy rate for binary prediction under the cut-off score as 0.5 and the area under ROC curve (AUC) for the latter.

4.2 Results

Experimental results demonstrated the performance of our classifiers using different sets of features showed in Table 2, 3 and 4. On the one hand, we consider the performance of the new method in estimating activation probability. For classification for topic *"Data Mining"* (Table 2), the performance of aggregated activation probability with amalgamation meta-path and textual information (AAP) is only revealed with Random Forest classifiers. However, the effectiveness of AAP is demonstrated comprehensibly in classification results on topic *"Machine Learning"* and *"Social Network"* (Table 3 and 4). For all three classification algorithms, we can see that AAP brings higher accuracy to compare with old activation probability (AP) which only based on meta-path information or textual information separately.

Table 2. Results of classification-topic: Data Mining

Features	Prediction accuracy					
	SVM		DT		RF	
	Accuracy	AUC	Accuracy	AUC	Accuracy	AUC
AP(MP)	0.609	0.704	0.623	0.639	0.609	0.694
AP(IS)	0.572	0.606	0.508	0.509	0.564	0.573
AAP(MP+IS)	0.582	0.664	0.555	0.555	**0.627**	**0.691**
AI	0.605	0.670	0.527	0.606	0.577	0.668
AP(MP)+AI	**0.636**	**0.701**	0.614	0.580	**0.618**	**0.722**
AP(IS)+AI	**0.614**	**0.703**	0.530	0.534	0.591	0.671
AAP(MP+IS)+AI	**0.632**	**0.678**	0.605	0.600	0.620	**0.730***

Table 3. Results of classification-topic: Machine Learning

Features	Prediction accuracy					
	SVM		DT		RF	
	Accuracy	AUC	Accuracy	AUC	Accuracy	AUC
AP(MP)	0.689	0.771	0.592	0.586	0.644	0.666
AP(IS)	0.668	0.753	0.511	0.511	0.567	0.716
AAP(MP+IS)	**0.690**	**0.781**	**0.661**	**0.661**	**0.667**	0.688
AI	0.611	0.708	0.568	0.596	0.589	0.680
AP(MP)+AI	**0.701**	**0.823**	0.703	0.690	0.689	0.789
AP(IS)+AI	**0.673**	**0.755**	0.569	0.589	0.715	0.787
AAP(MP+IS)+AI	**0.711**	**0.792**	**0.700**	**0.690**	**0.722***	**0.815***

On the other hand, classification results illustrated the significance of the author's interest feature and the effectiveness of amalgamation between external and intrinsic factors in topic diffusion prediction. We can see that combination feature AP(MP), AP(IS) or AAP with the author's interest in the topic (AI) almost obtained higher accuracy compare with used only AP(MP), AP(IS), AAP or AI. Especially, Random Forest with a combination of AAP and AI reached the highest accuracy for all topics. From that point out the significance of feature AI in predicting the topic's propagation. Figures 1, 2, and 3 demonstrate the performance of our Random Forest classifiers on the topics "Data Mining", "Machine Learning" and "Social Network" using different combinations of features respectively.

Table 4. Results of classification-topic: Social Network

Features	Prediction accuracy					
	SVM		DT		RF	
	Accuracy	AUC	Accuracy	AUC	Accuracy	AUC
AP(MP)	0.613	0.691	0.614	0.586	0.589	0.623
AP(IS)	0.620	0.664	0.643	0.643	0.625	0.694
AAP(MP+IS)	**0.621**	**0.686**	**0.654**	**0.654**	**0.688**	**0.695**
AI	0.650	0.681	0.609	0.633	0.621	0.682
AP(MP)+AI	**0.673**	**0.683**	0.536	0.541	**0.682**	**0.712**
AP(IS)+AI	**0.645**	**0.688**	0.623	0.623	**0.670**	**0.700**
AAP(MP+IS)+AI	**0.632**	**0.680**	**0.641**	0.629	**0.813***	**0.742***

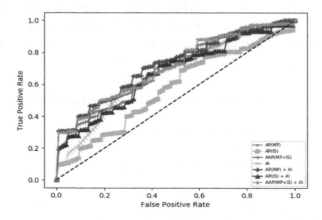

Fig. 1. ROC curve of Random Forest classifier on different feature sets for topic "Data Mining"

In these experiments, we see that the efficiency is expressed most clearly with Random Forest. Perhaps, Support Vector Machine is less sensitive to the selection of input parameters than Random Forest. Besides, Random Forest obtains typically higher accuracy than a single decision tree by two reasons that are diverse and unpruned. The diversity of trees is formed by each random forest tree in Random Forest is created from a random set of features. Additionally, while a single decision tree is often pruned, a random forest tree is fully grown and unpruned, the feature space is split into more and smaller regions.

In short, experimental results demonstrated that aggregated activation probability with amalgamation meta-path and textual information (AAP) can bring better performance in the topic's propagation prediction to compare with using old activation probability based on only meta-path or textual information separately. Moreover, the amalgamation between external factor (activation probability from active neighbors) and intrinsic factor (author's interest on-topic)

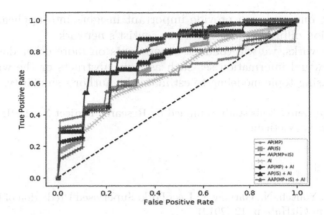

Fig. 2. ROC curve of Random Forest classifier on different feature sets for topic "Machine Learning"

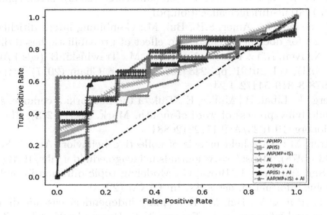

Fig. 3. ROC curve of Random Forest classifier on different feature sets for topic "Social Network"

in topic's spreading prediction on bibliographic network obtained higher accuracy compare with using the single feature. Particularly, the combination of AAP with AI for Random Forest reached the highest accuracy.

5   Conclusion and Future Work

This paper proposed a novel approach of identifying the active nodes in the diffusion of a topic in the bibliographic network. We carried out an analysis of meta-path and the textual information, from that calculating activation probability as an external factor. Furthermore, we exploited the author's preference for the topic as an intrinsic factor. We then trained a classifier using these features to classify various nodes into active or inactive for topic propagation. We believed that our work can provide important insights into applications using the information diffusion process in the scientist's network.

In future works, we will conduct experiments on more other datasets with the bigger textual information set such as from abstracts or the whole of the papers and using topic modeling to estimate the author's similarity.

Acknowledgement. This study is funded by Research Project No. DHH2020-01-164 of Hue University, Vietnam.

References

1. Akula, R., Yousefi, N., Garibay, I.: DeepFork: Supervised Prediction of Information Diffusion in GitHub, p. 12 (2019)
2. Blei, D.M., Ng, A.Y., Jordan, M.I.: Latent dirichlet allocation. In: Dietterich, T.G., Becker, S., Ghahramani, Z. (eds.) Advances in Neural Information Processing Systems, vol. 14, pp. 601–608. MIT Press, Cambridge (2002). http://papers.nips.cc/paper/2070-latent-dirichlet-allocation.pdf
3. Bui, Q.V., Sayadi, K., Amor, S.B., Bui, M.: Combining latent dirichlet allocation and k-means for documents clustering: effect of probabilistic based distance measures. In: Nguyen, N.T., Tojo, S., Nguyen, L.M., Trawiński, B. (eds.) ACIIDS 2017. LNCS (LNAI), vol. 10191, pp. 248–257. Springer, Cham (2017). https://doi.org/10.1007/978-3-319-54472-4_24
4. Goldenberg, J., Libai, B., Muller, E.: Talk of the network: a complex systems look at the underlying process of word-of-mouth. Mark. Lett. **12**(3), 211–223 (2001). https://doi.org/10.1023/A:1011122126881
5. Granovetter, M.: Threshold models of collective behavior. Am. J. Sociol. **83**(6), 1420–1443 (1978). https://www.journals.uchicago.edu/doi/abs/10.1086/226707
6. Gui, H., Sun, Y., Han, J., Brova, G.: Modeling topic diffusion in multi-relational bibliographic information networks. In: CIKM (2014)
7. Ho, T.K.T., Bui, Q.V., Bui, M.: Homophily independent cascade diffusion model based on textual information. In: Nguyen, N.T., Pimenidis, E., Khan, Z., Trawiński, B. (eds.) ICCCI 2018. LNCS (LNAI), vol. 11055, pp. 134–145. Springer, Cham (2018). https://doi.org/10.1007/978-3-319-98443-8_13
8. Kempe, D., Kleinberg, J., Tardos, É.: Influential nodes in a diffusion model for social networks. In: Caires, L., Italiano, G.F., Monteiro, L., Palamidessi, C., Yung, M. (eds.) ICALP 2005. LNCS, vol. 3580, pp. 1127–1138. Springer, Heidelberg (2005). https://doi.org/10.1007/11523468_91
9. Kempe, D., Kleinberg, J.M., Tardos, V.: Maximizing the spread of influence through a social network. In: KDD (2003)
10. Macy, M.W.: Chains of cooperation: threshold effects in collective action. Am. Sociol. Rev. **56**(6), 730–747 (1991). https://www.jstor.org/stable/2096252
11. Molaei, S., Babaei, S., Salehi, M., Jalili, M.: Information spread and topic diffusion in heterogeneous information networks. Sci. Rep. **8**(1), 1–14 (2018). https://www.nature.com/articles/s41598-018-27385-2
12. Molaei, S., Zare, H., Veisi, H.: Deep learning approach on information diffusion in heterogeneous networks. Knowl.-Based Syst., p. 105153 (2019). http://www.sciencedirect.com/science/article/pii/S0950705119305076
13. Rosen-Zvi, M., Griffiths, T., Steyvers, M., Smyth, P.: The Author-Topic Model for Authors and Documents. arXiv:1207.4169 [cs, stat] (2012)

14. Salton, G., Buckley, C.: Term-weighting approaches in automatic text retrieval. Inf. Process. Manag. **24**(5), 513–523 (1988). http://www.sciencedirect.com/science/article/pii/0306457388900210
15. Sun, Y., Han, J., Yan, X., Yu, P.S., Wu, T.: Pathsim: meta path-based top-k similarity search in heterogeneous information networks. In: VLDB 11 (2011)
16. Varshney, D., Kumar, S., Gupta, V.: Modeling information diffusion in social networks using latent topic information. In: Huang, D.-S., Bevilacqua, V., Premaratne, P. (eds.) ICIC 2014. LNCS, vol. 8588, pp. 137–148. Springer, Cham (2014). https://doi.org/10.1007/978-3-319-09333-8_16
17. Yang, H.: Mining social networks using heat diffusion processes for marketing candidates selection. ACM (2008). https://aran.library.nuigalway.ie/handle/10379/4164

Detecting the Degree of Risk in Online Market Based on Satisfaction of Twitter Users

Huyen Trang Phan[1], Van Cuong Tran[2], Ngoc Thanh Nguyen[3,4], and Dosam Hwang[1(✉)]

[1] Department of Computer Engineering, Yeungnam University, Gyeongsan, Republic of Korea
huyentrangtin@gmail.com,dosamhwang@gmail.com
[2] Faculty of Engineering and Information Technology,Quang Binh University, Dong Hoi, Vietnam
vancuongqbuni@gmail.com
[3] Department of Applied Informatics, Wroclaw University of Science and Technology, Wroclaw, Poland
[4] Faculty of Information Technology, Nguyen Tat Thanh University, Ho Chi Minh City, Vietnam
Ngoc-Thanh.Nguyen@pwr.edu.pl

Abstract. In recent years, companies have begun using social networks as a useful tool for marketing campaigns and communicating with their customers. Social networks are enormously beneficial for both sellers and buyers. For producers, the analysis of social content can provide immediate insight into people's reactions regarding products and services. Meanwhile, from such content, customers can know about products and services, and whether they are good or not. More importantly, users want to know about the degree of risk related to such products or services, which is a practical issue that needs to be resolved. Numerous studies have attempted to address this problem using a variety of methods. However, previous approaches have frequently predicted risk based on the user's satisfaction regarding a specific entity (product, service, etc.). Therefore, some information, such as the user's dissatisfaction and hesitation regarding an entity, has not yet been considered. In addition, there are very few methods for pointing out the aspects of an entity with a high degree of risk. These factors lead to low accuracy in terms of risk prediction. In this study, we introduce a method for detecting the degree of risk in an online market when considering not only the user's satisfaction but also their dissatisfaction and hesitation regarding the given entity based on tweets sentiment analysis. The results prove the efficacy of the proposed approach in terms of the F_1 score and received information.

Keywords: Tweet sentiment analysis · Risk prediction · User's satisfaction

© Springer Nature Switzerland AG 2020
N. T. Nguyen et al. (Eds.): ICCCI 2020, LNAI 12496, pp. 58–70, 2020.
https://doi.org/10.1007/978-3-030-63007-2_5

1   Introduction

Social networks have become a popular aspect of everyday life for people of all cultures and ages. Every day, millions of opinions are published on social networks, and most people willingly express their views and emotions over a particular product or topic. The viewpoints on social networks bring about enormous benefits for both sellers and buyers. Marketers can benefit tremendously from an analysis of such opinions; for instance, at the launch of a new marketing campaign, a study of social content can provide immediate insight regarding people's reactions. In addition, from such analyses, customers can learn about products and services, and whether they are good or not [15].

As the use and presence of social networking sites have grown, the amount of information available on such websites has also increased. Twitter is currently one of the most popular social networking sites [14,17]. Twitter's userbase has become overgrown, and approximately 500 million tweets are published every day[1]. According to available statistics[2], the monthly number of active users on Twitter worldwide has reached 326 million. According to eMarketer, nearly 66% of the businesses that have 100 or more employees have a Twitter account. Twitter is a source of available information, which, if we can properly exploit, will bring about numerous benefits, notably, the benefit of avoiding risk in an online market.

Various methods have been developed to automatically analyze personal reviews of products, services, events, and policies on Twitter that aim to help users avoid risk when using online buying and selling services [2,3], and [4]. However, existing methods only predict the risk based on the user's satisfaction regarding a specific entity (e.g., a product or service). Therefore, some information, such as the user's level of dissatisfaction and hesitation regarding an entity, has yet to be considered. These factors may affect the accuracy of the determination of risk related to the particular entity [11,12]. In addition, there are very few methods for indicating the aspects of an entity with a high degree of risk. These drawbacks motivated us to propose a way to detect the degree of risk in an online market based on the satisfaction of Twitter's users, with further consideration given to the user's level of dissatisfaction and hesitation. In the proposed method, a set of features related to the syntactic, lexical, semantic, and sentiment of words is first extracted. Second, tweet sentiments are determined. Third, the user's satisfaction, dissatisfaction, and hesitation are identified. Finally, the degree of risk related to the given entity is produced, and a list of aspects with a high degree of risk is determined.

2   Related Works

Many researchers have dealt with the application of a tweet sentiment analysis in solving practical problems. Claster and Cooper [5] mined more than 70 million tweets to conduct a sentiment analysis of tourism in Thailand. They filtered

---

[1] http://www.internetlivestats.com/twitter-statistics/.
[2] https://zephoria.com/twitter-statistics-top-ten/.

the messages to include only those with texts regarding Phuket or Bangkok, two important tourist areas in the country, and applied different algorithms to them. In addition, Ghiassi *et al.* [8] focused on Twitter to provide feedback to firms regarding their brands. They used supervised feature engineering and artificial neural networks, and concluded that feature representations with seven dimensions are highly effective in capturing indicators of Twitter sentiments. Other similar studies have been conducted in other contexts, including that by Amolik *et al.* [1], who dealt with reviews of upcoming Bollywood or Hollywood movies using a support vector machine and Naive Bayes. In addition, Wang *et al.* [18] worked on presidential election cycles and the sentiment of users toward them. The authors [19] built a novel domain-independent decision support model for research into customer satisfaction. This model was based on an in-depth analysis of consumer reviews posted on the Internet in natural language. Artificial intelligence techniques, such as web data extraction, sentiment analysis, aspect extraction, aspect-based sentiment analysis, and data mining have been used to analyze consumer reviews. This method evaluates customer satisfaction both qualitatively and quantitatively. The efficacy of the approach was assessed on two datasets related to hotels and banks. The results prove the efficacy of this approach for quantitative research on customer satisfaction. In addition, Phan *et al.* [16] proposed a way to support the decision-making process by combining a sentiment analysis with data mining. This method considers a set of features related to the syntactic, lexical, semantic, and sentiment aspects of the extracted words. Objects and their sentiments are then determined. Next, the results of the object sentiment analysis are converted into a Boolean value. Finally, a binary decision tree is built, and data mining is applied on this tree to estimate the significance of the objects in each topic.

From the above analysis, it can be seen that a tweet sentiment analysis can be applied through many practical applications. However, very few studies have considered detecting the degree of risk in an online market based on the satisfaction of Twitter users. In this study, we propose a method to solve this problem based not only on the user's satisfaction but also on the level of dissatisfaction and hesitation based on analyzing sentiment of tweets by combining the feature ensemble model and the convolutional neural network model.

3   Research Problem

Given a set of tweets $\mathcal{T} = \{t_1, t_2, ..., t_n\}$.

Let $\mathcal{L} = \{$ *"strong_positive"*, *"positive"*, *"neutral"*, *"negative"*, *"strong_negative"*$\}$ be a set of sentiment labels of tweets, where each tweet is assigned one label.

3.1   Definition of Tweet and Types of Tweet Sentiments

Definition 1. *A tweet t_i is a set of opinion words, emoticons, etc. to describe something regarding a subset of entities $e = \{e_i | e_i \in \mathcal{E}\}$, where $\mathcal{E}$ is the set of all entities. Each e_i can be a person, an organization, a location, a product, etc. Tweet t_i is denoted by $t = \{w_1, w_2, ..., w_m\}$.*

Definition 2. *Each tweet t can be classified into one type of sentiment, such as strong positive (SP), positive (P), neutral (Ne), negative (N), or strong negative (SN). The types of tweet sentiments (se_t) is defined as follows:*

$$se_t = \begin{cases} SP, & if(t \in T \land Lb(t) = \text{``strong\_positive''}), \\ P, & if(t \in T \land Lb(t) = \text{``positive''}), \\ Ne, & if(t \in T \land Lb(t) = \text{``neutral''}), \\ N, & if(t \in T \land Lb(t) = \text{``negative''}), \\ SN, & if(t \in T \land Lb(t) = \text{``strong\_negative''}). \end{cases} \tag{1}$$

where $Lb : T \to L$ be a mapping function that associates with every tweet t a label $Lb(t)$, called the sentiment label of tweet t.

3.2   Definition of Different Types of User Satisfaction

For $t \in T$:

let $T_{sp} = \{t | t \in T \land se_t = SP\}$ be a set of tweets with strong positive sentiment,

$T_p = \{t | t \in T \land se_t = P\}$ be a set of tweets with positive sentiment,

$T_{ne} = \{t | t \in T \land se_t = Ne\}$ be a set of tweets with neutral sentiment,

$T_n = \{t | t \in T \land se_t = N\}$ be a set of tweets with negative sentiment,

and $T_{sn} = \{t | t \in T \land se_t = SN\}$ be a set of tweets with strong negative sentiment.

Definition 3. *The user satisfaction for a specific entity, denoted by s_t, is calculated based on the strong positive and positive sentiments of users expressed through tweets. The user satisfaction s_t is defined by:*

$$s_t = \frac{Card(T_{sp}) + Card(T_p)}{Card(T)}. \tag{2}$$

Definition 4. *The user dissatisfaction for a specific entity, denoted by d_t, is calculated based on the strong negative and negative sentiments of users expressed through tweets. The user dissatisfaction s_t is computed by:*

$$d_t = \frac{Card(T_{sn}) + Card(T_n)}{Card(T)}. \tag{3}$$

Definition 5. *The user hesitation for a specific entity, denoted by h_t, is calculated based on the neutral sentiments users expressed through tweets. The user hesitation h_t through the following:*

$$h_t = \frac{Card(T_{ne})}{Card(T)}. \tag{4}$$

3.3   Definition of Different Degrees of Risk

Definition 6. *The degree of risk, denoted by d_r, is determined based on the satisfaction, hesitation, and dissatisfaction of users expressed in their tweets. The degree of risk is defined as follows:*

$$d_r = \frac{s_t - (h_t + d_t)}{s_t}. \tag{5}$$

Definition 7. *The kind of risk, denoted by k_r, is defined as follows:*

$$k_r = \begin{cases} low\ risk, & if\ 0 < d_r \leq 0.5, \\ intermediate\ risk & if\ d_r = 0, \\ high\ risk, & if\ -0.5 \leq d_r < 0. \end{cases} \tag{6}$$

Definition 8. *An aspect of an entity with a high degree of risk, which is called the high-risk aspect and denoted by a_i, is a noun in tweet t that characterizes a factor of this entity and has a high frequency of appearance. The high-risk aspect is defined as follows:*

$$a_i = \{w | tag(w) = \text{``noun''} \wedge w \in \mathcal{A} \wedge \mathcal{R}a(w) \leq \beta\}. \tag{7}$$

where $\mathcal{A}$ is a set of aspects of entity e; $\mathcal{R}a(w)$ is a mapping function from a word to a correspond ranking; β is a threshold to list the high-risk aspects.

3.4   Research Question

In this study, we endeavor to answer the following main research question: *How can we determine the degree of risk in an online market based on the level of satisfaction of Twitter users?.* This question is partitioned into the three following sub-questions:

- *Which features are extracted, and how should the sentiment of tweets be analyzed based on these features?*
- *How can we determine the level of user satisfaction, dissatisfaction, and hesitation based on their sentiment regarding a specific entity?*
- *Which aspects of a given entity have a high degree of risk?*

4   Proposed Method

In this section, we present the methodology used to implement our proposal. The workflow of the method is shown in Fig. 1.

Given a set of tweets $\mathcal{T}$ related to a given entity. Our proposed method consists of four main steps: First, the features regarding the lexical, word-type, sentiment score, semantic, and position of each word in a tweet are extracted to generate word embeddings. Second, a CNN model is used to classify the sentiment of tweets in $\mathcal{T}$ into five sets, such as strong negative tweets, negative tweets,

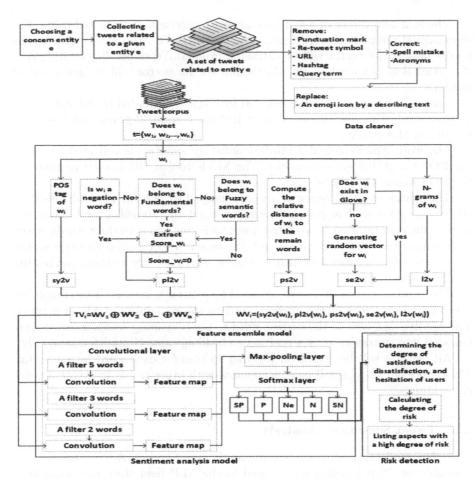

Fig. 1. Workflow of proposed method. (SP: Strong Positive; P: Positive; Ne: Neutral; N: Negative; SN: Strong Negative)

neutral tweets, positive tweets, and strong positive tweets. Third, the levels of user satisfaction, dissatisfaction, and hesitation are determined using tweet sentiments. Finally, the degree of risk related to the given entity is calculated, and the high-risk aspects are listed. The details of these steps are described in the next sub-sections.

4.1 Feature Extraction

In this study, features related to the information of a word, such as: lexical, word type, sentiment score, and semantic, are extracted and mapped into the vectors [13]. The steps used to identify and apply the features are explained as follows:

The semantic vector of a word, denoted by $se2v(w_i)$, is extracted using 300-dimensional pre-trained word embeddings from GloVe[3]. If a word exists in the GloVe dataset, its vector will be extracted from GloVe embeddings. Otherwise, if a word does not exist in the GloVe dataset, its vector will be generated at random.

The lexical vector of a word, denoted by $l2v(w_i)$, is created based on n-grams of this word. The n-grams of a word include 1-gram, 2-grams, and 3-grams started by this word.

The word-type vector of a word, denoted by $sy2v(w_i)$, is collected based on the POS tag of this word in tweet t. The NLTK toolkit [10] is used to annotate the POS tags of the words.

The sentiment score vector of a word, denoted by $pl2v(w_i)$, is built based on the type of word, such as positive, negative, negation, intensifier, and diminisher words. Such information is extracted using a window of one to three words before a sentiment word and through a search for these types of words. The appearance of these words in a tweet and their sentiment scores become features and feature values, respectively.

The position vector of a word, denoted by $ps2v(w_i)$, is created by computing the relative distances of the current word to the remaining words in a tweet. The relative distances of the current word to the remaining words in tweet t are encoded into vectors d_i using a position embedding table (Initialized randomly).

All features will be combined together to transfer each word into a vector. Then, all word vectors will be concatenated with other words to create a tweet embedding.

4.2 Tweet Sentiment Analysis

The CNN model is used to analyze the sentiment of tweets. A CNN has become a significant Deep learning model used in the NLP field since the research of Collobert *et al.* [6] are published and then Kim [9] who successfully applied a CNN in a sentiment analysis. The sentiment analysis model is built as the following steps:

Tweet embeddings layer: Each tweet will be represented by a vector $T2V$:

$$T2V_{1:n} \in \mathcal{R}^{d \times n} \wedge T2V_{1:n} = v_1 \oplus v_2 \oplus v_3 \oplus ... \oplus v_n \tag{8}$$

where $\oplus$ is the concatenation operator, d is the demension of v_i, v_i is i-th word vector, $v_i = l2v(w_i) \oplus se2v(w_i) \oplus sy2v(w_i) \oplus pl2v(w_i) \oplus ps2v(w_i)$.

Convolutional layer: This layer aims to create a feature map (c) from the tweet embedding layer. The feature map is created by using a window of length q words from i to $i + q - 1$ to slide and filter important features. Each time sliding of the window creates a new feature vector as follows:

$$c_i = \mathcal{R}e\mathcal{L}\mathcal{U}(\mathcal{M}.T2V_{i:i+q-1} + b) \tag{9}$$

---

[3] http://nlp.stanford.edu/projects/glove/.

where $ReLU$ is a rectified linear function. b is a bias term. $M \in R^{h \times qd}$ is a transition matrix created for each filter, h is the number of hidden units in the convolutional layer. Therefore, when a tweet is slided completely, the features map is generated as follows:

$$c = [c_1, c_2, .., c_{d-q+1}], c \in R^{d-q+1} \tag{10}$$

Max-pooling layer: The primary function of the max-pooling layer is to reduce the dimensional of the feature map by taking the maximum value $\hat{c} = max(c)$ as the feature corresponding to each filter. Assume that we use m filters, after this step the obtained new feature is $\hat{c} = [\hat{c}_1, \hat{c}_2, .., \hat{c}_m]$. Then this vector is fed into next layer.

Softmax layer: This layer uses a fully connected layer to adjust the sentiment characteristic of the input layer, and predict tweet sentiment polarity by using Softmax function as follows:

$$y = softmax(M\hat{c} + b) \tag{11}$$

where M is a transition matrix of Softmax layer.

The hyperparameters of the CNN model is presented in Table 1.

Table 1. Hyperparameters for CNN model

Hyperparameters	Values
# hidden layer	3
comma-separated filter sizes	5, 3, 2
# filters	128
l_2 regularization	0.0001
# epochs	150
dropout keep probability	0.1

4.3 Determining the User Satisfaction, Dissatisfaction, and Hesitation

After the sentiments of the tweets are classified, the results will be used to compute the degree of user satisfaction for the given entity. To understand more clearly how to conduct the calculation, we apply the following example.

Example 1: Assume that we have the results of a sentiment analysis step shown in Table 2.

Table 2. Example results of tweet sentiment analysis

$Card(T_{sp})$	$Card(T_p)$	$Card(T_{ne})$	$Card(T_n)$	$Card(T_{sn})$	$Card(T)$
12	10	8	15	5	50

From the data in Table 2, we can identify the satisfaction, dissatisfaction, and hesitation of users regarding the given entity by using Eqs. (2), (3), and (4) as follows:

$$s_t = \frac{12+10}{50} = 0.44, d_t = \frac{15+5}{50} = 0.40, h_t = \frac{8}{50} = 0.16$$

Therefore, 44% of users are satisfied, 40% of users are dissatisfied, and 16% of users are hesitant when evaluating the given entity.

4.4   Calculating the Degree of Risk

Example 2: From the results of Example 1, Eqs. (5) and (6) are applied to compute the degree of risk related to the given entity.

$$d_r = \frac{0.44 - (0.40 + 0.16)}{0.44} = -0.27 \in [-0.5, 0) \rightarrow k_r = \text{``high risk''}$$

It can be seen that, from a set of tweets regarding a given entity across the proposed model, we know that there will be many potential risks when users purchase this entity online. From this, users can have a reasonable choice when they make a decision related to this entity.

5   Experiment

5.1   Data Acquisition

In this study, we use 5350 English tweets in [16] as training data. The Python package Tweepy[4] is then applied to collect 1605 English tweets regarding the Phone topic on Twitter to use as the testing data. The elements in tweets of two datasets such as punctuation marks, re-tweet symbols, URLs, hashtags, and query term are extracted and removed. Next, a describing text replaces an emoji icon in tweets by using the Python emoji package[5]. In addition, tweets are informal in which the users can use the acronyms as well as make spelling mistake. These can affect the accuracy of the result. Therefore, the Python-based Aspell library[6] is employed to implement spell correction. Then, the tweets in both training data and testing data are assigned labels, such as *strong_positive, positive, neutral, negative* and *strong_negative* by three manual annotators. We annotated the testing set as the gold standard to assess the performance. The detail of the training and testing sets is presented in Table 3.

---

[4] https://pypi.org/project/tweepy/.
[5] https://pypi.org/project/emoji/.
[6] https://pypi.org/project/aspell-python-py2/.

Table 3. Tweets statistics by annotators.

Data	Training data	Testing data
#tweets	5350	1605
#strong positive tweets	1007	303
#positive tweets	1051	316
#neutral tweets	1271	382
#negative tweets	1116	333
#strong negative tweets	905	271

5.2 Evaluation Results

The metrics used to assess the proposed method include *Precision*, *Recall*, and $\mathcal{F}_1$. The values of *Precision*, *Recall*, and $\mathcal{F}_1$ are computed as follows:

$$Precision = \frac{\mathcal{TP}}{\mathcal{TP} + \mathcal{FP}} \tag{12}$$

$$Recall = \frac{\mathcal{TP}}{\mathcal{TP} + \mathcal{FN}} \tag{13}$$

$$\mathcal{F}_1 = 2 \times \frac{Precision \times Recall}{Precision + Recall} \tag{14}$$

where, assuming we have a given class C, $\mathcal{TP}$ (True Positive) refers to elements belonging to C and identified as belonging to C, $\mathcal{FP}$ (False Positive) refers to elements not belonging to C but classified as C, and $\mathcal{FN}$ (False Negative) is the number of elements belonging to C but not classified as C.

5.3 Results and Discussion

The results of the sentiment analysis step implemented by our system are shown in Table 4. Table 4 shows the confusion matrix of the sentiment analysis method on the tweets of nine users. Using the confusion matrix in Table 4 and Eq. 12, Eq. 13, and Eq. 14, we calculated the performance of the sentiment analysis in the tweets.

Table 4. Confusion matrix of the sentiment analysis step.

Actual		Predicted				
		strong positive	positive	neutral	negative	strong negative
	strong positive	249	33	21	0	0
	positive	23	275	18	0	0
	neutral	17	28	248	47	42
	negative	0	0	13	284	36
	strong negative	0	0	8	36	227

Table 5. Performance of the sentiment analysis step.

	strong positive	positive	neutral	negative	strong negative
TP	249	275	248	284	227
FP	40	61	60	83	78
FN	54	41	134	49	44
Precision	0.86	0.82	0.81	0.78	0.75
Recall	0.82	0.87	0.65	0.85	0.84
F_1	0.84	0.84	0.72	0.82	0.79

Looking at Table 5, we can see that the *strong positive* and *positive* classes performed better than the *negative*, *strong negative*, and *neutral* classes. Intuitively, one of the main reasons for the low performance is that the training data contain fewer tweets indicating a negative sentiment. We believe that, with the construction of a large data warehouse and a better balance between tweets indicating relevant factors, this result can be significantly improved. In addition, the algorithm used to classify the sentiment of tweets is quite good at analyzing the sentiment at a particular moment. The feature ensemble model also has a significant impact on the results of the sentiment analysis method.

In addition, To evaluate the performance of the sentiment analysis model by comparison to other methods, we conducted two more experiments on the same dataset as follows: First, we used a traditional lexicon-based approach (LBA), which means that we calculated the sentiment scores of a sentence as the mean value of the scores of its words. We then used the scaling method (SM) [7] to determine the polarity by comparing every word in the lexicon to every word in the tweet and assign the corresponding score of the word from the lexicon to the tweet, which means the tweet score will be updated by the process of summation from the scores of the words. The results of this are shown in Table 6.

Table 6. Performance comparison of the sentiment analysis step.

Method	Precision	Recall	F_1
LBA	0.70	0.72	0.71
SM	0.73	0.77	0.75
Our model	0.80	0.81	0.80

Table 6 shows that our method achieves the best results in comparison to two other methods in terms of a tweet sentiment analysis. This step is the most important in determining the performance of our model. According to our assessment, this performance was able to be achieved because the CNN model is quite a good algorithm in terms of analyzing sentiments. In addition, the extracted features also help the CNN model determine the sentiment of tweets more accurately. Using the data in Table 5, we can obtain tweet statistics similar to those in Table 7.

Table 7. Tweets statistics using the proposed method.

$Card(T_{sp})$	$Card(T_p)$	$Card(T_{ne})$	$Card(T_n)$	$Card(T_{sn})$	$Card(T)$
289	336	308	367	305	1605

From the data in Table 7, it can be seen that $d_r = -0.58 \in [-0.5, 0) \rightarrow k_r ='$ *high risk'*. This means that users should carefully consider whether they intend to buy a product or use services related to a given entity. If $\beta = 4$, four words with the POS tag "noun" and ranked as less than or equal to 4 will then be listed. These words, which are considered as the high-risk aspects, are *battery, style, GB, camera*. This means that if the users decide to buy this phone, they should check these aspects carefully.

6 Conclusion and Future Work

This work presented a generic framework for detecting the degree of risk in an online market based on a tweet sentiment analysis. The analysis results revealed that the proposed model predicts the degree of risk regarding the given entity with a significant performance. In addition, this model also provides a set of high-risk aspects. However, the main limitation of the proposed approach is that it is challenging to find a similar method to compare with our model results. Thus, the performance of the model has not been compared with other methods. In the future, we plan to find ways to compare the performance of our model with other methods to determine exactly the results of our framework.

References

1. Amolik, A., Jivane, N., Bhandari, M., Venkatesan, M.: Twitter sentiment analysis of movie reviews using machine learning techniques. Int. J. Eng. Technol. **7**(6), 1–7 (2016)
2. Casaló, L.V., Flavián, C., Guinalíu, M., Ekinci, Y.: Avoiding the dark side of positive online consumer reviews: enhancing reviews' usefulness for high risk-averse travelers. J. Bus. Res. **68**(9), 1829–1835 (2015)
3. Chang, W.L., Wang, J.Y.: Mine is yours? Using sentiment analysis to explore the degree of risk in the sharing economy. Electron. Commer. Res. Appl. **28**, 141–158 (2018)
4. Chang, Y.S., Fang, S.R.: Antecedents and distinctions between online trust and distrust: predicting high-and low-risk internet behaviors. J. Electron. Commer. Res. **14**(2), 149 (2013)

5. Claster, W.B., Cooper, M., Sallis, P.: Thailand-tourism and conflict: modeling sentiment from twitter tweets using Naïve Bayes and unsupervised artificial neural nets. In: 2010 Second International Conference on Computational Intelligence, Modelling and Simulation, pp. 89–94. IEEE (2010)
6. Collobert, R., Weston, J.: A unified architecture for natural language processing: Deep neural networks with multitask learning. In: Proceedings of the 25th International Conference on Machine learning, pp. 160–167. ACM (2008)
7. Dinakar, S., Andhale, P., Rege, M.: Sentiment analysis of social network content. In: 2015 IEEE International Conference on Information Reuse and Integration, pp. 189–192. IEEE (2015)
8. Ghiassi, M., Zimbra, D., Lee, S.: Targeted twitter sentiment analysis for brands using supervised feature engineering and the dynamic architecture for artificial neural networks. J. Manag. Inf. Syst. **33**(4), 1034–1058 (2016)
9. Kim, Y.: Convolutional neural networks for sentence classification. arXiv preprint arXiv:1408.5882 (2014)
10. Loper, E., Bird, S.: Nltk: the natural language toolkit. arXiv preprint cs/0205028 (2002)
11. Nguyen, N.T.: Using consensus methods for solving conflicts of data in distributed systems. In: Hlaváč, V., Jeffery, K.G., Wiedermann, J. (eds.) SOFSEM 2000. LNCS, vol. 1963, pp. 411–419. Springer, Heidelberg (2000). https://doi.org/10.1007/3-540-44411-4_30
12. Nguyen, N.T., Sobecki, J.: Using consensus methods to construct adaptive interfaces in multimodal web-based systems. Univ. Access Inf. Soc. **2**(4), 342–358 (2003)
13. Phan, H.T., Tran, V.C., Nguyen, N.T., Hwang, D.: Improving the performance of sentiment analysis of tweets containing fuzzy sentiment using the feature ensemble model. In: IEEE Access, p. 1 (2020)
14. Phan, H.T., Nguyen, N.T., Hwang, D.: A tweet summarization method based on maximal association rules. In: Nguyen, N.T., Pimenidis, E., Khan, Z., Trawiński, B. (eds.) ICCCI 2018. LNCS (LNAI), vol. 11055, pp. 373–382. Springer, Cham (2018). https://doi.org/10.1007/978-3-319-98443-8_34
15. Phan, H.T., Nguyen, N.T., Tran, V.C., Hwang, D.: A sentiment analysis method of objects by integrating sentiments from tweets. J. Intell. Fuzzy Syst. **37**(6), 7251–7263 (2019). https://doi.org/10.3233/JIFS-179336
16. Phan, H.T., Tran, V.C., Nguyen, N.T., Hwang, D.: Decision-making support method based on sentiment analysis of objects and binary decision tree mining. In: Wotawa, F., Friedrich, G., Pill, I., Koitz-Hristov, R., Ali, M. (eds.) IEA/AIE 2019. LNCS (LNAI), vol. 11606, pp. 753–767. Springer, Cham (2019). https://doi.org/10.1007/978-3-030-22999-3_64
17. Tran, V.C., Nguyen, N.T., Fujita, H., Hoang, D.T., Hwang, D.: A combination of active learning and self-learning for named entity recognition on twitter using conditional random fields. Knowl.-Based Syst. **132**, 179–187 (2017)
18. Wang, H., Can, D., Kazemzadeh, A., Bar, F., Narayanan, S.: A system for real-time twitter sentiment analysis of 2012 US presidential election cycle. In: Proceedings of the ACL 2012 System Demonstrations, pp. 115–120. Association for Computational Linguistics (2012)
19. Yussupova, N., Boyko, M., Bogdanova, D., Hilbert, A.: A decision support approach based on sentiment analysis combined with data mining for customer satisfaction research. Int. J. Adv. Intell. Syst **8**, 145–158 (2015)

Method of Detecting Bots on Social Media.
A Literature Review

Botambu Collins[1], Dinh Tuyen Hoang[1,2], Dai Tho Dang[1], and Dosam Hwang[1(✉)]

[1] Department of Computer Engineering, Yeungnam University, Gyeongsan, South Korea
botambucollins@gmail.com, hoangdinhtuyen@gmail.com,
daithodang@ynu.ac.kr, dosamhwang@gmail.com
[2] Faculty of Engineering and Information Technology,
Quang Binh University, Đồng Hới, Vietnam

Abstract. The introduction of the online social media system has unquestionably facilitated communication as well as being a prime and cheap source of information. However, despite these numerous advantages, the social media system remains a double-edged sword. Recently, the online social media ecosystem although fast becoming the primary source of information has become the medium for misinformation and other malicious attacks. These malicious attacks are further exacerbated by the use of social bots that have implacable consequences to victims. In this study, we examine the various methods employed by experts and academia to detect and curb Sybils attack. We define and explain three types of social bots such as the good, the bad and the ugly. We surmised that although the various social media giants have peddled in orthogonal techniques to uncloak and perturb Sybils activities, the adversaries are also working on a robust method to evade detection, hence, a heuristic approach including hybrid crowdsourced-machine learning technique is required to avert future attacks.

Keywords: Social bots · Bot detection · Sybil attacks · Types of bots

1 Introduction and Background

The rise in technological advancement has come as a blessing to our lives helping solve some of mankind's problems including not limited to health, economic, social as well as in the political domain [1]. Nowadays, people can take part in political processes online as well as engage in some important conferences with the aid of social media [2–4]. Citizens from certain countries where there are limited press freedom and oppressive regime can freely express their minds with the aid of social media [5]. The growing advancement of the internet and communication system is further enhanced with the introduction of online social media which has made communication not only easy [2] but has also emerged as a principal source of information owing to it less costly and easy accessibility as opposed to the traditional media. In today's contemporary society, the use of social media as a medium for information has skyrocketed [6] with Twitter and Facebook recording millions of users daily [1]. As these social media sites become

© Springer Nature Switzerland AG 2020
N. T. Nguyen et al. (Eds.): ICCCI 2020, LNAI 12496, pp. 71–83, 2020.
https://doi.org/10.1007/978-3-030-63007-2_6

increasingly popular, malicious users equally grow exponentially posing threats to honest users. World leaders and organization now uses social media as a means to give out important announcement ranging from sports club announcing the signing of a new player, government announcing relations with other states as well as an update during a crisis period.

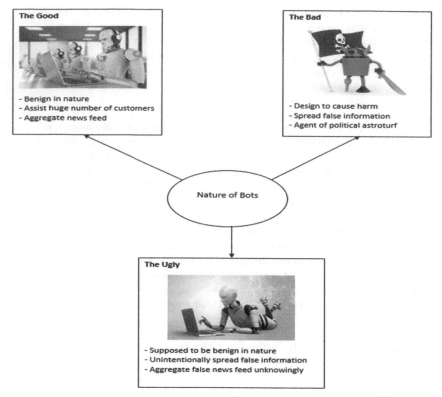

Fig. 1. Showing the nature of bots

The numerous advantages of social media as outlined above also came with a huge price, although used as a medium for information, there is a growing caveat concerning the use of the online social media amid it being a source of misinformation, malicious attacks, smear campaign, spam as well as spreading fake news. The prevalence of false contents and other malicious attack has had reverberations around the globe and mete untold damages to its victim and this is further exacerbated with the use of social bots as their automated nature give it high scalability. The use of social bots to spread false and unverified information online has not only abuse the notion of press freedom but has also affected democratic values and principles [7]. Social media play a crucial role in political campaigns [8] such as the Obama campaign during the 2008 US presidential election as well as the Trump campaign in the 2016 US election respectively [7, 9]. With the unscrupulous use of social bots, our polity is prone to having a candidate which was not chosen but was rather selected by bots. Bots are capable of enhancing both the success and failure of a political campaign [9].

Social bots have witnessed tremendous scholarly attention in recent years as they are capable of influencing public discourse in several domains such as politics including electioneering [8], public health [10]. As a result of their unhealthy nature, several methods have been proposed to detect and prevent social bots from polluting the online social media such as the use of centrality measures [11], wavelets [12], feature-based with the application of random forest [13], deep learning [5, 14].

Prior studies on various approaches to bots detection have witnessed a significant research boom, these include the work of Emilio Ferrara [15] who did an overview of bots detection models on social media by getting an insight into how bots are created while assessing some method of tracking them. Some authors focus on reviewing the general risk that online social media users are prone to face [16]. Furthermore, Sheharbano Khattak and colleagues [3] shed light upon the taxonomy of botnets. This method focus on giving an appraisal of the actions of botnets and how they operate. An analogous survey of bots detection techniques includes the work of Arzum Karataş and Serap Şahin [2] who examined vividly 3 main detection approaches such as the social network-based approach, crowdsourced-based as well as machine learning-based method which is geared towards gaining insight into bots detection models. Contrary to our work, we examine several models including expert model, the behavioral pattern approach as well as graphical modeling and we further examine the nature bots by gaining insights into their modus vivendi which is critical in any attempt to uncloak Sybils activities on social media.

Couple to the above, Bhise and Kamble [17] examine some literature on methods of mitigating Sybils attack. The authors did a general approach and give attention to network aspects such as wireless sensor networks as well as mobile application network. In contrast to us, we focus only on social media with users spanning hundreds of millions daily. In addition to our method, we focus only on those detection models which have proven to be successful by citing a working example rather than just a narrative approach.

The goal of this study is to examine social bots as tools use in spreading malicious propaganda which has invariably affected our online social media ecosystem negatively. For instance, Sneha Kudugunta and Emilio Ferrara [5] alluded that bots affected our online community negatively such as to "sway political elections by distorting online discourse, to manipulate the stock market, or to push anti vaccine conspiracy theories that may have caused health epidemics". In so doing, we discuss some models proposed in detecting and curbing the actions of these bots. The rest of this paper is organized as follows: Sect. 2 includes examining the type of social bots, while in Sect. 3 we elucidate on the various detective models, in Sect. 4, we shed light on the issues raised and open challenges and we made our concluding remarks in Sect. 5.

2 Type of Bots

Those who developed bots at the first did so with good intention to solve growing customer challenges faced within companies and brands where humans cannot respond to customers' inquiries within the appropriate time due to the voluminous nature of queries that some companies receive within a short time. Social bots, social cyborg or Sybil dates back to 1950 during the Alan Turing era in [7] such as chatbot which depicts an algorithm design to hold a conversation with humans. Conflict arises when bots are being use with evil intention. The work in [36] depicts a typical conflict situation between diverse views and there is need for consensus [35] to be reached. Yang and colleagues [18] opine that Sybils occurs when a malicious user creates multiple fake identities [19], to unfairly increase their power and influence within a target community. Social bots are social media accounts that are run by computer algorithms and they mimic real users [1, 7]. Some bots are benign in nature [7] such as those that automatically aggregate useful content from diverse sources like news feed, automatic response to inquiries by customers in their large volumes which is difficult to be done manually by humans. In the domain of speech recognition [20], benign bots also assist in automatic response to audio messages, give direction to customers as well as outline detail information regarding products or brand. The work of Perez-Soler et al. [6] focused on the benign nature of bot by modeling bot that can assist in processing messages through Natural Language. Given the good nature of bots described above, Ferrara et al. [7] argue that they are two categories of bots in which we have included the third category as seen in Fig. 1 above, the good bots or those which are benign in nature herein referred to as "the good" It is specifically designed out of goodwill but contrary it can also be harmful since it doesn't have the capacity to verify information as well as other content before sharing them. Even those in charge of automatically aggregating news content also aggregate fake contents unintentionally since it is a bot, it will eventually act like a bot and consequently, it also contributes to spreading untrue and false information unknowingly and in this situation, we refer to this type of bot as "the ugly".

The third category of bots involves those that are designed specifically for the purpose to harm and cause havoc within the social media ecosystem. We refer to it as "the bad" indicating those bots which spread false contents and unverified information online to influence public opinions as well as engage in smearing and character assassination [7, 21]. Ferrara and colleagues [7] posit that these "bad" bots cause chaos by manipulating social media discourse such as "misleading, exploiting, manipulating as well as spreading rumors, spam, malware, misinformation, slander" [7], and hence, tracking and curbing their activities becomes the ultimate goal of this study.

3 Method of Detecting Social Bots

The perennial nature of Sybils attacks has impelled some prominent social media firms including but not limited to Facebook, Twitter, Renren Inc, to work on orthogonal techniques to deal with Sybils attack, however, these models are ad-hoc as users are still prone to malicious attacks and these adversaries are also working tirelessly to come up with robust attacking techniques.

The introduction of these social media has not been for so long but the recurrent nature of Sybils attack has paved the way for researchers and other stakeholders to find a suitable solution in which users can evade malicious attacks. Social media has contributed to the acquisition of knowledge but problem may also occur when these

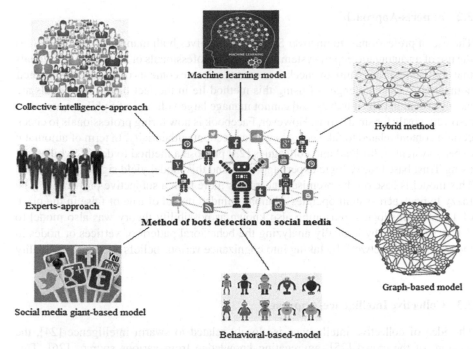

Fig. 2. Models of detecting Bots on social media

generated knowledge are inconsistent [34]. In the following paragraph, we will discuss vividly varied dynamic models aim at curbing social bots as well as uncloaking Sybils attacks on social media as seen in Fig. 2 above.

3.1 Social Media Giant Model

Almost all the online social media sites have developed and peddled in their own defense system that protects its users from possible malicious attacks. The Facebook Immune System [22] is a novel example by the social media giant to deal with Sybils attack by vividly giving a critique of their system performance, this help to boost some trust and confidence within its users but at the same time will help the attacker to develop different measures of bypassing it since every detail of the defense mechanism is available in the public sphere. The system model the social network into a graph and apply a heuristic approach in defending the graph against attacks, the social graph has information about users and attacker tries to steal information from users or act as creepers [22], if an account is compromised, it is returned to its real user. The users or accounts are the nodes or vertices and the Sybils also appear as nodes which makes it difficult to track reason being that attackers relate with other nodes as legitimate users. The success of a single algorithm or classifier is not the main tenet of the Facebook Immune System rather a combination of many classifiers such as random forests, Support Vector Machines, logistic regression as well as gradient boosting.

3.2   Experts-Approach

The use of professionals to uncover Sybils here involves both manual experts as well as the use of an automatic expert system. Experts are professionals or a group of individuals that companies usually hire to check the veracity of some contents or users to ensure their authenticity. The challenges of using this method lie in the fact that professionals are usually small in their numbers and cannot manage large volumes of Sybil accounts and also very costly for small firms. However, Facebook is now hiring professionals to check certain content related to fake news as well as account authenticity. In term of automatic experts system, Aditi Paul and colleagues [23] propose a method to detect Sybil attack using Trust based fuzzy logic expert approach and this model yield significant success. This model is base on the premise that trust is more than a subjective probability. The fuzzy logic expert system operates a human-minded model of true or false in the place of 1 and 0, this logical reasoning also known as possibility theory was also model to detect Sybil node by logically analyzing the behavioral pattern of vertices or nodes in the social media network by taking into cognizance various beliefs and trait personality [23].

3.3   Collective Intelligence-Approach

The idea of collective intelligence is closely related to swarm intelligence [24], the wisdom of the crowd [25], aggregating knowledge from various sources [26]. This approach seeks to get diverse and collective knowledge regarding an important and complex problem and it is base on the notion that the collective intelligence or efforts of groups yield better fruit than that of any single individual. James Surowiecki [25] opined that under a conducive atmosphere, the crowd is wiser than the smartest person in the society. Levy [27] surmises a widely accepted definition of collective intelligence as he alluded that "collective intelligence is groups of individuals doing things collectively that seem intelligent". This intelligent nature of the group has proven to aid in the milieu of Sybil tracking as individuals act autonomously from diverse backgrounds to predict if a user is Sybil or not. Gang Wang [28] is one of the authors to apply the wisdom of the crowd approach to detect Sybil. The author applies the collective knowledge of both experts, as well as "Turkers", hired from the AMT to detect Sybils on Facebook and Renren network and the result prove to be highly accurate as it indicates a significant correlation between experts as well the crowds.

3.4   Machine Learning Model

Early bots were very naïve in nature and perform literally just one function by generating and posting contents, this type could be easily detected by simply examining the volumes and nature of information posted within a short time. James Schnebly and Shamik Sengupta [29] championed a Random Forest machine-learning algorithm to track bot on Twitter and they observe that social bots have the potential to alter trending issues on social media by actively engaging in large volumes of retweeting. Using datasets from the Institute of Informatics and Telematics which include a list of hybrid crowdsourced as well as machine authentic bots accounts that are used to spread malicious content, their result got an exponential 90.25% accuracy rate. Ratkiewicz and colleagues [9] pioneered the method to detect and track political abuses on social media and they got a tremendous accuracy rate of 96%. The study is base on the premise that online social media such as Twitter play a very crucial role in grassroots mobilization during a political campaign to give useful information regarding party manifesto as well as policies. However, despite this, the same Twitter can also be used adversely to spread misinformation during grassroots mobilization and hence, there is a need to detect and track political abuses termed political astroturfing which is usher in through the social media. The author argues that political astroturf occurs when there is mass creation of accounts on social media including impersonation of certain users such those vying in for a political position and such accounts are used to post false and deceptive information [9], these accounts are trolls; a type of social bot control by humans. Using datasets from Twitter, they constructed a meme network graph with the user being the nodes with edges linking them together. The meme network was used to track users with several similar accounts link to the main account twitting several times to indicate that such a user is very popular. They discovered that meme account usually tweets with a link in their content prompting followers to click on such a link which has information smearing a given candidate.

3.5 Hybrid Method

The caveat of focusing on a single method remains a constellation issue. The employment of professionals, as well as crowdsourced, has not been able to perturb Sybil attack and consequently, a combination of heuristic models becomes necessary. Facebook is currently employing a hybrid-crowdsourced and automatic approach to detect social bots or Sybils account whereby users are allowed to comment or flag certain account or content as fake, once many users report or flag particular content or account, it is then passed on to a group of experts that will review such content or users and then decide on its authenticity. Furthermore, when many users flag or report a particular post, the ranking algorithm will send such content below the newsfeed of users. As a result, Facebook alluded it has suspended over 1.5 billion fake accounts just in 2018 [1]. The reason for this heuristic approach is that a service provider would preferably fail to detect a malicious or Sybil than inconvenience a real user with an erroneous account suspension [7] which is bad for business, knowing in mind that not all Sybils are harmful

3.6 Graphical Modeling to Detect Bots

The graphical modeling of social media accounts to uncloak Sybil chime in owing to the inability of the various machine learning approaches to curb Sybil attacks. With the application of a machine learning model, the adversary still finds ways to evade detection. The homophily nature of the social media online system makes graph-based a novel approach. This homophily nature of account pattern is base on the supposition that two connected accounts on social media are capable of having similar traits. Therefore an honest account link to another honest account will have a similar honest trait in nature and vice versa in terms of Sybils account. As a result, these accounts are model in a graph form considering honest nodes to refer to trusted users and Sybils to referring to untrusted accounts.

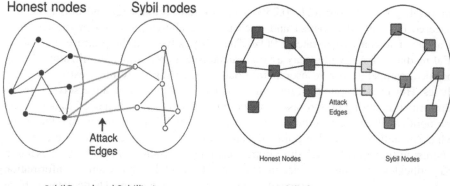

Honest nodes   Sybil nodes

Attack Edges

SybilGuard and Sybillimit   SybilInfer

Fig. 3. Illustration of social network random-walk system [31, 32]

The random-walk as opined by Qiang Cao and colleagues *SybilRank* [19], Danezis et al. *SybilInfer* [30], Yu et al. *SybilLimit* [31], and *SybilGuard* [32] respectively, holds that there exists a social network undirected graph G with user representing the nodes or vertices and they are linked together by edges E. Within this graph there exist two types of users, honest users and Sybils users between these two types of users there exist an attack edges as seen in Fig. 3 above. These attack edges are the location where the adversary will send the Sybil nodes. A set of honest nodes is then put on a sub-graph within the main graph, these honest nodes are determined by the social media meta-data which indicates that two honest nodes will have similar meta-data and dishonest nodes or Sybil will have similar meta-data. Therefore, the algorithm will perform a random-walk starting from a trusted node from point X with a probability of stopping at point Y which will normally be another honest node. If the algorithm traverses through Sybil there is also the probability that it will visit only Sybil nodes thereby pointing out dishonest nodes within the graph. It is assume that Sybils nodes are connected to each other within the network. The fundamental differences between these random-walk models are shown as seen in Table 1 below.

Table 1. Comparison of SybilGuard and Sybillimit [32]

Number of attack edges g (unknown to protocol)	SybilGuard accepts	SybilLimit accepts
$o(\sqrt{n}/\log n)$	$O(\sqrt{n}\log n)$	$O(\log n)$
$\Omega(\sqrt{n}/\log n)$ to $o(n/\log n)$	unlimited	$O(\log n)$
below $\sim 15,000$	~ 2000	~ 10
above $\sim 15,000$ and below $\sim 100,000$	unlimited	~ 10

George Danezis and Prateek Mittal [30] proposed a random-walk model to detect bots known as SybilInfer by employing a combination of methods including Bayesian inference and Monte-Carlo sampling techniques which predict a set of honest nodes and Sybil nodes. The main idea is the same as SybilGuard and Sybillimit but differs within the thresholds. It should be noted that both SybilGuard and Sybillimit are championed by the same authors [32], Sybillimit is the advanced version of the SybilGuard as postulated by Haifeng Yu et al. in [32] with differences surmised in Table 1 above. In SybilGuard there exist decentralize system which enables a vertex deemed to be honest referred to as the verifier which accept another vertex known as the suspect and accepting means that the verifier is ready to collaborate with the incoming nodes by taking a long random-walk within a particular rout whereas Sybillimit takes multiple routes within a probability that short random-walk will stay within honest nodes. SybilRank [19] is a robust system base on the features of the social network graph and label some real users as honest nodes and Sybils as dishonest, although analogous to the previously discussed methods, it was used to track down Sybils account in one of the largest popular online social networks in Spain known as Tuenti, it tries to minimize the computational complexity with an outstanding accuracy rate.

3.7 Behavioral Based-Model

The skillful action of Sybils operators has ushered in a new insight into tracking bots on social media based on the user's behavioral pattern. Everyone has a purpose of logging into their online social media sites, some just to spend time if they feel bored, while others will be chatting and exchanging messages with their friends, watching contents, as well as reading posts which are potential behavior of real and honest users of online social media sites. Yang and colleagues [18], Wang et al. [33], propounded a Sybil tracking model on Renren based on the user's behavioral pattern and observes that real user spend time doing human activities like messaging, commenting on friend's post and viewing post and media contents while bots spend a considerable time sending friend request as well as following others account and 67% of Sybils account after offline verification contains blacklisted URLs as well as banned keywords. The work of Yang et al. gave a high accuracy rate as just within 2010 and 2011 it led to the suspension of over 100,000 Sybil accounts on Renren Inc. The work of Wang [33] focuses on clickstream to uncover the behavioral nature of bots when compared to human and observes that bots have more clickstream pertaining to their goals on social media, the author contends that Sybils users have a specific goal that can be track with a series of clickstream activities while a human will have diverse clickstream.

4 Discussion and Open Challenges

The use of social media is fast becoming a double-edged sword, though being less costly and easily accessible, the social media ecosystem has witnessed a reverberation amid constant attacks from Sybils and uncloaking these malicious users remain a potent challenge. The adversary usually hides their patterns and tries to subverts all detection mechanisms. The major challenge is due to the fact that most models employ to uncloak and perturb Sybil activities on social media have their codes available online. The availability of these codes in the public arena gives the adversary the leverage to find loopholes in the process thereby employing a brute and stealthy measures that will remain opaque in our eyes as well as other means to bypass the algorithm designed to track and uncover them. The issue of privacy is not helping matters, this is one of the reasons why most of these social media giants are compelled to release their code or methods online as consumers fear that such a method may be designed to invade their privacy and hence most of these sites will rely heavily on crowdsource and human experts before automatically suspending user's account.

Another core issue here is the case of "puppet master", most of these Sybils are working for powerful and influential statesmen as well as politicians and even stock firm, therefore, these bots are deployed to work for their master meaning they are puppets and tracking these master becomes a crucial issue. The use of cyber warfare by some government as a means to foster their political quest is increasingly becoming a salient issue, research by [22] indicates that Sybil attackers are skillful and well funded. For instance, the Syrian Electronic Army that is supposedly working for the government of Assad in Syria poses a serious challenge cognizance of the fact that such agency will have enormous resources and backing. It is believed that the Internet Research Agency IRA which is a troll agency in Russia works for several officials across the globe influencing public opinions or acting as political astroturf, after the 2016 US election, twitter released a list of trolls account linked to IRA that was involved in political astroturfing against both Donald Trump and Hilary Clinton. Therefore, we can surmise that attacking the master may curb the activities of their puppets.

5   Conclusions and Future Directions

The discourse on uncovering Sybil attacks as well as other malicious activities on social media has been a challenging and complex issue. Despite the benign nature of some bots as seen in Fig. 1 above, the bad bots otherwise referred to as Sybils continue to post a serious threat to the online social media communities. Social bots, Social cyborg, trolls or Sybils activities have devastating and implacable consequences. These malicious users are capable of influencing even the stock market by spreading fake news which can hike the stock exchange or decrease its value as well which has great repercussions as was the case with the Syrian Electronic Army [7]. Although the owners of these social media giants have peddled in what is considered orthogonal techniques to deal with Sybils attack, users are still prone to a series of malicious attacks by adversaries. In this regard, we recommend that these firms employ a heuristic approach and limit the publication of their defense system to the public arena.

With respect to future work, we propose that future study is needed to examine the behavioral nature of bots by employing more crowdsourced as well as expert techniques. Also, in terms of tracking political astroturf, examining who they smear could uncloak their master.

Acknowledgment. This research was supported by the Basic Science Research Program through the National Research Foundation of Korea (NRF) funded by the Ministry of Science, ICT & Future Planning (2017R1A2B4009410), and the National Research Foundation of Korea (NRF) grant funded by the BK21PLUS Program (22A20130012009).

References

1. Yang, K., Varol, O., Davis, C.A., Ferrara, E., Flammini, A., Menczer, F.: Arming the public with artificial intelligence to counter social bots. Hum. Behav. Emerg. Technol. **1**(1), 48–61 (2019). https://doi.org/10.1002/hbe2.115
2. Karataş, A., Şahin, S.: A Review on social bot detection techniques and research directions. In: Proceedings of the International Information Security and Cryptology Conference, Turkey, no. i, pp. 156–161 (2017)
3. Khattak, S., Ramay, N.R., Khan, K.R., Syed, A.A., Khayam, S.A.: A taxonomy of botnet behavior, detection, and defense. IEEE Commun. Surv. Tutorials **16**(2), 898–924 (2014). https://doi.org/10.1109/SURV.2013.091213.00134
4. Grimme, C., Preuss, M., Adam, L., Trautmann, H.: Social bots: human-like by means of human control? Big Data **5**(4), 279–293 (2017). https://doi.org/10.1089/big.2017.0044
5. Kudugunta, S., Ferrara, E.: Deep neural networks for bot detection. Inf. Sci. (Ny) **467**, 312–322 (2018). https://doi.org/10.1016/j.ins.2018.08.019
6. Perez-Soler, S., Guerra, E., De Lara, J., Jurado, F.: The rise of the (modelling) bots: towards assisted modelling via social networks. In: ASE 2017 – Proceedings of the 32nd IEEE/ACM International Conference on Automated Software Engineering (ASE), pp. 723–728 (2017). https://doi.org/10.1109/ase.2017.8115683
7. Ferrara, E., Varol, O., Davis, C., Menczer, F., Flammini, A.: The rise of social bots. Commun. ACM **59**(7), 96–104 (2016). https://doi.org/10.1145/2818717
8. Yang, K.C., Hui, P.M., Menczer, F.: Bot electioneering volume: visualizing social bot activity during elections. In: Web Conference 2019 - Companion World Wide Web Conference WWW 2019, pp. 214–217 (2019). https://doi.org/10.1145/3308560.3316499
9. Ratkiewicz, J., Meiss, M., Conover, M., Gonçalves, B., Flammini, A., Menczer, F.: Detecting and tracking political abuse in social media. In: Proceedings of the Fifth International AAAI Conference on Weblogs and Social Media, p. 297 (2011)
10. Broniatowski, D.A., et al.: Weaponized health communication: Twitter bots and Russian trolls amplify the vaccine debate. Am. J. Public Health **108**(10), 1378–1384 (2018). https://doi.org/10.2105/AJPH.2018.304567
11. Mehrotra, A., Sarreddy, M., Singh, S.: Detection of fake Twitter followers using graph centrality measures. In: Proceedings of the 2016 2nd International Conference on Contemporary Computing and Informatics, IC3I 2016, September 2016, pp. 499–504 (2016). https://doi.org/10.1109/ic3i.2016.7918016
12. Barbon, S., et al.: Detection of human, legitimate bot, and malicious bot in online social networks based on wavelets. ACM Trans. Multimed. Comput. Commun. Appl. **14**(1s) (2018). https://doi.org/10.1145/3183506
13. Kaubiyal, J., Jain, A.K.: A feature based approach to detect fake profiles in Twitter. In: ACM International Conference Proceeding Series, pp. 135–139 (2019). https://doi.org/10.1145/336 1758.3361784
14. Luo, L., Zhang, X., Yang, X., Yang, W.: Deepbot: a deep neural network based approach for detecting Twitter Bots. IOP Conf. Ser. Mater. Sci. Eng. **719**(1) (2020). https://doi.org/10.1088/1757-899x/719/1/012063

15. Ferrara, E.: Measuring social spam and the effect of bots on information diffusion in social media. In: Lehmann, S., Ahn, Y.-Y. (eds.) Complex Spreading Phenomena in Social Systems. CSS, pp. 229–255. Springer, Cham (2018). https://doi.org/10.1007/978-3-319-77332-2_13. arXiv: 1708.08134v1

16. Fire, M., Goldschmidt, R., Elovici, Y.: Online social networks: threats and solutions. IEEE Commun. Surv. Tutor. **16**(4), 2019–2036 (2014). https://doi.org/10.1109/COMST.2014.232 1628

17. Bhise, A.M., Kamble, S.D.: Review on detection and mitigation of Sybil attack in the network. Phys. Procedia Comput. Sci. **78**, 395–401 (2016). https://doi.org/10.1016/j.procs.2016.02.080

18. Yang, Z., Wilson, C., Wang, X., Gao, T., Zhao, B.Y., Dai, Y.: Uncovering social network Sybils in the wild. ACM Trans. Knowl. Discov. Data **8**(1) (2014). https://doi.org/10.1145/ 2556609

19. Cao, Q., Sirivianos, M., Yang, X., Pregueiro, T.: Aiding the detection of fake accounts in large scale social online services. In: NSDI 2012 Proceedings of the 9th USENIX Conference on Networked Systems Design and Implementation, p. 15 (2012)

20. Lieto, A., et al.: Hello? Who am I talking to? A shallow CNN approach for human vs. bot speech classification. In: ICASSP, IEEE International Conference on Acoustics, Speech and Signal Processing - Proceedings, May 2019, pp. 2577–2581 (2019). https://doi.org/10.1109/ icassp.2019.8682743

21. Melmeti, K., Shannon, C., Asaf, V.: Visualization of the social bot's fingerprints. In: 4th International Symposium on Digital Forensics and Security, pp. 161–166 (2016)

22. Stein, T., Chen, E., Mangla, K.: Facebook immune system. In: Proceedings of the 4th Workshop on Social Network Systems, SNS 2011 (2011). https://doi.org/10.1145/1989656.198 9664

23. Paul, A., Sinha, S., Pal, S.: An efficient method to detect Sybil attack using trust based model. In: Proceedings of the International Conference on Advances in Computer Science AETACS, December 2013, pp. 228–237 (2013)

24. Glasgow, J.: Swarm intelligence: concepts, models and applications. Technical report 2012-585 (2012)

25. Surowiecki, J.: The Wisdom of Crowds, First Anch. Anchor Books, A Division of Random House Inc, New York (2004)

26. Dang, D.T., Nguyen, N.T., Hwang, D.: Multi-step consensus: an effective approach for determining consensus in large collectives. Cybern. Syst. **50**(2), 208–229 (2019). https://doi.org/ 10.1080/01969722.2019.1565117

27. Malone, T., Atlee, T., Lévy, P., Rt, T., Paul, H., Homer-dixon, T.: Collective Intelligence: Creating a Prosperous World at Peace. Earth Intelligence Network, Oakton (2008)

28. Wang, G., et al.: Social turing tests: crowdsourcing Sybil detection (2012)

29. Schnebly, J., Sengupta, S.: Random forest Twitter bot classifier. In: 2019 IEEE 9th Annual Computing and Communication Workshop and Conference CCWC 2019, pp. 506–512 (2019). http://doi.org/10.1109/CCWC.2019.8666593

30. Danezis, G.: SybilInfer: detecting Sybil nodes using social networks. In: Network and Distributed System Security Symposium (2009)

31. Yu, H., Gibbons, P.B., Kaminsky, M., Xiao, F.: SybilLimit: a near-optimal social network defense against Sybil attacks. IEEE/ACM Trans. Netw. **18**(3), 885–898 (2010). https://doi. org/10.1109/TNET.2009.2034047

32. Yu, H., Kaminsky, M., Gibbons, P.B., Flaxman, A.: SybilGuard: defending against Sybil attacks via social networks. IEEE/ACM Trans. Netw. **16**(3), 267 (2008). https://doi.org/10. 1145/1159913.1159945

33. Gang, W., Tristan, K., Christo, W., Haitao, Z., Zhao, B.Y.: You are how you click: clickstream analysis for Sybil detection. In: Proceedings of the 22nd USENIX Security Symposium, vol. 7, no. 2, pp. 95–112 (2013). https://doi.org/10.1111/j.1745-4522.2000.tb00164.x

34. Nguyen, N.T.: Advanced Methods for Inconsistent Knowledge Management. AIKP. Springer, London (2008). https://doi.org/10.1007/978-1-84628-889-0
35. Danilowicz, C., Nguyen, N.T.: Consensus-based methods for restoring consistency of replicated data. In: K'opotek et al. (eds.) Advances in Soft Computing, Proceedings of 9th International Conference on Intelligent Information Systems 2000, pp. 325–336. Physica (2000)
36. Nguyen, N.T.: Using consensus methods for solving conflicts of data in distributed systems. In: Hlaváč, V., Jeffery, K.G., Wiedermann, J. (eds.) SOFSEM 2000. LNCS, vol. 1963, pp. 411–419. Springer, Heidelberg (2000). https://doi.org/10.1007/3-540-44411-4_30

Using Interval-Valued Fuzzy Sets for Recommending Groups in E-Learning Systems

Krzysztof Myszkorowski$^{(\boxtimes)}$ (iD) and Danuta Zakrzewska (iD)

Institute of Information Technology, Lodz University of Technology,
Wolczanska 215, 90924 Lodz, Poland
{Krzysztof.Myszkorowski,Danuta.Zakrzewska}@p.lodz.pl

Abstract. To obtain required effects of Web-based learning process, teaching environment should be adjusted to student needs. Differentiation of the environment features can be received by grouping learners of similar preferences. Then each new student, who joins the community, should obtain the recommendation of the group of colleagues with similar characteristics. In the paper, we consider using fuzzy logic for modeling student groups. As the representation of each group, we assume fuzzy numbers connected with learner attributes ranked according to their cardinality. Recommendations for new students are determined taking into account similarity of their dominant features and the highest ranked attributes of groups. The presented approach is examined, for students described by learning style dimensions. The method is evaluated on the basis of experimental results obtained for data of different groups of real students.

Keywords: Recommender system · Fuzzy logic · Interval-valued fuzzy sets · Groups modeling

1 Introduction

Nowadays there is a big need of Web-based education process. However, its performance depends on the degree the learning environment is adjusted to learners needs. Dividing students into groups of similar preferences and tailoring learning resources appropriately may help to achieve assuming learning outcome. However, the group assignment of each new learner should guarantee his similarity to the members of the recommended group. Effectiveness of recommendations depends on accuracy of group modeling. However, if our knowledge concerning students' traits is imperfect one has to apply tools for describing uncertain or imprecise information. As the most consistent with human being decision making process Shakouri and Tavassoli [1] mentioned fuzzy logic methods, which are based on the fuzzy set theory [2].

A concept of a fuzzy set has been used in [3] for group recommending in e-learning systems. A fuzzy group representation has been defined with the use

© Springer Nature Switzerland AG 2020
N. T. Nguyen et al. (Eds.): ICCCI 2020, LNAI 12496, pp. 84–96, 2020.
https://doi.org/10.1007/978-3-030-63007-2_7

of linguistic terms corresponding to attribute values. The definition of fuzzy set contains a membership function which is a mapping $R \rightarrow [0,1]$. It indicates the membership grade by assigning to each element of a universe of discourse a number from the unit interval. However, in some circumstances traditional fuzzy sets (type-1 fuzzy sets) may appear an insufficient tool. Values of membership degrees are not always unique as it is required by the concept of the type-1 fuzzy set. To capture this kind of uncertainty one can apply its extension, known as an interval-valued fuzzy set, in which the membership grade is expressed by means of a closed subinterval of the interval $[0,1]$. The idea was proposed by Zadeh [4]. A place of interval-valued fuzzy sets among other extensions of the concept of fuzzy sets was shown in [5].

The current paper extends the idea presented in [3] by applying interval-valued fuzzy sets. The proposed method is examined for student traits based on their learning style dimensions. It is validated, on the basis of experiments, done for real students' clusters. The performance of the considered method is evaluated by experiments done on real student data. The results are compared with the ones obtained using traditional fuzzy sets. The remainder of the paper is organized as follows. The relevant research is described in the next section. Section 3 presents the basic notions related to interval-valued fuzzy sets. Then, the methodology for building recommendation based on probabilistic representation of groups is depicted. Section 5 discusses applying of interval-valued fuzzy sets in the considered problem. Section 6 focuses on application of the proposed methodology into attributes based on learning style dimensions. In the following section some experimental results are presented and discussed. Finally, concluding remarks and future research are outlined.

2 Related Work

Recommender systems are considered to be an important tool for improving e-learning courses. Numerous works discuss their adaptation to e-learning environments. A survey of the state-of-the-art in e-learning recommended systems was presented in [6]. Various challenges and techniques were discussed in [7]. An educational recommender system should take into account different preferences of learners and so it should be highly personalized [8]. Some authors proposed applying personal learning styles for building recommended systems [9,10]. Qomariyah and Fajar [9] implemented a system based on a logical approach. The proposed method helps students to choose the best material according to their preferences. Nafea et al. [10] elaborated a recommender algorithm for recommending personalized learning objects. Their approach is based on the Felder and Silverman learning style model [11]. Special attention was paid to using recommendations for group learning. Christodoulopoulos and Papanikolaou [12] discussed several factors that should be considered while assigning learners into groups. They investigated the choice of the best algorithms for creating student clusters. Masthoff [13] described using of group modeling and group recommendation techniques for recommending to individual users. A survey of the state-of-the-art in group recommendation was presented in [14].

In the design of e-learning systems researchers considered the use of fuzzy logic. Authors used fuzzy sets to describe reality by means of linguistic terms, which are close to human nature. Several researchers examined possibilities of using fuzzy logic for student modeling. Different aspects of the use of fuzzy techniques in e-learning were shown in [15]. Hogo [16] proposed applying fuzzy clustering methods for evaluation of e-learners behaviour. Similar analysis was presented in [17]. Limogneli and Sciarrone [18] applied fuzzy student modeling for personalization of e-learning courses. Goyal et al. [19] proposed student modeling based on learning style, personality and knowledge level which was evaluated with the use of the intuitionistic fuzzy approach. In [20] authors defined two metrics based on fuzzy logic for evaluation of different personal strategies. Modeling of educational data containing fuzzy classes for student performance assessment was applied in [21]. Using fuzzy logic for evaluation and classification of students performance was presented in [22]. Salmi et al. [23] used fuzzy sets in fuzzy evaluation of e-learning courses. Chen and Wang proposed methods for evaluating students' answerscripts based on interval-valued fuzzy grade sheets [24]. In order to improve recommendation of e-learning courses Lin and Lu [25] created an intuitionistic type-2 fuzzy inference system. A bidirectional approximate reasoning method based on interval-valued fuzzy sets was proposed in [26]. Fuzzy inference has also been used by Gogo et al. [27] in an inference engine which recommends relevant learning content to learners. In [28] Lu proposed a fuzzy matching method to find suitable learning materials. To handle uncertainties connected with e-learning environments and students Almohammadi et al. [29] proposed a type-2 fuzzy logic system which is able to estimate the engagement degree of students for both remote and on-site education.

3   Interval-Valued Fuzzy Sets

Since the first presentation of the fuzzy set theory [2] a number of its extensions have been proposed. One of them is the theory of interval-valued fuzzy sets.

Definition 1. *Let R be a universe of discourse. An interval-valued fuzzy set A in R is a set of ordered pairs:*

$$A = \{< x, \mu_A(x) >: x \in R, \quad \mu_A(x) : R \to \text{Int}([0,1])\}, \tag{1}$$

where $\mu_A(x) = [\mu_{A_L}(x), \mu_{A_U}(x)]$ is an interval-valued membership function, $Int([0,1])$ stands for the set of all closed subintervals of $[0,1]$: $Int([0,1]) = \{[a,b] : a, b \in [0,1]\}$.

Thus, the mapping $R \to [0,1]$ occurring in the definition of an ordinary fuzzy set has been replaced with the mapping $R \to \text{Int }[0,1]$. Each element x of R is associated with two membership functions $\mu_{A_L}(x)$ and $\mu_{A_U}(x)$, which are the bounds of the membership interval $\mu_A(x) = [\mu_{A_L}(x), \mu_{A_U}(x)]$. The basic characteristics of interval-valued fuzzy sets are defined with the use of the border type-1 fuzzy sets A_L and A_U which are determined by functions $\mu_{A_L}(x)$ and

$\mu_{A_U}(x)$. In the presented approach we use the cardinality concept. For a finite universe of discourse $R = \{r_1, r_2, \ldots r_n\}$ the cardinality $card(A)$ of an interval-valued fuzzy set A is defined by the interval $[card(A_L), card(A_U)]$, where:

$$card(A_L) = \sum_{x \in R} \mu_{A_L}(x), \;\; card(A_U) = \sum_{x \in R} \mu_{A_U}(x), \;\; R = \{r_1, r_2, \ldots, r_n\}. \qquad (2)$$

Wu and Mendel define the cardinality concept as [30]

$$card(A) = \frac{1}{2} \sum_{x \in R} (\mu_{A_L}(x) + \mu_{A_U}(x)). \qquad (3)$$

A support of an interval-valued fuzzy set A is determined by supports of A_L (lower support) and A_U (upper support):

$$supp(A)_L = supp(A_L) = \{x \in R : \mu_{A_L}(x) > 0\},$$
$$supp(A)_U = supp(A_U) = \{x \in R : \mu_{A_U}(x) > 0\}. \qquad (4)$$

The lower support is included in the upper support: $supp(A)_L \subseteq supp(A)_U$. A closeness measure, between two interval-valued fuzzy sets A and B, denoted by $\approx (A, B)$, is expressed by a subinterval of $[0, 1]$, with the bounds:

$$\approx (A, B)_L = \sup_x \min(\mu_{A_L}(x), \mu_{B_L}(x)),$$
$$\approx (A, B)_U = \sup_x \min(\mu_{A_U}(x), \mu_{B_U}(x)). \qquad (5)$$

4   Recommender System

Let us consider objects described by a set U of N categorical attributes $U = \{X_1, X_2, \ldots, X_N\}$. Domains of attributes, denoted by $D(X_i)$, $i = 1, \ldots, N$, are finite sets. Let us denote by p_i cardinality of $D(X_i)$: $p_i = card(D(X_i))$. Thus, $D(X_i) = \{x_{i,1}, x_{i,2}, \ldots x_{i,p_i}\}$. An object O is represented by a tuple t in the form

$$O = (t(X_1), t(X_2), \ldots, t(X_N)), \qquad (6)$$

where $t(X_i)$ denotes a value of X_i and $t(X_i) \in D(X_i)$.

Let us assume that there exist different groups of objects of similar features GO_k, $k = 1, \ldots, M$ with the set U of attributes. For each attribute one can determine a distribution of values occurring in a given group. Thus, one can indicate dominant values for every attribute. Probability $P_{i,j}$ that objects of the group GO_k are characterized by a certain value $x_{i,j}$ of X_i can be expressed by the following formula:

$$P_{i,j} = card(\{O \in GO_k : t(X_i) = x_{i,j}\})/card(GO_k), \;\; x_{i,j} \in D(X_i). \qquad (7)$$

The probabilistic representation of the group can be used to classify new objects to the closest groups. In order to find an appropriate group for a given object one should determine matching degrees. Let a tuple

$NO = (ox_1, ox_2, ..., ox_N)$, $ox_i \in D(X_i)$ represent a new object. The matching degree, of NO to GO_k, for the attribute X_i, denoted as S_i, is computed as the proportion of objects O belonging to the group, $O \in GO_k$, such that $O(X_i) = ox_i$ to the size of the group. Thus it equals $P_{i,j}$. The total matching degree S for the group is a minimal value of S_i, $i = 1, ..., N$:

$$S = \min_i S_i. \tag{8}$$

A group with maximal S should be chosen for NO. According to this methodology a value of S strongly depends on the "worst" attribute. For example, if $S_i = 0$ for a certain attribute X_i then also $S = 0$, regardless of other matching degrees. The described way of recommendation assumes that all attributes are of the equal importance. However, if an attribute with a low matching degree is less important the rejection of a given group could be unjustified. The choice may be improved by introduction of weights. Let $w_i \in [0, 1]$ denote the grade of importance of X_i. It is assumed that $\max_{1,2,...,N} w_i = 1$. The total matching degree takes the form:

$$S = \min_i \max(1 - w_i, S_i). \tag{9}$$

For the most important attributes $w_i = 1$. If $w_i = 1$ for every i the total matching degree is expressed by formula (8). If $w_i = 0$, then the attribute X_i in not considered.

5 Interval-Valued Fuzzy Sets in Building Recommendations

The recommendation procedure does not take into account closeness relationships which may be associated with elements of attribute domains. If the neighbouring values are close to one another the change of matching degrees should be considered. Otherwise, the recommendation result may be unsatisfactory.

Assumption of sharp boundaries between elements of attribute domains impose a unique qualification to the corresponding category. In the paper we introduce imprecision to the definition of the group representation. The existing uncertainty is modeled by means of interval-valued fuzzy sets.

Let us consider attribute X_i with $D(X_i) = \{x_{i,1}, x_{i,2}, ... x_{i,p_i}\}$. Let elements of $D(X_i)$ be linguistic terms represented by the following interval-valued fuzzy sets $FX_{i,j}$:

$$FX_{i,j} = \{< x, \mu_{FX_{i,j}}(x) >: x \in D(X_i), \ \mu_{FX_{i,j}}(x) : D(X_i) \to \text{Int}([0,1])\}, \tag{10}$$

where $i = 1, ..., N$ and $j = 1, ..., p_i$. Let $FX_{i,j_L}(x)$ and $FX_{i,j_U}(x)$ be lower and upper membership functions of $FX_{i,j}$, respectively. According to (5) the degree of closeness between interval-valued fuzzy sets $FX_{i,j}$ and $FX_{i,j+1}$ is an interval with the following bounds:

$$\approx (FX_{i,j}, FX_{i,j+1})_L = \sup_x \min(\mu_{FX_{i,j_L}}(x), \mu_{FX_{i,j+1_L}}(x)),$$
$$\approx (FX_{i,j}, FX_{i,j+1})_U = \sup_x \min(\mu_{FX_{i,j_U}}(x), \mu_{FX_{i,j+1_U}}(x)). \tag{11}$$

For every group GO_k, $k = 1, ..., M$ one can define fuzzy sets of objects $FO_{i,j}$ with corresponding values of attributes:

$$FO_{i,j} = \{< O, \mu_{FO_{i,j}}(O) >: O \in GO_k, \ \mu_{FO_{i,j}}(O) : GO_k \to Int([0,1])\} . \quad (12)$$

The membership function of $FO_{i,j}$ is as follows:

$$\mu_{FO_{i,j}}(O) = \mu_{FX_{i,j}}(O(X_i)). \quad (13)$$

As the representation of the attribute X_i for the group GO_k, $k = 1, ..., M$, we will consider probability $P_{i,j}$, $i = 1, ..., N$; $j = 1, ..., p_i$ that objects from GO_k, are characterized by the linguistic term $x_{i,j}$ represented by interval-valued fuzzy set (10). Probability $P_{i,j}$ belongs to the following interval:

$$P_{i,j} \in [card(FO_{i,j_L})/card(GO_k), card(FO_{i,j_U})/card(GO_k)] \quad (14)$$

In further considerations the definition (3) will be used. Thus

$$P_{i,j} = \frac{card(FO_{i,j_L}) + card(FO_{i,j_U})}{2 * card(GO_k)} \quad (15)$$

Matching degrees of a new object $NO = (ox_1, ox_2, ..., ox_N)$, to GO_k for respective attributes equal to the corresponding values of $P_{i,j}$. The total matching degree is expressed by formula (9).

Let us assume, that there are M groups, then the whole process of recommendation building will take place in the following way:

```
[Input]: A set of M groups GO_k, containing objects
         described by N nominal attributes; a new object NO;
Step 1: For each group GO_k, k = 1, 2, ..., M find
        its representation according to (15)
Step 2: For the object NO find the group GR_rec
        with the maximal value of the matching degree (9);
Step 3: Recommend GR_rec to the object.
```

6   Student Group Recommendation

For the purpose of the evaluation of the proposed method, we will consider a student model based on dominant learning styles [31]. We will apply Felder and Silverman [11] model, where learning styles are described by means of 4 attributes representing preferences for 4 dimensions from among excluding pairs: active or reflective (L_1), sensing or intuitive (L_2), visual or verbal (L_3), and sequential or global (L_4). A student without dominant preferences is called as balanced. The model takes the form of a vector SL of 4 integer attributes: $SL = (sl_1, sl_2, sl_3, sl_4)$, where $sl_i \in \{l_1, l_2, ..., l_{12}\}$, $l_j = 2j - 13$. Attribute values belong to the set of odd integers from the interval $[-11, 11]$, that represent student preferences. They are determined on the base of ILS questionnaire [32], filled by students.

Negative values of sl_1, sl_2, sl_3, sl_4 mean scoring for active, sensing, visual or sequential learning styles, respectively. Positive attribute values indicate scoring for reflective, intuitive, verbal or global learning styles. Values $-5, -7$ or $5, 7$ mean that a student learns more easily in a learning environment which favors the considered dimension; values $-9, -11$ or $9, 11$ mean that learner has a very strong preference for one dimension of the scale and may have real difficulty learning in an environment which does not support that preference.

For creating of the fuzzy group representation we will define in the domain of each attribute interval-valued fuzzy sets F_j with the border type-1 fuzzy sets F_{j_L} and F_{j_U}. Let us assume that the lower membership function $\mu_{F_{j_L}}(x)$ takes the value 1 for $x = l_j$ and $1/2$ for neighbouring elements. The lower supports of F_j are the following sets:

$$supp(F_1)_L = \{l_1, l_2\}, \quad supp(F_{12})_L = \{l_{11}, l_{12}\},$$
$$supp(F_j)_L = \{l_{j-1}, l_j, l_{j+1}\}, \text{ for } j = 2, 3...11. \tag{16}$$

The lower membership functions are as follows:

$$\mu_{F_{1_L}}(x) = -(x + 7)/4, \text{ if } x \in \{l_1, l_2\}, \tag{17}$$

$$\mu_{F_{12_L}}(x) = (x - 7)/4, \text{ if } x \in \{l_{11}, l_{12}\} \tag{18}$$

and for j = 2, 3, ..., 11

$$\mu_{F_{j_L}}(x) = \begin{cases} (x - 2j + 17)/4, & \text{if } x \in \{l_{j-1}, l_j\} \\ -(x - 2j + 9)/4, & \text{if } x \in \{l_j, l_{j+1}\} \end{cases}. \tag{19}$$

The upper support of F_j contains more elements. We will assume that the upper membership function $\mu_{F_{j_L}}(x)$ takes the value 1 for $x = l_j$, $3/4$ for l_{j-1} and l_{j+1}, $1/2$ for l_{j-2} and l_{j+2} and $1/4$ for l_{j-3} and l_{j+3}. The upper supports of F_j are the following sets:

$$supp(F_1)_U = \{l_1, ..., l_4\}, \quad supp(F_{12})_U = \{l_9, ..., l_{12}\},$$
$$supp(F_2)_U = \{l_1, ..., l_5\}, \quad supp(F_{11})_U = \{l_8, ..., l_{12}\},$$
$$supp(F_3)_U = \{l_1, ..., l_6\}, \quad supp(F_{10})_U = \{l_7, ..., l_{12}\},$$
$$supp(F_j)_U = \{l_{j-3}, ..., l_j, ..., l_{j+3}\}, \text{ for } j = 4, 5...9. \tag{20}$$

The upper membership functions are as follows:

$$\mu_{F_{1_U}}(x) = -(x + 3)/8, \text{ if } x \in \{l_1, l_2, l_3, l_4\}, \tag{21}$$
$$\mu_{F_{1_U}}(x) = (x + 3)/4, \text{ if } x \in \{l_9, l_{10}, l_{11}, l_{12}\}, \tag{22}$$

$$\mu_{F_{2_U}}(x) = \begin{cases} (x + 17)/8, & \text{if } x \in \{l_1, l_2\} \\ -(x + 1)/8, & \text{if } x \in \{l_2, l_3, l_4, l_5\} \end{cases}, \tag{23}$$

$$\mu_{F_{11_U}}(x) = \begin{cases} (x-1)/8, & \text{if } x \in \{l_8, l_9, l_{10}, l_{11}\} \\ -(x-17)/8, & \text{if } x \in \{l_{11}, l_{12}\} \end{cases}, \tag{24}$$

$$\mu_{F_{3_U}}(x) = \begin{cases} (x+15)/8, & \text{if } x \in \{l_1, l_2, l_3\} \\ -(x-1)/8, & \text{if } x \in \{l_3, l_4, l_5, l_6\} \end{cases}, \tag{25}$$

$$\mu_{F_{10_U}}(x) = \begin{cases} (x+1)/8, & \text{if } x \in \{l_7, l_8, l_9, l_{10}\} \\ -(x-15)/8, & \text{if } x \in \{l_{10}, l_{11}l_{12}\} \end{cases} \tag{26}$$

and for $j = 4, 5, ..., 9$

$$\mu_{FL_{i,j_U}}(x) = \begin{cases} (x-2j+21)/8, & \text{if } x \in \{l_{j-3}, l_{j-2}, l_{j-1}, l_j\} \\ -(x-2j+5)/8, & \text{if } x \in \{l_j, l_{j+1}, l_{j+2}, l_{j+3}\} \end{cases}. \tag{27}$$

Let fuzzy sets F_j represent linguistic terms f_j corresponding to attribute values. Thus, lower C_L and upper C_U closeness degrees between elements of attribute domains are as follows:

$$C_L(f_j, f_{j-1}) = C_L(f_j, f_{j+1}) = 1/2,$$
$$C_L(f_j, f_{j-k}) = C_L(f_j, f_{j+k}) = 0 \text{ if } k > 1$$
$$C_U(f_j, f_{j-1}) = C_U(f_j, f_{j+1}) = 3/4,$$
$$C_U(f_j, f_{j-2}) = C_U(f_j, f_{j+2}) = 1/2,$$
$$C_U(f_j, f_{j-3}) = C_U(f_j, f_{j+3}) = 1/4,$$
$$C_U(f_j, f_{j-k}) = C_U(f_j, f_{j+k}) = 0 \text{ if } k > 3 \tag{28}$$

The membership functions of interval-valued fuzzy sets $FSL_{i,j}(SL)$ of students with corresponding values of attributes L_i are determined by formulas (17–19) and (21–27). Probability $P_{i,j}$, $i = 1, 2, 3, 4$, $j = 1, ..., 12$, that students of the group GS, are characterized by the linguistic term f_j with respect to the attribute L_i equals

$$P_{i,j} = \frac{card(FSL_{i,j_L}) + card(FSL_{i,j_U})}{2 * card(GS)} \tag{29}$$

Let $jmax_i$ denotes the index j of f_j for which $P_{i,j}$ is maximal. As the fuzzy group representative we will consider four sets Rep_i, $1 \le i \le 4$, consisting of 3 elements, $Rep_i = \{rep_{i,1}, rep_{i,2}, rep_{i,3}\}$, such that

$$rep_{i,1} = f_1, \ rep_{i,2} = f_2, \ rep_{i,3} = f_3, \text{ if } jmax_i = 1, \tag{30}$$

$$rep_{i,1} = f_{10}, \ rep_{i,2} = f_{11}, \ rep_{i,3} = f_{12}, \text{ if } jmax_i = 12 \tag{31}$$

and for $jmax_i = 2, 3, ..., 11$

$$rep_{i,1} = f_{jmax_i-1}, \ rep_{i,2} = f_{jmax_i}, \ rep_{i,3} = f_{jmax_i+1}. \tag{32}$$

For the new student $NSL = (nsl_1, \ nsl_2, \ nsl_3, \ nsl_4)$, and each group GS_k, $k = 1, ..., M$ we can define a recommendation error Err_k as follows:

$$err_{k,i} = \begin{cases} 1 & \text{if } nsl_i \notin Rep_i \\ 0 & otherwise \end{cases}, \tag{33}$$

$$Err_k = \sum_{i=1}^{4} err_{k,i}. \tag{34}$$

7 Experiments

The performance of using interval-valued fuzzy sets for recommending student groups has been checked by experiments done on the real data sets. The effectiveness of the proposed method have been evaluated by recommendation error defined by (34) and compared to the results obtained by application of type-1 fuzzy sets presented in [3]. Tests have been conducted for different numbers of groups of different sizes and qualities.

We have considered two different datasets of real students' data represented by their dominant learning styles according to SL model (see (16)). The first set containing data of 194 Computer Science students from different courses has been used for building groups of similar students. The second set has comprised dominant learning styles of students, who were to learn together with their peers from the first dataset and whose data was used for evaluating the performance of the proposed recommendation method. This set consists of 31 data of students studying the master course of Information Systems in Management. The method of collecting learning styles data was described with details in [33].

The groups were created by different clustering techniques to obtain clusters of disparate structures and sizes. There were considered clusters built by three well known algorithms: partitioning - K-means, statistical - EM and hierarchical Farthest First Traversal (FFT) [34]. Such approach allows to examine the considered method for groups of different structures. To enable analysis of the performance of the proposed technique we investigated different data divisions, taking into account 3, 6 and 7 clusters, what enabled differentiating numbers and sizes of groups considered for recommendations. Recommendation accuracy has been measured by considering an error defined by (34). Additionally, every case has been examined to check if there exists better group for recommendation than the suggested one. The detail results of quantitative analysis for different group structures are presented in Table 1. The first two columns present clustering method and the number of clusters. Next columns show respectively the percentage of students of exact match (Err = 0), and of the ones for whom recommendation error was equal to $1, 2, 3, 4$. The results did not show dependency between clustering technique, group sizes and the percentage of properly assigned recommendations. The number of students of exact match was in most of the cases greater than the ones with recommendation error equal to 3. Mostly, recommendation errors take values 1 or 2. The average weighted error belongs to the interval $\langle 1.32; 1.58 \rangle$. An error equal to 4 concerned only 2 students, whose characteristics significantly differ from their peers. These students should be considered separately as outliers. Finally, all the students obtained the best group suggestions.

Table 1. Quantitative analysis for different group structures

Schema	Cl. no	Err = 0	Err = 1	Err = 2	Err = 3	Err = 4
KM	3	12.90%	35.48%	32.26%	19.35%	0%
	6	16.13%	41.94%	25.80%	9.68%	6.45%
	7	19.35%	38.71%	35.48%	3.23%	3.23%
EM	3	19.35%	32.26%	29.03%	16.13%	3.23%
	6	19.35%	32.26%	22.58%	22.58%	3.23%
	7	12.90%	41.93%	38.71%	6.45%	0%
FFT	3	19.35%	25.81%	41.93%	12.90%	0%
	6	19.35%	25.81%	38.71%	12.90%	3.23%
	7	19.35%	29.03%	41.94%	9.68%	0%

In the next step recommendation effectiveness, of the considered method (IVFS), was compared to the techniques using traditional fuzzy sets (TFS) to build group representations. Table 2 presents values of the average weighted errors, regarding error values and the respective number of students, for the both of the techniques. In the case of 10 from 12 clustering schemes the average weighted error values are less for recommendations build by using the current method. What is more, in all the considered clustering schemas, 1 to 4 students haven't obtained the best recommendations while traditional fuzzy sets have been applied.

Table 2. Average weighted error of the two methods

Schema	Cl. no	IVFS	TFS
KM	3	1.58	1.61
	6	1.48	1.32
	7	1.32	1.32
EM	3	1.516	1.45
	6	1.58	1.70
	7	1.39	1.45
FFT	3	1.48	1.68
	6	1.55	1.58
	7	1.42	1.48

8 Concluding Remarks

In the paper, fuzzy logic for building group recommendations for students was considered. We use interval valued fuzzy sets to build group representations. The proposed method shows good performance for students described by dominant learning styles. Experiments done for data sets of real students and different group structures showed that for all of the students the system indicated the best possible choice of colleagues to learn together. The comparison to the technique based on traditional fuzzy sets showed the advantage of the proposed method.

Future research will consist in further investigations of the recommendation tool, examination of other attributes and including to recommendations student historical activities as well as making group creating process more dynamic, by adding new learners each time the recommendation is accepted.

References

1. Shakouri, H.G., Tavassoli, Y.N.: Implementation of a hybrid fuzzy system as a decision support process: a FAHP-FMCDM-FIS composition. Experts Syst. Appl. **39**, 3682–3691 (2012)
2. Zadeh, L.A.: Fuzzy sets. Inf. Control **8**, 338–353 (1965)
3. Myszkorowski, K., Zakrzewska, D.: Using fuzzy logic for recommending groups in e-learning systems. In: Bădică, C., Nguyen, N.T., Brezovan, M. (eds.) ICCCI 2013. LNCS (LNAI), vol. 8083, pp. 671–680. Springer, Heidelberg (2013). https://doi.org/10.1007/978-3-642-40495-5_67
4. Zadeh, L.: The concept of a linguistic variable and its application to approximate reasoning. Inf. Sci. **8**(3), 199–249 (1975)
5. Deschrijver, G., Kerre, E.: On the relationship between some extensions of fuzzy set theory. Fuzzy Sets Syst. **133**(2), 227–235 (2003)
6. Klašnja-Milićević, A., Vesin, B., Ivanović, M., Budimac, Z., Jain, L.C.: Recommender systems in e-learning environments. In: E-Learning Systems. ISRL, vol. 112, pp. 51–75. Springer, Cham (2017). https://doi.org/10.1007/978-3-319-41163-7_6
7. Nath, S.A., Selvam, E.: A pragmatic review on different approaches used in e-learning recommender systems. In: International Conference on Circuits and Systems in Digital Enterprise Technology (ICCSDET) (2018)
8. Bobadilla, J., Serradilla, F., Hernando, A.: Collaborative filtering adapted to recommender systems of e-learning. Knowl.-Based Syst. **22**, 261–265 (2014)
9. Qomariyah, N., Fajar, A.N.: Recommender system for e-learning based on personal learning style. In: 2019 International Seminar on Research of Information Technology and Intelligent Systems (ISRITI), pp. 563–567 (2019)
10. Nafea, S.M., Siewe, F., He, Y.: A novel algorithm for course learning object recommendation based on student learning styles. In: 2019 International Conference on Innovative Trends in Computer Engineering (ITCE), pp. 192–201 (2019)
11. Felder, R.M., Silverman, L.K.: Learning and teaching styles in engineering education. Eng. Educ. **78**, 674–681 (1988)
12. Christodoulopoulos, C.E., Papanikolaou, K.A.: A group formation tool in an e-learning context. In: 19th IEEE ICTAI 2007, vol. 2, pp. 117–123 (2007)
13. Masthoff, J.: Group recommender systems: combining individual models. In: Ricci, F., Rokach, L., Shapira, B., Kantor, P.B. (eds.) Recommender Systems Handbook, pp. 677–702. Springer, Boston (2011). https://doi.org/10.1007/978-0-387-85820-3_21

14. Boratto, L., Carta, S.: State-of-the-art in group recommendation and new approaches for automatic identification of groups. In: Soro, A., Vargiu, E., Armano, G., Paddeu, G. (eds.) Information Retrieval and Mining in Distributed Environments. SCI, vol. 324, pp. 1–20. Springer, Heidelberg (2010). https://doi.org/10. 1007/978-3-642-16089-9_1

15. Guijarro, M., Fuentes-Fernández, R.: A comparative study of the use of fuzzy logic in e-learning systems. J. Intell. Fuzzy Syst. **29**(3), 1241–1249 (2015)

16. Hogo, M.: Evaluation of e-learners behaviour using different fuzzy clustering models: a comparative study. Int. J. Comput. Sci. Inf. Secur. **7**, 131–140 (2010)

17. Chen, J., Huang, K., Wang, F., Wang, H.: E-learning behavior analysis based on fuzzy clustering. In: 2009 Third International Conference on Genetic and Evolutionary Computing, pp. 863–866 (2009)

18. Limongelli, C., Sciarrone, F.: Fuzzy student modeling for personalization of e-learning courses. In: Zaphiris, P., Ioannou, A. (eds.) LCT 2014, Part I. LNCS, vol. 8523, pp. 292–301. Springer, Cham (2014). https://doi.org/10.1007/978-3-319-07482-5_28

19. Goyal, M., Yadav, D., Sood, M.: Decision making for e-learners based on learning style, personality, and knowledge level. In: 2018 5th IEEE Uttar Pradesh Section International Conference on Electrical, Electronics and Computer Engineering (UPCON) (2018)

20. Essalmi, F., Jemni, L., Ayed, B., Jemni, M., Kinshuk, Graf, S.: Evaluation of personalization strategies based on fuzzy logic. In: 2011 IEEE 11th International Conference on Advanced Learning Technologies, pp. 254–256 (2011)

21. Badie, F., Soru, T., Lehmann, J.: A fuzzy knowledge representation model for student performance assessment. In: 2014 IEEE 14th International Conference on Advanced Learning Technologies, pp. 539–540 (2014)

22. Vrettaros, J., Vouros, G., Drigas, A.: Development of an intelligent assessment system for solo taxonomies using fuzzy logic. In: Mellouli, K. (ed.) ECSQARU 2007. LNCS (LNAI), vol. 4724, pp. 901–911. Springer, Heidelberg (2007). https:// doi.org/10.1007/978-3-540-75256-1_78

23. Salmi, K., Magrez, H., Ziyyat, A.: A fuzzy expert system in evaluation for E-learning. In: 2014 Third IEEE International Colloquium in Information Science and Technology (CIST), pp. 225–229 (2014)

24. Chen, S., Wang, H.: Evaluating students' answerscripts based on interval-valued fuzzy grade sheets. Expert Syst. Appl. **36**, 9839–9846 (2009)

25. Lin, K., Lu, Y.: Applying intuitionistic type-2 fuzzy inference system for e-learning system. In: 2015 8th International Conference on Ubi-Media Computing (UMEDIA), pp. 282–284 (2015)

26. Chen, S., Hsiao, W.: Bidirectional approximate reasoning for rule-based systems using interval-valued fuzzy sets. Fuzzy Sets Syst. **113**(2), 185–203 (2000)

27. Gogo, K.O., Nderu, L., Mwangi, R.W.: Fuzzy logic based context aware recommender for smart e-learning content delivery. In: 2018 5th International Conference on Soft Computing and Machine Intelligence (ISCMI), pp. 114–118 (2018)

28. Lu, J.: Personalized e-learning material recommender system. In: Proceedings of the 2nd International Conference on Information Technology for Application, pp. 374–379 (2004)

29. Almohammadi, K., Yao, B., Alzahrani, A., Hagras, H., Alghazzawi, D.: An interval type-2 fuzzy logic based system for improved instruction within intelligent e-learning platforms. In: 2015 IEEE International Conference on Fuzzy Systems (FUZZ-IEEE) (2015)

30. Wu, D., Mendel, J.M.: A vector similarity measure for interval type-2 fuzzy sets. In: Proceedings of FUZZ-IEEE International Conference, London (2007)
31. Brusilovsky, P., Peylo, C.: Adaptive and intelligent web-based educational systems. Int. J. Artif. Intell. Educ. **13**, 156–169 (2003)
32. Index of Learning Style Questionnaire. http://www.engr.ncsu.edu/learningstyles/ ilsweb.html
33. Zakrzewska, D.: Student groups modeling by integrating cluster representation and association rules mining. In: van Leeuwen, J., Muscholl, A., Peleg, D., Pokorný, J., Rumpe, B. (eds.) SOFSEM 2010. LNCS, vol. 5901, pp. 743–754. Springer, Heidelberg (2010). https://doi.org/10.1007/978-3-642-11266-9_62
34. Han, J., Kamber, M.: Data Mining. Concepts and Techniques, 2nd edn. Morgan Kaufmann Publishers, San Francisco (2006)

Analysis of User Story Dynamics
on a Medium-Size Social News Site

Mariusz Kamola(✉)

NASK National Research Institute, Kolska 12, 01045 Warszawa, Poland
Mariusz.Kamola@nask.pl

Abstract. We propose a model of dynamics for stories posted by users on a social news site. The model is an adaptation of the classical epidemiological SIR model (susceptible-infectious-recovered), with initial linear phase added. The model was tested on a completely new dataset of stories reported on a local social news site. The model fits the real data well and makes it possible to parametrize a story by a point in low-dimensional space of parameters. However, it turns out that still more data records and more complete and accurate measurement approach are needed in order to use the model for prediction of story popularity or to detect untrue stories.

Keywords: SIR model · Social news · Natural language processing

1 Introduction

Social news websites operate by letting registered users report stories that wider audience might find interesting. The very concept of such website operation is deceptively simple, rooted in free market rules: let some users dig news, let some others rate their quality, let everyone read the best ones, let the operator make profit from careful advertisement placement. In fact, such seemingly trouble-free business model poses challenges of a classical news website and more. The operator has to balance the quantity (of views) against the quality (of served content) because both affect the volume and quotes of sold ads. But the difficulty is that while such editorial policy goes into effect directly in classical news websites, in social news websites it must be accomplished indirectly, by stimuli to users.

Therefore, social news operators put so much effort in fine tuning of systems of user rewards—be it a virtual badge, reputation score, or placement of a delivered story on a mirror premium channel (e.g. facebook.com). Also, this is why modeling and predicting of the ongoing phenomena in social news services is of much importance.

1.1 Social News and Its Problems

Social news operator controls dynamics of reported news mainly by defining the order in which they appear on the front page. That order depends on how

© Springer Nature Switzerland AG 2020
N. T. Nguyen et al. (Eds.): ICCCI 2020, LNAI 12496, pp. 97–109, 2020.
https://doi.org/10.1007/978-3-030-63007-2_8

many upvotes a story has got from other users. Usually, other factors are also taken into account, like the number of story views, user reputation, story source reputation etc., thus differentiating social news platforms behaviour.

The common idea of collapsing user's complex attitude towards a story onto one-dimensional binary scale of a single upvote or downvote makes analytical tasks difficult. Users may express their dislike because they do not like the topic, the style, the author or the source in general. They may envy the user who reported the story, they may find it manipulated or utterly made up. And so on. This is why consideration of user comments to findings as well as users' relationships provides so much insight into the processes and helps improving social news website operation.

Both classical and social news websites strive to separate the wheat from the chaff, i.e., to pick up objective and substantive comments, and suppress all the others. Automated comment moderation based on text analysis turned out successful for *Washington Post* and *The New York Times* [10]. The underlying algorithms are based on Coral Project, which uses artificial intelligence (AI) models to detect common misuses, like hate speech. However, this approach has not been adopted by the biggest social news sites (Digg.com, Slashdot.org, Reddit.com) because it cannot detect manipulation or disinformation that are related to deep sense of text and the context, and not just the writing style.

Not implementing AI-based comment moderation happens also because social media websites care much more about user comfort than the classical news websites, which comes from their business model. The comfort means that auto-mated moderation process must be clear for commenting users and easy to set up by a moderator who often has no information technology background. Therefore, Reddit.com uses a rule-based, fully explainable algorithm, called Automod [5]. It is based on regular expression content marking combined with a multitude of user metrics. The care about user comfort is not overrated; a study [7] shows that users are sensitive to news ranking algorithm deficiencies: behavioral (same or similar submissions not merged), structural (limit on title or news body length) and relational (unjust exclusion of posts). The research concerned Reddit.com platform and focused on distress scenarios (terrorist attacks, natural disasters).

1.2   Research Aims and Similar Work

Considering limitations and difficulty in text-based policing for stories listing, the analysis and modeling of social news activities makes wide use of user rela-tionship network. The work reported here also goes this way. We want to pro-pose an accurate model for news dynamics and point out the factors that model parameters depend on. Finally, we check if false news conform to that model.

A reliable model of user activity around a new story can be of paramount importance to social news operator. First, it may help to predict ad-driven rev-enue, and to adjust front page contents and timing optimally. Second, it may help to detect model outliers, analyse and treat them separately. In particular, it is expected that fake news will turn up as outliers and can be sifted out efficiently.

Models of news dynamics date back to 1960s, to Daley and Kendall's [4] adoption of epidemiological compartmental model back from 1927. The three classes of individuals in the original model, namely Susceptible, Infected and Recovered (SIR) were mapped onto equivalent classes in rumour spreading scenario, and named Ignorant, Spreader and Stifler (ISS). The underlying state equations stay the same:

$$\dot{x} = -\beta \frac{x}{N} y \tag{1a}$$

$$\dot{y} = \beta \frac{x}{N} y - \gamma y \tag{1b}$$

$$\dot{z} = \gamma y , \tag{1c}$$

where x is the number of individuals susceptible (prone to accept) the rumour; y is the number of those that have believed and spread the rumour, and z is the number of those that either lost interest or have not heard the rumour, stifling it anyhow. N is the population size. It is assumed that infection rate (1a) is determined by the product of a number of susceptible and infected individuals. Formula (1a) implies that the network of possible transmission paths between susceptible and infected is regular—otherwise the system (1) would not be invariant to the actual topology of links between infected and susceptible individuals. It is also worth to observe that infected people naturally "recover" from interest in the rumour (1c), and its dynamics is determined by γ.

The major point of research interest as regards model (1) and its successors is to determine the tipping point of epidemics, i.e. the conditions to be met in order to ignite spreading of rumour—and to estimate the fraction of individuals that get infected. Those can be computed from the initial condition, $\frac{x(0)}{N}$ and the coefficients. Successive works provide model extensions to account for more elaborate interaction scenarios as well as inhomogeneous interaction network between individuals.

Zhao et al. [15] observe that in case of rumours an infected individual (that is the one who believes the rumour is true) may change his/her opinion if s/he encounters i) a recovered or ii) another infected but with a different version of the rumour. Both encounters may undermine that individual's stance, and they are represented by introduction of new elements for state transitions in (1). Equilibrium properties of such system are examined by extensive numerical simulations for uniform network structure of individuals.

SIR model behaviour for non-uniform networks has been addressed by Leventhal et al. [9]. The authors verify earlier observations that reduced network homogeneity (in sense of greater node distribution variance) makes epidemic easier to trigger. Clustering coefficient, in turn, appears not to impact epidemic properties—because its working is different from classical information cascade model, where infection has to be triggered by majority of an individual's neighbours [2]. Moreover, a scenario of appearance of a new virus strain proposed in [9] can be an interesting and valuable analogy to distortions of rumours in the course of word-of-mouth transmission.

Recent effective disinformation campaigns make people realize the scale of damage fabricated news are able to inflict, and stimulates broad research in that field. Usability of our model in that context is discussed as a separate thread is Sect. 3.2. Now we present how original SIR model addresses that issue. In fact, unlike for pathogens, news spreading models have been from the beginning branded with "rumour" term [4], instead of "fact". This inherent distrust resulted in [15] in update of equations (1). Finally, Piqueira et al. [11] in their latest work extend SIR model by a new class of individuals called *checkers*, i.e. those in progress of checking rumour veracity after having heard it. Simulations show that such augmented model helps to keep more individuals away from being infected.

Research on SIR model and its variants focuses on finding conditions that trigger an epidemic, and on estimation of its scope. However, to trigger news spreading in infection-like manner is exactly the goal for a social news portal, contrary to the goal of containing a pathogen. Here we show that SIR model can be harnessed also for such purpose. The structure of this paper is as follows. In Sect. 2 we describe the original dataset and present the way SIR model was adopted. Results of model application to real data as well as the discussion about is usability to detect false stories are presented in Sect. 3. In Sect. 4 we discuss model usability to predict the total interest into the story. We conclude in Sect. 5.

2   Datasets and Descriptive Model of Dynamics

The main contributions of this paper are twofold. First, we perform analytic work on a new dataset from a social news website smaller than Reddit.com or Digg.com, and point out observed differences and similarities. Second, we adopt SIR model to account for phenomena specific for social news services.

2.1   Wykop.pl Public Data

The data source of our choice was Wykop.pl, the largest Polish social news website. With over 800,000 user profiles and 95 million page views monthly, the service aims to stimulate its community to promote valuable up-to-date news. Registered users can follow one another; also, all users get notified about news from the front page. Users can upvote or downvote provided stories, and those considered most popular make it to the front page and become visible to general audience. Users can place comments on stories and threaded replies to the comments. A user that submits a story may provide a short custom description as well as tags. Submitted stories must link to the original source, and if the source has any visual content its thumbnail gets embedded on the front page.

The data collected from the service consist of all stories that have appeared on front page in the period from 4th until 19th April 2020, which amounts to nearly 3,000 new stories. Dynamics of every story (number of up- and downvotes, number of views, posted comments) had been monitored for the following 72 h, i.e. when the all social buzz has well settled down.

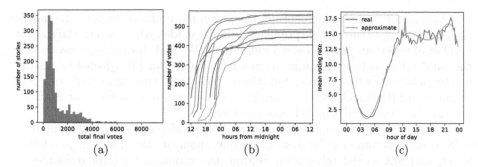

Fig. 1. a) Distribution of final votes count. b) Number of votes count for sample stories from dominant interval in Fig. 1a, w.r.t. time since midnight on day the story was reported. c) Average number of new votes per hour per single story, for subsequent hours of a day. (Color figure online)

Figure 1a provides histogram of the final number of votes (upvotes plus downvotes) for observed stories. Here we consider number of votes rather than a number of views as appropriate metrics of users' interest in a story for two reasons. First, granularity of views counter provided on website was very coarse, indicating only order of magnitude instead of exact figure, and therefore unsuitable for analytic purposes. Second, user's vote is indeed a sound indicator of his/her attitude and naturally filters out non-voting users who would stay as indifferent to served ads as they were towards the served content. Votes distribution shows a fat but short tail and a dominant bucket of 380 to 580 final votes count. A closeup on sample stories from that bucket is given in Fig. 1b. The graphs are anchored at midnight on their publication day to see daily seasonality effects.

We can see a number of interesting phenomena in the figure. Users effectively lose interest in a story after about 24 h after it is published on the front page. Most of the observed stories gain popularity very quickly just the moment they get discovered by us—but there are others (cf. lines in lilac, blue, khaki and cyan) that demonstrate quasi-linear initial phase of growth, before taking off seriously. Finally, independently how a story begins, the growth is substantially damped after the soonest midnight (denoted in Fig. 1b by first 00's).

2.2   SIR Model Modifications

Our observations on story dynamics generally agree with those reported by Lerman [8] for Digg.com where occasionally observed initial linear phase of votes growth was attributed to the period *preceding* story promotion to the front page. Note however, that in our case all recorded voting activity happened *after* the story had landed on front page (otherwise it would not be detected by the scanning software). Therefore, placing a story on a front page does not mean *per se* that its ratings will explode instantly; on the contrary, it may take hours (cf. e.g. the khaki scenario in Fig. 1b). It is an important finding, yet given the quality of our data we can only speculate about possible explanation of this fact.

Once a story gets its momentum, the graph of accumulated votes resembles the complement of susceptible population in SIR model, which equals the current number of infectious plus recovered individuals. We find this analogy reasonable: the total voting activity at time t comes from users who felt *affected* by a story to the point of casting a vote. Substitute "affected" with "infected" and here we go with SIR model. But not straight away, because we have to account for several other things SIR model does not have.

The first, the initial, optional linear phase with slope α, ending at some time τ from story submission by a user. At that moment, the infected population is $\alpha\tau$, and SIR model takes over. Second, the rationale for joint dynamics of infected and recovered, represented in our observation by the actual number of votes. Since a story at that time is on the front page, it is exposed to all users and therefore there is no reason to have infection rate dependent on actual number of infected users. Now our model could look like:

$$
\dot{v} = \begin{cases} \alpha & \text{if } t < \tau \\ \beta(N - v) & \text{otherwise} , \end{cases}
\tag{2}
$$

with $v(t_0) = 0$. The only variable v denotes number of votes, identified with the sum of infectious and recovered individuals in (1), $v \equiv y + z$. The number of susceptible, x, equals $N - v$. The meaning of transmission rate β is unchanged.

Next, we want to address the nightly drop in user activity. We propose to approximate the overall voting activity on the webpage with a polynomial, as it is presented in Fig. 1c. Separate weekday and weekend profiles are not needed in case of our data because they were collected at the height of Covid-19 lockdown, when users behaviour stayed quite uniform throughout the week. And finally, different radii of bends leading to votes saturation (cf. Fig. 1b) need to be addressed. We propose voting rate to depend on $N - v$ nonlinearly, and our final model is as follows:

$$
\dot{v} = \begin{cases} \alpha & \text{if } t < \tau \\ \beta r(t_0 + t)(N - v)^{\xi} & \text{otherwise} , \end{cases}
\tag{3}
$$

where ξ is the "boost" coefficient that accelerates reaching saturation level N. The function r is the general activity profile that dampers dynamics at night.

N, α, τ, β and ξ constitute a vector of model parameters that is individual for each story i, and denoted here by φ_i. Note that also N is specific for a story, unlike in SIR model. This assumption is based in multidimensional and unique meaning of every story. Stories are treated by us the same way as different viruses, each of them having different susceptible population, i.e. the group of users that find it interesting. The model has undergone verification and made it possible to examine properties of stories in 5-D space of model parameters.

3   Parametric Model Properties

Model fitting in terms of mean square error has been performed with an enhanced Simulated Annealing solver called Dual Annealing and available from Python scipy.optimize package. Quadratic regularization term was imposed on α parameter in order to prevent large α play as substitute for the proper nonlinear phase of the model. The number of stories subject to modeling has been limited to include only those younger than 1.5 h at the moment they had been detected by our software. This way, most of stories with only non-linear phase were discarded from further analysis. We find stories that miss the linear part deficient in context of our analytical goals. In particular, any forecasting for a new story makes sense in its early stage, hence linear phase must be present in the data. Consequently, our set of stories has been roughly sifted and has shrunk to the size of 650 samples. Average relative error of fitting a model to a scenario was satisfactory; it was less than 10% for more than 2/3 of stories.

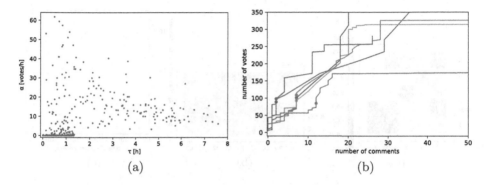

Fig. 2. a) Stories model parameters α vs. τ. b) Growth of number of votes and number of comments for sample stories. Transitions from linear to nonlinear phase at τ are marked with dots.

Figure 2a provides insight into location of models in subspace of parameters α and τ. Stories without linear phase have got $\alpha = 0$; they form thick blurred horizontal line at the origin of coordinate system. The rest of points represent scenarios with linear part. Note that the shape of populated area is limited (except 6 dots) with hyperbolic-like boundary. It means that a story goes into nonlinear phase having got some 100 votes at the latest. The mechanism of this phase transition is still to be explained; apparently, sheer promotion of a story to the front page does not do the job—or at least, not always.

3.1 Correlation with User Network Metrics

Linking epidemic model with network structure of a given population seems a natural research trail, and it has been followed in [9] for networks in general, and in [8] specifically for Digg.com. The latter study reports that users show affinity to like stories submitted or liked by those who they follow—namely, probability of a user having liked a story at random is lower than a user having liked a story by someone followed by him/her. This natural phenomenon, however, when combined with site's algorithm promoting *collectively filtered* stories, leads to dominance of news pushed by a few tightly knit communities. Such oligarchy is contrary to the original ideas and undermines operation of any social news site.

Wary of the impact of user network on news spreading, we examined it for Wykop.pl data. Unfortunately, the available data were unsuitable to keep record on identities of voters, so we used comments records as a substitute. Figure 2b shows that usually the number of comments is roughly proportional to the number of votes, and can be considered with caution as predictor for model (3) parameters. Having passed their tipping points marked with dots, the graphs fan out. As stories get older, they are taken off the front page and lose new votes—but commenting activity goes on (horizontal lines of the graphs).

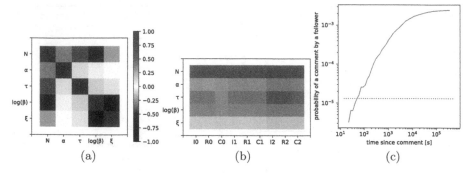

(a)   (b)   (c)

Fig. 3. a) Correlation coefficient matrix of model parameters. b) Correlation coefficient matrix between model parameters and aggregates of network metric of commenting users. c) Probability of a comment being responded by a comment author follower (solid) vs. probability of comments posted at random (dotted).

Figure 3 is a comprehensive report of relationships between model parameters and network metrics of users involved in commenting. Figure 3a shows that internal model parameters are largely uncorrelated, except for N, α and β, ξ pairs. Both relationships are reasonable: a quick uptake of comments can be a symptom of final story's popularity; also, negative coupling of β and ξ demonstrates that the nonlinear phase can be driven by either of the parameters, but not both. (We use $\log(\beta)$ to flatten its variability.)

Figure 3b provides correlation between model parameters and selected network metrics of users that commented on a story. We considered ego networks of actors (i.e. users that submitted a story and the commentators) of radius 0, 1 and 2; we considered a number of metrics for those ego network nodes: in-degree, Page Rank, clustering coefficient; we considered several ways to aggregate the metrics: the sum, the mean, the maximum value. Most of indicators calculated in various ways turned out to be weakly correlated with model parameters. Those with stronger correlation are based on sum of the metrics, calculated only for comments placed within 1 h after story publication. Such limit makes sense in context of dynamics prediction or content moderation, which should be done early. Metric codes in Fig. 3b stand for (I) in-degree, (R) Page Rank and (C) clustering coefficient, followed by ego network size: (0) only the actor, (1) actor followers and (2) actor followers' followers. One can notice considerable (0.6–0.65) correlation of the metrics with N, the highest one for clustering coefficient summed over ego-2 nodes of the early commenting users. It means, in the statistical sense, that stories promoted to front page by early commentators forming well connected communities are more likely to reach wider audience.

However consistent with earlier observations [8] this one is, one should not be very confident about its value for prediction. Figure 3c shows the real role of networking in the commenting process: we calculated fraction of one's followers that really responded to his/her comment within a given time. While it quickly grows with time over pure chance level (dotted line), it stays very small in absolute terms, reaching approximately 0.001 after 1 h. Networking role in social news popularity should not be overestimated, and its correlation with it (cf. Fig. 3b) can be an artefact of some underlying causality, invisible here.

3.2 Undesired Content Taxonomy and Mapping into Parameter Space

There is a number of reasons social news operator wants to get rid of a story or a comment. Posted stories may be duplicates of already reported news, leading to users' perplexity. Otherwise, the content may violate ethical norm in many ways. In terms of its effect on addressee, it can be upsetting, offending, misleading. The cases of journal sites provided in Sect. 1.1 show that automated detection of many of those categories can be a success. However, planned disinformation activities pose challenges of another magnitude to machine-run moderation. The now popular term *fake news* may encompass plain fabricated lies, lies bundled with truth, allegations and innuendos embedded in reported speech etc.

Current research activity on fake news classification takes structure of users network, message content and news dynamics as valuable model inputs. Many works, e.g. already mentioned [11], propose SIR model extensions to account for dynamics that is specific for fake news. Likewise, Yang et al. [14] divide infectious individuals into spreaders of true and false information, and change model equations accordingly. Results have been verified for Facebook.com network.

A common veracity classification approach is based on deep neural networks. For instance, Ajao et al. [1] detect fake news on Twitter.com with over 80% accuracy. Current research trends for fake news detection and containment, with special attention to embedding (projecting onto low dimensional space) of available data, as user info or message content, are summarized in [13].

Social news is inherently vulnerable to undesired content because it is somewhat complementary to "official" news. Social news users submit and promote news that are extreme in many aspects, as impact on daily life, funniness, incredibility. It is relatively easy in such setting to pass fake news. It is also equally easy to smear true news as fake by someone with opposing opinion. And there is ubiquitous irony in the texts, which in fact defines Wykop.pl's identity.

We have come across all the above features in our dataset while manually verifying a half of 650 samples that contained words like "fake" or "untrue" in the discourse. Sometimes it is really difficult for a human to tell apart fabricated news from true ones, let alone the machine. In the end, we have got two disjoint fake news subsets: one reported by moderators, and another one verified manually by us.

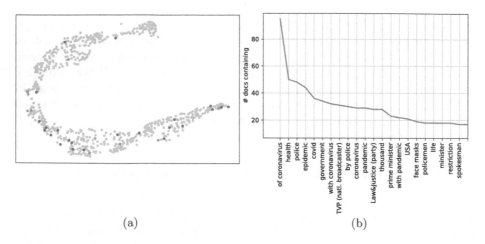

(a)   (b)

Fig. 4. a) Projection of t-SNE embedding of stories' attributes on 2D plane. False news reported by moderators are marked red; other verified false news are marked blue. b) Word frequency distribution in story titles and descriptions. (Color figure online)

Location of false stories of both kinds have been examined w.r.t. model parameters, however, they appear dispersed the same way as the true stories. So, there is no useful way to detect them using data and apparatus presented here. To give a concise idea how fake news are mingled with others, we applied t-distributed Stochastic Neighbor Embedding (t-SNE) projection of space of model parameters φ plus C2 network metrics (cf. Fig. 3b). Embedding results, cf. Fig. 4a, show that fake news tend to be located in lower half of the data but they are too much scattered to be useful in any fake news identification task.

4   Content Analysis and Predictive Models

Our final research question is about performance of typical predictive models fed with stories' attributes found so far as well as with text of the story and accompanying comments. Consistently, we define the goal to minimize predicted value of N within 1 h from story submission.

4.1   Approach to Natural Language Processing

Mixing numerical input, α and C2 in our case, with textual one requires vectorization of the latter. We apply binary vectorizer, i.e. procedure of finding M most frequent words in input text samples, and turning them into a binary vector of length M. Text samples can be just stories' titles with short descriptions. Optionally, we may append text of the comments. This way, we prepare a *corpus* of documents, subject to vectorization. A sample distribution of most frequent corpus words is given in Fig. 4b. From that, one can easily make out that Covid-19 epidemic was the main, if not the only, topic of the discourse. Moreover, keywords referring to politics (party names, the police, governmental positions) indicate that the way Covid-19 was handled by the government caused the biggest stir in users' community.

Our experiments were performed in the space of the following parameters: model types (linear regression, ridge regression, random forest regression, multilayer perceptron), text vector length (50, 100, 200) and kernel for predicted value of N (N, $\log N$, $\sqrt{N}$). Additionally, we considered inclusion or exclusion of comments in the corpus as well as the model parameters, α and C2.

4.2   Prediction Results

The prediction quality was measured by mean absolute percentage (MAPE) and root mean square (RMSE) errors w.r.t. N. Multilayer perceptron of plain N, with $M = 100$ and texts without comments provided best predictions in terms of MAPE: 92%. We consider it totally unsatisfactory as well as RMSE of 1148, obtained by random forest regressor. Interestingly, all four prediction models gave similar RMSE errors, which means in particular that the simpler and more transparent ones—ridge and linear regression—may still play a role in the future, once provided with better input data. This observation is consistent with [6] and [3] where plain models perform better and, moreover, provide explanation of their forecasts, e.g. text keywords that drive the forecast up.

5   Conclusion

Research reported in this paper extends prior works aiming to analyze [8,11,15] and forecast [6,12] dynamics of news diffused by social links. We provided and worked on a completely new dataset from local social news website. Unlike for big social news platforms, all stories on a smaller site get presented in one official channel, which makes text-based modelling more difficult.

Our key findings are as follows. We propose two-phase model of news dynamics (3), which proved to fit well scenarios from the dataset. We find that rapid increase of story's popularity does not have to happen immediately after its promotion to the front page—yet the reasons remain unknown. We also find that network properties of story authors and early commenting users do not impact story's future dynamics as much as reported elsewhere [8].

Our research has failed in application of the proposed model to fake news detection and to final popularity prediction. However, both goals are really difficult and have been approached here with many models. These failures point at directions of future work: to have more detailed data, to consider more elaborate text embeddings, to process graphical content provided in stories and comments, to distinguish between users. Most of the directions have been already postulated [13], yet they are out of the scope of this paper. Selection of the most prospective ones can be a challenging task itself.

References

1. Ajao, O., Bhowmik, D., Zargari, S.: Fake news identification on Twitter with hybrid CNN and RNN models. In: Proceedings of the 9th International Conference on Social Media and Society, pp. 226–230 (2018)
2. Banerjee, A.V.: A simple model of herd behavior. Q. J. Econ. **107**(3), 797–817 (1992)
3. Ciecierski, K.A., Kamola, M.: Comparison of text classification methods for government documents. In: Rutkowski, L., Scherer, R., Korytkowski, M., Pedrycz, W., Tadeusiewicz, R., Zurada, J.M. (eds.) ICAISC 2020. LNCS, vol. 12415, pp. 39–49. Springer, Cham (2020). https://doi.org/10.1007/978-3-030-61401-0_4
4. Daley, D.J., Kendall, D.G.: Epidemics and rumours. Nature **204**(4963), 1118 (1964)
5. Jhaver, S., Birman, I., Gilbert, E., Bruckman, A.: Human-machine collaboration for content regulation: the case of Reddit Automoderator. ACM Trans. Comput. Hum. Interact. **26**(5), 1–35 (2019)
6. Jones, M.S.: The Reddit self-post classification task (RSPCT): a highly multiclass dataset for text classification (2018). https://evolution.ai/blog_figures/reddit_dataset/rspct_preprint_v3.pdf
7. Leavitt, A., Robinson, J.J.: The role of information visibility in network gatekeeping: information aggregation on Reddit during crisis events. In: Proceedings of the 2017 ACM Conference on Computer Supported Cooperative Work and Social Computing, pp. 1246–1261 (2017)
8. Lerman, K.: Social networks and social information filtering on Digg. CoRR abs/cs/0612046 (2006). http://arxiv.org/abs/cs/0612046
9. Leventhal, G.E., Hill, A.L., Nowak, M.A., Bonhoeffer, S.: Evolution and emergence of infectious diseases in theoretical and real-world networks. Nature Commun. **6**, 6101 (2015). https://doi.org/10.1038/ncomms7101
10. Miroshnichenko, A.: AI to bypass creativity. Will robots replace journalists? (The answer is "yes"). Information **9**(7), 183 (2018). https://doi.org/10.3390/info9070183
11. Piqueira, J.R., Zilbovicius, M., Batistela, C.M.: Daley-Kendal models in fake-news scenario. Phys. A **548**, 123406 (2020)
12. Shen, L., Joshi, A.K.: Ranking and reranking with perceptron. Mach. Learn. **60**(1–3), 73–96 (2005). https://doi.org/10.1007/s10994-005-0918-9
13. Shu, K., Bernard, H.R., Liu, H.: Studying fake news via network analysis: detection and mitigation. In: Agarwal, N., Dokoohaki, N., Tokdemir, S. (eds.) Emerging Research Challenges and Opportunities in Computational Social Network Analysis and Mining. LNSN, pp. 43–65. Springer, Cham (2019). https://doi.org/10.1007/978-3-319-94105-9_3

14. Yang, D., Chow, T.W., Zhong, L., Tian, Z., Zhang, Q., Chen, G.: True and fake information spreading over the Facebook. Phys. A **505**, 984–994 (2018)
15. Zhao, L., Cui, H., Qiu, X., Wang, X., Wang, J.: SIR rumor spreading model in the new media age. Phys. A **392**(4), 995–1003 (2013)

Collective Decision-Making

Collective Decision-Making as a Contextual Multi-armed Bandit Problem

Axel Abels[1,2]([✉]) [iD], Tom Lenaerts[1,2] [iD], Vito Trianni[3] [iD], and Ann Nowé[2] [iD]

[1] Machine Learning Group, Université Libre de Bruxelles, Brussels, Belgium
{axel.abels,tom.lenaerts}@ulb.ac.be
[2] AI Lab, Vrije Universiteit Brussel, Brussels, Belgium
ann.nowe@ai.vub.ac.be
[3] Laboratory of Autonomous Robotics and Artificial Life, Institute of Cognitive Sciences and Technologies, National Research Council, Rome, Italy
vito.trianni@istc.cnr.it

Abstract. Collective decision-making (CDM) processes – wherein the knowledge of a group of individuals with a common goal must be combined to make optimal decisions – can be formalized within the framework of the deciding with expert advice setting. Traditional approaches to tackle this problem focus on finding appropriate weights for the individuals in the group. In contrast, we propose here meta-CMAB, a meta approach that learns a mapping from expert advice to expected outcomes. In summary, our work reveals that, when trying to make the best choice in a problem with multiple alternatives, meta-CMAB assures that the collective knowledge of experts leads to the best outcome without the need for accurate confidence estimates.

Keywords: Deciding with expert advice · Contextual bandits · Confidence · Noise · Collective decision-making

1 Introduction

When faced with complex decision-making problems, aggregating the advice of multiple experts before making a decision may be rewarding since individual errors may potentially be overcome by a collective judgement. Peer review processes for example combine the opinion of multiple experts with the goal of maximizing the quality of selected works from a pool of submissions [1]. In medical diagnostics, a group of medical experts may provide better advice on how to solve difficult patient cases [2].

Contextual multi-armed bandits (CMAB) [3] provide a formalization of decision problems [4,5]. For each situation entailing a decision, a CMAB presents a decision-maker with a set of options (i.e., the arms of the bandit) to which contexts (i.e., descriptive feature vectors) are associated. The decision-maker aims to make the best possible choice (i.e., to select the most rewarding arm) given the contextual information.

© Springer Nature Switzerland AG 2020
N. T. Nguyen et al. (Eds.): ICCCI 2020, LNAI 12496, pp. 113–124, 2020.
https://doi.org/10.1007/978-3-030-63007-2_9

To do so, either human experts or artificial systems (e.g., a pre-trained regressor) that have knowledge about the link between the contextual information and the potential reward can be consulted. Consequently an intelligent decision-support system can be designed to automatically exploit such knowledge, allowing to automatically find the best arm. As the exact performance of a set of experts can be difficult to estimate a-priori, the decision-support system needs to learn how to exploit their advice purposely. The problem of deciding with expert advice formalizes this learning (or optimisation) process.

The dominant approach in this setting is to compute a weighted sum of expert advice (i.e., probability distributions over the arms) and act according to the resulting probability distribution [6–8]. The seminal EXP4 algorithm [6], for instance, iteratively increases the importance of experts, i.e., the corresponding weights, whose advice leads to beneficial outcomes. In recent work on this algorithm, we showed that including experts' confidence estimates and value advice improves performance [9], particularly when more experts than choices are available. The confidence estimates provide the aggregating algorithm with prior information about which experts it should trust.

Here, we propose to resolve the CDM problem in a different manner by considering that such a problem can be directly transformed into a CMAB, making possible the use of established CMAB algorithms to solve the decision-making problem. We start from the assumption that there exists a mapping between experts' advice and actual outcomes, and that this mapping can be learned. We hence propose a higher-level or meta-CMAB, wherein the contexts are no longer the original problem's contexts, but rather the experts' advice about those contexts. We show that addressing this meta-problem through established CMAB algorithms provides a more robust solution than state-of-the-art approaches like EXP4, with respect to both variations in the quality of experts in the collective and to noisy confidence estimates.

In the following section we provide the background knowledge on MAB, CMAB and the problem of deciding with expert advice. We then present our main contribution, the meta-CMAB approach. Finally, we provide and discuss an experimental comparison of this approach with the state of the art.

2 Background

2.1 Contextual Multi-armed Bandits

In the (non-contextual) multi-armed bandit (MAB) problem, a learner repeatedly aims to pull the best arm from a set of arms. The quality of each of the K arms is determined by a function f which maps each arm to a reward distribution. Because f is unknown a priori, the learner must balance exploration – to reduce its uncertainty – and exploitation – to maximize its collected rewards – over time. Performance is typically measured in terms of regret, i.e., the difference between the learner's collected rewards and the rewards that would have been collected by only pulling the best arm $k^* = \arg\max_{k \in K} \mathbb{E}[f(k)]$.

Real-world problems are typically not as straightforward as MABs. Indeed, the context of a decision problem – the additional information about the problem that decision-makers take into account – is not captured in MABs.

By introducing context vectors – a set of features which are predictive of the arm's expected outcome – we obtain a contextual MAB (or CMAB).

We consider here stochastic CMABs [8], wherein at time t the set of all arms is characterized by K time-dependent d-dimensional context vectors $\{\vec{x}_{1,t}, ..., \vec{x}_{K,t}\} \in \mathbb{R}^{K \times d}$. Each context vector $\vec{x}_{k,t}$ is mapped to a reward by a fixed but unknown scalarization function $f : \mathbb{R}^d \to [0,1]$. Solving a CMAB requires iteratively improving a policy $\pi_t : \mathbb{R}^{K \times d} \to [0,1]^K$, i.e., a probability distribution over the arms according to which an arm $k_t \sim \pi_t(\mathbf{x}_t)$ is selected. In CMABs, the regret over T rounds of a learner pulling arm $k_t \sim \pi_t(\mathbf{x}_t)$ by following its policy π_t at each timestep t is the sum of reward differences between the pulled arm given the context at time t, i.e., $f(\vec{x}_{k_t \sim \pi_t, t})$, and the best arm at each time step t, i.e., $\max_{k=1}^{K} f(\vec{x}_{k,t})$;

$$R_T^\pi = \sum_{t=1}^{T} \left(\max_{k=1}^{K} f(\vec{x}_{k,t}) - f(\vec{x}_{k_t \sim \pi_t, t}) \right) \tag{1}$$

A good approximation of f is often required to make appropriate decisions in CMABs. As learning such an approximation inevitably takes times, it is desirable to exploit prior knowledge when possible. In *deciding with expert advice* [6] the approximation of f is foregone in favour of querying a set of experts for advice about the contexts. The complexity then no longer resides in approximating f, but rather in learning how to exploit expert advice. In the following section we elaborate on the problem of deciding with expert advice and we describe state-of-the-art approaches.

2.2   Approaches to Deciding with Expert Advice

The problem of deciding with expert advice [6] formalises a process wherein at each timestep t a set of N experts can observe the set of contexts of a CMAB and provide the learner with advice based on their prior knowledge about the problem. The learner must then exploit this advice to select arms and progressively update the policy that maps expert advice to probabilities over the arms. Concretely, the advice $\xi_{k,t}^n$ is expert n's recommended probability of pulling arm k at time t. The aim of the learner is to perform as well or better than the best available expert. We measure this performance in terms of regret with respect to the best expert:

$$R_T^{'\pi} = \max_{n=1}^{N} \sum_{t=1}^{T} \left(f(\vec{x}_{k_t \sim \vec{\xi}_t^n, t}) - f(\vec{x}_{k_t \sim \pi_t, t}) \right) \tag{2}$$

As outlined in Algorithm 1, algorithms solving the problem of deciding with expert advice should provide a concrete implementation of the policy which maps advice to selected contexts (Line 5), and how the policy is updated (Line 6).

A straightforward approach to this setting is the majority vote which considers all experts as equals, computes an average of their advice, and then selects the arm with the highest average.

As experts can differ in their competence, equally weighting their advice is not always appropriate. EXP4 [6] solves the problem outlined in Algorithm 1 by learning to weigh the advice provided by experts to minimize the regret. To identify the best expert(s), EXP4 maintains a weight w_t^n for each expert which it uses to compute a weighted average of expert advice. Based on this weighted average the learner pulls an arm k_t and collects a reward $r_t \sim f(\vec{x}_{k_t,t})$. The weights are then updated such that experts whose high probability arms match high expected rewards gain more influence and thus become more important in the aggregation. Because the trained weights are not conditioned on the context, EXP4 is of limited use when expertise is localized (e.g., when experts are trained on subsets of the context-space).

Algorithm 1. Deciding with expert advice

Require: N experts, contextual bandit with distribution function f and K arms of dimensionality d, learner with policy $\pi : [0,1]^{K \times N} \to [0,1]^K$
1: Each expert n has experience on P^n contexts sampled from its expertise region.
2: **for** $t = 1, 2, ..., T$ **do**
3:　　Observe context matrix $\mathbf{x}_t$ and share it with experts
4:　　Get expert advice vectors $\boldsymbol{\xi}_t = \{\vec{\xi}_t^1, ..., \vec{\xi}_t^N\}$
5:　　Pull arm $k_t \sim \pi_t(\boldsymbol{\xi}_t)$ and collect resulting reward r_t
6:　　$\pi_{t+1} = update(\pi_t, \boldsymbol{\xi}_t, k_t, r_t)$　　　▷ Learner updates its policy based on the received advice, the pulled arm and the observed reward

---

Confidence when Deciding with Expert Advice. If experts are given the opportunity to share how confident they are about their advice, the collective performance can be improved by increasing the importance of experts with high confidence. Straightforwardly, we can use these confidence estimates as weights in a weighted majority vote (WMV) [10]: $\sum_{n \in N} logit(c_{k,t}^n)\xi_{k,t}^n$, with $c_{k,t}^n$ the confidence of expert n for its advice about context $\vec{x}_{k,t}$ at time t. We then greedily select the arm with the highest weighted sum. The $logit$ term was introduced in [10] so that experts with worse-than-random confidence (<0.5) are weighted negatively, and experts with random confidence ($=0.5$) are ignored.

This method is however dependent on accurate confidence estimates, when estimates are noisy the weighted majority vote's performance degrades [9]. In such scenarios a more robust method such as EXP4.P+CON [9] is necessary. By using confidence estimates as priors for the expert weights, EXP4.P+CON improves the performance of a collective of experts when accurate confidence estimates are provided, but is also able to diverge from imperfect confidence estimates (e.g., if they are noisy).

Value Advice for Deciding with Expert Advice. When providing probability advice, uncertainty in some contexts affects the probability distribution of all arms. In contrast, the alternative of value advice [9] can prevent uncertainty about one arm from spreading to the advice about the other arms. The results given in [9] show that such value advice can improve the performance over the classical probability advice.

2.3   CDM as a Multi-armed Bandit

In [6], an unnamed alternative to EXP4 is proposed to identify the best expert, an approach which we will refer here to as meta-MAB. In essence, given N experts, each expert can be treated as an arm in an N-armed meta-bandit. Selecting an arm means we apply the corresponding expert's policy. Concretely, if at time t arm n of the meta-bandit is pulled, the policy of expert n is followed to pull an arm in the original CMAB. The arm's estimated value is then updated based on the reward observed by applying its policy. As expert advice is never combined, this approach's performance is bounded by the performance of the best expert. What's more, each timestep only updates the estimated value of one expert. These limitations motivated the introduction of EXP4 [6]. Note that when confidence estimates are available they can be used as priors on each expert's estimated value.

While the WMV is dependent on accurate confidence estimates, EXP4 (and its variants) and meta-MAB are limited to finding an appropriate weighted average of the expert's advice through reinforcement learning. In contrast to these methods we propose in the following section meta-CMAB, a method which learns an appropriate mapping of expert advice to expected outcomes without the need for confidence estimates and without being constrained by a weighted average model.

3   The Meta-Contextual Multi-armed Bandit

In the meta-contextual multi-armed bandit (meta-CMAB), the assumption is made that there exists a function $\mathcal{V}$ which maps the experts' advice and confidence for a given context to an expected reward. In other words, given a context $\vec{x}_{k,t}$ (i.e., a context for a given arm k at time t) and a set of N experts wherein each expert n provides advice $\xi_{k,t}^{n}$ and confidence $c_{k,t}^{n}$ about that context, we assume the scalarization function f can be approximated by

$$f(\vec{x}_{k,t}) \approx \mathcal{V}(\{\xi_{k,t}^{1}, c_{k,t}^{1}, ..., \xi_{k,t}^{N}, c_{k,t}^{N}\})$$

If such a $\mathcal{V}$ exists, minimizing regret in the CMAB with contexts $\vec{y}_{k,t} = \{\xi_{k,t}^{1}, c_{k,t}^{1}, ..., \xi_{k,t}^{N}, c_{k,t}^{N}\} \ \forall k \in K$ and distribution function $\mathcal{V}$ is equivalent to optimising the CDM process (i.e., minimizing regret in the deciding with expert advice setting).

This formulation makes it possible to select one of the many CMAB algorithms to solve the meta-CMAB, and consequently the original problem. Just as in standard CMAB, the choice of CMAB algorithm depends on the assumptions made about $\mathcal{V}$. For example, when solving a CMAB with context dimensionality d, LinUCB assumes there is a linear relation between contexts and expected rewards, in other words, it assumes there exists some parameter vector $\theta \in \mathbb{R}^d$ such that

$$\mathbb{E}[f(\vec{x}_{k,t})] = \vec{\theta} \cdot \vec{x}_{k,t} \qquad (3)$$

Selecting LinUCB to solve the meta-CMAB, assumes that $\mathcal{V}$ is linear, i.e., there exists some $\vec{\theta} \in \mathbb{R}^{2N}$ such that

$$\mathbb{E}[f(\vec{x}_{k,t})] = \mathbb{E}[\mathcal{V}(\vec{y}_{k,t})] = \vec{\theta} \cdot \vec{y}_{k,t} \qquad (4)$$

LinUCB provides a relatively easy to interpret linear relation between expert advice and expected reward, but other CMAB with less restrictive assumptions on $\mathcal{V}$ but harder to interpret mappings could be applied to solve the meta-bandit. A decision-tree approach to CMABs, as in [11] for example, can also provide understandable results. Alternatively, non-parametric approaches such as KernelUCB [12] might provide more powerful predictions at the expense of comprehensibility.

Algorithm 2 gives the meta-CMAB implementation for deciding with expert advice.

Algorithm 2. meta-CMAB for deciding with expert advice

Require: N experts, contextual bandit with distribution function f and K arms of dimensionality d
1: Each expert n has experience on P^n contexts sampled from its expertise region.
2: Initialize a CMAB algorithm learner $\pi_1, e.g., LinUCB$
3: **for** $t = 1, 2, ..., T$ **do**
4:     Observe context matrix $\mathbf{x}_t$ and share it with experts
5:     Get expert advice vectors $\boldsymbol{\xi}_t = \{\vec{\xi}_t^1, ..., \vec{\xi}_t^N\}$
6:     Get expert confidence vectors $\mathbf{c}_t = \{\vec{c}_t^1, ..., \vec{c}_t^N\}$
7:     $\vec{y}_{k,t} = \{\xi_{k,t}^1, c_{k,t}^1, ..., \xi_{k,t}^N, c_{k,t}^N\}$ ▷ construct meta-contexts
8:     Pull arm $k_t \sim \pi_t(\{\vec{y}_{1,t}, ..., \vec{y}_{K,t}\})$ and collect resulting reward r_t
9:     $\pi_{t+1} = update(\pi_t, \vec{y}_{k_t,t}, k_t, r_t)$ ▷ Update the policy according to the selected CMAB algorithm

---

Crucially, regardless of the chosen solver, meta-CMAB is as context-agnostic[1] as EXP4.P(+CON) [9].

4   Experiments

In what follows, the experimental setting is described. Afterwards, the performance of meta-CMAB is compared with the performance of three other

---

[1] Neither EXP4 (and derivatives) nor meta-CMAB make explicit use of the base contexts to solve the problem.

approaches, i.e., EXP4.P+CON, meta-MAB and WMV. First, the results for using value advice as opposed to probability advice are shown. Second, the effects of confidence estimates on the performance of all four algorithms are compared. Third, as perfect confidence estimates are often not available, the robustness of the methods towards noisy confidence is assessed[2].

4.1 Settings

Contextual Bandits. Following [9], we use artificial experts which solve an artificial CMAB. Two-dimensional contexts are sampled from the unit square. The value landscape is generated following Perlin noise [13]. The reward for pulling an arm with context $\vec{x}$ is sampled from a Bernoulli distribution with probability of success $p(r = 1; \vec{x}) = f(\vec{x})$, where $f(\vec{x})$ is the context's value in the sampled Perlin landscape.

Prior Information. A pool of N experts with differences in prior expertise is used here. We simulate prior knowledge by training each expert n to P^n experiences on contexts sampled from within its hyper-rectangle with origin $\vec{o}^n \in [0,1]^d$ and side lengths $\vec{s}^n \in [0,1]^d$ with $\vec{o}^n_d + \vec{s}^n_d \leq 1 \ \forall d$. For our simulations, experts are trained using KernelUCB. We fix $P^n = 100$, and train experts on hyper-squares covering (a possibly overlapping) 25% of the context space.

Noisy Confidence. To evaluate the effect of imperfect confidence, we follow the noisy model presented in [9]. Concretely, if a^n_T is expert n's true confidence, its reported confidence is sampled as follows: $c^n \sim \beta(1 + a^n_T/\eta, 1 + (1 - a^n_T)/\eta)$, with η the noise level.

Collective Decision Making. The results discussed in the following sections are aggregated over 1000 runs (or trials). Each run consists of one iteration of Algorithm 1, itself consisting of $T = 1000$ time-steps. The CMAB instance and experts are re-sampled at the start of each run. For any given run the algorithms discussed below share the same CMAB instance and pool of experts. Any difference in performance is a consequence of how expertise is exploited.

Meta Algorithms. Meta-MAB and meta-CMAB both require the selection of a (C)MAB algorithm. For the meta-MAB approach we applied Thompson Sampling [14] to find the best expert, as it has been shown to empirically outperform other MAB algorithms such as UCB [15]. As comprehensibility of the decision process is a desirable property of any CDM, we opt here for a simple model that can be easily interpreted to solve the meta-CMAB. More specifically, we make the assumption that there is a linear relation between expert advice and outcomes and apply LinUCB [16].

---

[2] Code available at https://github.com/axelabels/CDM.

4.2   Results

Due to space limitations, the performance for the two extreme cases of many arms with few experts, and, few arms with many experts are shown here. Results are given in terms of the distance between the best expert and the CDM's performance, i.e., regret in relation to the best expert. A negative regret indicates that the collective results are better than those produced by the best expert. As a comparison between EXP4.P(+CON) and WMV is extensively discussed in [9], the focus of the current discussion will be on meta-MAB and meta-CMAB, in relation to those two.

How Does Value Advice Affect the Meta Approaches? The top row of Fig. 1 plots the performance when no confidence estimates are available. In both plots and regardless of the advice type, meta-CMAB performs significantly better than EXP4.P or the majority vote (statistical significance based on a Wilcoxon rank-sum test with confidence level 5%). What's more, the performance of meta-CMAB improves when value advice is provided, significantly so when $K << N$. In contrast to meta-CMAB, meta-MAB performs badly when the number of experts is high. Furthermore, there is no distinction between meta-MAB's performance with value or probability advice.

As the regret of MAB algorithms such as Thompson Sampling, which is used to determine the best expert in meta-MAB, are bound by the number of arms (see for example [17]), the regret of meta-MAB in our results increases with the number of experts (i.e., the meta-arms, with each arm in meta-MAB matching one expert). Intuitively, if there are more experts it is harder to find the single best expert. The observation that there is no difference between value and probability advice is due the meta-MAB algorithm itself: the algorithm selects a single expert's advice and then acts greedily on this advice.

The lower regret in the $K << N$ case of meta-CMAB is due to the number of experts: having more experts leads to more features that can be exploited to identify the most interesting arm (or expert). Concerning the performance difference between value advice and probability advice, the latter gives the meta-CMAB algorithm an indication of relative performance, whereas the former provides an indication of absolute performance. As a result, the former is easier to map to value estimates. Independent of the advice type or number of arms/experts, one can observe that the proposed meta-CMAB significantly outperforms prior work (i.e., EXP4.P, WMV and Meta-MAB) in this scenario without confidence, with the exception of meta-MAB when the number of experts is low. While meta-MAB performs well when the number of experts is low, its high regret for the $K << N$ case limits its applicability to a small subset of CDM scenario's. We propose that large inter-quartile ranges in the $N = 2$ case are the consequence of the absence of intermediate experts, leading to performance close to either the best or the worst expert.

The Effect of Non-contextual Confidence on the Meta Approaches. When experts provide non-contextual confidence estimates they provide an indication of their expected overall performance over the whole context-space. The

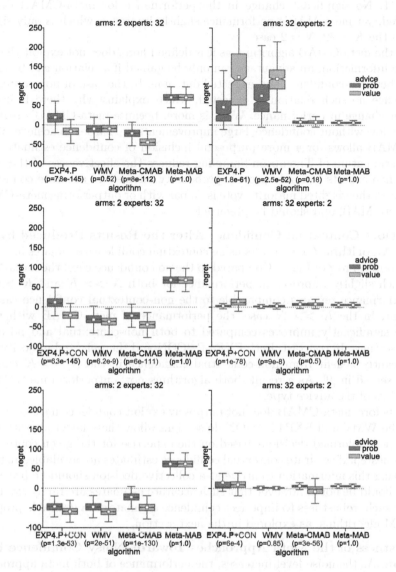

Fig. 1. Algorithm performances per advice and confidence type. Performance is measured in terms of regret, a regret below 0 means the algorithm performs better than the best expert. P-values are given for a Wilcoxon test between probability and value advice results. This plot presents performance when experts outnumber arms (left) and arms outnumber experts (right). (top) Performance without confidence, (middle) performance with non-contextual confidence, and (bottom) performance with contextual confidence.

results using non-contextual confidence estimates are given in the central row of Fig. 1. No significant change in the performance for meta-CMAB can be observed, yet meta-MAB's performance slightly improves, which is only significant in the $K = 32, N = 2$ case.

As the meta-CMAB algorithm, as it is defined here, does not exploit the confidence information, an advantage can only be gained if a relation can be established between confidence and expected outcome. In the case of non-contextual confidence no such relation is expected, which explains why there is no significant change in performance. What is more, because meta-CMAB's regret is already low without confidence, large improvements are harder to achieve. While meta-MAB allows for a more purposeful inclusion of confidence estimates, the stochastic nature of Thompson Sampling reduces the effectiveness of these priors. When experts can only provide probability advice and accurate confidence estimates, the weighted majority vote is on par with or outperforms meta-CMAB and meta-MAB, and should be preferred.

How Does Contextual Confidence Alter the Results Produced by the Meta Algorithms? The results using contextual confidence estimates are given in the bottom row of Fig. 1. Compared to the no confidence case, the meta-MAB approach slightly improves in performance for both $N >> K$ and $K >> N$. Its performance remains comparable to the non-contextual confidence case. In contrast, in the $K >> N$ case, the performance of meta-CMAB with value advice significantly improves compared to both non-contextual and no confidence settings. In contrast, both EXP4.P+CON and the weighted majority vote significantly benefit from non-contextual confidence in the $N >> K$ case, as was observed in [9]. As a result, both algorithms now outperform meta-CMAB regardless of the advice type.

As before, meta-CMAB does not purposely exploit confidence measures while both the WMV and EXP4.P+CON do so. This allow these latter algorithms to make more informed decisions based on the expertise for the given contexts at each timestep. If accurate contextual confidence estimates are available, methods exploiting this information to arrive at a collective decision should be preferred.

It should be noted however that such accurate estimates are rarely available, and as such, robustness to imperfect confidence estimates is a desirable property of CDM algorithms, as explored in the next section.

Robustness of the Meta Approaches Towards Noisy Confidence Estimation. As the noise level increases, the performance of both meta approaches is not significantly affected, as shown in Fig. 2. In contrast, the performance of EXP4.P+CON and WMV degrades significantly as the amount of noise increases. While EXP4.P+CON is more robust to noise than WMV, it still undergoes a slight degradation in performance. While their lack of explicit confidence exploitation hurts their performance when accurate confidence can be guaranteed, these results show that when no guarantees can be given on the accuracy of confidence, meta-CMAB should be preferred. Meta-MAB shows a similar robustness to noise, but its benefits are limited to cases with few experts.

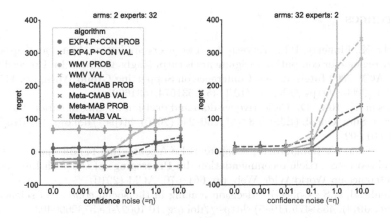

Fig. 2. Influence of noise on algorithm performance. Performance of different aggregation algorithms in function of (noisy) confidence estimates. For each noise level (η) confidence is sampled from the beta distribution $\beta(1 + a/\eta, 1 + (1 - a)/\eta)$. A value of 0 means the algorithm performs as well as the best expert. Dashed lines use value advice, full lines use probability advice. This plot presents performance when experts outnumber arms (left) and arms outnumber experts (right).

5 Conclusion

In this paper, a novel approach to tackle CDM problems is proposed. Decision-making with expert advice is formulated as a CMAB. More specifically, expert advice and confidence estimates are considered as predictive features for the context's expected reward. The assumption that there is a learnable mapping from these predictive features to the actual rewards motivates the construction of a meta-CMAB wherein each meta-context consists of an expert's advice and confidences for the base problem. Any of the existing CMAB algorithms can then be applied to minimize the regret for this meta-CMAB which is equivalent to optimizing the original CDM problem. Our results show that even the relatively simple LinUCB algorithm leads to performance that significantly improves on the results produced by state-of-the-art approaches. Finally, while meta-CMAB is slightly outperformed by existing methods for probability advice when accurate confidence estimates are available, its robustness to noisy confidence makes it preferable whenever confidence are expected to be imperfect. Future work should study whether confidence can be exploited more explicitly while limiting the influence of noise.

Acknowledgment. This publication benefits from the support of the French Community of Belgium in the context of a FRIA grant, and by the FuturICT2.0 (www.futurict2.eu) project funded by the FLAG-ERA Joint Transnational call (JTC) 2016.

References

1. Reily, K., Finnerty, P.L., Terveen, L.: Two peers are better than one: aggregating peer reviews for computing assignments is surprisingly accurate. In: Proceedings of the ACM 2009 International Conference on Supporting Group Work, pp. 115–124. ACM (2009). https://doi.org/10.1145/1531674.1531692
2. Robson, N., Rew, D.: Collective wisdom and decision making in surgical oncology. Eur. J. Surg. Oncol. (EJSO) 36(3), 230–236 (2010). https://doi.org/10.1016/j.ejso.2010.01.002
3. Li, L., Chu, W., Langford, J., Schapire, R.E.: A contextual-bandit approach to personalized news article recommendation. In: Proceedings of the 19th International Conference on World Wide Web, pp. 661–670. ACM (2010)
4. Aikenhead, G.S.: Collective decision making in the social context of science. Sci. Educ. 69(4), 453–475 (1985). https://doi.org/10.1002/sce.3730690403
5. Nitzan, S., Paroush, J.: Collective Decision Making: An Economic Outlook. CUP Archive, Cambridge (1985). https://doi.org/10.1016/0167-2681(87)90033-3
6. Auer, P., Cesa-Bianchi, N., Freund, Y., Schapire, R.: The nonstochastic multiarmed bandit problem. SIAM J. Comput. 32(1), 48–77 (2002). https://doi.org/10.1137/S0097539701398375
7. McMahan, H.B., Streeter, M.: Tighter bounds for multi-armed bandits with expert advice. In: Proceedings of the 22nd Annual Conference on Learning Theory (COLT) (2009)
8. Zhou, L.: A survey on contextual multi-armed bandits. CoRR abs/1508.03326 (2015)
9. Abels, A., Lenaerts, T., Trianni, V., Nowé, A.: How expert confidence can improve collective decision-making in contextual multi-armed bandit problems. In: Nguyen, T.N., Hoang, H.B., Huynh, P.C., Hwang, D., Trawiński, B., Vossen, G. (eds.) ICCCI 2020. LNCS, vol. 11683, pp. 125–138. Springer, Cham (2020)
10. Marshall, J.A., Brown, G., Radford, A.N.: Individual confidence-weighting and group decision-making. Trends Ecol. Evol. 32(9), 636–645 (2017). https://doi.org/10.1016/j.tree.2017.06.004
11. Elmachtoub, A.N., McNellis, R., Oh, S., Petrik, M.: A practical method for solving contextual bandit problems using decision trees. CoRR abs/1706.04687 (2017)
12. Valko, M., Korda, N., Munos, R., Flaounas, I.N., Cristianini, N.: Finite-time analysis of kernelised contextual bandits. CoRR abs/1309.6869 (2013)
13. Lagae, A., et al.: A survey of procedural noise functions. In: Computer Graphics Forum, vol. 29, pp. 2579–2600. Wiley Online Library (2010). https://doi.org/10.1111/j.1467-8659.2010.01827.x
14. Thompson, W.R.: On the likelihood that one unknown probability exceeds another in view of the evidence of two samples. Biometrika 25(3/4), 285–294 (1933). https://doi.org/10.2307/2332286
15. Agrawal, R.: Sample mean based index policies by o (log n) regret for the multi-armed bandit problem. Adv. Appl. Probab. 27(4), 1054–1078 (1995). https://www.jstor.org/stable/1427934
16. Chu, W., Li, L., Reyzin, L., Schapire, R.: Contextual bandits with linear payoff functions. In: Proceedings of the Fourteenth International Conference on Artificial Intelligence and Statistics, pp. 208–214 (2011)
17. Agrawal, S., Goyal, N.: Further optimal regret bounds for Thompson sampling. CoRR abs/1209.3353 (2012)

How Expert Confidence Can Improve Collective Decision-Making in Contextual Multi-Armed Bandit Problems

Axel Abels[1,2](✉) [iD], Tom Lenaerts[1,2] [iD], Vito Trianni[3] [iD], and Ann Nowé[2] [iD]

[1] Machine Learning Group, Université Libre de Bruxelles, Brussels, Belgium
{axel.abels,tom.lenaerts}@ulb.ac.be
[2] AI Lab, Vrije Universiteit Brussel, Brussels, Belgium
ann.nowe@ai.vub.ac.be
[3] Laboratory of Autonomous Robotics and Artificial Life, Institute of Cognitive Sciences and Technologies, National Research Council, Rome, Italy
vito.trianni@istc.cnr.it

Abstract. In collective decision-making (CDM) a group of experts with a shared set of values and a common goal must combine their knowledge to make a collectively optimal decision. Whereas existing research on CDM primarily focuses on making binary decisions, we focus here on CDM applied to solving contextual multi-armed bandit (CMAB) problems, where the goal is to exploit contextual information to select the best arm among a set. To address the limiting assumptions of prior work, we introduce confidence estimates and propose a novel approach to deciding with expert advice which can take advantage of these estimates. We further show that, when confidence estimates are imperfect, the proposed approach is more robust than the classical confidence-weighted majority vote.

Keywords: Deciding with expert advice · Contextual bandits · Confidence · Noise · Collective decision-making

1 Introduction

In CDM, a group (e.g. experts) aims to find collectively the best solution among a set of alternatives for a given problem [1–3]. Example applications are peer review processes, wherein the decisions of multiple expert reviewers are combined to ensure that the qualitatively best works are selected from a pool of submissions [4], and medical diagnostics, wherein a group of medical experts must decide on the best treatments for patients [5].

The quality of the decision produced in CDM depends strongly on the expertise of each person involved in the process. Participants in the CDM process should thus have the opportunity to provide an estimate of the confidence they have in their advice, as is now mandatory in many paper reviewing procedures,

© Springer Nature Switzerland AG 2020
N. T. Nguyen et al. (Eds.): ICCCI 2020, LNAI 12496, pp. 125–138, 2020.
https://doi.org/10.1007/978-3-030-63007-2_10

for instance. When confidence information is available, it should be considered by a CDM system to enhance decision accuracy based on expert advice [6].

The Exponential-weight Algorithm for Exploration and Exploitation using Expert advice (EXP4 for short [6]) is a state-of-the-art CDM solver that learns how to integrate the advice of a set of stationary experts, which can either be trained predictors or human experts. Although it is considered to be one of the key approaches to automatically infer collective decisions based on expert advice, it does not consider expert confidence in the learning process. This is a limiting assumption, as experts are likely to have expertise only for the region of the problem on which they were trained. In general, it is safe to assume experts will perform relatively well in settings for which they have prior experience. Querying human experts for (honest) confidence estimates about their given advice has been shown to improve performance on visual perception and value estimation tasks [1,3]. The dominant approach in these tasks is to use confidence-weighted majority votes [3]. The higher an expert's confidence, the higher its opinion (i.e., advice) will be weighted when aggregating.

We hypothesize that EXP4's performance can be improved by including such confidence information. We show how EXP4 can be adapted and under which conditions this hypothesis holds, considering two types of confidence, i.e., a global/non-contextual and a contextual one. Yet, as one cannot assume that an expert always provides correct confidence estimates, we also consider how imperfect confidence estimates affect CDM, revealing thus the robustness of the approach to noise.

Our analysis is performed in the framework of contextual multi-armed bandits (CMAB) [7], where each arm is identified by a combination of contextual features, associated in turn to a context-dependent reward retrieved from an a-priori unknown function. Most problems that can be solved through CDM naturally lend themselves to a formalization through CMABs. In medical decision-making [8] for example, the set of possible patient-treatment pairs is the set of arms and the contexts are pairwise patient-treatment characteristics (e.g. patient symptoms, the results of medical tests, treatment properties). The aim of every medical expert is to select the most appropriate treatment (i.e., the best arm) given the set of contexts and their associated information. Similarly, in a review process the best submission(s) (i.e., the best arm(s)) must be selected based on their context. Different from classic CMAB solving, CDM requires all experts to solve the same problem given their knowledge and combine their proposals/opinions in a way that maximizes expected outcome (e.g., maximizing the overall quality of accepted submissions by taking into account multiple reviewers). As the exact performance of a set of experts can be difficult to estimate a-priori, it is useful to learn to exploit their knowledge purposefully. EXP4 performs exactly this task.

Prior to reporting the methods used to generate the results of this paper, the next section provides first of all the background knowledge on CMAB and making decisions based on expert advice. The final section provides a discussion on the generated results and the conclusions that can be drawn. Note that within this work, we do not yet consider human experts. Experts are modelled as known stochastic contextual bandit algorithms [7], having different degrees of expertise on the CMAB problems for which they need to provide advice.

2 Background

2.1 Contextual Multi-Armed Bandits

We follow here the formalism for stochastic contextual bandits specified in [7], which associates to each individual arm a context vector. At time t, the set of all arms in a CMAB is characterized by K time-dependent d-dimensional context vectors $\{\vec{x}_{1,t}, ..., \vec{x}_{K,t}\} \in \mathbb{R}^{K \times d}$. A CMAB also possesses a fixed but unknown value function f which maps each arm context to a reward, $f : \mathbb{R}^d \rightarrow [0, 1]$. A policy $\pi : \mathbb{R}^{K \times d} \rightarrow [0, 1]^K$ maps all K arm contexts to a probability distribution according to which the learner chooses an arm.

When approximating f from scratch is infeasible, experts can provide the knowledge required to select the appropriate arms. Indeed, experts can reduce the complex contextual information into an advice about each arm that can be exploited for the arm choice. To this end, methods such as EXP4 – described in the following section – learn to identify the best performing experts.

2.2 EXP4: Deciding with Expert Advice

When deciding with expert advice [6], a learner can query a set of N stationary experts for their advice on which arm to select, with each expert having access to every context vector $\vec{x}_{k,t}$ associated with those arms. Each expert n has some expertise about these contexts which it uses to express advice $\xi^n_{k,t}$ for each arm k (i.e., the probability of pulling arm k). Such experts can be complex, time-intensive algorithms trained in advance on similar data as well as human experts that are able to infer relations beyond the reach of current algorithmic approaches (some human intuitions for example are hard to translate into an algorithm), or a mix of both. In this setting, the learner has no access to the information about the best arm, and should rely on the experts. Informally, a learner must identify which experts' advice to follow. The quality of this identification is measured in terms of regret (R'^{π}_T):

$$R'^{\pi}_T = \max_{n=1}^{N} \sum_{t=1}^{T} \left(f(\vec{x}_{k_t \sim \xi^n_t, t}) - f(\vec{x}_{k_t \sim \pi_t, t}) \right) \tag{1}$$

By combining the knowledge of multiple experts, algorithms can surpass the performance of the best single expert, generating a negative regret value.

Algorithm 1 outlines the problem of deciding with expert advice. Solvers for this problem provide a concrete implementation of (i) the policy which maps advice to selected arms (Line 5), and (ii) how the policy is updated based on the observed reward (Line 6). EXP4 [6] performs these tasks by maintaining a weight w^n_t for each expert which it uses to compute a weighted average of expert advice,

$p_{k,t} = softmax(\vec{w}_t) \cdot \vec{\xi}_{k,t}$, where w_t is the vector of expert weights at time t, and $\vec{\xi}_{k,t}$ is the vector of advices for arm k. Based on this weighted average, the learner pulls an arm k_t and collects a reward $r_t \sim f(\vec{x}_{k_t,t})$. Weights are updated based on the collected reward, the expert's advice and the aggregated probability, as follows:

$$w_{t+1}^n = w_t^n + \gamma r_t \xi_{k_t,t}^n \frac{1}{p_{k_t,t}}, \tag{2}$$

where γ is the learning rate. The factor $\frac{1}{p_{k_t,t}}$ is included to un-bias the estimator by increasing the weight of arms that were unlikely to be pulled. However, because of the factor's high variance, EXP4 is prone to instability [9]. EXP4.P [9] (see Algorithm 2), a later improvement on EXP4, reduces this instability by including an additional term in the weight update:

$$\hat{v}_t^n = \sum_{k=1}^{K} \xi_{k,t}^n / p_{k,t} \tag{3}$$

$$w_{t+1}^n = w_t^n + \frac{\gamma}{2} \left(r_t \xi_{k_t,t}^n \frac{1}{p_{k_t,t}} + \hat{v}_t^n \sqrt{\frac{\ln(N/\delta)}{KT}} \right) \tag{4}$$

Intuitively, the term in (3) measures how much each expert disagrees with the aggregated probabilities. For any given expert n this term will be large when there is an arm k such that $\xi_{k,t}^n >> p_{k,t}$ (in other words, if expert n disagrees with the aggregated probability $p_{k,t}$). The factor $\sqrt{\frac{\ln(N/\delta)}{KT}}$ weighs this additional term in function of the number of experts (N), the number of arms (K), the number of time-steps (T) and the parameter δ.

Neither EXP4 nor EXP4.P make use of contextual information when updating weights. As a consequence, the weight of an expert is uniform over the complete context space, which limits the usefulness of EXP4.P when expertise is localized (e.g., when experts provide good advice for subsets of the context-space, but do not show significant differences in performance when the whole context-space is considered).

Algorithm 1. Deciding with expert advice

Require: N experts, contextual bandit with distribution function f and K arms of dimensionality d, learner with policy $\pi : [0,1]^{K \times N} \rightarrow [0,1]^K$ which maps advice to a probability distribution over the arms
1: Each expert n has experience on P^n contexts sampled from its expertise region.
2: **for** $t = 1, 2, ..., T$ **do**
3:     Observe context matrix $\mathbf{x}_t = \{\vec{x}_{1,t}, ..., \vec{x}_{K,t}\}$ and share it with experts
4:     Get expert advice vectors $\boldsymbol{\xi}_t = \{\vec{\xi}_t^1, ..., \vec{\xi}_t^N\}$
5:     Pull arm $k_t \sim \pi_t(\boldsymbol{\xi}_t)$ and collect resulting reward r_t
6:     $\pi_{t+1} = update(\pi_t, \boldsymbol{\xi}_t, k_t, r_t)$ ▷ Learner updates its policy based on the received advice, the pulled arm and the observed reward

---

Algorithm 2. Description of the EXP4.P algorithm

Require: $\delta > 0$

1: Define $\gamma = \sqrt{\frac{\ln N}{KT}}$, set $\vec{w}_1 = \mathbf{1}$ of size N.
2: **for** $t = 1, 2, ...T$ **do**
3:      Get expert advice vectors $\boldsymbol{\xi}_t = \{\vec{\xi}_t^1, ..., \vec{\xi}_t^N\}$, each vector is of size K.
4:      **for** $k = 1, 2, ..., K$ **do**   ▷ compute weighted average
5:          $p_{k,t} = softmax(\vec{w}_t) \cdot \vec{\xi}_{k,t}$
6:      Draw arm k_t according to $\vec{p}_t$, and receive reward r_t.
7:      **for** $n = 1, ..., N$ **do**   ▷ Update weights

$$\hat{y}_t^n = \xi_{t,k_t}^n \cdot r_t / p_{k_t,t}$$

$$\hat{v}_t^n = \sum_{k=1}^{K} \xi_{k,t}^n / p_{k,t}$$

$$w_{t+1}^n = w_t^n + \frac{\gamma}{2}\left(\hat{y}_t^n + \hat{v}_t^n \sqrt{\frac{\ln(N/\delta)}{KT}}\right)$$

2.3 Weighted Majority Vote

To evaluate the results obtained for our adaptations of EXP4, we consider as a baseline a straightforward aggregation method consisting in computing a weighted average of all advices and acting greedily on this average, i.e., the Weighted Majority Vote (WMV) algorithm [3]. The weights used in the WMV can for example be based on experts' expressed confidence, with higher confidence resulting in a higher impact on the weighted aggregation. In binary decision-making the usage of confidence-based weights is optimal [3]. Building on that result we propose a rudimentary extensions of the weighted majority vote for the n-ary case by computing the weighted average of the advice vectors. If the confidence $c_{k,t}^n$ of an expert n at time t about context $\vec{x}_k$ is expressed in the range $[0, 1]$ wherein confidences of $1, 0.5$, and 0 correspond respectively to a perfect expert, a random expert, and the worst possible expert, we can weigh advice as follows: $\sum_{n \in N} logit(c_{k,t}^n)\xi_{k,t}^n$.

Given the weighted value, WMV greedily selects the arm with the highest resulting value. The $logit$ function provides optimal weights for the binary case [3], because experts with worse-than-random confidence ($c_{k,t}^n < 0.5$) are weighted negatively, and experts with random confidence ($c_{k,t}^n = 0.5$) are ignored. A further discussion on how the confidence estimates can be obtained for CMABs is given in Sect. 3.2. It should nevertheless be clear that this method heavily relies on accurate confidence estimates. To address this drawback we propose an expansion of EXP4.P in Sect. 3.4 which can take advantage of accurate confidence estimates but is robust to inaccurate values.

3   Implementation

In this section we introduce our extensions to EXP4.P as well as the two forms of confidence that will be used, i.e., contextual and non-contextual confidence, and how they intuitively can be incorporated in the algorithm. We also hypothesize that by using as advice the expected value obtained from pulling an arm as opposed to the probability distribution over the arms an additional boost in decision-making performance can be obtained. As already mentioned in the introduction, experts are considered here as instances of known stochastic contextual bandit algorithms [7].

3.1   Value Advice

When considering localized expertise in a CMAB problem, experts can be knowledgeable about a subset of the active contexts but agnostic about the remaining contexts. To provide probability advice, experts must make assumptions about unknown arms which affect the probability distribution over all the arms. Previous work on deciding with expert advice has been limited to advice in the form of probability distributions (see Sect. 2.2). In contrast, if advice consists of one value estimate per arm, the uncertainty about some contexts does not affect the given advice for the known arms. This is the main motivation behind our first contribution: the introduction of value advice and a straightforward extension of EXP4.P to this setting.

Concretely, in the case of value advice, if $\tilde{f}_t^n$ is expert n's approximation of f at time t, then its advice for context vector $\vec{x}_{k,t}^n$ at time t is: $\xi_{k,t}^n = \tilde{f}_t^n(\vec{x}_{k,t}^n)$

In the original algorithm, when using probability advice, EXP4.P computes the following unbiased gain for each expert which is used to increment expert weights: $\hat{y}_t^n = \xi_{k,t}^n r_t/p_{k,t}$, with $p_{k,t}$ the probability of pulling arm k at time t. When dealing with value advice we hypothesize that an expert with low prediction errors will have low regret and use the negation of (unbiased) squared error between the expert's predicted value and the outcome: $\hat{y}_t^n = -(\xi_{k,t}^n - r_t)^2/p_{k,t}$. This value iteratively increases the relative weight of the experts with the lowest mean square error. While value advice prevents the spread of uncertainty to all arms, the expression of confidence as we explore in the following section can further help the CDM algorithm in its decision-making.

3.2   Confidence in Contextual Multi-Armed Bandits

In what follows we propose two measures of confidence, i.e., non-contextual confidence, which is analogous to the accuracy measure used for weighted majority votes in binary classification [3], and contextual confidence, in which experts provide confidence for active contexts.

Non-contextual Confidence. The *non-contextual confidence* takes inspiration from the accuracy of experts in binary classification problems [3], wherein a perfect expert has confidence 1, a random expert has confidence 0.5 and the worst possible expert has confidence 0. Given an expert's confidence c^n (the probability that an expert n's advice is the right one), their advice can be optimally weighted by $ln(\frac{c^n}{1-c^n})$. The goal is to derive a similar measure for CMABS in CDM.

To this end one needs to derive a confidence for n-ary decisions similar to the binary classification accuracy, with similar mappings as for the binary classification, i.e., a measure of 1 for perfect performance or optimal policy π^*, a measure of 0 for the worst possible performance or worst policy π^-, and 0.5 for the performance of a random agent or uniform policy $\pi^{\mathcal{U}}$. Because rewards are not all-or-nothing as they are in binary classification, we define confidence in terms of regret. Given a policy π with regret R_T^π we derive its confidence over T steps by normalizing its regret with regards to the worst possible regret $(R_T^{\pi^-})$, the best possible regret $(R_T^{\pi^+})$, and random regret $(R_T^{\pi^{\mathcal{U}}})$ as

$c_T^\pi = ((R_T^{\pi^-} - R_T^\pi)/(R_T^{\pi^-} - R_T^{\pi^+}))^\rho$, where $\rho = log(0.5)/log(\frac{R_T^{\pi^-} - R_T^{\pi^{\mathcal{U}}}}{R_T^{\pi^-} - R_T^{\pi^+}})$ scales the regret such that a random policy is assigned a confidence of 0.5. Analogously to the binary classification setting, this confidence measure has the following properties: (i) $c_T^\pi \in [0,1]$ for every policy π, (ii) $c_T^\pi < c_T^{\pi'} \Leftrightarrow R_T^\pi > R_T^{\pi'}$, (iii) $c_T^{\pi^{\mathcal{U}}} = 0.5$, (iv) $c_T^{\pi^*} = 1$ and v) $c_T^{\pi^-} = 0$.

Note that, while determining the exact confidence of an expert a priori would be impossible, a reasonable assumption is that a confidence estimate is available based on prior experiences. Such (approximate) confidence measure reflects how confident a participant can be about its advice. This provides the aggregating algorithm with information on how to weigh expert advice. Such confidence is however limited in that it only captures a general trend rather than decision-specific confidence. A more appropriate form of confidence, would depend on the decision that needs to be made rather than on a sequence of decisions.

Contextual Confidence. It is reasonable to assume that expertise is not uniformly distributed over the context-space. Global confidence measures like the one discussed earlier fail to capture such a heterogeneous expertise distribution. When confidence can be considered on a case-by-case basis, i.e., based on the contexts for which a decision must be made, we refer to it as *contextual confidence*. Concretely, every time an expert n gives an advice $\xi_{k,t}^n$ for an arm k, she can also express a confidence measure $c_{k,t}^n$ related to that advice. We assume that this confidence is on average correlated to the expert's performance.

Confidences are expressed for the advice on the current context $\mathbf{x}_{k,t}$, which is, intuitively, how likely it is that following the expert's advice for that arm will help the learner pick the best arms. An expert's lack of confidence might reflect that the expert has spent little time solving problems in that region of the context space (e.g., a patient showing symptoms the doctor is not familiar with might reduce the doctor's confidence in which treatment is appropriate). Contextual confidence provides a convenient way of modelling for example a general practitioner as an expert whose prior experiences are spread out over most of the context-space as opposed to a specialist (e.g., an ophthalmologist) whose prior experience is focused on a small region of the context-space. The former will have a moderate confidence over most of the context space, the latter will have high confidence for that specific region on which she was trained.

Note that confidence is not always accurate. Humans also have a tendency to overestimate their confidence [10], and over-fitting is a well-known problem in algorithmic prediction wherein performance on training data (on which one might base confidence) does not translate to performance on the test data [11,12]. The noise model presented in Sect. 3.3 partially addresses this drawback.

Although human experts can readily provide contextual confidence our experimental results focus on CDM with CMAB-based algorithmic experts. The next section discusses how contextual confidence can be derived for some of the more common CMAB algorithms [7].

Deriving Confidence from Artificial Experts. CMAB algorithms make (explicit) use of an additional term that drives exploration. At time t, these algorithms generally select the arm k that maximizes $\tilde{f}_t(\vec{x}_{k,t}) + \alpha \sigma_{k,t}$, where $\tilde{f}_t$ is the learner's current approximation of f, $\sigma_{k,t}$ is the uncertainty around context $\vec{x}_{k,t}$ and α weighs this exploratory term. Thus, the higher the uncertainty about a context, the higher the exploratory drive. This measure of uncertainty is linked to a lack of confidence as one can consider that low uncertainty is correlated with a high accuracy and can be used as a proxy for perfect confidence.

Hence, since experts here correspond to CMAB algorithms (and more specifically KernelUCB [13]), we can exploit this uncertainty to obtain confidence estimates. In essence, when the uncertainty $\sigma_{k,t}$ around a context $\vec{x}_{k,t}$ is large, the expert's confidence should be low. Conversely, a small uncertainty should result in a high confidence. A high level of uncertainty for all contexts indicates an overall lack of knowledge. In such cases, performance is equivalent to a random policy and a confidence of 0.5 is appropriate. In all other cases more information than random is available, and the resulting confidence should reflect this by being superior to 0.5. Taking this into account, if $\sigma_{k,t}^n \in [0,1]$ is expert n's uncertainty for context vector $\vec{x}_{k,t}$, the expert's contextual confidence is defined as $c_{k,t}^n = 0.5 + \frac{1}{2}(1 - \sigma_{k,t}^n)$.

In the case of probability advice, the probabilities are expressed in function of multiple contexts. As a result, the expressed confidence should be a function of the confidences of these multiple contexts. When we need to combine multiple confidences we will use the geometric mean of individual confidences.

3.3   Noise Model

Experimental results have shown that humans have a tendency to show bias in self-reported confidence estimates [10]. Whether it is because of past experience which is no longer relevant or simply a tendency to over or under-estimate one's confidence, an estimated confidence which diverges from the expert's actual confidence can be counter-productive. It is therefore desirable to have CDM methods that are robust to the presence of noise in confidence estimates. To simulate the presence of imperfect confidence we propose the following noise model parametrized by a noise level η. Given an expert with true confidence c_T^n, we sample her noisy confidence from the Beta distribution $\beta(1+c_T^n/\eta, 1+(1-c_T^n)/\eta)$, which ensures one remains in the $[0, 1]$ interval. As Fig. 1 (left panel) illustrates, the lower the noise level, the more likely it is that the expert's sampled confidence equals its true confidence.

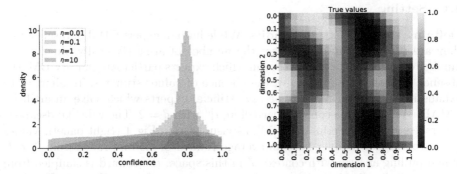

Fig. 1. Confidence distributions and reward values in 2-dimensional contextual bandit. (left) Confidence distribution in function of noise (η) levels for $c_T^e = 0.8$. Given an expert with true confidence c_T^n, the expert's noisy confidence is sampled from the beta distribution $\beta(1 + c_T^n/\eta, 1 + (1 - c_T^n)/\eta)$. As $\eta \to 0$ the sampled values converge to c_T^n. As $\eta \to \infty$, the confidence distribution converges to a uniform distribution over $[0, 1]$. (right) Example of the truth values of a 2-dimensional contextual bandit. Brighter values have a higher expected reward. This landscape is generated using the Perlin noise procedure described in Sect. 4.1.

3.4 Confidence-Weighted, Value-Based EXP4.P

Our implementation starts from EXP4.P [9], detailed in Algorithm 2, which builds on the assumption that expertise is equal over the complete context-space. To deal with more localized expertise with the help of confidence estimates we propose EXP4.P+CON. In its original description, EXP4.P assumes no prior knowledge about the performance of experts. Hence, weights are initialized uniformly. However, if a confidence estimate $c_{k,t}^n$ is available, we modify Line 5 in Algorithm 2 to integrate at each time-step the confidence estimate in the aggregation rule (the denominator ensures the weights add up to 1):

$$\sum_{n \in N} \frac{exp(w_{n,t})c_{k,t}^n/(1 - c_{k,t}^n)}{\sum_{n' \in N} exp(w_{n',t})c_{k,t}^{n'}/(1 - c_{k,t}^{n'})} \xi_{k,t}^n \tag{5}$$

4 Experiments

In what follows the experimental settings are defined. First, the performance of the different advice types, i.e., probability advice and value advice, is evaluated.

Second, the effect of (non-)contextual confidence estimates on performance are tested against the scenario without confidence. Third, as accurate confidence estimates are not always available, the impact of noisy confidence estimates is tested. EXP4.P+CON is compared to the WMV algorithm described earlier[1].

4.1   Setting

Defining the Contextual Bandits. While human expert CDM datasets exist, they are typically limited in either the number of arms (typically binary), the number of samples, the consistency in which experts participate in the CDM, the absence of confidence, or, finally, the absence of value estimates. To allow us to exhaustively test our methods we use artificial experts which solve an artificial CMAB. We consider a context space of $[0,1]^d$ with $d = 2$. The value landscape is generated following Perlin noise [14], as visualized in Fig. 1 (right panel). Values generated in this manner have an average reward of 0.5 and range from 0 to 1. When pulling an arm with context $\vec{x}$ in this space, the reward is sampled from a Bernoulli distribution with probability of success $p(r = 1; \vec{x}) = f(\vec{x})$, where $f : [0,1]^d \to [0,1]$ is the function mapping the context to its value.

Prior Expert Information. We simulate prior knowledge by introducing each expert n to P^n experiences on contexts sampled from within its hyper-rectangle with origin $\vec{o}^n \in [0,1]^d$ and side lengths $\vec{s}^n \in [0,1]^d$ with $\vec{o}^n_d + \vec{s}^n_d \leq 1 \ \forall \ d$. This allows us to model the case wherein experts come into play with (in)accurate prior knowledge. Increasing P^n improves the expert's performance, increasing side lengths increases the region of context-space for which the expert can provide relevant advice.

Expert Implementation. A pool of N experts with differences in prior expertise is used here. Each individual expert is implemented as a KernelUCB algorithm, as mentioned earlier, and exposed to a different subset of the context space. We fix $P^n = 100$, $\vec{s}^d = \vec{0.5}$ and randomly sample origins from $[0,0.5]^d$, meaning every expert covers (a possibly overlapping) 25% of the context space. The noisy confidence values are sampled following the noisy model discussed in Sect. 3.3.

Collective Decision Making. A trial or run is defined as one iteration of Algorithm 1. Within each trial, after each expert acquires experiences in its expertise range, collective decision-making occurs with $T = 1000$. The results discussed in the following sections are aggregated over 1000 runs. At the start of each run, a new CMAB instance and pool of experts is generated. For any given trial however, all algorithms considered here solve the same CMAB instance with the same pool of experts.

---

[1] Code available at https://github.com/axelabels/CDM.

4.2   Results and Discussion

Due to space limitations the results presented here are limited to two extreme bandit-arms/expert combinations, i.e., many arms ($K = 32$) few experts ($N = 2$), and few arms($K = 2$) many experts ($N = 32$).

How Does Value Advice Alter Probability Advice Results? The left-most column of Fig. 2 compares the performance of the different algorithms when no confidence is provided. It appears that EXP4.P with value advice performs better than probability advice when $K << N$, a tendency which inverses this condition is no longer met.

When the number of arms is high but the number of experts is low, it is easier for an expert's overestimation of a sub-optimal arm to affect the final decision. In contrast, when the number of experts outnumbers the number of arms, the collective variance is reduced (similarly to ensemble methods [15]). It's notable that EXP4.P's improvement on a non-adaptive weighted majority vote is not as large as one might expect. In part, this is due to the absence of worse than random experts, which is a well known condition for effective majority votes [16].

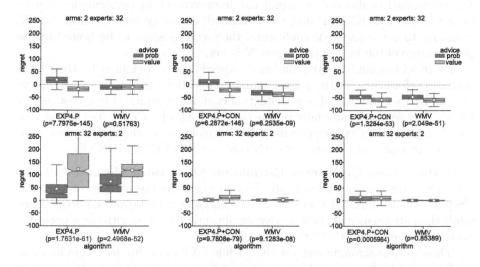

Fig. 2. Performance per advice and confidence type. Regret of different aggregation algorithms in function of advice and confidence type. A value of 0 means the algorithm performs as well as the best expert. White squares mark the mean. The given p-value results from a Wilcoxon test on the results for probability and value advice. This plot presents performance when experts outnumber arms (top) and arms outnumber experts (bottom). (left) Performance without confidence, (middle) performance with non-contextual confidence, and (right) performance with contextual confidence.

How Does Non-contextual Confidence Influence EXP4.P and WMV? Results using non-contextual confidence estimates are given in the central column of Fig. 2. Comparing these results with those obtained without confidence, a significant (Wilcoxon rank-sum test with confidence level 5%) increase in performance can be observed for both EXP4.P (with an exception for probability advice in the $N \gg K$ case) and the (weighted) Majority vote. We further note that the methods appear to be limited by the performance of the best expert when $K \gg N$.

While both methods can improve with the use of non-contextual confidence, the improvements for EXP4.P are less pronounced. This is in part due to how the confidence measures are exploited. In the case of EXP4.P, confidence is essentially used as a prior on the weights, and as such the EXP4.P algorithm can learn to diverge from the given confidence estimates. While this can be useful if confidence is inaccurate, it also reduces the performance benefits when confidence estimates are appropriate. Similar to results obtained in binary classification [16], increasing the number of experts increases the relative performance of the collective, as the lower regret when $N \gg K$ suggests.

How Does Contextual Confidence Influence the Outcome? The results using contextual confidence estimates are given in the right-most column of Fig. 2. Comparing these results with those obtained without confidence or with non-contextual confidence, a significant improvement in performance can be observed for both EXP4.P and the (weighted) Majority vote when $N \gg K$. Similarly to non-contextual confidence, the methods seem to be bound by the performance of the best expert when N is low.

By providing contextual confidence, experts can be weighted by their (estimated) performance for the given contexts. This allows the methods to improve beyond the performance of non-contextual confidence, which only give a general trend. This seems to especially be the case for EXP4.P+CON. We suggest that the change in priors can purposefully drive exploration in the early stages of the learning process and prevent the early convergence of EXP4.P+CON.

How Does Noisy Confidence Estimation Affect Both Methods? Plots in function of different noise levels are given in Fig. 3. As the noise levels increase, the performance of EXP4.P+CON and the Majority vote degrades. Furthermore, while the performance of the majority significantly degrades with large noise, the performance of EXP4.P+CON is less affected.

These results strongly suggest that, while EXP4 benefits less from accurate confidence, it is also more robust to noisy confidence estimates than the majority vote is. From this, a rule of thumb for the selection of the appropriate algorithm can be derived. If noisy confidence is expected, one should prefer EXP4.P. What's more, this confirms the intuition that if confidence is known to be extremely noisy, it should be ignored when making decisions.

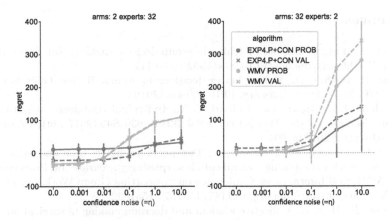

Fig. 3. Influence of noise on algorithm performance. For each noise level (η) confidence is sampled from the beta distribution $\beta(1 + a/\eta, 1 + (1 - a)/\eta)$. A value of 0 means the algorithm performs as well as the best expert. Dashed lines use value advice, full lines use probability advice. This plot presents performance when experts outnumber arms (left) and arms outnumber experts (right).

5 Conclusion

To reduce the influence of uncertainty, this paper proposed an alternative take on advice in the deciding with expert advice setting. More specifically, we introduced value advice and proposed an extension to EXP4.P to integrate such value advice as opposed to probability advice. Our results show such value advice can significantly improve performance when the number of experts is sufficiently bigger than the number of arms. What's more, to handle the problem of localized expertise, we proposed the addition of confidence estimates in the deciding with expert advice. By using these confidences as priors on EXP4.P's weights we obtain a method that can benefit from confidence and is more robust than the classical weighted majority vote when confidence is noisy. We also find that contextual confidence, which is straightforward to derive from existing CMAB experts can further improve the performance when compared to non-contextual confidence. As the latter only provides information on overall performance it is ineffective at determining optimal per-context weights. Confidence with high noise remains a problem however, suggesting that a method which purposefully identifies when confidence is noisy might provide further improvements. This lays the foundation for future work in which we aim to further explore the influence of noise (in the form of bias) on confidence and how it can be counteracted.

Acknowledgment. This publication benefits from the support of the French Community of Belgium in the context of a FRIA grant, and by the FuturICT2.0 (www.futurict2.eu) project funded by the FLAG-ERA Joint Transnational call (JTC) 2016.

References

1. Bang, D., et al.: Confidence matching in group decision-making. Nat. Hum. Behav. **1** (2017). https://doi.org/10.1038/s41562-017-0117
2. Bang, D., Frith, C.D.: Making better decisions in groups. R. Soc. Open Sci. **4**(8), 170,193 (2017). https://doi.org/10.1098/rsos.170193
3. Marshall, J.A., Brown, G., Radford, A.N.: Individual confidence-weighting and group decision-making. Trends Ecol. Evol. **32**(9), 636–645 (2017). https://doi.org/10.1016/j.tree.2017.06.004
4. Reily, K., Finnerty, P.L., Terveen, L.: Two peers are better than one: aggregating peer reviews for computing assignments is surprisingly accurate. In: Proceedings of the ACM 2009 International Conference on Supporting Group Work, pp. 115–124. ACM (2009). https://doi.org/10.1145/1531674.1531692
5. Robson, N., Rew, D.: Collective wisdom and decision making in surgical oncology. Eur. J. Surg. Oncol. (EJSO) **36**(3), 230–236 (2010). https://doi.org/10.1016/j.ejso.2010.01.002
6. Auer, P., Cesa-Bianchi, N., Freund, Y., Schapire, R.: The nonstochastic multiarmed bandit problem. SIAM J. Comput. **32**(1), 48–77 (2002). https://doi.org/10.1137/S0097539701398375
7. Zhou, L.: A survey on contextual multi-armed bandits. CoRR abs/1508.03326 (2015)
8. Villar, S., Bowden, J., Wason, J.: Multi-armed bandit models for the optimal design of clinical trials: benefits and challenges. Stat. Sci. **30**, 199–215 (2015). https://doi.org/10.1214/14-STS504
9. Beygelzimer, A., Langford, J., Li, L., Reyzin, L., Schapire, R.E.: An optimal high probability algorithm for the contextual bandit problem. CoRR abs/1002.4058 (2010)
10. Dunning, D.: The Dunning-Kruger effect: on being ignorant of one's own ignorance. In: Advances in Experimental Social Psychology, vol. 44, pp. 247–296. Elsevier (2011). https://doi.org/10.1016/B978-0-12-385522-0.00005-6
11. Scholkopf, B., Smola, A.J.: Learning with Kernels: Support Vector Machines, Regularization, Optimization, and Beyond. MIT Press, Cambridge (2001)
12. Zaremba, W., Sutskever, I., Vinyals, O.: Recurrent neural network regularization. arXiv preprint arXiv:1409.2329 (2014)
13. Valko, M., Korda, N., Munos, R., Flaounas, I.N., Cristianini, N.: Finite-time analysis of kernelised contextual bandits. CoRR abs/1309.6869 (2013)
14. Lagae, A., et al.: A survey of procedural noise functions. In: Computer Graphics Forum, vol. 29, pp. 2579–2600. Wiley Online Library (2010). https://doi.org/10.1111/j.1467-8659.2010.01827.x
15. Ueda, N., Nakano, R.: Generalization error of ensemble estimators. In: Proceedings of International Conference on Neural Networks (ICNN 1996), vol. 1, pp. 90–95. IEEE (1996). https://doi.org/10.1109/ICNN.1996.548872
16. Grofman, B., Owen, G., Feld, S.L.: Thirteen theorems in search of the truth. Theor. Decis. **15**(3), 261–278 (1983). https://doi.org/10.1007/BF00125672

Autonomous Hybridization
of Agent-Based Computing

Mateusz Godzik[(✉)] [ID], Michał Idzik[ID], Kamil Pietak[ID], Aleksander Byrski[ID],
and Marek Kisiel-Dorohinicki[ID]

AGH University of Science and Technology,
Al. Mickiewicza 30, 30-059 Krakow, Poland
{godzik,miidzik,kpietak,olekb,doroh}@agh.edu.pl

Abstract. Using agent-based systems for computing purposes, where
agent becomes not only driver for realizing computing task, but a part
of the computing itself is an interesting paradigm allowing for easy
yet robust design of metaheuristics, making possible easy paralleliza-
tion and developing new efficient computing methods. Such methods as
Ant Colony Optimization (ACO), Particle Swarm Optimization (PSO)
or Evolutionary Multi Agent-System (EMAS) are examples of such algorithms. In the paper novel approach to hybridization of such computing
systems is presented. A number of agents doing their computing task can
agree to run other algorithm (similarly to high level hybrid proposed by
Talbi). The paper focuses on presenting the background and the idea of
such algorithm along with firm experimental results.

Keywords: Agent-based computing · Hybrid metaheuristics ·
Nature-inspired algorithms.

1 Introduction

Wolpert and MacReady have confirmed [30] the necessity for tuning the existing
metaheuristics in order to solve the difficult computing problems. Such tuning usually comprises of choosing the parameters, following different well-known
methodologies to make sure the chosen values make the algorithm run really
efficacious (cf. iRace [19]). However, adaptation of the algorithms to a greater
extent, following e.g. hybridization (cf. Talbi [27]) may allow not only for finding
better metaheuristics, but also creating algorithms which will be easily paral-
lelized or run in hybrid environments. In particular, well-researched computing
methods, for which particular formal proofs were conducted (e.g. simple genetic
algorithm [29] or EMAS [2]), may become a good basis for further hybridizations.

EMAS is present in the state of the art since 1996 [6] and since then many
different versions and hybrids of this algorithm were proposed, yielding interesting results [4]. This computing method consists in putting together evolutionary
and agent-based computing paradigm, creating a system where agent becomes a

N. T. Nguyen et al. (Eds.): ICCCI 2020, LNAI 12496, pp. 139–151, 2020.
https://doi.org/10.1007/978-3-030-63007-2_11

part of the computing process and undergoes such processes as death and reproduction in order to participate in decentralized selection and produce offspring
that will be used for exploring and exploiting the search space. Minding that
EMAS was thoroughly analyzed from the theoretical point of view [2], it may
be viewed a good starting point for introducing hybrid versions.

Recently new hybrids of EMAS were proposed, comprising the already
researched, agent- and evolution-based synergetic metaheuristic with swarm
algorithm [21] and Differential Evolution (DE) [13]. Based on the experiences gathered during conducting of this research, a more general approach to
hybridization of EMAS was proposed, making the agents responsible for choosing a new metaheuristic, using it for improvement of their solution. Such an
autonomous approach for hybridization of metaheuristics is a main contribution
of this paper.

In the following sections, after presenting the basic structure and principles
of EMAS and related hybrid metaheuristics, the concept of autonomous hybrid
agent-based metaheuristic is presented, supported by experimental results and
their discussion. Finally the conclusion is given and the future work is sketched
out.

2   Evolutionary Multi Agent-Systems

EMAS [7] is metaheuristic which accurateness was proven with a proper formal background, moreover can be treated as interesting and quite effective [2].
Therefore, this algorithm was chosen to solve the problem presented in this
article.

Because evolutionary processes are by their very nature decentralized, they
can easily be implemented in a multi-agent process at the population level. This
means that agents can *reproduce* - in cooperation with other agents or be killed
(*die*) as a result of rivalry between agents (selection). A congruous model with
narrow autonomy of agents deployed in the planned positions on some lattice (as
in a model built from cellular of parallel evolutionary algorithms) was developed
by Zhong et al. [33]. However, the decentralized model of evolution in EMAS
[15] was created to ensure to give agents full independence.

Such a system is built of a big number of simple and homogeneous agents,
each of whom is trying to develop his solution to a common problem. The low
computational complexity and the ability to create separate subsystems (subpopulations) means that such systems can be efficiently used in large-scale distributed environments (see, e.g. [3]).

Each agent in EMAS can be seen as a representation of a single solution
to a given problem, while the islands on which the agents are located represent a distributed computational structure. The island is a local environment in
which agents can interact with each other. However, agents are not trapped on
the island - they can change location so that information and resources can be
exchanged throughout the entire system [15].

In EMAS, the main evolutionary factors - inheritance and selection - are
implemented through agents' activities related to *death* and *reproduction* (see

Fig. 1). Inheritance is the result of a properly defined reproduction - similar to classic evolutionary algorithms. The agent's basic features are recorded in its genotype, which inherits from the parent(s) as a result of mutation and recombination (variation operators). An agent can also gain knowledge (phenotype) during his existence. Such knowledge is not inherited by his descendants, but along with the genotype affects the behavior of the agent. It is worth noting here that it is relatively easy to influence the increase of diversity in EMAS by introducing algorithms such as allotropic speciation (cf. [5]). It introduces the population distribution and allows the agent to move from one evolutionary island to another (migration) (see Fig. 1). Assuming the lack of public knowledge and the automation of agents, a selection mechanism was introduced, which is based on the acquisition and exchange of non-renewable raw materials [7]. As a result, the quality of the solution presented by the agent can be expressed by the number of non-renewable resources owned by it. In other words, the agent gains resources as a result of effective ("good") actions or loses them as a result of wrong decisions ("bad actions"). "Bad" or "good" actions can be understood here as an attempt to find a good enough solution. Based on the amount of resources, selection is carried out - agents with more resources have a better chance to *reproduce*, while those who have gained little will increase their likelihood of death. Following the classic taxonomy of Franklin and Graesser - EMAS agents can be qualified as Artificial Life Agents (this is a kind of Computational Agents) [12].

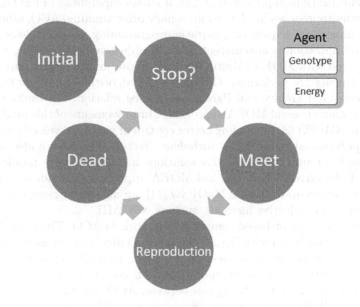

Fig. 1. Evolutionary multi-agent system (EMAS)

Many of the optimization problems that have been solved using EMAS and its versions have yielded better results than some classic approaches. They concern, for example, financial optimization, optimization of multiple goals and optimization of the neural network architecture. In this way, it was proved that in practice EMAS is applicable as a comprehensive optimization tool.

A summary of EMAS-related review has is given in [4]. EMAS can serve as an example of a cultural algorithm in which evolution is possible thanks to the interaction between agents and cultural knowledge is obtained from information related to non-renewable resources (energy). This approach makes it possible to determine which agent is better and which is worse, thus justifying decisions on which genes should remain in the pool. Therefore, knowledge about energy (non-renewable resources) is situational knowledge. Adding an appropriate local-search method to operators, EMAS easily change to memetic version.

3   Hybrid Agent-Based Computing Methods

PSO can be referred as agent-based systems. Their results are obtained by a cooperation of particles (agents), which form a population. There are also many examples of PSO and Genetic Algorithm (GA) hybridization. Basic GA-PSO approach was proposed in [14], where part of population is processed with evolutionary operators and then PSO method is used to adjust output set of individuals. Other GA/PSO solutions include hybrid for solving combinatorial problems, e.g. MPSO [1] (designed to solve Traveling Salesman Problem) or the algorithm for combinatorial vehicle routing optimization problem (VRP) [31]. An overview of PSO hybridizations is presented in [28]. It shows capabilities of PSO combined with multiple approaches like DE, evolutionary programming, ACO, tabu search, simulated annealing, sequential quadratic programming, gradient descend, etc.

PSO hybridization is also present in multi-objective optimization. Standard GA is replaced with MOEA (Multi-Objective Evolutionary Algorithm) and further adjustments are performed. OMOPSO [25] algorithm combines PSO technique, two-layered archive and Pareto dominance relation. Its results are competitive to other classical MOEA approaches. Improvements of this method were proposed in SMPSO [20], including better control of particles' velocity and incorporating polynomial mutation as turbulence factor. There were also attempts to combine PSO and many-objective solutions in order to solve problems with large set of objectives, where classical MOEA approaches are not sufficient. An example of such hybridization is MaOPSO [11], an algorithm using core ideas of well-known many-objective methods, such as NSGAIII.

Another set of agent-based computing methods is ACO. These methods are also very often combined with GA. In [23] an ACO algorithm is used to create an initial population for the subsequent phase, which uses EA operators to develop a solution (HRH). A hybrid incorporating both an ACO and a DE algorithm was proposed in [32]. DE is being run between ACO iterations, optimizing the pheromone trail deposited into the environment (LRH). ACO-EA hybrids for continuous optimization problems have also been designed. As an example, [8] proposes such an algorithm, where ACO_R and CGA_R (Conditionally Breeding Genetic Algorithm) execute their iterations and generations interchangeably, whilst sharing a population.

More generic GA hybridization can be achieved with multi-deme meta-heruristics. Hierarchical Genetic Strategy (HGS) introduced in [24] is an example of such model. HGS can be used to divide calculations into tree-like structure. Nodes closer to the tree root are responsible for more general calculations, while leaves evaluate detailed aspects of most promising search space areas. Sprout nodes are added to the tree when satisfactory results are found on parent node. Meanwhile, old or redundant nodes are cut and removed from the tree. HGS was combined with classical multi-objective algorithms (MOHGS [9]). This promising direction was further investigated in [17]. MO-mHGS, improved meta-model is able to connect with any single-deme MOEA algorithm as its driver. New nodes are created basing on progress ratio of popular MOEA quality indicator – hypervolume. In addition, fitness function can be adjusted to speed up calculations on lower tree levels. It was shown that MO-mHGS can significantly improve single-deme algorithm performance. Moreover, HGS model has natural capabilities to be treated as agent-based system and run in parallel environment.

EMAS was hybridized many times and different directions of such endeavors were undertaken. E.g. one of first EMAS hybrids were immunological-EMAS (proposed by Byrski) where the notion of immunological cells introduced among the evolutionary agents was used to remove non-promising individuals, speeding up the whole computing process. Other significant directions of hybridizing emas were co-evolutionary MAS (developed by Drezewski, introducing many sexes, niching and speciation mechanisms, aiming at improving the diversity and solving multi-modal optimiation problems). Elitist-EMAS was proposed by Siwik and was aimed at solving multi-criteria optimization problems by using a notion of elitist evolutionary island inside regular multi-deme population structure of EMAS. Those hybrids were summarized in [4].

Korczynski worked on memetic version EMAS where a dedicated buffering mechanism for fitness evaluation was constructed [16], so high-dimensional optimization problems could be addressed.

Finally, Godzik et al. worked on hybrids of evolutionary algorithms, in particular EMAS with PSO [21] and DE [13]. After abstracting of the mechanism uses for hybridizations in those papers, the higher-level hybridization was considered and a relevant algorithm is a main contribution of this paper.

4   Autonomous Hybrid Agent-Based Metaheuristic

Autonomous hybrid agent-based metaheuristic is a type of modified EMAS algorithm. It consists of the same steps as the base algorithm, except for one additional step. As shown in Fig. 2, an additional hybrid step is placed as the last step of the algorithm loop. In this step, three stages can be distinguished: checking the start condition, running support algorithms (e.g. PSO, DE) and adjusting the energy level of agents using redistribution. The steps are described in detail below.

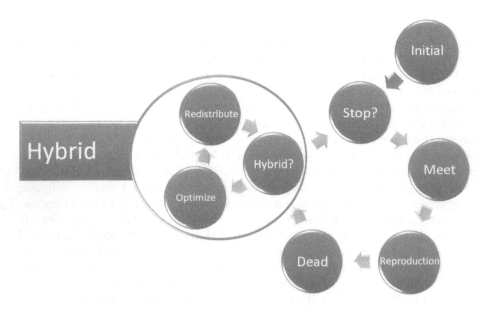

Fig. 2. Hybrid Evolutionary multi-agent system

4.1 Conditions for Running the Optimization

Agents can decide autonomously which optimization they would like to take part in. They may also decide not to participate in any of the optimizations. The terms of these decisions can be any and different for each optimization method and different for each agent. They may depend on the value of energy (e.g. agents with low energy scared to die; agents with average energy wanting to look for another area of solutions; agents with high energy wanting to improve their solution before reproduction). The decision may also depend on the random factor, the agent's life span or calculation time. During their life, agents can freely change their decisions about the desire to optimize.

Because running optimization algorithms is expensive (it consumes both a lot of computation time and calls to the evaluation function), hybrids are not run every algorithm cycle. Sometimes also running a given algorithm does not make sense because of the properties of the algorithm itself. Very often it is not correct to run the algorithm with only one or more willing agents. Therefore, at this stage it is checked if the remaining stages of this step will be started. Launch conditions include the number of cycles since the last launch, variety of solutions or the aforementioned condition of the minimum number of willing agents for a given hybrid. These are just examples, you can try others. Conditions can also be combined with each other (both by conjunction and alternative).

If the start condition is met, the next stage follows (Optimization algorithms). If not, the algorithm goes to the next step (checking the end of the algorithm). In both cases, the agents' decisions are not changed, and if agents do not change them themselves, they will again be considered in the next hybridization step.

4.2   Optimization Algorithms

If the algorithm requires creating new solutions (agents) and killing existing ones, it is worth considering when including such an algorithm. It is recommended to modify the steps of such an algorithm so as not to create/delete agents, but only to replace their solutions. Thanks to this, we will not lose energy and other parameters belonging to agents.

In our article we present the concept of the EMAS algorithm combined with PSO and DE. Previous attempts have already been made to improve EMASA by each of these algorithms separately. The results were promising, which is why we continued this direction of research and combined both ideas into one algorithm in which EMAS agents can choose between many algorithms. For the purposes of this paper, we used two algorithms to be able to examine the impact of this solution on results more easily. In further studies, you can try to use more algorithms. You can also try different algorithms or parameters, e.g. startup frequency or length of operation.

4.3   Redistribution Operator

The algorithms used in the hybrid step do not use agent energy. Therefore, after leaving these algorithms, agents have an energy level inadequate to the quality of the solution. To repair this condition, agents leave the energy redistribution operator after leaving the algorithms. You can use different redistribution operators. This article uses the proportional redistribution operator. It sets energy in proportion to agent solutions. Example: we have agent A and B. Agent A has twice the solution than agent B. As a result of the operator's action, agent A will have twice as much energy as agent B. The sum of the agents' energy before and after redistribution is constant.

5   Experimental Results

In this section, the experimental results obtained for EMAS and the proposed hybrid algorithm are presented and discussed.

All experiments were realized using a laptop with Intel i7-6700HQ 2.60 GHz processor and 32 GB of RAM. 64-bit Ubuntu system (ver. 18.04). For experiments, the jMetal platform[1] was used. This platform has been modified and improved by dr Leszek Siwik. On this platform a lot of calculations have been made such as [22] and [26]. All algorithms, problem definitions and other components come from this platform and can be found here: https://bitbucket.org/lesiwik/modelowaniesymulacja2018. The tests were realized using jMetal version 5.6 and Java 11.0.4.

---

[1] jMetal [10] is an object-oriented Java-based framework aimed at the development, experimentation, and study of metaheuristics for solving optimization problems. http://jmetal.github.io/jMetal/.

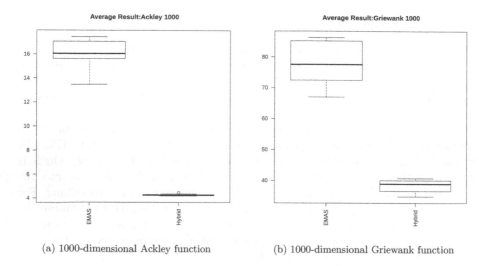

(a) 1000-dimensional Ackley function   (b) 1000-dimensional Griewank function

Fig. 3. Best fitness values for the selected benchmark functions.

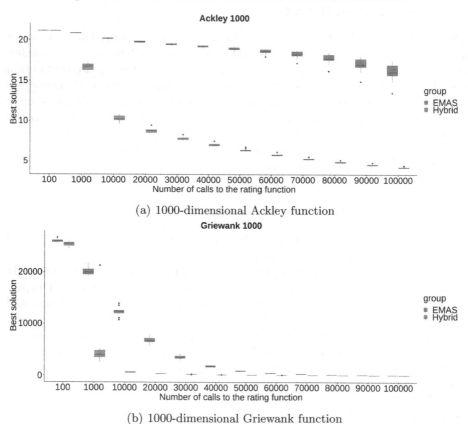

(a) 1000-dimensional Ackley function

(b) 1000-dimensional Griewank function

Fig. 4. Best fitness values in the time domain for the selected benchmark functions.

5.1   Benchmarks

In order to compare basic algorithm and hybrid was used implementation of problems from jmetal (Ackley, Griewank, Rastrigin) in two sizes (500D and 1000D) [10].

5.2   Configuration

The most important parameters set for the compared systems are bellow:

- EMAS parameters: Population size: 50; Initial energy: 10; Reproduction predicate: energy above 20; Death predicate: energy equal to 0; Crossover operator: SBXCrossover; Mutation operator: PolynomialMutation; Mutation probability: 0.01; Reproduction energy transfer: 10; Fight energy transfer: 1;
- Hybrid parameters: Hybrid predicate: algorithm calls frequency - every 500 EMAS cycles; Redistribution operator: Proportional redistribute operator;
- PSO parameters: Max iterations: 3; Optymalization predicate: energy below 3; Minimal population size: 20;
- DE parameters: Max iterations: 3; Optimilization predicate: energy more than 17; Minimal population size: 20;

For each variant of dimension and algorithm (EMAS or hybrid), optimization tests were carried out 10 times, and the stopping conditions were related to the number of calls of the evaluation function. Namely each experiment could cause a maximum of 100 * size of the problem (for 500 D it was 50,000) calls.

5.3   Discussion of the Results

Each of the charts presented in Fig. 3 consists a box plot describing the best values of an objective function obtained for all individuals in the population after calculations. On both charts left boxplot is for EMAS and right boxplot is from Hybrid algorith results. For both the 1000 dimensional Ackley function and the 1000 dimensional Griewank function the results of the Hybrid algorithm are better than the results of EMAS.

Figure 4 shows the successive stages of obtaining these results. Red color is the results of EMAS, blue of Hybrid algorithm. It can be seen that at the very beginning the values of the drawn solutions are comparable. Differences, however, appear from further stages. Two more things follow from this chart. The first is greater repeatability of hybrid results relative to EMAS. The hybrid achieves a significant improvement at the very beginning of the search, and then systematically improves the result. The quality of the solution can be controlled by extending or shortening the calculation time. The results of given stages and the shape of the function they make up are different for different problems. It depends on the problem and its difficulties.

Results of all problems and median, mean, standard deviation, maximum and minimum of results can be found in Table 1. From the value it contains, it can be seen that for each of the problems presented and its size, the hybrid algorithm finds better solutions. Often it is even an order of magnitude better solution.

Table 1. Results of EMAS and Hybrid algorithm for tested problems.

EMAS

	Mean	Median	SD	Minimum	Maximum
Griewank 500	36,53959	36,47595	2,465202	32,42908	40,19382
Griewank 1000	77,72416	77,59668	6,799436	67,00974	86,30626
Rastrigin 500	1230,133	1234,579	53,72975	1140,196	1312,001
Rastrigin 1000	2623,715	2624,648	80,49499	2497,007	2739,022
Ackley 500	13,58948	13,70353	2,301543	9,254563	17,67479
Ackley 1000	15,99848	16,05875	1,130237	13,47086	17,46292

Hybrid

	Mean	Median	SD	Minimum	Maximum
Griewank 500	24,43789	2,52E + 01	2,637139	21,17531	29,13334
Griewank 1000	38,32668	38,94534	2,002169	34,87153	40,72877
Rastrigin 500	879,7538	893,0913	73,14583	715,2792	972,8848
Rastrigin 1000	1622,948	1647,153	73,70861	1497,864	1741,93
Ackley 500	4,636582	4,611668	0,163013	4,330747	4,90088
Ackley 1000	4,240177	4,221788	0,075062	4,160407	4,42008

6   Conclusion

In this paper a concept of autonomous, agent-based hybrid metaheuristic algorithm rooted in EMAS was presented. The agents decide in an autonomous way, in which possible hybridization they would like to participate, and depending on their choice (e.g. based on the level of their energy) their solutions undergo optimization by one of possible hybrid algorithms. In this paper PSO and DE algorithms were used, while it is possible to extend this list so the proposed concept of hybridization is open. One has to remember that after completion of this hybrid step, the computing continues inside EMAS, therefore proper redistribution of energy is required, depending on the quality of the improved solutions.

The experiments conducted, presented in this paper, tackled selected benchmark problems and tested the efficacy of the introduced hybridizations. For three difficult benchmarks (Griewank, Rastrigin and Ackley) set in 500 and 1000 dimensions the experiments showed that the hybrid versions improve significantly the results obtained by classic, non-hybrid ones. This encourages us to further research the proposed metaheuristics and broaden the experiments and delve into detailed testing of different hybridization intrincacies, e.g. the mechanism of redistribution of energy or the mechanism of autonomous decision undertaken by the agents, whether to participate (or not) in a hybrid step.

The proposed metaheuristic can be further investigated by extending research area to multiobjective optimization problems. Standard, EMAS and PSO algorithms can be replaced with MOEA solutions and hybrids. Incorporating MO-mHGS [18] multi-deme model into multi-agent system environment is also worth considering.

Acknowledgments. The work presented in this paper was supported by Polish National Science Centre PRELUDIUM project no. 2017/25/N/ST6/02841.

References

1. Borna, K., Khezri, R.: A combination of genetic algorithm and particle swarm optimization method for solving traveling salesman problem. Cogent Math. **2**(1) (2015). http://doi.org/10.1080/23311835.2015.1048581
2. Byrski, A., Schaefer, R., Smołka, M.: Asymptotic guarantee of success for multi-agent memetic systems. Bull. Pol. Acad. Sci. Tech. Sci. **61**(1), 257–278 (2013)
3. Byrski, A., Debski, R., Kisiel-Dorohinicki, M.: Agent-based computing in an augmented cloud environment. Comput. Syst. Sci. Eng. **27**(1), 7–18 (2012)
4. Byrski, A., Dreżewski, R., Siwik, L., Kisiel-Dorohinicki, M.: Evolutionary multi-agent systems. Knowl. Eng. Rev. **30**(2), 171–186 (2015). https://doi.org/10.1017/S0269888914000289
5. Cantú-Paz, E.: A summary of research on parallel genetic algorithms. IlliGAL Report No. 95007. University of Illinois (1995)
6. Cetnarowicz, K., Kisiel-Dorohinicki, M., Nawarecki, E.: The application of evolution process in multi-agent world (MAW) to the prediction system. In: Tokoro, M. (ed.) Proceedings of the 2nd International Conference on Multi-Agent Systems (ICMAS 1996). AAAI Press (1996)
7. Cetnarowicz, K., Kisiel-Dorohinicki, M., Nawarecki, E.: The application of evolution process in multi-agent world (MAW) to the prediction system. In: Tokoro, M. (ed.) Proceedings of the 2nd International Conference on Multi-Agent Systems (ICMAS 1996), pp. 26–32. AAAI Press (1996)
8. Chen, Z., Wang, R.: GA and ACO-based hybrid approach for continuous optimization. In: 2015 International Conference on Modeling, Simulation and Applied Mathematics. Atlantis Press (2015). https://doi.org/10.2991/msam-15.2015.81
9. Ciepiela, E., Kocot, J., Siwik, L., Dreżewski, R.: Hierarchical approach to evolutionary multi-objective optimization. In: Bubak, M., van Albada, G.D., Dongarra, J., Sloot, P.M.A. (eds.) ICCS 2008. LNCS, vol. 5103, pp. 740–749. Springer, Heidelberg (2008). https://doi.org/10.1007/978-3-540-69389-5_82
10. Durillo, J.J., Nebro, A.J.: jMetal: a Java framework for multi-objective optimization. Adv. Eng. Softw. 42, 760–771 (2011). http://www.sciencedircct.com/science/article/pii/S0965997811001219. https://doi.org/10.1016/j.advengsoft.2011.05.014
11. Figueiredo, E.M., Ludermir, T.B., Bastos-Filho, C.J.: Many objective particle swarm optimization. Inf. Sci. **374**, 115–134 (2016)
12. Franklin, S., Graesser, A.: Is It an agent, or just a program?: a taxonomy for autonomous agents. In: Müller, J.P., Wooldridge, M.J., Jennings, N.R. (eds.) ATAL 1996. LNCS, vol. 1193, pp. 21–35. Springer, Heidelberg (1997). https://doi.org/10.1007/BFb0013570. http://dl.acm.org/citation.cfm?id=648203.749270
13. Godzik, M., Grochal, B., Piekarz, J., Sieniawski, M., Byrski, A., Kisiel-Dorohinicki, M.: Differential evolution in agent-based computing. In: Nguyen, N.T., Gaol, F.L., Hong, T.-P., Trawiński, B. (eds.) ACIIDS 2019. LNCS (LNAI), vol. 11432, pp. 228–241. Springer, Cham (2019). https://doi.org/10.1007/978-3-030-14802-7_20

14. Kao, Y.T., Zahara, E.: A hybrid genetic algorithm and particle swarm optimization for multimodal functions. Appl. Soft Comput. **8**(2), 849–857 (2008). http://dx.doi. org/10.1016/j.asoc.2007.07.002
15. Kisiel-Dorohinicki, M.: Agent-oriented model of simulated evolution. In: Grosky, W.I., Plášil, F. (eds.) SOFSEM 2002. LNCS, vol. 2540, pp. 253–261. Springer, Heidelberg (2002). https://doi.org/10.1007/3-540-36137-5_19
16. Korczynski, W., Byrski, A., Kisiel-Dorohinicki, M.: Buffered local search for efficient memetic agent-based continuous optimization. J. Comput. Sci. **20**, 112–117 (2017). https://doi.org/10.1016/j.jocs.2017.02.001
17. Lazarz, R., Idzik, M., Gadek, K., Gajda-Zagorska, E.: Hierarchic genetic strategy with maturing as a generic tool for multiobjective optimization. J. Comput. Sci. **17**, 249–260 (2016)
18. Lazarz, R., Idzik, M., Gadek, K., Gajda-Zagórska, E.: Hierarchic genetic strategy with maturing as a generic tool for multiobjective optimization. J. Comput. Science **17**, 249–260 (2016). https://doi.org/10.1016/j.jocs.2016.03.004
19. López-Ibáñez, M., Dubois-Lacoste, J., Cáceres, L.P., Birattari, M., Stützle, T.: The irace package: Iterated racing for automatic algorithm configuration. Oper. Res. Perspect. **3**, 43–58 (2016). https://doi.org/10.1016/j.orp.2016.09.002. http:// www.sciencedirect.com/science/article/pii/S2214716015300270
20. Nebro, A.J., Durillo, J.J., Garcia-Nieto, J., Coello, C.C., Luna, F., Alba, E.: SMPSO: a new PSO-based metaheuristic for multi-objective optimization. In: IEEE symposium on Computational Intelligence in Multi-Criteria Decision-Making, 2009. MCDM 2009, pp. 66–73. IEEE (2009)
21. Placzkiewicz, L., et al.: Hybrid swarm and agent-based evolutionary optimization. In: Shi, Y., et al. (eds.) ICCS 2018. LNCS, vol. 10861, pp. 89–102. Springer, Cham (2018). https://doi.org/10.1007/978-3-319-93701-4_7
22. Podsiadło, K., Łoś, M., Siwik, L., Woźniak, M.: An algorithm for tensor product approximation of three-dimensional material data for implicit dynamics simulations. In: Shi, Y., et al. (eds.) Computational Science - ICCS 2018, pp. 156–168. Springer, Cham (2018). https://doi.org/10.1007/978-3-319-93701-4_12
23. Rajappa, G.P.: Solving combinatorial optimization problems using genetic algorithms and ant colony optimization. Ph.D. thesis, University of Tennessee (2012). https://trace.tennessee.edu/utk_graddiss/1478
24. Schaefer, R., Kolodziej, J.: Genetic search reinforced by the population hierarchy. Found. Genet. Algorithms **7**, 383–401 (2002)
25. Sierra, M., Coello, C.: Improving PSO-based multi-objective optimization using crowding, mutation and e-dominance. In: Evolutionary Multi-Criterion Optimization, pp. 505–519 (2005)
26. Siwik, L., Los, M., Kisiel-Dorohinicki, M., Byrski, A.: Hybridization of iso-geometric finite element method and evolutionary multi-agent system as a tool-set for multiobjective optimization of liquid fossil fuel reserves exploitation with minimizing groundwater contamination. Procedia Comput. Sci. **80**, 792–803 (2016). https://doi.org/10.1016/j.procs.2016.05.369. http://www. sciencedirect.com/science/article/pii/S1877050916308444. International Conference on Computational Science 2016, ICCS 2016, 6–8 June 2016, San Diego, California, USA
27. Talbi, E.G.: A taxonomy of hybrid metaheuristics. J. Heuristics **8**, 541–564 (2002)
28. Thangaraj, R., Pant, M., Abraham, A., Bouvry, P.: Particle swarm optimization: Hybridization perspectives and experimental illustrations. Appl. Math. Comput. **217**(12), 5208–5226 (2011). https://doi.org/10.1016/j.amc.2010.12.053. http:// www.sciencedirect.com/science/article/pii/S0096300310012555

29. Vose, M.: The Simple Genetic Algorithm: Foundations and Theory. MIT Press, Cambridge, MA, USA (1998)
30. Wolpert, D., Macready, W.: No free lunch theorems for optimization. IEEE Trans. Evol. Comput. **67**(1), 67–82 (1997)
31. Xu, S.H., Liu, J.P., Zhang, F.H., Wang, L., Sun, L.J.: A combination of genetic algorithm and particle swarm optimization for vehicle routing problem with time windows. Sensors **15**(9), 21033–21053 (2015). https://doi.org/10.3390/s150921033. http://www.mdpi.com/1424-8220/15/9/21033
32. Zhang, X., Duan, H., Jin, J.: DEACO: hybrid ant colony optimization with differential evolution. In: Proceedings of the IEEE Congress on Evolutionary Computation, CEC 2008, 1–6 June 2008, Hong Kong, China, pp. 921–927 (2008). https://doi.org/10.1109/CEC.2008.4630906
33. Zhong, W., Liu, J., Xue, M., Jiao, L.: A multiagent genetic algorithm for global numerical optimization. IEEE Trans. Syst. Man Cybern. Part B Cybern. **34**(2), 1128–1141 (2004)

Using Neural Networks as Surrogate Models in Differential Evolution Optimization of Truss Structures

Tran-Hieu Nguyen[✉] [iD] and Anh-Tuan Vu

National University of Civil Engineering, Hanoi, Vietnam
hieunt2@nuce.edu.vn

Abstract. In this study, Differential Evolution, a powerful metaheuristic algorithm, is employed to optimize the weight of truss structures. One of the major challenges of all metaheuristic algorithms is time-consuming where a large number of structural analyses are required. To deal with this problem, neural networks are used to quickly evaluate the response of the structures. Firstly, a number of data points are collected from a parametric finite element analysis, then the obtained datasets are used to train neural network models. Secondly, the trained models are utilized to predict the behavior of truss structures in the constraint handling step of the optimization procedure. Neural network models are developed using Python because this language supports many useful machine learning libraries such as scikit-learn, tensorflow, keras. Two well-known benchmark problems are optimized using the proposed approach to demonstrate its effectiveness. The results show that using neural networks helps to greatly reduce the computation time.

Keywords: Structural optimization · Truss structure · Differential evolution · Machine learning · Neural network · Surrogate model

1 Introduction

Truss structures have been widely used in large-span buildings and constructions due to their advantages as lightweight, robustness, durability. However, because truss structures are intricate and complex with many individual elements, a good design requires a lot of human resources. The conventional process to design truss structures is the "trial and error" method where the result strongly depends on the designer's experience. Moreover, for large-scale trusses with a wide list of available profiles, the number of candidates becomes too prohibitive. For example, a simple 10-bar truss in which the cross-section of each member must be selected from a set of 42 available profiles has totally 42^{10} possible options [1]. In such cases, the "trial and error" method is impossible. In order to help a designer find the best choice, another approach called optimization-based design method was invented and has been constantly developed.

In recent decades, many optimization algorithms have been proposed and successfully applied to solve structural problems. Several algorithms are designed based on natural evolution such as Genetic Algorithm (GA) [1], Evolution Strategy (ES) [2],

© Springer Nature Switzerland AG 2020
N. T. Nguyen et al. (Eds.): ICCCI 2020, LNAI 12496, pp. 152–163, 2020.
https://doi.org/10.1007/978-3-030-63007-2_12

Differential Evolution (DE) [3]. Some other algorithms are inspired by the swarm intelligence like Particle Swarm Optimization (PSO) [4], Ant Colony Optimization (ACO) [5], Artificial Bee Colony (ABC) [6], etc. These algorithms use an effective "trial and error" method to find the minimum. In this way, the global optimum is usually found, but it requires a huge amount of function evaluation. This is further complicated for structural optimization problems where the function evaluation process is usually performed by the finite element analysis (FEA). To demonstrate this, the duration of a single analysis for the tied-arch bridge which consists of 259 members described in [7] is approximately 60 s but the optimization time is nearly 133 h. In recent years, the development of machine learning (ML) has shown a promising solution to this challenge. By building ML-based surrogate models to approximately predict the behavior of structures, the number of FEAs is greatly reduced and the overall computation time is consequently decreased.

The idea of using ML as surrogate models in structural optimization is not new. Many related studies have been previously published [8–11]. However, due to the recent development in the field of ML, this topic needs to be carefully considered. Among these evolutionary algorithms, DE is preferred because of its advantages [12]. On the other hand, while many ML algorithms exist, the capacity of the NN has been proved [13]. Therefore, an optimization approach that combines NN and DE is proposed in this study. The paper consists of five main sections. The background theory is briefly presented in Sect. 2. Based on the integration between NN and DE, an optimization approach is proposed in Sect. 3. Two computational experiments are performed in Sect. 4. The obtained results are compared with those of other algorithms. Finally, some main conclusions are pointed out in Sect. 5.

2 Background Theory

2.1 Optimization Problem Statement

The weight optimization problem of a truss structure can be stated as follows.

Find a vector of $\mathbf{A}$ representing the cross-sectional areas of truss members:

$$\mathbf{A} = [A_1, A_2, \ldots, A_n] \text{ where } A_i^{min} \leq A_i \leq A_i^{max} \tag{1}$$

$$\text{to minimize :} \qquad W(\mathbf{A}) = \sum_{i=1}^{n} \rho_i A_i l_i \tag{2}$$

$$\text{subject to:} \qquad \begin{cases} g_{i,s} = \sigma_i / \sigma_i^{allow} - 1 \leq 0 \\ g_{j,u} = \delta_j / \delta_j^{allow} - 1 \leq 0 \end{cases} \tag{3}$$

where: ρ_i, A_i, l_i are the density, the cross-sectional area and the length of the ith member, respectively; A_i^{min}, A_i^{max} are the lower and upper bounds for the cross-sectional area of the ith member; $\sigma_i, \sigma_i^{allow}$ are the actual stress and the allowable stress of the ith member; n is the number of members; $\delta_j, \delta_j^{allow}$ are the actual and the allowable displacements of the jth node; m is the number of nodes.

2.2 Differential Evolution Algorithm

DE was originally proposed by K. Price and R. Storn in 1997 [14]. Like many evolutionary algorithms, the DE comprises four basic operators namely initialization, mutation, crossover, and selection. They are briefly described as follows.

Initialization: a random population of Np individuals is generated. Each individual which is a D-dimensional vector represents a candidate of the optimization problem. Np is the number of candidates in the population and D is the number of design variables. The jth component of the ith vector can be generated using the following express:

$$x_{ij}^{(0)} = x_j^{min} + rand[0, 1]\left(x_j^{max} - x_j^{min}\right)$$ (4)

where: $rand[0,1]$ is a uniformly distributed random number between 0 and 1; x_j^{min} and x_j^{max} are the lower and upper bound for the jth component of the ith vector.

Mutation: a mutant vector $v_i^{(t)}$ is created by adding a scaled difference vector between two randomly chosen vectors to a third vector. Many different mutation strategies have been proposed like 'DE/rand/1/', 'DE/rand/2', 'DE/best/1', 'DE/best/2', etc. In this study, a powerful mutation strategy, called 'DE/target-to-best/1' is employed. This variant produces the mutant vector based on the best individual of the population $x_{best}^{(t)}$ and the target individual $x_i^{(t)}$ as follows:

$$v_i^{(t)} = x_i^{(t)} + F \times \left(x_{best}^{(t)} - x_i^{(t)}\right) + F \times \left(x_{r1}^{(t)} - x_{r2}^{(t)}\right)$$ (5)

where: $r_1 \neq r_2$ are randomly selected between 1 and Np; F is the scaling factor.

Crossover: a trial vector u_i is created by getting each variable value from either the mutant vector v_i or the target vector x_i according to the crossover probability.

$$u_{ij}^{(t)} = \begin{cases} v_{ij}^{(t)} & \text{if } j = K \text{ or } rand[0, 1] \leq Cr \\ x_{ij}^{(t)} & \text{otherwise} \end{cases}$$ (6)

where: $u_{ij}^{(t)}$, $v_{ij}^{(t)}$ and $x_{ij}^{(t)}$ are the jth component of the trial vector, the mutant vector, and the target vector, respectively; K is any random number in the range from 1 to D, this condition ensures that the trial vector differs the target vector by getting at least one mutant component; Cr is the crossover rate.

Selection: for each individual, the trial vector is chosen if it has a lower objective function value; otherwise, the target vector is retained. The selection operator is described as follows:

$$x_i^{(t+1)} = \begin{cases} u_i^{(t)} & \text{if } f\left(u_i^{(t)}\right) \leq f\left(x_i^{(t)}\right) \\ x_i^{(t)} & \text{otherwise} \end{cases}$$ (7)

where: $f(u_i^t)$ and $f(x_i^t)$ are the objective function value of the trial vector and the target vector, respectively.

For constrained problems, the mutation and crossover operators could produce infeasible candidates. In such case, the selection is based on three criteria: (i) any feasible candidate is preferred to any infeasible candidate; (ii) among two feasible candidates, the one having lower objective function value is chosen; (iii) among two infeasible candidates, the one having lower constraint violation is chosen [15]. For the implementation, the objective function is replaced by the penalty function:

$$f'(\mathbf{x}) = f(\mathbf{x}) + \sum_{i=1}^{n} r_i \times \max(0, g_i(\mathbf{x})) \tag{8}$$

where: r_i is the penalty parameter; g_i is the constraint violation.

The initialization operator is performed only one time at the initial iteration while three last operators are repeated until the termination criterion is satisfied.

2.3 Neural Networks

Neural networks (NNs) are designed based on the structure of the human brain. Many NN architectures have been developed, in which, the feedforward neural network (FFNN) is commonly used in the structural engineering field. In FFNN, the information moves through the network in a one-way direction as illustrated in Fig. 1 [16]. Neurons are organized into multiple layers including the input layer, the hidden layers, and the output layer. The outputs from previous neurons become the inputs of the current neuron after scaling with the corresponding weights. All inputs are summed and then transformed by the activation function.

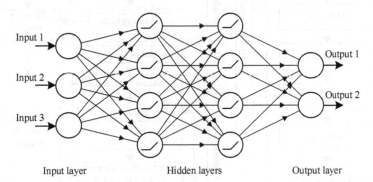

Fig. 1. Typical architecture of an FFNN

It can be expressed as follows. The neuron of jth layer u_j ($j = 1, 2, ..., J$) receives a sum of input x_i ($i = 1, 2, ..., I$) which is multiplied by the weight w_{ji} and will be transformed into the input of the neuron in the next layer:

$$x_j = f(u_j) = f\left(\sum_{i=1}^{I} w_{ji} x_i\right) \tag{9}$$

where $f(.)$ is the activation function. The most commonly used activation functions are: tanh, sigmoid, softplus, and rectifier linear unit (ReLU). The nonlinear activation function ensures that the network can simulate the complex data.

A NN can has more than one hidden layer, which increases the complexity of the model and can significantly improve prediction accuracy. The loss function is used to measure the error between predicted values and true values. The loss function is chosen depending on the type of task. For regression tasks, the loss functions can be Mean Squared Error (MSE), Mean Absolute Error (MAE) or Root Mean Squared Error (RMSE). To adapts NN for better predictions, the network must be trained. The training process is essentially finding a set of weights in order to minimize the loss function. In other words, it is an optimization process. In the field of machine learning, the commonly used optimization algorithms are stochastic gradient descent (SGD) or Adam optimizer. An effective technique, namely "error backpropagation", developed by Rumelhart et al. [17] is normally used for training.

3   Proposed Surrogate-Based Optimization Approach

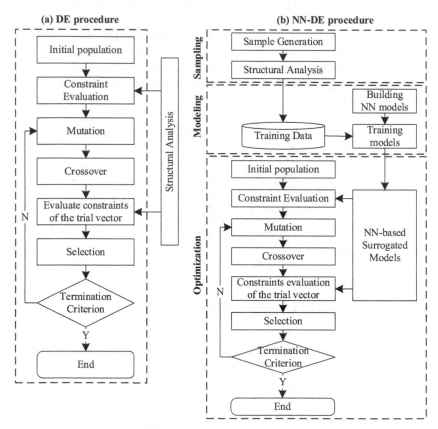

Fig. 2. Optimization workflows

According to the workflow of the conventional DE optimization (Fig. 2(a)), the structural analysis must be performed for every candidate. Consequently, the total number of structural analyses is too large, leading to time-consuming. To deal with this problem, NNs are used to approximately predict the behavior of the structure instead of FEA. The proposed optimization approach, called NN-DE, consists of three phases: sampling, modeling, and optimization as illustrated in Fig. 2(b).

First of all, some samples are generated. All samples are then analyzed using FEA. The second phase focuses on constructing accurate NN models. After selecting the suitable NN architecture, the models are trained with the datasets obtained from the sampling phase. The performance of the NN models is strongly influenced by the diversity of the training data, which also means depends on the sampling method. Therefore, a method, called Latin Hypercube Sampling, is used to produce the sample points. The NN models that are already trained will be used to evaluate the constraints in the optimization phase.

In this study, both DE and NN-DE approaches are implemented by Python language. The DE algorithm is written based on the code published on R. Storn's website [18]. The structural analysis is conducted with the support of the finite element library PyNiteFEA [19]. NN models are build using the library Keras [20].

4   Computational Experiments

4.1   10-Bar Truss

Design Data. The configuration of the truss are presented in Fig. 3. All members are made of aluminum in which the modulus of elasticity is $E = 10,000$ ksi (68,950 MPa) and the density is $\rho = 0.1$ lb/in^3 (2768 kg/m^3). The cross-sectional areas of truss members range from 0.1 to 35 in^2 (0.6 to 228.5 cm^2). Constraints include both stresses and displacements. The stresses of all members must be lower than ± 25 ksi (172.25 Mpa), and the displacements of all nodes are limited to 2 in (50.8 mm).

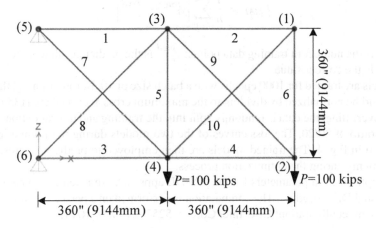

Fig. 3. 10-bar truss layout

Implementation. Firstly, the truss is optimized based on the conventional DE procedure. The design variables are the cross-sectional areas of the truss members. In this problem, each member is assigned to a different section. It means this problem has ten design variables ($D = 10$). The optimization parameters are set after a parameter sensitive analysis as follows: $F = 0.8$; $Cr = 0.7$, $Np = 5 \times D = 50$; maximum iterations $n = 1000$.

For the NN-DE approach, 1000 sample points are initially produced by LHS. Each sample point is a 10-dimensional vector representing the cross-sectional areas of ten corresponding members. Once the input data were generated, the outputs are determined based on FEA. The obtained results are the internal axial forces of members and the displacements of nodes. From the structural engineering point of view, for some sample points, the truss structures are close to being unstable, leading to the large values of the internal forces and the displacements. These sample points are meaningless and they can negatively affect the accuracy of surrogate models. Therefore, the sample points having maximum constraint violation $g(\mathbf{x}) > 1.0$ are removed from the dataset. The final dataset contains about 700 data points.

In the modeling phase, two surrogate models are developed. The first model named 'Model-S' will be used to predict the stresses inside the members while the second model named 'Model-U' will be used to predict the displacements of the free nodes. 'Model-S' has the architecture (10-40-40-40-10) in which ten inputs of the network are the cross-sectional areas of the ten truss members, ten outputs include stresses of ten members and three hidden layers with 40 neurons per layer. 'Model-U' has the architecture (10-20-20-20-4) where four outputs are vertical displacements of four free nodes (1, 2, 3, 4) [21]. ReLU is used as the activation function in this work.

Among available loss functions, MAE is useful if the training data is corrupted with outliers. Therefore, the loss function MAE is used in this work:

$$E_{MAE} = \frac{1}{n} \sum_{i=1}^{n} \left| y_i^{true} - y_i^{pred} \right| \tag{10}$$

where: n is the number of training data points; y_i^{pred} is the predicted value of the network and y_i^{true} is the correct value.

Models are trained for 1000 epochs with a batch size of 10. Before training, the input data should be normalized by dividing to the maximum cross-sectional area (35 in^2). To prevent overfitting, the data is randomly split into the training and the validation subsets with the ratio of 80/20. The loss curves of the two models during the training process are plotted in Fig. 4. The trained models are then employed to predict the stresses and displacements during the optimization process.

The optimization parameters for the NN-DE approach are taken the same as in the conventional DE procedure. The computation is performed on a personal computer with the following configuration: CPU Intel Core i5-5257 2.7 GHz, RAM 8.00 Gb.

Results. Because of the random nature of the search, the optimization is performed for 30 independent runs. The best results of both DE and NN-DE for 30 runs are presented in Table 1 in comparison with other algorithms taken from literature.

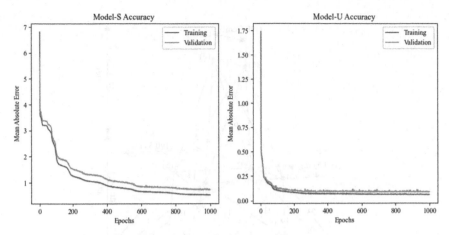

Fig. 4. Loss curves during the training process

Table 1. Comparison of optimum results for 10-bar truss

Member	GA [22]	PSO [22]	ALSSO [22]	DE	NN-DE
1 (in^2)	30.440	33.500	30.4397	30.5603	35.0000
2 (in^2)	0.100	0.100	0.1004	0.1000	0.1000
3 (in^2)	21.790	22.766	23.1599	23.1646	22.7771
4 (in^2)	14.260	14.417	15.2446	15.2025	12.5917
5 (in^2)	0.100	0.100	0.1003	0.1000	0.1000
6 (in^2)	0.451	0.100	0.5455	0.5440	0.1000
7 (in^2)	7.628	7.534	7.4660	7.4632	8.3957
8 (in^2)	21.630	20.392	21.1123	21.0501	22.2952
9 (in^2)	21.360	20.467	21.5191	21.5251	20.7936
10 (in^2)	0.100	0.100	0.1000	0.1001	1.0312
Weight (lb)	4987.00	5024.25	5060.885	5060.8087	5217.7381
Max. constraint violation	1.0140	1.0194	1.0000	1.0000	0.9958

4.2 25-Bar Truss

Design Data. The layout of the truss is presented in Fig. 5. The mechanical properties are the same as in the 10-bar truss. The allowable horizontal displacement in this problem is ±0.35 in (8.89 mm). Members are grouped into eight groups with the allowable stresses as shown in Table 2. Hence, the number of design variables in this problem $D = 8$. The cross-sectional areas of the members vary between 0.01 in^2 and 3.5 in^2. Two loading cases acting on the structure are given in Table 3.

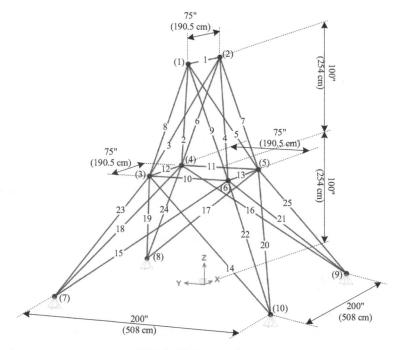

Fig. 5. 25-bar truss layout

Table 2. Allowable stresses for 25-bar truss - unit: ksi (MPa)

Group	Member	Allowable stress for compression	Allowable stress for tension
1	1	35.092 (241.96)	40.0 (275.80)
2	2, 3, 4, 5	11.590 (79.913)	40.0 (275.80)
3	6, 7, 8, 9	17.305 (119.31)	40.0 (275.80)
4	10, 11	35.092 (241.96)	40.0 (275.80)
5	12, 13	35.092 (241.96)	40.0 (275.80)
6	14, 15, 16, 17	6.759 (46.603)	40.0 (275.80)
7	18, 19, 20, 21	6.959 (47.982)	40.0 (275.80)
8	22, 23, 24, 25	11.082 (76.410)	40.0 (275.80)

Implementation. The DE approach and the proposed NN-DE approach are also implemented with the same parameters: $F = 0.8$; $Cr = 0.7$; $Np = 5 \times D = 40$; $n = 500$.

There are totally 5 NN models which are built in this case. Two models namely 'Model-S-min' and 'Model-S-max' with the architecture (8-50-50-50-25), are used to predict the maximum and the minimum values of stresses inside truss members. Eight inputs of the network are the cross-sectional areas of the eight groups while twenty-five

Table 3. Loading conditions for 25-bar truss - unit: kips (kN)

Node	Case 1			Case 2		
	P_X	P_Y	P_Z	P_X	P_Y	P_Z
1	0.0	20.0 (89)	−5.0 (22.25)	1.0	10.0 (44.5)	−5.0 (22.25)
2	0.0	−20.0 (89)	−5.0 (22.25)	0.0	10.0 (44.5)	−5.0 (22.25)
3	0.0	0.0	0.0	0.5 (2.22)	0.0	0.0
6	0.0	0.0	0.0	0.6 (2.67)	0.0	0.0

outputs are the stress values of 25 members. Three remaining models, namely 'Model-Ux', 'Model-Uy', and 'Model-Uz', have the architecture (8-20-20-20-6) in which six outputs are displacements of six free nodes (1, 2, 3, 4, 5, 6) along three directions (UX, UY, and UZ). Other parameters are completely similar to the 10-bar truss problem. The optimization is also performed for 30 independent runs.

Results. The optimization is also performed for 30 independent runs. The best result of DE, NN-DE, and other algorithms is presented in Table 4.

Table 4. Comparison of optimum results for 25-bar truss

Group	HS [22]	ABC [22]	ALSSO [22]	DE	NN-DE
1 (in^2)	0.047	0.011	0.01001	0.0100	0.0100
2 (in^2)	2.022	1.979	1.983579	1.9173	2.4118
3 (in^2)	2.950	3.003	2.998787	2.9793	3.2004
4 (in^2)	0.010	0.01	0.010008	0.0100	0.0100
5 (in^2)	0.014	0.01	0.010005	0.0100	0.0100
6 (in^2)	0.688	0.69	0.683045	0.6801	0.4485
7 (in^2)	1.657	1.679	1.677394	1.7217	1.6081
8 (in^2)	2.663	2.652	2.66077	2.6601	2.5083
Weight (lb)	544.38	545.193	545.1057	543.7736	545.9119
Max. constraint violation	1.0238	1.0212	1.0218	1.0000	1.0697

4.3 Performance Comparisons

The performances of the DE approach and the NN-DE approach are given in Table 5.
  Based on the obtained results, some observations can be summarized as follows.
  First of all, it can be noted that the DE algorithm is capable of finding the global optimum. The conventional DE optimization achieves the same results in comparison with

Table 5. Comparison of computation time

Problem	Approach	Number of FEA	Computation time (s)			
			FEA	Training	Optimization	Total
10-bar truss	DE	50,050	1,757	–	–	1,757
	NN-DE	1,000	36	234	54	324
25-bar truss	DE	20,040	4,426	–	–	4,426
	NN-DE	1,000	232	279	64	575

other algorithm like GA, PSO, HS, ALSSO, etc. Minor differences in results obtained from different algorithms due to the use of different FEA codes.

Secondly, the computation times of the NN-DE approach are very small compared to the conventional DE optimization. For the 10-bar truss, the computation times of the DE and NN-DE approaches are 1757 s and 324 s, respectively. These values are 4426 s and 575 s for the 25-bar truss. It means the NN-DE approach is more than 5 times faster than the conventional DE approach. It is achieved by a significant reduction in the number of FEAs.

Furthermore, the errors of the optimum weight between DE and NN-DE for two problems are 3.1% and 0.4%, respectively. The reason for the errors is the models' inaccuracy in predicting structural behavior. However, the coefficient of determination (R^2) between the cross-sectional areas found by DE and NN-DE for 10-bar truss and 25-bar truss are 0.981 and 0.971, respectively. It indicates a good similarity and linear correlation between the results of the DE and NN-DE approaches.

5 Conclusions

In this paper, a hybrid approach, called NN-DE, which is combined Neural Networks and Differential Evolution algorithm is proposed. By using Neural Networks as surrogated models instead of FEA, the computation times of the evolutionary optimization is significantly reduced. Thus, the proposed approach has a high potential for large-scale structures. Besides, the optimum results of the proposed approach have still slightly errors compared to the conventional procedure. Therefore, it is important to notice that the results obtained from the proposed approach are not exact, but it can be considered as a good suggestion in the practical design. In the future, the methods to improve the accuracy of the Neural Network models should be studied.

Acknowledgment. This work was supported by the Domestic Ph.D. Scholarship Programme of Vingroup Innovation Foundation.

References

1. Rajeev, S., Krishnamoorthy, C.S.: Discrete optimization of structures using genetic algorithms. J. Struct. Eng. **118**(5), 1233–1250 (1992)

2. Beyer, H.G.: The Theory of Evolution Strategies. Springer, Heidelberg (2001). https://doi. org/10.1007/978-3-662-04378-3s
3. Price, K.V., Storn, R.M., Lampien, J.A.: Differential Evolution: A Practical Approach to Global Optimization. Springer, Heidelberg (2005). https://doi.org/10.1007/3-540-31306-0
4. Eberhart, R., Kennedy, J.: Particle swarm optimization. In: Proceedings of ICNN 1995-International Conference on Neural Networks, vol. 4, pp. 1942–1948. IEEE (1995)
5. Dorigo, M., Stützle, T.: Ant Colony Optimization. MIT Press, Cambridge (2004)
6. Karaboga, D.: An idea based on honey bee swarm for numerical optimization. Technical report - TR06, vol. 200, pp. 1–10 (2005)
7. Latif, M.A., Saka, M.P.: Optimum design of tied-arch bridges under code requirements using enhanced artificial bee colony algorithm. Adv. Eng. Softw. **135**, 102685 (2019)
8. Papadrakakis, M., Lagaros, N.D., Tsompanakis, Y.: Optimization of large-scale 3-D trusses using evolution strategies and neural networks. Int. J. Space Struct. **14**(3), 211–223 (1999)
9. Kaveh, A., Gholipour, Y., Rahami, H.: Optimal design of transmission towers using genetic algorithm and neural networks. Int. J. Space Struct. **23**(1), 1–19 (2008)
10. Krempser, E., Bernardino, H.S., Barbosa, H.J., Lemonge, A.C.: Differential evolution assisted by surrogate models for structural optimization problems. In: Proceedings of the international conference on computational structures technology (CST), vol. 49. Civil-Comp Press (2012)
11. Penadés-Plà, V., García-Segura, T., Yepes, V.: Accelerated optimization method for low-embodied energy concrete box-girder bridge design. Eng. Struct. **179**, 556–565 (2019)
12. Vesterstrom, J., Thomsen, R.: A comparative study of differential evolution, particle swarm optimization, and evolutionary algorithms on numerical benchmark problems. In: Proceedings of the 2004 Congress on Evolutionary Computation (IEEE Cat. No. 04TH8753), Portland, USA, vol. 2, pp. 1980–1987. IEEE (2004)
13. Hieu, N.T., Tuan, V.A.: A comparative study of machine learning algorithms in predicting the behavior of truss structures. In: Proceeding of the 5th International Conference on Research in Intelligent and Computing in Engineering RICE 2020. Springer (2020). (accepted for publication)
14. Storn, R., Price, K.: Differential evolution–a simple and efficient heuristic for global optimization over continuous spaces. J. Glob. Optim. **11**(4), 341–359 (1997)
15. Lampinen, J.: A constraint handling approach for the differential evolution algorithm. In: Proceedings of the 2002 Congress on Evolutionary Computation (IEEE Cat. No. 02TH8600), Portland, USA, vol. 2, pp. 1468–1473. IEEE (2002)
16. Goodfellow, I., Bengio, Y., Courville, A.: Deep Learning. MIT Press, Cambridge (2016)
17. Rumelhart, D.E., Hinton, G.E., Williams, R.J.: Learning representations by back-propagating errors. Nature **323**(6088), 533–536 (1986)
18. Differential Evolution Code Homepage. https://www.icsi.berkeley.edu/~storn/code.html. Accessed 28 Jan 2020
19. PyNiteFEA Homepage. https://pypi.org/project/PyNiteFEA/. Accessed 22 Apr 2020
20. Keras Document Homepage. https://keras.io/. Accessed 22 Apr 2020
21. Lee, S., Ha, J., Zokhirova, M., Moon, H., Lee, J.: Background information of deep learning for structural engineering. Arch. Comput. Meth. Eng. **25**(1), 121–129 (2018)
22. Du, F., Dong, Q.Y., Li, H.S.: Truss structure optimization with subset simulation and augmented Lagrangian multiplier method. Algorithms **10**(4), 128 (2017)

Convergence Behaviour of Population Size and Mutation Rate for NSGA-II in the Context of the Traveling Thief Problem

Julia Garbaruk[✉][iD] and Doina Logofătu[✉][iD]

Department of Computer Science and Engineering, Frankfurt University of Applied Sciences, 60318 Frankfurt a.M., Germany
j.garbaruk@outlook.de, logofatu@fb2.fra-uas.de

Abstract. The so-called optimization problems are encountered by mathematicians and computer scientists everywhere. The probably simplest optimization problem is finding a minimum or maximum of an analytic one-dimensional function, which is usually accomplished by finding the roots of the first derivative. It is, however, not unusual that no efficient algorithm is known for a particular optimization problem. It gets even harder, when you combine two such problems to a multi-component optimization problem. Such multi-component optimization problems are difficult to solve not only because of the contained hard optimization problems, but in particular, because of the interdependencies between the different components. Interdependence complicates a decision making by forcing each sub-problem to influence the quality and feasibility of solutions of the other sub-problems.

The subject of the investigation of this work is the multi-component optimization problem called "Traveling Thief Problem", which combines two well-known optimization problems: The Knapsack Problem and the Traveling Salesman Problem. In particular, we want to examine how the mutation rate and population size affect the fitness achieved by the Non-dominated Sorting Genetic Algorithm II when applying it to the Traveling Thief Problem.

Keywords: Multi-objective optimization · Pareto optimization · Travelling Thief Problem · Evolutionary Algorithm · NSGA II · Convergence behaviour

1 Introduction

Multi-objective optimization has been applied in many fields of science, including engineering, economics and logistics where optimal decisions need to be taken in the presence of trade-offs between two or more conflicting objectives. Even in our everyday life we use the principles of multi-objective optimization, often without recognizing it. For example, when we buy a car, we often want to maximize some

© Springer Nature Switzerland AG 2020
N. T. Nguyen et al. (Eds.): ICCCI 2020, LNAI 12496, pp. 164–175, 2020.
https://doi.org/10.1007/978-3-030-63007-2_13

criteria like comfort while the costs should be minimized. To find the best car in this case, we have to compare the candidates. If two cars offer the same level of comfort but differ in price, we choose the car with the lower price. Similarly, if two cars have the same price, we choose the car with the higher level of comfort. At some point, we will probably come across the following case: Car A is more comfortable than Car B, but Car B has a better price than Car A. In this case we cannot say which car is the better one in sense of our objective functions. That is exactly what defines the target set of a multi-objective optimization problem (also called Pareto set): You need to identify the set of solutions, where you cannot improve or optimize solutions in one direction without simultaneously worsening them in the other direction.

In 2013, M. R. Bonyadi, Z. Michalewicz, and L. Barone have constructed another multi-objective optimization problem called "Traveling Thief Problem". This relatively new problem has so far been viewed primarily in a purely academic context, which makes it no less interesting for research. The goal of the Traveling Thief Problem is to provide to a thief a tour across all given cities and a packing plan that defines which items should be taken in which city. The two sub-problems are interdependent because the weight of the items slows the thief down and time is of importance since the knapsack can be rented.

In the end, we are dealing with two conflicting goals here: On the one hand, we want the thief to collect as many items as possible and to maximize his yield. On the other hand, the thief should visit all cities as quickly as possible. But the more there is in his knapsack, the slower he gets. So the task is to reconcile these conflicting goals. The following chapter describes the problem in more detail.

2   Problem Description

The Traveling Thief Problem consists of two sub-problems, which we want to describe individually in the first step (based on [1] and [2]). As next, the existing interdependencies between these two sub-problems are considered. Finally, we will present our research questions and the corresponding results.

2.1   Knapsack Problem (KNP)

For the Knapsack Problem a knapsack has to be filled with items without violating the maximum weight constraint. Each item j has a value $b_j \geq 0$ and a weight $w_j \geq 0$ where $j \in \{1, .., m\}$. The binary decision vector $z = (z_1, .., z_m)$ defines, if an item is picked or not. The search space of this problem contains 2^m combinations and the goal is to maximize the profit $g(z)$:

$$max\ g(z)$$

$$\text{s.t.}\ \sum_{j=1}^{m} w_j \leq Q$$

$$z = (z_1, ..., z_m) \in \mathbb{B}^m$$

$$g(z) = \sum_{j=1}^{m} z_j b_j$$

The solution of the knapsack is a binary vector z representing picked items which is called for items that show which item should be picked. Each element z_j is a bit $(0/1)$ which shows picking the item or not: $z = (z_1, ..., z_m)$.

2.2 Traveling Salesman Problem (TSP)

In the TSP a salesman has to visit n cities. The distances are given by a map represented as a distance matrix $A = (d_{ij})$ with $i, j \in \{1, .., n\}$. The salesman has to visit each city once and the result is a permutation vector $\pi = (\pi_1, \pi_2, ..., \pi_n)$, where π_i is the i-th city of the salesman. The distance between two cities divided by a constant velocity v results in the traveling time for the salesman denoted by $f(\pi)$. The goal is to minimize the total traveling time of the tour:

$$min\ f(\pi)$$

$$\text{s.t.}\ \pi = (\pi_1, \pi_2, ..., \pi_n) \in P_n$$

$$\pi_1 = 1$$

$$f(\pi) = \sum_{i=1}^{n-1} \frac{d_{\pi_i, \pi_{i+1}}}{v} + \frac{d_{\pi_n, \pi_1}}{v}$$

There are $\frac{(n-1)!}{2}$ different tours to consider, if we assume that the salesman has to start from the first city and travels on a symmetric map where $d_{i,j} = d_{j,i}$.

The solution for the problem is the tour $\pi = (\pi_1, \pi_2, ..., \pi_n) \in P_n$ where π_i is a city.

2.3 The Combination of KNP and TSP: Traveling Thief Problem

The Traveling Thief Problem is a combinatorial optimization problem that consists of two interweaving problems, TSP and KNP, that have just been presented separately. The Traveling Thief Problem combines the above defined subproblems and lets them interact with each other. The traveling thief can collect items from each city he is visiting. The items are stored in a knapsack carried by him. In more detail, each city π_i provides one or multiple items, which could be picked by the thief. There is an interaction between the subproblems: The velocity of the traveling thief depends on the current knapsack weight w, which is carried by him. It is calculated by considering all cities, which were visited so far, and summing up the weights of all picked items. The weight at city i given π and z is calculated by:

$$w(i, \pi, z) = \sum_{k=1}^{i} \sum_{j=1}^{m} a_j(\pi_k) w_j z_j$$

The function $a_j(\pi_k)$ is defined for each item j and returns 1 if the item could be stolen at city π_k and 0 otherwise. The current weight of the knapsack has an influence on the velocity. When the thief picks an item, the weight of the knapsack increases and therefore the velocity of the thief decreases. The velocity v is always in a specific range $v = [v_{min}, v_{max}]$ and could not be negative for a feasible solution. Whenever the knapsack is heavier than the maximum weight Q, the capacity constraint is violated. However, to provide also the traveling time for infeasible solutions the velocity is set to v_{min}, if $w > Q$:

$$v(w) = \begin{cases} v_{max} - \frac{w}{Q} \cdot (v_{max} - v_{min}) & \text{if } w \leq Q \\ v_{min} & \text{otherwise} \end{cases}$$

If the knapsack is empty the velocity is equal to v_{max}. Contrarily, if the current knapsack weight is equal to Q the velocity is v_{min}. Furthermore, the traveling time of the thief is calculated by:

$$f(\pi, z) = \sum_{i=1}^{n-1} \frac{d_{\pi_i, \pi_{i+1}}}{v(w(i, \pi, z))} + \frac{d_{\pi_n, \pi_1}}{v(w(n, \pi, z))}$$

The calculation is based on TSP, but the velocity is defined by a function instead of a constant value. This function takes the current weight, which depends on the index i of the tour. The current weight, and therefore also the velocity, will change on the tour by considering the picked items defined by z. In order to calculate the total tour time, the velocity at each city needs to be known. For calculating the velocity at each city the current weight of the knapsack must be given. Since both calculations are based on z and z is part of the knapsack subproblem, it is very challenging to solve the problem to optimality. In fact, such problems are called interwoven systems as the solution of one subproblem highly depends on the solution of the other subproblems.

Here, we leave the profit unchanged to be calculated as in the KNP problem. Finally, the TTP problem is defined by

$$min \; f(\pi, z)$$

$$max \; g(z)$$

$$f(\pi, z) = \sum_{i=1}^{n-1} \frac{d_{\pi_i, \pi_{i+1}}}{v(w(i, \pi, z))} + \frac{d_{\pi_n, \pi_1}}{v(w(n, \pi, z))}$$

$$g(z) = \sum_{j=1}^{m} z_j b_j$$

$$s.t. \; \pi = (\pi_1, \pi_2, ..., \pi_n) \in P_n$$

$$\pi_1 = 1$$

$$z = (z_1, ..., z_m) \in \mathbb{B}^m$$

$$\sum_{j=1}^{m} z_j w_j \leq Q$$

3 Related Work

Although the TTP was first introduced in 2013, much research has already been done in this field. An attempt was made to consider the two sub-problems separately. But as Bonyadi, Michalewicz and Barone have already shown in [2], solving each sub-problem does not provide any information about the optimal solution of the whole problem. Even if the shortest tour is found and the best picking plan is guaranteed in isolation (f is minimized and g is maximized), the final objective value is not necessarily the optimum solution.

Most of the publications aimed to solve these single-objective problems by using different types of algorithms: Heuristic Based, Local Search, Coevolution, Evolutionary Algorithm, Ant Colony Optimization [1,2,4,5]. The effects of population size and the mutation rate in this specific context have not yet been investigated.

4 Proposed Approach

4.1 Test Data (Input)

For our research we have used the test problems provided by the organizators of GECCO 2019 (Bi-objective Traveling Thief Competition). They are very versatile and provide all the information needed to construct a Traveling Thief Problem. First, the general parameters such as number of cities or items in the test instance are described. This is followed by a list with the coordinates of all cities as well as a list of profit, weight and the city of each item.

The 9 test instances differ in the following aspects:

- Number of cities (smallest value: 280 cities, highest value: 33810 cities)
- Number of items (smallest value: 279 items, highest value: 338090 items)
- Capacity of Knapsack (smallest value: 25936, highest value: 153960049)

- Knapsack data type (bounded strongly correlated, uncorrelated and similar weights or uncorrelated)

Moreover we have determined that we consider a maximum of 100 solutions in the Pareto front for each test instance.

4.2   Result Format (Output)

For each problem two output files are generated: One file containing the tour and packing plan and one file containing the time and profit for each solution.

4.3   Algorithm

NSGA II
Evolutionary algorithms are popular approaches to generate Pareto optimal solutions. The main advantage of evolutionary algorithms, when applied to solve multi-objective optimization problems, is the fact that they typically generate sets of solutions, allowing computation of an approximation of the entire Pareto front. The algorithm we used for solving the Traveling Thief problem is the NSGA-II.[?]

As usual for evolutionary algorithms all individuals in NSGA-II are factored and added to the population in the beginning. Then each individual gets a rank based on its level of domination and a crowding distance which is used as a density estimation in the objective space. The binary tournament selection compares rank and crowding distance of randomly selected individuals in order to return individuals for the recombination. After executing recombination and mutation the offspring is added to the population. In the end of each generation the population is truncated after sorting it by domination rank and crowding distance.

Non-dominated Sort
The-non dominated sort represents the core component of the whole algorithm. It splits the population into sets of non-dominated solutions and orders them into a hierarchy of non-dominated Pareto fronts. Based on this, the solutions in a Pareto front are assigned a rank. The rank is needed to calculate the fitness of a solution. Solutions with the highest rank (smallest rank number) are considered the fittest.

Crowding Distance
The Crowding Distance provides an estimate of the density of solutions surrounding a solution. The Crowding Distance of a particular solution is the average distance of the two adjacent solutions (along all objective functions (in this case time and profit)). Solutions with higher Crowding Distance are considered good, since it guarantees diversity and spread of solutions.

Tournament Selection

The tournament selection selects randomly two parents from the population. From these two parents, a winner is determined. With the probability p, the parent with the higher fitness will be selected. Accordingly, the worse solution is selected with the probability $1 - p$. It is important to give a worse solution a chance to witness offspring, because otherwise there is a risk of premature convergence because of too strong selective pressure towards best solution. If the Tournament Selection was done twice, we have two winners, which then produce the offspring.

Recombination

We have to keep in mind that each city in the path may only appear once. This condition applies both to parents and to newly created paths. If a city occurs several times as a result of the recombination and some another city does not occur at all, this must be repaired. We used a simple recombination method that ensures from the outset that each city occurs exactly once. One of the parents ($p1$) inherits a randomly selected area of its path to the child. The rest of the path is populated with the values from the other parent ($p2$). For this, the algorithm iterates through the entire path of $p2$ and check whether the currently viewed city is already included in the child path. If not, it will be added to the next free place in the child path. Of course, the packing plan must also be recombined. To do this, we performed a simple crossover operation at a random point of the packing list. After the recombination of the packing plan, the maximum capacity of the knapsack may have been exceeded. To fix this, randomly selected items are removed from the packing list until the knapsack has reached a permissible weight again.

Mutation

Since each city must be visited exactly once, it makes sense to simply swap two randomly chosen cities. This is possible without any problem, since there is a connection from every city to every other city. A mutation can also occur in the packing list. We opted for a simple mutation method in which a randomly determined bit that represents an item or rather its status (collected or not collected) is toggled. After the packing plan has been mutated, the maximum capacity of the knapsack may have been exceeded. To fix this, randomly selected items are removed from the packing list until the knapsack has reached a permissible weight again.

5   Experimental Results

In this chapter we present our questions in more detail, as well as the results of our experiments.

Our goal was to investigate how the population size and mutation rate affect the outcome of NSGA-II in the context of the TTP (Fig. 1).

The appropriate population size is still the subject of discussion. Many different approaches are known: For example, there is the $10\times$ *Dimensions* rule,

---

Algorithm 1. Fast Non-dominated Sort

Require: Popualtion P
  for each $p \in P$ **do**
    $S_p = \emptyset$ $\triangleright$ S_p: set of solutions that the solution p dominates
    $n_p = 0$ $\triangleright$ n_p: nr. of solutions which dominate the solution p
    for each $q \in P$ **do**
      if $p < q$ **then** $\triangleright$ if p dominates q
        $S_p = S_p \cup \{q\}$ $\triangleright$ add q to the set of solutions dominated by p
      else if $q < p$ **then**
        $n_p = n_p + 1$ $\triangleright$ increment the domination counter of p
    if $n_p = 0$ **then** $\triangleright$ p belongs to the first front
      $p_{rank} = 1$
      $F_1 = F_1 \cup \{p\}$
  $i = 1$ $\triangleright$ initialize the front counter
  while $F_i \neq \emptyset$ **do**
    $Q = \emptyset$ $\triangleright$ used to store the members of the next front
    for each $p \in F_i$ **do**
      for each $q \in S_p$ **do**
        $n_q = n_q - 1$
        if $n_q = 0$ **then** $\triangleright$ q belongs to the next front
          $q_{rank} = i + 1$
          $Q = Q \cup \{q\}$
    $i = i + 1$
    $F_i = Q$
  return $\{F_1, F_2, ...\}$ $\triangleright$ return all Pareto fronts in the population

---

Algorithm 2. Crowding Distance Assignment

Require: Front F
  $l \leftarrow |F|$ $\triangleright$ number of solutions in the front F
  for each i **do**
    $F[i]_{distance} = 0$ $\triangleright$ set the distance to 0 at the beginning
  for each objective m **do** $\triangleright$ for time and profit
    $F = sort(F, m)$ $\triangleright$ sort using each objective value
    $F[0]_{distance} = \infty$ $\triangleright$ so that boundary points are always selected
    $F[l-1]_{distance} = \infty$ $\triangleright$ so that boundary points are always selected
    for $i = 1$ to $l - 2$ **do** $\triangleright$ for all other points
      $F[i]_{distance} = F[i]_{distance} + (F[i+1].m - F[i-1].m)/(f_m^{max} - f_m^{min})$

---

according to which you get the right number of individuals for the population by multiplying the number of objectve functions by 10. Some others recommend large populations, which should be divided into subpopulations. The population size also does not always have to be static, but could, for example, shrink over time. However, the best way is always to test different population sizes and get a solution tailored to the specific problem and its parameters.

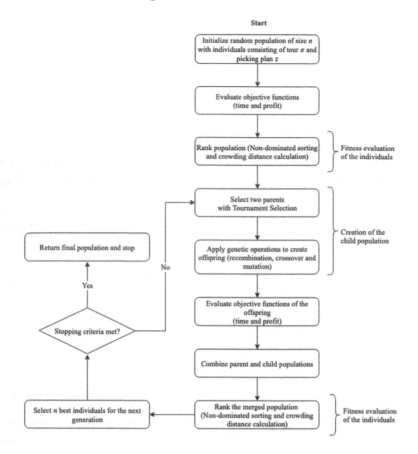

Fig. 1. NSGA-II procedure for Traveling Thief Problem

We decided to test different static population sizes, from 20 up to 500. We have set the number of generations to 10,000, since from there the changes take place more slowly and you can still see the tendency. The mutation rate remained constant at 4%. These are the results for our first test case with 280 cities, 279 items and a knapsack capacity of 25936 (Fig. 2):

For the first test case, it could be shown that the results increase significantly with increasing population size, but only up to a certain limit. Up to a population size of 100, the rule "the more the better" seems to apply. At a population size of 200, however, it turns out that the results are not getting much better and the range of values is also shrinking as the solutions seem to converge more and more. With a population size of 500, this problem becomes even clearer - the curve that forms the Pareto front is getting very short, which means is that the tours and packing plans are becoming increasingly similar. We therefore consider a population size of ca. 100 to be recommended in this case. For comparison, we want to show below our results for one of our largest test cases with 33810 cities,

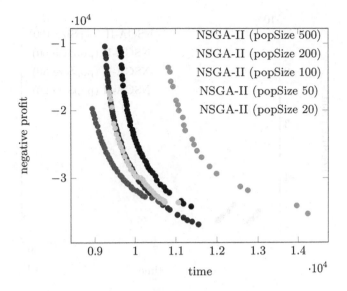

Fig. 2. Results of the NSGA-II for the Traveling Thief Problem depending on the population size after 10,000 generations (test case 1)

33809 items and a knapsack capacity of 2915215. In this test case, the number of generations was also 10,000 and the mutation rate 4%.

The problem of too fast convergence shows up even faster in larger test cases. In case of a population size of 50, the results for the test case 4 are already very similar: Almost all tours are the same and only differ in the packing plans. The other test cases show similar behavior. Generally one can say: The larger the test case was, the more harmful influence had a large population size on the result (Fig. 3).

Finally, we wanted to see how the results change when you change the mutation rate. From now on, we use the population size that has been found to be optimal for the respective test case.

The example of test case 1 shows that it is definitely advisable to play with the mutation rate. Increasing the mutation rate has an effect similar to increasing the population rate. Above a certain value, however, this has an adverse effect because too many good individuals are rejected, which leads to an overall deterioration in the gene pool.

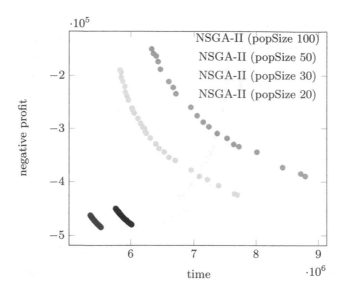

Fig. 3. Results of the NSGA-II for the Traveling Thief Problem depending on the population size after 10,000 generations (test case 4)

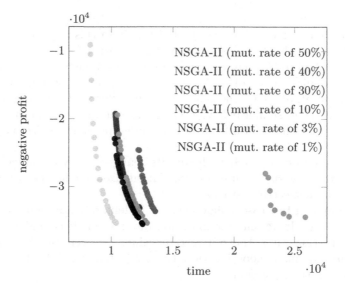

Fig. 4. Results of the NSGA-II for the Traveling Thief Problem depending on the mutation rate after 10,000 generations (test case 1)

6   Conclusion

This work should encourage to deal more with the parameters of an evolutionary algorithm when working with it. They have a huge impact on the result, which is often underestimated. For example, it could be shown that a large population does not necessarily have to be advantageous, but can even be harmful. Generally one can say: The larger the test case was, the more harmful influence had a large population size on the result. The solutions converged faster and were no longer meaningful. In addition, the computational effort increases with a large population, which is why a large population is also problematic.

We were also able to show that you don't have to be afraid of high mutation rates (e.g. 30%). This seems to prevent you from getting stuck in a local optimum too quickly (Fig. 4).

In this work we have shown an extract from our experiments. Next, we would like to examine the convergence behavior of the two parameters more systematically and try to work out specific laws and, based on this, formulate guidelines for the optimal determination of the two parameters.

References

1. Blank, J., Deb, K., Mostaghim, S.: Solving the bi-objective traveling thief problem with multi-objective evolutionary algorithms. In: Trautmann, H., et al. (eds.) EMO 2017. LNCS, vol. 10173, pp. 46–60. Springer, Cham (2017). https://doi.org/10.1007/978-3-319-54157-0_4
2. Bonyadi, M.R., Michalewicz, Z., Barone, L.: The travelling thief problem: the first step in the transition from theoretical problems to realistic problems. In: 2013 IEEE Congress on Evolutionary Computation, pp. 1037–1044. IEEE (2013)
3. Deb, K.: A fast elitist non-dominated sorting genetic algorithm for multi-objective optimization: NSGA-2. IEEE Trans. Evol. Comput. 6(2), 182–197 (2002)
4. Mei, Y., Li, X., Yao, X.: On investigation of interdependence between sub-problems of the travelling thief problem. Soft Comput. 20(1), 157–172 (2016)
5. Srinivas, N., Deb, K.: Muiltiobjective optimization using non-dominated sorting in genetic algorithms. Evol. Comput. 2(3), 221–248 (1994)
6. Zamuda, A., Brest, J.: Population reduction differential evolution with multiple mutation strategies in real world industry challenges. In: Rutkowski, L., Korytkowski, M., Scherer, R., Tadeusiewicz, R., Zadeh, L.A., Zurada, J.M. (eds.) EC/SIDE -2012. LNCS, vol. 7269, pp. 154–161. Springer, Heidelberg (2012). https://doi.org/10.1007/978-3-642-29353-5_18

Resource-Constrained Model of Optimizing Patient-to-Hospital Allocation During a Pandemic

Paweł Sitek[(⊠)] and Jarosław Wikarek

Department of Information Systems, Kielce University of Technology, Kielce, Poland
{sitek,j.wikarek}@tu.kielce.pl

Abstract. Healthcare management, in particular managing a hospital network, is a complex issue which requires taking into account the morbidity process dynamics, simultaneous administration of various therapies, preventive actions, drug supply and responding to emergencies, such as mass casualty traffic incidents, pandemics (e.g. SARS, MERS), etc. The overall objective is to provide appropriate, dedicated aid to patients and affected persons as quickly as possible. One of the aspects of key importance to achieving this objective is the issue of appropriate patient-to-hospital allocation within a specific area. Very often the allocation is determined by constrained resources which the healthcare facilities in the given area have at their disposal, i.e. the number of doctors with specific medical specialties, the number of nurses, the number of beds of specific types in individual hospitals, the number of available medical transportation vehicles, but most importantly, the time limits for initiating successful hospital treatment. Optimal use of constrained resources makes it possible/facilitates optimal allocation in patients, which is essential in emergency situations. The paper proposes a model of optimal patient-to-hospital allocation taking into account the constrained resources of the hospital network and emergency ambulance service which provides medical transportation. The proposed model is formulated using Binary Integer Programming (BIP).

Keywords: Optimization · Allocation problem · Emergency medical services · Patients · Pandemic

1 Introduction

Emergencies such as mass casualty traffic incidents, natural disasters or pandemics are major challenges for the healthcare system, local and state authorities, etc. In emergency situations, a large number of problems arise which must be solved simultaneously within a relatively short time. The most important problems include the appropriate triage of patients (affected/infected), ensuring quick and secure transportation to a specific hospital, providing appropriate hospital treatment and care, etc. Hospitals in a given area are very often unprepared for a large influx of a specific type of patients within a short period of time. For this reason, the so-called field hospitals are often set up,

© Springer Nature Switzerland AG 2020
N. T. Nguyen et al. (Eds.): ICCCI 2020, LNAI 12496, pp. 176–187, 2020.
https://doi.org/10.1007/978-3-030-63007-2_14

or selected hospitals are adapted for treating only a specific group of patients (from a disaster, pandemic, etc.).

Concerning patient triage in emergency situations, various methods are applied, such as Pandemic Influenza Triage Algorithm (PITA) [1], etc. The secure transportation of patients to the nearest appropriate hospital (i.e. one with available beds, medical specialists and equipment, such as ventilators, etc.) is usually the responsibility of the emergency ambulance service, which may be sometimes aided by military medical transportations services. Reorganization applies also to emergency departments which must be prepared for processing a larger influx of patients. Patient traffic within the hospital must also be modified accordingly.

Implementing the measures mentioned above is hindered by constrained resources, i.e. the number of doctors and nurses, the number of hospital beds of specific type, the number of ambulances and, last but not least, time. It should also be remembered that the hospitals and emergency ambulance service in a given area also provide treatment and transportation to other patients who are not casualties of a disaster or pandemic.

Consequently, the question arises: *How to optimally allocate (designate and transport) patients to hospitals in view of the abovementioned constraints?*

In order to answer this and similar questions, the paper proposes a mathematical model of optimizing patient allocation to the existing hospital network using medical transportation services, taking into account the existing constrained medical and logistic resources. To implement the model, GUROBI [2] mathematical programming and constrained programming environment and AMPL [3] modeling language were used.

2 Literature Review

Modeling the issues of resources allocation in healthcare has been broadly discussed in the literature of the subject, both in the context of pandemics of e.g. influenza-like diseases, and for situations not related to pandemics. Planning and responding during pandemics of diseases such as seasonal influenza, N1H1 or, most recently, the SARS-CoV-2 coronavirus, involves a number of aspects, including the disease spread forecast, organizing mass vaccinations (if a vaccine is available), planning and resupplying hospital resources, reorganizing the hospital network, or organizing medical transport. Mathematical models of the spread of influenza-like diseases have been presented in a number of studies [4, 5]. Hospital resources planning is another important area addressed in the literature of the subject. Using planning software, such as FluAid and FluSurge, to forecast the impact of a pandemic on the operation and resources of hospitals and other healthcare facilities was discussed in [6]. A model for optimizing nurse allocation in a hospital during an outbreak of influenza pandemic using FluSurge 2.0 software is presented in [7]. The literature concerning the issue of allocation in a hospital network (i.e. patient allocation, allocation/re-allocation of hospital resources, etc.) is quite broad and covers the issues of both long-term planning (e.g. planning for the hospital network) and short-term planning (e.g. ambulance allocation, emergency response to disasters, etc.). Concerning the former category, the literature of the subject provides a variety of location-allocation models (optimal healthcare facility locations and patient-to-facility allocation), e.g. in the studies in [8, 9]. In terms of short-term planning, there is a number of studies on modeling issues such as immediate emergency response following an earthquake, flood, hurricane or terrorist attack; ambulance allocation; allocation of the available medical resources to specific areas of operation, etc. The most interesting studies in this category include those in [10, 11]. The models related to the issues discussed herein are mostly focused on patient-to-hospital allocation/distribution, taking into account the availability of hospital beds and the patient transport time as the optimization criterion.

There are no models which would include not only the availability of hospital beds, but also of the healthcare staff, the type of available hospital beds, e.g. ventilator beds, patient classification, e.g. based on various types of TRIAGE, the medical transport capacity, etc.

The main contribution of the presented work is to propose a formal model of patient-to-hospital allocation during pandemic (Sect. 3) and an iterative method of solving it, which enables decision support in the field of patient transport and allocation (Sect. 4). The proposed model takes into account not only the limited availability of hospital beds, but also takes into account the type of available beds, the number of available healthcare staff with specific qualifications, the availability of a specific type of medical transport, etc. Moreover, the proposed model can be used both in reactive (decisions made immediately by the operator) and proactive (decisions related to the possibility of serving a specific group of patients at a specific time, moving equipment and personnel, etc.) mode. Given the high parameterization of the model, it is possible to easily improve its functionality by altering the values and meaning, and the structure of individual parameters.

3   State of the Problem and the Mathematical Model

The following assumptions were adopted in building the mathematical model of optimizing patient-to-hospital allocation:

1. A hospital network $h \in H$ is given in the specific area/metropolitan area or smaller towns and countryside – distances between healthcare facilities from several do several dozen kilometers.
2. The hospital has various types of beds $b \in B$, e.g. for general treatment, for pandemic patients, with ventilators, etc. The type of hospital bed is also the designation of the patient's category. Each hospital at the given time has a specific number of beds of the given type available $w_{h,b}$.
3. The hospital also has the fleet of available ambulances $a \in A$. The parameter $f_{a,b}$ specifies whether ambulance a can transport type b patients ($f_{a,b}= 1$ Yes; $f_{a,b}= 0$ No).
4. The hospital has employees with specific qualifications to which the relevant types of positions $g \in G$ are assigned. The applicable standards specify the maximum number of patients per the given g type employee; this is determined by the value of parameter d_g.
5. Each hospital h has a specific number of g type employees. This is determined by the value of parameter $u_{h,g}$. The parameter $\underline{z_h}$ determines the current number of patients treated in hospital h.

6. There is a given set of patients ($p \in P$). The patients are transported to the hospital by ambulances after calling the central emergency phone number, or, if the patient's condition allows it, they report directly to the emergency department. Each patient undergoes initial triage and is assigned a specific category b (type of hospital bed required).

7. In the case of patients reporting directly to the ED, if the hospital is full (no available beds of the required type b), the patients may be transported to another hospital.

8. The time of transporting each patient to each hospital $e_{p,h}$ is known, as is the required time in which the patient should be taken to the hospital j_p.

9. In order to ensure model cohesion and reduce its size, the so-called virtual ambulance (transporting the patient within the given hospital from the ED to the relevant ward) and virtual hospital (for all patients transported to the ED by ambulance) are introduced.

10. The developed model applies to a specific situation in time used for the so-called reactive planning. Therefore, the model can be run iteratively following an update of the resources in specified intervals, or after receiving a specific number of reports from the patients. It can also be used for proactive planning, i.e. simulating a pandemic threat in a given area, and relocating or resupplying resources as appropriate.

Considering the abovementioned assumptions for the modelled problem, a fundamental question emerges: *How to quickly and safely put the patients in the available hospitals?* Thus, two parameters are crucial: quickness, i.e. the time of transportation to the hospital, and safety, i.e. using the appropriate means of transport, and transporting the patient to the appropriate hospital, i.e. one with the available required medical personnel, hospital beds, etc. An overall diagram of the modelled problem for a case of 4 hospitals, 6 patients and transportation provided by the emergency ambulance service, is provided on Fig. 1.

On the basis of those premises, a model of optimizing patient-to-hospital allocation during a pandemic has been formulated in the form of a binary integer programming (BIP) model (1)…(10). Minimizing the patient transport time is adopted as the goal function (1). The goal function is complemented with penalties for failing to deliver the patient to the hospital (n_p), or failing to deliver the patient to the hospital on time (k_p). The model has significant constraints (2)…(9), discussed in Table 2. The key constraints arise from limited availability of resources such as hospital beds, healthcare staff, ambulances, etc. Table 1 presents indices, parameters and decisive variables of the model.

In the development of the model, an innovation in modeling decision variables of the problem was implemented. Basically, modeling the decision variable $X_{a,p,h,t}$ would suffice. With the introduction of two additional decision variables Y_p and U_p, the model will always have a solution. Obviously, if the additional variables are different than zero, the solution will not always be satisfactory, but with model of decision variables, we eliminate the risk of an "NSF" (no solution found) response of the solver and thus no information on the solution. Obtaining non-zero values of Y_p and U_p in the solution informs the decision-maker of specific missing resources, thus enabling them to make the decision on emergency resupplying and delivering the patient to the hospital.

$$\min \sum_{a \in A} \sum_{p \in P} \sum_{h \in H \cup s} \sum_{t \in T} e_{p,h} \cdot X_{a,p,h,t} + \sum_{p \in P} (k_p \cdot Y_p + n_p \cdot U_p) \tag{1}$$

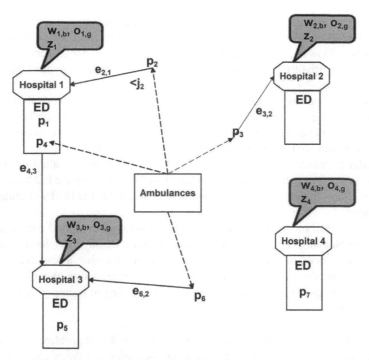

Fig. 1. Illustration of an example of data instance of the modelled problem (4 hospitals, 6 patients, centralized medical transportation

$$\sum_{a \in A \cup i} \sum_{p \in P} \sum_{h \in H \cup s} X_{a,p,h,t} + z_t \leq o_{t,g} \cdot d_g \forall t \in H \cup s, g \in G \qquad (2)$$

$$\sum_{p \in P} \sum_{h \in H \cup s} \sum_{t \in H} X_{a,p,h,t} \leq 1 \forall a \in A \qquad (3)$$

$$X_{a,p,h,t} = 0 \forall a \in A, p \in P, h \in H \cup s, t \in H \wedge s_{p,a} = 0 \qquad (4)$$

$$\sum_{a \in A \cup i} \sum_{h \in H \cup s} \sum_{t \in H} r_{p,h} \cdot X_{a,p,h,t} + U_p = 1 \forall p \in P \qquad (5)$$

$$X_{i,p,h,t} = 0 \forall p \in P, h \in H, t \in H \wedge h \neq t \qquad (6)$$

$$X_{a,p,h,t} \cdot e_{p,t} - m \cdot Y_p \leq j_p \forall a \in A \cup i, p \in P, h \in H \cup s, t \in H \cup s \qquad (7)$$

$$\sum_{a \in A} \sum_{p \in P} \sum_{h \in H \cup s} c_{p,b} X_{a,p,h,t} \leq w_{t,b} \forall t \in H, b \in B \qquad (8)$$

$$s_{p,a} = \sum_{b \in B} f_{a,b} \cdot c_{p,b} \forall p \in P, a \in A \qquad (9)$$

$$X_{a,p,h,t} \in \{0, 1\} \forall a \in A \cup i, p \in P, h \in H \cup s, t \in H \tag{10}$$

$$Y_p, U_p \in \{0, 1\} \forall p \in P$$

Table 1. Indices, sets, parameters and decision variables

Symbol	Description
Indices and Sets	
H	A set of hospitals
B	A set of bed's type
A	A set of all ambulances
G	A set of employee types
P	A set of patients
h,t	Hospital index $(h \in H)$
b	Type of bed index $(b \in B)$
a	Ambulance index $(a \in A)$
g	Employee type index $(g \in G)$
p	Patient index $(p \in P)$
i	Index of virtual ambulance traveling between the same hospital
s	Index of virtual hospital (patient reporting by phone)
Parameters	
$w_{t,b}$	The number of free beds type b in hospital t $(b \in B, t \in H)$
$f_{a,b}$	If an ambulance a can carry b-type patient $f_{a,b} = 1$ otherwise $f_{a,b} = 0$
d_g	How many patients can there be one employee of type g $(g \in G)$
$o_{t,g}$	How many employees of type g are in the hospital of t $(u \in U, t \in H)$
z_t	Current number of patients in the hospital t $(t \in H)$
$c_{p,b}$	If patient p has been classified as type b $c_{p,b} = 1$ otherwise $c_{p,b} = 0$
$r_{p,h}$	If the patient is in a hospital h $r_{p,h} = 1$ otherwise $r_{p,h} = 0$ $(p \in P, h \in H \cup \{s\})$
$e_{p,t}, e_{p,h}$	Time to bring the patient p to the hospital t $(p \in P, t \in H)$
j_p	Time required to deliver the patient p to the hospital
m	Very large constant
Calculated parameter	
$s_{p,a}$	If patient p can be overcome by ambulance a $(p \in H, h \in H)$
Parameters of the penalty function	
k_p	Penalty for failure to deliver the patient p within the required time $(p \in P)$
n_p	Penalty if the patient p cannot be delivered to the hospital
Decision variables	
$X_{a,p,h,t}$	If the ambulance a transports patient p from hospital h to hospital t $(a \in A, p \in P, h \in H \cup \{s\}, t \in T)$
Y_p	If the patient p cannot be delivered within the required time $Y_p = 1$ otherwise $Y_p = 0$ $(p \in P)$
U_p	If the patient p cannot be delivered to the hospital due to lack of places $U_p = 1$ otherwise $U_p = 0$ $(p \in P)$

Table 2. Description of the problem constraints

Con.	Description of constraints
(2)	The number of patients in a specific category delivered to the hospital does not exceed the number of hospital beds of the given type
(3)	Each ambulance is dispatched not more than once in the given time interval (with the exception of virtual ambulances)
(4)	The ambulance transports only patients belonging to specific categories.
(5)	Each patient is delivered to the hospital
(6)	The virtual ambulance moves within the hospital only
(7)	The patient is delivered to the hospital within the required time
(8)	The number of patients delivered to the hospital does not exceed the quantitative standards related to medical staff
(9)	The given patient can be transported by the given ambulance
(10)	Decision variables are binary

4 Methods and Implementation

The proposed mathematical model (1) .. (10) of the problem (Sect. 3) has become a central element of the decision support system regarding the allocation of patients in hospitals. In order to take into account the dynamics of changes in the availability of beds, medical transport and personnel, medical equipment etc., an iterative method of solving the modeled problem in successive time intervals (τ) was proposed with the simultaneous update of the model parameters resulting from the obtained solution. For this reason, all model parameters were divided into two sets. The first *parameter_1* specifies the parameters whose values change when the problem is solved for the period τ. The second set named *parameters_2* defines parameters with the same value for all periods τ. The diagram of the iterative approach is shown in Fig. 2. The methods of mathematical programming (including Branch & Bound method) and constraint programming (in particular constraint propagation as presolving method) were used to solve the model. Due to the nature of the modeled problem (NP-hard), with its larger size, the proposed methods may turn out to be ineffective. In the future, the hybrid approaches will be proposed, using dedicated heuristics, metaheuristics and exact methods and algorithms like constraint logic programming [12], accelerated cuckoo optimization algorithm [13], etc.

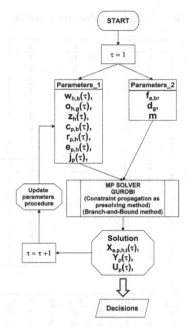

Fig. 2. Iterative approach to solving modeled problem and generate decisions in period τ

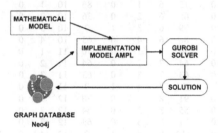

Fig. 3. Model implementation and optimization scheme

The model was implemented using AMPL modeling language, NoSQL graph database (Neo4j), into which the data instances of the modeled problem (parameters, obtained outcomes, etc.) were uploaded, and GUROBI mathematical and constraint programming solver. The method of implementation and optimization of the model is illustrated schematically on Fig. 3.

5 Computational Experiments

In order to verify the proposed model, a number of computational experiments were conducted. In the first phase, optimization was performed for the selected problem data instance *Example_1*(characterized by the following parameters: 4 hospitals, 15 patients, of which 7 reported to emergency departments by themselves, 10 ambulances, etc. – details are provided in Table 3). The results are provided in Table 4 and as a data base

Table 3. Parameter values for *Example_1*

h	z_h
1	400
2	768
3	456
4	989

b
1
2
3

g	d_g
1	50
2	50
3	70
4	80
5	80

h	b	$w_{h,b}$
1	1	6
1	2	4
1	3	4
2	1	3
2	2	3
2	3	3
3	1	2
3	2	2
3	3	3
4	1	1
4	2	1
4	3	3

h	g	$o_{h,g}$
1	1	8
1	2	9
1	3	8
1	4	7
1	5	7
2	1	20
2	2	20
2	3	15
2	4	12
2	5	12
3	1	18
3	2	29
3	3	10
3	4	8
3	5	8
4	1	20
4	2	22
4	3	17
4	4	16
4	5	16

a
1
2
3
4
5
6
7
8
9
10

a	b	$f_{a,b}$	a	b	$f_{a,b}$
1	1	1	6	1	1
1	2	1	6	2	1
2	1	1	7	1	1
3	1	1	7	2	1
3	2	1	8	3	1
3	3	1	9	3	1
4	3	1	10	2	1
5	3				

p	b	$c_{p,b}$	p	b	$c_{p,b}$
1	1	1	9	2	1
2	1	1	10	1	1
3	3	1	11	1	1
4	3	1	12	3	1
5	3	1	13	3	1
6	1	1	14	3	1
7	1	1	15	3	1
8	2	1			

p	j_p
1	100
2	100
3	70
4	70
5	70
6	100
7	100
8	880
9	80
10	100
11	100
12	70
13	70
14	70
15	701

p	h	$r_{p,h}$	$e_{p,h}$	p	h	$r_{p,h}$	$e_{p,h}$	p	h	$r_{p,h}$	$e_{p,h}$	p	h	$r_{p,h}$	$e_{p,h}$
1	1	1	0	5	1	0	60	9	1	0	70	13	1	0	15
1	2	0	53	5	2	0	68	9	2	0	64	13	2	0	65
1	3	0	86	5	3	0	75	9	3	0	63	13	3	0	99
1	4	0	70	5	4	0	18	9	4	1	0	13	4	0	85
2	1	0	15	6	1	0	86	10	1	0	69	14	1	0	58
2	2	0	65	6	2	0	36	10	2	0	73	14	2	0	9
2	3	0	99	6	3	1	0	10	3	0	77	14	3	0	38
2	4	0	86	6	4	0	63	10	4	0	15	14	4	0	73
3	1	0	70	7	1	0	70	11	1	0	69	15	1	0	70
3	2	0	64	7	2	0	64	11	2	0	51	15	2	0	64
3	3	0	63	7	3	0	63	11	3	0	48	15	3	0	63
3	4	1	0	7	4	1	0	11	4	0	14	15	4	1	0
4	1	0	91	8	1	0	70	12	1	0	81				
4	2	0	55	8	2	0	64	12	2	0	47				
4	3	0	71	8	3	0	63	12	3	0	68				
4	4	0	119	8	4	1	0	12	4	0	111				

graph on Fig. 4. Seven patients were transported to the hospitals, 2 were transported from the emergency departments to other hospitals, and the remaining 6 patients were admitted to the hospitals to which they reported. In the second phase of the experiments, the efficiency of the proposed model and implementation thereof was analyzed. The calculations were performed for 10 data instances which differed in terms of the number of hospitals, ambulances, patients, etc. The time of calculations turned out to be very short, i.e. 1–2 s. In some cases, the solution was not satisfactory, because the hospitals ran out of resources, as evident from the non-zero values of additional variables (instance 5, 7, 8 and 9). The results are provided in Table 5. Calculations were performed on a workstation with the following hardware configuration: Intel (R) core (TM) i5 4200 M CPU @ 2.50 GHZ processor, 8 GB RAM, Windows 10.

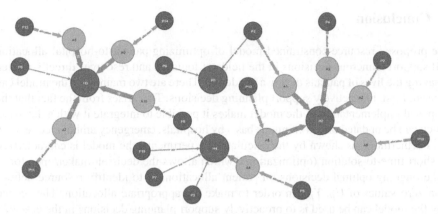

Fig. 4. Results for *Example_1* in the form of a database graph

Table 4. Results for *Example_1* (i-virtual ambulance, s-virtual hospital)

a	p	h	h	a	p	h	h
1	1	1	2	i	9	4	4
2	2	s	2	6	10	s	2
i	3	4	4	7	11	s	3
3	4	s	2	5	12	s	3
4	5	s	4	8	13	s	2
i	6	3	3	9	14	s	3
i	7	4	4	i	15	4	4
10	8	4	3				

Table 5. Results for second part of calculation experiments -number of non-zero additional variables in brackets (Y_p-U_p)

En	Number of hospitals	Number of patients	Number of ambulances	Calculation time	Number of variables	Additional variables
E1	4	6(1)	10	1	792	12(0-0)
E2	4	8(2)	10	1	1056	16(0-0)
E3	4	10(3)	10	1	1320	20(0-0)
E4	4	15(7)	10	1	1980	30(0-0)
E5	6	12(5)	10	1	3048	24(1-0)
E6	6	15(8)	10	2	3810	30(0-0)
E7	8	20(8)	20	2	13828	40(2-0)
E8	8	25(8)	20	2	15420	50(2-0)
E9	8	35(20)	20	2	16180	75(2-0)
E10	10	40(20)	25	2	28350	80(0-0)

6 Conclusion

The proposed resource-constrained model of optimizing patient-to-hospital allocation will support numerous decisions in the fields of logistics and resources directly related to saving the lives of patients during a pandemic. There are two main ways the model can be used. First, to reactively support planning decisions. This arises from the fact that the proposed implementation of the model makes it possible to integrate it with a database, which can be updated on a continuous basis by hospitals, emergency ambulance service, etc. Furthermore, as shown by the calculation experiments, the model is characterized by short time-to-solution (optimization), which allows the decision-maker/operator to make ongoing optimal decisions on patient allocation, or to identify resource deficits (non-zero values of U_p, Y_p), in order to make the appropriate allocation. The second way the model can be used is to proactively support planning decisions in the case of a hypothetical pandemic. It will be possible to determine which hospitals have sufficient resources, and identify and address potential deficits, whether the ambulance service has the necessary fleet of ambulances for a specific type of pandemic, i.e. a specific number of patients in a given category in subsequent periods of time.

In future studies, it is planned to introduce mechanisms to the model which will make it possible to take into account the potential absences of healthcare personnel (infections, work shifts, etc.). In subsequent versions of the implementation, it is also planned to use a proprietary hybrid approach [12, 14–16], fuzzy logic [17, 18], and neural networks [19] etc.

References

1. Pandemic Influenza Triage Tools. https://www.cdc.gov/cpr/healthcare/pan-flu-app/desktop/pita.html?fbclid=IwAR0mEaCLKvNm8oJn3hfuAhmZp04QmHISVNO3RoJp3ZeYRFzI4UxxUgjAomw. Accessed 8 May 2020
2. Gurobi. http://www.gurobi.com/. Accessed 8 May 2020
3. Home-AMPL. https://ampl.com/. Accessed 8 May 2020
4. Parker, J.: A flexible, large-scale, distributed agent based epidemic model. In: WSC 2007, pp. 1543–1547 (2007)
5. Larson, R.C.: Simple models of influenza progression within a heterogeneous population. Oper. Res. **55**(3), 399–412 (2007)
6. Lum, M.E., McMillan, A.J., Brook, C.W., Lester, R., Piers, L.S.: Impact of pandemic (HIN1) 2009 influenza on critical care capacity in Victoria. Med. J. Aust. **191**(9), 502–506 (2009)
7. Rico, F., Salari, E., Centeno, G.: Emergency departments nurse allocation to face a pandemic influenza outbreak. In: WSC 2009, pp. 1292–1298 (2007)
8. Gunes, E.D., Yaman, H.: Health network mergers and hospital re-planning. J. Oper. Res. Soc. **61**(2), 275–283 (2010)
9. Koyuncu, M., Erol, R.: Optimal resource allocation model to mitigate the impact of pandemic influenza: a case study for Turkey. J. Med. Syst. **34**(1), 61–70 (2008). https://doi.org/10.1007/s10916-008-9216-y
10. Yi, W., Ozdamar, L.: A dynamic logistics coordination model for evacuation and support in disaster response activities. EJOR **179**(3), 1177–1193 (2007)
11. Minciardi, R., Sacile, R., Trasforini, E.: Resource allocation in integrated preoperational and operational management of natural hazards. Risk Anal. **29**, 62–75 (2009)

12. Sitek, P., Wikarek, J.: A multi-level approach to ubiquitous modeling and solving constraints in combinatorial optimization problems in production and distribution. Appl. Intell. **48**(5), 1344–1367 (2017). https://doi.org/10.1007/s10489-017-1107-9

13. Goli, A., Aazami, A., Jabbarzadeh, A.: Accelerated cuckoo optimization algorithm for capacitated vehicle routing problem in competitive conditions. Int. J. Artif. Intell. **16**(1), 88–112 (2018)

14. Sitek, P., Wikarek, J.: Capacitated vehicle routing problem with pick-up and alternative delivery (CVRPPAD): model and implementation using hybrid approach. Ann. Oper. Res. **273**(1), 257–277 (2017). https://doi.org/10.1007/s10479-017-2722-x

15. Sitek, P., Wikarek, J., Nielsen, P.: A constraint-driven approach to food supply chain management. IMDS **117**, 2115–2138 (2017). https://doi.org/10.1108/IMDS-10-2016-0465

16. Wikarek, J.: Implementation aspects of hybrid solution framework. In: Szewczyk, R., Zieliński, C., Kaliczyńska, M. (eds.) Recent Advances in Automation, Robotics and Measuring Techniques. AISC, vol. 267, pp. 317–328. Springer, Cham (2014). https://doi.org/10. 1007/978-3-319-05353-0_31

17. Bocewicz, G., Banaszak, Z., Nielsen, I.: Multimodal processes prototyping subject to gridlike network and fuzzy operation time constraints. Ann. Oper. Res. **273**(1), 561–585 (2017). https://doi.org/10.1007/s10479-017-2468-5

18. Kłosowski, G., Gola, A., Świć, A.: Application of fuzzy logic in assigning workers to production tasks. Distributed Computing and Artificial Intelligence, 13th International Conference. AISC, vol. 474, pp. 505–513. Springer, Cham (2016). https://doi.org/10.1007/978-3-319-40162-1_54

19. Relich, M.: Computational intelligence for estimating cost of new product development. Found. Manage. **8**(1), 21–34 (2016)

Declarative UAVs Fleet Mission Planning: A Dynamic VRP Approach

Grzeogorz Radzki[1], Peter Nielsen[2], Amila Thibbotuwawa[3], Grzegorz Bocewicz[1(✉)], and Zbigniew Banaszak[1]

[1] Faculty of Electronics and Computer Science,
Koszalin University of Technology, Koszalin, Poland
radzki.grzegorz@gmail.com,
{grzegorz.bocewicz,zbigniew.banaszak}@tu.koszalin.pl
[2] Department of Materials and Production, Aalborg University, Aalborg, Denmark
peter@mp.aau.dk
[3] Department of Transport and Logistics Management, Faculty of Engineering,
University of Moratuwa, Moratuwa, Sri Lanka
amilat@uom.lk

Abstract. In this paper, we study the problem of dynamically routing Unmanned Aerial Vehicles (UAVs) taking into account not only the known requests, their type, pick-up, and delivery locations, and time windows, but also considering traffic, i.e., collision avoidance, and changing weather conditions as well as the arrival of new customer requests or request cancellation by impatient consumers and emergency departures caused by low battery. This problem can be viewed as the dynamic version of the well-known Vehicle Routing Problem with Time Windows (VRRTW), where current routings are subject to change at any time. Its NP-hard character following the vehicle routing and deadlock-avoidance problems implies the need to use a constraint programming based framework that has proven to be effective in various contexts, especially related to the nonlinearity of system characteristics. The approach has been tested on several examples, analyzing customer satisfaction, i.e., service level, throughput (number of serviced requests). Revenue maximization is influenced by different values of the mission parameters, such as the fleet size, travel distance, wind direction, and wind speed. Computational experiments show the results that allow assessing alternative strategies of UAV mission planning.

Keywords: UAV mission planning · Declarative modeling · Robust planning

1 Introduction

Fleet mission planning for Unmanned Aerial Vehicles (UAVs) creates flight plans for the specific sets of service times and travel times, typically over some time. However, there are often situations where not all information about the problem instance is known in advance. Such cases occur in situations related to the ordering of services carried out at strictly defined intervals, i.e., remaining active for a certain deterministic amount of

© Springer Nature Switzerland AG 2020
N. T. Nguyen et al. (Eds.): ICCCI 2020, LNAI 12496, pp. 188–202, 2020.
https://doi.org/10.1007/978-3-030-63007-2_15

time and then expire, which is the case with impatient customers [9]. In other words, in such cases where the fulfillment of an active service request enables one of the UAVs to visit the location of a new request [4, 5]. Dynamism is mostly considered for customer requests. Since the most common source of dynamism in UAVs routing is the online arrival of customer requests during the operation, i.e., the current routing is subject to change at any time. Hence, vehicles do not know their next destination until they finish serviced requests.

The UAVs mission planning problem specified above belongs to the class of Vehicle Routing Problems (VRP). Because possible occurrences are dynamically changing demands, service, and travel times, i.e., the input data revealing during the execution of the plan, is also referred to as online VRP or the dynamic VRP (DVRP) [4, 6, 12]. Because part or all of the inputs are unknown and revealed dynamically during the design or execution of the fleet mission plan, the UAV routes are redefined in an ongoing fashion that correspond to rapidly evolving problem constraints.

The DVRP and its related problems have been studied since the late eighties of the last century [1, 5]. The issues extensively studied in the literature cover various issues of modeling and planning mobile vehicle fleets in flying ones [3, 7, 8]. Excellent reviews on DVRPs and their taxonomy, are given in [2, 10, 12].

This research addresses the existing gap in the state-of-the-art of UAVs fleet mission planning concerning the changing weather conditions, and it allows generating alternative robust mission plans. Assuming limited battery capacity, any change in weather conditions results in a range change for a drone. In this context, it can be seen as the continuation of our previous works [11, 14] by assessing the possibility of using declarative modeling methods in order to provide a strategy for determining the minimum number of UAVs needed to ensure that a certain fraction of service requests is fulfilled in assumed time horizon. Our main contributions to considered dynamic and energy-dependent multi-route VRP with time windows problem can be summarized as follows:

1. The proposed approach considers multiple factors that influence the UAVs' ability to complete the missions, such as changing weather conditions, different UAVs energy consumption, and the possibility of an emergency interruption of the UAV's mission, that forces him to return to the depot.
2. The declarative modeling-driven approach is formulated, which allows for the assessment of alternative UAVs fleet routing and scheduling variants. The proposed Constraint Satisfaction Problem (CSP) based framework enables for predictive (i.e., considering forecasted weather conditions) and reactive (i.e., enabling UAVs emergency departure) planning of missions aimed at impatient customers service.
3. The proposed approach enables us to replace the usually used computer simulation methods of routes prototyping and UAVs scheduling by employing a constraint programming environment. Since CSP based framework allows us to search for the answer to the opposite question: what conditions do guarantee the success of a mission? In this context, the proposed solution can be recognized as an outperforming solution approach concerning those usually used for UAV mission planning.

The rest of the paper is organized as follows. In Sect. 2, using the illustrative example, the UAVs fleet mission planning problem was introduced. A dynamic programming approach, including the detailed description of the solution method adopted, is given in Sect. 3. Section 4 reports the computational experiments to assess the model behavior and evaluate the impact of some key input parameters. Concluding remarks are provided in Sect. 5.

2 Problem Formulation

As an example, let us consider a company that provides air transport services using a fleet of UAVs. In a case in point, the fleet $\mathcal{U} = \{U_1, U_2, U_3\}$ consists of three UAVs with identical technical parameters (Fig. 1). The UAVs deliver goods to 19 customers located in an area covering 100 km^2 – the network of connections is shown in Fig. 1. Node N_1 represents the location of the company (the depot which the UAVs take off from/land at), and nodes $N_2 - N_{20}$ represent the individual customers.

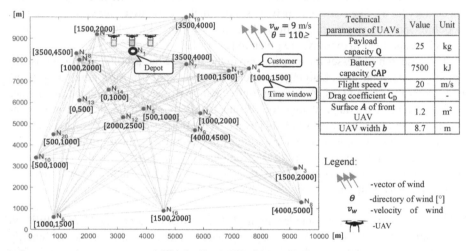

Fig. 1. Transportation network

Known is the demand z_i of the individual customers, they are respectively: $z_2 = z_3 = z_4 = z_5 = z_6 = 5$ [kg], $z_7 = 10$ [kg], $z_8 = 15$ [kg], $z_9 = 15$ [kg], $z_{10} = z_{11} = \ldots = z_{16} = 5$ [kg], $z_{17} = 10$ [kg], $z_{18} = z_{19} = 15$ [kg], $z_{20} = 5$ [kg]. It is also assumed that time windows tw_i are known in which the i-th consumers make the deliveries they have ordered. The considered time horizon for deliveries does not exceed 1.5 h ($t_{max} = 5400$ [s]). The problem under consideration boils down to seeking the answer to the following question: *Is the available fleet $\mathcal{U}$ able to guarantee the delivery of the required amount of goods $\{z_2, \ldots, z_{20}\}$, to the customers $\{N_2, \ldots, N_{20}\}$, in a given time horizon (t_{max})?* The answer to this question allows one to designate flight mission S carried out by the UAVs fleet, and more specifically, to designate the routes Π of individual UAV and the associated delivery schedules Y. The assessment of the feasibility of carrying out the planned mission takes into account the forecast of weather conditions. Weather conditions accompanying the mission are determined based on forecasts (Fig. 2a), enabling the determination of the so-called set of allowed weather conditions $\mathbb{Z}$ (Fig. 2b). $\mathbb{Z}$ is a set of forecasted weather conditions represented by the pairs: (wind's direction θ, a wind's speed vw), that may occur during the mission: $\mathbb{Z} = \{(\theta, vw)|\theta \in [0°, 360°), vw \leq Z(\theta)\}$. The set $\mathbb{Z}$ is determined by the function $Z(\theta)$ where: $\theta \in [0°, 360°)$ whose values determine the maximum forecasted wind speed for given direction θ. It is assumed that the function $Z(\theta)$ is known and determined based on available weather forecasts (e.g., see Fig. 2b).

a)

Forecasted weather conditions			θ	$Z(\theta)$
Wind direction		Wind speed		
E	east	0 … 8	0°	8
ENE	east northeast	0 … 8.5	22°30'	8.5
NE	northeast	0 … 9	45°	9
NNE	north northeast	0 … 9	67°30'	9
N	north	0 … 9	90°	9
NNW	north northwest	0 … 9.5	112°30'	9.5
NW	northwest	0 … 10	135°	10
WNW	west-northwest	0 … 10	157°30'	10
W	west	0 … 10	180°	10
WSW	west southwest	0 … 9.5	202°30'	9.5
SW	southwest	0 … 9	225°	9
SSW	south-southwest	0 … 9	247°30'	9
S	south	0 … 9	270°	9
SSE	south southeast	0 … 8.5	292°30'	8.5
SE	southeast	0 … 8	315°	8
ESE	east southeast	0 … 8	337°30'	8

b)

Fig. 2. Sample weather forecast a) and the corresponding function $Z(\Theta)$ b)

The variability of weather conditions (as part of the adopted set $\mathbb{Z}$) significantly affects the level of battery consumption [11, 13, 14] of UAVs carrying out the planned mission S and thus determines the possibility of its completion. In practice, there are situations when, when the wind is too strong. It is impossible to perform the planned mission within a given time horizon. This concept introduces the concept of the robustness of the mission plan S to the weather conditions $\mathbb{Z}$.

Let the set $\mathbb{Y}_{USG}$ determine the set of weather conditions (pairs (θ, vw)), for which the plan of mission S by fleet $\mathcal{U}$ in the distribution network $\mathcal{U}$ is feasible: $\mathbb{Y}_{USG} = \{(\theta, vw)|\theta \in [0°, 360°), vw \leq \Upsilon_{USG}(\theta)\}$, where: $\Upsilon_{USG}(\theta)$ – is the function determining the boundary weather conditions the exceeding of which would result in a situation that the battery of at least one UAV from the fleet $\mathcal{U}$ would be empty. Under these assumptions, it is assumed that a plan of mission S to be executed by fleet $\mathcal{U}$ in distribution network G is robust to forecasted weather conditions $\mathbb{Z}$ only when, $\mathbb{Z} \subseteq \mathbb{Y}_{USG}$.

According to the above definition, it possible to formulate a new class problem of searching for proactive plans of missions robust to given changes in weather conditions, i.e., the robust plans of mission (Fig. 3). It is assumed that a given set of forecast weather conditions $\mathbb{Z}$ is given, for fleet $\mathcal{U}$ and distribution network G. The answer to the following question is sought: *Does there exist a plan of mission S guaranteeing robustness to given weather* $(\Upsilon_{USG}(\theta) \geq Z(\theta))$? Such a form for the plan for mission S is sought (routes Π and related flight schedules Y) for fleet $\mathcal{U}$, which guarantees timely delivery (within a given time horizon) to all recipients in the G network. That is resistant to forecasted weather conditions $\mathbb{Z}$. Therefore, such a form for of plan of mission S, for which the condition is met $\mathbb{Z} \subseteq \mathbb{Y}_{USG}$ that means: $\forall_{\theta \in [0°, 360°)} \Upsilon_{USG}(\theta) \geq Z(\theta)$ and it is stated that for each direction θ the wind speed value $\Upsilon_{USG}(\theta)$ for which the plan of the mission is achievable exceeds the maximum forecast wind speed $Z(\theta)$ for the given direction. The problem considered assumes that:

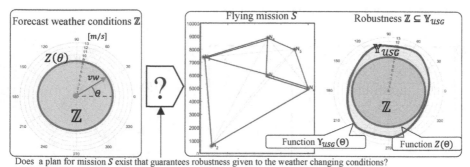

Does a plan for mission S exist that guarantees robustness given to the weather changing conditions?

Fig. 3. Illustration of UAVs fleet robust mission planning

- the set of forecasted weather conditions $\mathbb{Z}$ is known and constant,
- the structure G of the goods distribution network is known (Fig. 1),
- the goods are transported by the fleet $\mathcal{U}$ of the same UAVs (Fig. 1),
- all missions should be completed in the given time horizon (t_{max}),
- all UAVs are in the depot (N_1) before the start of the delivery mission,
- after returning to the depot and replacing the battery, the UAV is ready for the next flight,
- the same type of freight is delivered to all customers (demands z_i),
- during the flight, the total weight of the UAV is constant (67 kg),
- the UAVs ground speed are constant speed ($vg_{i,j} = 20$ m/s),
- a safe energy level (reserve) is known at the points served.

Due to the limitations related to the size of the available fleet and the constraints related to the limited capacity of the battery, i.e., the flight range, as well as the possibility of order cancellations and the occurrence of weather changes exceeding previously forecasted arrangements the DVRP based approach has been adopted. This approach implies that a plan of flying mission S is designated as a composition of successively designated sub-missions $^\alpha S$. In other words, it means that the decision to designate (a safe and collision-free mission) a new sub-mission $^\alpha S$ takes place in the distinguished states of the delivery process (see Fig. 4):

- during the UAV's stay in the depot (N_1): decision on a new mission plan,
- at delivery points: the decision to discontinue the mission and return to depot.

An example of a dynamic process of planning (determining) the flying mission S for a fleet of two UAVs are shown in Fig. 4. In the first step (moment t_1), a sub-mission was

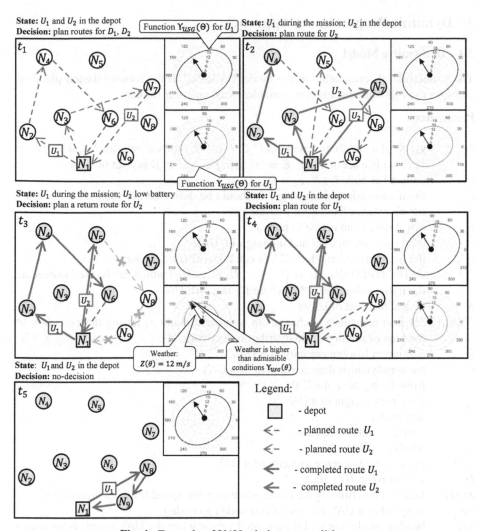

Fig. 4. Example of UAV mission accomplishment

set ^1S, under which UAVs make deliveries following routes: $\pi_1 = (N_1, N_2, N_4, N_6, N_1)$, $\pi_2 = (N_1, N_3, N_7, N_1)$. After U_2 return to the depot (moment t_2), a decision was made to start a new sub-mission ^2S for this UAV (planned route: $\pi_2 = (N_1, N_5, N_8, N_9, N_1)$). At t_3, it turned out that the weather conditions exceeded the allowable value (11 m/s), which resulted in the decision to discontinue the mission and return U_2 to the depot. Deliveries to N_8 and N_9 were carried out by U_1 (sub-mission ^3S: $\pi_1 = (N_1, N_8, N_9, N_1)$). Adopting the above approach to mission planning, S is conditioned by the possibility of effectively determining safe and collision-free (robust to forecasted weather conditions) sub-missions $^\alpha S$, at every stage of decision making. To this end, declarative programming techniques implementing the model proposed in the next section were used.

3 Dynamic Programming Approach

3.1 Declarative Model

The mathematical formulation of the model dedicated to the robust mission planning employs the following parameters, variables, sets, and constraints:

Parameters

$^{\alpha}G$ graph of a distribution network: $^{\alpha}G = (N, E)$ for sub-mission $^{\alpha}S$, where $N = \{1 \ldots n\}$ is a set of nodes, $E = \{\{i, j\} | i, j \in N, i \neq j\}$ is a set of edges

z_i demand at node $i \in N$, $z_1 = 0$

tw_i the time window in which goods should be delivered to node $i \in N$, $tw_1 = \emptyset$

$d_{i,j}$ travel distance from node i to node j

$t_{i,j}$ travel time from node i to node j

w time spent on take-off and landing of a UAV

ts the time interval at which UAVs can take off from the base

$^{\alpha}\mathcal{U}$ set (fleet) of UAVs: $^{\alpha}\mathcal{U} = \{U_1, \ldots, U_k, \ldots, U_K\}$ which can be used to execute the flying sub-mission $^{\alpha}S$, where U_k is a k-th UAV

K size of the fleet of UAVs

$^{\alpha}\Upsilon_{USG}$ $^{\alpha}\mathcal{U}$ fleet resistance to changes in weather conditions during the execution of the plan of mission $^{\alpha}S$ in distribution network $^{\alpha}G$

Q maximum loading capacity of a UAV

C_D the aerodynamic drag coefficient of a UAV

A front-facing area of a UAV

ep the empty weight of a UAV

D air density

g gravitational acceleration

b width of a UAV

CAP the maximum energy capacity of a UAV

H time horizon $H = [0, t_{max}]$

$Z(\Theta)$ function determining the upper value of wind speed for wind direction θ

$va_{i,j}$ airspeed of a UAV traveling from node i to node j

$\varphi_{i,j}$ heading angle, angle of the airspeed vector when the UAV travels from node i to node j

$vg_{i,j}$ ground speed of a UAV traveling from node i to node j

$\vartheta_{i,j}$ course angle, angle of the ground speed vector when the UAV travels from node i to node j

Decision Variables

$x_{i,j}^k$ the binary variable used to indicate if U_k travels from node i to node j

$$x_{i,j}^k = \begin{cases} 1 & \text{if } U_k \text{ travels from node i to node j} \\ 0 & \text{otherwise.} \end{cases}$$

y_i^k time at which U_k arrives at node i

c_i^k weight of freight delivered to node i by U_k
$f_{i,j}^k$ weight of freight carried from node i to node j by U_k
$P_{i,j}^k$ energy per unit of time, consumed by U_k during a flight from node i to j
bat^k total energy consumed by U_k
s^k take-off time of U_k
cp_i total weight of freight delivered to node i
π_k route of U_k, $\pi_k = (v_1, \ldots, v_i, v_{i+1}, \ldots, v_\mu)$, $v_i \in N$, $x_{v_i, v_{i+1}}^k = 1$

Sets

Y^k set of times y_i^k, schedule of U_k
$^{\alpha}Y$ family of Y^k, schedule of fleet $^{\alpha}\mathcal{U}$
C^k set of c_i^k, payload weight delivered by U_k
$^{\alpha}C$ family of C^k
$^{\alpha}\Pi$ set of UAV routes $\pi_{m,l}^k$
$^{\alpha}S$ plan of sub-mission: $^{\alpha}S = (^{\alpha}\Pi, {}^{\alpha}Y, {}^{\alpha}C)$

Constraints

1. Routes. Relationships between the variables describing drone take-off times/mission start times and task order:

$$s^k \geq 0; k = 1 \ldots K \tag{1}$$

$$\left(\left| s^k - s^q \right| \geq ts \right); k, q = 1 \ldots K; \quad k \neq q \tag{2}$$

$$\sum_{j=1}^{n} x_{1,j}^k = 1; k = 1 \ldots K \tag{3}$$

$$\left(x_{1,j}^k = 1 \right) \Rightarrow \left(y_j^k = s^k + t_{1,j} \right); j = 1 \ldots n; k = 1 \ldots K \tag{4}$$

$$\left(y_i^k \neq 0 \wedge y_i^q \neq 0 \right) \Rightarrow \left(\left| y_i^k - y_i^q \right| \geq w \right); i = 1 \ldots n; k, q = 1 \ldots K; \ k \neq q \tag{5}$$

$$\left(x_{i,j}^k - 1 \right) \Rightarrow \left(y_j^k = y_i^k + t_{i,j} + w \right); j = 1 \ldots n; i = 2 \ldots n; k = 1 \ldots K \tag{6}$$

$$\left(x_{i,j}^k = 1 \right) \Rightarrow \left(y_j^k \in tw_j \right); j = 1 \ldots n; i = 2 \ldots n; k = 1 \ldots K \tag{7}$$

$$y_i^k \geq 0; i = 1 \ldots n; k = 1 \ldots K \tag{8}$$

$$\sum_{j=1}^{n} x_{i,j}^k = \sum_{j=1}^{n} x_{j,i}^k; i = 1 \ldots n; k = 1 \ldots K, \tag{9}$$

$$y_i^k \leq t_{max} \times \sum_{j=1}^{n} x_{i,j}^k, i = 1 \ldots n; k = 1 \ldots K, \tag{10}$$

$$x_{i,i}^k = 0; i = 1 \ldots n; k = 1 \ldots K. \tag{11}$$

2. <u>Delivery of freight.</u> Relationships between the variables describing the amount of freight delivered to nodes by UAVs and the demand for goods at a given node:

$$c_i^k \geq 0; i = 1 \ldots n; k = 1 \ldots K \tag{12}$$

$$c_i^k \leq Q \times \sum_{j=1}^{n} x_{i,j}^k; i = 1 \ldots n; k = 1 \ldots K \tag{13}$$

$$\sum_{i=1}^{n} c_i^k \leq Q; k = 1 \ldots K \tag{14}$$

$$\left(x_{i,j}^k = 1 \right) \Rightarrow c_j^k \geq 1; k = 1 \ldots K; i = 1 \ldots n; j = 2 \ldots n \tag{15}$$

$$\sum_{k=1}^{K} c_i^k = cp_i; i = 1 \ldots n \tag{16}$$

$$cp_i \leq z_i; i = 1 \ldots n \tag{17}$$

$$\sum_{i=1}^{n} c_i^k = cs^k; k = 1 \ldots K \tag{18}$$

$$\left(x_{1,j}^k = 1 \right) \Rightarrow \left(fc_j^k = cs^k \right); j = 1 \ldots n; k = 1 \ldots K \tag{19}$$

$$\left(x_{i,j}^k = 1 \right) \Rightarrow \left(fc_j^k = fc_i^k - c_i^k \right); i, j = 1 \ldots n; k = 1 \ldots K \tag{20}$$

$$\left(x_{1,j}^k = 1 \right) \Rightarrow \left(f_{1,j}^k = cs^k \right); j = 1 \ldots n; k = 1 \ldots K \tag{21}$$

$$\left(x_{i,j}^k = 1 \right) \Rightarrow \left(f_{i,j}^k = fc_j^k \right); i, j = 1 \ldots n; k = 1 \ldots K \tag{22}$$

3. <u>Energy consumption.</u> The plan of sub-mission $^{\alpha}S$ is robust to weather conditions $Z(\theta)$. That means the amount of energy needed to complete tasks performed by an UAV cannot exceed the maximum capacity of its battery.

$$^{\alpha}\Upsilon_{USG}(\theta) \geq Z(\theta); \quad \forall \theta \in [0°, 360°) \tag{23}$$

$$^{\alpha}\Upsilon_{USG}(\theta) = \max \Gamma(\theta) \tag{24}$$

$$\Gamma(\theta) = \left\{ vw | vw \in R_+^0 \wedge \forall_{k \in \{1 \ldots K\}} bat^k(\theta, vw) \leq CAP \right\} \tag{25}$$

$$bat^k(\theta, vw) = \sum_{i=1}^{n} \sum_{j=1}^{n} x_{i,j}^k \times t_{i,j} \times P_{i,j}^k(\theta, vw) \tag{26}$$

$$P_{i,j}^k(\theta, vw) = \frac{1}{2} C_D \times A \times D \times \left(va_{i,j}(\theta, vw) \right)^3 + \frac{\left(\left(ep + f_{i,j}^k \right) \times g \right)^2}{D \times b^2 \times va_{i,j}(\theta, vw)} \tag{27}$$

where $va_{i,j}(\theta, vw)$ and $t_{i,j}$ depend on the assumed strategy for goods delivering. If the ground speed $vg_{i,j}$ is constant, then the air speed $va_{i,j}$ is calculated from:

$$va_{i,j}(\theta, vw) = \sqrt{\left(vg_{i,j} \times cos\vartheta_{i,j} - vw \times cos\theta\right)^2 + \left(vg_{i,j} \times sin\vartheta_{i,j} - vw \times sin\theta\right)^2}$$

(28)

$$t_{i,j} = \frac{d_{i,j}}{vg_{i,j}}.$$

(29)

4. Customer's satisfaction. For modeling purposes, we assume that the equitable aid distribution is measured by customer's satisfaction CSL expressing a percentage of the expected amount of goods delivered to the recipients:

$$\frac{\sum_{i=1}^{n} cp_i}{\sum_{i=1}^{n} z_i} \times 100\% \geq CSL.$$

(30)

3.2 Method

The adopted approach assumes that mission S consists of successively designated submissions: $^1S \ldots {}^\alpha S \ldots {}^L S$. The decision to designate the next α-submission is made after the UAV returns to the depot, or the mission is discontinued because of the prevailing weather conditions. Determining the submission $^\alpha S$ boils down to solving the following problem. Consider a fleet $^\alpha \mathcal{U}$ servicing customers allocated in the supply distribution network $^\alpha G$. *Does there exist a plan of sub-mission $^\alpha S$ (determined by variables $^\alpha \Pi, {}^\alpha Y, {}^\alpha C$) guaranteeing robustness to given weather ($\Upsilon_{USG}(\theta) \geq Z(\theta)$ (constraints (24)–(30)) while following customer's satisfaction level CSL (30)?* This kind of problem can be seen as recursive Constraint Satisfaction Problem (CSP) [14] given by the following formula (31):

$$^\alpha CP\left(^{(\alpha-1)}\Pi, {}^{(\alpha-1)}Y, {}^{(\alpha-1)}C\right) = \left(^\alpha \mathcal{V}, {}^\alpha \mathcal{D}, {}^\alpha C\left(^{(\alpha-1)}\Pi, {}^{(\alpha-1)}Y, {}^{(\alpha-1)}C\right)\right) \quad (31)$$

where:

$^\alpha \mathcal{V} = \left\{^\alpha \Pi, {}^\alpha Y, {}^\alpha C, {}^\alpha G\right\}$ -   a set of decision variables determining a plan of submission $^\alpha S$: $^\alpha \Pi$ - a set of UAV routes, $^\alpha Y$ - a schedule of a UAV fleet, $^\alpha C$ - a set of payload weights delivered by the UAVs, $^\alpha G$ – graph of a distributed network updated by completed deliveries.

$^\alpha \mathcal{D}$ -   a finite set of decision variable domain descriptions,

$^\alpha C\left(^{(\alpha-1)}\Pi, {}^{(\alpha-1)}Y, {}^{(\alpha-1)}C,\right)$ -   a set of constraints (1)–(30) parameterized by the solution of problem $^{(\alpha-1)}CP$

To solve the $^\alpha CP$ defined in formula (31), one must determine the values of the decision variables for which all the constraints are satisfied. By implementing $^\alpha CP$ in a constraint programming environment, such as IBM ILOG, it is possible to obtain the sub-mission $^\alpha S$ guaranteeing robustness to given weather conditions.

A dynamic mission $S = \left({}^{1}S \ldots {}^{\alpha}S \ldots {}^{L}S\right)$ algorithm based on the proposed concept ${}^{\alpha}CP$ is shown in Fig. 5. Mission S is determined in an iterative way wherein subsequent iterations (corresponding to the stages of deciding on a new route) the problem ${}^{\alpha}CP$ is solved (*solve* function). The existence of an acceptable solution (i.e. $\left({}^{\alpha}\Pi \neq \emptyset\right) \wedge \left({}^{\alpha}Y \neq \emptyset\right) \wedge \left({}^{\alpha}C \neq \emptyset\right)$), means that there is a sub-mission ${}^{\alpha}S$ ensuring delivery to selected points in the network ${}^{\alpha}G$. Subsequent sub-missions are set up until the demands of each customer z_i are met. In the absence of an admissible solution to the problem ${}^{\alpha}CP$, an increase in the UAVs fleet should be considered. If this is not possible ($\left|{}^{\alpha}\mathcal{U}\right| \geq LU$, where: LU – maximum fleet size), no solution is returned. The proposed algorithm has been implemented in the IBM ILOG environment.

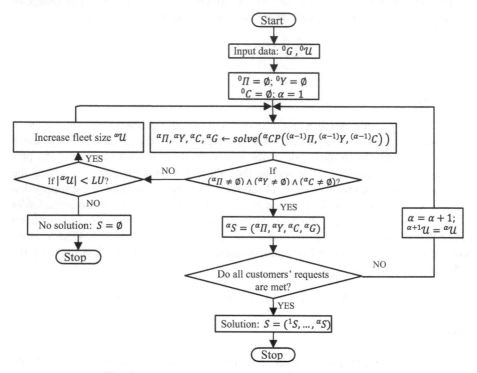

Fig. 5. Algorithm of dynamic flight mission S planning

4 Computational Experiments

Consider the case of UAVs fleet mission planning presented on Fig. 1. A plan of flight mission is sought such that it guarantees the completion of planned deliveries within a given time horizon (5400 s) in the given range of changing weather conditions. Parameters of the three UAVs forming the fleet are summarized in Fig. 1. In particular, the answer to the question is sought: *Is there a plan of mission S for fleet U that would* guarantee *timely delivery of expected essential goods in order to fulfill basic needs (CSL = 100%)*

if weather conditions would change to: $vw = 0\frac{m}{s} - 9\frac{m}{s}$; $\Theta = 0° - 360°$? In order to find the answer to the stated research question, the proposed algorithm (Fig. 5) was used. Due to the algorithm from Fig. 5 the plan sought was obtained within three iterations (28 s: 16 s for 1st iteration, 6 s for the 2nd iteration, 6 s for 3rd iteration) in the declarative programming environment IBM ILOG (Intel Core i7-M4800MQ 2.7 GHz, 32 GB RAM). Figure 6 shows the computed flight routes:

- first iteration ($\alpha = 1$): $^1\pi_1 = (N_1, N_{14}, N_{20}, N_6, N_3, N_{12}, N_1)$, $^1\pi_2 = (N_1, N_5, N_4, N_{11}, N_{17}, N_1)$, $^1\pi_3 = (N_1, N_{13}, N_{10}, N_{15}, N_2, N_{16}, N_1)$;
- second iteration ($\alpha = 2$): $^2\pi_2 = (N_1, N_7, N_{18}, N_1)$;
- third iteration ($\alpha = 3$): $^3\pi_1 = (N_1, N_{19}, N_8, N_9, N_1)$, $^3\pi_3 = (N_1, N_9, N_8, N_1)$;

guaranteeing that the demanded quantity of goods is delivered to customers under the given weather conditions and given horizon (5400 s).

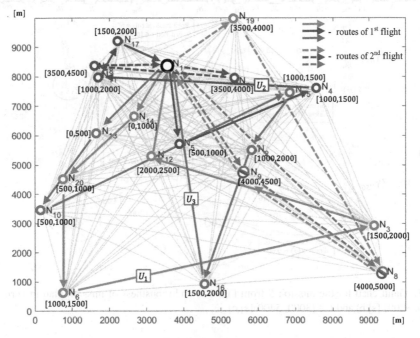

Fig. 6. Obtained routes

As can be seen, each UAV executes two flights (Fig. 6 and 7), robust to the given range of weather conditions ($vw \in \left[0\frac{m}{s}, 9\frac{m}{s}\right]$; $\theta \in [0°, 360°]$). Until the wind exceeds the permissible value of $vw > 9$ m/s, the implementation of the mission following the schedule in Fig. 7 is not threatened. The robustness of execution plans of individual UAVs is different and changes over time. Missions carried out by U_2 are characterized by the highest robustness level (see $^1_2\Upsilon_{USG}$ and $^2_2\Upsilon_{USG}$), in turn, missions carried out by U_1 have a lower level of robustness (see $^1_1\Upsilon_{USG}$ and $^2_1\Upsilon_{USG}$). In addition, the first part of the mission of each UAV covering routes $^1\pi_1$, $^1\pi_2$, $^1\pi_3$ carried out in the period $t \in [0, 3000)$ [s] have less robustness level than the second part of the mission cowering routes $^3\pi_1$, $^2\pi_2$, $^3\pi_3$) carried out in the period $t \in [3000, 5400)$ [s]. Therefore, the charts presented (see Fig. 7) show that UAV U_1, is the most exposed to changes in weather conditions in the period $t \in [0, 3000)$ [s].

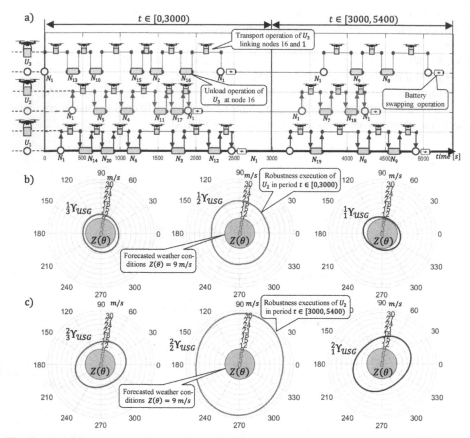

Fig. 7. Gantt chart for the mission S from Fig. 6 a) and robustness of mission plan in periods: $t \in [0, 3000)$ [s] b) and $t \in [3000, 5400)$[s] c)

5 Conclusions

The dynamic vehicle routing approach presented in this paper provides a new way of studying the fleet mission planning of UAVs in dynamically changing environments. Indeed, we presented the DVRP driven approach to the design of reactive flight mission planning, resulting in dynamic routing strategies for networks allowing the presence of impatient consumers awhile used in conditions of weather changes exceeding previously forecasted ones, i.e., forcing the emergence of emergency departures. It is worth noting that this approach extends reactive planning models (including weather forecasts) with elements of reactive planning (considering dynamically occurring changes of different nature).

The results of the conducted experiments were not compared with the results of other studies. Because there is currently no reference benchmark for DVRPs as well as there is a lack of work on the taxonomy of these problems [6, 10].

The conducted review of the existing literature revealed that a significant fraction of work done in the area of dynamic routing does not consider stochastic aspects. We are convinced that developing algorithms that make use of stochastic information will improve the fleet performance and reduce operating costs. Of course, many other key problems in UAVs systems implementation could benefit from being studied from the perspective of proactive-reactive fleet mission planning models presented in this paper. Some examples include search and rescue missions, force protection, map maintenance, and pursuit-evasion [6, 10]. Thus this line of research taking into account the specificity of these applications should become a priority in the near future.

References

1. Backer, B., Furnon, V., Shaw, P., Kilby, P., Prosser, P.: Solving vehicle routing problems using constraint programming and metaheuristics. J. Heuristics **6**(4), 501–523 (1999). https://doi.org/10.1023/a:1009621410177

2. Braekers, K., Ramaekers, K., Van Nieuwenhuyse, I.: The vehicle routing problem: state of the art classification and review. Comput. Ind. Eng. **99**, 300–313 (2016). https://doi.org/10.1016/j.cie.2015.12.007

3. Bullo, F., Frazzoli, E., Pavone, M., Savla, K., Smith, S.L.: Dynamic vehicle routing for robotic systems. Proc. IEEE **99**(9), 1482–1504 (2011). https://doi.org/10.1109/jproc.2011.2158181

4. Grippa, P.: Decision making in a UAV-based delivery system with impatient customers. In: 2016 IEEE/RSJ International Conference on Intelligent Robots and Systems (IROS), pp. 5034–5039 (2016). https://doi.org/10.1109/iros.2016.7759739

5. Holborn, P.L.: Heuristics for dynamic vehicle routing problems with pick-ups and deliveries and time windows. Ph.D. Thesis. School of Mathematics Cardiff University, Cardiff, UK (2013)

6. Khoufi, I., Laouiti, A., Adjih, C.: A survey of recent extended variants of the traveling salesman and vehicle routing problems for unmanned aerial vehicles. Drones **3**(3), 66 (2019). https://doi.org/10.3390/drones3030066

7. O'Rourke, K.P., Bailey, T.G., Hill, R., Carlton, W.B.: Dynamic routing of unmanned aerial vehicles using reactive Tabu search. In: 67-th MORS Symposium (1999)

8. Pavone, M., Bisnik, N., Frazzoli, E., Isler, V.: A stochastic and dynamic vehicle routing problem with time windows and customer impatience. Mob. Netw. Appl. **14**(3), 350–364 (2008). https://doi.org/10.1007/s11036-008-0101-1

9. Pillac, V., Gendreau, M., Guéret, C., Medaglia, A.L.: A review of dynamic vehicle routing problems. Eur. J. Oper. Res. **225**(1), 1–11 (2012). https://doi.org/10.1016/j.ejor.2012.08.015

10. Radzki, G., Nielsen, P., Bocewicz, G., Banaszak, Z.: A proactive approach to resistant UAV mission planning. In: Szewczyk, R., Zieliński, C., Kaliczyńska, M. (eds.) AUTOMATION 2020. AISC, vol. 1140, pp. 112–124. Springer, Cham (2020). https://doi.org/10.1007/978-3-030-40971-5_11

11. Ritzinger, U., Puchinger, J., Hartl, R.F.: A survey on dynamic and stochastic vehicle routing problems. Int. J. Prod. Res. **54**(1), 215–231 (2015). https://doi.org/10.1080/00207543.2015.1043403

12. Thibbotuwawa, A., Bocewicz, G., Nielsen, P., Banaszak, Z.: UAV mission planning subject to weather forecast constraints. In: Herrera-Viedma, E., Vale, Z., Nielsen, P., Martin Del Rey, A., Casado Vara, R. (eds.) DCAI 2019. AISC, vol. 1004, pp. 65–76. Springer, Cham (2020). https://doi.org/10.1007/978-3-030-23946-6_8

13. Thibbotuwawa, A., Bocewicz, G., Radzki, G., Nielsen, P., Banaszak, Z.: UAV mission planning resistant to weather uncertainty. Sensors **20**(2), str. 515 (2020). https://doi.org/10.3390/s20020515

14. Thibbotuwawa, A., Nielsen, P., Zbigniew, B., Bocewicz, G.: Energy consumption in unmanned aerial vehicles: a review of energy consumption models and their relation to the UAV routing. In: Świątek, J., Borzemski, L., Wilimowska, Z. (eds.) ISAT 2018. AISC, vol. 853, pp. 173–184. Springer, Cham (2019). https://doi.org/10.1007/978-3-319-99996-8_16

Applications of Collective Intelligence

Increasing Mutation Testing Effectiveness by Combining Lower Order Mutants to Construct Higher Order Mutants

Quang-Vu Nguyen[✉]

The University of Danang, Vietnam-Korea University of Information and Communication Technology, Da Nang, Viet Nam
nqvu@vku.udn.vn

Abstract. Researching and proposing the solutions in the field of mutation testing in order to answer the question of how to improve the effectiveness of mutant testing is a problem that researchers, who study in the field of mutation testing, are interested. Limitations of mutation testing are really big problems that prevent its application in practice although this is a promising technique in assessing the quality of test data sets. The number of generated mutants is too large and easy-to-kill mutants are two of those problems. In this paper, we have studied and presented our solution, as well as analyzed the empirical results for the purpose of introducing a way to improve the effectiveness of mutant testing. Instead of constructing higher order mutants by using and combining first-order mutants as previous studies, we propose a method to use higher-order mutants for creating mutants. In other words, we have combined two "**lower**" order mutants to construct "**higher**" order mutants, i.e., use two second order mutants to construct a fourth order mutant, guided by our proposed objective and fitness functions. According to the experimental results, the number of generated is reduced and number of valuable mutants is fairly large, we have concluded that our approach seems to be a good way to overcome the main limitations of mutation testing.

Keywords: Mutation testing · Limitations of mutation testing · Overcome · Reducing the cost · Harder to kill · Realistic faults

1 Introduction

In the field of Software Testing, Mutation Testing (MT), including First Order Mutation Testing (FOMT) and Higher Order Mutation Testing (HOMT), is an effectiveness approach (also high automation technique) which has been introduced to assess the quality of test suites.

Mutation Testing technique evaluates the quality of a given test suite by evaluating the test case ability to detect differences between the original program and its mutants. A mutant is another version of the original program, in which one or more different operators have been changed.

© Springer Nature Switzerland AG 2020
N. T. Nguyen et al. (Eds.): ICCCI 2020, LNAI 12496, pp. 205–216, 2020.
https://doi.org/10.1007/978-3-030-63007-2_16

Hamlet [1] and DeMillo et al. [2] are the first authors who present the idea of mutant testing and its related concepts. Whilst, the concepts and descriptions about higher order mutation testing as well as the distinction between First Order Mutants (FOMs) and Higher Order Mutants (HOMs) are firstly introduced by co-authors: Jia et al. [3] and Harman et al. [4].

Hitherto, there are many different interesting researches, such as [3–37], which have been proposed in the field of mutation testing. Some of these researches were developed to apply and improve the effectiveness of mutation testing and some others were proposed to overcome the problems of mutation testing. According to these researches result, mutation testing has a wide range of applications in software testing. It can be used with different programming languages for testing software at the unit level, the integration level or the specification level [5].

However, there are some really big barriers of mutation testing which are the main reasons to explain why mutation testing is not yet widely adopted in practice [5, 6].

- The first of them refers to the problem of high execution cost due to a large number of generated mutants. The execution cost of mutation testing includes not only the execution cost of software under test as well as all generated mutants against the given set of test cases but also the execution cost for their corresponding output results evaluations to determine that the mutant is "killed" or "alive" [1, 2].
- The second one is realism problem of generated mutants, in other words, the mutants do not denote realistic faults.
- And another is generated mutants are simple and so easy to kill. An easy-to-kill mutant is a mutant which is killed by all of given set of test cases.

In Mutation Testing, the quality of a set of test cases is evaluated by MS (Mutation Score) [1, 2] or MSI (Mutation Score Indicator) [11, 26–29] which is calculated based on number of generated mutants, number of **killed mutants**, number of **equivalent mutants** and number of **alive mutants**.

A mutant is called a **"killed mutant"** if its output results differ from the original program when they are executed with the same test case (in a given set of test cases). Conversely, if the mutant has the same output as the original program with all given test cases, it is called **"alive mutant"**. **Equivalent mutants** are the mutants which always produce the same output as the original program, so they cannot be killed.

As we mentioned before, there are so many researches, e.g., [3–37], which have been introduced to overcome the main problems of mutation testing including traditional mutation testing (also known as first mutation testing or traditional mutation testing) and higher order mutation testing. With those studies, besides the advantages which make mutation testing get more effectiveness while doing, there are also some disadvantages that need to be considered, i.e., the number of generated mutants is still very large and this leads to a high execution cost of mutation testing.

In the above-mentioned studies [3–37], the authors have focused on two main methods for constructing higher order mutants: (1) Insert n faults ($n = 1..70$) [18, 19, 23] to create a n-order-mutant; (2) Combine n first-order-mutants to produce a n-order-mutant [20–25].

Different from the 2 above-methods, we will propose the another: Combine two "**lower**" order mutants to construct "**higher**" order mutants (guided by our proposed objective and fitness functions) as follows:

- Use two first order mutants to construct a second order mutant.
- Use two second order mutants to construct a fourth order mutant.
- And so on.

In addition, based on our previous research results [20–25], we will only use **not-easy-to-kill mutants** (details are presented in Sect. 2) to construct the higher-order-mutants.

The purpose of this investigation is to focus on the way to overcome the aforementioned limitations as well as to improve the effectiveness of mutation testing by combining the lower order mutants to construct higher order mutants. In this study of the paper, we have focused on reducing the number of mutants generated while improving the quality of mutations.

In the next section, we will present in details the backgrounds as well as the hypotheses of research problem and from that introduce the idea for this study. Section 3 presents and analyzes empirical results to demonstrate the effectiveness of our solution. And the last section is used to give a conclusion and some ideas for future work.

2 Background and the Idea for Study

In our previous works [20–25], we have proposed and proved (through empirical results) the effectiveness of applying multi-objective optimization algorithms into higher order mutation testing based on our mutant classification as well as our objective and fitness functions.

According to our researches, there are some positive results that we will reuse as "hypotheses" for the study in this paper, specifically as follows:

- Our mutant classification consists of eleven kinds (**H1–H11**) of HOMs and can cover all of the available cases of generated HOMs [20–24]. The idea of our HOMs classification approach is based on the combination of a set of test cases which can kill HOM, and sets of test cases which can kill its constituent FOMs.
- **H1** is group of alive (potentially equivalent) mutant. Alive mutants can be "really equivalent mutants" or "difficult-to-kill mutant". This mean that, the mutants cannot be killed by the given set of test cases which are included in the project under test, but they perhaps could be killed by other new, better test cases in terms of fault detecting. Reduction of H1 mutants leads to reducing of mutation testing execution cost of the given set of test cases on those live mutants [20–24].
- **H4–H9** are groups of "**Reasonable mutants**". They are harder to kill and more realistic (reflecting real, complex faults) than their constituent FOMs [20–24].
- **H7** is group of "**High quality and reasonable mutants**" [20–24]. These mutations, in our study, are the best ones which can be used to replace the set of their constituent FOMs while ensuring the effectiveness of the test. In this case, the set of test cases can kill both HOMs and their constituent FOMs.

- **eNSGAII algorithm** is the best multi-objective optimization algorithm in terms of constructing the "H7 - High Quality and Reasonable HOMs" [24]. Approximately 12% of "reasonable HOMs" in our studies, which were found by eNSGAII algorithm, are classified as "high quality and reasonable HOMs".
- **Five** (5) a relevant upper bound on mutation order in higher order mutation testing [23, 24]. This conclusion of us based on the relationships between the order of mutation testing and the properties of mutants.
- The **not-easy-to-kill mutants** should be used to generate higher order mutants because it seems to be a promising method to improve the quality of test cases [22, 24].

   Easy-to-kill mutants are the mutants that are killed by all given test cases of project under test. The not-easy-to-kill mutants are the remaining ones of the set of all generated mutants after deleting all easy-to-kill mutants.

   From these hypotheses, in this study, we have proposed the solution for increasing the effectiveness (in terms of reducing the cost, generating valuable mutants and do not waste computational resources for creating mutants, which are easy to kill by most test cases) of mutation testing by combining two lower order mutants to construct higher order mutants (5 is upper bound order [23, 24]) as follows:

- Firstly, generate all possible FOMs, calculate number of generated FOMs, number of live (potentially equivalent) FOMs and MSI.
- Delete easy-to-kill-FOMs from the set of generated FOMs.
- From set of remaining-FOMs (The not-easy-to-kill FOMs), generate Second Order Mutants (SOMs) by combining two FOMs guided by our objective and fitness functions;
- Calculate number of H1, H4–H9, H7 and MSI of second order mutation testing.
- Delete easy-to-kill-SOMs from the set of generated SOMs.
- From set of remaining-SOMs (The not-easy-to-kill SOMs), generate Fourth Order Mutants (FOOMs) by combining two SOMs guided by our objective and fitness functions;
- Calculate number of H1, H4–H9, H7 and MSI of fourth order mutation testing.
- Evaluate and compare the obtained results.

   In our solution, we have focused on eliminating the easy-to-kill mutants before constructing the higher-order mutants due to many studies have been demonstrated that the majority (about 90%) of real faults of software are complex faults [18, 19].

   We have used (and extended) Judy [29] as a support tool to generate and evaluate FOMs and HOMs (SOMs and FOOMs) with the same full set of mutation operators of Judy. This is a tool that can be used to generate mutations, perform mutant testing, evaluate results and produce reports as well as support both first order and high order mutation testing.

   As described in Sect. 2, eNSGAII algorithm is the best multi-objective optimization algorithm in terms of constructing valuable mutants. That is why we continue to use this algorithm in our research of this paper.

   Selected projects under test, five open source projects (Barbecue, BeanBin, JWBF, Common Chain 1.2 and Common Validator 1.4.1) downloaded from SourceForge (https://sourceforge.net/), for experiment along with number of classes (NOC), number of lines of code (LOC) and number of build-in test cases (NOT) are shown in Table 1.

Table 1. Projects under test

PROJECT	NOC	LOC	NOT
Barbecue	57	23.996	190
BeanBin	72	5.925	68
JWBF	51	13.572	305
CommonChain 1.2	103	13.410	17
CommonValidator 1.4.1	144	25.422	66

These projects have a fairly large number of lines of code, as well as built-in test cases that are considered to be quality. Besides, these projects also include a test suite with a high number of test cases.

3 Empirical Results and Analysis

We have produced First Order Mutants, Second Order Mutants, Fourth Order Mutants as well as analyzed and calculated the corresponding parameters for each order of the generated mutants.

Experimental results of First Order Mutation Testing (FOMT), Second Order Mutation Testing (SOMT) and Fourth Order Mutation Testing (FOOMT) are shown in Table 2, 3 and 4 respectively.

Table 2. FOMT results

PROJECT	Number of FOMs	% of live (potentially equivalent) FOMs to all FOMs	MSI(%)
Barbecue	3.084	84,21%	15,79%
BeanBin	1.330	84,89%	15,11%
JWBF	1.482	87,04%	12,96%
CommonChain 1.2	1.476	57,35%	42,65%
CommonValidator 1.4.1	2.981	52,90%	47,10%

In this study, we have used the following parameters to confirm our proposed solution is good or not to improve the effectiveness of mutation testing (in terms of reducing the cost, generating valuable mutants and do not waste computational resources for creating mutants which are easy to kill by most of the test cases):

Table 3. SOMT results

PROJECT	Number of SOMs	% of H1 to all SOMs	% of H4–H9 to all SOMs	% of H7 to all SOMs	MSI(%)
Barbecue	678	37,61%	54,24%	6,25%	62,39%
BeanBin	297	37,89%	53,18%	6,12%	62,11%
JWBF	329	42,22%	40,09%	6,08%	57,78%
CommonChain 1.2	320	39,85%	51,12%	6,21%	60,15%
CommonValidator 1.4.1	656	36,10%	63,47%	6,25%	63,90%

Table 4. FOOMT results

PROJECT	Number of FOOMs	% of H1 to all FOOMs	% of H4–H9 to all FOOMs	% of H7 to all FOOMs	MSI
Barbecue	99	32,15%	66,19%	6,13%	67,85%
BeanBin	68	33,01%	58,24%	6,01%	66,99%
JWBF	71	34,83%	54,41%	6,05%	65,17%
CommonChain 1.2	78	38,95%	45,80%	6,14%	61,05%
CommonValidator 1.4.1	92	25,12%	60,94%	6,12%	74,88%

- Number of generated mutants;
- Number of "**Live**" mutants;
- Number of "**Reasonable**" mutants;
- Number of "**High Quality and Reasonable**";

In Table 2, the main parameters are followings:

- Number of generated first order mutants;
- Proportion of live (potentially equivalent) mutants (H1) to all generated mutants;
- MSI;

Whilst, in Table 3 and 4, the main parameters are followings:

- Number of generated second/fourth order mutants,
- The proportions of Live (potentially equivalent) mutants (H1) to all generated mutants;
- The proportions of group of reasonable mutants (H4–H9) to all generated mutants;
- "High Quality and Reasonable" mutants (H7) to all generated mutants.
- MSI;

From the obtained results shown in Tables 2, 3 and 4 above, we can see that the number of constructed mutations tends to significantly reduce in order from lower to higher (See Fig. 1 below).

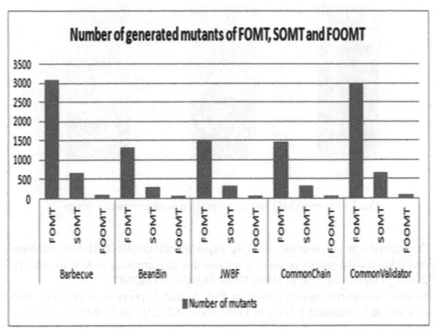

Fig. 1. Number or generated mutants of 1st, 2nd and 4th order mutation testing

Number of generated of FOMs (1st order) is about 4,5 times more than number of generated of SOMs (2nd order), and number of generated of SOMs (2nd order) is about 5,5 times more than number of generated of FOOMs (4th order).

In other words, the number of higher order mutants is reduced at least 70% compared to the adjacent lower order mutants. This is because we only use the set of not-easy-to-kill lower mutants instead of using all lower generated mutants to construct the higher mutants. In addition, we focus on constructing the valuable (H7 - High Quality and Reasonable) mutants instead of generating all possible mutants by applying our proposed objectives and fitness functions [20–24].

Reducing the number of generated mutants leads to reduce the execution cost of mutation testing. Therefore, it can be said that our solution in this paper is a promising method for overcoming the big problem (a very large number of generated mutants) of mutation testing in general and higher order mutation testing in particular.

Figure 2 shows that the number of H1 mutants decreases in orders (from 73.28% of FOMT to 38.73% of HOMT and 25.12% of FOOMT). This demonstrates that the higher order mutants are more complex and more realistic than their constituent lower order mutants. As mentioned above, H1 is the group of alive (potentially equivalent) mutants.

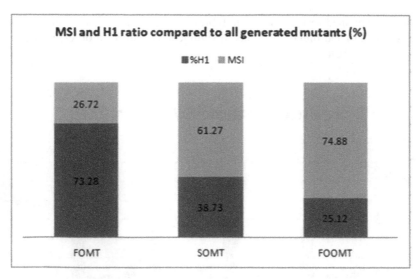

Fig. 2. The mean MSI and H1 proportion to all generated mutants

The second conclusion drawn from the experimental results is: Mutant combination does not decrease the quality of set of test cases due to increasing of MSI in order (from 26.72% of FOMT to 61.27% of HOMT and 74.88% of FOOMT).

Another noteworthy result, shown in Fig. 3, that is proportion of group H4–H9 mutants to total generated HOMs is high, about 52,42% (in SOMT) to 57,12% (in FOOMT).

As we mentioned in Sect. 2, H4–H9 are groups of reasonable mutants which are harder to kill and more realistic (reflecting real, complex faults) than their constituent. The term "Reasonable mutant" (harder to kill mutant), in our study, means that "*the set of test cases which kills mutant is smaller than the set of test cases which kills its constituent*".

Reducing number of needed test cases leads to reducing testing costs without loss of test effectiveness. Because, in mutation testing (including higher order mutation testing), the mutation testing cost covers not only the original program but also all of its mutants against all given set of test cases.

The number of test cases is smaller but still ensuring the quality is what we want in mutation testing. It can be said that overcoming the problem of mutation testing costs will lead to the widespread application of mutation testing techniques to reality.

According to experimental results, in both of SOMT and FOOMT, the mean ratio of H7 mutants to all generated mutants is about 6,2% and to all reasonable mutants (H4–H9) is about 11%.

This is a fairly high number because H7 mutant is a best one (**High Quality and Reasonable Mutant**) in our proposed approach [20–25] for constructing the quality mutants. In fact, they can be used to replace the set of their constituent mutants without lost of testing effectiveness. In other words, it helps to reduce the mutation testing cost

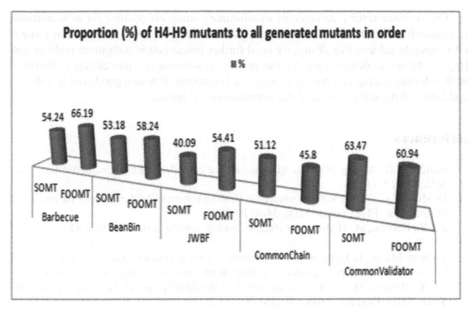

Fig. 3. Proportion (%) of H4–H9 mutants to all generated mutants in order

effectively. In our solution, although the number of higher-order mutants is always lower than the number of lower-order mutants, the rate of H7 is still high.

This, once again, demonstrates that this is a promising method that may need to be further researched and applied to not only reduce the number of produced mutants but also to construct a fairly large number of **High Quality and Reasonable Mutant**.

4 Conclusions

In this paper, through the approach of combining two lower order mutants to construct higher order mutants, we have investigated and presented a solution which can be used to overcome the main limitations of mutation testing. That are problems of large number of mutants and this also leads to have a very high execution cost; generated mutants are simple, easy to kill and do not denote realistic faults in practice.

Our empirical results indicate that the solution presented in this study is fairly good way to address the main limitations of mutation testing in terms of reducing the cost, generating valuable mutants and do not waste computational resources for creating mutants, which are easy to kill by most test cases.

Overcoming the mentioned main limitations of mutation testing will contribute to promote applying mutation testing into the field of software testing more widely and effectively. This applying will be very helpful for those who want to improve the quality of test cases (especially test data sets) for software testing because, it can be said up, mutation testing is considered as an automatic, powerful and effective technique to evaluate the quality of test suites.

Our research results, though only a preliminary study, are positive for us to continue to research and from that to promote the actual implementation of mutation testing. Of course, to achieve that desire, we need further investigation with more realistic and larger software to demonstrate that our proposing solution is really effective. Working with software testing companies or software companies is also a good way to validate and improve the effectiveness of this approach in the future.

References

1. Hamlet, R.G.: Testing programs with the aid of a compiler. IEEE Trans. Softw. Eng. (SE) **3**(4), 279–290 (1977)
2. DeMillo, R.A., Lipton, R.J., Sayward, F.G.: Hints on test data selection: help for the practicing programmer. IEEE Comput. **11**(4), 34–41 (1978)
3. Jia, Y., Harman, M.: Higher order mutation testing. Inform. Softw. Technol. **51**, 1379–1393 (2009)
4. Harman, M., Jia, Y., Langdon, W.B.: A manifesto for higher order mutation testing. In: Third International Conference on Software Testing, Verification, and Validation Workshops (2010)
5. Jia, Y., Harman, M.: An analysis and survey of the development of mutation testing. IEEE Trans. Softw. Eng. **37**(5), 649–678 (2011)
6. Nguyen, Q.V., Madeyski, L.: Problems of mutation testing and higher order mutation testing. In: van Do, T., Thi, H.A.L., Nguyen, N.T. (eds.) Advanced Computational Methods for Knowledge Engineering. AISC, vol. 282, pp. 157–172. Springer, Cham (2014). https://doi.org/10.1007/978-3-319-06569-4_12
7. Offutt, A.J.: Investigations of the software testing coupling effect. ACM Trans. Softw. Eng. Methodol. **1**, 5–20 (1992)
8. Polo, M., Piattini, M., Garcia-Rodriguez, I.: Decreasing the cost of mutation testing with second-order mutants. Softw. Test. Verification Reliab. **19**(2), 111–131 (2008)
9. Kintis, M., Papadakis, M., Malevris, N.: Evaluating mutation testing alternatives: a collateral experiment. In: Proceedings 17th Asia Pacifc Software Engineering. Conference (APSEC) (2010)
10. Papadakis, M., Malevris, N.: An empirical evaluation of the first and second order mutation testing strategies. In: Proceedings of the 2010 Third International Conference on Software Testing, Verification, and Validation Workshops, ser. ICSTW'10, Computer Society, pp. 90–99. IEEE (2010)
11. Madeyski, L., Orzeszyna, W., Torkar, R., Józala, M.: Overcoming the equivalent mutant problem: a systematic literature review and a comparative experiment of second order mutation. IEEE Trans. Softw. Eng. **40**(1), 23–42 (2014)
12. Omar, E., Ghosh, S.: An exploratory study of higher order mutation testing in aspect-oriented programming. In: IEEE 23rd International Symposium on Software Reliability Engineering (2012)
13. Jia, Y., Harman, M.: Constructing subtle faults using higher order mutation testing. In: Proceedings Eighth Int'l Working Conference Source Code Analysis and Manipulation (2008)
14. Omar, E., Ghosh, S., Whitley, D.: Constructing subtle higher order mutants for java and aspectJ programs. In: International Symposium on Software Reliability Engineering, pp. 340–349 (2013)
15. Omar, E., Ghosh, S., Whitley, D.: Comparing search techniques for fnding subtle higher order mutants. In: Proceedings of the 2014 Annual Conference on Genetic and Evolutionary Computation, pp. 1271–1278 (2014)

16. Belli, F., Güler, N., Hollmann, A., Suna, G., Yıldız, E.: Model-based higher-order mutation analysis. In: Kim, T., Kim, H.K., Khan, M.K., Kiumi, A., Fang, W., Ślęzak, D. (eds.) ASEA 2010. CCIS, vol. 117, pp. 164–173. Springer, Heidelberg (2010). https://doi.org/10.1007/978-3-642-17578-7_17

17. Akinde, A.O.: Using higher order mutation for reducing equivalent mutants in mutation testing. Asian J. Comput. Sci. Inform. Technol. 2(3), 13–18 (2012)

18. Langdon, W.B., Harman, M., Jia, Y.: Multi-objective higher order mutation testing with genetic programming. In: Proceedings Fourth Testing: Academic and Industrial Conference Practice and Research (2009)

19. Langdon, W.B., Harman, M., Jia, Y.: Efficient multi-objective higher order mutation testing with genetic programming. J. Syst. Softw. 83(12), 2416–2430 (2010)

20. Nguyen, Q.V., Madeyski, L.: Searching for strongly subsuming higher order mutants by applying multi-objective optimization algorithm. In: Le Thi, H.A., Nguyen, N.T., Do, T.V. (eds.) Advanced Computational Methods for Knowledge Engineering. AISC, vol. 358, pp. 391–402. Springer, Cham (2015). https://doi.org/10.1007/978-3-319-17996-4_35

21. Nguyen, Q.V., Madeyski, L.: Empirical evaluation of multi-objective optimization algorithms searching for higher order mutants. Cybern. Syst. Int. J. 47(1-2), 48–68 (2016)

22. Nguyen, Q.V., Madeyski, L.: Higher order mutation testing to drive development of new test cases: an empirical comparison of three strategies. In: Nguyen, N.T., Trawiński, B., Fujita, H., Hong, T.P. (eds.) ACIIDS 2016. LNCS (LNAI), vol. 9621, pp. 235–244. Springer, Heidelberg (2016). https://doi.org/10.1007/978-3-662-49381-6_23

23. Nguyen, Q.V., Madeyski, L.: On the relationship between the order of mutation testing and the properties of generated higher order mutants. In: Nguyen, N.T., Trawiński, B., Fujita, H., Hong, T.P. (eds.) ACIIDS 2016. LNCS (LNAI), vol. 9621, pp. 245–254. Springer, Heidelberg (2016). https://doi.org/10.1007/978-3-662-49381-6_24

24. Nguyen, Q.V., Madeyski, L.: Addressing mutation testing problems by applying multi-objective optimization algorithms and higher order mutation. J. Intell. Fuzzy Syst. 32, 1173–1182 (2017). https://doi.org/10.3233/jifs-169117

25. Nguyen, Q.V., Pham, D.T.H.: Is higher order mutant harder to kill than first order mutant. An experimental study. In: Nguyen, N.T., Hoang, D.H., Hong, T.P., Pham, H., Trawiński, B. (eds.) ACIIDS 2018. LNCS (LNAI), vol. 10751, pp. 664–673. Springer, Cham (2018). https://doi.org/10.1007/978-3-319-75417-8_62

26. Madeyski, L.: On the effects of pair programming on thoroughness and fault-finding effectiveness of unit tests. In: Münch, J., Abrahamsson, P. (eds.) PROFES 2007. LNCS, vol. 4589, pp. 207–221. Springer, Heidelberg (2007). https://doi.org/10.1007/978-3-540-73460-4_20

27. Madeyski, L.: The impact of pair programming on thoroughness and fault detection effectiveness of unit tests suites. Softw. Process Improv. Pract. 13(3), 281–295 (2008). https://doi.org/10.1002/spip.382

28. Madeyski, L.: The impact of test-first programming on branch coverage and mutation score indicator of unit tests: an experiment. Inform. Softw. Technol. 52(2), 169–184 (2010). https://doi.org/10.1016/j.infsof.2009.08.007

29. Madeyski, L., Radyk, N.: Judy - a mutation testing tool for java. IET Softw. 4(1), 32–42 (2010). https://doi.org/10.1049/iet-sen.2008.0038

30. Zhu, Q., Panichella, A., Zaidman, A., An investigation of compression techniques to speed up mutation testing. In: 2018 IEEE 11th International Conference on Software Testing, Verification and Validation (ICST), Vasteras, pp. 274–284 (2018)

31. Jimenez, M., et al.: Are mutants really natural. A study on how naturalness helps mutant selection. In: The International Symposium on Empirical Software Engineering and Measurement (ESEM) (2018)

32. Saber, T., Delavernhe, F., Papadakis, M., O'Neill, M., Ventresque, A.: A hybrid algorithm for multi-objective test case selection. In: 2018 IEEE Congress on Evolutionary Computation (CEC), Rio de Janeiro, pp. 1–8 (2018)
33. Abuljadayel, A., Wedyan, F.: An investigation of compression techniques to speed up mutation testing. In: International Journal of Intelligent Systems and Applications, January 2018
34. Lewowski, T., Madeyski, L.: Mutants as patches: towards a formal approach to mutation testing. Found. Comput. Decis. Sci. **44**(4), 379–405 (2019)
35. Zhang, J.M., Harman, M., Ma, L., Liu, Y.: Machine learning testing: survey, landscapes and horizons. In: IEEE Transactions on Software Engineering (2019). https://doi.org/10.1109/tse.2019.2962027
36. Bokaei, N.N., Keyvanpour, M.R.: A comparative study of whole issues and challenges in mutation testing. In: 2019 5th Conference on Knowledge Based Engineering and Innovation (KBEI), Tehran, Iran, pp. 745–754 (2019). https://doi.org/10.1109/kbei.2019.8735019
37. Naeem, M.R., Lin, T., Naeem, H., Ullah, F., Saeed, S.: Scalable mutation testing using predictive analysis of deep learning model. IEEE Access **7**, 158264–158283 (2019). https://doi.org/10.1109/access.2019.2950171

Spotted Hyena Optimizer: An Approach to Travelling Salesman Problems

Van Du Nguyen[1], Tram Nguyen[1,2], Tan Luc Nguyen[1], Van Cuong Tran[3], and Hai Bang Truong[4(✉)]

[1] Faculty of Information Technology, Nong Lam University, Ho Chi Minh City, Vietnam
{nvdu,ntptram}@hcmuaf.edu.vn, tanlucnguyenit@gmail.com
[2] Department of Computer Science, Faculty of Electrical Engineering and Computer Science, VŠB - Technical University of Ostrava, Ostrava, Czech Republic
[3] Faculty of Engineering and Information Technology, Quang Binh University, Dong Hoi City, Vietnam
vancuongqbuni@gmail.com
[4] Faculty of Information Technology, Nguyen Tat Thanh University, Ho Chi Minh City, Vietnam
thbang@ntt.edu.vn

Abstract. The traveling salesman problem (TSP) is a well-known NP problem. Its main objective is to find a shortest close trip that visits all given cities, once for each. In this paper, we present an approach to Travelling Salesman Problems (TSPs) using a novel swarm-based algorithm named Spotted Hyena Optimizer (SHO). The algorithm is inspired by the social relationship between spotted hyenas and their collaborative behavior. Experimental results with four benchmark datasets in TSPLIB (Burma14, Bays29, Att48, and Berlin52) indicated that SHO algorithm could provide optimal solutions to TSPs. Even in some cases, it outperforms other metaheuristic algorithms such as GA, ACO, and PSO.

Keywords: Spotted hyena optimizer · Swarm intelligence · Meta-heuristic · TSP

1 Introduction

To date, there exists ample evidence that metaheuristic algorithms are effective approaches to finding solutions to optimization problems in the real world. Accordingly, swarm-based algorithms - a sort of metaheuristic algorithms besides evolutionary, physics-based, bio-inspired, and nature-inspired algorithms have attracted much research attention. In 1989, Beni and Wang introduced a novel swarm-based algorithm, called *Swarm Intelligence*, which was based on the collective behavior of decentralized, self-organized systems [1]. According to [2], Swarm Intelligence was defined as *"The emergent collective intelligence of groups of simple agents"*. Even in [3], it was considered as a specific kind of collective intelligence which is considered as the intelligence emerging from the collaboration and competition of many individuals or groups of individuals which collectively do things that seem intelligent [4–6]. Individuals can be humans, agent systems, animals, or insects. In the case of Swarm Intelligence, it can be

© Springer Nature Switzerland AG 2020
N. T. Nguyen et al. (Eds.): ICCCI 2020, LNAI 12496, pp. 217–228, 2020.
https://doi.org/10.1007/978-3-030-63007-2_17

seen that collective intelligence is inspired by the interaction of swarm with each other and their environment. In [7], many characteristics of collective have been taken into account in analyzing their impact on collective performance. Later in [8], the authors have presented research challenges on the combination of collective intelligence and other research fields such as machine learning and social networks.

The most popular swarm-based algorithm is Particle Swarm Optimization (PSO), inspired by the social behavior of bird flocking or fish school [9]. The algorithm has been widely applied to a variety of optimization problems such as extracting multiple-choice tests [10, 11], timetable scheduling [12–14]. Another swarm-based algorithm is Ant Colony Optimization (ACO) which inspired by the foraging behavior of some ant species [15]. Accordingly, some ants will mark some favorable path by the behavior of depositing pheromone on the ground and other ants of the colony will follow that favorable path. To date, it can be seen that ACO has been widely applied to find solutions to many optimization problems including vehicle routing and scheduling [16].

The traveling salesman problem is a well-known optimization problem. Its main objective is to find a shortest close trip that visits all given cities, once for each. In the current literature, many metaheuristic algorithms such as GA, ACO, PSO, Artificial Bee Colony (ABC), Firefly Algorithm (FA) and Simulated Annealing (SA) have been investigated for such a task [17, 18]. In [19], another new metaheuristic algorithm named ABO (the African Buffalo Optimization), which is inspired by the behavior of the African buffalos in the African forests and savannahs, has been proposed for solving TSPs. An improved version of GA-based approach has been proposed in [20]. The experimental results showed the effectiveness of the proposed method in finding solutions to TSPs, even with larger datasets.

It can be seen that one optimizer cannot be effective in solving all optimization problems with different nature [21]. Therefore, in the current literature, applications of metaheuristic algorithms to finding solutions to optimization problems have attracted much research attention and it also motivated to propose new metaheuristic algorithms. Dhiman et al. [22, 23] introduced a novel swarm-based algorithm named SHO (Spotted Hyena Optimizer). This algorithm is mainly based on the social relationship between spotted hyenas and their collaborative behavior. Later, many SHO-based approaches have been proposed for finding solutions to multi-objective optimization, economic dispatch problems, discrete optimization problems [24–27]. Besides, most of the experimental results were conducted using 29 well-known benchmark test functions. In this paper, we introduce an application of SHO algorithm to TSPs. For such a task, we proposed an SHO-based approach aiming at determining a close trip of a given number of cities such that the total distance of the obtained trip is minimal as much as possible. Besides, experiments are conducted using some selected benchmark datasets from TSPLib [28] to evaluate the efficiency of the proposed method. Furthermore, we also present a comparison of the proposed method to other approaches such as GA, PSO, ACO-based algorithms to TSPs.

The rest of the paper is organized as follows. Some related works have been presented in Sect. 2. Next, we introduce an approach to the application of SHO algorithm to the TSPs. Section 4 describes the experimental results as well as their analysis. The paper is ended with some conclusions and future research.

2 Related Work

To date, there exists ample evidence that metaheuristic algorithms are effective approaches to finding solutions to TSPs such as GA-based, PSO-based, ACO-based methods. Genetic Algorithm (GA) is a sort of evolutionary algorithms, which is inspired by the process of natural selection. The solutions are represented as chromosomes, which are often evaluated by fitness functions. Besides, new solutions are generated based on the natural selection of living organisms with three genetic operators: selection, crossover, and mutation [29].

PSO was first introduced by Kennedy and Eberhart in 1995 [9]. It simulates the behavior of birds flocking, fish schooling, and social interaction within a population. Each solution, which is often referred to as a particle, is a "*bird*" in the search space. All particles come with their fitness values, which are evaluated by fitness functions to be optimized. The particles also exhibit random velocities that indicate in which direction they are moving. This velocity is adjusted according to the particle's own experience and that of its neighbors. Each particle is updated by the two best values in each iteration and keeps track of its coordinates in the search space which is associated with the best solution (fitness) that has been achieved (the fitness value is thus also stored by each particle). This value is called *pbest*. Another "best" value that is tracked by the PSO is the best value obtained so far by any particle in the swarm, and since this best value is global, it is called *Gbest*. Similarly, another swarm-based algorithm that has attracted much research attention and has been applied to find many solutions to optimization problems is An Colony Optimization (ACO). It is inspired by the foraging behavior of some ant species. Accordingly, some ants will mark some favorable path by the behavior of depositing pheromone on the ground and other ants of the colony will follow that favorable path [30]. In [17], the authors have presented an empirical comparison between ACO, PSO, Artificial Bee Colony (ABC), Firefly Algorithm (FA), and GA to solve TSP using some selected benchmark datasets including Burma14, Bayg29, Att48, Berlin52 [28]. The experimental results reveal that GA and ACO outperform to ABC, PSO, and FA in finding solutions to benchmark TSPs.

Referring to [19], a new metaheuristic algorithm named ABO (the African Buffalo Optimization) inspired by the behavior of the African buffalos in the African forests and savannahs, has been proposed for solving TSP. By means of experimental results, the ABO algorithm can provide the optimal or near-optimal solutions and outperform other popular algorithms including Ant Colony Optimization (ACO), Particle Swarm Optimization (PSO), Artificial Bee Colony Optimization (ABO)... In [18], the authors have presented a performance comparison of Genetic Algorithm (GA), Particle Swarm Optimization (PSO), and Simulated Annealing (SA) to TSP. The experimental results have indicated that the PSO is better than both GA and SA in finding the shortest close trips to TSP. In addition, in terms of execution time, the SA algorithm is better than GA and PSO algorithms. In [20], the authors presented an improved version of GA for solving TSP. The experimental results indicated that the improved GA can provide an optimal solution in 7 iterations while the standard genetic algorithm can get the optimal solution in 30 iterations. In the case of using larger datasets, only the improved GA can achieve optimal solutions.

As aformentioned Dhiman et al. [22, 23] have introduced a novel swarm-based algorithm named SHO, which is based on the behavior of spotted hyenas. The main concept behind this algorithm is the social relationship between spotted hyenas and their collaborative behavior. The three basic steps of SHO are searching for prey, encircling, and attacking prey and they are mathematically modeled and implemented. The experimental results with 29 well-known benchmark test functions indicated that the proposed algorithm outperforms other algorithms such as PSO, GA, GWO, MFO, MVO, SCA, GSA, and HS. Through the statistical analysis, the novel algorithm can be applied to find solutions to many optimization problems in the real world.

Later, a multi-objective version of SHO (called MOSHO) was proposed by Dhiman et al. [24]. Accordingly, optimal solutions are selected based on the use of a roulette wheel mechanism, which is then used to simulate the social and hunting behaviors of spotted hyenas. Experimental results on 24 benchmark test functions have revealed that the proposed method outperforms other approaches in finding optimal solutions with high convergence.

The authors in [25] have introduced an application of SHO algorithm to economic dispatch problems (for both convex and non-convex). The experimental results on 6, 10, 20, and 40 generators systems indicated the effectiveness and efficiency of the proposed method. Later, in [26], the authors have proposed an approach to improving the hunting prey of spotted hyenas by using PSO. The experimental results have revealed the efficiency of the proposed method in comparison to the traditional SHO, PSO, and GA approaches. Recently, Kumar et al. have proposed a binary version of SHO for dealing with discrete optimization problems [27]. In particular, the authors have used hyperbolic tangent function to discrete-continuous positions. The prey searching, encircling, and attacking are three main steps of binary spotted hyena optimizer. The proposed algorithm has been compared with six well-known meta-heuristic techniques over 29 benchmark test functions. The effects of convergence, scalability, and control parameters have been investigated. The statistical significance of the proposed approach has also been examined through ANOVA test. The proposed approach is also applied to the feature selection domain. The performance of the proposed approach has been compared with four well-known meta-heuristic techniques over 17 UCI repository datasets. The experimental results reveal that the proposed approach is able to search the optimal feature set than the others.

From the above analysis, it can be seen that research on SHO algorithms mainly focuses on experimenting with well-known benchmark test functions. Therefore, in this paper, we focus on the application of SHO to solve TSPs. Besides, we also present a comparison to other algorithms (i.e., GA, ACO, PSO) in finding solutions to TSPs.

3 The Proposed Method

3.1 Problem Statement

The problem statement of TSPs can be stated as follows: For a given number of cities: $X = \{x_1, x_2, \ldots, x_n\}$ and a function d measuring the distance between two cities. The main aim of TSPs is to find a close tour that visits all given cities, once for each so that the following objective function is minimal:

$$\min\left\{\sum_{i=1}^{n-1} d(x_i, x_{i+1}) + d(x_n, x_1)\right\} \tag{1}$$

where $d(x_i, x_{i+1})$ represents the distance between city x_i and city x_{i+1}.

According to Eq. (1), the fitness function of a given TSP is described as follows:

$$\mu = \sum_{i=1}^{n-1} d(x_i, x_{i+1}) + d(x_n, x_1) \tag{2}$$

In this case, it can be seen that the smaller the value of μ, the better the fitness value. In other words, the goal of any method for solving a given TSP is to minimize the value of μ as much as possible. Apart from the fitness function, some proposed methods also to reduce the execution time as well as the convergence rate [18, 20].

3.2 SHO for TSPs

As aforementioned, recent novel swarm-based algorithm, named SHO, was inspired by the social relationship between spotted hyenas and their collaborative behavior in hunting preys [22, 23]. Its three main steps include encircling prey, hunting prey, and attacking prey:

- Encircling prey: since the search space is not known in advance, the target prey (or objective) is assumed as the current best candidate solution which is close to the optimal solution. After the target prey is defined, other hyenas will try to update their positions toward the position of the prey.

$$\vec{D}_h = \left|\vec{B}.\vec{P}_p(i) - \vec{P}(i)\right| \tag{3}$$

$$\vec{P}(i+1) = \vec{P}_p(i) - \vec{E}.\vec{D}_h \tag{4}$$

where $\vec{D}_h$ presents the distance between the prey and hyenas, i represent the current iteration, $\vec{B}$ and $\vec{E}$ are coefficient vectors. $\vec{P}_p$ represents the position of the prey, $\vec{P}$ represents the position of hyenas. $\vec{B}$ and $\vec{E}$ are computed as follows:

$$\vec{B} = 2.\vec{rd}_1 \tag{5}$$

$$\vec{E} = 2\vec{h}.\vec{rd}_2 - \vec{h} \tag{6}$$

$$\vec{h} = 5 - (i * (5/Max_{Iteration})) \tag{7}$$

where $\vec{rd_1}$ and $\vec{rd_2}$ are random values belonging to [0, 1]. The value of $\vec{h}$ belongs to [0, 5] which is linearly decreased from 5 to 0 according to $Max_{Iteration}$.

- Hunting prey: in order to mathematically model the hunting behavior of spotted hyenas the best search agent is supposed having knowledge about the location of prey and other search agents try to update their positions based on the best solutions obtained so far. Concretely, such a mechanism is described as follows:

$$\vec{D_h} = \left| \vec{B}.\vec{P_h} - \vec{P_k} \right| \tag{8}$$

$$\vec{P_k} = \vec{P_h} - \vec{E}.\vec{D_h} \tag{9}$$

$$\vec{C_h} = \vec{P}_k + \vec{P}_{k+1} + \ldots + \vec{P}_{k+N} \tag{10}$$

Where $\vec{P}_h$ represents the position of the first best spotted hyenas, $\vec{P}_k$ represents the positions of other hyenas, N represents the number of spotted hyenas in the group.

$$N = count_{nos}\left(\vec{P}_h, \vec{P}_{h+1}, \vec{P}_{h+2}, \ldots, \left(\vec{P}_h + \vec{M} \right) \right) \tag{11}$$

Where $\vec{M}$ is a random vector belonging to [0.5, 1], nos represents the number of solutions, $\vec{C}_h$ represents the group of optimal solutions.

- Attacking prey: In order to mathematically model for attacking the prey, the value of $\vec{h}$ will be decreased from 5 to 0 over the course of iterations. The variation in values of $\vec{E}$ is also decreased to change the value of $\vec{h}$.

$$\vec{P}(i+1) = \frac{\vec{C}_h}{N} \tag{12}$$

where $\vec{P}(i+1)$ represents the best solution and the positions of other spotted hyenas will be updated based on the position of the best search agent (the closest spotted hyenas to the target prey).

Algorithm 1. SHO for TSPs.

Input: initialized random population ($P = \{P_1, P_2, ..., P_n\}$ - n tours

Output: optimal tour P_h

BEGIN
1: Initialize the parameters h, B, E, and N
2: Evaluate the fitness of each individual
3: P_h= the best individual
4: C_h= the group of optimal tours
5: while (i < MAX_ITERATIONS) do
6:     for each $p_i \in P$ do
7:             Update the position of p_i by Eq. (12)
8:     end for
9:     Update h, B, E, and N
10:    Update the position of individuals going beyond the given search space
11:    Evaluate the fitness of each individual
12:    Update P_h if there is a better solution than the previous one
13:    Update the group C_h regarding P_h
14:    i++
15: end while
16: return P_h
END

The most important issue in Algorithm 1 is updating the positions of individuals concerning the best solution. Example, for a given number of cities: $X = \{x_1, x_2, x_3, x_4, x_5\}$, the best solution so far is (x_1 - x_3 - x_5 - x_2 - x_4), then others hyenas will update their positions concerning the best solution by swap sequence including swap operators as follows:

$$SS = \{SO_1, \ SO_2, \ldots, \ SO_n\} \tag{13}$$

Each swap operator (SO_i) represents a pair of cities x_i and x_j that can be swapped with each other to generate a new solution. In the next section, we conduct experiments with some selected benchmark datasets (Burma14, Bays29, Att48, and Berlin52) in TSPLIB [28].

4 Experimental Results and Their Evaluation

4.1 Settings

Algorithms are implemented in Java and tested on a computer with the following configurations: Intel Core (TM) i7-5500U CPU 2.40 GHz/8 GB RAM Laptop. The parameters of selected metaheuristic algorithms are described in the following Table 1.

Accordingly, the proposed algorithm is stopped based on the predefined number of iterations. The benchmark datasets are chosen from TSPLib [28], and their properties are presented in Table 2.

Table 1. Experimental parameters

Parameter	GA	PSO	ACO	SHO
Population	100	100	100	100
Iterations	2000	2000	2000	2000
Crossover Rate	0.9	–	–	–
Mutation Rate	0.04	–	–	–
Ω	–	0.5	–	–
α	–	–	1	–
β	–	–	1	–
Total number of runs	50	50	50	50

– Not Applicable

Table 2. Experimental parameters

Dataset	Number of cities
Burma14	14
Bays29	29
Att48	48
Berlin52	52

4.2 Experimental Results

The experimental results are presented in Table 3. The *"relative error"* values are computed by using the following equation:

$$Rel.err(x) = \frac{|x - x_{opt.}|}{x_{opt.}} \times 100 \tag{14}$$

where x represents the distance of the final obtained tour and x_{opt} represents the distance of the optimal tour of each dataset.

As aforementioned, we performed 50 runs for each setting. The best values are selected from these 50 values and the mean values are the average of the corresponding 50 values.

According to Table 3, in the case of Burma14, all methods can provide optimal solutions (optimal tours). Other datasets, SHO method can outperform GA, PSO, and ACO methods in finding minimal tours (near-optimal tours). From these results, it can be stated that SHO can find competitive results with other metaheuristic algorithms. A visualization of these results is described in the following Fig. 1.

Table 3. Experimental results

Dataset	Opt.	Approach	Best	Rel. err	Mean	Rel. err
Burma14	30.88	PSO	30.88	0.00%	33.52	8.53%
		GA	30.88	0.00%	31.22	1.10%
		ACO	30.88	0.00%	30.88	0.00%
		SHO	30.88	0.00%	31.26	1.23%
Bays29	9,074	PSO	10,666.48	17.55%	13,487.05	48.63%
		GA	9,077.92	0.04%	9,849.58	8.55%
		ACO	9,108.77	0.38%	9,259.10	2.04%
		SHO	9,074.15	0.0016%	9074.15	0.0016%
Att48	33,522	PSO	63,095.26	88.22%	82,167.54	145.12%
		GA	37,193.37	10.95%	45,536.85	35.84%
		ACO	34,301.59	2.33%	35,313.91	5.35%
		SHO	33,523.71	0.01%	33,687.88	0.49%
Berlin52	7,542	PSO	12,661.03	67.87%	17,055.97	126.15%
		GA	8,569.75	13.63%	10,445.39	38.50%
		ACO	7,544.37	0.03%	7,782.07	3.18%
		SHO	7,544.37	0.03%	7,678.71	1.81%

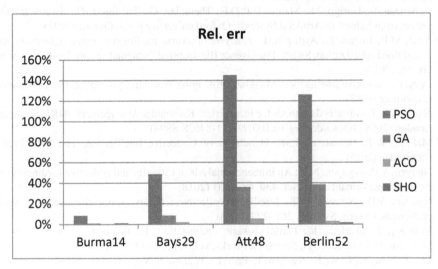

Fig. 1. Relative errors of mean values

5   Conclusions and Future Works

In recent years, applications of swarm-based algorithms to solve some common optimization problems have attracted much research attention. Many research results have revealed the efficiency of such approaches. In [22, 23], a novel swarm-based algorithm has been introduced based on the social relationship between spotted hyenas and their collaborative behavior (named SHO). In this paper, we have presented an application of SHO algorithm to solve TSPs using some selected benchmark datasets in TSPLIB (Burma14, Bays29, Att48, and Berlin52). The experimental results revealed that the proposed method could provide optimal or near-optimal solutions to TSPs. Even in some cases, it outperforms other metaheuristic algorithms such as GA, ACO, and PSO.

For future work, we will intensively analyze the efficiency of SHO algorithm in finding solutions to TSPs with larger datasets by taking into account other criteria such as the execution time as well as convergence rate. We also consider a hybrid approach to improve the hunting capacity of spotted hyenas using PSO.

Acknowledgment. This research is supported by project CS-CB19-CNTT-01.

References

1. Beni, G., Wang, J.: Swarm intelligence in cellular robotic systems. In: Dario, P., Sandini, G., Aebischer, P. (eds.) Robots and Biological Systems: Towards a New Bionics, pp. 703–712. Springer Berlin Heidelberg, Berlin (1993)
2. Bonabeau, E., Dorigo, M., Marco, D.R.D.F., Theraulaz, G., Théraulaz, G.: Swarm Intelligence: from Natural to Artificial Systems. Oxford university press, Oxford (1999)
3. Saka, M.P., Doğan, E., Aydogdu, I.: Analysis of swarm intelligence–based algorithms for constrained optimization. Swarm Intelligence Bio-Inspired Computation, pp. 25–48. Elsevier, Oxford (2013)
4. Levy, P.: Collective Intelligence: Mankind's Emerging World in Cyberspace. Perseus Books, Cambridge (1997)
5. Nguyen, N.T.: Advanced Methods for Inconsistent Knowledge Management. AIKP. Springer, London (2008). https://doi.org/10.1007/978-1-84628-889-0
6. Malone, W.T., Bernstein, S.M.: Handbook of Collective Intelligence. The MIT Press, Cambridge (2015)
7. Nguyen, V.D., Nguyen, N.T.: An influence analysis of diversity and collective cardinality on collective performance. Inf. Sci. **430**, 487–503 (2018)
8. Nguyen, V.D., Nguyen, N.T.: Intelligent collectives: theory, applications, and research challenges. Cybern. Syst. **49**, 261–279 (2018)
9. Kennedy, J., Eberhart, R.: Particle swarm optimization. In: Proceedings of ICNN'95 - International Conference on Neural Networks, vol. 4, pp. 1942–1948 (1995)
10. Bui, T., Nguyen, T., Vo, B., Nguyen, T., Pedrycz, W., Snásel, V.: Application of particle swarm optimization to create multiple-choice tests. J. Inf. Sci. Eng. **34**, 1405–1423 (2018)
11. Nguyen, T., Bui, T., Vo, B.: Multi-swarm single-objective particle swarm optimization to extract multiple-choice tests. Vietnam J. Comput. Sci. **06**, 147–161 (2019). https://doi.org/10.1142/S219688881950009X

12. Chu, S.C., Chen, Y.T., Ho, J.H.: Timetable scheduling using particle swarm optimization. In: Proceedings of First International Conference on Innovative Computing, Information and Control, Vol. 3, pp. 324–327. IEEE Computer Society (2006). https://doi.org/10.1109/icicic.2006.541

13. Montero, E., Riff, M.C., Leopoldo, A.: A pso algorithm to solve a real course + exam timetabling problem. In: International Conference on Swarm Intelligence, pp. 24–1-24-8 (2011)

14. Abayomi-Alli, O., Abayomi-Alli, A., Misra, S., Damasevicius, R., Maskeliunas, R.: Automatic examination timetable scheduling using particle swarm optimization and local search algorithm. In: Shukla, R.K., Agrawal, J., Sharma, S., Singh Tomer, G. (eds.) Data, Engineering and Applications, pp. 119–130. Springer, Singapore (2019). https://doi.org/10.1007/978-981-13-6347-4_11

15. Dorigo, M., Mauro, B., Thomas, S.: Ant colony optimization – artificial ants as a computational intelligence technique. IEEE Comput. Intell. Mag. 1, 28–39 (2006)

16. Mirjalili, S., Song Dong, J., Lewis, A.: Ant colony optimizer: theory, literature review, and application in AUV path planning. In: Mirjalili, S., Song Dong, J., Lewis, A. (eds.) Nature-Inspired Optimizers. SCI, vol. 811, pp. 7–21. Springer, Cham (2020). https://doi.org/10.1007/978-3-030-12127-3_2

17. Chaudhari, K., Thakkar, A.: Travelling salesman problem: an empirical comparison between ACO, PSO, ABC, FA and GA. In: Shetty, N.R., Patnaik, L.M., Nagaraj, H.C., Hamsavath, P.N., Nalini, N. (eds.) Emerging Research in Computing, Information, Communication and Applications. AISC, vol. 906, pp. 397–405. Springer, Singapore (2019). https://doi.org/10.1007/978-981-13-6001-5_32

18. Panda, M.: Performance comparison of genetic algorithm, particle swarm optimization and simulated annealing applied to TSP. Int. J. Appl. Eng. Res. 13, 6808–6816 (2018)

19. Odili, J.B., Kahar, M.N.M.: Solving the traveling salesman's problem using the african buffalo optimization. Comp. Int. Neurosc. vol. 2016 (2016). 1510256:1–1510256:12

20. Fu, C., Zhang, L., Wang, X., Qiao, L.: Solving TSP problem with improved genetic algorithm. AIP Conf. Proc. 1967, 40057 (2018)

21. Wolpert, D.H., Macready, W.G.: No free lunch theorems for optimization. IEEE Trans. Evol. Comput. 1, 67–82 (1997)

22. Dhiman, G., Kumar, V.: Spotted hyena optimizer: a novel bio-inspired based metaheuristic technique for engineering applications. Adv. Eng. Softw. 114, 48–70 (2017)

23. Dhiman, G., Kumar, V.: Spotted hyena optimizer for solving complex and non-linear constrained engineering problems. In: Yadav, N., Yadav, A., Bansal, J.C., Deep, K., Kim, J.H. (eds.) Harmony Search and Nature Inspired Optimization Algorithms. AISC, vol. 741, pp. 857–867. Springer, Singapore (2019). https://doi.org/10.1007/978-981-13-0761-4_81

24. Dhiman, G., Kumar, V.: Multi-objective spotted hyena optimizer: a multi-objective optimization algorithm for engineering problems. Knowl. Based Syst. 150, 175–197 (2018)

25. Dhiman, G., Guo, S., Kaur, S.: ED-SHO: a framework for solving nonlinear economic load power dispatch problem using spotted hyena optimizer. Mod. Phys. Lett. A 33, 1850239 (2018)

26. Dhiman, G., Kaur, A.: A hybrid algorithm based on particle swarm and spotted hyena optimizer for global optimization. In: Bansal, J.C., Das, K.N., Nagar, A., Deep, K., Ojha, A.K. (eds.) Soft Computing for Problem Solving. AISC, vol. 816, pp. 599–615. Springer, Singapore (2019). https://doi.org/10.1007/978-981-13-1592-3_47

27. Kumar, V., Kaur, A.: Binary spotted hyena optimizer and its application to feature selection. J. Ambient Intell. Humanized Comput. 11(7), 2625–2645 (2019). https://doi.org/10.1007/s12652-019-01324-z

28. Reinelt, G.: TSPLIB—a traveling salesman problem library. ORSA J. Comput. **3**, 376–384 (1991)
29. Mitchell, M.: An Introduction to Genetic Algorithms. MIT Press, Cambridge (1998)
30. Dorigo, M., Stützle, T.: Ant Colony Optimization. MIT Press, Cambridge (2004)

Anchor Link Prediction in Online Social Network Using Graph Embedding and Binary Classification

Vang V. Le[1]($\boxtimes$), Tin T. Tran[1], Phuong N. H. Pham[2]($\boxtimes$), and Vaclav Snasel[3]

[1] Artificial Intelligence Laboratory, Faculty of Information Technology,
Ton Duc Thang University, Ho Chi Minh City, Vietnam
{levanvang,trantrungtin}@tdtu.edu.vn
[2] Faculty of Information Technology,
Ho Chi Minh City University of Food Industry, Ho Chi Minh City, Vietnam
phuongpnh@hufi.edu.vn
[3] Department of Computer Science,
VSB-Technical University of Ostrava, Ostrava, Czech Republic
vaclav.snasel@vsb.cz

Abstract. With the widespread popularity as well as the variety of different online social networks. Today, each user can join many social networks at the same time for many different purposes. They can join Facebook to share and update status, join Instagram to share photos, join LinkedIn to share in work, etc. As the scale and number of online social networks grows, social network analysis has become a widespread problem in many scientific disciplines. One of the emerging topics in social network analysis is anchor link prediction problem which identifies the same user across different networks. In this paper, we propose an algorithm to predict the missing anchor links between users across source and target network. Our algorithm represents the vertices and the edges in source and target network as the represenation vectors, we then apply the binary classification algorithms to predict the matching score of all pairs of vertices between the source and target network. The experimental results show that our algorithm performs better traditional anchor link prediction algorithms.

Keywords: Anchor link prediction · Graph embedding · Word2vec · Online social network analysis

1 Introduction

Today, the online social networks such as Facebook, Twitter are increasingly popular and have become an indispensable spiritual food in everyone's life. Social network analysis is also a highly important research area. In recent years, the number of studies in the field of complex networks have attracted great amounts of awareness from the scientific community.

© Springer Nature Switzerland AG 2020
N. T. Nguyen et al. (Eds.): ICCCI 2020, LNAI 12496, pp. 229–240, 2020.
https://doi.org/10.1007/978-3-030-63007-2_18

One of the most important research in this area is anchor link prediction which involves inferring the same users between the source and target network based on currently network structure and the existing anchor links. Anchor link prediction plays an important role in understanding the functions of complex networks. How to predict efficiently the existence of anchor relationships across social networks is a major challenge up to the present.

Regard to the anchor link prediction problem there are many different methods, and we can divide into two difference approaches. The first approach is called network alignment which often determines the similarity of pairs of vertices between the source and target network based on the structure of vertices in each network. Those pairs of vertices with high similarity are more likely to form anchor links and vice versa. The second approach using the supervised methods to train the model based on the observed anchor links. Most of these approaches have problems with small and inbalance datasets because the overlap rate between different social networks is not high, leading to low accuracy prediction.

In this paper, we further propose a difference anchor link prediction method which combines the graph embedding algorithm and binary classification. The experiments on the dataset demonstrate that our method can significantly improve the F1 score of the traditional anchor link prediction techniques. Our algorithm is based on the idea:

(1) Embedding every vertice in source and target network into independent representation vectors but still preserve network information including the connections between the vertices in each network.
(2) Apply deep learning technique to classify the pair of vertices between source and target network. The output of the classification indicates whether this pair of vertices formed a link or not and then we can determine whether this pair of vertices is the same user.

The major contribution of our work is the enhancement of the accuracy, the F1 score of anchor link prediction acquired from our method is higher than the result acquired from traditional anchor link prediction methods. The rest parts of this paper are arranged as follows. We review the related work in Sect. 2. In Sects. 3, we propose our anchor link prediction method. Experiments are given in Sect. 4. Finally, we conclude the paper in Sect. 5.

2 Related Works

Anchor link prediction is widely used in practice and has many applications in many different fields. For example, it can be integrated into searching systems which allow users to search information of a person on various social networks based on their name. This is convenient in finding people on networks with little information. In addition, anchor link prediction is also used in studies of link prediction and community detection in online social networks, etc. This section presents briefly some related works that illustrate the anchor link prediction along with the graph embedding process that embedding the vertices in network into representation vectors.

2.1 Anchor Link Prediction Algorithm

There are many difference techniques in anchor link prediction analysis. We can divide them into three difference categories as below:

User profile-based approach, this method often uses user profile and additional information in the network to predict anchor links. Information that can be used to predict include username, email address, or avatar, etc. Daniele Perito et al. [1] proposed a method to predict the possibility of linking user profiles across multiple online social networks only by looking at their usernames. Beside usernames matching approach, Raad et al. [2] and Cortis et al. [3] proposed the methods to predict anchor links using additional textual information for improving the accuracy of the prediction. Liu et al. [4] proposed a method which uses user's face images to predict anchor links.

User behavior-based approach, this approach often uses the behavioral information and habits of users on social networks to predict anchor links. The behaviors that can be used to predict include: status postings, page likes, friends list, social network usage time, etc. This method predicts anchor links based on the assumption that the behavior of the same user on many different social networks is consistent with each other. Zafarani et al. [5] introduced a methodology (MOBIUS) for finding a mapping among identities of individuals across social media sites. This methodology is based on behavioral patterns that users exhibit in social media. Zheng et al. [6] developed a framework for authorship identification of online messages to address the identity-tracing problem. Kong et al. [7], Lu et al. [13] proposed the methods to infer anchor links across multiple heterogeneous social networks using check-in/check-out information. Liu et al. [4] proposed a method HYDRA, a solution framework automatically linking user accounts belonging to the same natural person across different social media platforms using user's posts.

Network structure-based approach, this method predicts anchor links based on the current topology of each network as well as information about the anchor links observed between networks, thereby making predictions about anchor links which are currently missing. This approach can be divided into 2 different approaches:

Network alignment approach, It works in an unsupervised manner and does not leverage the existing correspondence. Specifically, the type of methods aligns nodes by finding structural similarity between nodes across networks.

Supervised methods approach, which learns a predictor relying on the observed anchor links

2.2 Graph Embedding Algorithm

The graph embedded algorithms transform a graph into a vector space but preserve the original structure and properties of the graph. This transformation allows us to have a different perspective on the graph so we can apply the models on vector space to solve the graph problem such as node classification, recommendation, link prediction and more. This approach is also an effective way to solve graph analysis problems by embedding the graph information into a low dimensional space while preserving the structure and properties of the graph. There are many different graph embedded methods and we can categorize them into three groups: Matrix Factorization-based, random walk-based, and neural network-based:

Matrix Factorization based approach, MF has been widely applied in data analysis and graph analysis is not an exception. Basically, this approach converts an original data matrix into lower dimensional matrix but retains the hidden structure and topological attributes inside the original data matrix. In this direction, there are several pioneeer research in the early 2000s such as Tenenbaum et al. [21] proposed an algorithm Isomap to represent data points in the D-dimensional space into data points in the d-dimensional space (d < D) while preserving the shortest path distance between the data points on the original space; Roweis et al. [22] introduced an algorithm Locally Linear Embedding, an unsupervised learning algorithm that computes low-dimensional embedding from high-dimensional inputs but preserving the neighborhood; Ahmed et al. [8] propose a novel factorization strategy that depends on partitioning a graph in order to minimize the number of neighboring vertices instead of edges across partitions;

Traditional MF often focus on factorizing the first-order data matrix, such as graph factorization (GF), and singular value decomposition (SVD). More recently, Cao et al. [9] proposed a strategy name GraRep which focus on designing various high-order data matrices in order to preserve the graph structure, this model learns low dimensional vectors which integrate global structural information of the graph into the learning process; Ou et al. [10] proposed a method name HOPE which is adaptable to preserve high-order proximities of large scale graph and capable of fitting the asymmetric transitivity.

Random Walk based approach, this approach has been motivated by the word2vec model proposed by Mikolov, et al. [28], a famous word embedding method from Natural Language Processing (NLP), random walk-based techniques attempts to learn node representations by generating a sequence of vertices through random walks in graphs. Then apply the word2vec model on the generated sequences of nodes to learn embeddings while preserving the structural and topological knowledge. One of the early works in this research direction is DeepWalk proposed by Perozzi et al. [16] and node2vec proposed by Grover et al. [20]. There are several additional variants which extend random walks to jointly learn network structure and node attributes such as GenVector proposed by Yang et al. [17]; Discriminative Deep Random Walk (DDRW) proposed by Li et al. [18]; and TriDNR proposed by Pan et al. [19]. Moreover, struc2vec is proposed by Ribeiro et al. [15] to improve the modeling of structural identity.

Deep Learning based approach, Deep learning has been shown to be successful in many of domains such as natural language processing, computer vision, and recent years have been applied successfully into the research area of graph analysis. As general, we can divide the deep learning-based approach into four research directions: recurrent graph neural network (RecGNNs), convolutional graph neural network (ConvGNNs), graph autoencoders (GAEs), and spatial–temporal graph neural network.

Sperduti et al. [23], Micheli et al. [24] proposed an algorithm known as one of the earliest works towards RecGNNs. They apply the same set of parameters recurrently over nodes in a graph to extract high-level node representations. Due to the limitation of computational power, the pioneer research in this approach is mainly focused on directed acyclic graphs. Scarselli et al. [25] extended the prior works on RecGNNs to handle the complex types of graphs such as directed/undirected graphs, acyclic/cyclic graphs.

Encouraged by the success of CNNs in the natural language processing and computer vision domain, ConvGNNs and its variants have been widely adopted. Niepert et al.

[14] extended the concepts from convolutional neural networks for images to build a framework for learning representations for classes of directed and undirected graphs. ConvGNNs fall into two categories: spectral-based and spatial-based. Defferrard et al. [26] present an idea of CNNs in the contextual relationship of spectral graph principles, which provides the essential mathematical background and effective numerical strategy to design fastlocalized convolutional neural network on graphs. Kipf et al. [27] present a scalable technique for semi-supervised learning on graph-structured data that is built on an effective modification of convolutional neural networks which work directly on graphs

3   Proposed Model

3.1   Problem Formulation

Suppose we have 2 different social networks denoted G^s (V^s, E^s) and G^t (V^t, E^t) in which $V^s = \{v_1^s, v_2^s, \ldots, v_m^s\}$ is a set of vertices in the network G^s; $E^s = \left\{u_{ij}^s\right\}$ is the set of edges connecting vertex © and vertex j in the G^s network. Similarly, $V^t = \{v_1^t, v_2^t, \ldots, v_n^t\}$ is the set of vertices of the network G^t; $E^t = \{u_{ij}^t\}$ is the set of edges connecting the © and j vertices in the G^t network. Denote $A = \{(v_i^s, v_j^t)\}$ is a set of known anchor links between G^s and G^t networks in which v_i^s is a vertex belongs to G^s and v_j^t is a vertex belongs to G^t. The problem of predicting anchor links is to determine: $A^* = \left\{x = \left(v_i^s, v_j^t\right) \backslash x \not\subset A\right\}$.

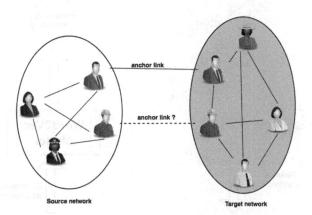

Fig. 1. Anchor link prediction problem example

The Fig. 1 illustrates the problem of anchor link predict between the source network G^s and target network G^t. The green line connecting a vertex in G^s to G^t represent the known anchor links (observed anchor links); and the dash line connecting the vertices between G^s and G^t are the links which we need to predict.

3.2 Graph Embedding

The first step in our approach is embedding vertices in source and target network into representation vectors but still preserve the connections between vertices in each network. As mentioned in the review, we have a lot of graph embedding algorithms to perform this conversion. In this paper, we select the node2vec algorithm proposed by Grover et al. [20] to do this task. The Fig. 3 illustrates the process of graph embedding using node2vec algorithm which I mentioned above.

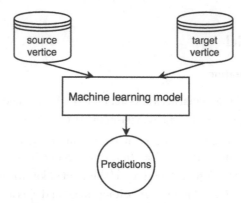

Fig. 2. Anchor link prediction model

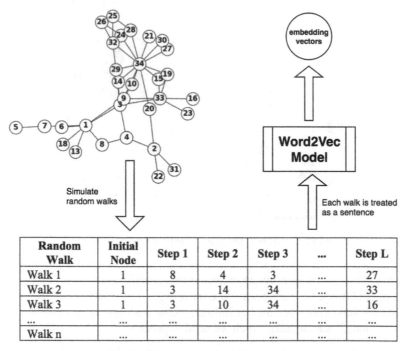

Random Walk	Initial Node	Step 1	Step 2	Step 3	...	Step L
Walk 1	1	8	4	3	...	27
Walk 2	1	3	14	34	...	33
Walk 3	1	3	10	34	...	16
...	...	...	...	...	...	...
Walk n	...	...	...	...	...	...

Fig. 3. The process of node2vec model

3.3 Anchor Link Prediction

In the next step, we will use a binary classification to predict the class of each pair of vertices between source and target network. We construct a neural network with 2 vectors as the input, hidden layers, and the output is the scalar value in the range of [0, 1] which represents the link formation probability between unconnected pair of vertices in the source and target network. We will then classify the output based on a threshold. As in the Fig. 2, the model receive two input vectors (one is the representation vector of vertice in source network, another one is the representation vector of vertice in target network).

Algorithm 1 Anchor Link Prediction

1: $G \leftarrow read\_graph()$
2: $S, T, anchor\_links \leftarrow gen\_subgraphs(G)$
3: $emb\_S \leftarrow node2vec(S)$
4: $emb\_T \leftarrow node2vec(T)$
5: $dataset \leftarrow gen\_dataset(emb\_S, emb\_T, anchor\_links)$
6: $under\_sampling(dataset)$
7: $train, test \leftarrow train\_test\_split(dataset)$
8: $model \leftarrow PredictModel()$
9: $model.fit(train)$
10: $model.save()$
11: $metrics \leftarrow model.evaluate(test)$

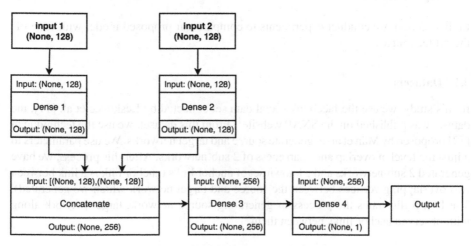

Fig. 4. Anchor link prediction detail model

The Fig. 4 presents more detail about the anchor link prediction learning model, each input vector is fed into the first and second hidden layer, the result of each input vector after passing through these hidden layers will be aggregated and put into the third and fourth hidden layer. In hidden layers we use the relu function as the activation function. In the output layer of our network, we use the sigmoid function to convert the hidden layer value into values within [0–1]. The *Algorithm 1* and *Algorithm 2* illustrates the pseudo code which presents the process of our neural network model.

Algorithm 2 Generate Dataset

Require: S - Source nodes, T - Target nodes, A - Anchor links
1: Initilize $dataset\_class\_0 = \emptyset$
2: Initilize $dataset\_class\_1 = \emptyset$
3: **for each** $s \in S$ **do**
4:     **for each** $t \in T$ **do**
5:         **if** $(s, t) \in A$ **then**
6:             $dataset\_class\_1 \leftarrow (s, t)$
7:         **else**
8:             $dataset\_class\_0 \leftarrow (s, t)$
9:         **end if**
10:     **end for**
11: **end for**

---

4 Experiments

In this section, we conduct experiments to compare our proposed model with state-of-the-art techniques.

4.1 Datasets

In this study, we use the facebook social data set collected by Leskovec et al. [11], the dataset was published on the SNAP website[1]. From this dataset, we use the technique in [12] proposed by Man et al. to generate source and target networks. We use parameters to adjust the level of overlap and sparseness of 2 sub-networks. After this process, we have generated 2 sub-networks and a known set of anchor links (anchor link is a link between two overlapping vertices between the source and target network which we generated). The Fig. 5 illustrates the process of generating source network, target network along with observed anchor links between them.

4.2 Experimental Results

To evaluate and compare the experimental results of our proposed model, we conduct experiments on many different datasets generated by changing the parameters in the level

---

[1] http://snap.stanford.edu/data/ego-Facebook.html.

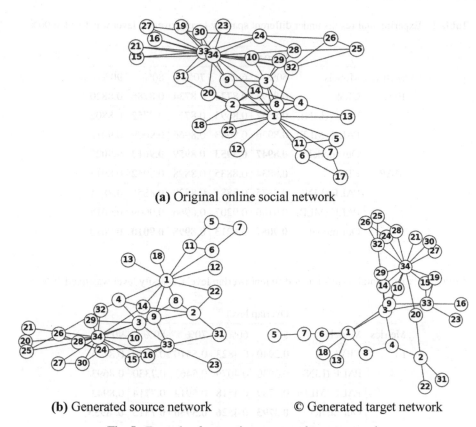

(a) Original online social network

(b) Generated source network   © Generated target network

Fig. 5. Example of generating source and target network

of overlap as well as the sparseness of source and target network. One of our difficulties when experimenting is the imbalance of the labeling dataset. It means that in the dataset we generate, there is only a small amount of data labeled "*yes*" (equivalent to 2 input vertices forming the anchor link), remaining most data labeled "*no*" (meaning that 2 input vertices are not forming the anchor link). To solve this problem, we use under-sampling or over-sampling technique to balance the training data set, this technique effectively improves the accuracy of the model.

After generating the data set by pairing each vertex in the source network connect to each vertex in the target network and assigning the label based on the pre-observed anchor links. We then processing the imbalance problem of datasets to make it balance between the labels. We carried out the division of the data set into 2 subsets at the rate of 75% for training and 25% for testing. The Table 1 and Table 2 shows that our proposed model exhibits the best performance on predicting anchor links in difference levels of sparsity and overlap.

Table 1. Experimental results under different sparsity levels, overlap level was fixed at 90%.

Metrics	Models	Sparsity level				
		50%	60%	70%	80%	90%
F1	CRW	0.8693	0.8724	0.8734	0.8786	0.8820
	PALE (LIN)	0.8652	0.8693	0.8713	0.8752	0.8802
	PALE (MLP)	0.8936	0.8943	0.8966	0.9009	0.9012
	Our model	**0.8947**	**0.8953**	**0.8959**	**0.9013**	**0.9027**
MAP	CRW	0.8834	0.8835	0.8898	0.8912	0.8915
	PALE (LIN)	0.8875	0.8881	0.8829	0.8856	0.8881
	PALE (MLP)	0.9100	0.9207	0.8966	0.9009	0.9012
	Our model	**0.9087**	**0.9213**	**0.8998**	**0.9010**	**0.9013**

Table 2. Experimental results under different overlap levels, sparsity level was fixed at 60%.

Metrics	Models	Overlap level				
		50%	60%	70%	80%	90%
F1	CRW	0.2940	0.3823	0.5510	0.7350	0.8724
	PALE (LIN)	0.3030	0.4079	0.5463	0.7330	0.8693
	PALE (MLP)	0.3789	0.4518	0.5914	0.7714	0.8943
	Our model	**0.3793**	**0.4526**	**0.5950**	**0.7813**	**0. 8953**
MAP	CRW	0.3245	0.4133	0.5998	0.7732	0.8835
	PALE (LIN)	0.3399	0.4432	0.5659	0.7756	0.8881
	PALE (MLP)	0.4197	0.4845	0.6224	0.8118	0.9207
	Our model	**0.4190**	**0.4854**	**0.6331**	**0.8213**	**0.9213**

5 Conclusion

In this paper we propose a model that predicts anchor links between two similar social networks. Different from previous studies, we approach this problem in the direction of a binary classification model. The input of the classification algorithm is a pair of two vectors which represents any two vertices (one in source network and one in target network). The output of the classification problem will determine whether these two vertices form an anchor link or not (if there is an anchor link, then these two vertices are the same person). Our approach is the combination method which combines the graph embedding algorithms and binary classification approach. Experiments on the dataset show that our approach can considerably improve the anchor link prediction accuracy compare with the traditional algorithms.

References

1. Perito, D., Castelluccia, C., Kaafar, M.A., Manils, P.: How unique and traceable are usernames. In: Fischer-Hübner, S., Hopper, N. (eds.) PETS 2011. LNCS, vol. 6794, pp. 1–17. Springer, Heidelberg (2011). https://doi.org/10.1007/978-3-642-22263-4_1
2. Raad, E., Chbeir, R., Dipanda, A.:User profile matching in social networks. In: 2010 13th International Conference on Network-Based Information Systems, pp. 297–304. IEEE (2010)
3. Cortis, K., Scerri, S., Rivera, I., Handschuh, S.: An ontology-based technique for online profile resolution. In: Jatowt, A., et al. (eds.) SocInfo 2013. LNCS, vol. 8238, pp. 284–298. Springer, Cham (2013). https://doi.org/10.1007/978-3-319-03260-3_25
4. Liu, S., Wang, S., Zhu, F., Zhang, J., Krishnan, R.: Hydra: large-scale social identity linkage via heterogeneous behavior modeling. In: Proceedings of the 2014 ACM SIGMOD International Conference on Management of Data, pp. 51–62. ACM (2014)
5. Zafarani, R., Liu, H.: Connecting users across social media sites: a behavioral-modeling approach. In: Proceedings of the 19th ACM SIGKDD International Conference on Knowledge Discovery and Data Mining, pp. 41–49. ACM (2013)
6. Zheng, R., Li, J., Chen, H., Huang, Z.: A framework for authorship identification of online messages: writing-style features and classification techniques. J. Am. Soc. Inf. Sci. **57**, 378–393 (2006). https://doi.org/10.1002/asi.20316
7. Kong, X., Zhang, J., Yu, P.S.: Inferring anchor links across multiple heterogeneous social networks. In: Proceedings of the 22nd ACM International Conference on Information & Knowledge Management, pp. 179–188. ACM (2013)
8. Ahmed, A., Shervashidze, N., Narayanamurthy, S., Josifovski, V., Smola, A.J.: Distributed large-scale natural graph factorization. In: Proceedings of the 22nd International Conference on World Wide Web, pp. 37–48. ACM (2013)
9. Cao, S., Lu, W., Xu, Q.: Grarep: learning graph representations with global structural information. In: Proceedings of the 24th ACM International on Conference on Information and Knowledge Management, pp. 891–900. ACM (2015)
10. Ou, M., Cui, P., Pei, J., Zhang, Z., Zhu, W.: Asymmetric transitivity preserving graph embedding. In: Proceedings of the 22nd ACM SIGKDD International Conference on Knowledge Discovery and Data Mining, pp. 1105–1114. ACM (2016)
11. Leskovec, J., Krevl, A.: SNAP Datasets: Stanford Large Network Dataset Collection (2015)
12. Man, T., Shen, H., Liu, S., Jin, X., Cheng, X.: Predict anchor links across social networks via an embedding approach. IJCAI **16**, 1823–1829 (2016)
13. Lu, C.T., Shuai, H.H., Yu, P.S.: Identifying your customers in social networks. In: Proceedings of the 23rd ACM International Conference on Conference on Information and Knowledge Management, pp. 391–400. ACM (2014)
14. Niepert, M., Ahmed, M., Kutzkov, K.: Learning convolutional neural networks for graphs
15. Ribeiro, L.F.R., et al.: struc2vec: learning node representations from structural identity. In: Proceedings of the 23rd ACM SIGKDD International Conference on Knowledge Discovery and Data Mining, Halifax, NS, Canada, pp. 385–394. ACM (2017)
16. Perozzi, B., Al-Rfou, R., Skiena, S.: DeepWalk: online learning of social representations. In: KDD, pp. 701–710 (2014)
17. Yang, Z., Tang, J., Cohen, W.: Multi-modal bayesian embeddings for learning social knowledge graphs. In: IJCAI, pp. 2287–2293 (2016)
18. Li, J., Zhu, J., Zhang, B.: Discriminative deep random walk for network classification. In: ACL (2016)
19. Pan, S., Wu, J., Zhu, X., Zhang, C., Wang, Y.: Tri-party deep network representation. In: IJCAI, pp. 1895–1901 (2016)

20. Grover, A., Leskovec, J.: node2vec: scalable feature learning for networks. In: Proceedings of the 22nd ACM SIGKDD International Conference on Knowledge Discovery and Data Mining, pp. 855–864. ACM (2016)
21. Tenenbaum, J.B., de Silva, V., Langford, J.C.: A global geometric framework for nonlinear dimensionality reduction. Science **290**(5500), 2319–2323 (2000)
22. Roweis, S.T., Saul, L.K.: Nonlinear dimensionality reduction by locally linear embedding. Science **290**, 2323–2326 (2000)
23. Sperduti, A., Starita, A.: Supervised neural networks for the classification of structures. IEEE Trans. Neural Netw. **8**(3), 714–735 (1997)
24. Micheli, A., Sona, D., Sperduti, A.: Contextual processing of structured data by recursive cascade correlation. IEEE Trans. Neural Netw. **15**(6), 1396–1410 (2004)
25. Scarselli, F., Gori, M., Tsoi, A.C., Hagenbuchner, M., Monfardini, G.: The graph neural network model. IEEE Trans. Neural Netw. **20**(1), 61–80 (2009)
26. Defferrard, M., Bresson, X., Vandergheynst, P.: Convolutional neural networks on graphs with fast localized spectral filtering. In: Proceedings of NIPS, pp. 3844–3852 (2016)
27. Kipf, T.N., Welling, M.: Semi-supervised classification with graph convolutional networks. In: Proceedings of ICLR, pp. 1–14 (2017)
28. Mikolov, T., et al.: Distributed representations of words and phrases and their compositionality. Advances in Neural Information Processing Systems 26: 27th Annual Conference on Neural Information Processing Systems, pp. 3111–3119. Lake Tahoe, Nevada (2013)

Community Detection in Complex Networks Using Algorithms Based on K-Means and Entropy

Phuong N. H. Pham[1](✉), Vang V. Le[2](✉), and Vaclav Snasel[3]

[1] Faculty of Information Technology, Ho Chi Minh City University
of Food Industry, Ho Chi Minh City, Vietnam
phuongpnh@hufi.edu.vn
[2] Artificial Intelligence Laboratory, Faculty of Information Technology,
Ton Duc Thang University, Ho Chi Minh City, Vietnam
levanvang@tdtu.edu.vn
[3] Department of Computer Science, VSB-Technical University of Ostrava, Ostrava,
Czech Republic
vaclav.snasel@vsb.cz

Abstract. Detecting community structures in complex networks such as social networks, computer networks, citation networks, etc. is one of the most interesting topics to many researchers, there are many works focus on this research area recently. However, the biggest difficulty is how to detect the number of complex network communities, the accuracy of the algorithms and the diversity in the properties of each complex network. In this paper, we propose an algorithm to detect the structure of communities in a complex network based on K-means algorithm and Entropy. Moreover, we also evaluated our algorithm on real-work and computer generate datasets, the results show that our approach is better than the others.

Keywords: Community detection · Social network analysis · K-means · Entropy

1 Introduction

Recently, complex network analysis is the most interesting research direction. Complex network analysis is the problem that scientific researchers quite concern. In real life, there are many areas related to complex networks such as biological cell networks, social networks, World Wide Web, Internet, etc. Therefore, the structure of the community is an important element in complex networks. Community structure is an element that consists of edges between vertices of network that form a tight structure between components. Not only the vertices and edges, community structure also related to many other factors such as direction, weight or general characteristics, etc. Because of the complex in the structure of community, so their analysis is also a complex problem. Moreover, the structure of network today provides a lot of useful information such as attributes of

© Springer Nature Switzerland AG 2020
N. T. Nguyen et al. (Eds.): ICCCI 2020, LNAI 12496, pp. 241–251, 2020.
https://doi.org/10.1007/978-3-030-63007-2_19

a user's location, behavior, preferences, and emotions in social networks, from which researchers discover community structures based on this useful information.

In this paper, we present a method to solve the problem of how to identify community numbers and categorize each vertex on their communities in a graph of vertices and edges. Currently, a simple graph with only vertices and edges also has many shortcomings to divide the community between them. Therefore, we studied an algorithm based on previous studies to make the most specific and accurate by determining the number of communities based on the method of calculating entropy, identifying the central vertices based on the importance and similarity between the vertices, finally gathering the remaining vertices into the community by calculating the similarity and reliability between them. Through it, we also offer a combined method to identify open communities in that graph.

The structure of this paper was organized into the following sections: part 1 introduces an overview of the complex network and community structure, related works introduced in Sect. 2. Our proposed algorithm is described in Sect. 3. Part 4 we experiment on real-work and computer-generated datasets. Finally, we summarize the content in the conclusion section.

2 Related Works

A community structure is generalized as a set of elements/entities that have similar properties or have similar roles. The complex network is referred to as the graph network $G = (E, V)$ where E is the set of edges/links, V is the set of vertices/nodes. For example, in social networks, communities are people with the same interest in watching movies, listening to music, reading books; in the citing network the communities are research scientists in the same field or related citation, or in society communities are groups of people who share their views, work goals or relationships. The importance of the community structure in the complex network can be found in order to find the relationships between the components of the complex network, identifying the elements that have important implications in the community and strong/weak relationships with surrounding components. In this section, we present related works on detecting community structures in complex networks because detecting communities is a (challenging task) challenge for researchers. Many methods of detecting community structure have been introduced in recent years with many different methods and different results. Methods for discovering common community structures include the following four types of methods: graph partitioning, hierarchical clustering, clustering by region and clustering by spectrum.

Girvan and Newman [4] introduced intermediate measurement between edges with the idea of finding and removing connections between communities that have a higher intermediate, after each removal of an edge we will recalculate the intermediate measurement of the remaining edges until no edges in the graph. Basically, Girvan and Newman algorithms have relatively good results but are limited in the number of communities and have a relatively high time complexity with $O(m^2n)$ and also cannot detect overlapping components. Newman and Girvan [5] provide a new concept of the largest modularity for better clustering. Modularity is a function that evaluates cluster quality to achieve good or bad results. The value of modularity ranges from [0.1], the greater the value of modularity, the higher the results of community clustering will be. However, this method also had many disadvantages in discovering the community, so the author proposed a method in Newman [6] to improve the modularity optimization to achieve better results.

Based on the method of Newman, Rattigan et al. [7] introduced a faster method of community detection by dividing graphs/networks into different regions and calculating the distance of nodes in each region. This method uses a network structure index instead of the largest modularity function. The results showed that Ratigan's method and his colleagues have the complexity of only O(m). Chen et al. [8] proposed a calculation method based only on unrelated links because of calculating the intermediate of edges by counting all the shortest paths that could lead to unbalanced partitioning means there are some communities with a size that is too large and vice versa. The results show that this method gives much better results than the methods proposed by Girvan-Newman. Dinh et al. [9], Blondel et al. [10] proposed a method to detect community structure in complex networks by optimizing the largest modularity (maximizing modularity) in the free-scale network. The result is much better than other methods for directional or scalar networks.

A new algorithm based on the edge structure and node attributes proposed by Yang and et al. [1] in 2014, this method overcomes the limitations of the Newman algorithm that detects the overlapping community. The approach of Yang and el's proposal is to be able to cluster in combination with other information from sources such as edge attributes, information diffusion. Ying Pan and el [2] proposed another method based on the similarity of the node by calculating the largest similarity of the pair of nodes and form the communities based on ZLZ measurement. This method has the advantage of low computational complexity and also does not need to know information about the number of communities. To verify the accuracy of algorithms in the detection of community structure, an LFR method [3] introduces a benchmark graph to verify the detection methods, modularity optimization, etc. Through this verification it is possible to know the size of the graph and the density of links between the nodes in that network. Caiyan et al. [13] introduced a method of detecting community structure based on the extension of node attribute, this method implemented on two algorithms kNN-nearest and kNN-Kmeans to detect community structure.

In addition, in recent years, researchers have introduced many methods of detecting community structure such as the works of Le et al. [16], Chun et al. [17] improved the Label propagation algorithms using LinkRank algorithm of Satrio et al. [14], Santo Fortunato et al. [18], community detection on large and flexible network [15], dynamic community detection [20]; evolutionary method based on the density of modularity of Caihong Liu et al. [19].

3   Proposed Model

The algorithm is developed based on methods of calculating Entropy of each node, calculating the similarity between any two nodes, and calculating the reliability of a node compare to a community in the network.

3.1 Entropy

Suppose that a graph G has n vertices and the total degrees of vertices is D. The minimum number of communities K of a graph G is calculated by n multiply with the average of entropy of graph divided by D. The Eq. 1 illustrates the calculation of value K. The value of K will be a real number, and the number of communities is determined by taking the upper bound of K.

$$K = N/(avgE(G) \times D) \tag{1}$$

To calculate the minimum number of communities K in the network we need the average Entropy of a graph G. The Eq. 2 illustrates the calculation of average Entropy value of a graph G.

$$avgE(G) = \frac{\sum_{i=1}^{n}(E(v_i) * d_i)}{D} \tag{2}$$

We use the Eq. 3 to calculate the entropy value of a vertex v_i in graph G. In which v_i is the vertex ith of graph G; d_i is the degree of v_i; and l is the max degree among the neigbors of v_i; k_t is the count of neigbours of v_i which has degree t.

$$E(v_i) = -\frac{d_i}{D} \times \sum_{t=1}^{l} \frac{k_t}{d_i} log_2 \frac{k_t}{d_i} \tag{3}$$

Algorithm 1 - Calculate the number of communities in graph G

```
Function NumOfCommunities (G)
Input:
    •  The input graph G.
Output: Number of Community in graph G
Begin
        V = nodes(G)
        N = len(V)
        D = total_degree(G)
        α = cal_alpha()
        E_avg = AverageEntropy(V, D)
        K =  N
            ―――――
            E_avg×α×D
        Return K
End
```

To explain more clearly about the counting of occurencies we use a example network as in Fig. 1. The degree value of each vertex was calculated in Table 1, We then calculate the occurencies of neigbors's degree in Table 2, (Fig. 2).

3.2 Clustering

From the number of communities K calculated based on entropy in Sect. 3.1, we proceed to identify central nodes. Here, to determine the central nodes, we improve the formula

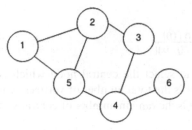

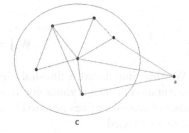

Fig. 1. Example graph to demonstrate the counting of occurencies

Fig. 2. Example graph to demonstrate the counting of occurencies

Table 1. The degree of each vertex in example graph

	Node v_1	Node v_2	Node v_3	Node v_4	Node v_5	Node v_6
Degree	2	3	2	3	3	1

Table 2. The count of occurencies of neigbors's degree in example graph

Nodes	Count of occurencies of neigbors
Node v_1	[(3:2)] means that node v_1 has 2 neigbors at degree 3 • 0 neigbor at degree 1; • 0 neigbor at degree 2; • 2 neigbors at degree 3
Node v_2	[(2:2) (3:1)] means that node v_2 has 2 neigbors at degree 2, and 1 neigbor at degree 3. • 0 neigbor at degree 1; • 2 neigbors at degree 2; • 1 neigbor at degree 3
Node v_3	[(2:1) (3:1)]
Node v_4	[(1:1) (3:2)]
Node v_5	[(2:1) (3:2)]
Node v_6	[(3:1)]

of Jaccard similarity between any 2 nodes. The Eq. 4 is the original Jaccard similarity formula proposed by Newman []. In which: Γ (i) is the neigbours of vertex i^{th} in graph.

$$Wij = \frac{|\Gamma(i) \cap \Gamma(j)|}{|\Gamma(i) \cup \Gamma(j)|} \qquad (4)$$

In Eq. 5, we then improve the original Jaccard similarity by adding node j to the denominator of Eq. 4. This means that we also include the node being considered with the node considering to increase the accuracy for the algorithm.

$$\mathbf{Wij} = \frac{|\,\Gamma(i) \cap \Gamma(j)\,|}{|\,\Gamma(i) \cup \Gamma(j)\,\cup j\,|} \tag{5}$$

We then introduced a threshold in Eq. 6 to select the central node which is the representation of each community. In which, N is the total number of vertices; k is the number of central vertices need to be selectd; ∂ is the ramain number of central vertices need to be selected.

$$Wij < \frac{degree(i)}{N - k + \partial} \tag{6}$$

Thus, here we have generated the number of K central nodes as accurately as possible. Next step, we need to gather the remaining nodes to their central nodes. The problem is how to determine which node will belong to the community of which central node? Here we offer a method to solve that problem. The method is divided into 2 steps:

Forming the primitive communities, The formation of primitive communities is done in a very simple way. We conducted the collection of nodes that only linked to one of the central nodes found in the above step into the same community.

Extending the community, we propose Eq. 7 to increase the accuracy when determining the cluster in which a node will belong to. In case the node being considered has the same number of connections to the cluster, then the clustering algorihm will be incorrect if only based on their associated number of connections. This formula attempts to calculate the weight of a node to each cluster. By applying this formula, we will calculate the link weight of that node to each cluster, we then are able to select the best suitable cluster which it will belong to. In Eq. 7, m is the number of neigbor nodes of node v in cluster C, u_i is the neighbor node i^{th} of node v in the cluster C; N is the total number of nodes in cluster C.

$$T(C_v) = \sum_{i=1}^{m} \left(\frac{\Gamma(u_i)}{N} \right) \tag{7}$$

Based on this formula, we iterate through the neighboring nodes of labeled nodes (nodes have been treated as the center nodes). We consider node aggregation according to α value (the percentage of links that can be used to collect, default 50% of links), so when the higher value of α then we will determine the larger Q value of the community, and discard more outbound links. In this section, we introduce method cluster nodes to the central node in the complex network based on the three main conditions such as

a. When finding enough links to communities. If the clustering process falls into the loop then the node will be clustered based on the number of links (the link is only counted with only the labeled nodes) to community of considering central node. We will then iterate to the next node when the node being considered is clustered to any community.
b. When the link number is the most with any case when there are not enough links yet. Switch to the next node when the node being considered is gathered with the center node.

c. When there exists only 1 link to a community in communities. Switch to the next node when the node being considered is gathered with the center node.

However, there is a problem that occurs here is that when browsing through pending nodes without gathering any nodes (no changes, falling into endless iterations), we will turn on the priority at condition a. When we turn on the priority, we only need to look at the names of the links we have found with the reviewing community without having to find enough links left. This priority mode ends when browsing through the list of pending nodes.

Algorithm 2 – Detect the communities

```
Function DetectCommunities (G)
Input:
    •  The input graph G to detect the communities.
Output: List of communities
Begin
      K = NumOfCommunities(G)
      centralNodes = CentralNodes(G, K)
      seedCommunities = InitCommunities(G, centralNodes)
      Return ExpandCommunities(G, seedCommunities)
End
```

In this study, we also introduce advantages over the state of the arts of community detection algorithms in that we identify the initial actions not described in Eq. 1. Then we use entropy to find the average entropy value of a graph as well as continue to calculate the entropy value of each vertex in the network described in Eq. 2 and Eq. 3. Finally, we define the community structure based on similarity between vertices in network graph. Morever, we improved the method of calculating similarity to Jaccard as well as proposed the method of selecting the central node in Eq. 6. In addition, we improved the method of calculating the accuracy of clustering of nodes in the community to expand. the network community effectively using Eq. 7. In addition, the implementation of the algorithm to collect cluster nodes also results in unexpected results and we have overcome them with conditions such as above thereby determine the effective community expansion. Therefore, we introduced the efficient algorithm by experimentally implementing it on the realworld datasets described in the next section.

4   Experiments

In this section, we experimented with our algorithm in Python programming language on the PC with the configuration of Core i7-7800X 3.5Ghz processor and 8 GB memory. We evaluate our algorithm on proven real-world grouth-truth datasets with other algorithms such as: Zachary club dataset Karate, Dolphins social network, American college football club network and network of political category books. In addition, we also tested our method on computer-generated data sets with the number of nodes N = 1000, 5000, 10000. Experimental results of our method initially give better results than other methods when comparing values of Modularity and NMI.

4.1 Datasets

We use the famous data sets that have been clarified the ground-truth, which are used by many algorithms to detect community structure, specifically including:

- Zachary karate club [11]: this is a social network model describing community structure with many algorithms evaluated, data model of karate club including 34 vertices representing members in the club, in which the members divided into two groups: a group supporting the coach and a group supporting the club president.
- Dolphin network [12]: this is a network describing dolphins living in Doubtful, Sound in New Zealand, which describes 62 dolphins symbolizing 62 vertices. Between two dolphins appear regularly close together will be represented by 01 edge connecting the two vertices.
- Network of political books (http://www-personal.umich.edu/~mejn/netdata/): A directed network of hyperlinks between weblogs on US politics, recorded in 2005 by Adamic and Glance. These books describe the American politics published in the presidential election, and are best-selling on the amazon.com e-commerce site.
- American College football club [4]: The dataset describing the match schedule between American college football teams in one season. It contains 115 teams and is divided into 12 groups. The experimental results on this dataset achieved Modularity $= 0.6006$ and NMI $= 0.8399$ are better than comparable methods as shown in Table 4.

4.2 Evaluation

In this paper, we verify the proposed algorithm on proven data sets such as Karate, Doolphin, Footballs, etc. The experiments show that our approach performs better than other algorithms (Table 3), (Fig. 3, 4).

In this experiment, we have also tested on real datasets all yield better results when evaluated by modularity measurement with NF algorithms, K-means adn ELM-CD algorithms, the result of modularity values to achieve high results at least 0.7966 on dataset

Table 3. The experiment results on difference real-world datasets

	Methods	Karate	Dolphins	Polbooks	Football
Modularity	NF	0.3807	0.4941	0.5019	0.5680
	K-Means	0.1071	0.2818	0.3360	0.5680
	ELM-CD	0.2374	0.2788	0.4861	0.5086
	Our method	**0.7126**	**0.6989**	**0.7966**	**0.6006**
NMI	NF	0.6925	0.5943	0.5282	0.7424
	K-Means	0.3960	0.3336	0.3739	0.8396
	ELM-CD	0.4340	0.5728	0.5461	0.8262
	Our method	**1.0**	**0.8859**	**0.5787**	**0.8399**

Table 4. Experimental results on computer generation dataset

Missing parameter	1000 nodes	5000 nodes	10000 nodes
0,05	0.8947	0.8908	0.8806
0,1	0.7908	0.7940	0.8090
0,15	0.7468	0.7228	0.7409
0,2	0.6725	0.6630	0.6713
0,25	0.5866	0.5878	0.6067
0,3	0.5529	0.5435	0.5420
0,35	0.4737	0.4784	0.4826
0,4	0.4310	0.4234	0.4274
0,45	0.3689	0.3802	0.3853
0,5	0.3672	0.3397	0.3251

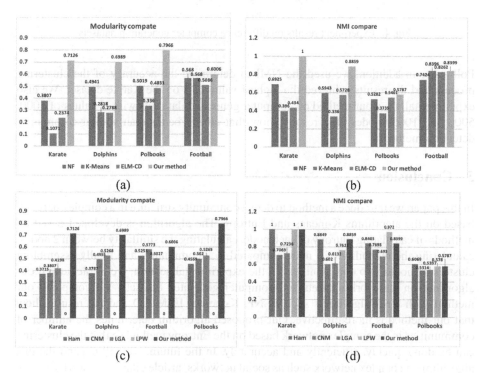

Fig. 3. Experiment results on difference real-world datasets

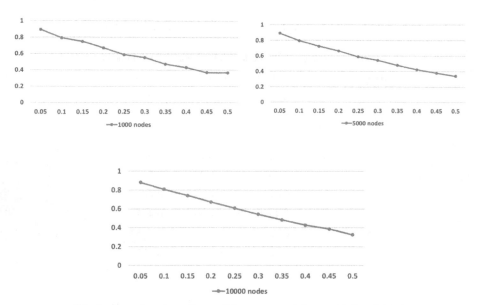

Fig. 4. Experiment results on difference computer generation datasets

Polbooks. In addition, we used the NMI to determine the accuracy of the clustering process and the results achieved the highest value of 1 on the Karate dataset. We also experimentally run our method on computer generated data sets with N values of 1000, 5000 and 10000 nodes. The results show that all are better than similar community detection methods.

5   Conclusion

In this paper, we introduce a method to detect community structure in a complex network based on the algorithms K-means and Entropy. The algorithm is developed based on methods of calculating Entropy of each node, calculating the similarity between 2 nodes, calculating the reliability of a node compared to a community and finally assembling clusters of nodes into communities. In the experimental section, we implemented our algorithm on real-work datasets and computer generated datasets. We compared our method with other algorithms such as NF, K-means, ELM-CD and the results show that our method is more effective. Our proposed algorithm determines the number of communities in the complex network based on the Entropy method so that the clustering can be done quickly, efficiently and accurately. In the future, we will expand the this algorithm on complex network such as social networks, article citation networks, online advertising networks to detect community structures.

References

1. Yang, J., McAuley, J., Leskovec, J.: Community detection in networks with node attributes. In: 2013 IEEE 13th International Conference on Data Mining, pp. 1151–1156. IEEE (2013)

2. Pan, Y., Li, D.H., Liu, J.G., Liang, J.Z.: Detecting community structure in complex networks via node similarity. Phys. A Stat. Mech. Appl. **389**(14), 2849–2857 (2010)
3. Lancichinetti, A., Fortunato, S., Radicchi, F.: Benchmark graphs for testing community detection algorithms. Phys. Rev. E **78**(4), 046110 (2008)
4. Girvan, M., Newman, M.E.J.: Community structure in social and biological networks. Proc. Nat. Acad. Sci. **99**(12), 7821–7826 (2002)
5. Newman, M.E.J., Girvan, M.: Finding and evaluating community structure in networks. Phys. Rev. E **69**(2), 026113 (2004)
6. Newman, M.E.J.: Modularity and community structure in networks. Proc. Nat. Acad. Sci. **103**(23), 8577–8582 (2006)
7. Rattigan, M.J., Maier, M., Jensen, D.: Graph clustering with network structure indices. In: Proceedings of the 24th International Conference on Machine Learning, pp. 783–790. ACM (2007)
8. Chen, J., Yuan, B.: Detecting functional modules in the yeast protein–protein interaction network. Bioinformatics **22**(18), 2283–2290 (2006)
9. Dinh, T.N., Thai, M.T.: Community detection in scale-free networks: approximation algorithms for maximizing modularity. IEEE J. Sel. Areas Commun. **31**(6), 997–1006 (2013)
10. Blondel, V.D., Guillaume, J.L., Lambiotte, R., Lefebvre, E.: Fast unfolding of communities in large networks. J. Stat. Mech Theory Exp. **2008**(10), P10008 (2008)
11. Zachary, W.W.: An information flow model for conflict and fission in small groups. J. Anthropol. Res. **33**(4), 452–473 (1977)
12. Lusseau, D.: The emergent properties of a dolphin social network. Proc. Roy. Soc. Lond. Ser. B Biol. Sci. **270**(suppl_2), S186–S188 (2003)
13. Jia, C., Li, Y., Carson, M.B., Wang, X., Jian, Y.: Node attribute-enhanced community detection in complex networks. Sci. Rep. **7**(1), 2626 (2017)
14. Yudhoatmojo, S.B., Samuar, M.A.: Community detection on citation network of DBLP data sample set using linkrank algorithm. Procedia Comput. Sci. **124**, 29–37 (2017)
15. Harenberg, S., et al.: Community detection in large-scale networks: a survey and empirical evaluation. Wiley Interdisc. Rev. Comput. Stat. **6**(6), 426–439 (2014)
16. Le, B.D., Shen, H., Nguyen, H., Falkner, N.: Improved network community detection using meta-heuristic based label propagation. Appl. Intell. **49**(4), 1451–1466 (2018). https://doi.org/10.1007/s10489-018-1321-0
17. Gui, C., Zhang, R., Zhao, Z., Wei, J., Rongjing, H.: LPA-CBD an improved label propagation algorithm based on community belonging degree for community detection. Int. J. Mod. Phys. C **29**(02), 1850011 (2018)
18. Fortunato, S.: Community detection in graphs. Phys. Rep. **486**(3–5), 75–174 (2010)
19. Liu, C., Liu, Q.: Community detection based on differential evolution using modularity density. Information **9**(9), 218 (2018)
20. Rossetti, G., Cazabet, R.: Community discovery in dynamic networks: a survey. ACM Comput. Surv. (CSUR) **51**(2), 35 (2018)

Data Mining Methods and Applications

Analysing Effects of Customer Clustering for Customer's Account Balance Forecasting

Duy Hung Phan[✉] and Quang Dat Do

FPT University, Hanoi, Vietnam
hungpd2@fe.edu.vn, dat18mse13010@fsb.edu.vn

Abstract. Forecasting deposits as balance in a customer's payment account is one of the most important bank problems. Accurate forecasting helps manage risks, plan investment policies, adjust interest rates, marketing and customer care. With the increasingly powerful application of information systems to collect full customer data and the miraculous ability of artificial intelligence, the problem of forecasting payment account balances can be solved. This paper used AutoRegressive Integrated Moving Average (ARIMA), Long short term memory (LSTM) and Hierarchical Forecasting (HF) methods to forecast customer account balance, while focusing on analysing effects from customer clustering on the predicted results. Research has shown that the forecast of the series of total balances can be based on the results of predictions on the group. At the same time, we can quickly detect anomalies in groups and devise appropriate remedies.

Keywords: Account balance forecasting · Customer clustering · AutoRegressive Integrated Moving Average · Long short term memory · Hierarchical Forecasting

1 Introduction

There is a lot of research on time series forecasting in different contexts. Many authors have studied innovation and financial risk, and have come up with several ways to calculate, assess and manage risk.

For the past few years, forecasting stock returns has become an important field of research. Debadrita Banerjee (2014) used the AutoRegressive Integrated Moving Average (ARIMA) model to the forecast of the Indian Stock Market [1]. The author collected data on the monthly closing stock indices of Sensex for six years (2007–2012) and based on these they have tried to develop an appropriate model which would help us to forecast the future unobserved values of the Indian stock market indices.

Ning Chen-xu et al. (2015) used ARIMA models as predict method of bank cash flow time series [2].

Zheng Wang and Yuansheng Lou (2019) used ARIMA model to fit and forecast the denoised data to obtain the fitting residuals and forecast results [3]. They experimented to shows that this model can be well adapted to the hydrological time series forecast and has the best forecast effect.

© Springer Nature Switzerland AG 2020
N. T. Nguyen et al. (Eds.): ICCCI 2020, LNAI 12496, pp. 255–266, 2020.
https://doi.org/10.1007/978-3-030-63007-2_20

Duraj Agnieszka et al. (2018) used ARIMA model for detecting outliers in the financial time series [4]. They have found that ARIMA models for forecasting were insufficient, as data with the effect of grouping variances requires models considering these effects, like ARCH, GARCH.

Hierarchical forecasting methods allow the forecasts at each level to be summed giving the forecasts at the level above. When the data are grouped, the forecasts of each group must be equal to the forecasts of the individual series making up the group. Forecasting a large set of time series with hierarchical aggregation constraints is a central problem for many organizations. In the current statistical literature, existing approaches to hierarchical time-series forecasting usually involve either a top-down method or a bottom-up method or a combination of both methods often referred to as the "middle-out" approach.

Souhaib Ben Taieb et al. (2019) used Hierarchical Forecasting forecasting method which relaxes these unbiasedness conditions, and gave the revised forecasts with the best tradeoff between bias and forecast variance [5]. They presented a regularization method which allows us to deal with high-dimensional hierarchies, and provided its theoretical justification then compare the proposed method with well-known methods both theoretically and empirically. Finally, they provided competitive results compared to the state-of-the-art methods.

Juan Pablo Karmy et al. (2019) used Hierarchical time series forecasting via Support Vector Regression in the European Travel Retail Industry [6]. They formalized three different hierarchical time series approaches: bottom-up SVR, top-down SVR, and middle-out SVR, and use them in a sales forecasting project for the Travel Retail Industry. Various hierarchical structures are proposed for the retail industry to achieve accurate product-level predictions.

Zitao Liu et al. (2015) used Hierarchical time series (HTS) to develop an efficient algorithm, HTSImpute, to accurately estimate the missing value in multivariate noisy web traffic time series with specific hierarchical consistency in HTS settings [7]. Their approach can provide more accurate and hierarchically consistent estimations than other baselines.

Henning Wilms et al. (2019) used convolutional long-short term recurrent neural networks (convLSTM) to improve forecasting wind power production using machine learning techniques [8]. Their advantage is the property of including temporal dependencies arising from the (wind) time-series as well as spatial dependencies obtained from geographically scattered wind forecasts. convLSTM shows promising results to modulate both temporal as well as spatial dependencies on wind power output time-series.

Irena Koprinska et al. (2018) showed that the convolutional and multilayer perceptron neural networks performed similarly in terms of accuracy and training time, and outperformed the other models [9]. This highlights the potential of convolutional neural networks for energy time series forecasting.

In banking, the customer's account balance forecasting is a typical problem. However, most of the forecasting methods for this are using static customer information like age, gender, job, salary, etc. and has not mentioned the use of customer account balance history. This paper uses the customer's balance history and applies ARIMA, LSTM or Hierarchical Forecasting models to find appropriate forecasting methods as well as analyse the effectiveness of time series clustering (Fig. 1). This result will be the input for marketing, risk management, etc. in banks. As an additional contribution, a dataset, which is stripped of customers' private information is available at Github [10], which can be used for other fields of research regarding time series and applications in banks, etc.

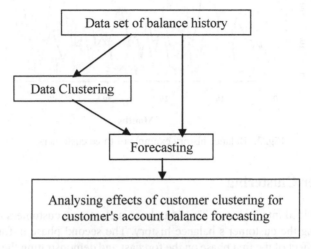

Fig. 1. Main flow of the study.

The remainder of the paper is organised as follows. Section 2 describes the data set. The customer clustering are analysed in Sect. 3. Methodology for forecasting and Analysing effects of customer clustering for customer's account balance forecasting discussed in Sect. 4. Then, conclusions and perspectives are made in Sect. 5.

2 Data Description

The data set is taken from a bank's deposit account information. Data is provided formally and is for research purposes only. For each account, there is data about balance history in 59 months from January 2013 to November 2017. We use data for the first 48 months for training and the last 11 months for testing. The total number of accounts collected is 976,289. However, 95% of the accounts are no longer active or the balance is very low, under 350 USD, and will not be used in this study because of their low significance. The number of remaining accounts with a high balance is 5,869. These accounts represent only 0.6% of the total but they contain 46.55% of the total balance of all deposit accounts.

For privacy reasons, all customer information and bank information have been discarded. Only the account balance details remain. Hence, the data for each customer is a sequence of 48 values, each being the balance at the beginning of the month. Figure 2 shows the balance history of three customers.

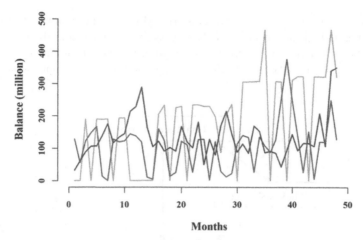

Fig. 2. Balance history example of three customers.

3   Customer Clustering

The work is divided into 2 phases. The first phase is clustering customers into a number of clusters using the customer's balance history. The second phase is forecasting and analysing the effect of the first phase on the forecast and demonstrating the effectiveness of clustering using customer balance history in forecasting.

This section presents the customer clustering, which is to divide customers into clusters, in each cluster the customers have the same behavior. This task is conducted with a number of related studies summarized as follows.

Customer information can be divided into two groups named "static" and "dynamic". The "static" customer information includes age, gender, job, salary, etc. This kind of information will stay consistent or rarely change. On the contrary, dynamic customer information will change frequently, for example, balance history, daily expenses.

Shiyang You et al. were interested in finding the clustering with potential value in financial time series. An experiment on ten-time segments showed that the obtained clusters were effective, in which both the whole similarity and the trend similarity on training data were markedly higher than that of randomized clustering [11]. Hanaa Talei et al. presented an end-to-end real-time architecture for analysing and clustering time-series sensor data using an IoT architecture [12]. The authors used the Euclidian distance (ED) to compute the distance between the time-series and Agglomerative Hierarchical Clustering (AHC) technique to cluster time-series. Another distance also used for the time-series data is the basic Dynamic Time Warping (DTW). Weizeng Wang et al. proposed a new time series distance calculation method that integrates the characteristics of DTW and ED as a distance calculation for K-means clustering [13].

In banking, customer clustering is a typical problem. However, most of the clustering methods for this are using static customer information, which may not provide an up-to-date picture of the customer.

This work uses the customer's balance history to cluster customers based on two types of distances: DTW and Soft-DTW (SDTW) [14]. First, the original data of the first 48 months is smoothed using the spline function to reduce sharp variations. Next, the data is normalized to the range of [0, 1]. The data corresponding to each account is a high-dimensional vector, reduced to two dimensions using principal component analysis. Then, filter out all anomalies [15]. This preprocessed data will be the input of the next clustering process.

Clustering strategies used are both Partitional (PAR) and Hierarchical (HIERAR). Two different centroid computation methods are explored: Partition Around Medoid (PAM) and DTW Barycenter Averaging (DBA) [16]. Performance evaluations are based on the three indexes, Silhouette [17], SF (Score Function) [18] and Davies-Bouldin (DB) [19]. The number of clusters in the study is limited to 8 so that it can be meaningful in practice. The results are shown in the following graphs.

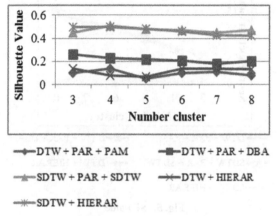

Fig. 3. Silhouette value.

In Fig. 3, the SDTW distance has the best Silhouette index with 4 as the number of clusters. The Silhouette value will decrease slightly when the number of clusters increases. As opposed to the Silhouette value, the DB value varies differently with the number of clusters and different methods (Fig. 4). For example, the DB value of SDTW using the AHC strategy increases fast when the number of clusters goes from 3 to 5 and decreased from 6. With the SF value, for easy visualization, the logarithmic scale is used (Fig. 5). SF values are almost unchanged when using the SDTW distance calculation method but will increase rapidly when using DTW.

From the analyses of the collected data set, the clustering is most optimal with the SDTW distance, the partitional clustering strategy and **4 clusters**. The number of time series in the four clusters obtained with this method are: 1483, 1125, 512 and 2132. The centroid lines for the different clusters are calculated and treated as time series representing each cluster to model and forecast for the next 11 months.

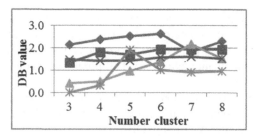

Fig. 4. DB value.

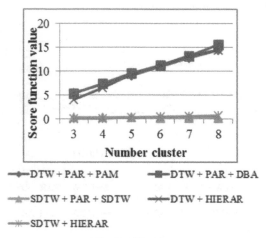

Fig. 5. SF value.

4 Forecasting Customer's Account Balance

4.1 Methodology

This section introduces the forecasting methods applied to the time series used in this study such as ARIMA (Autoregressive integrated moving average), LSTM (Long short term memory) and HF (Hierarchical Forecasting).

ARIMA is actually a class of models that explains a given time series based on its own past values, that is, its own lags and the lagged forecast errors, so that equation can be used to forecast future values [1, 2]. The notation for ARIMA is ARIMA (p, d, q). The "p" stands for the number of autoregressive terms, "d" is the number of differencing needed, and "q" is the number of lagged forecast errors in the prediction equation (of best fit).

LSTM is a network architecture of the regression neural network (RNN), often used in the field of Deep learning and suitable for time series data [3, 20]. When using unidirectional RNNs as generative models, it is straightforward to draw samples from the model in sequential order. However, the inference is not trivial in smoothing tasks, where we want to evaluate probabilities for missing values in the middle of a time series. In bidirectional RNNs, data processed in both directions processed with two separate hidden layers, which are then fed forward into the same output layer. Therefore, this can better exploit context in both directions, for e.g. bidirectional LSTMs perform better than unidirectional ones in forecasting customer's account balance.

HF is a method of time series forecasting using a hierarchical model. This hierarchical model often occurs when time series are aggregated from smaller time series components [6, 7]. In Sect. 3, customers are divided into 4 clusters. HF has several approaches such as bottom-up, top-down or middle-out. This study uses the middle-out approach, which allows analysing the effectiveness of forecasting on each cluster compared to all customers.

4.2 Analysing Effects of Customer Clustering

In order to reach the goal of the study, first, forecasting methods ARIMA and LSTM are applied to each time series (total balance of customers in each cluster), to find the forecast part of each cluster (11 months). Comparing the forecasted data with the actual data, we found the suitable method for forecasting each cluster as shown in Fig. 6.

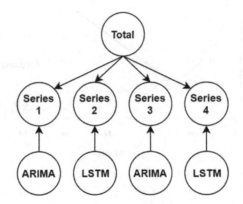

Fig. 6. Forecasting method suitable for each cluster.

The forecast on each cluster with the corresponding methods is shown in Fig. 7.

Performing the forecast for the next 1, 3, 6 and 11 months for each cluster, the key performance indicators (KPIs) are shown in Fig. 8, and for the total series, the KPIs are shown in Fig. 8.

From Fig. 9, the KPIs for each group show that cluster 4 has the highest error value in all forecast months. The actual cause can be seen from Fig. 6, during the period from the 45th month to the 48th month, this group had a very fast increase in the total balance and accounted for 56% of the total value of the balance.

Figure 9 shows that the forecast result on the total time series based on results from clusters (HF method) is similar to the result calculated directly on the total series (ARIMA, LSTM) in short periods (1, 3, 6 months). However, these results are clearly different over the long period (11 months).

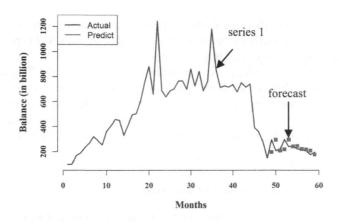

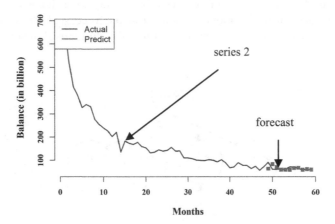

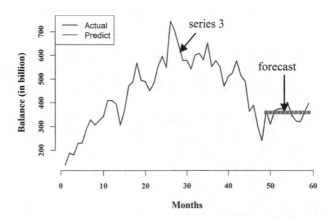

Fig. 7. Forecast on each cluster with the appropriate methods shown in Fig. 6.

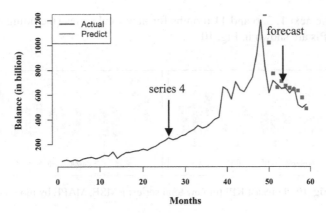

Fig. 7. (*continued*)

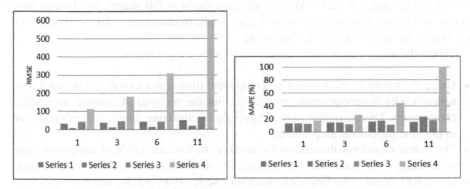

Fig. 8. Forecast KPI: RMSE, MAPE by month and by cluster.

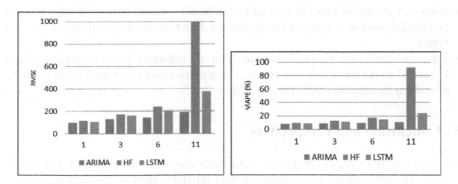

Fig. 9. Forecast KPI for total series: RMSE, MAPE by month

With the effects of cluster 4 as above on forecast output, we try to separate cluster 4 from the input, and conduct the forecast on the remaining 3 clusters. Performing the forecast for the next 1, 3, 6 and 11 months for new total series (including clusters 1, 2 and 3), the KPIs are shown in Fig. 10.

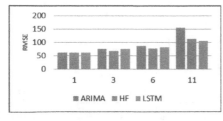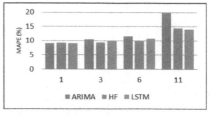

Fig. 10. Forecast KPI for new total series: RMSE, MAPE by month

Figure 10 shows that the values of Root Mean Squared Error (RMSE) and Mean Absolute Percentage Error (MAPE) of all three methods fell sharply on the new total series. In addition, results based on predictive results of component-time series (HF) are equivalent to ARIMA and LSTM methods.

From the above experiments, some conclusions are as follows:

- Using the results of the forecast on component time series to forecast the total time series results is very positive, especially after the removal of unusual time series components. This also confirms that the results of clustering time series are significant in the time series forecast problem.
- The forecast results on the total series based on the forecast results of component-time series may not be good when the forecast on one or more sub-series has bad results.
- Using KPI values of the forecast on each time series allow quickly identifying clusters with unusual characteristics, which can provide solutions to optimize the final forecast results.
- After eliminating the unusual time series, the forecast results by all methods are better and the HF method is equal or better than the direct forecasting methods on the total series.
- For an unusual time series, further analysis of customers in the respective cluster is needed to decide whether to continue using this cluster or find a more accurate, consistent forecasting model for this cluster.

5   Conclusion and Perspectives

The paper analyses the effectiveness of customer clustering for account balance forecasting. The research prepares a practical data set and conducts data preparation, preprocessing and then clustering. Experiments with different forecasting methods on component time series and on total time series gives that the clustering time series is significant in the time series forecast problem; using KPI values of the forecast on each time series allows to quickly identify clusters with unusual characteristics and need more analysis to decide whether to continue using this cluster or find a more accurate, consistent forecasting model for this cluster.

This result will be the input for marketing, risk management, etc. in banks. The paper is also a valuable reference for problems in areas such as Knowledge Representation, Prediction, Time Series Analysis, etc. It can also be applied when dealing with time-series data such as biomedical signals, insurance expenditures, etc.

References

1. Banerjee, D.: Forecasting of Indian stock market using time-series ARIMA model. In: Proceedings of the 2nd International Conference on Business and Information Management (ICBIM), Durgapur, pp. 131–135 (2014). https://doi.org/10.1109/icbim.2014.6970973
2. Chen-Xu, N., Jie-Sheng, W.: Auto regressive moving average (ARMA) prediction method of bank cash flow time series. In: Proceedings of the 34th Chinese Control Conference (CCC), Hangzhou, pp. 4928–4933 (2015). https://doi.org/10.1109/chicc.2015.7260405
3. Wang, Z., Lou, Y.: Hydrological time series forecast model based on wavelet de-noising and ARIMA-LSTM. In: Proceedings of the IEEE 3rd Information Technology, Networking, Electronic and Automation Control Conference (ITNEC), Chengdu, China, pp. 1697–1701 (2019). https://doi.org/10.1109/itnec.2019.8729441
4. Agnieszka, D., Magdalena, L.: Detection of outliers in the financial time series using ARIMA models. In: Proceedings of the Applications of Electromagnetics in Modern Techniques and Medicine (PTZE), Racławice, pp. 49–52 (2018). https://doi.org/10.1109/ptze.2018.8503260
5. Souhaib, B.T., Bonsoo, K.: Regularized regression for hierarchical forecasting without unbiasedness conditions. In: Proceedings of the 25th ACM SIGKDD International Conference on Knowledge Discovery and Data Mining (KDD 2019), pp. 1337–1347. ACM, New York (2019). https://doi.org/10.1145/3292500.3330976
6. Juan, P.K., Sebastián, M.: Hierarchical time series forecasting via support vector regression in the European travel retail industry. Expert Syst. Appl. **137**, 59–73 (2019). https://doi.org/10.1016/j.eswa.2019.06.060
7. Liu, Z., Yan, Y., Yang, J., et al.: Missing value estimation for hierarchical time series: a study of hierarchical web traffic. In: Proceedings of the IEEE International Conference on Data Mining, Atlantic City, NJ, pp. 895–900 (2015). https://doi.org/10.1109/icdm.2015.58
8. Wilms, H., Cupelli, M., Monti, A., et al.: Exploiting spatio-temporal dependencies for RNN-based wind power forecasts. In: Proceesings of the IEEE PES GTD Grand International Conference and Exposition Asia (GTD Asia), Bangkok, Thailand, pp. 921–926 (2019). https://doi.org/10.1109/gtdasia.2019.8715887
9. Koprinska, L., Wu, D., Wang, Z.: Convolutional neural networks for energy time series forecasting. In: Proceedings of the International Joint Conference on Neural Networks (IJCNN), Rio de Janeiro, pp. 1–8 (2018). https://doi.org/10.1109/ijcnn.2018.8489399
10. Data Set: (2019). https://github.com/ziczacziczac/customer-clustering/tree/master/data
11. You, S.Y., Wang, Y.D., Luo, L.D., et al.: Finding the clusters with potential value in financial time series based on agglomerative hierarchical clustering. In: Proceedings of the 11th International Conference on Computer Science and Education, Nagoya, pp. 77–81 (2016)
12. Talei, H., Essaaidi, M., Benhaddou, D.: An end to end real time architecture for analyzing and clustering time series data: case of an energy management system. In: Proceedings of the 6th International Renewable and Sustainable Energy Conference (IRSEC), Rabat, pp. 1–7 (2018)
13. Wang, W., Lyu, G., Shi, Y., et al.: Time series clustering based on dynamic time warping. In: Proceedings of the IEEE 9th International Conference on Software Engineering and Service Science, Beijing, China, pp. 487–490 (2018)
14. Cuturi, M., Blondel, M.: Soft-DTW: a differentiable loss function for time-series. arXiv preprint arXiv:1703.01541 (2017)

15. The R library for distance and density-based outlier detection (2019). https://cran.r-project. org/web/packages/DDoutlier/
16. Petitjean, F., Ketterlin, A., Gancarski, P.: A global averaging method for dynamic time warping, with applications to clustering. Pattern Recogn. **44**, 678–693 (2011)
17. Rousseeuw, P.J.: Silhouettes: a graphical aid to the interpretation and validation of cluster analysis. J. Comput. Appl. Math. **20**, 53–65 (1987)
18. Saitta, S., Raphael, B., Smith, I.F.: A bounded index for cluster validity. In: Proceedings of the International Workshop on Machine Learning and Data Mining in Pattern Recognition, pp. 174–187 (2007)
19. Arbelaitz, O., Gurrutxaga, I., Muguerza, J., et al.: An extensive comparative study of cluster validity indices. Pattern Recogn. **46**(1), 243–256 (2013)
20. Hua, Y., Zhao, Z., Li, R., et al.: Deep learning with long short-term memory for time series prediction. IEEE Commun. Mag. **57**(6), 114–119 (2019). https://doi.org/10.1109/mcom.2019. 1800155

Towards an Efficient Clustering-Based Algorithm for Emergency Messages Broadcasting

Faten Fakhfakh[1(✉)], Mohamed Tounsi[1,3], and Mohamed Mosbah[2]

[1] ReDCAD Laboratory, University of Sfax, Sfax, Tunisia
{faten.fakhfakh,mohamed.tounsi}@redcad.org
[2] University of Bordeaux, CNRS, Bordeaux INP, LaBRI, Bordeaux, France
mohamed.mosbah@labri.fr
[3] Common first year Deanship, Umm Al-Qura University, Mecca, Saudi Arabia

Abstract. Broadcasting urgent information is emerging as an important area of research. One of the issues posed by this subject is the delivery ratio and the transmission time that depend on several factors such as the mobility of persons, the battery of their mobile devices, etc. In this paper, we are interested in broadcasting emergency messages to inform persons in case of unexpected situation occurrence in a subway. In this regard, we introduce a new strategy which consists in applying a clustering mechanism before proceeding with the broadcasting phase. This mechanism is one of the most efficient techniques used in a large-scale network. To show the performance of the proposed approach, several simulation experiments are presented. The results of these experiments highlight the efficiency of our solution in terms of broadcasting delay, delivery ratio, and energy consumption.

Keywords: Broadcasting · Clustering · Persons · Emergency message

1 Introduction

The control of persons flowing in highly crowded areas has become a critical challenge in our daily life [1]. Indeed, these flows are often characterized by strong density and fast propagation of wrong information amongst persons. For instance, a woman fainting on the subway station of Shenzhen caused a grave stampede. The persons surrounding the woman moved back to give more space. Nevertheless, the other persons began to scream and ran because they were notified with false information.

Numerous research studies [2–6] have been proposed in the literature to ensure the broadcasting of emergency messages in the context of Vehicular Ad-hoc Networks (VANETs) [7]. In this respect, a large number of data broadcasting algorithms are based on Vehicle-to-Vehicle (V2V) communication. In fact, vehicles broadcast their presence to notify the available vehicles for the purpose of preventing road accidents. Most of the proposed algorithms are based on

© Springer Nature Switzerland AG 2020
N. T. Nguyen et al. (Eds.): ICCCI 2020, LNAI 12496, pp. 267–278, 2020.
https://doi.org/10.1007/978-3-030-63007-2_21

clustering techniques which are efficient to reduce overhead and avoid network congestion. Other works have focused on Vehicle-to-Pedestrian (V2P) communication [8–10] which allows to prevent accidents involving pedestrians who are equipped with mobile computing devices. Such communication is mainly beneficial to school kids, elderly persons and physically disabled persons. Only few works [11–13] have been interested in sharing data via mobile devices of persons in order to exchange safety information. At the best of our knowledge, only the work of Higuchi et al. [11] adopted a clustering mechanism before disseminating data between the network members.

In this work, we consider a subway which contains many passengers who are equipped with smartphones having a Bluetooth connection. The emergency of unexpected events can cause serious effects on materials and human losses. Then, it is necessary to disseminate emergency messages to the maximum number of persons in the subway. These messages need to be arrived in time. The main contributions of this paper consists of three stages. In the first stage, we introduce a distributed clustering algorithm, where nodes represent persons. It takes into account the residual battery power, the maximal number of nodes which can be handled by a clusterhead and the distance between nodes. We assume that the mobility of nodes is very low, thereby we will not consider the speed of nodes in our algorithm. In the second stage, we propose a broadcasting algorithm which ensures the exchange of information in case of an emergency situation. This algorithm is based on the clustering mechanism to handle the broadcast storm problem [14]. In such a problem, each node acquiring the same message further retransmits it, thus, causing a serious network congestion. In the third stage, we present the simulation experiments that we have conducted to evaluate the efficiency of the proposed algorithms in terms of the delivery ratio, delivery time of messages, and energy consumption. Simulation results demonstrate that our approach can quickly and reliably deliver emergency messages while reducing the redundancy of disseminated messages.

The rest of this paper will be divided into the following sections: In Sect. 2, we provide an overview of the related work. Section 3 introduces a detailed description of our clustering mechanism. Section 4 exhibits the proposed broadcasting algorithm. Then, Sect. 5 exposes the simulation setup and discusses the experimental results. Finally, the last section concludes and provides insights for future work.

2   Related Work

This section provides a review of the approaches focusing on broadcasting emergency messages in crisis situations. A large number of algorithms have been proposed to satisfy some requirements in the context of vehicular applications. The technique of clustering is considered as one of the most powerful methods that consists in dividing the network into clusters and electing clusterheads. This technique has several advantages such as decreasing the energy consumption, enhancing the network lifetime, reducing the overhead. For instance, In

[15], Benkerdagh et al. are interested in broadcasting emergency messages in VANETs based on two steps. The first one consists in proposing an encryption protocol which allows to decrease the number of the exchanged messages. In fact, vehicles exchange codes and pertinent data rather than entire messages. The second step aims at grouping vehicles depending on parameters that ensure clusters stability and messages routing in a minor time. Additionally, the approach presented by Ramakrishnan et al. [16] aims to introduce a broadcasting algorithm for danger messages using a clustering technique. A cluster consists of vehicles having the same road and the same direction. A vehicle can take one of these roles: The clusterhead manages the vehicles of the cluster. while preserving their specific cluster tables. The sub clusterhead nodes are responsible for transporting packages to the preceding vehicles. They incorporate the details of the ordinary vehicles surrounded by the same cluster. Moreover, to improve the quality of communications and reduce the overhead, Cheng et al. [17] introduced a clustering protocol for VANETs. This protocol construct and preserve stable clusters on highways to prevent continual cluster reconstructing. In each cluster, an appropriate clusterhead is elected based on the speed, position and maximal acceleration of vehicles. Furthermore, in [18], the authors aim to maintain the stability of vehicular networks while considering a tradeoff between mobility constraints and Quality of Service requirements which are essential for VANET safety and multimedia services. To do so, they proposed an extension of the QoS-OLSR protocol [19]. In fact, they added the distance and velocity that are the mobility metrics to the QoS function. After that, the cluster-heads are elected based the maximal value of QoS satisfying both routing and mobility constraints. The authors introduced a cheating prevention technique to ensure a reliable election procedure.

To exchange safety information and assess the crowd probability, only few works [12,13,20] have focused on the interaction between pedestrians using mobile devices. In [13], the authors of are interested in evaluating a new methodology of broadcasting information in a subway station. To do so, they produced traces of people mobility using a pedestrian simulator. They particularly concentrate on the evaluation of congested places where people can either join or quit the evaluated scenario. The recent work presented by Chen et al. [12] introduce a broadcasting algorithm which aims to reduce the number of messages transmission in duty-cycled networks. To do so, the authors propose an auxiliary graph that incorporates the active time slots of each node in the network. Next, a scheduling algorithm is presented to exploit these slots.

To our knowledge, only Higuchi et al. [11] adopted the clustering technique. They proposed an information diffusion algorithm for sensor data collection via an opportunistic network. This algorithm can identify groups of persons based on the radio connectivity history between the nodes. It also aims to maintain a local network among the members of the detected clusters. The link management of the cluster members is performed by discovering neighbours in a collaborative way in order to ameliorate the energy-efficiency and reduce the information delivery duration. Nevertheless, the proposed algorithm is not intended for distributed computing. In fact, it needs a server to collect sensor data from mobile devices of pedestrians. The main contribution of our work is to propose a distributed broadcasting algorithm which ensures the dissemination of urgent information between pedestrians equipped with mobiles devices. Our algorithm is based on the clustering mechanism to accelerate the messages exchange.

3 Clustering Mechanism

Clustering can be considered as a graph partitioning problem with some added constraints. In our work, a network is represented by a graph denoted G = (V, E), where V designates the set of nodes vi and E designates the set of links ei. Clusters are a set of virtual groups constructed through clustering algorithms. Each cluster contains one clusterhead (CH) and several cluster members (CM). Within a cluster, the CH is a representative node which is responsible for gathering the information of the cluster to organize the remaining members and maintain the topology of the network. A CM is a node that belongs to a given cluster and it regularly sends the data to its clusterhead. In what follows, we introduce the details of our proposed clustering mechanism.

3.1 Cluster Formation and Clusterhead Election Algorithm

Our algorithm is inspired from the Weighted Clustering Algorithm (WCA), proposed by Chatterjee et al. [21], allowing to get 1-hop clusters. Each cluster has one clusterhead (CH) which is selected based on its weight. The weight of each node is calculated taking into consideration three metrics which are:

- *Degree difference* (Δ_v): It represents the difference between the size of the cluster (S) and the number of neighbours. It is computed as follows:
  $\Delta_v = | d_v - S |$ where:
  - dv is the degree of the node v (the number of its neighbours).
  $d_v = | N(v) | = \sum_{v' \in V, v' \neq v} \{dist(v, v') < range\}$, where "$N(v)$" contains the set of neighbours of the node v, "*range*" is the transmission range of the node v and "$dist(v,v')$" is the distance between the nodes v and v'.
  - S is a threshold for the cluster's size in terms of the number of nodes.
- *Residual battery power* (B_v) : It designates the remaining battery power of the node v. A clusterhead must have more residual battery power than a cluster member since it has extra tasks to do for its members.
- *Distance* (D_v): It represents the sum of the distances between a node and all its neighbours. It is defined as follows: $D_v = \sum_{v' \in N(v)} \{dist(v, v')\}$.

These metrics are inspired from those utilized in WCA. However, we are interested in B_v instead of the consumed battery power adopted in WCA because it aims to extend the lifetime of nodes by abandoning the role of a CH when the battery power is insufficient. Also, we do not consider the speed metric since we assume that the mobility of persons is very low. The clusterhead election algorithm consists of five steps. Firstly, we calculate the degree difference Δ_v for each node v. Secondly, we compute the residual battery power B_v for the node v. In the third step, we calculate, for every node v, the total distance D_v between the node v and all its neighbours. The fourth step consists in calculating the combined weight Wv for each node v, where $W_v = w1*\Delta_v - w2*B_v + w3*D_v$ ($w1 + w2 + w3 = 1$). $w1$, $w2$ and $w3$ are the weighing factors for the corresponding system metrics. After that, the node with the smallest W_v is elected as the CH. All the neighbours of the selected CH can not participate in the election procedure. The steps already mentioned are repeated for the remaining nodes not yet selected as a CH or assigned to a cluster.

3.2 An Illustrative Example

We illustrate our clustering algorithm with the help of Fig. 1 and Fig. 2. We present in Fig. 1 the first configuration of the nodes which are identified by their unique ids. The dotted circles correspond to the transmission range for each node. A node is able to hear broadcast messages only from the nodes which belong to its transmission range. Two nodes are neighbours if there is an edge which joins them (see Fig. 2).

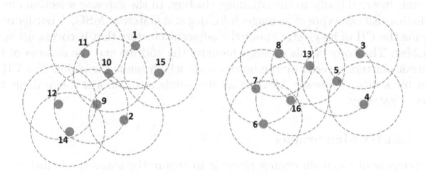

Fig. 1. Transmission range of each node of the graph

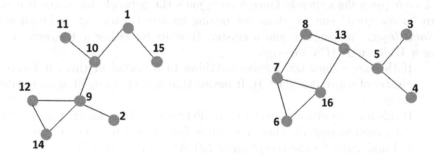

Fig. 2. Initial configuration of nodes

After identifying all the nodes of the graph, we calculate the weight Wv for each node based on the formula already presented. The weight value of each node in the graph is presented in Table 1. We mention that the weighing factors are chosen arbitrarily such that $w1 + w2 + w3 = 1$. For example, we consider that $w1 = 0.6$, $w2 = 0.1$ and $w3 = 0.3$. We note that there are no two CHs which are immediate neighbours. The election is done in a distributed manner.

Table 1. The weight value of each node in the graph

Nodes	1	2	3	4	5	6	7	8	9	10	11	12	13	14	15	16
Wv	2.49	2.22	2.55	2.225	1.47	2.16	1.56	10	2.5	11.2	10.2	5.6	8.4	1.5	9	9.8

3.3 Gateway Selection Method

If a node (noted v) belongs to a cluster and it is connected to one (or more) node(s) of another cluster, v is marked as a border node. If there are several border nodes in a cluster which are connected to another cluster, the node having the minimum value of W is marked as a gateway. The role of a gateway is to transmit internal traffic to the adjoining clusters. In the gateway selection phase, we distinguish two types of message: Info_Msg and Gateway_MSG. A border node informs the CH of its cluster about the adjacent clusters that it covers using an Info_Msg. The body of this message includes the address and the number of the adjacent clusters covered by the border node which sends the claim. The CH of a cluster sends a Gateway_MSG to all its members to inform them about the selected gateway.

3.4 Cluster Maintenance

The purpose of the maintenance phase is to ensure the stability of clusters. We identify different cases which require the maintenance phase:

- *A node joins the network*: Once a node joins the network, its status is equal to "unassigned" since it does not belong to any cluster. So, it broadcasts *Join_Request* message to join a cluster. It waits for either a *Welcome_ACK* or a *Welcome_NACK* message.
  - If this node does not receive anything in a period of time, it forms a cluster of which it is the CH. It means that it declares itself as an isolated node.
  - If this node receives more than one *Welcome_ACK*, it selects the one with the lowest weight W. Then, it sends a *Join_Accept* message to the chosen CH and waits for the reception of *CH_ACK* from this CH.
- *No Connections between a CM and its CH*: If a CM finds its CH node unreachable, it will change its status to "unassigned". This means that the CM has lost connection with its CH. So, it will be removed from the CH record and it will join another cluster (see the previous case "A node joins the network").

- *The residual battery power of the CH is less than a predefined threshold*: In this case, the CH sends a *Battery_Down* message to all its neighbours. All the member nodes participate in the re-election procedure using our clusterhead election algorithm and the node with the least weight is elected as the new CH.
- *The distance between two CHs is less than or equal to a predefined threshold value L*: In this case, the cluster having fewer nodes is omitted and each node of the omitted cluster must find a new cluster to join.

4   Broadcasting Algorithm

In the last section, the formation of clusters is performed and the CHs are elected. Now, it is necessary to apply a broadcasting algorithm to transmit an emergency message. In Fig. 3, we present the flowchart of our proposed algorithm. When a node v receives a broadcast message, there are two cases which are delineated as follows:

(1) The node v is a CH or a gateway: In this case, if the CH receives the message for the first time, it must broadcast the message to all its neighbours. Otherwise, the algorithm finishes its execution.
(2) The node v can be either a border node or a CM: If the node v is a CM, then it is required to verify whether the message is received from the CH. If that is the case, the algorithm is finished. Otherwise, v must send the message to the CH of its cluster and wait a period of time. If this message is received from the CH, then the neighbours are already aware of the message else the message will be transferred to all the adjacent nodes.

If the node v is a border node, then it is essential to check if the message is received from another cluster. If that is not the case, we deal with the same cases presented in the situations of a cluster member. Otherwise, v must transmit the message to the CH of its cluster and wait a period of time. If a message is returned from the CH, the cluster nodes are informed about the message, else the CH rebroadcasts this message to all the adjacent nodes.

5   Performance Analysis

In order to evaluate our proposed approach, we have implemented and conducted extensive simulation experiments. In this section we begin by presenting the simulation settings. After that, we describe and discuss our experimental results.

5.1   Simulation Settings

To evaluate the performance of our approach, we used the simulator CupCarbon[1] which is an open source tool devoted to wireless sensor networks [22]. It is

---

[1] http://cupcarbon.com/.

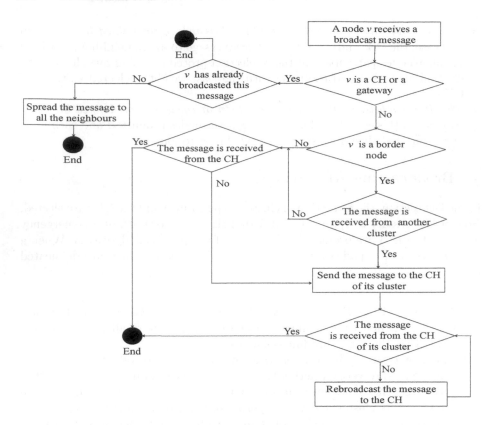

Fig. 3. An overview of our broadcasting process

adopted for scientific and educational goals. It focuses on designing, visualizing, debugging and validating distributed algorithms. It allows to create environmental scenarios such as gas, fires, mobiles, etc. To configure sensor nodes, CupCarbon offers a scripting language called SenScript. We implement our algorithm in CupCarbon. The nodes are placed randomly in the considered area. The different values for all the used parameters are mentioned in Table 2.

Table 2. Simulation settings

Parameter	Value
Area (m2)	40 m × 2.5 m
Number of nodes	from 10 to 100
Interface	Bluetooth
Range radius (m)	8

5.2 Simulation and Results

The most important goal of an emergency message broadcasting algorithm is to diffuse the message as often as possible and as soon as possible. The algorithm which has the highest delivery ratio in a short time is the most efficient one.

5.2.1 Evaluation of the Delivery Ratio

The delivery ratio is the most significant performance metric as it represents the ratio of nodes which receive the emergency message. In Fig. 4, we compare the delivery ratio of our algorithm with two other existing algorithms called ESS [20] and EpidemicX2 [13]. Each experiment runs for 50 times and the average value of these executions is reported. As illustrated in the figure, for all algorithms, the delivery ratio decreases when the number of network nodes increases. Nevertheless, the delivery ratio of our approach is bigger than the two competitive algorithms.

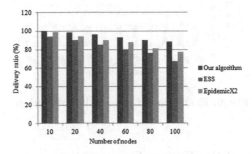

Fig. 4. Evaluation of the delivery ratio

5.2.2 Evaluation of the Delivery Time

We display in Fig. 5 the results obtained by the three algorithms when computing the average delivery time while increasing the number of nodes. The delivery time represents the time needed to send the message to persons. We can see that the

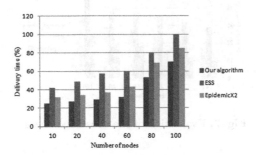

Fig. 5. Evaluation of the delivery time

result of our algorithm is significantly important compared to the others since it is based on the clustering mechanism that accelerates the communication between the nodes.

5.2.3   Evaluation of the Number of Clusters

In Fig. 6, we present the number of clusters during the simulation time. We assume that we have 80 nodes in the network. Initially, the number of clusters is 80 since each node represents a cluster formed by a single node. After that, the number of clusters gradually decreases by merging the clusters. Finally, the number of clusters converges between 18 and 22. As a result, our approach gives better performance in terms of cluster's stability.

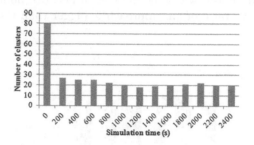

Fig. 6. Evaluation of the number of clusters

5.2.4   Evaluation of the Energy Consumption

Fig. 7 compares the percentage of the energy consumed by our proposed algorithm and the two existing algorithms while increasing the number of nodes. It can be observed that our algorithm consumes the least energy since it is based on clustering mechanism which reduces the communication between nodes.

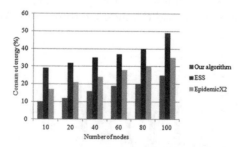

Fig. 7. Evaluation of the consumed energy

6   Conclusion and Future Work

In emergency situations, broadcasting alert messages is an essential task. Our proposed approach introduces a new algorithm that ensures the dissemination of emergency messages between pedestrians based on the clustering mechanism. This mechanism consists in computing the weight value for each node taking into consideration three metrics including the degree difference, residual battery power, and the distances between a node and all its neighbours. The election of the CH is based on the smallest weight value. Afterwards, the formation of clusters and the maintenance mechanism are performed. In order to avoid critical situations, the urgent messages will be transmitted to all the nodes in the network. To evaluate the efficiency of the proposed approach, we present a set of experiments with different simulation parameters.

In the future, we aim to formally verify our proposed algorithm using a formal method based on our previous works [23,24]. Also, it is interesting to use real pedestrian mobility datasets to illustrate the performance of our approach in real environments which are characterized by the inaccuracy of the estimated execution times and data. In addition, we intend to study the integration of this work in a Cloud-Fog environment which provides different types of resources and reduces unexpected delays and heavy communication.

References

1. Sharma, D., Bhondekar, A.P., Shukla, A., Ghanshyam, C.: A review on technological advancements in crowd management. Int. J. Ambient Intell. Humanized Comput. (JAIHC) 9(3), 485–495 (2018)
2. Liu, L., Chen, C., Qiu, T., Zhang, M., Li, S., Zhou, B.: A data dissemination scheme based on clustering and probabilistic broadcasting in VANETs. Veh. Commun. 13, 78–88 (2018)
3. Tian, D., et al.: A distributed position-based protocol for emergency messages broadcasting in vehicular ad HOC networks. IEEE Internet Things J. 5(2), 1218–1227 (2018)
4. Ramakrishnan, B., Selvi, M., Nishanth, R.B., Joe, M.M.: An emergency message broadcasting technique using transmission power based clustering algorithm for vehicular ad HOC network. Wireless Pers. Commun. 94(4), 3197–3216 (2017)
5. Naderi, M., Zargari, F., Ghanbari, M.: Adaptive Beacon broadcast in opportunistic routing for vanets. Int. J. Ad Hoc Netw. 86, 119–130 (2019)
6. Li, S., Liu, Y., Wang, J.: An efficient broadcast scheme for safety-related services in distributed TDMA-based VANETs. Int. J. IEEE Commun. Lett. 23, 1432–1436 (2019)
7. Tonguz, O., Wisitpongphan, N., Bait, F., Mudaliget, P., Sadekart, V.: Broadcasting in VANET. In: Proceeding of the Mobile Networking for Vehicular Environments, pp. 7–12. IEEE (2007)
8. Liu, Z., Liu, Z., Meng, Z., Yang, X., Pu, L., Zhang, L.: Implementation and performance measurement of a V2X communication system for vehicle and pedestrian safety. Int. J. Distrib. Sens. Netw. 12(9), (2016)
9. Eyobu, O.S., Joo, J., Han, D.S.: A broadcast scheme for vehicle-to-pedestrian safety message dissemination. Int. J. Distrib. Sens. Netw. 13(11), 1–19 (2017)

10. Wu, M., Ma, B., Liu, Z., Xiu, L., Zhang, L.: BLE-horn: a smartphone-based bluetooth low energy vehicle-to-pedestrian safety system. In: Proceeding of the 9th International Conference on Wireless Communications and Signal Processing (WCSP), pp. 1–6. IEEE (2017)
11. Higuchi, T., Yamaguchi, H., Higashino, T., Takai, M.: A neighbor collaboration mechanism for mobile crowd sensing in opportunistic networks. In: Proceeding of the IEEE International Conference on Communications (ICC), pp. 42–47. IEEE (2014)
12. Chen, Q., Wang, T., Cheng, L., Tao, Y., Gao, H.: Energy-efficient broadcast scheduling algorithm in duty-cycled multihop wireless networks. Int. J. Wireless Commun. Mobile Comput. (2019)
13. Chancay-García, L., Hernández-Orallo, E., Manzoni, P., Calafate, C.T., Cano, J.C.: Information dissemination using opportunistic networks in scenarios with people renewal. In: Proceeding of the 14th International Wireless Communications and Mobile Computing Conference (IWCMC), pp. 1351–1356. IEEE, 25–29 June 2018
14. Bhuiyan, M.M., Salim, S.M., Hasan, M.R.: Density aware broadcasting scheme for VANET. In: Proceeding of the 17th Asia-Pacific Conference on Communications (APCC), pp. 467–471. IEEE (2011)
15. Benkerdagh, S., Duvallet, C.: Cluster-based emergency message dissemination strategy for VANET using V2V communication. Int. J. Commun. Syste. **32**(5) (2019)
16. Jin, D., Shi, F., Song, J.: Cluster based emergency message dissemination scheme for vehicular ad HOC networks. In: Proceeding of the 9th International Conference on Ubiquitous Information Management and Communication (IMCOM). ACM (2015)
17. Cheng, X., Huang, B.: A center-based secure and stable clustering algorithm for VANETs on highways. Int. J. Wireless Commun. Mobile Comput. **2019**, 8415234:1–8415234:10 (2019)
18. Wahab, O.A., Otrok, H., Mourad, A.: VANET QoS-OLSR: Qos-based clustering protocol for vehicular ad hoc networks. Int. J. Comput. Commun. **36**(13), 1422–1435 (2013)
19. Otrok, H., Mourad, A., Robert, J.M., Moati, N., Sanadiki, H.: A cluster-based model for QoS-OLSR protocol. In: Proceeding of the 7th International Wireless Communications and Mobile Computing Conference (IWCMC), pp. 1099–1104. IEEE, 5–8 July 2011
20. Gorbil, G., Gelenbe, E.: Disruption tolerant communications for large scale emergency evacuation. In: Proceeding of the International Conference on Pervasive Computing and Communications Workshops (PERCOM), pp. 540–546. IEEE (2013)
21. Chatterjee, M., Das, S.K., Turgut, D.: WCA: a weighted clustering algorithm for mobile ad hoc networks. Int. J. Cluster Comput. **5**(2), 193–204 (2002)
22. Mehdi, K., Lounis, M., Bounceur, A., Kechadi, T.: CupCarbon: a multi-agent and discrete event wireless sensor network design and simulation tool. In: Proceeding of the 7th International Conference on Simulation Tools and Techniques (ICST), pp. 126–131 (2014)
23. Fakhfakh, F., Tounsi, M., Mosbah, M., Méry, D., Kacem, A.H.: Proving distributed coloring of forests in dynamic networks. Computación y Sistemas **21**(4) (2017)
24. Fakhfakh, F., Tounsi, M., Mosbah, M.: Formal modeling and verification of a distributed algorithm for constructing maximal cliques in static networks. Computación y Sistemas **23**(4) (2019)

Aspect Level Sentiment Analysis Using Bi-Directional LSTM Encoder with the Attention Mechanism

Win Lei Kay Khine[(✉)] and Nyein Thwet Thwet Aung[(✉)]

Faculty of Information Science, University of Information Technology, Yangon, Myanmar
`{winleikkhine,nyeinthwet}@uit.edu.mm`

Abstract. Aspect level sentiment analysis (ALSA) is a fine-grained task in sentiment analysis. It classifies the different polarities (positive, negative) for the specific aspects of each review. In general, document and sentence level sentiment analysis has achieved remarkable results, but they can't make the right prediction for the specific aspects in the given review. In the past few years, many researchers have worked sentiment analysis using machine learning approaches, but they have a problem in polarity detection for each aspect in the sentence. Therefore, this paper proposes to classify the sentiment polarity for each aspect by using Bi-directional LSTM (Bi-LSTM) encoder combining with the attention mechanism. The attention mechanism pays attention to the aspect of a specific target in the given review. It is a type of deep learning model and also an extension of the LSTM network, which can learn the long sequences of text. Deep learning models take a long time to train and when the network is deep, it encounters the vanishing gradient problem, a long-standing issue in the neural network model. This paper also considers the hyperparameter tuning approach to solve the vanishing gradient problem for ALSA task. Hyperparameter may be the weight, bias, the number of epochs, batch size, and so on. Experiments are conducted on IMDB and SemEval 2014 Task 4 datasets and the results show that the accuracy of our sentiment model reaches 88.5%, which is higher than other LSTM-based methods like standard AE-LSTM, AT-LSTM, standard LSTM, TC-LSTM, and TD-LSTM.

Keywords: Attention mechanism · Aspect Level Sentiment Analysis (ALSA) · Bi-directional LSTM (Bi-LSTM) encoder · Deep Learning (DL) · Recurrent Neural Network (RNN)

1 Introduction

Aspect level sentiment analysis (ALSA) is a essential task in sentiment classification and also a popular research topic in NLP. There are some issues in sentiment analysis like aspect extraction and polarity detection for each specific aspect in the review. There are two main tasks in aspect level sentiment analysis, they are aspect extraction and polarity detection.

In the past decades, many researchers are using machine learning for sentiment analysis which can provide complete and in-depth results. But, deep learning models

© Springer Nature Switzerland AG 2020
N. T. Nguyen et al. (Eds.): ICCCI 2020, LNAI 12496, pp. 279–292, 2020.
https://doi.org/10.1007/978-3-030-63007-2_22

are popular and implemented for AI application and it gains better performance than the traditional machine learning techniques. While the machine learning technique breaks down the problem into different parts at first and combines the results at the final stage, the deep learning technique solves the problem by using end to end approach. Machine learning considers not only for the feature extraction but also for classification method, but deep learning can learn the feature representation from the data without consideration feature engineering. As a consequence, deep learning methods reduce the processing steps than machine learning methods. One of the advantages of a deep learning algorithm is that if it trained well in the training time, then it takes much less time running in the testing time [13].

To classify the text in sentiment analysis, RNN models have difficulty in remembering the long sequences of text [11]. To overcome this issue, this paper presents a Bi-LSTM encoder with the attention mechanism between the aspect and context words. By using the attention mechanism, we can pay more attention to context words that are closer to the specific target aspect [2]. Using the attention model is to solve the problem of the ALSA task. The polarity of the sentence depends especially on aspect and if we didn't consider the aspect, the accuracy will not be correct. ALSA overcomes the limitations of the document and sentence levels when multiple aspects appear in one sentence. For example, a sentence, "Not only the food was great, but also the staff is very excellent". If we didn't consider the aspect, it is hard to determine the polarity of the given review because it says different polarities for aspects "food" and "staff" in one sentence. This problem always occurs in general sentiment analysis.

This paper aims to solve the problem of vanishing gradient. The vanishing gradient problem occurs when the gradient will be vanishingly small, it prevents the weight from changing the value. This may stop the neural network for further training. The solution to this problem is by using the Bi-LSTM neural network, which can learn long sequences but also the short-term. The main objectives are to predict the target aspect, classify the relevant sentiment polarity, and finally, compare the results with other LSTM methods by using the hyperparameter tuning approach.

The remainder of the paper is organized as follows: Sect. 2 discusses the related work of ALSA tasks using RNN-based methods like LSTM-based methods. Section 3 gives the system overview and Sect. 4 emphasizes the experiments, results, and evaluation. Finally, Sect. 5 finishes with the conclusion of the presented study.

2 Related Work

This section discusses the research works that are related to aspect level sentiment analysis using LSTM-based approaches. LSTM networks are generally used to tackle vanishing gradient problems when working with RNN. RNN models have challenges in a long sequence of data because they have a problem in carrying the information from earlier time steps to later ones. As a solution, LSTM helps to solve long term dependencies and can memorize previous data easily. In [1], the authors present the target-dependent LSTM approach for sentiment classification. They model the preceding and following contexts surrounding the target strings so that contexts in both directions could be used as feature representations for sentiment analysis. However, TD-LSTM is still not good enough because it does not capture the interactions between target words and their contexts. Based on its consideration, they develop a target-connection LSTM (TC-LSTM). The experiments are conducted on the Twitter benchmark dataset and compare the results with the adaptive recursive neural network, lexicon-enhance neural network, and feature-based SVM. The authors in [2] present an attention-based LSTM Network for aspect-level sentiment classification. The paper focuses on the contents and aspect words by using the LSTM network. For the embedding layer, they use Glove pre-trained word vectors with 300 hidden layers. Experiments are tested on Theano with the SemEval 2014 dataset. The results show the accuracy of their approaches AE-LSTM and ATAE-LSTM is higher than LSTM and TD-LSTM methods on three-way (3-class classification) and binary classification (Pos/Neg). Finally, they prove their attention mechanism works well on ALSA. The authors in [3] describe the SemEval 2016 task 5 on ABSA. It provides 39 datasets from 7 domains and 8 languages. The data are prepared in XML format. The participants in SemEval 2016 can choose the subtasks, languages, slots, and domains they want. It contains 3 subtasks: Subtask 1 (SB1), Subtask 2 (SB2), and Subtask 3 (SB3). SB1 is for sentence-level ABSA and it contains Slot1 (identifying aspect category), Slot2 (extraction opinion target expression - OTEs) and Slot3 (identified sentiment polarity). SB2 is text-level ABSA and its goal is to identify a set of {cat, pol} tuples and summarize the opinions of the review. SB3 is an out-of-domain ABSA in which the participants test their systems in the domain. The test data for SB3 were provided for the museums' domain in French. The evaluation shows with two phases: Phase A and Phase B. In the "Phase A", the participants returned the aspect categories (Slot1), (Slot2) and {Slot1, Slot2} tuples for SB1. For SB2, the respective text-level categories are identified. In the "Phase B", the annotation for the test sets of Phase A are provided. To evaluate sentiment polarity classification (Slot3) in Phase B, they use the accuracy measurement of each system. They trained with an SVM classifier for polarity detection. For the evaluation, Slot1 and Slot2 use F1 score measurement and Slot3 use the accuracy measurement. In [4], the authors present the creation of a new ABSA annotated dataset that is developed on the Foursquare[1] restaurant review. They annotate a new dataset from comments and the comments are about 215,000 user reviews during 2009–2018. In [5], the authors present an attention-based LSTM model, and experiments are tested on SemEval 2014, 2015, and 2016 datasets respectively, and explained with two novel approaches. The first approach is using target encoding to capture the semantics of the sentence and the second one is to construct a syntactic-based attention model that focuses on small subset words that are close to the target. Finally, the results show that the attention-based LSTM improves performance by incorporating two methods. The author in [9] describes bidirectional LSTM for emotional detection in textual conversations which is participated in SemEval-2019 Task 2 with the name "EmoContext". The result is measured with a micro-average F1 score and achieved 72.59% for emotional classes on the test dataset which is outperformed than the baseline methods. The authors in [10] discuss the ALSA with feature enhanced attention by using CNN and BiLSTM named FEA-NN. Instead of using aspect vectors to calculate the context attention, they use the combination model to enhance the feature extraction and semantic expression ability of the model. Using CNN is to extract the higher level of

---

[1] https://foursquare.com/toledonews/list/restaurant-reviews.

representation sequence from the embedding layer and BiLSTM is to capture the local feature, global feature, and sentence semantics. They evaluate their model on Twitter, Restaurant, and Laptop datasets and show the effectiveness of their FEA-NN model. They use improved word vector (IWV) [12] as the pre-trained word vector for sentiment analysis.

3 Methodology

This section explains the system overview including embedding layer, LSTM and Bidirectional LSTM Encoder layer, attention layer, and the case study for the aspect sentiment analysis will be presented.

3.1 Embedding Layer

Embedding layer is the basic layer in deep learning models. It captures the sentence and tokenizes into a sequence of words. After that, each word is mapped into a high-dimensional vector space through the embedding layer. In this paper, GloVe pre-trained word vector [6] and aspect vector is used for the word embedding layer. GloVe pre-trained vector is a fixed-length embedding vector for each word. Unlike word2vec, it relies not only on global statistics but also on local statistics. By using GloVe embedding, we can load the weights from this.

Firstly, the review data is passed to the embedding layer. A review may contain a sequence of sentences and a sentence consists of a sequence of words. For example, S $= \{w_1, w_2, ..., w_i, ..., w_n\}$ consists of an aspect, w_i in n sequence of words. And that, the input words are converted into corresponding word vectors $\{v_1, v_2, ..., v_i, ..., v_n\}$. The word vector for word embedding matrix, E_w is:

$$E_w \in \mathbb{R}^{d_v} \times |V| \tag{1}$$

where, d_v is the dimension of the word embedding vector and $|V|$ is the vocabulary size. For the embedding matrix, the paper uses 100-dimension and 300-dimension word embedding matrix.

3.2 Long Short-Term Memory

When we input a review for the sentiment classification, RNN may leave out some important information from the beginning. LSTM is used to solve the RNN problem like vanishing gradient and the challenges of a long sequence of data [8]. Standard LSTM has gates and these gates can learn which information is important to keep or throw away. They are forget gate (f_t), input gate (i_t), output gate (o_t), and cell states. Gates are the components of the neural network model and decide which information is allowed on the cell state. Cell state acts as the memory of the network and it multiplies the forget gate with the previous cell state and adds new information and produces the new cell state [8]. The illustration of LSTM architecture is shown in Fig. 1.

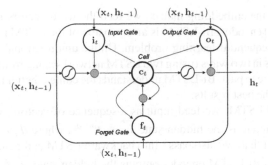

Fig. 1. General LSTM architecture.

The operations within the LSTM cell can be described as follows:

$$f_t = \sigma\left(W_f.[h_{t-1}, x_t] + b_f\right) \tag{2}$$

$$i_t = \sigma\left(W_i.[h_{t-1}, x_t] + b_i\right) \tag{3}$$

$$C_{t-1} = \tanh\left(W_C.[h_{t-1}, x_t] + b_C\right) \tag{4}$$

$$C_t = f_t \times C_{t-1} + i_t \times C_{t-1} \tag{5}$$

$$o_t = \sigma\left(W_o.[h_{t-1}, x_t] + b_o\right) \tag{6}$$

$$h_t = o_t \times \tanh(C_t) \tag{7}$$

where, C_{t-1} =memory cell of the previous block, C_t = memory cell from the current block, x_t = input vector, h_{t-1} = output of previous block, and h_t = output of current block. W is the weight matrices, b is bias vector and σ is denoted as the sigmoid function. Activation function *tanh* is used to calculate for the prediction. By combining all the mechanisms, the LSTM can choose which information is relevant to remember or forget during the processing. Firstly, the previous hidden state h_{t-1} and current input x_t are combined to form a vector. And then, the vectors are passed to the sigmoid activation function whereas the sigmoid produces the value between 0 and 1. Multiplying with the '0' becomes the value disappear or 'forget' and multiplying with '1' becomes the value stay the same or 'keep'.

3.3 Bi-directional LSTM Encoder

During the backpropagation, RNN suffers the vanishing gradient problem and it occurs when it back propagates through time. In RNN, layers that get a small gradient value can stop learning. To overcome this RNN problem, this paper uses the Bi-LSTM encoder for the solution of long and short-term sequences of text.

After creating the embedding matrix, we feed the word vectors into Bi-directional LSTM (Bi-LSTM) encoder. Bi-LSTM is an extension of the LSTM neural network and it is used for the sequential learning problem. Unlike unidirectional LSTM, Bi-LSTM manages the inputs in two ways (using two LSTM networks): one from past to future and the other from future to past. Bi-LSTM understands the context better than unidirectional LSTM and gives the best results.

In the forward LSTM, we feed input as a sequence of vectors, $s = [v_1, v_2,..., v_n]$ and it generates output as the hidden state $\overrightarrow{h_s} \in R^{n \times d_h}$, where d_h is the dimension of hidden states. After that, we also pass s into backward LSTM and generate another state sequence $\overleftarrow{h_s}$. Final Bi-LSTM encoder outputs the hidden state $\overrightarrow{h_s} \in R^{n \times 2d_h}$, where h_s is computed by concatenating $\overrightarrow{h_s}$ and $\overleftarrow{h_s}$.

$$h_{s=}\left[\overrightarrow{h_s} || \overleftarrow{h_s}\right]$$
(8)

In this model, we define 128 hidden layers in the Bi-LSTM layer. Bi-LSTM layer with 128 hidden neurons produces 128 features for the next layer. There is no rule on how many the number of hidden neurons should use. It depends on the training of the model and you can choose the best optimal size of your model. The following statement describes the Bi-LSTM layer creates a layer with 128 hidden layers.

```
model.add (Bidirectional (LSTM (128)))
```

The two output vectors (forward and backward) are concatenated and sent to the attention layer. The attention layer calculates the attention weight for the context words, after that, the output is passed to the dense layer for predicting the sentiment polarity. The Dense layer is also called Fully-connected (FC) layer which receives the neurons from the previous layer. In the experiment, we modify a dense layer with different neurons such as 128, 150, 300, 400, 500, 784, and 1000. Among them, 500 neurons give the best accuracy in the training and accurate result in the testing process. We can test with any number and choose the optimal size for our model. The number of neuron units is 500, then the output shape will be 500. Although the more hidden layers improve the accuracy, a dense layer with 500 neurons gives the best accuracy than 1000 neuron nodes in my model.

3.4   Attention Mechanism

In recent years, neural network models are getting more attention especially in sentiment classification. The attention mechanism is a way to capture the interactions between aspects and context words. The attention model addresses the limitations of encoder-decoder problems on long sequences. It does not focus on everything and focus only on specific aspects and polarity. So, it enables easier learning with high quality.

For example, the sentence: "I *like* this orange juice". In this sentence, the attention model focus on the sentiment polarity "*like*". This is the most important context in the sentence and it should have a larger weight than other context words. Output representation of the sequence encoding is attention weight such as $\alpha_1, \alpha_2, \alpha_3$, and so on. The attention layer combines all the attention weights for each context word w_i, where w_i is the right word to focus on when figuring out for the sentiment polarity of aspect. After that, the weight is calculated as a function of the hidden representation h_i of w_i and outputs all the products to the dense layer to do the sentiment classification. Finally, the

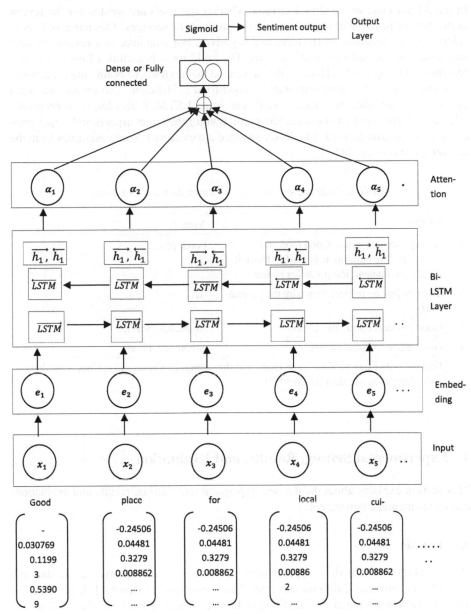

Fig. 2. Architecture for aspect level sentiment analysis using Bi-direction LSTM encoder with the attention mechanism.

output sentiment polarity is produced and the value may be a positive or negative value. The attention model with Bi-LSTM encoder for the ALSA task is shown in Fig. 2.

3.5 Case Study

In the ALSA task, we need to determine whether the users are written for the review as positive or negative or neutral on specific products or services. This paper only considers binary classification (positive and negative). For example, in a review "A very nice restaurant. Good food and delicious. The building is beautiful. I love it. I highly recommend Rangoon Tea House". When we read this review, our brain only remembers important words like "nice restaurant", "good food", "delicious", so on and we don't care much words like "a", "and", "The", etc. In an LSTM, it also learns to keep only relevant information to make sentiment prediction for the target aspects and forget irrelevant data. So, aspect words like food and place are extracted. Some examples from the test set are shown in Table 1.

Table 1. Example sentences of restaurant data and its aspects

	Sentences	Aspects
1	A very nice restaurant. Good food and delicious. The building is beautiful. I love it. I highly recommend Rangoon Tea House	Food, place
2	There is just no respect shown by the general staff	staff
3	Good ambience and fast service!	Ambience, Service
4	Good place for local cuisine	Ambience, Food
5	Burgers with extra pickles, onion rings, and the chocolate shake are the best ever!!!!:)	Burgers, Onion rings, Chocolate shake

4 Experimental Setting, Results, and Evaluation

This section explains about the dataset, hyperparameter tuning, results and evaluation, and experimental environment.

4.1 Dataset

Our neural sentiment model is applied on movie, restaurant, and laptop data. The datasets are collected from the IMDB movie review[2] and SemEval 2014 Task 4 [7]. The detailed datasets used in this paper are described in Table 2, which includes training, validation, and testing samples.

---

[2] https://www.kaggle.com/lakshmi25npathi/imdb-dataset-of-50k-movie-reviews.

Table 2. Datasets, its size, and the number of samples

Dataset	Data size	Training sample	Validation sample	Testing sample
IMDB movie review	50000	32000	8000	10000
Restaurant	4728	3608	–	1120
Laptop	2966	2328	–	638

4.2 Hyperparameter Tuning

For the experiments, we tune the training and testing dataset to (1) 80% and 20%, (2) 75% and 25%, and (3) 70% and 30% respectively on the datasets shown in Table 2. The authors in [7] classified the sentiment polarity on the same datasets using rule-based approach and machine learning approach (Support Vector Machines). Comparative results with our model are shown in Fig. 3. Firstly, we trained the embedding layer with 100 and 300 dimensional (whose size is about 840 billion) GloVe pre-trained word vector. In Table 3, we can see that the model is trained on 100-dimensional GloVe and use the Bi-LSTM network with different length of the input sentence. The result shows that trained with 150 words gives the highest accuracy. Therefore, we set the maximum length of the review size to 150 and if the review size is less than 150 words, we add '0' padding at the end of the review. Although training with 100-dimensional embedding performs pretty well and without taking too much time, but, 300 dimension GloVe gives the highest accuracy. The result is shown in Tables 3 and 4. We test on different hyperparameter such as embedding-dimension, batch size, epochs, optimizer, loss, and activation function on both LSTM and Bi-LSTM. The unique token size of the features are 92524 and the initial learning rate is set to 0.01 for Adam optimizer. Finally, we choose the best parameters for the sentiment model. The result shows that training with 128 batch size, 6 epochs, 128 hidden neurons, 300 high-dimensional embedding matrix on Bi-LSTM gives the highest accuracy for the aspect sentiment analysis. It needs around 1 h for training the whole model. But, it depends on parameter tuning.

The model is trained in an end-to-end backpropagation approach. The following statement describes for compiling the model. Accuracy is used for the measurement and the optimizer, loss, and activation function used are Adam, BCE (binary cross-entropy), and Sigmoid.

```
model.compile (optimizer = 'adam', loss = 'binary_crossentropy',
metrics = ['acc'])
```

4.3 Results and Evaluation

For the evaluation, we test on different LSTM and Bi-LSTM models and show the performance with the accuracy measurement. Firstly, we train the model with different lengths of words using Bi-LSTM on a 100 and 300-dimensional embedding matrix. After that, the result is compared with different LSTM-based methods. The result shows

Table 3. Hyperparameter tuning on 100-dimension embedding and Bi-LSTM with different lengths of the input sentence.

	Embed-dim	Max-len	Layer	Batch-Size	Epochs	Training-acc	Validating-acc	Testing-acc	Time
1	100	100	Bi-LSTM	128	6	87.21	84.84	83.87	4 min
2	100	150	Bi-LSTM	128	6	**89.55**	**87.65**	**87.93**	7 min
3	100	200	Bi-LSTM	128	6	87.39	87.28	87.09	9 min
4	100	250	Bi-LSTM	128	6	86.59	86.98	86.83	10 min
5	100	300	Bi-LSTM	128	6	89.37	87.11	87.18	15 min

Table 4. Hyperparameter tuning on 300-dimension embedding with Bi-LSTM encoder and the different sizes of the input sentence.

	Embed-dim	Max-len	Layer	Batch-Size	Epochs	Training-acc	Validating-acc	Testing-acc	Time
1	300	100	Bi-LSTM	128	6	89.26	86.84	86.87	5 min
2	300	150	Bi-LSTM	128	6	**90.71**	**88.65**	**88.50**	15 min
3	300	200	Bi-LSTM	128	6	87.39	87.78	87.09	10 min
4	300	250	Bi-LSTM	128	6	86.59	86.98	86.83	12 min
5	300	300	Bi-LSTM	128	6	89.37	88.11	88.18	29 min

Table 5. Accuracy of aspect level sentiment analysis on the IMDB dataset and SemEval 2014 task4 dataset (restaurant and laptop data).

	Models	Accuracy
1	LSTM	66.5
2	AE-LSTM	82.5
3	AT-LSTM	83.1
4	TC-LSTM	71.5
5	TD-LSTM	70.8
6	**Bi-LSTM-Att**	**88.5**

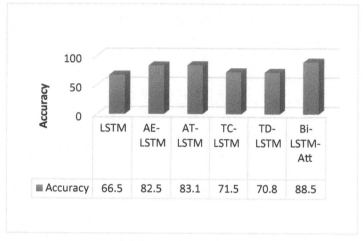

Fig. 3. Accuracy on different LSTM-based methods compared with attention Bi-LSTM encoder.

that Bi-LSTM gets 88.5% which is the highest accuracy among all LSTM models. It is shown in Table 5. We test all the methods on the same datasets. When we train the model, the training accuracy gets higher accuracy than the testing accuracy and it causes the overfitting problem. Because of overfitting, the model can't predict the right polarity. To overcome this problem, we train the model by adding many Bi-LSTM layers and tune the hyperparameter. Finally, the model can predict correctly and gets the best accuracy among all the networks. Overall accuracies for different models are shown in Fig. 3.

4.4   Experimental Environment

For the experimental setup, Keras framework 2.2.2 and Tensorflow 1.10.0 are used. Keras is a high-level neural network API and runs on top of Tensorflow, Theano, and CNTK. The model is developed using Python programming (Python version 3.7.4). All the implementations are tested on Google Colab which is a free cloud service. It provides free access to computing resources including GPUs.

5 Conclusions and Future Work

As a conclusion, this paper presents to develop a deep neural sentiment model for aspect level sentiment analysis using Bi-LSTM encoder combining with the attention mechanism. The result shows that adding attention mechanism to LSTM RNN is more robust and improve accuracy than other types of sentiment classification because the model focuses on the relationship between aspect target and its contexts. Aspect plays an important role in sentiment analysis. Therefore, this paper model on the ALSA task of the movie, restaurant, and laptop review. The goal is to classify the sentiment polarity for every detailed aspect of the target entity. Adding attention mechanisms generate a more accurate representation of the target aspect. Finally, experiments show that Bi-LSTM encoder using attention model and hyperparameter tuning approach gets higher accuracy than baselines models like TD-LSTM, TC-LSTM, AE-LSTM, and ATAE-LSTM. As future works, we plan to build the model on our language, Myanmar Language, and show the best performance on ALSA task by using automatic hyperparameter tuning, instead of manual hyperparameter tuning.

Acknowledgments. We thank anonymous reviewers for their valuable comments and suggestions. We would like to show our gratitude to the rector and course supervisor of the University of Information Technology (UIT), Yangon, Myanmar for submitting this paper.

References

1. Tang, D., Qin, B., Feng, X., Liu, T.: Effective LSTMs for target-dependent sentiment classification. In: Proceedings of COLING 2016, the 26th International Conference on Computational Linguistics, 11–17 December 2016, Osaka, Japan, pp. 3298–3307 (2016)
2. Wang, Y., Huang, M., Zhao, L., Zhu, X.: Attention-based LSTM for aspect-level sentiment classification. In: Proceedings of the 2016 Conference on Empirical Methods in Natural Language Processing, 1–5 November 2016, Austin, Texas, pp. 606–615 (2016)
3. Pontiki, M., et al.: SemEval-2016 task 5: aspect based sentiment analysis. In: Proceedings of SemEval-2016, 2016 Association for Computational Linguistics, 16–17 June 2016, San Diego, California, pp. 19–30 (2016)
4. Burn, C., Nikoulina, V.: Aspect based sentiment analysis into the wild. In: Proceedings of the 9th Workshop on Computational Approaches to Subjectivity, Sentiment and Social Media Analysis, Brussels, 2018 Association for Computational Linguistics, Belgium, pp. 116–122, 31 October 2018
5. He, R., Lee, W.S., Ng, H.T., Dahlmeier, D.: Effective attention modeling for aspect-level sentiment classification. In: Proceedings of the 27th International Conference on Computational Linguistics, 20–26 August 2018, Santa Fe, New Mexico, USA, pp. 1121–1131 (2018)
6. Pennington, J., Socher, R., Manning, C.: GloVe: global vectors for word representation. In: Proceedings of the 2014 Conference on Empirical Methods in Natural Language Processing (EMNLP), pp. 1532–1543 (2014)
7. Wagner, J., et al.: DCU: aspect-based polarity classification for SemEval task 4 (2014). In: Proceedings of the 8th International Workshop on Semantic Evaluation (SemEval 2014), 23–24 August 2014, Dublin, Ireland, pp. 223–229 (2014)
8. Hochreiter, S., Schmidhuber, J.: Long short-term memory. Neural Comput. **9**(8), 1735–1780 (1997)

9. Smetanin, S.: EmoSense at SemEval-2019 task 3: bidirectional LSTM network for contextual emotion detection in textual conversations. In: Proceedings of the 13th International Workshop on Semantic Evaluation (SemEval-2019), 2019 Association for Computational Linguistics, Minneapolis, Minnesota, USA, pp. 210–214, 6–7 June 2019

10. Meng, W., Wei, Y., Liu, P., hu, Z., Yin, H.: Aspect based sentiment analysis with feature enhanced attention CNN-BiLSTM. IEEE Access **7**, 167240–167249 (2019)

11. Dieng, A.B., Wang, C., Gao, J., Paisley, J.: TopicRNN: a recurrent neural network with long-range semantic dependency. In: ICLR (2017)

12. Rezaeinia, S.M., Rahmani, R., Ghodsi, A., Veisi, H.: Sentiment analysis based on improved pre-trained word embeddings. Expert Syst. Appl. **117**, 139–147 (2019)

13. Mahapatra, S.: Why deep learning over traditional machine learning? (2018). https://toward sdatascience.com/why-deep-learning-is-needed-over-traditional-machine-learning-1b6a99 177063

Predicting National Basketball Association Players Performance and Popularity: A Data Mining Approach

Nguyen Nguyen$^{(\boxtimes)}$, Bingkun Ma$^{(\boxtimes)}$, and Jiang Hu$^{(\boxtimes)}$

Texas Tech University, Lubbock, TX 79409, USA
{Nguyen-Hoang.Nguyen,bingkun.ma,jiang.hu}@ttu.edu

Abstract. Basketball is known for the vast amounts of statistics that are collected for each player, team, game, and season. As a result, basketball is an ideal domain to work on different data analysis techniques to gain useful insights. In this study, we reviewed some important factors to predict players' future performance and being selected in an All-Star game, one of most prestigious events, of National Basket Association league. Our result showed gradient boosting machine is more qualified to predict NBA players' future performance, and balanced undersampling random forest has better predictive ability compared to other algorithms for All-Star prediction. Cross Industry Standard Process for Data Mining (CRISP-DM) methodology is chosen as backbone of the project to tackle this data mining problem and provide a systematic process.

Keywords: Data mining · CRISP-DM · Imbalanced data · Machine learning

1 Introduction

This study focuses on National Basketball Association (NBA) league, which is one of the most popular leagues in America and the most well-known basketball league over the world. The most important goal of our study is to use individual data of each player to predict their -future performance and the popularity, so contributing to improve NBA-related decision making e.g. recruitment process. Through predicting players' future performance, team management and sport agency would negotiate and determine the most suitable compensation (salaries, bonus, image/name revenue ...) in players' contracts, which constitutes more than 50% of teams' expenditure [1].

For our second goal of forecasting players' popularity, the study paid attention on making the prediction if NBA players are chosen to play in NBA All-Star game in next season. NBA All-star game is an annual exhibition event hosted by NBA in February which 24 NBA star players are divided into 2 teams to compete other. The procedure to choose players participating in NBA All-star games involves a voting poll from fans, which has a vigorous influence on selection outcome. Thus, "Being selected in NBA All-star roster" is a good indicator for us to evaluate players' public popularity. In contrast to the effect of player's performance on the court, the benefit of player's popularity is

© Springer Nature Switzerland AG 2020
N. T. Nguyen et al. (Eds.): ICCCI 2020, LNAI 12496, pp. 293–304, 2020.
https://doi.org/10.1007/978-3-030-63007-2_23

not clear to recognize, so we would like to summarize briefly two essential aspects in perspective of business value creation from popular players.

First of all, popular or star players can have a significant contribution to their franchises' brands among the teams in league [2]. Athletes possessing strong on-field performance have a better ability to establish their star player's attributes into a realized equity for a team's brand, thus raising the awareness for a team, getting the public attention and assisting in reaching the new market.

Moreover, through different economic models, star players are proved to generate externalities that increase attendance and other revenue sources beyond their individual contributions to team success [3, 4]. In other words, they can not only lead their own teams to win games, but also attract more fans and gain public attention to increase overall league's business revenue and media coverage, even for their opponents'. The historical data showed the superstar effect on the economy throughout different eras.

With the rapid development of data science in recent years, Machine learning (ML) and Data mining (DM) have been applied in various fields. As a result of this movement, Sport Analytics, a field that ML methods and its implementations are used to gain the useful insights from sport data [5], has been emerging as one of the favorable areas for both business and academic research. As Sport Analytics has become more prominent and attainable, sport teams, coaches, players and companies are more likely to use its applications to improve their performance and operation on- and off-the court [6]. Among sports, there have been many academic studies and systematic frameworks developed in basketball domain using ML and DM techniques for long-term strategy, daily operation and prediction in professional leagues or college/high school [7–9].

CRISP-DM reference model is used as the structured guidance for this study to construct ML models. The greatest benefit of this methodology is to provide a common model for communication and document that help to connect different tools and people with a variety of skills and backgrounds to progress an efficient and effective project [10]. As a typical CRISP-DM model, our data mining study is divided into 6 phases: (1) Business understanding: understanding the issue from business perspective to define data mining goal and preliminary project plan; (2) Data understanding: collecting the data, learning data characteristics, data quality issues; (3) Data preparation: data cleaning and manipulation for modeling; (4) Modeling: several modeling algorithms are trained to choose the most qualified one; (5) Evaluation: based on the predetermined objectives, criteria and metrics, models are appraised; (6) Deployment: direction to deploy the ML model into production.

Our study concentrated mostly on first five steps with details while the final phase provides some limitations and recommendations for further improvement.

2 Business Understanding

2.1 Business Objectives

As indicated in Introduction part, the most important purpose of our study is to promote and advance models which can be used to forecast the NBA players' future performance and if they would be selected for NBA All-Star rosters. Based on these two purposes, three aiming objectives are detailed. First objective is to identify and provide insightful information about key factors affecting on the performance and popularity of NBA players. Secondly, it aims to improve team's success on- and off- the court through recruiting more qualified players in the future by predictive models. In addition, predictive models can also support the final objective of boosting business revenue for different stakeholders as NBA teams and sport sponsors would take advantage e.g. balancing between how much to pay and what can get from: brand reputation index, sales of tickets, subscribers, merchandises… or NBA current players, potential players or sport agencies can use the models as reference to understand the mechanisms behind the future performance and popularity to boost their competency of gaining more attention, enhancing playing style and advancing their earnings.

2.2 Data Mining Objectives

Based on the above business objectives, there are two data mining objectives for our study: (1) Predicting the players' Win Share (WS) score based on the previous regular season's statistics; and (2) Predicting players into All-star and non-All-star based on previous regular season's statistics. For the first objective, a new terminology *WS* is introduced to be used as Target variable for our regression model. *WS* is defined as a player statistic which attempts to summarize credit for team success to the individuals on the team.

Some popular evaluation metrics in ML field were selected to assess and compare our ML algorithms: (1) Root Mean Squared Error (RMSE) and Mean Absolute Error (MAE) for the first objective's regression models; (2) Accuracy, Precision, Recall, Receiver operating characteristic area under curve (ROC AUC) and F1 scores for the second objective's classification models.

3 Data Understanding

3.1 Data Sources

The first dataset is NBA players' stats since 1950 from Kaggle repository (https://www.kaggle.com/drgilermo/nba-players-stats), which was originally collected and published from website basketball-reference.com. There are originally 24,691 observations with 51 variables from Season 1949–1950 to 2016–2017. Since there are many unavailable and inconsistent data for variables, which were planned for being used in ML modeling development phase, in the past seasons, this study only considered data from Season 1982–1983 to Season 2016–2017 with 14,617 observations and 30 variables including players' personal information (name - *Player*, position on the court - *Pos*, team, season's year - *Year*) and their basketball KPIs in each season they played, which can be divided into 2 categories: "cumulative" variables: number of games played (*G*), total minutes played (*MP*), total points (PTS), field goals (*FG*), 2 points (*2P*), 3 points (*3P*), free throws (*FT*),… and its "percentage" variables: percentage of 2 points made on total attempts in given season (*%2P*), percentage of 3 points (*%3P*), percentage of field goals (*%FG*),… The dataset also includes our target variable for the first objective – *WS*.

The second dataset is from website basketball.realgm.com archiving all NBA All-star rosters in each year and it was merged with the first dataset in the Data Preparation step based on two mutual variables: year and players' names to find out if player was chosen to play in All-star games with total of 899 selected players from 1984-2018. As a result, the target variable – *AllStar*, for the second objective was created as binary variable coded as 1 if selected for NBA All-star roster in the following season and 0 if not.

3.2 Data Summary

Considering predictor variables, "cumulative" variables (*2P*, *3P*, *FG*, ...) are right skewed as some superior players had exceptional statistics compared to the majority. In contrast, variable for number of games played in given season is left skewed. "Percentage" variables (*2P%*, *3P%*, *FG%*, ...) are normally distributed and it is noteworthy that all missing values are from "percentage" variables.

In term of response variables, the variable *WS* is right skewed. Observing the variable for the second objective – *AllStar*, there is an issue with imbalanced data. After merging 2 datasets and removing outliers, there are 859 All-Star players compared to 13319 non-All-Star players, so the percentage of All-Star players is only 6%. Technically, imbalanced data exhibits an unequal distribution between its classes, or one class severely out-represents another, particularly between-class in this case [11], so dealing with imbalanced data was also one crucial challenge for this study. Two potential solutions were proposed to solve this problem: under-sampling and over-sampling techniques. Moreover, as our priority is to detect potential "All-Star" players, two metrics: ROC AUC and Recall scores, are our primary options for model evaluation and these metrics are also less sensitive than Accuracy metric to assess models trained by imbalanced data.

4   Data Preparation

The first step for data preparation was to merge the above first and second datasets so the target variable *AllStar* would be created. As there was no missing value and a unique combination, two variables: *Year* and *Player*, were used as primary and foreign keys among datasets. *Player* had to be standardized as "First name – Last name" format and any specialized symbol attached was removed.

The reason for missing values in "percentage" variables is that there was no attempt or success from players, so we assumed that no attempt was similar to no success and missing values for these variables were imputed by zero-value.

As we planned to use *Pos* (position) variable for our models, *Pos* were converted into 5 dummy variables for all on-court positions: *PG* (Point Guard), *SG* (Shooting Guard), *SF* (Small Forward), *PF* (Power Forward) and *C* (Center).

Our first objective is to predict the *WS* next year, so *WS* values had to be lagged back to the previous year and players' final career season's records were removed, resulting to number of observations at 11,959. *PTS*, *FT*, *FG* and *2P* have high correlations with *WS* and there are also high correlations between these variables, so we decided to keep *PTS* and removed *FT*, *FG* and *2P* because *PTS* has the highest correlation with *WS*. Dummy features for positions have low correlations with *WS*, so these were removed from our regression models. *Age* and *ORB%* were also discarded with low correlations. The variable *TOV* was not used instead *TOV%* was chosen as we believed it is more accurate to describe relationship between *WS* and "turnover" factor. In conclusion, there are 19 predictor variables used in our first objective's regression model: *G, MP, PTS, FG%, 2P%, 3P, 3P%, FT%, AST, AST%, BLK, BLK%, DRB, DRB%, ORB, STL, STL%, TOV%* and *PF*. For the purpose of our first objective, the original dataset was firstly partitioned into training-test sets with the ratio of 80–20. Then, our training set was divided again into train-valid sets with the ratio of 80–20. The train set was used to train the model with cross-validation technique. Then, train-valid sets were used to evaluate models under the potential overfitting condition. Test set would be used for our Evaluation phase to estimate how effective our final model is when they are used for unseen data. To eliminate the case when players' data in some periods of time were sampled into train/valid/test sets unevenly, stratified sampling technique was adopted, using Year ratio.

The train-valid-test splitting process was also used for our second objective. As mentioned in Data Summary section, one issue with the original data is class imbalance which can affect the model evaluation and performance, so two popular solutions: over-sampling and under-sampling, were applied for this study, which aims to ease the effect of imbalanced data distribution on learning process [12–14]. Beside random over-sampling, synthetic minority oversampling technique (SMOTE) was also used for over-sampling purpose, which is widely adopted in many applications for different domains e.g. network intrusion detection [15], breast cancer detection [16], or biotechnology [17]. Its methodology is to create new minority class examples through randomly choosing one (or more depending on the defined over-sampling ratio) of the k nearest neighbors (kNN) of a minority class instance and then generation of the new instance values from a random interpolation of both instances [18], so it would help to reduce the potential effect of over-fitting from random over-sampling. Another popular sampling technique used for our study is under-sampling, which targets to balance class distribution through the random elimination of majority class instances and is proved in many studies to out-perform SMOTE or random over-sampling in most situations for both low- and high-dimensional data [19–21].

5   Modeling

5.1   Objective 1

To select the best model for our first objective - *WS*, first six candidate models were trained with the train data using 10-fold cross-validation (CV). Then, all models were compared by its results on train and valid datasets, so we could find the most fitted model under different scenarios. RMSE and MAE are two metrics used for evaluation as mentioned in the Sect. 2.2.

Regression model types: Linear Regression (linear_model), Gradient Boosting Machine (gradient_boosting), Linear Support Vector Machine (linear_svm), Polynomial (Non-Linear) Support Vector Machine (poly_svm), Random Forest (random_forest), and Neural Net (neural_net); were used as the first candidate models. As shown in Fig. 1, using 10-fold cross-validation on train set, 3 models with the best results for RMSE and

MAE are: gradient_boosting, neural_net and poly_svm with lower means or ranges of their result distributions. The MAE's means of 3 best models range from 1.53 to 1.62 and they are around 2.12 to 2.15 for RMSE's means while the range of MAE is [1.47, 1.70] and [2, 2.27] for RMSE.

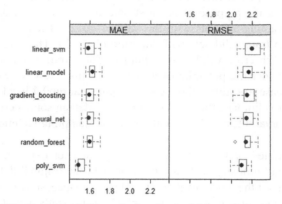

Fig. 1. Distributions of CV results for six candidate models on train data

Then, our 7 candidate models were evaluated on valid data. As shown in Fig. 2, gradient_boosting, neural_net and poly_svm are still the best three algorithms. However, neural_net and poly_svm results were worse in term of RMSE metric compared to its medians from CV on train data. On the other hand, gradient_boosting keeps a steady outcome with only small increases, 0.02 for RMSE and 0.01 for MAE.

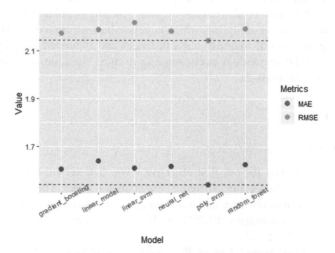

Fig. 2. MAE and RMSE results on valid dataset

In conclusion, we decided to use Gradient Boosting Machine as our final model because of the following three reasons: (1) Gradient Boosting Machine has decent and stable results with both train and valid data with small change of RMSE and MAE. (2) The differences between Gradient Boosting Machine and top performing models (usually Polynomial Support Vector Machines) at MAE and RMSE are small which is acceptable for our data mining's first objective. (3) Gradient Boosting Machine is less subjective to overfitting and performs much faster compared to Polynomial Support Vector Machines and Neural Net.

For model tuning, manual grid search was used with 135 combinations based on following four parameters: (1) Learning rate: [0.01, 0.1, 0.3]; (2) Depth of trees: [1–5]; (3) Minimum number of observations in the terminal nodes of the trees: [5, 10, 15]; (4) Subsampling: [0.65, 0.8, 1]. Model was tuned by all train and valid datasets with CV of 5 to find the optimal number of trees with maximum of 1000, and RMSE was used as primary metric. With lowest RMSE of 2.1467, these parameters: (1) learning rate = 0.1, (2) depth of trees = 4, (3) minimum number of observations = 15, (4) subsampling = 0.8, and the optimal number of trees of 358; were used to train our final regression model.

5.2 Objective 2

Firstly, popular ML classifiers: logistic regression (LG), Stochastic gradient descent (SGD), linear or polynomial support vector machine (LSVM or PSVM), random forest (RF) and Naïve Bayes (NB), were trained with both random and SMOTE over-sampling cases and were compared by Recall and ROC AUC scores. Two representative boosting algorithms: AdaBoost (AB) and Gradient Boosting Machine (GBM) were also employed for comparison. Boosting is constructed on the methodology of repeatedly a given weak learning algorithm on various distributions over the training data, and then combining the classifiers produced by the weak learner into a single composite classifier [22], which would benefit learning minority class through assigning weighted voting to outputs for each learner in the final prediction model to focus more on hard examples [23, 24].

As under-sampling technique has a drawback of potentially removing the useful information [18], under-sampling methodology was applied for two bragging-related algorithms: balanced bragging classifier (BB) and balanced random forest classifier (BRF). The core concept of these techniques is to use *bootstrap aggregating* [25] to construct ensembles where a classification tree is induced by draw a bootstrap sample from the minority class and same number of randomized drawn cases, with replacement, from the majority class [26]. Some research showed the effort of artificially balancing the classes provides some improving effective with respect to a given performance measurement for tree classifier and under-sampling seems to have advantage over over-sampling [21, 27, 28]. Besides, under-sampling boosting algorithm (BU) was also involved in our comparison.

The results of applying 5-fold CV on random and SMOTE over-sampling train data are shown on Table 1. Among over-sampling algorithms, RF classifier had exceptional outcomes compared to others with nearly perfect recall scores for both random and SMOTE over-sampling data and ROC AUC scores at 0.990 and 0.964 respectively, followed by GBM classifiers with recall and ROC AUC scores at around 0.94–0.97.

RF and GBM algorithms were then trained by two cases: random and SMOTE over-sampling, and made predictions on valid data, so we would compare their best results to under-sampling algorithms trained by original train data.

Table 1. Cross validation results on random-, SMOTE over-sampling and under-sampling

	Random over-sampling				SMOTE over-sampling			
	Precision	Recall	ROC AUC	F1	Precision	Recall	ROC AUC	F1
LG	0.892	0.920	0.900	0.910	0.900	0.936	0.918	0.916
SGD	0.890	0.910	0.900	0.900	0.883	0.951	0.913	0.916
LSVM	0.880	0.930	0.904	0.910	0.890	0.948	0.916	0.918
PSVM	0.885	0.930	0.904	0.907	0.901	0.954	0.924	0.927
RF	0.980	1.000	0.990	0.990	0.959	0.981	0.964	0.970
NB	0.806	0.910	0.845	0.855	0.810	0.921	0.852	0.862
AB	0.905	0.918	0.911	0.911	0.910	0.932	0.920	0.921
GBM	0.918	0.970	0.942	0.943	0.926	0.959	0.941	0.942

As shown in Table 2, with our priority to focus on capturing players selected for All-Star rosters through Recall and ROC AUC scores, Balanced Random Forest was chosen for the second objective with highest Recall and ROC AUC scores of 0.9 and 0.8855 in the order given.

Table 2. Results on valid data

	Valid data			
	Precision	Recall	ROC AUC	F1
RF	0.4881	0.6308	0.7953	0.5503
GBM	0.3518	0.8308	0.8689	0.4943
BB	0.3652	0.8231	0.868	0.5059
BRF	0.2977	0.9000	0.8855	0.4474
RU	0.2418	0.2846	0.6152	0.2615

Similar to our first objective, the second objective's classification model was also tuned on with CV of 5, primary metrics as Recall and ROC AUC and 1760 combinations for 4 parameters: (1) Max number of levels in each decision tree: [10, 20, 30, 40, 50, 60, 70, 80, 90, 100, 110]; (2) Min number of data points allowed in a leaf node: [2–5]; (3) Min number of data points placed in a node before the node is split: [6, 8, 10, 12]; (4) Number of trees in forest: [100, 200, 300, 400, 500, 600, 700, 800, 900, 1000] with default bootstrap. With highest Recall score of 0.9153 and ROC AUC score of 0.8914, these parameters: (1) max depth = 10, (2) min samples leaf = 4, (3) min samples split = 8, (4) number of trees = 700, were used to train our final model.

6 Evaluation

6.1 Objective 1

Final regression model was evaluated on test dataset (20% of the original data) and had results of 2.1969 for RMSE and 1.6465 for MAE. Compared to its RMSE on train-valid data, its RMSE result on test dataset is just over within 3% which can be considered satisfactory.

Observing Fig. 3 - Top 10 relative features of our regression model, *PTS* is the most important feature with the relative influence of 51.56 while the second one – *DRB* – defensive rebound, has only 9.78. It was a little surprised that there is not any 3-point variable in top 10 even it can be seen that 3-point play is really popular in NBA games nowadays when almost every team and player reply heavily on 3-point scoring. It can be explained that our analysis used many players' statistics in the past seasons while 3-point playing tactic has been only extremely popular for recently 10 years. Moreover, games are still dependent heavily on 2-point successful attempts as the ratio of total 2-point successful attempts on total 3-point successful attempts is at 3.63 from season 2012–2013 to season 2016–2017.

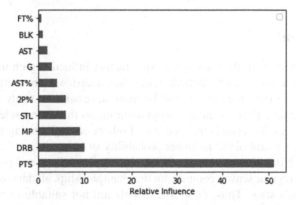

Fig. 3. Top 10 relative features for final regression model

6.2 Objective 2

Classification model was also appraised on test dataset and resulted at Recall score of 0.9657 and ROC AUC score of 0.9096, which is better than our expectation. This shows that balanced under-sampling random forest is suited for our second objective to capture NBA players with high potential to be selected for All-Star events. However, this also has one disadvantage of low Precision score of 0.3023, which may be needed to assess as economic factor if model is evaluated for production.

Based on Fig. 4 of Top 10 relative features of our classification model, it is surprised that the most relative feature is number of successful free throws *FT* at 0.21. This can be justified that best players from each team are more likely to be get fouled by other teams. *PTS* continues to be an important feature with relative influence of 0.19. Total minutes played – *MP*, has critical role in both objectives' models with relative influences ranking at third for both cases.

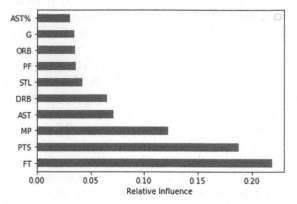

Fig. 4. Top 10 relative features for final classification model

7 Deployment

As a team-oriented sport, there are some other factors influencing on the players' performance and popularity: team's tactical style, coach decision, team chemistry…, which are not included in our study and would be more accessible to study to improve the models in the future. There is an additional assumption that being selected to play in All-star event for each season is independent of others or participating in previous All-star games does not contribute to higher probability of being selected to play in latter ones. Although NBA season includes 2 periods: regular season and playoff when the best 16 teams in regular season compete for the championship, all data used in our study is regular season's stats. Thus, these ML models are not suitable to predict players' performance in playoff and the effect of prior playoff performance on players' popularity is also overlooked in this study. Popularity is also affected by external non-sporting factors e.g. celebrity status in media, charisma, social media…than the pure quality of the game [29]. As these factors are perceived distinctively by public in term of time and geography, it is a complicated issue and further research is needed.

8 Conclusion

This study aims to provide a CRISP-DM approach to sport analytics and show the benefits that machine learning would bring to the evolution of sports and sport-related business.

CRISP-DM methodology provides a clear guidance to understand issues in both business and data mining perspectives, and to tackle problem with machine learning algorithms. Machine learning can give many advantages to sport teams and sport-related business e.g. marketing, betting, etc. with its proficient ability to predict the future outcomes, which can be seen through our study's results: RMSE of 2.1969 and MAE of 1.6465 for regression model, Recall of 0.9657 and ROC AUC of 0.9096 for classification model. Our study also confirms the importance of scoring ability in basketball for both on- and off-the court. One interesting topic mentioned in this study is imbalanced data, which has been popular in data mining field. Our result is consistent with many prior studies proving the better capability of under-sampling technique compared to over-sampling. Because our study used intensively pure basketball statistics for models, it possibly neglects the critical influence of external factors on popularity. Thus, it is suggested further studies in this domain with more external variables which would improve the predictive ability and provide more comprehensive understanding about the degree of importance of different factors.

References

1. Sport Illustrated Homepage. https://www.si.com/nba/2018/09/21/nba-teams-revenue-spe nding-breakdown-small-large-market. Accessed 1 Aug 2019
2. Pifer, N., Mak, J., Bae, W.-Y., Zhang, J.: Examining the relationship between star player characteristics and brand equity in professional sport teams. Mark. Manage. J. **25**, 88–106 (2015)
3. Humphreys, B.R., Johnson, C.: The effect of superstars on game attendance: evidence from the NBA. J. Sports Econ. **21**(2), 152–175 (2020). https://doi.org/10.1177/1527002519885441
4. Berri, D.J., Schmidt, M.B.: On the road with the national basketball association's superstar externality. J. Sports Econ. **7**(4), 347–358 (2006). https://doi.org/10.1177/1527002505275094
5. Apostolou, K., Tjortjis, C.: Sports Analytics algorithms for performance prediction. In: 2019 10th International Conference on Information, Intelligence, Systems and Applications (IISA), Patras, Greece, pp. 1–4 (2019). https://doi.org/10.1109/iisa.2019.8900754
6. Tichy, W.: Changing the Game: Dr. Dave Schrader (2016)
7. Thabtah, F., Zhang, L., Abdelhamid, N.: NBA game result prediction using feature analysis and machine learning. Ann. Data Sci. **6**(1), 103–116 (2019). https://doi.org/10.1007/s40745-018-00189-x
8. Miljković, D., Gajić, L., Kovačević, A., Konjović, Z.: The use of data mining for basketball matches outcomes prediction. In: IEEE 8th International Symposium on Intelligent Systems and Informatics, Subotica, pp. 309–312 (2010). https://doi.org/10.1109/sisy.2010.5647440
9. Zuccolotto, P., Manisera, M., Sandri, M.: Big data analytics for modeling scoring probability in basketball: the effect of shooting under high-pressure conditions. Int. J. Sports Sci. Coaching **13**(4), 569–589 (2018). https://doi.org/10.1177/1747954117737492
10. Wirth, R., Hipp, J.: CRISP-DM: towards a standard process model for data mining. In: Proceedings of the 4th International Conference on the Practical Applications of Knowledge Discovery and Data Mining, pp. 29–39. CiteSeer (2000)
11. He, H., Garcia, E.A.: Learning from imbalanced data. IEEE Trans. Knowl. Data Eng. **21**(9), 1263–1284 (2009). https://doi.org/10.1109/TKDE.2008.239
12. Batista, G.E.A.P.A., Prati, R.C., Monard, M.C.: A study of the behavior of several methods for balancing machine learning training data. SIGKDD Expl. Newslett. **6**, 20–29 (2004)

13. Chawla, N.V., Bowyer, K.W., Hall, L.O., Kegelmeyer, W.P.: SMOTE: synthetic minority over-sampling technique. J. Artif. Intell. Res. **16**, 321–357 (2002)
14. Chawla, N.V., Japkowicz, N., Kolcz, A. (eds.): Special issue learning imbalanced datasets. SIGKDD Explor. Newsl. **6**(1), 1–6 (2004)
15. Cieslak, D.A., Chawla, N.W., Striegel, A.: Combating imbalance in network intrusion datasets. Proceedings of IEEE International Conference on Granular Computing, Atlanta, Georgia, USA, pp. 732–737 (2006)
16. Fallahi, A., Jafari, S.: An expert system for detection of breast cancer using data preprocessing and bayesian network. Int J Adv Sci Technol. **34**, 65–70 (2011)
17. Batuwita, R., Palade, V.: microPred: effective classification of pre-miRNAs for human miRNA gene prediction. Bioinformatics **25**(8), 989–995 (2009). https://doi.org/10.1093/bioinform atics/btp107
18. Galar, M., Fernandez, A., Barrenechea, E., Bustince, H., Herrera, F.: A review on ensembles for the class imbalance problem: bagging-, boosting-, and hybrid-based approaches. IEEE Trans. Syst. Man, Cybern. Part C (Appl. Rev.) **42**(4), 463–484 (2011)
19. Hulse, J.V., Khoshgoftaar, T.M., Napolitano, A.: Experimental perspectives on learning from imbalanced data. In: Proceedings of the 24th International Conference on Machine Learning, Oregon State University, Corvallis, Oregon, pp. 935–942 (2007)
20. Blagus, R., Lusa, L.: SMOTE for high-dimensional class-imbalanced data. BMC Bioinform. **14**, 106 (2013). https://doi.org/10.1186/1471-2105-14-106
21. Drummond, C., Holte, R.C.: C4. 5, class imbalance, and cost sensitivity: why under-sampling beats over-sampling. In: Workshop on Learning from Imbalanced Datasets II, Washington DC, vol. 11. CiteSeer (2003)
22. Freund, Y., Schapire, R.E.: Experiments with a new boosting algorithm. In: ICML, vol. 96 (1996)
23. Schwenk, H., Bengio, Y.: AdaBoosting neural networks: application to on-line character recognition. In: Gerstner, W., Germond, A., Hasler, M., Nicoud, J.-D. (eds.) ICANN 1997. LNCS, vol. 1327, pp. 967–972. Springer, Heidelberg (1997). https://doi.org/10.1007/BFb002 0278
24. Guo, H., Viktor, H.L.: Learning from imbalanced data sets with boosting and data generation: the databoost-im approach. ACM SIGKDD Explor. Newsl. **6**(1), 30–39 (2004)
25. Breiman, L.: Bagging predictors. Mach. Learn. **24**, 123–140 (1996)
26. Chen, C., Liaw, A., Breiman, L.: Using random forest to learn imbalanced data. University of California, Berkeley, vol. 110, pp. 1–12 (2004)
27. Ling, C.X., Li, C.: Data mining for direct marketing: problems and solutions. In: KDD, pp. 73–79 (1998)
28. Kubat, M., Matwin, S.: Addressing the curse of imbalanced data sets: one-sided sampling. In: Proceedings of the 14th International Conference on Machine Learning, pp. 179–186. Morgan Kaufmann (1997)
29. Adler, M.: Stardom and Talent. Am. Econ. Rev. **75**(1), 208–212 (1985)

Efficient Method for Mining High-Utility Itemsets Using High-Average Utility Measure

Loan T. T. Nguyen[1,2], Trinh D. D. Nguyen[3], Anh Nguyen[4], Phuoc-Nghia Tran[5], Cuong Trinh[6], Bao Huynh[7], and Bay Vo[7(✉)]

[1] School of Computer Science and Engineering, International University,
Ho Chi Minh City, Vietnam
nttloan@hcmiu.edu.vn
[2] Vietnam National University,
Ho Chi Minh City, Vietnam
[3] Department of Information Technology, HCM Pre-University School, Ho Chi Minh City,
Vietnam
dzutrinh@hcmpreu.edu.vn
[4] Faculty of Computer Science and Management, Wroclaw University
of Science and Technology, Wroclaw, Poland
anh.nguyen@pwr.edu.pl
[5] Bac Lieu University, Bac Lieu, Vietnam
tpn_blu@yahoo.com.vn
[6] Artificial Intelligence Laboratory, Faculty of Information Technology,
Ton Duc Thang University, Ho Chi Minh City, Viet Nam
trinhphicuong@tdtu.edu.vn
[7] Faculty of Information Technology, Ho Chi Minh City University
of Technology (HUTECH), Ho Chi Minh City, Vietnam
{hq.bao,vd.bay}@hutech.edu.vn

Abstract. Mining high-utility itemsets (HUIs) based on high-average utility measure is an important task in the data mining field. However, many of the existing algorithms are performing the mining process sequentially and do not utilize the widely available multi-core processors, thus requiring long execution times. To address this issue, we propose an extended version of the HAUI-Miner algorithm, namely pHAUI-Miner. The algorithm applies multi-thread parallel processing to significantly reduce the mining time. Experimental evaluations on standard databases have shown the effectiveness of the proposed algorithm over the original and sequential method.

Keywords: High-average utility itemset · Data mining · Parallel computing · Multi-thread

1 Introduction

To discover the associations and the relations among the items within a transactional database, frequent itemset mining (FIM) [1] methods were applied. Companies have

© Springer Nature Switzerland AG 2020
N. T. Nguyen et al. (Eds.): ICCCI 2020, LNAI 12496, pp. 305–315, 2020.
https://doi.org/10.1007/978-3-030-63007-2_24

incorporated FIM onto their available databases to boost the executive performance. The analysis of the transactions helps put forth effective strategies in their business, such as catalog designing, marketing, customer behavior's analysis or basket analysis. FIM analyzes the customer's shopping habit, and then discover the associations among the items that were selected by the customer. Retailers use the discovered knowledge to develop effective strategies to boost their sales.

Some algorithms to perform this task are Apriori [1], AprioriTid [1], Eclat [2], FP-Growth [3], etc. Of them, the FP-Growth only requires two database scans to construct the FP-tree and directly extracts frequent itemsets from the tree. Thus, discovering the complete set of frequent itemsets (FIs). FIM only considers the existence of the items within transactions and treats all items equally. It completely ignores other important information such as the purchase quantity of items, item's profit, etc. In real-word applications, every item has its own value (unit profit), and in most cases, frequent patterns might not be the ones that yield high profit, or the usefulness to the users. Briefly, the generated profit of an item when purchased, called utility, is the product of the purchase quantity and its unit profit. Patterns or itemsets that generate high profit and satisfy a user-specified threshold are called high-utility patterns (HUPs) or itemsets (HUIs).

In HUIM, utility of an item or itemset is the sum of its utility in the database. This traditional utility calculation has a major drawback: it ignores the length of the itemset and thus the longest itemsets has higher utility value. Thus, it is not fair when applying this utility calculation on to all itemsets. To address this drawback, a new utility measure, called average utility (au) measure [4], was proposed to better assess the utility of itemsets. It is defined as the sum of the utilities of the itemset in transactions that contain it, divided by its length or the number of items in that itemset. If an itemset has its au value no less than a user-specified threshold, called the minimum average utility threshold ($minAU$), then it's called high-average utility itemset (HAUI). However, the downward closure property does not hold for this new utility measure. An itemset whose au value does not satisfy the threshold may be combined with one or more items to form a HAUI. This might generate a large number of candidates and the process of checking all the generated candidates is time consuming. A new upper-bound was proposed to address this issue and called average utility upper-bound ($auub$). Lan et al. has applied this new upper-bound to prune candidates [5, 6]. Lan et al. also proposed new index-table structure to speed up the mining process [7].

The rest of the paper is organized as follows: Sect. 2 surveys related works on HUIs and average utility itemsets mining. Section 3 describes definitions and propose methods on average utility itemsets mining. Experimental results will be showed in Sect. 4. Finally, Sect. 5 presents conclusion and future improvements.

2 Related Work

Extending from FIM, the task of mining the complete set of HUIs is called high-utility itemset mining (HUIM). The problem of mining HUIs was first proposed in Yao et al. 2004 [8]. The authors presented the concepts of utility and high-utility measure. HUIM is considered a challenging task since the utility measure does not satisfies the downward closure property [1], which original states in FIM that all subsets of a frequent itemset must also be frequent. In 2005, Liu et al. presented an algorithm to mine HUIs in two phases [9], namely Two-Phase. In the first phase, the algorithm computes the downward closure on utility of itemsets in transactions to prune the search space. This novel upper-bounds on utility is called Transaction Weighted Utility (TWU). Second phase scans the database again to calculate the exact utility value of itemsets to determine which one is HUI. However, TWU is not tight enough to effectively prune the search space, leaving a huge number of candidates for the algorithms to check. Thus, to reduce further the generated candidates and database scans, Lin et al. proposed a tree structure, called HUP-tree [10], to effectively mine HUIs. It first calculates the utility values for 1-itemsets and uses them to construct the HUP-tree. Then the algorithm recursively traverses the tree to extract HUIs based on a header table. The algorithm requires only two database scans to discover the complete set of HUIs in a database. In 2016, Zida et al. proposed a single phase for effectively mining HUIs, namely EFIM [11]. The algorithm using new and tighter upper-bounds to prune a large number of candidates, thus significantly reduce the mining time. To achieve better performance and to utilize the full power of the modern processors, Nguyen et al. has proposed a parallel version of EFIM, named pEFIM [12]. The algorithm partitions the search space in to separated sub-spaces and assigned each execution thread to a sub-space, thus dramatically reduce time needed to mine HUIs.

Lan et al. proposed an algorithm which incorporated index-table and the average utility upper-bound (*aub*) to mine HAUIs in 2012 [7]. The algorithm presented an effective pruning strategy using indices to reduce the execution time and memory consumption. Lin et al. proposed a single phase algorithm to efficiently mine HAUIs, named HAUI-Miner [13]. Also in 2016, Lu et al. proposed an algorithm and a tree structured, named HAUI-tree to quickly generate candidates and mine HAUIs [14]. The algorithm consists of two steps: (i) calculates the utility values of 1-itemsets in transactions to identify the maximum utility value for each transaction, then calculates the *aub* for each item. (ii) From the list of all 1-itemsets that satisfied the threshold, construct the list of 2-itemsets using the downward closure property based on the HAUI-tree. The process repeats until no new candidates generated. To mine HAUIs using multiple *minAU* thresholds, Lin et al. proposed the algorithm HAUIM-MMAU with two pruning strategies, known as the improved EUCP strategy (IEUCP) and Prune Before Calculation strategy (PBCS) [15]. However, the HAUIM-MMAU uses the generate-and-test approach, which is time consuming. In 2018, Lin et al. proposed another algorithm named MEMU [16] and three pruning strategies to increase the performance of the mining process. Experiments show MEMU has better performance compare to HAUIM-MMAU in terms of runtime, memory usage, candidates and scalability.

3   Proposed Algorithm

This section presents preliminary concepts and problem statement. Many of the definitions and theorems were given in detail and proved in [13].

3.1 Preliminaries

Let $\mathcal{I} = \{i_1, i_2, \ldots, i_m\}$ is the finite set of m distinct items. A transaction database $\mathcal{D}$ is a set of transactions $\mathcal{D} = \{T_1, T_2, \ldots, T_n\}$. In which, each transaction $T_q \in \mathcal{D}$ and $T_q \subseteq \mathcal{I}$ $(1 \leq q \leq n)$. Each transaction T_q has a unique identifier q, called its *TID*.

Definition 1. The utility of an item i_j in a transaction T_q is the product of its purchase quantity and its unit profit, denoted as $u(i_j, T_q)$ [13].

$$u(i_j, T_q) = q(i_j, T_q) \times p(i_j) \tag{1}$$

Whereas, $q(i_j, T_q)$ is the purchase quantity of item i_j in transaction T_q; positive integer $p(i_j)$ is the unit profit of item i_j, which is given in the unit profit table $\mathcal{PT}$.

Given set of k distinct items $X = \{i_1, i_2, \ldots, i_k\}$, $X \subseteq \mathcal{I}$ and is called k-itemset where k is the length of X, $k = |X|$.

Definition 2. The average utility of a k-itemset X in a transaction T_q, denoted as $au(X, T_q)$, is defined as follows [13].

$$au(X, T_q) = \frac{\sum_{i_j \in X \wedge X \subseteq T_q} q(i_j, T_q) \times p(i_j)}{k} \tag{2}$$

When $k = 1$, X becomes a single item $i_j \in \mathcal{I}$, and thus the average utility of this 1-itemset in transaction T_q can be calculated as follows [13].

$$au(i_j, T_q) = \frac{q(i_j, T_q) \times p(i_j)}{1} = u(i_j, T_q) \tag{3}$$

Definition 3. Average utility of itemset X in database $\mathcal{D}$, denoted as $au(X)$, is defined as follows [13].

$$au(X) = \sum_{X \subseteq T_q \wedge T_q \in \mathcal{D}} au(X, T_q) \tag{4}$$

Definition 4. Utility of transaction T_q, denoted as $tu(T_q)$, is defined as follows [13].

$$tu(T_q) = \sum_{i_j \in T_q} u(i_j, T_q) \tag{5}$$

Definition 5. Total utility of database $\mathcal{D}$, denoted as TU, and is defined as follows [13].

$$TU = \sum_{T_q \in \mathcal{D}} tu(T_q) \tag{6}$$

Definition 6. The transaction-maximum utility of transaction T_q, denoted as $tmu(T_q)$, is defined as follows. [13].

$$tmu(T_q) = \max\{u(i_j, T_q) | i_j \in T_q\} \tag{7}$$

Definition 7. Average-utility upper-bound of an itemset X, denoted as $auub(X)$, is the sum of all the transaction-maximum utilities of transactions containing X [13].

$$auub(X) = \sum_{X \subseteq T_q \wedge T_q \in \mathcal{D}} tmu(T_q) \tag{8}$$

Definition 8. An itemset X is called a high average-utility upper-bound itemset, denoted as $HAUUBI(X)$, if its average-utility upper-bound is no less than $minAU$. $HAUUBI(X)$ is defined as follows [13].

$$HAUUBI(X) = \{X \mid auub(X) \geq TU \times minAU\} \tag{9}$$

Theorem 1. The $auub$ measure is downward closed. The transaction-maximum-utility downward closure ($TMUDC$) property holds for any $HAUUBIs$ [13].

The proof of this theorem is given in detail in [13]. From Theorem 1, we have two corollaries as follows:

Corollary 1. Given a k-itemset X^k, if X^k is a $HAUUBI$, then all subsets of X^k are also $HAUUBIs$.

Corollary 2. If an itemset X^k is not a HAUUBI, then all supersets of X^k are not $HAUUBIs$.

Theorem 2. The $TMUDC$ property ensures that $HAUUBIs \subseteq HAUIs$. Thus, if an itemset is not a $HAUUBI$, then none of its supersets are HAUIs. If an itemset is not a $HAUUBI$, it is also not a HAUI [13].

By using Theorem 2, we can prune a large number of unpromising candidates from the search space and thus, reduce the mining time.

3.2 Problem Statement

Given a user-specified minimum average-utility threshold ($minAU$), $minAU$ is a positive integer. The problem of mining high-average utility itemsets in database $\mathcal{D}$ is the task of discovering the complete set of HAUIs. An itemset X is a HAUI if and only if its utility is no less than $minAU$. The problem can be defined as follows.

$$HAUIs = \{X \mid au(X) \geq TU \times minAU\} \tag{10}$$

3.3 The Revised Database

The original algorithm HAUI-Miner [13] requires two database scans. The first scan discovers the set of high average-utility upper-bound 1-itemsets (1-$HAUUBIs$). The second scan constructs the average-utility list (AU-list) of 1-itemsets. In this second scan, all 1-itemsets that are non-HAUUBIs will be removed from the database. The database obtained after removing all these non-HAUUBIs is called revised database $\mathcal{D}'$. The pseudo-code of the construction of $\mathcal{D}'$ (**InitRevisedDatabase**) is given in Algorithm 1.

3.4 The Average-Utility List (AU-List) Structure

The AU-list of an item or an itemset X is a list of elements, such that each element represents a transaction $T_q \in \mathcal{D}'$ and $X \subseteq T_q$. Each element consists of three fields, as follows:

- The *tid* field indicates the transaction T_q.
- The *iu* field indicates the utility of X in T_q, $u(X, T_q)$.
- The *tmu* field indicates the transaction-maximum-utility of X in T_q, $tmu(X, T_q)$.

To construct the AU-list for k-itemset with $k \geq 2$, it is not necessary to rescan the database. They can be constructed by intersecting the AU-list of smaller itemsets. By using the AU-list, the search space of the whole algorithm can be modelled as a set-enumeration tree. In which, each node represents an itemset. The HAUI-Miner explores the tree using depth-first search and prune the unpromising child nodes early using Theorem 3. This can be done by using the sum of *iu* and *tmu* field in the designed AU-list.

Algorithm 1. The construction of $\mathcal{D}'$ and obtain 1-*HAUUBIs*

```
Input:    transaction database D, minAU threshold
Output:   D' and set of all 1-HAUUBIs, total utility TU.
1: for each transaction T_q ∈ D do
2:     scan T_q to calculate tmu(T_q) and TU.
3: for each item i ∈ D do
4:     calculate auub(i)
5: 1-HAUUBIs ← { i | auub(i) ≥ TU × minAU}
6: scan D to remove each item i such that i ∉ 1-HAUUBIs and
   obtain D'.
7: for each T_q ∈ D' do
8:     sort T_q in ascending order < of auub(i).
9: return D', 1-HAUUBIs, TU.
```

Algorithm 2. AU-list construction

```
Input: AU-list of itemset P, P_x, P_y: P.AUL, P_x.AUL, P_y.AUL
Output: AU-list of itemset P_xy: P_xy.AUL
1: P_xy.AUL ← null
2: for each E_x ∈ P_x.AUL do
3:     if ∃E_y ∈ P_y.AUL ∧ E_x.tid = E_y.tid then
4:         if P.AUL = null then
5:             E_xy ← ⟨E_x.tid, E_x.u + E_y.u, E_y.tmu⟩
6:         else
7:             if exists E ∈ P.AUL such that E.tid = E_x.tid then
8:                 E_xy ← ⟨E_x.tid, E_x.u + E_y.u, E_y.tmu⟩
9:     P_xy.AUL ∪ E_xy
10: return P_xy
```

Algorithm 3. DFS-based search space exploration algorithm

```
Input:   AU-list of itemset P: P.AUL, list of AU-list of all
         P's 1-extension: AULs, minAU threshold, TU of D
Output:  all HAUI with prefix P
```
1: **for each** $Y.AUL \in AULs$ **do**
2:   **if** $\frac{SUM.Y.iu}{|Y.AUL|} \geq minAU \times TU$ **then**
3:     $HAUIs \leftarrow HAUIs \cup Y$
4:   **if** $SUM.Y.tmu \geq minAU \times TU$ **then**
5:     $extAULs \leftarrow null$
6:     **for each** $Z.AUL$ after $Y.AUL, Z.AUL \in AULs$ **do**
7:       $extAULs \leftarrow extAULs \cup \textbf{Construct}(P.AUL, Y.AUL, Z.AUL)$
8:       $\textbf{Search}(Y.AUL, extAULs, minAU, TU)$

Theorem 3. Given an itemset X, if the sum of it's *tmu* in all transactions containing X, using the AU-list, is less than *minAU*, all extensions of X are not HAUIs [13].

The pseudo-code of the AU-list construction (**Construct**) is given in Algorithm 2, the pseudo-code of the DFS based search process (**Search**) is given in Algorithm 3.

Algorithm 4. The pHAUI-Miner algorithm

```
Input:  transaction database D, minAU threshold.
Output: D' and set of all 1-HAUUBIs.
```
1: $D', 1\text{-}HAUUBIs, TU \leftarrow \textbf{Init}(D, minAU)$
2: **for each** $T_q \in D'$ **do**
3:   sort T_q in ascending order $<$ of $auub(i)$.
4: **for each** item $i \in 1\text{-}HAUUBIs$ **do parallel**
5:   scan D' to construct $AULs$ containing AU-list of all
     1-extensions of i
6:   $\textbf{Search}(i.AUL, AULs, minAU, TU)$

3.5 The PHAUI-Miner Algorithm

The original algorithm HAUI-Miner, obtained from the SPMF open-source package [17], perform several database scans when processing each item in the set of all 1-*HAUUBIs*, which is not efficient. To relieve the algorithm from this bottleneck, parallel processing should be considered. Modern processors are now containing multiple cores to handle many tasks simultaneously. To speed-up the process of mining HAUIs, increase the response time and to utilize widely available multi-core processors, we apply multi-thread parallel processing into this phase. The load balance strategy used in our proposed algorithm is Task Parallelism. In detail, we partition the search space into separated sub-search spaces and assign to them a DFS-based search thread using divide and conquer strategy. Each thread in turn will recursively explore down its sub-search space in parallel. Consider the search space of the algorithm as shown in Fig. 1, the search space is partitioned at the level of all items contained in the 1-*HAUUBIs*. Thus, significantly reduce the time needed to discover the complete set of HAUIs.

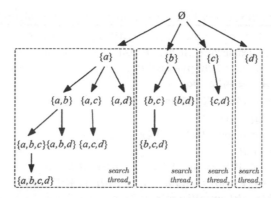

Fig. 1. Partition search space of the pHAUI-Miner algorithm

The pseudo-code of the Algorithms 1 to 3 remains unchanged as in the sequential version. We incorporated them in to a parallel version and name it pHAUI-Miner, whose pseudo-code is shown in Algorithm 4. In which, the parallel processing of each item in the 1-*HAUUBIs* is given from line #4 to #6. Each call of the **Search** function in line #6 operates in its own sub-search space with respect to an item *i*.

4 Experimental Studies

This section presents the experiments of the proposed algorithm on the standard databases to evaluate its performance and effectiveness. All the experiments were conducted on a workstation equipped with an Intel® Xeon® E5-2678 v3 processor (12-core/24-thread) clocked at 2.5 Ghz, 32 GB DDR4 ECC of internal memory and running Windows 10 Pro Workstation. All the algorithms used in the experiments were developed using the Java programming language (JDK8). The HAUI-Miner source code can be obtained from the SPMF package [17].

The databases used in the experiments are standard databases which are used in many data mining researches [17], and can be downloaded at https://bit.ly/2vixvH0. Their characteristics are given in Table 1.

Table 1. Database characteristics

Database	#Transactions	#Items
Mushroom	8,124	119
Retail	88,163	16,470
Kosarak	990,003	41,270
Chainstore	1,112,949	46,086

We compare the runtime of the proposed algorithm, pHAUI-Miner, using 4 threads and 24 threads against the original and sequential algorithm HAUI-Miner on all the test databases. Runtime comparison on the *Mushroom, Retail, Kosarak* and *Chainstore* database are given from Fig. 2a *to* Fig. 2d, respectively. Furthermore, the average speed-up factors of the pHAUI-Miner algorithm over the original HAUI-Miner algorithm on all the databases are also provided in Fig. 3.

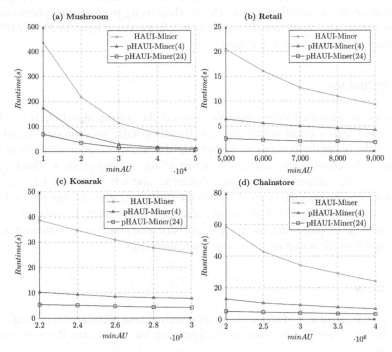

Fig. 2. Runtime comparisons on four databases for various *minAU* thresholds

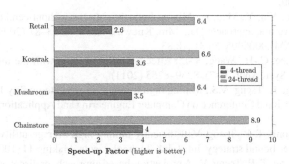

Fig. 3. Average speed-up factor on all test databases

It can be seen in Fig. 2 that the parallel versions pHAUI-Miner dominate all the tests. With the speed-up factor using 4 threads is up to 4 times faster, and with 24 threads, the factor is over 6 to 8 times faster. It can be observed from Fig. 3 that by using 4 threads on the test system, the speed-up factor is the most ideal since the speed-up factor is up to 4 times, while using 24 threads, the speed-up factor is only over 8 times. Considering

4 threads, the highest factor is observed on the *Chainstore* database, the largest one, and the lowest factor is on the *Retail* database. There are several factors that could affect the speed-up when using more processing cores. First, it can be seen in line #5 of Algorithm 4 each thread performs a full scan of the revised database $\mathcal{D}'$, thus using more processing threads would cause excessive scans on $\mathcal{D}'$ and reduce the effectiveness of the algorithm. Next, to discover the complete set of HAUIs while using parallelism, synchronization between threads is required to maintain the processing order of items in the 1-*HAUUBIs*, thus increased the overhead of the algorithm.

5 Conclusions

In this work, we identified and analyzed the issues of the original algorithm HAUI-Miner when mining high-average utility itemsets. Based on this, we proposed an extended version of the original algorithm, named pHAUI-Miner, which address all these issues to improve the effectiveness and performance of the mining process. The proposed algorithm handles effectively all the test databases and has much better performance in terms of runtime than the original one. In the future, we want to improve further the algorithm to further reduce cost of database scans; apply new utility calculations to make it work on dynamic profits databases; applied distributed computing framework such as Apache Spark to allow mining from large-scale databases.

References

1. Agrawal, R., Srikant, R.: Fast algorithms for mining association rules in large databases. In: Proceedings of the 20th International Conference on Very Large Data Bases, pp. 487–499 (1994)
2. Zaki, M.: Scalable algorithms for association mining. IEEE Trans. Knowl. Data Eng. **12**(3), 372–390 (2000)
3. Han, J., Pei, J., Yin, Y., Mao, R.: Mining frequent patterns without candidate generation: a frequent-pattern tree approach. Data Min. Knowl. Disc. **8**(1), 53–87 (2004). https://doi.org/10.1023/B:DAMI.0000005258.31418.83
4. Hong, T.-P., Lee, C.-H., Wang, S.-L.: Effective utility mining with the measure of average utility. Expert Syst. Appl. **38**(7), 8259–8265 (2011)
5. Lan, G., Hong, T., Tseng, V.S.: Mining high transaction-weighted utility Itemsets. In: 2010 Second International Conference on Computer Engineering and Applications, vol. 1, pp. 314–318 (2010)
6. Lan, G.-C., Hong, T.-P., Tseng, V.: Efficiently mining high average-utility itemsets with an improved upper-bound strategy. Int. J. Inf. Technol. Decis. Making **11**, 1009–1030 (2012)
7. Lan, G.-C., Hong, T.-P., Tseng, V.: A projection-based approach for discovering high average-utility itemsets. J. Inf. Sci. Eng. **28**, 193–209 (2012)
8. Yao, H., Hamilton, H., Butz, C.: A foundational approach to mining itemset utilities from databases. In: Proceedings of the Fourth SIAM International Conference on Data Mining, vol. 4, pp. 22–24 (2004)
9. Liu, Y., Liao, W., Choudhary, A.: A two-phase algorithm for fast discovery of high utility itemsets. In: Proceedings of the 9th Pacific-Asia Conference on Advances in Knowledge Discovery and Data Mining, pp. 689–695 (2005)

10. Lin, C.-W., Hong, T.-P., Lu, W.-H.: An effective tree structure for mining high utility itemsets. Expert Syst. Appl. **38**(6), 7419–7424 (2011)
11. Zida, S., Fournier-Viger, P., Lin, J.C.-W., Wu, C.-W., Tseng, V.S.: EFIM: a fast and memory efficient algorithm for high-utility itemset mining. Knowl. Inf. Syst. **51**(2), 595–625 (2016). https://doi.org/10.1007/s10115-016-0986-0
12. Nguyen, T.D.D., Nguyen, L.T.T., Vo, B.: A parallel algorithm for mining high utility itemsets. In: Świątek, J., Borzemski, L., Wilimowska, Z. (eds.) ISAT 2018. AISC, vol. 853, pp. 286–295. Springer, Cham (2019). https://doi.org/10.1007/978-3-319-99996-8_26
13. Lin, J.C.-W., Li, T., Fournier-Viger, P., Hong, T.-P., Zhan, J., Voznak, M.: An efficient algorithm to mine high average-utility itemsets. Adv. Eng. Inform. **30**(2), 233–243 (2016)
14. Lu, T., Vo, B., Nguyen, H., Hong, T.-P.: A new method for mining high average utility itemsets. In: Computer Information Systems and Industrial Management, pp. 33–42 (2014)
15. Lin, J.C.-W., Li, T., Fournier-Viger, P., Hong, T.-P., Su, J.-H.: Efficient mining of high average-utility itemsets with multiple minimum thresholds. In: Advances in Data Mining. Applications and Theoretical Aspects, pp. 14–28 (2016)
16. Lin, J.C.-W., Ren, S., Fournier-Viger, P.: MEMU: more efficient algorithm to mine high average-utility patterns with multiple minimum average-utility thresholds. IEEE Access **6**, 7593–7609 (2018)
17. Fournier-Viger, P., Gomariz, A., Gueniche, T., Soltani, A., Wu, C.-W., Tseng, V.S.: SPMF: a Java open-source pattern mining library. J. Mach. Learn. Res. **15**(1), 3389–3393 (2014)

Efficient Method for Mining Maximal Inter-transaction Patterns

Thanh-Ngo Nguyen[1], Loan Thi Thuy Nguyen[2,3], Bay Vo[4(✉)], and Adrianna Kozierkiewicz[1]

[1] Department of Applied Informatics, Faculty of Computer Science and Management, Wroclaw University of Science and Technology, Wrocław, Poland
{thanh-ngo.nguyen,AdriannaKozierkiewicz}@pwr.edu.pl
[2] School of Computer Science and Engineering, International University, Ho Chi Minh City, Vietnam
nttloan@hcmiu.edu.vn
[3] Vietnam National University, Ho Chi Minh City, Vietnam
[4] Faculty of Information Technology, Ho Chi Minh City University of Technology (HUTECH), Ho Chi Minh City, Vietnam
vd.bay@hutech.edu.vn

Abstract. Frequent Maximal Pattern (FMP) mining is an interesting topic in data mining. So far, many algorithms have been proposed for mining frequent maximal patterns of items occurring within transactions, but there is no method for mining FMPs across transactions in the database. In this study, we propose an efficient algorithm, namely tMITP-Miner, for mining frequent maximal inter-transaction patterns (FMITPs). The proposed method uses tidset to store the information of patterns for efficient mining FMITPs. Besides, we also proposed effective pruning strategies help reducing the search space to speed up the runtime and to cut down the memory usage. Experiments have been conducted to compare the effectiveness between the tMITP-Miner and the post-processing method in terms of runtime and memory usage.

Keywords: Pattern mining · Inter-transaction pattern mining · Maximal itemset mining · Frequent maximal inter-transaction pattern mining

1 Introduction

Frequent pattern mining (FPM) is one of the essential tasks of data mining. Since Agrawal et al. presented the Apriori [1] method for mining FPs, many algorithms have been proposed to mine frequent patterns (FPs) from large databases, such as Eclat [2], dEclat [3], FP-Growth [4], FP-Growth* [5], etc. Moreover, many algorithms have also been proposed for mining various patterns, among them are some typical mining algorithm groups such as MEFIM and iMEFIM [6], HMiner-Closed [7], dHAUIM [8], HAUP-growth [9] for mining high-utility patterns, DBV-Miner [10] and NFWI [11] for frequent weighted itemset mining.

© Springer Nature Switzerland AG 2020
N. T. Nguyen et al. (Eds.): ICCCI 2020, LNAI 12496, pp. 316–327, 2020.
https://doi.org/10.1007/978-3-030-63007-2_25

In addition, association rule mining (ARM) from a very large number of FPs would generate a lot of redundant association rules, which will make us harder to predict and make decisions. To solve this problem, condensed representations are used to not only reduce the overall size of frequent patterns collection but also obtain non-redundant association rules. The two main types of condensed representation are maximal frequent patterns (FMPs) [12] and frequent closed patterns (FCPs) [13]. Although a set of FMPs is a subset of FPs, it still has necessary properties for generating essential association rules that helps significantly reduce search space, computation time, and memory usage. So far, many methods have been proposed for mining FMPs, consisting of MaxMiner [14], DepthProject [14], GenMax [12], dGenMax [12], MAFIA [15], TDM-MFI [16], INLA-MFP [17].

However, most of the previous studies only consider FPM of items occurring within transactions of database (Frequent Intra-Transaction Patterns, FIaTPs) and can only predict rules like *R1*. One of the major drawbacks of the FIaTP approaches is that they do not take into account FPM of items occurring across several different transactions in the database (Frequent Inter-Transaction Patterns, FITPs), so they cannot predict rules like *R2*, which is generated from FITPs.

R1: *If a customer purchases a smartphone, a phone case is usually purchased with it.*
R2: *If a customer purchases a smartphone, the customer will be able to purchase a phone battery one year later.*

In this study, we propose an efficient algorithm for mining FMITPs, called tMITP-Miner. Our proposed algorithm has the following main contributions. We apply our proposed theorem that helps fast pruning infrequent 1-patterns. Then, tMITP-Miner algorithm applies the theorem to reduce the search space in order to quickly find all FITPs at the 1-pattern level with their tidsets. Next, the proposed algorithm uses DFS (Depth First Search) traversing to generate all FMITPs with their tidset. Finally, experiments are conducted to prove the effectiveness between dMITP-Miner and post-processing method in terms of runtime and memory usage.

The remainder of this article is organized into 4 sections. Section 2 describes basic concepts and relevant works. Section 3 discusses the proposed algorithm (tMITP-Miner) for mining FMITPs. Experimental results are presented in Sect. 4. Section 5 concludes the paper and shows future works.

2   Basic Concepts and Related Works

A transaction database (*TDB*) is defined as follows. A *TDB* consists of n transactions, $T = \{T_1, T_2, ..., T_n\}$, in which each transaction is defined as a subset of a set of distinct items, $I = \{i_1, i_2, ..., i_m\}$, where m is the number of items. A *tidset* is a subset of a set of transaction identifiers (*tid*) of *TDB*, $tidset \subseteq \{tid_1, tid_2, ..., tid_n\}$. Therefore, a *TDB* can be expressed as a set of tuples $< tid, T_{tid} >$, where $T_{tid} \subseteq I$, and T_{tid} is a pattern occurring at *tid* transaction. The support of pattern X, denoted by *support*(X), is the number of transactions in *TDB* containing the pattern X. Assuming that α, T_α and β, T_β are two transactions of *TDB*. The value of $(\alpha - \beta)$ is called relative distance between α and β, where $\alpha > \beta$, and β is called the reference point. With respect to β, an item

i_k, where $k \in \{1, \ldots, m\}$ at α is called an extended item, denoted by $i_k(\alpha - \beta)$, where $(\alpha - \beta)$ is called the *Span* of the extended item. In the same way, with respect to the transaction at β, a transaction T_α at α is called an extended transaction and denoted as $T_\alpha(\alpha - \beta)$. Therefore, $T_\alpha(\alpha - \beta) = \{i_1(\alpha - \beta), \ldots, i_p(\alpha - \beta)\}$, where p is the number of items in T_α.

An example database *TDB* consisting of 6 transactions ($n = 6$) and $I = \{A, B, C, D, E\}$ is shown in Table 1. This database is used in illustrative examples throughout this article. Therefore, with respect to the transaction at $tid = 1$ in the example database in Table 1, the extended transaction of the transaction at $tid = 2$ is $\{B(1), C(1), E(1)\}$.

Assuming that $x_i(\omega_i)$ and $x_j(\omega_j)$ are two extended items that satisfy the following criteria: $x_i(\omega_i) < x_j(\omega_j)$ if $(\omega_i < \omega_j)$ or $(\omega_i = \omega_j$ and $x_i < x_j)$. In addition, $x_i(\omega_i) = x_j(\omega_j)$ if $\omega_i = \omega_j$ and $x_i = x_j$. For instance, $C(0) < C(1)$, $C(0) < D(0)$, and $C(1) = C(1)$. An inter-transaction pattern (ITP) is defined as a set of extended items, $\{x_1(\omega_1), x_2(\omega_2), \ldots, x_k(\omega_k)\}$, where $\omega_1 = 0$, $\omega_l \leq maxSpan$, *maxSpan* is a maximum *Span* given by user, $x_i(\omega_i) < x_j(\omega_j)$, and $1 \leq i < j \leq l$. A pattern is called a *l*-pattern, a pattern of length l, if it contains l extended items. For example, $\{A(0), T(0), W(1)\}$ is a 3-pattern. Let X be an ITP. X is called an FITP if $support(X) \geq minSup$, where *minSup* is a minimum support given by user. An FITP X is called an FMITP if it does not have any superset. For instance, using example *TDB* in Table 1 with $minSup = 3$, we have only two frequent maximal patterns (FMPs) *ABDE* and *BCE*. Any other FP in the example *TDB* must be a subset of one of these FMPs. We can say that *ABE* is a FP, since $ABE \subset ABDE$, and we also have $sup(ABE) \geq sup(ABDE) = 3$.

Table 1. Example database

Tid	Items
1	$\{A, B, D, E\}$
2	$\{B, C, E\}$
3	$\{A, B, D, E\}$
4	$\{A, B, C, E\}$
5	$\{A, B, C, D, E\}$
6	$\{B, C, D\}$

Applications of ITP mining in predicting the movements of stock prices were presented by Lu et al. [18], and studying meteorological data has also been proposed by Li et al. [19]. Several other algorithms based on Apriori have also been proposed to mine FITP, such as E/EH-Apriori [20] and FITI [21]. Expanding the scope of the association rules mined from traditional one-way internal transaction association rules to multi-dimensional inter-transaction association rules was also introduced by Li et al. [22]. Lee et al. recently presented two algorithms ITP-Miner [23] and ICMiner [24] to mine FITPs and FCITPs. ITP-Miner is based on IT-Tree and DFS traversing to mine FITPs. While ICMiner, which is based on IT-Tree and CHARM properties, is used to mine all frequent closed inter-transaction patterns. Wang et al. proposed the PITP-Miner [25] algorithm, which relies on tree projection to mine entire sets of FITPs in a database. In addition, FITP mining has been applied to mine profit rules from stock databases by Hsieh et al., with approaches such as PRMiner [26], JCMiner and ATMiner [27]. The authors also presented ITR-Miner and NRIT [28] to mine redundant inter-union association rules. Nguyen et al. recently proposed two efficient methods, DITP-Miner [29] and FCITP [30], to effectively mine FITPs and FCITPs, respectively.

3   The Proposed Algorithm (TMITP-Miner) for Mining FMITPs

Definition 1. Let X be a frequent inter-transaction pattern (FITP) with $0 \leq Span \leq maxSpan$. If there does not exist a FITP Y that is a superset of X, $(X \not\subseteq Y)$, X is a frequent maximal inter-transaction pattern (FMITP).

Definition 2 (*maxpoint*). Let x be an item occurring at the transactions with the set of transaction identifications, $tidset = \{t_1, \ldots, t_k\}$, where $k = 1 \ldots n$. The *maxpoint* of item x is defined as the order of the last element t_k of $tidset$ and $maxpoint(x)$ is also the $support(x)$.

For example, item A occurs in the example database in Table 1 at the transactions $<1,3,4,5>$ in turn. According to Definition 2. $maxpoint(A) = support(A) = 4$.

Theorem 1 [30]. Let $x(0)$ be an inter-transaction 1-pattern of item x at $Span = 0$ with $tidset(x(0)) = \{t_1, t_2, \ldots, t_u\}$, where $t_i \in T$ and $x(k)$ be an inter-transaction 1-pattern of item x at $Span = k$, where $0 \leq Span \leq maxSpan$ and $1 \leq k \leq maxSpan$. If $t_{u\text{-}minSup+1} \leq k$ or $maxpoint(x(0)) - minSup + 1 \leq k$, where $minSup$ is a minimum support threshold and $maxpoint(x(0)) = support(x(0))$, then $x(k)$ cannot be a frequent inter-transaction (FIT) pattern.

The proof of this theorem is given in [30].

The proposed algorithm, tMITP-Miner, is shown in Fig. 1. In step 1, tMITP-Miner algorithm applies the theorem 1 to reduce the search space to quickly create all FITPs with the length of 1-pattern. In step 2 and step 3, tMITP-Miner method generates FIT 2-patterns with $(0 \leq Span \leq maxSpan)$. Next, the algorithm recursively invokes the procedure FMITP_DFS to generate all FMITPs. In the procedure FMITP_DFS, the proposed algorithm also uses the function to check whether the FITPs are FMITPs or not, before adding them to the collection of FMITPs. Eventually, all of the FMITPs are obtained in Step 5.

The post-processing method for FMITP mining is described in Fig. 2. First of all, in step 1, the algorithm scans the database to find all FIT 1-patterns with $(0 \leq Span \leq maxSpan)$. Step 2, the post-processing algorithm insert FIT 1-patterns ($Span = 0$) into the set of FITPs. Step 3, post-processing algorithm generates FIT 2-patterns. And then, Step 4 uses the DFS traversing to scan the nodes of FIT 2-patterns to generate all of FIT k-patterns ($k \geq 2$). After recursively invoking the DFS procedure for the next equivalence classes, we can obtain all of FITPs in Step 5. Step 6, post-processing collects FITPs meet the maximal definition (Definition 1). Therefore, all of FMITPs are obtained in Step 7.

Algorithm: tMITP-Miner(*TDB, minSup, maxSpan*)
Input: A transaction *TDB, minSup, maxSpan*.
Output: all of FMITPs.
Method:
Step 1. Scan *TDB* to generate all FIT *1*-patterns and their *support* (0 ≤ *Span* ≤ *maxSpan*) by applying theorem 1.
Step 2. Add FIT 1-patterns (*Span* = 0) with their tidsets into the set of FMITPs.
Step 3. Produce FIT 2-patterns with the given *Span* values (0 ≤ *Span* ≤ *maxSpan*) by combinining FIT 1-patterns (*Span* = 0) with FIT 1-patterns (1≤ *Span* ≤ *maxSpan*).
Step 4. Perform FMITP_DFS(FIT 2-patterns, *minSup, maxSpan*) to generate the set of FMITPs
recursively.
Step 5. Output all of FMITPs.
Function: FMITP_DFS
Input: [P_2], *minSup, maxSpan*. //([P_2] is the equivalence class of FIT *k*-patterns, *k* = 2)
Output: the newly updated for next level
Step 1. Sort the list of IT 2-patterns in the processing class in increasing order of their support.
Step 2. Add X_i to FMITPs if it cannot be subset by any other patterns. // X_i is a FMCITP at the [P_i]
Step 3. FMITP_DFS([P_k],*minSup,maxSpan*) //([P_k] is the equivalence class of FIT *k*-patterns, *k* > 2)

Fig. 1. The proposed algorithm tMITP-Miner for mining FMITPs.

Algorithm: post-processing(*TDB, minSup, maxSpan*)
Input: A transaction *TDB, minSup, maxSpan*.
Output: all of FMITPs.

Method:
Step 1. Scan *TDB* to generate all FIT *1*-patterns and their *support* (0 ≤ *Span* ≤ *maxSpan*)
Step 2. Add FIT 1-patterns (*Span* = 0) with their tidsets into the set of FITPs.
Step 3. Generate frequent inter-transaction 2-patterns.
Step 4. Generate all of frequent inter-transaction *k*-patterns (*k* ≥ 2) by applying DFS strategy.
Step 5. All of FITPs from the database *TDB* are mined and added to the set of FITPs.
Step 6. Collect all of FITPs meet the maximal properties and add to the set of FMITPs.
Step 7. Output all of FMITPs.

Fig. 2. The post-processing algorithm for mining FMITPs.

To illustrate tMITP-Miner and post-processing algorithms, an example is given by using an example database in Table 1 with *minSup* = 3 and *maxSpan* = 0. With respect to tMITP-Miner, after scanning the database, the obtained FIT 1-patterns are *A*(0), *B*(0), *C*(0), *D*(0), *and E*(0), in which their supports are 4, 6, 4, 4, and 5, respectively. Then, the proposed algorithm generates FIT 2-patterns at the equivalence class

$P[A(0)]$, and then recursively invokes the procedure FMITP_DFS from the FIT 2-pattern level onwards. The FMITPs were added to the set of FMITPs during the mining process (backtracking processing). Likewise, we apply the method at the nodes $B(0)$, $C(0)$, $D(0)$, and $E(0)$. Finally, all of FMITPs are added to the set of FMITPs consisting of $A(0)B(0)D(0)E(0)$ and $B(0)C(0)E(0)$ out of 19 FITPs $\{B(0), E(0), A(0), C(0), D(0), B(0)E(0), A(0)B(0), A(0)E(0), B(0)C(0), B(0)D(0), A(0)D(0), C(0)E(0), D(0)E(0), A(0)B(0)E(0), A(0)B(0)D(0), A(0)D(0)E(0), B(0)C(0)E(0), B(0)D(0)E(0), A(0)B(0)D(0)E(0)\}$.

More generally, another example is illustrated on the example database in Table 1 with $maxSpan = 1$ and $minSup = 5$. After scanning the database, there are four FIT 1-patterns satisfying the $minSup$ such as $E(0)$, $B(0)$, $E(1)$, and $B(1)$, of which only $E(0)$ and $B(0)$ are inserted into the set of FITPs. The entire mining process is shown in Fig. 3 as follows

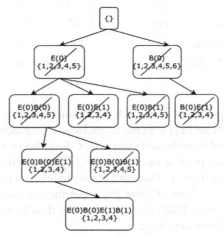

Fig. 3. An example of performance of the tMITP-Miner algorithm on the example database with $minSup = 5$ and $maxSpan = 1$.

Through the two examples above, it is easy to realize that number of FITPs is many times as much as that of FMITPs. The proposed algorithm exploits FMITPs during the mining process, in which it applies the pruning strategies to reduce the search space, which makes tMITP-Miner more efficient in terms of runtime and memory usage. Otherwise, the post-processing algorithm mines FMITPs via two phases, mining all of FITPs and collecting FMITPs from the completed set of FITPs. The completed FITP set is usually a massive one, from which the set of mined FMITPs consumes a large amount of resources, which makes the post-processing method inefficient.

4   Experimental Results

The algorithms used in our experiment were implemented in Microsoft Visual C# 2019 for Mac. The evaluations were conducted on a Macbook Pro 13″ Early 2015 equipped with an Intel 2.9 GHz Dual-Core Intel i5-5287U @ 2.90 GHz, 8.00 GB RAM DDR3 and running macOS Catalina 10.15.2.

Databases used to conduct experiments have been downloaded from the link (http://fimi.uantwerpen.be/data/). The features of the databases are described in Table 2.

Table 2. Features of the databases used for experimentation

Dataset	#distinct items	#records	#Average length
Chess	76	3,196	37
Connect	129	67,557	43
T10I4D100K	870	100,000	10
T40I10D100K	942	100,000	40

The post-processing method for FMITP exploitation is carried out in two stages. In the first stage, it exploits all FITPs. In the second stage, it selects all FMITPs from the FITP collection extracted from the first stage. Since the collection of FITPs is extremely huge, the post-processing method has to scan the FITP collection to select FMITPs at a very high computationally cost. Therefore, it consumes a lot of memory and runtime resources. Figures 4, 5, 6, 7 and 8 show the experimental results indicating that the proposed algorithm discovers FMITPs more efficiently than the post-processing method in terms of runtime and memory usage.

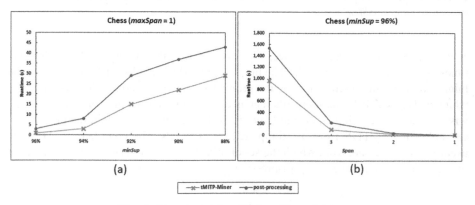

Fig. 4. Experimental runtime on Chess database.

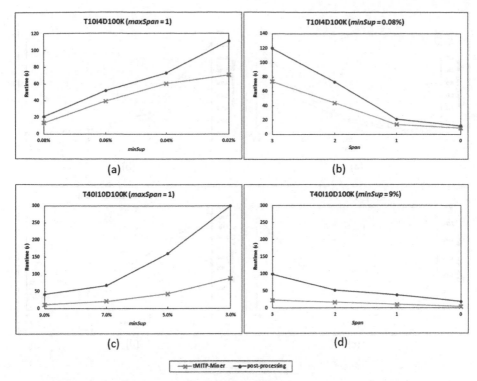

Fig. 5. Experimental runtime on T10I4D100K and T40I10D100K databases.

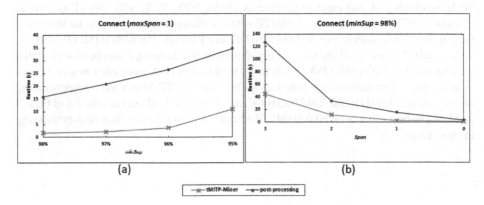

Fig. 6. Experimental runtime on Connect database.

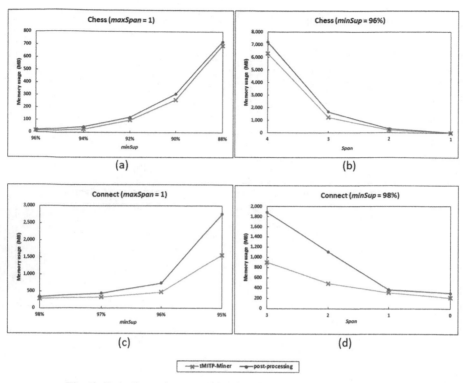

Fig. 7. Experimental memory usage on Chess and Connect databases.

It can be seen in Fig. 4 (Chess database) that tMITP-Miner dominates in most cases. With *maxSpan* = 1 and *minSup* ranging in {88%, 90%, 92%, 94%, 96%} as well as *minSup* = 96% and *maxSpan* = 4, tMITP is faster than post-processing more than two-fold. It can also be seen in Fig. 5 (T10I4D100K and T40I10D100K) that tMITP-Miner is up to nearly 2 times on all the tests. In Fig. 6 (Connect database), It can be observed that the execution speed of tMITP-Miner is faster than that of post-processing nearly 3 times in most cases. Comparison on memory usage between tMITP-Miner and post-processing on the Chess, T10I4D100K, T40I10D100K, and Connect databases are shown in Figs. 7 and 8. It can be easily observed that tMITP-Miner uses less memory than post-processing in most cases.

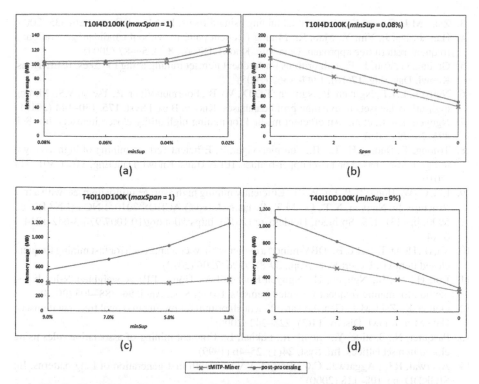

Fig. 8. Experimental memory usage on T10I4D100K and T40I10D100K databases.

5 Conclusion and Future Works

In this study, we proposed an efficient algorithm for mining FMITPs, in which we adopted theorems and proposed pruning strategies applied to reduce the search space and quickly determine the frequency of ITPs as well as the maximal ITPs. We also conducted experiments on real datasets that are widely used in the data mining research community. The proposed algorithm, tMITP-Miner, is then compared with the post-processing method in terms of runtime and memory usage. Our algorithm for both criterias and for all tested databases is clearly shown to be better.

In future works, we will develop efficient methods for mining FMITPs, and FCITPs as well as FITPs on incremental databases and consensus system for solving conflicts in distributed systems [31]. Besides, it could be worth applying parallelism and cloud computing platform to these algorithms to make them feasible on the massive databases.

References

1. Agrawal, R., Ramakrishnan, S.: Fast algorithms for mining association rules. In: VLDB, pp. 478–499 (1994)
2. Zaki, M.J.: Scalable algorithms for association mining. IEEE Trans. Knowl. Data Eng. 12(3), 372–390 (2000)

3. Zaki, M.J., Gouda, K.: Fast vertical mining using diffsets. In: SIGKDD, pp. 326–335 (2003)
4. Han, J., Pei, J., Yin, Y., Mao, R.: Mining frequent patterns without candidate generation: a frequent-pattern tree approach. Data Min. Knowl. Discov. **8**(1), 53–87 (2004)
5. Grahne, G., Zhu, J.: Fast algorithms for frequent itemset mining using FP-trees. IEEE Trans. Knowl. Data Eng. **17**(10), 1347–1362 (2005)
6. Nguyen, L.T.T., Nguyen, P., Nguyen, T.D.D., Vo, B., Fournier-Viger, P., Tseng, V.S.: Mining high-utility itemsets in dynamic profit databases. Knowl. Based Syst. **175**, 130–144 (2019)
7. Nguyen, L.T.T., et al.: An efficient method for mining high utility closed itemsets. Inf. Sci. **495**, 78–99 (2019)
8. Truong, T., Duong, H., Le, B., Fournier-Viger, P.: Efficient vertical mining of high average-utility itemsets based on novel upper-bounds. IEEE Trans. Knowl. Data Eng. **31**(2), 301–314 (2019)
9. Lin, C.-W., Hong, T.-P., Lu, W.-H.: Efficiently mining high average utility itemsets with a tree structure. In: Nguyen, N.T., Le, M.T., Świątek, J. (eds.) ACIIDS 2010. LNCS (LNAI), vol. 5990, pp. 131–139. Springer, Heidelberg (2010). https://doi.org/10.1007/978-3-642-12145-6_14
10. Vo, B., Hong, T.-P., Le, B.: DBV-miner: a dynamic bit-vector approach for fast mining frequent closed itemsets. Expert Syst. Appl. **39**(8), 7196–7206 (2012)
11. Bui, H., Vo, B., Nguyen, H., Nguyen-Hoang, T.A., Hong, T.P.: A weighted N-list-based method for mining frequent weighted itemsets. Expert Syst. Appl. **96**, 388–405 (2018)
12. Gouda, K., Zaki, M.J.: GenMax: an efficient algorithm for mining maximal frequent itemsets. Data Min. Knowl. Discov. **11**(3), 223–242 (2005)
13. Pasquier, N., Bastide, Y., Taouil, R., Lakhal, L.: Efficient mining of association rules using closed itemset lattices. Inf. Syst. **24**(1), 25–46 (1999)
14. Agarwal, R.C., Aggarwal, C.C., Prasad, V.V.V.: Depth first generation of long patterns. In: SIGKDD, pp. 108–118 (2000)
15. Burdick, D., Calimlim, M., Flannick, J., Gehrke, J., Yiu, T.: MAFIA: a maximal frequent itemset algorithm. IEEE Trans. Knowl. Data Eng. **17**(11), 1490–1504 (2005)
16. Liu, X., Zhai, K., Pedrycz, W.: An improved association rules mining method. Expert Syst. Appl. **39**(1), 1362–1374 (2012)
17. Vo, B., Pham, S., Le, T., Deng, Z.H.: A novel approach for mining maximal frequent patterns. Expert Syst. Appl. **73**, 178– 186 (2017)
18. Lu, H., Feng, L., Han, J.: Beyond intratransaction association analysis: mining multidimensional intertransaction association rules. ACM Trans. Inf. Syst **18**(4), 423–454 (2000)
19. Feng, L., Dillon, T., Liu, J.: Inter-transactional association rules for multi-dimensional contexts for prediction and their application to studying meteorological data. Data Knowl. Eng. **37**(1), 85–115 (2001)
20. Feng, L., Yu, J.X., Lu, H., Han, J.: A template model for multidimensional inter-transactional association rules. VLDB J. **11**(2), 153–175 (2002)
21. Tung, A.K.H., Lu, H., Han, J., Feng, L.: Efficient mining of intertransaction association rules. IEEE Trans. Knowl. Data Eng. **15**(1), 43–56 (2003)
22. Li, Q., Feng, L., Wong, A.: From intra-transaction to generalized inter-transaction: Landscaping multidimensional contexts in association rule mining. Inf. Sci. (Ny) **172**(3–4), 361–395 (2005)
23. Lee, A.J.T., Wang, C.S.: An efficient algorithm for mining frequent inter-transaction patterns. Inf. Sci. **177**(17), 3453–3476 (2007)
24. Lee, A.J.T., Wang, C.S., Weng, W.Y., Chen, Y.A., Wu, H.W.: An efficient algorithm for mining closed inter-transaction itemsets. Data Knowl. Eng. **66**(1), 68–91 (2008)
25. Wang, C.S., Chu, K.C.: Using a projection-based approach to mine frequent inter-transaction patterns. Expert Syst. Appl. **38**(9), 11024–11031 (2011)

26. Hsieh, Y.L., Yang, D.L., Wu, J.: Effective application of improved profit-mining algorithm for the interday trading model. Sci. World J. **2014**, 13 (2014). ID 874825

27. Hsieh, Y.L., Yang, D.L., Wu, J., Chen, Y.C.: Efficient mining of profit rules from closed inter-transaction itemsets. J. Inf. Sci. Eng. **32**(3), 575–595 (2016)

28. Wang, C.: Mining non-redundant inter-transaction rules. J. Inf. Sci. Eng. **31**(6), 1521–1536 (2015)

29. Nguyen, T.N., Nguyen, L.T.T., Nguyen, N.T.: An improved algorithm for mining frequent Inter-transaction patterns. In: INISTA, pp. 296–301 (2017)

30. Nguyen, T., Nguyen, L.T.T., Vo, B., Nguyen, N., Member, S.: An efficient algorithm for mining frequent closed inter- transaction patterns. In: SMC, pp. 2019–2024 (2019)

31. Nguyen, N.T.: Consensus system for solving conflicts in distributed systems. Inf. Sci. **147**(1–4), 91–122 (2002)

Outlier Detection, Clustering, and Classification – Methodologically Unified Procedures for Conditional Approach

Piotr Kulczycki[1,2(✉)] and Krystian Franus[1]

[1] Polish Academy of Sciences, Systems Research Institute, Warsaw, Poland
`kulczycki@ibspan.waw.pl, kulczycki@agh.edu.pl,`
`krystian.franus@gamil.com`
[2] Faculty of Physics and Applied Computer Science, AGH University
of Science and Technology, Kraków, Poland

Abstract. The subject of the study are three fundamental procedures of contemporary data analysis: outliers detection, clustering and classification. The issue is considered in a conditional approach – introduction of specific (e.g. current) values to the model allows in practice a significantly precise description of the reality under research. The same methodology has been used for all three above tasks, which considerably facilitates the interpretations, potential modifications and practical applications of the material investigated. Using non-parametric methods frees the procedures under investigation from a distribution in the considered dataset.

Keywords: Data analysis · Data mining · Outliers detection · Clustering · Classification · Conditional approach · Distribution free methods · Numerical algorithm

1 Introduction

The tasks:

(a) outlier detection – indication of elements that are considerably different from the remainder [1],
(b) clustering – grouping of elements in relatively homogenous subsets [4],
(c) classification – assignment of the tested element to one of the distinguished classes [3],

are fundamental problems in the majority of practical issues of data analysis and data mining. Moreover, in many of these applications, the above procedures (a)–(c) constitute a skeleton for the whole concept of the solution being designed.

In many practical tasks, the information possessed in the form of data may be made considerably more precise by measurement and introduction to the model, the specific values of the factors having significant impact on the phenomenon under investigation.

© Springer Nature Switzerland AG 2020
N. T. Nguyen et al. (Eds.): ICCCI 2020, LNAI 12496, pp. 328–340, 2020.
https://doi.org/10.1007/978-3-030-63007-2_26

Such a factor can be, for example, the current temperature of a device in engineering or a weekday in marketing. From a formal perspective this goal may be achieved by the application of a probabilistic conditional approach [2]. Then the basic attributes, called describing, are dependent on conditioning attributes, whose measured and introduced concrete values may give meaningfully precise information concerning the considered object. Such an approach, applied to outlier detection, clustering, and classification problems constitutes the subject of researches presented in this publication. For defining characteristics of data, the nonparametric methodology of kernel estimators [6, 13, 15] is used, which freed the investigated procedures from distributions characterizing both the describing and conditioning attributes. This concept will be used for all three procedures (a)–(c). The homogeneity of the methodology obtained in this way simplifies understanding, interpretation, implementation and conformity to individual research circumstances.

The research concerning the unconditional case was summarized in the publication [7]. It has been extended in the presented paper to a conditional approach, potentially very valuable in many practical tasks of engineering, marketing, natural sciences, and others. Further details are found in the full paper [9], where whole the material is presented in the ready-to-use form.

2 Kernel Estimators

Consider the m-elements set of n-dimensional vectors with continuous attributes:

$$x_1, x_2, \ldots, x_m \in \mathbb{R}^n. \tag{1}$$

The kernel estimator $\hat{f} : \mathbb{R}^n \to [0, \infty)$ of the density of a dataset (1) distribution, is defined as

$$\hat{f}(x) = \frac{1}{m} \sum_{i=1}^{m} K(x, x_i, h), \tag{2}$$

where after separation into coordinates

$$x = \begin{bmatrix} x_1 \\ x_2 \\ \vdots \\ x_n \end{bmatrix}, x_i = \begin{bmatrix} x_{i,1} \\ x_{i,2} \\ \vdots \\ x_{i,n} \end{bmatrix} \text{ for } i = 1, 2, \ldots, m, \ h = \begin{bmatrix} h_1 \\ h_2 \\ \vdots \\ h_n \end{bmatrix}, \tag{3}$$

while the positive constants h_j are the so-called smoothing parameters; the kernel K will be used here in the product form:

$$K(x, x_i, h) = \prod_{j=1}^{n} \frac{1}{h_j} K_j \left(\frac{x_j - x_{i,j}}{h_j} \right), \tag{4}$$

whereas the one-dimensional kernels $K_j : \mathbb{R} \to [0, \infty)$, for $j = 1, 2, \ldots, n$, are measurable with unit integral $\int_{\mathbb{R}} K_j(y)dy = 1$, symmetrical with respect to zero, and non-increasing for $x \in [0, \infty)$; (in consequence, non-decreasing in $(-\infty, 0]$). A broader description of the kernel estimators methodology, in particular rules for selection of the kernel K_j form and procedures for calculating of the smoothing parameter h_j value, can be found in the classic books [6, 13, 15]. In practical applications one can also use specific concepts, generally improving the estimator properties, and others optionally fitting the model to a considered reality. In the first group, a so-called modification of the smoothing parameter [6, Section 3.1.6; 13, Section 5.3.1], while the support boundary [6, Section 3.1.7; 13, Section 2.10], belonging to the second group, should be particularly mentioned.

The fundamental concept of the kernel estimator (2) will now be generalized for the conditional approach. Let the basic (describing) attributes be given as the n_Y-dimensional vector Y, and moreover the conditioning attributes create the conditioning n_W-dimensional vector W. Denote their composition as the $(n_Y + n_W)$-dimensional vector $X = \begin{bmatrix} Y \\ W \end{bmatrix}$. Now, an equivalent of the dataset (1) is

$$\begin{bmatrix} y_1 \\ w_1 \end{bmatrix}, \begin{bmatrix} y_2 \\ w_2 \end{bmatrix}, \ldots, \begin{bmatrix} y_m \\ w_m \end{bmatrix}. \tag{5}$$

Its particular elements can be interpreted as the describing values y_i taken in measurements when the conditioning vector W assumed the respective values w_i. On the basis of the sample (5) one can calculate $\hat{f}_X$, i.e. the kernel estimator of the vector $X = \begin{bmatrix} Y \\ W \end{bmatrix}$ distribution density, while the set $w_1, w_2, \ldots, w_m$ gives $\hat{f}_W$ – the kernel estimator for the conditioning vector W. Assume that the second estimator be constructed using a kernel with positive values. Let also be given the so-called conditioning value, i.e. the fixed value $w^* \in \mathbb{R}^{n_W}$. Finally, the kernel estimator of conditional density of the vector Y distribution for the above conditioning value w^* can be defined then as the function $\hat{f}_{Y|w^*} : \mathbb{R}^{n_Y} \rightarrow [0, \infty)$ given by

$$\hat{f}_{Y|w^*}(y) = \frac{\hat{f}_X\left(\begin{bmatrix} y \\ w^* \end{bmatrix}\right)}{\hat{f}_W(w^*)}. \tag{6}$$

The conditional density can so be treated as a 'standard' (unconditional) density, whose form has been made more accurate in practice with w^* – a concrete conditioning value adequate in a given situation under research.

In the case when for the estimators $\hat{f}_X$ and $\hat{f}_W$ the product kernel (4) is used, applying the same kernels to the estimator $\hat{f}_W$ and for conditioning coordinates of $\hat{f}_X$, then the expression for the kernel estimator of conditional density becomes particularly helpful for practical applications. Assume the natural notations

$$y = \begin{bmatrix} y_1 \\ y_2 \\ \vdots \\ y_{n_Y} \end{bmatrix}, w^* = \begin{bmatrix} w_1^* \\ w_2^* \\ \vdots \\ w_{n_W}^* \end{bmatrix} \text{ and } y_i = \begin{bmatrix} y_{i,1} \\ y_{i,2} \\ \vdots \\ y_{i,n_Y} \end{bmatrix}, w_i = \begin{bmatrix} w_{i,1}^* \\ w_{i,2}^* \\ \vdots \\ w_{i,n_W}^* \end{bmatrix} \text{ for } i = 1, 2, \ldots, m, \tag{7}$$

and next, define the positive parameters d_i, for $i = 1, 2, \ldots, m$, by

$$d_i^* = K_{n_Y+1}\left(\frac{w_1^* - w_{i,1}}{h_{n_Y+1}}\right)K_{n_Y+2}\left(\frac{w_2^* - w_{i,2}}{h_{n_Y+2}}\right)\ldots K_{n_Y+n_W}\left(\frac{w_{n_W}^* - w_{i,n_W}}{h_{n_Y+n_W}}\right). \tag{8}$$

Let us norm them

$$d_i = \frac{m d_i^*}{\sum_{i=1}^{m} d_i^*}, \tag{9}$$

to obtain $\sum_{i=1}^{m} d_i = m$; therefore, arithmetic mean of d_i equals 1. So the kernel estimator of the conditional density (6) can be finally presented in the convenient form

$$\hat{f}_{Y|w^*}(y) = \frac{1}{m(\prod_{j=1}^{n_Y} h_j)} \sum_{i=1}^{m} d_i K_1\left(\frac{y_1 - y_{i,1}}{h_1}\right)K_2\left(\frac{y_2 - y_{i,2}}{h_2}\right)\ldots K_{n_Y}\left(\frac{y_{n_Y} - y_{i,n_Y}}{h_{n_Y}}\right). \tag{10}$$

The parameter d_i value characterizes the 'distance' of the given conditioning value w^* from w_i, i.e. that of the conditioning vector for which the i-th element of the dataset (5) was obtained. Then the estimator (10) can be interpreted as the linear combination of kernels mapped to particular elements of a dataset obtained for the describing vector Y, when the coefficients of this combination d_i characterize how representative particular elements are for the current conditioning value w^*.

3 Outliers (Atypical Elements) Detection

There is no universal definition of atypical elements. In the following, the frequency approach will be applied, whereby atypical elements are understood as those which rarely appear. In this way, one can find atypical observations not only on the peripheries of the population, but in the case of multimodal distributions with wide-spreading segments, also those lying in between these segments, even if they are close to the 'center' of the set. In the conditional case the fact of recognizing the tested element as atypical will be significantly dependent on the fixed conditioning value w^*.

Consider the data set (5) representative for a studied population (containing both atypical and typical elements), whose particular elements $\begin{bmatrix} y_i \\ w_i \end{bmatrix}$ consist of the describing attributes y_i obtained for the conditioning vector w_i, respectively. Denote also a tested element as

$$\begin{bmatrix} y^* \\ w^* \end{bmatrix} \in \mathbb{R}^{n_Y+n_W}, \tag{11}$$

interpreted as the describing attributes y^* obtained for the conditioning vector w^*. The aim of the procedure is to ascertain if the element y^* should be considered as atypical (in the sense of rare occurrences), or not, for the value w^*, based on the set (5).

First, applying the material from Sect. 2, one should calculate the conditional density $\hat{f}_{Y|w^*}$. The value $\hat{f}_{Y|w^*}(y)$ refers to the frequency of occurrence of the describing vector y when the conditioning value is w^*. Therefore let us treat as typical such elements for which the density $\hat{f}_{Y|w^*}$ value is bigger than a given limit value, while atypical – those for which it is smaller.

To establish this limit value, one should first fix a sensitivity of the procedure, given in the form of the number

$$r \in (0, 1) \tag{12}$$

defining a desired proportion of atypical to typical elements, more accurately the share of atypical elements in the set (5). For justification of the assumption (12), note that for $r \geq 0.5$ elements recognized as atypical would become *de facto* typical. In practice the values $0.1, 0.05, 0.01$ are commonly used.

Next, consider the following set calculated for the particular elements of the set (5):

$$\hat{f}_{Y|w^*,-1}(y_1), \hat{f}_{Y|w^*,-2}(y_2), \ldots, \hat{f}_{Y|w^*,-m}(y_m), \tag{13}$$

where $\hat{f}_{Y|w^*,-i}$ denotes the kernel estimator $\hat{f}_{Y|w^*}$ (10) calculated excluding i-th element from the set (5). The value $\hat{f}_{Y|w^*,-i}(y_i)$ refers to the frequency of occurrence of the describing vector y_i when the conditioning value is w^*; therefore, as the sought above limit one can naturally treat a conditional quantile of the order r for the conditioning value w^*; its estimator is denoted hereinafter as $\hat{q}_{r|w^*}$. Finally, if for the fixed value w^*, the inequality

$$\hat{f}_{Y|w^*}(y^*) \leq \hat{q}_{r|w^*} \tag{14}$$

is fulfilled, then the tested element should be ascertained as atypical, while in the opposite case

$$\hat{f}_{Y|w^*}(y^*) > \hat{q}_{r|w^*} \tag{15}$$

as typical.

It remains, however, to calculate the above mentioned value of conditional quantile estimator $\hat{q}_{r|w^*}$. The concept of the two-factors quantile positional estimator [12] will be fitted to the conditional approach being investigated here. Thus, assume the m-elements set of real numbers

$$\{u_1, u_2, \ldots, u_m\} \tag{16}$$

and order it non-decreasingly to the set

$$\{v_1, v_2, \ldots, v_m\}, \tag{17}$$

i.e. $\{u_1, u_2, \ldots, u_m\} = \{v_1, v_2, \ldots, v_m\}$ with $v_1 \leq v_2 \leq \ldots \leq v_m$. Next, calculate the index k such that

$$\sum_{i=1}^{k} d_i \leq mr < \sum_{i=1}^{k+1} d_i. \tag{18}$$

If $d_1 \leq mr$, then (thanks to the truthfulness of the relations $d_i > 0$ and $d_1 \leq mr < m = \sum_{i=1}^{m} d_i$) such a number exists and it is unique; note also that $k \leq m - 1$. To avoid zero-index, which is theoretically possible here, define therefore additionally $\hat{q}_r = v_1$ if $mr < d_1$, and finally we obtain the conditional quantile estimator

$$\hat{q}_{r|w^*} = \begin{cases} v_1 & \text{when } mr < d_1 \\ \frac{\left(\sum_{i=1}^{k+1} d_i\right) - mr}{d_{k+1}} v_k + \frac{mr - \sum_{i=1}^{k} d_i}{d_{k+1}} v_{k+1} & \text{when } mr \geq d_1 \end{cases} \tag{19}$$

To interpret the second part of the above formula, note that mr plays the role of 'ideal' position of a quantile estimator in the set (17), with respect to representativeness (characterized by the parameters d_i) of particular elements for the conditioning value w^*. The value of the quantile estimator $\hat{q}_{r|w^*}$ is therefore a linear combination of the elements smaller and greater than this position, with coefficients equal relative distances to them: $(mr - \sum_{i=1}^{k} d_i)/d_{k+1}$ from v_k and $(\sum_{i=1}^{k+1} d_i - mr)/d_{k+1}$ from v_{k+1}. Both belong to the interval $[0, 1]$, while their sum amount to 1.

In the procedure for outliers detection investigated here, the role of the set (16) introduced above, plays the set (13), while its every element has mapped the parameter d_i. Thus one should non-decreasingly order the set (13) obtaining the set (16) with the parameters d_i (these must not be ordered!) mapped to particular its elements, next calculate the value of the conditional positional estimator (19), and finally verify the conditions (14)–(15).

The above idea, combined with the properties of kernel estimators, allows in the multidimensional case for inferences based not only on values for specific describing coordinates of a tested element, but above all, on the relationships between them. Thanks to the strong averaging properties of such a kind of estimators, inference takes place not only for data obtained exactly with w^* (among the values w_i there may be some too small for reliable consideration or even not at all) but also for neighboring values proportional to their 'closeness' with respect to the conditioning value.

Unconditional version of the above procedure has been exhaustively presented in the paper [11], also with the fuzzy form of evaluation, which may be directly applied in the conditional version presented here.

4 Clustering

Consider, as previously, the dataset (5). The most intuitive and natural concept is the assumption that specific clusters are related to modes (local maxima) of distribution density; thus, its 'valleys' become the borders of the resulting clusters [5]. Thus, for this purpose, applying the methodology described in Sect. 2, one can create the kernel estimator $\hat{f}_{Y|w^*}$ characterizing the density of the describing vector Y distribution for the fixed conditioning value w^*. After assuming that subsequent clusters are mapped to the local maxima of the above function, the elements of the dataset (5) can be shifted in the direction of the gradient $\nabla \hat{f}_{Y|w^*}$ by the following iterative algorithm:

$$y_i^0 = y_i \text{ for } i = 1, 2, \ldots, m \tag{20}$$

$$y_i^{k+1} = y_i^k + b * \frac{\nabla \hat{f}_{Y|w*}(y_i^k)}{\hat{f}_{Y|w*}(y_i^k)} \quad \text{for } i = 1, 2, \ldots, m \text{ and } k = 0, 1, \ldots, k^*, \quad (21)$$

whereas $b > 0$, $k^* \in \mathbb{N}\setminus\{0\}$ denotes the number of steps, and the operator $* : \mathbb{R}^n \times \mathbb{R}^n \to \mathbb{R}^n$ is understood in the sense of products of particular coordinates of vectors from $\mathbb{R}^n$, e.g. in the case $n = 2$ one has $\begin{bmatrix} y_1 \\ y_2 \end{bmatrix} * \begin{bmatrix} z_1 \\ z_2 \end{bmatrix} = \begin{bmatrix} y_1 z_1 \\ y_2 z_2 \end{bmatrix}$. Based on an optimizing criterion [5], the following can be proposed

$$b = \frac{1}{n+2} \begin{bmatrix} h_1^2 \\ h_2^2 \\ \vdots \\ h_{n_Y}^2 \end{bmatrix}, \quad (22)$$

where h_j denotes the smoothing parameter value of the j-th coordinate.

Next, it is assumed that the algorithm (20)–(21) needs to be completed, when the following inequality is fulfilled after the subsequent k-th step

$$|D_k - D_{k-1}| \le a D_0, \quad (23)$$

in which $a > 0$ and

$$D_0 = \sum_{i=1}^{m-1} \sum_{j=i+1}^{m} \text{dist}(y_i, y_j),$$
$$D_{k-1} = \sum_{i=1}^{m-1} \sum_{j=i+1}^{m} \text{dist}(y_i^{k-1}, y_j^{k-1}), \quad D_k = \sum_{i=1}^{m-1} \sum_{j=i+1}^{m} \text{dist}(y_i^k, y_j^k), \quad (24)$$

where 'dist' denotes Euclidean metric in $\mathbb{R}^{n_Y}$. Therefore, D_0 and D_{k-1}, D_k mean the sums of the distances between describing vectors during the starting of the algorithm and following the $(k-1)$-th and k-th steps, respectively. Initially, one can suggest $a = 10^{-6}$; raising this value increases the calculation speed, but creates the risk of mutual inability to draw together elements from potential clusters, while lowering threatens that the criterion (23) will not be fulfilled in the acceptable time. To counteract the above dangers, the additional introduction of boundaries in the last step

$$1,000 \le k^* \le 10,000 \quad (25)$$

is proposed. The left inequality preserves against the case when the criterion (23) will be fulfilled as if accident, before the points undergo sufficient attraction to the modal value. The right blocks potential redundant calculations – in practice, after 10.000 steps they are already drawn together sufficiently even if the criterion (23) is not fulfilled. It is worth noting that particularly difficult conditions occur in practice especially with large values of the parameters h and c – the kernel estimator $\hat{f}_{Y|w*}$ is then excessively flattened in sparse areas, which may result in, for example, the elements y^k are not drawn together to local maxima or, in contrast, their 'jumping' from side to another. Finally, if $k \ge 1,000$ and the condition (23) is fulfilled, or when $k = 10,000$ (independently on the condition (23)), one should finish the calculations and accept $k^* = k$ as the final step.

The procedure now needs to be applied to the creation of clusters and assign particular elements to them. The following set comprising elements of the dataset (5) submitted to k^* steps of the algorithm (20)–(21) is considered below to achieve this objective:

$$y_1^{k^*}, y_2^{k^*}, \ldots, y_m^{k^*}. \tag{26}$$

Now, define the set of their mutual distances

$$\left\{ \text{dist}(y_i^{k^*}, y_j^{k^*}) \right\}_{\substack{i=1,2,\ldots,m-1 \\ j=i+1,i+2,\ldots,m}} . \tag{27}$$

Considering the set (27) as the one-dimensional dataset (1), establish the auxiliary kernel estimator $\hat{f}_d$ of density of the mutual distances (27). Finding, with appropriate accuracy, the 'first' (in the sense of the lowest argument value) local minimum of the function $\hat{f}_d$ in the interval $(0, D)$, where

$$D = \max_{\substack{i=1,2,\ldots,m-1 \\ j=i+1,i+2,\ldots,m}} \left\{ \text{dist}(y_i^{k^*}, y_j^{k^*}) \right\} \tag{28}$$

is the next task. For this purpose, one can calculate the standard deviation $\hat{\sigma}_d$ for the dataset (27), and subsequently take the values y from the set

$$\left\{ 0.01\hat{\sigma}_d, 0.02\hat{\sigma}_d, \ldots, 0.01\hat{\sigma}_d \left(\text{int} \left[\frac{100D}{\hat{\sigma}_d} \right] - 1 \right) \right\}, \tag{29}$$

where int[a] means an integer of the number a, until the condition

$$\hat{f}_d (y - 0.01\hat{\sigma}_d) > \hat{f}_d(y) \text{ and } \hat{f}_d(y) \leq \hat{f}_d (y + 0.01\hat{\sigma}_d) \tag{30}$$

is fulfilled. The first (the smallest) value will be treated as the half of the smallest distance between cluster centers, and denoted as y_d hereinafter. In the event that such a value does not exist, the presence of one cluster should be recognized and the procedure completed. Similarly one should accept the existence of one cluster if $y_d \leq 10^{-12}D_0$, where D_0 is given by the formula (24); the aim is here to avoid a possible accidental minimum connected with a random 'astray' of the sequence (20)–(21) elements around the function $\hat{f}_{Y|w^*}$ maximum, which may appear in the case of one cluster.

The final step is the creation of the clusters. It is achieved by the following procedure:

1. from the set (26) elements produce an initial form of a list of the elements to be clustered, named LEC in the following;
2. take any element of LEC, remove it from this list, and primarily produce a (one-element) newly create cluster (called NCC hereinafter) including this element;
3. search the list LEC and find an element which is nearer than y_d to at least one element of NCC; if such an element exists, add it to NCC, remove from LEC, and repeat point 3 from the beginning of the list LEC (not only for those elements which follow the one just found);
4. add the obtained cluster NCC to a 'cluster list'; if LEC remains not empty, go to point 2, otherwise, finish the algorithm.

The final 'cluster list' thus obtained contains all clusters defined during the above procedure. Herein the clustering procedure has been completed.

Note that the clustering procedure investigated above did not necessitate any initial, often arbitrary, assumption regarding the number of clusters – it mainly depends on the internal data structure. In the elementary form presented above, the parameters are calculated based on the optimizing criteria, but in practical applications, it can be beneficial to suitably change the values of kernel estimator parameters, in consequence, influencing the cluster number. Namely, the result of increasing the values of the smoothing parameters h_j is the occurrence of fewer clusters; conversely, decreases to this value yield more clusters. In both cases, one can emphasize that despite influencing the number of clusters, it still solely depends on the data's internal structure.

A similar effect can be obtained using the procedure of the smoothing parameter modification [6, Section 3.1.6; 13, Section 5.3.1]. Increase of its intensity sharpens the kernel estimator in the dense regions of the dataset and also smooths in the sparse areas, and as a consequence, the number of clusters in dense areas rises and simultaneously diminishes in sparse regions. These effects are reversed in the event of this parameter value decrease.

Moreover, combining the aforementioned considerations from the last two paragraphs, one can leave the cluster number in dense data regions unchanged and at the same time lower or even eliminate clusters in sparse areas, which is frequently desired in practice.

These properties are particularly worthwhile to highlight as being practically absent in other clustering methods.

The above results will be obtained with the assumption of the specific conditioning value w^*, and therefore for a model made precise through its introduction. The division into obtained clusters becomes more appropriate for the i-th element of the dataset under research, the more its conditioning value w_i is closer to w^*.

Details for unconditional case of the procedure presented in this section, with visual aids, are presented in the article [8].

5 Classification

Consider conditional patterns, analogous to the set (5):

$$\begin{bmatrix} y_1' \\ w_1 \end{bmatrix}, \begin{bmatrix} y_2' \\ w_2 \end{bmatrix}, \ldots, \begin{bmatrix} y_{m_1}' \\ w_{m_1} \end{bmatrix} \tag{31}$$

$$\begin{bmatrix} y_1'' \\ w_1 \end{bmatrix}, \begin{bmatrix} y_2'' \\ w_2 \end{bmatrix}, \ldots, \begin{bmatrix} y_{m_2}'' \\ w_{m_2} \end{bmatrix} \tag{32}$$

$$\vdots$$

$$\begin{bmatrix} y_1''^{\cdots'} \\ w_1''^{\cdots'} \end{bmatrix}, \begin{bmatrix} y_2''^{\cdots'} \\ w_2''^{\cdots'} \end{bmatrix}, \ldots, \begin{bmatrix} y_{m_J}''^{\cdots'} \\ w_{m_J}''^{\cdots'} \end{bmatrix}, \tag{33}$$

characterizing J assumed classes. The sizes $m_1, m_2, \ldots, m_J$, need to be proportional to the share of specific classes within the investigated datasets. The aim of classification is to map the tested element

$$\begin{bmatrix} y^* \\ w^* \end{bmatrix} \in \mathbb{R}^{n_Y + n_W} \tag{34}$$

to one of the classes. A supplementary element which makes the model considered much more precise in the conditional approach constitutes the conditioning parameter w^* value, proper for the tested element.

Among the many algorithms of classification, special admission of practitioners is enjoyed by the Bayesian approach [3]. In the case of apply the methodology presented in Sect. 2, one can specify $\hat{f}_{Y_1|w^*}, \hat{f}_{Y_2|w^*}, \ldots, \hat{f}_{Y_J|w^*}$ – kernel estimators successively calculated on the basis of the patterns (31)–(33) treated as the dataset (5) each time. The classified element (34) needs then to be assigned to that class in which the value

$$m_1 \hat{f}_{Y_1|w^*} \left(y^* \right), m_2 \hat{f}_{Y_2|w^*} \left(y^* \right), \ldots, m_J \hat{f}_{Y_J|w^*} \left(y^* \right) \tag{35}$$

is the largest. By introducing the positive coefficients $z_1, z_2, \ldots, z_J$, the above can be generalized to

$$z_1 m_1 \hat{f}_{Y_1|w^*} \left(y^* \right), z_2 m_2 \hat{f}_{Y_2|w^*} \left(y^* \right), \ldots, z_J m_J \hat{f}_{Y_J|w^*} \left(y^* \right). \tag{36}$$

Giving the values $z_1 = z_2 = \ldots = z_J = 1$, the formula (36) reduces to the form (35). By applying a suitable rising the value z_i, one introduces a decrease to the probability of mistakenly assigning the i-th class elements to another, incorrect class; however, the slight growing in the overall quantity of misclassifications then appears. Bearing this in mind, note that it is possible to increase the values of even a few coefficients z_i. Joining the effective Bayes method with the nonparametric method of kernel estimators gives a unique opportunity to fit the classifier to the reality under research, especially for the cases of irregular patterns forms, also with shapes 'C' or 'O' types, or even incoherent (composed of many parts). The number of class is also unbounded. Moreover, the above idea, combined with the properties of kernel estimators, allows in the multidimensional case for inferences based not only on values for specific coordinates of a tested element, but above all, on the relationships between them. The inference takes place not only for data obtained exactly with w^* but also for neighboring values proportional to their 'closeness' to this value.

An example of the universality of the above method may be its easy extension into the classification of an interval information, which for the unconditional case is presented in the paper [10].

6 Exemplary Application for Data Analysis

The material presented in this work provides convenient apparatus for multilateral practical analysis of real data. To serve an illustrative example applying benchmark data, *The World Happiness Report* [14] will be used here. It concerns filling of happiness and various aspects that influences it in 156 countries. Each record consists of following factors: country name, year of studies, happiness, GDP per capita, generosity, healthy life expectancy, social support, perceptions of corruption, freedom to make life choices, and others. Such a convention, in which every record characterizes a specific country, is particularly convenient for illustrative analysis, and especially multilateral interpretations. Not all records are complete.

For the research presented below 118 full records concerning 2018 have been selected. A colorful and close intuition of the relationship between generosity and well-being will be presented in detail. Generosity is defined as the national average of response to the question "Have you donated money to a charity in the past month?" referring to average of similar countries (thus the values of this factor may be negative and positive). Well-being is straightforwardly assumed as GDP per capita, or specifically its logarithm.

Three values of conditioning attribute (well-being) have been chosen: quantiles of the orders of 0.15, 0.5, 0.85, characterizing non-wealthy, averagely-wealthy and wealthy countries, respectively. The values of these quantiles amounted successively to 7.63, 9.43, 10.51. Although the procedure was conducted for the full 118-elements dataset, for clarity of interpretation, the clustering results are presented below restricted to the categories of non-wealthy, averagely-wealthy and wealthy countries. As a border between them, the values of quantiles of the order of 0.25 and 0.75, amounting to 8.28 and 10.18, respectively, was assumed.

In the group of 30 non-wealthy countries, one cluster with the center around zero was obtained. The only atypical element for the level $r = 0.1$ was Haiti (on the side of high generosity values), which is an effect of the critical economic situation in that country in association with the extreme class division in society.

In the group of 58 averagely-wealthy countries, one main cluster (56 countries) with a center around –0.15, was obtained. A lower generosity level than in non-wealthy countries draws the attention. This is a well-known sociological attitude, when middle-class in its belief more eagerly looks at hard work (overvaluing its own) than 'handouts'. The second, considerably smaller, 2-elements cluster, with the center located at the value as high as 0.5, consists of Burma (Myanmar) and Indonesia, charming countries famous for the benevolence and friendliness of populations. At the level of $r = 0.1$, 6 outliers have been identified: for small values Greece as well as for large Laos, Thailand, Uzbekistan and the aforementioned Burma and Indonesia. Indication of Greece is the consequence of the current extremely painful financial crisis in this country; in turn, the addition similar and close Laos and Thailand to Burma and Indonesia does not seem to be coincidental.

And finally, in the group of 30 wealthy countries, two clusters of similar sizes were formed. The first with its center as previously around –0.15 (Belgium, Czech Republic, Estonia, Finland, France, Italy, Japan, Latvia, Lithuania, Luxemburg, Portugal, Slovakia, Slovenia, South Korea, Spain) and the second with the center around 0.1 (Australia, Austria, Canada, Denmark, Germany, Ireland, Israel, Malaysia, Nederland, New Zealand, Norway, Sweden, Switzerland, United Kingdom, USA). It is easy to observe that the first cluster comprises wealthy countries, a large part of them in the development phase, while the second mostly contains the absolutely richest countries. The first cluster is somehow an extension of the mentality of averagely-wealthy countries, whereas the second results from a broad range of eccentric behaviors, not always positive, such as for example image building megaphilanthropy or the tax optimization through fictional foundations. On the level of $r = 0.1$ the atypical element on the side of the large values of generosity turn out to be United Kingdom, where charity and voluntary work have a long and well-grounded tradition.

In the group of wealthy countries, the classification procedure was verified. All countries were sequentially subjected to this, while in accordance with the leave-one-out concept, the characteristics were constructed excluding this country. A 100% correct results were obtained, which is not surprising since the patterns were defined by clustering, but it also confirms the potential profits obtained by applying unified methodology for different procedures of data analysis.

Finally note that for specific applications the additional procedure of support boundary [6, Section 3.1.7; 13, Section 2.10] can be especially valuable, in particular used with respect to those describing attributes, which values are positive by their nature, e.g. time, height, pollution.

7 Summary

This paper presents methodologically uniform material for three fundamental procedures of data analysis: outliers (atypical elements) detection, clustering, and classification in the conditional approach. Correct definition of factors and conditioning values may considerably increase the possibility of data analysis, in particular the interpretation of the results. In turn, thanks to this uniformity and ease of interpretation of universal mathematical apparatus applied here, the presented concept becomes convenient for individual adaptations towards specific conditionings of the issues under investigation. Due to the use of the nonparametric kernel estimators method, the worked out procedures are independent of the distributions of the dataset being studied. They can be multimodal and even their supports may consist of several different parts. Except for the necessity of providing an appropriate dataset size and calculation time, there are no limits on the dimensionality of dataset elements. Especially in the case of multidimensionality of descriptive attributes the results are impacted not only by the values of particular coordinates but rather relations between them.

The extended version of this text can be found as the full paper [9], where the material is presented in the ready-to-use form. A detailed numerical examination and further investigations concerning fertility and pollution in Kraków, Poland, are also presented.

References

1. Aggarwal, C.C.: Outlier Analysis. Springer, New York (2013)
2. Casella, G., Berger, R.L.: Statistical Inference. Duxbury Press, Pacific Grove (2002)
3. Duda, R.O., Hart, P.E., Storck, D.G.: Pattern Classification. Wiley, New York (2001)
4. Everitt, B.S., Landau, S., Leese, M., Stahl, D.: Cluster Analysis. Wiley, Chichester (2011)
5. Fukunaga, K., Hostetler, L.D.: The estimation of the gradient of a density function, with applications in pattern recognition. IEEE Trans. Inf. Theory **21**, 32–40 (1975)
6. Kulczycki, P.: Estymatory jadrowe w analizie systemowej. WNT, Warsaw (2005)

7. Kulczycki, P.: Methodically unified procedures for outlier detection, clustering and classification. In: Arai, K., Bhatia, R., Kapoor, S. (eds.) FTC 2019, pp. 460–474. Springer, Cham (2020)
8. Kulczycki, P., Charytanowicz, M.: A complete gradient clustering algorithm formed with kernel estimators. Int. J. Appl. Math. Comput. Sci. **20**, 123–134 (2010)
9. Kulczycki, P., Franus, K.: Methodically unified procedures for a conditional approach to outlier detection, clustering, and classification. Inf. Sci. (2020). (in press)
10. Kulczycki, P., Kowalski, P.A.: Bayes classification for nonstationary patterns. Int. J. Comput. Methods **12**, 1550008 (2015)
11. Kulczycki, P., Kruszewski, D.: Identification of atypical elements by transforming task to supervised form with fuzzy and intuitionistic fuzzy evaluations. Appl. Soft Comput. **60**, 623–633 (2017)
12. Parrish, R.: Comparison of quantile estimators in normal sampling. Biometrics **46**, 247–257 (1990)
13. Silverman, B.W.: Density Estimation for Statistics and Data Analysis. Chapman and Hall, London (1986)
14. The World Happiness Report: United Nations Sustainable Development Solutions Network Network in partnership with the Ernesto Illy Foundation (2019). https://worldhappiness.report/. Accessed 29 June 2019
15. Wand, M.P., Jones, M.C.: Kernel Smoothing. Chapman and Hall, London (1995)

Sequential Pattern Mining Using IDLists

Huy Minh Huynh[1], Nam Ngoc Pham[1], Zuzana Komínková Oplatková[1],
Loan Thi Thuy Nguyen[2], and Bay Vo[3]([✉])

[1] Faculty of Applied Informatics, Tomas Bata University in Zlín, Nám. T.G. Masaryka,
5555 Zlín, Czech Republic
{huynh,npham,oplatkova}@utb.cz
[2] School of Computer Science and Engineering, International University - VNU-HCM,
Ho Chi Minh City, Vietnam
nttloan@hcmiu.edu.vn
[3] Faculty of Information Technology, Ho Chi Minh City University of Technology (HUTECH),
Ho Chi Minh City, Vietnam
vd.bay@hutech.edu.vn

Abstract. Sequential pattern mining is a practical problem whose objective is to discover helpful informative patterns in a stored database such as market transaction databases. It covers many applications in different areas. Recently, a study that improved the runtime for mining patterns was proposed. It was called pseudo-IDLists and it helps prevent duplicate data from replicating during the mining process. However, the idea only works for the special type of sequential patterns, which are clickstream patterns. Direct applying the idea for sequential pattern mining is not feasible. Hence, we proposed adaptions and changes to the novel idea and proposed SUI (Sequential pattern mining Using IDList), a sequential pattern mining algorithm based on pseudo-IDLists. Via experiments on three test databases, we show that SUI is efficient and effective regarding runtime and memory consumption.

Keywords: Sequential pattern mining · Vertical format · Pseudo-IDList · Data-IDList

1 Introduction

Discovering useful informative patterns among data is the job of pattern mining. One of the most popular and basic branches of pattern mining is sequential pattern mining, first proposed by Agrawal and Srikant [1]. The main purpose of the problem is to extract common and frequently occurring sequential patterns (patterns in which their elements occur in order) in databases. Besides this problem, there are many other branches of the problem that have been presented such as [2–9]. They also have been applying to various real-life applications, ranging from analyzing and mining patterns such as learning resource recommendations [10], to analyzing clickstream-type patterns [11, 12] such as DNA sequences, event sequences or clickstream sequences on online stores.

© Springer Nature Switzerland AG 2020
N. T. Nguyen et al. (Eds.): ICCCI 2020, LNAI 12496, pp. 341–353, 2020.
https://doi.org/10.1007/978-3-030-63007-2_27

Many algorithms have been proposed for sequential pattern mining such as GSP [13], PrefixSpan [14], or SPADE [15]. They can be fit into mainly two groups, which are vertical format (data structure) algorithms or horizontal format (data structure) algorithms. The former group consists of some popular algorithms such as SPADE [15] and the improved version CM-SPADE [16]. The latter group also includes some well-known algorithms such as PrefixSpan [14]. Based on the works in [15, 16], the vertical group has overall good performance as well as some advantages over the horizontal groups such as support counting without re-scanning the databases. According to [16], CM-SPADE was the most efficient algorithm for mining sequential patterns in the vertical group. Recently, an algorithm named CUP [17] using pseudo-IDList was proposed to avoid the data duplicate disadvantage of the vertical group algorithms. However, its idea only works for a special type of sequential patterns, which are clickstream patterns. Directly using CUP for sequential pattern mining does not fully work and can produce wrong results because clickstream can not contain two events happening at the same time. Unlike clickstream patterns, sequential patterns allow those events (which are called items) to happen at the same time. Those groups of items are called itemset, and they break the logic behind the idea of the CUP algorithm. The details are given more in Sect. 3.3.

In this paper, we address the aforementioned issues via our proposed methods. Our contributions are as follows:

- We propose adaptations for the idea of the pseudo-IDList [17], which was made specifically for clickstream patterns, to work for sequential pattern mining.
- Based on the proposed method, we present SUI (Sequential pattern mining Using IDList) for mining sequential patterns.
- We perform an experimental evaluation of our proposed methods on three databases and prove that SUI is effective.

The rest of the paper is organized as follows. Sections 2 gives some definitions, existing concepts, and defines the problem of sequential pattern mining. Section 3 presents our proposed algorithm and data structures. Section 4 shows the experiment and the results. The last section is our summary and future work.

2 Problem Definitions

In this section, we define the problem of sequential pattern mining and present some related definitions.

Let $I = \{i_1, i_2, ..., i_n\}$ be a set of integer values, in which each value represents an id (identification) of an item (e.g. an egg or a candle). A set of item ids $E \subseteq I$ is called an **itemset** and **a sequence** $s = <E_1, E_2, ..., E_m>$ is a sequence of itemsets, where $E_i \subseteq I$ ($1 \leq i \leq m$). The number of item ids in an itemset E is denoted as $|E|$. Assume that $|E| = k$ ($k \leq n$), E is called a k-itemset (i.e. E contains k item ids and the length of E is k). Without the loss of generality, we assume that there exists a total order $<_I$ on items such as lexicography order or numerical order. In our case, the total order is just normal integer order (e.g. $1 <_I 2 <_I 3 <_I 4 <_I 5$). For example, assume that we have $I = \{1,$

2, 3, 4, 5} as a set of identifications of items being sold in an online store, two possible itemsets can be {1, 2, 4} and {2, 4, 5}. Both of them are 3-itemset as there are three items in each itemset. **A transaction sequence** is a sequence generated by customers' purchasing items in a store. For example, $<\{1, 2, 4\}, \{1\}, \{5\}, \{2, 5\}, \{2, 4, 5\}>$ is a transaction sequence, in which there are five itemsets. Each itemset is enclosed in curly brackets and a sequence enclose itemsets with "$<$" and "$>$" symbols. The transaction sequence expresses that a user purchased 1, 2, and 4 together, then 1, then 5, then 2 and 5, and lastly 2, 4, and 5 together. If there are l items in the sequences, that sequence can be called an l–sequence. For example, the previous sequence $<\{1, 2, 4\}, \{1\}, \{5\}, \{2, 5\}, \{2, 4, 5\}>$ is called a 10-sequence.

A **sequence database** $SDB = \{S_1, S_2, ..., S_q\}$ is a collection of transaction sequences and each sequence is numbered with a user transaction sequence id (TSID). For example, Table 1 shows a sequence database with five user transaction sequences. Those given user transaction sequences express sequences of purchased merchandise by five different customers.

Let $s_x = <X_1, X_2, ..., X_n>$ and $s_y = <Y_1, Y_2, ..., Y_m>$ to be two sequences, $n \leq m$. Sequence s_x is a **subsequence** of s_y (i.e. s_x **appears** in s_y) or s_y is a **supersequence** of s_x if there exist integers $1 \leq i_1 < i_2 < ... < i_n \leq m$ such that $X_1 \subseteq Y_{i1}, X_2 \subseteq Y_{i2}, ..., X_n \subseteq Y_{in}$. The subsequence relation is denoted by $s_x \subseteq s_y$. For example, a sequence $<\{1\}, \{1, 2\}>$ is a subsequence of the first sequence $<\{1, 3, 4\}, \{1, 2\}, \{3, 4\}, \{1, 2, 3\}>$ in Table 1.

A sequence is called a **pattern** if it appears in at least one transaction sequence. A **support of a (sequential) pattern** s, denoted by $supp(s)$, is the number of user transaction sequences that are supersequence of s. A **candidate pattern** is a sequence that may or may not appear in the database. Provided that δ is an integer value acting as a given frequent support threshold (or **minimum support threshold**), any pattern with its support $\geq \delta$ is called **a frequent (sequential) pattern**.

Let $X = <X_1, X_2, ..., X_n>$ and $Y = <Y_1, Y_2, ..., Y_m>$ to be two sequences and $n < m$, X is a **prefix** of Y if $X_1 = Y_1, X_2 = Y_2, ..., X_m = Y_m$. For example, sequences $<\{1\}>$ and $<\{1\}, \{1, 5\}, \{3, 4\}>$ are both prefixes of $<\{1\}, \{1, 5\}, \{3, 4, 5\}>$. The prefix concept is used in generating candidate patterns for enumerating all frequent patterns in the mining process. We consider that a pattern can have either an **s-extension** or an **i-extension**. If the last itemset of a pattern contains a single item, that pattern is an s-extension type. Otherwise, it has an i-extension type. For example, if $X = <\{1, 3\}, \{4\}>$ and $Y = <\{1\}, \{2, 5\}>$, X is an s–extension and Y is an i-extension.

Problem Statement. The purpose of frequent sequential pattern mining is to find all frequent patterns in frequent sequential database SDB with their supports $\geq$ a given minimum support threshold δ.

Table 1. An example of a sequential transaction database.

TSID	Transaction sequences
100	$\{1, 3, 4\},\{1, 2\},\{3, 4\}, \{1, 2, 3\}$
200	$\{1, 2\},\{1, 3\}$
300	$\{1\},\{1, 2, 3\}$
400	$\{3\},\{2, 4\}$
500	$\{2, 3\},\{1, 2, 3\},\{1, 3\}$

Example 1. Given a minimum support threshold $\delta = 3$ and an *SDB* in Table 1, the first transaction sequence (with TSID = 100) is $<\{1, 3, 4\},\{1, 2\}, \{3, 4\}, \{1, 2, 3\}>$. Patterns $<\{3, 4\}, \{1\}>$ and $<\{2\}, \{3\}, \{3\}>$ are both sub-sequence of transaction sequence 100 and are 3-patterns, whereas $<\{2, 4\}, \{3\}, \{1\}>$ is not. The pattern $<\{2\}, \{3\}>$ have its support $= 3$ $(= \delta)$ because it appears in transaction sequences 100, 200 and 500, thus it is considered frequent. The pattern $<\{3, 4\}, \{1\}>$ only appears in transaction sequence 100, thus its $supp(\{3, 4\}, \{1\}) = 1 < \delta = 3$ and it is infrequent.

3   The SUI Algorithm

In this section, we present SUI (Sequential pattern mining Using IDLists) and its structure. Most of the general sequential mining algorithms must replicate data multiple times during execution, while our algorithm extends the ideas from [17] to avoid this issue. However, directly applying the ideas into sequential pattern mining encounter some obstacles due to the characteristics of general sequential patterns. Clickstream patterns only have one item per itemset in their patterns, while sequential patterns can have multiple items per itemset. This means a clickstream pattern is always an *s*-extension, meanwhile, a sequential pattern can be either an *s*-extension or *i*-extension. Hence, their idea is only compatible with *s*-extension patterns, but not *i*-extension patterns. We propose a method (Sect. 3.3) to adapt their ideas to sequential pattern mining.

Our primary data structures for storing patterns' information are data-IDList and pseudo-IDList, depending on which type of candidate pattern. Data-IDLists are used to store the real positions of sequential patterns, while pseudo-IDLists are collections of indices from which we can use them to retrieve necessary pattern positions from referenced data-IDLists.

3.1 Data-IDList

A data-IDList [17] stores the positions of which a pattern appears in the horizontal database. Those positions are the *TSID* of transaction sequences contain the pattern and where the pattern appears in those sequences. Based on [15], only the positions of the last item of the sequential pattern need storing. For example, provided that we have a sequential pattern $X = <\{1, 3\}, \{2\}>$, and a transaction sequence $Y = <\{2\}, \{1, 3\}, \{2\}, \{2\}>$, the position list of X in Y is $<3, 4>$. A data-IDList is made from three different elements P, M, and *supp*.

- P: the pattern that is associated with this data-IDList.
- M: a table with three columns {*Data id, TSID, Position list*}. *TSID* is the id of the transaction sequence. All the positions of the pattern's last item are store in the *position list*. For each transaction sequence, there is an assigned *data id* in the IDList, they act as row indices for pseudo-IDList. The same transaction sequence may have different *data id* in different Data-IDLists. For example, the transaction sequence 500 may have a data id of 4 in data-IDList of $<\{1\}>$ but it has a data id of 5 in data-IDList of $<\{3\}>$.
- *Supp*: the support count of the pattern. It is the number of rows in M (Fig. 1).

M ⎨

Pattern: <{1}>		
Data id	TSID	Position list
1	100	1, 2, 4
2	200	1, 2
3	300	1, 2
4	500	2, 3

Pattern: <{3}>		
Data id	TSID	Position list
1	100	1, 3, 4
2	200	2
3	300	2
4	400	2
5	500	2, 3

Fig. 1. Data IDLists of frequent 1-patterns (i.e. the vertical format database).

Pattern: <{1, 3}>		
Data id	TSID	Position list
1	100	1, 4
2	200	2
3	300	2
4	500	2, 3

Pattern: <{1}, {3}>		
Data id	TSID	Position list
1	100	3, 4
2	200	2
3	300	2
4	500	3

Fig. 2. Data-IDLists of $<\{1, 3\}>$ and $<\{1\}, \{3\}>$, which some frequent 2-patterns that share prefix $<\{1\}>$. $<\{1, 3\}>$ is an *i*-extension pattern and $<\{1\}, \{3\}>$ is *s*-extension.

Pattern: <{1}, {3}>		
DIP: <{3}>		
Local id	Data id	Start index
1	1	2
2	2	1
3	3	1
4	5	2

M —

Fig. 3. The respective pseudo-IDLists of s-extension patterns <{1}, {3}> in Fig. 2.

3.2 Pseudo-IDList

A pseudo-IDList does not hold explicitly the positions of their associated pattern. It retrieves actual positions of the associated pattern via the data of another data-IDList. It has four elements from data-IDList as follows (Fig. 3).

- P: the pattern that is associated with this pseudo-IDList.
- DIP (data IDList pointer): a pointer to a data IDList where it can retrieve the position data for P. The referenced data-IDList is always of a frequent 1-pattern formed from the last item in P. For example if the pattern is <{1, 2}, {3}>, DIP would point to the data-IDList of 1-pattern <{3}>
- M: an index matrix contains indices of the data IDList in three columns {$Local\ id$, $Data\ id$, $Start\ index$}. In a similar way to IDList, a local id is a locally assigned id for the corresponding transaction sequence in this pseudo-IDList. A data id is a value that matches a corresponding data id in the data-IDList. A start index is the start index location in a position list, where we can retrieve the continuous sub-list (i.e., suffix) from the start index to the end of the position list.
- $Supp$: the support count of the pattern. It is the number of rows in M.

3.3 Adapting Pseudo-IDList for Sequential Pattern Mining

The novel idea of pseudo-IDLists is to prevent duplication data, however, there are some reasons that the idea can not fully work for sequential patterns. Let X be a clickstream pattern and Y be the frequent 1-pattern that is formed from the last item of X. Every position list in X's data-IDList is always a continuous sub-list (or a suffix) of a position list with the same $TSID$ in Y's data-IDList. A clickstream is a sequential pattern that all of its itemsets contain only one item, thus, the idea fully works in the situation where a pattern has all of its itemsets contain one item. For example, let X = <{1}, {3}> and Y = <{3}>, considering the position list L_X = <3, 4> for $TSID$ = 100 in X's data-IDList and the position list L_Y = <1, 3, 4> for $TSID$ = 100 in Y's data-IDList. Because L_X = <3, 4> ⊆ L_Y = <1, 3, 4>, L_X is a suffix and a continuous sub-list of L_Y. It also works for the situations where a pattern is just an s-extension such as X = <{1, 2}, {2, 4}, {3}> and Y = <{3}>.

Another example with $X = <\{1, 3\}>$ and $Y = <\{3\}>$, the position list $L_X = <1,$ $4>$ for $TSID = 100$ in X's data-IDList and the position list $L_Y = <1, 3, 4>$ for $TSID = 100$ in Y's data-IDList. In this case $L_X = <1, 4> \subseteq L_Y = <\underline{1}, 3, \underline{4}>$, however, L_X is not a suffix of L_Y. Therefore, L_X is only a sub-list of L_Y, not a suffix of L_Y. This happens for i-extension patterns, so the idea of pseudo-IDList does not work for i-extension patterns. To adapt the idea for sequential patterns, we proposed the following changes:

- For generated s-extensions patterns, pseudo-IDLists are created and associated with the patterns. This case happens when the two parent patterns are both s-extensions, or one of them is s-extension and the other one is i-extension.
- For generated i-extensions patterns, data-IDLists are created and associated with the patterns. This case happens when the two parent patterns are both i-extensions or both s-extensions.

Candidate Generation. To discover all frequent patterns, most algorithms traverse search space that is a lattice. The tree starts with patterns with length one (level one) and longer patterns (or higher level) on the lattice are formed level by level by adding one item to each existing pattern. The process producing longer patterns from shorter ones is called candidate generation. In this paper, we use the SPADE [15] method because it is more close to our algorithm.

IDList Creation. Unlike the original idea in [17], in which the process of IDList generation always produce pseudo-IDLists. In our case, our IDList creation generates pseudo-IDList if the candidate pattern is an s-extension or data-IDList if the candidate is an i-extension. Algorithm 1 illustrates the process of creating pseudo-IDList for s-extensions and Algorithm 2 shows the process of generating data-IDLists of i-extensions for k-patterns ($k \geq 2$). In Algorithm 1, two cases can happen. One is that X and Y are both s-extensions, then IDList of both X and Y are pseudo-IDLists. The second case is that one of them is i-extension and the other or one is s-extension. In this case, we assume that X always is the i-extension and Y is always the s-extension. For Algorithm 2, there are also two cases. X and Y are either both s-extensions or both i-extensions.

Algorithm 1. Pseudo-IDList creation for s-extension candidate pattern

Input: IDList of X and Y
Output: pseudo-IDList of Z

1: **if** X is an s-extension //IDList of X is a pseudo-IDList
2:      $M_X \leftarrow$ the matrix M in pseudo-IDList of X
3:      $Data\_M_X \leftarrow$ the matrix M in data IDList that DIP of X points to
4: **else**
5:      $Data\_M_X \leftarrow$ the matrix M in data IDList of X
6: $M_Y \leftarrow$ the *matrix* M in pseudo-IDList of Y
7: Initialize the pseudo-IDList of Z to initial values
8: $M_Z \leftarrow$ the matrix M in pseudo-IDList of Z
9: $Data\_M_Y \leftarrow$ the matrix M in data IDList that DIP of Y points to
10: $local\_id_Z \leftarrow 1$
11: $row_X \leftarrow 1$ // An index variable that iterates all rows in $Data\_M_X$ or M_X
12: $row_Y \leftarrow 1$ // An index variable that iterates all rows in M_Y
13: **while** row_X does not exceed the number of rows in M_X (or $Data\_M_X$) **do**
14:      **while** row_Y does not exceed the number of rows in M_Y **do**
15:          **if** X is an s-extension
16:              $\{local\_id_X, data\_id_X, start\_index_X\} \leftarrow$ the row at row_X in M_X
17:              $TSID_X \leftarrow TSID$ *value* of the row containing $data\_id_X$ in $Data\_M_X$
18:          **else**
19:              $\{data\_id_X, TSID_X, plist_X\} \leftarrow$ the row *at* row_X in $Data\_M_X$
20:          $\{local\_id_Y, data\_id_Y, start\_index_Y\} \leftarrow$ the row at row_Y in M_Y
21:          $TSID_Y \leftarrow TSID$ value of the row containing $data\_id_Y$ in $Data\_M_Y$
22:          **if** $TSID_X < TSID_Y$ **then**
23:              $row_X \leftarrow row_X + 1$
24:          **else if** $TSID_X > TSID_Y$ **then**
25:              $row_Y \leftarrow row_Y + 1$
26:          **else if** $TSID_X = TSID_Y$ **then**
27:              **if** X is an s-extension
28:                  $plist_X \leftarrow$ the position list with the *data id* $= data\_id_X$ in $Data\_M_X$
29:                  $e_X \leftarrow$ the element at start_$index_X$ in $plist_X$
30:              **else**
31:                  $e_X \leftarrow$ the first element in $plist_X$
32:              $plist_Y \leftarrow$ the position list with the *data id* $= data\_id_Y$ in $Data\_M_Y$
33:              **for** each element e_Y starting at $start\_index_Y$ in $plist_Y$ **do**
34:                  **if** $e_Y > e_X$ **then** // Found the start index of duplicate data
35:                      $start\_index_Z \leftarrow$ the index of e_Y in $plist_Y$
36:                      Add a row $\{local\_id_Z, data\_id_Y, start\_index_Z\}$ to M_Z
37:                      Break;
38:              $row_X \leftarrow row_X + 1$
39:              $row_Y \leftarrow row_Y + 1$
40:              $local\_id_Z \leftarrow local\_id_Z + 1$
41: DIP *of pseudo-IDList of* $Z \leftarrow DIP$ *of pseudo-IDList of* Y
42: **return** pseudo-IDList of Z

Algorithm 2. Data-IDList creation for *i*-extension candidate pattern

---

Input: IDList of X and Y
Output: Data-IDList of Z

1:    **if** X and Y are *s*-extensions //IDList of X is a peudo-IDList
2:      $Data\_M_X \leftarrow$ the matrix M in data IDList that DIP of X points to
3:      $Data\_M_Y \leftarrow$ the matrix M in data IDList that DIP of Y points to
4:    **else**
5:      $Data\_M_X \leftarrow$ the matrix M in data IDList of X
6:      $Data\_M_Y \leftarrow$ the matrix M in data IDList of Y
7:    Initialize the data-IDList of Z to initial values
8:    $M_Z \leftarrow$ the matrix M in pseudo-IDList of Z
9:    $row_X \leftarrow 1$ // An index variable that helps iterate all rows in $Data\_M_X$
10:   $row_Y \leftarrow 1$ // An index variable that helps iterate all rows in $Data\_M_Y$
11:   **while** row_X does not exceed the number of rows in $Data\_M_X$ **do**
12:      **while** row_Y does not exceed the number of rows in $Data\_M_Y$ **do**
13:        $\{data\_idx, TSID_X, plist_X\} \leftarrow$ the row at row_X in $Data\_M_X$
14:        $\{data\_id_Y, TSID_Y, plist_Y\} \leftarrow$ the row at row_X in $Data\_M_Y$
15:        **if** $TSID_X < TSID_Y$ **then**
16:          $row_X \leftarrow row_X + 1$
17:        **else if** $TSID_X > TSID_Y$ **then**
18:          $row_Y \leftarrow row_Y + 1$
19:        **else if** $TSID_X = TSID_Y$ **then**
20:          $plist_Z \leftarrow \emptyset$
21:          **for** each element e_X starting in an ascending order in $plist_X$ **do**
22:            **for** each element e_Y starting in an ascending order in $plist_Y$ **do**
23:              **if** $e_X = e_Y$ **then**
24:                Add e_X to $plist_Z$
25:          **if** $plist_Z$ is not empty **then**
26:            Add a row $\{data\_idx, TSID_X, plist_Z\}$ to M_Z
27:          $row_X \leftarrow row_X + 1$
28:          $row_Y \leftarrow row_Y + 1$
29:   **return** data-IDList of Z

3.4 An Example of the SUI Algorithm

In this section, we give an example of how SUI's process work. Using the database *SDB* in Table 1 and a minimum support threshold $\delta = 3$. A part of the lattice is shown in Fig. 4 and the mining process executes as follows.

Step 1. The whole database is scanned to identify the set of frequent 1-patterns $=$ $\{<\{1\}>, <\{2\}>, <\{3\}>\}$ and their respective support is 4, 5, and 5. All of the frequent 1-patterns have their IDLists (both pseudo-IDLists and data-IDLists) created.

Step 2. The 2-candidate set $\{<\{1\}, \{1\}>, <\{1\}, \{2\}>, <\{1\}, \{3\}>, <\{1, 2\}>, <\{1, 3\}>\}$ that shares the same 1-prefix $<\{1\}>$ is generated. The process is done by joining $<\{1\}>$ with $<\{1\}>$, $<\{1\}>$ with $<\{2\}>$ and $<\{1\}>$ with $<\{3\}>$.

Step 3. In this step, based on the IDLists of $<\{1\}>$, $<\{2\}>$ and $<\{3\}>$, we construct pseudo-IDLists for *s*-extension candidates $<\{1\}, \{1\}>$, $<\{1\}, \{2\}>$ and $<\{1\}, \{3\}>$ and data-IDLists for *i*-extension candidates $<\{1, 2\}>$ and $<\{1, 3\}>$. After creating their

IDLists, the candidate supports are calculated as {4, 2, 4, 4, 4} respectively. We discard candidate <{1}, {2}> of <{1}> because $supp(<\{1\}, \{2\}>) = 2 < \delta = 3$. SUI repeats back step 2 and this time, 3-candidates { <{1, 2}, {1}>, <{1, 2}, {3}>, <{1,2,3}> } are generated based on frequent 2-patterns { <{1}, {1}>, <{1}, {3}>, <{1, 2}>, <{1, 3}> }. The algorithm repeats those steps and stops after no more candidates can be found in the <{3}> branch.

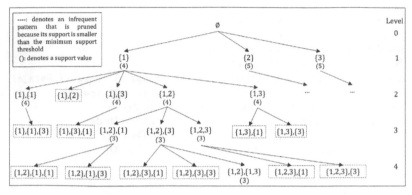

Fig. 4. A part of the lattice based on the example database.

4 Experimental Results

In this section, we report our SUI algorithm performance in comparison to the other two state-of-the-art sequential pattern mining algorithms, PrefixSpan [14], and CM-SPADE [16]. Both are reported as very effective algorithms for mining sequential patterns by [16]. All algorithms are implemented in Java, and PrefixSpan (version 2016) and CM-SPADE come from the SPMF package [18]. The hardware specification of the computer used for running the experiments is Intel Core I7 8750H 2.2 GHz and 16 GB RAM. The computer was installed with Windows 10 64 bits and JDK 8.

Table 2. Summary of databases for experiments

Database	Database size	Distinct items
C50S15T3	50,000	3,000
C150S40T2	150,000	1,000
C200S12T5	200,000	2,000

The three synthetic test databases used for experiments are following the standard generator in [1]. The summary of the databases is given in Table 2. To test those algorithms, we executed them on all databases while decreasing the minimum support threshold δ to measure the algorithms' runtime (Fig. 5) and maximum memory consumption

(Fig. 6). For optimization reasons, we also integrate the CMAP data structure [16] and DUB heuristic [17] to prune candidates in our SUI algorithm.

Performance Comparison. On all test databases, SUI generally performs better than both PrefixSpan and CM-SPADE regarding runtime execution. When the minimum support threshold δ becomes smaller, differences in runtime become more noticeable. The runtime of SUI increases slower than the other two towards the smaller δ. Typically, on the C200S12T5 dataset, PrefixSpan has lower runtime on higher δ but towards the lower δ, both CM-SPADE and SUI surpass PrefixSpan's runtime performance. The reason SUI works better was that it did not have to replicate duplicate data multiple times during the mining process by using pseudo-IDLists. Even SUI and CM-SPADE share several mining processes, but the differences in data structures for storing position information denote the differences in performance. This is shown in Fig. 6, the maximum memory consumption by CM-SPADE, while PrefixSpan and SUI have a similar memory consumption. This means SUI is efficient regarding runtime while it can manage a low memory consumption.

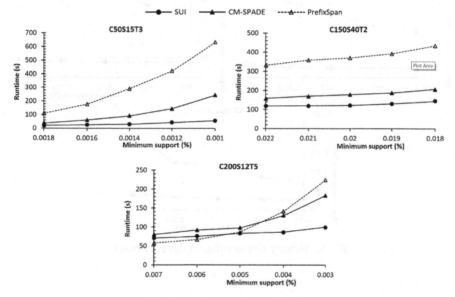

Fig. 5. Runtime on three databases

5 Summary and Future Work

Sequential pattern mining has various potential applications and many vertical algorithms have proposed for the problem. However, one issue is that they keep duplicating data information during the mining process. Pseudo-IDList and CUP were proposed to deal with this, however, they only work for a specific case of sequential patterns, which are clickstream patterns. In this paper, we proposed methods to adapt the idea of pseudo-IDLists for sequential pattern mining. We also present SUI, an algorithm for mining sequential patterns based on pseudo-IDLists and data-IDLists. Via three test databases, we showed that the SUI algorithm is efficient and effective and has a better performance than CM-SPADE and PrefixSpan, which are considered the two efficient algorithms for sequential pattern mining.

In future work, we plan to develop other algorithms based on pseudo-IDLists for other branches of the problem such as weighted or high utility sequential pattern mining or parallelize the algorithms to work in highly parallelism environments. Furthermore, even pseudo-IDList help avoiding duplicate data, a portion of duplicate information still exists via i-extension patterns and their data-IDLists. We plan to study this issue further to propose a method that can improve the capability to avoid data duplicate for i-extension patterns.

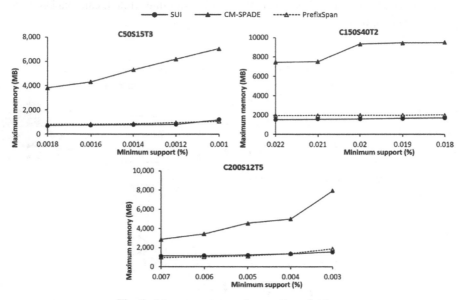

Fig. 6. Memory consumption on three databases

Acknowledgements. This work was supported by the Internal Grant Agency of Tomas Bata University under the Projects no. IGA/CebiaTech/2020/001. The work was further supported by resources of A.I.Lab at the Faculty of Applied Informatics, Tomas Bata University in Zlin (ailab.fai.utb.cz).

References

1. Agrawal, R., Srikant, R.: Mining sequential patterns. In: Proceedings of the International Conference on Data Engineering (ICDE), pp. 3–14 (1995)

2. Van, T., Vo, B., Le, B.: Mining sequential patterns with itemset constraints. Knowl. Inf. Syst. **57**(2), 311–330 (2018). https://doi.org/10.1007/s10115-018-1161-6

3. Huynh, B., Trinh, C., Huynh, H., Van, T.T., Vo, B., Snasel, V.: An efficient approach for mining sequential patterns using multiple threads on very large databases. Eng. Appl. Artif. Intell. **74**, 242–251 (2018)

4. Gan, W., Lin, J.C.-W., Fournier-Viger, P., Chao, H.-C., Yu, P.S.: HUOPM: high-utility occupancy pattern mining. IEEE Trans. Cybern. **50**, 1195–1208 (2020)

5. Ao, X., Luo, P., Wang, J., Zhuang, F., He, Q.: Mining precise-positioning episode rules from event sequences. IEEE Trans. Knowl. Data Eng. **30**, 530–543 (2018)

6. Cule, B., Feremans, L., Goethals, B.: Efficiently mining cohesion-based patterns and rules in event sequences. Data Min. Knowl. Disc. **33**(4), 1125–1182 (2019). https://doi.org/10.1007/s10618-019-00628-0

7. Rahman, M.M., Ahmed, C.F., Leung, C.K.-S.: Mining weighted frequent sequences in uncertain databases. Inf. Sci. (Ny) **479**, 76–100 (2019)

8. Mudrick, N.V., Azevedo, R., Taub, M.: Integrating metacognitive judgments and eye movements using sequential pattern mining to understand processes underlying multimedia learning. Comput. Hum. Behav. **96**, 223–234 (2019)

9. Lee, G.H., Han, H.S.: Clustering of tourist routes for individual tourists using sequential pattern mining. J. Supercomput. **76**(7), 5364–5381 (2019). https://doi.org/10.1007/s11227-019-03010-5

10. Tarus, J.K., Niu, Z., Yousif, A.: A hybrid knowledge-based recommender system for e-learning based on ontology and sequential pattern mining. Futur. Gener. Comput. Syst. **72**, 37–48 (2017)

11. Dalmas, B., Fournier-Viger, P., Norre, S.: TWINCLE: a constrained sequential rule mining algorithm for event logs. Procedia Comput. Sci. **112**, 205–214 (2017)

12. Huynh, H.M., Nguyen, L.T.T., Vo, B., Nguyen, A., Tseng, V.S.: Efficient methods for mining weighted clickstream patterns. Expert Syst. Appl. **142**, 112993 (2019)

13. Srikant, R., Agrawal, R.: Mining sequential patterns: generalizations and performance improvements. In: Apers, P., Bouzeghoub, M., Gardarin, G. (eds.) EDBT 1996. LNCS, vol. 1057, pp. 1–17. Springer, Heidelberg (1996). https://doi.org/10.1007/BFb0014140

14. Pei, J., Han, J., Chen, Q., Hsu, M.-C., Mortazavi-Asl, B., Pinto, H., Dayal, U.: PrefixSpan: mining sequential patterns efficiently by prefix-projected pattern growth. In: Proceedings of the International Conference on Data Engineering (ICDE), pp. 215–224 (2001)

15. Zaki, M.J.: SPADE: An efficient algorithm for mining frequent sequences. Mach. Learn. **42**, 31–60 (2001). https://doi.org/10.1023/A:1007652502315

16. Fournier-Viger, P., Gomariz, A., Campos, M., Thomas, R.: Fast vertical mining of sequential patterns using co-occurrence information. In: Proceedings of the Pacific-Asia Conference on Knowledge Discovery and Data Mining. pp. 40–52 (2014)

17. Huynh, H.M., Nguyen, L.T.T., Vo, B., Yun, U., Oplatková, Z.K., Hong, T.-P.: Efficient algorithms for mining clickstream patterns using pseudo-IDLists. Futur. Gener. Comput. Syst. **107**, 18–30 (2020)

18. Fournier-Viger, P., Lin, J.C.W., Gomariz, A., Gueniche, T., Soltani, A., Deng, Z., Lam, H.T.: The SPMF open-source data mining library version 2. In: Proceedings of the Joint European Conference on Machine Learning and Knowledge Discovery in Databases, pp. 36–40 (2016)

Machine Learning Methods

A Method for Building Heterogeneous Ensembles of Regression Models Based on a Genetic Algorithm

Bartosz Kardas[1], Mateusz Piwowarczyk[1] ⓘ, Zbigniew Telec[1] ⓘ,
Bogdan Trawiński[1(✉)] ⓘ, Patient Zihisire Muke[1] ⓘ, and Loan Thi Thuy Nguyen[2] ⓘ

[1] Department of Applied Informatics, Wrocław University of Science and Technology,
Wrocław, Poland
{mateusz.piwowarczyk,zbigniew.telec,bogdan.trawinski,
patient.zihisire}@pwr.edu.pl
[2] School of Computer Science and Engineering, International University,
Ho Chi Minh City, Vietnam
nttloan@hcmiu.edu.vn

Abstract. This paper focuses on the use of evolutionary methods to generate ensembles of regression models. A novel method for building heterogeneous and homogeneous ensembles using a genetic algorithm was presented in the paper. It consists in generating an excess number of component models and selecting from them a subsets which provides the best performance. A series of experiments was conducted to examine its properties as well as the impact of its various hyperparameters on the accuracy of models created. A real-world data of sales transactions of apartments completed in a Polish city was employed to the evaluation procedure. Results of the statistical analysis applied to compare the proposed method with classic bagging, AdaBoost and single regressors revealed that it outperformed significantly the tested algorithms but bagging.

Keywords: Machine learning · Regression models · Heterogeneous ensembles · Genetic algorithms · Real estate appraisal

1 Introduction

Over the years, it has been proven many times that machine learning ensembles reveal better accuracy and stability compared to single component models. According to Polikar [1], the first work using model ensemble methods was [2] by Dasarathy and Sheel from 1979. They used the divide and conquer method to split the space of features into subsets, which were then used to train two and more classifiers. After more than ten years, Hansen and Salamon [3] demonstrated that models using multiple classifiers (in the form of many similarly configured neural networks) have variance-reducing properties and better generalize. In 1990 Schapire [4] showed that several weak classifiers can be combined into one strong classifier. Thanks to this work, many researchers began to intensively explore the field of machine learning model ensembles.

© Springer Nature Switzerland AG 2020
N. T. Nguyen et al. (Eds.): ICCCI 2020, LNAI 12496, pp. 357–372, 2020.
https://doi.org/10.1007/978-3-030-63007-2_28

Up to date a large number of various approaches have been devised to create ensembles of classification and regression models. The best-known are mixture of experts [5], stacked generalization [6], dynamic model selection [7], fusion of classifiers [8]. Many predictive regression models for auto- mated property valuation are generated using multiple learning algorithms. Our research we have conducted so far in the field of real estate valuation has been based on various advanced techniques of machine learning, including ensemble learning [9–11], evolutionary fuzzy systems [12] as well as evolving fuzzy systems [13]. We have developed and tested several multiple learning methods employing bagging with decision trees, support vector machines, artificial neural networks, and fuzzy systems as base learners [14, 15] as well as bagging combined with fuzzy genetic systems [16, 17].

A new method for creating heterogeneous ensembles is presented in the paper. It includes a genetic algorithm applied to compose an ensemble from a subset of models whose weighted combination provides the best performance. A series of experiments was conducted to compare the proposed method with single models and standard ensembles: bagging and AdaBoost. A real-world dataset containing the sales/purchase transaction of apartments derived from a cadastral system was employed.

2 Related Works

The method for creating a neural network ensemble based on genetic algorithm GEASEN devised by Wu et al. [18, 19] for regression problems was the one which inspired the authors to develop the method presented in this paper. There are also several methods, similar to GASEN, that address classification problems. The first is GA-EoC [20]. It is a heterogeneous ensemble consisting of 20 algorithms divided into 5 families (bayesian algorithms, function approximations, k-nearest neighbors, rule-based algorithm and decision trees). In addition, this method uses only the binary representation of the chromosome. The second method described in [21], a genetic algorithms-based coverage optimization system for ensemble learning, uses similar solutions to GA-EoC.

Other approaches consisted in the selection of component models employing various representations of individuals and different fitness functions. An additional gene was used in [22], which determined the method of combination of results - voting and meta-classifier. In [23], multi-criteria optimization was used. The first criterion was the error produced by an ensemble, while the second was a specially defined measure of diversity between the component models.

Liu et al. [24] explicitly use the properties of methods based on negative correlation (NCL). At first, the models are generated according to the NCL algorithm. Then, parents are selected randomly from among them for the individuals in the next generation. After crossover and mutation operations, these individuals are combined with their parents into a set on which the fitness function based on the negative correlation is calculated. As a result, the weakest individuals are discarded and the set returns to its original size. This process is repeated until a stopping condition is reached.

The most advanced method is presented in [25]. It involves improving the combination of individual neural networks and the cooperative evolution of such networks. For this purpose, a number of criteria are designed that the genetic algorithm is to optimize.

Some of them relate to individual networks, i.e. criteria of performance, regularization, diversity and cooperation. For the evaluation of the ensemble as a whole, the criteria of performance and ambiguity are applied.

Kuncheva and Jain in [26] proposed a method of building ensembles based on genetic selection of feature sets for individual models. As a result of optimization, each model uses different parameters. Such a method allows for obtaining an appropriate variety, and also prevents dimensional curvature.

Methods of fuzzy logic, machine learning ensembles and genetic optimization can also be interconnected to create effective systems. Specific coding of the ensemble model and a criterion based on entropy was proposed in [27]. Multi-criteria optimization was used also in [28] to create classifier ensemble based on fuzzy reasoning. Optimization in this case was based on the creation of a set of models using rules with the widest possible diversity. Similarly, in [29] a hierarchical method of evolution to create nondominant fuzzy classifiers with the diversity and interpretability requirement is presented.

One of the most important characteristic of well performing in terms of prediction accuracy ensemble machine learning models is diversity of a model. Diettrich and Tang et al. underlined the importance of this concept in [30] and [31] respectively. Diversity can be established in many different ways, and can be measured differently according to its way of creation. We can achieve diversity of ensemble model mainly in three ways, that is: data diversity, parameter diversity and structural diversity.

In data diversity we try to ensure diversity by splitting original dataset on multiple, diverse subsets of sample data and train multiple diverse predictors of the same type using this different subsets.

One of the most popular methods for creating data diverse models using input training data are: bagging [32], adaptive boosting (AdaBoost) [33], random subspace [34] and random forest [35]. On the other hand it is possible to manipulate output data, to achieve diversity in terms of data. One of the most popular technique using this approach is 'output smearing' [36].

Another way of creating diverse ensemble models is parameter diversity and it is achieved by generating diverse set of models using the same base predictor, but with different parameters. In parameter diversity outputs of the base predictor with diverse set of its parameters may vary even on the same training dataset on the input. One of the most popular method that use parameter diversity is the Multiple Kernel Learning [37]. In this technique multiple kernels are combined together, to provide accurate prediction.

The third of the main ways to create diverse prediction ensemble models is called structural diversity and it uses method based on creating ensemble models that are diverse in a sense of their structure of base predictors. Several base predictors, that could be different in size, parameters and architecture, are used in this method. This approach is applied to generate heterogeneous ensemble models [38]. In fact, we can distinguish many other methods for achieving diversity among prediction ensemble models, and they can be, for example, the "divide and conquer" technique, which is widely used in time series analysis and forecasting, multi-objective optimization, where we can have several goals and we need to find the optimal Pareto solution, as in the case of the bias-variance trade-off [39]. There are also techniques based on fuzzy sets or fuzzy logic that are widely used to deal with missing values or any other data imperfection.

Because we cannot strictly define diversity [31], each measure of diversity depends on the context. Below are some of the most intuitive measures that rely on comparing diversity among many base classifiers. First, it is the disagreement measure that was proposed by Skalak [40]. It assumes that different classifiers should produce different results on the same training data. The disagreement measure is in base words the ratio of the number of classifications that were not consistent between the measured models to the number of all classifications. Another measure of diversity that we can suggest is the double-fault measure introduced by Giacinto and Roli in 2001 [41]. In this measure, we only count the ratio of incorrect classifications to the number of all classifications.

3   Algorithm Description

The proposed method consists of two main phases. The first is to generate an excess number of component models. The process consists in creating a model, training it and validating it. Then, the genetic algorithm is applied to select a subset of models whose weighted combination achieves the best performance with a specific fitness function. The method is outlined in Fig. 1. The individual steps are described in detail below.

Algorithm 1: Outline of Evolutionary Method

Data: T - set of model types
D - set of diversity ensuring techniques
Dataset split into $X_{train}, X_{validation}, X_{test}$
Result: m_{best} - the best genetically generated solution
Initialization;
$M \longleftarrow trainedmodelsset$ **for** $d \in D$ **do**
    for $t \in T$ **do**
        $m_i \longleftarrow trainModel(t, d, X_{train}, X_{validation})$
        $M.add(m_i)$

for $m_i \in M$ **do**
    if $isOutlier(m_i.error)$ **then**
        $M.remove(m_i)$
$m_{best} \longleftarrow generateBestGenetically(M, X_{train}, X_{validation}, X_{test})$

Fig. 1. Outline of the proposed evolutionary method.

3.1   Model Parameter Selection

The composition of a heterogeneous set of models may include one of K different types of models. In our research we employed five types of component models built with *polynomial regression (poly), k-nearest neighbors (knn), decision tree (tree), support vector regression (svr), multilayer perceptron neural network (mlp)*. Every component model was generated using randomly selected diversity ensuring technique. We used four such techniques, i.e. random parameters (*PARAM*), random training samples (*BAG*), random attribute subspace (*SUB*), and random forest (*RAN*) as the combination of *SUB* and *BAG*. The *PARAM* technique consists in a random selection of hyperparameters for a given type of algorithm. The list of the ranges of hyperparameters which values were randomly chosen in this process is presented in Table 1. For the *BAG*, *SUB* and *RAN* techniques the hyperparameters are selected by the *PARAM* method for a given model type and then used by training with one of the other techniques for ensuring diversity. The hyperparameters at this step are the types of models used, techniques for ensuring diversity, and the target size of the set of candidate models.

Table 1. Ranges of hyperparameter values used in the experiment: *len(X)* is the size of the training set, n_{i-1} is the number of neurons in the preceding layer

Algorithm	Parameter name	Possible values
poly	degree of polynomial	*{1, 2, ..., 5}*
poly	bias	*{true, false}*
poly	unique monomials	*{true, false}*
knn	Minkowski metric (p)	*{1, 2}*
knn	number of neighbors	*{2, ..., len(X)/4}*
knn	weights	*{uniform, distance}*
poly	degree of polynomial	*{1, 2, ..., 5}*
tree	maximum depth	*{1, 2, ..., 10}*
tree	number of features	*{1, 2, ..., 5}*
tree	division criterion	*{mae, mse}*
tree	division	*{best, random}*
svr	gamma	*<0.1, 0.9>*
svr	epsilon	*<0.1, 0.9>*
svr	C	*<0.5, 5.0>*
svr	kernel	*{sigmoid, rbf}*
mlp	activation function	*{identity, logistics, tanh, relu}*
mlp	optimizer	*{adam, sgd, lbfgs}*
mlp	learning rate	*{fixed, inverse, adaptive}*
mlp	number of layers	*{1,2,..., 10}*
mlp	number of neurons in a layer	*{$n_{i-1}/2$, ..., $n_{i-1} - 1$}*

3.2 Training

In the next step, all models are built over the training dataset using the selected parameters. Then, they are evaluated over the validation dataset using the mean absolute error

(*MAE*). The results produced by individual models are saved and used in the evolutionary process.

Outliers are removed from the set of trained models. Outliers are those models for which the mean absolute error exceeded the following value: $MAE_{Value} > Q3 + 1.5 *$ $(Q3 - Q1)$, where $Q1$ and $Q3$ stand for lower quartile and upper quartile respectively. At this stage, the neural networks that have not achieved convergence are also removed from the set of trained models.

3.3 Genetic Algorithm

Chromosome Representation. A single chromosome is a vector of real numbers from the range <0, 1> or in the second variant taken from the set of integer numbers: {0, 1} as binary representation. For binary representation some mutation parameters were turned off. Each number in the vector represents the weight of influence of a component model on the final result. The higher weight, the greater influence of the component model. Additionally, the method was enriched with a two- stage genetic algorithm which, in the first stage, works on the binary representation of chromosomes, and in the second one (after finding the best subset of base models) on real number representation in order to modify the weights of selected models.

Crossover. Uniform crossover was used, where each bit is chosen from either parent with given probability. In our case this process occurs for a pair of chromosomes with a 50% probability.

Mutation. Three types of mutations were implemented. They are all point mutations which means, that individual values (x_i) in genotype are the subject of random changes. Used mutation functions are:

- Negation: $f(x_i) = 1 - x_i$
- Random real: $f(x_i) = uniform(0,1)$
- Random integer: $f(x_i) = randint(0,1)$

The *uniform* and *randint* functions choose random number from the uniform distribution of real numbers and binary integer respectively. Each of the above mutations occurs in two stages with appropriate probabilities. In the first stage, mutations that are likely to occur with a 15% probability are determined. In the second stage, if a given mutation occurs, each element of the genotype is mutated with a 50% secondary probability. The type of mutation is selected evenly among the three possible ones described above.

Selection. Tournament selection was used. It involves random creation of a subset of individuals of a given size, and then choosing the best of them. The bigger the tournament group, the greater the favouritism of the best individuals in the population. In our research 5 individuals were chosen for the tournament group.

Fitness Function. During the preliminary experiments we tested a few fitness functions, namely maximum value, average and median of square errors, absolute errors, and absolute percentage errors. The Mean Absolute Error (*MAE*) was chosen as the final fitness function.

4 Experimental Setup

The evaluation experiments aimed to examine the performance of the proposed method applied to generate homogeneous and heterogeneous ensembles. We compared our method to single models as well as to the ensemble models created with two standard approaches: bagging [32] and AdaBoost [33].

4.1 Implementation

The method presented in the paper was implemented in Python environment using the *scikit-learn* library. It is one of the most popular Python extensions containing machine learning tools. It provides implementation of all algorithms described in previous chapters employed to build both component models and classic ensembles.

The genetic algorithm has been implemented using the *DEAP* library. It contains a number of tools for the development of evolutionary algorithms in the Python environment, such as the most popular genetic operators and selection methods. Other parts of the experiments, including statistical tests, have been implemented using the *SciPy* library.

4.2 Dataset

The experiments were conducted on a real-world dataset derived from the cadastral system of one of the major Polish cities. It contains 16 605 records of sale/purchase transactions concluded in 2007–2015. Each transaction was described by 31 attributes such as: number of cadastral region, number of expert zone, distance from the city center, parks, and shopping centers, year of construction, floor, number of rooms and others. In addition, an analysis of the description of the property was carried out, on the basis of which further attributes were extracted, such as the type of kitchen or balcony, the number of rooms, the presence of a garage, mezzanine and others. Five the most important attributes according to the real estate market expert opinion were selected: usable area of apartment, number of floors in the building, year of construction, distance from the city center and distance from the shopping center. Base models were then generated using these attributes but in the case of attributes randomizing methods (random subspace, random forest) all 31 available attributes were utilized. In turn, price per square metre in PLN was taken as the output variable. Data standardization was used to transform each attribute so that its average value is 0.0 and the standard deviation is 1.0. As a result, problems related to the data scale, to which some basic algorithms are sensitive, such as k-nearest neighbors and neural networks, were eliminated.

The dataset was randomly split into subsets for training, validation, and testing accounting for 50%, 25% and 25% of the full data set, respectively. To avoid uneven partition of apartments within the city area, this division took into account expert zones.

Instances were randomly selected from each zone and divided between sets according to the above proportions. The training set was used to generate component models, validation set to estimate the fit of individuals in the evolution process, while the test set served to the final assessment of the found solution.

4.3 Scope

The scope of the experiments is presented in Table 2, briefly describing their names, goals and hypotheses. To achieve the goals of our research a series of preliminary experiments was conducted to examine such model hyperparameters as population size, fitness function, diversity ensuring technique, mutations, and types of base algorithms to build models with the best possible configuration of them.

Table 2. Scope of experiments

Experiment	Goal	Hypotesis
Size of the set of models	Does the size of a set of component models have a significant impact on the accuracy of the generated ensemble?	No significant differences in MAE values among ensembles built with different number of base models
Techniques for ensuring diversity	Does a technique for ensuring diversity have a significant impact on the accuracy of the generated model?	No significant differences in MAE values among ensembles built with different diversity ensuring techniques
Mutation	Does the type of mutation have a significant impact on the accuracy of the generated model?	No significant differences in MAE values among ensembles built with different mutation types
Homo- vs. heterogeneity	Does the ensemble composed of different type models outperforms ensembles comprising models of the same type?	No significant differences in MAE values between heterogeneous and homogeneous ensembles
Single models	Does the ensemble built with the proposed method outperforms single component models?	No significant differences in MAE values between the ensemble built with the proposed method and single component models
Ensembles	Does the proposed method outperforms classic bagging and AdaBoost?	No significant differences in MAE values between the ensemble built with the proposed method and classic bagging and AdaBoost ensembles

The following hyperparameter values were used in the experiment: population size - 200 individuals, fitness function mean absolute error (*MAE*), diversity ensuring technique parameter randomization, mutations - binary, integer representation, types of base algorithms – *all, poly, knn, tree, svr, mlp*, number of generations - 400, tournament size - 5 individuals, crossover probability - 75%, negation mutation probability - 15% (real number representation), real number probability mutation - 15% (real number representation), integer mutation probability - 15%, single event in the mutation - 15%. In the comparative experiments with single models and classic ensembles, the parameters that provided the best performance in the first four experiments were used.

4.4 Statistical Analysis

The statistical analysis was conducted on a test set divided into 100 random subsets by drawing them randomly from the test set without replacement. Thus, each subset consisted of 41 or 42 data points. Next, prediction accuracy in terms of the mean absolute error was computed for every subset. In this way for each tested algorithm a sample of 100 MAE values was obtained. These values were used to examine differences in performance of individual models employing parametric and non-parametric statistical tests for multiple comparison as shown in Table 3. To determine what type of statistical significance tests should be used, the normality and equality of variance of the individual samples were examined. In the event that at least one of the null hypotheses in the Shapiro-Wilk test and Bartlett's test was rejected, nonparametric tests were used in the further procedure. On the other hand, if there was no evidence for rejecting both null hypotheses, parametric tests were applied. The level of significance was set to 0.05 in each test.

Table 3. Summary of statistical tests employed

Feature examined	Test	
Normality of distribution	Shapiro–Wilk test	
Feature examined	*Normal distribution*	*Non normal distribution*
Equality of variances	Bartlett's test	Levene's test
Feature examined	*Parametric tests*	*Nonparametric tests*
Means/Medians	Student's t-test	Wilcoxon test
Multiple comparison	ANOVA test	Friedman test
Post-hoc procedure	Tukey's test	Nemenyi test

5 Analysis of Experimental Results

The results of six experiments are illustrated in the form of box plots in Figs. 2, 3, 4, 5, 6 and 7. In turn, their rank according to the mean absolute error is presented in Table 4. We denoted the individual models as follows:

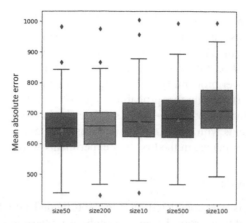

Fig. 2. Box plot of results for examining sizes of model sets.

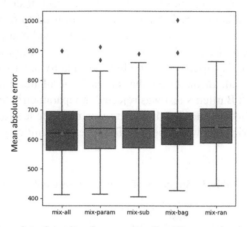

Fig. 3. Box plot of results of comparing diversity ensuring techniques.

sizeN –   ensemble model built with N base models,
mix-all –   ensemble built with all methods for diversity ensuring,
mix-bag –   ensemble built with bagging method,
mix–param –   ensemble built with random hyperparameters,
mix-ran – e   nsemble built with random forest,
mix-sub –   ensemble built with random subspace,
bin –   ensemble built with binary genes,
real –   ensemble built with real number genes,
two–stage –   ensemble built with combination of *bin* and *real*,
evo –   model built by our method presented in this paper,
knn –   k-nearest neighbors algorithm,
lin –   linear regression,
mlp –   multilayer perceptron neural network,
svr –   support–vector regression,

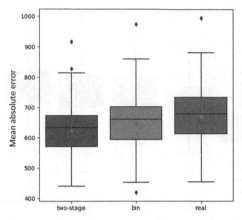

Fig. 4. Box plot of results of comparing mutation types.

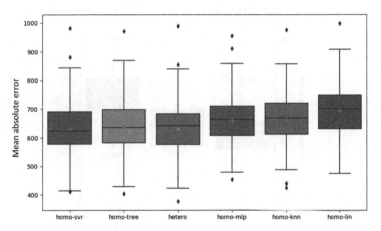

Fig. 5. Box plot of results of comparing heterogeneous and homogeneous ensembles.

tree –	decision tree,
hetero –	heterogeneous ensemble,
homo-model-name –	homogeneous ensemble consisting of *model–name* types,
ada –	ensemble built with AdaBoost method,
bag –	ensemble built with bagging method

The goal of the first experiment was to examine if the size of the set of component models significantly affect the performance of generated ensembles. The ensembles composed of 50 and 200 models provided the lowest MAE value (see Table 4). However, based on the Tukey's test, they turned out statistically significant better than only the *size100* ensemble. No statistically significant difference in performance was observed, between *size50* and *size200* ensembles. The results of this experiment are presented in Fig. 2.

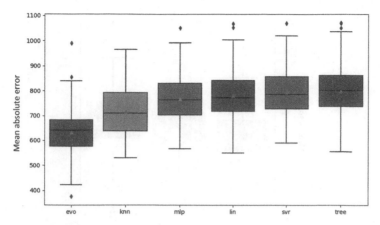

Fig. 6. Box plot of results of comparison with single models.

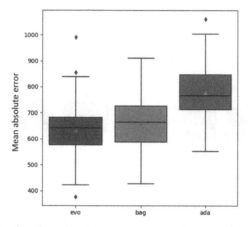

Fig. 7. Box plot of results of comparison with classic ensemble methods.

The second experiment aimed at comparison of diversity ensuring techniques. The models built with *mix-all* and *mix-param* revealed the best accuracy. However, according to the Nemenyi test, they outperformed significantly the *mix-ran* model. Moreover, the *mix-all* model surpassed significantly the *mix-bag* one. The results of this experiment are depicted in Fig. 3.

In the mutation experiment the *two-stage* method produced the smallest MAE and this method was significantly better than the *real* one in the Tukey's test. The results of this experiment are shown in Fig. 4.

In the experiment comparing homogeneous and heterogeneous ensembles the *hetero* and *homo-svr* ensembles produced the lowest value of MAE. Based on the Nemenyi test, they turned out significantly better than the *homo-knn, homo-mlp,* and *homo-tree* ensembles. No statistically significant difference in MAE was detected between *hetero* and *homo-svr* ensembles. The results of this experiment are displayed in Fig. 5.

Table 4. Performance of models in individual experiments

Experiment	Rank by Mean Absolute Error for prices in PLN					
	1st	2nd	3rd	4th	5th	6th
Size	size50	size200	size10	size500	size100	
	645.38	649.31	675.19	678.4	709.26	
Diversity	mix-all	mix-param	mix-sub	mix-bag	mix-ran	
	623.24	624.43	632.4	636.37	645.23	
Mutation	two-stage	bin	real			
	626.17	648.06	671.23			
Homo-vs heterogeneity	hetero	homo-svr	homo-tree	homo-mlp	homo-knn	homo-lin
	632.54	632.76	638.82	664.24	664.43	695.9
Single models	evo	knn	mlp	lin	svr	tree
	632.54	713.43	766.66	780.34	794.15	798.36
Ensembles	evo	bag	ada			
	632.54	661.69	776.92			

In the last two experiments we evaluated the *evo* heterogeneous ensemble built using our proposed method which the features were selected based on the results of the first four experiments. The features providing the best performance, presented in the 1st column of Table 4, were employed. The *evo* ensemble outperformed significantly all compared single models, namely the *knn, lin, mlp, svr,* and *tree* models as well as the *ada* classic ensemble. Only no statistically significant difference in performance was observed between the *evo* and *bag* ensembles. The results of this comparative experiments are presented in Figs. 6 and 7.

6 Conclusions

A new method for creating heterogeneous machine learning ensembles based on a genetic algorithm was devised in the paper. Its selected hyperparameters and features were examined and compared with single component models and classic methods for ensemble creation. The statistical analysis provided a lot of useful information about the differences in the analyzed algorithms.

In the first stage, the influence of individual hyperparameters on the results of the proposed method was examined, including the size of the set of component models, methods of ensuring diversity and types of mutations. It was shown that the proposed method achieved the best results on sets of 50 and 200 models. Among the methods of ensuring diversity, the best results were obtained by the mixed method, but compared to methods based on randomizing parameters and attributes these differences were not statistically significant. By intuition, the two-step method of mutation was most accurate, with the difference between it and the binary representation not being statistically significant.

In the second stage, homogeneous and heterogeneous ensembles, single models and classical methods were compared with each other. The experiments showed that the proposed heterogeneous method achieved comparable results to the homogeneous version of the same method employing support vector regression and decision trees. Compared to the methods based on single models, the proposed algorithm showed a significantly lower mean absolute error. The implemented method obtained similar results in comparison to the classic methods of generating regression ensembles, such as bagging and AdaBoost. However, the statistical analysis revealed that the differences between the proposed method and bagging were not statistically significant.

Further research is planned, including checking whether the proposed method is equally effective on other datasets. In addition, the proposed method can be further improved in many places, for example, instead of a random generation of base models, a method based on negative correlation could be used. Such a procedure could improve results while reducing processing time. Another interesting extension could be the use of dynamic model selection, which could ensure the optimal composition of the algorithms depending on the test examples.

References

1. Polikar, R.: Ensemble based systems in decision making. IEEE Circuits Syst. Mag. **6**(3), 21–45 (2006)
2. Dasarathy, B.V., Sheela, B.V.: A composite classifier system design: concepts and methodology. Proc. IEEE **67**(5), 708–713 (1979)
3. Hansen, L.K., Salamon, P.: Neural network ensembles. IEEE Trans. Pattern Anal. Mach. Intell. **12**(10), 993–1001 (1990)
4. Schapire, R.E.: The strength of weak learnability. Mach. Learn. **5**(2), 197–227 (1990)
5. Jacobs, R.A., Jordan, M.I., Nowlan, S.J., Hinton, G.E.: Adaptive mixtures of local experts. Neural Comput. **3**(1), 79–87 (1991)
6. Wolpert, D.H.: Stacked generalization. Neural Networks **5**(2), 241–259 (1992)
7. Woods, K., Kegelmeyer, W.P., Bowyer, K.: Combination of multiple classifiers using local accuracy estimates. IEEE Trans. Pattern Anal. Mach. Intell. **19**(4), 405–410 (1997)
8. Kuncheva, L.I., Bezdek, J.C., Duin, R.P.: Decision templates for multiple classifier fusion: an experimental comparison. Pattern Recogn. **34**(2), 299–314 (2001)
9. Woźniak, M., Graña, M., Corchado, E.: A survey of multiple classifier systems as hybrid systems. Inf. Fusion **16**, 3–17 (2014)
10. Jędrzejowicz, J., Jędrzejowicz, P.: A family of GEP-Induced ensemble classifiers. In: Nguyen, N.T., Kowalczyk, R., Chen, S.-M. (eds.) ICCCI 2009. LNCS (LNAI), vol. 5796, pp. 641–652. Springer, Heidelberg (2009). https://doi.org/10.1007/978-3-642-04441-0_56
11. Burduk, R., Baczyńska, P.: Dynamic ensemble selection using discriminant functions and normalization between class labels – approach to binary classification. In: Rutkowski, L., Korytkowski, M., Scherer, R., Tadeusiewicz, R., Zadeh, L.A., Zurada, J.M. (eds.) ICAISC 2016. LNCS (LNAI), vol. 9692, pp. 563–570. Springer, Cham (2016). https://doi.org/10.1007/978-3-319-39378-0_48
12. Fernández, A., López, V., José del Jesus, M., Herrera, F.: Revisiting evolutionary fuzzy systems: taxonomy, applications, new trends and challenges. Knowl. Based Syst. **80**, 109–121 (2015)
13. Lughofer, E., Cernuda, C., Kindermann, S., Pratama, M.: Generalized smart evolving fuzzy systems. Evolving Syst. **6**(4), 269–292 (2015). https://doi.org/10.1007/s12530-015-9132-6

14. Lasota, T., Telec, Z., Trawiński, B., Trawiński, K.: A multi-agent system to assist with real estate appraisals using bagging ensembles. In: Nguyen, N.T., Kowalczyk, R., Chen, S.-M. (eds.) ICCCI 2009. LNCS (LNAI), vol. 5796, pp. 813–824. Springer, Heidelberg (2009). https://doi.org/10.1007/978-3-642-04441-0_71

15. Krzystanek, M., Lasota, T., Telec, Z., Trawiński, B.: Analysis of bagging ensembles of fuzzy models for premises valuation. In: Nguyen, N.T., Le, M.T., Świątek, J. (eds.) ACIIDS 2010. LNCS (LNAI), vol. 5991, pp. 330–339. Springer, Heidelberg (2010). https://doi.org/10.1007/978-3-642-12101-2_34

16. Lasota, T., Telec, Z., Trawiński, B., Trawiński, K.: Exploration of bagging ensembles comprising genetic fuzzy models to assist with real estate appraisals. In: Corchado, E., Yin, H. (eds.) IDEAL 2009. LNCS, vol. 5788, pp. 554–561. Springer, Heidelberg (2009). https://doi.org/10.1007/978-3-642-04394-9_67

17. Lasota, T., Telec, Z., Trawiński, G., Trawiński, B.: Empirical comparison of resampling methods using genetic fuzzy systems for a regression problem. In: Yin, H., Wang, W., Rayward-Smith, V. (eds.) IDEAL 2011. LNCS, vol. 6936, pp. 17–24. Springer, Heidelberg (2011). https://doi.org/10.1007/978-3-642-23878-9_3

18. Zhou, Z.-H., Wu, J.-X., Jiang, Y., Chen, S.F.: Genetic algorithm based selective neural network ensemble. In: Proceedings of the 17th International Joint Conference on Artificial Intelligence, vol. 2, pp. 797-802 (2001)

19. Zhou, Z.-H., Wu, J., Tang, W.: Ensembling neural networks: many could be better than all. Artif. Intell. **137**(1–2), 239–263 (2002)

20. Haque, M.N., Noman, N., Berretta, R., Moscato, P.: Heterogeneous ensemble combination search using genetic algorithm for class imbalanced data classification. PLoS ONE **11**(1), e0146116, 1–28 (2016)

21. Kim, M.-J., Kang, D.-K.: Classifiers selection in ensembles using genetic algorithms for bankruptcy prediction. Expert Syst. Appl. **39**(10), 9308–9314 (2012)

22. Ordonez, F.J., Ledezma, A., Sanchis, A.: Genetic approach for optimizing ensembles of classifiers. In: Proceedings of the Twenty-First International FLAIRS Conference, pp. 89-94. AAAI Press (2008)

23. Kadri, C., Tian, F., Zhang, L., Peng, X., Yin, X.: Multi-objective genetic algorithm based selective neural networks ensemble for concentration estimation of indoor air pollutants using electronic nose. Int. J. Comput. Sci. Issues **10**(3), 105–112 (2013)

24. Liu, Y., Yao, X., Higuchi, T.: Evolutionary ensembles with negative correlation learning. IEEE Trans. Evol. Comput. **4**(4), 380–387 (2000)

25. Garcia-Pedrajas, N., Hervas-Martinez, C., Ortiz-Boyer, D.: Cooperative coevolution of artificial neural network ensembles for pattern classification. IEEE Trans. Evol. Comput. **9**(3), 271–302 (2005)

26. Kuncheva, L.I., Jain, L.C.: Designing classifier fusion systems by genetic algorithms. IEEE Trans. Evol. Comput. **4**(4), 327–336 (2000)

27. Nojima, Y., Ishibuchi, H.: Designing fuzzy ensemble classifiers by evolutionary multiobjective optimization with an entropy-based diversity criterion. In: Sixth International Conference on Hybrid Intelligent Systems (HIS 2006), pp. 59–59, IEEE (2006)

28. Ishibuchi, H., Yamamoto, T.: Evolutionary multiobjective optimization for generating an ensemble of fuzzy rule-based classifiers. In: Cantú-Paz, E., et al. (eds.) GECCO 2003. LNCS, vol. 2723, pp. 1077–1088. Springer, Heidelberg (2003). https://doi.org/10.1007/3-540-45105-6_117

29. Cao, J., Wang, H., Kwong, S., Li, K.: Combining interpretable fuzzy rule-based classifiers via multi-objective hierarchical evolutionary algorithm. In: 2011 IEEE International Conference on Systems, Man, and Cybernetics, pp. 1771–1776 (2011)

30. Dietterich, T.G.: Ensemble methods in machine learning. In: Kittler, J., Roli, F. (eds.) MCS 2000. LNCS, vol. 1857, pp. 1–15. Springer, Heidelberg (2000). https://doi.org/10.1007/3-540-45014-9_1

31. Tang, E.K., Suganthan, P.N., Yao, X.: An analysis of diversity measures. Mach. Learn. **65**(1), 247–271 (2006)

32. Breiman, L.: Bagging predictors. Mach. Learn. **24**(2), 123–140 (1996)

33. Schapire, R.E.: Explaining AdaBoost. In: Schölkopf, B., Luo, Z., Vovk, V. (eds.) Empirical Inference. LNCS, pp. 37–52. Springer, Heidelberg (2013). https://doi.org/10.1007/978-3-642-41136-6_5

34. Tan, C., Li, M., Qin, X.: Random subspace regression ensemble for near-infrared spectroscopic calibration of tobacco samples. Anal. Sci. **24**(5), 647–653 (2008)

35. Breiman, L.: Random forests. Mach. Learn. **45**(1), 5–32 (2001)

36. Breiman, L.: Randomizing outputs to increase prediction accuracy. Mach. Learn. **40**(3), 229–242 (2000)

37. Gonen, M., Alpaydin, E.: Multiple kernel learning algorithms. J. Mach. Learn. Res. **12**, 2211–2268 (2011)

38. Mendes-Moreira, J., Soares, C., Jorge, A.M., Sousa, J.F.D.: Ensemble approaches for regression: a survey. ACM Comput. Surv. **45**(1), 1–40 (2012)

39. Geman, S., Bienenstock, E., Doursat, R.: Neural networks and the bias/variance dilemma. Neural Comput. **4**(1), 1–58 (1992)

40. Skalak, D.B.: The sources of increased accuracy for two proposed boosting algorithms. In: Proceedings of American Association for Artificial Intelligence, AAAI 1996, vol. 1129, pp. 120–125 (1996)

41. Giacinto, G., Roli, F.: Design of effective neural network ensembles for image classification purposes. Image Vis. Comput. **19**(9), 699–707 (2001)

A Combined Learning-Based Bagging Method for Classification Improvement

Chau Vo[(✉)] [iD] and Hua Phung Nguyen[(✉)] [iD]

Faculty of Computer Science and Engineering, Ho Chi Minh City University of Technology,
Vietnam National University-HCMC, Ho Chi Minh City, Vietnam
{chauvtn,nhphung}@hcmut.edu.vn

Abstract. Classification is one of the most popular and important data mining tasks. It has been resolved by many various machine learning approaches. Combining different learning approaches has been considered in many existing works to take advantages of each learning approach and to suit a particular application domain. At this moment, their methods have been mainly defined with unsupervised learning and supervised learning. However, they are quite complex with data space exploration and parameter settings. As a result, they are non-trivial to be brought to various application domains. Different from the existing works, in this paper, we propose a combined learning-based bagging method for classification improvement in a simple but effective manner. In our method, partitional clustering and k-Nearest Neighbors (k-NN) are combined with each other to form a base classifier. This base classifier is then a component of a final ensemble model designed in a bagging mechanism. Three new design points that make our method effective are: (1). tackling the difficulties of k-NN by means of cluster-based nearest neighbors, (2). defining a new distance that can take into account both nearest neighbors and density of neighborhoods, and (3). conducting a bagging mechanism to form a better classifier from many ordinary classifiers based on individual combinations. Via an empirical evaluation on several datasets in education and medicine, our method outperforms its variants and other baseline ones with better Accuracy and F-measure results. The method can thus be applied in practical applications for more effectiveness.

Keywords: Bagging · Ensemble model · Unsupervised learning · Local learning

1 Introduction

Nowadays, classification is one of the most important and popular data mining tasks. It has been applied in many various application domains, e.g. education, medicine, (e) commerce, finance, (e) marketing, etc. Some applications are listed as follows. In education, student classification is used to identify if a student belongs to any predefined study group. In medicine, label prediction is used to diagnose if a person is a patient. In e-commerce, classification is applied to categorize customers into appropriate customer segments. In order to perform this task, many various machine learning approaches have been used. They are listed as unsupervised learning, supervised learning, semi-supervised learning,

© Springer Nature Switzerland AG 2020
N. T. Nguyen et al. (Eds.): ICCCI 2020, LNAI 12496, pp. 373–387, 2020.
https://doi.org/10.1007/978-3-030-63007-2_29

transfer learning, and so on. Combining different learning approaches has been considered in many existing works to take advantages of each learning approach so that the task can be solved more effectively in a particular application domain. Some typical works proposed with such a combined approach are [4, 6, 9, 16]. At this moment, their methods have been mainly defined with unsupervised learning and supervised learning. They are dedicated to classification on imbalanced overlapping datasets. Such data characteristics make the task challenging. For data imbalance, SMOTE and its variants as those discussed in [7] can support the task, while for data overlapping, new representation in other spaces where there exists no overlapping might be needed. Each of these two problems is non-trivial and thus, handling both of them simultaneously is harder. For such reasons, the solutions defined in the related works are quite complex with data space exploration and parameter settings. As a result, it is not straightforward to bring them to a domain of interest.

Indeed, in [4], a binary classification task is supported with cluster-based support vector machines (SVMs). The proposed method in [4] needs to explicitly identify overlapping and non-overlapping regions so that statistical learning models can be constructed on such regions. If those regions are not large enough, their models might not be effective. As for [6], unsupervised learning is also combined with any existing supervised learning algorithm. However, it is used in the preprocessing phase to resize the training dataset with undersampling so that a more balanced dataset can be obtained to build a classifier. Furthermore, [9] used k-NN along with fuzzy SVMs in the proposed overlap-sensitive margin classifier. On the other hand, [9] is similar to [4] when dealing with data overlapping in terms of soft-overlap and hard-overlap regions. Based on these so-called regions, new instances can be classified accordingly. Their final predictions are then decided by combining overlap-sensitive margin and 1-NN classifiers. In addition, in [16], a soft-hybrid algorithm was proposed with RBFN, dDBSCAN, and kernel learning models for obviously non-overlapped, borderline, and overlapped regions, respectively. In short, it is realized that, in these works, only binary classification has been demonstrated with different data characteristics inherent in each domain and the complexity with various parameter settings.

Different from the existing works, in this paper, we propose a new combined learning-based bagging method for classification improvement in a simple but effective manner. In our method, partitional clustering and k-Nearest Neighbors (k-NN) are combined with each other to form a base classifier. This base classifier is then a component of a final ensemble model designed in a bagging mechanism. The rationales behind our method design are given as follows. Firstly, partitional clustering is chosen to generate homogeneous groups of the instances of the same class which are the most similar to each other. They are then used as cluster-based instances in local learning of k-NN. Secondly, k-NN is used because of its simplicity and applicability in practice. However, it has several challenges with specifying the number of the nearest neighbors for local learning in order to avoid the influence of noisy instances. Aware of its challenges, our method tackles the corresponding difficulties by means of cluster-based nearest neighbors and a new distance that can count both nearest neighbors and density of neighborhoods. Thirdly, bagging is defined for our method because of its aggregation of many weak classifiers for a final stronger classifier.

Via an empirical evaluation on several datasets in education and medicine, our method outperforms its variants and other baseline ones with better Accuracy and F-measure results. All the differences in Accuracy values between our method and the others have been statistically tested. The statistical test results have confirmed the significant performance improvement of our method on the experimented datasets. The method can thus be applied in practical applications for more effectiveness.

2 Classification Task

Classification is one of the most popular and important data mining tasks with many practical applications. This task is often detailed with two phases: construction and classification. It is normally resolved by machine learning algorithms in many various approaches: unsupervised learning, supervised learning, semi-supervised learning, etc. In our work, a combined approach is proposed with the unsupervised learning approach for the construction phase and the supervised learning approach for the classification phase of the task. Its formal definition is stated for each phase as follows.

Let D_t be a training dataset of n_t instances corresponding to n_t recorded objects in a domain of interest, D_u be a dataset of n_u new instances corresponding to n_u objects to be predicted, and Y be a set of predefined classes of the task. In case of binary classification, Y is $\{0, 1\}$ where 1 is used for positive class and 0 for negative class.

$$D_t = \{X_i, \text{ for } i = 1..n_t\}$$

where X_i is a vector defined as $(x_{i1}, .., x_{ip})$, each x_{id} $(d = 1..p)$ is a numeric value, and p is the number of attributes characterizing each instance. p is also the dimensionality of the data space. Each instance X_i is associated with a predefined class y_i in Y.

$$D_u = \{Z_j, \text{ for } j = 1..n_u\}$$

where Z_j is a vector defined as $(z_{j1}, .., z_{jp})$ and each z_{jd} $(d = 1..p)$ is a numeric value.

The problem of the task is to predictably assign a class y_j in Y to each instance Z_j.

In the construction phase, let h be a classifier obtained with a learning algorithm *learning*() on D_t. It is derived as follows.

$$h = learning(D_t)$$

In the classification phase, h is used for each prediction in the task shown below.

$$y_j = h(Z_j) \text{ for every } Z_j \in D_u$$

Different from the existing solutions to classification, our work proposes a novel combined learning solution that uses partitional clustering for *learning*() of the construction phase and local learning of k-NN for lazy predictions of the classification phase. Moreover, this combination is then repeated in a bagging mechanism for a resulting ensemble model. Its details are given in the next section.

3 The Proposed Combined Learning-Based Bagging Method

3.1 Method Descriptions

The proposed combined learning-based bagging method is described below with two main parts: combining partitional clustering and local learning of k-Nearest Neighbors and bagging for final predictions. They also consist of the construction and classification phases of the task when taking both training and new datasets into account. In the first part of our method, partitional clustering like k-means [11] is used because the space needs to be divided into separate regions which are then used for local learning. Local learning of k-NN [5] is preferred because whenever each new instance is predicted, its characteristics can be examined with respect to its only surrounding region. In the second part of our method, bagging is used because partitional clustering has randomness in its initialization and converges with local optimization. Combining their locally optimized results might bring out a globally optimized one. These properties ensure the diversity of the components of an ensemble model which is required for performance improvement as compared to its individual components.

With the aforementioned foundations, our proposed method is sketched as follows.

Input:
- D_t: a training set of instances X_i with classes y_i,
- D_u: a set of new instances Z_j,
- k: a predefined number of clusters,
- b: a bagging size,
- *clustering*(): a partitional clustering algorithm.

Output:
- Predicted class y_j of Z_j for every $Z_j \in D_u$.

Process:
```
(1).  for t = 1..b
(2).      clusters ← clustering (Dt)
(3).      homo_groups ← class_assigning (clusters, Dt)
(4).      for each Zj ∈ Du
(5).          yj,t ← k_NN (Zj, homo_groups)
(6).      end for
(7).  end for
(8).  for each Zj ∈ Du
(9).      yj ← argmaxc∈Y {∑t=1..b {1 | c = yj,t}}
(10). end for
```

With no loss of generality, it is supposed that our bagging model has b components. For each component built in each round, the unsuperivsed learning process on line (2) is conducted with *clustering*(). For partitional clustering, the following objective function of k-means is typically minimized for the compactness of each cluster. Other partitional clustering algorithms with different objective functions can be used. When there is almost no change on this objective function's value, the process is terminated.

$$F = \sum_{j=1..k} \sum_{i=1..n_t} \gamma_{i,j} d^2(X_i, C_j) \tag{1}$$

where $\gamma_{i,j}$ is the membership of X_i to the cluster whose center is C_j: 1 if a member; otherwise, 0; and $d(X_i, C_j)$ is a distance between X_i and the center C_j. Normally, Euclidean distance is used for partitional clustering in the data space.

Once a clustering model is achieved, *class_assigning*() on line (3) is performed to obtain homogeneous groups from each cluster. All the homogeneous groups are handled in *homo_groups*. A homogeneous group *HG* is a group of the instances that belong to the same cluster with the same class label. Generally speaking, at most $|Y|$ homogeneous groups can be derived from each cluster. Moreover, each homogeneous group is labeled with the same class label as its members. By doing that, all the members of each homogeneous group are unified to be a bigger cluster-based instance which is then used for local learning of k-NN.

Besides unsupervised learning, supervised learning is executed on line (5) with k-NN. In our work, the number of the nearest neighbors, k, is 1 because instead of individual instances, the aforementioned cluster-based instances, which are homogeneous groups, are examined for local learning. With k-NN, the nearest neighbor is selected if the distance between it and the new instance is the smallest. Moreover, we prefer a denser neighborhood so that noisy instances can have less impact on a corresponding prediction. This implies that our method favors a homogeneous group with the larger number of the members. Putting them altogether, we come up with a new distance that can enhance the contributions of the nearest neighbors and the density of its neighborhood to a choice of the nearest cluster-based instance for each new instance.

$$d(Z_j, HG_h) = d(Z_j, C\_HG_h) / |n_h| \tag{2}$$

Where HG_h is a homogeneous group of n_h members of the same class in such a way that: $HG_h \in homo\_groups$ and $n_h = |HG_h|$. In addition, C_HG_h is a mean vector of HG_h, which is a representative of all the members X_i in HG_h, computed as follows.

$$C\_HG_h = \sum_{i=1..n_h} X_i/n_h \tag{3}$$

Besides, in Eq. (2), $d(Z_j, C\_HG_h)$ is a distance between the new instance Z_j and the representative C_HG_h of the homogeneous group HG_h. This can be calculated in a data space or a feature space depending on data characteristics of each domain.

In iteration t corresponding to the t-th component of our ensemble model, on line (5), a class label decided for the new instance Z_j after local learning of k-NN is the class label of the nearest homogeneous group as follows.

$$y_{j,t} = argmin_{HG_h \in homo\_groups}\{d(X_j, HG_h)\} \tag{4}$$

As soon as all the components have been completely created, on lines (8)–(10), bagging is applied with the majority voting scheme to determine a final class y_j for each new instance Z_j. The predicted final class y_j is the most common class predicted by the components of this ensemble model as follows.

$$y_j = argmax_{c \in Y} \left\{ \sum_{t=1..b} \left\{ 1 \mid c = y_{j,t} \right\} \right\} \tag{5}$$

As previously mentioned, the diversity of this ensemble model is highly attained because partitional clustering is normally converged with local optima, caused by alternative optimization with random initialization. Besides, one prediction by this ensemble model is wrong if and only if more than half the predictions from its components are wrong in the case of binary classification. Otherwise, bagging leads to a performance improvement as compared to its base models. Other ensemble approaches like those introduced in [18] instead of bagging can be considered for our method.

3.2 Method Characteristics

From the theoretical perspectives, our work is different from [14]. Firstly, its combination is conducted in two separate phases of the classification task while [14] only focuses on the classification phase. Secondly, our method is defined as an ensemble one while the one in [14] is not. Thirdly, [14] was dedicated to educational data while this work is more general-purpose, not only for education but also other domains.

Compared to other existing works, our work has addressed the difficulties of k-NN and further combined partitional clustering with its local learning. Firstly, the number of the nearest neighbors for each prediction is not required. Secondly, noisy instances are included in a larger group so that our cluster-based k-NN can be performed instead of traditional instance-based k-NN which is delicately influenced by noisy instances. If noisy instances exist, our local learning does not take them into account individually. Thirdly, bagging is used for our method to aggregate many various combinations for each final prediction. This ensemble can increase a chance of a correct prediction. As a result, our method is designed for more expected effectiveness.

As for the existing works in [4, 6, 9, 16], their proposed methods contrast with ours in several aspects. First of all, all of them supported only binary classification while our method is generally defined for multi-class classification. Different from [4], local learning performed on the cluster-based regions, which can be seen as non-overlapping regions in our work, is not impacted by region sizes compared to global learning like SVMs. Compared to [6], our work similarly reduces the number of instances in the training dataset to the number of clusters after unsupervised learning. Nonetheless, no instance is removed from our training dataset. Instead, the contribution of each instance to the later supervised learning process is preserved in its own cluster. In our case, no matter is raised with the size of datasets as no data reduction is made, while this issue needs to be checked with the method proposed in [6]. Different from [9], our ensemble combines many combined learning processes each of which includes homogeneous groups generated by partitional clustering and individual predictions made by cluster-based 1-NN. In comparison with [16], our method is more general with no such explicitly-defined regions. Instead, only local learning is conducted for any region depending on the own data characteristics of new instances and the training ones. As a result, our method is more flexible for any domain of interest.

Besides, a large number of the works exist for classification nowadays. Nevertheless, it is non-trivial to make the most of their solutions for a specific domain due to different data characteristics inherent in each domain and the complexity of each method with many various parameter settings. How challenging these data characteristics are for the task can be referred in [10]. By contrast, our method is simply defined with k-NN, applicable in many practical applications like the one in [3].

4 Empirical Evaluation

4.1 Experiment Settings

Firstly, we state the following questions for empirical evaluation on our method.

Question 1: Does our method outperform its variants and other baseline methods?

Question 2: Are differences in performance between our method and the others statistically significant?

For Question 1 (Q1), our proposed method is implemented in Java with two various partitional clustering algorithms: k-means and an ensemble of k-means in [14]. More recent ensemble methods like the one in [15] can be used for more effectiveness instead. Its corresponding algorithms are named KK-Bagging and eKK-Bagging, respectively. The variants are also implemented in Java with the same clustering algorithms and parameter settings. They are different from our algorithms in such a way that bagging is not applied. Their corresponding algorithms are named KK and eKK, respectively. In addition, the normal use of partitional clustering for 1-Nearest Neighbor (1-NN) classification is implemented as each cluster is regarded an object for the nearest neighbor search. The resulting algorithms are named non-KK and non-eKK, respectively. Besides these variants, k-Nearest Neighbors (k-NN), C4.5, and Naïve Bayesian (NB) are used as baseline methods. 1-NN and the best k-NN are included for comparison because they lay the foundations of our method. The best k-NN is the one providing the best results among k-NN with different values of k in $\{1, 3, 5, 7, 9\}$. C4.5 and NB are selected because of their simplicity and popularity with no parameter settings. In our work, we reused their implementations from Weka library [17].

Furthermore, for the parameter settings of our method, we use $\{2, 10, 20\}$ for varying values of k, the number of clusters in k-means, $\{10, 30, 50\}$ for varying values of bagging sizes, and 50 for an ensemble size. The values for k are selected for the smaller to the larger number of clusters generated as the objects given to the local learning process of 1-NN, regarding the number of classes in the datasets. The values for bagging sizes are set according to the large numbers for statistics where a smaller one, ten (10), is included to check its impact on the final results. It is also worth noting that the ensemble size is fixed at 50 because slight changes were found with many various values for the ensemble size of the resulting model constructed by the weighted object-cluster association-based ensemble method in [15].

For Question 2 (Q2), Paired-Samples T-Test is conducted to check if the mean differences in accuracy between our method and the others are statistically significant. The tests were performed with 95% confidence interval of the difference. In Table 3, we use "X > Y" to denote if the results of X algorithm is really better than those of Y algorithm. Values of Sig. (2-tailed) (Sig. for short) are also reported.

Secondly, we used several datasets in education and medicine in the experiments. The medicine dataset about diabetic (non)patients, Diabetic_All, is stratified into two folds, Diabetic_F1 and Diabetic_F2, which are then used for both training and testing alternatively in turn. It was downloaded from UCI Machine Learning repository [13] and originally prepared in [2]. All the other datasets about students are prepared from a virtual learning environment and the normal one. DDD_2013J, DDD_2014B, FFF_2013B, and FFF_2013J were from the Open University Learning Analytics Dataset in [8]. They include the assessment results from two courses, DDD and FFF, in two different periods of time in years, 2013 and 2014, starting in February (B) and October (J). For each course, the past dataset is used for training and its corresponding later one for testing. In addition to these datasets, PPL_2010 and PPL_2011 are two educational datasets obtained from Principles of Programming Languages course in 2010 and 2011, respectively, and prepared in [12]. Year 3_2007 and Year 3_2008 are two other educational datasets with the course grades of the third-year students enrolling in 2007 and 2008, respectively. All these datasets were with the regular students at Faculty of Computer Science and Engineering, Ho Chi Minh City University of Technology, Vietnam National University-Ho Chi Minh City, Vietnam [1]. Similar to the previous educational datasets, the previous datasets are used for training and the later ones for testing. Furthermore, for early predictions, only assessments before the middle points in time are used in the course-level datasets. For more information, the descriptions of all the datasets are given in Table 1. In an overall view on these datasets, they are different from each other in terms of the number of attributes (Att #), the number of instances (Ins #), and class distribution for positives (P) and negatives (N) to check how well our method is generalized in different contexts.

Table 1. Data descriptions.

Dataset	Role	Domain	Att #	Ins #	P #	P %	N #	N %
Diabetic_All	Training, Testing	Medicine	19	1151	611	53.08	540	46.92
Diabetic_F1	Training, Testing	Medicine	19	576	306	53.13	270	46.87
Diabetic_F2	Training, Testing	Medicine	19	575	305	53.04	270	46.96
DDD_2013J	Training	Education	4	1082	352	32.53	730	67.47
DDD_2014B	Testing	Education	4	572	212	37.06	360	62.94
FFF_2013B	Training	Education	6	1031	367	35.6	664	64.4
FFF_2013J	Testing	Education	6	1351	444	32.86	907	67.14
PPL_2010	Training	Education	5	289	73	25.26	216	74.74
PPL_2011	Testing	Education	5	264	73	27.65	191	72.35
Year 3_2007	Training	Education	43	223	56	25.11	167	74.89
Year 3_2008	Testing	Education	43	235	67	28.51	168	71.49

Thirdly, for comparison, Accuracy (A) is used in range [0, 100] for overall performance of each prediction model, while Recall (R), Precision (P), and F-measure (F) in range [0, 1] for specific performance of each prediction model on the instances of the positive class. Their higher values imply the better models.

Finally, the hold-out validation scheme is used to measure the values of each measure instead of the k-fold cross validation scheme because of temporal aspects. In this scheme, only the past data are used to build prediction models to predict those in the later periods of time. Moreover, each experiment is carried out 30 times due to random initializations in partitional clustering. The values of each measure were recorded and averaged for the final results in Tables 2 and 3. For simplicity, the best Accuracy and F-measure results are presented in bold and the second best ones in italic.

Table 2. Experimental results on different datasets from 1-NN, k-NN, C4.5, and our methods.

Dataset		1-NN	k-NN	C4.5	NB	KK-Bagging	eKK-Bagging
Diabetic_F1	A	57.99	63.54	64.24	58.33	*68.64*	**68.91**
	R	0.57	0.64	0.50	0.25	0.67	0.67
	P	0.61	0.66	0.75	0.88	0.72	0.72
	F	0.59	0.65	0.60	0.39	*0.69*	**0.70**
Diabetic_F2	A	59.30	63.83	61.22	55.13	**64.45**	*64.21*
	R	0.59	0.61	0.71	0.21	0.61	0.60
	P	0.62	0.68	0.62	0.80	0.69	0.68
	F	0.61	*0.64*	**0.66**	0.33	*0.64*	*0.64*
DDD_2014B	A	76.92	83.57	84.97	85.49	**86.66**	*86.64*
	R	0.76	0.81	0.79	0.80	0.78	0.78
	P	0.67	0.76	0.80	0.81	0.85	0.85
	F	0.71	0.78	*0.80*	*0.80*	**0.81**	**0.81**
FFF_2013J	A	84.16	88.53	88.53	88.97	*89.62*	**89.64**
	R	0.85	0.84	0.87	0.86	0.82	0.82
	P	0.72	0.82	0.80	0.81	0.86	0.86
	F	0.78	*0.83*	*0.83*	**0.84**	**0.84**	**0.84**
PPL_2011	A	83.33	89.02	89.39	88.26	**89.86**	*89.84*
	R	0.67	0.74	0.64	0.82	0.74	0.73
	P	0.71	0.84	0.96	0.77	0.87	0.88
	F	0.69	*0.79*	0.77	*0.79*	**0.80**	**0.80**
Year 3_2008	A	85.96	89.36	80.43	82.98	**90.30**	*90.24*
	R	0.93	0.98	0.83	0.95	0.99	0.98
	P	0.88	0.88	0.89	0.84	0.89	0.90
	F	0.90	*0.93*	0.86	0.89	**0.94**	*0.93*

Table 3. Experimental results on different datasets from non-KK, non-eKK, KK, eKK, and our methods.

Dataset		non-KK	non-eKK	KK	eKK	KK-Bagging	eKK-Bagging
Diabetic_F1	A	64.70	64.39	67.66	66.38	*68.64*	**68.91**
	R	0.62	0.58	0.67	0.66	0.67	0.67
	P	0.69	0.70	0.70	0.69	0.72	0.72
	F	0.65	0.63	*0.69*	0.68	*0.69*	**0.70**
Diabetic_F2	A	60.40	59.50	62.72	62.78	**64.45**	*64.21*
	R	0.63	0.58	0.59	0.60	0.61	0.60
	P	0.63	0.63	0.67	0.67	0.69	0.68
	F	0.63	0.60	0.63	0.63	*0.64*	*0.64*
DDD_2014B	A	83.95	83.98	85.27	85.13	**86.66**	*86.64*
	R	0.74	0.78	0.77	0.75	0.78	0.78
	P	0.81	0.79	0.83	0.83	0.85	0.85
	F	0.77	0.78	0.79	0.79	**0.81**	**0.81**
FFF_2013J	A	86.79	86.69	89.40	89.02	*89.62*	**89.64**
	R	0.86	0.86	0.77	0.82	0.82	0.82
	P	0.78	0.78	0.89	0.84	0.86	0.86
	F	0.81	0.81	*0.83*	*0.83*	**0.84**	**0.84**
PPL_2011	A	82.08	82.20	87.27	88.06	**89.86**	*89.84*
	R	0.56	0.50	0.59	0.72	0.74	0.73
	P	0.70	0.70	0.92	0.83	0.87	0.88
	F	0.57	0.54	0.72	0.77	**0.80**	**0.80**
Year 3_2008	A	86.24	86.79	88.48	88.98	**90.30**	*90.24*
	R	0.94	0.92	1.00	0.98	0.99	0.98
	P	0.88	0.90	0.86	0.88	0.89	0.90
	F	0.90	0.90	*0.93*	*0.93*	**0.94**	*0.93*

4.2 Experimental Results and Discussions

Firstly, for Q1, according to the experimental results in Table 2, our algorithms, KK-Bagging and eKK-Bagging, have made more correct predictions for all the datasets in the experiments as compared to its variants and other baseline ones. Compared to 1-NN and k-NN with k in $\{1, 3, 5, 7, 9\}$ providing the best results, KK-Bagging and eKK-Bagging can improve their performance. This shows the advantages of our algorithms over k-NN when no specification of the number of the nearest neighbors is needed and noisy instances are restricted in their clusters. Moreover in Table 3, KK-Bagging and eKK-Bagging outperform KK and eKK, while KK and eKK outperform non-KK and non-eKK, respectively. Their corresponding better results reflect the appropriate design of our method when the unsupervised learning process of a partitional clustering algorithm and the local learning process of k-Nearest Neighbors is reasonably combined and bagging is then applied. Furthermore, KK-Bagging and eKK-Bagging are more effective than some typical baseline algorithms like C4.5 and Naïve Bayesian.

Less or much difference in performance depends on the characteristics of data in classification. It is realized that dimensionality needs to be taken into account for our method because our method belongs to the distance-based learning method category. Indeed, it is non-trivial for our method to tackle Year 3_2007 and Year 3_2008 datasets in a 43-dimensional space, while more improvement can be obtained with DDD_2013J and DDD_2014B datasets in a 4-dimensional space.

In addition, data imbalance has a strong impact on most of the methods. Our method is also influenced by this characteristic. Little difference is found for our method on PPL_2011 and Year 3_2008 as compared to more differences on the other datasets. Nonetheless, homogeneous clusters from partitional clustering help us constrain this characteristic. Using homogeneous clusters, the nearest denser neighborhood is more reliable for class prediction of each new instance than just the individual nearest neighbors which might be noisy. Such a better choice in our method is proved with the better results of KK-Bagging and eKK-Bagging as compared to those of non-KK and non-eKK.

On the other hand, when we change individual neighbors which are true instances into cluster-based neighbors which are groups of the instances in the same class, our method depends on clustering models. Most of the partitional clustering algorithms are designed with a local optimization process. Consequently, the prediction results of our method might vary with the various convergences of clustering models. If a more advanced clustering algorithm is employed, the complexity of the method needs to be considered as soon as our method follows the lazy approach of k-Nearest Neighbors.

This can be seen as a trade-off in method design. For our method, bagging is included so that both effectiveness and efficiency can be preserved. As a result, bagging brings many combinations which might be associated with the results from a local optimization process to form a final model with better results. However, our bagging method is different from the traditional ensemble ones when no data sampling is required. Instead, correlation between the individual models of our bagging method can be controlled with randomness in partitional clustering. Eventually our resulting method can classify new instances better than its variants with no bagging. It is shown in Table 3 with higher Accuracy and F-measure values from KK-Bagging and eKK-Bagging in comparison with those from KK and eKK.

Secondly, for Q2, Table 4 shows that there is no significant difference between KK-Bagging and eKK-Bagging from all the results on all the datasets used in our experiments. This can be explained in such a way that we have no tuning on the unsupervised learning process when the ensemble of k-means is simply chosen with no various parameter settings. Therefore, their experimental results are comparable to each other. In the future, the unsupervised learning process can be adjusted for more effectiveness with other partitional clustering algorithms which should be different from k-means and its ensemble. For example, kernel k-means can be explored.

Table 4. Statistical test results with Paired-Samples T-Test.

Dataset	Diabetic_F1	Diabetic_F2	DDD_2014B	FFF_2013J	PPL_2011	Year3_2008
eKK-Bagging > KK-Bagging	*No* (Sig. = .075)	*No* (Sig. = .153)	*No* (Sig. = .654)	*No* (Sig. = .593)	*No* (Sig. = .855)	*No* (Sig. = .776)
eKK-Bagging > eKK	Yes (Sig. = .002)	Yes (Sig. = .000)	Yes (Sig. = .000)	Yes (Sig. = .005)	Yes (Sig. = .000)	*No* (Sig. = .070)
KK-Bagging > KK	Yes (Sig. = .000)	Yes (Sig. = .000)	Yes (Sig. = .000)	*No* (Sig. = .116)	Yes (Sig. = .000)	Yes (Sig. = .000)
eKK-Bagging > k-NN	Yes (Sig. = .000)	Yes (Sig. = .000)	Yes (Sig. = .000)	Yes (Sig. = .000)	Yes (Sig. = .000)	Yes (Sig. = .000)
KK-Bagging > k-NN	Yes (Sig. = .000)	Yes (Sig. = .000)	Yes (Sig. = .000)	Yes (Sig. = .000)	Yes (Sig. = .000)	Yes (Sig. = .000)
eKK-Bagging > non-eKK	Yes (Sig. = .000)	Yes (Sig. = .000)	Yes (Sig. = .000)	Yes (Sig. = .000)	Yes (Sig. = .000)	Yes (Sig. = .037)
KK-Bagging > non-KK	Yes (Sig. = .000)	Yes (Sig. = .000)	Yes (Sig. = .000)	Yes (Sig. = .000)	Yes (Sig. = .000)	Yes (Sig. = .008)
eKK-Bagging > C4.5	Yes (Sig. = .000)	Yes (Sig. = .000)	Yes (Sig. = .000)	Yes (Sig. = .000)	Yes (Sig. = .000)	Yes (Sig. = .000)
eKK-Bagging > NB	Yes (Sig. = .000)	Yes (Sig. = .000)	Yes (Sig. = .000)	Yes (Sig. = .000)	Yes (Sig. = .000)	Yes (Sig. = .000)
KK-Bagging > C4.5	Yes (Sig. = .000)	Yes (Sig. = .000)	Yes (Sig. = .000)	Yes (Sig. = .000)	Yes (Sig. = .000)	Yes (Sig. = .000)
KK-Bagging > NB	Yes (Sig. = .000)	Yes (Sig. = .000)	Yes (Sig. = .000)	Yes (Sig. = .000)	Yes (Sig. = .000)	Yes (Sig. = .000)

On the other hand, in most of the cases, KK-Bagging and eKK-Bagging have significant differences in performance as compared to its variants and other baseline ones. Such statistical test results are consistent with the aforementioned experimental results regardless of little or much improvement we have achieved. In some cases with FFF_2013J and Year 3_2008, it is found that eKK-Bagging and KK-Bagging do not really outperform eKK and KK, respectively. The rationale behind these statistical test results stems from the parameter settings with their corresponding experimental results. In these cases, the bagging size is 10 for FFF_2013J and Year 3_2008, while 30 and 50 for other datasets. Therefore, more parameter tuning is needed for more effectiveness. This also leads to a growing need of parameter-free methods so that they can be adaptive to data characteristics. Moreover, data distribution with these datasets is different from the others. Both of them have more new objects in testing datasets as compared to those in training datasets with more imbalance. Although our method has coped with them better than other methods, bagging can not cover all the cases for our method. Semi-supervised learning thus becomes more potential to take more new instances into account during the learning process. Our method can be revised with semi-supervised learning for tackling these data characteristics better.

5 Conclusions

In this paper, we have proposed a combined learning-based bagging method for a classification task. This method is novel in such a way that it provides a nested learning method to build a more effective classifier than its corresponding individual learning methods. First, it combines an unsupervised learning process of partitional clustering with a local learning process of k-nearest neighbors. This combination can deal with the difficulties of k-nearest neighbors such as influence of noises and parameter settings. Second, a bagging mechanism is defined with our method so that randomness from the unsupervised learning process can be exploited for final predictions. Such an ensemble learning process wraps the previous learning combinations and approaches the final predictions in a more global optimization manner as compared to the one with no bagging. Indeed, its higher effectiveness has been confirmed in an empirical evaluation on several different datasets in education and medicine with its variants and the baseline ones. Better Accuracy results have been achieved for all the classes while better F-measure results for the positive class in particular.

For future works, our method can be extended to incorporate more characteristics of the new instances in a semi-supervised learning mechanism so that the clustering model can be adjusted effectively in the expanded space. Parameter-free setting is also of our interest to make our method more practical in the applications. Last but not least, applying our method to other application domains in addition to education and medicine is taken into consideration.

References

1. Academic Affairs Office, Ho Chi Minh City University of Technology, Vietnam. http://www.aao.hcmut.edu.vn, 29 June 2017
2. Antal, B., Hajdu, A.: An ensemble-based system for automatic screening of diabetic retinopathy. Knowl.-Based Syst. **60**, 20–27 (2014)
3. Bertsimas, D., Kallus, N., Weinstein, A.M., Zhuo, Y.D.: Personalized diabetes management using electronic medical records. Diabetes Care **40**, 210–217 (2017)
4. Chujai, P., Chomboon, K., Chaiyakhan, K., Kerdprasop, K., Kerdprasop, N.: A cluster based classification of imbalanced data with overlapping regions between classes. In: Proceedings of the International MultiConference of Engineers and Computer Scientists I, pp. 1-6 (2017)
5. Cover, T., Hart, P.: Nearest neighbor pattern classification. IEEE Trans. Inf. Theory **13**, 21–27 (1967)
6. Das, B., Krishnan, N.C., Cook, D.J.: Handling class overlap and imbalance to detect prompt situations in smart homes. In: Proceedings of the 2013 IEEE 13th International Conference on Data Mining Workshops, pp. 1–8 (2013)
7. Fernández, A., García, S., Herrera, F., Chawla, N.V.: SMOTE for learning from imbalanced data: progress and challenges, marking the 15-year anniversary. J. Artif. Intell. Res. **61**, 863–905 (2018)
8. Kuzilek, J, Hlosta, M., Herrmannova, D., Zdrahal, Z., Wolff, A.: OU analyse: analysing at-risk students at the open university. Learning Analytics Review, no. LAK15–1, March 2015
9. Lee, H.K., Kim, S.B.: An overlap-sensitive margin classifier for imbalanced and overlapping data. Expert Syst. Appl. **98**, 72–83 (2018)
10. López, V., Fernández, A., Moreno-Torres, J.G., Herrera, F.: Analysis of preprocessing vs. cost-sensitive learning for imbalanced classification. Open problems on intrinsic data characteristics. Expert Syst. Appl. **39**, 6585–6608 (2012)
11. MacQueen, J.: Some methods for classification and analysis of multivariate observations. In: Proceedings of the 5th Berkeley Symposium Math. Stat. Prob., pp. 1:281–297 (1967)
12. Nguyen, H.G.P., Vo, C.T.N.: A CNN model with data imbalance handling for course-level student prediction based on forum texts. In: Proceedings of the 10th International Conference on Computational Collective Intelligence, pp. 479–490 (2018)
13. UCI Machine Learning Repository. http://archive.ics.uci.edu/ml. Accessed June May 2016
14. Vo, C.T.N., Nguyen, H.P.: A class-cluster k-nearest neighbors method for temporal in-trouble student identification. In: Proceedings of the 11th Asian Conference on Intelligent Information and Database Systems, pp. 219–230 (2019)
15. Vo, T.N.C., Nguyen, H.P.: A kernel-induced weighted object-cluster association-based ensemble method for educational data clustering. J. Inform. Telecommun. **8**, 1–21 (2019)

16. Vorraboot, P., Rasmequan, S., Chinnasarn, K.: Improving classification rate constrained to imbalanced data between overlapped and non-overlapped regions by hybrid algorithms. Neurocomputing **152**, 429–443 (2015)
17. Weka 3. http://www.cs.waikato.ac.nz/ml/weka. Accessed 2 June 2017
18. Zhou, Z.H.: Ensemble Methods: Foundations and Algorithms. Chapman and Hall/CRC (2012)

A Modified I2A Agent for Learning
in a Stochastic Environment

Constantin-Valentin Pal and Florin Leon[✉]

Department of Computer Science and Engineering, "Gheorghe Asachi"
Technical University of Iaşi, Iaşi, Romania
valentin.pal@gmail.com, florin.leon@tuiasi.ro

Abstract. The paper proposes and analyses the evolution of a deep reinforcement learning agent in a stochastic environment that represents a simple game. We investigate the use of an embedded planning loop in the training of a model free agent, using a learned model in the style of I2A (Imagination-Augmented Agent), to solve a stochastic grid environment. The performance of the proposed agent architecture is compared against a baseline A2C (Advantage Actor Critic) agent.

Keywords: Imagination-Augmented agent · Advantage actor critic · Deep reinforcement learning · Games

1 Introduction

A characteristic of the human brain is the ability to learn an abstract model of the environment with which it interacts. In reinforcement learning (RL), the class of algorithms where the agent has access to a model of the environment, either given or learned, is called model-based RL. This is in contrast to model-free RL, where an agent learns to act based directly on observations from the environment.

Model-free agents do not use a model and they are very sample-inefficient, but they are easier to implement and tune to great success, e.g. TRPO [1], PPO [2], A3C [3], SAC [4], DQN [5] or DDPG [6]. On the other hand, model-based RL is much more sample-efficient, because agents can use the model to plan instead of planning by interacting with the real world. Besides, sometimes learning directly in the real environment is simply not affordable, and models learned in simulated environments become much more attractive if they can be used in the real world. Some relatively recent impressive achievements in the model-based area are AlphaGo Zero [7] and AlphaZero [8], which has achieved superhuman performance at the games of go, chess and shogi. But one big disadvantage of this class of algorithms is that a ground-truth model of the environment is often unavailable to the agent. Still, the agent can try to learn it, just from interacting with the environment. The main drawback here is that the learned model can be imperfect, and this can degrade the performance of the agent that plans and acts according to the learned model in the real environment [9, 10]. I2A (Imagination-Augmented Agent) [11] makes use of imperfect environment models to embed planning loops in the policy learning of a

© Springer Nature Switzerland AG 2020
N. T. Nguyen et al. (Eds.): ICCCI 2020, LNAI 12496, pp. 388–399, 2020.
https://doi.org/10.1007/978-3-030-63007-2_30

model free agent. Learning to plan is achieved by learning to extract relevant information from "imagined" trajectories in an end-to-end way.

In the rest of this paper, we analyze the application of the I2A method in a stochastic grid environment. We make some changes to the convolutional layers used in the various components of the algorithm, to increase its efficiency for the proposed environment. We compare the performance with a regular A2C (Advantage Actor Critic) agent. A2C is an algorithm that tries to collect experiences from multiple instances of the same environment, but sequentially, instead of in parallel; its results are close to those of the A3C (Asynchronous Advantage Actor-Critic) [3] algorithm.

2 Problem Description

The environment, implemented as a standard *OpenAI Gym*[1] environment, is a simple grid environment like in Fig. 1.

Fig. 1. Sample observation (Color figure online)

The grid in the image is of the size 5×5, but in the algorithm the size is configurable. The agent, or hero, is represented by the blue dot. It can move one square at a time, in the directions up, down, left or right, coded by actions $a = 0, 1, 2$ or 3. When it is touching the edge of the grid and executes an action that moves it towards that specific edge, the agent will remain in the same position. In the example above, if the agent wants to go right, the blue square will remain in the same position. The goal of the agent is to collect as many green squares as possible, while avoiding the red squares. When the agent moves over a green square, it receives a reward of $+1$, and a reward of -1 for touching a red square. The red or green square, once touched by the agent, will be relocated to a random position in the grid that will not overlap with any other existing green or red square. The environment provides observations in the form of RGB images like the one in Fig. 1. After 50 steps (actions) the environment resets, concluding a full game *episode*. The implementation for this paper is available on Github [17] and the I2A training steps were inspired by [13].

3 I2A Architecture

The high-level architecture of the original paper was kept, but changes were made to the convolutional networks from the various components in the I2A architecture. The general architecture of the I2A agent is presented in Fig. 2.

---

[1] https://gym.openai.com/.

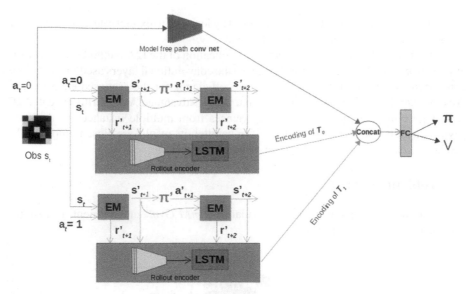

Fig. 2. High level I2A architecture

Observation s_t goes into the two separate paths, colored with blue and green. The blue one is the model-free path of the I2A agent, which is a convolutional neural network (CNN) used to extract relevant features from the input state s_t. The green path represents the imagined trajectories, one for every of the 4 possible actions the agent can execute. The Fig. 2 shows just two out of four actions, actions 0 (up) and 1 (down) to save space. The input state s_t, together with action a_i, start the imagined trajectory T_i by going into the *Environment Model* (EM). EM makes a prediction about the next state s'_{t+1} and the reward r'_{t+1}, which are then being fed as the input to a *Rollout Encoder*. This encoder concatenates s'_{t+1} and r'_{t+1}, passes them through a CNN and a recurrent neural net (LSTM). It does this sequentially for an entire trajectory (s'_{t+1}, r'_{t+1}, s'_{t+2}, r'_{t+2}, s'_{t+3}, r'_{t+3}, …) and outputs a fixed size vector encoding for the entire trajectory. The trajectory length (number of time steps) is configurable, and in Fig. 2 only the first 2 steps of the trajectories are represented to save space. The encoded trajectories for the four actions are concatenated with the output of the model-free CNN. The concatenation goes into a fully connected layer of the I2A agent which then produces both a policy π and value estimation $V(s)$, like a standard A2C agent.

The *rollout policy π'* used for the rollout of the imagined trajectory is not the same policy network of the I2A agent. A cross-entropy loss between the I2A loss and this rollout policy loss is added to the regular loss of the rollout policy network. This ensures that the rollout policy is close to the I2A agent policy and produces similar trajectories.

The *rollout encoder* uses the same CNN as the one used in the model-free path of the I2A agent, and the same one used in the baseline A2C agent. The CNN layers are tuned to this problem and are different than in the I2A paper [11].

4   Environment Model

The EM receives an action and the current state as the input and concatenates them, after the action has been first one-hot encoded and then broadcasted into a matrix shape that corresponds to the one-hot encoding, like in Fig. 3. Broadcasting means to take each element of the one hot encoding vector and transform it into a corresponding full matrix of the size of the observation. This matrix has on all its elements the same value as the element from the one hot encoding vector.

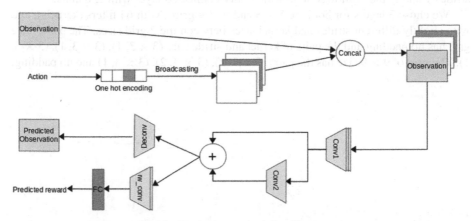

Fig. 3. Environment model architecture

In the original paper [11], multiple sequential input observations are stacked together before the concatenation with the actions. But in this environment, the historical information of the moving objects is not very useful for solving the problem. Therefore, only one observation is stacked together with the broadcasted action. The concatenated action and observation/state are then fed into a CNN that outputs a prediction of the next state and the reward for the action taken.

Also in [11], after each convolutional layer from the *rw_conv* part of the network, there was a max pooling layer. In the proposed setup, those layers were removed, because there is no need to further reduce the dimensionality of the input image, because it already has a small resolution.

Each entry in the training set of the EM network consists of the current observation, the next one, the action taken, and the reward obtained. The optimized loss is a weighted sum of the mean squared error (MSE) observation loss and the MSE reward loss. A weighted loss is used so that it can give more emphasis either to the observation or the reward loss.

5   Experimental Results and Discussion

5.1   A2C Choice of Convolutional Network and Comparison with I2A mini-pacman

The *mini-pacman* environment from I2A [11] has a similar resolution, 15×19 pixels, as both our 5×5 grid environment, which is 14×14, and the 9×9 one, which is 22×22. For the A2C baseline, and for the I2A model-free path CNN, the authors of I2A chose a structure with two layers, both with 3×3 kernels, 16 output channels and strides 1 and 2; they followed it up with a fully connected layer with 256 units.

We chose 3 layers for both the 5×5 and 9×9 grids, with 64 filters (kernels), and with slightly different strides and kernel sizes between the 2 grid sizes. The 5×5 size grid has no padding and the pairs of kernel and strides are $(3 \times 3, 1)$, $(3 \times 3, 1)$, $(3 \times 3, 1)$. The grid of 9×9 size has the pairs $(5 \times 5, 2)$, $(3 \times 3, 2)$, $(3 \times 3, 1)$ and no padding.

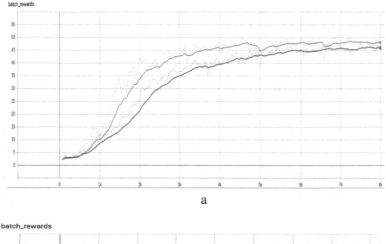

a

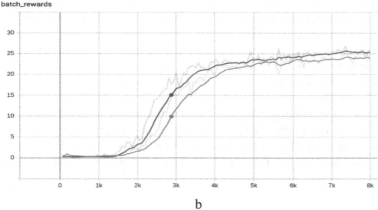

b

Fig. 4. a. Our convolutional network choice for 9×9 grid, compared to the *mini-pacman* choice, also yields a significantly better learning curve. b. Our choice of convolutional network for 5×5 grid yields significantly better learning compared with the I2A author's choice of convolutional network for similarly sized environment

Our choices also lead to smaller sized networks in terms of total learnable parameters, due to a reduced dimensionality of the post-convolutional layers. Figure 4 shows the learning comparison of the learning curves between the two choices of convolutional networks.

This difference also reflects in the I2A agent learning curves; it improves them as well in a similar fashion.

5.2   Environment Model Predictions for Reward and Next Observation

The best results we obtained in training the EM were by using an "almost random" A2C agent to produce the rollout trajectories. An almost random agent is an agent trained very little, that performs slightly better than what an agent with randomly chosen actions will achieve. A fully trained agent will not allow the EM to learn to predict negative rewards, because the agent would avoid them. Also, a half-trained agent did not produce the best results, possibly because it does not sufficiently explore the states where the agent is far from the rewards. Predicting the reward, be it positive, negative or none, is a straightforward task for the agent because there is no stochasticity in terms of reward. A random agent will explore the state space very well to learn to predict positive, negative and absence of reward (Fig. 5).

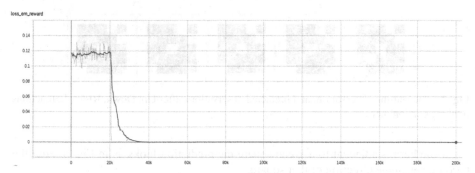

Fig. 5. Reward loss in EM

For the larger grids that we tested, of 9×9 or 13×13, the rewards get sparser, because the number of green and red squares is kept unchanged. But, for the EM to learn to predict the reward in these cases, the size of the fully connected output layer (FC) in Fig. 2 had to be increased to 256 and 512 respectively. For a grid environment of the size 5×5, the loss quickly gets close to zero ($\sim 10^{-7}$).

The observation loss is not that small, it is a few orders of magnitude higher than the reward loss ($\sim 10^{-4}$) suggesting less accurate prediction (Fig. 6).

loss_em_obs

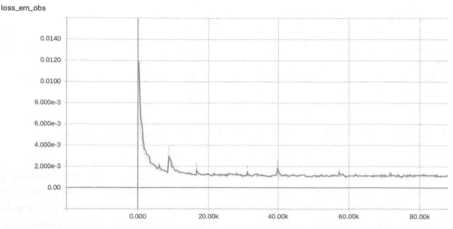

Fig. 6. Observation loss in EM

Let us see a few examples of predicted next rewards for all possible actions for some random starting observation where the agent is not adjacent to any of the green or red squares (Fig. 7).

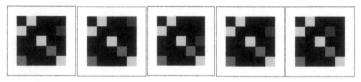

Fig. 7. The starting observation, and predicted observations after Up, Down, Right, Left actions (Color figure online)

If the hero is adjacent to a green square the prediction looks as in Fig. 8, after the hero moves in the direction of that square.

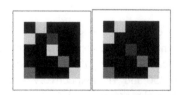

Fig. 8. Next observation prediction when the hero collects a green reward (Color figure online)

The green square apparently disappeared. But on a closer inspection of the Green channel of the RGB image, the intensity of all pixels where there is no square changed from $\sim 10^{-4}$ (almost perfect black) to $\sim 10^{-2}$ (very dark green). Since the replacement of the green square by the environment is made uniformly random, any of the unoccupied spots in the grid could be a candidate for replacement, and the agent cannot guess anything other than some mean value for the background pixels encountered in all the next observations following the same starting observation.

5.3 I2A Agent Learning Performance

The I2A agent for a grid of 5×5, with rollout trajectories of length 1, and observation loss weight 10x higher than the reward loss weight, compared to a very well parameterized baseline A2C agent has the following *batch_rewards* (3-step discounted reward per 32 environments) graph during learning (Fig. 9).

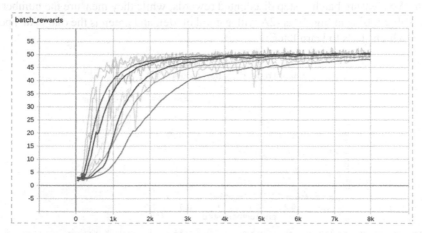

Fig. 9. I2A with imagined trajectories of length 1 through 4 vs. baseline A2C. Batch rewards represent 3-step discounted rewards as per n-step TD method, but on 32 parallel game environments. This means ~100,000 environment interactions in 1000 epochs.

The slowest, in orange, is the baseline A2C agent. The fastest to learn, in magenta, is the I2A with rollout trajectories of 1 step. The second fastest learner, in blue, is the one with imagined trajectories of size 2. The next, in red, uses trajectories of size 3, and the gray one uses trajectories of size 4.

The I2A agent learns significantly better than the baseline A2C. This happens even with trajectories of 3 and 4, despite the predictions for the next observation and reward being worse the longer the imagined trajectory, due to the combined effect of the inaccurate predictions at each step. Despite using more imprecise trajectories, agents with rollouts of 3 or 4 are still better than the baseline. So, an inaccurate trajectory is likely still useful, and an I2A agent learns to discard trajectory information that is not useful for learning in a stochastic environment like this. Longer trajectories, though, seem not as useful as the shorter ones because the longer a trajectory is, the more imprecise it is because of stochasticity. Agents with rollout trajectories of 1 and 2 are very close, while the ones with 3 and 4 are significantly worse, but still better than the baseline A2C agent.

The best learner reaches the maximum performance of the A2C baseline agent in 2000 epochs, compared to 8000 epochs for the A2C agent. All I2A agents manage to reach a better top performance too, with an average of **27** reward points in 50 steps in the test environment for the grid of 5 × 5, compared to the baseline A2C agent which averages **24** in 50 steps. The biggest difference in the learning curve is in the beginning of the learning and not in the maximum performance, possibly because this environment seems to be easy to learn.

In the I2A paper [11], in the Sokoban environment, which is a deterministic environment, when using a poorly learned model, the starting of the learning is poorer compared to the I2A agent with a better model. This happens in our case as well, because the agents with longer trajectories can be thought to use a poorer model if we look at how precise the entire trajectory is estimated in terms of observations and rewards. So, from this perspective, our results are similar, even though we measure learning differently per epoch. We measure batch 3-step discounted rewards, while they measure the number of levels solved. Blue in Fig. 10 is I2A with a good model, and green is the one with a poor model, which starts to learn later.

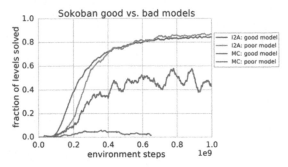

Fig. 10. Comparison of Monte-Carlo (MC) search and I2A when using either the accurate or the noisy model for rollouts [11] (Color figure online)

On the other hand, in Sokoban, which is a deterministic environment, longer "imagined" trajectories produce better results later in the training. This is opposite to our results. The I2A authors posit this as learning to plan, because Sokoban is the type of environment that requires planning ahead. This corroborated with a very well-trained Environment Model leads to longer "imagined" trajectories being more useful, unlike our case. Though, in their case, the initial part of the learning curve does not show precise separation between agents with various trajectories depth. Even the standard A2C agent starts to go up in learning faster than an I2A agent, in the first 100 million interactions with the environment.

Since our environment is not very difficult to learn, even if the longer rollouts agents learn to discard not useful information, they do not do it fast enough in the beginning of the learning, where the agents with smaller rollout trajectories seem to have an edge.

Experiments with grid sizes of 9 × 9 and 13 × 13 produced similar results, only that the trajectories that are longer are slightly less stable in learning. The observation and reward losses of the Environment Model are worse than the smaller 5 × 5 grid, and from the first step of the trajectory small artifacts in some positions of the grids may be seen.

5.4 Grad-CAM Visual Explanations from Baseline and I2A Agents in the Convolutional Networks

Grad-CAM [12] is a method that produces visual explanations for the decisions of CNN based models, including deep reinforcement learning models, that can give us some hints about what parts of the grid observation is the agent "interested" in when deciding about a specific action. The method produces a "heatmap" that is superimposed on the input observation. This heatmap is created by combining the activations of the last convolutional layer with the gradients of a target concept (like a specific action) flowing back into the last convolutional layer.

Figure 11 *Left* shows the area of interest for the A2C agent when choosing action "down". The brown area is not useful to the agent, despite the observation showing some other rewards farther away from the "interest" area, possibly suggesting that the agent collects rewards in a greedy fashion rather than by using a plan.

Fig. 11. *Left:* A2C Grad-CAM for the action "down". *Right:* I2A Grad-CAM for action "left" (Color figure online)

In the I2A agent in Fig. 11 *Right*, we obtain similar results, although the entire architecture is much more complicated than the simple A2C agent. The I2A agent "focuses" on the area of the observation that is immediately close to the hero, despite positive and negative reward being placed in the upper left corner, or bottom center area of the observation. This seems to suggest that, at least in terms of feature extraction from the model free CNN, the I2A agent is more of a greedy agent type than a planning agent. This could explain the fact that longer trajectories are not as useful as an imagined trajectory of size 1.

5.5 Generalization in a Deterministic Environment

We trained the A2C and I2A agents using a rollout trajectory of 1 step in the stochastic environment and then tested their generalization power in a deterministic environment. The deterministic environment is different in that the positive or negative reward, once collected by the hero, is not replaced back into the grid. An episode ends when there is no more positive reward to collect, making the episodes shorter than in the stochastic environment. In the path to the first reward, the observations seen by the agent are not new. But, once a reward is collected and not replaced into the grid, all the subsequent observations until the end of the episode are new for the agent. We ran 1000 episodes and calculated the rewards per step and the results are in the table below, and we can see that the stochastic I2A agent is getting very close to a regular A2C agent trained in the deterministic environment (Table 1).

Table 1. Generalization power of stochastic A2C and I2A

	Deterministic A2C	Stochastic A2C	Stochastic I2A
Rewards per step	**0.32**	0.21	0.30

6 Conclusions and Future Work

From the experiments, one can see that I2A agents are very effective in this type of stochastic environment, compared to a baseline A2C agent, even if the environment is relatively easy to learn by a regular A2C agent, and may also not require planning in order to be learned very well. The Grad-CAM method showed some possible evidence for the idea that this agent does not need to plan, and when choosing an action, it is interested only in the rewards closest to the hero. This is why it is able to generalize in the deterministic environment.

Playing ourselves the small game, we managed to match the A2C performance of ~24 rewards per episode of 50 steps. The I2A agent obtains a significantly larger maximum reward than an A2C agent. The fact that, on average, the trajectories with just one step are the fastest learners, makes the I2A even more efficient in this type of environment, because longer rollouts make the forward step of the I2A much more expensive. It also means that the LSTM could be replaced with a fully connected layer in the Rollout Encoder, further increasing the effectiveness of the I2A agent. The I2A agent with longer trajectories can be thought of as an I2A agent with a poor model, and the I2A agent is able to discard useless information, albeit at a penalty in learning ramp-up, compared to smaller imagined trajectory agents.

The convolutional network structure that we proposed for extracting features from the observations shows better results in learning of both A2C baseline agent and I2A agent.

Some interesting future research would be to make more experiments in a similar but deterministic environment, to confirm whether planning to collect all rewards with the shortest path is learned or not by the I2A agent in this type of environment. Larger grids could be used, with sparser rewards and longer imagined trajectories to see if more stable and higher performance agents could be trained. Another idea to reduce stochasticity would be to replace only some of the squares that the agent gets to, and not all of them.

Another direction of investigation would be to compare the proposed approach with other methods of "planning from pixels", such as PlaNet [14], World Models [15], MuZero [16].

References

1. Schulman, J., Levine, S., Abbeel, P., Jordan, M., Moritz, P.: Trust region policy optimization. In: International Conference on Machine Learning, pp. 1889–1897 (2015)
2. Schulman, J., Wolski, F., Dhariwal, P., Radford, A., Klimov, O.: Proximal policy optimization algorithms (2017). https://arxiv.org/abs/1707.06347
3. Mnih, V., et al.: Asynchronous methods for deep reinforcement learning. In: International Conference on Machine Learning, pp. 1928–1937 (2016)

4. Haarnoja, T., Zhou, A., Abbeel, P., Levine, S.: Soft actor-critic: off-policy maximum entropy deep reinforcement learning with a stochastic actor (2018). https://arxiv.org/abs/1801.01290
5. Mnih, V., Kavukcuoglu, K., Silver, D., Graves, A., Antonoglou, I., Wierstra, D., Riedmiller, M.: Playing Atari with Deep Reinforcement Learning. Preprint at: https://arxiv.org/abs/1801.01290 (2013)
6. Lillicrap, T.P., et al.: Continuous control with deep reinforcement learning (2015). https://arxiv.org/abs/1509.02971
7. Silver, D., et al.: Mastering the game of go without human knowledge. Nature **550**(7676), 354–359 (2017). https://doi.org/10.1038/nature24270
8. Silver, D., Hubert, T., Schrittwieser, J., Antonoglou, I., Lai, M., Guez, A., Lanctot, M., Sifre, L., Kumaran, D., Graepel, T., Lillicrap, T.: A general reinforcement learning algorithm that masters chess, Shogi, and go through self-play. Science **362**(6419), 1140–1144 (2018)
9. Talvitie, E.: Model regularization for stable sample rollouts. In: Thirtieth Conference on Uncertainty in Artificial Intelligence, pp. 780–789 (2014)
10. Talvitie, E.: Agnostic system identification for monte carlo planning. In: Twenty-Ninth AAAI Conference on Artificial Intelligence (2015)
11. Racanière, S., et al.: Imagination-augmented agents for deep reinforcement learning. In: Advances in Neural Information Processing Systems, pp. 5690–5701 (2017)
12. Selvaraju, R.R., Cogswell, M., Das, A., Vedantam, R., Parikh, D., Batra, D.: Grad-Cam: visual explanations from deep networks via gradient-based localization. In: Proceedings of the IEEE International Conference on Computer Vision, pp. 618–626 (2017)
13. Lapan, M.: Deep Reinforcement Learning Hands-On: Apply Modern RL Methods, with Deep Q-networks, Value Iteration, Policy Gradients, TRPO, AlphaGo Zero and More. Packt Publishing, Birmingham (2018)
14. Hafner, D., et al.: Learning latent dynamics for planning from pixels (2018). https://arxiv.org/abs/1811.04551
15. Ha, D., Schmidhuber, J.: World models (2018). https://arxiv.org/abs/1803.10122
16. Schrittwieser, J., et al.: Mastering Atari, go, chess and shogi by planning with a learned model (2019). https://arxiv.org/abs/1911.08265
17. Pal, C.V.: I2AGrid. Online source code (2020). https://github.com/ValentinPal/I2AGrid

Evaluation of the Cleft-Overstep Algorithm for Linear Regression Analysis

Duy Hung Phan[✉] and Le Dinh Huynh

FPT University, Hanoi, Vietnam
hungpd2@fe.edu.vn, huynhldmse0083@fpt.edu.vn

Abstract. Optimization algorithms have been applied to improve the learning speed of machine learning. In the backpropagation phase, the weights of the neural network will be updated in each epoch with the purpose that the difference between the actual output and predicted one will be reached to a value smaller than a predefined number epsilon. In essence, the backpropagation process only uses the idea of optimization algorithm to formulate a weighted update formula, rather than a complete optimization problem. The enhancement of machine learning speed is meaningful when the application of artificial intelligence is rising. The cleft-overstep optimal algorithm has been introduced since the 1990s and implemented in optimal control, which has not been popularized and evaluated in other fields. This paper aims to use the idea of cleft-overstep method, also apply and program probing in linear regression analysis - a simple machine learning algorithm. Results were compared with classic gradient descent method based on the known problem and showed a significant learning speed improvement.

Keywords: Optimization algorithm · Cleft-overstep · Linear regression · Gradient descent · Machine learning speed

1 Introduction

Studies of optimization theory are essential in many fields such as economic, engineering, biology, chemistry, etc. Optimization is an inmost part of life and human activity. For example, coordinators need to optimize scheduling process, hotel room reservation or optimize the places in a warehouse, containers in port to lead up the most convenient of importing and exporting merchandise.

In many IT problems and with the booming period of Industry 4.0, the application of artificial intelligence and machine learning has been developing rapidly and has brought about miraculous results. For machine learning, optimization methods play a particularly important role in learning backward propagation and to update weights in the network. Gradient descent is a classical and popular optimization algorithm [1]. There has been much research on speeding up machine learning based on mathematical optimization methods. Speeding up machine learning algorithms will save time and improve the performance of hardware computation [2, 3].

© Springer Nature Switzerland AG 2020
N. T. Nguyen et al. (Eds.): ICCCI 2020, LNAI 12496, pp. 400–411, 2020.
https://doi.org/10.1007/978-3-030-63007-2_31

The theory of nonlinear function optimization methods is nonlinear planning. Its main content is to study the properties of object functions and build interactive algorithms, starting from an initial position and then gradually approaching the optimal solution. This type of interactive optimization algorithm is built on two basic concepts moving direction and moving step length. In each moving step, the starting, the moving direction, and the moving step length are appropriately determined in order to guarantee the convergence of the algorithm and its convergence speed. Direction and step, in general, are of equal significance in ensuring the convergence as well as the speed of iteration optimization.

The method of determining the length of a displacement step is called the step adjustment rule. To formulate an iterative algorithm, it is possible to combine a method of determining the direction of motion with different step adjustment rules. In contrast, a step adjustment rule can be combined with many methods of determining the direction to form different algorithms. If the combination of movement direction and step adjustment rule is chosen properly, it is possible to build an efficient and converged algorithm at high speed. There are currently hundreds of optimization algorithms proposed, but they mostly differ in how the motion is determined.

It can be seen that the general principle of applying optimization in machine learning is quite simple but the specific implementation when programming is not simple, it depends on the complexity of the algorithm, the working way of each machine learning method. In addition, each optimization method will suit the data type/nature, machine learning method, so it is needed evaluation and study in detail.

The paper will continue with the following content: Sect. 2 summaries basic optimization algorithms being used in machine learning. Afterward, Sect. 3 presents the method and variations of the cleft-overstep algorithm. Section 4 is to implement, evaluate and compare cleft-overstep methods, and to compare with the classical method stochastic gradient descent in basic machine learning problem which is linear regression analysis. The results of this section are seen as the beginning of the application of the cleft-overstep algorithm in machine learning. Finally, conclusions and future development directions of the study will be introduced.

2 Survey Well-Known Optimization Algorithms

2.1 Gradient Descent

Gradient Descent is the most common optimization algorithm for machine learning and deep learning [4]. It is a first-order optimization algorithm. The frequent approach is to start from a point we consider to be close to the solution, then use an iterative operation to get to the closest point we are looking for until the loss is close to 0. We can have a simple update formula.

$$\omega_{k+1} = \omega_k - \alpha \frac{\partial L}{\partial \omega_k} \tag{1}$$

where:

k – time step

ω – weight/parameter which we want to update

α – learning rate

$\partial L/\partial \omega$ – gradient of L, the loss function to minimize, w.r.t. to ω

The convergence speed is depended on the initial point and learning rate. The fact that the learning rate α is too small, it would take a long time to converge, even never reaching the destination. If α is large, the algorithm moves very quickly to its destination after a few iterations. However, the algorithm does not converge because of the jump (step) is too large, making it hang around at the destination.

2.2 Momentum

In lieu of depending only on the current gradient to find in formula (1), started by the current gradient with velocity V as the exponential moving average of current and past gradients. Gradient descent with momentum could be described [4, 5]:

$$\omega_{k+1} = \omega_k - \alpha V_k \tag{2}$$

where $V_k = \beta V_{k-1} + (1 - \beta)\frac{\partial L}{\partial \omega_k}$ and V initialized to 0. Common default value: $\beta = 0.9$. Momentum helps the moving cross the local minimum slope. However, there is a limitation when in near destination, momentum still takes quite a bit of time before stopping.

2.3 Nesterov Accelerated Gradient (NAG)

Nesterov accelerated gradient (NAG) is a way to reduce the restriction of Momentum [5]. The basic idea is to predict future moving direction. The comparison of Momentum and NAG is shown in Fig. 1. NAG could reduce the 'zigzag' effect, improve convergence speed compare to momentum.

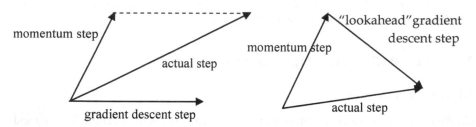

Fig. 1. Gradient descent with momentum and NAG update

2.4 AdaGrad

AdaGrad or Adaptive Gradient is initiated by Duchi et al 2011 [6]. It adapts the learning rate by dividing the rate by the square root of S which is the cumulative sum of current and past squared gradients.

$$\omega_{k+1} = \omega_k - \frac{\alpha}{\sqrt{S_t} + \varepsilon}\frac{\partial L}{\partial \omega_k} \tag{3}$$

where $S_k = S_{k-1} + \left[\frac{\partial L}{\partial \omega_k}\right]^2$ and S initialized to 0. The main benefit of AdaGrad is the rule-set tune learning rate which means we do not need to set the learning rate manually. And one of the weakness is its accumulation of the squared gradients in the denominator, can cause the learning rate to become infinitesimally small, let the algorithm no longer able to acquire additional knowledge.

2.5   RMSprop

Root mean square prop or RMSprop is another adaptive learning rate that is an improvement of AdaGrad [7]. Instead of taking cumulative sum of squared gradients like in AdaGrad, we take the exponential moving average of these gradients.

$$\omega_{k+1} = \omega_k - \frac{\alpha}{\sqrt{S_t + \varepsilon}} \frac{\partial L}{\partial \omega_k} \tag{4}$$

where $S_k = \beta S_{k-1} + (1 - \beta)\left[\frac{\partial L}{\partial \omega_k}\right]^2$ and S initialized to 0.

3   Cleft-Overstep Algorithms

In 1999, N. V. Manh in his doctoral dissertation presented the cleft-overstep algorithm and applied it to control problems [8]. A number of subsequent studies he presented the improvements of the original algorithm in more detail [9–11]. According to the cleft-overstep principle, the starting and ending points of each iteration are always on either side of the minimum point of the objective function in the searching direction. That movement creates a geometric picture that is like on each iteration, the searching point always "step over" through the "cleft" of the object function. The "overstep" movement passing the minimum point (in the direction) on each iteration creates the ability to analyze the "terrain" of the "cleft" region and receive specific information about the "cleft" characteristics of the object function. That allows building the most effective searching strategy, leading to the optimal solution.

Examining the unconstrained optimization problem:

$$J(x) \rightarrow \min, x \in E^n \tag{5}$$

The optimization algorithm to solve (5) has the iteration formula:

$$x_{k+1} = x_k + \alpha_{k+1}s_k, k = 0, 1, 2, \ldots \tag{6}$$

α_{k+1} is called the **moving step**; s_k is called **moving direction.**

To determine the moving step, consider the function of the variable α defined at step $k + 1$:

$$h(\alpha) = J(x_k + \alpha s_k) \tag{7}$$

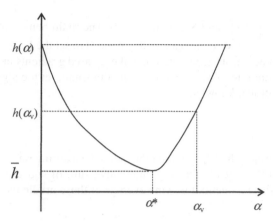

Fig. 2. The cleft-overstep principle

If $J(x)$ is continuously differentiable everywhere, $h(\alpha)$ is also continuously differentiable. Since s_k is the direction of reducing the object function, the derivative in the direction satisfies the condition:

$$h'(\alpha)|_{\alpha=0} = \frac{d}{d\alpha} J(\mathbf{x}_k + \alpha \mathbf{s}_k)|_{\alpha=0} = \langle \nabla J(\mathbf{x}_k), \mathbf{s}_k \rangle < 0 \qquad (8)$$

This inequality proves that $h(\alpha)$ is a reduction function by a. If $J(x)$ is blocked below, then $h(\alpha)$ is also blocked below. In addition, if $\lim\limits_{\|\mathbf{x}\|\to\infty} J(\mathbf{x}) = \infty$, there exists a local minimum α^* of $h(\alpha)$ (Fig. 2). Thus, the condition for determining the moving step α_v is:

$$h'(\alpha)|_{\alpha=\alpha_v} > 0, \ h(\alpha_v) \leq h(0). \qquad (9)$$

Let a, b are vectors n-dimensional Euclidean Space E^n. We have calculated directions.

Algorithm 1: Moving Directions Of Cleft-overstep Algorithm

$$d_{bisector} = \frac{a}{\|a\|} + \frac{b}{\|b\|} \qquad (10)$$

Where $\|x\| = \sqrt{\sum\limits_{i=1}^{n} x_i^2}$, a and b are gradient vectors at x_{k+1} and x_k.

$$d_{perpendicular} = \frac{\langle a,(a-b)\rangle}{\langle b,(a-b)\rangle} b + a \qquad (11)$$

Where $\langle x, y \rangle$ is scalar product of vector x and y

---

Assume, we have last consecutive iteration r $(r{\leq}n)$ gradient of the object function $g^k, g^{k-1}, ..., g^{k-r+1}$

$$d_{Affin} = -\sum_{i=0}^{r-1} \gamma_i g^{k-i}, \sum_{i=0}^{r-1} \gamma_i = 1 \qquad (12)$$

The moving direction is improved if the objective function decreases with a certain moving step. There are 3 moving directions that are used in cleft-overstep: bisector, perpendicular, and Affin.

The rule to determine the moving step α is described as the pseudocode:

Algorithm 2: Determine Cleft-overstep Moving Step Algorithm	
Input:	x_0, s_0
Output:	α
Parameters: $a=0.5, \varepsilon=0.01, \gamma=0.10$	

Step 1	1. ASSIGN $\alpha = a$
	2. COMPUTE: $h_\alpha = h(x + as)$
	3. IF $h_\alpha \geq h_0$ THEN
	    a. ASSIGN $\alpha = 0, \beta = a$
	    b. GOTO Step 2
	ELSE
	    c. REPEAT
	        ASSIGN $\alpha = \beta, \beta = 1.5\beta$
	        UNTIL $h_\alpha \leq h_\beta$
	    d. GOTO Step 2
	ENDIF

Step 2	1. IF $\|\beta - \alpha\| \leq \varepsilon$ THEN
	    a. GOTO Step 3
	ELSE
	    b. ASSIGN $\theta = \alpha + \gamma(\beta - \alpha)$
	ENDIF
	2. IF $h_\theta \leq h_\alpha$ THEN
	    a. ASSIGN $\alpha = \theta$
	ELSE
	    b. ASSIGN $\beta = \theta$
	ENDIF
	3. GOTO Step 2

Step 3	1. ASSIGN $\alpha = \beta$ 2. RETURN α

In the next section, the authors would like to evaluate optimal via linear regression analysis.

4 Implementation and Analysis Results

Linear regression is an approach for modeling the relationship between the dependent variable y and one or more explanatory variables denoted X [12, 13]. Let's start with the problem formulation.

With the response variable y and n features i.e. $(x_1, x_2, \ldots, x_N)$ the parameters $[\omega_1, \omega_n, \ldots, \omega_N]$ are learnt through the estimation techniques.

$H_\omega(X) = \omega^T X$ is the hypothesis function that will be learned from the data. The cost function is the squared error in prediction. That is the deviation from the actual value of y_i and the value computed from the model.

The formal mathematical representation is as follows:

$$J(\omega) = \frac{1}{2N} \sum_{i=1}^{N} (y_i - h_\omega(x_i))^2 \tag{13}$$

Objective of solving would be to identify the values for parameters i.e. ω that will minimize the value of $J(\omega)$.

Broadly there are two different classes of ways to solve this. One of them is called analytical or closed-form solution. And the other one is called iterative solution (like gradient descent). The analytical solution works fine in most of the cases except when the number of features are large or when $X^T X$ becomes non-invertible. The iterative solution comes into rescue, in these scenarios where analytical solution fail.

In this section, the work will address the iterative solution for linear regression in order to evaluate the optimal algorithm. We perform all three variations of cleft-overstep algorithm and the gradient descent algorithm.

When the gradient descent is used for iterations, the ω values are updated:

$$\omega = \omega - \alpha \frac{\partial J}{\partial \omega} \tag{14}$$

α is the learning rate. Gradient descent can let the computation start with any arbitrary point and the derivative in ω of the loss function [14].

$$\frac{\partial L(\omega)}{\partial \omega} = X^T (X\omega - y) \tag{15}$$

When the cleft-overstep is used for iterations, the ω values are updated:

$$\omega_{k+1} = \omega_k + \alpha_{k+1} s_k, k = 0, 1, \ldots \tag{16}$$

α_{k+1} is the **moving step**; s_k is **moving direction.**

Table 1 below is novel parametrization using for valuation.

100 data sets and 1000 data points/1 set for the evaluation are generated randomly. Each data point is a 2D feature vector. To make the evaluation intuitive and impartial, we have given the same initialization value ω_0. In code, data generation looks something like this [15].

```
(X, y) = make_blobs(n_samples=1000, n_features=2, centers=2, clus-
ter_std=1.5, random_state=1)
W0 = np.random.randn(np.c_[X, np.ones((X.shape[0]))].shape[1], 1)
```

This work then performs algorithms and compares the speed between them for the linear regression problem.

Table 1. Operation parameters of train.

Definition	Symbol	Value
Alpha	α	0.01
Beta	β	0.01
Epsilon	ε	0.01
Gamma	γ	0.13
Gamma-i	γ_i	$\frac{1}{n}$
Learning-rate (14)	α	0.01
Epoch	–	100

4.1 Bisector Direction Method

Applying the bisector direction as formula (10) nearly all experiments, loss-epoch graphs decreased linearly.

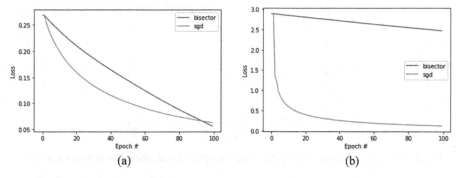

(a)   (b)

Fig. 3. Training loss of Bisector direction optimal and stochastic gradient descent

Figure 3 pointed out that the loss of the bisector direction method is almost linear. Most of the epoch, loss of SGD is better than bisector but in the end, bisector direction has better results.

A problem of bisector direction through experiments showed that the loss does not decrease too much from the starting to the ending point. Sometimes it got an ideal result for accuracy, precision, recall, and f1 score if the initiation point w_0 is close enough to the solution (Fig. 3.a) otherwise the result is very underprivileged (Fig. 3.b).

4.2 Perpendicular Direction Method

Through testing over 100 prepared datasets, Perpendicular is much better than Bisector. There are 33 situations that the final loss value of Perpendicular is smaller (better) than SGD. Sift into the rest of 67 cases, by calculating the difference between two last values

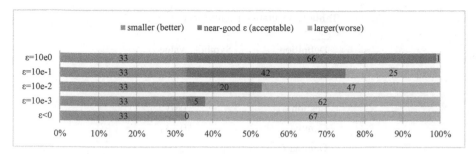

Fig. 4. Perpendicular and SGD final loss value comparison.

compare within the epsilon $\varepsilon = 0.01$, we obtained 20 near-good situations. Continue to adjust epsilon ε through $10e$–3, $10e$–2, $10e$–1, the comparison is shown in Fig. 4.

Perpendicular and SGD, they were well matched. Figure 5 below describes a situation that Perpendicular and SGD are overlapping each other, however, Perpendicular has a faster reduction in epoch from 0 to 20.

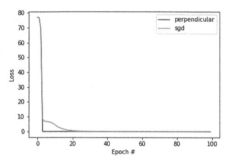

Fig. 5. Training loss of perpendicular direction optimal and stochastic gradient descent.

4.3   Affin Direction Method

Affin has a much better case than Perpendicular (Fig. 6). The number situation with a better result after 100 epochs is relatively equal to SGD (46 cases vs 54 cases).

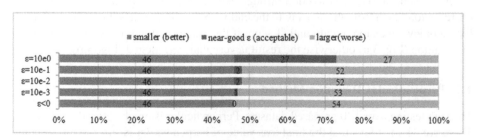

Fig. 6. Affin and SGD final loss value comparison.

The graphs decrease more naturally and smoothly compared with Bisector and Perpendicular methods (Fig. 7). The averaging computing $\gamma_i = \frac{1}{n}$ (Table 1) might be the reason to make the direction of motion smoother, more stable, and not impulsive like the other two methods.

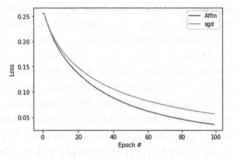

Fig. 7. Affin and SGD loss-epoch.

4.4 Summary

We have given the same initialization value w_0, used predefined hyper-parameters (Table 1) to create an equitable evaluation. Perpendicular and Affin directions have the stability and efficiency equivalent to basic gradient descent, sometimes event superior. Bisector in this evaluation did not get the outstanding optimal but it has some acceptable case (Fig. 8).

One of the most important factors that have not been mentioned yet is the number of time "step over" the "cleft". The ability of cleft-overstep algorithm is to survey the entire surface of "cleft" and having steps to overcome. It is the main highlight that makes the difference. This evaluation has an observation of the maximum number of "overstep" per epoch of 40 and minimum of 1 for Bisector, Perpendicular, and Affin. Their average moving step values are 1.44, 1.05 and 2.17 respectively. Compared with SGD (default unit as 1), each epoch needs more calculations, but on the general problem, calculating a finite one or more does not make sense. Figure 9 attempts to show "overstep" efforts, by experimentally proving the correctness of method.

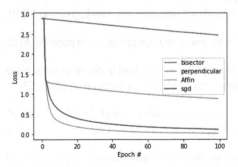

Fig. 8. Three methods cleft-overstep and SGD.

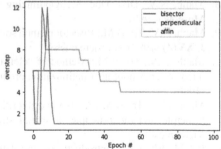

Fig. 9. "Overstep" efforts over epoch.

5 Conclusions and Perspectives

Optimal methods are an especially important part of machine learning. Speeding up machine learning speed will save time, save energy consumption, and improve hardware performance. This paper is the initial study to implement and evaluate the cleft-overstep optimization in machine learning. The research has introduced the theory, implemented and compared variations of cleft-overstep algorithm and the stochastic gradient descent optimizer into Linear Regression problem. 100 dummy datasets are generated randomly in which data point is a 2D feature vector. The experimental results have been proved that Perpendicular and Affin optimization methods are the most dominant. Subjectively, Affin improves outstanding speed, compared to stochastic gradient descent.

The research will continue with the complete integration into the well-known machine learning frameworks Keras, and evaluation on various machine learning models, a benchmark on diverse data types and deep learning methods to gain a comprehensive view of efficiency of the cleft-overstep optimization algorithm. The paper is also a good reference for research on machine learning, deep learning applications [16, 17].

References

1. Ruszczyński, A.: Nonlinear Optimization, vol. 13. Princeton University Press, Princeton (2006)
2. Zouggar, S.T., Adla, A.: Optimization techniques for machine learning. In: Kulkarni, A.J., Satapathy, S.C. (eds.) Optimization in Machine Learning and Applications. AIS, pp. 31–50. Springer, Singapore (2020). https://doi.org/10.1007/978-981-15-0994-0_3
3. Ezquerro, J.A., Grau-Sánchez, M., Grau, A., et al.: On iterative methods with accelerated convergence for solving systems of nonlinear equations. J. Optim. Theory Appl. **151**, 163–174 (2011)
4. Ruder, S.: An overview of gradient descent optimization algorithms, pp. 1–14 (2016). https://arxiv.org/abs/1609.04747
5. Botev, A., Lever, G., Barber, D.: Nesterov's accelerated gradient and momentum as approximations to regularised update descent. In: Proceedings of the International Joint Conference on Neural Networks, pp. 1899–1903 (2017)
6. Zhang, N., Lei, D., Zhao, J.F.: An improved Adagrad gradient descent optimization algorithm. In: Proceedings Chinese Automation Congress, CAC 2018, no. 3, pp. 2359–2362. IEEE (2019)
7. Park, H., Lee, K.: Adaptive natural gradient method for learning of stochastic neural networks in mini-batch mode. Appl. Sci. **9**, 4568 (2019)
8. Manh, N.V.: Diss. Doc. Sc.: Optimizing methods of uncertainty control systems. MPEI, Moscow (1999)
9. Manh, N.V., Tri, B.M.: Bisector method solves the unconstraines optimization problem. Math J. **XV**(4) (1987). (in Vietnamese)
10. Manh, N.V., Tri, B.M.: Method of "cleft-overstep" by perpendicular direction for solving unconstraines nonlinear optimization problem. Acta Mathematica Vietnamica **15**(2), 73–83 (1990)
11. Manh, N.V., Tri, B.M.: An extreme algorithm based on a combination of the "cleft-overstep" principle and the principle of spatial stretching. J. Sci. Technol. (12), 1–6 (1996). (in Vietnamese)
12. Pal, M., Bharati, P.: Introduction to correlation and linear regression analysis. Applications of Regression Techniques, pp. 1–18. Springer, Singapore (2019). https://doi.org/10.1007/978-981-13-9314-3_1

13. Perron, P., Yamamoto, Y.: Pitfalls of two-step testing for changes in the error variance and coefficients of a linear regression model. Econometrics **7**, 22 (2019)
14. Jon, D.: Appendix D matrix calculus. In: Convex Optimization & Euclidean Distance Geometry. Meboo Publishing (2018). https://ccrma.stanford.edu/~dattorro/matrixcalc.pdf
15. Scikit-learn   (2019).   https://scikit-learn.org/stable/modules/generated/sklearn.datasets.make_blobs.html
16. Hung, P.D., Su, N.T., Diep, V.T.: Surface classification of damaged concrete using deep convolutional neural network. Pattern Recogn. Image Anal. **29**(4), 676–687 (2019). https://doi.org/10.1134/S1054661819040047
17. Nam, N.T, Hung, P.D.: Padding methods in convolutional sequence model: an application in Japanese handwriting recognition. In: Proceedings of the 3rd International Conference on Machine Learning and Soft Computing (ICMLSC 2019), pp. 138–142. Association for Computing Machinery, New York (2019)

Deep Learning and Applications for Industry 4.0

Early Unsafety Detection in Autonomous Vehicles

Thuy Pham[1,2], Tien Dang[1], Nhu Nguyen[1,2], Thao Ha[1,2],
and Binh T. Nguyen[1,2(✉)]

[1] AISIA Research Lab, Ho Chi Minh City, Vietnam
ngtbinh@hcmus.edu.vn
[2] VNU HCM University of Science, Ho Chi Minh City, Vietnam

Abstract. Autonomous vehicles have been investigated broadly during the last decade and predicted to decrease road fatalities by shifting control of safety-critical tasks from humans to machines. An early unsafety detection consequently becomes a key feature in every self-driving cars and trucks. In this paper, we present a promising approach for the safety prediction problem in autonomous vehicles by using one dataset collected from the competition CMDC 2019, which can capture multiple safe or unsafe situations from a front car camera put in different autonomous buses. We consider various ways to extract potential features from images provided and apply numerous machine learning techniques to learn an efficient detection algorithm. The experimental results show that by combining Histogram-of-Gradients (HOG) features as well as deep-learning ones computed from both ResNet50 and our proposed deep neural networks (MRNets), we can achieve an auspicious performance in terms of both micro-averaged F1-score and macro-averaged F1-score. The outcome of our papers can give an additional contribution to the current study of the problem.

Keywords: Autonomous vehicles · Safety detection · Deep neural networks

1 Introduction

Nowadays, there have been more and more companies making autonomous vehicles (AVs) in developing countries, especially in the United States of America, Germany, Japan, and Korea. Fully autonomous cars and trucks that can operate independently instead of us driving them are going to become a reality. Consequently, better road safety has also become one of the essential features of these self-driving cars, particularly for public transportation. There exist a lot of studies related to the improvement of road safety during recent years [4,12,13].

Two first authors have equal contribution.

© Springer Nature Switzerland AG 2020
N. T. Nguyen et al. (Eds.): ICCCI 2020, LNAI 12496, pp. 415–426, 2020.
https://doi.org/10.1007/978-3-030-63007-2_32

Autonomous vehicles can presently be equipped with a combination of hardware (sensors, cameras, and radar) and software, which can increase sophisticated safety and crash avoidance technology. Using multiple cameras with diverse views can enhance the chance of early unsafety identification to save lives and prevent injuries. Interestingly, several brand-new motor vehicles have driver assistance technologies that can help drivers avoid drifting into adjacent lanes or making unsafe lane changes. They can also inform drivers of other cars behind them when they are backing up or automatically brake in case that one vehicle ahead of them suddenly stops or slows [16].

Implementing an efficient algorithm that can quickly help vehicles identify certain safety risks from signals of hardware provided is hugely significant for warning the driver to act to avoid a crash. Althoff et al. [1] propose a probabilistic approach for collision detection for a given trajectory of the autonomous car under different uncertainties and possible behaviors of other traffic participants. Kabeer and colleagues [6] present an efficient autonomous simulator for supporting to pre-train the autonomous vehicles in the real world. Riaz et al. [14] introduce a new approach to improve the collision avoidance of Autonomous Vehicles (AVs) by using human social norms and human emotion, that provides a better alternative for tailoring the autopilots of future self-driving vehicles. Tian et al. [17] provide a powerful systematic testing tool, namely DeepTest, for automatically discovering erroneous behaviors of Deep Neural Networks (DNN)-driven vehicles that can potentially lead to fatal crashes under different driving conditions.

Fig. 1. An illustration for two categories in the SADAVS dataset. The left image is a safety case while the remaining one is an unsafe situation.

In this paper, we aim at investigating a vehicle-based accident detection system that can monitor a network of sensors to determine if an accident is going to occur shortly. Instances of high acceleration/deceleration are due in no small change in velocity over a short period. In the context of an autonomous car, the speed may be hard to attain as a human driver does not control a vehicle. For studying an appropriate algorithm for the problem, we use one dataset, namely SADAVS dataset, provided by organizers of the competition CDMC 2019[1]. They created this dataset by employing one front car camera located in front of several public vehicles facing forward in New Zealand. It is worth noting that people always drive on the left-hand side of the road in New Zealand, and when someone is driving, the person must be seated in the middle of the road as well as the front seat passenger should be the on the edge of the street. After that, the organizers collected videos and then extract real-time images of size 160×144 with the corresponding labels in monitoring the status of moving vehicles. There are only two labels in this dataset, which are safe (1) or unsafe (-1). Interestingly, the objective of this competition task is for the early detection of any potential road accidents in two different scenarios.

There are two specific tests in this competition, including scenario A and scenario B. Notably, scenario A has 416 records in the testing data; meanwhile, there are 850 ones in the testing data for the scenario B. It is vital to note that the raw dataset is a matrix of float numbers with a size of 160×144. After carefully analyzing the dataset, we find out that the sensor array provided contains not only signals from multiple sensors but also images captured from the front camera in each vehicle. Therefore, we convert float matrix data to image data, as shown in Fig. 1, and turn the initial problem into an image classification problem with two labels.

To solve this problem, we use the training dataset provided from the competition (973 samples) and apply various machine learning methods and different types of features, including hand-crafted features and deep-learning features. Also, we consider a hybrid network, which is a combination of both those features. For hand-crafted features, we use Histograms of Oriented Gradients (HOG) [2] and SIFT [9] for extracting potential factors from each image. We apply deep neural networks to obtain deep-learning features by utilizing the pre-trained model ResNet50 [5] and our proposed deep neural network, namely MRNet. To compare the performance of different approaches, we use the following metrics: Micro averaged F1-score and Macro averaged F1-score. The experimental results show that the hybrid method can obtain an auspicious performance of 98% for both Micro averaged F1-score and Macro averaged F1-score, and outperforms other techniques. These outcomes can give an additional contribution to the current research of building an early unsafety detection problem for AVs.

The rest of this article can be organized as follows. In Sect. 2, we present our proposed methods and feature-engineering step. All experimental results are presented in Sect. 3. Finally, the paper ends with conclusions and future works.

2   Our Proposed Methods

In this section, we present our approaches to build a binary classification model for a vehicle-based accident detection system using a camera. As depicted in

---

[1] http://www.csmining.org/cdmc2019/index.php?id=5.

Fig. 2, our proposed hybrid network is a combination among HOG [2] features and deep features extracted from deep neural networks.

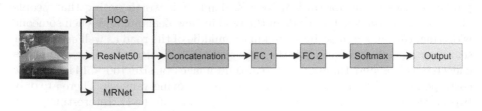

Fig. 2. The data pipelines of our proposed hybrid network.

2.1 Hand-Crafted Features

Hand-crafted features (such as color, texture, and shape) are traditional types of features, which are used a lot in object recognition. In this work, we employ HOG and SIFT to extract potential features from images captured from the front car camera.

Typically, SIFT [9] can generate a collection of interesting key points which are mostly invariant with image translation, scaling, and rotation. Calculating SIFT features of a given image includes four main steps: scale-space extreme detection using Difference of Gaussian (DoG) [9], localizing key-points which ignore low contrast candidates by Hessian matrix, orientation assignment, and key-point descriptors. Figure 3 illustrates a SIFT descriptor.

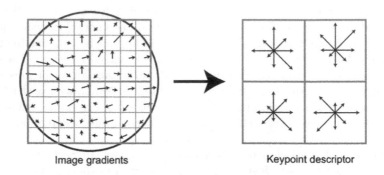

Image gradients   Keypoint descriptor

Fig. 3. A 2 × 2 SIFT descriptor that can be computed from an 8 × 8 block [9].

Meanwhile, HOG [2] can illustrate the shape of an object by calculating a histogram of oriented gradients for small squared cells in images and then normalize histogram values by using a block-wise pattern. Figure 4 shows features derived by SIFT and HOG. Moreover, combining HOG features and SIFT features can also be useful in the experiments.

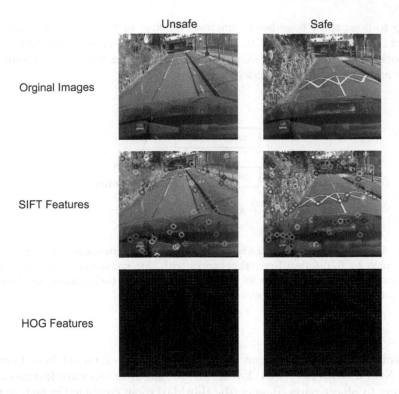

Fig. 4. An example of features extracted by SIFT and HOG.

2.2 Deep-Learning Features

For deep-learning features, we apply transfer-learning techniques by fine-tuning ResNet50 [5] model with initial weights as ImageNet weights. Furthermore, we design and implement a new architecture based on the multi-level convolutional neural networks (MLCNN) [10], namely MRNet, in our experiments.

ResNet Architecture. In a traditional neural network, outputs of the current layer can be fed into the next layer. However, the network cannot keep the information about low-level features that can be valuable for the final outputs. In 2015, Kaiming He and co-workers develop ResNet [5], which is the winning solution of both ILSVRC [15] and MS COCO 2015 competitions [8]. Notably, the fundamental idea of ResNet is a deep residual framework. As depicted in Fig. 5, a network with residual blocks has skip-connections that are used to clone the features from the previous layer to the next layer. Therefore, it can solve the existent drawbacks in traditional neural networks.

Up to now, there have been numerous versions of ResNet models, including ResNet18, ResNet34, ResNet50, ResNet101, ResNet152, and ResNeXt [18]. In our work, we decide using ResNet50 as it can fit better with a small dataset to create an efficient learning model for the problem.

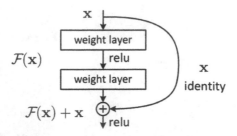

Fig. 5. A residual block in a ResNet architecture. The formulation of $\mathcal{F}(\mathbf{x}) + \mathbf{x}$ can be obtained by feed-forward neural networks with skip-connections. In this case, the skip-connections simply perform an identity mapping, and their outputs can be added to the outputs of the stacked layers [5].

MRNet Architecture. Figure 6 presents features extracted from Convolutional Neural Networks (CNN) layers. The second layer can learn features corresponding to object parts. Besides, the third layer can combine the feature parts extracted from previous layers to represent the object with higher-level features [7]. Therefore, it is significant to build a model that can mix multi-level features on CNNs.

To detect a safety or unsafety status for autonomous vehicles, we concentrate not only on the whole image extracted from the camera but also on small regions inside the image. Consequently, it is reasonable to develop an architecture adapting these conditions. MLCNN [10] is a decent idea for overcoming these challenges as MLCNN considers a combination of mid-level features and high-level features. Thus, MLCNN architecture can conform to these conditions.

In this study, we propose to use an MRNet architecture that is a combination of residual blocks [5] and MLCNN [10]. As illustrated in Fig. 7, the proposed model has seven blocks and residual-connections (skip-connections) among these blocks. Interestingly, each block contains two, three, or four convolutional layers followed by the max-pooling layer. The skip-connections are used to copy features from the previous block to later block.

Mainly, we also apply the global average pooling (GAP) at the end of each block (except the 1st block) to obtain useful features as many as possible and concatenate all of these features into the final vector of features. The input of MRNet is a 224 × 224 grayscale image, and the last layer is a Softmax layer consisting of two nodes, which corresponds to two categories: safe and unsafe.

faces   cars

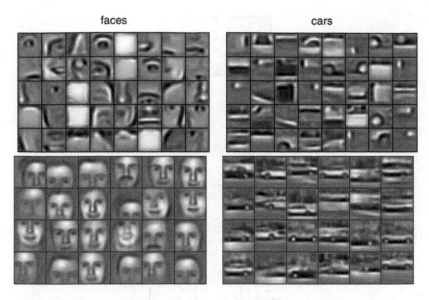

Fig. 6. The second layer bases (top) and the third layer bases (bottom) learned from specific object categories [7].

2.3   The Fusion Technique

It is worth emphasizing that ResNet50 [5] and MRNet can generate powerful features that are a combination of multi-level features on CNNs. Furthermore, HOG features can well represent the main shape and the contextual information of objects. It turns out that mixing features computed between CNNs and HOGs can take the main advantages of these approaches and become a more powerful one. Figure 2 illustrates the whole pipeline of our proposed hybrid network. Here, one can deduce HOG, ResNet50, and MRNet features from the initial image. Subsequently, these features are mixed up as the final feature vector, and then one can use it to predict the final output.

For the implementation, we train both ResNet50 [5] and MRNet by using the SADAVS training set [11]. Next, we use the best model learned from each architecture, and then we concatenate them for the fusion model. Assume that F_{HOG}, F_{ResNet} and F_{MRNet} are the corresponding features extracted from HOG, ResNet50, and MRNet, respectively. Then, one can determine the fusion feature, which is F_{Fusion}, as follows

$$F_{Fusion} = F_{HOG} \oplus F_{ResNet} \oplus F_{MRNet} \tag{1}$$

Finally, we use the multi-layer perceptron (MLP) as a learning model to predict the final output. We call the fusion model as "Fusion" and measure the performance of each proposed method in the following section.

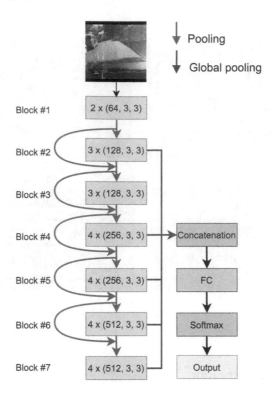

Fig. 7. MRNet architecture.

3   Experiments

We operate all experiments on a computer with Intel(R) Core(TM) i7 2 CPUs running 2.4 GHz with 8 GB of RAM and an Nvidia GeForce RTX 2080Ti GPU. In what follows, we present all necessary settings and experiments for the early unsafety detection problem.

3.1   Dataset

The SADAVS [11] training dataset (973 samples) includes two classes with the following distribution: safe (602 samples) and unsafe (371 samples). To pre-process data, we convert the raw data to image data. Images are then resized by padding zeros to remain the same ratio between the length and the width. After that, we split the SADAVS training set into three parts, which are training, validation, and testing datasets. We use two different ratios for these three parts, including (a) 7:1:2 and (b) 6:1:3, to carefully check the stability of our models. More information related to these datasets can be found in Table 1.

Table 1. The distribution of training, validation, and testing datasets with different separation ratios: 7:1:2 and 6:1:3.

Ratio	Training (No. samples)	Validation (No. samples)	Testing (No. samples)
7:1:2	682	97	194
6:1:3	613	68	292

3.2   Experimental Results

Hand-Crafted Features. For hand-crafted features, we resize all images into the size of 200×200 pixels and compare the performance of using SIFT and HOG. SIFT features may have different numbers of key-points in various images. Therefore, we apply a Bag of Words (BoW) to extract final feature vectors that have the same size. In this approach, we chose the number of words (number of clusters) is from 10 to 40. For HOG, computing feature vectors depend on the number of cells/blocks and the size of each cell/block as well as the overlapping region between two neighborhood blocks but have the same length for given image size. In detail, the cell size is selected between 32×32 and 64×64, while we choose the block size from 2 to 4 and the bin as 9.

With these hand-crafted features, we apply Support Vector Machines [3] (SVM) model with radial basis function (RBF) kernel, $\gamma = [0, 10]$, and $C = [0, 10]$ for modeling.

Table 2. The performance of hand-crafted features in different scenarios.

Ratio	Learning model	Micro-averaged F1-score (%)	Macro-averaged F1-score (%)
7:1:2	SIFT	58.25	58.24
	HOG	95.88	95.53
	SIFT + HOG	95.88	95.53
6:1:3	SIFT	62.33	61.45
	HOG	96.23	96.03
	SIFT + HOG	96.23	96.03

Deep-Learning Features. For implementation, we use the Keras deep learning framework for all of our experiments. We measure the performance of ResNet50 [5], MRNet, and the fusion method on the SADAVS dataset. We apply the class weights and data augmentation to deal with the imbalance occurring in the dataset. To achieve the best results, we tune all necessary hyper-parameters such as learning rate, drop out, and the number of hidden units. Specifically, the learning rate belongs to the interval $[0.0001, 0.003]$, the drop-out value varies from 0 to 0.5, and the number of hidden units can be picked from 510 to 4096.

Tables 2 and 3 describe the performance of different methods in terms of the micro-averaged F1-score and macro-averaged F1-score among hand-crafted and deep-learning features.

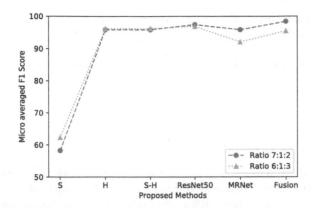

Fig. 8. The performance of different approaches on the testing set (S: SIFT, H: HOG, S-H: Combine SIFT and HOG, ResNet50: ResNet50, MRNet: MRNet, Fusion: Fusion).

Table 3. The performance of deep-learning methods in different scenarios.

Ratio	Model	Micro-averaged F1-score (%)	Macro-averaged F1-score (%)
7:1:2	ResNet50	97.42	97.33
	MRNet	95.88	95.61
	Fusion	98.45	98.36
6:1:3	ResNet50	96.92	96.72
	MRNet	92.12	91.79
	Fusion	95.55	95.33

3.3   Discussion

We have presented our experiments on two different separation ratios for training, validation, and testing datasets. We have compared two types of useful features, including hand-crafted and deep-learning features. Figure 8 visualizes the results of various models considered. The experimental results show that using the SVM model as well as hand-crafted features, can obtain a lower performance in comparison with deep-learning methods (about 2%). Table 2 depicts the performance of SVM model with various hand-crafted features. It is interesting to observe that using SVM models with SIFT features has the lowest performance compared to the others. Among hand-crafted features, using the HOG features can achieve the highest performance in our experiments (96.23% in micro-averaged F1-score and 96.03% in macro-averaged F1-score corresponding to the separation ratio as 6:1:3).

The experimental results in Table 3 implies that the performance of the fusion technique outperforms other deep-learning models as expected. The ResNet50 [5] with ImageNet weights can work well and give a stable performance. Moreover, MRNet is also a promising learning model, and it can provide an essential impact on the fusion model. The best performance in our experiments belongs to the fusion method, where the micro-averaged F1-score is 98.45% and the macro-averaged F1-score is 98.36% corresponding to the separation ratio as 7:1:2.

Afterward, our experiments prove that the initial weights are imperative. That is, if one does not have good initial weights (e.g. ImageNet weights), one may need more data to obtain an efficient classification method.

4   Conclusion and Further Works

We have presented a novel approach for the quick unsafety detection problem for self-driving cars by using the SADAVS training dataset. We have considered different methods by extracting both hand-crafted and deep-learning features as well as the fusion technique. The experiment results show that by combining HOG features with deep-learning ones obtained from ResNet50 and our proposed MRNets, we can achieve the highest performance in terms of both micro-averaged and macro-averaged F1-scores. These outcomes of the paper can contribute to the current research of the crash detection problem for autonomous vehicles. In the future, we aim to apply other deep-learning approaches for enhancing the performance of learning models and collect more datasets related to the problem.

Acknowledgement. This research is funded by Vietnam National University HoChiMinh City (VNU-HCM) under grant number NCM2019-18-01.

References

1. Althoff, M., Stursberg, O., Buss, M.: Model-based probabilistic collision detection in autonomous driving. IEEE Trans. Intell. Transp. Syst. **10**(2), 299–310 (2009). https://doi.org/10.1109/TITS.2009.2018966
2. Dalal, N., Triggs, B.: Histograms of oriented gradients for human detection. In: Proceedings of the 2005 IEEE Computer Society Conference on Computer Vision and Pattern Recognition (CVPR 2005) - Volume 1 - Volume 01, CVPR 2005, pp. 886–893. IEEE Computer Society, Washington, DC (2005). https://doi.org/10.1109/CVPR.2005.177
3. Gunn, S.R., et al.: Support vector machines for classification and regression. ISIS Tech. Rep. **14**(1), 5–16 (1998)
4. Hancock, P.A., Nourbakhsh, I., Stewart, J.: On the future of transportation in an era of automated and autonomous vehicles. Proc. Nat. Acad. Sci. **116**(16), 7684–7691 (2019). https://doi.org/10.1073/pnas.1805770115. https://www.pnas.org/content/116/16/7684
5. He, K., Zhang, X., Ren, S., Sun, J.: Deep residual learning for image recognition. In: Proceedings of the IEEE Conference on Computer Vision and Pattern Recognition, pp. 770–778 (2016)
6. Kabeer, M., Riaz, F., Jabbar, S., Aloqaily, M., Abid, S.: Real world modeling and design of novel simulator for affective computing inspired autonomous vehicle. In: 2019 15th International Wireless Communications Mobile Computing Conference (IWCMC), pp. 1923–1928, June 2019. https://doi.org/10.1109/IWCMC.2019.8766745

7. Lee, H., Grosse, R., Ranganath, R., Ng, A.Y.: Convolutional deep belief networks for scalable unsupervised learning of hierarchical representations. In: Proceedings of the 26th Annual International Conference on Machine Learning, pp. 609–616 (2009)

8. Lin, T.-Y., et al.: Microsoft COCO: common objects in context. In: Fleet, D., Pajdla, T., Schiele, B., Tuytelaars, T. (eds.) ECCV 2014. LNCS, vol. 8693, pp. 740–755. Springer, Cham (2014). https://doi.org/10.1007/978-3-319-10602-1_48

9. Lowe, D.G.: Distinctive image features from scale-invariant keypoints. Int. J. Comput. Vis. **60**(2), 91–110 (2004). https://doi.org/10.1023/B:VISI.0000029664.99615.94

10. Nguyen, H.D., Yeom, S., Lee, G.S., Yang, H.J., Na, I.S., Kim, S.H.: Facial emotion recognition using an ensemble of multi-level convolutional neural networks. Int. J. Pattern Recognit Artif Intell. **33**(11), 1940015 (2019). https://doi.org/10.1142/S0218001419400159

11. Pang, S., Huang, B.: Sensor array data for autonomous vehicle incident detection. In: The 10th International Cybersecurity Data Mining Competition (CDMC 2019) (2019)

12. Penmetsa, P., Adanu, E.K., Wood, D., Wang, T., Jones, S.L.: Perceptions and expectations of autonomous vehicles – a snapshot of vulnerable road user opinion. Technol. Forecast. Soc. Change **143**, 9–13 (2019). https://doi.org/10.1016/j.techfore.2019.02.010. http://www.sciencedirect.com/science/article/pii/S0040162518316603

13. Rajasekhar, M.V., Jaswal, A.K.: Autonomous vehicles: the future of automobiles. In: 2015 IEEE International Transportation Electrification Conference (ITEC), pp. 1–6, August 2015. https://doi.org/10.1109/ITEC-India.2015.7386874

14. Riaz, F., Jabbar, S., Sajid, M., Ahmad, M., Naseer, K., Ali, N.: A collision avoidance scheme for autonomous vehicles inspired by human social norms. Comput. Electr. Eng. **69**, 690–704 (2018). https://doi.org/10.1016/j.compeleceng.2018.02.011. http://www.sciencedirect.com/science/article/pii/S0045790617327039

15. Russakovsky, O., et al.: ImageNet large scale visual recognition challenge. Int. J. Comput. Vision **115**(3), 211–252 (2015). https://doi.org/10.1007/s11263-015-0816-y

16. Stilgoe, J.: Machine learning, social learning and the governance of self-driving cars. Soc. Stud. Sci. **48**(1), 25–56 (2018). https://doi.org/10.1177/0306312717741687. pMID: 29160165

17. Tian, Y., Pei, K., Jana, S., Ray, B.: DeepTest: automated testing of deep-neural-network-driven autonomous cars. In: Proceedings of the 40th International Conference on Software Engineering, ICSE 2018, pp. 303–314. Association for Computing Machinery, New York (2018). https://doi.org/10.1145/3180155.3180220

18. Xie, S., Girshick, R., Dollár, P., Tu, Z., He, K.: Aggregated residual transformations for deep neural networks. In: Proceedings of the IEEE Conference on Computer Vision and Pattern Recognition, pp. 1492–1500 (2017)

Sentence Compression as Deletion with Contextual Embeddings

Minh-Tien Nguyen[1,2(✉)], Cong Minh Bui[1], Dung Tien Le[1],
and Thai Linh Le[1,3]

[1] CINNAMON LAB, 10th Floor, Geleximco Building, 36 Hoang Cau,
Dong Da district, Hanoi, Vietnam
{ryan.nguyen,matthew,nathan,linhlt}@cinnamon.is
[2] Hung Yen University of Technology and Education, Hung Yen, Vietnam
tiennm@utehy.edu.vn
[3] The University of Queensland, Brisbane, Australia

Abstract. Sentence compression is the task of creating a shorter version of an input sentence while keeping important information. In this paper, we extend the task of compression by deletion with the use of contextual embeddings. Different from prior work usually using non-contextual embeddings (Glove or Word2Vec), we exploit contextual embeddings that enable our model capturing the context of inputs. More precisely, we utilize contextual embeddings stacked by bidirectional Long-short Term Memory and Conditional Random Fields for dealing with sequence labeling. Experimental results on a benchmark Google dataset show that by utilizing contextual embeddings, our model achieves a new state-of-the-art F-score compared to strong methods reported on the leader board.

Keywords: Sentence compression · Summarization · Transformers

1 Introduction

Sentence compression is a standard task of natural language processing (NLP), in which a long original sentence is compressed into a shorter version. The compression tries to retain important information, which can be used to reflect the original sentence. Table 1 shows an example of compression.

The output of compression models can be used in NLP systems, e.g. compression of summarization [14] or dialog summary generation [12].

Over two decades, there are a lot of studies focusing on sentence compression. Although compression may differ lexically and structurally from the source sentence, there are two main approaches to this task. The first approach is extractive by deleting unimportant tokens from the original sentence [2,4,6,7,14–16]. The tokens can be defined as words [6,14–16] or phrases from parsed trees [2,7]. By contrast, the abstractive compression approach crates compression by paraphrasing tokens from the original sentence. Therefore, tokens of the compression do not need to be similar to those in the original sentence. To do that, many

© Springer Nature Switzerland AG 2020
N. T. Nguyen et al. (Eds.): ICCCI 2020, LNAI 12496, pp. 427–440, 2020.
https://doi.org/10.1007/978-3-030-63007-2_33

Table 1. An example of sentence compression. We can observe that the compression is created by deleting unnecessary words from the original sentence.

Original sentence	Floyd Mayweather is open to fighting Amir Khan in the future, despite snubbing the Bolton-born boxer in favour of a May bout with Argentine Marcos Maidana, according to promoters Golden Boy
Compression	Floyd Mayweather is open to fighting Amir Khan in the future

neural machine translation models can be utilized [3]. However, the quality of abstractive compression models is still far from human satisfaction.

In this paper, we study the task of sentence compression by deletion. The idea of our study comes from the fact that compression can be created by removing unnecessary tokens [6,7,15,16]. To do that, we formulate the compression as a sequence labeling task and introduce a sequence labeling model. More precisely, inspired by the recent success of contextual embeddings [1,5], we employ contextual embeddings as word embeddings. The contextual concept enables our model to exploit word contextual transformation for word representation. To learn hidden representation, we stack bidirectional Long-short Term Memory (BiLSTM) on the embedding layer. The sequence tagging is done by using Conditional Random Fields (CRFs) to take into account global optimization over the whole sequence. This paper makes two main contributions as the following:

- It introduces a neural-based deletion model for sentence compression. The model exploits contextual embeddings from transformers, which allow our model to encode the contextual aspect of input words. It efficiently facilitates learning the hidden representation of data.
- It validates the efficiency of the model on the Google dataset, a benchmark corpus of sentence compression. Experimental results show that our model with contextual embeddings achieves a new state-of-the-art F-score compared to previous strong methods reported on the leader board.

We review related work of compression in Sect. 2. We next introduce our model, including data preparation, layers, and the training process in Sect. 3. Settings and evaluation metrics are showed in Sect. 4. Comparison and observation are reported in Sect. 5 . We finally draw conclusions in Sect. 6.

2   Related Work

The compression task has been addressed in two main directions: deletion and abstraction. The deletion approach usually treats the compression as an extraction or a sequence labeling task, in which unnecessary words or tokens are removed. The removal can be done on several level of word units [2,4,6,7]. For example, Kirkpatrick et al. introduced a model for jointly learning sentence extraction and compression for multi-document summarization [2]. The model used n-grams and compression features to score extraction candidates. The model infers to extract candidates by using Integer Linear Programming (ILP). By jointly learning, the model achieved the highest ROUGE-scores of TAC 2008. Filippova and Altun addressed the lack of data for sentence compression by introducing a new dataset [7]. The dataset was created by using deletion-based algorithms on hundreds of thousands of instances. To do that, the authors used ILP on syntactic trees. In extension work, Filippova et al. employed Long-short Term Memory (LSTM) for word deletion [6]. The model used LSTM to learn the hidden representation of input tokens. Labels of tokens in the final layer were predicted by using softmax. Experimental results show that this simple model is better than baselines in terms of readability and informativeness. Wang et al. improved the domain adaptability of a deletion-based LSTM for sentence compression [15]. The authors assumed that syntactic information helps to make a robust model. To do that, the authors defined syntactic features and introduced syntactic constraints solved by ILP. The evaluation shows that this method is better than a traditional non-neural-network in a cross-domain setting. Zhao et al. exploited a neural language model as an evaluator for deletion-and-evaluation [16]. To do that, a reward function was defined by using a series of trial-and-error deletion operation on the source sentence to obtain the best target compression. Vanetik et al. presented an unsupervised constrained optimization method for summarization compression by iteratively removing redundant parts from original sentences [14]. The model used constituency-based parse trees and hand-crafted rules for creating elementary discourse units. To do that, the authors defined a weighted function computed by a parse tree gain for assigning weights into tokens. Experimental results confirm the efficiency of the model in the task of single-document summarization. The relation of our model to existing work is that we share the idea of sentence compression as a deletion task. However, we also enrich the task by introducing a model based on contextual embeddings.

There is little research on abstractive compression. A very close research direction is machine translation, in which a translator receives an original sentence and translates it into a shorter version. From this formulation, we can utilize many sophisticated neural machine translation (NMT) models for compression as a sequence-to-sequence problem [3]. However, even with the recent success of abstractive compression models, their quality is still quite far from human expectation. Therefore, we focus on sentence compression by deletion.

3   Sentence Compression with Contextual Embeddings

This section shows our proposed model of the sentence compression task. We introduce the general process of our model in Fig. 1. The data alignment prepares training data for training the sequence labelling model. After training, the trained model is applied to testing samples to compress raw sentences. We first describe data preparation and next introduce our compression model.

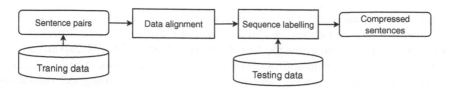

Fig. 1. The process of our model.

3.1 Data Preparation

Dataset. We used the Google dataset[1] for the sentence compression task [7]. To create pairs of sentences, the headline and the first sentence of each article collected from Google News service were extracted. Instead of directly using headline-first-sentence pairs, the authors used the headline to find our proper extractive compression of the sentence by a matching algorithm. This is because headlines are syntactically different from the first sentences. So directly using headlines makes a challenge for compression by deleting words. We used a new version of the dataset. It includes automatic generated 200,000 pairs for training and 10,000 pairs generated by humans for testing. Each pair contain an original sentence and a shorter version. Table 2 shows data observation.

Table 2. Data observation counting on works.

	Longest	Shortest	Average	#_all_words
Original sentences	1019	5	27.4	156,565
Compression	40	2	10.4	89,238

We can observe that the longest sentence is more than 1000 words while the longest of compression is 40. Generally, compression compresses a lot of unnecessary words. The shortest sequences of both original and compression sentences are quite short. The trend of the number of all words is quite similar to the average, in which original sentences are nearly twice longer than compressions, showing that a good model can reduce to nearly half of the words.

Data Alignment. The original data includes pairs of sentences. To train our compression model, we followed Filippova et al. to align original sentences and compressed sentences [6]. This is because we formulate the compression task as a sequence labeling task, in which unnecessary words are marked by a label, i.e. deletion or no-deletion and our model learns to remove deletion words.

---

[1] http://nlpprogress.com/english/summarization.html.

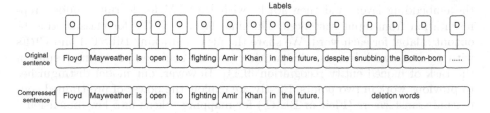

Fig. 2. An alignment example. D denotes deletion and O is for no-deletion words.

The alignment was done in two steps. The first step is word segmentation, which segments a sentence into a set of words. The second step aligns words of original and compressed sentences. If a word in the original sentence appears in the gold compressed sentence, this word is kept (no-deletion); otherwise, it is deleted (deletion). Figure 2 shows an example of the alignment.

We can observe that miss-matched words are labeled by "D", showing that these words should be deleted from the compression model. After alignment, original sentences with labels are input for our model.

3.2   The Proposed Model

As mentioned, we formulated the compression as a sequence labeling task. Given an input sequence of words, our model learns to predict whether a word should be deleted or not. More precisely, this is a binary classification task. Given a word, our model needs to classify this word into deletion or non-deletion labels.

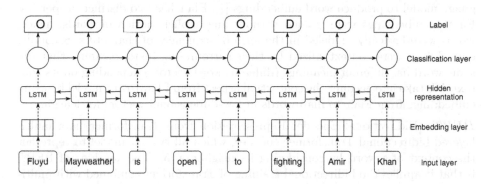

Fig. 3. The overview of our model. The model outputs a label for each word. We put two incorrect labels (D) to show that in training, these output labels were used to compute the loss with the ground-truth data in Fig. 2.

From this formulation, we introduce our model in Fig. 3. The main idea of our model is that it exploits the efficiency of pre-trained language models for the embedding layer, and then stacks with BiLSTM for learning hidden representation from input sentences. The final layer is CRFs for classification to output a label for each word. We share the idea of stacking BiLSTM and CRFs with previous work because this architecture has achieved promising results in the task of named entity recognition [9,11]. However, our model distinguishes to previous work in two points. Firstly, we exploit the power of pre-trained contextual transformers (Flair or BERT) for mapping tokens into low-dimensional vectors, instead of using word embeddings (Word2Vec or Glove) [9,11]. It enables our model to encode the context aspect of a sequence into the learning process. Secondly, we design a flat structure, instead of using a nested structure [9]. It facilitates the learning process in a simple fashion. Our model also shares the idea of deleting unnecessary words as Filippova et al. [6]; however, exploiting pre-trained contextual embeddings from transformers makes a different point of our model compared to [6]. Also, we add one CRF layer for classification, instead of directly using softmax. It allows our model utilizing global optimization on a whole sequence. We next describe each layer of our model.

Embedding Layer. The embedding layer is to use for mapping tokens into low-dimensional vectors. It is possible to employ any embedding method such as Word2Vec, Glove, or fastText; however, we utilized pre-trained contextual embeddings from transformers. This is because such transformers were trained with the consideration of the context of tokens on a huge amount of data. As a result, these models output high-quality embeddings compared to other word embedding methods (Glove). Inspired by the recent success of transformers in many NLP tasks [1,5], we exploited Flair and BERT as our embedding layer.

Flair. Flair is contextual string embeddings, which were from a character language model to produce word embeddings [1]. Flair has two distinct properties. Firstly, embeddings were trained without any explicit notion of words, hence, words were basically modeled in the form of sequences of characters. Secondly, embeddings were contextualized by their surrounding texts, meaning that the same word has different meanings (different word vectors) depending on its context. We take into account the contextual aspect from Flair to our model by using embeddings from Flair to map words in low-dimensional vectors for learning.

BERT. (Bidirectional Encoder Representation from Transformer) is a multilayered bidirectional Transformer encoder, which allows our model to represent the context of a word by considering its neighbors [5]. The key idea of BERT is that it applies the bidirectional training of Transformer combined with multihead attention to learn contextual relationships among words in a sequence. It includes two separate mechanisms: an encoder that reads the text input and a decoder that produces a prediction given an input sequence. Due to the purpose of building a language model, BERT only needs the encoder.

Different from directional models, which read the text input sequentially (left-to-right or right-to-left), the transformer encoder of BERT reads the entire sequence of words. With the combination of a large number of layers and multihead attention, BERT can deeply capture the meaning of words based on their context. For example, considering the word "bank" in two sentences "I went to the bank to deposit some money" and "I went to the bank of the river", the representations of "bank" are identical for a left-context unidirectional model, but they are distinguished with the use of BERT. This characteristic is appropriate with our task, in which our model needs to understand the context of a sequence for the deletion of words, i.e. detecting deletion or no-deletion words.

We employed a pre-trained BERT as the embedding layer due to two reasons: (i) BERT has achieved promising results on 11 NLP tasks, including sequence tagging [5,13] and (ii) BERT was contextually trained on a huge amount of data, so it can encode word meaning, which is important for machine learning models.

Hidden Representation. The hidden representation layer receipts output from the embedding layer to learn the hidden representation of input tokens. To do that, we stacked a layer by using LSTM [8] on the embedding layer.

LSTM is a variation of recurrent neural networks. It was designed to tackle long-term dependency of words and vanishing gradient descent in training deep learning models. Each LSTM cell uses the gate mechanism to decide whether input information is kept or ignored. The gate mechanism allows our model capturing the hidden representation of a long sequence. In practice, we employed BiLSTM for training our model. This is because BiLSTM encodes information from forward and backward directions, showing higher efficiency in learning data representation compared to LSTM [5,9].

Classification. The final layer is classification to predict labels of each word represented from the hidden presentation layer. In order to do that, we utilized CRFs as the final layer for prediction. This is because CRFs were designed for the sequence labeling task [10] and stacking CRFs on the top of BiLSTM has achieved promising results for the task of named entity recognition [9,11].

CRFs were designed to globally predict label sequences of any given sequences. Given an input sequence $X = (x_1, x_2, ..., x_n)$ which is the output from the BiLSTM layer, CRFs learn to make the prediction of x_i by maximizing the log probability during training. More precisely, given a sentence sequence $X = (x_1, x_2, ..., x_n)$ and the corresponding state of sequence (labels) $Y = (y_1, y_2, ..., y_n)$, the probability of Y conditioned on X was defined as $P(Y|X)$. When making prediction of y_i, CRFs consider the current input x_i (the current word) and previous states of previous words as $P(y_i = 1|X)$. For example, in Fig. 3, the label of ''fighting" is decided by using information from previous words. In practice, we consider the last one or two steps because using all information has a higher computational cost for training and inference.

Training. Our model was trained in an end-to-end fashion. The classification layer predicts a label of each word. Predicted labels were used to compare to ground-truth labels of training data to compute the cross-entropy loss. Error loss was updated for training by using back-propagation.

We used the BERT-large cased model trained for English with the BookCorpus (800M words) and English Wikipedia (2,500M words) as mentioned in [5]. For Flair, we used the English language models in both forward and backward directions trained on 1-billion words corpus mentioned in [1]. To increase the representation, we concatenated word vectors from Glove to word vectors from Flair or BERT in the embedding layer. This is because we want to increase the data representation of our model for learning.

4   Settings and Evaluation Metrics

4.1   Settings

We used a new version of the dataset, which includes 200,000 pairs for training our model. We randomly selected 1000 pairs [6,15,16] from 10,000 pairs of human annotation for automatic evaluation and the rest for validation. We used Adam optimizer for training in 100 epochs with gradient clipping at 5, except for BERT-MLP in which we found performed best with 10 epochs of training. LSTM layers have 256 hidden states. For Flair's language models, each composed of one-layered LSTM with 2048 hidden states. The BERT-large model has 24 layers, a hidden layer of 1024 neurons, 16 heads and 340M parameters.

4.2   Evaluation Metrics

We used F-score and compression rate for evaluation [6,7] as follows.

F-Score. We used recall and precision to compute the F-1 of compression and ground-truth data. These metrics were computed as follows.

$$R = \frac{\#correct\_del\_words}{\#all\_del\_words}; \quad P = \frac{\#correct\_del\_words}{\#del\_words}; \quad \text{F-1} = \frac{2 \times R \times P}{R + P}$$

where: $\#correct\_del\_words$ is the number of correct deletion words from the compression model compared to the ground-truth data; $\#all\_del\_words$ is all deletion words in ground-truth data; and $\#del\_words$ is the number of deletion words processed by the compression model.

Compression Rate considers the length aspect of compression. It was computed by dividing the length of the compression over the original sentence length.

4.3   Baselines

We compared our model to several strong methods of sentence compression. F-score of several models can be found in the leader board (http://nlpprogress.com/english/summarization.html).

- **ILP+features:** uses Integer Linear Programming with a set of features to find out optimal paths on syntactic trees [7]. The compressions are sub-trees generated from the optimization algorithm.
- **BiRNN+LM:** uses a language model as an evaluator to supporting BiRNN trained by a reinforcement learning fashion for sentence compression [16].
- **LSTM:** is the extension work of [7]. The authors treated compression a deletion task [6]. To do that, the authors used LSTM to deal with the sequence labeling task, in which the model tries to delete unnecessary words.
- **BiLSTM:** is the same with LSTM but using a bi-directional LSTM cell for learning hidden representation [15].
- **BiLSTM-CRF:** We implemented BiLSTM-CRF as a baseline of our model. It uses Glove for the embedding layer and BiLSTM to learn hidden representation. The final layer uses CRFs for classification. This model does not use Flair or BERT embeddings.
- **BERT+MLP:** We utilized BERT as the embedding layer and multi-layer perceptron (MLP) for classification.
- **BERT+BiLSTM-CRF:** It uses BERT as an embedding layer and stacks BiLSTM. It finally uses CRFs for classification to detect unnecessary words.

5   Results and Discussion

This section first reports the comparison of our model with baselines. It next shows the observation of embeddings and error analysis.

5.1   F-Score Comparison

Table 3 shows the comparison of our model and baselines. We can observe that our model is better than baselines in terms of F-score with quite large margins. For example, our model is significantly better than BiLSTM-CRF (0.889 vs. 0.820 with p-value ≤ 0.05 with pairwise t-test)[2] even they share the same hidden representation and classification layers. The improvement comes from two points. Firstly, we exploit contextual embeddings from transformers instead of directly using word embeddings (Glove) for the embedding layer. Using these embeddings allows our model taking into account the contextual aspect of words trained on a huge amount of data. From that, our model can correctly distinguish necessary and unnecessary words of input sequences. This again confirms the efficiency of transformers for NLP tasks [1,5]. By contrast, BiLSTM-CRF directly uses Glove as the embedding layer, which somehow limits the model in learning context among words. Another reason is that we also exploit the power of word embeddings by concatenating word vector from Glove with vector generated from transformers. This combination enables our model to increase data representation, leading to improvements.

---

[2] https://docs.scipy.org/doc/scipy-0.19.0/reference/generated/scipy.stats.ttest_ind.html.

Table 3. Comparison of sentence compression models. † shows that our model is significantly better with p-value ≤ 0.05.

Model	Embedding	F-score	Compression Rate
ILP+features [7]	—	0.843	—
BiRNN+LM [16]	—	0.851	0.39
LSTM [6]	Word2Vec	$0.820^\dagger$	0.38
BiLSTM [15]	—	$0.800^\dagger$	0.43
BiLSTM-CRFs	Glove	$0.820^\dagger$	0.40
BERT(original)+MLP	BERT	0.867	0.38
BERT+BiLSTM-CRF (Ours)	BERT+Glove	*0.883*	0.39
Flair+BiLSTM-CRFs (Ours)	FLair+Glove	**0.889**	0.39

For variants of LSTM (BiRNN, LSTM, and BiLSTM), our model still achieves better F-score from 3–5% points. This supports our idea that using contextual embeddings for word representation. Compared to BiLSTM and BiLSTM-CRF, the model using CRFs for prediction is 2% points better than that of only using BiLSTM. This shows the contribution of CRFs for making global label sequence prediction. The ILP model obtains a promising F-score because it uses features for weighting concepts. The features help to increase the quality of deletion based on constraints. Compared to the original BERT, our model is still better, but the margins among compression models are small. This is because the original BERT takes into account the contextual aspect of words for learning. We can also observe the contribution of BiLSTM-CRF, in which BERT with this architecture gives a better F-score than BERT using MLP (Tables 3 and 5). The model using Flair is slightly better than that using BERT (0.889 vs. 0.883). A possible reason is that BERT may be appropriate for quite long documents while the dataset includes short sentences. As a result, the BERT-based method is challenged to encode short separated texts. However, the gap is tiny, showing that the contextual embeddings from BERT can still contribute to our model.

The compression rate (CR) of compression models is quite similar, even they yield different F-scores. BiLSTM outputs the longest sequences, followed by BiLST-CRFs. Our model is not the best in terms of CR, compared to BERT+MLP. A possible reason may come from BiLSTM because BiLSTM-based methods tend to output longer sequences compared to LSTM or RNN.

To avoid over-fitting, we tested our model five times on the test set. In each time, we randomly selected 1000 samples from 10,000 pairs created by humans for testing and the rest for validation. We also used the same data segmentation to train BiLSTM-CRFs and BERT+MLP. We did not compare to other methods due to the different setting. The F-score was the average of our model in five times. Table 4 shows that our model consistently achieves better F-scores than BiLSTM-CRFs and the original BERT after testing in five times. This again confirms the efficacy of our model. Comparing to results in Table 3, F-scores are slightly different due to the average on five times.

Table 4. The F-score of testing three models in five times.

Model	Embedding	F-score	Compression Rate
BiLSTM-CRFs	Glove	0.820[†]	0.40
BERT(original)+MLP	BERT	0.863	0.38
Flair+BiLSTM-CRFs (Ours)	FLair+Glove	**0.887**	0.39

5.2 Glove Contribution

As mentioned, we concatenated embeddings from Glove to word vectors from Flair and BERT. To observe the contribution of Glove, we compared contextual-based compression models using with/without word vectors from Glove.

Table 5. The contribution of Glove.

Model	Embeddings	F-score	Compression rate
BERT(w/o Glove)+BiLSTM-CRF	BERT+Glove	0.875	0.39
BERT(with Glove)+BiLSTM-CRF	BERT+Glove	**0.883**	0.39
Flair(w/o Glove)+BiLSTM-CRF	Flair+Glove	0.877	0.38
Flair(with Glove)+BiLSTM-CRF	Flair+Glove	**0.889**	0.39

From Table 5, we can observe that models using Glove obtain better F-cores than those which do not use Glove. This is because the concatenation of embeddings from Glove and contextual embeddings enriches the data representation of sentences, hence, it improves the learning quality of our model. However, the margins are small, showing the efficiency of contextual embeddings from Flair and BERT [1,5]. The compression rate of transformer variants is similar, which is consistent with the compression rate of transformer-based models in Table 3.

5.3 Output Observation

We observed the outputs of (i) BiLSTM-CRF, (ii) BERT+MLP, (iii) BERT+BiLSTM-CRF, and (iv) our model. We can observe that for the first output (the half of the table), all models give correct compression. A possible reason is that the input sequence is quite short and simple, so all the models can correctly predict deletion words. For the second output, our model outputs correct compression. This supports our idea in exploiting contextual embeddings for word representation and confirms F-scores in Table 3. BiLSTM-CRF shares one incorrect phrase ("as Matthew Wuss") with BERT-MLP. The reason may come from the use of BiLSTM-CRF, which may be limited for learning data representation of long sequences. In addition, BiLST-CRF does not use contextual embeddings, so it makes a challenge to capture the meaning of words from input sequences. As a result, it predicts two wrong phrases. It again confirms F-scores in Table 3, in which the BiLSTM-CRF compression model yields a quite low F-score (Table 3).

Table 6. Output samples. Incorrect phrases are mark by strike-through words.

Original	Vine, the mobile app owned by Twitter, has banned sexually explicit content, effective immediately
Gold-comp	Vine has banned sexually explicit content
(i)	Vine has banned sexually explicit content
(ii)	Vine has banned sexually explicit content
(iii)	Vine has banned sexually explicit content
Our model	Vine has banned sexually explicit content
Original	A man found dead in a Fairfield hotel room on Sunday, Sept. 1 has been identified as Matthew Wuss, 20, of Chester
Gold-comp	A man found dead in a Fairfield hotel room has been identified
(i)	A man found dead in a Fairfield hotel room ~~on Sept. 1~~ has been identified ~~as Matthew Wuss~~
(ii)	A man found dead in a Fairfield hotel room has been identified ~~as Matthew Wuss~~
(iii)	A man found dead in a Fairfield hotel room ~~on Sunday~~ has been identified
Our model	A man found dead in a Fairfield hotel room has been identified

6   Conclusion

This paper introduces a model for sentence compression as deletion. Our model utilizes the power of contextual embeddings for capturing the context aspect of input words for learning. The embeddings combined with BiLSTM and CRF allow our model efficiently learning hidden representation from data. Experimental results on a benchmark dataset show two points. Firstly, contextual embeddings contribute to the compression model. This leads to a new state-of-the-art F-score on the Google dataset. Secondly, by adding word vectors from Glove, our model improves the quality of deletion compared to the model without using Glove.

One possible direction is to analyze syntactic features that can be integrated into our model. Also, parsed tree representation may be helpful for deep learning.

Acknowledgement. This research is funded by Hung Yen University of Technology and Education under the grant number UTEHY.L.2020.04.

References

1. Akbik, A., Blythe, D., Vollgraf, R.: Contextual string embed-dings for sequence labeling. In: Proceedings of the 27th International Conference on Computational Linguistics, pp. 1638–1649 (2018)
2. Berg-Kirkpatrick, T., Gillick, D., Klein, D.: Jointly learning to extract and compress. In: Proceedings of the 49th Annual Meeting of the Association for Computational Linguistics: Human Language Technologies-Volume 1, pp. 481–490 (2011)
3. Cho, K., et al.: Learning phrase representations using RNN encoder-decoder for statistical machine translation. In: Proceedings of the 2014 Conference on Empirical Methods in Natural Language Processing, pp. 1724–1734 (2014)
4. Clarke, J., Lapata, M.: Global inference for sentence compression: An integer linear programming approach. J. Artif. Intell. Res. **31**, 399–429 (2008)
5. Devlin, J., Chang, M.W., Lee, K., Toutanova, K.: Bert: pre-training of deep bidirectional transformers for language understanding. In: Proceedings of the 2019 Conference of the North American Chapter of the Association for Computational Linguistics: Human Language Technologies, vol. 1, pp. 4171–4186 (2019)
6. Filippova, K., Alfonseca, E., Colmenares, C.A., Kaiser, L., Vinyals, O.: Sentence compression by deletion with LSTMs. In: Proceedings of the 2015 Conference on Empirical Methods in Natural Language Processing, pp. 360–368 (2015)
7. Filippova, K., Altun, Y.: Overcoming the lack of parallel data in sentence compression. In: Proceedings of the 2013 Conference on Empirical Methods in Natural Language Processing, pp. 1481–1491 (2013)
8. Hochreiter, S., Schmidhuber, J.: Long short-term memory. Neural Comput. **9**(8), 1735–1780 (1997)
9. Ju, M., Miwa, M., Ananiadou, S.: A neural layered model for nested named entity recognition. In: Proceedings of the 2018 Conference of the North American Chapter of the Association for Computational Linguistics: Human Language Technologies, Volume 1 (Long Papers), pp. 1446–1459 (2018)
10. Lafferty, J., McCallum, A., Pereira, F.: Conditional random fields: probabilistic models for segmenting and labeling sequence data. In: Proceedings of the 18th International Conference on Machine Learning, pp. 282–289 (2001)
11. Lample, G., Ballesteros, M., Subramanian, S., Kawakami, K., Dyer, C.: Neural architectures for named entity recognition. In: NAACL-HLT, pp. 260–270 (2016)
12. Liu, C., Wang, P., Xu, J., Li, Z., Ye, J.: Automatic dialogue summary generation for customer service. In: Proceedings of the 25th ACM SIGKDD International Conference on Knowledge Discovery & Data Mining, pp. 1957–1965 (2019)
13. Nguyen, M.T., et al.: Transfer learning for information extraction with limited data. In: Proceedings of 16th International Conference of the Pacific Association for Computational Linguistics (2019)
14. Vanetik, N., Litvak, M., Churkin, E., Last, M.: An unsupervised constrained optimization approach to compressive summarization. Inf. Sci. **509**, 22–35 (2020)

15. Wang, L., Jiang, J., Chieu, H.L., Ong, C.H., Song, D., Liao, L.: Can syntax help? improving an LSTM-based sentence compression model for new domains. In: Proceedings of the 55th Annual Meeting of the Association for Computational Linguistics (Volume 1: Long Papers), pp. 1385–1393 (2017)
16. Zhao, Y., Luo, Z., Aizawa, A.: A language model based evaluator for sentence compression. In: ALC (Volume 2: Short Papers), pp. 170–175 (2018)

Robust Discriminant Network for Gait Recognition on Low-Resolution Input

Viet-Ha Ho[1]([⊠]) and Huu-Hung Huynh[2]([⊠])

[1] Danang Vocational Training College, Da Nang, Vietnam
viethait@gmail.com
[2] The University of Danang, University of Science and Technology,
Da Nang, Vietnam
hhhung@dut.udn.vn

Abstract. Gait recognition is one of the main challenges in surveillance systems due to the high diversity of possible factors affecting the accuracy. We propose a convolutional neural network addressing this task that requires only inputs of small resolution. Our method can also adapt with scenarios where there are many identified subjects in the system's database but each subject has very few gait samples for generalizing a recognition model. Our network can be trained end-to-end with an optimization strategy that processes just a small portion of training data while still provides good results. The experiments are performed on the largest and most challenged OU-MVLP Gait Database under 4 different major camera angles (0°, 30°, 60°, 90°) and demonstrate a competitive performance with respect to related studies.

Keywords: Gait recognition · CNN · Small resolution ·
Optimization · GEI pair · Balance sets · Sampling · Inception

1 Introduction

Human gait is one of the most common factors that are considered in automatic surveillance systems. Therefore, the problem of gait recognition is widely being studied in the research field of computer vision. This is challenging due to the high diversity of possible effects such as view point (of the camera), clothing, walking velocity, and even surface of the subject. Under application aspect, a system of gait recognition usually requires a huge amount of gait data of known subjects (gallery) to guarantee a reasonable accuracy. Besides, the resolution of system input is required to be in medium or big size since a small one usually loses useful information.

In this paper, we propose a method of gait recognition using convolutional neural network (CNN) that attempts to overcome the two mentioned limitations. First, our method is appropriate to work in realistic scenarios where the gallery data contain a huge number of subjects but with very few gait samples for each one. Second, our algorithm can provide competitive recognition accuracies

© Springer Nature Switzerland AG 2020
N. T. Nguyen et al. (Eds.): ICCCI 2020, LNAI 12496, pp. 441–452, 2020.
https://doi.org/10.1007/978-3-030-63007-2_34

(compared with related studies) while working on inputs of just a few dozens of pixels for each input's spatial dimension. In addition, such accuracies can be obtained when we trained our model with a small portion of available training data (the details are provided in Sect. 3.2).

The contributions in this paper can be summarized as follows:

- Our network works well on inputs of a significantly smaller resolution compared with other studies on gait recognition.
- We propose an optimization strategy that requires just a small portion of available training data but still provides acceptable results.
- Our model can be trained end-to-end without using any additional machine learning algorithm for post-processing.

The remainder of the paper is organized as follows: a brief description of related studies is provided in Sect. 2; Sect. 3 describes the two main factors in our work: network structure and optimization strategy; the experiments on the largest (and most challenged) gait dataset OU-MVLP [23] and discussions are presented in Sect. 4; and Sect. 5 is the conclusion.

2   Related Work

Since the problem of gait recognition has been studied for a long time, there are various studies have been proposed. In this section, we summarize two typical categories: (1) exploring hand-crafted features as gait descriptions and (2) let the models (CNNs) find their desired gait characteristics.

2.1   Hand-Crafted Features

Recently, some studies attempted to extract useful information from individual silhouettes and then combine them along the temporal axis. For example, Euclidean distance transform was applied on 2D silhouettes in [6,7] to replace the raw input gait representation. Another approach is to accumulate silhouettes together to provide a gait signature describing its properties in both spatial and temporal dimensions. There are typically various gait signatures such as Gait Energy Image (GEI) [9], Motion History Image (MHI), Motion Energy Image (MEI), Motion Silhouettes Image (MSI), Gait History Image (GHI), forward Single-step History Image (fSHI), backward Single-step History Image (bSHI), and Active Energy Image (AEI). An overview of these gait signatures can be found in [11]. A common property of these features is that they are quite simple, the models thus need to be carefully selected and designed to obtain acceptable execution results.

2.2   CNN Approaches

Differently from the methods indicated above, other researchers used CNNs to automatically extract useful features that are significantly more complicated than gait signatures. The input of CNNs may be raw images, silhouettes, or even hand-crafted features. The advantage of CNNs compared with manual descriptions is the embedding of information abstraction inside the feature maps in each CNN layer. Such level-based abstractions provided very good results in a wide range of applications such as image classification [5,20], segmentation [4,10], gait index estimation [16,17], and anomaly detection [15,18]. Regarding to gait recognition, various CNNs have been proposed in [19,26,27]. These models are employed to provide a comparison in Sect. 4.

3   Proposed Method

As mentioned in Sect. 1, our model is a convolutional neural network (CNN). There are many CNNs that were proposed to deal with tasks of recognition. Such models usually follow the same prototype where a number of convolutional layers (together with their activations) are arranged into a stack and the last layer is fully-connected containing m units corresponding to m classes of the classification problem. For datasets of gait recognition, the number of classes (i.e. m) may be very great (thousands) while each one contains very few samples. The lack of training data for each class would significantly reduce the efficiency of a CNN that is designed in the mentioned way.

To deal with this limitation, we apply the strategy of few-shot learning. In detail, instead of feeding a single walking gait into the network and then predicting its class (i.e. the subject's ID), our model considers a pair of gaits and assesses whether they are come from the same class. Since the objective is binary (either the same or different subject's IDs), the last fully-connected layer just consists of only one unit indicating a probability, i.e. we have only two classes for a typical recognition. The architecture of our CNN is presented in detail in the next section.

3.1   Network Architecture

An overview of the proposed network is shown in Fig. 1. The input is a tensor of shape $(b, 2c, h, w)$ where b is the batch size, c is the number of channels of a single gait representation (e.g. 3 for a RGB image and 1 for a gray one), h and w respectively indicate the corresponding spatial height and width. There are $2c$ channels for the input because we feed a pair of gaits into the network.

The convolutional part is a stack of two Inception modules that were introduced in [21,22]. Differently from that original GoogleNet, we do not use any auxiliary classifiers since our network is much shallower and thus does not need to encourage discrimination in far away stages. The use of Inception module in our CNN is inspired from [15] in order to let the network automatically select its desired convolutional streams. In other words, there are multiple convolutional paths inside the module and the network can prefer appropriate ones by itself. Notice that each module is followed by a convolution (that can be alternatively replaced by a pooling operation to avoid learnable parameters) to reduce the

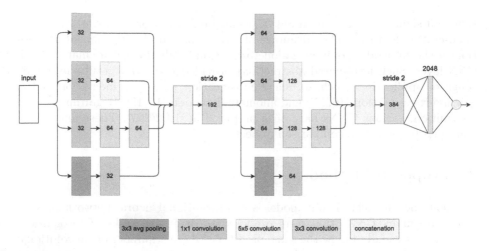

Fig. 1. Structure of our proposed network that predicts whether an input pair of gait representations is from the same subject. The number inside each convolutional layer indicates that of output channels. Convolutions with stride 2 are to reduce the spatial dimensions of feature maps in their outputs.

spatial dimensions of feature maps. The activation function is ReLU [3,14] for each convolutional layer. These features are then converted into a 2048-element vector before estimating a probability at the last layer of one unit with the support of sigmoid activation. The next section presents our strategy of optimizing the network given a training dataset with the lack of samples for each subject.

3.2 Optimization Strategy

As mentioned in the description of our network architecture, the input is a tensor of shape $(b, 2c, h, w)$ where $2c$ indicates the pairing (concatenation) of two gait representations along the channel dimension. Beside the significantly reduction of CNN's classes, such pairing also increases the number of available training samples. Let us denote n as the number of subjects in training data and each one has up to k gait samples, there would be $O(kn)$ individual training gaits for a typical classification described in the beginning of Sect. 3. By coupling gaits as the input of our CNN, such number of possible training samples significantly increases to be $O(k^2n^2)$.

However, it should be noticed that the pairing of gaits leads to an imbalanced training data since the number of pairs corresponding to the same subject (denoted as class 1) is significantly smaller than ones of the other class (denoted as class 0), i.e. $O(k^2n) \ll O(k^2n^2)$ because n may be thousands in realistic datasets. Therefore, a strategy of adapted optimization is necessary to deal with this problem.

The optimization is performed in our work with the idea that the whole training samples are not fed into the network in an epoch. Instead, all the patterns in class $\mathbb{1}$ always appear in each epoch together with the same number of patterns sampled from the other class $\mathbb{0}$. This strategy keeps the balance of data during the optimization stage while still guarantees the generalization of the method. We use the binary cross entropy loss for the optimization as

$$\mathcal{L}(p) = -[p \in \mathbb{1}] \log f(p) - [p \notin \mathbb{1}] \log(1 - f(p)) \tag{1}$$

where p is an input pair of gait representations, and $[\circ]$ is a function returning 1 if the condition $\circ$ is true and 0 otherwise.

A pseudo code of our training procedure is presented in Algorithm 1.

Algorithm 1. Optimization strategy with batch size b

1: Given training samples of gait pairs $\{p_1\}$ and $\{p_0\}$ corresponding to classes $\mathbb{1}$ and $\mathbb{0}$, respectively.
2: $c = |\{p_1\}|$ // get number of samples in class $\mathbb{1}$
3: for $e = 1$ to n do begin   // optimizing with n epochs
4:     $\{p_0^*\} = \mathbf{sampling}(\{p_0\})$ s.t. $|\{p_0^*\}| = c$ // sampling c samples from class $\mathbb{0}$
5:     $\{x\} = \{p_1\} \cup \{p_0^*\}$ // forming training data for current epoch
6:     for $i = 1$ to $2c/b$ do begin   // process each batch
7:         Calculating loss for batch i in $\{x\}$
8:         Update network weights
9:     end
10: end

---

4 Experiment

We present in this section details of experiments including the considered gait dataset, the evaluation metric and the obtained results.

4.1 Dataset

Regarding to the problem of gait recognition, there are some public datasets acquired in different environments. In this paper, we consider the OU-MVLP gait dataset [23] because of the following factors.

Firstly, it contains a huge number (10,307) of subjects that is significantly greater than other datasets (that are usually around or less than 100 subjects). This diversity of gaits can guarantee the generalization ability of the proposed method. Secondly, the OU-MVLP has a wide range of view angles, the dependency and/or the ability of adaptation of the proposed method to each camera view angle can thus be evaluated. Thirdly, each view consists of 2 gait sequences, in which a subject appears only once in each sequence. In other words, there are up to 2 gait samples for each subject of a camera view angle. This lack of data is a real challenge for the task of gait recognition, especially for CNNs.

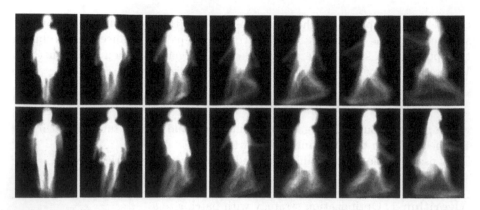

Fig. 2. Some GEIs corresponding to different camera view angles provided in the OU-MVLP gait dataset. We randomly selected them from the dataset for the illustration.

The gait sample in the OU-MVLP dataset is represented as a Gait Energy Image (GEI) [9] since this is the most common gait representation that combines the spatial and temporal information. Some GEIs are visualized in Fig. 2. The original resolution of each GEI in the dataset is 128×88. As an attempt to reduce the computational cost as well as demonstrate the ability of our CNN on small inputs, we scale-down the GEI so that the number of pixels decreases 16 times, i.e. we deal with GEIs of resolution 32×22. Such reduction of spatial resolution enhances the challenge of the dataset since typical CNNs may encounter difficulties when working on small images that lose some information. Our model, however, still provided competitive results as shown in Sect. 4.3.

4.2 Evaluation

The proposed method is evaluated by the rank-1 recognition accuracy in typical cooperative setting. In detail, all subjects in the dataset are divided into two disjoint groups. The first group includes GEIs of 5153 subjects that are used as training samples. The other group consists of GEIs of the remaining 5154 subjects for testing. The evaluation is performed independently on each camera view angle. As suggested in [23], we focus on 4 major angles including $0°$, $30°$, $60°$, and $90°$. The split of data into training and test sets for a camera view angle is illustrated in Fig. 3.

According to Fig. 3, each pair of GEIs in the training stage is formed as $\{s_P, s_G\}$ where s_P and s_G are sampled from the probe A and gallery C subsets, respectively. In the evaluation stage, assume that we have the identities of subjects in D, our task is to identify the subject of each GEI in B. In other words, we need to assign each unknown GEI in B to a known subject in D. The rank-1 recognition accuracy is calculated according to the Algorithm 2, in which the notation i (e.g. i_B, i_D) indicates an array index, and the function $(u == v)$ returns 1 if u is equal to v and 0 otherwise.

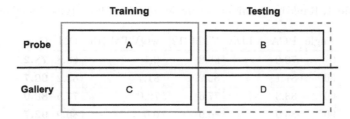

Fig. 3. Data splitting into training and test subsets for a camera view angle. Data of each camera view contain two sequences of GEIs: gallery and probe. $\{A, C\}$ indicates the gaits of training subjects in the two sequences, and $\{B, D\}$ gaits are used for testing.

Algorithm 2. Estimation of rank-1 recognition accuracy

1: Given our trained convolutional neural network f
2: Given arrays of GEIs B and D as in Fig. 3
3: Given array id_D of already known identities of D (the same order of elements).
4: Given array id_B of identities of B, used only for accuracy calculation.
5: $b = |B|, d = |D|$ // get number of samples in each subset
6: $t = 0$ // counting number of true identifications provided by our CNN
7: for $i_B = 1$ to b do begin   // identify each probe GEI
8:     $prob = [\ ]$ // initialize array of probabilities for this probe GEI
9:     for $i_D = 1$ to d do begin
10:       $p = \{B[i_B], D[i_D]\}$ // forming a pair of GEIs
11:       $o = f(p)$ // calculate output of the CNN
12:       $prob = \mathbf{append}(prob, o)$ // adding the output to array of probabilities
13:     end
14:     $i_D^* = \mathbf{argmax}(prob)$ // getting index of subject with highest probability
15:     $t = t + (id_D[i_D^*] == id_B[i_B])$ // checking result and count
16: end
17: $accuracy = t/b$

4.3   Results

Beside presenting the experimental results of our method, we also provide a comparison with related studies that are grouped into 2 categories: (1) methods with typical machine learning algorithms and (2) approaches using CNNs. Their implementations are referred from the publication of OU-MVLP dataset [23].

Comparison with Typical Methods: We consider the base line approach with principal component analysis (PCA) for GEI dimension reduction followed by linear discriminant analysis (LDA) to obtain gait features. Besides, we also focus on the view transformation model (VTM) in [12] and another improved model named wQVTM [13]. The trivial direct matching (DM) using L2 distance is also taken into account since many studies considered GEI as their final gait feature. The rank-1 recognition accuracies of these method and ours on 4 major camera view angles are presented in Table 1. This shows that our

Table 1. Rank-1 recognition accuracies obtained from typical methods

Angle	PCA + LDA	VTM [12]	wQVTM [13]	DM	Ours
0°	70.0	68.8	0.1	68.8	**78.2**
30°	87.1	82.2	81.7	82.2	**90.7**
60°	83.3	77.6	78.0	77.5	**88.0**
90°	85.9	80.9	0.0	80.9	**92.7**

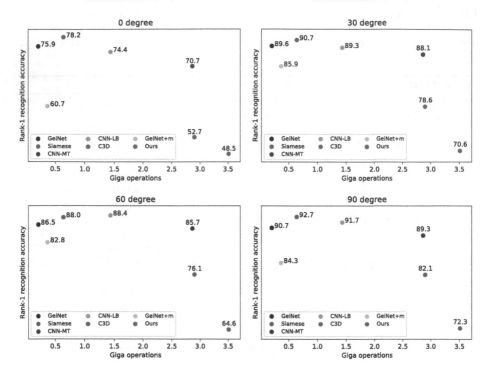

Fig. 4. Rank-1 recognition accuracies of experimented CNNs together with their number of operations that need to perform for a propagation.

approach outperforms the experimented methods belonging to the category of typical algorithms. A closer look on our experiments with CNNs is presented in the next section.

Comparison with CNN Approaches: In order to provide a comparison with related methods that used CNNs, we focus on some models as follows. We first consider the GeiNet [19] which has a typical architecture of CNNs. The number of units in the last fully-connected layer corresponds to the number of subjects since this model mainly focuses on extracting features from GEIs, i.e. the last classification layer could be removed in the inference stage. A modification [1] of this model using multiple losses, denoted as GeiNet+m, is also taken into account. Some other CNNs that deal with or can be adapted to the task of checking pairs of GEIs are also included in our comparison: Siamese network [27], CNN-MT and CNN-LB [26], and C3D [24]. The differences between our network and these CNNs are as follows. While GeiNet [19] performs a typical classification on an input GEI, ours works as a binary classifier on a pair of GEIs. The Siamese [27] and CNN-MT [26] require a couple of GEIs but they are independently processed on different streams while our CNN concatenates the input as an image of 2 channels and the further convolutions consider the spatial correspondence between these two GEIs. In addition, our network uses Inception modules with parallel convolutions of various kernels as an alternative of network depth adaptation [15]. Some other recent studies also employed the OU-MVLP dataset in their experiments but we do not take them into account in this comparison since they exploited the dataset under other perspectives such as silhouette sequence reconstruction [25] or cross-view camera setting [2, 8, 28].

Beside the rank-1 recognition accuracy, we also consider the number of operations that need to perform throughout each network. In realistic applications, this is an important factor because the high computational cost will limit the ability of model adaptation on common systems. The details of experimental results on CNNs are shown in Fig. 4.

It is obvious that our model provided competitive results compared with the others while requires significantly smaller number of operations, recall that our network is shallow and deals with input of small resolution (32×22 vs. original 128×88 GEIs).

It is also noticeable that our model was trained with a couple of dozens epochs which means that we used only a very small portion of available training data (according to the rule of sampling in Algorithm 1). Therefore, the approach presented in this paper has a great potential to be extended and/or improved in further studies.

4.4 Discussion

According to the promising rank-1 recognition accuracies obtained from our method, GEIs of low-resolution are still appropriate for representing individual gaits. Differently from common CNNs requiring high spatial dimensions (e.g. a few hundreds pixels for each), the proposed approach reasonably exploit the input GEIs of size 32×22 because of the following factors. First, a GEI contains only a single channel and does not have plentiful textures compared to natural color images. Therefore, down-scaling such original GEIs (128×88 to 32×22) almost does not affect the information within. Second, the use of Inception modules can help the network capturing appropriate features in image patches of various sizes, contrarily to others that focus only on fixed-size patches.

In practical situations, the recognition is performed according to pairs of GEIs in which each one is formed by a GEI in database and the considering (unknown) one. The resulted identity corresponds to the GEI that provides the pair of highest network output. In that way, our method can be extended to perform experiments on other gait datasets as long as gait samples of the identities are provided. This requirement is mostly satisfied since we can simply keep training samples as the reference of identities (gallery data).

For gait recognition, typical classification methods are usually used, in which a gait sample is fed and a corresponding ID is outputted. A limitation of such approaches is that the inference must be performed on known classes (i.e. subjects). For example, when they are applied on different ensembles of subject identities (such as various places), their models need to be trained on the corresponding collection of subjects before performing the gait recognition. On the contrary, our pre-trained network can continue to perform the identification without adapting its weights for each scenario (e.g. place). Since our network is not trained on such identities, it requires their gait samples as the gallery data and recognizes an unknown gait into one of these identities.

In the case where the gait of interest is obtained from an unknown subject, i.e. its identity is not in the database, using a threshold for the similarity probability outputted from the network may help to determine it. In other words, the maximum similarity between that gait and the ones in database is expected to not exceed a specific threshold.

5   Conclusion

In this paper, we present a convolutional neural network that focuses on the problem of gait recognition. The model is designed as a stack of two Inception modules where each one is followed by a dimensional-reduction convolution, and the output is a probability predicting whether the input pair of gaits comes from the same subject. An optimization strategy is also proposed to deal with the problem of imbalanced classes in the training data. According to experimental results on the challenge OU-MVLP gait dataset, our CNN provided competitive rank-1 recognition accuracies on 4 major camera view angles while just working on small resolution input (32×22 vs. original 128×88). In further studies, we plan to expand the network to increase its capacity for generalizing various gaits from different camera view angles in the same model.

Acknowledgement. We would like to thank Trong-Nguyen Nguyen (DIRO, University of Montreal) for his helpful discussions and support in model implementation. We also thank The Institute of Scientific and Industrial Research (Osaka University) for acquiring and sharing their gait dataset.

References

1. Carley, C., Ristani, E., Tomasi, C.: Person re-identification from gait using an autocorrelation network. In: IEEE Conference on Computer Vision and Pattern Recognition Workshops, CVPR Workshops 2019, Long Beach, CA, USA, 16–20 June 2019. Computer Vision Foundation/IEEE (2019)
2. Chao, H., He, Y., Zhang, J., Feng, J.: GaitSet: regarding gait as a set for cross-view gait recognition. In: Proceedings of the AAAI Conference on Artificial Intelligence, vol. 33, pp. 8126–8133 (2019)

3. Glorot, X., Bordes, A., Bengio, Y.: Deep sparse rectifier neural networks. In: Gordon, G., Dunson, D., DudíÂk, M. (eds.) Proceedings of the Fourteenth International Conference on Artificial Intelligence and Statistics. Proceedings of Machine Learning Research, vol. 15, pp. 315–323. PMLR, Fort Lauderdale, 11–13 April 2011
4. He, K., Gkioxari, G., Dollár, P., Girshick, R.B.: Mask R-CNN. In: IEEE International Conference on Computer Vision, ICCV 2017, Venice, Italy, 22–29 October 2017, pp. 2980–2988. IEEE Computer Society (2017)
5. He, K., Zhang, X., Ren, S., Sun, J.: Deep residual learning for image recognition. In: The IEEE Conference on Computer Vision and Pattern Recognition (CVPR), June 2016
6. Ho, V., Huynh, H., Ngo, V.: Direction-free person identification with distance transform and random forest. In: 2019 IEEE-RIVF International Conference on Computing and Communication Technologies (RIVF), pp. 1–6, March 2019
7. Ho, V.H., Vo, D.H., Ngo, V.S., Huynh, H.H.: Person identification based on Euclidean distance transform. J. Eng. Appl. Sci. **14**(13), 4312–4316 (2019)
8. Huang, Y., Zhang, J., Zhao, H., Zhang, L.: Attention-based network for cross-view gait recognition. In: Cheng, L., Leung, A.C.S., Ozawa, S. (eds.) ICONIP 2018. LNCS, vol. 11307, pp. 489–498. Springer, Cham (2018). https://doi.org/10.1007/978-3-030-04239-4_44
9. Han, J., Bhanu, B.: Individual recognition using gait energy image. IEEE Trans. Pattern Anal. Mach. Intell. **28**(2), 316–322 (2006)
10. Long, J., Shelhamer, E., Darrell, T.: Fully convolutional networks for semantic segmentation. In: IEEE Conference on Computer Vision and Pattern Recognition, CVPR 2015, Boston, MA, USA, 7–12 June 2015, pp. 3431–3440. IEEE Computer Society (2015)
11. Lv, Z., Xing, X., Wang, K., Guan, D.: Class energy image analysis for video sensor-based gait recognition: a review. Sensors **15**(1), 932–964 (2015)
12. Makihara, Y., Sagawa, R., Mukaigawa, Y., Echigo, T., Yagi, Y.: Gait recognition using a view transformation model in the frequency domain. In: Leonardis, A., Bischof, H., Pinz, A. (eds.) ECCV 2006. LNCS, vol. 3953, pp. 151–163. Springer, Heidelberg (2006). https://doi.org/10.1007/11744078_12
13. Muramatsu, D., Makihara, Y., Yagi, Y.: View transformation model incorporating quality measures for cross-view gait recognition. IEEE Trans. Cybern. **46**(7), 1602–1615 (2016)
14. Nair, V., Hinton, G.E.: Rectified linear units improve restricted Boltzmann machines. In: Proceedings of the 27th International Conference on International Conference on Machine Learning, ICML 2010, pp. 807–814. Omnipress, Madison (2010)
15. Nguyen, T.N., Meunier, J.: Anomaly detection in video sequence with appearance-motion correspondence. In: The IEEE International Conference on Computer Vision (ICCV), October 2019
16. Nguyen, T.N., Meunier, J.: Applying adversarial auto-encoder for estimating human walking gait abnormality index. Pattern Anal. Appl. **22**(4), 1597–1608 (2019)
17. Nguyen, T.N., Meunier, J.: Estimation of gait normality index based on point clouds through deep auto-encoder. EURASIP J. Image Video Process. **2019**, 65 (2019)
18. Nguyen, T.N., Meunier, J.: Hybrid deep network for anomaly detection. In: British Machine Vision Conference 2019, BMVC 2019, Cardiff University, Cardiff, UK, 9–12 September 2019. BMVA Press (2019)

19. Shiraga, K., Makihara, Y., Muramatsu, D., Echigo, T., Yagi, Y.: GeiNet: view-invariant gait recognition using a convolutional neural network. In: International Conference on Biometrics, ICB 2016, Halmstad, Sweden, 13–16 June 2016, pp. 1–8. IEEE (2016)
20. Simonyan, K., Zisserman, A.: Very deep convolutional networks for large-scale image recognition. In: Bengio, Y., LeCun, Y. (eds.) 3rd International Conference on Learning Representations, ICLR 2015, San Diego, CA, USA, 7–9 May 2015, Conference Track Proceedings (2015)
21. Szegedy, C., et al.: Going deeper with convolutions. In: The IEEE Conference on Computer Vision and Pattern Recognition (CVPR), June 2015
22. Szegedy, C., Vanhoucke, V., Ioffe, S., Shlens, J., Wojna, Z.: Rethinking the inception architecture for computer vision. In: The IEEE Conference on Computer Vision and Pattern Recognition (CVPR), June 2016
23. Takemura, N., Makihara, Y., Muramatsu, D., Echigo, T., Yagi, Y.: Multi-view large population gait dataset and its performance evaluation for cross-view gait recognition. IPSJ Trans. Comput. Vis. Appl. **10**(1), 4 (2018)
24. Tran, D., Bourdev, L.D., Fergus, R., Torresani, L., Paluri, M.: Learning spatiotemporal features with 3d convolutional networks. In: 2015 IEEE International Conference on Computer Vision, ICCV 2015, Santiago, Chile, 7–13 December 2015, pp. 4489–4497. IEEE Computer Society (2015)
25. Uddin, M.Z., Muramatsu, D., Takemura, N., Ahad, M.A.R., Yagi, Y.: Spatiotemporal silhouette sequence reconstruction for gait recognition against occlusion. IPSJ Trans. Comput. Vis. Appl. **11**(1), 9 (2019)
26. Wu, Z., Huang, Y., Wang, L., Wang, X., Tan, T.: A comprehensive study on cross-view gait based human identification with deep CNNs. IEEE Trans. Pattern Anal. Mach. Intell. **39**(2), 209–226 (2017)
27. Zhang, C., Liu, W., Ma, H., Fu, H.: Siamese neural network based gait recognition for human identification. In: 2016 IEEE International Conference on Acoustics, Speech and Signal Processing, ICASSP 2016, Shanghai, China, 20–25 March 2016, pp. 2832–2836. IEEE (2016)
28. Zhang, Y., Huang, Y., Yu, S., Wang, L.: Cross-view gait recognition by discriminative feature learning. IEEE Trans. Image Process. **29**, 1001–1015 (2020)

Finding the Best k for the Dimension of the Latent Space in Autoencoders

Kien Mai Ngoc[1,2] and Myunggwon Hwang[1,2(✉)]

[1] University of Science and Technology, Daejeon, Korea
https://www.ust.ac.kr
[2] Korea Institute of Science and Technology Information, Daejeon, Korea
{kienmn,mgh}@kisti.re.kr
https://www.kisti.re.kr

Abstract. In machine learning, one of the most efficient feature extraction methods is autoencoder which transforms the data from its original space to a latent space. The transformed data is then used for machine learning downstream tasks rather than the original data. However, there is little research about choosing the best number of latent space dimensions (k) for autoencoders that can affect the result of these tasks. In this paper, we focus on the impact of k on the accuracy of a downstream task. Concretely, we survey recently developed autoencoders and their characteristics, and conduct experiments using different autoencoders and k for extracting information from different datasets. We then present the accuracy of a classifier on the extracted datasets and the reconstruction error of the autoencoders according to k. From the empirical results, we recommend the best k of the latent space dimension for each dataset and each autoencoder.

Keywords: Autoencoder · Neural network · Latent space · Feature engineering

1 Introduction

In practice, machine learning often requires feature selection or feature extraction in order to pre-process the dataset before building a model on it. The reason is that the raw data is sometimes too complicated and may contain noise or redundant information, which can make machine learning models complex but return poor results. Hence, feature selection or feature extraction attempts to find a better representation of the raw data which can reduce computation while maintaining or improving the accuracy [2].

Among plenty of feature reduction methods proposed, autoencoder, which makes use of neural network [2], is one of the most efficient feature extraction methods. It extracts information from the original feature space to a latent space with a smaller number of dimensions. The autoencoder tries to eliminate redundancy or noise in the original data while keeping useful information for

© Springer Nature Switzerland AG 2020
N. T. Nguyen et al. (Eds.): ICCCI 2020, LNAI 12496, pp. 453–464, 2020.
https://doi.org/10.1007/978-3-030-63007-2_35

downstream tasks. As a consequence, the selection of the number of dimensions of the latent space depends on the datasets and the downstream tasks.

To our best knowledge, there is little research about choosing the best number of latent space dimensions (denoted by k). Therefore, the goal of this research is to find the best value of k for autoencoders to extract information from the original dataset. Concretely, we survey a few well-known autoencoders, investigate their characteristics and compare their performance on data extraction. We conduct experiments using different autoencoders and values of k to extract information from different datasets. We report reconstruction error to assess the result of training the autoencoders. The extracted information is then used for a simple Gaussian Naïve Bayes classifier to evaluate the accuracy. The result gives some recommendation for the best number of latent space dimensions for each pair of autoencoder and dataset.

In the following sections, we provide an overview of feature reduction methods and autoencoder. Then, we present our experiments with description about procedures, datasets, and different types of the autoencoders. From the result acquired, we come to discussion about the selection of the latent space dimension.

For simplicity, some notations should be defined. We denote x as the input vectors, and z as the latent code vectors which is the information extracted by the autoencoder.

2 Related Work

2.1 An Overview of the Feature Reduction Methods

The goal of feature reduction is mapping the original feature space to a space with a smaller or equal number of dimensions. While *feature selection* finds an inclusive subset of the original features, *feature extraction* extracts a completely new set of features from the pattern of data [2].

In *feature selection*, the evaluation of the subset is based on some criteria, which are used to categorize a method as a *filter* or *wrapper* method. According to the paper [2], *filter methods* consider a ranking mechanism used to grade the features. These methods are based on *relevance* (the dependence or correlation of the features with the target feature) and *redundancy* (whether the features share redundant information). Meanwhile, *wrapper methods* integrate the model within the feature subset search. In this way, different subsets of features are found or generated and evaluated through the model.

The main goal of *feature extraction* is usually to construct either better representation/discrimination or easier visualization of the data. It can be categorized into 2 main categories: *supervised* and *unsupervised* feature extraction methods. The *supervised* methods take into account the labels and classes of data samples while the *unsupervised* methods are based on the variation and pattern of the data [2]. Autoencoder is initially an unsupervised feature extraction method as it does not make use of the label of the dataset. It is described in the next subsection.

2.2 Autoencoder in Feature Reduction

The idea of **autoencoder** has been a part of the historical landscape of neural networks for decades. Traditionally, autoencoders were used for dimensionality reduction or feature learning. Recently, theoretical connections between autoencoders and latent variable models have brought autoencoders to the forefront of generative modeling [3].

The goal of autoencoder is to learn a mapping from high-dimensional observations to a lower-dimensional representation space such that the original observations can be reconstructed (approximately) from the lower-dimensional representation [9].

In feature reduction, autoencoder, which makes use of neural network, is an unsupervised feature extraction method. The form of an autoencoder consists an encoder and a decoder having hidden layers. The input is fed to the encoder in order to produce latent code and the output is extracted from the latent code by the decoder. Conventional autoencoder tries to minimize the discrepancy between the input and the decoded output, or in other words, to learn an identity function. Through training, the autoencoder is expected to discover a more efficient and compressed representation of the data (presented by the latent code). Once the network is trained, the decoder part is discarded and the output of the innermost hidden layer is used for feature extraction from the input [2].

Recent advances in autoencoder try to apply *prior knowledge* on the latent space in order to learn useful representations of the data [9].

However, there is still little effort has been spent on choosing the number of latent space dimensions. This paper aims to find the best k for each autoencoder, which is the best suited number of latent space dimension used for classification on different datasets. Our work is described in detail in the following section.

3 Finding the Best k for the Autoencoders

3.1 The Procedure

The goal of using autoencoder for feature extraction is to reduce the dimension of the feature space while keeping enough useful information for subsequent tasks. As a first step of feature extraction, we want to find the best k of the latent space by conducting experiments on different datasets using autoencoders with different configurations.

The overall procedure is from extracting the original dataset by autoencoder to evaluating the performance of a classifier on the extracted dataset, as shown in Fig. 1. For each type of autoencoders, we use different values of k to extract useful information from the original data. The extracted information is then used for downstream tasks to evaluate the efficiency of the autoencoder. For the sake of simplicity of the downstream task, we employ Gaussian Naïve Bayes classifier only. Finally, we compare the accuracy of the classification among the values of the latent space dimension (k).

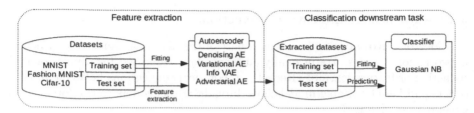

Fig. 1. Process of experiments.

More specifically, each dataset consists of a training and test set. The original training set is used for training the autoencoders in the unsupervised way. Particularly, the autoencoders try to reconstruct the original input after encoding it into the latent code, without using any information about the label of the input. To assess the reconstruction, we report the reconstruction error of the autoencoders in term of **mean square error** (MSE) between the original input and the reconstructed output on the test dataset. After being trained, the autoencoders transform the original training and test dataset (not including their labels) into a reduced training and a test dataset. At this step, these two extracted datasets and their associated labels are used as the training and test set for Gaussian Naïve Bayes classification.

The Gaussian Naïve Bayes classifier is trained using the extracted training set and makes prediction for the extracted test set. The ratio between the number of right predicted labels and the number of total labels is reported as the **accuracy**. Since the datasets in this paper are evenly distributed among classes, we only report the accuracy of the classifier.

The datasets and autoencoders will be described in more detail in following subsections.

3.2   Datasets

The dataset used in this paper includes: MNIST [7], Fashion MNIST [11], and Cifar-10 [6].

- MNIST is a dataset of handwritten digits, has a training set of 60,000 examples, and a test set of 10,000 examples. Each example is a 28×28 grayscale image, associated with a label of a digit.
- Fashion MNIST is a dataset of Zalando's article images consisting of a training set of 60,000 examples and a test set of 10,000 examples. Each example is a 28×28 grayscale image, associated with a label from 10 classes.
- The Cifar-10 dataset consists of 60,000 32×32 color images in 10 classes, with 6,000 images per class. There are 50,000 training images and 10,000 test images.

Table 1 summarizes information about the datasets.

Table 1. Summary about the datasets

Summary	MNIST	Fashion MNIST	Cifar-10
Training examples	60,000	60,000	50,000
Test examples	10,000	10,000	10,000
Image size	28×28	28×28	32×32
Image type	Gray	Gray	Color
No. of channel	1	1	3

3.3 Autoencoders

In this section, we review a few variations of basic autoencoder developed for dimensional reduction.

Denoising Autoencoder (DAE). The traditional autoencoder faces the risk of overfitting. Since the autoencoder learns the identity function, if the encoder and decoder are allowed too much capacity (informally, a model's capacity is its ability to fit a wide variety of functions [3]), the autoencoder can learn to perform the copy task without extracting useful information about the distribution of the data.

To avoid this problem, Denoising Autoencoder [10] proposed a modification to the basic autoencoder. The input is partially corrupted by adding noise or masking in a stochastic manner. Concretely, a fixed proportion of input dimensions are selected randomly and their values are forced to 0. Then the model is trained to recover the original input (not the corrupted one).

In our experiments, the Denoising Autoencoders have hidden layers 1000-500-250-k-250-500-1000 and the corruption proportion of 0.1 for MNIST and Fashion MNIST dataset (according to the paper [10]), and 0.2 for Cifar-10 dataset (the corruption proportion of 0.1, 0.2, and 0.5 give similar performance).

Variational Autoencoder (VAE). The difference of Variational Autoencoder is that instead of mapping the input into a fixed vector of latent space, we want to map it into a distribution. Variational Autoencoders aim to learn a parametric latent variable model by maximizing the marginal log-likelihood of the training data [9]. We denote that the prior distribution of latent space is $p(z)$ and the posterior distribution learned by the autoencoder model is $q_x(z)$. We also denote the distribution of the reconstruction of the input from latent code as $p(x|z)$.

The loss function is the evidence lower bound (ELBO) which has a formula

$$ELBO = -\log p(x|z) + KL(q_x(z)|p(z)) \tag{1}$$

In the first term of the loss function, we want to maximize the probability of the reconstruction. While in the second term, we can use Kullback-Leibler divergence to quantify the distance between the prior and posterior distributions of the latent space, which force the posterior distribution to be close to the prior distribution. The prior distribution is usually standard normal distribution $p(z) \sim \mathcal{N}(0, 1)$.

The training steps require sampling $z \sim q_x(z)$ (since the input is reconstructed from the latent code z, not the parameters of the distribution) which is a stochastic process and can not be backpropagated. To make it trainable, the sampling can be replaced by "parameterization trick" described in [5].

Our experiments use the model similar to that in paper [1]. The autoencoders have hidden layers 1000-500-250-k-250-500-1000.

Info Variational Autoencoder (Info VAE). According to [12], the KL divergence in equation (1) suffers from 2 problems: uninformative latent code and variance over-estimation in feature space. Therefore, they use Maximum mean discrepancy [4] (MMD) instead.

MMD is based on the idea that two distributions are identical if and only if all their moments are the same. Hence, we can define a divergence by measuring how different the moments of two distributions $p(z)$ and $q(z)$ are. Using MMD in Info Variational Autoencoder will maximize mutual information between the input x and the latent code z.

Our Info Variational Autoencoder models use 2 convolution layer with 64 and 128 filters, 1 hidden layer with 1024 units and latent space with k units for the encoder and the reverse structure for the decoder.

Adversarial Autoencoder (AAE). Adversarial Autoencoders (AAEs) [8] turn a standard autoencoder into a generative model by imposing a prior distribution $p(z)$ on the latent variables by penalizing some statistical divergence between $p(z)$ and $q_x(z)$ using a GAN [9].

In addition to minimizing the reconstruction discrepancy, these autoencoders have an additional discriminator part to ensure that the encoded latent codes are similar to samples sampled from the prior distribution. As in Variational Autoencoder, the prior distribution is usually standard normal distribution. In all experiments in [8], the encoder and decoder are taken to be deterministic.

In our experiments, the autoencoder has hidden layers 1000-1000-k-1000-1000 while the discriminator network has layers k-1000-1000-1 (the last layer indicates whether the latent code is from the encoder or sampled from the prior distribution).

3.4   Result

We conduct experiments on different datasets using different autoencoders[1] (as described in Sect. 3.1) and visualize the result here.

---

[1] The source code is available at: https://github.com/KienMN/Autoencoder-Experiments.

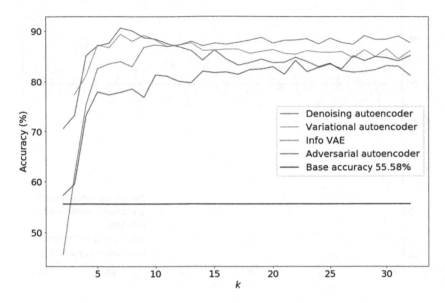

Fig. 2. Accuracy of classification on MNIST dataset.

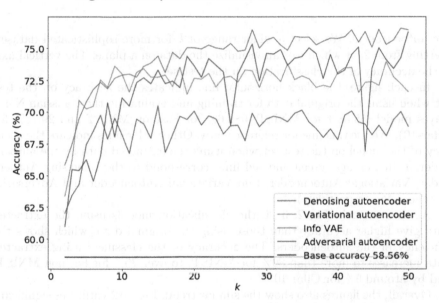

Fig. 3. Accuracy of classification on Fashion MNIST dataset.

Figure 2, 3, 4 illustrate the accuracy of the classification on the test set of the datasets (MNIST, Fashion MNIST and Cifar-10 dataset, respectively) depending on the number of the latent space dimensions (k). The horizontal axis is the values of k, which is the number of dimensions of the latent code encoded by

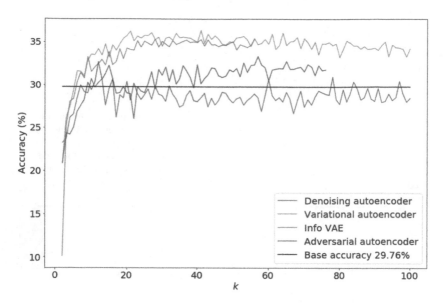

Fig. 4. Accuracy of classification on Cifar-10 dataset.

the autoencoders. We select a wider range of k for more sophisticated dataset, starting from 2, at which we can visualize the data on a plane. The vertical axis is the accuracy of the classification on the test set.

In each figure, the black horizontal line indicates the accuracy on the test set when using the original data for training and evaluating the Gaussian Naïve Bayes model (55.58% for MNIST, 58.56% for Fashion MNIST and 29.76% for Cifar-10). We use this line for reference only. Other color lines indicate the accuracy of the model on the test set when using the extracted data by the autoencoders (blue, orange, green and red lines correspond to the Denoising Autoencoder, Variational Autoencoder, Info Variational Autoencoder and Adversarial Autoencoder, respectively).

As illustrated in Fig. 2, 3, 4, the classification models using the extracted data give higher accuracy than those using the original data, which shows the efficiency of the autoencoders. The accuracy of the classifiers using extracted data increases to more than 80% for MNIST, to over 70% for Fashion MNIST, and by around 5% for Cifar-10.

Overall, the figures also show the similar trend. Figure 2 witnesses significant upward trend in all color lines, followed by slight increase or decrease when k keeps increasing. The lines in Fig. 3 rise when k is small and fluctuate slightly when k becomes large. In Fig. 4, apart from Denoising Autoencoder which shows poor performance, other autoencoders give small boost to the accuracy when k is large enough.

The similar trend is possibly due to a couple of reasons. Intuitively, the increase of k allows more information encoded in the latent code, which results in the increase of the accuracy. However, at some points, the encoded information becomes redundant and the useful information is blurred among dimensions of the space, which makes classification harder. As a consequence, the accuracy levels off or drops. Apart from k, the fluctuation on the accuracy lines can comes from the stochasticity of training and the selection of hyperparameters such as learning rate, number of epochs and batch size.

According to the comments above, we suggest a way to select the best k for each type of autoencoder on each dataset. Our selection is the point to which the accuracy rises significantly and after that, the accuracy varies slightly when increasing k. Such points are more probable to guarantee the improvement in the performance of the model while less likely to suffer from the stochasticity which is the nature of training machine learning models.

Applying to the figures, we recommend the best k for each type of autoencoder on each dataset in Table 2.

Table 2. Recommendation of k for each autoencoder on each dataset

Dataset	VAE	Info VAE	AAE	DAE
MNIST	7	9	10	7
Fashion MNIST	9	25	19	7
Cifar-10	20	20	12	10

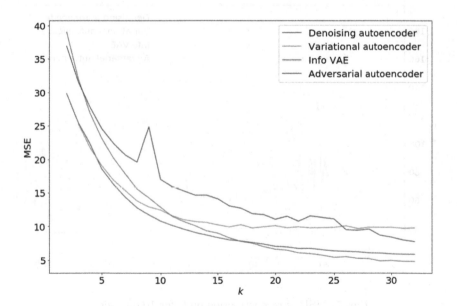

Fig. 5. MSE of reconstruction on MNIST dataset.

Additionally, we report mean square error (MSE) between the original input and the reconstruction output of the autoencoders, according to the number of latent space dimension k in Fig. 5, 6, 7.

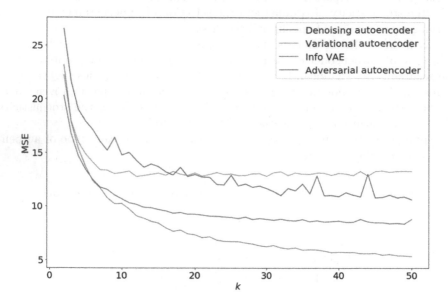

Fig. 6. MSE of reconstruction on Fashion MNIST dataset.

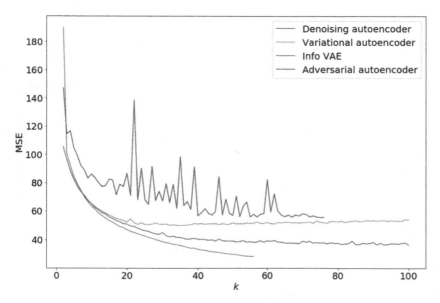

Fig. 7. MSE of reconstruction on Cifar-10 dataset.

Figure 5, 6, 7 show MSE of the reconstruction of the autoencoders on the test set of the datasets (MNIST, Fashion MNIST and Cifar-10 dataset, respectively) depending on the number of the latent space dimensions (k). Similarly to Fig. 2, 3, 4, the horizontal axis is the values of the dimension of the latent code encoded by the autoencoders, k, and the color lines indicate different types of autoencoder. The vertical axis is the MSE on the test set.

Overall, the MSE of reconstruction decreases when k keeps increasing and more information is encoded, which is consistent with the trend of accuracy. However, the best k (mentioned above) is not the point at which the autoencoders perform reconstruction best, which indicates that perfect reconstruction output is less likely to guarantee the discriminant effect in the latent code. Hence, we need develop more advanced loss function or training mechanism that can affect the result of the downstream task, rather than reconstruction error only.

4 Conclusion

Autoencoder as well as other feature reduction methods is the technique used in feature engineering to extract useful features from raw data. These features can then be used in order to improve the performance of machine learning algorithms.

In this paper, we reviewed feature reduction methods and autoencoders. Subsequently, we discussed different types of autoencoder and then conducted experiments using each type and various numbers of latent space dimension (k) on different datasets. After fitting the classifier using the extracted dataset, we visualized the connection between the accuracy and the value of k. From the experimental results, we pointed out the overall trend of the accuracy with regards to k and suggested a selection way of k and the value accordingly. We also reported the reconstruction error of the autoencoders and show that perfect reconstruction output is less likely to guarantee the discriminant effect in the latent code.

This paper is limited in terms of the dataset, classifier and metrics which can be improved in future research. We will try to apply autoencoders with different loss function, training mechanism and metrics on more sophisticated datasets with large number of dimensions in order to determine the impact of selection of k on those datasets and a general dataset. Besides, we will also combine autoencoder with other advanced classifiers in order to increase the accuracy of the end tasks.

Last thing to note is that the variation of the best value of k varies among datasets and autoencoders is still open problem. Hence, this work can be extended to let the model learn the selection of k by itself, which is an end-to-end approach in machine learning community.

Acknowledgement. This research was supported by Korea Institute of Science and Technology Information (KISTI).

References

1. Doersch, C.: Tutorial on variational autoencoders. arXiv preprint arXiv:1606.05908 (2016)
2. Ghojogh, B., et al.: Feature selection and feature extraction in pattern analysis: a literature review. arXiv preprint arXiv:1905.02845 (2019)
3. Goodfellow, I., Bengio, Y., Courville, A.: Deep Learning. MIT Press (2016). http://www.deeplearningbook.org
4. Gretton, A., Borgwardt, K., Rasch, M., Schölkopf, B., Smola, A.J.: A kernel method for the two-sample-problem. In: Schölkopf, B., Platt, J.C., Hoffman, T. (eds.) Advances in Neural Information Processing Systems 19, pp. 513–520. MIT Press (2007). http://papers.nips.cc/paper/3110-a-kernel-method-for-the-two-sample-problem.pdf
5. Kingma, D.P., Welling, M.: Auto-encoding variational Bayes. arXiv preprint arXiv:1312.6114 (2013)
6. Krizhevsky, A.: Learning multiple layers of features from tiny images. Technical report (2009)
7. LeCun, Y., Cortes, C., Burges, C.: MNIST handwritten digit database. ATT Labs 2 (2010). http://yann.lecun.com/exdb/mnist
8. Makhzani, A., Shlens, J., Jaitly, N., Goodfellow, I., Frey, B.: Adversarial autoencoders. arXiv preprint arXiv:1511.05644 (2015)
9. Tschannen, M., Bachem, O., Lucic, M.: Recent advances in autoencoder-based representation learning. arXiv preprint arXiv:1812.05069 (2018)
10. Vincent, P., Larochelle, H., Bengio, Y., Manzagol, P.A.: Extracting and composing robust features with denoising autoencoders. In: Proceedings of the 25th International Conference on Machine Learning, pp. 1096–1103 (2008)
11. Xiao, H., Rasul, K., Vollgraf, R.: Fashion-MNIST: a novel image dataset for benchmarking machine learning algorithms. CoRR abs/1708.07747 (2017). http://arxiv.org/abs/1708.07747
12. Zhao, S., Song, J., Ermon, S.: InfoVAE: information maximizing variational autoencoders. arXiv preprint arXiv:1706.02262 (2017)

A Graph-Based Approach for IoT Botnet Detection Using Reinforcement Learning

Quoc-Dung Ngo[1]([⊠]), Huy-Trung Nguyen[2,4]([⊠]), Hoang-Long Pham[1],
Hoang Hanh-Nhan Ngo[3], Doan-Hieu Nguyen[2], Cong-Minh Dinh[2],
and Xuan-Hanh Vu[5]

[1] Posts and Telecommunications Institute of Technology, Hanoi, Vietnam
dungnq@ptit.edu.vn
[2] People's Security Academy, Hanoi, Vietnam
huytrung.nguyen.hvan@gmail.com
[3] Academy of Cryptography Techniques, Hanoi, Vietnam
[4] Institute of Information Technology, Vietnam Academy of Science and Technology,
Hanoi, Vietnam
[5] Faculty of Information Technology, Hanoi Open University, Hanoi, Vietnam

Abstract. In recent years, the strong development of the Internet of Things (IoT) has resulted in an unprecedented rise in the number and variation of IoT malware. One of the most common malware on IoT devices today is the bot malware, popularly referred to as Botnets. This type of malware has been used to carry out many network attacks such as a denial of service, fraud, user data theft, etc. Over time, IoT botnets have been crafted with a higher level of complexity and danger, so existing researches based on non-graph structure features typically incur a high computational overhead and do not completely explore the relationship between behaviors, which can expose further characters of a botnet. Recently, to cope with these limitations, the approach of detecting IoT botnet based on structured-graph features using machine learning has gained its popularity. However, most of the existing graph-based approach has not fully explored the malicious behavior characteristics of IoT botnet yet. In this paper, we propose an effective method to classify executables as either IoT malware or IoT benign based on mining graph feature. Firstly, generating PSI-walks from PSI graphs via Reinforcement learning to form a dataset of PSI-walks before feeding it into a shallow LSTM network for IoT botnet detection. The methodology is verified using a dataset consisting of 6165 IoT botnet samples and 3845 benign samples. Experimental results indicate that the proposed approach can efficiently detect IoT botnets with achieving high accuracy as 97.14% and a low false-positive rate of 2.7%.

Keywords: IoT botnet detection · PSI-graph · Static analysis · Cyber security · Reinforcement-learning

1 Introduction

The fourth industrial revolution known as Industry 4.0 is backed by the outstanding development in physics, digitalization, biology, and having a great impact on other

© Springer Nature Switzerland AG 2020
N. T. Nguyen et al. (Eds.): ICCCI 2020, LNAI 12496, pp. 465–478, 2020.
https://doi.org/10.1007/978-3-030-63007-2_36

fields as well as the economic platform of every country. This trend explicitly causes the immense growing scale of the Internet of Things at a global scope. For instance, a recent report [1] forecasted that the estimated number of connected devices would be roughly 75.4 billion by 2025. This means that the usage of IoT systems is increasing dramatically all over the world. IoT applications have been applied in almost every aspect of daily life. However, this popularization poses a lot of critical information security issues including privacy, authentication, data storing and management, etc. Among these topics, malware attacks have been receiving a great deal of public attention. There have been a whole host of malware attacks which originate from IoT devices. For example, the biggest DDoS attack launched by Mirai botnet from 1.2 million infected devices [2] in the last quarter of 2016 had rocketed an enormous bandwidth capacity of 1.5 Tbps [3]. Furthermore, two successors of Mirai known as Hajime and Reaper also infected vulnerable IoT devices at first then used them as bots to launch several massive DDoS attacks [4]. As a result, to mitigate this kind of attack, researchers have been continuously investigating malware detection techniques. For instance, detecting botnet attacks by applying association rule learning to analyzing darknet traffic [5], and classifying between malware and benign by applying Machine Learning techniques on specific set of features of executables namely opcodes [6], processor information [7] etc.,. From the perspective of malware analysts, there are two approaches in malware detection known as static and dynamic analysis.

Dynamic analysis [8] is equivalent to detect abnormal behaviors while executing and monitoring executables based on a list of features namely system calls, network traffic, and register value in a supervised environment. The most critical part in the process of dynamic analysis is building a suitable environment that allows the malware to activate all of their malicious behaviors. Nevertheless, IoT malware can operate with tricky activating conditions on multiple architectures such as MIPS, ARM, SPARC, PowerPC. Therefore, it is costly to virtualize an entire compatible system that satisfies all the activation conditions of IoT malware. In other words, the critical drawbacks of dynamic analysis are technical difficulties in constructing a suitable environment for the full activation of malicious samples and an expensive monitoring process. On the other hand, static analysis [9] includes a wide range of techniques to detect malicious samples without executing them. Static approach relies on the extraction of known features from executables such as operation code sequences (opcode), printable string information, grayscale image and control flow graph (CFG), etc. The merits of this method are the ability to illustrate the structure and functionality of multi-architecture malware. Moreover, static analysis can analyze malicious files without executing, which reduces the cost of computational resources and ensures the safety of the system as well as. Therefore, the static analysis method is considered as a compatible solution in the problem of detecting IoT malware [9]. Although static analysis has limitations in dealing with encrypted or obfuscated files, there are several approaches to address this issue and these methods achieved satisfactory results. In the previous study, we proposed a graph-based structure feature that was effective in the problem of detecting IoT botnet malware, called PSI-graph [10]. In this study, H.T Nguyen et al. found that the malicious behavior of IoT botnets often took place according to a certain infectious process known as the law of action. On that basis, the authors came up with a graphical feature called PSI-graph efficiency in the problem of detecting IoT botnet. However, the study only focuses on the overall structure of the PSI graph and does not explore the information on the path and subgraph in the PSI graph. According to the research hypothesis, the PSI graph contains many executable paths of the executable file, including the path of maliciousness and also the normal path. Therefore, based on the characteristic of PSI graphs, if it is possible to trim and eliminate unnecessary paths, then it is possible to keep the routes with behavioral characteristics of malicious code or those with the greatest probability of malicious behavior only. Therefore, this method will contribute to the improvement of efficiency in IoT botnet detection. Thus, the issue that plays an important role here is how to determine the path in the graph that reveals the most highlighted characteristics of IoT botnet. In other words, this is the problem of path-finding in a graph.

Many existing algorithms [11, 12] was designed to handle the path-finding tasks in a graph, but those algorithms often require a defined and fixed environment. With the constantly evolving characteristics of malware, it is costly to fulfill these requirements, so those algorithms are not feasible in this case. In recent years, an effective method of finding and predicting behaviors that satisfy a certain purpose, called reinforcement learning. Reinforcement learning (RL) [13] is a branch of machine learning-based methods that implements dynamic learning by adjusting actions when interacting with the environment. Therefore, it maximizes the performance of systems based on continuous feedback to maximize a reward. Therefore, to reduce the complexity in graph analysis for IoT botnet malware detection problems based on structure-graph features, in this work, we propose an effective method that utilizes RL in finding the suspicious path that has many characteristics of a IoT botnet. These paths will be the most effective representation of the IoT botnet malware detection problem. The fundamental contributions of this work are summarized as follow:

- To the best of our knowledge, our research is one of the first approaches to IoT botnet detection with a combination of RL and graph mining techniques.
- We evaluate our approach on large datasets achieving high accuracy as 97.14% and a low false-positive rate of 2.7% for IoT botnets detection.

To achieve these contributions, the rest of this paper is organized as follows: Sect. 2 lists several significant researches which also leverages reinforcement learning in malware detection. Section 3 describes our proposed method in detail as well as the evaluations. Finally, we conclude the paper in Sect. 4.

2   Related Works

According to the characteristics of features which are extracted from malicious executables, malware detection techniques can be classified into dynamic analysis and static analysis.

Dynamic analysis focuses on inspecting the run-time behaviors of malwares by activating malicious samples in an appropriate environment [14]. On the contrary, static analysis includes a whole host of techniques to depict the structure as well as the malicious characteristics of malwares without any execution [10]. Generally, IoT devices adopt various processor architectures which are costly to virtualize precisely. Therefore, static analysis is often leveraged to deal with multi-architecture issues and tackle down the drawbacks of dynamic analysis in detecting IoT botnet. However, the malware is growing immensely in both number and complexity, so researchers have come up with machine learning based detection methods [15, 16] because of its natural advancement in detecting novel samples, fast processing, real-time predictions, improved detection accuracy and much more. Generally, machine learning has three basic learning paradigms namely supervised learning, unsupervised learning and reinforcement learning [17]. Supervised and unsupervised learning algorithms [18] such as DBN, SAE, Decision Tree and SVM are often utilized as classifiers which directly take part in the process of detecting malicious samples. In comparison, reinforcement learning is leveraged swiftly as an optimization method to maximize the accuracy and minimize the false-positive rate in recent malware detection proposals. There are a number of recent proposals which leverage reinforcement learning in distinct steps of the detection process such as [19–21].

Blount et al. proposed a method along with its proof of concepts for adaptive rule-based malware detection employing learning classifier systems, which combines a rule-based expert system with evolutionary algorithm based reinforcement learning [19]. This proposal suggested and implemented a self-training adaptive malware detection system which dynamically evolves detection rules. As described, the main responsibility of a Q-Learning Reinforcement Technique in this paper is to evolve rules of a LCS system to identify malwares based on function name and library name which were extracted in the Import Address Table of PE files. The best detection rate of this method is 96.1% with False Alarm Rate of 0.02. The drawbacks of this modified LCS system are the inability to process packed PE samples and PE files which have corrupt or missing IATs.

While most malware detectors simply leverage the power of Machine Learning into their classifier [22, 23] without any significant optimization, Cangshuaiwu et al. [21] proposed gym-plus, which based on an unique solution that includes utilizing Reinforcement Learning to create new malwares then labeled them as training data for their ML classifier. This creative architecture takes advantage of a malware generating system which is built on top of Reinforcement Learning algorithms and accumulates new malware manipulating functions into the proposed feature sets of gym-malware to increase the evasion rate of incoming generated malwares. The improvements made by Cangshuai Wu et al. were implemented on 4 different Reinforcement Learning agents namely Acer, DQN, Double DQN, Sarsa and have the best evasion rate of 47.5%. Therefore, after being trained with these samples, the detection rate of the LightGBM model achieves its best value at 93.5% compared to 15.75% before training with newly generated malwares. However, this solution has not proved its efficiency against novel IoT botnet.

Reinforcement Learning can also be leveraged to indirectly speeding up the process of malware detection. Liang Xiao et al. formulates a static malware detection game and follows up with a malware detection scheme with Reinforcement Learning [24]. There are a number of Reinforcement Learning algorithms modifications that have been applied in this research. Firstly, Q-learning algorithm is applied to achieve the optimal offloading rate without knowing the trace generation and radio bandwidth model of the neighboring IoT devices [24]. This scheme improves the detection accuracy by 40% and reduces the detection latency by 15% and increases the utility of the mobile devices by 47% compared with the benchmark offloading strategy in [15]. Secondly, by utilizing both the real defense and virtual experiences generated by the Dyna architecture, Dyna-Q-based malware detection scheme as proposed in [24] not only improves learning performance but also reduces the detection latency by 30% and increases the accuracy up to 18% compared to the detection with Q-learning. In addition, PDS-based malware detection scheme as developed in [24] leverages the known radio channel model to accelerate the learning speed as well as utilizing Q-learning to study the remaining unknown state space. Therefore, the detection accuracy was increased by 25% compared with the Dyna-Q based scheme in a network consisting of 200 mobile devices. Conversely, this scheme and its modifications only leverage reinforcement learning techniques during the data transferring process, not directly into the classification task.

Detecting IoT malwares has gained its popularity. Several feasible solutions have taken advantage of diverse Machine Learning techniques in combination with distinct feature sets to accomplish the malware classification tasks. Beside, several studies of malware detection have shown that methods based on structured features (i.e. graph) are more effective than using unstructured features in malware detection [25]. A typical example is the study of H.T Nguyen et al. [10] presented a lightweight method for detecting IoT botnet based on a graphical feature called PSI-graph. This feature shows the effectiveness of solving the multi-architecture problem of IoT botnet, and the experimental results on the data set of more than 11,000 samples achieved high accuracy at 98.7%. However, graphs are often complex and diverse. It involves restoring a significant number of subgraphs or paths as features, and the processing of those features can be very time-consuming. As the above studies, it seems that none of the above studies solved the problem of graph mining to extract the optimal and effective features in IoT botnet detection. Therefore, in this work, we propose an approach using reinforcement learning in graphical structured data mining, bringing high efficiency and low time-consuming when compared with other methods based on PSI-graph for detecting IoT botnet [10, 26]. Method details are presented in Sect. 3.

3 Proposed Method

We propose an effective method to classify execution files into IoT malware or IoT benign based on graph feature mining. The flow of this method is generating PSI-walks from PSI graphs via Reinforcement learning to form a dataset of PSI-walks before feeding it into a shallow Long Short Term Memory (LSTM) network for IoT botnet detection. In this section, we present the structure of our proposed method including the main components as well as the preprocessing steps. Our proposed method consists of three main steps as described in Fig. 1. First of all, we collect PSI graph dataset generated by H. Trung et al. [10] and feed it into a reinforcement learning block. Reinforcement learning considers each PSI graph as an environment and uses agents to interact with it and find an optimal policy with maximum expected return, then the algorithm generates a PSI-walk which best represents the features of an executable. Next, PSI-walk data is augmented so as to increase the total number of samples. This stage is done by processing self-loops in each node of the PSI-walk. Finally, we apply a shallow LSTM network which is described later to the augmented dataset for classification tasks (Fig. 3).

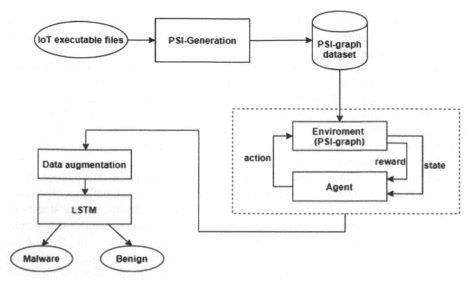

Fig. 1. Overview of proposed method.

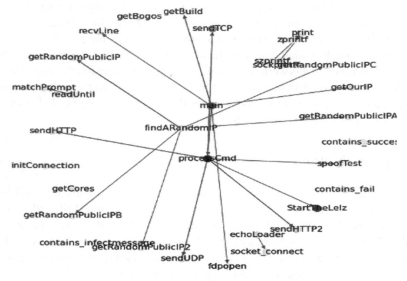

Fig. 2. An example of a simple PSI graph in our dataset.

3.1 PSI-Walk

We have inherited the approach to represent IoT executable files with PSI-graphs [10]. However, the authors in [10, 26] focus on the structure of the whole PSI graph or a subset of it called the PSI-rooted subgraph. These approaches can achieve a good classification benchmark, but the used features do not figure out the most significant characteristics of the IoT botnet. In this paper, we focus on a different way to process PSI graphs by extracting the most informative walk in this type of graph. That means some walks in the PSI graph of IoT botnet are more valuable than the others. Therefore, these walks can represent the executable with its highlighted characteristics at its best.

Definition 1: PSI-walk is a directed walk defined as a finite sequence of edges $(e_1, e_2, \ldots, e_{m-1})$ which joins a sequence of vertices $(v_1, v_2, \ldots, v_m)$ such that e_i connects v_i and v_{i+1}. Whereas $(v_1, v_2, \ldots, v_m)$ is the vertex sequence of the directed walk and is the way we store a PSI-walk in our dataset.

Obviously, in an executable, there are many good walks which can show the feature of that ELF (Executable and Linkable Format). We do not explicitly point out which walk is the best or the most significant. An optimal or near-optimal walk is enough for us to achieve a good result in the classification task.

3.2 Reinforcement Learning in PSI-Walks Generation

In order to find the expected PSI-walk of a PSI graph, we apply Q-learning [13] – a simple reinforcement learning algorithm. Q-learning is an off-policy reinforcement learning algorithm that seeks to find the best action to take given the current state. More specifically, Q-learning seeks to learn a policy that maximizes the total reward. In order to solve the problem of PSI-walk, we consider our model as a robot finding the most optimal walk to achieve as high reward as possible. Thereforew, main components of the inforcement learning model are defined as below.

- *Agent is* the robot standing in one vertex of the PSI-graph. Agent takes actions by travelling to a neighbor vertex. In the end, by following the optimal found policy, agent generates the PSI-walk.
- *Action is* a set of all possible moves the agent can make. Therefore, the action space is all vertices in PSI-graph. However, we control that agent can only take valid actions by moving to a neighbor vertex of the current vertex. Note that, to avoid stucking in one vertex's self-loop, the algorithm does not allow the agent to move into its self-loop
- *Environment* is the world through which the agent moves, and which responds to the agent. This includes a PSI graph and a mechanism to take the agent's current vertex and the vertex it wants to move to and return the agent's reward and its next state.
- *State* is the current situation which includes the current vertex and a list of visited edges. When the environment returns the agent's next state, the state is updat-ed by changing the current node and appending the edge to the list of visited edges.
- *Reward* is how we measure the success or failure of an agent's action in a given state. We define some rules below to give each action a weight of I portance as well as the reward.

To some extent, an important function in a program often calls many other functions. For example, the function "processCmd" of BASHLITE source code is in charge of receiving command input from the main function and depends on that command input, the function triggers attack by calling "sendTCP", "sendUDP", v.v. Moreover, the bigger a function is, the more external library functions it usually calls. Therefore, the weight of each vertex is depending on the out-degree of that vertex.

Definition 2: Outdegree of a vertex v in graph $G = (V, E)$, $(v \in V)$ is defined as the number of tail ends adjacent to a vertex and is denoted $deg^+(v)$

- a vertex with $deg^+(v) = 0$ is called a sink, since it is the end of each of its incoming arrows. This is the situation of such functions as "printf".
- The degree sum formula states that:

$$\sum_{v \in V} deg^+(v) = |E|$$

However, the PSI-graph is a directed multigraph, so a vertex may have all of its out-degree coming from its self-loops. Self-loops are not as much informative as connections to other vertices. Therefore, a vertex with a lot of self-loops will receive less reward than one with few of self-loops, and a vertex whose edges are all loops will receive nothing. Moreover, a vertex's reward must be as big as its out-degree and its real out-degree (eliminating self-loops).

In summary, given the number of self-loops of a vertex v $loops(v)$, moving from vertex u to vertex v in PSI-graph will receive a reward of R, where:

$$R = \begin{cases} 2 * deg^+(v) - loops(v) \ if \ deg^+(v) \neq loops(v) \\ 1 \qquad\qquad\qquad if \ deg^+(v) = loops(v) \end{cases}$$

Additionally, due to name convention, a vertex whose name starts with "_" or "__" may not be one of the main function of a program, so these vertices only receive a reward of 1 like the case $deg^+(v) = loops(v)$ above. Besides, moving to a vertex having self-loops is more promising than moving to one having no self-loops. Therefore, a vertex with self-loops will have a reward of $R' = 2 * R$.

Finally, when travelling in PSI-graph, agent may go into some cycles. In order to break cycle at some points and try some other walks, we reduce the reward of a visited edge. It means that moving to a vertex that agent has already visited that edge will receive only a reward of $R' = \lfloor \frac{R}{2^{m_e}} \rfloor$. Where m_e is the number of times agent repeat visiting that egde e. The formula means that the longer staying in a cycle, the smaller reward the agent receives. We apply Q-learning algorithm with epsilon-greedy algorithm to each PSI-graph with a number of episodes of 1000. When the algorithm ends iterating, using the learned Q table, we get the optimal PSI-walk. As we state earlier, we do not travel into self-loops. As a result, to show these self-loops, we duplicate vertices having self-loops in the final PSI-walk.

3.3 Data Augmentation

One problem of the generated PSI-walks is that many PSI-graphs can generate the same PSI-walk, therefore, the dataset shrinks. A small number of samples of PSI-walk in dataset may influence the performance of machine learning classifiers. A small dataset can be prone to overfitting or data mismatch problem. In our case, a lot of vertices is just found in only one PSI-walk. That can cause data distribution of training set is too much different from development/testing set.

Besides, self-loops are not processed completedly in previous reinforcement learning model. A program can be inside a loop for multiple times before breaking it and do something else. For example, IoT botnet will try to connect to C&C server and only continue after a connection is accepted.

To solve those problems above, we apply data augmentation to the PSI-walk dataset. Data augmentation helps to improve the performance of classification problems. Algorithm 1 takes each PSI-walk and generates an augmented PSI-walk by randomly repeating a vertex having self-loops. In our case, we limit the maximum number of times repeating is r.

Algorithm 1: $Random\_augment(W, r)$	
Input	$W = [v_i]$: list of vertices in PSI-walk
	r: maximum number of loops
Output	$W_a = [v_i']$: PSI-walk after data augmentation
1:	$Initialization$: $W_a = \emptyset, prev = None$
2:	$for\ each\ v \in W\ do$
3:	$\quad W_a := W_a \cup \{v\}$
4:	$\quad if\ v = prev\ then$
5:	$\quad\quad for\ i = 0\ to\ random(0, r)\ do$
	$\quad\quad\quad W_a := W_a \cup \{v\}$
6:	$\quad prev := v$
7:	$return\ W_a$

By applying the data augmentation algorithm described above, we managed to make our dataset fifth times bigger. That can prevent overfitting as well as data mismatch in the classification task.

3.4 Classification

As noted previously, PSI-walk is a sequence of vertices. Therefore, PSI-walk can be regarded as a sequence of words and the problem of malware classification can be considered as sentiment analysis. Since vertex data is text data, words in sequence, we can use a LSTM - advanced version of Recurrent neural network (RNN) to build a powerful model that does not only consider the individual words, but the order they appear in. It is reasonable because PSI-walk is a directed walk.

In this work, we utilize the shallow many-to-one LSTM model, as shown in Fig. 3. First, vertices have to be preprocessed so that we can get them into the network. We use embedding layers to encode each word with a vector. Then, these word embedding vectors are fed into LSTM and trained as a binary classification task. The output layer contains only one neuron whose output is the probability of being malware or benign. We also apply dropout technique to avoid overfitting.

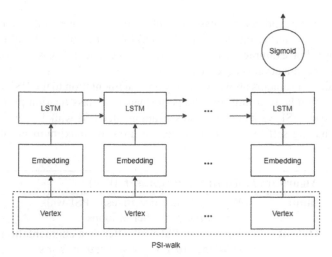

Fig. 3. LSTM model's architecture

3.5 Experimental Result

In this section, we evaluate the proposed method by experiment. We inherit the multi-architecture PSI-graph dataset from previous research of PSI-graph. This dataset contains 10010 PSI-graph samples including 6165 IoT botnet samples and 3845 samples. Experiment is conducted with a desktop with the following configuration: Windows 10 Pro 64-bit, Intel Core i5, 8 Gb RAM. Source codes are written in Python language. We divide the dataset into three sections including training set, test set, and validation set at the rate of 70%, 15%, and 15%, respectively. Validation set are used to evaluate the performance of model during hyperparameter tuning. After that, we use the final model to predict on the testing set.

a. *Augmented corpus*

The Reinforcement learning model extracts PSI-walk from PSI-graph dataset. It is obvious that multiple IoT botnet samples which belong to the same family or are cross-compiled version of the same botnet have the same sequence of PSI-walk. The reason is that all these botnets have a similar source code. Table 2 show the number of PSI-walks generated by Reinforcement learning model before and after data augmentation. In classification task, we only consider binary classfication problem, so we group three malware classes into one malware class.

From Table 1, we can see that data augmentation helps to generate new dataset approximately 5 times bigger than the original one. The augmented PSI-walk is just a modification of loops of the original PSI-walk so that it can represent well PSI-graph's features. Table 2 below shows some information about length of PSI-walk after augmented. Note that PSI-graphs having cycle are limited to travel in 50 steps for each episode of Reinforcement learning.

Table 1. Comparation of number of samples before and after data augmention

	Malware	Benign	Total
Before	1703	2857	4560
After	8350	10734	19084

Table 2. Length of PSI-walks

	Malware	Benign
Minimum	2	2
Maximum	157	166
Average	14	19

Table 3. Result of LSTM model

Metrics	LSTM
Accuracy (%)	97.14
FPR (%)	2.70
ROC AUC (%)	97.11

b. *Evaluation metrics*

The following terms are used to evaluate the precision-efficiency of the proposed method: True positive (TP) is the number of predicted malware samples correctly classified as malware; True negative (TN) is the number of predicted benign samples correctly classified as benign; False positive (FP) is the number of predicted malware samples incorrectly tagged as benign; False negative (FN) is the number of predicted benign samples incorrectly tagged as malware. The following metrics are used to evaluate the precision-efficiency of the proposed method: FPR = FP/(FP + TN); ACC = (TP + TN)/(TP + TN + FP + FN)

c. *Result and evaluation*

Table 3 shows detailed result of LSTM model in IoT botnet detection. The experimental results show that the proposed method has a satisfactory benchmark. The model has both high detecion rate and low false-alarm rate of 2.70%. Therefore, the model is robust to have a high ROC AUC score.

Comparing with some recent approaches on PSI-graph for IoT botnet detection, we can see that our proposed method outperforms graph-based methods with Deep Graph Convolutional Neural network and achieve a high detection rate as PSI-rooted subgraph approach. Besides, the model shows a lower false-alarm rate than the subgraph-based model. It is obvious that PSI-walk can cluster IoT botnets into families, while PSI-rooted subgraph can not represent. Compared to the study [10, 26], the PSI-walk is less accurate due to the paths found by RL are near-optimal. As, there are a few cases where the psi-walk is not the best abstract, and the algorithm used in this research is that Q-learning is quite simple. The existing PSI graph-based methods [10, 26] focus on the brute-force PSI-graphs approach to identify the malicious behavior of IoT botnet to detect IoT botnet malware. Meanwhile, the malicious behavior of IoT botnet only appears in some paths or subgraphs of the PSI-graph. Therefore, brute-force PSI-graphs traversal makes it highly complex to visit redundant paths or subgraphs. In addition, our model is compared with a promising method proposed by Hamed et al., [27]. This method also uses static features as well as machine learning classifiers to detect IoT botnet. Nevertheless, this method only applies to ARM samples. Table 4 shows that our multi-architecture model can generalize even better than single-architecture method. All of these papers are using the same exact training and testing datasets.

Table 4. A comparative summary of some malware detecion approach on IoT devices.

Methods	Accuracy (%)	FPR (%)
Ours	97.1	2.7
PSI-rooted subgraph based [26]	97.3	4.0
PSI-graph [10]	98.7	0.78
Hamed et al. [27] (ARM only)	96.35	–

4 Conclusions

With the gradual development pace and the ubiquitous nature of IoT, cybercriminals are always aiming to exploit, attack, and abuse IoT applications. Moreover, the threats that violate privacy when transmitted/received, and processed via the IoT network is also an endless race between security researchers and malicious code authors. In this paper, we have presented a novel PSI-walk based approach for IoT botnet detection. We propose a method to use a reinforcement learning model to extract the PSI-walk features and effective classify IoT botnet malware. In summary, our main contributions are the following: (1) we present a PSI-walk based effective feature for IoT botnet detection as a proper representation ELF files; (2) we proposed a reinforcement learning model and a LSTM model to achieve high accuracy and precision in classifying malicious and benign samples which achieved high accuracy as 97.14% and low false positive rate of 2.7%. However, the proposed method depends on the name of functions or vertices of PSI-graph, so attackers have their chance to bypass this method by changing the function name. Therefore, in the future work, we will try to embed the structure of PSI-graph to create more robust novel features.

Acknowledgement. This research was partially funded by Hanoi Open University in Vietnam with project MHN 2020-02.09.

References

1. Internet of Things - number of connected devices worldwide 2015–2025. https://www.statista.com/statistics/471264/iot-number-of-connected-devices-worldwide/. Accessed 3 May 2020

2. Antonakakis, M., et al.: Understanding the mirai botnet. In: Proceedings of the 26th {USENIX} Security Symposium ({USENIX} Security 2017, pp. 1093–1110 (2017)
3. Bertino, E., Islam, N.: Botnets and Internet of Things security. Computer **50**(2), 76–79 (2017). https://doi.org/10.1109/MC.2017.62
4. Flashpoint: Mirai Botnet Linked to Dyn DNS DDoS Attacks. https://www.flashpoint-intel.com/blog/cybercrime/mirai-botnet-linked-dyn-dns-ddos-attacks. Accessed 2 May 2020
5. Ozawa, S., Ban, T., Hashimoto, N., Nakazato, J., Shimamura, J.: A study of IoT malware activities using association rule learning for darknet sensor data. Int. J. Inf. Secur. **19**(1), 83–92 (2019). https://doi.org/10.1007/s10207-019-00439-w
6. Peters, W., Dehghantanha, A., Parizi, R.M., Srivastava, G.: A comparison of state-of-the-art machine learning models for OpCode-based IoT malware detection. In: Choo, K.-K.R., Dehghantanha, A. (eds.) Handbook of Big Data Privacy, pp. 109–120. Springer, Cham (2020). https://doi.org/10.1007/978-3-030-38557-6_6
7. Takase, H., Kobayashi, R., Kato, M., Ohmura, R.: A prototype implementation and evaluation of the malware detection mechanism for IoT devices using the processor information. Int. J. Inf. Secur. **19**(1), 71–81 (2019). https://doi.org/10.1007/s10207-019-00437-y
8. Chang, K.-C., Tso, R., Tsai, M.-C.: IoT sandbox: to analysis IoT malware Zollard. In: Proceedings of the Second International Conference on Internet of things, Data and Cloud Computing, pp. 1–8 (2017). https://doi.org/10.1145/3018896.3018898
9. Ngo, Q.-D., et al.: A survey of IoT malware and detection methods based on static features. ICT Express (2020). https://doi.org/10.1016/j.icte.2020.04.005
10. Nguyen, H.-T., Ngo, Q.-D., Le, V.-H.: A novel graph-based approach for IoT botnet detection. Int. J. Inf. Secur. **19**(5), 567–577 (2019). https://doi.org/10.1007/s10207-019-00475-6
11. Pohl, I.: Heuristic search viewed as path finding in a graph. Artif. Intell. **1**, 193–204 (1970)
12. Anbuselvi, R., Phil, M.: Path finding solutions for grid based graph. Adv. Comput. Int. J. **4**(3), 51–60 (2013)
13. Yousefi, S., Derakhshan, F., Karimipour, H.: Applications of big data analytics and machine learning in the Internet of Things. In: Choo, K.-K.R., Dehghantanha, A. (eds.) Handbook of Big Data Privacy, pp. 77–108. Springer, Cham (2020). https://doi.org/10.1007/978-3-030-38557-6_5
14. Islam, R., Tian, R., Batten, L.M., Versteeg, S.: Classification of malware based on integrated static and dynamic features. J. Netw. Comput. Appl. **36**, 646–656 (2013)
15. Xiao, L., Wan, X., Lu, X., Zhang, Y., Wu, D.: IoT security techniques based on machine learning. IEEE Signal Process. Mag. **35**(5), 41–49 (2018)
16. Souri, A., Hosseini, R.: A state-of-the-art survey of malware detection approaches using data mining techniques. Hum.-Centric Comput. Inf. Sci. **8**(1), 1–22 (2018). https://doi.org/10.1186/s13673-018-0125-x
17. Truong, T.C., et al.: Intelligence in the cyber domain: offense and defense. Symmetry **12**(3), 410 (2020)
18. Xin, Y., et al.: Machine learning and deep learning methods for cybersecurity. IEEE Access **6**, 35365–35381 (2018)
19. Blount, J.J., et al.: Adaptive rule-based malware detection employing learning classifier systems: a proof of concept. In: 35th Annual Computer Software and Applications Conference Workshops, pp. 110–115 (2011)
20. Urbanowicz, R.J., et al.: Learning classifier systems: a complete introduction, review, and roadmap. J. Artif. Evol. Appl. **2009**(1), 1–25 (2009). https://doi.org/10.1155/2009/736398
21. Wu, C., et al.: Enhancing machine learning based malware detection model by reinforcement learning. In: Proceedings of the 8th International Conference on Communication and Network Security, pp. 74–78 (2018)

22. Su, J., Vargas, D.V., Prasad, S., Sgandurra, D., Feng, Y., Sakurai, K.: Lightweight classification of IoT malware based on image recognition. In: IEEE 42nd Annual Computer Software and Applications Conference (COMPSAC), vol. 2, pp. 664–669 (2018)
23. Pektaş, A., et al.: Classification of malware families based on runtime behaviors. J. Inf. Secur. Appl. **37**, 91–100 (2017)
24. Xiao, L., et al.: Cloud-based malware detection game for mobile devices with offloading. IEEE Trans. Mob. Comput. **16**(10), 2742–2750 (2017)
25. Du, Y., et al.: An android malware detection approach using community structures of weighted function call graphs. IEEE Access **5**, 17478–17486 (2017)
26. Nguyen, H.-T., et al.: PSI-rooted subgraph: a novel feature for IoT botnet detection using classifier algorithms. ICT Express **6**(2), 128–138 (2020)
27. HaddadPajouh, H., Dehghantanha, A., Khayami, R., Choo, K.-K.R.: A deep recurrent neural network based approach for Internet of Things malware threat hunting. Future Gener. Comput. Syst. **85**, 88–96 (2018). https://doi.org/10.1016/j.future.2018.03.007

Vietnamese Food Recognition System Using Convolutional Neural Networks Based Features

Hieu T. Ung[1,2], Tien X. Dang[1], Phat V. Thai[4], Trung T. Nguyen[1,2,3], and Binh T. Nguyen[1,2,3(✉)]

[1] AISIA Research Lab, Ho Chi Minh City, Vietnam
ngtbinh@hcmus.edu.vn
[2] University of Science, Ho Chi Minh City, Vietnam
[3] Vietnam National University, Ho Chi Minh City, Vietnam
[4] Nanyang Technology University, Singapore, Singapore

Abstract. Food image recognition has been extensively investigated during the last decade and had multiple useful applications for monitoring food calories and analyzing people's eating habits to ensure better health. In this paper, we study a Vietnamese food recognition system using Convolutional Neural Networks (CNNs) based features. We manually collect one dataset for Vietnamese food classification with 13 categories and 8903 images. For learning a proper food classifier, we conduct brief analytics by comparing hand-crafted features and CNNs based features (including AlexNet, GoogleNet, ResNet50, ResNet101v2, and InceptionResnetv2) and choosing top K accuracy for measuring the performance of each model. The experimental results show that Inception-Resnetv2 can achieve the best performance among all these techniques. We aim at publishing our codes and datasets for giving and additional contribution to the research community related to the Vietnamese food recognition problem.

Keywords: Food recognition · CNNs · ResNet · AlexNet · GoogleNet

1 Introduction

The World Health Organization has indicated that the overall increment of non-communicable diseases is a significant issue; for instance, premature heart diseases, diabetes, and cancer [24]. Up to now, worldwide obesity has been increasing nearly three times since 1975, and there are 38 million children under the age of five were overweight or obese in 2019. Notably, most people live in countries where overweight and obesity kill more people than underweight. For this reason, preventing health problems from overweight and obesity has been one of the critical issues in different countries. Personalized nutrition has become a hot issue and received a great deal of public attention. Personalized nutrition is healthy eating advice based on genetic data, personal health status, lifestyle,

© Springer Nature Switzerland AG 2020
N. T. Nguyen et al. (Eds.): ICCCI 2020, LNAI 12496, pp. 479–490, 2020.
https://doi.org/10.1007/978-3-030-63007-2_37

Fig. 1. Different foods in our dataset (8903 images with 13 categories).

nutrient intake, and phenotypic data [5] besides doing exercises as much as possible and controlling calorie intake. Typically, this process can be accomplished by manually logging all food items, tracking food amounts for each meal, and estimating the caloric intake after each day. However, it is very time-consuming and not an excellent choice for many busy people. Using smart wearable devices with high-resolution cameras becomes popular in many countries, which requires multiple kinds of research related to building a system for food intake monitoring and action recommendations (Fig. 1).

Food image recognition and retrieval have become one of the promising applications of computer vision to make people easier to estimate food calories and analyze people's eating practices for better healthcare. There have been a lot of studies related to this field. Liu et al. [14] propose a deep learning-based food image recognition algorithms for implementing computer-aided technical solutions to improve the accuracy of current measurements of dietary intake. By applying Convolutional Neural Networks (CNNs) [13], they can achieve better results than previous techniques on two food image datasets: UEC-256 and Food-101. Mezgec and colleagues [17] a new deep CNN, namely "NutriNet", for the food and drink image recognition problem and achieve promising results in one real-word dataset with 225,953 images of 520 different food and drink items. Shimoda et al. [20] present a new approach for estimating food image similarity by using CNNs and show potential applications on food image retrieval. Other results can be found at [7,12,16], and [23].

In this work, we investigate a Vietnamese food recognition system as follows: for a given food image, the proposed system is able to predict the top N relevant foods. To learn an appropriate model, we analyze different approaches, including hand-crafted features and convolutional neural networks. We manually collect one dataset from various resources, which has 8903 food images with 13 distinct categories and use the top K accuracy for measuring the performance of different models. For hand-crafted features, we choose Histogram of Gradients (HOG) [4] to extract meaningful features from each food image and choose Support Vector Machines (SVMs) [6] and Extreme Gradient Boosting (XGBoost) [3] for training a suitable model. For deep learning approach, we compare the performance among five different deep neural networks, including AlexNet [13], GoogleNet [22], Resnet50 [8], ResNet101v2 [9], and InceptionRes-Netv2 [21]. The experimental results show that InceptionResNetv2 can obtain the best performance and outperform all other techniques with the top 3 accuracy 99.0% and top 5 accuracy 99.78%. We aim to publish our methods and datasets for giving and additional contribution to the research community in the Vietnamese food recognition problem.

2 Methodology

2.1 Hand-Crafted Features

Hand-crafted features are traditional techniques in object recognition that extract meaningful information from images such as color, texture, and shape.

In this work, we only select HOG as one popular feature to compare with other deep learning methods. The main reason is that deep learning features have been proven for both efficiency and accuracy compared to other traditional ones, and choosing a particular feature like HOG can be suitable for this illustration.

It is worth noting that HOGs are similar to that of edge orientation histograms, scale-invariant feature transform descriptors (SIFT [15], SURF[1]). Typically, HOGs compute a histogram of oriented gradients for small squared cells in images and normalize histogram values using a block-wise pattern similar to a sliding window. In detail, one can first preprocess each image by converting it to the grayscale channel and following by contrast and brightness adjustment. Next, one can calculate HOG feature vectors from the processed image. Notably, this computation depends on the number of cells/blocks and the size of each cell/block and the overlapping region between two neighborhood blocks. Therefore, these hyper-parameters are tuning by using a grid search method to maximize accuracy. Usually, the features computed can be fed into an appropriate classifier for prediction. In our approach, we consider two classifiers, SVMs and XGBoost, for learning a food classifier (Fig. 2).

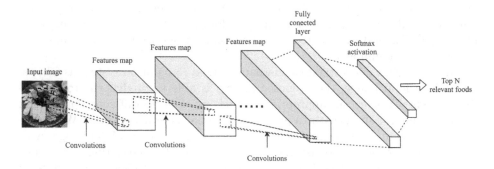

Fig. 2. A proposed CNN architecture in the Vietnamese food recognition system.

2.2 Convolutional Neural Networks

Overview. CNN is a particular deep neural network. Unlike other methods, it helps to focus on finding meaningful features in different regions of the input image, instead of only considering the whole area and sharing weights for all different input regions. Consequently, CNNs can have fewer parameters than neural networks and can easily stack more convolutional layers to build a more robust learning model. Experimental results [25] show that by training deep CNNs on a large amount of data, such as ImageNet, shallow filters usually extract low-level shapes. In contrast, deeper filters can obtain higher and more abstract features. Therefore, one can regard CNNs as a hierarchy of filters learned to calculate both low-level and high-level factors that are important to distinguish different visual concepts.

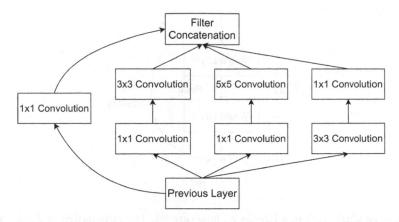

Fig. 3. Inception module with dimensionality reduction [22]. In the experiment, we use this approach as one of chosen deep learning methods for comparison.

Architectures. AlexNet[13] is one of the first convolutional neural networks that won the ImageNet Large Scale Visual Recognition Competition [19] in 2012. Its architecture consists of five convolutional layers, some of which are followed by max-pooling layers. Meanwhile, the classifier component has three fully connected layers with ReLU [18] activation in the first two and a Softmax activation in the final one.

GoogleNet [22] or InceptionV1, is the winner of the competition ILSVRC 2014. GoogleNet advances AlexNet by replacing large filter sizes in AlexNet by an inception module [22]. Here, the inception module is a composition of submodules such as filters of different sizes, especially the 1×1 fitters size and average pooling. Then, one can concatenate each submodule's outputs to obtain the final output. Figure 3 shows an example of an inception module. It is important to note that GoogleNet uses two auxiliary classifiers [22] to avoid vanishing gradient issues. Also, it has fewer parameters in comparison with AlexNet but achieves a superior performance [22].

To better deal with the vanishing gradient problem, Resnet [8] with a deep residual framework was first presented by Kaiming He and his co-workers, which can have more than 100 layers, five times deeper than GoogleNet. One of the main components in a ResNet architecture is a deep residual framework, as visualized in Fig. 4. Up to now, there many variants of ResNet models, including ResNet18, ResNet-34, ResNet50, ResNet101, ResNet152. The number in each name presents for the number of layers in the corresponding model. In our work, we choose ResNet50 and an upgrade version of ResNet, which is ResNet101v2 [9]. The primary difference between ResNetV2 and the original ResNet is that V2 uses the batch normalization before each weight layer in the residual block.

With the success of both inception and residual techniques, it is reasonable to combine them for a better one. Inception-ResNet [21] is a combination of the Inception and Residual networks to boost the performance further. Incep-

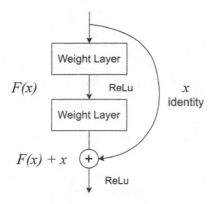

Fig. 4. A residual block in a ResNet architecture [8]. The formulation of $\mathcal{F}(\mathbf{x}) + \mathbf{x}$ can be obtained by feed-forward neural networks with skip-connections. In this case, the skip-connections simply perform an identity mapping, and their outputs can be added to the outputs of the stacked layers.

tionResNet using 3 different residual-inception blocks [21] and a stem block [21]. Figure 5 is a residual-inception block using InceptionResNet. InceptionResNetv2 using three residual-inception blocks from InceptionResNetv1 and the stem block from the Inceptionv4 model [21]. Table 1 describes all CNNs used in our experiments.

Table 1. Five different CNNs used in the experiments.

CNNs	Number of layers	Number of parameters
AlexNet	8	60 Million
GoogleNet	22	5 Million
Resnet50	50	26 Million
Resnet101v2	101	44 Million
InceptionResnetv2	164	55.97 Million

3 Experiments

In this section, we describe our datasets, the implementation of the proposed techniques, and experimental results in detail. We conduct all experiments on a workstation with Intel Core i9-7900X CPU, 128GB RAM, and two GPUs RTX-2080Ti.

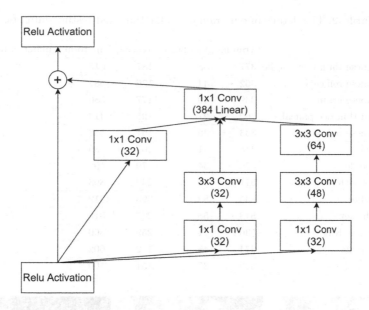

Fig. 5. Residual Inception Block (Inception-ResNet-A) [21].

3.1 Dataset

We manually collect one dataset containing 8903 images of 13 different Vietnamese dishes by various websites and photos taken in many meals we had for three consecutive months. After that, we manually find an appropriate label or delete images with no food inside. Table 2 presents the distribution of food images in different categories. One can see that our dataset is a bit unbalanced. For example, steamed thin rice pancakes have the smallest number of photos, while the rice dishes have the highest number. The average number of pictures of other foods is about 600–800. In our experiment, we randomly divide the dataset into three parts: training, validation, and testing sets, with the ratio 7:1:2, respectively.

In experiments, we train a model on the training set, evaluate the performance after each epoch on the validation set, choose the snapshot obtaining the lowest validation loss, and measure each model's performance on the testing dataset by using top K accuracy ($K = 1, 3, 5$).

3.2 Model Settings

Hand-Crafted Features. For hand-crafted features, we resize all images into the size of 200×200 pixels then convert color image to grayscale image. Using HOG extractors implemented in our system, we obtain a feature vector with M dimensions. Figure 6 visualizes HOG features in one food image.

After calculating HOG features from food images, we select two SVM and XGBoost for training a food classifier. For each classifier, we try finding the

Table 2. The details of our training, validation, and testing datasets.

Food	Training	Validation	Testing	The total number of images
Vietnamese thick rice noodle	377	53	187	617
Vietnamese roll cake	362	44	176	582
Vietnamese bread	369	40	177	586
Steamed thin rice pancake	260	27	125	412
Vietnamese roll pancake	333	39	161	533
Beef stew	438	41	207	686
Beef noodle	379	34	179	592
Noodles with fired tofu	511	50	242	803
Rice dishes	835	82	395	1312
Fried chicken	513	58	247	818
Vietnamese Kuy teav	530	71	259	860
Fried noodle	374	46	182	602
Pho	312	37	151	500

Fig. 6. Visualization of HOG features with image size 400 × 400, 20 pixels per cells, 1 cells per blocks, 9 orientations.

best parameters by tuning its parameters. We choose ones with the best performance on validation data and apply these best parameters to measure the testing dataset's performance. Precisely, we select the cell size between 20 × 20 and 50 × 50 and the block size from 2 to 6. Finally, we choose the value of bins between 9 and 18.

We compare SVMs with linear, polynomial, and RBF kernels. More clearly, we pick the kernel coefficient γ from 0 to 10, the regularization parameter C from 0 to 10, and the degree of polynomial kernels from 2 to 5. For XGBoost, we select the number of trees from 2 to 10, while the learning rate varies from 0.1 to 1. The maximum depth is from 3 to 12.

CNNs Based Features. We measure the performance of AlexNet, GoogleNet, ResNet50, ResNet101v2, and InceptionResnetv2 methods on our dataset.

In the preprocessing step, we resize the image to the required input size for CNNs and maintain the ratio between the length and the images' width by padding zeros. After that, we normalize the input image and use data augmentation to avoid overfitting. To augment the data, for each batch, we generate new samples by randomly flipping the image, rotating or shifting with the corresponding predefined angles and distance, whose values are 90° and a ratio of 0.2 of total width and height, respectively.

For fine-tuning each chosen model, after loading the model and weights, we replace the last fully connected layer in each model with a randomly initialized one as the number of classes in our experiment is different from that of the ImageNet data.

To train the model, we use Adam optimizer[11] with the initial learning rate is $1e − 3$, and the batch size of 64. During experiments, learning schedule and early stop are exploited. The learning rate can decrease ten times when validation loss does not reduce after three epochs. If validation loss does not drop after ten epochs, the training process is stopped.

4   Experiment Results

Table 3 and Fig. 7 show the performance of all models on the testing dataset. Among two approaches using HOG features, using SVMs for training the corresponding model is better than using XGBoost in terms of top K accuracy, $K = 1, 3, 5$. Also, CNNs perform much better than hand-crafted features, and the performance varies among different models' architecture. The deeper the model is, the better the performance is.

AlexNet has the smaller top K accuracy than GoogleNet, Resnet 50, Resnet101v2, and InceptionResnetv2. Meanwhile, InceptionResnetv2 achieves the highest performance where it gets the top K accuracy ($K = 1, 3, 5$) as 92.0%, 99.0%, and 99.78%, consecutively. Using HOG features and XGBoost model achieves the worst performance, 35.38%, 61.21%, and 75.63%, in terms of top 1, 3, 5 accuracy.

Table 3. Top K accuracy of different models, including hand-craft features and CNNs based features.

Model	Top 1 (%)	Top 3 (%)	Top 5 (%)
HOG + SVM	41.24	67.29	80.25
HOG + XGBoost	35.38	61.21	75.63
AlexNet	49.22	75.41	87.20
GoogleNet	63.36	85.79	94.12
Resnet50	75.0	92.0	97.0
Resnet101v2	87.0	97.0	99.0
InceptionResnetv2	**92.0**	**99.0**	**99.78**

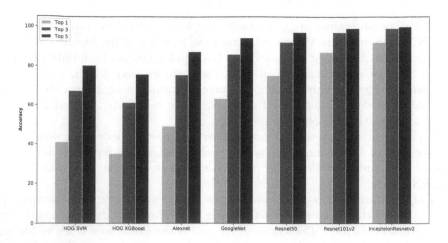

Fig. 7. Top K accuracy of different models in our experiments.

4.1 Discussion

From the experimental results, one can see that hand-craft features are not comparable with CNNs-based features as expected. The main reason is Vietnamese food, in general, are diverse in shapes, therefore, changing the angle of the image disturbs the local features, resulting in poor classification results. The CNN models can achieve superior performance due to their robustness and ability to learn essential features, although the dataset is complicated adaptively. Moreover, with aggressive regularization: using dropout in the pre-trained CNN models can achieve good generalization by having low error rates on both training, validation, and testing datasets.

5 Conclusion

In this paper, we have presented a promising approach for implementing a Vietnamese food recognition system using Convolutional Neural Networks. We also introduce a dataset for Vietnamese food classification with various categories and images. We have conducted extensive experiments using both hand-crafted features and CNNs based features to build the classification system. The experimental results show that InceptionResnetv2 outperforms other techniques of both top 3 and top 5 accuracies. We aim at publishing all implementing codes and datasets later to give an additional contribution to the research community. One can find our codes and datasets at the following Github repository: https:// github.com/BinhMisfit/vietnamese-food-recognition-v2.

Our work is just one of the first steps for building an autonomous system that assists people in managing their food intake to avoid health-related problems. In the future, we plan to collect more samples to extend the current dataset, annotate the food recipes or calorie, continue improving food recognition models, and try implementing an application on mobile devices.

Acknowledgement. This research is funded by Vietnam National University Ho Chi Minh City (VNU-HCM) under grant number NCM2019-18-01. We would like to thank the University of Science, Vietnam National University in Ho Chi Minh City and AISIA Research Lab in Vietnam for supporting us throughout this paper.

References

1. Bay, H., Tuytelaars, T., Van Gool, L.: SURF: speeded up robust features. In: Leonardis, A., Bischof, H., Pinz, A. (eds.) ECCV 2006. LNCS, vol. 3951, pp. 404–417. Springer, Heidelberg (2006). https://doi.org/10.1007/11744023_32
2. Bossard, L., Guillaumin, M., Van Gool, L.: Food-101 – mining discriminative components with random forests. In: Fleet, D., Pajdla, T., Schiele, B., Tuytelaars, T. (eds.) ECCV 2014. LNCS, vol. 8694, pp. 446–461. Springer, Cham (2014). https://doi.org/10.1007/978-3-319-10599-4_29
3. Chen, T., Guestrin, C.: XGBoost: a scalable tree boosting system. In: Proceedings of the 22nd ACM SIGKDD International Conference on Knowledge Discovery and Data Mining, pp. 785–794 (2016)
4. Dalal, N., Triggs, B.: Histograms of oriented gradients for human detection. In: 2005 IEEE Computer Society Conference on Computer Vision and Pattern Recognition (CVPR 2005), vol. 1, pp. 886–893. IEEE (2005)
5. Gibney, M.J., Walsh, M.C.: The future direction of personalised nutrition: my diet, my phenotype, my genes. Proc. Nutr. Soc. **72**(2), 219–225 (2013)
6. Gunn, S.R., et al.: Support vector machines for classification and regression. ISIS Technical report, vol. 14, no. 1, pp. 5–16 (1998)
7. Hassannejad, H., Matrella, G., Ciampolini, P., De Munari, I., Mordonini, M., Cagnoni, S.: Food image recognition using very deep convolutional networks. In: Proceedings of the 2nd International Workshop on Multimedia Assisted Dietary Management, pp. 41–49 (2016)
8. He, K., Zhang, X., Ren, S., Sun, J.: Deep residual learning for image recognition. In: Proceedings of the IEEE Conference on Computer Vision and Pattern Recognition, pp. 770–778 (2016)
9. He, K., Zhang, X., Ren, S., Sun, J.: Identity mappings in deep residual networks. In: Leibe, B., Matas, J., Sebe, N., Welling, M. (eds.) ECCV 2016. LNCS, vol. 9908, pp. 630–645. Springer, Cham (2016). https://doi.org/10.1007/978-3-319-46493-0_38
10. Kawano, Y., Yanai, K.: Food image recognition with deep convolutional features. In: Proceedings of the 2014 ACM International Joint Conference on Pervasive and Ubiquitous Computing: Adjunct Publication, pp. 589–593 (2014)
11. Kingma, D.P., Ba, J.: Adam: a method for stochastic optimization. arXiv preprint arXiv:1412.6980 (2014)
12. Kiourt, C., Pavlidis, G., Markantonatou, S.: Deep learning approaches in food recognition. arXiv preprint arXiv:2004.03357 (2020)
13. Krizhevsky, A., Sutskever, I., Hinton, G.E.: ImageNet classification with deep convolutional neural networks. In: Advances in Neural Information Processing Systems, pp. 1097–1105 (2012)
14. Liu, C., Cao, Yu., Luo, Y., Chen, G., Vokkarane, V., Ma, Y.: DeepFood: deep learning-based food image recognition for computer-aided dietary assessment. In: Chang, C.K., Chiari, L., Cao, Yu., Jin, H., Mokhtari, M., Aloulou, H. (eds.) ICOST 2016. LNCS, vol. 9677, pp. 37–48. Springer, Cham (2016). https://doi.org/10.1007/978-3-319-39601-9_4

15. Lowe, D.G.: Distinctive image features from scale-invariant keypoints. Int. J. Comput. Vision **60**(2), 91–110 (2004). https://doi.org/10.1023/B:VISI.0000029664.99615.94

16. Martinel, N., Foresti, G.L., Micheloni, C.: Wide-slice residual networks for food recognition. In: 2018 IEEE Winter Conference on Applications of Computer Vision (WACV), pp. 567–576. IEEE (2018)

17. Mezgec, S., Koroušić Seljak, B.: NutriNet: a deep learning food and drink image recognition system for dietary assessment. Nutrients **9**(7), 657 (2017)

18. Nair, V., Hinton, G.E.: Rectified linear units improve restricted Boltzmann machines. In: Proceedings of the 27th International Conference on Machine Learning (ICML 2010), pp. 807–814 (2010)

19. Russakovsky, O., et al.: ImageNet large scale visual recognition challenge. Int. J. Comput. Vision **115**(3), 211–252 (2015). https://doi.org/10.1007/s11263-015-0816-y

20. Shimoda, W., Yanai, K.: Learning food image similarity for food image retrieval. In: 2017 IEEE Third International Conference on Multimedia Big Data (BigMM), pp. 165–168. IEEE (2017)

21. Szegedy, C., Ioffe, S., Vanhoucke, V., Alemi, A.A.: Inception-v4, Inception-ResNet and the impact of residual connections on learning. In: Thirty-First AAAI Conference on Artificial Intelligence (2017)

22. Szegedy, C., et al.: Going deeper with convolutions. In: Proceedings of the IEEE Conference on Computer Vision and Pattern Recognition, pp. 1–9 (2015)

23. Van Phat, T., Tien, D.X., Pham, Q., Pham, N., Nguyen, B.T.: Vietnamese food recognition using convolutional neural networks. In: 2017 9th International Conference on Knowledge and Systems Engineering (KSE), pp. 124–129 (2017)

24. Yera Toledo, R., Alzahrani, A.A., Martínez, L.: A food recommender system considering nutritional information and user preferences. IEEE Access **7**, 96695–96711 (2019)

25. Zeiler, M.D., Fergus, R.: Visualizing and understanding convolutional networks. In: Fleet, D., Pajdla, T., Schiele, B., Tuytelaars, T. (eds.) ECCV 2014. LNCS, vol. 8689, pp. 818–833. Springer, Cham (2014). https://doi.org/10.1007/978-3-319-10590-1_53

Bidirectional Non-local Networks
for Object Detection

Xuan-Thuy Vo, Lihua Wen, Tien-Dat Tran, and Kang-Hyun Jo$^{(\boxtimes)}$

School of Electrical Engineering, University of Ulsan, Ulsan, Korea
{xthuy,wenlihua,tdat}@islab.ulsan.ac.kr, acejo@ulsan.ac.kr

Abstract. The convolutional neural networks have reached great achievements in solving the challenging problems of computer vision tasks, such as image classification, object detection, semantic segmentation. The core element of CNNs is the convolution operation, which gathers important features by constructing pixel relationships in a local region. Even though CNNs are universally exploited in visual feature understanding, they still have drawbacks due to that the receptive field is restrained inside local neighborhoods by the physical construction of the convolution layer. The Non-local Network introduces a novel method for modeling long-range dependencies to remedy the local neighborhood problem, which computing the correlations between the query position and all positions to capture global context features and then performing a weighted sum of the features at all positions. As a complementary part of the Non-Local Network, the proposed method called Bidirectional Non-local operation designs the bidirectional relationship, which the informative feature at a specific-query position is gathered and distributed to all positions. Notably, this work relaxes the Bidirectional Non-local complexity by simplifying the network based on the same attention maps for different query positions. To evaluate the effectiveness of the proposed method, the Bidirectional Non-local block is embedded into the backbone network of the detector Mask R-CNN. Without bells and whistles, the integrated network achieves 0.9 points higher Average Precision than Global Context Network on the major baseline.

Keywords: Bidirectional non-local networks · Non-local networks · Object detection

1 Introduction

Object detection is one of the most vital and challenging problems in understanding the visual world. Object detection consists of two tasks. The first task is to classify what objects inside the given images. The second task is to determine where objects locate. Object detection has been widely utilized in many applications, such as autonomous cars, robot vision, intelligent surveillance systems.

© Springer Nature Switzerland AG 2020
N. T. Nguyen et al. (Eds.): ICCCI 2020, LNAI 12496, pp. 491–501, 2020.
https://doi.org/10.1007/978-3-030-63007-2_38

Currently, the rapid development of deep learning techniques, remarkably Convolutional Neural Networks (CNNs), has brought a bright future in the computer vision task (e.g., image classification, object detection, instance segmentation), as an efficient approach for automatically extracting feature representations from the visual world (e.g., images, videos).

Due to the physical design of the convolution operation, the receptive field is constrained to the local regions. To remedy this problem, capturing long-range dependency is helpful for extracting the global contextual feature of visual data. In CNNs, long-range dependencies are modeled by deeply stacking many convolutional layers to enlarge the receptive field. Nonetheless, repeating many convolutional layers is not an effective way, increasing the computational cost. Furthermore, this strategy leads to the difficult optimization that is time-consuming to converge to global points.

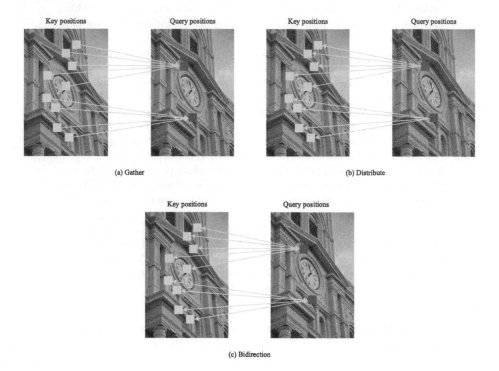

Fig. 1. Illustration of bidirectional information paths. They gather the features of all key positions to form an attention map. Another information flow distributes the information of query positions to all key locations.

The non-local network NLNet [16] introduces the non-local block inspired by non-local operation [1], modeling the long-range dependency. A non-local operation calculates the correlation between a query position and all positions and then gathers the feature of all positions by weighted average (Fig. 1(a)).

Therefore, the relationship between each pairwise is not bidirectional. As a complementary of the non-local block, the proposed method, named BNL, presents the bidirectional information paths (Fig. 1(c)) for understanding complex visual world, not only aggregates the feature of all query position to model global context but also distributes the important information at each position to key positions globally.

The global context network GCNet [2] investigates the simplified version of the non-local block based on the query-independent attention map for all positions. This simplified network dramatically reduces the number of parameters when compared with the non-local network but still maintaining accuracy. Based on the study of the global context network, this paper also relaxes the computation cost of the non-local block but surpasses the efficiency of the global context network and non-local network with only a slight increase of the computational cost.

The Bidirectional Non-local (BNL) block applies to any existing architecture of the backbone networks. To perform the improvement of the proposed method, this block is inserted into the residual block of the ResNet [5]. This work conducts the experiment on the MS-COCO dataset [10] for the object detection task. As mentioned, the proposed method achieves significant improvement, outperforming the Mask R-CNN [4] + GC block, Mask R-CNN + NL block by 0.9% in Average Precision (AP).

2 Related Work

CNNs have been one of the most popular research in the computer vision field since acceptably designing networks guarantee a significant improvement in image classification [5,6,14], object detection [4,7,9–13], segmentation [4,17].

With the accelerated development of deep learning, object detection has improved both accuracy and speed. The goal of object detection is to classify what objects inside the given images and localize where objects on. Based on the number of networks, object detection task consists of two types, the two-stage method, and the one-stage method. The two-stage method [4,12,13] first creates a set of proposals by region proposal networks (i.e., uses the anchor generator on each center of sliding window) and assigns each ground-truth to each proposal identifying negative proposals or positive proposal. Then the second network classifies each anchor by classification networks and refines coordinates of the proposals by learning offset. Whereas the two-stage method, one-stage method instead of region proposal network creating anchors, they densely place anchors with different size and aspect ratio on each position. Then the classification network and localization network form the final detection with a specific class and bounding boxes. Faster R-CNN [13] is the two-stage method, one of the most popular architectures in the computer vision task related to detection. Inspired by the Faster R-CNN method, many architectures such as Mask R-CNN [4], Libra R-CNN [12], TridentNet [7] have introduced. Mask R-CNN adds one branch into Faster R-CNN to predict the mask for the segmentation task. In this paper, the BNL inserts into the backbone ResNet [5] for object detection based on the detector Mask R-CNN method.

Owning to the restricted receptive field of convolution operation, Non-local network [16] proposes a new method capturing long-range dependencies based on the attention mechanism [15] and the non-local filter [1] to extract the global understanding of the visual world. The relationship between key-query position and query position is not bidirectional, gathering the information at each query position from all key-query position. Although this operation is effective, but still a high computational cost. Global context [2] studies the query-independent attention map for all positions. They only use one query position to form one attention map (i.e., corresponding to one output channel of the kernel) that represents all attention maps for other positions. From this characteristic and inspired by SENet [6], GCNet drastically reduces the number of parameters of the non-local block but still maintains the accuracy of non-local networks. Different from the non-local block and global context block, the proposed method introduces a bidirectional non-local (BNL) block that aggregates the feature at each position from all positions vice-versus distributes the information path at each query position to all positions (Fig. 1). Moreover, this work, inheriting the observation of GCNet, relaxes the high computational cost but surpasses the accuracy of the non-local network and global context network with a slight increase of the computational cost.

3   The Proposed Method

3.1   Non-local Network

To design the BNL, this section visits the non-local block [16]. As mentioned in Sects. 1 and 2, the non-local block gathers the feature information at each query position from all key positions. Equation 1 expresses this relationship as

$$\mathbf{z_i} = \mathbf{x_i} + \mathbf{W_z} \sum_{j=1}^{H*W} \omega_{i,j} \left(\mathbf{W_v} \, \mathbf{x_j} \right) \tag{1}$$

where $\mathbf{x_i}$ denotes the query position, $\mathbf{x_j}$ is the key query positions. H*W is the number of key positions in the input feature map. $\mathbf{W_z}$ and $\mathbf{W_v}$ are a 1×1 convolution operation. $\mathbf{z_i}$ presents the output of this block. $\omega_{i,j}$ is the correlation between the query position $\mathbf{x_i}$ and $\mathbf{x_j}$, presents four types, namely Gaussian function, Embedded Gaussian, Dot product, and Concatenation. In this paper, BNL inherits the advantage of Embedded Gaussian that forms the attention map (i.e., highlights the important regions and suppresses the unnecessary parts). The Embedded Gaussian is calculated as Eq. 2.

$$\omega_{i,j} = \frac{exp(\langle \mathbf{W_q x_i}, \, \mathbf{W_k x_j} \rangle)}{\sum_m exp(\langle \mathbf{W_q x_i}, \, \mathbf{W_k x_m} \rangle)} \tag{2}$$

where $\mathbf{W_q}$, $\mathbf{W_k}$ is 1×1 convolution operation. The overall computation of non-local block, as shown in Fig. 2(a). The non-local block models the global contextual feature, which performs a weighted sum from all key positions based on query attention maps to each query position. Hence, the relationship at pairwise positions is not bidirectional. From this observation, the proposed network constructs the bidirectional relationship between query positions and key positions.

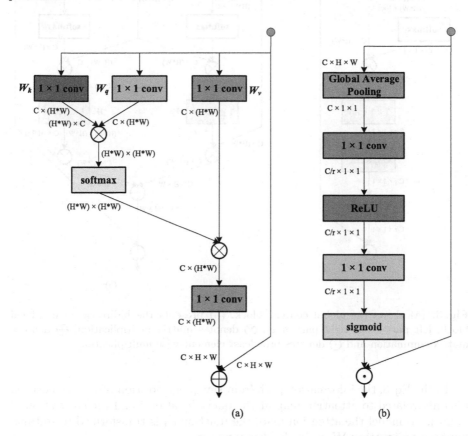

Fig. 2. (a) shows the non-local block. (b) expresses the squeeze-excitation network [6]. ⊗ denotes matrix multiplication, ⊕ denotes matrix summation and ⊙ denotes broadcast element-wise multiplication.

3.2 Bidirectional Non-local Network

In the Eq. 2, there are many key query positions and query positions in the feature map. It leads to a large number of the computation between $\mathbf{x_i}$ and $\mathbf{x_j}$. Hence, the non-local block is simplified by approximation strategy. The first, the function $\omega_{i,j}$ is converted as

$$\omega_{i,j} \approx \omega_i = \frac{exp(\mathbf{W_q x_i})}{\sum_m exp(\langle \mathbf{W_q x_i}, \mathbf{W_k x_m} \rangle)} \quad (3)$$

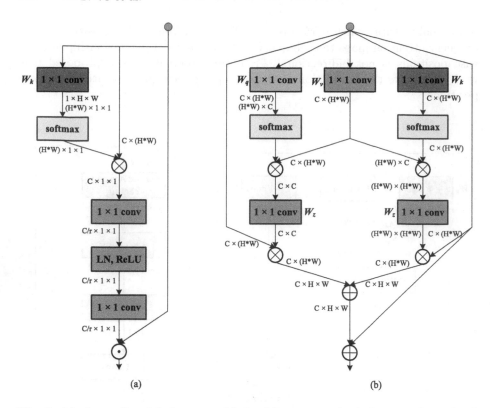

Fig. 3. (a) shows the global context block. (b) presents the bidirectional non-local block, left part is ω_i, right part is ω_j. $\otimes$ denotes matrix multiplication, $\oplus$ denotes matrix summation and $\odot$ denotes broadcast element-wise multiplication.

In the Eq. 3, the information path from key query position j to query position i is only related to attention map at the query location i and the correlation of i and j. To model the attention map, the function ω_i is transformed to softmax function by ignoring $\mathbf{W_q x_i}$ in the denominator.

$$\omega_{i,j} \approx \omega_i = \frac{exp(\mathbf{W_q x_i})}{\sum_m exp(\mathbf{W_k x_m})} \qquad (4)$$

Correspondingly, the function $\omega_{i,j}$ is simplified as

$$\omega_{i,j} \approx \omega_j = \frac{exp(\mathbf{W_k x_j})}{\sum_m exp(\mathbf{W_k x_m})} \qquad (5)$$

In the Eq. 5, the information path from key query position j to query position i is only related to attention map at the key query location j and the correlation of i and j. Especially, the function ω_j is the same formula of the global context block [2] (Fig. 3(a)). It means that the global context block is a special case of the proposed method named bidirectional non-local network (BNL).

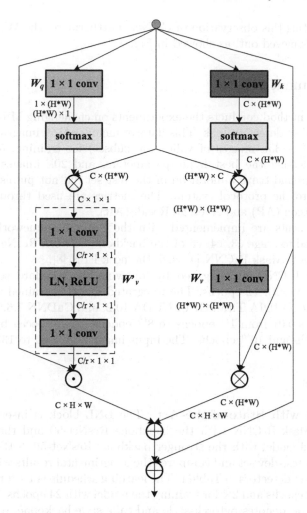

Fig. 4. Illustration of simplified bidirectional non-local block. $\otimes$ denotes matrix multiplication, $\oplus$ denotes matrix summation and $\odot$ denotes broadcast element-wise multiplication.

Finally, the bidirectional information path is formed as

$$\mathbf{z_i} = \mathbf{x_i} + \mathbf{W_z} \sum_{j=1}^{H*W} \omega_i \left(\mathbf{W_v}\, \mathbf{x_j} \right) + \mathbf{W_z} \sum_{j=1}^{H*W} \omega_j \left(\mathbf{W_v}\, \mathbf{x_j} \right) \tag{6}$$

The second term shows that each query position gathers the feature from other positions. The third term presents that each query position distributes the feature to other positions. Figure 3(b) shows the bidirectional non-local block.

Notably, the global context network [2] proposed the query-independent attention map for all positions. The proposed method relaxes the computational cost by inheriting this observation of GCNet. Furthermore, the $\mathbf{W_z}$ is removed, and the $\mathbf{W_v}$ is moved out, as showed in Fig. 4.

4 Experiment Setup

The proposed method conducts the experiments on challenging MS-COCO 2017 [10] for the object detection task. This dataset includes 115k images (80k images of training set + 35k images of validation subset) for training, 5k validation images for selecting the best hyper-parameters, and 20k images for testing. Because the ground-truth annotation of the test set did not publish, the result is submitted to the protocol system. The metrics are used through standard Average Precision (AP) and Average Recall (AR).

All experiments are implemented with the Pytorch framework. The BNL block is applied to stage c3, c4, c5 of the backbone network ResNet-50 [5]. The object detector is Mask R-CNN [4] with the neck FPN [8].

The Mask R-CNN is configured by following the standard setting of the mmdetection [3] with 12 epochs. The integrated model is trained with a batch size of 8 on one NVIDIA Titan GPU, CUDA 10.2, and CuDNN 7.6.5. The initial learning rate is 0.01 from 1st epochs to 8th epochs. It will decay by a factor of 10 at 9th epochs and 10th epochs. The input image is resized to 1333×800.

5 Results

Comparison with State-of-the-Art. The BNL block is inserted into the architecture Mask R-CNN with the backbone ResNet-50 and the neck FPN. The integrated model with the stronger backbone ResNet-50 + BNL evaluates on MS-COCO test-dev set and compares the experimental results with the state-of-the-art object detectors in Table 1. The learning schedule is $1\times$ for training the model with 12 epochs and $2\times$ for training the model with 24 epochs. The ResNet-50, ResNet-50(a) denotes pytorch-style and caffe-style backbone, respectively.

The proposed method, BNL block embedded into the backbone network ResNet-50 (i.e., ResNet-50+BNL) of the object detectors Mask R-CNN achieves 39.3 AP, which increases 0.9% higher AP than GCNet with the backbone ResNet-50+GC achieves 38.4 AP without bells and whistles. Especially, the integrated method outperforms the baseline Mask R-CNN with an improvement rate of 2%. Furthermore, the proposed method has surpassed most object detectors with the same backbone, neck FPN, and learning schedule, e.g., AP of Faster R-CNN [13] with ResNet-50 is 36.4, AP of RetinaNet [9] is 35.6, AP of [4] is 37.3. The performance on test-dev set pointed out that the strong baselines are boosted by a large margin when applying the GNL block to stage c3, c4, c5 of the backbone ResNet-50. These results prove the efficiency of the proposed method.

Figure 5 visualizes the qualitative results of the proposed method on the MS-COCO validation set with three levels of the dataset.

Table 1. Results on test-dev set 2017.

Method	Backbone	Schedule	AP	AP^{50}	AP^{75}	AP^S	AP^M	AP^L
Faster R-CNN [13]	ResNet-50	1×	36.4	58.4	39.1	21.5	40.0	46.6
Faster R-CNN	ResNet-50(a)	1×	36.6	58.5	39.2	20.7	40.5	47.9
Faster R-CNN	ResNet-50	2×	37.7	59.2	41.1	21.9	41.4	48.7
RetinaNet [9]	ResNet-50	1×	35.6	55.5	38.3	20.0	39.6	46.8
RetinaNet	ResNet-50(a)	1×	35.8	55.5	38.3	20.1	39.5	47.7
RetinaNet	ResNet-50	2×	36.4	56.3	38.7	19.3	39.9	48.9
Mask R-CNN [4]	ResNet-50	1×	37.3	59.0	40.2	21.9	40.9	48.1
Mask R-CNN	ResNet-50(a)	1×	37.4	58.9	40.4	21.7	41.0	49.1
Mask R-CNN	ResNet-50	2×	38.5	59.9	41.8	22.6	42.0	50.5
GCNet [2]	ResNet-50+GC	1×	38.4	59.3	41.8	21.6	41.7	49.8
Ours	**ResNet-50+BNL**	**1×**	**39.3**	**61.6**	**42.7**	**22.8**	**42.0**	**49.2**

Fig. 5. The qualitative results of the proposed method on MS-COCO validation set.

Ablation Study. This work studies the importance of each component in the BNL block. The proposed method consists of gathered information block ω_i and distributed information block ω_j. The first, the BNL module investigates the efficiency of the gathered information block by removing the distributed information block and otherwise.

Table 2 analyzes the impacts of each component in the BNL module. This experiment gradually inserts the gathered block and distributed block on the ResNet-50 Mask R-CNN baseline. The gathered component inheriting the advantage of the global context block improves 1.1% higher AP than the ResNet-50 Mask R-CNN baseline. The distributed component increases 0.5% from 37.2 AP to 37.7 AP. This block is lightweight due to that this component only used two 1 × 1 convs with a little of parameter. When combining gathered block and distributed components into the BNL block, the accuracy of the integrated model is gained by a large margin of 1.9% over the baseline.

Table 2. The impacts of each component in the BNL block. The result reports on the validation set.

Gathered	Distributed	AP^{bbox}	AP^{50}	AP^{75}	AP^{mask}	AP^{50}	AP^{75}
		37.2	59.0	40.1	34.8	55.4	35.9
✓		38.1	60.0	41.2	34.9	56.5	37.2
	✓	37.7	59.4	40.6	34.5	56.0	36.1
✓	✓	39.1	61.4	42.3	35.3	57.7	37.3

6   Conclusion

In this paper, the proposed Bidirectional Non-local (BNL) block studies the effectiveness of the gathered information block and the distributed information block. The gathered information block gathers the feature of all query position to capture long-range dependencies. The distributed block distributes important information at each position to key positions globally. By fusing two information propagation flows, the proposed methods not only encodes long-range dependencies by computing the correlation between each pair of query position but also considers the relative location of it. The experimental results demonstrate the significant improvement of the BNL block when applying to the backbone ResNet-50 of detectors Mask R-CNN baseline. Without bells and whistles, the integrated model brings 0.9 points higher AP than the GCNet and 2.0 points higher AP than the Mask R-CNN baseline.

Acknowledgement. This work was supported by the National Research Foundation of Korea (NRF) grant funded by the Korea government. (MSIT) (2020R1A2C2008972).

References

1. Buades, A., Coll, B., Morel, J.M.: A non-local algorithm for image denoising. In: 2005 IEEE Computer Society Conference on Computer Vision and Pattern Recognition (CVPR 2005), vol. 2, pp. 60–65. IEEE (2005)
2. Cao, Y., Xu, J., Lin, S., Wei, F., Hu, H.: GCNet: non-local networks meet squeeze-excitation networks and beyond. In: Proceedings of the IEEE International Conference on Computer Vision Workshops (2019)
3. Chen, K., et al.: MMDetection: Open MMLab detection toolbox and benchmark. arXiv preprint arXiv:1906.07155 (2019)
4. He, K., Gkioxari, G., Dollár, P., Girshick, R.: Mask R-CNN. In: Proceedings of the IEEE International Conference on Computer Vision, pp. 2961–2969 (2017)

5. He, K., Zhang, X., Ren, S., Sun, J.: Deep residual learning for image recognition. In: Proceedings of the IEEE Conference on Computer Vision and Pattern Recognition, pp. 770–778 (2016)
6. Hu, J., Shen, L., Sun, G.: Squeeze-and-excitation networks. In: Proceedings of the IEEE Conference on Computer Vision and Pattern Recognition, pp. 7132–7141 (2018)
7. Li, Y., Chen, Y., Wang, N., Zhang, Z.: Scale-aware trident networks for object detection. In: Proceedings of the IEEE International Conference on Computer Vision, pp. 6054–6063 (2019)
8. Lin, T.Y., Dollár, P., Girshick, R., He, K., Hariharan, B., Belongie, S.: Feature pyramid networks for object detection. In: Proceedings of the IEEE Conference on Computer Vision and Pattern Recognition, pp. 2117–2125 (2017)
9. Lin, T.Y., Goyal, P., Girshick, R., He, K., Dollár, P.: Focal loss for dense object detection. In: Proceedings of the IEEE International Conference on Computer Vision, pp. 2980–2988 (2017)
10. Lin, T.-Y., et al.: Microsoft COCO: common objects in context. In: Fleet, D., Pajdla, T., Schiele, B., Tuytelaars, T. (eds.) ECCV 2014. LNCS, vol. 8693, pp. 740–755. Springer, Cham (2014). https://doi.org/10.1007/978-3-319-10602-1_48
11. Liu, W., et al.: SSD: single shot MultiBox detector. In: Leibe, B., Matas, J., Sebe, N., Welling, M. (eds.) ECCV 2016. LNCS, vol. 9905, pp. 21–37. Springer, Cham (2016). https://doi.org/10.1007/978-3-319-46448-0_2
12. Pang, J., Chen, K., Shi, J., Feng, H., Ouyang, W., Lin, D.: Libra R-CNN: towards balanced learning for object detection. In: Proceedings of the IEEE Conference on Computer Vision and Pattern Recognition, pp. 821–830 (2019)
13. Ren, S., He, K., Girshick, R., Sun, J.: Faster R-CNN: towards real-time object detection with region proposal networks. In: Advances in Neural Information Processing Systems, pp. 91–99 (2015)
14. Russakovsky, O., et al.: ImageNet large scale visual recognition challenge. Int. J. Comput. Vision 115(3), 211–252 (2015). https://doi.org/10.1007/s11263-015-0816-y
15. Vaswani, A., et al.: Attention is all you need. In: Advances in Neural Information Processing Systems, pp. 5998–6008 (2017)
16. Wang, X., Girshick, R., Gupta, A., He, K.: Non-local neural networks. In: Proceedings of the IEEE Conference on Computer Vision and Pattern Recognition, pp. 7794–7803 (2018)
17. Zhao, H., et al.: PSANet: point-wise spatial attention network for scene parsing. In: Ferrari, V., Hebert, M., Sminchisescu, C., Weiss, Y. (eds.) ECCV 2018. LNCS, vol. 11213, pp. 270–286. Springer, Cham (2018). https://doi.org/10.1007/978-3-030-01240-3_17

Computer Vision Techniques

Automated Grading in Diabetic Retinopathy Using Image Processing and Modified EfficientNet

Hung N. Pham[1], Ren Jie Tan[2], Yu Tian Cai[2], Shahril Mustafa[2],
Ngan Chong Yeo[2], Hui Juin Lim[2], Trang T. T. Do[3], Binh P. Nguyen[4(✉)],
and Matthew Chin Heng Chua[2]

[1] Hanoi University of Science and Technology, Hanoi, Vietnam
hungpn@soict.hust.edu.vn
[2] National University of Singapore, Singapore, Singapore
mattchua@nus.edu.sg
[3] Wellington Institute of Technology, Lower Hutt, New Zealand
trang.do@weltec.ac.nz
[4] Victoria University of Wellington, Wellington, New Zealand
binh.p.nguyen@vuw.ac.nz

Abstract. We present our approach in achieving the Quadratic Weighted Kappa (QWK) score of 0.90 on the retinal image dataset from the APTOS 2019 Blindness Detection Kaggle challenge. We analysed various image preprocessing techniques then classified the images with a modified EfficientNet deep learning model. Our image preprocessing techniques helped to bring out the cell loss to the retina, highlight blood vessels, and centering the retina. We found that subtracting the average local color using a Gaussian mask was the most effective preprocessing technique, improving the QWK score by 0.03. We modified the EfficientNet-B5 network with the Batch Normalization layers replaced with Group Normalization and trained the network using the Rectified Adam (RAdam) optimizer. Group Normalization was found to do better for the batch size of 4 and RAdam trained the network better than Adam. This led to an increment of the QWK score by 0.02.

Keywords: Diabetic Retinopathy · Classification · Retinal images · EfficientNet · Deep learning

1 Introduction

Over the last two decades, decreasing physical activity and increasing obesity, combined with a constantly aging population has led to the proliferation of diabetes. Diabetes currently affects one in eleven adults [1,2] and is expected to double by year 2030 [3]. One of the major diseases resulting from diabetes is Diabetic Retinopathy (DR), which is the most common cause of blindness in adults [4]. Although treatment for the disease is usually effective when detected

© Springer Nature Switzerland AG 2020
N. T. Nguyen et al. (Eds.): ICCCI 2020, LNAI 12496, pp. 505–515, 2020.
https://doi.org/10.1007/978-3-030-63007-2_39

early, symptoms are rarely obvious until late in the disease process. In fact, fewer than half of DR patients are aware of their condition before visual impairment occurs [5]. Thus, early detection of this disease has been of interest to many healthcare professionals in recent years. Traditionally, ophthalmologists would determine the presence and severity of DR by visually recognizing its features such as microaneurysms, red lesions, and white exudates. However, this process is time consuming [6] and diagnosis of severity can be subjective with differing views across various studies [7]. To address these shortcomings, considerable research has been put into the design and implementation of automated solutions for retinal diseases diagnoses from colour images [8,9]. Generally, such automated solutions are made up of a series of operations, with low-level image processing operations acting as a basis for higher level recognition tasks. A typical sequence would consist of preprocessing the images, followed by image segmentation, feature extraction and finally classification. In this paper, we adapted a state-of-the-art deep learning architecture to accurately classify the presence and severity of DR in fundus images.

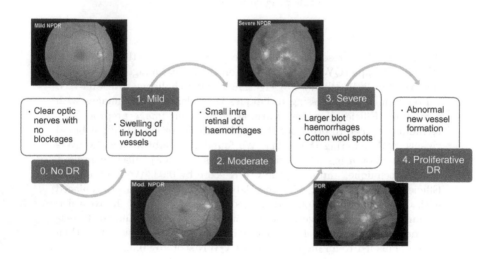

Fig. 1. Stages of diabetic retinopathy.

Figure 1 shows stages of DR with corresponding labelled sample images.

The paper will be organized as follows. Section 2 provides a review of current research in automatic detection of DR. Section 3 introduces the dataset used and the preprocessing techniques applied. Section 4 presents our classification model for retina images and provides a detailed explanation on EfficientNet, Rectified Adam and Group Normalization techniques used in the classification model. Section 5 then provides our experimental results. Section 6 concludes the study and discusses some potential improvements which can be done in future.

2   Literature Review

2.1   Preprocessing of Retina Images

Good quality retinal images are necessary for any meaningful analysis to be carried out effectively. However, studies have shown that 12% of retinal images cannot be analysed because of inferior quality [10]. One of the main reasons for this is the non-uniform illumination and poor contrast across images, which alters the local statistical characteristics of image intensity including mean, median and variance. This reduces the reliability of subsequent feature extraction and classification techniques applied to the images [9]. To combat this problem, different techniques have been used by various authors. Histogram specification techniques were usually used as the first step of preprocessing in some studies [11]. The distribution of each colour is interpolated to match with a reference model obtained from an image deemed by an expert to be outstanding in terms of contrast. However, one limitation is that there is a potential for specific lesion characteristics to be masked within the histogram. Cree et al. proposes a solution to this by using both shade correction and histogram normalization [12].

Retinal images acquired from clinics often have a higher contrast in the center of the image with lower contrast moving outwards from the center [13]. Local contrast enhancement methods are often used to enhance the local contrast in small regions. One popular technique used is the contrast limited adaptive histogram equalization (CLAHE) [14]. While CLAHE uses small windows as local transforms, Sinthanayothin et al. proposed an adaptive contrast enhancement transformation, which is dependent on mean and variance of the intensities [15]. Other contrast enhancement techniques include multilevel histogram equalization [16], colour remapping after single channel enhancement [17], and more recently, using high-pass filtering and mathematical modelling of the non-uniformity followed by subtraction from the observed image.

2.2   Segmentation of Optic Disk and Blood Vessels

Localization and segmentation of the optic disk is a key component of DR classification as it is connected to the major retinal vessels. Segmentation of the disk also helps by establishing a reference point for computation and vessel tracking methods [18]. The size and shape of the optic disk varies amongst individuals, but a clear distinguishing feature is that it is brighter than the surrounding area with a clearly visible elliptical contour. However, the optic disk is often obscured by vessel edges, yellow lesions and bright features [19], making segmentation a challenging task. Some of the common segmentation techniques explored include using the Hough transform [20], the principle component analysis (PCA) [21, 22], and neural networks [23]. Despite the great amount of research into this field, the main drawback is that all these methods require domain expert input, which is expensive and time consuming, thus further highlighting the need for a fully automated recognition system.

2.3 Automatic Classification Models

Several studies have been carried out using various classification techniques. These are presented in Table 1.

Table 1. Literature review of classification models

Study	Description	Performance
Grassmann et al. [24]	Random Forest ensemble of 6 different neural network architectures	QWK 0.92
Krause et al. [25]	Deep convolutional neural network	QWK 0.84
Habib et al. [26]	Tree Ensemble classifier	ROC 0.415
Gulshan et al. [27]	Inception-v3	Sensitivity 97.5%, Specificity 93.4%
Akram et al. [28]	Hybrid	Accuracy 99.4%
Oliveira et al. [29]	Two-step approach	Sensitivity 95.8%, Specificity 63.2
Ram et al. [30]	Similarity computation is applied using an SVM	Sensitivity 0.706%, ROC 0.264
Walter et al. [31]	Bayesian risk minimization with kernel density estimation	Sensitivity 88.5%
Usher et al. [13]	Unspecified neural network	Sensitivity 94.8%, Specificity 52.8%
Nguyen et al. [32]	Transfer learning	Accuracy 82%, Sensitivity 80%, Specificity 82%

3 Preprocessing of Retina Images

3.1 Dataset and Implementation

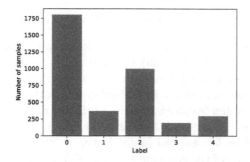

Fig. 2. Distribution of classes in the training set.

Experiments are conducted in this paper using a dataset from Kaggle [33]. 3662 (training set) and 1928 (test set) retina images are provided by Aravind Eye Hospital, which obtained using fundus photography. The test set is obscured as part of the competition's scoring and only used for testing performance of the model. A clinician has rated each image for the severity of diabetic retinopathy, from 0 (no DR), 1 (mild), 2 (moderate), 3 (severe) and 4 (proliferative DR). The distribution of these labels in the training set is shown in Fig. 2. The training set is highly unbalanced with 1805 images rated "0", 370 images rated "1", 999 images rated "2", 193 images rated "3" and 295 images rated "4". The images in the dataset differ widely in resolution, contrast, lighting conditions and dynamic range as different personnel using different equipment took the images.

Fig. 3. Sampled images from each severity class, from "0" leftmost to "4" at rightmost. Note the range difference in resolution and lighting conditions.

Figure 3 shows a series of sampled images from each severity class from label "0" leftmost to "4" rightmost.

3.2   Applying Preprocessing Techniques on Retina Images

To bring out the cell loss to the retina and highlight blood vessels more clearly, image colour editing is needed. There is also a need to standardize the resolution and shapes. We implemented an image preprocessing flow before feeding them to the model:

1. Crop out black non-useful areas from the original images
2. Perform a circular crop around the image center
3. Resize images to 600 × 600 pixels
4. Create a Gaussian blur mask of the image from above step
5. Merge the images from step 3 and 4 together; however, step 4 image has negative weights attached to it

This image processing flow effectively subtracts the local colour around each pixel. It brings out the cell losses, damages and blood vessels more clearly.

Figure 4 shows the result images of labelled samples after the preprocessing V1 which includes the operations: subtract local average colour and circular cropping.

Figure 5 shows the result images of labelled samples after the preprocessing V2 which includes the operations: subtract Gaussian blurred background with alternate mask parameters and alternate cropping (closer to original images and minimal warping)

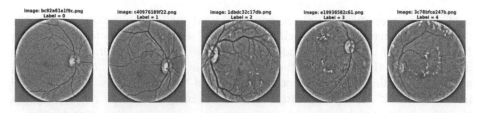

Fig. 4. Preprocessing V1: Subtract local average colour + Circular cropping.

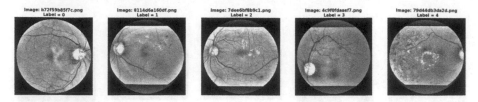

Fig. 5. Preprocessing V2: Subtract Gaussian blurred background with alternate mask parameters and alternate cropping (closer to original images and minimal warping).

Figure 6 shows result images of labelled samples after the of preprocessing V3 with the operation: applying contrast limited adaptive histogram equalization (CLAHE) on colour images including steps:

1. Convert to LAB colour space,
2. Apply CLAHE to L layer
3. Merge back, then convert back to RGB

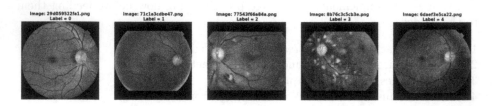

Fig. 6. Preprocessing V3: Contrast limited adaptive histogram equalization (CLAHE).

Figure 7 shows the result images of labelled samples after the preprocessing V4 which includes the operation: subtract local average colour + circular cropping + Kirsch operator (edge detection).

Figure 8 is applying CLAHE first, then subtracting local colour to bring out features.

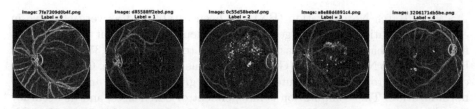

Fig. 7. Preprocessing V4: Subtract local average colour + Circular cropping + Kirsch operator (edge detection).

Fig. 8. Applying CLAHE first, then subtracting local colour to bring out features.

4   Classifying Retina Images with Modified EfficientNet

After preprocessing retina images, we built the classifying model by using a modified EfficientNet architecture. We evaluated the performance of EfficientNet-B5 [34] with modifications in its architecture on the data set of pre-processed retina images. The changes include

1. Use of RAdam as learning rate optimizer
2. Replaced all Batch Normalization layers with Group Normalization layers [35]
3. Change the final classification layer to predict a value from 0 to 4

EfficientNetis first conceptualized as way to scale up convolutional neural networks (CNN) in a structured way, using a compound coefficient, in order to increase accuracy while making the best use of available computing resources. The baseline network (EfficientNet-B0) is developed by performing a neural network architecture search using the AutoML MNAS [36] framework. The resulting architecture uses mobile inverted bottleneck convolution (MBConv), similar to MobileNetV2 and MnasNet, but is slightly larger due to an increased computational budget.

Rectified Adam (RAdam) [37] is an improvement of Adam [38]. Adam has a problematically large learning rate variance in the early stages of training, which can lead to potentially bad local optima. RAdam rectifies the adaptive learning rate, through a dynamic algorithm, so that the variance is consistent. This reduces the need for manual tuning involved with a warm-up during training. In addition, RAdam is shown to be more robust to learning rate variations and provides better generalization on a variety of datasets and when applied to a variety of neural network architectures [37].

While Batch Normalization (BN) has been established as very effective in easing optimization and convergences of deep neural networks, it requires a sufficiently large batch size (at least 16) in order to be accurate [35]. For smaller batches, Group Normalization (GN) [35] serves as an alternative. GN divides the channels into groups and computes within each group the mean and variance for normalization. This computation is independent of batch sizes, and its accuracy is stable in a wide range of batch sizes. On ResNet-50 trained in ImageNet, GN has 10.6% lower error than its BN counterpart when using a batch size of 2.

With modified EfficientNet-B5, we trained the model on the training set. The final prediction is a rounded integer value for the each of the 5 severity classes.

5   Experimental Results

5.1   Evaluation Metrics

The same metric, Quadratic Weighted Kappa (QWK) [39], was used in this experiment as well as in the Kaggle competition. QWK compensates for classifications that may be due to chance. It measures the agreement between the predictions and the actual severity, with the best score being 1.0 and worst being zero. The formula to compute QWK score is

$$QWK = \frac{1}{n} \sum_{i=1}^{n} (Y_i - \hat{Y}_i)^2, \tag{1}$$

where n is the number of data points, Y_i represents observed values, and $\hat{Y}_i$ represents predicted values.

We benchmarked our proposed model against EfficientNet-B5 with its default design, and ResNet-50, a commonly used image classification design with similar number of parameters (20+ million).

5.2   Results

Table 2 shows the QWK scores of the different models on the Kaggle dataset. Comparing the performance of Resnet-50 and EfficientNet-B5, without any modifications, EfficientNet-B5 has better performance of 0.03 QWK score. EfficientNet architecture is shown here to perform better in real life dataset, while shown in its original paper also performing better in synthetic common benchmark datasets such as ImageNet.

Image processing, through the subtraction of local color average of each pixel, improved the prediction performance by 0.03 QWK. Applying modification to the training optimizer (RAdam) and normalization layers (Group Normalization) also improved the QWK score by 0.02.

Table 2. Performance of different models on the Kaggle dataset

Architecture	Modification	Performance (QWK)
Resnet50	None (baseline)	0.82
Resnet50	Image preprocessing	0.88
EfficientNet-B5	None (baseline)	0.85
Modified EfficientNet-B5	Image preprocessing	0.90

6   Discussion and Conclusion

In this paper, we demonstrated an application of a state-of-the-art image classification model on real life medical dataset. Through image preprocessing using local average colour subtraction, more damages to the retina are revealed and hence increasing the QWK score by 0.03. Further improvement is done through optimization of the training optimizer and normalization layers.

Our work can be extended by using other deep learning architectures such as the capsule neural networks [40] which are suitable for small datasets [41] and by applying ensemble learning with different classifiers on the last feature map of the deep learning network. Ensemble learning often works well when the classifiers are diverse.

References

1. The International Diabetes Federation: IDF Diabetes Atlas 7th Edition (2015)
2. Nguyen, B.P., Pham, H.N., et al.: Predicting the onset of type 2 diabetes using wide and deep learning with electronic health records. Comput. Methods Programs Biomed. **182**, 105055 (2019)
3. Wild, S., Roglic, G., et al.: Global prevalence of diabetes: estimates for the year 2000 and projections for 2030. Diabetes Care **27**(5), 1047–1053 (2004)
4. Wilkinson, C., Ferris III, F.L., et al.: Proposed international clinical diabetic retinopathy and diabetic macular edema disease severity scales. Ophthalmology **110**(9), 1677–1682 (2003)
5. Beagley, J., Guariguata, L., et al.: Global estimates of undiagnosed diabetes in adults. Diabetes Res. Clin. Pract. **103**(2), 150–160 (2014)
6. Ozieh, M.N., Bishu, K.G., et al.: Trends in health care expenditure in US adults with diabetes: 2002–2011. Diabetes Care **38**(10), 1844–1851 (2015)
7. Sellahewa, L., Simpson, C., Maharajan, P., Duffy, J., Idris, I.: Grader agreement, and sensitivity and specificity of digital photography in a community optometry-based diabetic eye screening program. Clin. Ophthalmol. **8**, 1345 (2014)
8. Mookiah, M.R.K., Acharya, U.R., et al.: Computer-aided diagnosis of diabetic retinopathy: a review. Comput. Biol. Med. **43**(12), 2136–2155 (2013)
9. Winder, R.J., Morrow, P.J., et al.: Algorithms for digital image processing in diabetic retinopathy. Comput. Med. Imaging Graph. **33**(8), 608–622 (2009)
10. Teng, T., Leey, M., Claremont, D.: Progress towards automated diabetic ocular screening: a review of image analysis and intelligent systems for diabetic retinopathy. Med. Biol. Eng. Comput. **40**(1), 2–13 (2002)

11. Wisaeng, K., Hiransakolwong, N., Pothiruk, E.: Automatic detection of retinal exudates using a support vector machine. Appl. Med. Inform. **32**(1), 33–42 (2013)
12. Cree, M.J., Gamble, E., Cornforth, D.J.: Colour normalisation to reduce inter-patient and intra-patient variability in microaneurysm detection in colour retinal images. In: APRS Workshop on Digital Image Computing, pp. 163–168, February 2005
13. Usher, D., Dumskyj, M., et al.: Automated detection of diabetic retinopathy in digital retinal images: a tool for diabetic retinopathy screening. Diabetic Med. **21**(1), 84–90 (2004)
14. Zuiderveld, K.: Contrast limited adaptive histograph equalization. In: Graphic Gems IV, pp. 474–485. Academic Press Professional, San Diego (1994)
15. Sinthanayothin, C., Boyce, J.F., Cook, H.L., Williamson, T.H.: Automated locali-sation of the optic disc, fovea, and retinal blood vessels from digital colour fundus images. Br. J. Ophthalmol. **83**(8), 902–910 (1999)
16. Rapantzikos, K., Zervakis, M., Balas, K.: Detection and segmentation of drusen deposits on human retina: potential in the diagnosis of age-related macular degen-eration. Med. Image Anal. **7**(1), 95–108 (2003)
17. Marrugo, A.G., Millán, M.S.: Retinal image analysis: preprocessing and feature extraction. J. Phys. Conf. Ser. **274**, 012039 (2011)
18. Lowell, J., Hunter, A., et al.: Optic nerve head segmentation. IEEE Trans. Med. Imaging **23**(2), 256–264 (2004)
19. Goldbaum, M., Moezzi, S., et al.: Automated diagnosis and image understanding with object extraction, object classification, and inferencing in retinal images. In: Proceedings of the 3rd IEEE International Conference on Image Processing, vol. 3, pp. 695–698 (1996)
20. Ege, B.M., Hejlesen, O.K., et al.: Screening for diabetic retinopathy using computer based image analysis and statistical classification. Comput. Methods Programs Biomed. **62**(3), 165–175 (2000)
21. Li, H., Chutatape, O.: Automated feature extraction in color retinal images by a model based approach. IEEE Trans. Biomed. Eng. **51**(2), 246–254 (2004)
22. Sánchez, C.I., Hornero, R., Lopez, M.I., Poza, J.: Retinal image analysis to detect and quantify lesions associated with diabetic retinopathy. In: Proceedings of the 26th Annual International Conference in Medicine and Biology, vol. 1, pp. 1624–1627 (2004)
23. Gardner, G., Keating, D., Williamson, T.H., Elliott, A.T.: Automatic detection of diabetic retinopathy using an artificial neural network: a screening tool. Br. J. Ophthalmol. **80**(11), 940–944 (1996)
24. Grassmann, F., Mengelkamp, J., et al.: A deep learning algorithm for prediction of age-related eye disease study severity scale for age-related macular degeneration from color fundus photography. Ophthalmology **125**(9), 1410–1420 (2018)
25. Krause, J., Gulshan, V., et al.: Grader variability and the importance of refer-ence standards for evaluating machine learning models for diabetic retinopathy. Ophthalmology **125**(8), 1264–1272 (2018)
26. Habib, M., Welikala, R., et al.: Detection of microaneurysms in retinal images using an ensemble classifier. Inform. Med. Unlocked **9**, 44–57 (2017)
27. Gulshan, V., Peng, L., et al.: Development and validation of a deep learning algo-rithm for detection of diabetic retinopathy in retinal fundus photographs. JAMA **316**(22), 2402–2410 (2016)
28. Akram, M.U., Khalid, S., Khan, S.A.: Identification and classification of microa-neurysms for early detection of diabetic retinopathy. Pattern Recogn. **46**(1), 107–116 (2013)

29. Oliveira, C.M., Cristovao, L.M., Ribeiro, M.L., Abreu, J.R.F.: Improved automated screening of diabetic retinopathy. Ophthalmologica **226**(4), 191–197 (2011)
30. Ram, K., Joshi, G.D., Sivaswamy, J.: A successive clutter-rejection-based approach for early detection of diabetic retinopathy. IEEE Trans. Biomed. Eng. **58**(3), 664–673 (2010)
31. Walter, T., Massin, P., et al.: Automatic detection of microaneurysms in color fundus images. Med. Image Anal. **11**(6), 555–566 (2007)
32. Nguyen, Q.H., Muthuraman, R., et al.: Diabetic retinopathy detection using deep learning. In: Proceedings of the 4th International Conference on Machine Learning and Soft Computing, pp. 103–107 (2020)
33. APTOS: APTOS 2019 blindness detection (2019). https://www.kaggle.com/c/aptos2019-blindness-detection
34. Tan, M., Le, Q.V.: EfficientNet: rethinking model scaling for convolutional neural networks. arXiv preprint arXiv:1905.11946, November 2019
35. Wu, Y., He, K.: Group normalization. In: Ferrari, V., Hebert, M., Sminchisescu, C., Weiss, Y. (eds.) ECCV 2018. LNCS, vol. 11217, pp. 3–19. Springer, Cham (2018). https://doi.org/10.1007/978-3-030-01261-8_1
36. Tan, M., Chen, B., et al.: MnasNet: platform-aware neural architecture search for mobile. arXiv preprint arXiv:1807.11626, July 2018
37. Liu, L., Jiang, H., et al.: On the variance of the adaptive learning rate and beyond. arXiv preprint arXiv:1908.03265, August 2019
38. Kingma, D.P., Ba, J.: Adam: a method for stochastic optimization. arXiv preprint arXiv:1412.6980, December 2014
39. Ben-David, A.: Comparison of classification accuracy using Cohen's Weighted Kappa. Expert Syst. Appl. **34**(2), 825–832 (2008)
40. Sabour, S., Frosst, N., Hinton, G.E.: Dynamic routing between capsules. In: Guyon, I., et al. (eds.) Advances in Neural Information Processing Systems 30, pp. 3856–3866 (2017)
41. Nguyen, B.P., Nguyen, Q.H., et al.: iProDNA-CapsNet: identifying protein-DNA binding residues using capsule neural networks. BMC Bioinformatics **20**(Suppl 23), 1–12 (2019)

Retinal Image Segmentation Through Valley Emphasis Thresholding of the Gabor Filter Response

Mandlenkosi Victor Gwetu$^{(\boxtimes)}$, Jules-Raymond Tapamo, and Serestina Viriri

University of KwaZulu-Natal, Private Bag X54001, Durban 4000, South Africa
gwetum@ukzn.ac.za

Abstract. The quest for automated diagnosis of diabetic retinopathy continues due to increasing prevalence coupled with scarcity of skilled medical experts, especially in the third world. Due to the significant role that retinal image analysis plays in such diagnosis, there is a need for effective segmentation methods that accurately isolate the various retinal components, whose attributes have diagnostic relevance. Previous work has mainly focused on improving accuracy rates without much regard for algorithm efficiency. This study explores the use of Gabor features and Valley Emphasis (VE) thresholding for efficient and effective retinal image segmentation. Pre-processing is optimized through the squared magnitude Gabor response, prior to enrolling a selective VE thresholding approach. Experiments on the DRIVE and STARE datasets demonstrate significant reduction in computational overhead coupled with a minor improvement in segmentation accuracy.

Keywords: Retinal image segmentation · Gabor filter · Valley emphasis thresholding · Selective · Squared magnitude

1 Introduction

To facilitate effective visual tissue analysis in medical image segmentation, the region representing biological tissue of interest is normally isolated from its background digitally. Although this task can be accomplished through manual interaction with an image histogram, the automated approach may be preferred due to its potential for autonomous and scalable operation.

The Otsu method [19] is a widely used automatic thresholding algorithm which, despite being relatively simple, is reliable in the context of images with well formed bimodal distributions. The effectiveness of this method is however significantly reduced when it is presented with image histograms that tend towards unimodal distributions.

The Valley Emphasis (VE) method [12] improves the Otsu method by exaggerating valley points which are likely candidates for optimal thresholds in both unimodal and bimodal distributions. It has been found to be effective in industrial defect detection applications and competes favourably with other Otsu

© Springer Nature Switzerland AG 2020
N. T. Nguyen et al. (Eds.): ICCCI 2020, LNAI 12496, pp. 516–527, 2020.
https://doi.org/10.1007/978-3-030-63007-2_40

method adaptations. This study explores some recent improvements to the VE method and applies them to the challenging context of retinal blood vessel segmentation.

An attempt is made to build a simplified hybrid of VE adaptations so as to leverage their individual strengths. We note that the VE bears the computational overhead of considering all possible thresholds in search for the optimal candidate. We argue that since emphasis is ultimately placed on gray levels with lowest probability, it might be worthwhile excluding the highest peaks in the histogram from the search. We formulate the following research question to guide this study: can the proposed hybrid approach jointly improve the effectiveness and efficiency of VE in the context of Gabor filtered retinal images?

The remainder of this paper is structured as follows. Section 2 gives a brief description of Gabor filters while Sect. 3 outlines the Otsu method and various VE variations including our hybrid approach. Section 4 stipulates the experimental details of the study while Sect. 5 presents the results. We conclude by reflecting on our research question in the light of the reported findings.

2   Gabor Filters

Gabor filters convolve images with a sinusoidal Gaussian modulated function that is sensitive to orientation, frequency and bandwidth [4]. The filter response is a complex number with real and imaginary components that are orthogonal [8]. This results in four options for representing the filter response, namely the real, imaginary, phase and magnitude components. The real component can be represented as follows:

$$g_{real}(x', y', \lambda, \theta, \psi, \sigma, \gamma) = G(x', y', \sigma, \gamma)W_1(x', \lambda, \psi), \tag{1}$$

where G, W_1, x' and y' are defined by the respective Eqs. (2–6) below.

$$G(x', y', \sigma, \gamma) = \exp\left[-\pi\left(\frac{x'^2}{\sigma} + \frac{\gamma y'^2}{\sigma}\right)\right]. \tag{2}$$

$$W_1(x', \lambda, \psi) = \cos\left(2\pi\frac{x'}{\lambda} + \psi\right). \tag{3}$$

$$W_2(x', \lambda, \psi) = \sin\left(2\pi\frac{x'}{\lambda} + \psi\right). \tag{4}$$

$$x' = x\cos\theta + y\sin\theta. \tag{5}$$

$$y' = -x\sin\theta + y\cos\theta. \tag{6}$$

The imaginary component, $g_{imaginary}$ is defined in a similar manner to Eq. 1, except W_1 is replaced with W_2. The phase (g_{phase}) and magnitude ($g_{magnitude}$) are calculated by $\arctan\frac{g_{imaginary}}{g_{real}}$ and $\sqrt{g_{real}^2 + g_{imaginary}^2}$ respectively. The Gaussian envelope is represented by G while the sinusoidal wave is represented

518   M. V. Gwetu et al.

by W. The wavelength and phase-offset of the sinusoidal wave are symbolized by λ and ψ respectively. The angle of orientation is represented by θ while the sigma and aspect ratio of the Gaussian envelope are represented by σ and γ respectively. The co-ordinates of the point to be filtered are represented by x and y.

Gabor filters are suited for texture segmentation and are known to be a good model of how the human visual system processes light signals [3]. Cross sections of blood vessels which are perpendicular to the direction of blood flow usually have a Gaussian gray level distribution. As such, Gabor filters are seen as effective features for vessel detection. Previous applications of Gabor filters to retinal image segmentation [1,16,17,20] have typically made used of a bank of filters, each with varying orientation and scale. Vessel enhancement is generally achieved at pixel level by superimposing the maximum real or wavelet response over an entire bank of filters.

3 Automatic Thresholding Methods

The following notation is assumed in our descriptions of various automatic thresholding methods. Given an $M \times N$ gray level image G, $G(x, y) = g$ represents the intensity of a pixel within the image, where $0 \leq x < M$, $0 \leq y < N$ and $0 \leq g < L$. The image has $n = M \times N$ pixels and L different gray level intensities. These intensities are represented by indexes as opposed to actual pixel values. The frequency/likelihood of a gray level g in a normalized histogram of G is represented by:

$$h(g) = \frac{n_g}{n},\tag{7}$$

where n_g is the number of pixels with such an intensity in the image. Furthermore the average gray level within a portion of the image histogram is represented by $\mu_{(l_0,l_1)}$ where $0 \leq l_0 < l_1 < L$. Likewise the probability of a portion of the histogram is $p_{(l_0,l_1)}$, such that $p_{(0,L-1)} = 1$. In both cases, the portion of the histogram under consideration, is the range $[l_0, l_1]$ of gray levels.

3.1 Otsu Method

Although a variety of automatic thresholding techniques have been proposed [2], the Otsu method is still widely used to date due to its simplicity and moderate effectiveness. We outline its main concepts below.

If the image G is binarized using a threshold t, the probabilities and mean values of the two segments can be calculated as follows:

$$p_{(0,t)} = \sum_{g=0}^{t} h(g),\tag{8}$$

$$p_{(t+1,L-1)} = \sum_{g=t+1}^{L-1} h(g),\tag{9}$$

$$\mu_{(0,t)} = \sum_{g=0}^{t} \frac{gh(g)}{P_{(0,t)}}, \tag{10}$$

$$\mu_{(t+1,L-1)} = \sum_{g=t+1}^{L-1} \frac{gh(g)}{P_{(t+1,L-1)}}, \tag{11}$$

while the mean value of the whole image is:

$$\mu_{(0,L-1)} = \sum_{g=0}^{L-1} gh(g). \tag{12}$$

The between-class variance $\sigma_O^2(t)$ which ultimately measures the disparity between two classes is then calculated as follows:

$$\sigma_O^2(t) = P_{(0,t)}(\mu_{(0,t)} - \mu_{(0,L-1)})^2 + P_{(t+1,L-1)}(\mu_{(t+1,L-1)} - \mu_{(0,L-1)})^2. \tag{13}$$

This representation can be further simplified to:

$$\sigma_O^2(t) = P_{(0,t)}\mu_{(0,t)}^2 + P_{(t+1,L-1)}\mu_{(t+1,L-1)}^2. \tag{14}$$

The optimal threshold t^* which maximizes $\sigma_O^2(t)$, is defined as follows:

$$t^* = \underset{0<t<L-1}{\operatorname{argmax}} \, \sigma_O^2(t). \tag{15}$$

3.2   Valley Emphasis Method

Ng proposed the VE method [12] as an improvement to the Otsu method, that accommodates the automatic selection of optimal thresholds within unimodal distributions. This adaptation is facilitated by simply scaling the between-class variance with a weight that favours low thresholds as shown below:

$$\sigma_V^2(t) = (1 - h(t))(P_{(0,t)}\mu_{(0,t)}^2 + P_{(t+1,L-1)}\mu_{(t+1,L-1)}^2), \tag{16}$$

$$t^* = \underset{0<t<L-1}{\operatorname{argmax}} \, \sigma_V^2(t). \tag{17}$$

3.3   Valley Emphasis Method Adaptations

One of the recent adaptations of the VE method is by Fan and Lei [5] who note its weakness in scenarios where the variance of the object is significantly different from that of the background. This is said to be pronounced where the proportion of the object/foreground is small in comparison to that of the background. In such situations where the background has a high mean gray level intensity, the scaling factor in the VE method is insufficient to favour thresholds with low probabilities. This finding is of particular interest to us, since the context of our thresholding is dominated by a low proportion of blood vessels in comparison to the retinal background.

The proposed adaptation, Neighbourhood Valley Emphasis (NVE) method, modifies the scaling factor $(1 - h(t))$ such that it considers the valley as a neighbourhood instead of a point. The probability of the valley is expressed as follows:

$$\hat{h}(t) = h(t - m) + \cdots + h(t - 1) + h(t) + h(t + 1) + \cdots + h(t + m), \qquad (18)$$

where its neighbourhood is of size $z = 2m + 1$. The corresponding objective function and optimal threshold are defined by:

$$\sigma_N^2(t) = (1 - \hat{h}(t))(p_{(0,t)}\mu_{(0,t)}^2 + p_{(t+1,L-1)}\mu_{(t+1,L-1)}^2), \qquad (19)$$

$$t^* = \underset{0<t<L-1}{\operatorname{argmax}} \ \sigma_N^2(t). \qquad (20)$$

The new scaling factor $(1 - \hat{h}(t))$ ensures that t^* will always be at a value which is not only low but occurs in a neighbourhood of low probabilities. The authors however note the influence of z on the quality of segmentation and advise against using low or high neighbourhood lengths. From the conducted experiments, the recommended setting is $z = 11$ while threshold values such as 3 and 35 are considered to be too small or too big respectively. We argue that the choice of z should not be generalized but should instead, be based on the context under consideration. For example, low neighbourhood sizes could be suited for images with a small gray level range and low histogram variance. In such cases, it is likely that the valley separating classes is narrow. The total probability of such a narrow valley would still be favoured when faced with a high average background gray level, since the image intensity range is small.

Ng et al. subsequently proposed an alternative way [13] of incorporating the neighbourhood of a valley in the scaling factor, by introducing a Gaussian weighting mechanism as shown below.

$$\tilde{h}(t) = \sum_{i=-m}^{m} h(t - i) \exp^{-\frac{(t-i)^2}{2\sigma^2}} \qquad (21)$$

$$\sigma_G^2(t) = (1 - \tilde{h}(t))(p_{(0,t)}\mu_{(0,t)}^2 + p_{(t+1,L-1)}\mu_{(t+1,L-1)}^2), \qquad (22)$$

$$t^* = \underset{0<t<L-1}{\operatorname{argmax}} \ \sigma_G^2(t). \qquad (23)$$

This approach which we refer to as the Gaussian Valley Emphasis (GVE) method also considers gray levels within a valley neighbourhood but differs in that proximity to the valley-centre is taken into account. It also has the benefit of removing noise from the image histogram due to the smoothing effect of its Gaussian function. The details of the Gaussian window size and the preferred σ are however not specified and left for experimental determination.

A recent alternative approach which employs the concept of valley deepness, has been proposed by Ng et al. [14]; we refer to it as the Deepened Valley Emphasis (DVE) method. Given a prospective histogram valley-point b, the points a and c which represent the highest points to the left and right of b

respectively, will be higher than b, if b is indeed a valley-point. In other words, $h(a) > h(b)$ and $h(c) > h(b)$ if b is a valley point. Equation 24 shows that, if b is a confirmed valley point, then its valley-depth $\breve{h}(b)$ can be modelled as the average between the heights of the peaks at a and c, relative to $h(b)$, otherwise there is no valley-depth to measure.

$$\breve{h}(b) = \begin{cases} \dfrac{\max\limits_{0 \le a < b} (h(a)-h(b)) + \max\limits_{b < c < L} (h(c)-h(b))}{2}, & \text{if } h(a) > h(b) \text{ and } h(c) > h(b) \\ 0, & \text{otherwise.} \end{cases}$$

$$(24)$$

A new objective function was proposed, based on a scaling factor which incorporates how low and how deep a valley point is, as shown in Eq. 25.

$$\sigma_D^2(t) = (1 - h(t) + \breve{h}(b))(p_{(0,t)}\mu_{(0,t)}^2 + p_{(t+1,L-1)}\mu_{(t+1,L-1)}^2), \qquad (25)$$

$$t^* = \operatorname*{argmax}_{0 < t < L-1} \sigma_D^2(t). \qquad (26)$$

In a nutshell, the between class variance $\sigma_D^2(t)$, defaults to $\sigma_V^2(t)$ when t is not a true valley point but adds $\breve{h}(t)$ to $\sigma_V^2(t)$ for true valley points, in order to favour points with low $h(t)$ values. Due to the sensitivity of this approach to noise in the image histogram, a 1-Dimensional Gaussian filter is proposed for smoothing the histogram before this objective function can be applied. The main drawback of this approach is its computational overhead due to the consideration of all possible permutations of the points a, b and c. Since we seek to improve the efficiency of the automatic thresholding, we have therefore not incorporated the features of this method in our proposed approach.

3.4   Proposed Methods

Although adaptations to the VE method are reported to generally improve the effectiveness of automatic segmentation in various contexts, they do so at the expense of additional computation. Based on the observation that all VE methods typically favour thresholds that have low $h(t)$ values, we anticipate that it may not be necessary to consider all possible values of t when searching for t^*. We propose sorting candidate thresholds in ascending order of their $h(t)$ values and then only focusing on a portion at the top of the list. On the one hand, this line of reasoning may exclude potentially good thresholds that lie outside the focus area, on the other hand, it may do well by excluding potential false positives in terms of optimal thresholds.

In order to test the viability of our proposal, which we call the Selective Valley Emphasis approach, we apply it to two extensions of the VE method that have different levels of complexity as follows.

– **Selective VE** (SVE): creates a list of candidate thresholds sorted in ascending order of $h(t)$, then maximizes $\sigma_V^2(t)$ over the top half of the sorted list.

– **Selective Gaussian Neighbourhood VE** (SGNVE): creates a new between-class variance $\sigma^2_{GN}(t)$ which is a blend of the Gaussian and Neighbourhood VE methods. This variance is maximized over the top quarter of the sorted thresholds list with the lowest $h(t)$ values. We use a fixed Gaussian window with the following weights: $\left[\frac{1}{4}, \frac{1}{2}, \frac{1}{4}\right]$, such that $\hat{h}(t) = \frac{1}{4}h(t-1) + \frac{1}{2}h(t) + \frac{1}{4}h(t+1)$. Missing boundary values are compensated for by reflecting the existing neighbouring values of t.

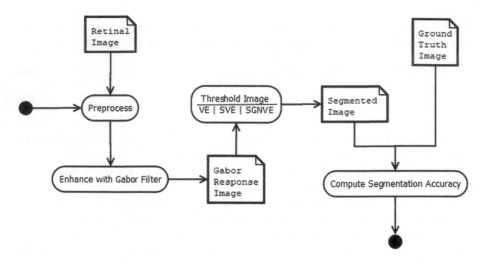

Fig. 1. Retinal image segmentation steps

4   Experiment Details

We evaluate the comparative effectiveness of our proposed VE methods by following the sequence of steps shown in Fig. 1. Colour retinal input images are preprocessed by extracting the green channel, which is known to preserve the most detail for use in gray level mode [18]. We are primarily interested in determining whether selective thresholding can improve the efficiency of VE method and if so, whether there is any compromise in effectiveness. The enhanced Gabor images are thresholded using the VE, SVE and SGNVE methods while noting running times and segmentation effectiveness. Although we adopt the Gabor filter parameters used in previous work [7], we explore the viability of the maximum Gabor magnitude response of each retinal image pixel instead of the real component. We propose a minor alteration to the calculation of the Gabor filter magnitude, instead of the conventional euclidean distance, we take its squared value. Thus, the alteration is simply a matter of dropping the square root function in the calculation of $g_{magnitude}$. This alteration yields a simpler computation while retaining the integrity of the ($\leq$ and $\geq$) boolean relational operators. It does however affect the granularity of the response values and it would be interesting to note whether there is a significant influence on automatic thresholding. Experiments are conducted on the DRIVE and STARE datasets, and results are evaluated using the sensitivity, specificity and accuracy metrics; to enable objective comparison with previous studies [6].

5 Results

Table 1. VE Algorithm execution times (ms)

Image	DRIVE			STARE		
	VE	SVE	SGNVE	VE	SVE	SGNVE
1	25	25	151	35	34	212
2	29	27	146	32	31	192
3	28	22	127	31	32	204
4	36	32	165	28	29	163
5	24	25	156	41	36	190
6	26	28	148	39	41	231
7	29	26	149	34	35	195
8	24	24	149	32	33	212
9	26	26	166	46	34	188
10	27	22	129	35	34	201
11	37	30	154	38	36	206
12	25	23	140	34	37	204
13	24	23	136	35	34	189
14	24	22	153	34	34	200
15	26	23	155	36	33	191
16	25	25	137	28	32	193
17	25	23	147	38	34	211
18	31	30	158	32	32	197
19	23	22	132	32	32	174
20	26	30	158	33	31	174
μ	27	25.4	147.8	34.65	33.7	196.35

Table 1 shows the processor clock times for calls to functions implementing VE, SVE and SGNVE algorithms. The average execution time of SVE is less than that of VE on both the DRIVE and STARE datasets, with the paired t-test yielding p-values of approximately 0.007% and 0.11% respectively. The difference in execution times between VE and SVE is thus significant for the DRIVE

Table 2. Results of retinal image thresholding

Approach			Sensitivity	Specificity	Accuracy
DRIVE	VE	Real [7]	68.3	97.22	93.54
		Magnitude	61.73	97.94	93.3
		Squared Magnitude	66.8	97.82	**93.84**
	Previous Work	Human observer[6]	77.63	97.23	94.70
		Yin et al. [21]	62.52	97.10	92.67
		Zhang et al. [22]	71.20	97.24	93.82
		Niemeijer et al. [15]	68.98	96.96	94.17
		Neto et al. [11]	79.42	96.31	–
STARE	VE	Real [7]	68.85	96.15	93.2
		Magnitude	69.16	96.07	93.2
		Squared Magnitude	68.6	96.39	**93.58**
	Previous Work	Human observer [6]	77.63	97.23	94.70
		Hoover et al. [9]	67.51	95.67	92.67
		Zhang et al. [22]	71.77	97.53	94.84
		Mendonca et al. [10]	69.96	97.3	94.4
		Neto et al. [11]	76.95	95.37	–

and not for the STARE dataset. We also note that the STARE dataset execution times are consistently greater than those of the DRIVE dataset. This leads us to assume the impact of the SVE is more prominent in the context of lower VE computation overhead[1]. Although an attempt was made to improve the efficiency of SGNVE, its execution times were consistently greater than those of VE and SVE algorithms. Although the average execution times of these three algorithms differ, their thresholded output was identical in all cases, leading us to prefer the SVE algorithm since it is as effective as the other approaches but more efficient. Table 2 compares our final segmentation results with those of previous work. It is interesting to note that the squared magnitude response yields a higher average accuracy than the magnitude and real response approaches, in both the DRIVE and STARE datasets. It is observed that the squared magnitude response value ranges are generally narrower than those of the magnitude response; this effect seems to favour the former approach. The results of the present study compare favourably with previous work; in some cases superior results are achieved. Sensitivity and specificity outcomes of up to 76.8% and 97.9% as well as 78.8% and 97.8% are achieved on normal images in the DRIVE and STARE datasets respectively; images exhibiting pathological traits remain a challenge. It is worth noting that although the most recent work of Neto et al. reports a very high sensitivity which surpasses that of the human observer, those

---

[1] DRIVE images have smaller dimensions than STARE images.

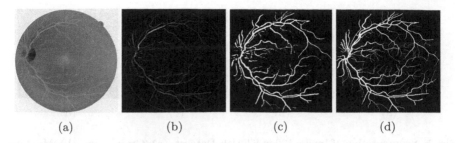

(a)   (b)   (c)   (d)

Fig. 2. Segmentation of Image 1 in DRIVE Dataset. (a): Gray Image, (b): Maximum Squared Magnitude, (c): SVE Segmentation, (d): Ground Truth

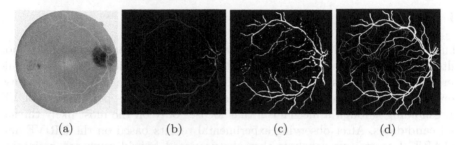

(a)   (b)   (c)   (d)

Fig. 3. Segmentation of Image 8 in DRIVE Dataset. (a): Gray Image, (b): Maximum Squared Magnitude, (c): SVE Segmentation, (d): Ground Truth

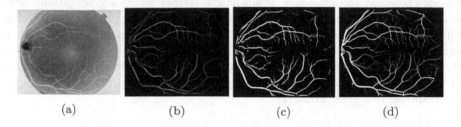

(a)   (b)   (c)   (d)

Fig. 4. Segmentation of Image 77 in STARE Dataset. (a): Gray Image, (b): Maximum Squared Magnitude, (c): SVE Segmentation, (d): Ground Truth

results are obtained using a different gold standard called the average human observer.

We conclude our results section by exhibiting some visual segmentations achieved by our approach on normal and pathological images in Figs. 2, 3, 4 and 5. A notable strength of our approach is the effective suppression of the optic disk and fovea regions. Although thick vessels are well located, thin vasculature remains a challenge. Image 8 of the DRIVE dataset and image 139 of the STARE dataset presented some microaneurysms. Although these were largely detected as blood vessels, further processing using shape features could possibly isolate them as pathological landmarks.

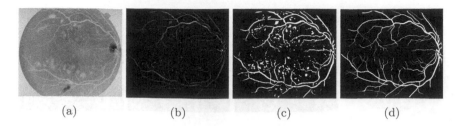

(a)   (b)   (c)   (d)

Fig. 5. Segmentation of Image 139 in STARE Dataset. (a): Gray Image, (b): Maximum Squared Magnitude, (c): SVE Segmentation, (d): Ground Truth

6   Conclusion

This study presented a retinal image segmentation approach based on Gabor filters and VE thresholding. In contrast to previous applications of Gabor filters in retinal image segmentation, we used a variant of the magnitude response for pixel enhancement. We sought an improvement in the performance of VE thresholding through a mechanism that focuses only on the most likely threshold candidates. After observing experimental results based on the DRIVE and STARE datasets, we conclude that the proposed hybrid approach maintains segmentation effectiveness while improving efficiency.

Although this study may be useful as a first step towards jointly improving the effectiveness and efficiency of automatic retinal image segmentation, more work needs to be done to overcome the limitations encountered by our Gabor filter preprocessing method. We have only observed marginal improvement in accuracy over some previous studies. It seems necessary to gain a better understanding of the contextualized costs and benefits of the Gabor filter responses alternatives, then perhaps formulate a dynamic filter which enlists the appropriate response in a given context.

References

1. Akram, M.U., Khan, S.A.: Multilayered thresholding-based blood vessel segmentation for screening of diabetic retinopathy. Eng. Comput. **29**, 165–173 (2013). https://doi.org/10.1007/s00366-011-0253-7
2. Chang, C.I., Du, Y., Wang, J., Guo, S.M., Thouin, P.: Survey and comparative analysis of entropy and relative entropy thresholding techniques (2006)
3. Daugman, J.: Complete discrete 2-D Gabor transforms by neural networks for image analysis and compression. IEEE Trans. Acoust. Speech Signal Process. **36**(7), 1169–1179 (1988). https://doi.org/10.1109/29.1644
4. Daugman, J.G., et al.: Uncertainty relation for resolution in space, spatial frequency, and orientation optimized by two-dimensional visual cortical filters. Opt. Soc. Am. J. A: Opt. Image Sci. **2**(7), 1160–1169 (1985)
5. Fan, J.L., Lei, B.: A modified valley-emphasis method for automatic thresholding. Pattern Recogn. Lett. **33**(6), 703–708 (2012)

6. Fraz, M., et al.: Blood vessel segmentation methodologies in retinal images - a survey. Comput. Methods Programs Biomed. **108**(1), 407–433 (2012)
7. Gwetu, M.V., Tapamo, J.R., Viriri, S.: Segmentation of retinal blood vessels using normalized Gabor filters and automatic thresholding. S. Afr. Comput. J. **55**(1), 12–24 (2014)
8. Henriksen, J.J.: 3D surface tracking and approximation using Gabor filters. South Denmark University, 28 March 2007 (2007)
9. Hoover, A., Kouznetsova, V., Goldbaum, M.: Locating blood vessels in retinal images by piecewise threshold probing of a matched filter response. IEEE Trans. Med. Imaging **19**(3), 203–210 (2000)
10. Mendonca, A.M., Campilho, A.: Segmentation of retinal blood vessels by combining the detection of centerlines and morphological reconstruction. IEEE Trans. Med. Imaging **25**(9), 1200–1213 (2006)
11. Neto, L.C., Ramalho, G.L., Neto, J.F.R., Veras, R.M., Medeiros, F.N.: An unsupervised coarse-to-fine algorithm for blood vessel segmentation in fundus images. Expert Syst. Appl. **78**, 182–192 (2017)
12. Ng, H.F.: Automatic thresholding for defect detection. Pattern Recogn. Lett. **27**(14), 1644–1649 (2006)
13. Ng, H.F., Jargalsaikhan, D., Tsai, H.C., Lin, C.Y.: An improved method for image thresholding based on the valley-emphasis method. In: Signal and Information Processing Association Annual Summit and Conference (APSIPA), 2013 Asia-Pacific, pp. 1–4. IEEE (2013)
14. Ng, H.F., Kheng, C.W., Lin, J.M.: A weighting scheme for improving Otsu method for threshold selection, vol. 27, no. 2, pp. 12–21 (2016)
15. Niemeijer, M., Staal, J., van Ginneken, B., Loog, M., Abramoff, M.D.: Comparative study of retinal vessel segmentation methods on a new publicly available database. In: Medical Imaging 2004, pp. 648–656. International Society for Optics and Photonics (2004)
16. Osareh, A., Shadgar, B.: Automatic blood vessel segmentation in color images of retina. Iran. J. Sci. Technol. Trans. B Eng. **33**(B2), 191–206 (2009)
17. Rangayyan, R., Oloumi, F., Oloumi, F., Eshghzadeh-Zanjani, P., Ayres, F.: Detection of blood vessels in the retina using Gabor filters. In: 2007 Canadian Conference on Electrical and Computer Engineering. CCECE 2007, pp. 717–720 (2007). https://doi.org/10.1109/CCECE.2007.184
18. Ricci, E., Perfetti, R.: Retinal blood vessel segmentation using line operators and support vector classification. IEEE Trans. Med. Imaging **26**(10), 1357–1365 (2007)
19. Vala, M.H.J., Baxi, A.: A review on Otsu image segmentation algorithm. Int. J. Adv. Res. Comput. Eng. Technol. (IJARCET) **2**(2), 387 (2013)
20. Wu, D., Zhang, M., Liu, J.C., Bauman, W.: On the adaptive detection of blood vessels in retinal images. IEEE Trans. Biomed. Eng. **53**(2), 341–343 (2006). https://doi.org/10.1109/TBME.2005.862571
21. Yin, Y., Adel, M., Bourennane, S.: Retinal vessel segmentation using a probabilistic tracking method. Pattern Recogn. **45**(4), 1235–1244 (2012)
22. Zhang, B., Zhang, L., Zhang, L., Karray, F.: Retinal vessel extraction by matched filter with first-order derivative of Gaussian. Comput. Biol. Med. **40**(4), 438–445 (2010)

Macroscopic Skin Lesion Segmentation Using GrabCut

Verosha Pillay, Divyan Hirasen, Serestina Viriri[✉],
and Mandlenkosi Victor Gwetu

School of Mathematics, Statistics and Computer Science,
University of KwaZulu-Natal, Durban, South Africa
{214539347,215018696,viriris,gwetum}@ukzn.ac.za

Abstract. Melanoma is one of the most dangerous forms of skin cancer with an apace increase in death rates each year. One major problem in Artificial Intelligence and Machine Learning is the issue of racial disparities. This leads to myriad problems in association with medical image analysis as the data fed to these algorithms are biased. Accurate and concise segmentation is an imperative requirement when developing a computer assisted diagnostic support system. In order to surmount the problems caused by the lack of a diverse set of images, we look at initially segmenting lesions, using the GrabCut method, from the surrounding skin. This lets us focus on the skin lesion and remove potential colour confusion associated with the mixture of the lesion colour and skin tones. Thereafter, we make use of 14 pre-trained transfer learning models. The experimental results achieve the following: Dice index 0.93, Jaccard index 0.88, Matthew Correlation Coefficient 0.87, Sensitivity 0.92, Specificity 0.95 and an Accuracy rate of 0.93.

Keywords: Melanoma · Skin tones · GrabCut method · Skin lesion segmentation

1 Introduction

Skin cancer begins when there is an out of control growth of cells in the body [1]. Melanoma is a very critical form of skin cancer which occurs in the melanocyte skin cells [2]. Melanocytes are cells found in the upper layer of the skin which give our skin its colour. According to the World Health Organization (WHO) there are currently 132,000 melanoma skin cancers globally occurring each year [3]. Nevertheless, melanoma skin cancer is highly curable provided is it diagnosed and treated at its early stages. However, if undetected, melanoma spreads to other parts of the body or gets deeper into the skin resulting in a life-threating situation.

For this study, it is of paramount importance to understand the key differences that exist between dark and fair skinned people. People of colour tend to have more eumelanin while fair skinned people have substantially more pheomelanin [2]. Eumelanin has the potential to inoculate the skin from sun damage

© Springer Nature Switzerland AG 2020
N. T. Nguyen et al. (Eds.): ICCCI 2020, LNAI 12496, pp. 528–539, 2020.
https://doi.org/10.1007/978-3-030-63007-2_41

while pheomelanin does not have this ability [2]. This results in white racial ethnic groups to be more susceptible to melanoma skin cancer. However, be that as it may, people of all colours can be diagnosed with skin cancer. Generally, people with darker skin tend to be diagnosed at a later stage (fatal stage) causing an ineffectual prognosis as this type of cancer spreads rapidly to different areas of the body.

Visual screening by oncologists for melanoma detection may not guarantee a patient of 100% detection [4]. In addition, due to possible uncertainties, it may be necessary to undergo more tests and procedures causing potential harm to the patient. To overcome this problem, we look to Computer Aided Diagnostic (CAD) support systems to assist physicians in the detection of early skin cancer. Computer Vision has become a cornerstone in intelligent medicine [5] and plays an imperative role in medical image diagnosis. The first step in computer vision is to acquire data, in our case the data consists of multiple macroscopic image datasets. Unfortunately, the available datasets solely consists of fair skinned people which results in biased data. As far as we know, no datasets of macroscopic images containing all skin tones exist.

Another crucial step in image processing is proper segmentation of the skin lesion. Improper or poor segmentation can result in misclassification causing an incorrect diagnosis. Hence, it is of utmost importance to ensure the precise segmentation of the lesion from the surrounding skin. There are an immense range of segmentation techniques proposed and implemented in literature for the detection of skin cancer which include clustering methods, threshold-based segmentation, artificial neural networks etc. Albeit, these segmentation techniques have a handful of downfalls such as inefficiency, low accuracy rates, poor performance, requiring tremendous amounts of data, etc. [4].

To overcome the problem of the lack of data, we propose using the Grabcut segmentation technique on the available datasets by extracting and primarily analysing the lesion to remove the issue of the surrounding skin (skin colour) which poses as potential confusion in the diagnosis of melanoma. This segmentation technique demonstrates capabilities for handling extremely textured, noisy and colour images which are present in macroscopic images [4].

2   Image Segmentation

Before diving into the GrabCut segmentation technique, we need to understand the Graph-Cut method. Essentially, the GrabCut technique is an image segmentation method based on graph cuts. A graph-based approach utilizes efficient solutions of the maxflow/mincut problem between source and sink nodes in a directed graph [19]. Consider a directed graph $G = (V, E)$, where V represents the vertices and E denotes the edges of the graph, with non-negative edge weights that has two special vertices i.e.: the source s and the sink t. An s-t cut also known as a cut $C = S, T$ a partition of the vertices into disjoint sets S and T such that $s \varepsilon S$ and $t \varepsilon T$. In the image the s node denotes the object while t denotes the background [4,14]. The cost of each $s - t$ cut is the sum of all edges that go from S to T shown in (1). The minimum $s - t$ cut problem is to find a cut C with the smallest cost. Due to the theorem of Ford and Fulkerson [15], this is equivalent to computing the maximum flow from the source to sink [13]

$$c(S,T) = \sum_{u\varepsilon S, v\varepsilon T (u,v)\ \varepsilon s} c(u,v) \tag{1}$$

The Graph-Cut segmentation technique is viewed as a rapid algorithm for binary labelling problems [6] where a set of pixels in an image $I = I_{i,j}$ A common strategy is to find the global optimum of the cost function based on the region and boundary properties of an image [7]. Several of the pixels are marked as foreground and the rest are marked as background. The labelling of the pixels is completed by making use of an energy function [9] which is depicted in (2).

$$E = (I_{i,j}, S, C, \lambda) \tag{2}$$

Where S takes values 0 for background and 1 for foreground to perform hard segmentation (algorithms that produce a binary map, i.e. a pixel belongs to either foreground or background).C represents the colour parameter and λ represents the coherence parameter [8]. When working with colour images a Gaussian Mixture Model (GMM) is employed for assisting or guiding the segmentation process [8] where a parametric probability density function represented as a weighted sum of Gaussian component densities [10]. The interactive Graph-Cut segmentation technique allows the user to draw a rectangle surrounding the macroscopic image of the suspected infected lesion. This then allows automatic segmentation to take place, as the selected lesion now becomes the foreground while the rest of the image becomes the background [4]. A likelihood ratio is utilized to calculate the relative probability of each pixel being foreground or background which is based on the GMM [7].

In 2004, Rother et al. [11] introduced the GrabCut segmentation technique which is an iterative and interactive image segmentation tool [7]. The authors look at the problem of efficient and interactive extraction of the foreground object in an involuted environment where the background cannot be easily segmented [11]. This technique aids in reducing the user interaction by using mechanisms called "iterative estimation" and "incomplete labelling" [7]. The GrabCut algorithm estimates the colour distribution of the target (lesion within the rectangle) and the background by making use of a Gaussian Mixture Model (GMM) shown in calculation (3). This is used to construct a Markov random field over the pixel labels, with an energy function that prefers connected regions having the same label, and running a graph cut based optimization to infer their values.

$$p(x) = \sum_{i=1}^{M} \pi_i N_i(x|u_i c_i) \tag{3}$$

where $N_i(x|u_i c_i)$ denotes a bivariate or trivariate normal distribution with mean vector u_i and a covariance matrix $C_i \times \pi$ is a mixture proportion for each group and it is regarded as the ith prior probability of Gaussian distribution that data sample produces. These prior probabilities should satisfy (4):

$$\sum_{i=1}^{M} \pi_i \ and \ 0 \leq \pi_i \leq 1 \tag{4}$$

The GrabCut technique allows for a variety of user inputs such as a bounding box (usually a rectangle) to enclose the foreground object and , a boundary brush for matting (border information that is employed to retrieve foreground colour information which is free of colour bleeding from the background information) and foreground and background strokes for local editing [12]. Labels are allocated by making use of "Iterative estimation" which assigns temporary labels to some pixels (in the foreground) that can be successively withdrawn [7]. Figure 1. depicts examples of segmentation results.

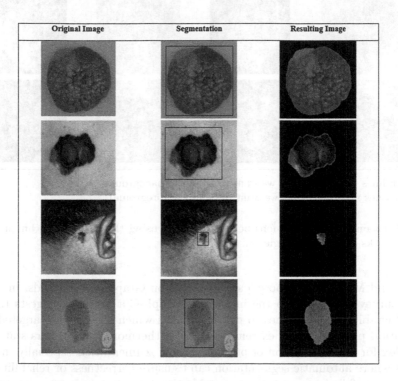

Fig. 1. Examples of skin lesions being segmented using the GrabCut technique

The GrabCut technique allows us to segment images in colour since it employs an energy minimization approach to segment an image which takes colour and contrast information into account [16]. Moreover, it works well for highly textured and noisy images as macroscopic images show the presence of noise such as hair, illumination variation etc. This technique is able to segment an area of the skin where more than one suspected mole/lesion is present whereas other techniques fail [17] (shown in Fig. 3). We can segment images in 3 ways for accurate results: I. Segmentation by drawing a rectangle around the lesion (shown in Fig. 1.), II. Segmentation by using masks to set background and foreground (Depicted in Fig. 3) and III. Rectangle + Masks (depicted in Fig. 2).

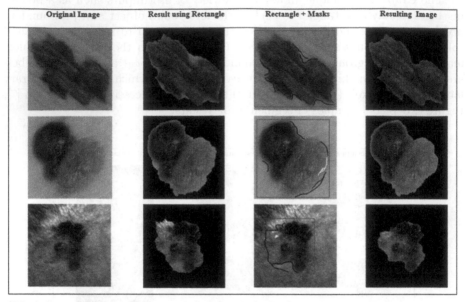

*Black lines represent what we want to be in the background
White lines represent what we want to be in the foreground

Fig. 2. Examples of skin lesions being segmented using the GrabCut technique with use of masks and the rectangle

Yi and Moon [14] propose a survey paper on Graph-Cut methods. In short, their survey pertaining to the interactive Graph-Cut method suggests that it is ineluctable when it comes to natural images which require the targeted segmentation precision to be extremely high. Furthermore, the authors state it is complex for the application of pure automatic segmentation especially in situations where automatic segmentation can't ensure correctness or reliability [18] resulting in failed segmentations or suboptimal results. As a consequence, an expert has to rectify the incorrect segmented solution manually [17]. However the automatic Graph-Cut method can rapidly segment images. On the other hand, the interactive technique ensures flexibility by allowing the user to select seed points which comes in handy for analysis in isolation of the lesion [19]. The interactive GrabCut segmentation technique is able to segment an area of the skin in which more than one suspected mole is present whereas other techniques may fall short.

3 Evaluation Metrics

The evaluation metrics employed include: Matthew Correlation Coefficient (MCC), Dice (DSC) and Jaccard (JAC) index, Sensitivity (SN), Specificity (SP) and Accuracy (ACC).

4 Initial Results

We make use of the three datasets i.e.: MED-NODE, DermQuest and DermIS, which are publically available. The combined dataset is randomly split into test and training data, i.e.: the train and test ratio are 80% to 20%. There are two kinds of experiments performed with the combined dataset. The first one is to evaluate the proposed method using the original datasets without image segmentation. The second one is to evaluate the proposed method with the use of image segmentation. Results of the two experiments are depicted in Fig. 3, Fig. 4 and Fig. 5. Images are segmented in colour with the use of the GrabCut segmentation technique. Thereafter, images are then tested on 14 pre-trained models which include: Resnet18, Resnet34, Resnet50, Resnet101, Resnet152, VGG16, VGG19, AlexNet, DenseNet201, Densenet121, DenseNet161, Densenet169, Squeezenet1-0 and Squeezenet1-1. In order to evaluate the performance of our segmentation technique i.e. GrabCut technique, the values of the three metric measures are computed which include the Matthew Correlation Coefficient, Jaccard and Dice Index (results are depicted in Table 1). Furthermore, in order to perform a quantitative evaluation of the proposed method, three traditionally used metrics for classification problems are employed which include: accuracy, sensitivity and specificity.

From Fig. 3. we can see the accuracy of the segmented images outperformed 13 of the 14 transfer learning models. Hence, the need to segment images to ensure improved accuracy rates. The transfer learning model for unsegmented images namely Densenet201 achieved a higher accuracy by 1.38%. Taking a closer look at this result by looking at Fig. 4 and Fig. 5. we see that even though Densenet201 achieved a higher accuracy rate, this model falls short with respect to its sensitivity and specificity results. Densenet201 for unsegmented images was fairly unbalanced when comparing its sensitivity (93.33%) and specificity (76.09%) results. Although, Fig. 3. reveals segmented images surpasses unsegmented images with regards to accuracy rates, Fig. 4. and Fig. 5. reflects some models such as Resnet34, Resnet10, Densenet121, Densenet169 and Densenet201 deviates when comparing sensitivity and specificity results.

Table 1 depicts the segmentation performance of the GrabCut technique for the top five performing transfer learning models. The Jaccard and Dice Index fall between the 0 and 1 range. The value 0 indicates no overlap or no similarly, whereas the value of 1 corresponds to a perfect match/agreement. According to the results depicted in Table 1 we observe the DSC is implementing much better than JAC. MCC returns a value between −1 and 1, where −1 indicates

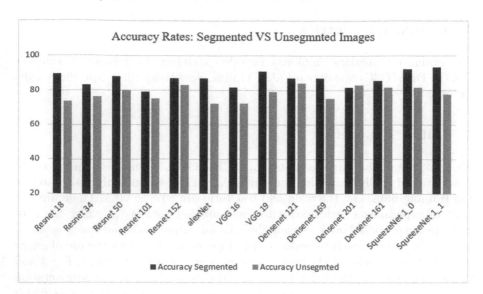

Fig. 3. Bar graph showing the comparison of Accuracy rates between segmented and unsegmented images

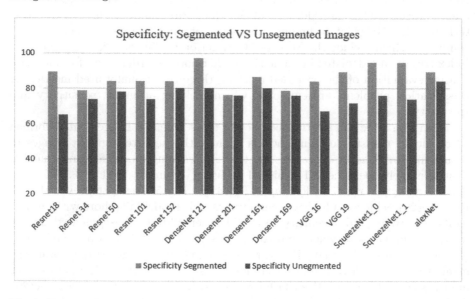

Fig. 4. Bar graph denoting the comparison of Specificity between segmented and unsegmented images

the dissimilarity that exits between the prediction and observation, 0 is considered a random predication and 1 indicates an ideal or perfect predication. Squeezenetnet1-1 achieved the best segmentation results with regards to DSC (0.93), JAC (0.88) and MCC (0.87).

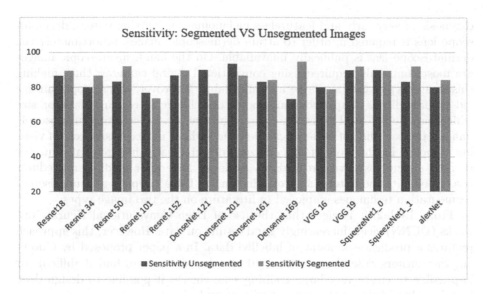

Fig. 5. Bar graph showing the comparison of Sensitivity between segmented and unsegmented images

Table 1. Quantitative comparison of lesion segmentation results

Segmentation performance						
Model	Dice index*	Jaccard index*	MCC*	Accuracy(%)	Specificity(%)	Sensitivity(%)
Squeezenet1-1	0.93	0.88	0.87	93.42	94.74	92.11
Squeezenet1-0	0.92	0.85	0.84	92.11	94.74	89.47
VGG19	0.9	0.83	0.82	90.79	89.47	92.11
Resnet18	0.89	0.81	0.79	89.47	89.47	89.47
Resnet50	0.87	0.80	0.75	88.00	84.21	92.11

*Jaccard and Dice index values fall within the range of [0, 1] and MCC falls within the range of [-1, 1]

5 Discussion

Segmentation of skin lesions plays a vital role in the precise detection and diagnosis of melanoma by CAD systems. Prominent and distinctive features of skin lesion are crucial in the classification of melanoma skin cancer. These features can only be procured by proper segmentation of the lesion from surrounding skin. There are a multitude of segmentation techniques (thresholding, edge-based, clustering etc.) implemented and tested using dermoscopic images (microscopic images) for the identification of skin cancer. However, not much attention has been given to macroscopic images in literature. This is largely due to the lack of available data. Both image types come with its own set of limitations and benefits. Dermoscopic images provide medical professionals with a more detailed view of the visual characteristics of the lesion. However, these images are highly dependent on the long-established dermoscopic features which in turn limits the

diagnosis of very early and featureless melanomas [4]. Furthermore, a dermatoscope lens is required in order to attain dermoscopic images, unfortunately the
dermatoscope lens is publically unavailable. On the hand, macroscopic images
are most commonly acquired using conventional digital cameras; thus, making
this image type easily available and affordable. Moreover, macroscopic images
aid in providing a simple comparison for the change in colour, shape or size
which may be potential signs of early malignancy [4],. By selecting macroscopic
images, pre-screening of patients can be done without the expensive cost of visiting a doctor. Furthermore, if skin cancer is detected early, it is generally curable
thereby saving costs with regards to a biopsy and other medical procedures
associated with the latter stages of skin cancer. Table 2 depicts a comparison of
segmentation techniques employed in literature on the two image types.

From Table 2, it is clear that the use of Deep Convolutional Neural Networks (DCNN) yields increasingly good results on data. However, this approach
requires a prodigious amount of labelled data. In a paper proposed by Guo et
al., the authors raise the question: "If the domain experts find it difficult or
impossible to create very large training sets, then is it possible to design deep
learning algorithms which require fewer examples"

Comparing papers from the Table 2 which make use of the macroscopic image
type, we notice paper [21] and [22] achieve superior results in terms of accuracy
and specificity. The authors in paper have demonstrated staggering results; however, when comparing results to those in paper [21], it must be pointed out, the
dataset employed consisted of only 126 digital images, where 66 of images are
melanoma cases and the others are non-melanoma. Contrary to the findings of
paper [22], we notice the sensitivity results are drastically lower than those of
the proposed method, resulting in the model being able to better detect patients
who are correctly identified as healthy. Whereas, the proposed model is more
or less balanced in terms of specificity and sensitivity, having a better chance
at correctly classifying the skin lesion in either case. It is important to highlight the fact that the papers [4,20] that make use of the Graph-Cut technique,
achieved a lower Dice and Jaccard index results than the proposed method. This
is particularly important when investigating the benefits the Grabcut technique
possess over the Graph-Cut technique. It is notable that the Grabcut method is
a semi-interactive version of the Graph-Cut technique allowing for more precise
results since the user marks the background and foreground pixels, thereafter,
the Grabcut method sorts out the rest. The proposed method yields superior
results for the Dice index when compared to the other mentioned papers in the
table.

Table 2. Comparison of segmentation in literature

Paper	Image Type	Segmentation	Accuracy	Sensitivity	Specificity	JAC	DSC
2019 [20]	Dermo	DCNN+Grabcut	93.39%	90.28%	92.68%	0.7481	0.8426
2017 [23]	Dermo	Deep ResNets	93.40%	80.20%	98.50%	0.7600	0.8420
2019 [4]	Macro	Graph-cut method	–	–	–	0.5532	0.7123
2016 [21]	Macro	DCNN	98.5%	95.0%	98.9%	–	–
2010 [24]	Macro	OSTU-R 84.9%	89.4%	92.7%	–	–	–
2018 [25]	Dermo	Fully-convolutional residual network	93.20%	82.00%	97.80%	0.7620	0.8470
2011 [22]	Macro	OSTU-PCA	98.1%	79.6%	99.6%	–	–
2018 [26]	Dermo	U-Net based model	-	–	–	0.477	–
2018 [26]	Dermo	R-CNN	–	–	–	0.233	–
2018 [27]	Dermo	Fuzzy entropy with A level-set thresholding	98.75%	83.78%	99.59%	0.9515	0.8768
Proposed	Macro	GrabCut technique	93.42%	92.11%	94.74%	0.8750	0.9333

*Proposed refers to the top performing transfer learning model i.e.: Squeezenet1-1 with GrabCut segmentation technique.Macro - Macroscopic images and Dermo - Dermoscopic Images

6 Conclusion

Medical images of skin lesions play a vital role and can have a significant impact on the detection and diagnosis of a patient. When conducting image processing, one of the predominant steps include segmentation. Accurate and precise segmentation can greatly improve the overall results for skin cancer identification. In this paper, we make use of the Grabcut segmentation technique to accurately segment lesions from the surrounding skin for the classification and detection of melanoma from all skin tones. The GrabCut technique is a popular segmentation method which is based on graph cuts. Colour is one of the pivotal components used by dermatologists in the identification of melanoma. The Graph-Cut method is appraised as one of the most powerful futuristic segmentation techniques employed for colour image segmentation [4]. Furthermore, we show the significant difference in results when testing segmented images versus unsegmented images.

References

1. American Cancer Society: About Melanoma Skin Cancer. https://www.cancer.org/cancer/melanoma-skin-cancer/about/what-is-melanoma.html. Accessed 7 Sep 2019
2. Skin Cancer Foundation. https://www.skincancer.org/skin-cancer-information/melanoma/. Accessed 7 Sep 2019
3. World Health Organization. https://www.who.int/uv/faq/skincancer/en/index1.html. Accessed 7 Sep 2019
4. Pillay, V., Viriri, S.: Skin cancer detection from macroscopic images. In: Conference on Information Communications Technology and Society, pp. 1–9 (ICTAS) (2019)

5. Applications of Computer Vision in Healthcare. https://medium.com/optima-ai/applications-of-computer-vision-in-healthcare-5651208b3539. Accessed 7 Sep 2019
6. Zhou, H., Zheng, J., Wei, L.: Texture aware image segmentation using graph cuts and active contours. Pattern Recogn. **46**, 1719–1733 (2013)
7. Kulkarni, M., Nicolls, F.: Interactive image segmentation using graph cuts. In: Proceedings of 20th Annual Symposium of the Pattern Recognition Association of South Africa (PRASA2009), Stellenbosch, South Africa (2009)
8. Raghunandanan, P., John, L.: A Review on Various Graph Cut Based Image Segmentation Schemes (2013)
9. Graph cuts in computer vision. https://en.wikipedia.org/wiki/Graph_cuts_in_computer_vision. Accessed 27 July 2019
10. Reynolds, D.: Gaussian Mixture Models, pp. 1–5 (2009)
11. Carsten, R., Vladimir, K., Andrew, B.: GrabCut: interactive foreground extraction using iterated graph cuts. ACM Trans. Graph. **23**(3), 309–314 (2004)
12. Yang, W., Cai, J., Zheng, J., Luo, J.: User-friendly interactive image segmentation through unified combinatorial user inputs. IEEE Trans. Image Process. 19, 2470–2479 (2010). https://doi.org/10.1109/TIP.2010.2048611. A publication of the IEEE Signal Processing Society
13. Kolmogorov, V., Ramin, Z.: What energy functions can be minimized via graph cuts. IEEE Trans. Pattern Anal. Mach. Intell. **26**, 147–59 (2004). https://doi.org/10.1109/TPAMI.2004.1262177
14. Yi, F., Moon, I.: Image segmentation: a survey of graph-cut methods. In: 2012 International Conference on Systems and Informatics (ICSAI2012), pp. 1936–1941 (2012). https://doi.org/10.1109/ICSAI.2012.6223428
15. Ford, L., Fulkerson, D.: Flows in Networks. Princeton University Press, Princeton (1962)
16. Franke, Markus: Color Image Segmentation Based on an Iterative Graph Cut Algorithm Using Time-of-Flight Cameras. In: Mester, Rudolf, Felsberg, Michael (eds.) DAGM 2011. LNCS, vol. 6835, pp. 462–467. Springer, Heidelberg (2011). https://doi.org/10.1007/978-3-642-23123-0_49
17. Nammalwar, P., Ghita, O., Whelan, P.F.: Segmentation of Skin Cancer Images. Vision Systems Group. Centre for Image Processing and Analysis. School of Electronic Engineering. Dublin City University. Ireland (2009)
18. Camilus, K., Govindan, V.K.: A review on graph based segmentation. Int. J. Image Graph. Signal Process. **4** (2012). https://doi.org/10.5815/ijigsp.2012.05.01
19. Oyebode, K.O., Du, S., Wyk, B.J., Djouani, K.: Investigating the relevance of graph cut parameter on interactive and automatic cell segmentation. Comp. Math. Methods Med. (2018)
20. Ünver, H., Ayan, E.: Skin lesion segmentation in dermoscopic images with combination of YOLO and GrabCut algorithm. Diagnostics **9**, 72 (2019). https://doi.org/10.3390/diagnostics9030072
21. Jafari, M.H., et al.: Skin lesion segmentaion in clinical images using deep learning. In: IEEE International Conference on Pattern Recognition (ICPR), Cancun, Mexico (2016)
22. Cavalcanti, P.G., Scharcanski, J.: Automated pre-screening of pigmented skin lesions using standard cameras. Comput. Med. Imaging Graph. **6**, 481–491 (2011)
23. Bi, L., Kim, J., Ahn, E., Feng, D.: Automatic skin lesion analysis using large-scale dermoscopy images and deep residual networks. arXiv arXiv:1703.04197 (2017)
24. Cavalcanti, P., Yari, Y., Scharcanski, J.: Pigmented skin lesion segmentation on macroscopic images. In: Proceedings 25th International Conference on Image Vision Computing, pp. 1–7 (2010)

25. Li, Y., Shen, L.: Skin lesion analysis towards melanoma detection using deep learning network. Sensors **18**, 556 (2018)
26. Chen, E.Z., Dong, X., Wu, J., Jiang, H., Li, X., Rong, R.: Lesion Attributes Segmentation for Melanoma Detection with Deep Learning. bioRxiv, p. 381855 (2018)
27. Maolood, I., Alsalhi, Y., Lu, S.: Thresholding for medical image segmentation for cancer using fuzzy entropy with level set algorithm. Open Med. **13**, 374–383 (2018). https://doi.org/10.1515/med-2018-0056

Biosensors and Biometric Techniques

Machine Learning Modeling of Human Activity Using PPG Signals

Anastasios Panagiotis Psathas⬤, Antonios Papaleonidas(✉)⬤, and Lazaros Iliadis⬤

Department of Civil Engineering, Democritus University of Thrace, 67100 Xanthi, Greece
{anpsatha,papaleon,liliadis}@civil.duth.gr

Abstract. The use of wearables is contributing towards the decrease of risk for chronic diseases related to cardiovascular or diabetes problems. Most wearables measure heart rate and the majority of them uses a *Photoplethysmography* (PPG) sensor. A serious limitation of the PPG sensors is their sensitivity to Motion Artifacts (MAs) which can severely corrupt the raw signal. Accurate estimation of the PPG signal as it is recorded from the subject's wearables while performing various physical activities, is a challenging task. This research introduces a novel Human Activity Recognition (HAR) approach that determines the subject's activity, by considering the respective PPG signal. It considers the public *PPG-DaLiA* dataset, for 15 persons, related to 9 activities. Totally, 24 Machine-Learning (ML) techniques were used. The weighted k-Nearest Neighbors (k-NN), the Cubic Support Vector Machines C-SVM and the Bagged Trees (BGT) have achieved the best performance.

Keywords: Bagged Trees · Cubic SVM · Human Activity Recognition (HAR) · Multi-classification · PPG-DaLiA · Wearables · Weighted k-NN

1 Introduction

Heart rate estimation is one of the most important application areas [27, 28] which can prove useful for healthcare or fitness [7, 8]. *Photoplethysmography* (PPG) sensors are among the most popular ones, as they are embedded in modern smart watches and wristbands. PPG signals are *plethysmograms* obtained optically and they are capable of detecting blood volume changes, in the microvascular bed of tissues [6]. They monitor heart rate (HR) and blood flow by diffusing light into the body and by measuring the amount of light that is reflected back. *Electrocardiography* (ECG) is a precise method of determining the heart rate, but is cumbersome under every-day life settings. Unlike the ECG monitoring, that requires placements of sticky metal electrodes on the body skin in order to monitor electrical activity from heart and muscles, PPG monitoring can be performed at peripheral sites of the body [3]. HAR applies ML models to recognize the underlying activity using the features extracted from the raw sensor traces [6]. It promotes healthy living and prevents obesity and physical inactivity (e.g., sitting and being still, or the lack of movement) [20].

© Springer Nature Switzerland AG 2020
N. T. Nguyen et al. (Eds.): ICCCI 2020, LNAI 12496, pp. 543–557, 2020.
https://doi.org/10.1007/978-3-030-63007-2_42

1.1 Literature Review

There are similar HAR researches in the literature [4]. Most of them are using a limited number of subjects or they are performed on groups of activities. In *Pirttikangas et al.* [22] data were recorded from13 subjects trying to recognize 17 different activities. Multilayer Neural Networks (NN) and k-NN were employed. The k-NN (with 4-fold cross validation) achieved an overall recognition accuracy of 90.61%.

Casale et al. [12], introduced a wearable system that applied an accelerometer on users' chest. They *manually* obtained 319 features from the signals. Random forest was employed in order to model *walking, climbing stairs, talking with a person, staying standing, and working at computer* [12]. The overall accuracy was 90%. Ahmed and Loutfi [1] used *Case Based Reasoning*, SVM and NN and achieved overall accuracy equal to 0.86, 0.62 and 0.59 respectively. Totally, 24 subjects participated in this project, performing 3 categories of activities (*breathing, walk or run, sitting and relaxing*). *Brophy et al.* [11], proposed a Convolutional NN-SVM model with overall accuracy equal to 92.3%. The dataset consisted of 8 participants performing 4 activities (*walking and running on a treadmill, low and high resistance bike exercise*). A more recent research was made by *Mehdi et al.* [6], where a deep NN was developed. Totally 12 subjects participated, trying to model 5 activities (*Standing, Walking, Jogging, Jumping and Sitting*). The model had an F1-score equal to 0.86 when predicting if the participants are in a *stationary state, walking, or jogging/jumping*.

1.2 Dataset - Innovation

This paper has used the public PPG-DaLiA dataset [23] which contains extended data records for motion recognition and heart rate estimation in Daily Life Activities. Its advantage is the fact that it comprises of data related to a very wide range of activities performed under natural conditions. It contains data from 15 subjects wearing physiological and motion sensors. It was chosen due to its large number of measurements related to long periods of time (2.5 h for each subject). It comprises of 9 specific activities *under close to real-life conditions (URLC)*, instead of groups of activities technically developed (e.g. static states, small motion, large motion). This increases modeling complexity, as there may not be significant variation in the number of pulses during the transition from one activity to another, or important changes might take a while. An important aspect is that the developed model is based on the contribution of every heart beat within every single activity. To the best of our knowledge, it is the first time in the literature that a HAR research considers such an extended URLC dataset having all of the above characteristics obtained automatically. This effort has used 24 different algorithms to determine the optimal one.

The achieved goal is the identification of each activity in real time so as to avoid any abnormalities and to protect human health. The focus is on the unexplored usability of PPG for HAR, and the determination of the way to use different components of PPG to predict human activities. Personalization has been managed, as the developed model not only considers PPG plus accelerometers' data, but it also accepts and considers data related to breathing condition and body temperature. Thus, it considers the fact that the pattern of potential changes in blood pressure, breathing and body temperature, according to the difficulty of a physical activity, distinguishes a slim and fit person from another.

2 Data

The physiological and motion data, were recorded from a wrist- and a chest-worn device of 15 subjects while performing a wide range of activities under close to real-life conditions. The data collection took approximately 2.5 h for each subject. PPG-DaLiA was introduced to public by Reiss *et al.* [23]. It is publicly available and it can be downloaded from: https://archive.ics.uci.edu/ml/datasets/PPG-DaLiA [25].

2.1 Dataset Description

The PPG_DaLiA contains data for 7 males and 8 females, aged between 21 and 55. Their respective characteristic are: *age, gender, height, weight, skin type* (according to the Fitzpatrick scale [17]) and *fitness level* (FL) which is an index on a scale 1–6, related to how often the subject exercises. A FL value of 1 is assigned to a person that exercises less than once a month, whereas a value of 6 corresponds to 5–7 times a week. The profiles of the subjects are presented in Table 1.

Table 1. Characteristics of Subjects $S_{i,j}$ where i = 1 to 15, j = {m (for Male), f (for Female)} SKT is Skin Type, FNT is Fitness Type

$S_{i,j}$	Age	Height	Weight	SKT	FNT	$S_{i,j}$	Age	Height	Weight	SKT	FNT
$S_{1,m}$	34	182	78	3	6	$S_{5,f}$	21	180	70	3	4
$S_{2,m}$	28	189	80	3	5	$S_{6,f}$	37	176	70	3	1
$S_{3,m}$	25	170	60	3	5	$S_{7,f}$	21	168	58	3	2
$S_{4,m}$	25	168	57	4	5	$S_{9,f}$	28	167	60	4	5
$S_{8,m}$	43	179	70	3	5	$S_{10,f}$	55	164	56	4	5
$S_{12,m}$	43	195	105	3	5	$S_{11,f}$	24	168	62	3	5
$S_{15,m}$	28	183	79	2	5	$S_{13,f}$	21	170	63	3	6
						$S_{14,f}$	26	170	67	3	4

Weight is measured in Kg, Height in cm and Age in years. Raw data was recorded with two devices: a chest-worn device (RespiBAN Professional, [16]) and a wrist-worn device (Empatica E4, [25]) (Table 2). Data collection was performed during a series of specific activities. Participants were instructed to carry out the activities as naturally as possible. In total, the data collection process took approximately 2.5 h for each subject. Further details on the hardware setup, participants, the data collection protocol and the dataset characteristics can be found in [23]. Regarding technical malfunctions, according to the developers of the dataset, there has only been one major hardware issue, due to which the recorded data in the case of person S_6 is only valid for the first 1.5 h.

Table 2. Raw data from sensors in RespiBAN and Empatica E4 devices

Feature	Device	Sampled at (Hz)	Description
Electrocardiogram (ECGchest)	RespiBAN	700	ECG-signal acquired via a standard three-point ECG
Three-axis accelerometer Chest-device (ACCchestx, ACCchesty, ACCchestz)	RespiBAN	700	Three-axis acceleration acquired via a 3D-accelerometer, into the RespiBAN wearable device
Respiration (Resp)	RespiBAN	700	Respiration signal acquired with an inductive respiration sensor
Blood Volume Pressure (BVP)	Empatica E4	64	Data from PPG. The PPG system consists of four LEDs (two green and two red) and two photodiode units. The PPG sensor output is the difference of light between oxygenated and non-oxygenated peaks
Three-axis accelerometer Wrist-device (ACCwristx, ACCwristy, ACCwristz)	Empatica E4	32	3 data columns refer to the 3 accelerometer channels
Electrodermal Activity (EDA)	Empatica E4	4	EDA reflects the output of integrated attentional and affective and motivational processes within the central nervous system acting on the body
Body Temperature (TEMP)	Empatica E4	4	Temperature of the body

2.2 Data Handling

The Python file *Si.pkl* includes all of the above serialized described data, and their corresponding labels-classes as well. The first step of this research effort was the development of the *Read_Pkl.py* Python script that reads the data vectors from the Si.*pkl* file and writes the respective content in plain *txt (text)* files. Activity details are presented in Table 3. The script *Mat_Trans.m* was written in Matlab. It was used to transfer the data from the text files that emerged in step 1, in Matlab for further processing. The goal of this research is to determine the type of activity for each window segment lasting 8 s (sec). The use of a **Sliding Window** with *Length* equal to 8 s and with a *Shift* value of 2 s is common practice in related work [23, 24, 27, 28] and it has also been adopted in this endeavor. Every attribute was segmented by employing this sliding window. After processing the emerged dataset, the independent and the dependent variables were determined. The *Read_Pkl.py* and the *Mat_Trans.m* Scripts are presented in the form of natural language, in Algorithms 1 and 2 respectively. The distribution of instances for each activity-class are presented in Table 4. The distribution of classes does not correspond to a characteristic case of a balanced dataset.

Table 3. Description of the eight Classes corresponding to respective Activities (AC)

Class/Activity	AC ID	Duration (min)	Description
Sitting still	1	10	Sitting still while reading. (motion artefact-free baseline)
Ascending/Descending stairs	2	5	Climbing six floors up and going down again, repeating this twice
Table soccer	3	5	Playing table soccer, 1 vs. 1 with the supervisor of the data collection
Cycling	4	8	Performed outdoors, around research campus, following a defined route of about 2 km length with varying road conditions (gravel, paved)
Driving car	5	15	Started at the parking ground of our research campus and was carried out within the area nearby. Subjects followed a defined route which took about 15 min to complete. The route included driving on different streets in a small city as well as driving on country roads
Lunch break	6	30	This activity was carried out at the canteen of research campus. The activity included queuing and fetching food, eating, and talking at the table
Walking	7	10	Walking back from the canteen to the office, with some detour
Working	8	20	Subjects returned to their desk and worked on a computer
Transient Periods	0		Before and after each activity, a transient period was included, in order to arrive at the starting location of the next activity

Table 4. Number of Instances (8 s window) for each subject (S_i) and class-activity (ACT)

S_i	ACT_0	ACT_1	ACT_2	ACT_3	ACT_4	ACT_5	ACT_6	ACT_7	ACT_8	Instances per Subject
S_1	1,141	349	143	172	205	444	1,178	377	594	4,603
S_2	1,260	300	133	152	194	460	610	345	645	4,099
S_3	1,005	300	218	146	189	455	1,080	369	605	4,367
S_4	1,260	284	261	163	237	503	948	297	619	4,572
S_5	1,287	300	232	144	215	415	1,127	295	634	4,649
S_6	1,145	317	215	155	266	524	0	0	0	2,622
S_7	1,095	309	203	137	251	518	1,212	355	588	4,668
S_8	1,042	300	206	161	209	384	900	240	595	4,037
S_9	1,001	300	241	142	277	478	921	295	622	4,277
S_{10}	1,772	298	233	152	243	468	1,042	541	572	5,321
S_{11}	1,014	300	228	162	245	430	1,205	327	610	4,521
S_{12}	994	301	242	140	240	445	730	265	597	3,954
S_{13}	1,191	302	248	145	249	449	1,014	355	612	4,565
S_{14}	1,282	303	227	162	250	477	866	307	602	4,476
S_{15}	1,026	306	209	177	203	393	721	329	602	3,966
Instances per ACT	17,515	4,569	3,239	2,310	3,473	6,843	13,554	4,697	8,497	**64,697**

There are enough records from each class that can be considered for the performance of a reliable classification and there are no extreme deviations.

Algorithm 1. The Read_Pkl.py Python Script

Script 1: *Read_Pkl.py*
Inputs: The serialized *.pkl* files, 15 in total, one for each subject (see figure 1a)
　　　　Step 1: *Deserialize* and read each one of the 15 *.pkl* files
　　　　Step 2: *Write* the respective content in the *.txt files, for each *.pkl file, 135 in total

　　　　　　　　(see figure 1b). All text files have 1 column, except for the *i_ACC_chest.txt*

　　　　and the *i_ACC_wrist.txt*, that have 3 columns.

Algorithm 2. The *Mat_Trans*.m Matlab Script

Script 2: *Mat_Trans.m*

Inputs: The 135 *.txt files exported from Script 1 (see figure 1b)

> **Part 1:**
>
> > **Step 1:** Read and convert each *.txt file to a Matlab table. The
>
> *i_ACC_chest.txt*
>
> > and the i_*ACC_wrist.txt*, have been converted to 3 tables,
>
> one for every
>
> > column (see figure 1c)
>
> **Part 2:**
>
> > **Step 1:** Every feature, except from the *ECG_bpm_i*, is segmented with
>
> a sliding
>
> > window of 8 seconds and a window shift of 2 seconds. (see
>
> figure 1d)
>
> > **Step 2:** For each time-series segment of *Activity_i*, the dominant value is
>
> held
>
> > (see figure 1d)
> >
> > **Step 3:** Fast Fourier Transform (FFT) is applied on each time series
>
> segment
>
> > of the rest features (see figure 1d)
>
> **Part 3:**
>
> > **Step 1:** A table of 12 independent and 1 dependent values is assembled
>
> from the
>
> > modified features of all 15 subjects (see figure 1e)
>
> **Step 2:** Save the tables in both .mat and .csv form for processing

A **Fast Fourier Transform** (**FFT**) has been performed on the original dataset. It computes the Discrete Fourier Transform (DFT) of a sequence, or its inverse one (IDFT) [2]. It converts a signal from its original domain (often time or space) to a representation in the frequency domain and vice versa. Any periodic function g(x) integrable in the domain D = $[-\pi, \pi]$ can be written as an infinite sum of sine and cosine as follows:

$$g(x) = \sum_{k=-\infty}^{\infty} \tau_k e^{jkx} \tag{1}$$

$$\tau_k = \frac{1}{2\pi} \int_D g(x) e^{-jkx} dx \tag{2}$$

Where $e^{i\theta} = \cos(\theta) + j\sin(\theta)$. *The idea that a function can be broken down into its constituent frequencies is powerful one and forms the backbone of the FFT* [14]. An FFT rapidly computes such transformations by factorizing the DFT matrix into a product of sparse (mostly zero) factors. As a result, it manages to reduce the complexity of computing the DFT from $O(N^2)$, which arises if one simply applies the definition of DFT, to $O(N.logN)$, where N is the data size. The FFT is an extension of the above

Fourier series to non-periodic functions. It is an *extremely* powerful mathematical tool that allows one to view the obtained signals in a different domain, inside which several difficult problems become very simple to *analyze.m.*

If x(t) is a continuous integrable signal, its FFT, X(f) is given by Eq. 3.

$$X(f) = \int_{\mathbb{R}} x(t)e^{-j2\pi ft}dt, \forall f \in \mathbb{R} \tag{3}$$

The inverse transformation is given by Eq. 4.

$$X(t) = \int_{\mathbb{R}} x(f)e^{-j2\pi ft}df, \forall f \in \mathbb{R} \tag{4}$$

FFT operates by decomposing an N point time domain signal, into N time domain signals each composed of a single point. The second step is to calculate the N frequency spectra corresponding to these N time domain signals. Finally, the N spectra are synthesized into a single frequency spectrum. It's ubiquity in nearly every field of engineering and physical sciences. The abbreviation Dominant is only for the variable Activity. The processing of every 8 s window of Activity is applied through the retention of the dominant value. The following Fig. 1 is a graphical representation of the overall algorithm. The FFT abbreviation is for those variables that have undergone FFT for a window of 8 s.

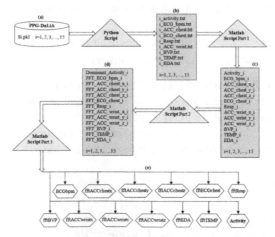

Fig. 1. The data cannot be separated by a hyperplane in the two-dimensional space (left). By using a kernel function the data becomes linearly separable in a higher dimensional feature space (right).

3 Classification Methodology

The independent variables used for the classification are the following: The processed signals from *RespiBAN* Professional [16] and *Empatica E4* [25] (fftACCchestx, fftACC-chesty, fftACCchestz, fftECGchest, fftResp, fftBVP, fftACCwristx, fftACCwristy, fftAC-Cwristz, fftEDA, fftTEMP) applying FFT in each variable, using a sliding window with length of 8 s and shift of 2 s. The ECGbpm was used as an independent feature, provided by the developers of the dataset. A total of 23 classification algorithms have been employed namely: *Fine Tree, Medium Tree, Coarse Tree, Linear Discriminant, Quadratic Discriminant, Linear SVM, Quadratic SVM, Cubic SVM, Fine Gaussian SVM, Medium Gaussian SVM, Coarse Gaussian SVM, Cosine KNN, Cubic KNN, Weighted KNN, Fine KNN, Medium KNN, Gaussian Naive Bayes, Kernel Naïve Bayes, Boosted Trees, Bagged Trees, Subspace Discriminant, Subspace KNN, RUSBoost Trees.* Only the architecture and the results of the three most robust algorithms with the highest values of performance indices, are described herein.

3.1 Brief Description of the Best Performing Algorithms

Weighted k-Nearest-Neighbors (Weighted k-NN). Given a set X of n points and a distance function, k-NN search finds the k closest points to a query point or set of them [19]. Dunami [15] first introduced a weighted voting method, called the *distance-weighted (DW) k-nearest neighbor rule* (Wk-NN). The closer neighbors are weighted more heavily than the farther ones, using the DW function. The weight w_i for the i-th nearest neighbor of the query x' is defined following function 5:

$$w_i' = \begin{cases} \frac{d(x'x_k^{NN})-d(x'x_i^{NN})}{d(x'x_k^{NN})-d(x'x_1^{NN})}, & if \quad d(x'x_k^{NN}) \neq d(x'x_1^{NN}) \\ 1 & , if \quad d(x'x_k^{NN}) = d(x'x_1^{NN}) \end{cases} \tag{5}$$

The classification result is determined by the majority weighted voting (function 6):

$$y' = \arg\max_{y} \sum_{(x_i^{NN}, y_i^{NN}) \in T'} w_i' \times \delta\left(y = y_i^{NN}\right) \tag{6}$$

Cubic SVM. Support Vector Machines [5] are a supervised ML approach [18]. They treat each of the observations as an n-dimensional vector, in order to find out if these observations can be separated in two classes by an $n - 1$ dimensional hyperplane (Fig. 2).

The optimum hyperplane maximizes the distance between the two classes and it is defined by only a small number of data points which are called support vectors (SV) which are derived through a minimization procedure.

Bagged Trees. Bagging is a ML method of combining multiple predictors. It is a model averaging approach. Bagging is a technique generating multiple training sets by sampling with replacement from the available training data [9, 10]. It reduces variance and helps to avoid overfitting. The bagging method creates a sequence of classifiers H_m m = 1, ..., M in respect to modifications of the training set, which are combined into a compound one.

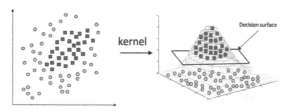

Fig. 2. By using a kernel function the data becomes linearly separable in a higher dimensional feature space (right).

It is a voting procedure discussed in [29]. Parameters α_m, m = 1, ..., M are determined in such way that more precise classifiers have stronger influence on the final prediction than less precise classifiers. Bagged trees use Breiman's 'random forest' algorithm [26].

4 Evaluation of the Activity Model Classifiers

Additional indices have been used to estimate the efficiency of the algorithms. The "One Versus All" Strategy [21, 26] was used. Table 5 presents the calculated validation indices Table 5.

Table 5. Calculated indices for the evaluation of the multi-class classification approach

Index	Abbreviation	Calculation
Sensitivity (also known as True Positive Rate or Recall)	**SNS, REC, TPR,**	**SNS = TP/(TP + FN)**
Specificity, (also known as True Negative Rate)	SPC, TNR	SPC = TN/(TN + FP)
Accuracy	ACC	ACC = (TP + TN)/(TP + FP + FN + TN)
F1 Score	F1	F1 = 2 * TP/(2 * TP + FP + FN)
Precision (also known as Positive predictive value)	PREC	PREC = TP/(TP + FP)

4.1 Experimental Results

The experiments were performed with the use of Matlab R2019a. The options and hyperparameters set for each algorithm are presented in Table 6. The weighted k-NN, Cubic SVM and Bagged Trees algorithms achieved an accuracy equal to 80%, 81.1% and 92.8% respectively. The Confusion Matrix (CM) and the ROC Curve for each algorithm are presented in the following Figs. 3, 4 and 5 below.

Table 6. Tuning Algorithms' hyperparameters

Algorithm	Hyperparameters	Optimal Values- functions
Weighted k-NN	**Number of neighbors**	**10**
	Distance metric	Euclidean
	Distance weight	Squared inverse
Cubic SVM	Box constraint level (C)	1
	Kernel scale	1
Bagged Trees	Maximum number of splits	10,000
	Number of learners	200
	Learning rate	0.1
	Subspace dimension	1

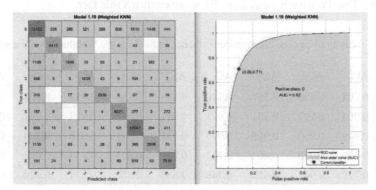

Fig. 3. Confusion Matrix and ROC Curve of the weighted k-NN algorithm

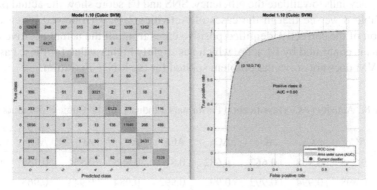

Fig. 4. Confusion Matrix and ROC Curve of the Cubic SVM

Table 7 shows, that for all classes, the vast majority of negatives are correctly identified. In the cases of Activities 2, 7 (followed by the cases 0 and 3) the proportion

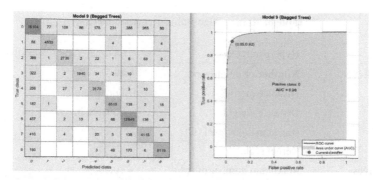

Fig. 5. Confusion Matrix and ROC Curve of the Ensemble Bagged Trees algorithm

of the correctly identified positive cases from all the actual positive cases is Low. The performance of the k-NN for the positive cases is below our expectations. For Activities 2 and 7 the True Positive Rate is Low. F1 score confirms this fact.

Table 7. Activity (AC) classification Performance Indices for the Weighted k-NN algorithm

Index	AC_0	AC_1	AC_2	AC_3	AC_4	AC_5	AC_6	AC_7	AC_8
SNS	0.708	0.966	**0.557**	0.710	0.844	0.880	0.889	**0.638**	0.885
SPC	0.905	0.992	0.991	0.991	0.991	0.985	0.927	0.961	0.972
ACC	0.849	0.990	**0.965**	0.979	0.981	0.971	0.918	**0.934**	0.958
PREC	0.750	0.918	0.807	0.792	0.867	0.893	0.794	0.602	0.856
F1	0.729	0.942	**0.659**	0.748	0.855	0.886	0.839	**0.620**	0.870

Accuracy fails to validate the efficiency. SNS and F1 score show the actual problem.

In Table 8 we see that in the cases of Activities 2, 3, 7 (followed by case 0) the proportion of the correctly identified positive cases from all the actual positive cases is Low. This is confirmed by F1 score which has slightly higher value for these cases. The use of SVM does not solve the problem spotted for the k-NN algorithm.

Table 8. Activity (AC) classification Performance Indices for the Cubic SVM algorithm

Index	AC_0	AC_1	AC_2	AC_3	AC_4	AC_5	AC_6	AC_7	AC_8
SNS	0.738	0.968	**0.662**	**0.682**	0.870	0.895	0.851	**0.730**	0.862
SPC	0.898	0.994	0.992	0.992	0.992	0.984	0.943	0.963	0.976
ACC	0.852	0.992	0.972	0.979	0.984	0.973	0.921	0.944	0.958
PREC	0.741	0.943	0.838	0.803	0.880	0.893	0.823	**0.648**	0.868
F1	0.740	0.955	**0.740**	**0.738**	0.875	0.894	0.837	**0.687**	0.865

Table 9. Activity (AC) classification Performance Indices for the Bagged Trees algorithm

Index	AC_0	AC_1	AC_2	AC_3	AC_4	AC_5	AC_6	AC_7	AC_8
SNS	**0.919**	0.986	**0.845**	**0.840**	0.913	0.952	0.948	**0.877**	0.956
SPC	0.952	0.999	0.998	0.998	0.995	0.993	0.982	0.991	0.997
ACC	0.943	0.998	0.989	0.992	0.991	0.989	0.975	0.983	0.991
PREC	0.880	0.983	0.950	0.947	0.922	0.948	0.938	0.894	0.981
F1	0.899	0.984	0.894	0.890	0.917	0.950	0.943	0.885	0.968

The values of all indices in Table 9 shows a very good performance. The Bagged Trees algorithm is the optimal approach.

5 Discussion and Conclusions

We have achieved successful human activity recognition, by considering a physiometry dataset, obtained from RespiBAN [22] and Empatica E4 [13] devices. We obtained 9 classes close to real-life conditions. The best 3 models were the weighted k-NN, Cubic SVM and Bagged Trees (BGT) with accuracy as high as **80%, 81.1% and 92.8% respectively. BGT' accuracy was the highest** [1, 11, 12, 22]. The Accuracy values have proven to be misleading as they did not spot the below average performance of k-NN and SVM for the negatives in the cases of Activities 2, 7. This problem was solved by the employment of the Bagged Trees which has achieved very high Sensitivity indices for the negatives of the problematic cases 2, 7, 0, 3. Also it achieved very high F1-score values (ranging from 0.885 to 0.968 for all classes) much higher than respective values reported in [6]. BGT produces very high values for all indices even for Class 0, which is the transition period from activity to activity. This class is a combination of other activities (e.g. walk to the stairs at the main building, or walk from the parking ground to the canteen). Sometimes the algorithms got confused and classified Class 0 as other classes or vice versa. This research has proven that we can overcome this obstacle.

References

1. Ahmed, M.U., Loutfi, A,.: Physical activity identification using supervised machine learning and based on pulse rate. Int. J. Adv. Comput. Sci. Appl. 4(7), 210–217 (2013)
2. Beerends, R.J., ter Morsche, H.G., Van den Berg, J.C., Van de Vrie, E.M.: Fourier and Laplace Transforms, p. 458. Cambridge University Press, Cambridge (2003). ISBN 0521534410
3. Bhowmik, T., Dey, J., Tiwari, V.N.: A novel method for accurate estimation of HRV from smartwatch PPG signals. In: 2017 39th Annual International Conference of the IEEE Engineering in Medicine and Biology Society (EMBC), pp. 109–112. IEEE, July 2017
4. Biagetti, G., Crippa, P., Falaschetti, L., Orcioni, S., Turchetti, C.: Human activity recognition using accelerometer and photoplethysmographic signals. In: Czarnowski, I., Howlett, R.J., Jain, L.C. (eds.) IDT 2017. SIST, vol. 73, pp. 53–62. Springer, Cham (2018). https://doi.org/10.1007/978-3-319-59424-8_6

5. Boser, B.E., Guyon, I.M., Vapnik, V.N.: A training algorithm for optimal margin classifiers. In: Proceedings of the Fifth Annual Workshop on Computational Learning Theory, pp. 144–152. ACM, July 1992
6. Boukhechba, M., Cai, L., Wu, C., Barnes, L.E.: ActiPPG: using deep neural networks for activity recognition from wrist-worn photoplethysmography (PPG) sensors. Smart Health **14**, 100082 (2019)
7. Boukhechba, M., Chow, P., Fua, K., Teachman, B.A., Barnes, L.E.: Predicting social anxiety from global positioning system traces of college students: feasibility study. JMIR Ment. Health **5**(3), e10101 (2018)
8. Boukhechba, M., Daros, A.R., Fua, K., Chow, P.I., Teachman, B.A., Barnes, L.E.: DemonicSalmon: monitoring mental health and social interactions of college students using smartphones. Smart Health **9**, 192–203 (2018)
9. Breiman, L.: Arcing the edge. Technical report 486, Statistics Department, University of California at Berkeley (1997)
10. Breiman, L.: Bagging predictors. Technical report 421, Department of Statistics, University of California at Berkeley (1994)
11. Brophy, E., Veiga, J.J.D., Wang, Z., Smeaton, A.F., Ward, T.E.: An interpretable machine vision approach to human activity recognition using photoplethysmograph sensor data. arXiv preprint arXiv:1812.00668 (2018)
12. Casale, P., Pujol, O., Radeva, P.: Human activity recognition from accelerometer data using a wearable device. In: Vitrià, J., Sanches, J.M., Hernández, M. (eds.) IbPRIA 2011. LNCS, vol. 6669, pp. 289–296. Springer, Heidelberg (2011). https://doi.org/10.1007/978-3-642-21257-4_36
13. Cochran, W.T., et al.: What is the fast Fourier transform? Proc. IEEE **55**(10), 1664–1674 (1967)
14. Cooley, J.W., Lewis, P., Welch, P.: Application of the fast Fourier transform to computation of Fourier integrals, Fourier series, and convolution integrals. IEEE Trans. Audio Electroacoust. **15**(2), 79–84 (1967)
15. Dudani, S.A.: The distance-weighted k-nearest neighbor rule. IEEE Trans. Syst. Man Cybern. **8**(4), 311–313 (1978)
16. Empatica E4 wristband (2019). https://www.empatica.com/en-eu/research/e4/. Accessed 20 Sept 2019
17. Fitzpatrick, T.B.: The validity and practicality of sun-reactive skin types I through VI. Arch. Dermatol. **124**(6), 869–871 (1988)
18. Gogas, P., Papadimitriou, T., Sofianos, E.: Money neutrality, monetary aggregates and machine learning. Algorithms **12**(7), 137 (2019)
19. Hechenbichler, K., Schliep, K.: Weighted k-nearest-neighbor techniques and ordinal classification (2004)
20. Incel, O.D., Kose, M., Ersoy, C.: A review and taxonomy of activity recognition on mobile phones. BioNanoScience **3**(2), 145–171 (2013). https://doi.org/10.1007/s12668-013-0088-3
21. Joutsijoki, H., Juhola, M.: Comparing the one-vs-one and one-vs-all methods in benthic macroinvertebrate image classification. In: Perner, P. (ed.) MLDM 2011. LNCS (LNAI), vol. 6871, pp. 399–413. Springer, Heidelberg (2011). https://doi.org/10.1007/978-3-642-23199-5_30
22. Pirttikangas, S., Fujinami, K., Nakajima, T.: Feature selection and activity recognition from wearable sensors. In: Youn, H.Y., Kim, M., Morikawa, H. (eds.) UCS 2006. LNCS, vol. 4239, pp. 516–527. Springer, Heidelberg (2006). https://doi.org/10.1007/11890348_39
23. Reiss, A., Indlekofer, I., Schmidt, P., Van Laerhoven, K.: Deep PPG: large-scale heart rate estimation with convolutional neural networks. Sensors **19**(14), 3079 (2019)

24. Reiss, A., Schmidt, P., Indlekofer, I., Van Laerhoven, K.: PPG-based heart rate estimation with time-frequency spectra: a deep learning approach. In: Proceedings of the 2018 ACM International Joint Conference and 2018 International Symposium on Pervasive and Ubiquitous Computing and Wearable Computers, pp. 1283–1292. ACM, October 2018
25. RespiBAN Professional (2019). https://www.biosignalsplux.com/index.php/respiban-profes sional. Accessed 20 Sept 2019
26. Rifkin, R., Klautau, A.: In defense of one-vs-all classification. J. Mach. Learn. Res. 5(Jan), 101–141 (2004)
27. Salehizadeh, S., Dao, D., Bolkhovsky, J., Cho, C., Mendelson, Y., Chon, K.H.: A novel time-varying spectral filtering algorithm for reconstruction of motion artifact corrupted heart rate signals during intense physical activities using a wearable photoplethysmogram sensor. Sensors 16(1), 10 (2016)
28. Schäck, T., Muma, M., Zoubir, A.M.: Computationally efficient heart rate estimation during physical exercise using photoplethysmographic signals. In: 2017 25th European Signal Processing Conference (EUSIPCO), pp. 2478–2481. IEEE, August 2017
29. Schapire, R.E., Freund, Y., Bartlett, P., Lee, W.S.: Boosting the margin: a new explanation for the effectiveness of voting methods. Ann. Stat. 26(5), 1651–1686 (1998)

A Variational Autoencoder Approach for Speech Signal Separation

Hao D. Do[1,2,3]($\boxtimes$), Son T. Tran[1,2], and Duc T. Chau[1,2]

[1] University of Science, Ho Chi Minh City, Vietnam
{ttson,ctduc}@fit.hcmus.edu.vn
[2] Vietnam National University, Ho Chi Minh City, Vietnam
[3] OLLI Technology JSC, Ho Chi Minh City, Vietnam
hao@olli-ai.com.vn

Abstract. Speech separation plays an important role in a speech-related system since it can denoise, extract, and enhance speech signals. In recent years, many methods are proposed to separate the human voice of noise and other sounds. To separate the speech from a complicated signal, we propose a more powerful method by using a VAE model and then post-processing with a bandpass filter. This combination can use to extract the original human speech in the mixture with not only high-frequency noise but also many different sounds. Our approach can be flexibly applied for the new background sounds.

Keywords: Bandpass filter · Variational autoencoder · Frequency domain · Speech separation

1 Introduction

The quality of data is very important for every machine learning applications, including speech-related applications. For an instant, speech recognition in a clean environment is much easier than in a noise environment. Because noised data can generate bad features for the learning model, the process of cleaning data is very important. With the speech data, this problem becomes more serious because noises and interference always exist. The signal we input to the model is the mixture of human speech and many other elements. If this mixture is separated into many independent frequency elements, the main signal can be extracted and reconstructed from some of them while the remaining ones are ignored because they are noises.

In this research, we suggest an approach to filter only human speech in the recorded sound. We combine a variational autoencoder (VAE) [1,2] - a machine learning model, and bandpass filter (BPF) [3] - a powerful tool in signal processing. In the frequency domain, we design a variational autoencoder network to capture the main behavior of human speech including intonation and content. The reconstructed signal via the variational autoencoder will be post-processed by a bandpass filter to hold only the harmonic elements which belong to the

N. T. Nguyen et al. (Eds.): ICCCI 2020, LNAI 12496, pp. 558–567, 2020.
https://doi.org/10.1007/978-3-030-63007-2_43

speech range. The whole solution includes a non-deep variational autoencoder and a Chebyshev filter, so it run too fast. On the other hand, this combination can clear most of the background sound and noise from the recorded sound, and hold most of the important information need for high-level applications.

We show that our approach can reduce perfectly out of range frequency elements and mostly intersect elements. We firstly apply a neural network architecture with the variational autoencoder style. This approach can be extended to apply to many similar applications related to speech or signal analysis to enhance the input signal. Because using the strength of the neural network, we interfere with all frequency of a signal to keep the speech signal and reduce the background signal. Our experimental results show that we reduce mostly background elements. This is a good achievement in comparison with the works by Wolf [4] and Ning Yang [5] in 2016 and 2017, respectively.

The proposed approach is a good solution for speech-related applications. Firstly, the model separates speech from the signal very fast, so it can use in real-time applications like voice bot or voice translator. Next, because the two main parts of the model are only small and not complicated, so it can be deployed into not only the server but also the edge devices such as the microphone. Lastly, and the most important, the proposed improves performance a lot in many applications.

The paper is organized as follows. Section 2 presents the related researches to this work. Then we describe our proposed model clearly in Sect. 3. In Sect. 4, we present our experimental results and compare them with the previous researches.

2 Related Works

There are many techniques proposed to due with the BSS problem. After the 2000s, because of the fast developments of artificial intelligence in general, machine learning methods, and computing infrastructure like GPUs, related-speech real-time applications are created more and more. This motivates that many methods are researched to extract, preprocess, and enhance the input speech signal. They are explored deeply to reconstruct or extract the main information from signal mixtures.

In the non-deep machine learning field, there are many effective algorithms for BSS and the most popular methods include Principal Component Analysis (PCA) [6], Independent Component Analysis (ICA) [8], and Singular Value Decomposition (SVD) [7]. These algorithms have been used in many applications, not only in speech signal processing but also in wireless communication and electrocardiogram technologies [9].

To describe the input signal, time-domain frequency representation is the original form of any kind of signal. This form is suitable to show the mixture and its components. With this waveform, the signal can be used in some applications in digital speech processing [10]. In these applications, many convolutional methods are used to deal with continuous signals BSS problem. However, these solutions work with an expensive computational cost and require hardware resources for implementation [11].

On the other hand, the behavior of the input signal in the frequency domain is shown by Short-Time Fourier Transform (STFT) [12]. The STFT firstly uses the Fourier spectrum to present the signal [13]. Then it applies the Time Window (TW) functions [14] to separate the signal into many time frames. Finally, the signal is analyzed in both the time and the frequency domain [15,16].

3   Variational Autoencoder for Speech Separation

3.1   Blind Source Separation and Speech Separation

In many speech-related applications, the main signal is usually impacted by noises and other signal sources. They can be the fan sounds, wind sounds, traffic sounds, or the sounds produced by other people. These unexpected signals distort the spectral of the speech. This causes a significant problem because a distorted signal cannot be recognized correctly by any machine learning models.

To clean the input source before we push it into the main model, the signal should be separated into its original elements including speech and the others. This description is very similar to the BSS problem.

The BSS problem is formulated to due with the Cocktail party problem, which is a classic issue in signal processing [17]. Assuming there are m people talking in the party, we use n devices to record the sounds and then use the recorded sounds to reconstruct the original voices separately.

Let s, x, γ denote the human speeches, recorded sounds, and noises in the party, we can formulate the relation as follow:

$$x(t) = A_{M \times N} \times s(t) + \gamma(t) \tag{1}$$

with A called the mixing matrix.

With the given signal $x(t)$, the path to restore the $s(t)$ includes two phases. The first phase filter the noises $\gamma(t)$ to hold the only human speech in the signal. The remaining phase uses a model to separate the mixture into the original human speeches. This is the reason we combine a machine learning model as VAE and a filter for BSS problem. These two elements are used in two phases separately to clean and reconstruct the speeches.

In this work, we focus on a special case of BSS where there are only two signals in the mixture including a human speech and another background sound. This means that our problem is the traditional BSS at $m = 2$.

3.2   Short Time Fourier Transform

The main properties of human speech include intonation, tone, stress, prosody, and sound. All these aspects are shown clearly in the frequency domain because they are caused by the vibration of the vocal track. This fact motivates us to use the frequency domain to present the input data for the processing model.

Fourier transform (FT) presents the signal as a summary of many sinusoidal elements while each element is corresponding with a particular frequency. Here is the formula for FT of $y[n]$, a discrete signal with N elements:

$$Y[k] = \sum_{n=0}^{N-1} y[n] \times e^{-j2\pi kn/N} \tag{2}$$

These factors show the power of sinusoidal waves and hence the properties of the signal. FT only shows the global attributes of the signal because each sub-wave is computed from the whole signal. That causes the development of Short-Time Fourier Transform (STFT), a transform that can show the values of sinusoidal waves and their changes by the time.

$$Y[m, k] = \sum_{n=0}^{N-1} y[n] \times w[n - m] \times e^{-j2\pi kn/N} \tag{3}$$

In the formula below, $Y[m, k]$ is the value in the time-frequency domain. The function $w[t]$ presents the way a window function masks the signal. There are many different window functions including rectangle, Gaussian, Harris window, etc. [18]. We choose the Blackman - Harris window for our work [19] because it minimizes the side-slope levels of the window by adding three more sinusoidal elements.

To convert the signal from the frequency domain to the time domain, we use the Invert Short Time Fourier Transform (ISTFT), named Filter Bank Summation (FBS) [20]:

$$y[n] = \frac{1}{w[0] \times N} \times \sum_{k=0}^{N-1} Y[m, k] \times e^{-j2\pi kn/N} \tag{4}$$

3.3 Variational Autoencoder

The main work in a BSS solution is phase two. That means we should build a model to convert the mixture to the original human speech. The model should identify which harmonic elements should be held to reconstruct human speech. In this research, we design a variational autoencoder as a separator. This model learns the features of human speech and uses them to decide whether a harmonic term is held or ignored.

Autoencoder [21,22] and its extended version variational autoencoder (VAE) are multi-layer neural network. These designs can be applied in many issues such as signal denoising or data compressing.

To mathematically define the VAE model, the input and output are denoted by $x, f(x)$, the encoder and decoder are denoted by $Q(.), P(.)$, and the code vale is denote by z (as in Fig. 1). Different with traditional autoencoder, z is a result of the fomula $z = Q(x)$, in variational autoencoder [1,2], z is supposingly created by sampling from $Q(x)$. If $Q(.)$ forms a Gaussian distribution, z is sampled from $N(\mu, \Sigma)$.

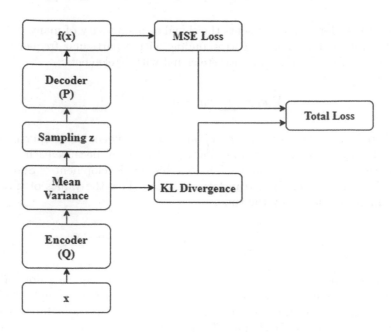

Fig. 1. Work flow of a Variational Autoencoder

When training the VAE, z is computed as follow:

$$z = \mu + \epsilon \times \Sigma \tag{5}$$

with ϵ is sampled from the normal distribution $N(0,1)$. This is called the reparameterization trick. In the original form of VAE, a sampling step cannot be back-propagating the error. When using this trick, two variable μ, Σ are updated easily and then being pushed into the optimal value.

There are two main purposes of variational autoencoder [23]. The first is how to reconstruct the original voice. The second is how to maintain the normal distribution for z. Let $q(.), p(.)$ denote the original and the reconstructed distributions of signal. The objective function is:

$$Loss_{\phi,\theta}(x_i) = E_{z \sim q\theta(x_i|z)} \log p_\phi(x_i|z) - KL(q_\theta(z|x_i), p_\phi(z)) \tag{6}$$

with $KL(q(.), p(.))$ presents the KL divergence [24] [25] of two distribution:

$$KL(q(x), p(x)) = \sum_{-\infty}^{\infty} (q(x) \times \log \frac{q(x)}{p(x)}) \tag{7}$$

We apply the reparameterization trick with ϵ is sampled from a normal distribution, then:

$$Loss_{\phi,\theta}(x_i) = \frac{1}{L} \sum_{l=1}^{L} \log p_\phi(x_i|z_i^l) + \frac{1}{2} \sum_{j=1}^{J} (1 + \log((\Sigma_i^j)^2) - (\mu_i^j)^2 - (\Sigma_i^j)^2) \tag{8}$$

when L, J denote the size for code layer and output layer.

Finally, the total loss of variational autoencoder is computed by:

$$Loss_{VAE} = Loss_{MSE}(x_i) + Loss_{\phi,\theta}(x_i) \tag{9}$$

with

$$Loss_{MSE}(x_i) = ||x_i - P(Q(x_i))||^2 \tag{10}$$

To train the VAE network, We apply the Back-propagation algorithm [26]. When the model is trained, we apply it to separate the mixture of signals in the inferring phase.

3.4 Bandpass Filter

Because the main content of human speech mostly spreads from 50 5000 Hz in the frequency domain, we apply a bandpass filter to clear all out-of-range harmonic elements. We use the Chebyshev filter for this process because this filter is the most suitable choice when filtering sine shape elements.

$$G_n(\omega) = H_n(j\omega) = \frac{1}{\sqrt{1 + r^2 T_n^2(\frac{\omega}{\omega_0})}} \tag{11}$$

with r, T, ω denote the ripple factor, order, and the cutoff frequency.

3.5 The Combination of VAE and Bandpass Filter for BSS

In this paper, we combine a VAE and a Chebyshev filter to due with two phases in a BSS problem. Figure 2 [27] illustrates our whole solution.

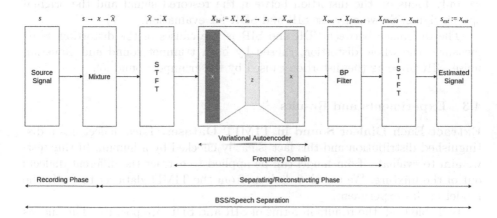

Fig. 2. BSS problem with VAE and bandpass filter

We use the time-frequency domain to present the data, that is the reason we apply STFT and ISTFT at the beginning and end of the process. The central block is a VAE, which is in charge of separating the mixture into the original sources and then keeping the human speech signal. The bandpass filter holds only the harmonic in the frequency range of speech. Finally, the last block is the estimated or the reconstructed voice.

4   Experimental Result

4.1   Dataset

In this work, we use the TIMIT dataset [28] as the data for the main speech signal and trumpet sounds for background sounds. TIMIT is a well-known data set for speech processing tasks. It includes 630 voices, corresponding with 630 speakers. Each person was recorded with ten sentences. Totally, TIMIT contains exactly 6300 audio files and we use all of them for our experiments.

The trumpet sounds are the second signal for our testes. We firstly collect 20 short audio files. Then we change the amplitudes of these files randomly by multiplying the original value with a random number in $[0, 1]$. Finally, we achieve a collection of 100 audio files for trumpet with many different amplitudes.

To get the data set for our experiments, we mix randomly a signal in TIMIT with a trumpet signal. Then we add Gaussian noise to form the mixture. Finally, our data set contains 6300 mixed signals. We use 90% of them for the training phase and 10% remaining for the inferring phase.

4.2   Evaluation Method

Vincent [29] suggested that we should use many measures including SDR, SIR, SNR, and SAR to verify the performance of a BSS solution. But in our research, we only focus on the distortion between the restored signal and the original speech signal. So we only use SIR and SDR for evaluation.

The difference between SDR and SIR is the causes of the distortion. SDR measures the whole distortion, caused by both trumpet sound and Gaussian noise. SIR presents the distortion caused by the trumpet sound [5].

4.3   Experiments and Results

Extract Each Dialect Sound in TIMIT Dataset. Each dialect has a distinguished distribution and this fact is easily checked by a human. In this test, we aim to evaluate if our model can be applied to extract the different dialects our of the mixture. We use all 8 dialects from the TIMIT data set to verify the model in this experiment.

In Table 1, all the results in terms of SIR and SDR are positive. This means that the noise is removed partly (SIR is positive) and the reconstructed sound looks like the original speech (SDR is positive). We can also see that the results are not stable between all 8 dialects. Some dialects get better results while some dialects get worst. This means that with each particular dialect, or voice, the design for VAE should not be the same.

Table 1. The results for 8 dialects separately in TIMIT

Dialect	SIR (db)	SDR (db)
1	8.75	11.02
2	6.11	8.20
3	6.80	7.54
4	12.34	13.02
5	2.28	2.15
6	9.61	10.11
7	9.36	8.69
8	4.14	4.92
Average	7.42	8.2

Extract Speech with Many Dialects from TIMIT Dataset. In this experiment, we aim to evaluate our approach when there are many dialects in the input. This task is more difficult than the test in Sect. 4.3 because the distribution of the input diverse. We use all samples in the TIMIT dataset for this experiment. Because the model was trained with a much bigger data set, the results (Table 2) is improved in comparison with the first experiment (Table 1).

Table 2. Results with whole TIMIT data set

Measure	SIR (dB)	SDR (dB)
Proposed method	9.81	17.51
Wolf [4] (2016)	7.56	16.22
Ning Yang [5] (2017)	9.47	21.09

In comparison with the works by Wolf [4] and Ning Yang [5], our model achieve the highest score in SIR and the second highest in SDR. This means that the reconstructed sound from our model is clearer than all the others, or the clearest sound. On the other hand, because the SDR score of us is lower than the research by Ning Yang, the remaining content in our output sound is incomplete.

5   Conclusion

We have suggested an effective approach for the BSS problems. We use the variational autoencoder to extract the original human speech out of the mixture and then use a bandpass filter to remove high-frequency noises. The experimental results prove that the combination in this research works well for the BSS problem.

References

1. Kingma, D.P., Welling, M.: Auto-encoding variational Bayes. In: International Conference on Learning Representations (2014)
2. Diederik, P.: Kingma and Max Welling: an introduction to variational autoencoders. Found. Trends Mach. Learn. **12**(4), 307–392 (2019)
3. Shenoi, B.A.: Introduction to Digital Signal Processing and Filter Design. Wiley, Hoboken (2006)
4. Wolf, G., Mallat, S., Shamma, S.: Rigid motion model for audio source separation. IEEE Trans. Signal Process. **64**(7), 1822–1831 (2016)
5. Yang, N., Usman, M., He, X., Jan, M.A., Zhang, L.: Time-frequency filter bank: a simple approach for audio and music separation. IEEE Access **5**, 27114–27125 (2017)
6. Serviere, C., Fabry, P.: Principal component analysis and blind source separation of modulated sources for electromechanical systems diagnostic. Mech. Syst. Signal Process. **19**, 1293–1311 (2005)
7. Lee, S., Pang, H.-S.: Multichannel non-negative matrix factorisation based on alternating least squares for audio source separation system. Electron. Lett. **51**(3), 197–198 (2015)
8. Chien, J., Hsieh, H.: Convex divergence ICA for blind source separation. IEEE Trans. Audio Speech Lang. Process. **20**(1), 302–313 (2012)
9. Fu, G.-S., Phlypo, R., Anderson, M., Li, X.-L., Adal, T.: Blind source separation by entropy rate minimization. IEEE Trans. Signal Process. **62**(16), 4245–4255 (2014)
10. Liu, B., Reju, V.G., Khong, A.W.H., Reddy, V.V.: A GMM post-filter for residual crosstalk suppression in blind source separation. IEEE Signal Process. Lett. **21**(8), 942–946 (2014)
11. Hosseini, S., Deville, Y.: Blind separation of parametric nonlinear mixtures of possibly auto correlated and non-stationary sources. IEEE Trans. Signal Process. **62**(24), 6521–6533 (2014)
12. Allen, J.B.: Short time spectral analysis, synthesis, and modification by discrete Fourier transform. IEEE Trans. Acoust. Speech Signal Process. **25**(3), 235–238 (1977)
13. Okopal, G., Wisdom, S., Atlas, L.: Speech analysis with the strong uncorrelating transform. IEEE/ACM Trans. Audio Speech Lang. Process. **23**(11), 1858–1868 (2015)
14. Kabal, P.: Time Windows for Linear Prediction of Speech. McGill University (2009)
15. Le Roux, J., Vincent, E.: Consistent Wiener filtering for audio source separation. IEEE Signal Process. Lett. **20**(3), 217–220 (2013)
16. Mai, V.-K., Pastor, D., Aïssa-El-Bey, A., Le-Bidan, R.: Robust estimation of non-stationary noise power spectrum for speech enhancement. IEEE/ACM Trans. Audio Speech Lang. Process. **23**(4), 670–682 (2015)
17. Parande, P.G., Thomas, T.G.: A study of the cocktail party problem. In: International Conference on Electrical and Computing Technologies and Applications (ICECTA), pp. 1–5 (2017)
18. Oppenheim, A.V., Schafer, R.W., Buck, J.A.: Discrete-Time Signal Processing. Prentice Hall, Upper Saddle River (1999)
19. Blackman, R.B., Tukey, J.W.: The Measurement of Power Spectra from the Point of View of Communications Engineering. Dover Publications Publishing House, New York (1959)

20. Quatieri, T.F.: Discrete-Time Speech Signal Processing: Principles and Practice. Prentice Hall Publishing House, Upper Saddle River (2001)
21. Kramer, M.A.: Nonlinear principal component analysis using autoassociative neural networks. AIChE J. **37**(2), 233–243 (1991)
22. Hinton, G.E., Zemel, R.S.: Autoencoders, minimum description length and Helmholtz free energy. In: Advances in Neural Information Processing Systems 6, pp. 3–10 (1994)
23. Doersch, C.: Tutorial on variational autoencoders. arXiv:1606.05908 (2016)
24. Kullback, S., Leibler, R.A.: On information and sufficiency. Ann. Math. Stat. **22**(1), 79–86 (1951)
25. Kullback, S.: Information Theory and Statistics. Wiley, Hoboken (1959)
26. Rumelhart David, E., Hinton Geoffrey, E., Williams, R.J.: Learning representations by back-propagating errors. Nature **323**(6088), 533–536 (1986)
27. Do, H.D., Tran, S.T., Chau, D.T.: Speech source separation using variational autoencoder and bandpass filter. IEEE Access **8**, 156219–156231 (2020)
28. Fisher William, M., Doddington George, R., Goudie-Marshall, K.M.: The DARPA speech recognition research database: specifications and status (1986)
29. Vincent, E., Gribonval, R., Févotte, C.: Performance measurement in blind audio source separation. IEEE Trans. Audio Speech Lang. Process. **14**(4), 1462–1469 (2006)

A Concurrent Validity Approach for EEG-Based Feature Classification Algorithms in Learning Analytics

Robyn Bitner, Nguyen-Thinh Le[✉], and Niels Pinkwart

Humboldt-Universität zu Berlin, Unter den Linden 6, 10099 Berlin, Germany
{nguyen-thinh.le,niels.pinkwart}@hu-berlin.de

Abstract. Learning analytics applications exploit data about learners. In addition to cognitive and physical data about learners, recent research is motivated by the correlation between data on the physiological dimension and the cognitive performance. In order to collect physiological data, different types of physiological sensors can be used, among which the popularization of brain-computer interfaces using wearable EEG sensors has sparked the interest of research in the field of education. The affective, attentional or motivational state of an individual can be determined using physiological parameters. The research question to be investigated is: How accurate are the algorithms (e.g., classifying attentional states) implemented in wearable EEG devices in a learning setting? This paper proposes a concurrent validity approach to verify the accuracy of the algorithms integrated in EEG devices, i.e., comparing the classifying output against the response of EEG band power. For this purpose, a wearable EEG device of NeuroSky has been deployed and attention was taken as a physiological metric of interest. In order to investigate the accuracy of NeuroSky's attention algorithms in the context of learning, an experiment was conducted with 23 subjects, with mean age 24.17 ± 3.68, who utilized a pedagogical agent to learn Java syntax while having their attention measured by the NeuroSky's EEG device. The results of the experiment support the claim that the device does in fact represent a user's attention accurately in a learning setting.

Keywords: Brain-computer interface · Attention · EEG · NeuroSky · Concurrent validity · Physiological computing

1 Introduction

Learning analytics is concerned with collecting and analyzing data during the learning process of learners in order to predict, inform the stakeholders timely, and consequently improve learning outcomes [31]. Thus, one of the challenges of learning analytics is collecting data about learners and developing data-intensive analytics methods [18]. In addition to cognitive data, physical data (e.g., clicks), or social network data (i.e., data related to building communities [16]), learning analytics may exploit physiological data in order to better understand the cognitive learning process of learners. For example,

N. T. Nguyen et al. (Eds.): ICCCI 2020, LNAI 12496, pp. 568–580, 2020.
https://doi.org/10.1007/978-3-030-63007-2_44

Brain-Computer Interaction (BCI) applications [25] can be utilized in order to visualize the attentional state of each individual learner and promote focused learning in (and outside) the classroom. This bio-cybernetic loop of a BCI application corresponds to the retrieval and processing of physiological signals, in this case the electroencephalography (EEG) signals indicating attention, and the subsequent production of biofeedback. The learner could, prompted by the biofeedback, change behaviour and consequently, their cognitive state. Furthermore, using physiological technology that can measure a learner's physiological state could appropriately guide how the learning style should be adapted, e.g., to increase attention and therefore deliver optimized results for the individual. This design demonstrates the great potential in measuring physiological signals to be integrated in learning analytics applications. Recently, some physiological sensors (e.g., ECG, EEG) have been designed to be more comfortable and wearable or even integrated in smartphones. Wearable physiological devices have the potential to help bring educational technology to a wider range of users.

With the focus on the type of EEG sensor, many wearable EEG devices are available on the market today including NeuroSky, Emotiv EPOC, Muse [9]. These devices not only provide us with raw EEG data, but also with some built-in algorithms that claim to assess physiological states of users. The accuracy of such algorithms is of utmost importance as its application is increasing in popularity in many disciplines, e.g. education, psychology, marketing. However, up until this point, very little testing has been conducted on the accuracy of algorithms implemented in these technologies. Thus, the research question addressed in this paper is: Do wearable EEG devices accurately measure and represent a user's physiological state (e.g., attention) whilst conducting tasks in a learning setting?

2   State of the Art

D'Mello [7] discussed the importance of emotion related to learning. The author pointed out four themes that illustrate the use of learning analytics and educational data mining methods to study affect during learning. The first theme is represented by studies of Sinha and colleagues [32], and Bosch and D'Mello [5] that use the rich stream of data (including instructional activities such as coding, reading text, testing code, receiving errors, videos of students' faces and computer screens) generated during interactions with learning technologies in order to analyze students' affect, and thus, understand learners' cognitive processes. The second line of work is referred to as sensor-free affect detection that infers learners' affect by analyzing the unfolding context of learning and learner actions. The third theme refers to affect detection from bodily signals, e.g. facial features, raised brow, tightened lips, head pose and position [4]. The last theme includes works that integrate techniques of the second (sensor-free affect detection) and third theme (bodily signals) into an affect model for adaptive learning technologies. From this recent discussion of emotional learning analytics, we can learn that physiological data about learners has not been extensively researched in the educational technology sector until now. An exceptional case is the work of Fortenbacher et al. [10] who used the physiological metrics like skin conductance and heart rate to develop a learning companion that visualizes sensor data, provides awareness/feedback and learning analytics services to the learner.

In order to determine physiological states of learners, wearable EEG technology is gaining popularity and researchers' attention. EEG devices collect neural signals via sensors placed on the head and this stream of physiological data is filtered and processed using software. Usually, some physiological computing algorithms (e.g., attention, stress, emotion) are integrated in these devices as black boxes and we rely on their accuracy. Concerning the reliability of these algorithms several studies have been conducted.

Rebolledo-Mendez et al. [28] conducted a study to assess NeuroSky's EEG usability as well as the accuracy of its attention metric. An experiment was conducted with 40 undergraduate university students between the ages of 18 and 20. An artificial avatar was used to measure the user's level of attention whilst conducting a multiple-choice questionnaire. The number of correct answers the user chose was recorded and feedback was given by the avatar to the user throughout the experiment. Before and after the task was completed, user feedback, in the form of a self-report questionnaire based on the DSM-IV criteria for ADHD [34], was collected and analyzed. This self-report was used to assess the user's general attention during class as well as their attention during the experiment. Positive correlations between the attention metric, the results of the multiple-choice questionnaire, and the self-assessment of attention, concluded that the attention algorithm does indeed prove to be accurate. However, insufficient data collection in terms of frequency of data sent from the headset to the client proved to be a hindrance in the accuracy of data. Moreover, there was a seemingly lengthy recalibration after a loss of connection. These factors could have an effect on results as the data collected did not always accurately represent the level of attention in real time.

Another study that evaluated the accuracy of the attention algorithm implemented in the NeuroSky's EEG concluded that an accuracy of 78% was reached while conducting a psychological stress-inducing test [6]. Despite this, no correlation between low cognitive performance (i.e. making errors during the test) and the change in attention was found.

A study evaluating both the NeuroSky's EEG and the Emotiv's EEG tested the accuracy of attention and meditation algorithms in consumer-grade EEG devices [21]. A deduction that resulted from the study was contrary to that of Rebolledo-Mendez and colleagues. The alleged adaptability of the NeuroSky's EEG to accommodate for the differences of attention, as claimed by NeuroSky developers [22] was refuted in the study from Maskeliunas et al. [21]. The results of the attention values across all participants were not normally distributed, demonstrating the wide range of average attention across users. Additionally, it was found with the use of a simple control task that the attention and meditation algorithms from NeuroSky were only of an accuracy of 22.2%.

In addition to this study from Maskeliunas et al. [21], some others also suggested similar conclusions. NeuroSky's attention algorithm was deemed as inaccurate as blinking proved to interfere with the attention value [33].

Other studies pertaining to NeuroSky technologies were conducted evaluating only the raw data that can be processed with fast Fourier transformations. These then in turn display the values for alpha oscillations, beta oscillations, etc. Examining the raw data is useful to investigate as they are what the attention and meditation algorithms are presumably based off of. If the base measurements captured by the device are not accurate, these errors can then aggregate to other values leading to inaccurate values for the algorithms, including attention and meditation, among others. Sałabun [30] conducted a study testing the accuracy of the raw EEG signals in the NeuroSky's EEG headset. With his findings, the raw data seemed to correspond with the theoretical foundations of alpha, beta, delta, theta, and gamma waves, demonstrating the potential use of the device in BCIs. One must consider, though, that the attention and meditation algorithms themselves were not thoroughly evaluated.

Accuracy evaluation studies for wearable EEG technology have been conducted in the context of multiple-choice test and stress induced situations. Yet, to our knowledge, the accuracy of those devices in a learning setting either in a classroom or in a technology-enhanced learning environment has not been investigated yet. Thus, this paper aims to address the research question whether wearable EEG devices accurately measure and represent a user's physiological state whilst conducting tasks in a learning setting.

3 Methodology

In order to investigate the specified research question, NeuroSky's MindWave Mobile 2^1 has been decided to be deployed because it is comfortable for learners in a learning setting. The NeuroSky MindWave Mobile 2 is a commercial EEG consisting of one dry electrode situated on the forehead, located at Fp1 of the international 10–20 system, as well as the reference and ground electrodes on the left ear. Its advantages include its affordability as well as its unobtrusive nature in comparison to other EEGs which use wet electrodes.

The physiological metric that is considered relevant and related to learning analytics is "attention" due to the following reasons. It has been shown in various studies [11, 12], not to mention from common human experience, that being able to focus and concentrate on a task results in greater task performance, whether this is at school, on the job, during free time, while driving, etc. Attention is a crucial factor in the advancement of an individual's cognitive skills, being a reason as to why it has been extensively studied and researched in the fields of psychology, neurology, biology, and physiology.

Existing studies in neuroscience regarding attention give us hints to focus on relevant EEG signals. Multiple authors concur that alpha activity is related to sustained attention [1, 3, 26]. It was also concluded that increasing beta reflects an increase in sustained attention [19, 24]. Oken et al. [24] and Linden et al. [19] agreed that theta increases with increased attention. There has been extensive research on the connection between EEG signals and selective attention. Concerning the alpha wave metric, alpha desynchronization (the decrease in the amplitude of the alpha waves) is said by most authors to reflect attentional processes [1, 11, 14, 17]. Other studies concluded that alpha activity increases when rejection tasks are performed whereby one completes a cognitive task and is internally attentive [26]. An increase in delta indicates internal attention and is present when completing cognitive tasks [13]. Gamma waves are said to increase as a result of cognitive processing in response to a stimulus [14, 15]. The form of attention that is of utmost importance to the study presented in this paper is sustained attention because in the context of solving problems in a learning setting, one must maintain focus

---

[1] https://store.neurosky.com/pages/mindwave (Accessed on 3rd February 2020).

on a stimulus over a period of time while performing a cognitive task [24, 27]; sustained attention is then implied in the act of concentration which NeuroSky's attention algorithm is said to measure. Based on findings in neuroscience, the following hypotheses are proposed:

1. The attention value measured by NeuroSky's MindWave Mobile 2 will be positively correlated to delta power as delta power increases with cognitive tasks and internal concentration [13].
2. Theta power and attention will have a negative correlation as theta power decreases with the increase of attention. It was observed that theta frequencies increase with the decline in cognitive performance [19, 24].
3. Attention will be negatively correlated to the alpha power as the alpha frequency decreases with the increase of attention [1].
4. The attention value will have a positive correlation to the beta power value as beta thresholds increase with neurofeedback treatment to enhance attention [19]. Beta frequency also decreases with decline in performance related to tasks requiring sustained attention [24].

Therefore, the corresponding null hypotheses are the following:

1. Delta power and attention will not have a positive correlation
2. Theta power and attention will not have a negative correlation.
3. Alpha power and attention will not have a negative correlation.
4. Beta power and attention will not have a positive correlation.

3.1 Materials

Data was to be collected from the NeuroSky's MindWave Mobile 2, by which the neural oscillations were captured from the user's scalp. The ThinkGear Connector software development kit then sent the digitized neural data from the serial port to an open network socket where the open source software, [29], was used to display band power and attention as well as record the data with the accompanying timestamps into CSV files. These CSV files had to be made more compact as each session lasted around 10 min (600 s) and the data was collected (and therefore recorded in the CSV file) at a rate of 512 Hz resulting in around 300,000 lines per file. As the attention algorithm, as well as the EEG power algorithms, were only calculated at a rate of 1 Hz, there existed a plethora of redundant information. Nevertheless, there was an easy solution to this problem. Using time-based epoching (1 s interval, 1 s length) while recording the data, the duplicates were easily removed, since only one data sample per epoch was retained.

In order to induce mental effort and sustained attention, a cognitive task was required that could be performed over an extended period of time. As mentioned earlier, in the field of education, measuring attention and incorporating its metric into biofeedback can be used to enhance learning abilities and increase concentration and focus in students. It was then deemed a good choice to utilize a pedagogical agent to conduct the experiment.

The pedagogical agent chosen is called "SYNJA". It aims to teach Java syntax to those without prior experience. It consists of explanations and clarifications of concepts along with follow up tasks such as multiple-choice questions, fill in the blanks, and coding exercises. SYNJA can be interacted with in either the German or English language. Two parameters from the pedagogical agent, a timestamp and a Boolean value, were recorded in a separate CSV file. These parameters pertain to the time in which a question was answered and if it was answered correctly or incorrectly while using the pedagogical agent. This data was recorded in each session to be later cross-referenced with the CSV file from OpenViBE.

Additionally, a self-report for the user was used to evaluate the user's subjective attention. The pre-test was completed before and the post-test after the interaction with the pedagogical agent. The pre-test and post-test questionnaires consisted of six questions which were in accordance with the Diagnostic and Statistical Manual of Mental Disorders (DSM-IV) [34] pertaining to ADHD. The pre-test questions pertained to the user's general qualities and behaviours as well as how they would gauge themselves, with respect to attention, in everyday tasks. The post-test questions pertained to the user's behaviours specifically while using SYNJA. Google Forms was used to record the results of the pre- and post-test questionnaires.

3.2 Participants

Although the trial originally consisted of 27 volunteers in total, 23 trials were deemed valid to be further evaluated. This was due to the fact that no tasks were completed by two of the participants while using the pedagogical agent SYNJA; there was an extended loss of connection experienced during the interaction for one subject; and one participant withdrew consent to have data used. 14 of these remaining participants were females and 9 males. The participants were between the ages of 19 and 30 with the mean age being 24.17 ± 3.68 years of age. Around two thirds of the participants were university students. Four of the 23 subjects chose to interact with SYNJA in the German language, all being native speakers, and the remaining 19 chose to use the English version of SYNJA. 14 of those participants speak English at a native level.

In order to have optimal results, only individuals with little to no Java experience were considered to ensure that the task would not be repetitive or familiar, implying "automatic processing" [23] which could decrease the potential of the individual's full concentration while completing the tasks. All participants claimed to be mentally healthy and none of the participants had ever been diagnosed with ADHD. Before completing the trial, each participant was asked to give consent to having their information and data used for this experiment. This consent form included information about the experiment and how it would be conducted as well as how the physiological data collected from the device and the results of the pre- and post-tests would remain anonymous when being analyzed and published.

3.3 Procedure

In order to have consistent results across trials, a quiet and solitary place was provided for each participant to complete the questionnaires and interact with the pedagogical agent. Each trial was conducted the following way:

1. The participant was instructed on how to use the pedagogical agent. (10 min)
2. The participant filled out the pre-test questionnaire. (2 min)
3. The device was placed on the participant's head and OpenViBE Acquisition Server was opened. The preferences were set to ensure the proper ports were being used as well as ensuring the metrics attention and band power were being collected by the MindWave Mobile 2. The user ID was assigned. OpenViBE Designer was opened, and the program was run to collect neural waves and record them in a CSV file labeled with the ID of the participant at the process. (2 min)
4. The participant interacted with the pedagogical agent and learned one to two concepts. (10 min)
5. The retrieval of cerebral oscillations was stopped and the CSV file from OpenViBE was written.
6. The participant completed the post-test questionnaire. (2 min)

In order to test the reliability and effectiveness of the procedure, a pilot test was conducted with two subjects. Trials of the procedure were run so that potential technical difficulties could be anticipated and an approach to deal with faulty data could be established.

3.4 Data Analysis

This paper proposes a concurrent validity method to validate test results based on a similarly conducted test with previously validated measures. This principle was used to support or reject the hypotheses proposed pertaining to the attention level measured by the MindWave Mobile 2 and different band powers.

Attention and Band Powers. Band power reflects the dominance of a certain band wave, or frequency, in a signal and the unit is expressed in volts squared per Hertz. Attention values resulted by MindWave Mobile 2 ranges between 0 (lowest) and 100 (highest). The best fitting statistical method to analyze the relationship between the various band powers and attention is correlation as what is being sought is the association between the band power value and the attention value. A model is not needed to be established as no predictions are to be made for random variables to fit this model, rather it is being inquired if the variation in band power is related to the variation in attention in accordance with previous studies. This attention value has unknown composition and therefore it is being examined if its values correspond to previous research. In order to obtain a normal distribution of the band power values for each sample, a log transformation is performed on the set of band powers. A Pearson correlation is then used to compare the attention and the respective band power with one another. To determine what kind of a relationship attention has with each of the respective band powers, the correlation coefficient and p-value will be calculated for each subject, as the datasets are very large with over 600 entries per subject.

Pre-Test and Post-Test. The pre-test and post-test questionnaires are used to later aid in providing explanations as to why certain phenomena occurred. In order to analyze the questionnaires completed by the subjects, each category in the Likert-type scale is assigned a number (Very often: 5; Often: 4; Sometimes: 3; Rarely: 2; Never: 1). The higher the score, the less attentive the subject judged them self to be. A paired two-sampled t-test will be performed with the scores of the pre-test, considering attention in general circumstances, and the post-test, considering attention while interacting with SYNJA, for each participant.

4 Results

As the datasets for each subject, which included the band power as well as the attention values recorded at a rate of 1 Hz, were relatively large (on average more than 620 entries per subject), the correlation coefficient was calculated for each subject. 23 subjects' data was used to conduct the analysis; subjects 4, 17, 21 and 23 were excluded.

Delta Band Power. The correlation coefficient of attention and delta band power was significantly different than 0 for each subject; the p-value was less than 0.05, showing the clear correlation between attention and delta band power. As the results indicated a negative correlation between the delta band power and the attention level, Hypothesis 1 can be rejected, that the attention algorithm correlates positively to the delta band power as implemented in the NeuroSky MindWave Mobile 2. Therefore, the null hypothesis, that delta band power and attention are not positively correlated, is supported.

Theta Band Power. The theta band power is expected to decrease with an increase in attention, and therefore result in a negative correlation coefficient. As the correlation coefficient for all 23 subjects was below zero and the p-value was less than 0.05, it can be deduced from the data that Hypothesis 2 is supported, and the null hypothesis is rejected.

Low Alpha Band Power. Low alpha band power is expected to decrease with an increase in attention. In order to find the significance of the relationship between the attention value and low alpha band power, the p-value was examined, and it was concluded that for subjects with IDs 6, 9, 10, and 14, the relationship was not strong enough to confirm Hypothesis 3, that there is a significant negative correlation between low alpha power and attention. For the other 19 subjects, Hypothesis 3 was confirmed. In the two subjects, 6 and 10, where a positive correlation was calculated, the significance, indicated by the values of $p = 0.463 > 0.05$ and $p = 0.427 > 0.05$, respectively, was not sufficient to confidently confirm the nature of the relationship. Therefore, it can be deducted from the rest of the results, that the correlation between low alpha band power and attention is negative. This concords with the assumption made based on previous studies leading us to reject the null hypothesis.

High Alpha Band Power. The hypothesis regarding the high alpha band power is that it is negatively correlated to attention. The subjects 6, 10 and 13 displayed correlation coefficients of a positive sign. Nonetheless, all three of these subjects had a p-value of greater than 0.05, indicating that these results were not significant. Besides these three subjects, subjects 11 and 14 also did not show significant correlations. Therefore, Hypothesis 3, that there is a significant negative correlation between attention and high alpha band power, for the subjects 6, 10, 11, 13, and 14 can be rejected. The remaining 18 subjects did indeed display a significant negative correlation. The results of these subjects confirm Hypothesis 3 and reject the corresponding null hypothesis.

Low Beta Band Power. The low beta band power is expected to increase with the increase of attention. Significant results were only found for roughly half of the subjects. Subjects 2, 5, 6, 7, 8, 10, 12, 14, 16, 18, 19, 26, and 27 had significant correlations where the p-value was less than 0.05. The remaining subjects' results were unable to confirm Hypothesis 4 based on the p-value. Of the subjects named with significant correlation coefficients, those with negative correlations were subjects 2, 7, 8, 12, 16, 18, 19, 26, and 27, and those with positive correlations were subjects 5, 6, 10, and 14. Based on this data, a definite conclusion cannot be drawn as 9 of 23 correlation coefficients were not significant, and those that were indeed significant, did not share the same results. Therefore, in this case, the null hypothesis supported.

High Beta Band Power. Lastly, high beta band power is expected to increase with the increase of attention. For all subjects, the correlation coefficient was positive, and 19 from 23 subjects had a significant correlation with the p-value being lower than 0.05. These results are in keeping with Hypothesis 4 with regards to the high beta band power; the hypothesis can be confirmed for these subjects and the null hypothesis be rejected. Subjects 7, 16, 18 and 27, did not have a significant correlation coefficient and therefore Hypothesis 4 cannot be confirmed for these. Nonetheless, as the vast majority of values were significant, there is strong evidence of a positive correlation.

Regarding results of the Pre-Test and the Post-Test, subjects 8, 11, 15, 18, 22, and 24 perceived attention to be significantly lower which using SYNJA than in normal circumstances. Seven subjects perceived their attention to be slightly lower while using SYNJA. Conversely, subject 7 perceived their attention to be significantly higher while using SYNJA than usual. Another seven subjects perceived their attention to be slightly higher. Two subjects had no perceived change (Table 1).

The Pearson's correlation coefficient to a precision of three significant figures for each subject (ID) for attention and the respective log normalized band power. Values in bold represent the correlation coefficient having the same sign as hypothesized as well as having a p-value < 0.05.

5   Discussion

The results of the testing of association between certain band powers were to an extent inconsistent with the hypotheses proposed. When taking delta band power into consideration, there was a significant negative correlation with attention for every subject. This is inconsistent with previous research from Harmony [13] where delta power is said to increase with internal concentration. However, as delta oscillations have an inhibitory effect, as demonstrated in the case of deep sleep [2] different attentional networks are inhibited while others are not. As in the studies mentioned, the internal processing was favoured while external stimuli were inhibited. Depending on the task at hand, and subsequent activation of different areas of the brain, an inhibitory effect can be observed where the sensor is measuring the brain oscillations. As in the case of the attention algorithm from NeuroSky, it can then be assumed that this inhibitory effect was anticipated.

As for the band powers of theta, low alpha and high alpha, the majority of the subjects' results, and in the case of theta, all the subjects' results, were significant enough

Table 1. Correlation values for eSense attention values and respective log normalized band powers

ID	Delta	Theta	Low Alpha	High Alpha	Low Beta	High Beta
1	-0.225	-0.326	-0.168	-0.108	-0.00517	0.206
2	-0.376	-0.414	-0.202	-0.0981	-0.0861	0.125
3	-0.419	-0.356	-0.132	-0.136	-0.0123	0.0756
5	-0.175	-0.238	-0.134	-0.0727	0.0708	0.212
6	-0.0807	-0.132	0.00371	0.0254	0.0794	0.181
7	-0.468	-0.429	-0.270	-0.198	-0.0729	0.0496
8	-0.467	-0.475	-0.287	-0.196	-0.0941	0.121
9	-0.200	-0.190	-0.0621	-0.0302	-0.00177	0.227
10	-0.246	-0.205	0.00746	0.0357	0.128	0.232
11	-0.292	-0.345	-0.255	-0.168	0.00135	0.193
12	-0.391	-0.330	-0.182	-0.150	-0.106	0.0792
13	-0.311	-0.298	-0.0741	0.0133	0.0473	0.297
14	-0.116	-0.117	-0.0554	-0.0203	0.0673	0.251
15	-0.225	-0.259	-0.179	-0.0950	-0.0369	0.206
16	-0.363	-0.409	-0.244	-0.178	-0.140	0.0541
18	-0.430	-0.449	-0.247	-0.249	-0.191	0.0143
19	-0.390	-0.400	-0.210	-0.106	-0.0680	0.142
20	-0.567	-0.498	-0.297	-0.298	-0.0770	0.183
22	-0.361	-0.309	-0.0968	-0.0631	-0.0510	0.159
24	-0.295	-0.316	-0.142	-0.0301	0.0266	0.191
25	-0.472	-0.293	-0.210	-0.141	-0.0391	0.282
26	-0.367	-0.356	-0.224	-0.252	-0.0764	0.158
27	-0.426	-0.389	-0.274	-0.257	-0.153	0.0505

to confirm the hypothesis, indicating that these did indeed correlate to attention as seen in previous studies. The attention algorithm implemented by NeuroSky does indeed display the relationship between these band powers and attention.

Regarding low beta band power, only 4 of 23 subjects had significant results that support the alternative hypothesis. To speculate as to why such weak results were obtained from the data, one must consider that NeuroSky differs between low and high beta band power values whereas previous studies did not. As the high beta band power did indeed significantly positively correlate to attention in the majority of the cases, supporting the alternative hypothesis, an explanation is needed as to why low beta band powers did not correlate in the same way. Perhaps the developers did not take low beta into consideration when calculating the attention value. Another study suggested that attention could be measured using a ratio between the sum of the power spectral densities of the alpha and beta bands, respectively [20]. It was also suggested that beta does not directly have an effect on attentiveness but rather, the relationship between the alpha and beta bands is of high importance. In the case of the MindWave Mobile 2, this could be an explanation for the unexpected results of the correlation between low band power and attention since the alpha band power was not taken into consideration when observing the beta band power. In conclusion, to account for the discrepancy between the expected and actual correlation between low beta power and attention, the developers of NeuroSky may have laid more importance on the high beta band rather than the lower to compute the attention value, or, as mentioned by Liu et al. [20], a ratio rather than a direct relationship between band powers and attention may have been considered.

Based on the results regarding the anticipated relationships between band powers and attention and considering the potential reasons for discrepancies with the proposed hypotheses, the accuracy of the attention algorithm can be validated. Regarding the pre-test and post-test results, approximately two thirds of the subjects perceived attention to be lower while using SYNJA than when conducting normal everyday tasks. A reason for this could be a lack of interest or motivation to learn Java syntax. "Subjects who are uninterested in the environment or apathetic will not be as vigilant as those with high motivation." [24, p. 1888].

In conclusion, the results based on the relationship between the attention metric and band powers are in favour of the accuracy of the NeuroSky MindWave Mobile 2.

6 Conclusion

In a learning analytics setting, the physiological state of the learner can be interpreted based on physiological signals. In order to collect and analyze physiological states of learners, wearable physiological devices (e.g., ECG, EEG) can be used. However, the accuracy of classification algorithms of those devices should be concurrently validated. This paper has proposed a concurrent validity approach using findings in neuroscience regarding the physiological metric "attention". This proposed approach has been demonstrated with the wearable EEG device, NeuroSky MindWave Mobile 2, and is, thus, the second contribution of the paper. Based on the results of the correlation between the different band powers and the attention values calculated by the device, it can be concluded that the NeuroSky's attention algorithm accurately classifies attentional states of learners. The NeuroSky's EEG device has been validated the first time in the context of learning, being the third contribution of this paper.

With the increased use of commercial EEG devices in fields of education, it seemed appropriate to utilize a pedagogical agent to test the attention metric and examine its usability for such application. Nonetheless, some things in the experiment would need to be altered in order to more suitably test wearable EEG devices in the future. A pedagogical agent should be used that does not overload the subject with cognitive tasks and is sufficiently long to collect enough data to analyze and compare with other subjects'. If the tasks differ in difficulty, this should also be accounted for in order to gauge cognitive task load as well as the expected amount of time needed in order to complete tasks.

Advantages of the concurrent validity approach include flexibility of the choice of task to induce attention, or other physiological states. In this case, it proved to be a good choice to hone in on the use of EEGs in the sector of education and being able to compare the neurological signals to performance tasks related to attention. A disadvantage in this method is that the user's perception of their attention may be different than the value as calculated causing discrepancies in the analysis of the accuracy of such algorithms.

In order to take advantage of the great potential of using physiological data to improve learning, more research and testing should be conducted regarding classification algorithms implemented in BCIs, including attention and meditation, among others. The use of concurrent validity, such as in the experiment conducted, is a good starting point to further assess, and therefore make improvements on, more commercial EEG devices, as well as other BCIs, as their use in educational settings is gaining popularity with good reason.

References

1. Aftanas, L., Golocheikine, S.: Human anterior and frontal midline theta and lower alpha reflect emotionally positive state and internalized attention: high-resolution EEG investigation of meditation (2001)
2. Banquet, J.-P., Sailhan, M.: Quantified EEG spectral analysis of sleep and Transcendental Meditation (1974)
3. Başar, E.: A review of alpha activity in integrative brain function: fundamental physiology, sensory coding, cognition and pathology (2012)
4. Bosch, N., et al.: Using video to automatically detect learner affect in computer-enabled classrooms (2016)
5. Bosch, N., D'Mello, S.: The affective experience of novice computer programmers. Int. J. Artif. Intell. Educ. **27**(1), 181–206 (2015). https://doi.org/10.1007/s40593-015-0069-5
6. Crowley, K., et al.: Evaluating a brain-computer interface to categorise human emotional response (2010)
7. D'Mello, S.: Emotional learning analytics. In: Handbook of Learning Analytics (2017)
8. Fairclough, S.H.: Fundamentals of physiological computing (2009)
9. Farnsworth, B.: Top 14 EEG Hardware Companies [Ranked]
10. Fortenbacher, A., et al.: Sensor Based Adaptive Learning-Lessons Learned (2019)
11. Gould, I.C., et al.: Indexing the graded allocation of visuospatial attention using anticipatory alpha oscillations (2011)
12. Guich, S.M., et al.: Effect of attention on frontal distribution of delta activity and cerebral metabolic rate in schizophrenia (1989)
13. Harmony, T.: The functional significance of delta oscillations in cognitive processing (2013)
14. Herrmann, C.S., et al.: EEG oscillations: from correlation to causality (2016)
15. Herrmann, C.S., Knight, R.T.: Mechanisms of human attention: event-related potentials and oscillations (2001)
16. Hoppe, H.U.: Computational methods for the analysis of learning and knowledge building communities (2017)
17. Jensen, O., et al.: Temporal coding organized by coupled alpha and gamma oscillations prioritize visual processing (2014)
18. Knight, S., Buckinghamm Shum, S.: Theory and learning analytics (2017)
19. Linden, M., Habib, T., Radojevic, V.: A controlled study of the effects of EEG biofeedback on cognition and behavior of children with attention deficit disorder and learning disabilities. Biofeedback Self-Regulation **21**, 297 (1996). https://doi.org/10.1007/BF02214740
20. Liu, N.-H., et al.: Recognizing the Degree of Human Attention Using EEG Signals from Mobile Sensors (2013)
21. Maskeliunas, R., et al.: Consumer grade EEG devices: are they usable for control tasks? (2016)
22. NeuroSky Inc.: eSense(tm) Meters, ATTENTION eSense. http://developer.neurosky.com/docs/doku.php?id=esenses\%20tm

23. Norman, D., Shallice, T.: Attention to action: willed and automatic control of behavior (1986)
24. Oken, B.S., et al.: Vigilance, alertness, or sustained attention: physiological basis and measurement (2006)
25. Pope, A.T., Stephens, C.L., Gilleade, K.: Biocybernetic adaptation as biofeedback training method. In: Fairclough, S.H., Gilleade, K. (eds.) Advances in Physiological Computing. HIS, pp. 91–115. Springer, London (2014). https://doi.org/10.1007/978-1-4471-6392-3_5
26. Ray, W.J., Cole, H.W.: EEG alpha activity reflects attentional demands, and beta activity reflects emotional and cognitive processes (1985)
27. Raz, A., Buhle, J.: Typologies of attentional networks (2006)
28. Rebolledo-Mendez, G., et al.: Assessing NeuroSky's usability to detect attention levels in an assessment exercise. In: Jacko, J.A. (ed.) HCI 2009. LNCS, vol. 5610, pp. 149–158. Springer, Heidelberg (2009). https://doi.org/10.1007/978-3-642-02574-7_17
29. Renard, Y., et al.: OpenViBE: an open-source software platform to design, test, and use brain–computer interfaces in real and virtual environments (2010)
30. Sałabun, W.: Processing and spectral analysis of the raw EEG signal from the MindWave (2014)
31. Siemens, G., et al.: Open Learning Analytics: an integrated & modularized platform. Open University Press (2011)
32. Sinha, T., et al.: Your click decides your fate: Inferring information processing and attrition behavior from mooc video clickstream interactions (2014)
33. Classification of EEG signals in a brain-computer interface system. Institutt for Datateknikk og Informasjonsvitenskap (2011)
34. Diagnostic and Statistical Manual of Mental Disorders (1994)

A Hybrid Method of Facial Expressions Recognition in the Pictures

Julita Bielaniewicz and Adrianna Kozierkiewicz[✉]

Faculty of Computer Science and Management, Wroclaw University of Science and Technology, Wybrzeze Wyspianskiego 27, 50-370 Wroclaw, Poland
{julita.bielaniewicz,adrianna.kozierkiewicz}@pwr.edu.pl

Abstract. The following article gives an insight into a new hybrid method of facial expression recognition and its usage on an open-source Google dataset. The paper also explains chosen methods of picture analysis that are generally known and available, which correctly recognize the specific facial expression shown on the face of a photographed person. The conducted experiments proved the effectiveness of the developed approach in comparison with the naive Bayes Classifier, Support Vector Classifier, and Convolutional Neural Network in terms of F1 measure.

1 Introduction

Emotions play a crucial part in humanity as a species. Through the centuries and evolution, they create a certain environment that can make us understand one another and almost read what a person can think and do. As metaphysical as they are, we generally try to express them in certain ways, whenever it is through our body language, the art we create, certain words we use or behaviors we show. The expression itself may or may not be intentional, but if not forcefully faking it, this certainly reflects our intentions and emotions and that fact can be used to contribute to making our life easier. This is the main reason why the topic of face recognition attracted significant interest in the scientific community during the past two decades.

Simultaneously, the expansion of research regarding the sub-tasks of mimicry recognition was being held, too. To recognize the facial expression, we first need to recognize a face in the picture. If we are certain what we have is a face, we can see many possible applications for such a state, most popular being the censorship of one's face, identity detection, and finally the facial expressions.

It is arguable if the face truly is the best source of facial expression detection. Possible sources of input for emotion recognition include different types of signals, such as audio, biosignals, text, or visual signals (image/video). The vision-based emotion recognition, many visual cues such as human action, pose or a scene context can provide a couple of useful information as well. Nevertheless, the facial expression is arguably the most important visual cue for analyzing the underlying human emotions.

© Springer Nature Switzerland AG 2020
N. T. Nguyen et al. (Eds.): ICCCI 2020, LNAI 12496, pp. 581–590, 2020.
https://doi.org/10.1007/978-3-030-63007-2_45

Despite the continuous research efforts, accurate facial expression recognition under an uncontrolled environment remains quite a challenge. Many early facial recognition datasets [1,3,8,15,16,18,20,23] were being made under a controlled environments where subjects were asked to artificially generate certain expressions [4]. This deliberate behavior often results in different visual appearances, audio profiles as well as timing [20], and is therefore by no means a good representation of natural facial expressions [4]. On the other hand, recognizing facial expressions in the wild can be considerably more difficult due to the visually varying and sometimes even ambiguous nature of the problem. Other adverse factors may include poor illumination, low resolution, blur, occlusion, as well as cultural/age differences.

The main aim of this paper focuses on developing an efficient method for facial expression recognition. In our work, we will try to combine some well-known approaches from the literature and examine the effectiveness of obtained results in comparison with other single algorithms. We will propose a hybrid method based on Convolutional Neural Network (CNN) and the Haar classifier. Based on the dataset provided by Google [24] we examine our algorithm, Naïve Bayes Classifier (NBC), Support Vector Classifier (SVC), and Convolutional Neural Network (CNN) in terms of F1 measure.

The remaining part of this article is organized as follows. In the next section, a summary of related work is given. Section 3 describes the main task we want to solve along with the proposed hybrid solution of a problem related to facial expression recognition. In Sect. 4 we provide results of an experiment we conducted. Section 5 gives brief summary and overviews our upcoming research plans.

2   Related Works

Several research works regarding facial expression recognition are known to classify the basics for the means of expanding further research. Examples being the definition of a set of six basic human emotions expressed through mimicry, being the following: anger, disgust, fear, happiness, sadness, and surprise [6]. This is a standard that will be applied in our research. As far as the standardization goes, the topic of human face muscles came through the surface, which sparked the creation of a set of muscle movements which are known as Facial Action Units (FAUs) that produce each facial expression of a human and though this formed the Facial Action Coding System (FACS) [10]. In the [17] we are presented how the FAUs are combined to make rules responsible for the formation of each facial expression on the human face.

Facial expression recognition is a difficult and error-prone process. Correct recognition of facial expressions can be difficult even for human experts. In the study of [5], 60 human non-expert subjects were asked to rate each facial image for the content of the six basic facial expressions. In 20.2% of all cases, the category which received the highest rating (averaged over all subjects) disagreed with the expression label of the image. This is similar to the results reported in the literature but with different image databases [2,11]. Several sources of this disagreement may be identified. The expresser may have posed the expression inaccurately or even incorrectly in some cases. The experimental subjects may have confused one expression with another when performing the rating task (for example, fear may be confused with surprise and anger with disgust). Finally, in a small percentage of cases, there is also a possibility that the images were mislabelled by the experimenter.

Current research focuses on an automated system for facial expression recognition. Most often those systems apply various types of artificial intelligence and machine learning methods. In recent years, approaches based on deep learning algorithms have gained popularity. Facial expression and emotion recognition with deep learning methods were reported in [9,12–14,19]. In particular, position [19] reported a deep CNN learned with a linear support vector machine (SVM) output. This method achieved first place on both public (validation) and private data on the FER-2013 Challenge [7]. [13] proposed a facial expression recognition framework with 3DCNN and deformable action parts constraints in order to jointly localizing facial action parts and learning part-based representations for expression recognition. In addition, [14] included the pre-trained Caffe CNN models to extract image-level features.

Our goal is to develop a recognition model that works well on the training data but most importantly, gives good predictions for new data. The Google dataset was used to train the CNN network [24]. That dataset happens to be created through another research [21] that provides more natural-sourced data that will show more specific results of our facial recognition methods.

3   A Hybrid Method for Facial Expressions Recognition

The main goal of the following research is to construct an effective hybrid of a CNN model together with the Haar Classifier. Our exploratory method will be created through a CNN+Haar hybrid. Convolutional Neural Networks largely outperform cascade classifiers. Haar cascade classifiers used to be the best tools for object detection. When computer vision met convolutional neural networks, cascade classifiers became the second-best alternative. But to see if it also applies for the face expression detection, we wanted to make sure it will still hold the best results.

The research gathered in order to successfully combine those two models, was specifically:

1. Choosing a training dataset
2. Building a Haar Classifier
3. Building a Convolutional Neural Network

The general idea of our CNN+Haar method is presented in Fig. 1.

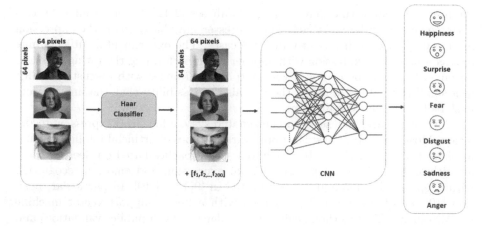

Fig. 1. CNN+Haar hybrid method

3.1 Dataset

The dataset [21] is an open-sourced, downloadable file that contains annotated face image triplets, each annotated by 60 human raters. Each triplet specifies which two faces in the triplet form the most similar pair in terms of facial expression. As authors say, this dataset is quite different from existing expression datasets that focus mainly on discrete emotion classification or action unit detection. The content is a .csv file with each line corresponding to a single data sample. The dataset contains more emotions that the standard chosen in this research, which is why we will select the data only corresponding to our 6 positions.

3.2 Haar Classifier

The Haar classifier certainly needs to go through the training phase with a few hundred sample views of a particular emotion, called positive examples. Then we let it work with some of the negative examples, arbitrary images. Both of those two examples need to have one size, which in our case will be 64×64 pixels to avoid any possible case of overflow.

After a classifier is trained, it can be applied to a region of interest (of the same size as used during the training) in an input image. The classifier outputs a "1" if the region is likely to show a certain emotion, and "0" otherwise. This is why our exact input needs to be according to the following schema: [picture, 64 pixels, 64 pixels, value = 0,1]. To search for the object in the whole image one can move the search window across the image and check every location using the classifier. The classifier is designed so that it can be easily "resized" to be able to find the objects of interest at different sizes, which is more efficient than resizing the image itself. So, to find an object of unknown size in the image the scan procedure should be done several times at different scales.

The Haar Classifier procedure consists of four stages [22]:

1. Haar Feature Selection
2. Creating Integral Images
3. Adaboost Trainings
4. Cascading Classifiers

The idea of Haar's filters is to use simple images, usually rectangular, in which bright and black areas are defined, and then we calculate substractions between the sums of the pixels in the respective areas. Those substractions are called descriptors. Haar filter owe its popularity to the ease of implementation and speed of determining features using so-called integral images. However, the number of determined features is huge, thus a machine learning algorithm called Adaboost is used to limit and select the most significant ones.

Haar-like features scanning is done on the image to detect human faces, starting from the upper left corner and ending in the lower right corner of the image. Scanning is done several times to detect human faces in an image.

3.3 Convolutional Neural Network

A Convolutional Neural Network is a class of deep neural networks consists of an input and output layer, as well as multiple hidden layers. The hidden layers of a CNN typically consist of convolutional layers, pooling layers, fully connected layers, and normalization layers. In our research, we assumed the following architecture of CNN which is visualized in Fig. 2.

1. The input layer receives the 64×64 image, where each pixel is defined with 200 values. Those 200 values are 200 features from Haar filters. This layer performs a 2-dimensional convolution with the number of filters equal to 64. The kernel size has a value of (2, 2) and there is a Rectified Linear Unit (ReLU) activation function.
2. The second layer consists of a 2-dimensional MaxPooling, with a pool size of (2, 2).
3. The Third layer is the convolutional layer. The number of filters is equal to 64 and the kernel size is (2, 2), there is the activation function ReLU.
4. The fourth layer consists of a 2-dimensional MaxPooling, with a pool size of (2, 2).
5. The fifth layer is a 2-dimensional convolutional layer, a number of filters is equal to 64, the kernel size is (2, 2) and the activation function is ReLU .
6. The sixth layer consists of a 2-dimensional MaxPooling, with a pool size of (2, 2).
7. The seventh layer, which is responsible for the flattening to reduce the dimensionality of the feature matrix describing the image to a one-dimensional vector for fully connected layers.
8. The eighth layer is a dense layer- it consists of 64 neurons and a ReLU activation function.
9. The output layer consists of 6 neurons representing the 6 possible classes (the types of facial expression) with the softmax activation function.

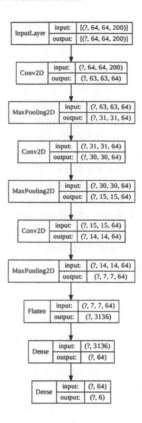

Fig. 2. Visualization of the CNN model.

4   The Results of Experiments

The dataset that we used was a Google-provided Dataset [24]. This dataset is a large-scale facial expression dataset consisting of face image triplets along with human annotations that specify which two faces in each triplet form the most similar pair in terms of facial expression. It contains around 500K triplets, with 156K face images, weighting around 200 MB. Its Authors are Raviteja Vemulapalli and Aseem Agarwala, who published the dataset in 2018.

Our CNN+Haar hybrid approach described in the previous Section will be compared with 3 chosen methods of face recognition: Naïve Bayes Classifier (NBC), Support Vector Classifier (SVC) and Convolutional Neural Network (CNN).

All of our models, together with the experimental one, went through the following process. We divided our dataset to train/validity/test (in proportion accordingly: 80%/10%/10%). We chose a specific amount of layers and then inserted the size of an input image (64 × 64). For methods assessment, we have chosen an F1-score measure which is the harmonic mean of the precision and recall.

We used the cross-validation technique to test different configurations of our CNN+Haar hybrid model. Thus, the result for each configuration shown below is the average of the results produced by 100 trained CNN+Haar models.

In order to investigate the appropriate dimension to code the facial expression, we vary the number of hidden units from 1 to 20. The models with NBC, SVC, and CNN alone were trained by running 250 cycles through all the training data, while the CNN+Haar was trained by running only 100.

The collection of all obtained F1 scores in % are presented in the Table 1 and in Fig. 3.

Table 1. The comparison of methods of facial expressions recognition

Classifier	Happiness	Surprise	Fear	Distgust	Sadness	Anger	Average F-1
NBC	50.8	56.6	67.2	63.4	71.1	82.3	65.2
SVC	69.8	66.6	75.2	77.8	78.4	79.1	74.5
CNN	80.4	79.2	**83.7**	69.2	74.8	85.3	78.7
CNN+Haar	**82.6**	**96.2**	80.7	**88.4**	**79.1**	**88.9**	**85.9**

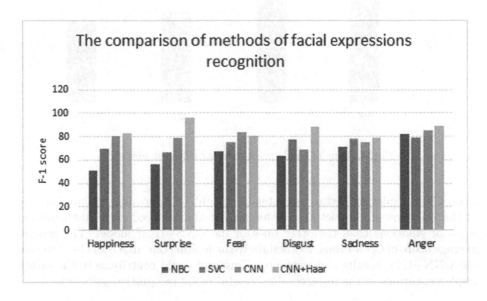

Fig. 3. The comparison of methods of facial expressions recognition

Table 2 and Fig. 4 present times of prediction for different methods.

Our results of experiments show that a CNN+Haar Classifier outperformed all of the previous methods with a higher F1 score, as well as shorter time in most cases. In 5 out of 6 cases (83,3%) our model showed a significant advantage over the rest of the researched models. Although there were cases where the

Table 2. The comparison of time (in seconds) of prediction for different methods

Classifier	Single prediction [sec]	Whole dataset [sec]
NBC	0.402	20525.72
SVC	0.388	19810.89
CNN	0.362	18483.36
CNN+Haar	**0.359**	**18330.18**

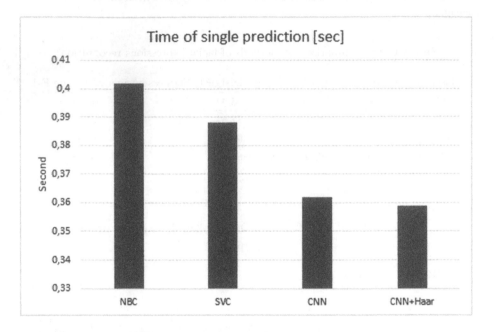

Fig. 4. Time of single prediction for different methods

plain CNN model showed to advantage, it could be happening mainly because of the selection of the pictures of the dataset that showed more distinguished signs of emotions than the other ones in the CNN+Haar model. The general average score of CNN+Haar was definitely the leading one above all else. Overall, the CNN+Haar results look very promising and could contribute to the future implementations in the research of successful facial recognition software.

5   Future Works and Summary

In this paper, we have proposed a hybrid method with a deep convolutional neural network-based facial expression recognition method with the Haar classifier to further boost the performance. We compared it with 3 well-known models and outperformed them. Our proposed method achieves excellent results on the Google-provided dataset, indicating the considerable potential of our facial expression recognition method.

CNN+Haar model can detect more information from the pictures, and even though the CNN model had similar times with the hybrid model, it never outperformed it. The final scores were always better on our CNN+Haar model. CNN can perform better when we have a dataset with fewer amount of data.

As far as the subject of facial recognition goes, we think the hybrid combination can achieve excellent practical applications that could apply not only to the expression classifier but also the subtasks of facial recognition, such as identity detection and the face censorship.

In our future works, we want to examine our hybrid method on different datasets. In this paper, we have tried to recognize only six basic human emotions expressed through mimicry like anger, disgust, fear, happiness, sadness, and surprise. Researches focus on the wider range of facial expressions may bring new challenges worth exploring.

References

1. Banziger, T., Scherer, K.R.: Introducing the geneva multimodal emotion portrayal (GEMEP) corpus. In: Scherer, K.R., Banziger, T., Roesch, E.B. (eds.) Blueprint for Affective Computing: A Sourcebook, pp. 271–294. Oxford University Press, Oxford (2010)
2. Bartlett, M., Viola, P., Sejnowski, T., Larsen, L., Hager, J., Ekman, P.: Classifying facial action. In: Touretzky, D., Mozer, M., Hasselmo, M. (eds.) Advances in Neural Information Processing Systems, vol. 8. MIT Press, Cambridge (1996)
3. Bartlett, M.S., Littlewort, G.C., Frank, M.G., Lainscsek, C., Fasel, I.R., Movellan, J.R.: Automatic recognition of facial actions in spontaneous expressions. J. Multimed. 1(6), 22–35 (2006)
4. Dhall, A., et al.: Collecting large, richly annotated facial-expression databases from movies. IEEE Multimedia 3, 34–41 (2012)
5. Daugman, J.: Complete discrete 2-D Gabor transforms by neural networks for image analysis and compression. IEEE Trans. Acoust. Speech Signal Process. 36(7), 1169–1179 (1988)
6. Ekman, P., Friesen, W.V.: Emotion in the Human Face. Prentice-Hall, Englewood Cliffs (1975)
7. Goodfellow, I.J., et al.: Challenges in representation learning: a report on three machine learning contests. In: Lee, M., Hirose, A., Hou, Z.-G., Kil, R.M. (eds.) ICONIP 2013. LNCS, vol. 8228, pp. 117–124. Springer, Heidelberg (2013). https://doi.org/10.1007/978-3-642-42051-1_16
8. Gross, R., Matthews, I., Cohn, J., Kanade, T., Baker, S.: Multi-pie. Image Vis. Comput. 28(5), 807–813 (2010)
9. Kahou, S.E., et al.: Combining modality specific deep neural networks for emotion recognition in video. In: Proceedings of the 15th ACM on International Conference on Multimodal Interaction, pp. 543–550. ACM (2013)
10. Kanade, T., Cohn, J., Tian, Y.: Comprehensive database for facial expression analysis. In: Proceedings of IEEE International Conference Face and Gesture Recognition, March 2000, pp. 46–53 (2000)

11. Lanitis, A., Taylor, C., Cootes, T.: Automatic interpretation and coding of face images using flexible models. IEEE Trans. Pattern Anal. Mach. Intell. **19**(7), 743–756 (1997)
12. Liu, P., Han, S., Meng, Z., Tong, Y.: Facial expression recognition via a boosted deep belief network. In: 2014 IEEE Conference on Computer Vision and Pattern Recognition (CVPR), pp. 1805–1812. IEEE (2014)
13. Liu, M., Li, S., Shan, S., Wang, R., Chen, X.: Deeply learning deformable facial action parts model for dynamic expression analysis. In: Cremers, D., Reid, I., Saito, H., Yang, M.-H. (eds.) ACCV 2014. LNCS, vol. 9006, pp. 143–157. Springer, Cham (2015). https://doi.org/10.1007/978-3-319-16817-3_10
14. Liu, M., Wang, R., Li, S., Shan, S., Huang, Z., Chen, X.: Combining multiple kernel methods on Riemannian manifold for emotion recognition in the wild. In: Proceedings of the 16th International Conference on Multimodal Interaction, pp. 494–501. ACM (2014)
15. Lucey, P., Cohn, J.F., Kanade, T., Saragih, J., Ambadar, Z., Matthews, I.: The extended Cohn-Kanade dataset (CK+): a complete dataset for action unit and emotion-specified expression. In: Computer Vision and Pattern Recognition Workshops (CVPRW). IEEE (2010)
16. McKeown, G., Valstar, M.F., Cowie, R., Pantic, M.: The semaine corpus of emotionally coloured character interactions. In: 2010 IEEE International Conference on Multimedia and Expo (ICME), pp. 1079–1084. IEEE (2010)
17. Pantic, M., Rothkrantz, L.J.M.: Expert system for automatic analysis of facial expressions. Image Vis. Comput. **18**(11), 881–905 (2000)
18. Pantic, M., Valstar, M., Rademaker, R., Maat, L.: Web-based database for facial expression analysis. In: IEEE International Conference on Multimedia and Expo 2005, ICME 2005, p. 5. IEEE (2005)
19. Tang, Y.: Deep learning using linear support vector machines. arXiv preprint arXiv:1306.0239 (2013)
20. Toole, A.J., et al.: A video database of moving faces and people. IEEE Trans. Pattern Anal. Mach. Intell. **27**(5), 812–816 (2005)
21. Vemulapalli, R., Agarwala, A.: A compact embedding for facial expression similarity. In: Proceedings of the IEEE Conference on Computer Vision and Pattern Recognition, pp. 5683–5692 (2019)
22. Viola, P., Jones, M.: Rapid object detection using a boosted cascade of simple features, In: Proceedings of the 2001 IEEE Computer Society Conference on Computer Vision and Pattern Recognition, CVPR 2001, vol. 1. IEEE (2001)
23. Wallhoff, F.: Facial expressions and emotion database. Technische Universitat Munchen (2006)
24. Google facial expression comparison dataset. https://research.google/tools/datasets/google-facial-expression/. Accessed 15 July 2020

Innovations in Intelligent Systems

Intelligent System for Early Detection and Classification of Breast Cancer: Data Driven Learning

Praveen Kokkerapati[1], Abeer Alsadoon[1], SMN Arosha Senanayake[2],
P. W. C. Prasad[1(✉)], Abdul Ghani Naim[2], and Amr Elchouemi[3]

[1] Study Group Australia, Sydney, Australia
pwcp111@yahoo.com, {aalsadoon,cwithana}@studygroup.com
[2] Universiti Brunei Darussalam, Gadong 1410, BE, Brunei Darussalam
{arosha.senanayake,ghani.naim}@ubd.edu.bn
[3] American Public University System, Charles Town, USA
Amr.elchouemi@mycampus.apus.edu

Abstract. Data driven learning models have not been successfully implemented due to higher rate of false positive in the detection of breast cancer lesions using mammograms. This research aims to decrease the false positive and increase the accuracy and to keep the independent features as they are. The intelligent system designed uses Fuzzy C as the morphological operators to eliminate the undesired elements of a mammogram. The embedded intelligence for breast cancer in this work has increased the accuracy rate of ~96% compared to existing rate of ~91% leading to the average processing time 0.459S with respect to current timing of 0.598S. Data driven model introduced targets on improving the detection of mass lesions by forcing to ignore undesired texture patterns. Hence, the intelligent system improves the positive rate of mammogram screening by decreasing the false positive rate. Data driven point of care system has been built using convolutional neural networks by applying the Rectifier Liner Unit (ReLU) activation function based on the personalized features extracted for early detection and classification of breast cancer.

Keywords: Breast cancer · Computer-Aided Diagnosis (CAD) · Mammograms · Masses · Micro-calcification · Segmentation

1 Introduction

Detection of breast cancer has been a major healthcare issue and solutions have been evolving in order to make the identification at an early stage. Recently, data drive learning models have been introduced to personalize the breast cancer using deep learning techniques [1]. Intelligent detection systems have been applied in the context of image archiving and communication systems [2, 3]. Data driven deep learning models provide the capacity to superimpose classification of lesions in the mammograms, which are critical identifying the lesions impacting benign or malignant at the early stages. The

© Springer Nature Switzerland AG 2020
N. T. Nguyen et al. (Eds.): ICCCI 2020, LNAI 12496, pp. 593–605, 2020.
https://doi.org/10.1007/978-3-030-63007-2_46

embedded intelligence for early detection and classification introduced in [2, 3] imposes the texture featuring mammograms by applying Convolutional Neural Network (CNN) layers improving the accuracy from 87.15 to 90.7%.

Data driven model is guided using mammograms. Mammograms are images that are used to identify and classify breast lesions; benign or malignant. This provides a clear view of the cancer detections with high accuracy in detecting and preventing the patients to undergo further painful processes detecting breast cancer. During the initial phase, mammograms are screened. Then, noise reduction process with augmentation is applied to improve the dataset prior to process using CNN subject to deep learning algorithms implemented. This technique is useful for clear classification of lesions. Hence, patient's time, effort, cost incurred will be saved avoiding mental stress during personalized cancer detection [4]. Data driven deep learning has the capability to observe each and every pixel of the image captured and to process the image area subject to baseline set.

The interactive detection-based lesion locator (IDBLL) provides an accuracy of 91% and a processing time of 12 to 15 frames per second. Hence, the accuracy can be accepted, but two critical factors; specificity and sensitivity shall be improved [1].

The solution proposed in [2] provides a cluster group in mammograms during the early signs of cancer. The major goal is to detect the microcalcification of clusters in digital mammograms.

Digital Breast Mammogram (DBT) images using the faster region-based convolutional neural network (faster-RCNN) introduced in [5] provides a solution to the problem by applying Convolutional Feature map and bounding network, thus it is in an acceptable range of Standard mean values with 94.5% accuracy.

Enhanced the screening of mammograms using H-measure method based on age risk factors in [6] is to identify the individual risk of possibilities determined by the risks prone at the highest possibility based on their age.

Improving the performance of some pre-trained CNN models and based on the medical image processing techniques the parasitic metric net may inspire a way of updating the strategy on other computing tasks as described in [7].

In [8], Mammogram of automated pipeline image processing is proposed and pectoral breast boundary is to be calculated with a novel filter texture. The solution provides an accuracy improved by 2% compared to existing system's accuracy of 95%. This solution provides accuracy with high processional values with boundary fitting and skin gradient filtering that would have been enhanced.

Computer-Aided Diagnosis (CAD) using deep learning technique is the best way of detecting and classifying the Breast cancer masses as reported in [9]. This solution provides an accuracy of 93% which is improved by 2% from the existing system of 91% and the processing time of 18 frames per second was improved to 14 frames per second.

The Solution provided in [10] DenseNet II improved the calculation speed and efficiency of the network.

The solution provided in [11] is the sum of all the four cardinalities $T\mu$, $T\eta$, $F\eta$, $F\mu$ which provide the desired segmentation value with the absolute measurement. The solution given is in an acceptable range of standard mean values with 96.5% accuracy.

Enhanced values of incoming characteristics of the clustering accuracy and performance are the visible results reported in [12]. Z-scores methods and image detection algorithms are used to identify and classify to obtain the optimal solution by using image processing and filtered images. Noise filtering is a major step introduced in [12].

Early detection of cancer helps in reducing the cost and multiple screening techniques as reported in [13]. The sensitivity reported is a sub optimal solution.

Data augmentation is the process in identifying the image as a typical mammogram which is used to identify the lesions of the cancer using GoogleNet, VGGNet, and other models extended till Fn values with 96% accuracy over 91% in the existing system in order to obtain the best CNN ratio values as discussed in [14].

Fuzzy C-Means & region-growing (FCMRG) is introduced in [15] to resolve and to identify the abnormality using breast mammography images.

2 State of the Art

Interactive detection-based lesion locator (IDBLL) introduced as a novel technique in [3, 16] to improve the accuracy of breast cancer classification. The solution was based on the integration of feature extraction preprocessed by using IDBLL. The accuracy obtained was 91% and a processing time of 12 to 15 frames per second. While the true positive mammogram's accuracy was improved to 91% and the processing time 12 to 15 frames per second. This model consists of three phases; pre-processing, feature extraction and classification.

Pre-processing: In the pre-processing step we use mammograms and apply the data augmentation technique using the algorithm feature-wise data augmentation. [2] In this step, mammogram images are tilted and rotated to increase the dataset and obtain a huge dataset for processing the convolutional neural network models.

Feature Extraction: In this step, there are multiple convolutional and pooling layers that are combined with a fully connected layer. The pooling layer plays an important role in CNNI-BCC. Multiple functions are applied to enhance the pooling and max pooling is the best function applied to this area. This function computes and divides the mammogram into multiple small rectangular non-overlapping structures. The computational burden and cost will be reduced by this pooling step. Thus, the grouping operation provides type translation invariance [12]. After that, the soft max function is applied to round the values to 1 or 0 to classify the mammograms.

Limitation: The experiment result illustrates that the state-of-art solution has achieved remarkable cancer detection and classification accuracy, with 90.5% in MIAS Dataset, respectively. However, the sigmoid function is used as the activation function in the convolutional layer, which is prone to the reduction in featuring mammograms [17].

Classification Stage: The convolutional neural network provides the extracted features from the input. CNN learns the value of the filters during training process and resulting the best image classifier [15]. In this Feature-wise data augmentation algorithm (FWDA algorithm) and Interactive detection-based lesion locator, the geometric error denotes with the sigmoid function where the depth is calculated for each neuron using the Eq. (1).

$$\int_{\infty}^{-\infty} TPR(T) - (-FPR(T))dT$$

$$f\left(\sum_i w_i x_i + b\right)$$

$$\int_{\infty}^{-\infty} \int_{\infty}^{-\infty} I(T' > T)f_0(T)dT - dT = P(X_1 > X_0) \tag{1}$$

where,

TPR is the total positive rate.   FPR is the false positive rate.

T is the positive probability score T' is the negative probability score.

X1 is the score for a positive instance X0 is the score for a negative instance.

w_i is the axon neuron x_i is the synapse   B is the cell body vector.

The error metric is identified in neuron arrangement of Convolutional Neural Networks which is determined as an exponential form is below as Eq. (2).

$$\sigma(z) = \frac{e^{z_j}}{\sum_{k=1}^{k} e^{z_{k1}}} \tag{2}$$

where,

z defines a vector of the inputs j indexes the output unit   k is the number of layers

3 Proposed System

Preprocessing: In the proposed solution Fuzzy C Means Region growing algorithm the feature texturing uses the ReLU Function which is less complex and processes less cost in performing the computations [5]. The pre-processing stage in the state of art runs using the data augmentation where the images are flipped, and the large dataset is being produced to process and produce higher accuracy rates and higher true positives [12]. In the proposed solution the pre-processing is done using Regions of extraction and fuzzy c means region growing algorithm.

Feature Extraction: After the Mammograms are pre trained, unique features are extracted using the classification based on the representations and passes through the pre trained dataset.

Feature Selection: After the data extracted from CNN, this step involves identification of critical and distinct elements using Local Binary Pattern Gray-Level Co-occurrence Matrix (LBP-GLCM) and Local Phase Quantization (LPQ). The hybrid features are obtained from these techniques.

Classification: This process is to improve the performance of the neural network. Firstly, the modified Sigmoid function is used to calculate the output of neurons as shown in the Eq. (3). It is based on the modified ReLU function as the activation function instead of the sigmoid function. The purpose is to prevent time taking the process and the performance of the function. The model is simpler and is more powerful to recognize the unseen data thus has higher classification accuracy and faster convergence speed [2]. In addition, the ReLU function enhances performance by defining the most appropriate point for classes and provide more accurate classification.

$$u_j = \sum_{i=1}^{l} \sum_{j=1}^{p} r_{ij}^{m} \|x_j - c_i\|^2 \tag{3}$$

where,

r_{ij}^{m} – Random Cluster values x_j – The intensity of the values

c_i – Compute clusters z - defines a vector of the inputs

j - indexes the output units k - is the number of layers

Novel equations are proposed in order to improve the learning capabilities using neural networks. In the proposed system the sigmoid function is replaced with ReLU function Which is denoted in (4):

$$u_j = \sum_{i=1}^{l} \sum_{j=1}^{p} r_{ij}^{m} \|x_j - c_i\|^2 \tag{4}$$

where,

r_{ij}^{m} – Random Cluster values x_j – The intensity of the values

c_i – Compute clusters z - defines a vector of the inputs

j - indexes the output units k - is the number of layers

P - for every image instance I - For every layer in neural network

The ReLU function in (4) works on achieving the exact probability of the convolutional layer for the Mammogram classification. However, the performed ReLU function is an estimated probable value so that the enhanced ReLU function is considered to be as (5).

$$u_j = \sum_{i=1}^{l} \sum_{j=1}^{p} r_{ij}^{m} \|x_j - c_i\|^2 \tag{5}$$

For every layer of the convolutional layer, there are multiple cluster images which are clusters using pixels. Hence, to obtain the unique interest of quadratic function for each image, we obtain it from Eq. (5) The modified function is as shown in (6),

$$u_j = \sum_{i=1}^{l} r_{ij}^{m} \|x_j - c_i\|^2 \tag{6}$$

For each image, the value for j will be incremental for every convolutional layer. The activation function which ignores the overfitting of mammogram datasets and also provides the long-term gradient features, will enhance the mammogram boundaries so, the convolution quadratic function changes with the activation function as shown in (7)

$$Mu_j = \frac{\sum_{i=1,j=1}^{l} r_{ij}^m \left\| x_j - c_i \right\|^2}{\sum_{k=1}^{k} e^{z_{k'}}} \tag{7}$$

where,

r_{ij}^m – Random Cluster values $\qquad$ x_j – The intensity of the values

c_i – Compute clusters $\qquad\qquad$ z defines a vector of the inputs

j indexes the output units $\qquad\qquad$ k is the number of layers

The membership value of a pixel j to cluster is r_{ij}^m, x_j denotes the intensity value of pixel j and c_i which represent the centre of its cluster so the contribution of all cluster variables on a single layer is modifies quadratic equation as illustrated in (8).

$$Mu_j = \sum_{i=1,j=1,k=1}^{k} \frac{r_{ij}^m \left\| x_j - c_i \right\|^2}{e^{z_k^1}} \tag{8}$$

4 Area of Improvement

The proposed system in this study is to improve the performance of the neural network by introducing a sigmoid function to calculate the output of neurons. It uses the modified ReLU function as the activation function instead of the sigmoid function. The purpose is to prevent time taking to process and to improve the performance of the function. The model proposed is simpler and is more powerful to recognize the unseen data, thus leads to higher classification accuracy and faster convergence speed [8, 10]. In addition, the ReLU function enhances performance by defining the most appropriate point where the common classes formed leading to accurate classification.

Fuzzy C means Region growing algorithm the feature texturing uses the ReLU Function which is less complex and processes less cost in performing the computations. The pre-processing stage is run using the data augmentation and K- means prediction where the images are flipped and the large dataset is been produced to process and produce higher accuracy rates and higher true positives [1, 12]. In the proposed solution the pre-processing is done using Regions of extraction and fuzzy c means region growing algorithm. This enhances the accuracy with less dataset and the ReLu function produces the best accuracy in the proposed solution.

5 Results

Matlab R2019b was used in the implementation of the Breast cancer classification using deep learning and convolutional neural networks based on the mammogram unique features dataset. The mammogram features that are taken to process are 32 different futuristic measurements that describe the mammogram; malignant and benign. The calculations performed are related to the prediction model and Polack-Ribiere flavor of conjugate gradients in order to compute the linear search based on quadratic and cubic polynomial approximations. The quality of parameters was taken from the university medical center. The Convolutional Neural Network is used for the implementation which consists of deep learning algorithm. For the experiment, 2.8 GHz of intel core i7 8th gen processor with 16 GB RAM (Random Access Memory) is used. There are three different classifications which are used for testing the dataset benign, malignant and normal. Table 1 illustrates the regions of extraction and fuzzy c means region growing novel algorithm implemented which enhances the accuracy with less dataset and the ReLu function produces the best accuracy.

Table 1. Fuzzy C Means Regions Growing (FCMRG) algorithm

Algorithm: Fuzzy C Means Region growing algorithm (FCMRG)   **Input:** Noise filtered Mammograms   **Output:** Provides an output of the pattern lesions
Begin   1 ROI Extraction is done   2. r_{ij} Randomly initialized values.   (a) ROI mass of MIAS   (b) FCM output   (c) Morphological operation result   (d) Region growing output.   3 Compute the cluster centers: c_i 4 Update r_{ij} as per the following: r_{ij} 5 Compute the objective function, j_m 6 Repeat steps 2–4 until j_m improves by less than a specified minimum threshold or until a specified maximum number of iterations are reached   7 Cluster p= $[(x_1, y_1), (x_2, y_2), \ldots\ldots (x_n, y_n)]$ Where p_x, represents the pixel having the highest value at x, y   8 Find (Cluster p) such that x, y $\in$ Cluster p   9 Use morphological operation to extract tumor part   10 Apply region growing algorithm on extracted tumor part by t = 0.2   11 Set size for IDBLL Bounding Box   12 Read Data Testing   13 For every point p of Data Test (R [i,j] x C [i, j] x No.of Pixel),   14 Apply IDBLL Bounding Box   15 Check if the Pixel Surround match the features   16 Compare the pixel feature with Trained CNNBS   End

The Mean and Standard deviation of the sample data are induced using multiple functions; COSTFUNCTION () Gradients () PREDICT () RANDINITIALIZEWEIGHTS (). The true positive of accuracy for breast cancer classification is ~91%. Similarly, for the proposed solution, the accuracy for the breast cancer classification is ~96%.

During the intraoperative phase, the mammogram is processed in order to calculate the convolution and pooling and updated with the latest closest value.

Figure 1 is extracted from Google search for the experiment and as well as for comparative analysis of results based on the work reported previously [18].

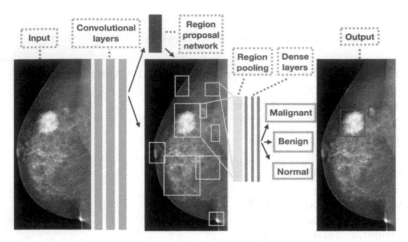

Fig. 1. Identification of cancerous lesion

The result is compared to the mammograms which are classified as benign or malignant based on the feature extraction and region pooling.

All samples provided were compared with the proposed solutions. All the data obtained are during the classification of mammograms. The results were divided and provided based on average data samples collected as reported in Tables (2) and (3). Here, the results from the dataset are considered in terms of processing time and accuracy. Accuracy is calculated by True positives and false positives, i.e. the difference between the total number of samples and the true positives obtained. and the processing time is the time taken to complete the processing of the mammogram. We have considered 20 samples of normal, benign & malignant samples. The accuracy was calculated by taking the average result of each test case.

Table 2. Accuracy and processing time comparison table for state of art & proposed solution. Classification representations based on women aged between 45–65: (Benign = 1).

	State of Art			Proposed Solution		
Images	Results	Accuracy	Time (Sec)	Results	Accuracy	Time (sec)
		90.5%	0.554		94.14%	0.416
		91.04 %	0.550		94.96%	0.351
		92.17 %	0.527		96.36%	0.457
		91.37 %	0.515		94.12%	0.481
		89.32 %	0.587		95.87%	0.438
		89.54 %	0.654		95.83%	0.517

Table 3. Accuracy and processing time comparison for state of art & proposed solution. Classification representations based on women aged between 45–65: Malignant = 2.

Images	State of Art			Proposed Solution		
	Samples	Accu-racy	Time (sec)	Samples	Accura-cy	Time (sec)
		91.35 %	0.545		95.24%	0.437
		92.01 5%	0.553		96.64%	0.425
		90.23 %	0.534		94.53%	0.413
		89.67 4%	0.521		92.23%	0.324
		92.23 %	0.587		94.34%	0.308
		91.54 6	0.512		95.64%	0.425

6 Discussion

The results of the proposed system prove the improvement in classification accuracy and processing time compared to the state-of-art solution using Convolution Neural Networks (CNN). With the modified activation function model, the system provides the average classification accuracy of 95.63% which is 3% higher than the current solution [9]. At the same time, the proposed model is required less convergence time to achieve optimization. In addition, the proposed solution decreases the average processing time to 0.459 s which is 0.224 s less than the current solution. The accuracy for each sample is obtained using the Polack-Ribiere flavor of conjugate gradients method using Matlab functions. The overall degree of improvement in classification accuracy and processing time is quantified by running the state-of-art and proposed solutions in the system respectively. The accuracy is calculated using Eq. (9) (Fig. 2).

$$\text{Accuracy} = \frac{Total\ True\ positives\ +\ Total\ False\ positives}{No.\ of\ samples} \tag{9}$$

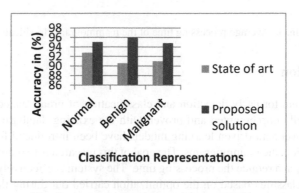

Fig. 2. Average accuracy based on true positives

where,

Total True Positives: the number of correctly identified positive samples
Total True Negatives: the number of correctly identified negative samples.

Using the modified ReLU function as the activation function in the CNN prevents gradient saturation and improves the performance. This new feature is inspired from [6]. The Activation loss function is another feature of our proposed solution, which is adapted from State-of-art solutions. It helps to reduce the bias in the imbalanced data and provides enhanced accuracy. In summary, the proposed system provides improved classification accuracy and reduced processing time compared to the state-of-art solution. Hence, combination of CNN and the proposed ReLU & Region growing algorithm are proven the Breast cancer classification with an enhanced accuracy of 95.63% and processing time of 0. 459 s.

The data driven learning technique proposed in this research consistently achieves higher classification accuracy while using lower processing time. The limitation of the existing/current solution has been successfully solved with an average accuracy of 95.63% against the existing/current accuracy of 89%. The results are also proven the average processing time to 0.459 ms against the current processing time of 0.598 ms. This is due to the improvement in the ReLU function to minimize the risk of gradient saturation and the weighted loss function in order to reduce the bias value. Hence, the proposed solution performs efficiently in different data scenarios (Fig. 3).

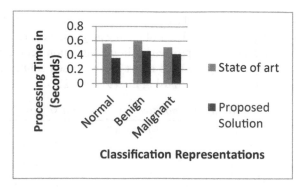

Fig. 3. Average processing time of the mammogram classification

7 Conclusion

Intelligent system for early detection and classification of breast cancer patients have been successfully implemented and proven with the existing databases of breast cancer images. Novel data-driven learning models have been introduced for breast cancer classification from the mammograms. The goal of this research is to increase the classification accuracy and reduce the processing time. The system is effectively and efficiently detecting and classifies based on the optimization carried out during the learning process of Convolutional Neural Network (CNN) with relevant learning algorithms used. In Future work, Breast cancer detection in mammograms can be detected by using texture and thermal characteristics using extensive learning based on different neural networks architectures, topologies and hybrid learning algorithms that can be considered for the best optimal solution. Accuracy and processing time are critical as major challenges in determining the benefits of the algorithms of the proposed intelligent system is critically analyzed with a limited but extensive dataset. However, there are major challenges, but an unlimited scope to improve the area of detection and classification of breast cancer using the synergy of human intelligence and artificial intelligence recently addressed as hybrid intelligent systems.

References

1. Valerie, M.: Breast density and parenchymal patterns as markers of breast cancer risk: a meta-analysis. Cancer Epidemiol. Biomark. Prev. **15**(6), 1159–1169 (2006)
2. Wen, H.-C., Chuu, C., Chen, C.: Elevation of soluble guanylate cyclase suppresses proliferation and survival of human breast cancer cells. PlosOne **12**, e0125518 (2015)
3. Chougrad, H., Zouaki, H., Alheyane, O.: Multi-label transfer learning for the early diagnosis of breast cancer. Neurocomputing **392**, 168–180 (2018)
4. Guo Yanhui, S.A.I., Amin, K.M., Sharawi Amr, A.: Breast cancer detection using convolutional deep neural learning networks. Comput. Methods Programs Biomed. **168**, 69–80 (2019)
5. Fana, M., Lia, Y., Zhenga, S., Pengb, W., Tangb, W., Lia, L.: Computer-aided detection of mass in digital breast tomosynthesis using a faster region-based convolutional neural network. Methods **166**, 103–111 (2019)

6. Fan, W., Shengfan, Z.: Adaptive decision-making of breast cancer mammography screening: a heuristic-based regression model. Omega **76**, 70–84 (2019)
7. Jiao, Z., Gao, X., Wang, Y., Li, J.: A parasitic metric learning net for breast mass classification based on mammography. Pattern Recogn. **75**, 292–301 (2018)
8. Peng, S., Zhong, J., Rampun, A., Wang, H.: A hierarchical pipeline for breast boundary segmentation and calcification. Comput. Biol. Med. **96**, 178–188 (2018)
9. Al-masni, M., et al.: Simultaneous detection and classification of breast masses in digital. Comput. Methods Programs Biomed. **157**, 85–94 (2018)
10. Hua, L., Shasha, Z., Deng-ao, L., Jumin, Z., Yanyun, M.: Benign and malignant classification of mammogram images based. Biomed. Signal Process. Control **51**, 347–354 (2019)
11. Araujo, T., Aresta, G., Castro, E., Rouco, J., Aguiar, P., Eloy, C.: Classification of breast cancer histology images using convolutional neural. PLoS ONE **126**(10), 324–396 (2017)
12. Kumar, S.M., Mainak, J., Karale, V., Anup, S.: Mammogram segmentation using multi-atlas deformable registration. Comput. Biol. Med. **110**, 244–253 (2019)
13. Gonzalez-Hernandez, J.L., Recinella, A.N., Kandlikar, S.G.: Technology, application and potential of dynamic breast thermography for the detection of breast cancer. Int. J. Heat Mass Transf. **131**, 558–573 (2018)
14. Basilea, T.M.A., Fanizzic, A., Losurdoc, L., Bellottia, R., Bottiglid, U., Dentamaroc, R.: Microcalcification detection in full-field digital mammograms: a fully automated computer-aided system. Physica Med. **64**, 1–9 (2019)
15. Sadad, T.: Fuzzy C-means and region growing based classification of tumor from mammograms using hybrid texture feature. J. Comput. Sci. **29**, 34–45 (2018)
16. Ting, F.F., Tan, Y., Sim, K.: Convolutional neural network improvement for breast cancer classification. Experts Syst. Appl. **120**, 103–115 (2018)
17. Ha, R., Chang, P., Karcich, J., Mutasa, S.: Convolutional neural network based breast cancer risk stratification using a mammographic dataset. Acad. Radiol. **26**(4), 544–549 (2019)
18. Mughal, B., Muhammad, N., Shariff, M.: Adaptive hysteresis thresholding segmentation technique for localizing the breast masses in the curve stitching domain. Int. J. Med. Inform. **126**, 26–34 (2019)

Integrating Mobile Devices with Cohort Analysis into Personalised Weather-Based Healthcare

Sin-Ban Ho[1]([⊠]) [iD], Radiah Haque[1], Ian Chai[1], Chin-Wei Teoh[1], Adina Abdullah[2] [iD],
Chuie-Hong Tan[3], and Khairi Shazwan Dollmat[1]

[1] Faculty of Computing and Informatics, Multimedia University, 63100 Cyberjaya, Malaysia
`{sbho,ianchai,shazwan.dollmat}@mmu.edu.my, radumoni2@gmail.com,`
`cwtewen@gmail.com`
[2] Department of Primary Care Medicine, Faculty of Medicine, University of Malaya,
50603 Kuala Lumpur, Malaysia
`adina@ummc.edu.my`
[3] Faculty of Management, Multimedia University, 63100 Cyberjaya, Malaysia
`chtan@mmu.edu.my`

Abstract. Mobile healthcare applications can empower users to self-monitor their health conditions without the need to visit any medical centre. However, the lack of attention on engagement aspects of mobile healthcare applications often result in users choosing to uninstall the application after the first usage experience. This results in failure of effective prolonged personalised healthcare, especially for users with chronic disease related to weather conditions such as asthma and eczema which require long-term monitoring and self-care. Therefore, this paper aims to identify the pattern of application user engagement with a weather-based mobile healthcare application through cohort retention analysis. Enhancement features for improving the engagement of personalised healthcare can provide meaningful insight. The proposed application allows the patient to conduct disease control tests to check the severity of their condition on a daily basis. To measure the application engagement, we distribute the mobile application designed for primary testing over a period of ten days. Based on the primary testing, data related to retention rate and the number of control test reported were collected via Firebase Analytic to determine the application engagement. Subsequently, we apply cohort analysis using a machine learning clustering technique implemented in Python to identify the pattern of the engagement by application users. Finally, useful insights were analysed and implemented as enhancement features within the application for improving the personalised weather-based mobile healthcare. The findings in this paper can assist machine learning facilitators design effective use policies for weather-based mobile healthcare with fundamental knowledge enhanced with personalisation and user engagement.

Keywords: Intelligent management information systems · Mobile intelligence · Mobile devices · Weather based healthcare · Personalisation

© Springer Nature Switzerland AG 2020
N. T. Nguyen et al. (Eds.): ICCCI 2020, LNAI 12496, pp. 606–618, 2020.
https://doi.org/10.1007/978-3-030-63007-2_47

1 Introduction

With the rise of smart devices and applications of machine learning, we expect a shift from the traditional healthcare model to digital health. In particular, with the ever-increasing costs of chronic condition treatments and an imminent shortage of doctors, personalized mobile healthcare applications are being developed to self-monitor such chronic conditions [1]. In Malaysia, mobile healthcare has become a significant trend as recent surveys record exponential growth in smartphone ownership [2]. This comes from the fact that many smartphone users appear to utilize mobile communication and social networking tools such as Facebook to consult with doctors and healthcare workers for self-care, and patients with chronic conditions seek to engage with their physicians to monitor their condition triggers [3]. Consequently, patients, especially the millennium generation in Malaysia, are highly reliant on their smartphones for health-related services to control and monitor their disease triggers [4].

However, personalized mobile healthcare application prolonged usage is still an issue, particularly in Malaysia. Typically, smartphone users require a few seconds of consideration to decide whether to download a mobile application (app) [5]. At the same time, it is undeniable that the user can also decide in a few seconds to uninstall a mobile application from their smartphone. The statistic via emarketer.com has proven that the probability for users to return to use a mobile application after first day of installation decreases as the time progress [6]. Most of the app providers give lots of attention to the strategy on finding a new customer to download the app but failed to identify this phenomenon immediately after the user downloads the app where none of the quick solutions is implemented to retain the app users. Furthermore, a study showed that smartphone users demand a usable application to sustain lasting engagement for prolonged self-care and monitoring. This is because, the majority of the mobile healthcare application design is unintuitive, which causing difficulty in searching correct healthcare information [7]. In consequence, most of the app users tend to uninstall the application and return to the traditional healthcare method.

To provide a platform to solve user engagement problems and address the user retention rate in mobile healthcare applications, this paper presents the outcome of the project which was divided into two sections; developing a mobile application for personalized weather-based healthcare and conducting quantitative analysis on the application engagement data. The mobile healthcare application was developed using Android Studio, which it utilizes XML to define the application layout and Java to provide the functionality of the application. This mobile weather-based healthcare application was developed to allow patients with asthma and eczema to monitor the effect of weather forecast on their disease condition. Next, quantitative data of the application engagement was collected via UX Cam Analytic, which was then cohort analysis was performed using the Jupyter Notebook Integrated Development Environment (IDE) with Python.

2 Related Work

Haenssgen and Ariana [8] identified the need for mobile healthcare applications among users by examining the relationship between smartphones and healthcare access among users in middle-income countries. However, it did not investigate the lifespan of those applications nor user engagement. Because of this, the challenge in accounting user engagement and user retention measurement of the mobile healthcare applications has been cited as one of the main limitations of literature on investigating success factors for prolonged use. The literature of mobile healthcare shows that previously developed applications were focused on various areas of personalized healthcare such as self-care and monitoring applications [9, 10], weight loss and fitness applications [11]. Typically, a mobile healthcare application is built with various features and functionalities to give sufficient information for users to manage their health conditions independently anywhere and at any time. A mobile healthcare application can provide the following features: check for disease symptoms, search for professional healthcare services, education and management procedures to prevent disease, self-monitoring, information to conduct rehabilitation for recovery and guideline for prescriptions to be taken [12].

User engagement with a mobile application refers to the procedure of creating and nurturing a valuable relationship with the mobile application users to ensure the target audience keeps using the application effectively for a long period of time. Different user levels of utilizing the healthcare services provided could influence the engagement trend within a mobile healthcare application. As such, a user with a lower level of app utilization is likely to rely on the doctor rather than engaging with the available mobile healthcare application. On the other hand, a user with a higher level of app utilization tends to behave independently or be proactive to obtain information about self-care, self-medication, self-monitoring and prevention steps. Moreover, a mobile healthcare application with more interactive elements, especially gamification of health activities and more communication support with others, is more likely to increase the level of user engagement for the group of patients with a low retention. Additionally, a previous study suggested that developers of mobile healthcare applications must create a custom feature to keep track of the behaviour of the user in application, as well as their preferences and demands. This mechanism will allow application developers to identify the features with content for specific users, and then create an experience that builds a positive relationship with those users [13]. Consequently, it will enhance user engagement with the mobile healthcare application.

Cohort Analysis is a technique applied to conduct behavioural analysis by measuring user retention rates. It is originated from social science as a part of the machine learning clustering technique and is considered a powerful data exploration technique for finding unusual user behavioural trends in large activity datasets using the concept of the cohort [14]. Cohort analysis performs a function to select a certain group of data from a large dataset based on a certain period of time. This reduces the analysis time of a large dataset by dividing it into smaller related groups (i.e. cohorts). A cohort study often starts with at least one hypothesis based on the case study. Thus, the outcome of cohort analysis can help to identify patterns of whether to support or reject the hypothesis. With cohort analysis, the trend of user engagement can be studied in three steps. First, users are assigned to various cohorts based on the period of time when users take an action for the first time. In the second step, the activity tuples are partitioned accordingly so that tuples of a user are assigned to the same cohort as the user. Finally, in the third step, to capture the aging effect, the tuples of each cohort are further split into smaller sub-partitions based on time in the application. The desired aggregate is then applied to each sub-partition [15].

Finding retention is a process to measure the percentage of application users who return to use the application after the first visit and thus group them into cohorts for analysis. A retention study is also useful for a developer to identify whether the feature within the application is working effectively over time. Two important procedures can be followed to implement an effective cohort retention analysis. Firstly, it is important to identify user retention metrics and construct the retention curve based on the requirement desired. Secondly, it is important to take proactive action to promote a marketing solution to build a strong relationship between application value and target audience [14]. Methods to calculate retention rates can be classified into two types: classic retention and range retention. In the classic retention method, the rate is calculated daily. In this case, the percentage of application users who come back on a specific day after first use can be measured. The range retention method, on the other hand, promotes the measurement of retention based on an interval of time such as 7 days for a weekly range or 30 days for a monthly range [15]. The following Eq. (1) and Eq. (2) are the equations for both classic retention and range retention.

$$Classic\ Retention\ Rate = (X\,/\,Y) \tag{1}$$

X = Number of users who open the app in the Nth day after day 0
Y = Number of users who first used the app on day 0

$$Range\ Retention\ Rate = (P\,/\,Q) \tag{2}$$

P = Number of users who open the app at least once at any time during an equal interval.
Q = Number of users who first use the app within an initial interval of the time.

3   Methodology

Initially, a mobile application related to weather-based healthcare was developed to self-monitor asthma and eczema conditions and triggers. The reason for selecting these diseases is their chronic nature, which requires prolonged healthcare and monitoring. Asthma is a disease that can be triggered by changes in weather temperature and humidity. Weather conditions such as high and low weather temperatures, an increase in wind speed, barometric pressure, and humidity can cause asthmatic attacks easily [16]. On the other hand, eczema patients suffer damage of the skin barrier, which can lead to reduced skin immunity and difficulty adapting to changes in the weather. The study has found that eczema patients suffer more itchiness in winter [17]. Thus, the mobile application developed includes weather information sourced from OpenWeather. The user can monitor the daily and hourly weather conditions around their location at any time.

Once the mobile application development was completed, pilot testing was performed for ten days where the application was deployed and distributed to mobile application users who have asthma or eczema. The primary user engagement data was collected via UX Cam Analytic. Exploratory data analysis was performed with Python in Jupyter Notebook. Then, the cohort analysis was constructed to study engagement patterns on each day of primary testing (i.e. classic retention rate). At the end of the study, the findings are discussed to identify useful insight.

4   Conceptual Representation, Results and Analysis

4.1   Conceptual Representation

Figure 1 shows how machine learning was used to give recommendations for patients based on the current weather forecast. The machine learning algorithm predicts how weather conditions affect a person's health. The algorithm and prediction was measured through the outcome of user-reported data and weather forecast data analysis respectively.

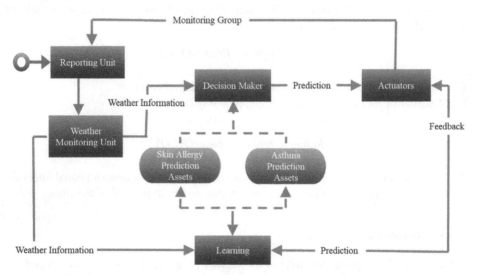

Fig. 1. Conceptual representation of the weather-based healthcare system

The use case diagram for the mobile application Weather Eczema Asthma (WEA) is shown in Fig. 2. The WEA application is built for a user who has eczema or asthma. The user is able to access weather forecasts and Air Quality Index (AQI) information within the mobile application. However, the user needs to register for a valid account before accessing the control test and report weather condition functionalities. The User Interface (UI) of these app activities was designed based on the F-shaped pattern. The weather information and location name is displayed on the left side of the screen, as inspired by the intuition that people tend to read and focus more on the information displayed on the left side than the right side [18].

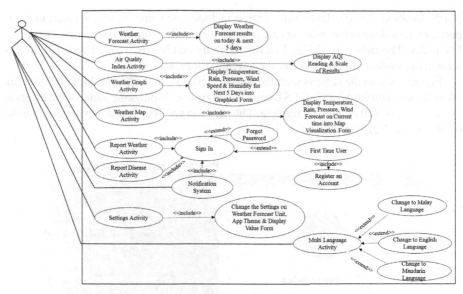

Fig. 2. Use case diagram for Weather Eczema Asthma (WEA)

4.2 Results of the Intelligent Management Information System

The left part of Fig. 3 shows the opening screen of the WEA application. At the top of screen, the weather forecast is retrieved based on device's *Global Positioning System*

Fig. 3. Weather forecast activity for the application

(*GPS*) location. The displayed information includes the name of city or location, temperature, rain description, wind speed, pressure, humidity, sunrise time, sunset time and UV index. The right part of Fig. 3 shows the daily and hourly weather forecast. In this screen, the system displays the five days weather forecast.

Figure 4 shows the screens with the AQI retrieved from the World Air Quality Index (WAQI) based on the device's GPS location. The system displays the name of the location and country as well as the AQI reading. The user can scroll up and down to compare the results to the AQI standard scale.

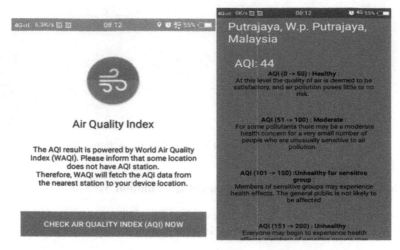

Fig. 4. The display AQI reading activity for the information system

Figure 5 shows the screens for graphs of weather metrics. There are five types of weather metrics converted into graphical form, i.e. temperature, wind speed, rain amount, pressure and humidity. Each graph shows the forecast result for the current day and the following five days. In Fig. 5, each graph displays interim vertical grey bars in the background across different intervals of metrics to allow the user to view and compare all weather metrics relationships easily.

Figure 6 shows the screen design for reporting disease activity. In this module, the system has two control test activities, asthma and eczema control test. The user selects the type of disease to conduct a control test of the disease. If the user selects asthma, the system will switch to the screen that displays the questions of asthma control test. If the user selects eczema, the system will switch to the screen that displays the questions of eczema control test.

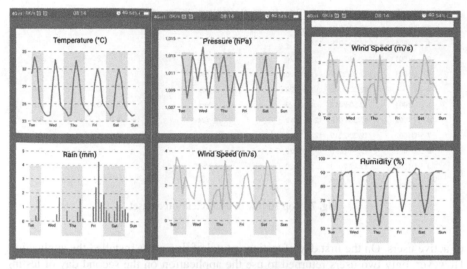

Fig. 5. Graphs of weather metrics

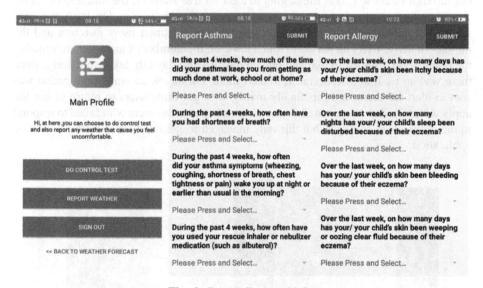

Fig. 6. Report disease activity

4.3 Cohort Analysis

User engagement data was collected with an automated software tool called UX cam. Figure 7 shows the dataset from the retention result of the ten days of preliminary testing. Five users were involved in this preliminary analysis.

The finding was constructed in cohort analysis form as illustrated in Fig. 8. The number of active users returned to use the application in pilot testing can be differentiated through the density of colour. In this case, the brighter the colour, the higher the number

	UserID	App Install Date	Visit Date	Number of control test	Number of report weather	Session Length
0	U1001	12/30/2019	12/30/2019	Yes	3	420
1	U1001	12/30/2019	12/31/2019	Yes	1	311
2	U1001	12/30/2019	1/2/2020	Yes	2	205
3	U1001	12/30/2019	1/3/2020	Yes	1	72
4	U1001	12/30/2019	1/6/2020	Yes	2	84
5	U1001	12/30/2019	1/8/2020	Yes	0	83
6	U1002	12/30/2019	12/30/2019	Yes	4	411
7	U1002	12/30/2019	12/31/2019	Yes	0	95
8	U1002	12/30/2019	1/4/2020	Yes	1	81
9	U1002	12/30/2019	1/5/2020	Yes	0	77
10	U1002	12/30/2019	1/8/2020	Yes	2	111

Fig. 7. Top 10 row of user retention dataset

of active users. On the first day of testing, a total of five users installed the application. However, only two users returned to use the application on the second day of testing and this dropped to zero on the third day of testing. Then, a push notification was sent out through Firebase Cloud Messaging to alert all five users on the morning of fourth day. This managed to get three users to return to use the application. On day 6, the same strategy of sending a push notification was applied to attract users to return and the number of active users increased to four. However, the number of users who returned to the application dropped to two and one on day 7th and day 8th day respectively, since there was no push notification sent to alert them. On day 9, an email notification was sent to alert all users, and this finally managed to get three users to return to use the application. On day 10, an email notification was sent to the users who failed to respond to the notification on day 9, but this only managed to get one user to return to use the application.

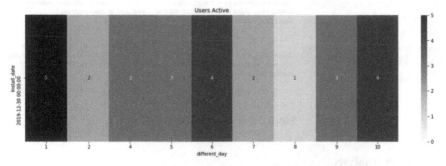

Fig. 8. Cohort analysis on users active on number of day difference

The retention rate in Fig. 9 shows the percentage of the users who returned to use the application. The basic calculation of retention rate is the number of users who returned on the Nth day divide by total number of users who installed the application on the first day. This means that only 40% of users returned to use the application on the second day. The retention percentage increased when push notifications and email notifications were sent to alert the users.

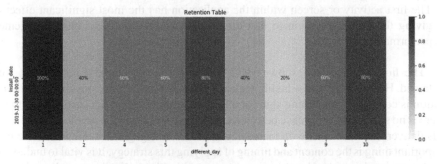

Fig. 9. Cohort analysis on users active on number of day difference (%)

Figure 10 represents the result of the activity-based engagement. This shows that the main screen (A1001), which is the first screen of the app, which focuses on delivering the weather forecast information, has the highest overall engagement time. After the main screen, the next most frequented screens are profile (A1002), login (A1003), and report asthma (A1004). The overall engagement time of the weather map (A1010), Air Quality Index (A1005), and graph (A1006) screens have an approximate of engagement time lower than 500 s in the ten days. A1010 has a much higher engagement time than A1005 and A1006.

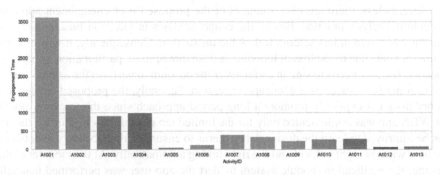

Fig. 10. Engagement time comparison on each activity (or screen) within app

5 Conclusions

Cohort analysis is an essential tool to measure mobile app engagement as it can help app providers or those responsible for in-app marketing to identify the pattern of app user engagement. Based on the user engagement testing in this paper, the following three hypotheses were assessed.

- The users spend less time on return days than on the first day of application installation.
- Email notification is more effective to encourage the user to return to use the application again than a push notification.
- The first activity or screen within the application has the most significant effect on giving the first impression to first-time users, which can affect their engagement performance.

The first hypothesis is shown valid based on the engagement results that were obtained. However, the cause is still unclear and left for further investigation. This implication is considered a warning sign for a low retention rate. For the second hypothesis, there is no significant difference between email or push notification methods. Both methods delivered similar results in increasing application engagement. However, the most important thing is the content and timing of applying this strategy. It is vital to understand the behavioural aspect of how the user engages with this application to deliver the right content at the right timing to attract the attention of the user.

For the third hypothesis, the main activity or screen, which provides the weather forecast information, has the highest engagement time among all activities. Hence, we conclude that the user will spend most of the time on the first screen of the application. Thus, it is important to study how to design an effective first screen of the application, which manages to deliver the core value of the application to the user in a short time. Throughout the analysis, it is crucial to monitor the level of app engagement on the first three days after the user first downloads the app. Although the proposed app can provide a great first experience to the user after the first download, the challenge is to sustain app usage. Therefore, it is important to monitor and collect information regularly to understand user behaviour.

Nevertheless, there are disadvantages of the proposed user engagement approach via cohort analysis practice. Firstly, the cohort analysis is selection bias, namely can happen when responders seldom follow the instruction. Consequently, it will give rise to missing data due to the loss of individuals from one or more participation groups. For instance, the user needs to sign in and register the account to perform the asthma control test in order for a successful data capture session. Secondly, the proposed engagement theory does not explicitly promote a long period approach since the tracking module for WEA app was implemented only for the limited ten days duration. Thirdly, the app can be improved to learn the device data patterns to ensure further accuracy in notifying the user with the right content and the right timing automatically. At the moment of this writing, the notification module system to alert the app user was performed manually with human intervention.

In conclusion, the proposed theory and practice impacts show that user interface design on the first screen on the app is a crucial determinant to the app retention rate, as the majority of app engagement time is focused on the first screen. Our cohort analysis further supports that it is crucial to maintain a good usability design on the first screen of the app because this gives the first impression to the first-time app user on how useful the app is to them. Future work on this study is to integrate a wider variety of machine learning techniques to predict the churn rate of the mobile healthcare app.

Acknowledgments. The authors would like to thank the financial support given by the Malaysian Fundamental Research Grant Scheme, FRGS/1/2019/SS06/MMU/02/4.

References

1. Bertalan, M., Zsofia, D., Éva, B., Bence, G., Zsuzsa, G.: Digital health is a cultural transformation of traditional healthcare. mHealth **3**(9), 38 (2017). https://doi.org/10.21037/mhealth. 2017.08.07
2. Fatin, A., Nobuaki, M.: Smartphone-based healthcare technology adoption in Malaysian public healthcare services. Int. J. Jpn. Assoc. Manage. Syst. **10**(1), 95–104 (2018). https://doi. org/10.14790/ijams.10.95
3. Hammer, R.: 30 amazing mobile health technology statistics for today's physicians (2015). https://getreferralmd.com/2015/08/mobile-healthcare-technology-statistics
4. Abdullah, N.: The uberisation of healthcare in Malaysia (2019). https://www.theedgemarkets. com/article/uberisation-healthcare-malaysia
5. Enberg, J.: What makes smartphone owners download (2016). https://www.emarketer.com/ Article/What-Makes-Smartphone-Owners-Download-App/2
6. Tom, S.: Tactics for combining UX and CX to get clinicians and IT working together (2017). https://www.healthcareitnews.com/news/tactics-combining-ux-and-cx-get-clinicians-and-it-working-together
7. Varabyova, Y., Blankart, C., Greer, A., Schreyögg, J.: The determinants of medical technology adoption in different decisional systems: a systematic literature review. Health Policy **121**(3), 230–242 (2017). https://doi.org/10.1016/j.healthpol.2017.01.005
8. Haenssgen, M., Ariana, P.: The social implications of technology diffusion: uncovering the unintended consequences of people's health-related mobile phone use in rural India and China. World Dev. **94**, 286–304 (2017). https://doi.org/10.1016/j.worlddev.2017.01.014
9. Zarka, N., Hinnawi, M., Dardari, A., Tayyan, M.: Patient keeper medical application on mobile phone. In: Proceedings of the 2004 International Conference on Information and Communication Technologies: From Theory to Applications (ICTTA), Damascus, Syria, pp. 19–23. IEEE (2004). https://doi.org/10.1109/ICTTA.2004.1307599
10. Mielnik, P., Tokarz, K., Mrozek, D., Czekalski, P., Fojcik, M., Hjelle, A.M., Milik, M.: Monitoring of chronic arthritis patients with wearables - a report from the concept phase. In: Nguyen, N.T., Chbeir, R., Exposito, E., Aniorté, P., Trawiński, B. (eds.) ICCCI 2019. LNCS (LNAI), vol. 11684, pp. 229–238. Springer, Cham (2019). https://doi.org/10.1007/ 978-3-030-28374-2_20
11. Mosa, J., Yoo, I., Sheets, L.: A systematic review of healthcare applications for smartphones. BMC Med. Inform. Decis. Mak. **12**, 67 (2012). https://doi.org/10.1186/1472-6947-12-67
12. Chekati, A., Riahi, M., Moussa, F.: Framework for self-adaptation and decision-making of smart objects. In: Nguyen, N.T., Chbeir, R., Exposito, E., Aniorté, P., Trawiński, B. (eds.) ICCCI 2019. LNCS (LNAI), vol. 11684, pp. 297–308. Springer, Cham (2019). https://doi. org/10.1007/978-3-030-28374-2_26
13. Diakou, C.M., Kokkinaki, A.I., Kleanthous, S.: A methodological approach towards crisis simulations: qualifying ci-enabled information systems. In: Nguyen, N.T., Papadopoulos, G.A., Jędrzejowicz, P., Trawiński, B., Vossen, G. (eds.) ICCCI 2017. LNCS (LNAI), vol. 10448, pp. 569–578. Springer, Cham (2017). https://doi.org/10.1007/978-3-319-67074-4_55
14. Guisado-Clavero, M., Roso-Llorach, A., López-Jimenez, T.: Multimorbidity patterns in the elderly: a prospective cohort study with cluster analysis. BMC Geriatr. **18**, 16 (2018). https:// doi.org/10.1186/s12877-018-0705-7

15. Gueye, M.L.: Modeling a knowledge-based system for cyber-physical systems: applications in the context of learning analytics. In: Nguyen, N.T., Chbeir, R., Exposito, E., Aniorté, P., Trawiński, B. (eds.) ICCCI 2019. LNCS (LNAI), vol. 11684, pp. 568–580. Springer, Cham (2019). https://doi.org/10.1007/978-3-030-28374-2_49
16. Zhang, Y., et al.: Effects of meteorological factors on daily hospital admissions for asthma in adults: a time-series analysis. PLoS ONE **9**(7), e102475 (2014). https://doi.org/10.1371/journal.pone.0102475
17. Engebretsen, K.A., Johansen, J.D., Kezic, S., Linneberg, A., Thyssen, J.P.: The effect of environmental humidity and temperature on skin barrier function and dermatitis. J. Eur. Acad. Dermatol. Venereol. **30**(2), 223–249 (2016)
18. Pernice, K.: F-shaped pattern of reading on the web: misunderstood, but still relevant (even on mobile) (2017). https://www.nngroup.com/articles/f-shaped-pattern-reading-web-content

Sharing Secured Data on Peer-to-Peer Applications Using Attribute-Based Encryption

Nhan Tam Dang[1](✉), Van Sinh Nguyen[1], Hai-Duong Le[2](✉),
Marcin Maleszka[3], and Manh Ha Tran[2]

[1] International University–HCMC Vietnam National University,
Block 6, Linh Trung Ward, Thu Duc District, Ho Chi Minh City, Vietnam
{dtnhan,nvsinh}@hcmiu.edu.vn
[2] Hong Bang International University,
215 Dien Bien Phu, Ward 15, Binh Thanh District, Ho Chi Minh City, Vietnam
{duonglh,hatm}@hiu.vn
[3] Wroclaw University of Science and Technology, Wybrzeże Wyspiańskiego 27,
50-370 Wroclaw, Poland
marcin.maleszka@pwr.edu.pl

Abstract. The strong growth of communication and storage gives rise to the significantly increasing demand for storing and sharing big data on networks. Research studies and industry applications can apply analytic techniques for exploiting data, or Internet users can exchange data on social networks or peer-to-peer networks. However, securing this shared data is a challenging problem that attracts much attention to researchers. Sharing data with a group of users on peer-to-peer faces the unavailability problem of peer-to-peer nodes, so that users cannot download the shared data. This affects an application class of sharing and storing online services. In this paper, we propose a solution for sharing secured data on peer-to-peer applications using blockchain and attribute-based encryption. The attribute-based encryption guarantees sharing keys among a group of users, while blockchain guarantees keys distribution. We implement the solution on the mobile peer-to-peer network that provides services for sharing and storing data securely.

Keywords: Data security · Data sharing · Attribute-based encryption · Blockchain · Peer-to-Peer network

1 Introduction

Peer-to-peer (P2P) technology provides a platform for sharing a large volume of data on networks. While decentralized P2P systems face the unavailability problem of P2P nodes for sharing data on a group of users. Securing this data on available P2P nodes is a challenging problem because P2P nodes can be unavailable, while data is not allowed to share with all users. There have been

N. T. Nguyen et al. (Eds.): ICCCI 2020, LNAI 12496, pp. 619–630, 2020.
https://doi.org/10.1007/978-3-030-63007-2_48

many data sharing services working with impressive performance and integrated features that greatly improve user experiences and ease the anxious feeling of security problems. However, many potential and unseen risks cause significant damage. For example, Facebook is one of the largest social networks and one of the most influential platforms for e-commerce. Still, it cannot have the most secure system to protect its content. This one shows that even one of the most reliable, secure data sharing services still has many risks. Even when people are vulnerable to many threats using data storage and sharing services, we still need to compromise our safety and using those services. Data storage and sharing services have become one of many pillars supporting people, society, and government.

Most data sharing system can be categorized into two types: centralized data sharing and P2P distributed system. Centralized data sharing is limited by trust and authority. For example, a Facebook user posted an article on Facebook and only want a group of users to be notified about the presence of the published article. Facebook will base on the request of the users and enforce the policy on the corresponding data. P2P file sharing is a process of sharing digital data from one end-user's computer connected to the other computer via the Internet without going through any intermediary server. Peers using P2P file-sharing software, e.g., Gnutella program, for this process. To get the data, a peer will query to other peers to get the location and download the data.

Both types of file-sharing systems have many disadvantages. Centralized data sharing often gets less efficiency compared to its counterpart P2P distributed system because all operations rely on the central server. While P2P data sharing often causes disorganized management and an insecure environment because of the difference in security standard, configuration and security awareness in each peer.

In this paper, we proposed a solution for data sharing service using blockchain, P2P, and attribute-based encryption (ABE). We have decided to use P2P over-centralized system for data storage because we do not need to pay a large sum of money to obtain and maintain hardware; implement authentication and security policies and data manipulation by having many copies in different P2P systems can minimize the chance of services shutdown peers. Blockchain will help our proposed scheme on the encrypted sharing data; We are using ciphertext-policy attribute-based encryption (CP-ABE) [1] for our cryptography scheme.

The rest of the paper is structured as follows: the next section introduces some background of data security and sharing, and research activities related to ABE, P2P and blockchain. Section 3 describes applying the ABE scheme to P2P system: workflow and functions. Some mathematical formulas and explanations are referred from the study [1]. Section 4 provides security evaluation for the ABE scheme of P2P system, some cryptography schemes applied in P2P systems, and reports the preliminary results with some lessons learned before the paper is concluded in Sect. 5.

2   Background

In this section, we review the fields in which this paper is related to data security, ABE, blockchain, and the P2P distributed system. We also present some related works and give some problems those researches faced. Later in the next section, we will go into detail why we use the blockchain and ABE instead of some other alternative options in the data security subsection.

2.1   Data Security

Data security is a must-have in any organization and becomes the research field that attracts many researchers and companies. The basic idea is to make sure that the data absolutely cannot be stored as full plaintext but in a form that no one can understand. Even if the system is compromised and data got stolen, it is still considered to be somewhat rather safe if no one can devise a way to transform the scrambled data back into the original state.

There are two conventional approaches to achieve the goal of transforming plaintext into rubbish data: hash functions and cryptography. In this paper, we focus on using cryptography to secure our data. Generally, we are well accustomed to two types of cryptography: symmetric cryptography and asymmetric cryptography. Symmetric cryptography like AES [2] using only one key to do both tasks: encryption and decryption. Because the key for encryption and decryption is the same, and so the name symmetric cryptography for that reason. Asymmetric cryptography like RSA [3] using two different keys for two tasks: encryption and decryption. Asymmetric cryptography introduces two kinds of keys: the private key for decryption and public key for encryption.

Centralized data sharing can be done through data access control, for example, Facebook. Shanker *et al.* in their work [4] provide fine-grained data access control with encryption to boost security on centralized storage server based on the work of Flank *et al.* [5]. However, there was not much discussion on what cryptography scheme the authors used and if the system can resist collusion attacks and protect user access privilege.

2.2   P2P System

P2P and centralized system both can be distributed computing systems. Both models can have multiple physical computers working together. The main difference is that in a centralized system, all physical computing devices all under the control policy of one organization or one person in P2P, each computing device is under control by a different owner. Ideally, the number of computing devices is the same as the number of the owner. They are peers with no one who can impose policy or control over others.

Napster, which has been nicely summarized in [6] and BitTorrent [7], are among the famous name built on the P2P system. Napster, in its prime age very renowned for being able to share and download music using the peer-to-peer model. There would be not much to debate about Napster if not for the interests of involved parties got violated. Many big shots in the music industry when the Napster still well-known among all people such as Metallica, Madonna, Nirvana, etc. suffers a massive loss of income while underground music bands steadily get their name widely spread because users share and download their music.

BitTorrent later learns from Napster and instead store a whole full-size data on one node, Bit Torrent divide data into many parts, and each node will only hold a fraction of a fully complete data. Bit Torrent argues that just a fraction cannot be considered as original data, even if those are copyrighted data, and BitTorrent has been working fine for many years with that logic. Soon, the law starts changing to deal with the case of BitTorrent, and the access to BitTorrent start restricted little by little.

Heng He *et al.* [8] proposed a secure, efficient, and fine-grained data access control on P2P storage cloud using ABE as a cryptography scheme and proxy re-encryption (PRE) [9] to achieve efficient user revocation. Their work also achieves higher performance and efficiency compared to the previous research on attribute revocation of ABE conducted by Yu *et al.* [10] and Liang *et al.* [11]. Heng He *et al.* research also includes many considerations and configurations to ensure the security standards are to be met. However, re-encryption is not suitable for large data file, re-encryption also have another apparent obstacle which is unavailability problem of the P2P system. To revoke a user, all the records of the encrypted data across the P2P network must be re-encrypted. The re-encryption process must be executed in a timely fashion which requires full cooperation and availability of all peers. To achieve this, it is challenging. Thus, the re-encryption may not be executed in all nodes and old records still retain. So even if a user is revoked, the chance to get the data remains positively high.

2.3   Blockchain

Blockchain first introduced by Satoshi Nakamoto [12] is a fact-based peer-to-peer replicated to several nodes connect to a network. Facts could be anything. A classic example would be cash transactions. All members of the system are anonymous; all communication use cryptography to reliably identify senders, receivers while still retain the unidentified property. When a new fact appears and needs to be added to the chain, a consensus is formed to determine where this fact should be presented and resolve all conflicts. This is called a block.

In the blockchain, a P2P network is just one of many components tightly integrated to make blockchain working. The others being cryptography, consensus mechanism, incentivization scheme, etc. Blockchain involves many processes that make it slow, and because of that, we have the size restriction of the block. Many blockchains have been implemented and used in various application domains: Bitcoin [12], Ethereum [13], Tomochain [14], etc.

2.4   Attribute-Based Encryption

As mentioned above, all theory and algorithm formulas are described in [1]. In this subsection, we only generally summarize the ABE. Amit Sahai and Brent Waters first introduced the current notion, ABE, in [15], and then later in [16]. Many ABE schemes have been proposed which extend upon the functionality of Sahai and Waters' original scheme. The study [17] provides an overview of applied ABE schemes and information about implemented libraries.

ABE is a form of asymmetric cryptography; messages are encrypted under an arbitrary number of attributes or a policy decided by users. Users can encrypt different parts of data with different sets of attributes or policies, so the owner can now selectively share data with other users in a fine-grained way. A policy can be interpreted as a set of rules needed to be satisfied to guarantee a successful encryption and decryption process. It is easier to understand the term of the attribute by referring to the notion in software engineer where the system actor specifies the role played by a user or any other system interacted with the main one. These actors or objects have their properties defined by using attributes. Ultimately, we could say that the according attributes signify the according to a group of people.

In ABE, encryption of data is specified by a set of attributes or a policy that defines the attributes that users need to possess. There are mainly two variants of ABE: Ciphertext-Policy ABE (CP-ABE) and Key-Policy (KP-ABE). Four main basic functions of CP-ABE are:

- Parameters Setup: This is a randomized algorithm that takes no input other than an implicit security parameter. This function generates a random public parameter (PK) and an associated secret master key (MK).
- Encryption: This is also a randomized algorithm that takes PK, the access structure (number of policies to be met for the decryption, and the message to be encrypted).
- Key generation: This function generates a private key (SK) by using the list of attributes that must satisfy the access structure tree to successfully decrypt a message, and generated MK during the parameters setup function.
- Decryption: The algorithm takes the ciphertext of encryption, the PK, and the SK as inputs. The decryption process happens successfully if and only if the list of attributes of the decryption key satisfies the enforcement policy.

3   ABE Scheme for P2P System

3.1   Workflow of the ABE Scheme on P2P System

To address the insecure environment in the P2P distributed sharing system, we use ABE to encrypt the data file before sending it to the network. Thus, it is imperative to transfer the private key reliably and securely to users who got sharing permission from the data owner. The data transmission problem is one of the main problems in the network's functioning. To solve the secure and reliable data transmission problem, we use blockchain to deliver the ABE private key. Blockchain using asymmetric cryptography to reliably identity users, and using the P2P system to replicate data. The ABE private key will be encrypted by the public key of asymmetric cryptography and got duplicated in all nodes of the blockchain. Users can later get the ABE private key by requesting the closet peer and using the private key from public-private key pair to get the plain text content of the ABE private key. We can use the symmetric cryptography instead of ABE to have higher performance whilst maintaining secure key transportation. However, the only approach for revocation in symmetric cryptography is re-encryption and re-distribute the key while with ABE, we can have an easier method for revocation. ABE has one problem which can be called labeling policy-how to attach attributes to the key and create a corresponding policy on the document. Coming up with a good set of attributes and good policy is tedious. We use the public key of the blockchain as explicit attributes to easily create data permission for documents.

Five entities will directly be involved in our system processes: data owner, data requester, centralized server, P2P data storage, and blockchain. Users must first create wallets on blockchain supported by our system. The public address and private key from blockchain will be used later on as we discuss how our system works. A particular user, for instance, A sends a request to create a new pair public parameter and secret key for encryption. Our system has a centralized server to handle this task. A can use the new public parameter to encrypt his data with an access structure is his public address. A then sends his encrypted data to the server for the request of storing it in a P2P system and can notify the server if the data is allowed to be shared. If A wants to share his data, he will leave some overview of his data and his public address. The server will publish these overview along with the public address and the data holder in the P2P model. Our system will not involve in verifying if the data is as precisely as the owner said and check whether the content is appropriate for simplicity.

User B and E see the information and want to download A's data. B and E will request directly to A, if A gives his consent, he will send his request to the server for creating ABE private key along with public addresses A agree to share and sign it. In our scenario, A agrees to share with B but not E. The server will then verify the request to check the genuineness of the message. Our system requires the consent of the data owner before generating a new private key. The ABE private key will have the public address of A and users who A agree to share data as embedded attributes. If there are multiple parties in A request, the server will generate the corresponding number of ABE private key. The server will use B public address to encrypt the ABE private key and then distribute it on a blockchain. After a new block appears on a public ledger, everyone can see, but only B can decrypt the content to use the key. Then B can download A data from the data holder in P2P and decrypt it with ABE private key.

The key generation process can occur on the local peer's machine without the intervention of any intermediary server. However, each peer has to manage their private keys, which documents encrypted under which public parameters.

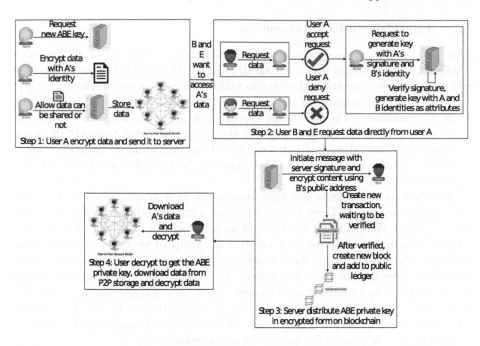

Fig. 1. ABE workflow for P2P system

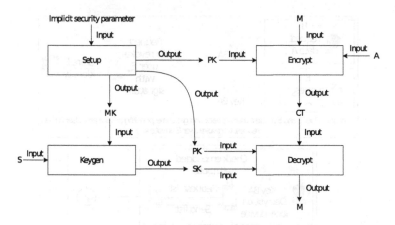

Fig. 2. CP-ABE fundamental functions

We use a centralized server to restrict the public parameter-secret key pair and safeguard the secret key to ensure users cannot massively generate private keys and mismanage them. The server is also a user of the blockchain. The work-flow of our proposed system can be visualized as in Fig. 1.

Our system used Charm [18] as a base to set up tests for ABE with four fundamental functions: parameters setup, encryption, key generation, decryption. The detail of the inputs and outputs of four functions are described in Fig. 2.

3.2   ABE Private Key Revocation

The usual attribute revocation requiring re-encryption is not suitable for large data and has a problem with the unavailability of the P2P network. Our system will be based on a centralized server to tackle the revocation problem.

To revoke the validity of a private key, we need to pinpoint the key we want to invalidate. The attributes represent a group of people or a role, so to further distinguish the individual in the group, we need more attributes or unique attributes. More attributes will affect the performance of ABE. Unique attributes usually contain personal information, and people are reluctant to give such information.

Blockchain public addresses that serve as explicit attributes to easily create data permission for ABE are enough to define a group and specify the individual in the group. We are using the two public addresses of the requester and data owner. Two public addresses for creating a group of users who request data and have the consent of the data owner and separate each requester since public addresses given to each wallet are unique. The scenario of denying the decryption process on the user machine can be summarized as in Fig. 3. Just as private key generation, the deny of decryption must first be approved by the data owner. The method to check the genuineness of data owner requests is the same as generating a new private key process in our system.

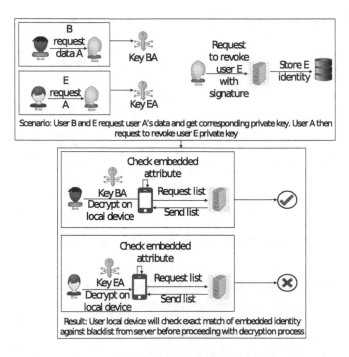

Fig. 3. ABE private key rejection process

This method does not involve re-encrypt files, re-distribute keys. However, this approach misguided people into thinking there is a big serious security issue as one can bypass this mechanism easily by performing a collusion attack to generate a new private key which has embedded attributes different from the list stored in the server. ABE is proven to overcome this adversity, as described in [1]. We observe that in the key generation process, each user is assigned a random parameter value, which is then embedded in the private key. So using different private keys means different parameter values in the decryption process, thus yields in failure when trying to combine to generate a new private key.

The set of attributes in CP-ABE is represented as a list of string without regard to order. Our revocation process will fail in some scenarios because it will revoke the wrong key. For example, user A request and get the private key from user B while user B request and get the private key from user C. If we blacklisted user B to revoke private key of user B, the private key from user A also got affected. The problem can be solved by adding more symbols or words in the attribute to distinguish the difference. For example, user A requests user B; then, we can present it as 'A+B'. In a string, 'B+A' is different from 'A+B', and we check with exact matching embedded attributes, we can differentiate private keys. The database also needs to be kept safe and can be bulged quickly as the number of negative attributes is infinite. The number of attributes required for denying services, the storage capacity is beyond our scope.

Our method does not solve the case of a user already decrypt the encrypted file and get the plaintext to distribute to others without the consent of the data owner. Our method currently works for CP-ABE.

4   Security Evaluation and Preliminary Results

The selling point of blockchain is that cryptographically secured distributed ledgers are virtually unbreakable under normal circumstances. However, the quantum computer is said to be capable of breaking blockchain. Aggarwal et al. learned on the attacks of blockchain using quantum computer [19] but still agreed that blockchains have some time-varying within around seven or more years before the quantum computer can pose a threat to blockchains' integrity. Later, Kiktenko et al. studied on a quantum-secured blockchain. In conclusion, key distribution using blockchain is secure within a short time frame before researchers moving on to quantum secured cryptography.

CP-ABE is provably secure under the standard security model and can resist collusion attacks and protect user access privilege [1]. The studies of [20–22] show that lattice-based cryptography had been resistant to a quantum computer; lattice-based CP-ABE had already been studied and implemented.

The centralized server is under the assumption of being trusted and secured. We will apply other researches, and methods to make the centralized server secure and trusted. User anonymity in the centralized server is secure as the only identity our proposed scheme requires is public address when a user creates a wallet on a blockchain. The public address is used for mapping data and data

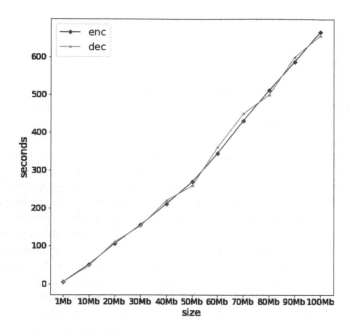

Fig. 4. ABE encryption and decryption performance.eps

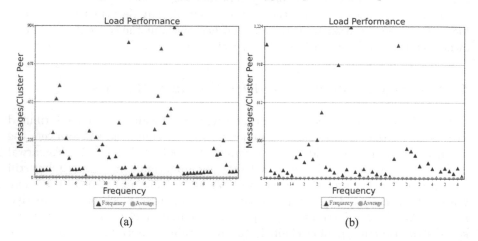

Fig. 5. The distribution of messages on P2P systems: (a) 3000 nodes and (b) 5000 nodes

owner so other users can directly request to data owner; and to prove authenticity on the request to the centralized server for some sensitive, crucial tasks which required the consent of data owner.

The implementation of ABE is under the symmetric curve with 512 bit (SS512) which provide 80 security strength level in bits. We test the performance of both encryption and decryption on data file size of 1 Mb, 10 Mb, 20 Mb, 30 Mb,

40 Mb, 50 Mb, 60 Mb, 70 Mb, 80 Mb, 90 Mb, 100 Mb. The result is as shown in Fig. 4. Time consumption linearly increases as file size increases and it approximately takes 700 s for encrypting or decrypting 100 Mb data.

We have tested load balance on simulated P2P networks with 3000 nodes and 5000 nodes. Load balance increases optimal utilization of distributed resources that include storage, data access, message forwarding, computation on peers. The number of messages per peer is as shown in Fig. 5. There is a small number of peers exchanging more than 450 messages for the 3000-node network, and more than 300 messages for the 5000-node network, i.e., except for only a few peers with high load, the other peers share load on the networks.

5   Conclusions

This paper aims at providing secure data sharing on peer-to-peer applications using attribute-based encryption. To achieve the goal of efficient data sharing, we design a system with the help of an additional component: blockchain. Our system provides user anonymity and fairly simple ABE private key denial on the request of the data owner. Our system also achieves secure key distribution on blockchain and secure data encryption on P2P storage under standard security model and can resist collusion attacks on the encrypted data and protect user access privilege. Blockchain has been long categorized as only digital money like stock for easy investing in harvesting a massive amount of profit by the mass media. Some even deemed that blockchain is only used by the criminal to hide their activities. Cryptography usually is used as the only means for protection, not as a factor to boost the business value. We are sure that with our experiments, we can provide some different insights on the purpose of blockchain and cryptography. Our future work includes deploying in real word P2P applications, securing the centralized server, testing lattice-based CP-ABE, and designing a scheme to detect peers got attacked by the botnet, virus, malware to protect the network.

Acknowledgement. This research activity is funded by Hong Bang International University under the grant number GV2025.

References

1. Bethencourt, J., Sahai, A., Waters, B.: Ciphertext-policy attribute-based encryption. In: IEEE Symposium on Security and Privacy (SP 2007), pp. 321–334 (2007)
2. Jamil, T.: The Rijndael algorithm. IEEE Potentials 23(2), 36–38 (2004)
3. Rivest, R.L., Shamir, A., Adleman, L.: A method for obtaining digital signatures and public-key cryptosystems. Commun. ACM 21(2), 120–126 (1978)
4. Shankar, U., Kulik, A., Moller, B., Patel, A., Bershad, B.N., Erb, D.: Storing encrypted objects, December 2013
5. Flank, J.H., Klinkner, S.R., Swartzlander, B.B., Thompson, T.J., Yoder, A.G.: Centralized role-based access control for storage servers, March 2011
6. Greenfeld, K.T., Taro, K.: Meet the Napster. Time Mag. 2, 998068 (2000)

7. Cohen, B.: Incentives build robustness in BitTorrent. In: Proceedings of the Workshop on Economics of Peer-to-Peer systems, vol. 6, pp. 68–72 (2003)

8. He, H., Li, R., Dong, X., Zhang, Z.: Secure, efficient and fine-grained data access control mechanism for P2P storage cloud. IEEE Trans. Cloud Comput. 2(4), 471–484 (2014)

9. Blaze, M., Bleumer, G., Strauss, M.: Divertible protocols and atomic proxy cryptography. In: Nyberg, K. (ed.) EUROCRYPT 1998. LNCS, vol. 1403, pp. 127–144. Springer, Heidelberg (1998). https://doi.org/10.1007/BFb0054122

10. Yu, S., Wang, C., Ren, K., Lou, W.: Attribute based data sharing with attribute revocation. In: Proceedings of 5th ACM Symposium on Information, Computer and Communications Security, pp. 261–270 (2010)

11. Liang, X., Cao, Z., Lin, H., Shao, J.: Attribute based proxy re-encryption with delegating capabilities. In: Proceedings of 4th International Symposium on Information, Computer, and Communications Security, pp. 276–286 (2009)

12. Nakamoto, S.: Bitcoin: a peer-to-peer electronic cash system (2008). https://bitcoin.org/bitcoin.pdf

13. Buterin, V., et al.: Ethereum white paper: a next generation smart contract & decentralized application platform. First version 53 (2014)

14. TomoChain R&D.: TomoChain: masternodes design technical white paper version 1.0. (2018)

15. Sahai, A., Waters, B.: Fuzzy identity based encryption. In: IACR Cryptology ePrint Archive (2004)

16. Goyal, V.K., Pandey, O., Sahai, A., Waters, B.: Attribute-based encryption for fine-grained access control of encrypted data. In: IACR Cryptology ePrint Archive, vol. 2006, p. 309 (2006)

17. Zickau, S., Thatmann, D., Butyrtschik, A., Denisow, I., Küpper, A.: Applied attribute-based encryption schemes. In: Proceedings of 19th International Conference-Innovations in Clouds, Internet and Networks (ICIN 2016), pp. 88–95 (2016)

18. Akinyele, J.A., et al.: Charm: a framework for rapidly prototyping cryptosystems. J. Cryptogr. Eng. 3(2), 111–128 (2013)

19. Aggarwal, D., Brennen, G.K., Lee, T., Santha, M., Tomamichel, M.: Quantum attacks on bitcoin, and how to protect against them. arXiv preprint arXiv:1710.10377 (2017)

20. Wang, Y.: Lattice ciphertext policy attribute-based encryption in the standard model. Int. J. Netw. Secur. 16(6), 444–451 (2014)

21. Agrawal, S., Boyen, X., Vaikuntanathan, V., Voulgaris, P., Wee, H.: Functional encryption for threshold functions (or fuzzy IBE) from lattices. In: Fischlin, M., Buchmann, J., Manulis, M. (eds.) PKC 2012. LNCS, vol. 7293, pp. 280–297. Springer, Heidelberg (2012). https://doi.org/10.1007/978-3-642-30057-8_17

22. Qiao, Z., Liang, S., Davis, S., Jiang, H.: Survey of attribute based encryption. In: Proceedings of 15th IEEE/ACIS International Conference on Software Engineering, Artificial Intelligence, Networking and Parallel/Distributed Computing (SNPD 2014), pp. 1–6. IEEE (2014)

Assessment of False Identity by Variability in Operating Condition for Memristor Write Time-Based Device Fingerprints

Ha-Phuong Nguyen[1], The-Nghia Nguyen[2], Nhat-An Nguyen[2], SungHyun Park[3], Yeong-Seok Seo[1], Dosam Hwang[1], and Donghwa Shin[3(✉)]

[1] Department of Computer Engineering, Yeungnam University, Gyeongsan, South Korea
nguyenphuong18285@gmail.com, ysseo@yu.ac.kr, dosamhwang@gmail.com
[2] Department of Software Convergence, Soongsil University, Seoul, South Korea
thenghianguyen@soongsil.ac.kr, nhatan147@gmail.com
[3] Department of Smart Systems Software, Soongsil University, Seoul, South Korea
{sunghyunpark,donghwashin}@soongsil.ac.kr

Abstract. The variability in manufacturing process and operating conditions has a significant impact on the operation of memristor devices, since it is usually implemented in nano-scale for higher density. The variability in thickness and area can be regarded as a source of variations in read and write times of memristor when using the device as a memory cell. Recently, there have been efforts to utilize this feature as a unique device ID (or so-called fingerprint) similar to its counterparts in static random-access memory (SRAM) and other non-volatile memories. In real systems, bit flips in the fingerprint caused by variability in the operating condition may increase the probability of false identity. In this study, we assess the effect of timing variability on false identity in write time-based random device fingerprint of memristor memory.

Keywords: Memristor · Device fingerprint · Variability

1 Introduction

Memristors have become candidates for future memory devices owing to their advantages such as high density, low power consumption, and non-volatility [10]. The memristor can be regarded as an electrical element that is able to retain its internal resistance state according to the history of applied voltage and current even when power is turned off [9]. The resistance states can be toggled by applying voltage with a proper magnitude and duration. This unique property makes memristor a promising candidate for next-generation non-volatile memories (NVMs).

Generally, the memristor is employed in nano-scale systems. Therefore, a small variability is likely to have considerable impact on parameters as well as

© Springer Nature Switzerland AG 2020
N. T. Nguyen et al. (Eds.): ICCCI 2020, LNAI 12496, pp. 631–639, 2020.
https://doi.org/10.1007/978-3-030-63007-2_49

behavior of a device. Hence it requires a careful consideration of the variability when using the memristor in practical systems. The variability in thickness and area is translated to variations in read and write times of memristor when using the device as a memory cell. The variation in thickness and area affects the resistance value related to the supplied voltage and current across the device [7]. Furthermore, the supply voltage for each device is also variable based on physical connection through the power distribution network. The dependence of domain-wall mobility on temperature is another well-known source of variability.

For conventional memory applications, the effect of variability should be suppressed lower than a certain level to guarantee the timing requirement. Nevertheless, we can utilize the variability feature in the fields of sensor and security applications. There have been some approaches that attempt to measure the variation of the write time to obtain the temperature [4,6]. For security applications, the variability in device thickness and area can be regarded as a source of randomness in read and write times of memristor when using the device as a memory cell. Recently, there have been efforts to utilize this feature as a unique device ID (fingerprint) similar to its counterparts in static random-access memory (SRAM) and other NVMs.

The device-dependent random and unique fingerprint generation is essential for the realization of physically-unclonable functions (PUF). A PUF is a physical entity with features that are practically impossible to duplicate. Such features usually result from the manufacturing process of individual devices. PUFs depend on the uniqueness of their physical microstructures obtained from random physical factors introduced during manufacture. These factors are expected to be unpredictable and uncontrollable to make the function unclonable.

An intuitive approach to obtain the random result in memristor array is the write interruption [5]. In the controlled condition, we can obtain 50% aliased random bit results in the digital value of the array. Ideally, the probability to have two identical fingerprints in the population is expected to be negligible when the total bit width of the fingerprint is sufficiently long. It is inversely proportional to the exponential of the total bit width of the fingerprint. However, it is feasible to have another source of variability in real operating conditions such as temperature and supply voltage. The bit flips in the fingerprint due to the variability in operating condition may increase the probability of false identity. Each of these multiple sources of variability in manufacturing and operating conditions needs to be carefully processed individually. In this study, we assess the effect of timing variability on the false identity in write time-based random device fingerprint of memristor memory.

2   Backgrounds

2.1   Memristor Cell Model with Variability

The memristor cell is typically modeled by a variable resistor with dividing position (domain wall) and two resistance states: a high resistance state and a low resistance state. The resistance state can be changed by moving the position of

Table 1. Constants and parameters of the proposed model [4].

Parameters	Values	Description (Unit)
a	0.15	Ion jump distance (nm)
E_A	0.18	Ion activation energy (eV)
k_B	8.6173303×10^{-5}	Boltzmann constant (eV K^{-1})
f	10	Ion jump frequency (THz)
q_I	2	Ion charge
V_w	10	Voltage for write (V)
Variables	Values	Description (Unit)
T	300–400	Temperature (K)
D	10	Thickness of memristor (nm)
R_{on}	100	Turn on resistance (Ω)
R_{off}	16000	Turn off resistance (Ω)
$R_{pulldown}$	1000	Pull-down resistance (Ω)
x_0	0	Initial state of memristor
x_f	1	Final state of memristor

the domain wall by applying voltage with a proper magnitude and duration. This domain wall position-based behavior of memristor can be given as follows [5]:

$$\frac{dx(t)}{dt}) = \frac{\mu_I R_{on}}{D^2} i_m(t),$$
$$v_m(t) = [R_{on}x(t) + R_{off}(1 - x(t))]i_m(t), \tag{1}$$

where D represents the length of device and $x(t)$, the domain wall position. Here, $v_m(t)$ and $i_m(t)$ are voltage and current applied to the memristor respectively. Temperature dependent mobility, $mu_I(T)$, and $D_I(T)$, relations is denoted as follows [5]:

$$\mu_I(T) = \frac{q_I D_I(T)}{k_B T},$$
$$D_I(T) = fa^2 exp\left(\frac{-E_A}{k_B T}\right), \tag{2}$$

where k_B is Boltzmann constant, q_I is ion charge, f is jump frequency, a is crystal geometry, E_A is ion activation energy, T is temperature.

And we have the equation about the write time of memristor cells in Eq. 3 as follows [5]:

$$t_{write} = \frac{D^2}{\mu_I(T)v_w}\left(\frac{r_1 - 1}{2}(x_0^2 - x_f^2) + (r_1 + r_2)(x_f - x_0)\right), \tag{3}$$

where parameters r_1, r_2 depend on R_{off}, R_{on}, $R_{pulldown}$ and they are calculated as follow: $r_1 = R_{off}/R_{on}$, $r_2 = R_{pulldown}/R_{on}$, D represents the length of device and $x(t)$ is the domain wall position, $\mu_I(T)$ is the mobility. The write time is related to temperature. When temperature increases, the write time decreases simultaneously.

The parameters used in this paper are summarized in Table 1 [5]. The write time is usually modeled according to a Gaussian distribution [3,6] that is similar to other physical parameters used in the semiconductor manufacturing process. Figure 1 shows the variation in write time with the thickness and the temperature.

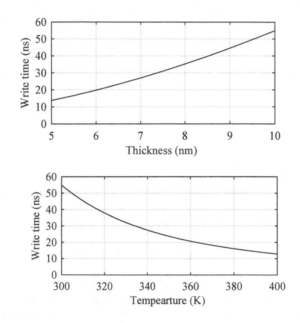

Fig. 1. Variation of write time with thickness and temperature.

2.2 Memristor Array Model

Figure 2 presents the circuit used in this study. An usual N-bit memristive PUF (M-PUF) circuit with N memristive devices, N challenge bits, N response bits used in related studies [5,8] is adopted for the model. The circuit is the combination between a challenge for memristive PUF and a random output of the memristive device cell implemented using XOR gate which produces the response bit of the PUF cell. As the challenge-response pair is unique, it identifies the integrated circuit that contains M-PUF. Hence, two different challenges cannot produce the same responses and the write time of cells of two different memmristor PUFs cannot be the same.

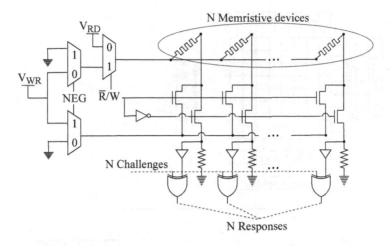

Fig. 2. An N-bit write-time based M-PUF [5].

2.3 Random Device Fingerprint Generation in Memristor Array

We need a desirable source of randomness in cryptographic applications for security to ensure uniqueness linked to a device. A random key generation based on the process variation of integrated circuits such as SRAM and NVM has been studied in this context so far [2]. These keys are unique depending on the device and therefore, it can be regarded as a fingerprint to identify the specific device. NVM-based applications are often regarded as vulnerable for advanced security applications due to its non-volatility. However, the smaller footprint and higher reliability of NVMs are still attractive to simple applications with basic security requirements [1].

Figure 3 illustrates the process of the memristor-based device fingerprints. The logical value of memristor cells in the array is determined by the access time and supply voltage. The length of the programming pulse and amplitude of programming current are determined in advance to ensure the change of logical state after the programming operation in memory applications. However, the programming pulse is interrupted in the intermediate epoch to obtain the random values as device fingerprints. With the variability in manufacturing process, the states of the memristor cells are partly changed only if the length of the programming pulse or amplitude of the current pulse is sufficient. In this study, we evaluate the value of the memristor cell and array by using the models presented in Sects. 1 and 2 when considering the process variability in thickness. We assume that the programming process can be halted using timing controller in a given error range.

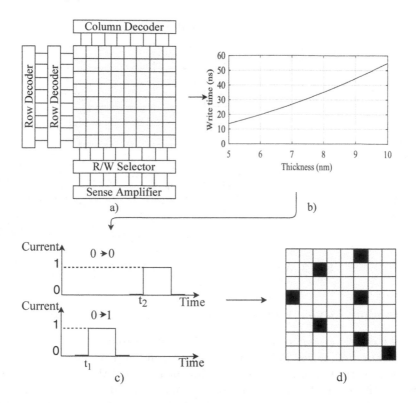

Fig. 3. Enrollment process of the memristor-based PUF. a) Memristor memory structure (initial state) b) Write time variation via the temperature c) applying programming pulse d) Randomly generated result for PUF

3   Timing Variability and False Identity

As shown in the procedure to check the device fingerprint in Fig. 2, the exact matching of the fingerprints from two different devices happens with the probability inversely proportional to the exponential of bit length of the fingerprint ($\propto 1/2^{N_{bits}}$). The probability of the exact match of the original and fake ones is expected to be substantially low with sufficiently long bit length. However, when we consider the effect of timing variability in the enrollment process, the probability of the false identity indicates significantly higher value in real systems [11].

Figure 4 summarizes the probability of the false identity with respect to timing error in the enrollment process. To assess the impact of variability, we have generated 10000 samples of 64-bit memristor-based fingerprint with ±3% of standard deviation for thickness D variability in our experiment. It represents the manufacturing process variability that is essential for the randomness in the fingerprints. To obtain the original fingerprint the ideal interruption epoch is set atc 7.1 μs for the balanced logic values (i.e. 50% of 1 and 50% of 0). We have selected a fingerprint as the original one, and then compared the challenging results of the remaining samples to the original value while applying the timing variability in the regeneration.

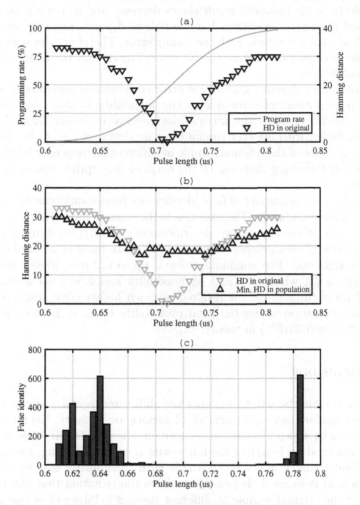

Fig. 4. (a) Array programming rate and change of original sample in Hamming distance vs. timing variability (b) Hamming distance in original device and minimum Hamming distance in population (c) Number of false identity with timing variability

In simple authentication applications, the device fingerprint is authenticated if the regenerated response is sufficiently close to the provisioned response in Hamming distance. Otherwise, the device fingerprint is used as a random seed to generate a public-private key pair in cryptographic applications. In the both cases, the noisy bits should be accepted or corrected. Figure 4 (a) indicates that the completion rate of programming and the average Hamming distance of the original fingerprint at different timings.

As the length of programming pulse increases around the ideal epoch, the rate of programming in the array increases. The Hamming distance of the original sample from the balanced result shows decrease and increase patterns since the original fingerprint is obtained at the balanced point. Even the original fingerprint has a noisy response with the timing error. Therefore, the system should be capable to correct or tolerate the bit errors larger than the expected error in the original device.

The tolerable range or capability of error correction is determined according to the expected range of error due to the variability in operating conditions. However, the bit error in the original device may be larger than that found in the population with a larger timing error as shown in Fig. 4 (b). Hence, the Hamming distance of the original sample at different timings may be larger than the minimum Hamming distance to the original fingerprint among the sample population.

Figure 4 (c) is the number of false identity candidates satisfying the look-alike condition in the population. The situation is the same as having higher number of candidates when there is a relaxed description of figures. If the figure is described as having worn glasses or not, we would have more number of candidates who can be the right one. The maximum value is up to 622 over 10000 samples and the average is 94, which is 6.22% at maximum and 0.94% on average. Only with 0.07 µs of timing error, it resulted in much higher error compared to the theoretical estimation where the ideal probability to have the false identity is merely $1/2^{16}$ ($\approx 0.0015\%$) in theory.

4   Conclusions

This paper reveals the effect of timing variability on the false identity in write time-based random device fingerprint of memristor memory. Even though the probability to have two identical fingerprints in the population is ideally negligible when the total bit length of the fingerprint is sufficiently long, the simulation result indicates that it is not much simple with the multiple sources of variability in practical systems. It is possible to have the situation that the Hamming distance of the original sample at different timings is larger than the minimum Hamming distance to the original fingerprint among the sample population without proper management of timing. Based on the simulation result, the maximum number of false identity in the population is significantly higher than the ideal value only with 0.07 ms of timing error. The result can be applied for other sources of variability such as temperature and voltage in similar manner provided the way to affect the write time is similar. The results obtained herein provides insights into the development of a practical method to generate the device fingerprint taking into account the variability in operating conditions.

References

1. Che, W., Plusquellic, J., Bhunia, S.: A non-volatile memory based physically unclonable function without helper data. In: Proceedings of the 2014 IEEE/ACM International Conference on Computer-Aided Design, pp. 148–153. IEEE Press (2014)
2. Eiroa, S., Castro, J., Martínez-Rodríguez, M.C., Tena, E., Brox, P., Baturone, I.: Reducing bit flipping problems in sram physical unclonable functions for chip identification. In: 2012 19th IEEE International Conference on Electronics, Circuits, and Systems (ICECS 2012), pp. 392–395. IEEE (2012)
3. Li, H., Hu, M.: Compact model of memristors and its application in computing systems. In: 2010 Design, Automation & Test in Europe Conference & Exhibition (DATE 2010) pp. 673–678. IEEE (2010)
4. Merkel, C.: Thermal profiling in CMOS/memristor hybrid architectures (2011)
5. Nguyen, H.P., Nguyen, T.N., Seo, Y.S., Hwang, D., Shin, D.: Correction of bit-aliasing in memristor-based physically unclonable functions with timing variability. IEEE Access (2019)
6. Nguyen, T.N., Shin, D.: Statistical memristor-based temperature sensors without analog-to-digital conversion. In: 2018 IEEE 7th Non-Volatile Memory Systems and Applications Symposium (NVMSA), pp. 99–104. IEEE (2018)
7. Rajendran, J., Maenm, H., Karri, R., Rose, G.S.: An approach to tolerate process related variations in memristor-based applications. In: 2011 24th International Conference on VLSI Design, pp. 18–23. IEEE (2011)
8. Rose, G.S., McDonald, N., Yan, L.K., Wysocki, B.: A write-time based memristive PUF for hardware security applications. In: 2013 IEEE/ACM International Conference on Computer-Aided Design (ICCAD), pp. 830–833. IEEE (2013)
9. Strukov, D.B., Snider, G.S., Stewart, D.R., Williams, R.S.: The missing memristor found. Nature 453(7191), 80 (2008)
10. Yang, J.J., Strukov, D.B., Stewart, D.R.: Memristive devices for computing. Nat. Nanotechnol. 8(1), 13 (2013)
11. Yu, M., Devadas, S.: Secure and robust error correction for physical unclonable functions. IEEE Des. Test Comput. 27(1), 48–65 (2010)

Analysis of Segregated Witness Implementation for Increasing Efficiency and Security of the Bitcoin Cryptocurrency

Michał Kędziora[1](✉), Dawid Pieprzka[1], Ireneusz Jóźwiak[1], Yongxin Liu[2], and Houbing Song[2]

[1] Faculty of Computer Science and Management,
Wroclaw University of Science and Technology, Wroclaw, Poland
michal.kedziora@pwr.edu.pl
[2] Department of Electrical Engineering and Computer Science, Embry-Riddle
Aeronautical University, Daytona Beach, FL 32114, USA

Abstract. The purpose of this paper is to present mechanisms and algorithms for improving Bitcoin cryptocurrency efficiency, security along with the block propagation times. Specifically, Segregated Witness Implementation (SWI) issues are verified based on both the simulation and real data from the Bitcoin network. Based on the block propagation times calculated in the simulator and real-world bitcoin network, the efficiency and safety of Bitcoin has been analysed and validated.

Keywords: Cryptocurrency · Blockchain efficiency · Segregated witness

1 Introduction

The time efficiency of algorithms is very important in Blockchain networks. Excessive block extraction together with long latency can cause security vulnerabilities and problems when accepting newly created chains. It leads to security issues and can harden the use of Blockchain technology [7,8]. Therefore shortening the propagation times in the network is of great significance [4,5]. Over the years, many solutions have been developed to improve the time efficiency of propagation and block capacity. One of them is, among other solutions, Segregated Witness, or SegWit, is an implementation of the protocol that allows to process a greater number of transactions by increasing the block's capacity and providing protection against bitcoin transaction malleability.

The highlight of SegWit is its ability to increase block capacity [6]. SegWit was initially published in 2015. Its primitive principle is to separate transactions on the Blockchain with signatures. The early version of SegWit can be blocked by miners who exploited the vulnerabilities in BIP-9. To increase the robustness,

© Springer Nature Switzerland AG 2020
N. T. Nguyen et al. (Eds.): ICCCI 2020, LNAI 12496, pp. 640–651, 2020.
https://doi.org/10.1007/978-3-030-63007-2_50

a strategy namely Soft Fork before SegWit is implemented in BIP-148, where the ominous miners can be bypassed as long as decisions are made by the majority. Thanks to this improvement, Bitcoin community has introduced SegWit in 2017.

Other important improvements of SegWit in Bitcoin network are: BIP91 - implemented on June 23, 2017 with the change concerned temporary software, which forced the obligatory upgrade of the node to SegWit; BIP148 - implemented on August 1, 2017 for Changing the mandatory SegWit updates on the node from August 1 was required for another 2 weeks and BIP141, 143, 147 - implemented on August 24, 2017 with the change updated the node to the latest version of SegWit [17]. The purpose of this work is to present SegWit mechanisms and to examine performance of Bitcoin network after its implementation.

The rest of the paper is organized as follows. Section 2 presents related work. SegWit implementation analysis is presented in Sect. 3. And Sect. 4 concludes this paper.

2   Related Work

A typical research on the simulation-based Bitcoin network is presented in [1]. The paper aims to investigate how consensus parameters, network characteristics and protocol modifications affect the scalability, security and performance of Proof of Work in the Blockchain. Specifically, the study was conducted on the proprietary Bitcoin simulator. It was built on the NS3 network simulator, One of the authors' goals is to create a realistic simulator incorporating with collected real network statistics. In addition, the authors collected data from popular Bitcoin websites to estimate block size distribution, blocks quantity, the scale of the Blockchain networks along with geographical distribution of peers. Their study was conducted from March 2015 to October 2016 and evaluated the performance of different Blockchain instances. The tests were not on a direct network due to the insufficient availability of nodes.

Authors in [2] present an empirical analysis of announcing and block propagation that led to the Bitcoin forks. They have shown that the block propagation delay between miners have a order similar to the delay in processing the Bitcoin network. The study was conducted in the period from January 2016 to March 2018 using Bitcoin network data. The study shows that on the basis of propagation time and forks, the first block advertisement has not only a meaning in which it becomes part of the main chain, but also the time of data propagation. However, the influence on whether a block will become an orphan or will be accepted by the main chain is insignificant.

The research in [3] presents the way in which data is spread and propagated on the Bitcoin network to identify critical weaknesses. In particular, information synchronization analysis was performed. This is one of the early studies closely related to block propagation in the Bitcoin network. The study was conducted in 2013. The research explains the way block propagation was calculated. The propagation time results show that the block size matters for propagation: the median propagation is 6.5 s and the average is 12.5 s. It has been proven that the larger the block, the longer the propagation time, which gives the network attackers a chance.

3   SegWit Implementation Analysis

The aforementioned researches allow us to draw conclusions related to blockchain and data propagation. And, by configuring the Bitcoin network simulator's input data, we can simulate a large number of nodes.

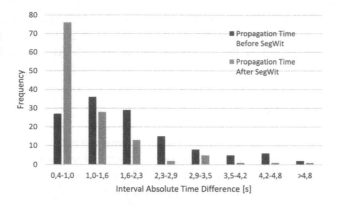

Fig. 1. Histogram of block propagation times from the last 127 days before and after the implementation of Segregated Witness.

Nowadays, we have up to 9,000 nodes available on Bitcoin [9], so we use the simulator's operation and results to assess its correctness and its potential to simulate Bitcoin with Segregated Witness. Previous researches on performance, security and forks based on block propagation times in the Bitcoin network, omit the information of where large time fluctuations come from. They focused on how block propagation affects forks and their orphaning, and no conclusions were drawn to answer why fluctuations in block propagation time exist in the network. More recent study in [2] on block propagation took place in 2013 and 2017, with the goal being analysis of changes in the propagation response against the network background. The authors proved that the SegWit provides real benefits to the Blockchain network.

3.1   Testing Environment

In our testbed, a virtual machine is created in Windows 10 along using Hyper-V with Ubuntu 18.04.2. The next step is to set up the simulation. To achieve this, there are three ways: the first is to edit existing simulator files, the second is to set the input data directly on the simulation start command, the third is to create your individual parameter to overwrite the default values. In this research, first option is utilized.

Table 1. Ordered simulation results.

Interval	mean	median	10%	25%	75%	90%	Sr	Bandwidth
1500	0,968	0,999	0,692	0,829	1,157	1,278	0,00%	10,0251
600	0,985	0,984	0,702	0,84	1,148	1,268	0,21%	25,0627
150	0,977	0,019	0,661	0,843	1,182	1,315	0,82%	100,251
60	0,992	0,971	0,683	0,84	1,171	1,282	0,85%	250,627
30	0,979	1,006	0,675	0,85	1,17	1,302	3,95%	501,627
20	0,983	1,034	0,653	0,839	1,199	1,33	4,20%	759,475
10	0,994	1,04	0,681	0,851	1,205	1,3	7,65%	1566,12
5	1,002	0,861	0,654	0,861	1,23	1,345	17,96%	3132,83
2	1,017	1,051	0,741	0,886	1,217	1,336	33,87%	8359,56
1	1,114	1,169	0,776	0,98	1,33889	1,457	45,80%	15389,6
0,5	11,734	12,562	11,788	12,398	12,723	12,829	66,80%	53642,2

Simulation parameters are: 1000 blocks, block size of 1,000,000 bytes (1 MB) and 6,000 nodes. These values are selected to check the correct operation of the simulator. The total simulation takes 17 h and sample results of block propagation times are presented in Table 1, with all unit in seconds (Fig. 2).

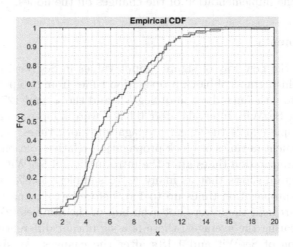

Fig. 2. Cumulative distribution of samples analyzed.

3.2   Network Analysis

The implementation of the SegWit is associated with emerging changes in the network. One of the most critical weaknesses killed by SegKit is the "malleability" of transactions. This issue allows the malicious to modify transaction signatures using a 64-digit hexadecimal hash called the identifier (txid). This vulnerability makes it possible to conduct double-spending activities. SegWit protects against third-party attackers and malicious scripts by enabling susceptible parts of transactions to be transferred to the transaction witness (SegWit) and limits the impact of the witness on the txid calculation [10,11].

The second benefit is the repair of scaling linear signature mixing operations - the main problem of increasing blocks is that there are transactions that scale squarely rather than linearly. This state of affairs can double the size of the transaction. It is easy to guess that this can be used by intentional, proper implementation of the transaction [12]. On average, a single block needs about 12.5 s for confirmation on the node, while a maliciously created transaction can take up to 3 min. SegWit solves the problem by changing the transaction hash calculation for the signature per each byte, allowing only a maximum of two transaction bytes to be mixed. Swap allows the same operation, but with much greater efficiency while being resistant to malicious transactions created [13].

The third benefit is a new way of signing input values - SegWit allows us to securely sign transactions by receiving only the transaction, index, and value abbreviation. Earlier, it requires checking the hash of a full copy of the transaction to perform this type of operation. This is problematic because some transactions are very large, making the whole process very time-consuming, even with a small amount of transactions. The change has significantly accelerated this process [15]. As depicted in Fig. 3, the propagation times of blocks have been reduced after the implementation of the changes on the nodes.

3.3 Experiments

To verify that the new way of signing input values in SegWit are effective, we compared two histograms of block propagation times from two periods. The first of 127 days before the introduction of SegWit and the second 127 days after the introduction of SegWit. Intervals after 0.632 s were adopted. 127 samples are used; each sample equals the mean propagation block times per day. Figure 1 shows improvement in times of block propagation relative to each other. Orange indicates the propagation times after the introduction of SegWit. It can be seen that the histogram shows that as many as 76 samples (59.8%) are in the first compartment (propagation times up to 1 s), before introducing this solution in the first compartment there were not even half of the samples (27 samples, 21.3 %). Also comparing the averages, there is a significant difference, 1.97 s before the introduction of SegWit and 1.18 s after the changes. As shown in Fig. 4, the impact of the change implementation on the nodes had a very significant impact on the decrease in block propagation times. The next part of the work will present a detailed analysis of the wider period of introducing changes on the nodes, including the Bitcoin version in the network. Both manufacturers and portfolio users benefited from the introduced changes by faster transaction confirmation.

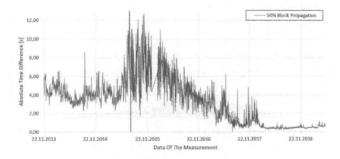

Fig. 3. Block propagation times in 2015–2019.

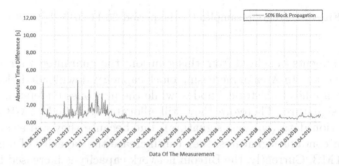

Fig. 4. Blocks propagation times from August 23, 2017–May 17, 2019

UTXO (Unspent Transaction Output) growth reduction is the next benefit of SegWit. A given database is used when validating whether the new transaction is valid or false. To be efficient, the base should work in the main RAM memory. Maintaining the database in such a small size becomes problematic when Bitcoin is growing. The increasing number of users means that every user must have their entry to ensure transaction security. SegWit solves this problem by using minimizing transactions. Thanks to this solution, signature data that does not affect the UTXO size cost 75% less. The goal is to encourage users to use this solution to minimize fees and encourage programmers to implement features that implement the least impact on UTXO, and to design smart contracts. People benefiting from a given shift are miners, companies, and users who have full nodes. They benefit from lower fees than people who do not use this solution. Besides, faster use of UTXO encourages more people to have full nodes, which increases network security. In terms of increased security, SegWit solved the problem for the payment of multisig contracts, which, using P2SH, enabled the funds to be stolen by an attacker with very large power resources, who was able to find an address conflict with part of the multisig script. In SegWit, it is decided to implement a change that the used HASH160 algorithm would be used only for direct payments only for a single public key using SHA256. In this case, this type of attack is useless and impossible to execute. Everyone using

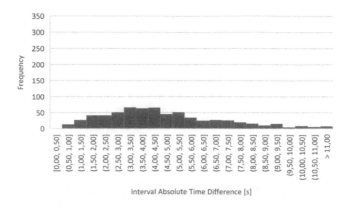

Fig. 5. Histogram samples for the period 30.11.2015–22.08.2017

multisig payments benefited from this solution; the guarantee guarantees additional protection. In Area of increasing block capacity, downloaded block without a signature applies to historical nodes, while the new ones understand that they contain a signature. Therefore they still allocate by default 1 MB of a block for transaction data (without signature), but because they are aware that the transaction contains signatures, they can increase the capacity of a given block to nearly 4 MB. Currently, the Bitcoin network capacity is increased from about 1.6 MB to about 2.4 MB. The main reason for only such a small increase in block capacity is the growing time of block propagation, which pays to large miners to jump to a different field than to fight to improve protocol performance [14]. Performance improvement was achived by segregation of signature data that allows nodes not interested in signatures to cut them on disk or only downloads them in the second place. Previously, the signature data was part of the transaction and had to be used in calculating the hash function. The solution saves disk space and works with lower bandwidth. SegWit introduced script versioning that solved the problem of the lack of script implementation in other than only backward compatible with soft forks. Adding the version number to the scripts has solved this problem, which makes it possible to handle them with the required hard forks by simply increasing the version of the script. The last concept introduced was Lightning Network, which is a network with very high bandwidth. Until recently, it is thought that the Bitcoin network had too complicated structure, mechanisms, and algorithms, which made it impossible to pursue this concept. The introduction of SegWit has simplified many algorithms and solutions due to the possible implementation of the Ligthning Network in the near future [16].

3.4   Bitcoin Data Analysis

Thanks to previously obtained results of block propagation times for individual days from 2013–2019, some of whose results are presented in Fig. 5 and Fig. 6.

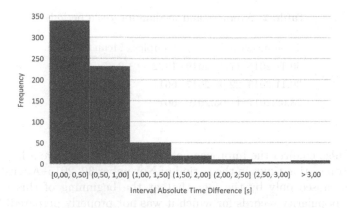

Fig. 6. Histogram of samples for the period 23.08.2015 to 17.05.2019

It was possible to analyze the impact of SegWit on the network. To this end, samples were checked to confirm the correctness of the data. Matlab version 9.0 was used to perform the analysis. For the purpose of analysis, 100 collected samples from two available sets were selected for comparison. The samples come from the period from July 15,2015 to October 27, 2019. First, the previously prepared block propagation samples from the Bitcoin network were loaded with a total of 200 observations, each observation with 100 samples. We see that the data sets fit in quite well with the cumulative distribution function. The next step was to check whether we would receive similar conclusions using the K-S test analysis. This will answer whether the difference between the two samples is not statistically significant to be able to conclude that the two sets are not different. Therefore, we should accept the null hypothesis that p-value is greater than 0.5, which is the default value of significance level. Thus, according to tests, the differences between the two samples are not statistically significant to be able to conclude that both these distributions are different. The obtained results of block propagation times are presented in Fig. 3.

The resulting Fig. 3 is hardly legible, therefore it was decided to change the scope of research from August 10, 2015 to May 17, 2019. The new data range given will allow to divide block propagation times into two equal samples after 661 days from the date of SegWit introduction (Fig. 4). It should be noted that not all nodes will immediately implement it, which will be shown later in this paper.

Based on the charts before and after the introduction of SegWit, one can observe that a very large improvement in block propagation times, which proves faster network performance and mechanisms implemented in it. In addition, to confirm the numbers, the means and medians for these two periods were counted, as well as for the whole range. The results are presented in Table 2.

The calculated medians and averages also confirm that the network has improved since the introduction of SegWit. We can see a clear decrease in block propagation times. Also comparing with the average times given in [2], which

Table 2. Averages and median for given periods.

Time inverval	Samples	Mean	Median
30.11.2015–17.05.2019	1322	2,65	1,49
30.11.2015–22.08.2017	661	4,63	4,2
23.08.2017–17.05.2019	661	0,68	0,49

are 12.5 s, also confirm the improvement. One can also observe a large decrease in block propagation times in the period of November 30, 2015–August 22, 2017, which was caused only by the fact that at the beginning of this period Bitcoin broke popularity records for which it was not properly prepared. Hence the average time was increased than the time from the older period despite newer versions of the Bitcoin network on the nodes. To illustrate the distribution of samples, this is best represented by the histogram for the two time intervals. Each histogram has 0.5 s intervals with 661 samples each.

Analyzing two histograms, it can be seen that after the introduction of SegWit (Fig. 6.) in the first two intervals (time up to 1 s), there are as much as 86.38% (571 samples) of measurements where before the implementation of this solution only 1.97% (13 samples). In addition, in the first interval of 0.5 s before the introduction of SegWit there is not a single sample from the analyzed period that would meet this condition. It was decided to supplement Fig. 7, which contains block propagation times after the implementation of SegWit with available versions of Bitcoin Core, and with introduced changes in the network.

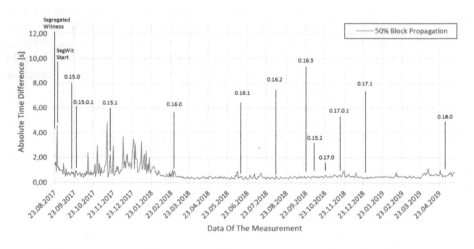

Fig. 7. Blocks propagation times from August 23, 2017–May 17, 2019

In Fig. 7, it can be seen that after the start of SegWit, there was a sudden drop in block propagation times. At that time, there was no official version that allowed SegWit support, but the network still reacted. The reason for this could be the fact that Bitcoin Core is an open-source program, so everyone has access to it, even in a not yet ready version. Most likely, large mines have prepared themselves and sooner implemented SegWit implementations. After entering version 0.15.0 there is a period of very large time deviations. This was due to many bugs in the software and the fact that not all functions were completed. The most serious error was the bug in version 0.15.0.1, which caused the Bitcoin Core environment to be blocked, which can be seen in the chart. After the repair version 0.15.1 and with many performance improvements, there has been an improvement, but not immediately. The main reason for this was that not all nodes immediately uploaded the implementation of the new version. Lack of conviction and the time needed to implement the solution meant that not everyone uses Segregated Witness immediately, this affects propagation times, because nodes with the old implementation (without SegWit) still take a 1 MB block, therefore the network must deal with blocks larger than 1 MB, sent to nodes able to accept only 1 MB. Backward compatibility has been maintained on the network at the expense of propagation times. The final implementation of SegWit has been published in version 0.16.3. All versions above also have previously implemented Segregated Witness. About 19.8% of nodes still do not have even the oldest version of the software that would support Segregated Witness. Noting that the stable version is 0.16.3 and above, currently as many as 21% of nodes do not have a SegWit implementation, which gives 2060 nodes with old software at 9450. Looking at the data when Segregated Witness was introduced, you can see that the more people on the network has a version larger than 0.15.0, the smaller is the block propagation time and network stability increases. It can be seen that the stability of block propagation times and very small times was achieved only after the implementation of the official version 0.16.0, which was used by more users because it had a full set of functions and support. This fact is followed by minimal jumps in time, but they are caused by small errors in the software that were repaired on a regular basis and did not significantly affect the operation of the network. Currently, block propagation times in the Bitcoin network have remained stable for less than a year, below one second, which also greatly increases network security.

4 Conclusion and Future Work

The purpose of this work was to present mechanisms improving Bitcoin cryptocurrency and to examine the block propagation time from a selected period, verifying both on the simulator and actual data of the Bitcoin network. In order to analyze the effectiveness of implemented implementations and confirm that SegWit is a good solution for the Bitcoin network, reactions of block propagation times for individual introduced network changes were examined. Based on the results obtained from the analysis of the Bitcoin network, an improvement in performance after the introduction of SegWit was demonstrated, by reducing the average propagation times of the block to 0.68 s, and for the entire period

(02.2013–05.2019) the average time fell to 3.2 from 12.5 s. Significant changes are also illustrated by the median, which for the whole period was 3.2 s from 6.5. The low level of block propagation time protects the network against frequent orphans of blocks and shows that the change in block capacity does not significantly affect the measurement times, which have remained below 1 second for a year. Stable network, code facilitation and implementation bug fixes have increased security, reducing the chance of an effective attack. It has been proved in the paper that the use of the Bitcoin Core version with the SegWit implementation in the stable version 0.16.3 or higher significantly improves the performance and security of the Bitcoin network. The above considerations show that the introduction of SegWit to the Bitcoin network was a very good decision. Therefore, it is recommended to deploy it to all nodes. This will increase the performance and security of the Bitcoin network, but also opens the door to the introduction of a wide-bandwidth Lightning Network.

Acknowledgements. This work was partially supported by the European Union's Horizon 2020 research and innovation programme under the grant agreement No. 825183.

References

1. Gervais, A., Karame, G.O., Wüst, K., Glykantzis, V., Ritzdorf, H., Capkun, S.: On the security and performance of proof of work blockchains. In Proceedings of the 2016 ACM SIGSAC Conference on Computer and Communications Security, pp. 3–16 (2016)
2. Neudecker, T., Hartenstein, H.: Short paper: an empirical analysis of blockchain forks in bitcoin. In: Goldberg, I., Moore, T. (eds.) FC 2019. LNCS, vol. 11598, pp. 84–92. Springer, Cham (2019). https://doi.org/10.1007/978-3-030-32101-7_6
3. Decker, C., Wattenhofer, R.: Information propagation in the Bitcoin network. In: IEEE P2P 2013 Proceedings, pp. 1–10. IEEE (2013)
4. Kuzuno, H., Karam, C.: Blockchain explorer: an analytical process and investigation environment for Bitcoin. In 2017 APWG Symposium on Electronic Crime Research (eCrime), pp. 9–16. IEEE (2017)
5. Rudlang, M.: Comparative analysis of Bitcoin and Ethereum (Master's thesis, NTNU), Norwegian Univeristy of Science and Technology (2017)
6. Song, J.: Understanding Segwit Block Size–Jimmy Song–Medium (2017)
7. Kedziora, M., Kozłowski, P., Szczepanik, M., Jóźwiak, P.: Analysis of Blockchain Selfish Mining Attacks. In: Borzemski, L., Światek, J., Wilimowska, Z. (eds.) ISAT 2019. AISC, vol. 1050, pp. 231–240. Springer, Cham (2020). https://doi.org/10.1007/978-3-030-30440-9_22
8. Kedziora, M., Gorka, A., Marianski, A., Jóźwiak, P.: Anti-Cheat tool for detecting unauthorized user interference in the unity engine using Blockchain. In: Poniszewska-Marańda, A., Kryvinska, N., Jarzabek, S., Madeyski, L. (eds.) Data-Centric Business and Applications. LNDECT, vol. 40, pp. 191–209. Springer, Cham (2020). https://doi.org/10.1007/978-3-030-34706-2_10
9. BTC.TOP: btc.com Mining Pool Statistics (2018). https://btc.com/stats/pool/BTC.TOP. Accessed Feb 2018

10. Antonopoulos, A.M.: Mastering Bitcoin: Unlocking Digital Cryptocurrencies. O'Reilly Media Inc., Sebastopol (2014)
11. Antonopoulos, A.M.: Mastering Bitcoin: Programming the Open Blockchain. O'Reilly Media Inc., Sebastopol (2017)
12. Nakamoto, P.: Bitcoin: Ultimate Guide to Understanding Blockchain, Bitcoin, Cryptocurrencies, Smart Contracts and the Future of Money. CreateSpace Independent Publishing Platform, Scotts Valley (2017)
13. Nakamoto, S.: The Book of Satoshi: The Collected Writings of Bitcoin Creator Satoshi Nakamoto. Phil Champagne. e53 Publishing LLC (2014)
14. Song, J.: Programming Bitcoin: Learn how to Program Bitcoin from Scratch. O'Reilly Media, Inc., Sebastopol (2019)
15. Drescher, D.: Blockchain Basics, vol. 276. Apress, Berkeley (2017)
16. Core, B.: Segregated witness benefits (2016). https://Bitcoincore.org/en/2016/01/26/segwit-benefits/
17. Fry, S.: BIP 148: Mandatory Activation of Segwit Deployment, GitHub, 12 March 2017

Natural Language Processing

Enrichment of Arabic TimeML Corpus

Nafaa Haffar[1,2]([✉]), Emna Hkiri[2]([✉]), and Mounir Zrigui[2]([✉])

[1] University of Sousse, ISITCom, 4011 Hammam Sousse, Tunisia
nafaa.haffar.5@gmail.com
[2] Research Laboratory in Algebra, Numbers theory and Intelligent Systems,
University of Monastir, Monastir, Tunisia
emna.hkiri@gmail.com, mounir.zrigui@fsm.rnu.tn

Abstract. Automatic temporal information extraction is an important task for many natural language processing systems. This task requires thorough knowledge of the ontological and grammatical characteristics of temporal information in the text as well as annotated linguistic resources of the temporal entities. Before creating the resources or developing the system, it is first necessary to define a structured schema which describes how to annotate temporal entities. In this paper, we present a revised version of Arabic TimeML, and we propose an enriched Arabic corpus, called "ARA-TimeBank", for events, temporal expressions and temporal relations based on the new Arabic TimeML. We describe our methodology which combines a pre-annotation phase with manuel validation and verification. ARA-TimeBank is the first corpus constructed for Arabic, which meets the needs of TimeML and addresses the limitations of existing Arabic TimeBank.

Keywords: Temporal information · Arabic corpus · Temporal expression · Events · Temporal relations · TimeML

1 Introduction

The automatic extraction of temporal information in texts has recently become an active field for scientific research. Likewise, It has become a useful technique for a lot of natural language processing (NLP) applications such as question answering and machine translation. From the computational viewpoint, temporal information processing consists of three processes presented as follows:

– Task 1: **Events** or situation expressions that occur instantaneously or that last for a period of time.
– Task 2: **Temporal expressions**, which describe the time or period in the real or virtual world.
– Task 3: **Temporal relations**, which describe the ordering relation between an event expression and a temporal expression, between two event expressions or between two temporal expressions.

© Springer Nature Switzerland AG 2020
N. T. Nguyen et al. (Eds.): ICCCI 2020, LNAI 12496, pp. 655–667, 2020.
https://doi.org/10.1007/978-3-030-63007-2_51

These three phenomena have attracted a lot of attention in the field of NLP, in particular within TempEval evaluation exercises [23–25]. These challenges have provided an essential framework for the automatic extraction of temporal information, and they are highly based on the ISO-TIMEML specification [20]. This latter is an annotation language whose purpose is the explanation of the temporal information contained in texts. This annotation schema was first used to annotate English [6], then it has been applied and adapted to other languages such as French, Italian, Korean, Romanian, Spanish, Portuguese and Basque, and with a low frequency for Arabic. Several corpora have been created based on the TimeML schema which fully satisfy TimeML needs. We can cite TimeBank1.1 which was created at the beginning of TimeML based on TimeML specifications1.1. This attempt has been used in several research studies and has played an important role in the creation of many other corpora and in the compilation of the task of extracting temporal information. This initiative has been the subject to give rise to a new corpus named Timebank 1.2[1] based on new TimeML specification 1.2.[2] This corpus was the building block of many other corpora in several languages such as Italian, French [5], Romanian [11] and Spanish.[3] In the same vein, TimeML has been adapted to the Arabic language, but the founded corpus presented by Haffar et al. [13] needed a deep modification and amelioration to satisfy TimeML specification as well as the Arabic characteristics.

In this paper, we argue that the Arabic TimeML corpus has some limitations, and we propose a revised version. Our new Arabic Timebank (ARA-Timebank) overcomes using our new specifications for the Arabic temporal information. We utilize for that the open source tool "Gate" [10] and other NLP tools. The rest of the paper is organized as follows: Sect. 2 presents the specificities of the TimeML standard. Section 3 provides the details (advantages and limitations) of the previous Arabic TimeML and presents our new Arabic TimeML. In Sect. 4, the methodology implemented to construct the new corpus is described. Section 5 is devoted to the representation of the statistics of our corpus as well as a comparison with the existent corpora. Finally, we conclude our work with a few perspectives.

2   TimeML: Temporal Markup Language

TimeML is a temporal information markup language for natural language texts. It allows tagging with a surface viewpoint the events and temporal expressions, as well as the different relations between them.

Table 1 presents the definition of TimeML tags. "EVENT", "TIMEX3" and "MAKEINSTANCE" tags mark temporal entities such as event expressions and temporal expressions. The "SIGNAL" tag identifies textual elements that determine the interpretation of the temporal expression.

---

[1] http://timexportal.wikidot.com/corpora-timebank12.

[2] http://www.timeml.org/publications/timeMLdocs/timeml_1.2.1.html.

[3] https://catalog.ldc.upenn.edu/LDC2012T12.

Table 1. TimeML tags

Tags	Definition
EVENT	Situations that happen or occur, includes verbs, nouns and adjectives
TIMEX3	Temporal expressions include date, time and duration
SIGNAL	Used to annotate textual elements that make explicit the relation holding between two temporal entities
MAKE-INSTANCE	It indicates different instances of a given event
LINKs	
TLINK	Represents temporal relations held between two temporal entities (Event and Event, TIMEX3 and Event or Timex and Timex)
SLINK	Represents context introducing relations between two events.
ALINK	Represents relations between an aspectual event and its argument

It is generally defined as [15]:

- **(1) Temporal conjunctions:** at (في), from (من), to (إلى)
- **(2) Temporal prepositions:** before (قبل), after (بعد), while (حين).
- **(3) Subordinators :** if (إذا).

Table 1 provides three types of relations which present the links between entities. The first tag is "TLINK" which represents the temporal relation between two entities. The definition of temporal relations using the "TLINK" tag is based on Allen's temporal relations [1]. The second tag is "SLINK", which annotates the relations between a main event and its subordinate event. This type of relations interacts with some event classes such as "Modal", "Reporting", "Perception", "I-State" and "I-Action". The third tag is "ALINK", which describes the aspectual relation between an aspectual event and its argument event.

3 Arabic TimeML

ISO-TimeML is a recent standard, first developed for English, and then adapted to other languages, such as French, Italian, Chinese and Korean. In this context, TimeML is also adapted for the Arabic language, but with several limitations because of its complexity. As an annotation language for Arabic, the existing Arabic TimeML was the first adaptation of TimeML for the Arabic language, and its contributions can be briefly resumed as follows:

- It contains surfacing annotations of events and temporal expressions.
- It employs the head-only tagging method of TimeML.

– It proposes that an event in Arabic can be expressed by a verb, a noun or an adjective.

For that, we will present in this section the limitation of existent Arabic TimeML specifications [12, 13] and we will also introduce Arabic TimeBank constructed based on the new Arabic TimeML specifications.

3.1 Limitations of Previous Arabic TimeML

Arabic is a complex language which needs a deep understanding of text. A large number of NLP tasks aims to represent data in a form that can be efficiently analyzed and to improve the annotated data quality by reducing the quantity of trivial noise [14, 27]. We argue that the previously proposed Arabic TimeML has many advantages and some limitations. The event annotation phase is the most relevant phase in the proposed annotation scheme. It satisfies the specifications of TimeML and it is well analyzed and detailed [12]. On the contrary, the part of temporal expressions misses some characteristics of Arabic and requires several improvements to satisfy TimeML needs. We can cite several limitation as follows:

– It expresses the temporal expressions for the Gregorian calendar but several temporal expressions can only be expressed and normalized by the Hijri calendar. given the following example

Albert Einstein was born on [Friday], <u>20 Rabi Al-Awwal 1296</u>.

ولد ألبيرت أينشتاين [يوم الجمعة] ٢٠ <u>ربيع الأول ١٢٩٦</u>.

The normalized value of the Hijri date "20 Rabi Al-Awwal 1296" is "14 March 1879" for the Gregorian date, but the normalization of the "20th day of the 3rd month" differs from year to year from the Gregorian calendar. For example, "20 Rabi Al-Awwal 1296" is 14/March/1879, but "20 Rabi Al-Awwal 1297" is 02/March/1880.

– It does not allow annotating temporal expressions related to holidays and islamic dates such as ("Eid al-Adha عيد الإضحى with the hijry date: 10/dhu-alhajja ذو الحجة ١٠").

– It does not allow to annotate temporal expressions related to the agricultural seasons المواسم الفلاحية, which present dates or durations: (It is desirable to plow the land in <u>black nights</u>." يستحب حرث الأرض في الليالي السود")

In this example, black nights (الليالي السود)" describes the duration from 14 January to 02 February.

– It does not allow annotating temporal expressions in a complete way; i.e. several attributes for annotating time expressions according to TimeML are missing such us: "beginPoint", "endPoint", "freq", "quant" and "mod".

– Similarly, the previous Arabic TimeML does not allow the annotation of TimeML signals, makeinstances and relations.

3.2   Our Schema for New Arabic TimeML Specifications

As it can be sees from the literature, the creation of a TimeML corpus has been the subject of enormous efforts to meet the specifications of the TimeML standard. We propose to extend the first adaptation of the TimeML standard for Arabic and to enrich the existing TimeML corpus. For this, we put forward the freely Arabic TimeBank based on the new Arabic TimeML specifications, which may avoid all the deficiencies noted in the previous Arabic TimeML. Our suggested annotation method is therefore as follows[4]:

```
EVENT < eid, Class >
MAKEINSTANCE < EventInstanceID, eid, sid, Tense, Aspect, Moods,
               Pos, Modality, Polarity, Stem, card >
SIGNAL < sid ::= S<INTEGER_ID >
TIMEX3 < Tid, Type, Value, beginPoint, endPoint,TypeOfCalendar,
         quant, freq, mod >
TLINK < TLid, EntitysourceID, timeID,signalID, EntityTargetID,
        relatedToTime, relType >
ALINK < ALid, EntitysourceID, signalID, EntityTargetID, relType >
SLINK < SLid, EntitysourceID, signalID, subordinat-EntityTargetID,
        relType >
```

Table 2 describes the relations tags and attributes of the new Arabic TimeML schema:

Table 2. Tags of new Arabic TimeML schema.

Attributes	Values
TIMEX3	
Type	Date, Time, Duration, Set
TypeOf-Calendar	Lunar, Gregorian, None (default)
Value	Duration, Date, Time, WeekDate, WeekTime, Season, PartOfYear
mod	Before, After, ON-OR-Before, ON-OR-After, Less-Than, More-Than, Equal-OR-Less, Equal-OR-More, Start, MID, END, Approx
TLINK	
related-To-Time	Before, After, Begins, Ends, Includes, Is-included, During, During-INV, Overlaps, Overlapped-by, I-after, I-before, Begun-BY, Ended-BY, Simultaneous
ALINK	
relType	Modal, Evidential, Neg-Evidential,Factive, Counter-Factive, Conditional
SLINK	
relType	Initiates, Culminates, Terminates, Continues, Reinitiates

---

[4] To fully understand the other attributes such as EVENT and MAKEINSTANCE tags, please see the proposed schema in [13].

4   Methodology

Many automatic approaches can be used to annotate corpora, but manual annotation is one of the first methods that gives effective results because it requires
the intervention of annotators who are proficient in the target language. To speed
up the annotation process, we carry out the automatic pre-annotation of tags
(temporal expressions, signals and some links), followed by manual correction.

4.1   Automatic Pre-annotation

For this pre-annotation phase, we describe in the following our developed modules.

TIMEX3 Extraction: In the literature, there have been several tools for
extracting temporal expressions, such as: "ZamAn and Raqm" [21], which extract
time sentences and numerical expressions using a machine learning approach.
This tool does not support the specifications of either TIMEX2 or TIMEX3 for
the extraction phase, and the normalization phase is not addressed. "ATEEMA"
[26] presents a temporal expression extraction technique from Arabic text based
on morphological analysis and finite state transducers. However, like "ZamAn
and Raqm", the extraction is not based on TIMEX2 or TIMEX3, and the normalization phase is not addressed. In addition, these tools are not publicly available.
Another tool for temporal expressions is called "HeidelTime" [22]. It is a multi-
lingual, domain-sensitive temporal tagger that currently contains hand-crafted
resources for 13 languages. The most recent version contains automatically created resources for more than 200 languages, which includes Arabic and follows
the TimeML standard. Up to our knowledge, HeidelTime[5] is the only publicly
accessible tool that performs the full task of temporal tagging for Arabic texts.
It marks temporal expressions <TIMEX3> in a NEWS dataset with an F-score
of 79.42%, and it normalizes them with an F-score of 71.54%. We note on the
other hand that HeidelTime does not support the temporal expressions referring
to the Hijri calendar. In addition, there is the problem of the extraction and normalization of temporal expressions that express holiday dates. In this way and
to meet the limitations of Heideltime, Aratimex [7] is presented. It is developed
with the aim of having an efficient, extensible and fast temporal tagger dedicated
for the Arabic language with an F-score of 96% for the extraction task and an
F-score of 94/% for normalisation, but this tool is not public for use.

Hence, for this step, we use the Heideltime tool, which is promoted as the
best tool in the tempEval-3. we utilize the GATE tool, which is an open source
tool that includes the Heideltime plugin. For that, our methodology is based on
the creation of some extraction and normalization rules to support Heideltime
limitations mentioned previously. However, in Arabic, ambiguity is a primary
cause of difficulties [17,18]. Sometimes we find that some names of months in
the Hijri calendar are used as people names, for example "رمضان, RAMADHAN"

---

[5] https://heideltime.ifi.uni-heidelberg.de.

could be the name of a person or the eighth month of the Hijri calendar (The family is happy, Since RAMADHAN's arrival, العائلة سعيدة منذ وصول رمضان). Another problem of ambiguity is that the names of days (الإثنين, AL-ITHNAYN) can mean either "Monday" or the number "two"; and the word "قرن, qrn" can mean either "century" or "horn". This phase requires the manual intervention of experts to solve certain difficulties in the Arabic language. For the extraction of public holidays, International days, agricultural seasons and complex events that express temporal information, GATE does not have a predefined gazetteer for the Arabic text. For this step, we enrich GATE with a new gazetteer[6] collected from the mapped DBpdia with SPARQL query, Arabic WordNet [3,4] and Arabic dictionary (See Table 3).

Table 3. Enrichment of GATE gazetteers.

Gazetteers	Predefined entries	Enriched entries
Temporal expressions	0	5760
Signals	0	19
Total	**0**	**5797**

Signal Extraction: As mentioned above, a signal is a textual element that makes explicit the relations between two entities such as Event-Event, Timex-Event or Timex-Timex. For that, we use the GATE Gate tool to mark signal entities. Nevertheless, GATE does not have a predefined gazetteer for signals. That is why we creat a new gazetteer for Arabic signals (See Table 3). With this gazetteer, we create some jape rules for GATE to annotate signals in the right way:

- Signal + Temporal expression

The player arrived <u>on</u> [Monday].

وصل اللاعب في [يوم الإثنين].

- Signal + Event

She lavished praise, on embassy staffers **before** [meeting] with bombing victims.

لقد أثنت على موظفي السفارة قبل [لقائها] بضحايا القصف.

---

[6] https://github.com/nafaa5/Arabic-event-timex-gazetteers-.

Makeinstance Annotation: This step is based on the previous labeled event corpus which contains the event tagger with the necessary attributes. To do this, we implement a simple JAVA code to analyze and add the necessary attributes of the event tag to the Makeinstance tag because the events in the previous Arabic TimeML corpus are well defined and tagged. Each Makeinstance tag takes a unique automatic ID.

Relation Annotation: In this step, we use GATE and some jape rules (15 rules) to annotate some relations between entities. We note that the annotated relations are between: **(1)** two events in the same sentence **(2)** an event and Timex in the same sentence. Some used temporal rules are presented below:

(*) If there is a Temporal Signal (TS) between an event and a temporal expression:

– If TS = (في, "at") Then Relation = TLINK and Type = is-included(E,T)
– If TS = (قبل, "before") Then Relation = TLINK and Type = Before(E,T)
– If TS = (بعد, "after") Then Relation = TLINK and Type = After(E,T)

(*) If there is no direct dependency path between E1 and E2:

– If [((E1 = Verb),(Tense = Present)) and ((E2 = Verb),(Tense = Past))] Then Relation = Tlink and Type = After(E1,E2)
– **If** { ((E1 = Verb), (Tense = Present)) and ((E2 = Verb), (Tense = future)) } **Then** Type = before(E1,E2)

4.2   Manual Annotation and Validation

In this step, the previously annotated texts are corrected by human expert annotators. Moreover, the rest of the TimeML tags are annotated manually based on the new Arabic TimeML specifications.

Relation Annotation: During this step, six human expert annotators are divided into three groups (G1, G2, G3) to correct and annotate relations between entities according to our schema (See Sect. 3.2). This manual annotation is based on the expertise of the annotators and the dependency path[7] between the two target entities in the same sentence. Some used temporal rules for the same sentence are presented below:

(*) If E2 is an adverbial clause modifier (Tag= advcl) or is an argument (Tag= obl/obj) of E1:

– If (E1 = Aspectual Verb for continuation (واصل, "Continue")) Then Relation = Alink and Type = continuation(E1,E2)
– If ((E1 = General Verb) and (aspect = Perfective)) Then Relation = Tlink and Type = simultaneous(E1,E2)

---

[7] The dependency path is analysed by udpipe tool: http://lindat.mff.cuni.cz/services/udpipe/.

(*) If E2 is a complement (Tag= ccomp/xcomp) of E1:

- If [(E1 = verb),(class = reporting/perception)] Then Relation = Slink and Type = Evidential(E1,E2)
- If [((E1 = verb), (class = Modal)) and (E2-class = I-action/I-state)] Then Relation = Slink and Type = Modal(E1,E2)

To calculate the inter annotator agreement, and instead of Cohen's kappa coefficient, the dice coefficient is used. This choice is made because the annotators can mark any word in sentences, which leads to a very large number of possibilities. Table 4 shows the results of the inter-coder agreement (G1|G2, G1|G3, G2|G3), which is calculated in pairs with the dice coefficient (Dice).

$$Dice(Gi, Gj) = 2 * \frac{|Gi \cap Gj|}{|Gi| + |Gj|} \tag{1}$$

where $|Gi \cap Gj|$ is the number of annotated relations common to Gi and Gj, and $|Gi|$ (resp. $|Gj|$) is the number of annotated relations of Gi (resp. Gj).

Table 4. Relation agreement results.

Annotators	Agreement		
	TLINKs	SLINKs	ALINKs
G1|G2	0.97	0.94	1.00
G1|G3	0.98	0.98	1.00
G2|G3	0.96	0.96	1.00
Average	**0.97**	**0.96**	**1.00**

Verification and Validation of the Annotated Texts: The challenge becomes enormous when we try to automatically create a corpus for a complex natural language like Arabic. This complexity is generally due to the inflexible nature of Arabic. Therefore, to solve this problem, most researchers have used a manual annotation method with a verification phase by the intervention of experts. For this step, and in the same context, a manual verification and validation phase is performed by three human super experts in the Arabic language to resolve the errors made by the automatic pre-annotation phase.

5   Annotated Data: Statistics, Comparison and Distribution

5.1   Statistics and Comparison of Our Corpora

Our objective with this methodology is to create an Arabic TimeML corpus of a comparable size to the existing resources for the other languages. Table 5 depicts a simple comparison between our corpus and the existing TimeML corpora.

Table 5. Comparison of our corpus versus other TimeML corpus

Corpora	Language	Tokens	Events	Timex	Signals	LINKS	Make-Instance
1. TimeBank 1.2	English	61,418	7,935	1,414	688	9,615	7,940
2. AQUAINT TB	English	34,154	4,432	605	268	6,111	4,432
3. EusTimeBank [2]	Basque	26,214	5,273	897	204	7,628	NA
4. FR-TB	French	61,000	2,100	608	2,88	2,408	2,100
5. Korean TB [16]	Korean	–	11,522	2,552	NA	3,985	11,577
6. Spanish TB	Spanish	68,000	12,385	2,776	NA	21,541	NA
7. IT-TimeBank [8]	Italian	280,379	26,817	6,453	3,523	18,285	NA
8. TimeBank-PT [9]	Portuguese	69,702	7,887	1,409	NA	6,539	NA
9. Persian [19]	Iranian	26,949	4,237	–	401	1,613	NA
10. Ro-TimeBank	Romanian	65,375	7,926	1,414	669	9,481	NA
11. Our corpora	**ARABIC**	**95,782**	**15,730**	**5,930**	**1,758**	**13,496**	**15,730**

5.2   Distribution of Temporal Tags in Arabic TimeBank Corpus

Table 6 presents the distribution of temporal expressions and relations annotated in the ARA-TimeBank. It is shown that the "DATE" type has increased from 2,015 tags in the old corpus to 3,035 tags in the new corpus but it has decreased in comparison with the other tags from 88% to 51%.

On the contrary, the other types have increased from 6% for the "DURATION" type (159 tags) to 25% (1,469 tags), from 4% for the "TIME" type (69 tags) to 13% (768) and from 2% for the "SET" type (49tags) to 11% (658 tags). For LINKs, we can see that the temporal links "TLINK" represent 69% of all annotated LINKs, almost three times more than the second most frequent type, "SLINK", with a rate of 22%. The "ALINK" type is ranked third with 9%. This representation suggests that temporal information is a crucial characteristic of the language used in many NLP tools.

Table 6. Statistics of Timex and LINKs in our corpus.

TIMEX		SLINK		TLINK	
		Conditional	27	After	1590
		Evidential	1050	Before	1785
		Neg-Evidential	22	Begins	71
		Factive	530	Begun-by	97
		Modal	1290	Ends	120
DURATION	1,469	Counter-Factive	40	Ended-by	184
SET	658	Negative	37	During	490
DATE	3,035	**TOTAL**	**2996**	I-After	151
TIME	768	ALINK		I-Before	143
TOTAL	**5,930**	Initiates	198	Includes	582
		Continues	465	IS-Included	1530
		Culminates	176	Simultaneous	730
		Reinitiates	234	Overlaps	870
		Terminates	107	Overlapped-by	347
		TOTAL	**1180**	During-Inv	630
				TOTAL	**9320**

6   Conclusion and Future Work

In this paper, we have presented the first free resource for Arabic language based on the TimeML specifications. Arabic TimeBank "ARA-TimeBank" represents a large corpus annotated with temporal information, which can be used in many NLP tools and which represents a case study for the creation of Arabic annotated resources. This work has been the result of a well studied methodology, based on an annotation pipeline combining an automatic pre-annotation task, a manual annotation step and a manual verification and correction step by experts. This methodology has been the most interesting part of this work. It proves that the manual annotation is time-consuming and expensive, but it gives a relevant result because of the intervention of experts. However, the automatic pre-annotation, with the manual annotation, followed by the manual evaluation and correction by human experts, represents a good solution.

As future work, we will build our automatic system for extracting temporal relations between entities based on the ARA-TimeBank corpus. We believe that the Ara-TimeBank will be widely used for a lot of Arabic-based research and automatic applications related to temporal information.

References

1. Allen, J.F.: Maintaining knowledge about temporal intervals. Commun. ACM **26**(11), 832–843 (1983)

2. Altuna, B., Aranzabe, M.J., Díaz de Ilarraza, A.: Adapting TimeML to Basque: event annotation. In: Gelbukh, A. (ed.) CICLing 2016. LNCS, vol. 9624, pp. 565–577. Springer, Cham (2018). https://doi.org/10.1007/978-3-319-75487-1_43

3. Batita, M.A., Ayadi, R., Zrigui, M.: Reasoning over Arabic WordNet relations with neural tensor network. Computación y Sistemas **23**(3), (2019)

4. Batita, M.A., Zrigui, M.: The enrichment of Arabic WordNet antonym relations. In: Gelbukh, A. (ed.) CICLing 2017. LNCS, vol. 10761, pp. 342–353. Springer, Cham (2018). https://doi.org/10.1007/978-3-319-77113-7_27

5. Bittar, A., Amsili, P., Denis, P., Danlos, L.: French TimeBank: an ISO-TimeML annotated reference corpus. In: The 49th Annual Meeting of the Association for Computational Linguistics, Portland, Oregon, United States, pp. 130–134 (2011)

6. Boguraev, B., Pustejovsky, J., Ando, R., Verhagen, M.: TimeBank evolution as a community resource for TimeML parsing. Lang. Resour. Eval. **41**, 91–115 (2007)

7. Boudaa, T., El Marouani, M., Enneya, N.: Arabic temporal expression tagging and normalization. In: Tabii, Y., Lazaar, M., Al Achhab, M., Enneya, N. (eds.) Big Data, Cloud and Applications, pp. 546–557 (2018)

8. Caselli, T., Bartalesi Lenzi, V., Sprugnoli, R., Pianta, E., Prodanof, I.: Annotating events, temporal expressions and relations in Italian: the It-TimeML experience for the Ita-TimeBank. In: Proceedings of the 5th Linguistic Annotation Workshop (2011)

9. Costa, F., Branco, A.: TimeBankPT: a TimeML annotated corpus of Portuguese. In: LREC, pp. 3727–3734 (2012)

10. Derczynski, L., Strötgen, J., Maynard, D., Greenwood, M.A., Jung, M.: GATE-time: extraction of temporal expressions and event. In: LREC 2016, pp. 3702–3708 (2016)

11. Forăscu, C., Tufiş, D.: Romanian TimeBank: an annotated parallel corpus for temporal information. In: LREC, pp. 3762–3766 (2012)

12. Haffar, N., Hkiri, E., Zrigui, M.: Arabic linguistic resource and specifications for event annotation. In: Proceedings of the 34th International Business Information Management Association Conference (IBIMA), Vision 2025: Education Excellence and Management of Innovations through Sustainable Economic Competitive Advantage, pp. 4316–4327 (2019)

13. Haffar, N., Hkiri, E., Zrigui, M.: TimeML Annotation of events and temporal expressions in Arabic texts. In: Nguyen, N.T., Chbeir, R., Exposito, E., Aniorté, P., Trawiński, B. (eds.) ICCCI 2019. LNCS (LNAI), vol. 11683, pp. 207–218. Springer, Cham (2019). https://doi.org/10.1007/978-3-030-28377-3_17

14. Haffar, N., et al.: Pedagogical indexed arabic text in cloud e-learning system. IJCAC **7**(1), 32–46 (2017). https://doi.org/10.4018/IJCAC.2017010102

15. Hkiri, E., Mallat, S., Zrigui, M.: Events automatic extraction from arabic texts. IJIRR **6**(1), 36–51 (2016)

16. Jeong, Y.S., Joo, W.T., Do, H.W., Lim, C.G., Choi, K.S., Choi, H.J.: Korean TimeML and Korean TimeBank. In: LREC, pp. 356–359 (2016)

17. Mahmoud, A., Zrigui, A., Zrigui, M.: A text semantic similarity approach for Arabic paraphrase detection. In: CICLing, pp. 338–349 (2017)

18. Mahmoud, A., Zrigui, M.: Deep neural network models for paraphrased text classification in the Arabic language. In: NLDB, pp. 3–16 (2019)

19. Mirzaei, A., Moloodi, A.: Persian proposition bank. In: LREC, pp. 3828–3835 (2016)

20. Pustejovsky, J., Lee, K., Bunt, H., Romary, L.: Iso-TimeML: an international standard for semantic annotation. In: LREC (2010)

21. Saleh, I., Tounsi, L., van Genabith, J.: ZamAn and Raqm: extracting temporal and numerical expressions in Arabic. In: Salem, M.V.M., Shaalan, K., Oroumchian, F., Shakery, A., Khelalfa, H. (eds.) AIRS 2011. LNCS, vol. 7097, pp. 562–573. Springer, Heidelberg (2011). https://doi.org/10.1007/978-3-642-25631-8_51
22. Strötgen, J., Gertz, M.: Multilingual and cross-domain temporal tagging. Lang. Resour. Eval. **47**, 269–298 (2013)
23. UzZaman, N., Llorens, H., Derczynski, L., Allen, J., Verhagen, M., Pustejovsky, J.: SemEval-2013 task 1: TempEval-3: evaluating time expressions, events, and temporal relations. In: SemEval 2013, vol. 2, pp. 1–9 (2013)
24. Verhagen, M., Gaizauskas, R., Schilder, F., Hepple, M., Katz, G., Pustejovsky, J.: SemEval-2007 task 15: TempEval temporal relation identification. In: SemEval 2007, pp. 75–80 (2007)
25. Verhagen, M., et al.: Automating temporal annotation with TARSQI. In: ACLDEMO 2005, pp. 81–84 (2005)
26. Zaraket, F.A., Makhlouta, J.: Arabic temporal entity extraction using morphological analysis. Int. J. Comput. Linguist. Appl. **3**, 121–136 (2012)
27. Zrigui, M., Ayadi, R., Mars, M., Maraoui, M.: Arabic text classification framework based on latent dirichlet allocation. CIT **20**(2), 125–140 (2012)

Automated Bilingual Linking of Wordnet Senses

Maciej Piasecki[✉], Roman Dyszlewski, and Ewa Rudnicka

Faculty of Computer Science and Management, Wrocław University of Science
and Technology, Wrocław, Poland
{maciej.piasecki,roman.dyszlewski,ewa.rudnicka}@pwr.edu.pl

Abstract. Wordnets for different languages are linked through synsets
- sets of synonymous word senses. We present a method of automated
transforming synset mapping to sense mapping to build a network of
translational equivalents. Two heuristics based on a cross-lingual distributional similarity model are compared with several variants of machine
learning based approach exploring different descriptive features. The features are extracted from bilingual and monolingual dictionaries and distributional semantics models, interpreted against wordnets.

Keywords: Wordnet · Translation equivalence · Bilingual sense
mapping

1 Introduction

Wordnets are built of synsets – sets of synonymous word senses, e.g. {*movie* 1,
film 1, *picture* 6}, representing the same concept. Most wordnets are linked
to at least one wordnet in another language, usually WordNet [6]. The linking
is done through synsets to show the identity of concepts across languages, e.g.
EN:{*movie* 1, *film* 1, *picture* 6} – PL:{*film* 1}. Yet, no fine-grained links between
words in their specific meanings are provided. Thus, though useful for many
applications, such as mapping between different wordnet-based resources, cross-
lingual Word Sense Disambiguation and Information Retrieval, the linking is
not precise enough for machine and human translation, emotive annotation and
knowledge transfer. It is less suitable than bilingual dictionaries.

There are also other problems with synset mapping. First, as early as in
EuroWordNet [17] it was noticed that inter-lingual linking may require more relations than simple equivalence. It was confirmed during the mapping of plWord-
Net [5] onto WordNet which showed that only one third of synsets[1], cf [5], can
be linked by the inter-lingual synonymy and for the remaining ones several more
types of inter-lingual relations are needed. Secondly, with the development of

---

[1] http://plwordnet.pwr.edu.pl/.

Co-financed by the Polish Ministry of Education and Science, CLARIN-PL Project.

N. T. Nguyen et al. (Eds.): ICCCI 2020, LNAI 12496, pp. 668–681, 2020.
https://doi.org/10.1007/978-3-030-63007-2_52

wordnets, synset building blocks – word senses called lexical units (LUs)[2] have received their own description in almost all wordnets, including special relations, glosses and register markers. Thirdly, in translation we deal with words, not their synonym sets. Thus, there is a clear need for a more elaborated wordnet interlingual mapping that goes beyond the coarse-grained 'concept level' mapping towards more linguistically informed inter-lingual linking of LUs. However, works on direct sense alignment are rare. One of the few exceptions is our work on manual sense alignment relying on the synset mapping between plWordNet and WordNet [15]. Still, the workload required is substantial. In order to reduce it, we experimented with an automated method for sense linking [13] on limited training data and feature sets. The initial results encouraged its further development. Our ultimate goal is to develop an automated method for linking word senses of two languages on the basis of manual synset mapping and corpus-based knowledge sources. In this paper, we propose an elaborated version of the preliminary work [13] based on a larger training-testing data set of better quality, a wider variety of features derived from wordnets, distributional model and bilingual dictionaries and improved classification methods based on machine learning. We also investigate limitations of possible features and available bilingual language resources for this task.

2   Interlingual Mapping of Wordnets

plWordNet was linked to WordNet via an extensive manual mapping, partly supported by an automatic prompt system, cf [16] and [8]. Such mapping was needed, because unlike many other wordnets, plWordNet is not an expanded copy of WordNet content and structure, but an independently built, large corpus based resource [14]. The mapping relied on a comparison of relation structures and glosses of Polish and English synsets to be linked. Depending on the type and degree of interlingual-correspondence, one of interlingual relations was chosen as a link between a given synset pair. A set of 10 inter-lingual (I-) relations was defined subsuming I-synonymy, I-partial synonymy, I-inter-register synonymy, I-hyponymy, I-hypernymy, I-meronymy, I-holonymy, I-instance, I-type, and I-cross-categorial synonymy. These were later supplemented by meaning-specifying verbal relations. Currently, the mapping covers 99% of Polish and English nouns, 99% of Polish adjectives and adverbs, about 50% of English adjectives and adverbs and about 10% of Polish and English verbs.

Recently, works have started on extending the existing noun synset mapping to a more fine-grained sense-level mapping [15]. The method takes as input pairs of Polish-English LUs extracted from synsets linked by I-synonymy, I-partial synonymy and I-hyponymy. It relies on a manual comparison of values of equivalence features such as: number, countability, gender, sense, lexicalisation of concepts, register, collocations, dictionary listing, and translation probability. Depending on the degree of compatibility between the values of equivalence features, three types of links are distinguished: *I-strong-equivalence*, *I-regular-equivalence* and

---

[2] Lexical units are lemma-grammatical category-sense number triples.

I-weak-equivalence. Strong equivalence is meant to express the closest type of equivalence link requiring identity or very high compatibility in feature values. Regular equivalence has slightly relaxed conditions, while weak equivalence is established for pairs of LUs that can function as translational equivalents, although they do not fully meet the requirements for regular equivalence. The model was applied to a sample of plWordNet inter-lingual mapping to create a bilingual sense-level linked resource. In addition, all errors spotted in the wordnets and their mapping, as well the lack of equivalence were recorded, too. The former have been already corrected in the version 4.1 of plWordNet. As a result, 9,998 instances of *I-strong-equivalence* and 1,139 of *I-regular-equivalence* were annotated.

3   Related Works

Several approaches were proposed for automatic wordnet mapping on synset level. plWordNet-WordNet mapping in [8] followed a relaxation labelling scheme. Potential translation lemma pairs and both structures of synset relations were used as input to constraints defining preferred connections. The method achieved ≈70% accuracy on the level of inter-lingual synset relations. However, such methods can be applied only on synset level, as there are too few relations linking LUs.

Automated construction of bilingual dictionaries was studied many times. [4] proposed a method for searching translation equivalents in Machine Readable Dictionaries. [10] followed this approach and presented the construction of a translation graph (nodes – words, arcs – translations) from 630 dictionaries and used to infer potential translation equivalents. However, such approaches work on bilingual dictionaries entries implicitly by described word senses and do not refer to wordnets. Bilingual dictionaries focus on dictionary entries, while wordnets describe sense and lexico-semantic relations, but provide a limited use context characterisation. [1] proposed to use information from inter-lingually linked synsets together with statistics from parallel, sentence aligned corpora and form similarity (the Levenshtein distance) in search for lexical translations that are most probable in the given context. We focus on finding translation equivalents that are more context-independent.

An elaborated method for the exploration of monolingual corpora in search of translational equivalents was presented in [7]. Words from different languages are described by several similarity features, such as: contextual (mapped on a common vector space), temporal, orthographic (i.e. the Levenshtein distance), frequency and burstiness (based on IDF). The method is able to link words not aligned in parallel corpora, but does not provide any way of linking words to their wordnet representations.

4   Problem and Knowledge Sources

Our methods are aimed at refining an existing interlingual synset-level mapping into a more precise sense-level mapping, i.e. linking LUs. Thus, the input to all methods are two wordnets mutually mapped on synset level. No restrictions are assumed for the number of different inter-lingual relation types, as well as for the way in which the mapping was built. However, a precise inter-lingual mapping between synsets and distinguishing between different types of synset correspondence by different I-relations should improve the performance of inter-lingual sense linking. Thus, the task is:

- for a pair of synsets S_p and S_e linked by an interlingual relation R,
- to find all pairs of LUs: $\{\langle x_i, y_j \rangle : x_i \in S_p \land y_j \in S_e\}$ that are linked by *strong-equivalence* and *regular-equivalence*,
- in addition, $\forall x_i \in S_p$ there can be at most one $y_j \in S_e$ that is linked to x_i.

The *strong* and *regular* equivalence relations have similar defining properties, and lexicographers had bigger problems in distinguishing between them than in the case of weak equivalence cf [15]. Thus, for the purposes of automated recognition, we have grouped them into one coarse-grained relation of *significant equivalence*, cf [13]. *Weak* equivalence and lack of equivalence are treated as negative cases. In [15], it was observed that significant equivalence is more often found within synsets linked by stronger types of I-relations, so we focus on *I-synonymy*, *I-partial-synonymy* and *I-hyponymy*.

Even the strongest I-relation, i.e. *I-synonymy*, does not guarantee that all pairs of LUs from the linked synsets represent the *strong* equivalence. Quite contrary, 1–2 pairs of equivalents can be observed on average for a pair of synsets. In the case of the weaker relations, i.e. *I-partial-synonymy* and *I-hyponymy*, even smaller numbers of equivalents should be expected. In order to identify them we need to go beyond the I-relations and look for additional information characterising pairs of LUs: word form similarity, linguistic characteristics, similarity of distributional vector representation, translation pairs from dictionaries, and bilingual corpus alignment.

English and Polish differ significantly, as they belong to different language groups. However, both are Indo-European languages that inherited many words from Latin. Also, Polish has borrowed a lot of words from English recently. Thus, the identity or similarity of word forms can be helpful to a surprising extent.

The model of translational equivalence of [15] refers to several linguistic characteristics of LUs such as gender, countability or stylistic register. Their automated extraction from corpora is a difficult task and they are not encoded in WordNet. Some of them, like gender, can be read from the Polish morphological dictionary, but not for English. Such features were not fully explored in [13]. In this paper, we survey existing mappings of WordNet on the linguistic resources and focus on mapping onto *Wiktionary*.[3]

Distributional models can provide insight into the meaning of LUs and enable measuring their semantic similarity, but the majority of methods are bound to data from one language. To cross the language barrier we need to transfer two distributional models into one common space.

---

[3] https://en.wiktionary.org.

Translation pairs from dictionaries are a basic knowledge source for translation. However, the availability of bilingual dictionaries may be a problem. The quality of the available ones must be high enough to make them useful, as well as their size. Moreover, bilingual dictionaries typically connect words, not senses, also it is hard to evaluate the strength of connection between two words on the basis of dictionary data alone.

Finally, frequent word alignment pairs from parallel corpora express similar properties to dictionary pairs, but are based on the actual language use and provide insight into the contextual translation choices. Unfortunately, the publicly available parallel corpora are of limited size, and, even worse, they cover only selected domains.

Summing up, the limited coverage and quality of the available knowledge sources cause that we need to combine them for the sense mapping task. Because distributional methods provide models of the largest coverage we selected them as a basis, and next expanded them with other types of knowledge sources.

A distributional semantics model can be simultaneously built as a common vector space for two languages, but a parallel corpus must be used as a basis. As parallel Polish-English corpora do not provide sufficient coverage for vocabulary and senses in the analysed wordnets, we explored an alternative approach, in which two distributional models, built separately on two monolingual corpora, are next mapped on a common vector space. We use the MUSE method [3], in which one vector space is mapped onto the second one using a linear transformation. We analysed a few other methods in preliminary experiments (see Sec. 6), some of them based on a more complex non-linear transformation, but they brought worse results in bilingual sense-to-sense mapping. The transformation is constrained by a dictionary of translations of the most frequent lemmas – a default dictionary is provided with the MUSE source.[4] In addition, we also built a bilingual Polish-English dictionary of monosemous words from both wordnets that have only one translation.

For both wordnets, we used basic distributional models of as large coverage as possible, built on very large corpora. We selected *fastText* – a sub-word algorithm capable of building vectors for out-of-vocabulary words, e.g. derivational word forms. Two pre-trained monolingual distributional models were used: English – a ready-to-use *fastText* [2] model built on the Common Crawl corpus[5] of 600 billion tokens which describes 2,000,000 words by vectors of 300 elements; Polish – a *fastText* model [9] extracted from the plWordNet Corpus 10.0 (>4 billion words) which describes 2,136,145 words by vectors of the size 300. The generated models were tested according to the scheme proposed in [3]. Since the model constrained by the dictionary built by us expressed the best performance, we used it in all experiments in this paper.

In spite of the large size of the source corpora and large dictionaries of both models, the overlap with words described in both wordnets is not perfect: plWordNet: the overlap: 134,434 words (lemmas) from 191,858 described in

---

the wordnet, including 108,511 single words (76.45% coverage) and 25,923 multi-word expressions (lexicalised and described in the wordnet) (41.98% coverage), WordNet: the overlap: 81.89% coverage single word lemmas and 77.85% for all lemmas (28.45% for multiword lemmas).

5 Datasets

We used two gold-standard datasets describing examples of translation equivalents – bilingual LU pairs – of different types: a large testing-training *Development Set*, and a small *Test-only Set*. The first is based on manual annotations made during building the first version of bilingual sense-to-sense mapping between plWordNet and WordNet [15]: 9,998 strong equivalence links and 1,139 regular equivalence ones are included in the mapping. We group them into **11,137 significant equivalence links**, and this is the maximal set of *positive* examples. There are two main problems with this set: it is not balanced according to the characteristics of the examples, and only a small number of negative examples are manually described.

Lexicographers were working on pre-selected bilingual LU pairs, so mostly only one pair of LUs from two synsets is annotated, while [15] allows for more than one significant equivalence link for a pair of synsets. This makes generation of negative cases harder. Moreover, several first subsets of LUs selected for the manual mapping were relatively easy cases with many identical words in Polish and English or words with only one translation. These phenomena definitely positively biased the results obtained by [13]. Here, we try to compensate for this problem by building Development Set as a subset of the maximal set.

From all positive cases we selected only those that were annotated with the same type of translational equivalence by all lexicographers. Most cases of identical Polish and English lemmas were filtered out and only 200 kept in Development Set. Finally, we selected 4,685 positive cases to be included in Development Set. We also tried to cover different wordnet domains during the selection of positive cases.

The shortage of negative examples is an even more serious problem. There are 384 manually annotated instances of the lack of equivalence and no examples of weak equivalence. Thus, the majority of negative cases had to be acquired automatically from LU pairs that were very likely to be non-equivalent. Pairs from synsets not linked by any I-relation are considered first, as the mapping on the synset level is very comprehensive and our goal is to find equivalents among LUs from the synsets already connected. However, such pairs are too simple for a classifier. It gives high results on *Development Set* and poor results on *Test-only Set*. As a result, we had to look for sources of more problematic negative cases to pose a more difficult classification problem. First, we considered **non-connected LUs** – if two synsets are linked by a stronger I-relation and include some strong translational equivalents, all pairs of LUs from these synsets that are not marked as equivalents become negative cases. Second, we examined **non-linked synsets** – from synsets not linked by any I-relation two are randomly selected and next an LU pair is randomly drawn as a negative example. However, such cases are mostly extremes and trivially different from positive cases, as they are not similar to positive ones with respect to the features. Third, we took **hypernyms of the** k **level** – for a pair of synsets linked by I-synonymy, an indirect hypernym in the distance of $k = 3$ of one of them is selected and one of its LUs is linked with an LU from the other synset into a negative pair. Hypernyms were selected on both sides: Polish and English to create negative examples. The intuition is that a hypernym in some semantic distance is too general to be a source of good translation equivalents, but also semantically close enough to be a problem for a classifier. Fourth, we looked at **meronyms and holonyms** – in a similar way to the use of hypernyms, we choose synsets linked by meronymy and holonymy as potential sources for negative cases. Fifth, we turned to **identical lemmas** – LUs from two languages with the same lemma from synsets not linked by any I-relation. The final set of negative examples of the size equal to the number of positive examples was randomly drawn. *Test-only Set* is a randomly selected sample of 449 bilingual LU pairs from synsets linked by an I-relation that was manually evaluated by lexicographers. It includes: 203 positive examples (significant equivalence pairs) and 246 negative ones.

6   Methods for Interlingual Sense Mapping

Maximum Similarity Heuristic – selecting an LU as an equivalent to the most similar one according to a bilingual, common space distributional model – is a simple heuristic baseline method (*MaxSim*) for the identification of equivalence links:

– for a pair of synsets S_p and S_e linked by one of the selected I-relation R:
   • for every LU $x_i \in S_p$ identify $\langle x_i, y_j \rangle : argmin_{y_j}(1 - bsim(x_i, y_j))$ as representing a *significant equivalence* instance

where $bsim(x_i, y_j)$ is a cosine measure of semantic relatedness based on mapping two monolingual distributional models onto a common vector space. As Development Set proposed in this paper is different than the one used in the preliminary work [13], *MaxSim* is the main reference point to compare both approaches.

In the evaluation, *MaxSim* was applied to all bilingual pairs of synsets that include LUs belonging to the two data sets (i.e. Development and Test-only Sets). The results obtained by *MaxSim* are presented in Table 1. Test-only-Set is more difficult, as it consists of pairs with high similarity. Moreover, Development Set includes many generated negative pairs that are loosely connected and relatively easy. However, *MaxSim* produces a potential link for every LU in the source synset, so it is prone to over-generation.

Similarity Threshold Cut-off Heuristic. (*MaxSimT*) – is *MaxSim* cut off by a threshold for the maximal semantic distance (i.e. 1 - the cosine measure). *MaxSim* produces a potential link for every LU in a processed synset, while we could expect only a few links per synset. The results of this heuristic, henceforth

Table 1. Extraction of equivalence links from synsets – 10-fold cross-validation on *Development Set* and *Test-only Set*. Basic features: 1 – 13 were used in all experiments, and expanded in other experiments by additional ones namely: 18 – cos. of differences with the synset vectors, 19+20 – dot products with the synset vectors, 14 – cos. of differences with the head vectors, and 15+16 – dot products with the head vectors. '(R)' – synset vectors were built in a contextual way.

Method	Threshold	Development set				Test-only-Set			
		Acc	P	R	F1	Acc	P	R	F1
MaxSim	–	85.01	91.48	77.20	**83.74**	61.02	58.33	48.28	52.83
MaxSimT	0.95	84.95	91.68	76.88	83.63	60.80	58.08	47.78	52.43
	0.90	84.57	91.88	75.84	83.09	61.47	59.26	47.29	52.60
	0.85	83.55	92.14	73.36	81.69	62.36	61.18	45.81	52.39
	0.80	80.96	92.50	67.39	77.97	63.70	64.93	42.86	51.63
	0.75	77.04	92.92	58.55	71.83	65.48	75.00	35.47	48.16
	0.70	71.40	**93.76**	45.85	61.58	63.70	81.25	25.62	38.95
	Features								
MLP	Basic	79.86	80.28	79.22	79.72	71.16	70.79	61.67	65.90
	18+(R)	79.87	80.28	79.29	79.73	71.16	70.43	62.61	66.19
	18	79.86	80.12	79.52	79.78	71.07	71.65	59.75	65.08
	19+20(R)	79.97	80.49	79.19	79.80	71.74	71.10	63.25	66.89
	19+20	79.93	80.04	79.81	79.89	71.07	70.69	61.82	65.82
	14	80.32	80.55	80.01	80.24	72.49	70.70	67.09	68.79
	15+16	80.10	80.32	79.80	80.03	70.56	70.22	60.64	65.04
	19+20+14(R)	80.42	80.89	79.74	80.28	**72.90**	**71.21**	67.29	**69.18**
	19+20+14	80.37	80.63	80.05	80.29	72.81	72.07	65.27	68.41
	19+20(R)+17	**80.45**	**80.73**	**80.09**	**80.37**	72.74	70.81	**67.68**	**69.18**

MaxSimT, are presented in Table 1 for different maximal thresholds. Concerning precision, *MaxSimT* must show some improvement starting from some threshold value in relation to *MaxSim*. However, in the case of F1 measure *MaxSimT* only comes close to *MaxSim* on both datasets. This is in contrast to [13] and signals that the proposed Development Set is now more similar to test samples in which all examples, positive and negative, are manually annotated.

Multi-Criteria Equivalent Extraction. As in [13], both heuristics: *MaxSim* and *MaxSimT* express relatively good performance. Thus, a bilingual distributional semantics model represents a good amount of knowledge about translational equivalence, but not sufficient. To improve the recognition of translational equivalents, we need to broaden the amount of knowledge sources describing LUs. From the set of features used in [13], we preserved 4 of 8 with small changes. Let x and y be two LUs to be compared:

1. cosine measure for vectors of x and y,
2. word frequency for Polish $log_{10}(x)$,
3. word frequency for English $log_{10}(y)$,
4. the level of *the cascade dictionary*[6] on which $\langle lem(x), lem(y)\rangle$ was found as a translation – normalised by 12, i.e. the number of levels,
5. whether both x and y are from the same wordnet domain – a binary feature.

The feature of the normalised difference of word frequency from [13] has been exchanged by two features better showing the frequency of compared lemmas. Frequency in a large general corpus provides insight into possible polysemy of a word. Thus, the presentation of such information separately for both lemmas supports classification. The logarithm is used to emphasise the main distinctions in the frequencies of words.

In comparison to [13], several features have been dropped out as less effective. The Levenshtein distance of word forms puts too much strength on the identity of word forms which biased classifiers. Features referring to the frequency of translation and/or alignment in *Paralela*, a large Polish-English parallel corpus [12], do not work as expected, as the extracted alignments do not provide sufficient coverage for word pairs or even words. Finally, the number of translations in the cascade dictionary seems to be an accidental property of the dictionary composition.

The reduction in the number of features resulted in decreasing noise in the training data. Nevertheless, we still need additional knowledge to enhance the bilingual distributional similarity. First of all, we tried to explore Wiktionary to extract *gender* of English LUs and *stylistic register* of both Polish and English LUs. In order to link Wiktionary to wordnets, we used the automated mapping proposed in the UBY dataset [11]. However, the coverage was only partial. Thus, we built our own parsers for the Polish and English versions of Wiktionary. Two separate procedures for comparing Wiktionary entries with plWordNet and WordNet synsets were developed. Both took into account descriptive content of the entries and their links in comparing them to synsets (including glosses and use examples) and their contexts (especially semantic relation links).

As for gender, only partial information could be extracted, so it was not used as a feature. Description of stylistic registers appeared to be much more informative. We extracted stylistic register for 24,899 out of 50,244 Polish noun senses in Wiktionary and 29,959 from 82,163 English noun senses. Stylistic register codes were automatically mapped to the system of 11 stylistic registers of plWordNet. We also added information about the capitalisation of Polish and English lemmas.

Bilingual distributional similarity appeared to be the most comprehensive knowledge source, but not flawless. A word vector may not be precise enough, e.g. it merges different senses; many less frequent senses are barely represented; also infrequent word vectors may have very poor ratio of meaning representation to noise. Differences in cosine measure values for different LU pairs may be

---

[6] In the work of [8], several bilingual dictionaries were collected and organised into a cascade: from the most reliable on the top to the lowest quality at the bottom.

very small or accidental. Quality of a word vector (i.e. the faithfulness of sense distinction representation) depends on the word frequency in the corpus, but also on the number of its meanings. Moreover, different number of meanings in the case of equivalent candidates may be helpful information, too. Thus, we added features representing the number of senses per word, and also the size of the synset which a considered LU belongs to.

There is partial information about sense frequency available in WordNet, but not in plWordNet. Theoretically, synsets are 'sets', i.e. without any internal structure. In practice, in both wordnets synsets are not only presented as ordered lists, but also they are mostly built in an incremental way by editors. A synset is usually started with one LU and next expanded with further ones. The first added LU is mostly kept on the first position which is often referred to as a 'synset head'. It somehow signals the main meaning of a synset and seems to influence the following editing decisions related to the given synset. Our hypothesis is that the less similar a given LU is to the 'head', the further it is from the I-relation describing the given synset. Thus, we introduced features based on the comparison of an LU and head vectors.

In spite of the suspected significant role of synset 'heads', a synset may consists of several LUs. I-relations should be defined on the basis of the analysis of the whole synset content, but also its location in the wordnet graph of lexico-semantic relations. A synset vector generated on the basis of vectors of its LUs, as well LUs from its context may represent the synset meaning. Next, by comparing the vector of an LU considered with the synset vector, we can obtain some insight into the correspondence of the LU meaning to the I-relation link of this synset. To obtain synset vectors, we experimented with four potential components assembled later in different combinations: (1) lemmas belonging to the synset; (2) lemmas from synsets directly linked by hypernymy and hyponymy, (3) lemmas from the glosses (of LUs in plWordNet or the synset in WordNet)[7], (4) lemmas from use examples (of Polish LUs or the English synset).

First, we collect a lemma set from the chosen components. A synset vector is calculated as an average of the lemma vectors. Different variants of synset vector composition were experimentally analysed: only synset elements: (1); synset elements + direct links: (1+2), synset elements + direct links + gloss(es): (1+2+3), synset elements + direct links + gloss(es) + use example(s): (1+2+3+4).

Finally, the basic set of features – inherited from the preliminary work – has been expanded with the following:

6. *stylistic register of the Polish LU*: a vector of 11 binary values representing possible registers – one LU can be assigned to several registers in Wiktionary,
7. *English LU stylistic registers*: 11 binary values,
8. *capital letter* of the Polish lemma (if it starts with a capital letter) – a binary feature,
9. *capital letter* of the English lemma – a binary feature,
10. *synset size* of the Polish LU: $log_{10}|S|$,
11. *synset size* of the English LU: $log_{10}|S|$,

---

[7] Glosses and use examples are defined in plWordNet for LUs, not for synsets.

12. *number of senses* of the Polish lemma (i.e. the number of LUs of the given lemma in plWordNet),
13. *number of senses* of the English lemma,
14. *similarity of differences from heads* =
    $cos((SrcHead - SrcLemma), (TrgtHead - TrgtLemma))$
15. *dot product with the head vector* on the Polish side = $SrcHead \cdot SrcLemma$
16. *dot product with the head vector* on the English side = $TrgtHead \cdot TrgtLemma$
17. *head present* – is any of the compared LUs a synset head – a binary feature,
18. *similarity of differences from synset vectors* =
    $cos((SrcSyn - SrcLemma), (TrgtSyn - TrgtLemma))$
19. *dot product with the synset vector* on the Polish side = $SrcSyn \cdot SrcLemma$
20. *dot product with the synset vector* on the English side = $TrgSyn \cdot TrgLemma$

The defined features (not all were used in all experiments, explained below) and Development Set were used to train a classifier. On the basis of the results obtained in the preliminary research, we chose a Multilayer Neural Network, implemented in *TensorFlow*[8] and *Keras*[9] and concentrated on it. The applied setting and architecture was as follows: architecture: 3 hidden layers with 500 neurones in each (2 layers were also tested), activation function in the hidden layers: *relu*, activation function in the output layer: *sigmoid*, dropout: 0.2, l2 regularization: 0.02, number of epochs: 100, loss: binary cross-entropy, optimizer: adam, metrics: accuracy.

It was trained and tested on Development Set according to the $k = 10$ fold cross-validation scheme: random division into k parts, one for testing and 10 iterations (repetitions) of tests. The average results from all iterations are presented in Table 1. The parameters of the training algorithm were set prior to the experiments and were not changed during them. In addition, the trained classifier, unchanged, was applied to Test-only Set, too. The results are shown in Table 1.

7   Results

In general, the results obtained for Development Set are much higher than the ones for Test-only Set, see Table 1. A similar situation was observed in the preliminary work, cf [13]. Negative samples were collected in fundamentally different ways in both datasets. In the case of Test-only Set, all examples, both positive and negative ones, came from human annotators. Development Set includes only a small portion of manually annotated negative samples, the rest were automatically inferred from the structure of the interlingual mapping between plWordNet and WordNet. Moreover, all samples in Test-only Set were drawn from a bilingual set of LUs of higher cross-lingual distributional similarity, while many negative pairs in Development Set express low values of similarity. However, the method

---

[8] https://www.tensorflow.org/.
[9] https://keras.io/.

for the generation of Development Set proposed in this paper resulted in better generalisation ability of classifiers trained on it, as they achieved substantially better results on Test-only Set than both heuristics.

Cross-lingual distributional similarity, used in *MaxSim*, despite of being generated by an imperfect transformation method, appeared to be a good basis for finding potential translational equivalents. The cut-off threshold (*MaxSThre* method) brought almost no improvement in terms of the F1 measure. First of all, the general level of the distributional similarity values may be significantly different for different words (e.g. it is typically lower for more frequent words in a given language), so it is difficult to find one threshold value for all cases. Moreover, the measure is used in this task in a relative way: to find the best fitting one among the members of the other synset. In many cases it is the first LU in a synset presented as a list, the so called 'head' of a synset.

Similarity-based heuristics (*MaxSim* and *MaxSThre*) have to assign some equivalent to every LU in a synset. There is no simple way to filter out spurious links. However, experiments with a neural network as a classifier showed that by delivering carefully selected additional knowledge, we can improve the recognition performance much beyond the performance of the similarity-based heuristics. Here, in spite of a much larger (more than four times) and more difficult Test-only Set, we managed to reduce the error of the F1 measure by 34.7%, while in the preliminary work the reduction was only 26%.

Several feature types were found not helpful, like Levenshtein distance between lemmas or statistics based on word-level alignment in a large bilingual corpus. The first showed a tendency to wrongly bias training process on Development Set, while the second revealed data sparseness of the corpus. Thus, finally, the basic set of 14 features now represents only: cross-lingual similarity, word frequency, (partially) translation pairs from a dictionary, partial information about stylistic registers and information about synset sizes and polysemy from wordnets. A classifier trained on the basic set significantly outperforms the similarity heuristics on Test-only Set.

Further improvement was achieved by comparing LU vectors with vectors of their synsets. Such feature shows how central the given LU is in relation to the synset and it is especially important if we take into account that the input is wordnet mapping on the synset level. Experiments with introducing features based on a comparison to the vectors of synset 'heads' suggest that these elements are somehow distinguished in synsets, while in theory synsets are sets of LUs without any internal structure.

Several more types of classifiers were trained on Development Set and tested, namely: SVM, GaussianNB Stochastic gradient, KNN and Decision Tree. They also achieved their best performance on the combination of the basic features, dot products with the synset vectors and the binary features signalling the presence of a synset head in the processed pair of LUs. However, their F1 measure was in the range 33.20 (GaussianNB) to 62.28 (Decision Tree), so much below the results of MLP.

8   Further Works

The samples include synsets with single and multiple LUs – the former ones immediately suggest a translational equivalent, if it is connected by I-synonymy, so the suggested linking can only be 'spoiled' by an automated linking. We plan to enhance the training-testing data sets with many more examples of translational equivalents coming from non-singleton synsets, e.g following a general scheme of Active Learning. The lack of positive influence of features based on a large parallel corpus means that we need to look for a more diversified corpus or to try to use comparable corpora that can be much bigger. More sophisticated methods for building cross-lingual common distributional semantics models may improve the performance.

References

1. Angelov, K., Lobanov, G.: Predicting translation equivalents in linked WordNets. In: Proceedings of the Sixth Workshop on Hybrid Approaches to Translation (HyTra6). ACL (2016)
2. Bojanowski, P., Grave, E., Joulin, A., Mikolov, T.: Enriching word vectors with subword information. arXiv preprint arXiv:1607.04606 (2016)
3. Conneau, A., Lample, G., Ranzato, M., Denoyera, L., Jegou, H.: Word translation without parallel data. In: Proceedings of the 7th International Conference on Learning Representations (2018)
4. Copestake, A., et al.: Acquisition of lexical translation relations from MRDS. Mach. Transl. **9**, 183–219 (1994). https://doi.org/10.1007/BF00980578
5. Dziob, A., Piasecki, M., Rudnicka, E.: plWordNet 4.1 - a linguistically motivated, corpus-based bilingual resource. In: Fellbaum, C., Vossen, P., Rudnicka, E., Maziarz, M., Piasecki, M. (eds.) Proceedings of the Tenth Global WordNet Conference, pp. 353–362 (2019)
6. Fellbaum, C. (ed.): WordNet - An Electronic Lexical Database. The MIT Press, Cambridge (1998)
7. Irvine, A., Callison-Burch, C.: A comprehensive analysis of bilingual lexicon induction. Comput. Linguist. **43**(2), 273–310 (2017)
8. Kędzia, P., Piasecki, M., Rudnicka, E., Przybycień, K.: Automatic prompt system in the process of mapping plWordNet on Princeton WordNet. Cognitive Studies | Études cognitives (2013)
9. Kocoń, J.: KGR10 FastText polish word embeddings (2018). http://hdl.handle.net/11321/606, CLARIN-PL digital repository
10. Soderland, S., et al.: Panlingual lexical translation via probabilistic inference. Artif. Intell. **174**(9), 619–637 (2010)
11. Miller, T., Gurevych, I.: WordNet-Wikipedia-Wiktionary: construction of a three-way alignment. In: Calzolari, N., et al (eds.) Proceedings of the 9th International Conference on Language Resources and Evaluation (LREC 2014), pp. 2094–2100. European Language Resources Association (ELRA), May 2014
12. Pęzik, P.: Exploring phraseological equivalence with paralela. In: Gruszczyńska, E., Leńko-Szymańska, A. (eds.) Polish-Language Parallel Corpora, pp. 67–81. Instytut Lingwistyki Stosowanej UW, Warszawa (2016)

13. Piasecki, M., Dyszlewski, R., Rudnicka, E.: Towards automated extraction of translational equivalents from interlingual synset relations. In: Vetulani, Z., Paroubek, P. (eds.) Human Language Technologies as a Challenge for Computer Science and Linguistics, pp. 67–71. Wydawnictwo Nauka i Innowacje, Poznań (2019)
14. Piasecki, M., Szpakowicz, S., Broda, B.: Toward plWordNet 2.0. In: Bhattacharyya, P., Fellbaum, C., Vossen, P. (eds.) Proceedings of 5th Global Wordnet Conference, pp. 263–270. Narosa Publishing House (2010)
15. Rudnicka, E., Bond, F., Grabowski, Ł., Piotrowski, T., Piasecki, M.: Sense equivalence in plWordNet to Princeton WordNet mapping. Int. J. Lexicograph. **32** (2019)
16. Rudnicka, E., Maziarz, M., Piasecki, M., Szpakowicz, S.: A strategy of mapping polish WordNet onto Princeton WordNet. In: Proceedings of COLING 2012, posters, pp. 1039–1048 (2012)
17. Vossen, P. (ed.): EuroWordNet: A Multilingual Database with Lexical Semantic Networks for European Languages. Kluwer, Dordrecht (1998)

Evaluation of Knowledge-Based Recognition of Spatial Expressions for Polish

Michał Marcińczuk[(✉)] [iD], Marcin Oleksy [iD], and Jan Wieczorek [iD]

Department of Computational Intelligence, Wrocław University of Science and Technology, Wrocław, Poland
{michal.marcinczuk,marcin.oleksy,jan.wieczorek}@pwr.edu.pl

Abstract. In the paper, we deal with the problem of spatial expression recognition. The goal of this task is to recognize in text information structures that represent a relative spatial relationship between two objects (a trajector and a landmark) indicated by a preposition of location, for example, *a book* on *the table*. We used the Corpus of Polish Spatial Texts (PST) to evaluate the knowledge-based approach to spatial expression recognition. We focused on the evaluation of the recall of the method for filtering candidates of spatial expressions. Our goal was to identify the bottlenecks of the existing preprocessing pipeline and the knowledge-based approach. We have shown that it is necessary to focus on three main areas, i.e., coreference resolution (relations from implied subjects and pronouns to nouns and named entities), word sense disambiguation, and cognitive schemas.

Keywords: Information extraction · Evaluation · Spatial information · Ontology · SUMO · Polish spatial texts · Polish

1 Introduction

Information extraction systems are composed of many components that perform core tasks of natural language processing. The most commonly used modules are text segmentation, morphological analysis and disambiguation, shallow parsing, word sense disambiguation, and others. In the paper, we deal with the problem of recognition of spatial relations between entities. The task includes a morphological analysis of the text, the recognition of object mentions, a parsing of the text, the recognition and categorization of named entities, a co-reference resolution, and the identification and interpretation of semantic relations. The problem with such an approach is that the feasibility and the quality of the analysis depend on the performance of specific natural language processing tools and the quality of the resources, knowledge bases used by the tools. We evaluated the existing

Work financed as part of the investment in the CLARIN-PL research infrastructure funded by the Polish Ministry of Science and Higher Education.

N. T. Nguyen et al. (Eds.): ICCCI 2020, LNAI 12496, pp. 682–693, 2020.
https://doi.org/10.1007/978-3-030-63007-2_53

approach to spatial expression recognition presented by [16] on the Polish Spatial Corpus [20]. In the evaluation, we focused on the knowledge-based approach to filtering candidates of spatial expressions in terms of two factors: the coverage of the template-based filtering method in terms of a different combination of categories of spatial objects, and the performance of mapping of spatial objects on SUMO concepts.

In Sect. 2, we briefly present existing applications of knowledge-based system to the problem of recognition of spatial relations. In Sect. 3, we present the existing preprocessing pipeline and the procedure for recognition of spatial expressions for Polish. Section 4 contains a description of the Corpus of Polish Spatial Texts used in the evaluation. In Sect. 5, we present the findings from the evaluation. The analysis consists of three parts: analysis of missing concepts, preprocessing errors, and impact of coreference resolution.

2   Related Work

There are several systems that use a formal description of knowledge, such as ontologies in spatial expressions automatic extraction and analysis. A combined approach to the automated analysis of intelligence reports [7] focused on verbs and their complements using an OWL-based ontology influenced by the FrameNet [1]. Ontological information about semantic frames of actions enabled among others to map spatial constituents to spatial roles. In [3] the authors performed an analysis of the semantics of linguistic expressions that are used to describe the relative location of objects in visual contexts. Clustering the target and landmark objects that occur with a given preposition into conceptual categories served to verify the correlation between the semantics of the objects and the sensitivity to the functional meaning of the preposition. Typical classes of the landmark and the target objects related by a preposition were predicted using an algorithm for class-labeling of words backed by the WordNet ontology [4]. Parts of spatial expressions extracted from a dataset were the basis for patterns development. Ontological information may be both a means of achieving the goals of automatic analysis and a goal itself. In [27] the authors introduced a method aimed at gaining a complete semantic understanding of consumer language. Automatically recognized spatial relations between disorders and anatomical structures were normalized to their appropriate UMLS CUIs.

The interpretation of spatial prepositions is context related. [5] showed that a complex ontology of object properties associated with spatial prepositions is needed to define a particular preposition sense. On the other hand, they conclude that "whereas the precise position of eyes relative to nose and mouth may be crucial in discriminating between faces, precisely where a pear lies relative to a bowl is not so crucial for determining whether it is in the bowl or not" [5, p. 188].

3   Recognition of Spatial Expressions

3.1   Preprocessing Pipeline

Diversity of expressing spatial relations between objects requires specialized tools and resources to make the task feasible. The elementary text processing, which includes text segmentation, morphological analysis, and disambiguation, can be performed with any of the existing taggers for Polish, i.e., WCRFT [25], Concraft [28] or Pantera [2]. The accuracy of the taggers is satisfactory and varies between 89–91%.

Identification of relevant entity mentions is the basis for the recognition of spatial relations. The mentions can be named entities, nominal phrases, pronouns, and null verbs (verbs which do not have an explicit subject cf. [8]). The spans of entity mentions can be recognized using a shallow parser for Polish, e.g., Spejd [22] with a NKJP grammar [6] or IOBBER [26]. According to [24], the NKJP grammars evaluated on the NKJP corpus obtained 78% of precision and 81% of recall in recognition of NGs, PrepNGs, NumNGs and PrepNumNGs. IOBBER evaluated on the KPWr corpus obtained 74% of precision and 74% of recall in recognition of NPs [26].

The next step is the division of entities into physical and non-physical. Using WoSeDon [12] for word sense disambiguation and then a mapping between plWordNet [18] and the SUMO ontology [21] is one of the solutions. The mapping contains more than 175 000 links between synsets from plWordNet and SUMO concepts. Other types of mentions (i.e., named entities, pronouns and null verbs) require additional processing. Named entities can be mapped by their categories which can be recognized using one of the named entity recognition tools for Polish, i.e., Liner2 [14], Nerf [28] or PolDeepNer[1] [17]. Liner2 and PolDeepNer provide a fine-grained model recognizing 82 categories of named entities that is more suitable than the coarse-grained models. The fine-grained model obtained 74% of precision and 72% of recall. Nevertheless, a mapping of named entity categories onto SUMO is required. We used NE SUMO PlWn mapping [29].

Pronouns and null verbs do not contain any semantic information about the entity they refer to. They require a coreference resolution to a nominal phrase or a named entity. In the initial analysis, we ignored coreference resolution to investigate how much information about the object can be drawn from their mentions. To analyze to what extent the missing information about the spatial object can be acquired from coreference resolution, we used Mention Detector [11] and Bartek [10] to find groups of mentions referring to the same entity.

Table 1 contains a sample sentence with all the information layers provided by the language processing tools. Column *Orth* represents the input text and the *Spatial* column contains gold-standard annotation of spatial components.

---

[1] https://github.com/CLARIN-PL/PolDeepNer.

Table 1. Result of an analysis of a sample sentence with NLP components.

No	Orth	Base	Ctag	Group	NE	WSD	SUMO	Spatial
1	Ze	z	prep:gen:wok	PrepNG	-	-		
2	stacyjki	stacyjka	subst:sg:gen:f	NGa	-	stacyjka.1(3:wytw)	EngineeringComponent, AutomobileIgnitionSystem	TR
3	kolejowej	kolejowy	adj:sg:gen:f:pos	NGa	-	kolejowy.1(43:rel)		TR
4	w	w	prep:loc:nwok	PrepNG	-	-		SI
5	Nowyn	nowy	adj:sg:loc:n:pos	NGa	CITY	nowy.2(42:jak)		LM
6	Mieście	miasto	subst:sg:loc:n	NGa	CITY	gród.2(12:msc) miasto.1(12:msc)	city, SubjectiveAssessmentAttribute	LM
7	podążamy	podążać	fin:pl:pri:imperf	-	-	podążać.1(36:ruch) zmierzać.1(36:ruch) iść.2(36:ruch)		
8	ulicami	ulica	subst:pl:inst:f	NGg	-	ulica.1(12:msc)		
9	miasta	miasto	subst:sg:gen:n	NGg	-	gród.2(12:msc) miasto.1(12:msc)		
...								

3.2   Recognition Procedure

Recognition of spatial expressions consists of two main stages: generation of spatial expression candidates and filtering of spatial expression candidates. We briefly describe both stages in the following subsections.

Generation of Spatial Expression Candidates—in this step, a set of manually crafted patterns is used to generate potential spatial expressions. For example, the most frequent pattern is „NG Prep NG", where NG is a *nominal group* and Prep is a preposition. The phrases are recognized by the Spejd tool. Other possible patterns are presented in [16].

In our analysis, we focus on the other part of the recognition process. Thus, we used gold annotation as spatial expression candidates.

Filtering of Spatial Expression Candidates—a set of 121 ontological schemas based on the semantic restrictions expressed with the SUMO classes are used to verify if a given triple of a trajector (TR), a spatial indicator (SI), and a landmark (LM) is a valid spatial expression. Each schema consists of the following elements: preposition, description, example, a set of valid concepts for trajector, and a set of valid concepts for the landmark. A sample schema for preposition *on* is presented on Fig. 1. The set of schemas defines 1484 distinct combinations of prepositions and SUMO concepts, for example, { *#Region, on, #LandForm*}.

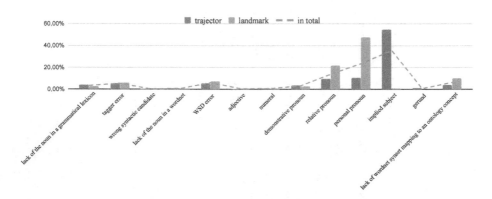

Fig. 1. Schema #1 for preposition ON (Pol. "NA")

4   Data

In the experiments, we used PST 2.0 (Corpus of Polish Spatial Texts) – a corpus designed for training and testing the tools for spatial expression recognition [20]. Texts derived from polish travel blogs manually annotated with spatial expressions using Inforex system [15] according to the guidelines [19] basing on three existing specifications for English (SpatialML [13], SpatialRole Labelling from SemEval-2013 Task 3 [9] and ISO-Space1.4 [23]). The PST corpus consists of 99 annotated documents with 2 035 spatial expressions. 1 474 of them consist of a landmark, a trajector, and a spatial indicator—these are the expressions that are subjected to evaluation. Moreover, we have divided the corpus into two subsets: training and testing (see Table 2). We conducted the analyses on the training subset and the test was left for future evaluation.

Table 2. Number of spatial expressions in the subsets of the PST corpus.

Metric	Training	Testing	Total
Documents	71	28	99
Spatial expressions	1 702	333	2 035
Spatial expressions with TR, LM and SI	1 200	274	1 474

5 Evaluation

5.1 Introduction

We used the existing preprocessing pipeline described in Sect. 3.1 to process the training subset of the Corpus of Polish Spatial Texts. Then we selected the manually annotated spatial expressions containing a trajector, a landmark and a spatial indicator, and applied the knowledge-based filtering procedure described in Sect. 3.2. 375 out of 1200 (31%) expressions were correctly classified as spatial. The remaining 825 (69%) expressions were incorrectly classified as non-spatial. We found out that 497 (60%) of the misclassified expressions were missing a concept for either trajector or landmark. Due to the missing SUMO concept, the knowledge-based approach could not be applied and the expressions were automatically discarded. In Sect. 5.2, we present the major reasons why the concepts were missing. For the remaining 328 (40%) with assigned concepts, the miss-classification was due to an incorrect assignment of SUMO concept or missing spatial schema. We discussed the results in Sect. 5.3.

5.2 Missing Concepts

Assigning the concepts to trajector and landmark is one of the main tasks of the system for spatial expression recognition, but the tools did not always achieve this goal. It was the reason for 497 of 824 failures (60%) in automatic matching cognitive schemas for the spatial expressions.

In Table 3, we present the most frequent reasons of why the concept was not assigned to either trajector or landmark. The preprocessing stage errors (unknown words, tagger errors, WSD errors) were, to a small extent, linked to the failures in concepts assigning. They were responsible for 15.72% cases in total.

Lack of concept assignment was most often related to the grammatical class of the spatial component. The meaning of the words belonging to some classes is based on indexing, which applies especially to pronouns. They, therefore, are not a part of plWordNet. This, in turn, makes it impossible to assign SUMO concept to a word, as the mapping plWordNet onto SUMO ontology is the crucial element of the process. Pronouns (mostly personal and relative pronouns) as spatial components caused 37% failures in concepts assignment.

Table 3. The reasons for missing concepts for trajectors or landmarks

Error type	Number of expressions	
Implied subjects	184	37.0%
Personal pronouns	105	23.6%
Relative pronouns	62	13.3%
Missing synset to concept mapping	28	6.3%
WSD errors	27	6.1%
Tagger errors	24	5.4%
Unknown words	15	3.4%
Demonstrative pronoun	14	3.2%
Other	38	
Total	497	100.0%

In some ways, the same problem concerns some grammatical classes (especially particles) and uses of verbs, which were annotated as spatial components. According to the annotation guidelines, the verbs could play the role of trajector when implied subjects or nominal sentences occurred, and a verb (null verb) was the only word referring to a spatial object—the „doer". In relatively rare cases, verbs could refer to landmarks. The problem with referring to the spatial object in the case of implied subjects and nominal sentences caused 37% errors in total.

Implied subjects, personal pronouns, and relative pronouns do not hold semantic information. Therefore, they cannot be directly mapped to a SUMO concept. This means that 365 (73%) cases cannot be handled. They require additional preprocessing, which is an coreference resolution. As mentioned in the Sect. 3.1, the coreference resolution was not included in the initial analysis. It was not a part of the original pipeline presented in [16]. We decided to analyze the impact of coreference resolution on concept mapping in a separate experiment. We presented the findings in the Sect. 5.4.

5.3 Spatial Objects with Concepts

In this section, we analyze expressions for which both spatial objects (the trajector and the landmark) were assigned SUMO concepts Table 4. The detailed breakdown of the analysis is presented in Table 4. 53% of spatial expressions with assigned concepts were correctly classified as spatial. In the remaining 46.7% (375 cases), we have identified two main groups of errors. The first one is related to errors generated during the preprocessing (tagger, WSD, or SUMO mapping), and it concerns 20.9% of the expressions. The majority of errors are related the word sense disambiguation (17.5%). Below are sample WSD errors:

- *mur* and *ściana* (a wall) were disambiguated as an obstacle, i.e. ,,something immaterial that stands in the way and must be circumvented or surmounted",
- *ruina* (a ruin) was disambiguated as disrepair, i.e. ,,in need of repairs",
- *drzewo* (a tree) was disambiguated as a wood.

The other group of errors is related to the incompleteness of ontological schemas. Despite the existing set of schemas consists of 121 elements with a total of 1484 distinct combinations of prepositions and SUMO concepts, 181 cases were not matched, for example:

- {*#CorpuscularObject, in, #City*},
- {*#Hill, in, #City*},
- {*#City, from, #City*}.

Table 4. Types of problems of not matching the expressions to cognitive scheme.

Group of spatial expressions	Count	% of all
Expressions with both concepts	703	100.0%
+ Correctly classified	375	53.3%
+ Incorrectly classified	328	46.7%
++ Preprocessing errors	147	20.9%
+++ Tagger errors	10	1.5%
+++ WSD errors	123	17.5%
+++ SUMO mapping errors	14	2.0%
++ Missing schema	181	25.7%

5.4   Impact of Coreference Resolution

70% of spatial expressions consist of an implied subject or a pronoun. To be able to determine a SUMO concept for them, it is required to resolve their coreference relations. For example, the following sentences ,,Give me a book. It is on the table." contains spatial expression {it, on (the) table}. Pronoun *it* refers to *a book*. In order to validate the expression {it, on (the) table} it is required to resolve the reference between *it* and *a book*.

As mentioned in Sect. 3.1, the coreference resolution consists of two steps. The first one is the recognition of mentions, i.e., phrases which refer to some entities. In the second step, the mentions are grouped. Each group refers to a distinct entity.

648 out of 3388 spatial objects are implied subjects or pronouns. 375 out of them were marked as a mention. Than 192 out of them were grouped with any other mention. In many cases, pronouns are grouped with other pronouns or verbs with other verbs. 85 out of 192 spatial objects were assigned SUMO concepts based on other mentions in the cluster. Only 46 spatial objects have been assigned a correct SUMO concept, which is only 7% of all implied subjects and pronouns (see Table 5). Below we present a sample sentence in which coreference resolution helped in determining the SUMO concept. Below we present samples of correctly and incorrectly recognized coreference relations.

Table 5. Number of implied subjects and pronouns as spatial objects correctly handled by coreference resolution.

Spatial object	Count	% of all
Implied subjects and pronouns	648	100.0%
+ Marked as mention	375	58.0%
++ Clustered with other mentions	192	29.0%
+++ Assigned SUMO concept	85	13.0%
+++++ Valid SUMO concept	47	7.0%

Samples of correctly recognized coreference relations:

- "Surprisingly, Garmin saw this forest path, and it led to this main road" (Pol. *O dziwo Garmin widział tę leśną dróżkę, i prowadziła ona do tej główniejszej drogi*)
- "I have chosen the 'CESARKA' Recreation and Training Centre as my target. It is located quite close to Łódź" (Pol. *Na celowniku obrałem sobie Ośrodek Wypoczynkowo-Szkoleniowy ,CESARKA'. Znajduje się on dość blisko Łodzi (...)*)
- "(...) a kiosk, with newspapers in it (...)" (Pol. *(...) kiosk, a w nim gazety (...)*)

Samples of incorrectly recognized coreference relations:

- "(...) a pond surrounded by a forest. On its shores, fishermen (...)" (Pol. *(...) staw otoczony lasem. Na jego brzegu wędkarze (...)*)—*its* should be linked with *pond*,
- "(...) a nice panorama of the valley of Węgierska Górka and the Silesian Beskid Mountains behind it (...)" (Pol. *(...) ładną panoramę na dolinę Węgierskiej Górki oraz znajdujący się za nią Beskid Śląski (...)*)—*it* should be linked with *valley*.

6   Conclusions

The existing preprocessing pipeline and the knowledge-based approach covers only 31% (375 out of 1200) spatial expressions from the training subset of Polish Spatial Texts Corpus. The remaining 825 expressions are not covered due to several reasons. The analysis showed that the largest loss is on cases which require coreference resolution—365 cases (44%). The available tool for coreference resolution was able to handle only 7% of the cases. The second-largest source of errors is word sense disambiguation—173 cases (21%). The third-largest source of errors is the incompleteness of cognitive schemas—146 cases (18%). The remaining 18% of errors have many different sources, i.e. tagger errors, missing words in the lexicon or in the word.

The analysis showed that to achieve improvements in the recall of spatial expression recognition, it is necessary to focus on three areas, i.e., coreference resolution (from implied subjects and pronouns to nouns and named entities), word sense disambiguation and cognitive schemas.

References

1. FrameNet: http://framenet.icsi.berkeley.edu/. Accessed 3 Jan 2020
2. Acedański, S.: A morphosyntactic brill tagger for inflectional languages. In: Loftsson, H., Rögnvaldsson, E., Helgadóttir, S. (eds.) NLP 2010. LNCS (LNAI), vol. 6233, pp. 3–14. Springer, Heidelberg (2010). https://doi.org/10.1007/978-3-642-14770-8_3
3. Dobnik, S., Kelleher, J.: Exploration of functional semantics of prepositions from corpora of descriptions of visual scenes. In: Proceedings of the Third Workshop on Vision and Language, pp. 33–37, Dublin City University and the Association for Computational Linguistics, Dublin, Ireland, August 2014. https://doi.org/10.3115/v1/W14-5405, https://www.aclweb.org/anthology/W14-5405
4. Fellbaum, C., Miller, G.: The Lexical Database. MITP (1998)
5. Garrod, S., Ferrier, G., Campbell, S.: In and on: investigating the functional geometry of spatial prepositions. Cognition **72**(2), 167–189 (1999). https://doi.org/10.1016/S0010-0277(99)00038-4,http://www.sciencedirect.com/science/article/pii/S0010027799000384
6. Głowińska, K.: Anotacja składniowa NKJP. In: Przepiórkowski, A., Bańko, M., Górski, R.L., Lewandowska-Tomaszczyk, B. (eds.) Narodowy Korpus Języka Polskiego, pp. 107–127. Wydawnictwo Naukowe PWN, Warsaw (2012)
7. Jenge, C., Kawaletz, S., Schade, U.: Combining different NLP methods for HUMINT report analysis (2009)
8. Kaczmarek, A., Marcińczuk, M.: Heuristic algorithm for zero subject detection in polish. In: Král, P., Matoušek, V. (eds.) TSD 2015. LNCS (LNAI), vol. 9302, pp. 378–386. Springer, Cham (2015). https://doi.org/10.1007/978-3-319-24033-6_43
9. Kolomiyets, O., Kordjamshidi, P., Bethard, S., Moens, M.: SemEval-2013 task 3: spatial role labeling. Second joint conference on lexical and computational semantics (SEM). In: Proceedings of the Seventh International Workshop on Semantic Evaluation (SemEval 2013), East Stroudsburg, PA, ACL, Atlanta, USA, June 2013
10. Kopeć, M., Ogrodniczuk, M.: Creating a coreference resolution system for polish. In: Proceedings of the Eighth International Conference on Language Resources and Evaluation, LREC 2012. ELRA, Istanbul, Turkey, pp. 192–195 (2012)

11. Kopeć, M.: Zero subject detection for polish. In: Proceedings of the 14th Conference of the European Chapter of the Association for Computational Linguistics, Short Papers, vol. 2, pp. 221–225. Association for Computational Linguistics, Gothenburg (2014)

12. Kędzia, P., Piasecki, M., Orlińska, M.: WoSeDon (2016). http://hdl.handle.net/11321/290, CLARIN-PL digital repository

13. Mani, I., et al.: SpatialML: annotation scheme, resources, and evaluation. Lang. Resour. Eval. **44**, 263–280 (2010)

14. Marcińczuk, M., Kocoń, J., Janicki, M.: Liner2 – a customizable framework for proper names recognition for Polish. In: Bembenik, R., Skonieczny, Ł., Rybiński, H., Kryszkiewicz, M., Niezgódka, M. (eds.) Intelligent Tools for Building a Scientific Information Platform, Studies in Computational Intelligence, vol. 467, pp. 231–253. Springer (2013). https://doi.org/10.1007/978-3-642-35647-6_17, http://dblp.uni-trier.de/db/series/sci/sci467.html#MarcinczukKJ13

15. Marcińczuk, M., Oleksy, M.: Inforex – a collaborative system for text corpora annotation and analysis goes open. In: Proceedings of the International Conference Recent Advances in Natural Language Processing, RANLP, pp. 711–719 (2019)

16. Marcińczuk, M.M., Oleksy, M., Wieczorek, J.: Towards recognition of spatial relations between entities for polish. Cognitive Studies—Études cognitives (16), 119–132 (2016)

17. Marcińczuk, M.: Fine-grained named entity recognition for polish using deep learning. In: Proceedings of PP-RAI 2019 Conference, Department of Systems and Computer Networks, Faculty of Electronics, Wroclaw University of Science and Technology, Wrocław, pp. 219–222 (2019)

18. Maziarz, M., Piasecki, M., Szpakowicz, S.: Approaching plWordNet 2.0. In: Proceedings of the 6th Global Wordnet Conference, Matsue, Japan, January 2012

19. Oleksy, M., Marcińczuk, M., Bernaś, T., Wieczorek, J., Kocoń, J.: KPWr annotation guidelines - spatial expressions (2.0) (2019). http://hdl.handle.net/11321/719, CLARIN-PL digital repository

20. Oleksy, M., Wieczorek, J., Bernaś, T., Marcińczuk, M.: Polish Spatial Texts (PST) 2.0 (2019). http://hdl.handle.net/11321/721, CLARIN-PL digital repository

21. Pease, A., Niles, I., Li, J.: The suggested upper merged ontology: a large ontology for the semantic web and its applications. In: In Working Notes of the AAAI-2002 Workshop on Ontologies and the Semantic Web (2002)

22. Przepiórkowski, A.: Powierzchniowe przetwarzanie języka polskiego. Problemy współczesnej nauki, teoria i zastosowania: Inżynieria lingwistyczna, Akademicka Oficyna Wydawnicza "Exit" (2008). https://books.google.pl/books?id=V076OgAACAAJ

23. Pustejovsky, J., Moszkowicz, J., Verhagen, M.: A linguistically grounded annotation language for spatial information. TAL **53**(2), 87–113 (2012). http://atala.org/Extraction-de-dates-saillantes

24. Radziszewski, A.: Metody znakowania morfosyntaktycznego i automatycznej płytkiej analizy składniowej języka polski. Ph.D. thesis, Politechnika Wrocławska, Wrocław (2012)

25. Radziszewski, A.: A tiered CRF tagger for Polish. In: Bembenik, R., Skonieczny, L., Rybiński, H., Kryszkiewicz, M., Niezgódka, M. (eds.) Intelligent Tools for Building a Scientific Information Platform: Advanced Architectures and Solutions. Springer Verlag (2013). https://doi.org/10.1007/978-3-642-35647-6_16

26. Radziszewski, A., Pawlaczek, A.: Large-scale experiments with np chunking of Polish. In: Sojka, P., Horák, A., Kopeček, I., Pala, K. (eds.) TSD 2012. LNCS (LNAI), vol. 7499, pp. 143–149. Springer, Heidelberg (2012). https://doi.org/10.1007/978-3-642-32790-2_17

27. Roberts, K., Rodriguez, L., Shooshan, S.E., Demner-Fushman, D.: Automatic extraction and post-coordination of spatial relations in consumer language. In: AMIA ... Annual Symposium Proceedings. AMIA Symposium 2015, pp. 1083–1092 (2015)

28. Waszczuk, J.: Harnessing the CRF complexity with domain-specific constraints. The case of morphosyntactic tagging of a highly inflected language. In: Proceedings of COLING 2012, pp. 2789–2804, December 2012 . http://cse.iitk.ac.in/users/cs671/2013/hw3/waszczuk-12coling_CRF-w-domainspecific-constraints-for-morpho-tagging.pdf

29. Wieczorek, J., Oleksy, M.: NE_SUMO_PLWN_mapping (2016). http://hdl.handle.net/11321/286, CLARIN-PL digital repository

Low Resource Languages Processing

Development of Kazakh Named Entity Recognition Models

Darkhan Akhmed-Zaki[1,2] ⓘ, Madina Mansurova[1(✉)] ⓘ, Vladimir Barakhnin[3,4] ⓘ,
Marek Kubis[5] ⓘ, Darya Chikibayeva[1], and Marzhan Kyrgyzbayeva[1]

[1] Al-Farabi Kazakh National University, Almaty, Kazakhstan
darhan_a@mail.ru, mansurova.madina@gmail.com,
dashachikibaeva@gmail.com, marzhan.kyrgyzbaeva@gmail.com
[2] University of International Business, Almaty, Kazakhstan
[3] Institute of Computational Technologies, Siberian Branch of the Russian
Academy of Sciences, Novosibirsk, Russian Federation
bar@ict.nsc.ru
[4] Novosibirsk State University, Novosibirsk, Russian Federation
[5] Faculty of Mathematics and Computer Science, Adam Mickiewicz University, Poznań, Poland
mkubis@amu.edu.pl

Abstract. Named entity recognition is one of the important tasks in natural language processing. Its practical application can be found in various areas such as speech recognition, information retrieval, filtering, etc. Nowadays there are a variety of available methods for implementing named entity recognition. In this work we experimented with three models and compared the performances of machine learning based models and probabilistic sequence modeling method on the task of Kazakh language named entity recognition. We considered three models based on BERT, Bi-LSTM and CRF baseline. In the future these models can be parts of an ensemble learning system for name entity recognition in order to achieve better performance results.

Keywords: Named entity recognition · Conditional random fields · BERT · Bi-LSTM

1 Introduction

In the information age with the increasing amount of digital data the need for automatic information extraction tools is bigger than ever. While there is a large number of information extraction tools available now for such languages as English or Russian, the situations with Kazakh differs. Kazakh is one of the low-resourced languages and it belongs to the group of agglutinative languages. In this paper we experiment on Kazakh data using different named entity recognition methods.

Currently, there are various approaches for extracting information. They are diverse and it is difficult to say that one is better than the other, since one or another shows good results in different situations. Information retrieval approaches can be classified into the following categories:

© Springer Nature Switzerland AG 2020
N. T. Nguyen et al. (Eds.): ICCCI 2020, LNAI 12496, pp. 697–708, 2020.
https://doi.org/10.1007/978-3-030-63007-2_54

- rule-based approaches. The experts manually create the rule sets needed to extract certain data.
- knowledge-based approaches. These include models based on ontologies [1], models based on thesauri [2].
- statistical approaches. They include hidden Markov models [3–5], conditional Markov models [6], conditional random fields [7].
- machine learning based approaches [8].

One of the foundational tasks in the process of information extraction is the recognition of named entities, i.e. spans of text that are proper names of people, organizations, locations and other objects[1]. The task consists of identifying the location of names in text and recognizing their type, as illustrated in Fig. 1.

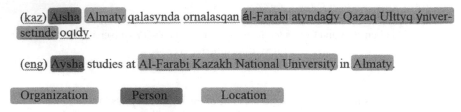

Fig. 1. A sentence with the proper names and their types denoted by square brackets.

Named entity recognition is an important preliminary step in a significant number of extraction tasks such as entity linking, relation extraction, event extraction and template filling (see [9]). Thus, having an accurate model for detecting and classifying proper names is not only significant on its own, but it also contributes to the performance of all the downstream tasks in the process of information extraction.

The existing methods for recognizing named entities can be divided into two categories:

- Rule-based methods. These are the earliest systems for recognizing named entities. Rules are based on lexico-syntactic patterns specific to a particular language.
- Supervised methods. These techniques y require training data, manually labeled by experts. Then, on the basis of the annotated data, the system learns the rules for recognizing named entities.

In recent years state-of-the-art models for the named entity recognition task are based on pre-trained language models. They include ELMo [10] and BERT [11]. BERT is a language representation model developed and pre-trained by Google. It is based on transformers and unlike other language representation models designed to "pre-train

---

[1] In a broad sense it can also encompass recognition of temporal and numerical expressions and identification of terms specific to a particular subject area, such as names of chemical compounds in the biological domain.

deep bidirectional representations from unlabeled text by jointly conditioning on both left and right context in all layers" [11]. In this paper we compare three different models. One is based on our previous work [12], the second one is based on BERT and the third is based on CRF. Furthermore, we juxtapose results of neural network models with the output of a non-neural named entity recognizer in order to verify, if the amount of training data that we have collected so far enables neural models to achieve state-of-the-art results in named entity recognition for Kazakh.

2 Related Work

Classical systems for extracting named entities use manually selected properties [13]. Some early systems used manual rules [14, 15], but the vast majority of modern systems rely on machine learning models [16], such as conditional random field (CRF) [17, 18], Hidden Markov model (HMM) [19], the support vector method (SVM). Although traditional machine learning models are not based on manual rules, they require a manual function development process, which is quite expensive and depends on the domain and language. Recently, many works using neural networks have surpassed classical systems [20–22]. In recent years, models with a recurrent neural network (RNN) such as Long-Short-Term-Memory (LSTM) [23], Gated Recurrent Unit (GRU) [24] have been very successful in sequence modeling problems, for example, Language Modeling [25, 26], machine translation [27], Dialog Act classification [28, 29]. One of the strengths of RNN models is their ability to learn from the main components of the text (i.e. words and symbols). This generalization feature facilitates the construction of language-independent NER models [30, 31], which are based on an uncontrolled study of properties and a small annotated case.

The first use of neural models in the task of marking a sequence was proposed by Collobert et al. [32]. However, there are some limitations to this model. Firstly, a simple neural network with direct connection is used here, which limits the range of the considered context around words. The model forgets the useful relationships between words over a long distance. Secondly, due to the dependence solely on the vectorization of words, it is impossible to define and use properties represented at the symbol level, such as suffixes and prefixes.

Later, modified models using bidirectional LSTM or Stacked LSTM were proposed [33, 34]. For example, in [33], architecture based on bi-LSTM and CRF is used. The authors of [35] use the bi-LSTM-CNNs architecture. To vectorize characters, they suggest the use of convolutional neural networks. New approaches have been found that use CNN or LSTM to extract subword information from input characters, the results of which are superior to other models [33]. Rei et al. [36] proposed a model, in which words and symbols are fed as input.

3 Models

3.1 Bi-LSTM

The model is based on a bi-LSTM block using vectorization of characters and words (see Fig. 2).

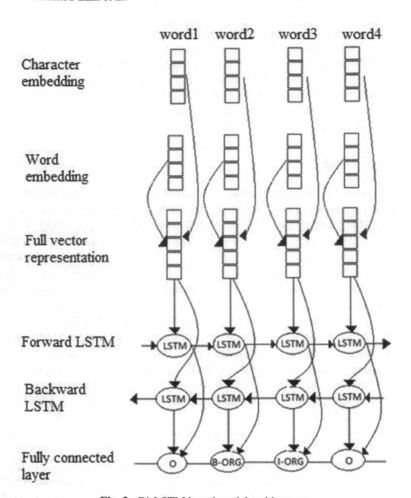

Fig. 2. Bi-LSTM based model architecture.

LSTM (Long Short-Term Memory) is a type of recurrent neural network. Recursive neural networks have the ability to remember the results of past iterations, but they are not able to remember them long-term. The problem of the disappearance of the gradient appears [37]. LSTM networks [35] are designed to combat this problem. They contain three main blocks that control which information will be forgotten and which will be transmitted to subsequent iterations.

3.2 BERT

BERT (Bidirectional Encoder Representations from Transformers) is a natural language processing method based on the use of new architecture neural networks for working with sequences known as "transformers" [11]. BERT features consist in the fact that the technology is trained based on the entire set of words in a sentence or request. Previously, neural networks were trained on an ordered sequence of words (from left to right or from right to left). BERT allows the language model to examine the context of a word based on all the words surrounding it. For example, the word "бет" (which can be translated from Kazakh as "face" or "surface") will have the same context-free representation in "адамның беті" (person's face) and "ыстелдің беті" (surface of a table). At the same time, BERT considers word context and represents "бет" using both the previous and the following surrounding word sequences.

In this paper BERT is used for the single sentence tagging task (see Fig. 3). In our work the model architecture consists of the BERT model followed by classifier (see Fig. 4). In this work BERT used twice. First time we use it to represent sentence as tokens and then BERT is used to get encoded representations of spans. The sentence is represented as sequence of words (w_1, w_2,...,w_n). BERT takes as input sequences of up to N tokens. The output is the last hidden state of the sequence with dimension H. Classifier constitutes of linear layer which takes as input that last hidden state.

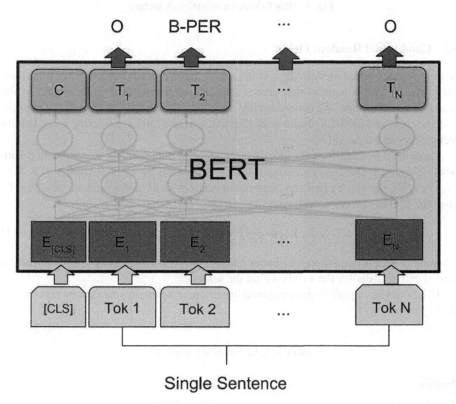

Fig. 3. BERT for single sentence tagging task [11].

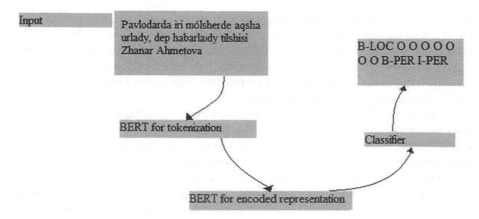

Fig. 4. BERT-classifier model architecture.

3.3 Conditional Random Fields

Neural network based models are data intensive, therefore we decided to confront their performance with a method that attains satisfactory results even with respect to the modest amount of data. We choose for this purpose Conditional Random Fields, a probabilistic sequence modeling framework [38] that was used for constructing named entity recognizers in the past [17].

As defined by Laferty et al. [38], for a sequence of data points X in conjunction with labels Y and a graph G = (V, E) such that Y is indexed by vertices from V (i.e. Y = (Y_v), v $\in$ V), the (X, Y) pair is a conditional random field, if the random variables Y_v obey the Markov property with respect to G, i.e.

$$p(Y_v \vee X, Y_w, w \neq v) = p(Y_v \vee X, Y_w, w \sim v) \quad (1)$$

where w~v means that (w, v) $\in$ E. In our case X represents a sentence and Y consists of named entity labels for the words within the sentence.

CRF models require feature engineering in order to attain satisfactory results (see Table 1).

Table 1. CRF baseline feature set.

Feature	Examples
Current word	word[0] = Tailandta
Prefixes and sufffixes of the current word	p[1] = T p[2] = Ta p[3] = Tai s[1] = a s[2] = ta s[3] = dta
Word shapes	shape[0] = ul shape [1] = 1
Predecessors and successors of the current word	word[1] = su

The model inherits the set of features from the Named Entity Recognizer developed for [39] with exception of lemmata and part-of-speech based features that are not available in our corpus.

4 Training and Evaluation

The experiments were conducted on data collected from Kazakh online news sources. The volume of the data was 7153 sentences. The dataset was labeled manually with 4 entity classes (Location, Organization, Person and Other). IOB scheme was used to denote boundaries of entities. The data were partitioned into training, validation and test sets with [6507, 2531 and 3015 sentences, respectively. The distribution of entities among classes is shown in Table 2.

Table 2. Entity class distribution

Enttiy class	Sample count
Location	4763
Organization	1650
Person	4352
Other	99650

For the purpose of training we used BERT$_{BASE}$ model with the following parameters: $H = 768$, $S = 512$, Total Parameters $= 110$ M. The pre-trained "bert-base-multilingual-cased" model that covers 104 languages was used for initialization. Parameters of the CRF model were estimated using the Passive Aggressive algorithm [39] with the maximum number of iterations set to 25. The CRFsuite library [40] was used for training the model.

We followed the established practice to compute precision, recall and F_1 scores with respect to the explicitly defined testset for the models under evaluation [41]. The metrics are computed according to the following formulas.

$$Precision = \frac{tp}{tp + fp}, \tag{2}$$

$$Recall = \frac{tp}{tp + fn}, \tag{3}$$

$$F_1 = \frac{2 * Precision * Recall}{Precision + Recall} \tag{4}$$

where tp means true positives (number of correctly recognized entities), fp means false positives (number of tokens that were mistakenly recognized as named entities) and fn means false negatives (number of named entities that were not recognized).

5   Results

The main results of the paper are presented in Table 3. As it can be seen from the table the BERT-classifier model outperforms simple Bi-LSTM system and shows better results in precision, recall and F_1 metrics. However, it does not surpass the CRF baseline.

Table 3. Comparison of the results on the test set.

Architecture	Precision	Recall	F_1
Bi-LSTM	86.81	83.94	85.31
BERT-classifier	98.93	97.07	97.99
CRF baseline	97.73	91.32	94.27

Tables 4 and 5 present the detailed results of the experiments. In Table 4 we report the precision, recall and F_1 scores obtained for the entity classes separately. Table 5 shows per tag results according to the IOB scheme that was used for training.

Table 4. Per class results on the test set.

Architecture	Entity class	Precision	Recall	F_1
Bi-LSTM	LOC	0.8573	0.8464	0.8525
	ORG	0.8735	0.8253	0.8456
	PER	0.8693	0.8577	0.8618
BERT-classifier	LOC	0.9791	0.9858	0.9872
	ORG	0.9539	0.8465	0.9406
	PER	0.9680	0.9642	0.9627
CRF baseline	LOC	0.9776	0.9839	0.9807
	ORG	0.9488	0.8268	0.8836
	PER	0.9676	0.9555	0.9615

Table 5. Per tag results on the test set.

Architecture	Tag	Precision	Recall	F_1
Bi-LSTM	B-LOC	0.8759	0.8654	0.8702
	B-ORG	0.9043	0.8783	0.8893
	B-PER	0.8614	0.8521	0.8582
	I-LOC	0.8675	0.8445	0.8579
	I-ORG	0.8564	0.8359	0.8431
	I-PER	0.8955	0.8852	0.8903
BERT-classifier	B-LOC	0.9973	0.9825	0.9899
	B-ORG	1.0000	0.9795	0.9896
	B-PER	0.9971	0.9663	0.9815
	I-LOC	1.0000	0.9545	0.9767
	I-ORG	0.9535	0.9535	0.9535
	I-PER	0.9881	0.9881	0.9881
CRF baseline	B-LOC	0.9899	0.9863	0.9881
	B-ORG	0.9840	0.8280	0.8993
	B-PER	0.9871	0.9656	0.9762
	I-LOC	0.9697	0.9412	0.9552
	I-ORG	0.9506	0.7857	0.8603
	I-PER	0.9825	0.9722	0.9773

6   Conclusion

In this paper we applied current state-of-the-art language representation model BERT to the Kazakh NER task and compared the results with the models based on Bi-LSTM module and CRF baseline. Despite the fact that the task of extracting named entities has many approaches to solving, the most popular are the approaches based on machine learning using contextual information. The Bi-LSTM algorithm uses the two-sided environment of the target word (before and after it) as contextual information, and as shown by the experiments, it demonstrates relatively high accuracy and completeness results, but it does not surpass the CRF baseline in our task. We found out that BERT-based model achieves significantly better results on the standard evaluation than both Bi-LSTM and CRF models. The results are especially notable in the case of ORG entities where neither Bi-LSTM model nor the CRF baseline get close to the performance of the BERT-based model.

Acknowledgements. This work was supported in part under grants of Foundation of Ministry of Education and Science of the Republic of Kazakhstan AP05132933 – "Development of a system for knowledge extraction from heterogeneous data sources to improve the quality of decision-making" (2018–2020) and O.0856 BR05236340 – «Creation of high-performance intelligent technologies for analysis and decision making for the "logistics-agglomeration"; system in the framework of the digital economy of the Republic of Kazakhstan» (2018–2020).

References

1. Embley, W.D., Campbell, M.D., Smith, D.R.: Ontology-based extraction and structuring of information from data-rich unstructured documents. In: Information and Knowledge Management (1998)
2. Cardie, C.: A case-based approach to knowledge acquisition for domain-specific sentence analysis. In: Eleventh National Conference on Artificial Intelligence, pp. 798–803. AAAI Press (1993)
3. Scheffer, T., Decomain, C., Wrobel, S.: Active hidden Markov models for information extraction. In: International Symposium on Intelligent Data Analysis (2001)
4. Scheffer, T., Wrobel, S., Popov, B., Ognianov, D., Decomain C., Hoche, S.: Learning hidden Markov models for information extraction actively from partially labeled text. K¨unstliche Intelligenz (2) (2002)
5. Skounakis, M., Craven, M., Ray, S.: Hierarchical hidden Markov models for information extraction. In: IJCAI (2003)
6. McCallum, A.K., Freitag, D., Pereira, F.: Maximum entropy Markov models for information extraction and segmentation. In: ICML (2000)
7. McCallum, A.K., Jensen, D.: A note on the unification of information extraction and data mining using conditional-probability, relational models. In: IJCAI'03 Workshop on Learning Statistical Models from Relational Data (2003)
8. Mansurova, M., Barakhnin, V., Khibatkhanuly, Y., Pastushkov, I.: Named entity extraction from semi-structured data using machine learning algorithms. In: Nguyen, N.T., Chbeir, R., Exposito, E., Aniorté, P., Trawiński, B. (eds.) ICCCI 2019. LNCS (LNAI), vol. 11684, pp. 58–69. Springer, Cham (2019). https://doi.org/10.1007/978-3-030-28374-2_6
9. Jurafsky, D., Martin, J.H.: Speech and Language Processing: An Introduction to Natural Language processing, Computational Linguistics, and Speech Recognition. Pearson Prentice Hall, Upper Saddle River (2009)
10. Peters, M., Neumann, M., Iyyer, M., et. al.: Deep contextualized word representations. In: 2018 Conference of the North American Chapter of the Association for Computational Linguistics: Human Language Technologies, vol. 1 (Long Papers), pp. 2227–2237 (2018)
11. Devlin, J., Chang, M., Lee, K., Toutanova, K.: Bert: Pre-training of deep bidirectional transformers for language understanding. Computing Research Repository (2018)
12. Chikibayeva D., Mansurova M., Nugumanova A., Kyrgyzbayeva M.: Named entity recognition from news sources based on BI-LSTM. In: 2019 IICT Conference, pp. 519–525 (2019)
13. Luo, G., Huang, X., Lin, C., Nie, Z.: Joint entity recognition and dis-ambiguation. In: 2015 Conference on Empirical Methods in Natural Language Processing, Lisbon, Portugal, pp 879–888. Association for Computational Linguistics (2015)
14. Rau, L.F.: Extracting company names from text. In: Seventh IEEE Conference on Artificial Intelligence Applications, vol. 1, pp. 29–32. IEEE (1991)
15. Sekine, S., Nobata, C.: Definition, dictionaries and tagger for extended named entity hierarchy. In: LREC, pp. 1977–1980 (2004)
16. Nadeau, D., Sekine, S.: A survey of named entity recognition and classification. In: Lingvisticae Investigationes (2007)

17. McCallum, A., Li, W.: Early results for named entity recognition with conditional random fields, feature induction and web-enhanced lexicons. In: The seventh conference on Natural language learning at HLT-NAACL 2003, vol, 4, pp. 188–191. Association for Computational Linguistics (2003)
18. Kubis, M.: Quantitative analysis of character networks in polish XIX and XX century novels. In: Digital Humanities 2019 Conference, Utrecht, The Netherlands (2019)
19. Bikel, D.M, Miller, S., Schwartz, R., Weischedel, R.: Nymble: a high-performance learning name-finder. In: Fifth Conference on Applied natural language processing, pp. 194–201. Association for Computational Linguistics (1997)
20. Nugumanova, A., Baiburin, Y., Apaev, K.: A new text representation model enriched with semantic relations. In: ICCAS 2015 – 2015 15th International Conference on Control, Automation and Systems, Proceedings (2015)
21. Nugumanova, A.B., Apayev, K.S., Baiburin, Y.M., Mansurova, M.Y.: A contrastive approach to term extraction: case-study for the information retrieval domain using BAWE corpus as an alternative collection. Eurasian J. Math. Comput. Appl. **5**, 73–86 (2017)
22. Asahara, M., Matsumoto, Y.: Japanese named entity extraction with redundant morphological analysis. In: 2003 Conference of the North American Chapter of the Association for Computational Linguistics on Human Language Technology, vol. 1, pp. 8–15. Association for Computational Linguistics (2003)
23. Hochreiter, S., Schmidhuber, J.: Long short-term memory. In: Neural Computation, pp. 1735–1780 (1997)
24. Chung, J., Gulcehre, C., Cho, K., Bengio, Y.: Empirical evaluation of gated recurrent neural networks on sequence modeling (2014)
25. Mikolov, T., Karafi, M., Burget, L., Cernock'y, J., Khudanpur, S.: Recurrent neural network based language model. In: Interspeech, vol. 2, p. 3 (2010)
26. Sundermeyer, M., Schl'uter, R., Ney, H.: LSTM neural networks for language modeling. In: Interspeech, pp. 194–197 (2012)
27. Bahdanau, D., Cho, K., Bengio, Y.: Neural machine translation by jointly learning to align and translate (2014)
28. Kalchbrenner, N., Blunsom, P.: Recurrent convolutional neural networks for discourse compositionality (2013)
29. Tran, Q., Zukerman, I., Haffari, G.: A hierarchical neural model for learning sequences of dialogue acts. In: 15th Conference of the European Chapter of the Association for Computational Linguistics, vol. 1, Long Papers, pp. 428–437. Association for Computational Linguistics, Valencia (2017)
30. Ma, X., Hovy, E.: End-to-end sequence labeling via bi-directional LSTM-CNNs-CRF (2016)
31. Lample, G., Ballesteros, M., Subramanian, S., Kawakami, K., Dyer, C.: Neural architectures for named entity recognition. In: 2016 Conference of the North American Chapter of the Association for Computational Linguistics: Human Language Technologies, pp. 260–270. Association for Computational Linguistics, San Diego (2016)
32. Collobert, R., Weston, J., Bottou, L., Karlen, M., Kavukcuoglu, K., Kuksa, P.: Natural language processing (almost) from scratch. Journal of Machine Learning Research **12**, 2493–2537 (2011)
33. Lample, G., Ballesteros, M., Subramanian, S., Kawakami, K., Dyer, C.: Neural Architectures for Named Entity Recognition. CoRR (2016)
34. Huang, Z., Xu, W., Yu, K.: Bidirectional LSTM-CRF models for sequence tagging (2015)
35. Jason, P.C., Nichols, E.: Named Entity Recognition with Bidirectional LSTM-CNNs (2016)
36. Rei, M., Crichton, G., Pyysalo, S.: Attending to characters in neural sequence labeling models. In: 26th International Conference on Computational Linguistics, pp. 309–318 (2016)
37. Pascanu, R., Mikolov, T., Bengio, Y.: On the difficulty oftraining recurrent neural networks (2012)

38. Lafferty, J., McCallum, A., Pereira, F.: Conditional random fields: probabilistic models for segmenting and labeling sequence data. In: 18th International Conference on Machine Learning, pp. 282–289 (2001)

39. Crammer, K., Dekel, O., Keshet, J., Shalev-Shwartz, S., Singer, Y.: Online passive-aggressive algorithms. J. Mach. Learn. Res. 7(Mar), 551–585 (2006)

40. Okazaki, N.: CRFsuite: a fast implementation of Conditional Random Fields (CRFs) (2007). http://www.chokkan.org/software/crfsuite/. Accessed 14 Feb 2020

41. Tjong, E.F., Sang, K., Meulder, F.D.: Introduction to the CoNLL-2003 shared task: language-independent named entity recognition. In: CoNLL-2003, Proceedings, Edmonton, Canada, pp. 142–147 (2003)

Creation of a Dependency Tree for Sentences in the Kazakh Language

Darkhan Akhmed-Zaki[1,2] ⓘ, Madina Mansurova[1](✉) ⓘ, Nurgali Kadyrbek[1],
Vladimir Barakhnin[3,4] ⓘ, and Armanbek Misebay[1]

[1] Al-Farabi Kazakh National University, Almaty, Kazakhstan
darhan_a@mail.ru, mansurova.madina@gmail.com,
nurgaliqadyrbek@gmail.com, armanbek128@mail.ru
[2] Astana IT University, Nur-Sultan, Kazakhstan
[3] Institute of Computational Technologies, Siberian Branch of the Russian
Academy of Sciences, Novosibirsk, Russian Federation
bar@ict.nsc.ru
[4] Novosibirsk State University, Novosibirsk, Russian Federation

Abstract. In the semantico-syntactic analysis of great importance is understanding of its formal structure. For this, in the text it is necessary to distinguish units of lexical meaning and designate the types of relations between them. The dependency tree is an indispensable tool for parsing sentences and determination of hierarchical relationships between the main components in it. In this work, an algorithm for constructing a dependency tree for sentences in the Kazakh language using the filter method is proposed. The dependency tree was created on the basis of the spinning tree from the oriented graph constructed according to the rules of syntactic relationship in the Kazakh language.

Keywords: Dependency tree · Dependency grammar · Corpus linguistics · Syntactic structure · Phrase structure rule

1 Introduction

When studying syntax which is an integral part of grammar, the main subject of research is the syntactical structure of the language. The syntactic structure is a set of system rules and laws of composing sentences. In its turn, a sentence is a single language unit organized according to grammatical rules in a particular language which is the main means of expressing thoughts, messages. Sentences are characterized by the following features: expressiveness, predicate relation, intonation consisting of separate words, word combinations [1–3]. In the research of the speech syntax in general linguistics, special attention is paid the sentence structure in the approach of a predicative construction which is a formal structure of a sentence. In this work, the authors consider the syntactical structure of a sentence for the description of which dependency trees were chosen as a basis. Let us consider this concept in more detail.

To present a formal structure in language, with a loose word order and case marking, a syntax of dependency trees is used [4]. A dependency tree is the most graphic and

© Springer Nature Switzerland AG 2020
N. T. Nguyen et al. (Eds.): ICCCI 2020, LNAI 12496, pp. 709–718, 2020.
https://doi.org/10.1007/978-3-030-63007-2_55

wide spread method of representing the syntactical structure of a sentence. Formalism of dependency trees presupposes construction of a graph of syntactic relationships between the words of a sentence. However, this graph, unlike the graph of a model tree of direct components, is not hierarchical [5]. The graph which serves as a basis for formalism of dependency trees must meet the following requirements: the graph has directed relationships between the sentence words - from the principal word to the dependent one; each word has only one parent; The graph does not contain cycles, syntax relations may be named termed but it is optional.

In this case, a sentence is presented as a linearly ordered set of elements (derivations forms) in which one can create an oriented tree with nodes from the elements of this set. Each rib connecting a pair of nodes indicates a subordinate relation between the main (subordinating) and dependent (subordinate) word corresponding to the direction of this rib.

Algorithms for creation of dependency trees are usually made up using the rules based on the strategy "it…,then…". These rules allow realizing a free logic concept mechanism, therefore they are widely used when representing knowledge in expert systems.

At present, two main methods of constructing a dependency tree based on the rules the method of fulcrums and the method of filters are used. The method of fulcrums [6] is used to search for the so-called fulcrums, i.e. the roots of syntax trees or some key supporting words according to the established rules. The filter method [7, 8] is based on the extraction of all possible phrases while applying the rules of syntactic relations after which a filter is used to the obtained structure (an oriented graph). It should be noted that the dependency tree like structures are a dispensable tool in solving the problems of syntactic analysts, machine translation, removal of homonymy, formal presentation of a speech construction [9–12]. The aim of this research is to develop an algorithm of building a dependency tree for sentences in the Kazakh language using the filter method. The dependency tree was created on the basis of the spinning tree from the oriented graph constructed according to the rules of syntactic relationships in the Kazakh language. This work is continuation of the authors investigations in the field of NLP for the Kazakh language [13, 14].

2 The Main Types of Syntactic Relationships of Words in Phrases for the Kazakh Language

According [15], there are 5 main types of syntactical connection of the words in the phrases in Kazakh language (see Fig. 1):

- *Kiyisu* – negotiation
- *Menggeru* – domination
- *Matasu* – subordination
- *Kabysu* – adjunction
- *Zhanasu* – convergence

Kiyisu (negotiation). In the Kazakh language, this type of connection is mostly used to connect subject and predicate. Kiyisu is the interconnection of subject and predicate

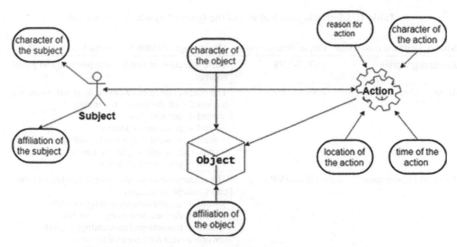

Fig. 1. Scheme of sentence and relations between the words.

in the level of person and plurality. In the word combination the subject initial and the predicative is narrative. Therefore, predicative would be the same form as subject. For example: *Men keldim, sen aittyn, biz erten baramyz.* The personal endings help words connect in the meaning of numeric meanings, and grammatical representation [16].

Mengeru (domination). Menggeru is the one of the main types of syntactical connection of the word phrases in which words are divided into initial and narrative. In this type of connection the form of the narrative depends on the ending of the initial word. But there is a big difference between kiyisu and menggeru. The interconnection of the initial word in the phrase with the narrative part in the level of case ending is menggeru. For example: *Kalammen zhazdy, dapterge zhazdy, kokzhiekten koterildi.* Narrative words with the case endings mostly are object or the object of preposition in the sentence.

Matasu (subordination). One of the forms of syntactic connection of words is matasu. It comes among the determined combinations of words, pronounced on 1 side (usually 3rd party) connection. For example: *Kunnin zhyluy, agamnyn balasy, ertennin isi.*

Kabysu (adjunction). The interconnection of the words in the phrase without any ending is called kabysu. Most conjugated words do not change the word order. A number of adjacent words change their place in the sentence and are removed from the words under which they obey. Such remote communication is subject to contact. It is not allowed to give other words between related combinations. At the same time, the syntactic relations of word combinations are changing. Adjacent phrases are words defined by the directory, worked out refined, supplemented. The first word, the connecting link, is the noun, the adjective, the demonstrative pronouns, the verbs, the adverbs, the adverbs of the verbs, the leader, and the second is the noun or verb. For example: Adal adam, zhauapty tulga, beibit el, aitylgan soz.

Zhanasu (convergence). The interconnection of the initial word and the narrative word without any ending despite its position in the sentence is called zhanasu. In this type of connection, the words can be objects of the preposition objects of the preposition. They are used in such samples below:

Table 1. Morphological features of the types of syntactic connection

Kind of syntactic connection	Phrase structure rules	Morphological features of syntactic connection
Kiyisu negotiation	<SP>–<VP>	The connection of words using personal and plural endings
Matasu subordination	<N>–<SP>	The connection of the word in the genitive case and the word with the possessive ending <word + genitive case> <word + possessive ending> <word > < word + possessive ending> <verb + participle + genitive case> <word + possessive ending>
Menggeru domination	<OP>–<VP>	The connection of words using the endings of the cases except the genitive <word + accusative case ending><verb> <word + dative case ending><verb> <word + instrumental case ending><verb> <word + locative case ending><verb> <word + nominative case ending><verb>
Kabysu adjunction	<ADJ>–<SP> <ADJ>–<OP>	The connection of words without any postpositions only due to word order. Usually no other words between them. <noun><noun> <adjective><noun> <numeral><noun> <locative><noun> <noun + dative case ending><participle> <noun + accusative/locative/nominative/ instrumental case ending><participle> <adverb><noun/adjective/numeral/pronoun>
Zhanasu convergence	<ADV>–<VP>	The connection of words without any postpositions. Basically, the combination of adverb and verb is formed by participation < adverb><verb> < participle><verb>

Here SP – subject predicative phrase structure, a description/qualification of the sub-ject. Adjectival or nominal;
OP – object predicative phrase structure, a description/qualification of the direct ob-ject. Adjectival or nominal;
VP – verb phrase structure;
N – noun; NUM – numeral; ADJ – adjective; ADV – adverb; CONN – conjunction; AUX – auxiliary verb.

- Objects of time adverbs.
- Objects with the case endings.
- Objects of preposition.

For example: *Biyl bitirdi, erten keledi, aptyga soiledi.*

At present, syntactic dependencies in word combinations for the Kazakh language are determined according to the main rules using phrase structure elements (Table 1) to describe a given languages syntax and are closely associated with the early stages of transformational grammar proposed by Noam Chomsky [17].

Phrasal structures of the Kazakh language can take the following forms:

```
<SP>::=<N>|<ADJ><SP>|<NUM><SP>|<N><SP>|<SP><CONN><SP>
<OP>::=<N>|<ADJ<OP>|<NUM><OP>|<OP><CONN><OP>
<VP>::=<VP>|<AUX><VP>|<ADV><VP>
```

3 Construction Dependency Trees for Simple Sentences of the Kazakh Language

The dependency grammar deals with taxanomic units. All relationships in the dependency grammar are considered subordinate. Analysis of syntactic relationships in word combinations and simple sentences in the Kazakh language is presented in [18]. The author notes that in the Kazakh language the arrangement of tokens in a sentence obeys a strict law.

The process of a dependency tree construction consists of several stages (see Fig. 2).

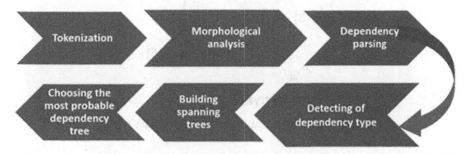

Fig. 2. The process of constructing a dependency tree.

For example: Korshiles turgyndar gimarattyn tobesinde ornalaskan agashtan zhasalgan kyzyl shatyry ortengenin anyktady. Figure 3 shows the dependency tree of this sentence, the vertices are tokens with their indices in the sentence.

A linear order of words in the tree is not reblected and one and the same tree may correspond to several orders. However, the ratio of syntactic dependencies and the order of words is not arbitrary. One to the property of sentences in a natural language- their projectivity was discovered [19]. A sentence is called projective if all dependency arrows are drawn on one side of the line on which the sentence is written and:

- none of the arrows crosses any other arrow,
- none of the arrows covers the root node (the principle of not projectivity is also preserved for the word order in phrases).

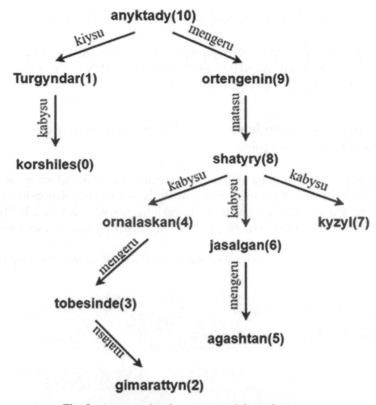

Fig. 3. An example of a constructed dependency tree.

Example 1.
Korshiles (0) turgyndar (1) gimarattyn (2) tobesinde (3) ornalaskan (4) agashtan (5) zhasalgan (6) kyzyl (7) shatyry (8) ortengenin (9) anyktady (10).
Phrase model of the sentence: <SP><OP><VP> (see Fig. 4).

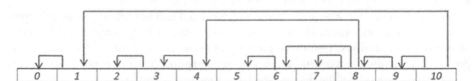

Fig. 4. Phrasal model of the sentence indicating the direction of syntactic connection for example 1.

Example 2.
Gimarattyn (0) tobesinde (1) ornalaskan (2) agashtan (3) zhasalgan (4) kyzyl(5) shatyry (6) ortengenin (7) korshiles (8) turgyndar (9) anyktady (10).
Phrase model of the sentence: <OP><SP><VP> (see Fig. 5).

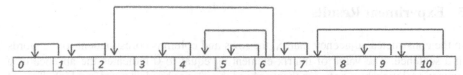

Fig. 5. Phrasal model of the sentence indicating the direction of syntactic connection for example 2.

The property of projectivity may be used in problems of automatic detection of syntactic relationships. It allows avoiding the detection of false relationships. Besides, the property of syntactic relationships. The conditions of projectivity and poor projectivity allow predicting the relationships between words or exclude impossible relationships [20].

There are two approaches to construction of a dependency tree: via building a spinning tree and using the formal model of Backus [21]. In the work, the approach of building a spinning tree was used.

4   The Algorithm of Building a Spinning Tree

The spinning tree is a tree covering all vertices of graph $G<V,E>$, where V – vertices of the graph a set of tokens in the sentence, E – ribs of the graph, and indicating the dependency between word combinations. The authors of [22] shows the method of obtaining the spinning tree from the oriented graph as well as obtaining several spinning trees from one graph. This multiplicity is due to the fact that the path to some vertices of the graph can be constructed in several ways.

The spinning tree algorithm [23]:

1) from graph G, we choose vertex u_1 which can become a tree forming an inner graph, for example, let us suppose that i = 1 (usually the main pair of word combinations forming the relationships is chosen);
2) if i = n(G), the found spinning tree. In the other case, we pass to step 3;
3) let us suppose that graph G_i covering vertices u_1, u_2, ... u_i is created which will be an inner graph of G where $1 \leq i \leq n-1$. Then adding a new vertex $u_{i+1} \in V$ adjacent to the vertex u_i of the graph G_i, create the graph G_{i+1}, thus adding an edge $\{u_{i+1}, u_i\}$. In addition, G_{i+1} is a tree, since the graph G_i did not cover the cycle. We perform i: = i + 1 and continue further, that is, go to step 2.

Dependency search rules:

1. Search for relationships kosymsha: identify all words adjacent to the prepositions;
2. To search for relations kiyisu: determine the root of the tree - the word at the beginning of the sentence, the verb;
3. Perform a kabysu relationship search;
4. Perform a matasu relationship search;
5. Perform a zhanasu relationship search.

5 Experiment Results

In the constructed adjacency matrix, the rows and columns corespondent to the words in a sentence. The value of matrix element a_{ij} equal to 0 indicates the absence of a syntactic relationships between the word and the ith word and j^{th} word in which i^{th} word a principal. The value of matrix element a_{ij} which is not equal to 0 indicates the fact that the ith word is principal in the syntactic relationships with the jth word and the value of a_{ij}, indicates the type of relationships (see Fig. 6):

$$
A = \begin{matrix}
0\,0\,0\,0\,0\,0\,0\,0\,0\,0 \\
5\,0\,0\,0\,0\,0\,0\,0\,0\,1 \\
0\,0\,0\,0\,0\,0\,0\,0\,0\,0 \\
0\,0\,3\,0\,0\,0\,0\,0\,0\,0 \\
0\,0\,0\,2\,0\,0\,0\,0\,0\,0 \\
0\,0\,0\,0\,5\,0\,0\,0\,0\,0 \\
0\,0\,0\,2\,0\,2\,0\,0\,0\,0 \\
0\,0\,0\,0\,0\,0\,0\,0\,0\,0 \\
0\,0\,0\,0\,0\,0\,5\,3\,0\,0\,0 \\
0\,0\,0\,0\,0\,2\,0\,0\,2\,0\,0 \\
0\,0\,0\,0\,0\,0\,0\,0\,2\,0 \\
\end{matrix}
\qquad
\begin{matrix}
1-\text{kiysu} \\
2-\text{mengeru} \\
3-\text{matasu} \\
4-\text{zhanasu} \\
5-\text{kabysu} \\
6-\text{kosymsha}
\end{matrix}
$$

Fig. 6. Adjacency matrix (on the left), types of syntactic connections (on the right).

The analyzer returns 4 types of spanning tree for the considered example 1 (see Fig. 7):

1) the graph is:	2) the graph is:	3) the graph is:	4) the graph is:
vertex 0 : []	vertex 0 : []	vertex 0 : []	vertex 0 : []
vertex 1 : [10, 0]	vertex 1 : [10, 0]	vertex 1 : [10, 0]	vertex 1 : [10, 0]
vertex 2 : []	vertex 2 : []	vertex 2 : []	vertex 2 : []
vertex 3 : [2]	vertex 3 : [2]	vertex 3 : [2]	vertex 3 : [2]
vertex 4 : [3]	vertex 4 : [3]	vertex 4 : []	vertex 4 : []
vertex 5 : []	vertex 5 : []	vertex 5 : []	vertex 5 : []
vertex 6 : [5]	vertex 6 : []	vertex 6 : [5, 3]	vertex 6 : [3]
vertex 7 : []	vertex 7 : []	vertex 7 : []	vertex 7 : []
vertex 8 : [4, 6, 7]	vertex 8 : [4, 6, 7]	vertex 8 : [4, 6, 7]	vertex 8 : [4, 6, 7]
vertex 9 : [8]	vertex 9 : [8, 5]	vertex 9 : [8]	vertex 9 : [8, 5]
vertex 10 : [9]	vertex 10 : [9]	vertex 10 : [9]	vertex 10 : [9]

Fig. 7. Spanning trees generated for example 1.

Variant 1 correspondents to the expected results: coincidence – 100%, variant2: coincidence – 90%, variant 3: coincidence – 90%, variant 4: coincidence – 80%. The shortcoming at the given moment in the system of presentation of syntactic structures in the form of a dependency tree are:

1. a strict requirement to consider each token (parenthesis, isolated part of a sentence, idioms) as a separate element of a sentence. The cases of automatic representation of relationships between the following components of a sentence: idioms, parentheses, verbose expressions are not considered. For example: *Adam balasy garyshka zhyyrmasynshy gasyrda ayak basti.*
2. all relation in word combinations are considered as subordinate.

6 Conclusion

The work presents an algorithm for construction a dependency tree for sentences in the Kazakh language using the filter method and the dependency tree is created on the basis of the spinning tree from the oriented graph built according to the rules of syntactic relationships in the Kazakh language. Dependency trees are an indispensable tool in solution of the problems of syntactic analysis, machine translation, removal of homonymy, formal representation of a speech construction. The authors will go on with the investigations in this field including the task of detecting parenthetical words, isolated parts of a sentence, idioms.

Acknowledgements. This work was supported in part under grant of Foundation of Ministry of Education and Science of the Republic of Kazakhstan BR05236340 – «Creation of high-performance intelligent technologies for analysis and decision making for the "logistics-agglomeration" system in the framework of the digital economy of the Republic of Kazakhstan» (2018-2020).

References

1. Chomsky, N.: Aspects of the Theory of Syntax. The MIT Press, Cambridge (1965)
2. Chomsky, N.: Some Concepts and Consequences of the Theory of Government and Binding. MIT Press, Cambridge (1982)
3. Belletti, A.: Structures and Beyond: The Cartography of Syntactic Structures, vol. 3. Oxford University Press, Oxford (2004)
4. Mel'čuk, I.: Dependency Syntax: Theory and Practice. State University of New York Press, New York (1988)
5. Carnie, A.: Syntax: A Generative Introduction. Blackwell Publishing, Malden (2007)
6. McNamara, T.: Applied linguistics: the challenge of theory. Appl. Linguist. **36**(4), 466–477 (2015)
7. Leserf, I.: Application of the program and model of a specific situation to automatic syntactic analysis. NTI, no. 11, pp. S. 42–50. VINITI, Moscow (1963)
8. Fundel, K., Küffner, R., Zimmer, R.: RelEx – relation extraction using dependency parse trees. Bioinformatics **23**(3), 365–371 (2007)
9. Baiburin, Y., Zhantassova, Z., Nugumanova, A., Syzdykpayeva, A., Bessmertny, I.: The case study approach to learning Text Mining. In: AICT 2016 - Conference Proceedings on Application of Information and Communication Technologies (2016)
10. Nugumanova, A., Baiburin, Y., Apaev, K.: A new text representation model enriched with semantic relations. In: ICCAS 2015 – 2015 15th International Conference on Control, Automation and Systems, Proceedings (2015)

11. Mansurova, M., Barakhnin, V., Khibatkhanuly, Y., Pastushkov, I.: Named entity extraction from semi-structured data using machine learning algorithms. In: Nguyen, N.T., Chbeir, R., Exposito, E., Aniorté, P., Trawiński, B. (eds.) ICCCI 2019. LNCS (LNAI), vol. 11684, pp. 58–69. Springer, Cham (2019). https://doi.org/10.1007/978-3-030-28374-2_6
12. Nugumanova, A.B., Apayev, K.S., Baiburin, Y.M., Mansurova, M.Y.: A contrastive approach to term extraction: Case-study for the information retrieval domain using BAWE corpus as an alternative collection. Eurasian J. Math. Comput. Appl. (2017)
13. Alimzhanov, Y., Mansurova, M.: An approach of automatic extraction of domain keywords from the kazakh text. In: Nguyen, N.-T., Manolopoulos, Y., Iliadis, L., Trawiński, B. (eds.) ICCCI 2016. LNCS (LNAI), vol. 9876, pp. 555–562. Springer, Cham (2016). https://doi.org/10.1007/978-3-319-45246-3_53
14. Mansurova, M., Madiyeva, G., Aubakirov, S., Yermekov, Z., Alimzhanov, Y.: Design and development of media-corpus of the kazakh language. In: Nguyen, N.T., Papadopoulos, G.A., Jędrzejowicz, P., Trawiński, B., Vossen, G. (eds.) ICCCI 2017. LNCS (LNAI), vol. 10449, pp. 509–518. Springer, Cham (2017). https://doi.org/10.1007/978-3-319-67077-5_49
15. Ashirova, A.T.: Approaches of word combinations and connection forms. In: Proceedings of International scientific-methodical online conference «Modern Kazakh language in the conditions of competitiveness of civilization: research paradigms and mobile technologies of teaching» dedicated to the 80th anniversary of the Doctor of Philological Sciences, Professor Talgat Sairambaev Almaty, 28–29 April 2017 (2017)
16. Grammar, K.: Phonetics. Wordable Word. Morphology. Syntax.In: Zhanpeisov, O.E. (ed.) Astana, p. 784 (2002)
17. Chomsky, N.: Syntactic Structures. Mouton, The Hague/Paris (1957)
18. Sairanbaev, T.: Problems of Kazakh linguistics. Almaty, Abzal ay, p. 640 (2014)
19. Testelets, Y.G.: Introduction to General Syntax. Russian State University for the Humanities (2001)
20. Batura, T.V.: Mathematical linguistics and automatic word processing: textbook. In: Batura, T.V. (ed.) Novosib. RIC NSU, state un-t - Novosibirsk, p. 166 (2016)
21. Mehler, A., Lücking, A., Banisch, S., Blanchard, P., Job, B. (eds.): Towards a Theoretical Framework for Analyzing Complex Linguistic Networks. Springer-Verlag, Heidelberg (2016). https://doi.org/10.1007/978-3-662-47238-5
22. Uno, T.: An algorithm for enumerating all directed spanning trees in a directed graph. In: ISAAC'96: Proceedings of the 7th International Symposium on Algorithms and Computation, pp. 166–173 (1996)
23. Chakraborty, M., Chowdhury, S., Chakraborty, J., Mehera, R., Pal, R.K.: Algorithms for generating all possible spanning trees of a simple undirected connected graph: an extensive review. Complex Intell. Syst. **5**(3), 265–281 (2019)

Approach to Extract Keywords and Keyphrases of Text Resources and Documents in the Kazakh Language

Diana Rakhimova$^{(\boxtimes)}$ and Aliya Turganbayeva ⓘ

Al-Farabi Kazakh National University, Almaty, Kazakhstan
di.diva@mail.ru, turganbaeva.aliya@bk.ru

Abstract. In this paper authors propose a hybrid approach for extracting keywords and keyphrases of text resources and documents in Kazakh. Direct application of the statistical method tf-idf is not the optimal solution to the question of extracting keywords and phrases in the Kazakh language, since the Kazakh language is an agglutinative type of language. The authors developed and used the stemming algorithm in the pre-processing process taking into account the grammatical features of the Kazakh language. In the extraction, we also take into account the syntactic feature of the words or phrases using the morphological analyzer of the Kazakh language. During extraction, the restrictions indicated by the authors are observed as well, as not all words may be key words. When choosing keywords or a phrase, their features are considered (for example, some words that are a numeral name in combination with a noun are selected). The extraction of keywords and phrases specifically for the Kazakh language is an urgent task in classification, clustering, abstracting the text, and searching the information. The results of the research indicate that the presented approach is the best solution on extracting keywords and phrases from texts in the Kazakh language.

Keywords: Keyword extraction · TF-IDF · Lemmatization · Kazakh language

1 Introduction

Currently, the volumes and dynamics of information that is to be processed in lexicography and information retrieval make the task of automatically extracting keywords and keyphrases that can be used to create and develop terminological resources, as well as for efficient processing of documents: indexing, summarizing, clustering and classifying.

The analysis of a huge amount of data can be simplified if we have keywords or keyphrases that can provide us with the basic characteristics, concept, etc. of a document. The relevant keywords and keyphrases can serve as a summary of the document and help us easily organize documents and extract them based on their contents [1]. It is necessary to distinguish two main approaches to solving the problem of automating the selection of keywords and keyphrases: the assignment of keywords and keyphrases and their extraction [2, 3]. The main difference is that the first approach allows to select only

© Springer Nature Switzerland AG 2020
N. T. Nguyen et al. (Eds.): ICCCI 2020, LNAI 12496, pp. 719–729, 2020.
https://doi.org/10.1007/978-3-030-63007-2_56

those keywords and keyphrases that are contained in some provided dictionary, and the second approach involves the selection of key information directly from the text.

Keywords can be assigned manually or automatically, but the first approach is very time-consuming and expensive. Thus, there is a need for an automated process that extracts keywords from documents. There are ready-made software solutions to this problem for common languages (English, Russian, Spanish, etc.), and for the Kazakh language there are only a few and they are not in open access.

2 Researching of Keyword Extraction Approaches

Keyword assignment methods can be divided into two categories: (1) keyword assignment and (2) keyword extraction [4]. Both revolve around the same problem - choosing the best keyword. The words found in the document are analyzed to identify the most representative words, usually exploring the properties of the source (that is, frequency, length) [5]. Existing methods for automatically extracting keywords at the suggestion of Ping-I and Shi-Jen can be divided into [6]: statistical approaches and machine learning approaches.

It is also necessary to focus on four categories proposed by the author of Zahang et al. In [5]: 1) simple statistical approaches; 2) linguistic approaches; 3) machine learning approaches; 4) other approaches.

Simple statistical approaches include simple methods that do not require training data. In addition, the methods are language and domain independent. Word statistics from a document can be used to identify keywords: n-gram statistics, word frequency, TF-IDF, PAT tree (Patricia tree; suffix tree or position tree), etc. The disadvantage is that in some professional texts, such as health and medicine, the most important keywords can appear only once in an article. The use of statistically authorized models may inadvertently filter out these words [6].

The paper [7] proposes a method for evaluating terminology based on the contrast approach. The method takes as a basis the well-known TF-IDF word-weighting formula. According to this formula, the higher the word weight in a document, the higher the frequency of the use of a word in the document is, and the lower its scatter throughout the collection. In the new version of the formula, which the author calls "term frequency - inverse domain frequency", the word weight is estimated not in the document, but in the target collection. According to the new formula, the higher the weight of the word, the higher the relative frequency of its use in the target collection and the lower its relative spread across all collections:

$$TF * IDF = TF(t, D) * IDF(t) = \frac{n_{t,D}}{\sum_k n_{k,D}} * \log\left(\frac{|TS|}{|\{d : t \in d\}|}\right) \tag{1}$$

where $n_{t,D}$ is the number of occurrences of the word t in the target collection D, $\sum_k n_{k,D}$ is the sum of the occurrences of all words in the target collection D, $|TS|$ is the number of documents in all used collections, $|\{d : t \in d\}|$ is the number of all documents that include the word t at least once. Thus, the authors consider in terms all words with a high concentration within a narrow subset of documents.

The authors [8] also propose to evaluate the terminology of words based on the formula TF-IDF. They call their own version of this formula the contrastive weight and define it as a measure, which is higher, the higher the frequency of use of the word in the target collection is and the lower the relative frequency of its use in contrast collections:

$$Contrastive\ Weight = TF(t, D) * IDF(t) = loglog\left(f_t^D\right) * \log\left(\frac{F_{JC}}{\sum_j f_t^i}\right) \qquad (2)$$

where f_t^D is the frequency of the word in the target collection, $\sum_j f_t^j$ is the sum of the frequencies of all uses of the word in contrast collections, $F_{TC} = \sum_{i,j} f_i^j$ is the sum of the frequency of use of all words in all collections, including the target. As the authors themselves note, the contrasting weight assesses the terminology of words much better than the pure frequencies, however, the overall effectiveness of the method, determined using the F-measure, according to them, is not striking.

In paper [9] also develops the idea of fines and rewards inherent in the basic construction of the TF-IDF formula, and proposes a new version of this formula, which called "term frequency - disjoint corpora frequency". As a reward, the absolute frequency of word use in the target collection is used, and as a fine, the product of the absolute frequency of word use in contrast collections is used:

$$TF * DCF = \frac{f_t^D}{\prod_{g \in G} 1 + \log\left(1 + f_t^g\right)} \qquad (3)$$

where f_t^D and f_t^g is the frequency of use of the word t in the target and contrast collections, respectively, G is the set of all contrast collections.

Linguistic approaches use the linguistic feature of words mainly, sentences and documents. Lexical, syntactic, semantic and discursive analysis are some of the most common, but complex analyzes.

Machine learning approaches consider supervised or unsupervised learning with examples, but the related work of extracting keywords prefers a supervised approach. Controlled machine learning approaches create a model that learns based on a set of keywords. They require manual annotation in the training dataset, which is extremely tedious and inconsistent (sometimes asks for a predefined taxonomy). Unfortunately, authors usually assign keywords to their documents only when they are forced to do so. Thus, the induced model is used to extract keywords from a new document. This approach includes the naive Bayes method, SVM, C4.5, Bagging, etc. Thus, methods require training data and often depend on the subject area. The system needs to re-examine and install the model every time a domain changes [10, 11]. Induction of the model can be very complex and time consuming for massive data sets.

Other keyword extraction approaches generally combine all the methods mentioned above. In addition, they sometimes include heuristic knowledge such as position, length, layout features of terms, HTML and similar tags, text formatting for combining.

The vector space model (VSP) is well known and the most used model for representing text in text mining approaches [12, 13]. In particular, documents presented in the form of feature vectors are located in multidimensional Euclidean space. This model is suitable for capturing the frequency of simple words, but structural and semantic information is not usually taken into account. Therefore, the vector space model has several drawbacks because of its simplicity [14]: 1) the meaning of the text and structure cannot be expressed, 2) each word is independent of the other, the sequence of occurrence of words or other relationships are not required, 3) if two documents have the same meaning but different words, the similarity cannot be easily calculated.

The graph-based textual representation is known as one of the best solutions to solve these issues effectively [14]. The graph is a mathematical model that allows to explore relationships and structural information efficiently. The taxonomy of the basic methods for extracting keywords is presented in a hierarchical form in Fig. 1 and 2. Figure 1 presents the classic classification of keyword extraction, where the methods are divided into supervised, semi-supervised, unsupervised. Figure 2 shows graph-based analysis methods where different types of computation can be performed to rank the vertices or to measure the topological properties of the graph.

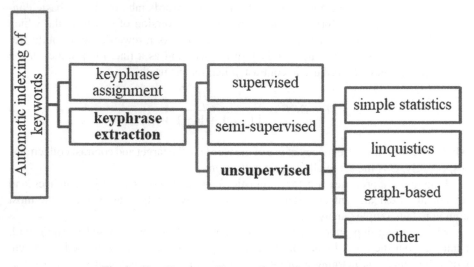

Fig. 1. Classification of keyword extraction methods [3]

The boundary relationship between the two terms can be established on many principles, using a different area of the text or relationship to construct the graph [14, 15]: 1) words found together in a sentence, paragraph, section or document added to the graph in the form of a click; 2) intersecting words from a sentence, paragraph, section or document; 3) words found in a fixed window in the text; 4) semantic relations - connecting words that have the same meaning, words written the same but with different meanings, synonyms, antonyms, etc.

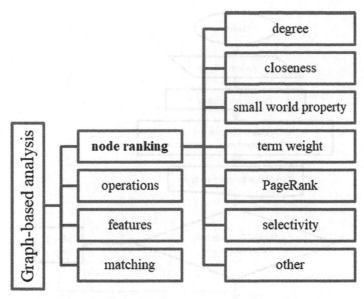

Fig. 2. Classification of methods based on the graph [3]

3   An Algorithm for Extracting Keywords Based on Linguistic and Statistical Data

The algorithm in Fig. 3, 4 of extracting keywords from documents in the Kazakh language includes 3 stages: 1. finding candidates for keywords; 2. selection of signs; 3. ranking.

At the first stage, 2 tasks are solved: preliminary word processing; and the division of the text into separate words and keyphrases.

The first task is language-dependent, therefore, the Kazakh language morphological feature is taken into account here. To solve this problem, a system of complete endings of the Kazakh language is used (through the morphological analyzer of the Kazakh language developed on the platform Apertium, we perform markup of the document), the algorithm for stemming and lemmatization for the Kazakh language (implemented in the Python3 programming language). Then, a simple approach was used - the tokenization procedure, which helps to divide the whole text into separate words.

At the second stage, each candidate for keywords is distinguished by features which help to assess the degree of its importance. The distinguished features can be divided into 3 categories: syntactic, statistical and structural features.

To highlight the syntactic features, we used a morphological analysis of the Kazakh language. And the TF-IDF (Term Frequency - Inverse Document Frequency) algorithm for determining the frequency, that is, to highlight statistical features. In the program for the bigram word, the following features were indicated: noun + noun (N + N), adjective + noun (Adj + N), noun + verb (N + V), noun + noun (Np + N), numeral + noun (just some words) (Num + SomeWordsOfTime).

At the third stage, we rank the results according to a statistical feature and the text volume to appropriate extent.

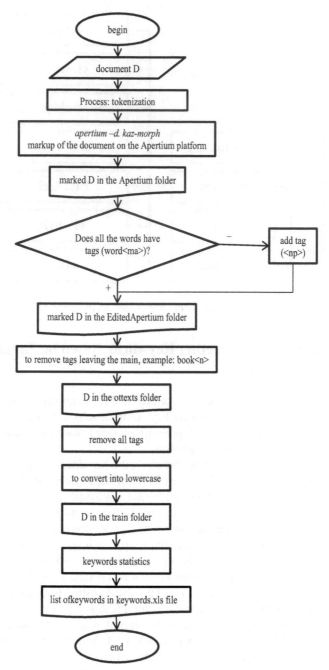

Fig. 3. The block diagram of the algorithm for extracting keywords from documents in the Kazakh language

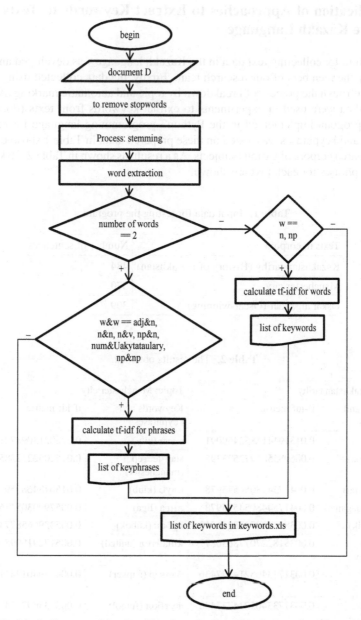

Fig. 4. The block diagram of the algorithm for calculating the keyword metric and keyphrase

4 Application of Approaches to Extract Keywords to Texts in the Kazakh Language

An algorithm for collecting text data in the Kazakh language was developed and implemented by the members of our research team. Firstly, the data collected using this tool first went through the process of breakdown by topic and automatic marking. And these prepared data were used in experiments to extract keywords from texts (documents), that is, a program implemented in the Python3 programming language for extracting keywords and keyphrases was tested on these prepared data. In Table 1 showed one part of the prepared corpora of various subjects. As a result, as shown in Table 2, 10 keywords and 5 key phrases for each text are shown.

Table 1. Input data for testing the program.

Texts in corpora	Number of sentences
Kazakhstan tarihy (History of Kazakhstan)	484
Manchester city	370
Oskar algandar (Oscar-winning)	309

Table 2. The results obtained.

Topic: Kazakhstan tarihy		Topic: Manchester city	
Keywords and keyphrases	tf-idf metric	Keywords and keyphrases	tf-idf metric
ғұн (gun)	0.013194415852460091	сити (city)	0.02602130987211911
тайпа (taipa)	0.006085581972523395	манчестер (manchester)	0.01520522323852743
қытай (qytai)	0.004175448054575978	клуб (klub)	0.015048468359779727
қағанат (qaganat)	0.004175448054575978	лига (liga)	0.005799930513665103
тырік (turik)	0.0038034887328271213	кубок (kubok)	0.0053296658774219866
мемлекет (memleket)	0.0035182270778650877	юнайтед (united)	0.005172910998674281
кылтегін (kultegin)	0.0031733405214777436	бапкер (bapker)	0.0048594012411788704
тоныкөк (tonykok)	0.0031733405214777436	футбол (futbol)	0.00313509757495411
ескерткіш (eskertkish)	0.002672286754928626	маусым (mausym)	0.0029450594945452436
жорық (zhoryq)	0.002672286754928626	ойыншы (oiynshy)	0.002855815267437812
тырік қағанат (turik qaganat)	0.0033403584436607825	манчестер сити (manchester city)	0.009405292724862329

(*continued*)

Table 2. (*continued*)

Topic: Kazakhstan tarihy		Topic: Manchester city	
Keywords and keyphrases	tf-idf metric	Keywords and keyphrases	tf-idf metric
ғұн мемлекет (gun memleket)	0.002839304677111665	манчестер юнайтед (Manchester united)	0.0047026463624311645
қола дәуір (qola dauir)	0.001336143377464313	есеп жең (esep zheng)	0.0029783426962064043
қазақстан жер (qazakhstan zher)	0.0011691254552812739	есеп жеңіл (esep zengil)	0.0021945683024678767
тас дәуір (tas dauir)	0.0010021075330982347	роберто манчини (roberto manchini)	0.0020378134237201712

The obtained experimental results were performed on the corpora shown in Table 3. And the results were analyzed taking into account the boundary coefficient of the find by volume and it was revealed that the keywords and phrases were selected correctly. The results of the analysis are shown in Table 4.

Table 3. The volume of corpora by topic.

Topics	Number of sentences
Geography	99 659
Space	12 658
Computer science	26 886
Psychology	20 940
Sport	482
History	37 574
Equipment	708

Table 4. Experimental results of the developed algorithm for determining keywords for the Kazakh language.

Document's name	The volume of the document (sentences)	Boundary coefficient of keywords	Number of keywords	Accuracy of finding
futbol.txt	58	3–8	8	85,71%
boks.txt	59	3–8	8	75%
Samsung.txt	67	3–8	8	87,5
7tarihitulga.txt	75	3–8	8	100%
LG.txt	97	9–11	10	90%
ginnes.txt	103	9–11	10	80%
imidj.txt	122	12–14	12	50%
2018biznesmen.txt	152	12–14	12	58,33%
oskaralganjuldyzdar.txt	309	15–17	15	93,33%
GenriFord.txt	343	15–17	15	93,33%
ttrening	366	15–17	15	86,67%
manchestercity.txt	370	15–17	15	86,67%
BilGeits.txt	452	15–17	15	100%
Kazakhstantarihy.txt	484	15–17	15	100%
AppleInc.txt	531	15–17	15	100%
geoinformatika.txt	821	15–17	15	100%

5 Conclusion and Future Work

According to the results of scientific research work, the following results were obtained:

– Methods and modern approaches to extracting keywords and semantic analysis of texts are investigated;
– The modified approach has been developed for extracting keywords and keyphrases, which will be applied to solve the problem of abstracting texts in the Kazakh language;
– The developed approaches and algorithms were applied for processing texts in the Kazakh language.

Our approach to extracting keywords and phrases is suitable for low resource language processing and is flexible in terms of data volume. According to the results of the experiment, you can see that the keywords and phrases are precisely selected.

In the future, the authors plan to develop the method using machine learning technology. The training data which is necessary to complete this task will be collected using the presented method of extracting keywords and marking them up. The method also finds its continuation in the problem of summarizing text.

Acknowledgments. The study was supported by the Ministry of Education and Science of the Republic of Kazakhstan within the framework of the AP05132950 and AP08052421 scientific projects.

References

1. Sheremeteva, S.O., Osminin, P.G.: Methods and models for automatic keyword extraction (resource language – Russian). Bull. South Ural State Univ. 1(12), 76–81 (2015)
2. Effective Approaches for Extraction of Keywords. http://www.ijcsi.org/papers/7-6-144-148.pdf. Accessed 25 July 2019
3. Keyword extraction a review of methods and approaches. http://langnet.uniri.hr/papers/beliga/Beliga_KeywordExtraction_a_review_of_methods_and_approaches.pdf. Accessed 05 July 2019
4. Keyword extraction. https://en.wikipedia.org/wiki/Keyword_extraction. Accessed 16 June 2019
5. Zahang, C., Wang, H., Liu, Y., Wu, D., Liao, Y., Wang, B.: Automatic keyword extraction from documents using conditional random fields. J. CIS **4**(3), 1169–1180 (2008)
6. Chen, P., Lin, S.: Automatic keyword prediction using Google similarity distance. Expert Syst. Appl. **37**(3), 1928–1938 (2010)
7. Kim, S.N., Baldwin, T., Kan, M.-Y.: An unsupervised approach to domain-specific term extraction. In: Proceedings of the Australasian Language Technology Association Workshop, pp. 94–98 (2009)
8. Ngomo, N.A.-C., Křemen, P.: Knowledge engineering and semantic web. In: Proceedings of the 7th International Conference, KESW 2016, Prague, Czech Republic, pp. 104–109 (2016)
9. Lopes, L., Fernandes, P., Vieira, R.: Estimating term domain relevance through term frequency, disjoint corpora frequency-tf-dcf. Knowl.-Based Syst. **97**, 156–187 (2016)
10. Siddiqi, S., Sharan, A.: Keyword and keyphrase extraction techniques: a literature review. Int. J. Comput. Appl. **109**(2), 18–23 (2015)
11. Jean-Louis, L., Gagnon, M., Charton, E.: A knowledge-base oriented approach for automatic keyword extraction. Computacion y Sistemas **17**(2), 187–196 (2013)
12. Zhao, Y., Shi, X.: The application of vector space model in the information retrieval system. In: Zhang, W. (ed.) Software Engineering and Knowledge Engineering: Theory and Practice, Advances in Intelligent and Soft Computing, vol. 162, pp. 43–49. Springer, Heidelberg (2012). https://doi.org/10.1007/978-3-642-29455-6_6
13. Hanumanthappa, M., Narayana, Swamy M., Jyothi, N.M.: Automatic keyword extraction from dravidian language. Int. J. Innov. Sci. Eng. Technol. **1**(8), 87–92 (2014)
14. Sonawane, S.S., Kulkarni, P.A.: Graph based representation and analysis of text document: a survey of techniques. Int. J. Comput. Appl. **96**(19), 1–8 (2014)
15. Mihalcea, R., Radev, D.: Graph-Based Natural Language Processing and Information Retrieval, 1st edn, p. 202. Cambridge University Press, Cambridge (2011)

UIT-ViIC: A Dataset for the First Evaluation on Vietnamese Image Captioning

Quan Hoang Lam[1,2(✉)], Quang Duy Le[1,2], Van Kiet Nguyen[1,2],
and Ngan Luu-Thuy Nguyen[1,2]

[1] University of Information Technology, Ho Chi Minh City, Vietnam
{15520673,15520687}@gm.uit.edu.vn, {kietnv,ngannlt}@uit.edu.vn
[2] Vietnam National University, Ho Chi Minh City, Vietnam

Abstract. Image Captioning (IC), the task of automatic generation of image captions, has attracted attentions from researchers in many fields of computer science, being computer vision, natural language processing and machine learning in recent years. This paper contributes to research on Image Captioning task in terms of extending dataset to a different language - Vietnamese. So far, there has been no existed Image Captioning dataset for Vietnamese language, so this is the foremost fundamental step for developing Vietnamese Image Captioning. In this scope, we first built a dataset which contains manually written captions for images from Microsoft COCO dataset relating to sports played with balls, we called this dataset UIT-ViIC (University Of Information Technology - Vietnamese Image Captions). UIT-ViIC consists of 19,250 Vietnamese captions for 3,850 images. Following that, we evaluated our dataset on deep neural network models and did comparisons with English dataset and two Vietnamese datasets built by different methods. UIT-ViIC is published on our lab website (https://sites.google.com/uit.edu.vn/uit-nlp/) for research purposes.

Keywords: Image Captioning · Vietnamese · Deep neural network

1 Introduction

Generating descriptions for multimedia contents such as images and videos, so called Image Captioning, is helpful for e-commerce companies or news agencies. For instance, in e-commerce field, people will no longer need to put much effort into understanding and describing products' images on their websites because image contents can be recognized and descriptions are automatically generated. Inspired by Horus[1], Image Captioning system can also be integrated into a wearable device, which is able to capture surrounding images and generate descriptions as sound in real time to guide people with visually impaired.

---

[1] https://italianinnovationday.weebly.com/horus-technology.html.

© Springer Nature Switzerland AG 2020
N. T. Nguyen et al. (Eds.): ICCCI 2020, LNAI 12496, pp. 730–742, 2020.
https://doi.org/10.1007/978-3-030-63007-2_57

Image Captioning has attracted attentions from researchers in recent years [6,17,18], and there has been promising attempts dealing with language barrier in this task by extending existed dataset captions into different languages [7,18].

In this study, generating image captions in Vietnamese language is put into consideration. One straightforward approach for this task is to translate English captions into Vietnamese by human or by using machine translation tool, Google Translation. With the method of translating directly from English to Vietnamese, we found that the descriptions are sometimes confusing and unnatural to native people. Moreover, image understandings are cultural dependent, as in Western, people usually have different ways to grasp images and different vocabulary choices for describing contexts. For instance, in Fig. 1, one MS-COCO English caption introduced about "a baseball player in motion of pitching", which made sense and captured accurately the main activity in the image. Though it sounds sensible in English, the sentence became less meaningful when we tried to translate it into Vietnamese. One attempt of translating the sentence was performed by Google Translation, and the result was not as expected.

COCO: baseball player in motion picthing at a game
Google Translated: cầu thủ bóng chày trong chuyển động ném bóng trong một trò chơi

Fig. 1. Example of MS-COCO English caption compared with Google translated one

Therefore, we came up with the approach of constructing a Vietnamese Image Captioning dataset with descriptions written manually by human. Composed by Vietnamese people, the sentences would be more natural and friendlier to Vietnamese users. The main resources we used from MS-COCO for our dataset are images. Besides, we considered having our dataset focus on ball sports category due to several reasons:

- By concentrating on a specific domain we are more likely to improve performance of the Image Captioning models. We expected our dataset can be used to confirm or reject this hypothesis.
- ball sports Image Captioning can be used in certain sport applications, such as supporting journalists describing great amount of images for their articles.

Our primary contributions of this paper are as follows:

- Firstly, we introduce UIT-ViIC, the first Vietnamese dataset extending MS-COCO with manually written captions for Image Captioning. UIT-ViIC is published for research purposes.
- Secondly, we introduce our annotation tool for dataset construction, which is also published to help annotators conveniently create captions.
- Finally, we describe our experiments to evaluate state-of-the-art models (evaluated on English dataset) on UIT-ViIC dataset, and the analysis of performance results to have insights into our corpus.

The structure of the paper is organized as follows. Related documents and studies are presented in Sect. 2. UIT-ViIC dataset creation is described in Sect. 3. Section 4 introduces briefly the models we did experiment on. The experimental results and analysis are presented in Sect. 5. Conclusion and future work are deduced in Sect. 6.

2   Related Works

We summarized in Table 1 an incomplete list of published Image Captioning datasets, in English and in other languages. Several image caption datasets for English have been constructed, the representative examples are Flickr3k [5,12]; Flickr 30k [19]—an extending of Flickr3k and Microsoft COCO (Microsoft Common in Objects in Context) [9].

Besides, several image datasets with non-English captions have been developed. Depending on their applications, the target languages of these datasets vary, including German and French for image retrieval, Japanese for cross-lingual document retrieval [3] and image captioning [10,18], Chinese for image tagging, captioning and retrieval [7]. Each of these datasets was built on top of an existing English dataset, with MS-COCO as the most popular choice.

Our dataset UIT-ViIC was constructed using images from Microsoft COCO (MS-COCO). MS-COCO dataset includes more than 150,000 images, divided into three distributions: train, vailidate, test. For each image, five captions were provided independently by Amazon's Mechanical Turk. MS-COCO has been the most popular dataset for Image Captioning thanks to the MS-COCO challenge (2015) and it has a powerful evaluation server for candidates.

Regarding to the Vietnamese language processing, there were quite a number of research works on other tasks such as word segmentation, part-of-speech, named entity recognition, parsing, sentiment analysis, question answering. However, to the extent of our knowledge, there have been no research publications on

Table 1. Published english and other languages image captioning datasets.

Dataset	Release	Data source	Languages	Images	Sentences	Application
IAPR TC-12	2006	Internet	English/German	20,000	100,000	Image retrieval
Pascal sentences	2015	Pascal sentences	Japanese/English	1,000	5,000	Cross-lingual document retrieval
YJ Captions	2016	MS-COCO	Japanese/English	26,500	131,470	Image Captioning
MIC test data	2016	MS-COCO	French/German/ English	1,000	5,000	Image retrieval
Bilingual caption	2016	MS-COCO	German/English	1,000	1,000	Machine translation - Image Captioning
Multi30k	2016	Flickr30k	German/English	21,014	186,084	Machine translation - Image Captioning
Flickr8k-CN	2016	Flickr8k	Chinese/English	8,000	45,000	Image Captioning
AIC-ICC	2017	Internet	Chinese	240,000	1,200,000	Image Captioning
Flickr30k-CN	2017	Flickr30k	Chinese/English	1,000	5,000	Image Captioning
STAIR Captions	2017	MS-COCO	Japanese/English	164,062	820,310	Image Captioning
COCO-CN	2018	MS-COCO	Chinese/English	20,342	27,128	Image tagging - captioning - retrieval
COCO 4K	N/A	MS-COCO	Vietnamese/ English	4,000	20,000	Image Captioning
UIT-ViIC	2019	MS-COCO	Vietnamese/ English	3,850	19,250	Image Captioning

image captioning for Vietnamese. Therefore, we decided to build a new dataset of Vietnamese image captioning for Image Captioning research community and evaluated the state-of-the-art models on our corpus. In particular, we validated and compared the results by BLEU [11], ROUGE [8] and CIDEr [16] metrics between Neural Image Captioning (NIC) - Show and Tell model, Image Captioning model from the Pytorch-tutorial [2] by Yunjey on our corpus as the pioneering results.

3   Dataset Creation

This section demonstrates how we constructed our new Vietnamese dataset. The dataset consists of 3,850 images relating to sports played with balls from 2017 edition of Microsoft COCO. Similar to most Image Captioning datasets, we provided five Vietnamese captions for each image, summing up to 19,250 captions in total.

3.1   Annotation Tool with Content Suggestions

To enhance annotation efficiency, we present a web-based application for caption annotation. Figure 2 is the annotation screen of the application.

Our tool assists annotators conveniently loading images into a display and storing captions they created into a new dataset. With saving function, annotator

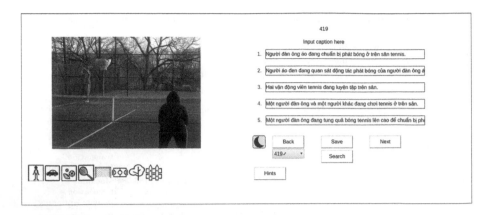

Fig. 2. Annotation screen of UIT-ViIC Image Captioning tool.

can save and load written captions for reviewing purposes. Furthermore, users are able to look back their works or the others' by searching image by image ids.

The tool also supports content suggestions taking advantage of existing information from MS-COCO. First, there are categories hints for each image, displaying as friendly icons. Second, original English captions are displayed if annotator feels their needs. Those content suggestions are helpful for annotators who can't clearly understand images, especially when there are issues with images' quality.

3.2   Annotation Process

In this section, we describes procedures of building our ball sports Vietnamese dataset, called UIT-ViIC.

Our human resources for dataset construction involved five writers, whose ages are from 22–25. Being native Vietnamese residents, they are fluent in Vietnamese. All five UIT-ViIC creators first researched and were trained about sports knowledge as well as the specialized vocabulary before starting to work.

During annotation process, there are inconsistencies and disagreements between human's understandings and the way they see images. According to Micah Hodosh et al. [5], most images' captions on Internet nowadays tend to introduce information that cannot be obtained from the image itself, such as people name, location name, time, etc. Therefore, to successfully compose meaningful descriptive captions we expected, their should be strict guidelines.

Inspired from MS-COCO annotation rules [1], we first sketched UIT-ViIC's guidelines for our captions:

1. Each caption must contain at least ten Vietnamese words.
2. Only describe visible activities and objects included in image.
3. Exclude name of places, streets (Chinatown, New York, etc.) and number (apartment numbers, specific time on TV, etc.)
4. Familiar English words such as laptop, TV, tennis, etc. are allowed.

5. Each caption must be a single sentence with continuous tense.
6. Personal opinion and emotion must be excluded while annotating.
7. Annotators can describe the activities and objects from different perspectives.
8. Visible "thing" objects are the only one to be described.
9. Ambiguous "stuff" objects which do not have obvious "border" are ignored.
10. In case of 10 to 15 objects which are in the same category or species, annotators do not need to include them in the caption.

In comparison with MS-COCO [1] data collection guidelines in terms of annotation, UIT-ViIC's guidelines has similar rules (1, 2, 8, 9, 10) . We extended from MS-COCO's guidelines with five new rules to our own and had modifications in the original ones.

In both datasets, we would like to control sentence length and focus on describing important subjects only in order to make sure that essential information is mainly included in captions. The MS-COCO threshold for sentence's length is 8, and we raised the number to 10 for our dataset. One reason for this change is that an object in image is usually expressed in many Vietnamese words. For example, a "baseball player" in English can be translated into " vận động viên bóng chày" or " cầu thủ bóng chày", which already accounted for a significant length of the Vietnamese sentence. In addition, captions must be single sentences with continuous tense as we expect our model's output to capture what we are seeing in the image in a consise way.

On the other hand, proper name for places, streets, etc must not be mentioned in this dataset in order to avoid confusions and incorrect identification names with the same scenery for output. Besides, annotators' personal opinion must be excluded for more meaningful captions. Vietnamese words for several English ones such as tennis, pizza, TV, etc are not existed, so annotators could use such familiar words in describing captions. For some images, the subjects are ambiguous and not descriptive which would be difficult for annotators to describe in words. That's the reason why annotators can describe images from more than one perspective.

3.3 Dataset Analysis

After finishing constructing UIT-ViIC dataset, we had a look in statistical analysis on our corpus in this section. UIT-ViIC covers 3,850 images described by 19,250 Vietnamese captions. Sticking strictly to our annotation guidelines, the majority of our captions are at the length of 10–15 tokens. We are using the term "tokens" here as a Vietnamese word can consist of one, two or even three tokens. Therefore, to apply Vietnamese properly to Image Captioning, we proposed a tokenization tool - PyVI [15], which is specialized for Vietnamese language tokenization, at words level. The sentence length using token-level tokenizer and word-level tokenizer are compared and illustrated in Fig. 3, we could see there are variances there. So that, we could suggest that the tokenizer performs well enough, and we could expect our Image Captioning models to perform better with Vietnamese sentences that are tokenized, as most models perform more efficiently with captions having fewer words.

Table 2. Statistics on classes of Vietnamese words.

Verbs	Nouns	Adjectives
cầm (hold): 3,344	bóng (ball): 7,686	tennis: 3,005
chơi (play): 2,760	sân (pitch): 6,725	bóng chày (baseball): 880
đánh bóng (hit): 2,581	cầu thủ (player): 2,635	cao (tall): 687

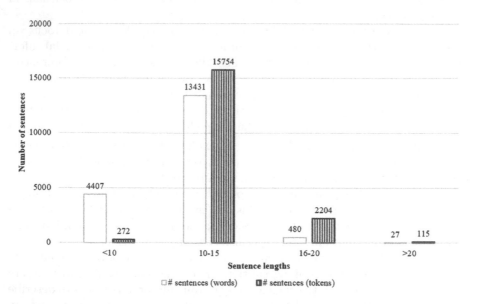

Fig. 3. UIT-ViIC dataset analysis by sentences length.

Table 2 summarizes top three most occuring words for each part-of-speech. Our dataset vocabulary size is 1,472 word classes, including 723 nouns, 567 verbs, and 182 adjectives. It is no surprise that as our dataset is about sports with balls, the noun "bóng" (meaning "ball") occurs most, followed by "sân" and " cầu thủ" ("pitch" and "athlete" respectively). We also found that the frequency of word "tennis" stands out among other adjectives, which specifies that the set covers the majority of tennis sport, followed by "bóng chày" (meaning "baseball"). Therefore, we expected our model to generate the best results for tennis images.

4   Image Captioning Models

Our main goal in this section was to see if Image Captioning models could learn well with Vietnamese language. To accomplish this task, we trained and evaluated our dataset with two published Image Captioning models applying encoder-decoder architecture. The models we proposed are Neural Image Captioning (NIC) model, Image Captioning model from the Pytorch-tutorial [2] by Yunjey.

Overall, Convolutional Neural Network (CNN) is first used for extracting image features for encoder part. The image features which are presented in vectors will be used as layers for decoding. For decoder part, Recurrent Neural Network - Long short-term memory (RNN - LSTM) are used to embed the vectors to target sentences using words/tokens provided in vocabulary.

4.1 Model from Pytorch Tutorial

Model from pytorch-tutorial by Yunjey applied the baseline technique of CNN and LSTM for encoding and decoding images. Resnet-152 [4] architecture was proposed for encoder part, and we used the pretrained one on ILSVRC-2012-CLS [13] image classification dataset to tackle our current problem. LSTM was then used in this model to generate sentence word by word.

4.2 NIC - Show and Tell Model

NIC - Show and Tell used CNN model which was currently yielding the state-of-the-art results. The model achieved 0.628 when evaluating on BLEU-1 on COCO-2014 dataset. For CNN part, we utilized VGG-16 [14] architecture pretrained on COCO-2014 image sets with all categories. In decoding part, LSTM was not only trained to predict sentence but also to compute probability for each word to be generated. As a result, output sentence was chosen using search algorithms to find the one that have words yielding the maximum probabilities.

5   Experiments

5.1   Experiment Settings

Dataset Preprocessing. As the images in our dataset were manually created by human, there were mistakes including grammar, spelling or extra spaces, punctuation. Sometimes, the Vietnamese's accent signs were placed in the wrong place due to distinct keyboard input methods. Therefore, we eliminated those common errors before working on evaluating our models.

Dataset Preparation. We conducted our experiments and did comparisons through three datasets with the same size and images of ball sports category: Two Vietnamese datasets generated by two methods (translated by Google Translation service and annotated by human) and the original MS-COCO English dataset. The three sets were distributed into three subsets: 2,695 images for the training set, 924 images for validation set and 231 images for test set.

5.2   Evaluation Measures.

To evaluate our dataset, we used metrics proposed by most authors in related works of extending Image Captioning dataset, which are BLEU [11], ROUGE [8] and CIDEr [16]. BLEU and ROUGE were often used mainly for text summarization and machine translation, whereas CIDEr was designed especially for evaluating Image Captioning models.

Comparison Methods. We did comparisons with three ball sports datasets, as follows:

– **Original English (English-ball sports):** The original MS-COCO English dataset with 3,850 ball sports images. This dataset was first evaluated in order to have base results for following comparisons.
– **Google-translated Vietnamese (GT-ball sports):** The translated MS-COCO English dataset into Vietnamese using Google Translation API, categorized into ball sports.
– **Manually-annotated Vietnamese (UIT-ViIC):** The Vietnamese dataset built with manually written captions for images from MS-COCO, categorized into ball sports.

5.3   Experiment Results

The two following tables, Table 3 and Table 4, summarize experimental results of Pytorch-tutorial, NIC - Show and Tell models. The two models were trained with three mentioned datasets, which are English-ball sports, GT-ball sports, UIT-ViIC. After training, 924 images from validation subset for each dataset were used to validate the our models.

Table 3. Experimental results of pytorch-tutorial models.

Dataset	Tokenizer	BLEU-1	BLEU-2	BLEU-3	BLEU-4	ROUGE-L	CIDEr-D
English-ball sports	nltk	**0.761**	0.562	0.405	0.289	0.560	0.668
GT-ball sports	PyVI	0.596	0.455	0.341	0.254	0.522	0.578
UIT-ViIC	PyVI	0.710	0.575	0.476	0.394	0.626	**1.005**

Table 4. Experimental results of NIC - Show and Tell models.

Dataset	Tokenizer	BLEU-1	BLEU-2	BLEU-3	BLEU-4	ROUGE-L	CIDEr-D
English-ball sports	nltk	**0.689**	0.501	0.355	0.252	0.585	0.667
GT-ball sports	PyVI	0.643	0.481	0.368	0.281	0.565	0.567
UIT-ViIC	PyVI	0.682	**0.561**	**0.411**	**0.327**	0.599	**0.818**

As can be seen in Table 3, with model from Pytorch tutorial, MS-COCO English captions categorized with ball sports yielded better results than the two Vietnamese datasets. However, as number of consecutive words considered (BLEU gram) increase, UIT-ViIC's BLEU scores started to pass that of English ball sports and their gaps kept growing. The ROUGE-L and CIDEr-D scores for UIT-ViIC model proved the same thing, and interestingly, we observed that the CIDEr-D score for the UIT-ViIC model surpassed English-ball sports counterpart.

The same conclusion can be said from Table 4. Show and Tell model's results show that MS-COCO ball sports English captions only gave better result at BLEU-1. From BLEU-3 to BLEU-4, both GT-ball sports and UIT-ViIC yielded superior scores to English-ball sports. Besides, when limiting MS-COCO English dataset to ball sports category only, the results were higher (0.689, 0.501, 0.355, 0.252) than when the model was trained on MS-COCO with all images, which scored only 0.629, 0.436, 0.290, 0.193 (results without model fine tuning in 2018) from BLEU-1 to BLEU-4 respectively.

When the two Vietnamese datasets are compared, we found that UIT-ViIC models performed better than ball sports dataset translated automatically, GT-ball sports. The gaps between the two results sets were more trivial in NIC model, and the numbers got smaller as the BLEU's n-gram increase.

English output:
a group of young men playing a game of soccer .

GT – sportball output:
một nhóm các cô gái trẻ chơi một trận bóng đá .

UIT – ViIC output:
những cô gái đang chơi bóng đá ở trên sân .

English output:
a baseball player is in the process of throwing a ball .

GT – sportball output:
một cầu thủ bóng chày đang vung gậy bóng chày .

UIT – ViIC output:
một người đàn ông đang chuẩn bị ném quả bóng chày .

Fig. 4. Examples of captions generated by models from pytorch-tutorial trained on the three datasets that yieled expected outputs.

In Fig. 4, two images inputted into the models generate two Vietnamese captions that were able to describe accurately the sport game, which is soccer. The two models could also differentiate if there were more than one person in the images. However, when comparing GT-ball sports outputs with UIT-ViIC ones in both images, UIT-ViIC yielded captions that sound more naturally, considering Vietnamese language. Furthermore, UIT-ViIC demonstrated the specific action of the sport more accurately than GT-ball sports. For example, in the below image of Fig. 4, UIT-ViIC tokd the exact action (the man is preparing to throw the ball), whereas GT-ball sports was mistaken (the man swing the bat). The confusion of GT-ball sports happened due to GT-ball sports train set was translated from original MS-COCO dataset, which had been annotated in more various perspective and wider vocabulary range with the dataset size was not big enough.

There are cases when the main objects are too small, both English and GT - ball sports captions told the unexpected sport, which was tennis instead of baseball, for instance. Nevertheless, the majority of UIT-ViIC captions could tell the correct type of sport and action, even though the gender and age identifications still need to be improved.

6   Conclusion and Further Improvements

In this paper, we constructed a Vietnamese dataset with images from MS-COCO, relating to the category within ball sports, consisting of 3,850 images with 19,250 manually written Vietnamese captions. Next, we conducted experiments on two famous existed Image Captioning models to evaluate their efficiency when learning with two Vietnamese datasets. The results are then compared with the original MS-COCO English categorized with ball sports category.

Generally, we saw that the English set only outperformed Vietnamese ones in BLEU-1 metric, rather, the Vietnamese sets produced better scores basing on BLEU-2 to BLEU-4, especially CIDEr. On the other hand, when UIT-ViIC was compared with the dataset having captions translated by Google, the evaluation results and the output examples suggested that Google Translation service was able to perform acceptably, though most translated captions were not perfectly natural and linguistically friendly. As a result, we proved that manually written captions for Vietnamese dataset was currently preferred.

For future improvements, extending the UIT-ViIC's category into all types of sport to verify how the dataset's size and category affect the Image Captioning models' performance is our highest priority. Moreover, the human resources for dataset construction will be expanded. Second, we will continue to fine tune our experiments to find out proper parameters for models, especially with encoding and decoding frameworks, for better learning performance with Vietnamese dataset, especially when the categories are limited.

References

1. Chen, X., et al.: Microsoft coco captions: Data collection and evaluation server (2015). arXiv preprint arXiv:1504.00325
2. Choi, Y.: Yunjey/Pytorch-Tutorial (2018). https://github.com/yunjey/pytorch-tutorial/tree/master/tutorials/03-advanced/image_captioning. Accessed 1 Feb 2020
3. Funaki, R., Nakayama, H.: Image-mediated learning for zero-shot cross-lingual document retrieval. In: Proceedings of the 2015 Conference on Empirical Methods in Natural Language Processing (2015). http://dx.doi.org/10.18653/v1/d15-1070
4. He, K. et al.: Deep residual learning for image recognition. In: 2016 IEEE Conference on Computer Vision and Pattern Recognition (CVPR) (2016). https://doi.org/10.1109/cvpr.2016.90
5. Hodosh, M., Young, P., Hockenmaier, J.: Framing image description as a ranking task: data, models and evaluation metrics. J. Artif. Intelli. Res. 47, 853–899 (2013). https://doi.org/10.1613/jair.3994
6. Karpathy, A., Fei-Fei, L.: Deep visual-semantic alignments for generating image descriptions. In: 2015 IEEE Conference on Computer Vision and Pattern Recognition (CVPR) (2015). https://doi.org/10.1109/cvpr.2015.7298932
7. Li, X., et al.: COCO-CN for cross-lingual image tagging, captioning, and retrieval. IEEE Trans. Multimedia 21(9), 2347–2360 (2019). https://doi.org/10.1109/tmm.2019.2896494
8. Lin, C.-Y.: ROUGE: a package for automatic evaluation of summaries. In: Proceedings of Workshop on Text Summarization Branches Out, Post-Conference Workshop of ACL 2004, Barcelona, Spain (2004)
9. Lin, T.-Y., et al.: Microsoft COCO: common objects in context. In: Fleet, D., Pajdla, T., Schiele, B., Tuytelaars, T. (eds.) ECCV 2014. LNCS, vol. 8693, pp. 740–755. Springer, Cham (2014). https://doi.org/10.1007/978-3-319-10602-1_48
10. Miyazaki, T., Shimizu, N.: Cross-lingual image caption generation. In: Proceedings of the 54th Annual Meeting of the Association for Computational Linguistics (Volume 1: Long Papers) (2016). http://dx.doi.org/10.18653/v1/p16-1168
11. Papineni, K., et al.: BLEU. In: Proceedings of the 40th Annual Meeting on Association for Computational Linguistics - ACL 2002 (2001). https://doi.org/10.3115/1073083.1073135
12. Rashtchian, C., Young, P., Hodosh, M., Hockenmaier, J.: Collecting image annotations using Amazon's mechanical turk. In: Proceedings of the NAACL HLT 2010 Workshop on Creating Speech and Language Data with Amazon's Mechanical Turk, pp. 139–147. Association for Computational Linguistics, June 2010
13. Russakovsky, O., et al.: ImageNet large scale visual recognition challenge. Int. J. Comput. Vis. 115(3), 211–252 (2015). https://doi.org/10.1007/s11263-015-0816-y
14. Simonyan, K., Zisserman, A.: Very deep convolutional networks for large-scale image recognition (2014). arXiv preprint arXiv:1409.1556
15. Tran Viet, T.: Trungtv/Pyvi (2019). https://github.com/trungtv/pyvi. Accessed 1 Feb 2020
16. Vedantam, R., Zitnick, C.L., Parikh, D.: CIDEr: consensus-based image description evaluation. In: 2015 IEEE Conference on Computer Vision and Pattern Recognition (CVPR) (2015). https://doi.org/10.1109/cvpr.2015.7299087
17. Vinyals, O., et al.: Show and tell: a neural image caption generator. In: 2015 IEEE Conference on Computer Vision and Pattern Recognition (CVPR) (2015). https://doi.org/10.1109/cvpr.2015.7298935

18. Yoshikawa, Y., Shigeto, Y., Takeuchi, A.: STAIR captions: constructing a large-scale Japanese image caption dataset. In: Proceedings of the 55th Annual Meeting of the Association for Computational Linguistics (Volume 2: Short Papers)(2017). https://doi.org/10.18653/v1/p17-2066
19. Young, P., et al.: From image descriptions to visual denotations: new similarity metrics for semantic inference over event descriptions. Trans. Assoc. Comput. Linguist. **2**, 67–78 (2014). https://doi.org/10.1162/tacl_a_00166

Detection of Extremist Ideation on Social Media Using Machine Learning Techniques

Shynar Mussiraliyeva[1][✉], Milana Bolatbek[1], Batyrkhan Omarov[1,2][✉], and Kalamkas Bagitova[1]

[1] Al-Farabi Kazakh National University, Almaty, Kazakhstan
mussiraliyevash@gmail.com, batyahan@gmail.com
[2] International Kazakh-Turkish University, Turkistan, Kazakhstan

Abstract. At present, the number of terrorist attacks carried out by lone terrorists under the influence of propaganda and extremist ideology, as well as by organized terrorist communities with a network and poorly connected structure, is increasing. The main means of information exchange, recruitment and promotion for such structures is the Internet, namely web resources, social networks and e-mail. In this regard, the task of detecting, identifying topics of communication, connections, as well as monitoring the behavior and forecasting of threats emanating from individual users, groups and network communities that generate and distribute terrorist and extremist information on the Internet arises.

The paper is devoted to the research and application of machine learning methods aimed at solving the problems of detecting potentially dangerous information on the Internet. The study examines the development of a corpus in Kazakh language for detecting extremist messages, and explores machine learning algorithms that used to detect content that contains calls for terrorist attacks and propaganda materials.

Keywords: Extremist ideation detection · Machine learning · Natural language processing · Classification

1 Introduction

The Internet is one of the main means of information exchange and propaganda for terrorist and extremist communities. The paper develops the proposed methods based on machine learning, using a sample search script to detect electronic messages, documents, and web resources containing extremist information, as well as users and communities in social networks that distribute such information. In this scenario, material with extremist content is available, and you need to find semantically similar materials in a social network. Using the method of semantic analysis based on orthonormal non-negative matrix factorization, the sample keywords that form search queries for the social network and the characteristic topics of the sample are highlighted. Based on orthonormal nonnegative matrix factorization, the semantic analysis method identifies the sample keywords that form search queries for the social network, and the characteristic topics

© Springer Nature Switzerland AG 2020
N. T. Nguyen et al. (Eds.): ICCCI 2020, LNAI 12496, pp. 743–752, 2020.
https://doi.org/10.1007/978-3-030-63007-2_58

of the sample. Search results for keywords in the social network contain a lot of "noise" – documents containing keywords, but semantically far from the original sample [1]. To filter noise, an estimate of the relevance of the found documents to the sample is calculated using a projection on the topics identified in the sample. Documents with extremist content are characterized by multilingualism, accidental and deliberate grammatical errors, deliberate distortion of semantically important words, and the presence of links and hashtags, which significantly complicates semantic analysis [2]. To solve these problems, we use n-gram representation of documents and "enrichment" of document texts (pumping out and automatically annotating information by links and hashtags and including them in the document body). The software prototype, which implements the described approaches, is applied to the analysis of real data from social networks.

2   Related Works

Over the past decade, terrorist and extremist organizations have significantly increased their presence on the Internet and social networks, actively using these tools to recruit new members and train them, prepare and organize terrorist attacks, promote violence, distribute extremist literature, etc. [3–5]. Using the Internet-a free and open resource-allows you to quickly and anonymously distribute any information, address directly to the audience of social networks and forums, without fear of censorship, present in traditional mass media. Activities aimed at identifying terrorists and related individuals, preventing the spread of extremist materials, and preventing upcoming terrorist attacks require analysis of all information received from representatives of extremist groups [6, 7]. In this context, the analysis of Internet resources comes to the fore. Due to the huge volume of information distributed over the Internet, its linguistic diversity and the requirement to monitor it in real time, it is necessary to use automatic text analysis procedures to identify potentially dangerous users, timely removal of extremist materials, and analysis of information about terrorists and upcoming terrorist attacks [8]. The main tasks in creating automatic tools for analyzing terrorist information are to select suitable data for testing algorithms and to develop algorithms that are suitable for solving the problem of detecting terrorist activity.

2.1   Development and Analysis of the Extremist Text Corpus

Chen et al. provides examples of collecting, analyzing, and visualizing publicly available terrorist materials using the so – called "shadow Internet" - a segment of the network that can only be accessed using special SOFTWARE and remain completely anonymous [9]. For the study, the authors took lists of terrorist groups (664 organizations) and their sites from US government sources, and downloaded their contents (3.6 million web pages) in English, Arabic, and Spanish. The finished corpus of extremist texts in English is described in [10]. All texts were written in Arabic and later translated into English. The case has a diverse markup (syntactic, semantic, anaphoric markup, as well as temporary markers and events), which was carried out automatically, and then checked manually.

In [11], a corpus of texts was created containing illegal texts of seven categories (terrorism, ideological texts, religious hatred, separatism, nationalism, aggression and calls for unrest, fascism) and neutral texts with similar vocabulary. Various extensions of the standard corpus platform for studying specialized text corpora have been proposed [12, 13]. In [14], research is conducted on the use of methods for analyzing the corpus of illegal texts.

2.2 Extremist Ideation Detection

According to a study [15], the use of social networks to track the spread of radical ideas and extremist threats has attracted the attention of researchers for more than 10 years. In the last 3 years, there has been a surge in research interest in identifying and predicting the text content of messages in open social networks. The authors [16] note that Twitter is the most common data source, and various methods of information retrieval and machine learning are used for content analysis. Clustering, logistic regression, and dynamic Query Expansion are more suitable for predicting terrorist attacks, riots, or protests. A common component of various approaches and methods is named Entity Recognition (NER), which allows you to extract structured information from unstructured or semi-structured documents. To detect radicalism and extremism in real time, the K-Nearest neighbor method, the Naive Bayes classifier, the support Vector Machine (SVM) method, decision trees, Topical Crawler/Link Analysis, and others are most often used [17, 18].

In works based on the analysis of publicly available information on the Internet (Twitter, text documents of free access), one of the main tasks is to identify terrorist bandits and other terrorists. The difficulty lies in the fact that, first, communication on forums is carried out in different languages, and also, perhaps, in their combination (the same applies to documents posted on the Internet). And secondly, the fact that a simple search for keywords or specific phrases does not allow you to distinguish terrorist attacks from, for example, news agencies. In addition, terrorist sites are often disguised as news sites and religious forums. The number of sites is huge, which makes their analysis in manual mode ineffective, so for the correct identification of real sites and forums associated with certain terrorist groups, automatic means of effective selection and filtering are necessary. It is more difficult to determine whether the information being distributed belongs to one of the terrorist groups, since different terrorist groups may be ideologically close and use similar vocabulary [19].

In [20], authors investigated the possibility of creating methods for automatically detecting aggressiveness in social media texts. Identification of psycholinguistic characteristics of the text and determination of the percentage of words and phrases from the specified dictionaries is performed. In [21], the analysis of texts with extremist content is carried out, on the basis of which psychological criteria are derived, according to which the expert should evaluate the text.

In [22], decision trees to classify texts presented as graphs to classify texts. The subgraphs obtained as a result of the analysis of documents allow you to select several words, the presence of which in the text clearly determines its belonging to the terrorist site. At the same time, the absence of all these words means that the document is not exactly a terrorist document.

A similar problem, for which several different approaches are used, is considered in [23]. This is an attempt to automatically identify radical content released by jihadist groups on Twitter. To do this, we compare the results of classifying tweets into radical and non – radical using SVM methods with linear kernel functions, AdaBoost, and the naive Bayesian classifier.

In [24], the problem of identifying tweets that promote hatred and extremism is solved as a binary classification problem using the k-neighbor and LIBSVM methods. It is shown that the classification using LIBSVM is more accurate.

Another area of research on extremist texts on the Internet is to determine the type of Internet user activity. In this work [25], the task of identifying extremist users is solved based on Twitter records, and it is also evaluated whether an ordinary user will choose extraterritorial materials and whether users will respond to contacts initiated by extremists. In this case, the analysis can be performed on aggregated data after the fact or in real-time forecast mode.

In [26], we present the Advanced Terrorist Detection System (ATDS), which is designed to track real-time access to anomalous content, which may include websites created by terrorists, by analyzing the content of information received by users via the Internet. ATDS functions in learning and recognition mode. In training mode, ATDS determines the typical interests of a pre-defined group of users by processing web pages that these users have accessed for some time. In recognition mode, ATDS monitors real-time Internet traffic generated by the controlled group, analyzes the content of web pages, and signals if the information received is not part of the group's typical range of interests and is similar to the interests of terrorists. The system analyzes arbitrary text data, which is used to determine the typical interests of users (groups of users) using the k-means clustering method.

As you can see, the development of approaches to the presentation of text information, its processing, building effective and accurate algorithms for analyzing texts, identifying their topics is an important and relevant scientific direction, which is paid much attention in the world. It should be noted that there are practically no researches devoted to the analysis of terrorist information for Kazakh language. Apparently, this is due to the lack of systematized data for testing algorithms, and the lack of expressed need for automatic processing and searching for information on the Internet (since such processing is performed manually by experts).

Thus, the development of automatic tools for thematic analysis will significantly improve the efficiency of solving problems of searching the Internet for documents and individual messages of terrorist and extremist orientation, which, in turn, will lead to the possibility of preventing upcoming terrorist attacks, reducing the influence of extremist groups and increasing the level of national security.

3   Development of the Extremist Intended Texts Corpus

Text data is necessary for analyzing what is said, thought, or felt in texts. Unfortunately, when it comes to analyzing extremist behavior, it is difficult to find a suitable selection of texts. Many document collections from social networks and media, are shared collections and should be filtered according to the research area. Because of the complexity and lack of an appropriate subject area of the corpus in the Kazakh Language we decided to create our own corpus of extremist intended texts. The corpus consists of several parts as extremist intended posts that contains 3000 words and 15 000 words with non-extremist posts, which include religious texts and texts from news portals.

In order to collect data we use Vkontakte social network that is popular in Commonwealth of Independent States. Figure 1 illustrates a schema of the data collection process. We use Python 3.6 to create a parser for data collection. Interaction with the social network API was performed using the requests library. The Pycharm Community Edition 2018 software was chosen as the development environment. To get the data we use The Vkontakte API that is a ready-made interface that allows to get the necessary information from the Vkontakte social network database using https requests to the server. Components of the request were given in Table 1.

Table 1. Query components.

Component	Value
https://	Connection protocol
Api.vk.com/method	Address of the API service
User.get	Name of the Vkontakte API method
?user_id = 210700286&v = 5.92	Query parameters

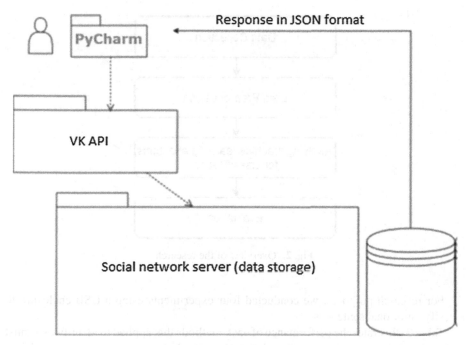

Fig. 1. Data collection schema

Methods are conditional commands that correspond to a specific database operation. For example, users.get-method for getting information about the user, account.getinfo-method for returning information about the current user, etc.

All methods in the system are divided into sections. In the transmitted request, after the method name, you must pass the input data as GET parameters in the http request. If the request is processed successfully, the server returns a JSON object with the requested data. The response structure for each method is strictly defined. The rules are specified on the pages describing the method in the official documentation.

4 Experiment Results

In order to test the corpus, we approached the extremist text detection problem as a classification task. We performed the step-by-step process outlined in Fig. 2. We analyse and do primary pre-processing the collected data. In this step, we labeled all the texts to two classes, that class 1 means extremist behavior, and class 0 means non-extremist behavior. To preprocess the data we applied StringToWordVector that fulfills tokenization, stemming, and stop/frequent word removal.

To classify documents into two classes, we experimented with machine learning models as Gradient boosting with word2vec, Random forest with word2vec, Gradient boosting with tf-idf, and Random forest with tf-idf. The selected algorithms have demonstrated their efficiencies in various studies of text classification.

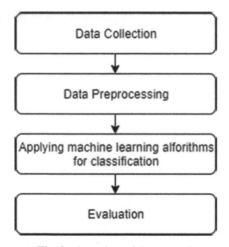

Fig. 2. Overview of the research

For research purposes, we conducted four experiments using a USB enclosure to classify emotional sentences.

Table 2 illustrates the performance of each methods that applied to identify extremist texts using the extremist texts corpus. For each method we compare accuracy, precision, recall, F1 score, and AUC to evaluate quality of corpus and performance of the algorithms. All the methods shown precision around 90%. Table 2 confirms that, the models classify extremist and non-extremist texts very good showing more that 90% accuracy. It means that, quality of the extremist texts corpus is quite good. In spite of this

Table 2. Comparison of different machine learning models on the corpus

Model	Accuracy	Precision	Recall	F1 score
Gradient boosting with word2vec	89	87	86	86
Gradient boosting with tf-idf	85	84	84	85
Random forest with word2vec	87	86	84	85
Random forest with tf-idf	83	84	83	81

result, we should complement the corpus in order to get more precision in identifying extremist texts. The experimental results illustrate that from our collected corpus, we can successfully classify extremist behavior in the texts.

Table 3. TF-IDF values of most frequently used words in the corpora

Keyword	TF-IDF value
allah (аллаһ)	25.62
jihad (жиһад)	22.62
alla (алла)	19.92
djihad (джихад)	17.1
allah (аллах)	16.72
sog'ys (соғыс)	14.3
jihad (жихад)	11.43
sogys (согыс)	8.4
ka'pir (кәпір)	7.98
tozaq (тозақ)	6.28
tozak (тозак)	5.88
kafir (кафир)	3.4

Table 3 shows the TF-IDF values of most frequently used words in the corpora. These words can be used to improve the reliability of detecting the extremist orientation in the text. In the future it is planned to assign emotional tones to the revealed words, which will later be used to create algorithms and software for analyzing the tonality of the text (sentiment analysis) [27].

For classification authors applied machine learning methods such as linear SVC, multinomial naive Bayes, logistic regression, classification trees and random forest. For this experiment authors used open source library of machine learning methods - Scikit-learn. Classification results are given in Table 4.

Table 4. Text classification results

Model	Accuracy
Linear SVC	0.61
Multinomial naive Bayes	0.81
Logistic regression	0.70
Classification trees	0.51
Random forest	0.83

5 Conclusion and Future Work

In this paper, we applied text classification techniques using natural language processing technologies for the detection of extremist behavior. To complete our task, we applied various classification algorithms.

Our experimental results show that the problem can be successfully solved. Experiments show that we can achieve high accuracy in extremist text classification using the collected corpus.

In this article, we used individual words as attributes without any additional syntactic or semantic knowledge. In the future, we plan to include information about emotions that can positively affect the accuracy of the task.

Ideally, text analysis methods are applied to cases containing thousands or even millions of documents. In this case, less than 200 records were used that can be identified with certainty as extremist behavior. Further analysis of language models will require a larger corpus. To achieve a larger corpus, we will use internal semi-automatic methods that will ensure sufficient representation of each topic in the corpus.

Using a large corpus, researchers can identify features such as the presence of emotions, cause-and-effect relationships, or language models associated with extremist behavior that can be used to teach machine learning algorithms. The main purpose of the case is to use it as an ML resource.

However, despite these limitations, the created corpus proved to be effective in training ML algorithms.

In the next step of this research we are going to supply the corpus with new texts, make balanced corpus, tonality of posts in social media, and increase the accuracy of extremist text classification.

Acknowledgements. This research has been funded by the Ministry of Digital Development, Innovations and Aerospace industry of the Republic of Kazakhstan (Grant No. AP06851248, "Development of models, algorithms for semantic analysis to identify extremist content in web resources and creation the tool for cyber forensics").

References

1. Pande, N., Karyakarte, M.: A Review for Semantic Analysis and Text Document Annotation Using Natural Language Processing Techniques. Available at SSRN 3418747 (2019)

2. Alshemali, B., Kalita, J.: Improving the reliability of deep neural networks in NLP: a review. Knowl. Based Syst. **191**, 105210 (2019)
3. Yankah, S., Adams, K.S., Grimes, L., Price, A.: Age and online social media behavior in prediction of social activism orientation. J. Soc. Media Soc. **6**(2), 56–89 (2017)
4. Costello, M., Hawdon, J.: Who are the online extremists among us? sociodemographic characteristics, social networking, and online experiences of those who produce online hate materials. Violence Gend. **5**(1), 55–60 (2018)
5. Ferrara, E.: Contagion dynamics of extremist propaganda in social networks. Inf. Sci. **418**, 1–12 (2017)
6. Awan, I.: Cyber-extremism: Isis and the power of social media. Society **54**(2), 138–149 (2017)
7. Chetty, N., Alathur, S.: Hate speech review in the context of online social networks. Aggress. Violent. Beh. **40**, 108–118 (2018)
8. Kruglanski, A., Jasko, K., Webber, D., Chernikova, M., Molinario, E.: The making of violent extremists. Rev. Gen. Psychol. **22**(1), 107–120 (2018)
9. Chen, H.: Exploring extremism and terrorism on the web: the dark web project. In: Yang, Christopher C., et al. (eds.) PAISI 2007. LNCS, vol. 4430, pp. 1–20. Springer, Heidelberg (2007). https://doi.org/10.1007/978-3-540-71549-8_1
10. Finlayson, M.A., Halverson, J.R., Corman, S.R.: The N2 corpus: a semantically annotated collection of Islamist extremist stories. LREC, pp. 896–902 (2014)
11. Chepovskiy, A., Devyatkin, D., Smirnov, I., Ananyeva, M., Kobozeva, M., Solovyev, F.: Exploring linguistic features for extremist texts detection (on the material of Russian-speaking illegal texts). In: 2017 IEEE International Conference on Intelligence and Security Informatics: Security and Big Data, ISI 2017, pp. 188–190. Institute of Electrical and Electronics Engineers Inc. (2017)
12. Ménard, P.A., Barriere, C.: PACTE: a colloaborative platform for textual annotation. In: Proceedings of the 13th Joint ISO-ACL Workshop on Interoperable Semantic Annotation (ISA-13) (2017)
13. Anthony, L.: Visualisation in corpus-based discourse studies, pp. 197–224. A Critical Review, Corpus Approaches to Discourse (2018)
14. Wolfe, C.R., Dandignac, M., Reyna, V.F.: A theoretically motivated method for automatically evaluating texts for gist inferences. Behav. Res. Methods **51**(6), 2419–2437 (2019). https://doi.org/10.3758/s13428-019-01284-4
15. Danekenova, A., Zhussupova, G., Nurmagambetov, R., Shunayeva, S., Popov, V.: The most used forms and methods of citizens involvement in terrorist and extremist activity. J. Pol. & L. **12**, 1 (2019)
16. Nicholls, T., Bright, J.: Understanding news story chains using information retrieval and network clustering techniques. Commun. Methods Measures **13**(1), 43–59 (2019)
17. Tulkens, S., Hilte, L., Lodewyckx, E., Verhoeven, B., Daelemans, W.: The automated detection of racist discourse in dutch social media. Comput. Linguist. Netherlands J. **6**, 3–20 (2016)
18. Narynov, S., Mukhtarkhanuly, D., Omarov, B.: Dataset of depressive posts in Russian Language collected from social media. Data Brief **29**, 105195 (2020)
19. Ahmad, S., Asghar, M.Z., Alotaibi, F.M., Awan, I.: Detection and classification of social media-based extremist affiliations using sentiment analysis techniques. Hum. Centric Comput. Inf. Sci. **9**(1), 24 (2019)
20. Scrivens, R., Gaudette, T., Davies, G., Frank, R.: Searching for extremist content online using the dark crawler and sentiment analysis. In: Methods of Criminology and Criminal Justice Research. Sociology of Crime, Law and Deviance, vol. 24, pp. 179–194. Emerald Publishing Limited (2019)
21. Asif, M., Ishtiaq, A., Ahmad, H., Aljuaid, H., Shah, J.: Sentiment analysis of extremism in social media from textual information. Telematics and Informatics, p. 101345 (2020)

22. Last, M., Markov, A., Kandel, A.: Multi-lingual detection of terrorist content on the web. In: Chen, H., et al. (eds.) WISI 2006. LNCS, vol. 3917, pp. 16–30. Springer, Heidelberg (2006). https://doi.org/10.1007/11734628_3

23. Enghin Omer Using machine learning to identify jihadist messages on Twitter. http://uu.div aportal.org/smash/get/diva2:846343/FULLTEXT01.pdf

24. Sureka, A., Agarwal, S.: Learning to classify hate and extremism promoting tweets intelligence and security. In: 2014 IEEE Joint Year Informatics Conference (JISIC), 2014, pp. 320–320 (2014). https://doi.org/10.1109/jisic.2014.65

25. Ferrara, E., Wang, W.-Q., Varol, O., Flammini, A., Galstyan, A.: Predicting online extremism, content adopters, and interaction reciprocity arXiv:1605.00659 [cs.SI] (2016)

26. Elovici, Y., et al.: Detection of access to terrorrelated Web sites using an Advanced Terror Detection System (ATDS). J. Am. Soc. Inf. Sci. **61**, 405–418 (2010). https://doi.org/10.1002/asi.21249

27. Bolatbek, M., Mussiraliyeva, S., Tukeyev, U.: Creating the dataset of keywords for detecting an extremist orientation in web-resources in the Kazakh language. J. Math. Mech. Comput. Sci. Farabi Kazakh National Univ. **1**(97), 134–142 (2018)

Development of Real Size IT Systems with Language Competence as a Challenge for a Less-Resourced Language

Zygmunt Vetulani[1($\boxtimes$)] and Grażyna Vetulani[2]

[1] Faculty of Mathematics and Computer Science, Adam Mickiewicz University in Poznań,
Ul. Uniwersytetu Poznańskiego 4, 61-614 Poznań, Poland
vetulani@amu.edu.pl
[2] Faculty of Modern Languages and Literatures, Adam Mickiewicz University in Poznań,
Al. Niepodległości 4, 61-874 Poznań, Poland
gravet@amu.edu.pl

Abstract. In this paper, based on the example of our early works for Polish, we want to share our experience in the challenging task of developing NLP-based technologies in the situation of initial scarcity of digital language resources that ranked Polish among the Less-Resourced Languages. We present some of our projects aiming at language resources and tools we had to develop in order to be able to process text in Polish and to develop real-scale systems with language understanding competence. The case study we present here is the rule-based system POLINT-112-SMS for improving information management in emergency situations. We argue in favor of the lexicon-grammar approach to formal description of highly inflected languages and present our current work on this grammatical paradigm.

Keywords: Applications with NL competence · Language resources and tools · Language technology · Less-Resourced Language · Dictionaries · Lexicon-grammar

1 Introduction

Using the example of our early works for Polish, we should like to share our experience of the last three decades in the challenging task of developing NLP based technologies in the situation of initial shortages of digital language resources. Our objective behind this overview is to contribute to the discussion of possible solutions of scarcity of resources and tools for the low-resourced languages.

For a long time, from the 15th till the 18th centuries, Polish was a lingua franca over a large part of Central and Eastern Europe. During the Renaissance and Baroque periods there was intensive literary production in Poland followed by the first dictionaries and grammars. Still, until recently descriptions of the Polish language were addressed to human users for teaching and translation purposes. For this reason they were of little use to the language industries because of lack of precision.

© Springer Nature Switzerland AG 2020
N. T. Nguyen et al. (Eds.): ICCCI 2020, LNAI 12496, pp. 753–764, 2020.
https://doi.org/10.1007/978-3-030-63007-2_59

Polish was considered as a "less-resourced-language" at least until the end of the twentieth century. The negative effects of this deficiency at this time may still be observed. The awareness actions undertaken by the EU followed by appropriate funding measures in the 1990s were important milestones in the development of human language technologies in Central Europe. The new bridges emerging between the technologically advanced research communities and the newcomers often stimulated the appearance of new original ideas. International grants bringing together partners from various language communities representing different linguistic traditions were often oriented to the creation of basic language resources and tools in order to serve the dynamically growing language industries, including in Poland. The general condition of language technologies for Polish is now good enough for Polish to be no longer classified as "less-resourced". Nevertheless, there are still many gaps to fill.

The paper is organized into five sections followed by the references. After this introduction and a brief reference to the beginnings of our research, we present an overview of some of our projects related to the language resources and tools we had to develop in order to be able to process text in Polish and to develop real-scale systems like POLINT-112-SMS (Sect. 3.3), with language understanding competence. Particular attention is paid to electronic dictionaries, WordNet-inspired lexical ontologies, collocations, and the organization of grammatical data into a lexicon-grammar.

2 Early Works

Among the first attempts to use computers in processing Polish text and speech noteworthy is research conducted in 1970s in Warsaw and Poznań (L. Bolc, S. Szpakowicz for text, W. Jassem, M. Steffen-Batóg for speech processing). In the late 1970s and early 1980s the first attempts to implement systems that understood Polish were carried out (independently) e.g. by W. Lubaszewski, St. Szpakowicz and Z. Vetulani.

Typical of these early works was the unavailability of real-size electronic language resources as well as of NLP dedicated tools for Polish. These early studies on NL parsing and logic-based question-answering were to appear inspiring two decades later when we started working on real size applications (Vetulani 2012). However, real size applications require real scale resources.

3 Basic Resources for Text Processing

During our first attempts to design non-trivial rule-based question-answering systems with deep understanding[1] (Vetulani 1988) we identified the most urgent needs: electronic dictionaries, computer processible grammars and corpora (for general language, but also application-domain-specific ones). Several national and European projects contributed to partially fill the gaps in resources and tools.

---

[1] See e.g. (Vetulani 1988) reporting our results obtained already in 1984 at GIA, Marseille.

3.1 Dictionary Project POLEX (1994–1996)

Polish is a highly inflected language and therefore it has a relatively free word order. Consequently, the simple adaptation of processing algorithms that are efficient for English or French appeared hard to apply. This is so, because the information concerning the function of a word in the sentence is typically encoded in the word form, independently of its linear position in the sentence. The evidence forced us to propose our own algorithms, e.g. parsers (Vetulani 1988) that require a precise description of Polish grammar.

In the field of morphology, a huge amount of work by lexicographers until the 1990s did not lead to a standard for the description of Polish words that would eliminate the individual linguistic competence of users to interpret dictionaries. We proposed an unambiguous inflectional description system[2] capable of eliminating the need for human linguistic competence to interpret word-forms and therefore appropriate for the development of machine-processing software (Vetulani et al. 1998a).

POLEX is a morphological dictionary of core Polish words of general interest included in a large traditional paper dictionary (Szymczak 1995). It uses a precise machine-interpretable formalism (coding system), which is the same for all categories (classes of speech) (Vetulani et al. 1998a).

The dictionary entries are described as a list of four parameters: *basic form, list of stems, paradigmatic code*, and *distribution of stems*. Two of these parameters, the *paradigmatic inflection code* and *distribution of stems*, describe how to associate endings to stems to obtain the required forms of the word (distribution associates stems to the paradigmatic positions).

The first public release of the resource contained (2007) over 42,000 nouns, 12,000 verbs, 15,000 adjectives, 25,000 participles, and about 200 pronouns[3].

3.2 First Steps Towards Lexicon-Grammars for Polish

In the 1970s Maurice Gross (LADL, Paris 7) proposed a grammatical lexicon based on the idea of storing words together with possibly all relevant syntactic and semantic information (Gross 1975). Lexicon-Grammars were developed first for French, then for other languages. Consequently, predicative words were studied from the point of view of their aptitude to form elementary sentences. Gross introduced the term lexicon-grammar (fr. *lexique-grammaire*) in the sense of the method of describing the meaning of predicative words by providing descriptions of how these words form simple sentences. What distinguishes lexicon grammars from traditional grammatical descriptions of a language is that lexicon grammar entries contain exhaustive grammatical description (on syntactic and semantic levels) of well-defined senses of words. This property renders lexical-grammars well-suited for NLP applications.

---

[2] This system is an outcome of the POLEX Polish Lexicon Project ("POLEX - Polska Leksykalna Baza Danych No KBN8S50301007") realised by Z. Vetulani, B. Walczak, T. Obrębski, G. Vetulani and other team members during 1994–1996 (Vetulani et al. 1998a).

[3] The resource is distributed through ELRA. ISLRN: 147-211-031-223-4; ID: ELRA-L0047.

The EUREKA Project GENELEX (1990–1994). GENELEX[4] was an initiative – which first addressed some Western-European languages, starting with English, French, German, and Italian – to realize the idea of lexicon-grammar in the form of a generic model for lexicons and to propose software tools for lexicon management (Antoni-Lay et al. 1994). The first of the two reasons given by Antoni-Lay for large-size lexicons was that when Natural Language applications left the research labs for world of practical applications, they were required to cover a wide variety of language phenomena, and this implied real scale resources such as electronic dictionaries, grammars and corpora. The second reason was the tendency observed already in the eighties (and even before[5]) to put a large amount of grammatical information into a lexicon. This tendency finally led to grammatical systems with relatively few grammar rules and more complex lexicon instead (Gross (1975) and Polański (1980–1992)).

Although Polish was not covered by the GENELEX project, it was studied in two EU projects, GRAMLEX and CEGLEX, aimed at testing the potential of the novel GENELEX-based LT solutions to some languages not represented in GENELEX.

PECO-COPERNICUS Project 1032 CEGLEX (1995–1996). The main goal of the CEGLEX consortium[6] (Vetulani et al. 1995) was to test the GENELEX proposal of a generic model for reusable lexicons for three official languages spoken in Central Europe: Czech, Hungarian and Polish.

The CEGLEX/GENELEX model claims to be theory-welcoming, complete, (i.e. to cover all relevant phenomena on three classical layers: morphological, syntactic, and semantic), as well as easily applicable to different languages.

The three layers of the CEGLEX/GENELEX model were confronted with the data for languages under consideration with generally positive results, especially for Czech and Polish. In particular, the model had to be adapted to accept language data for the Polish language. On this occasion some modifications were proposed concerning the representation of the inflection phenomena specific to the Polish language.

PECO-COPERNICUS Project 621 GRAMLEX (1995–1998). "The aim of GRAM-LEX was to facilitate the initiation, coordination and standardization of the construction of morphological dictionary packages"[7] for the following European languages: French, Hungarian, Italian and Polish[8], including a detailed formal description of the morphology of the Polish language. The intention of the GRAMLEX tasks for Polish was to contribute to the improvement of the situation concerning language engineering tools

---

[4] GENELEX was continued by LE-PAROLE (1996–1998), LE-SIMPLE (1998–2000) and GRAAL (1992–1996) projects.

[5] See e.g. Maurice Gross (1975) and Polański (1980–1992).

[6] CEGLEX Consortium: AMU, Poznań/Poland/, Charles University, Prague/Czech Rep./, GSI-ERLI, Charenton/France/(coordinator), Lingware, Szeged/Hungary/.

[7] From the GRAMLEX project description by Eric Laporte, project coordinator. Quoted by (Vetulani et al. 1998b).

[8] GRAMLEX Consortium: AMU, Poznań/Poland/, ASSTRIL, Marne la Vallée/France/ (coordinator), CLR, Salerno/Italy/, Hungarian Academy of Science, Budapest/Hungary/.

and resources. Among the main achievements was a corpus-based morphological dictionary (for over 22.500 entries derived from POLEX) as well as the related tools and applications (lemmatizer, inflected form generator, concordance generator and others[9]) in the GENELEX format (Vetulani et al. 1998b). The project GRAMLEX was related to the two projects mentioned above POLEX and CEGLEX lexemes.

3.3 Further Steps Towards Lexicon Grammars for Polish. PolNet 3.0 as Lexicon-Grammar

The IT applications with language competence we were able to develop until 1990 were all classified as toy-systems. This was caused by the lack of real-size digital, easily machine processable electronic resources. This problem was addressed in the R&D grant "Text Processing Technologies for Homeland Security Purposes"[10].

POLINT-SMS-112 – A System with Natural Language Competence (2006–2010). Within the above mentioned grant we created a prototype of the system that was designed to assist the monitoring of mass events and to enhance real-time identification of potentially dangerous situations in the crowd of fans in order to fix processes with a high degeneration risk (early prevention). This application required a powerful natural language competence to understand and to process SMS messages exchanged between the security staff agents in uncontrolled natural language, cf. (Vetulani and Osiński 2017). The understanding module of the system is rule-based because the need to obtain a very precise representation of the utterance content that is crucial in processing sensitive information. Messages were supposed to be written in standard, correct and unconstrained Polish. Resources essential for this project, besides the machine-readable grammar and dictionaries, were ontologies for knowledge representation and logic-based reasoning, and text and dialogues corpora to support the implementation of the language processing model of the application.

Corpora. Text and speech corpora have numerous applications in language processing. First of all they constitute an empirical foundation on which to construct language models. The elementary application of a corpus consist in identifying and cataloging language use phenomena important for further text processing (like parsing, understanding, etc.). Several corpora were used to implement the POLINT-112-SMS system. For purposes such as concepts acquisition for ontology building or creating frequency-based heuristics for language processing, it is common to apply large corpora. In our case we used the open version of the Polish National Corpus, (Przepiórkowski 2004).

---

[9] These tools and applications were: (i) a lemmatizer/tagger (LEXAN) (Vetulani et al. 1997, 1998b), (ii) a generator of inflected forms for simple and compound lexemes (Vetulani et al. 1998b), (iii) a syntactic concordance generator (SCON) (Vetulani et al. 1998b), (iv) a tool for the extraction of compound terms and terminology from texts (EXTRACT) (Vetulani et al. 1998b), (v) an application for the structure analysis of dictionary entries (VERBAN) (Vetulani et al. 1998b), (vi) an application for acquisition of the lexicon from dictionary definitions (NOUNAN) (Vetulani et al. 1998b), (vii) an application for interactive analysis of dictionary definitions (NOUNDAN) (Vetulani et al. 1998b).

[10] Grant of Ministry of Science and Higher Education (MNiSzW) Nr R0002802 (2006–2010).

In cases where project specific linguistic information was necessary, we were obliged to collect the necessary corpora. Some of them were:

– the experimentally collected St. Claus Corpus of informative dialogs (Vetulani 1989, 1990), (Vetulani et al. 2004),
– the corpus of 1700 private SMS messages (Walkowska 2009), (Vetulani et al. 2010),
– corpus of experimental *Role Playing Game* dialogs (Vetulani et al. 2010)/1374 dialogs/,
– experimental Wizard_of_Oz – supported dialogs (Vetulani et al. 2010)/1198 dialogs/,
– a juridical text corpus (papers/23/, books/2/, documents/80/) (Vetulani et al. 2010),
– speech corpus – emergency line 997[11] (24 h of recording for 1818 calls, partially transcribed into text and tagged/58,935 words/).

PolNet - Polish Wordnet as Lexical Ontology (Since 2006).[12] The absence on the market of lexical ontologies reflecting conceptualization typical of Polish[13] speakers inspired us to develop PolNet Polish Wordnet – a lexical database of the type of Princeton Word-Net[14]. We built it from scratch according to the so-called "merge model" methodology[15]. Creation of PolNet started in 2006 and continues. The resource development procedure was based on the exploration of traditional dictionaries and the use of available language corpora such as the IPI PAN Corpus (Przepiórkowski 2004). Incremental development of PolNet started with general and frequently used vocabulary[16]. We decided to selected the most widely used words found in a reference corpus of Polish language (Vetulani et al. 2007), with an important exception made for methodological reasons: even though we intended PolNet to be a resource of general interest, we assumed its possibly early validation in the real-size applications for which to have a domain-specific terminology represented in the system was crucial.

By 2008, the initial PolNet version based on noun synsets related by hyponymy/hyperonymy relations was already large enough to serve as a core lexical ontology for real-size applications. However, in order to develop a POLINT-112-SMS system prototype, an extension of the core set of nouns with domain terminology was necessary. Further extension with verbs and collocations transformed PolNet into a lexicon-grammar (Vetulani and Vetulani 2014a) bringing to PolNet various new possibilities, such as facilitating the implementation of parsers. By including the verb category in PolNet we brought ideas inspired by FrameNet (Fillmore et al. 2002) and VerbNet

---

[11] Emergency telephone service maintained by the Polish Police (equivalent to tel. 112).

[12] See (Vetulani Z. 2014) for the core PolNet bibliography until 2014.

[13] At about the same time, Wrocław Technical University started another successful wordnet project plWordnet (pl. Słowosieć) (Piasecki et al. 2009) based on a different methodology.

[14] In the Princeton WordNet the basic entities are synsets, i.e. classes of synonyms related by semantic relations of which the most important are hyponymy and hyperonymy.

[15] Princeton WordNet (Miller et al. 1990) was used as a formal ontology to implement systems with language understanding functionality. In order to respect a specific Polish conceptualization of the world, we decided to build PolNet from scratch rather than merely translate the Princeton WordNet into Polish.

[16] See (Vetulani et al. 2007) for PolNet development algorithm.

(Palmer 2009) projects to PolNet. The verbal part was at the heart of the entire network. Its organizing backbone was the system of semantic roles (Palmer 2009).

First Step from PolNet to Lexicon-Grammar PolNet 1.0. Already in the early 1980s information typically contained in lexicon-grammar entries for predicative words, simple or compound, was considered useful for parsing and generating natural language sentences. Lexical entries used in the PROLOG code of the demonstration system ORBIS[17] (Colmerauer and Kittredge 1982), were in fact lexicon-grammar units describing syntactic and sematic valency of words. The syntactic/semantic valency (valency structure) appeared useful to avoid the acceptance of incorrect sentences by a parser and the production of incorrect sentences by a generation algorithm. It is also helpful to build error-correcting software. The qualitative evolution of PolNet, initially conceived as lexical ontology, towards a lexicon-grammar of Polish took place between the release of PolNet 0.1 (2009) and the version PolNet 3.0. (2014). The pragmatic reason to substantially enrich PolNet was the need of an efficient parsing engine to support the understanding module.

In addition to noun synsets that make of PolNet 0.1 (2009) a lexical ontology, we decided to enrich PolNet with verb synsets containing syntactic/semantic information in the form of valency structure. The valency structure of a predicative word provides the morpho-syntactic and semantic constraints on the acceptable fillers of the argument positions opened by this word (like *case, number, gender, preposition, register* etc. for morpho-syntactic constraints and semantic roles (Palmer 2009) like *agent, patient, beneficiary,* etc. for semantic ones). Later, we decided to refine our idea of verb synsets taking into account the granularity issues related to synonymy. We focused on verb-noun constraints corresponding to the particular argument positions of the verb. For our purposes we proposed the following definition: verb+meaning pairs are only synonymous when they take the same semantic roles and the same concepts as values (see more in (Vetulani and Vetulani 2014b) and (Vetulani 2015).). In particular, the valency structure of a verb is one of the indices of meaning (i.e. all members of a synset share the valency structure).

Verb synsets appeared already in the first public release of PolNet in 2011 (PolNet 1.0) (Vetulani et al. 2016). This extension opened a new generation of PolNet systems that we call now "PolNet – Polish Lexicon-Grammar systems". The expansion of PolNet to the Lexicon Grammar of Polish was based on the results of research on predicative verbs assembled in the Dictionary of Polish Verbs (Polański 1980–1992) where linguistic descriptions were provided for 7000 Polish predicative verbs.

The valency information permitted us to make a smart use of PolNet as it was enriched with lexicon-grammar features when implementing the POLINT-112-SMS system. In addition to using PolNet as a lexical ontology in the World Knowledge and Situation Analysis Modules, we made use of the valency information to enhance the efficiency of the parser as part of the Text Understanding Module. In this module, syntactic/semantic valency information stored in the lexicon-grammar rules was used to control parsing

---

[17] ORBIS, an interface to a database on planets, was implemented in PROLOG to show the qualities of the declarative programming paradigm. The initially bilingual system was extended with a module for Polish by Z. Vetulani while his research fellowship at GIA, the University Aix-Marseille II in 1984 (Vetulani 1988).

execution by heuristics[18] in order to speed-up parsing due to additional information gathered at the pre-analysis stage. The effect of substantially reducing the processing time was due to the reduction of search space.

Collocations in PolNet 2.0 - PolNet 3.0. As the usefulness of PolNet as lexical ontology in the development of real-size systems was positively verified by the above-mentioned application, we decided to take the next steps towards the full lexicon-grammar. The versions PolNet 2.0 and PolNet 3.0 were important milestones in this process. The passage from PolNet 1.0 to PolNet 2.0 (Vetulani and Vetulani 2014b) was marked by inclusion of a set of verb-noun collocations from the syntactic dictionary of verb-noun collocations (Vetulani 2000 and 2012)[19] or directly from corpora described in (Vetulani et al. 2010)[20]. Verb-noun collocations, typically composed of a noun (playing the role of predicate) and a predicatively empty support verb[21] (Vetulani 2000), play in the sentence the same role as simple predicative verbs in other cases. By playing the role of the logical center of the sentence, these collocations attribute some properties to the sentence arguments (subject, complements) and fix relationships between the subject and its complements. Thus the role of predicative collocations[22] in the lexicon-grammar is equally as important as the role of simple predicative verbs, especially when for purposes of further processing[23], information carried by predicative elements appears useful.

Being predicatively empty, the support verb in Polish still plays a significant auxiliary function in the interpretation of the predicates. This is due to its possible emotional and metaphorical aspect. A support verb may provide information on the language register, aspect (*perfective/imperfective*), action mood (*inchoative, terminative, progressive* etc.) or pragmatic/situational meaning (as *politeness* or *informality*). The "predicatively empty" support verb contributes to the sense of the collocation and to its disambiguation.

The study of predicative collocations is equally important for language technology as for the traditional domains of language teaching and translation. This is because of the conventional nature of collocations whose structure and lexical selection are

---

[18] In (Vetulani 1994) we described the switch technique which combined with appropriate heuristics permits, on the ground of morphological and valency information, the reduction of the complexity of parsing sometimes down to linear.

[19] This dictionary is described in two monographs. The first one (2000) describes the initial phase of work on a dictionary of verb-noun collocations together their usage in sentences as predicates (2862 predicative nouns). This work was done manually. The extension of the resource to 14.600 collocations was described in the second book (2012) reporting further, computer-assisted work. A part of this resource was integrated with PolNet.

[20] In (Vetulani et al. 2010) we described a computer-assisted algorithm to extract collocations directly from text corpora. Still, involvement of qualified lexicographers is necessary.

[21] The term *support verb* was first introduced to linguistics by Harris (1964), on the occasion of his research on nominalisation. Gross (1975) used the term *verb support (French)* in his work on lexicon-grammars, while Ch. Fillmore (Filmore et al. 2002) preferred to use the word *light verb* in the project VerbNet. G. Vetulani (Vetulani 2000) uses the term *czasownik podporowy (Polish)*.

[22] Here support verb + predicative noun, but more generally any other predicative word (such as an adjective or adverb) instead of a noun.

[23] Eg. in order to seed-up parsing (Vetulani 1991).

unpredictable. This is one more reason to have all the varieties of predicative collocations included in the lexicon-grammar with as complete a description as possible.

Adding verb-noun collocations to PolNet appeared a non-trivial task because of specific morpho-syntactic phenomena related to collocations such as syntactic synonymy[24] (Vetulani et al. 2016), as well as the problem of (optimal) granularity of verbal synsets. In (Vetulani, Z., Vetulani, G., 2014b) we observed that granularity is directly related to *synonymy which is the basis of the organization of the wordnet database in synsets,* (i.e. that synonyms should belong to the same synset (see above). Our approach differs from the one of Miller and Fellbaum (in Vossen et al. 1998) who postulate a very weak understanding of this concept (based on *an invariability test with respect to just one linguistic context*) often leading to very large synsets

Version 3.0 of PolNet was meticulously cleaned and extended[25] with respect to the Version 2.0. It has been user-tested as a resource for modeling semantic similarity between words (Kubis 2015).

4 Last but not Least: Human Resources

The possibility of gaining the status of a High-Resourced Language depends on the existence of a research community of experts qualified to create NLP resources and tools. For Polish this difficult requirement was satisfied from the very beginning due to the existence of well qualified computer science manpower and very competent descriptive linguists. This fact made possible the creation of crucial language resources independently in several research centers throughout the country[26].

The increase in the volume of R&D work in Poland is correlated with the progress of Polish computational linguistics. The Language and Technology Conferences (LTC) organized in Poznań mobilized since 1995 over 1.360 authors from over 60 countries (see http://www.ltc.amu.edu.pl). For 25 years LTC was for Polish authors a natural forum to present research about Polish. More than 300 LTC contributors representing national and private institutions of fundamental research, R&D groups and companies testify to the creation in Poland of a strong community of HLT developers.

This means the promotion of Poland to the small number of countries with solid human capital in the area of Language Technologies who are well prepared to develop language technologies for their mother tongue.

5 Conclusions

In this paper we presented some of our achievements in the field of Language Engineering over more than 30 years (cf. references below). These achievements, in parallel with

---

[24] In Polish we observe the phenomenon of syntactic synonymy (Jędrzejko 1993) where for some predicative verbs their morpho-syntactic structure varies from the morpho-syntactic structure of their semantic synonyms in the form of verb-noun collocation (e.g. for the direct complement). For consistency with our methodological assumptions, we range these synonymous forms in distinct synsets interconnected by a special semantic similarity relation.

[25] From 14.400 in PolNet 2.0 to 17.564 in PolNet 3.0.

[26] In Kraków, Poznań, Rzeszów, Śląsk (Silesia), Warszawa, Wrocław, and other places.

those of other Polish academic centers, mean that Polish is no longer considered as belonging to the class of Less-Resourced Languages as it was in the 1990s. Not being exhaustive, this presentation aims to show the nature of the challenges to be faced when developing sophisticated systems for language processing for Less-Resourced Languages. It is fundamental to possess text (or/and speech where necessary) corpora to serve as an empirical basis for the computer modelling of language competence, and to create tools to build and process these corpora (such as lemmatizers, taggers, concordance creators, electronic dictionaries and lexicons, grammars, parsers and text (voice) generators, etc.). The acquisition of such an instrumentarium is a *conditio sine qua non* for leaving the group of Less-Resourced Languages, and thereby acquiring the necessary potential for creating advanced applications on an industrial scale.

To start working to join the still small group of High-Resourced Languages it is essential to dispose of initial manpower composed of researchers and engineers with a linguistic or/and IT background. In our case this pre-condition was satisfied, although initially only very few were experts in both domains.

The need to acquire a solid empirical basis for computer processable resources and related tools for creating non-trivial systems with human language competence was obvious for us from the beginning, but, nevertheless only work on real-size systems with language competence (such as POLINT-112-SMS) would appear to be a key milestone in the understanding of the scale of the problem. An important side-effect of this project was the creation of a strong multidisciplinary group of well-trained experts in language related technologies capable of facing operational challenges. These practical works confirmed our understanding of the problems of the scarcity of tools, but first of all permitted us to identify our priorities on the way to enriching our instrumentarium. Among these priorities there is the further development of the Polish lexicon-grammar integrated with the PolNet lexical basis. This long-term project is currently being realized.

We hope that this paper will appear interesting for people taking on the challenge facing the Less-Resourced Languages.

References

Antoni-Lay, M.-H., Francopoulo, G., Zaysser, L.: A Generic Model for Reusable Lexicons: The Genelex Project. Literary and Linguistic Computing, vol. 9, no 1, pp. 47–54. University Press, Oxford (1994)

Colmerauer, A., Kittredge, R.: ORBIS. In: J. Horecký, J. (ed.) Proceedings of the 9th COLING Conference (1982)

Fillmore Ch.J., Baker C.F., Sato H.: Seeing arguments through transparent structures. In: Proceedings of Third International Conference on Language Resources and Evaluation, Proceedings, vol. III, Las Palmas, pp. 787–791 (2002)

Gross, M.: Méthodes en syntaxe. Hermann, Paris (1975)

Harris, Z.S.: The Elementary Transformations. Transformations and Discourse Analysis Papers No. 54. University of Pennsylvania, Philadelphia (1964)

Jędrzejko, E.: Nominalizacje w systemie i w tekstach współczesnej polszczyzny. Wydawnictwo Uniwersytetu Śląskiego, Katowice (1993)

Kubis, M.: A semantic similarity measurement tool for WordNet-like databases. In: Vetulani, Z., Mariani, J. (eds.) Proceedings of the 7th Language and Technology Conference, Poznań, Poland, 27–29 November 2015. FUAM, Poznań, pp. 150–154 (2015)

Miller, G.A., Beckwith, R., Fellbaum, C.D., Gross, D., Miller, K.: WordNet: an online lexical database. Int. J. Lexicograph. 3(4), 235–244 (1990)

Palmer, M.: Semlink: Linking PropBank. VerbNet and FrameNet. In: Proceedings of the Generative Lexicon Conference, Pisa, Italy, September 2009

Piasecki, M., Szpakowicz, S., Broda, B.: A Wordnet from the Ground Up. Oficyna Wydawnicza Politechniki Wrocławskiej, Wrocław (2009)

Polański, K. (ed.): Słownik syntaktyczno-generatywny czasowników polskich. vol. I-IV, Ossolineum, Wrocław, 1980–1990; vol. V, IJP PAN, Kraków (1992)

Przepiórkowski, A.: Korpus IPI PAN. Wersja wstępna (The IPI PAN Corpus: Preliminary version). IPI PAN, Warszawa (2004)

Szymczak, M. (ed.): Słownik Języka Polskiego (Polish Dictionary). Państwowe Wydawnictwo Naukowe, Warszawa (1995)

Vetulani, G.: Rzeczowniki predykatywne języka polskiego. W kierunku syntaktycznego słownika rzeczowników predykatywnych na tle porównawczym. (Predicate nouns of Polish. Towards a syntactic dictionary of predicate nouns), AMU Press, Poznań (2000)

Vetulani, G.: Kolokacje werbo-nominalne jako samodzielne jednostki języka. Syntaktyczny słownik kolokacji werbo-nominalnych języka polskiego na potrzeby zastosowań informatycznych. Część I (Verb-noun collocations as language units. Syntactic dictionary of Polish verb-noun collocations for NLP applications. Part I). AMU Press, Poznań (2012)

Vetulani, Z.: PROLOG implementation of an access in polish to a data base. In: Studia z automatyki, XII, Państwowe Wydawnictwo Naukowe, pp. 5–23 (1988)

Vetulani, Z.: Linguistic problems in the theory of man-machine communication in natural language. A study of consultative question answering dialogs. Empirical approach. Brockmeyer, Bochum (1989)

Vetulani, Z.: Corpus of consultative dialogs. Experimentally collected source data for AI applications. Adam Mickiewicz University Press, Poznań (1990)

Vetulani, Z.: Lexical preanalysis in a DCG parser of POLISH. In: Klein, E., et al. (eds.) Betriebslinguistik und Linguistikbetrieb. Akten des 24 Linguistischen Kolloquiums, Bremen 1989, (Ling. Arbeiten 260/261), Max Niemeyer, Tübingen, pp. 389–395 (1991)

Vetulani, Z.: SWITCHes for making Prolog more Dynamic Programming Language, Logic Programming, The Newsletter of the Association for Logic Programming, vol 7/1, p. 10, February 1994

Vetulani, Z., Martinek, J., Vetulani, G.: The CEGLEX dictionary model for Polish. In: Bazylewicz, R., Kossak, O. (eds.) Proceedings of the 4th and 5th International Conferences UKRSOFT (Lviv, 1994, 1995), SP «BaK», Lviv, 1995, pp. 144–150 (1995)

Vetulani, Z., Martinek, J., Obrębski, T., Vetulani, G.: Lexical Resources and Tools for Tagging Polish Texts within GRAMLEX. In: Linguisticae Investigationes, XXI:2, John Benjamins B.V, Amsaterdam 401–416 (1997)

Vetulani, Z., Walczak, B., Obrębski, T., Vetulani, G.: Unambiguous coding of the inflection of Polish nouns and its application in the electronic dictionaries - format POLEX. Adam Mickiewicz University Press, Poznań (1998a)

Vetulani, Z., Martinek, J., Obrębski, T., Vetulani, G.: Dictionary Based Methods and Tools for Language Engineering. Adam Mickiewicz University Press, Poznań (1998b)

Vetulani, Z.: Komunikacja człowieka z maszyną. Komputerowe modelowanie kompetencji językowej (Man-machine communication. Computer modelling of language competence), Akademicka Oficyna Wydawnicza EXIT, Warszawa (2004)

Vetulani, Z., Walkowska, J., Obrębski, T., Marciniak, J., Konieczka, P., Rzepecki, P.: An algorithm for building lexical semantic network and its application to PolNet - polish WordNet project. In: Vetulani, Z., Uszkoreit, H. (eds.) LTC 2007. LNCS (LNAI), vol. 5603, pp. 369–381. Springer, Heidelberg (2009). https://doi.org/10.1007/978-3-642-04235-5_32

Vetulani, Z., et al.: Zasoby językowe i technologie przetwarzania tekstu. POLINT-112-SMS jako przykład aplikacji z zakresu bezpieczeństwa publicznego (Language resources and text processing technologies. POLINT-112-SMS as example of homeland security oriented application). AMU Press, Poznań (2010)

Vetulani, Z.: Language resources in a public security application with text understanding competence. A Case Study: POLINT-112-SMS. In: Proceedings of the LRPS Workshop at LREC 2012, May 27, 2012. Istanbul, Turkey, ELRA, Paris, pp. 54–63 (2012)

Vetulani, Z.: PolNet – Polish WordNet. In: Vetulani, Z., Mariani, J. (eds.) LTC 2011. LNCS (LNAI), vol. 8387, pp. 408–416. Springer, Cham (2014). https://doi.org/10.1007/978-3-319-08958-4_33

Vetulani, Z., Vetulani, G.: Through Wordnet to Lexicon Grammar. In: Kakoyianni Doa, F. (ed.) Penser le lexique grammaire: perspectives actuelles, pp. 531–543. Editions Honoré Champion, Paris (2014a)

Vetulani, Z., Vetulani, G.: Verb-Noun Collocations in PolNet 2.0. In: Henrich, V., Hinrichs, E., (eds.) Proceedings of the Workshop on Computational Cognitive and Linguistic Approaches to the Analysis of Complex Words and Collocations (CCLCC 2014), Tübingen, Germany, pp. 73–77 (2014b)

Vetulani, Z., Vetulani, G.: Synonymie et granularité dans les bases lexicales du type Wordnet. Studia Romanica Posnaniensia, vol. 42/1, WN UAM, Poznań, pp. 113–127 (2015)

Vetulani, Z., Vetulani, G., Kochanowski, B.: Recent advances in development of a lexicon-grammar of polish: PolNet 3.0. In: Calzolari, N., et al. (eds.) The 10th Conference on Language Resources and Evaluation, pp. 2851–2854. Paris, France, ELRA (2016)

Vetulani, Z., Osiński, J.: Intelligent information bypass for more efficient emergency management. Comp. Methods in Science and Technology 23(2), 105–123 (2017)

Vossen, P., Bloksma, L., Rodriguez, H., Climent, S., Calzolari, N., Peters, W.: The euro WordNet base concepts and top ontology, final version (1998). https://www.researchgate.net/publication/228594694_The_EuroWordNet_Base_Concepts_and_Top_Ontology

Walkowska, J.: Gathering and analysis of a corpus of polish SMS dialogs. In: Kłopotek, M.A., et al. (eds.) Challenging Problems of Science, pp. 145–157. Publishing House EXIT, Warszawa, Computer Science. Recent Advances in Intelligent Information Systems (2009)

Computational Collective Intelligence and Natural Language Processing

Towards a Context-Aware Knowledge Model for Smart Service Systems

Dinh Thang Le[1]($\boxtimes$) (iD), Thanh Thoa Pham Thi[2] (iD), Cuong Pham-Nguyen[3] (iD),
and Le Nguyen Hoai Nam[3]

[1] Université du Québec à Trois-Rivières, C.P 500, Trois-Rivières, Québec, Canada
thang.ledinh@uqtr.ca
[2] Technological University Dublin, Aungier St., Dublin 2, Ireland
thoa.pham@tudublin.ie
[3] Faculty of Information Technology, VNUHCM-University of Science,
Ho Chi Minh City, Vietnam
{pncuong, lnhnam}@fit.hcmus.edu.vn

Abstract. The advancement of the Internet of things, big data, and mobile computing leads to the need for smart services that enable the context awareness and the adaptability to their changing contexts. Today, designing a smart service system is a complex task due to the lack of an adequate model support in awareness and pervasive environment. In this paper, we present a context-aware knowledge model for smart service systems that organizes the domain and context-aware knowledge into knowledge components based on the three levels of services: Services, Service system and Network of service systems. The context-aware knowledge model for smart service systems integrates all the information and knowledge related to smart services, knowledge components and context awareness that can play a key role for any framework, infrastructure, or applications deploying smart services. To demonstrate the approach, a case study about a chatbot as a smart service for customer support is presented.

Keywords: Smart services · Smart service systems · Knowledge component · Context-aware · Chatbot

1 Introduction

The advancement of the Internet of things, big data, and mobile computing leads to the need for smart services that enables the context awareness and the adaptability to their changing contexts. Consequently, the information technology paradigm shifts to a smart service environment, as ubiquitous technologies are used in the latest industry trend. The major features of smart services are high dynamism and heterogeneity of their environment and the need for context awareness (Oh et al. 2009).

Smart services are services that are capable of actively adapting and responding based on the circumstance of interests. A smart service, as is evident from its name, is a context-aware connected service (Geum et al. 2016). Therefore, to smart services,

© Springer Nature Switzerland AG 2020
N. T. Nguyen et al. (Eds.): ICCCI 2020, LNAI 12496, pp. 767–778, 2020.
https://doi.org/10.1007/978-3-030-63007-2_60

the service context plays a key role that influences the service behaviors. From another perspective, smart services are considered as suitable knowledge provided to consumers and smart objects based on their circumstances. However, designing a smart service system is a complex task due to the lack of an adequate model support in awareness and pervasive environment (Gu et al. 2005).

Therefore, the paper presents an approach based on a context-aware knowledge model for smart service systems. This approach aims at organizing the domain and context-aware knowledge of smart service systems into knowledge components based on the three levels of services: Services, Service system and Network of service systems (Le Dinh and Pham Thi 2012). The context-aware knowledge model for smart service systems integrates all the information and knowledge related to smart services, knowledge components and context awareness that can play a key role for any framework, infrastructure, or applications for deploying smart services.

The rest of the paper is organized as follows. Section 2 provides the background of contexts, service systems, and smart service systems. Section 3 proposes a context-aware knowledge model for smart service systems. Section 4 illustrates our proposed approach with a specific case of smart services for a software support center. Section 5 provides some conclusions and future research work.

2 Background

2.1 Context-Aware Systems

Context. "Context" is defined as "the situation within which something exists or happens, and that can help explain it" in Cambridge dictionary. In the computing field, context is defined as "any information that can be used to characterize the situation of an entity. An entity is a person, place, or object that is considered relevant to the interaction between a user and an application" (Abowd et al. 1999). Contexts can be classified such as computing context, physical context, time context, and user context (Chen and Kotz 2000). In the context of smart services, there are certain types of context that are, in practice, more important than others such as *location, identity, activity* and *time*. Those types of context are the primary context types for characterizing the situation of a particular entity and can be used to find the secondary context for that same entity as well as primary context for other related entities (Abowd et al. 1999). Consequently, the questions of who, what, when, and where are often used to identify other sources of contextual information.

Context-Aware Systems. A system is context-aware if it uses context to provide relevant information and/or services to the user, where relevancy depends on the user's task (Abowd et al. 1999). A context-aware system refers to a general class of systems that can sense their environment, and adapt their behavior accordingly (Bellavista et al. 2012). The main features of context-aware systems are: i) Presentation of information and services to users; ii) Execution automatically of a service; and iii) Tagging of context to information for later use.

2.2 Services, Service System and Network of Service Systems

Services. In the service-dominant logic, services are defined as the use of an economic entity's specific competencies, such as knowledge, skills and technologies, for the benefit of another economic entity (Lusch and Vargo 2008). Services include all economic activities in which individuals, organizations and technologies work together, apply specialized competences and capabilities to co-create business value.

Service Systems. Value creation occurs when a resource is turned into a specific benefit, called resourcing, that is performed by a service system. A service system is defined as a "value-coproduction configuration of people, technology, other internal and external service systems, and shared information." (Spohrer et al. 2007). Service systems have been getting smarter overtime as new trends such as big data and business analytics have been used to generate information and automate business operations to create more value for customers.

Network of Service Systems. Besides, the traditional supply chain is re-conceptualized as a *network of service systems*, also called a *service value creation network*, which is a group of autonomous organizations working together to achieve not only their own goals, but also a collective goal (Lusch et al. 2008; Le Dinh and Léonard 2009).

2.3 Smart Service and Smart Service Systems

Smart Services. Services delivered to or through intelligent products that feature awareness and connectivity are called "smart services" (Lim and Maglio 2018). Smart services are services that are capable of actively adapting and responding based on the circumstance of interests. A smart service, as is evident from its name, is a context-aware connected service (Geum et al. 2016).

Smart Service Systems (SSS). A smart service system is a service system, which is "capable of learning, dynamic adaptation, and decision-making based upon data received, transmitted, and/or processed to improve its response to a future situation" (Medina-Borja 2015). Furthermore, smart service systems are instrumented, interconnected, and intelligent (Spohrer 2013). Instrumented means sensors that capture more real-time and historical information that stakeholders need to make better decisions. Interconnected means people have easy access to information about a particular service system, as well as others that interact with it. Intelligent means recommendation algorithms that work to provide stakeholders best choices. There are several types of smart service systems such as Smart home, Smart energy, Smart building, Smart transportation, Smart logistics, Smart farming, Smart security, Smart health, Smart hospitality, Smart education, and Smart city and government (Lim and Maglio 2018).

Indeed, the field of smart service systems is still an emerging field that covers different research topics (Lim and Maglio 2018). One of the most important topics is how to "design of smart service systems" which addresses knowledge for the design of these systems, including design model, approach, and process. For this reason, this paper addresses this challenge and presents a context-aware knowledge model for designing and building a smart service system in the following sections.

3   CAK Model for Smart Service Systems

3.1   Research Design

3.1.1   Research Question

This paper seeks to answer the following research question: *"How to design a context-aware smart service system based on knowledge components?"*

In order to respond to this question, the paper proposes the Context-Aware Knowledge (CAK) model, called CAK model, which can be used to design and build context-aware smart service systems. Indeed, a smart service system (SSS) must be capable of learning, dynamic adaptation, and decision-making. Therefore, a SSS needs a knowledge structure, including a knowledge management system for its operations as well as a knowledge development process to facilitate the transformation of data into information and then from information into knowledge (Le Dinh et al. 2014). The underlying research design consists of two phases. Firstly, the paper aims at the construction of the research artefacts of the proposed model and then continues with the subsequent evaluation and applicability check of these artefacts with the case study.

3.1.2   Definition of a Context

After reviewing the relevant thematic and methodological literature (Le Dinh et al. 2014), the paper considers a context is all the formation that can be used to describe a situation of a smart service and its interactions with the environment. Based on the perspective of knowledge components (Le Dinh et al. 2014), a context is defined by a set of knowledge components, including know-with, know-who, know-where, know-when, know-what, know-how, and know-why.

A typical expression of a context is as the following: *A «stakeholder» (know-who) performs «operations» (know-how) on «objects» (know-what) at «time» (know-when) in «a location» (know-where) because of «a contract» (know-with) to be consistent with «a business rule» (know-why).*

3.1.3   Service and Its Context

The proposed approach considers that a service consists of three service elements: service proposal, service consumption, and service operation (Le Dinh and Pham Thi 2012). At the Network of service systems level, the *service proposal* element uses the knowledge and understanding to create and increase the values of business services in a service value creation network by applying effective management practices. At the Service system level, the *service consumption* element aims at organizing services in a service system and supporting consumers in consuming services. At the service level, the *service operation* element improves the quality of services. Accordingly, the focal points of the CAK model could involve different knowledge components (Le Dinh et al. 2015) at different levels of services (Table 1).

At the Network of service systems level, the *Know-who* and *Know-with* knowledge components aim at capturing knowledge about the relationship and interaction between stakeholders of the network and at determining the process of value proposition and

Table 1. Knowledge components of the CAK model.

Level	Objective	Knowledge components	Corresponding types of context
Network of service systems	Service proposal	Know-with	Secondary context
		Know-who	Identity (primary context)
Service system	Service consumption	Know-where	Location (primary context)
		Know-when	Time (primary context)
Service	Service operation	Know-what	Activity (primary context)
		Know-how	
		Know-why	

cocreation. At the Service systems level, the *Know-where* and *Know-when* knowledge components focus on the knowledge about strategies and implementation of business services to create more value. At the Service level, the *Know-what*, *Know-how* and *Know-why* knowledge components concentrate on the knowledge related to the use of new technologies and knowledge to improve the quality of business services.

3.2 Context-Aware Knowledge Model

3.2.1 CAK Model at the Network of Service Systems Level

The Network of service systems level focuses on the service proposal, which aims at modelling services as a chain of value creation and exchange in which service systems co-produce common results (Le Dinh and Pham Thi 2012). This level relates to the knowledge about the business ecosystem and relationships between its members, which is represented by the Know-who and Know-with knowledge components (John-son et al. 2004; Le Dinh et al. 2014). **Know-who** knowledge component refers to "a combination of knowledge and social relationship about resources such as individuals, groups, or organizations" that provide or consume a service (Le Dinh and Pham Thi 2012). **Know-with** is the relational knowledge that concerns with the knowledge in the relationships between stakeholders inside a network of service systems such as knowledge about the interactions in partner relationships, knowledge about the management of supply chain functions, and knowledge about its external operating environment (Johnson et al. 2004; Le Dinh et al. 2014). Those two knowledge components facilitate the process of value co-creation in a network of service systems (Le Dinh and Pham Thi 2012).

In the CAK model, know-who is represented by *Entity*; meanwhile, know-with is represented by *Contract*. Table 2 presents the concepts of the CAK model at the Network of service systems level.

In order to illustrate the concepts of our model, we use an example of a smart software support service. The Adobe Photoshop had been chosen to develop the service based on its popularity and available resources. A service is required and begun when

Table 2. Concepts of the CAK model at the Network of service systems level.

Concept	Knowledge component	Definition
Entity	Know-who	A stakeholder of the network and has distinct goals
Resource		Having the responsibility to carry out a contract related to a service
Contract	Know-with	Defining what to offer and to whom, such as a SLA (service level agreement)

a photographer, as a Photoshop's customer, wants to use an online Image processing tool for his work. The service proposal value is to help him to complete the work with high quality. The entities included in the service are the photographer as a service consumer, Adobe and Adobe partners are the service provider. This service disposes of some different resources such as the software itself, documentations, community forum, and customer support center. The photographer needs to buy a license to use the service. The license, which is associated with a price and a specific type of usage, is considered as a contract between the service consumer and the service provider.

3.2.2 CAK Model at the Service System Level

The service system level concerns the service consumption that involves the configuration, implementation and use of business services in a service system. This level focuses on the knowledge that ensures all the services have adequate resources and sufficient technological support. The knowledge at this level determines what resources will be consumed, where and when it will take place, and who will be consumers. Firstly, **Know-where** indicates the locations related to resources of the service provider and the service consumer. **Know-when** indicates the time frame in which certain services are expected to offer or in which consumers are expected to consume services. According to the view of the service consumer, know-where and know-when help consumers find the right information in the right place at the right time.

In the CAK model, know-where is represented by Location and know-when is represented by Time frame. Table 3 presents the concepts of the CAK model at the Service system level.

Table 3. Concepts of the CAK model at the Service system level.

Concept	Knowledge component	Definition
Location	Know-where	Situational knowledge about positional relationships of resources that indicates where to request and consume services
Time frame	Know-when	Situational knowledge representing the period in which certain services are expected to offer or in which consumers are expected to consume services

Regarding our example, in order to use the Image processing tool, the user needs to access the Adobe Photo link and sign in. The tool is available for 24/7. In relation to the help center and the community forum, the service time frame is also 24/7 or the office hours 9–6 if the user wants to contact a support staff based on his location. On the other hand, the history of the usages of the service based on the location and time frame also helps the service provider to allocate their resources efficiently.

3.2.3   CAK Model at the Service Level

The Service level, concerning the service operation, emphasizes what is provided to consumers and how it is provided (Le Dinh and Pham Thi 2012). This level also concerns the governance so that a service is operated smoothly by enforcing a set of rules. There are three types of knowledge components at this level: know-what, know-how and know-why (Le Dinh et al. 2014). **Know-what** refers to objects relating to a service. **Know-how** refers to the understanding of the operations constituting a service. **Know-why** refers to the understanding of the service quality.

In the CAK model, know-what is described by Object, know-how by Operation, and know-why by Rule. Table 4 presents the concepts of the CAK model at the Service level.

Table 4. Concepts of the CAK model at the Service level.

Concept	Knowledge component	Definition
Object	Know-what	A thing or product that consumers can use or consume
Attribute		A piece of information determining the properties of an object
State		Conditions, modes or situations during which certain business activities are "enabled" and others "disabled"
Operation	Know-how	An operation of a service that is used to transit from a state to another state of an object
Rule	Know-why	A rule represents the implementation of a business rule in a service system

Some concepts related to the service operation in our example can be described as follows. Firstly, the main objects of Adobe Photoshop are Images and Video. The attributes of images are Color, Shape, Background, Texture, Brightness, and Contrast; meanwhile, the attributes of videos are Length, Size, File Format, Timeline, Motion, and Layer. Each object may have several states. For instance, the states of images are Original, Edited, Undone, and Finished. The operations are used to change the states of objects. Concerning the Image object, there are operations such as Edit, Undo, Set color, Crop, and Purge. To conform to the contract, some rules are required to help users getting a high-quality image and good experience during the image processing.

3.2.4 Elements of the CAK Model and Their Interrelationships

Figure 1 presents the elements of the CAK model and the corresponding knowledge components using the notation of UML (Rumbaugh et al. 1999).

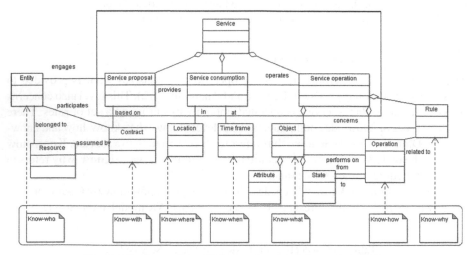

Fig. 1. Elements of the CAK model and their interrelationships

Firstly, a service consists of service proposals, service consumption and service operations. Economic entities (know-who) can engage in a service such as service provider or service consumers. A service proposal is based on a contract (know-with) that indicates the resources must be assumed by corresponding entities. Secondly, a service consumption is allowed based on a service proposal. A consumer can consume the services at one or different locations (know-where) at different time frames (know-when). Lastly, a service operation supports the process of a service consumption. A service operation can be performed a set of operations (know-how) on a set of objects (know-what). To guarantee the quality of the services, a set of rules (know-why) are taken into account. The scope of a rule covers a subset of relative objects, and the influence of a rule may lead to fail points of certain operations.

4 Chatbot as a Smart Service for Customer Support

To illustrate and evaluate the approach, a smart service for customer support based on the CAK model, called *Adobot*, is proposed as part of the applicability check. The paper continues to use the Adobe Photoshop software to demonstrate the implementation of the approach. This case study has selected the specific knowledge components of the CAK model that fit to its application domain and requirements for the time being.

In the case of Adobot, only the key knowledge components related to the customer support application are selected, including *know-what, know-how, know-where* and *know-when*, to support Photoshop's users.

Concerning the service operation, Adobot aims at building a chatbot-based interactive question-answering (QA) to provide the technical support with the focus on what – and how- questions. Concerning the service consumption, the context information related to know-where and know-when are used to refine the responses by increasing the accuracy and quality when answering the users' queries. Concerning the service proposal, the chatbot can be used as a new resource to provide customized services in order to increase the customer satisfaction. Moreover, the interaction between users and the service system can help to build a knowledge base that can co-create more value for customer support services. Finally, to demonstrate the implementability of the approach, an ontology-based model is used for implementing the context-aware knowledge model, and the RASA framework[1] is used for building the Adobot at the Service system and Service levels.

4.1 Adobot at the Network of Service Systems Level

Customers are always eager to get accurate and timely supports from companies when they encounter problems on products, especially complex products such as software products. Therefore, most software companies heavily invest in customer support services such as building websites showing product information, even assigning employees to answer online. One of the effective solutions is to build chatbots for customer technical support as a key resource (Skianis 2017). Consequently, companies can save training and operating costs for customer care staff as well as meet customer expectations and increase customer satisfaction.

4.2 Adobot at the Service System Level

At the Service system level, the implementation of the CAK model in this case is based on a combination of ontologies for the representation of contextual knowledge and advanced chatbot technologies. In particular, to validate and experiment this chatbot in practice, the knowledge model is built from the questions and answers related to Adobe Photoshop software. The abundant data obtained by the Photoshop's forum facilitates the construction of a contextual knowledge base that reflects the operations in Photoshop (Dulceanuy et al. 2018). In this knowledge base, the *know-what* component represents the definition of objects that users want to ask about, such as "What is the recoding tool in CS6?" or "What is the back ground layer?". Thus, the *know-how* component represents the questions that users ask about operations, such as "How to paint 3D images?" or "Yesterday, I opened my Photoshop to use the paint 3D image, but it doesn't work?". The *know-when* component represents the time frame and version (as its enhanced concept, such as CS5, CS6); meanwhile, the *know-where* component describes the context for location and environment (e.g. Window, Mac OS, Ubuntu, etc.).

To construct the knowledge base, the questions related to Photoshop are manually analyzed and then classified into 557 what- and 1,334 how-questions, in which the content explaining about a definition of objects is classified into *know-what* component; and the content guiding the operations is classified into *know-how* component.

---

[1] https://rasa.com/.

4.3   Adobot at the Service Level

The ontology-based contextual knowledge presented above plays an important role in the architecture of Adobot, which includes the CAK based ontology, the NLP (Natural Language Processing) and GUI (Graphical User Interface) components (Fig. 2).

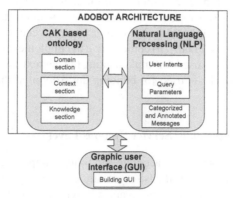

Fig. 2.   Architecture of adobot

The CAK based ontology includes three sections: i) *Domain section* represents the knowledge related to the service proposal such as the Photoshop product of the Adobe company; ii) *Context section* represents the knowledge related to the service consumption, which can be a version, an environment, or an agent, etc. There are two context types such as "Context-When" related to the time, version (CS6, CS5) and "Context-Where" related to location, environment (Window, Mac OS, Ubuntu, etc.); and iii) *Knowledge section* represents the knowledge related to the service operation such as know-what and know-how.

Concretely, for each user's message, the Adobot performs user message analysis, including user intent classification, and then query parameter extraction. Based on this information, the system interacts with the ontology to respond to the user. A process view of Adobot presented in the Fig. 2 demonstrates how Adobot components combine with each other to deal with user messages. Firstly, the NLP component based on Rasa NLU receives a user message. Then, the user intent and the context information are identified and stored. This information is processed to decide which next action is called. If Adobot cannot fully extract the required information, the system responds to the user by asking additional information via the GUI component. Otherwise, it sends via APIs all the context information to the Ontology component to query and give feedback.

Models for user intent classification and query parameter extraction are learned from the categorized and annotated messages, called the training corpus. The training corpus is formed by 3,000 questions collected from the Photoshop's forum. The user intent classification is performed by supervised embedding (Wu et al. 2018) while query parameter extraction (including context information) is performed by ner_spacy[2] (Luong et al. 2020).

---

[2] https://spacy.io/usage/training#ner.

5 Conclusion

This paper proposes an approach for context-aware knowledge model for smart service systems based on the knowledge components. We believe that the proposed knowledge model can capture all the information and knowledge related to smart services and their environment to provide the right information in the right circumstances for a right person. The proposed model is being tested and experimented in a chatbot application as a smart service for a customer support center.

Compared with the similar approach, such as the 5W1H context (Kim and Son 2012), our proposed approach disposes the following advantages: i) It can cover various context environments; therefore, it can be used to determine the unified context that describes context-aware information without dependence on purpose of any service; ii) It shows the relationship between contexts thanks to its related concepts in the knowledge model that allows to further exploitation and better understanding of user contexts; iii) By keeping context information in a knowledge repository, it helps to further analysis for better service quality and improving user satisfaction.

Concerning the implications of our work in practice, the proposed knowledge model can be extended and adapted for different types of services, especially knowledge-intensive services so that knowledge about services can be linked and used based on corresponding user-centric contexts in order to implement effectively and efficiency smart services. Concerning the implications for research, this approach needs to be validated and experimented on a broader scale. Moreover, our future researches aim at enhancing the approach for complicated and more elaborate smart services, as well as at integrating the knowledge model with current artificial intelligence techniques such as deep learning and reinforcement learning.

References

Abowd, Gregory D., Dey, Anind K., Brown, Peter J., Davies, N., Smith, M., Steggles, P.: Towards a better understanding of context and context-awareness. In: Gellersen, Hans-W. (ed.) HUC 1999. LNCS, vol. 1707, pp. 304–307. Springer, Heidelberg (1999). https://doi.org/10.1007/3-540-48157-5_29

Altinok, D.: An ontology-based dialogue management system for banking and finance dialogue systems. arXiv preprint arXiv:1804.04838 (2018)

Wu, L.Y., Fisch, A., Chopra, S., Adams, K., Bordes, A., Weston, J.: Starspace: embed all the things!. In: Thirty-Second AAAI Conference on Artificial Intelligence (2018)

Bellavista, P., Corradi, A., Fanelli, M., Foschini, L.: A survey of context data distribution for mobile ubiquitous systems. ACM Comput. Surv. (CSUR) 44(4), 24 (2012)

Chen, G., Kotz, D.: A survey of context-aware mobile computing research. Dartmouth Computer Science Technical report TR2000-381 (2000)

Dulceanuy, A., et al.: PhotoshopQuiA: a corpus of natural language for why-question answering. In: Dulceanuy, A., Le Dinh, T., Chang, W., Bui, T., Kim, D.S., Vu, M.C., Seokhwan. In: 11th edition of the Language Resources and Evaluation Conference, Miyazaki, Japan (2018)

Geum, Y., Jeon, H., Lee, H.: Developing new smart services using integrated morpho-logical analysis: integration of the market-pull and technology-push approach. Serv. Bus. 10(3), 531–555 (2016)

Gu, T., Pung, H.K., Zhang, D.Q.: A service-oriented middleware for building context-aware services. J. Network Comput. Appl. **28**(1), 1–18 (2005)

Johnson, J.L., Sohi, R.S., Grewal, R.: The role of relational knowledge stores in interfirm partnering. J. Mark. **68**(3), 21–36 (2004)

Kim, J.D., Son, J., Baik, D.K.: CA 5W1H onto: ontological context-aware model based on 5W1H. Int. J. Distrib. Sens. Netw. (2012), [247346]. https://doi.org/10.1155/2012/247346

Le Dinh, T., Leonard, M.: A conceptual framework for modelling service value creation networks. In: 2009 International Conference on Network-Based Information Systems (2009)

Le Dinh, T., Pham Thi, T.T: Information-driven framework for collaborative business service modelling. Int. J. Serv. Sci. Manage. Eng. Technol. (IJSSMET) **3**(1), 1–18 (2012)

Le Dinh, T., Rickenberg, T.A., Fill, H.G., Breitner, M.H.: Towards a knowledge-based framework for enterprise content management. In: Proceedings of the 2014 47th Hawaii International Conference on System Sciences, pp. 3543–3552. IEEE Computer Society (2014)

Lim, C., Maglio, P.P.: Data-driven understanding of smart service systems through text mining. Serv. Sci. **10**(2), 154–180 (2018)

Luong, H.T., Ly Tran, T.L., Pham Nguyen, C., Le Dinh, T., Gia, T.H., Le Nguyen, H.N.: Towards Chatbot-based Interactive What- and How-Question Answering Systems: the Adobot Approach. To be published in IEEE-RIVF (2020)

Lusch, R.F., Vargo, S.L., Wessels, G.: Towards a conceptual foundation for service science: contributions from service-dominant logic. IBM Syst. J. **47**(1), 5–14 (2008)

Medina-Borja, A.: Smart things as service providers: a call for convergence of disciplines to build a research agenda for the service systems of the future. Serv. Sci. **7**(1), ii–v (2015)

Oh, J.S., Park, J.S., Kwon, J.R.: Design middleware platforms for ubiquitous smart service on city gas environment in Korea. In: Ślęzak, D., Kim, T.-h., Ma, J., Fang, W.-C., Sandnes, F.E., Kang, B.-H., Gu, B. (eds.) UNESST 2009. CCIS, vol. 62, pp. 90–97. Springer, Heidelberg (2009). https://doi.org/10.1007/978-3-642-10580-7_14

Rumbaugh, J., Jacobson, I., Booch, G.: The Unified Modeling Language Reference (1999)

Skianis, K.: The Question-Answering and Chatbot challenges (2017)

Spohrer, J., Maglio, Paul P., Bailey, J., Gruhl, D.: Steps towards a science of service systems. IEEE Comput. **1**, 71–77 (2007)

Spohrer, J.C.: NSF virtual forum: platform technologies and smart service systems (2013). http://service-science.info/archives/3217. Accessed 14 Nov 2017

Vargo, S.L., Lusch R.F.: Evolving to a new dominant logic for marketing. J. Mark. **1**, 1–17 (2004)

Towards Learning to Read Like Humans

Louise Gillian Bautista[✉] and Prospero Naval Jr.

University of the Philippines, Quezon City, Philippines
{lcbautista1,pcnaval}@up.edu.ph

Abstract. Previous NLP works were successful in using human gaze behavior to improve task performance on their data sets. However, having to repeatedly collect gaze data for every new data set is impractical. Thus, there is a need for a method that will allow the utilization of available gaze data without the overhead. Our work presents a novel attempt to directly predict gaze features for each word with respect to its sentence. We take on a multi-corpus and task-agnostic approach: using four different eye-tracking data sets, regardless of reading task, material, and experiment design. Using only the word sequence as input to a 2-layer bidirectional LSTM, we achieve R^2 scores in the range of 76.80 to 95.59 for the following five gaze features: Number of Fixations (NFIX), First Fixation Duration (FFD), Total Reading Time (TRT), Go-Past Time (GPT), and Gaze Duration (GD). In addition, we use the model to predict gaze features for words in seen and unseen sentences in an attempt to improve performance in two NLP tasks. This led to a slight increase in performance, supporting the potential of such a model. Our paper presents an exploratory experiment into this methodology.

Keywords: Eye-tracking · Gaze features · Natural Language Processing · Recurrent Neural Network

1 Introduction

Learning from experience, humans can comprehend everyday scenes and text almost unconsciously. For example, reading sentences has become a trivial task over time: we intuitively know which words are important and needs more attention. Human reading patterns can represent a person's cognitive process [19]. These patterns are therefore beneficial in teaching machines to achieve human-level text understanding. These can be captured by using eye-trackers to measure the amounts of attention, or reading times, that humans give to certain words. Transferring these measurements to machine learning models have been attempted in previous Natural Language Processing (NLP) tasks, and have shown to improve model performance. Such tasks are sarcasm detection [14,15], sentiment classification [3,8,14,16,17], sentence complexity [20], and text readability [6].

These works used eye-tracking data that were particularly collected for their respective text corpora. If this methodology is to be extended to other corpora,

© Springer Nature Switzerland AG 2020
N. T. Nguyen et al. (Eds.): ICCCI 2020, LNAI 12496, pp. 779–791, 2020.
https://doi.org/10.1007/978-3-030-63007-2_61

then there would be a need to repeatedly gather data. This is a tedious process due to subject recruitment, data collection, and data preprocessing. Therefore, to build on this area of research and further explore the utilization of human gaze patterns for NLP, our work asks: *can we instead predict the measures of time that a person reads a word in any given sentence?* We hypothesize that the reading time measurements (e.g. fixation duration) of a word can be predicted given the context of its sentence.

These predicted measurements can then be used in place of actual data and reduce the need for extensive data collection. In general, creating such a model opens the following possibilities:

- An out-of-the-box method to increase performance of NLP tasks by having a model predict gaze features for sentences.
- The development of embedding models that take into account the amount of attention a word typically receives during reading, effectively endowing human knowledge to the embedded context.
- The usage of gaze features to train, augment, or replace attention mechanisms such that it learns to attend to the same words that humans attend to. [3]

To this end, we view the prediction of reading time measurements, from hereon called gaze features, as a sequence labeling task. We use a Recurrent Neural Network (RNN) and train on sentences from different data sets. The features are predicted directly i.e., the main and only task of the network is to output gaze feature predictions. This is in contrast to some of the earlier works that learned gaze features in a multi-task setting [6,8,17]. Furthermore, to validate the usefulness of the predictions, we test the model for use on downstream NLP tasks by predicting gaze features for words in seen and unseen sentences to augment their word embeddings.

This work presents an exploration into creating a general model that can endow machine learning models with human attention to improve their sentence understanding.

2   Gaze Features

Eye-tracking devices track a subject's eye movements and maps them to corresponding locations on the stimuli. Raw eye movement data collected during reading are commonly processed into per-word measures such as fixation count and duration. Because the processing of eye-tracking data into gaze features is a wide topic by itself, we describe only the features that will be mentioned in this paper.

- Number of Fixations (NFIX) is the number of times a subject fixates on the word.
- First Fixation Duration (FFD) is the duration with which the subject fixates on the word for the first time.
- Gaze Duration or First Pass Duration (GD) is the sum of all fixation durations on the current word before moving to any other word.

- Total Reading Time or Total Fixation Duration (TRT) is the sum of all fixation durations on the word.
- Mean Fixation Duration (MFD) is the mean of all fixation durations on the word.
- Regression Path Duration or Go-Past Time (GPT) is the sum of all fixation durations on the word starting from when it was first entered until moving to any word on its right.

For further reading on eye movements during reading, refer to the work of Rayner et al. [19]. For this work, we predict the following features for each word in a given sentence: NFIX, FFD, GD, TRT, and GPT. We select these features because most of them are already available in the eye-tracking data sets.

3   Related Work

3.1   Gaze Feature Prediction as Auxiliary Task

The first known work attempting to predict gaze features on the word-level is that of Singh et al. [20]. To improve the task of assessing sentence complexity, they used the Dundee corpus and predicted four gaze features: FFD, GD, GPT, and TRT. They performed linear regression using extracted linguistic features (e.g. word lengths, frequencies). They achieved R^2 scores of 64.9, 60.0, 57.0, and 51.0, respectively. Using the automatically predicted gaze features, they were able to achieve competitive results with models that used extensive syntactic features.

Garduno et al. used native speakers' gaze patterns to improve readability predictions [6]. They treated gaze feature prediction as an auxiliary task for their multi-task multilayer perceptron (MLP), assuming that readability and gaze feature prediction tasks are related. They find that gaze information improves the main task, and that based on 50 word instances, gaze features can be predicted to an extent.

Mishra et al. [17] aimed to improve document sentiment classification. They discretized FFD values into bins, and used FFD classification and POS tagging as auxiliary tasks for a bidirectional LSTM. This allowed their model to achieve competitive results with state-of-the-art approaches for sentiment analysis.

3.2   Gaze Feature Transfer to an Unseen Data Set

Barrett et al. [3] considered MFD as a measure of human attention. They trained a network using two alternating loss functions: given an RNN with attention mechanism, one loss function measures the task loss using cross entropy, while the second loss function measures the MSE between the attention score and MFDs of each word. Training the model in this way helps the attention mechanism learn using human heuristics, and led to a higher accuracy.

Hollenstein et al. [8,10] constructed a lexicon of observed word types and their corresponding gaze features averaged across subjects. They formed a lookup table using the available words, and gave random values to unseen ones. Using this method led to a minor but significant increase in the F1 score on an NER task.

3.3 Contributions

In this work, we utilize a Recurrent Neural Network (RNN), a machine learning model that is commonly used for modelling sequential data. It passes information from timestep to timestep, allowing it to learn the temporal dependencies of the data. We use a variant of RNN called the Long Short-Term Memory (LSTM) Network [7], which incorporate additional operations in each timestep, allowing it to support long-term dependencies.

To perform gaze feature prediction, we treat each word in a sentence as a timestep, and use them as inputs to an LSTM. The task of the LSTM is to output the gaze features for each word. Intuitively, the LSTM should understand the context of a sentence such that it can predict the gaze features that each word elicits from human readers. Our work is different from the previous works because of the following reasons:

1. For each word, we aggregate the gaze features and predict them on the sentence-level, instead of globally. We hypothesize that certain sentence structures and word combinations elicit certain gaze patterns that can be predicted.
2. We do not construct a set of linguistic features for each word and instead use only the word sequence. This bypasses the need for feature selection and makes our approach straightforward.
3. Our approach is task-agnostic, i.e., we predict gaze features independent of any task. This allows our method to be general and highly extensible.

4   Methodology

4.1   Data Sets

In this section, we briefly describe the eye-tracking data sets used for the experiment. Unless otherwise stated, the five gaze features to be predicted are already pre-extracted by the providers.

1. **ZuCo.** The Zurich Cognitive Language Processing Corpus (ZuCo) [9] consists of eye-tracking and EEG data of 12 subjects given three reading tasks. Task 1 is to rate the sentiment of 400 one-sentence movie reviews. Task 2 is to answer a question based on each of the 300 sentences, and Task 3 is to answer a question on relation types (e.g. award, education, employer) based on each of the 407 sentences. Sentences for task 2 and 3 are taken from Wikipedia, and have 48 overlapping sentences. However, because they are different reading tasks, we consider them disjoint and do not filter the overlapping sentences out. In total, ZuCo provides 1,107 sentences with eye tracking data. We utilize only the data of 11 subjects, because the file for one of the subjects was corrupt. Note that from hereon, we consider each task as a separate data set.

Table 1. Comparison of eye-tracking data sets. For ZuCo, the same 12 subjects participated in all tasks. WPS: words per sentence.

	# Subj.	# Sent.	%	Ave. WPS	Text Data
ZuCo-1 [9]	12	400	5.9	17.70	movie reviews
ZuCo-2 [9]	12	300	4.5	21.29	Wikipedia
ZuCo-3 [9]	12	407	6.0	20.06	Wikipedia
Provo [12]	84	134	2.0	13.3	articles, fiction
UCL [5]	43	205	3.0	13.7	novel
GECO [4]	14	5,284	78.5	10.29	novel
Total	153	6,730	100		

2. The **Provo** Corpus [12] provides eye tracking data for 55 paragraphs read by 84 subjects. In total, data is available for 134 sentences. The material is obtained from news articles, science magazines, and works of fiction, and the subjects did not have to answer any question after reading the sentence.
3. The **UCL** Corpus [5] provides eye tracking data for 205 sentences read by 43 subjects. Based on a word frequency criteria, the sentences are chosen from three publicly available novels. Because this corpus does not provide NFIX and TRT, we manually calculate for their values using their provided fixation data.
4. **GECO.** The Ghent Eye-Tracking Corpus [4] provides eye tracking data of 14 subjects reading Dutch and English text. We use only the data for the English text, where they were tasked to read the novel "The Mysterious Affair at Styles" by Agatha Christie. From this data set, we extracted 5,284 sentences based on unique sentence IDs.

Table 1 presents a summary of the data sets.

4.2 Preprocessing

We use six different data sets with different distributions, but we perform only standard preprocessing per gaze feature: we normalize the values to zero mean and unit variance.

The vocabulary is constructed from the available words in the data set. We do not lowercase the words, but clean special characters except for apostrophes. If a word is found in the GoogleNews word2vec [13] model, it is automatically included in the vocabulary. Otherwise, we represent numbers or floats as a special token <NUM>, and include words occurring more than 100 times in the vocabulary. For a word that occurs less than 100 times, we convert it to another special token <ENTITY> if it starts with a capital letter, else, it is represented using <UNK>. We believe using the first two placeholders help capture human intuition while reading: numerical texts represent quantitative information about a subject, and words with capitalized first letters represent proper nouns. This makes most use

of the data and more effectively preserves the contextual information that may
be useful for predicting gaze features.

4.3 Gaze Feature Prediction

To predict the gaze features, we use a two-layer bidirectional LSTM. This processes the input sequence in a forward and backward manner, improving its
capacity to capture the context of a sequence.

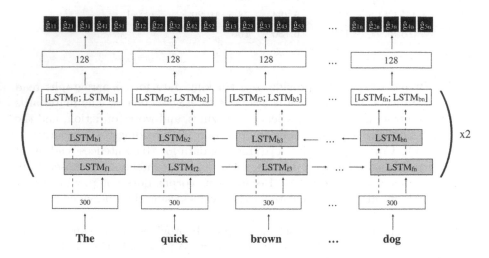

Fig. 1. A visualization of the 2-layer Bi-LSTM network for predicting gaze features

Our input to the LSTM is a sequence of words encoded using word2vec
embeddings trained on GoogleNews corpus [13]. This gives each word a 300-
dimensional vector representation, which are passed on to a 2-layer bidirectional
LSTM.

Concretely, given a sentence s with tokens $t_1, t_2, ..., t_n$, the ground truth gaze
features g_{1i}, g_{2i}, g_{3i}, g_{4i}, and g_{5i} for each token t_i are predicted as follows:

$$s' = \texttt{word2vec}(s)$$
$$x_i = [L_{fi}; L_{bi}] = LSTM(s')_i$$
$$\hat{g}_{1i}, \hat{g}_{2i}, \hat{g}_{3i}, \hat{g}_{4i}, \hat{g}_{5i} = h(x_i)$$

where the $LSTM$ has 64 units and Dropout [21] with $p = 0.5$ after the first
and second layer. x_i is the concatenation of the forward and backward outputs
of $LSTM$ for the token t_i in s. h is a linear layer that outputs predictions for
the gaze features for each word representation x_i. Figure 1 visualizes this model.

For all experiments, the ground truth of each word is the mean values of the
gaze features calculated across subjects. The mean-aggregation reduces noise,

and is done on per-word and per-sentence basis. For example, a word w_i that occurs in two sentences s_a and s_b will have two separate sets of ground truths.

$$rMSE = \sqrt{\frac{\sum\limits_{i=1}^{n}\sum\limits_{j=1}^{5}(\hat{g}_{ji} - g_{ji})^2}{5n}} \qquad (1)$$

$$R^2 = \left(1 - \frac{\sum\limits_{i=1}^{n}(\hat{g}_i - g_i)^2}{\sum\limits_{i=1}^{n}(\bar{g}_i - g_i)^2}\right) * 100 \qquad (2)$$

We optimize the model with Adam [11] using root Mean Squared Error (rMSE) loss. The rMSE for each sample, given in Eq. 1, is calculated from all the gaze feature predictions of all the words in the sentence.

For analysis, we also calculate the R^2 score for each gaze feature, given in Eq. 2. The R^2 of a model indicates the percentage of the variation in the data that it can explain, i.e. a perfect model has an R^2 of 100.

We train seven models: one for each of the six data sets, and another using all 6,730 sentences from all the data sets, which we will refer to as the Full model. Normalization of data is done respectively.

For all the models, the batch size is set to 32, the learning rate is initialized to 1e−3, and is decayed by a factor of 0.1 with a patience of 3. We perform 10-fold cross validation, and report the mean error metric.

The models trained on individual data sets were trained for a maximum of 30 epochs, while the full model was trained for a maximum of 10 epochs. All hyperparameters are chosen based on experiments. Random states were kept consistent to ensure fair comparison and reproducibility.

5   Results and Discussion

The raw prediction test results are summarized in Table 2, and charts of the mean R^2 scores for each data set and each gaze feature are shown in Fig. 2. First, we observe that the R^2 values are promising despite a relatively simple model. The highest individual value is 95.91, and the lowest is 57.85. At best, the model can explain most of the variance in the data, and at worst, it can still explain more than half of the variance.

Second, based on the R^2 scores, the two features easiest to predict are FFD and GD, followed by TRT, NFIX, and GPT. This finding is consistent with that of Singh et al.'s work [20] even though we use a different corpus and prediction method. This may be because FFD and GD are early measures, while TRT and GPT are late measures, making them more difficult to predict. This validates both our results and highlights the consistent predictability of the gaze features.

Lastly, as recently pointed out, ZuCo-3 consistently achieves lower scores than the other data sets. Recall that ZuCo-3 collected data in a task-specific

Table 2. Test metrics obtained from 10-fold cross validation. rMSE values are in their original scales.

		ZuCo-1	ZuCo-2	ZuCo-3	Provo	UCL	GECO	Full
NFIX	rMSE	.5606	.5299	.4085	.3301	.3492	.2798	.3406
	R^2	76.35	79.44	74.01	84.67	82.03	88.85	86.74
FFD	rMSE	25.20	26.76	31.59	26.80	35.09	39.59	36.3
	R^2	92.07	90.99	86.64	95.39	85.14	95.91	95.59
TRT	rMSE	68.12	71.48	58.71	74.54	75.81	67.00	66.31
	R^2	81.67	82.49	79.53	83.09	83.31	92.75	91.56
GD	rMSE	38.02	39.67	39.01	45.56	48.34	47.66	45.02
	R^2	87.95	87.51	84.49	93.02	82.68	94.99	94.42
GPT	rMSE	125.5	131.5	147.7	107.4	99.59	152.5	149.7
	R^2	72.68	75.46	57.85	84.90	81.22	78.89	76.80

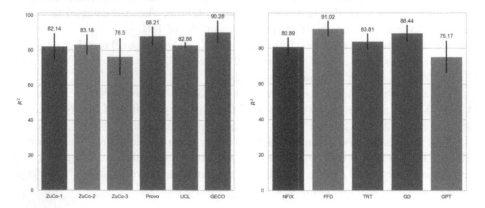

Fig. 2. Mean R^2 scores per data set (left) and per gaze feature (right). Error bars represent standard deviation.

reading setup: subjects had to correctly answer a question based on the text. It may be that the subjects had to forego the usual sequential reading style and scanned the sentence using different cognitive strategies [9,19]. Thus, gaze patterns across sentences and subjects may be less coherent, and consequently harder to predict.

6 Evaluation on Downstream Use

To further assess our proposed methodology, we use trained models to predict gaze features for each word and for each sentence in a seen and an unseen data set. The predicted gaze features are concatenated to their respective words, adopting the method used by Hollenstein et al. [8]. As a result, each word's embedding is extended by 5 dimensions. We retrain the ZuCo-1 model and the Full model for a number of epochs equal to the average number of epochs it took to overfit during cross-validation in Sect. 4.3. Because learning about feature importance is outside our scope, we use the gaze features as they are.

6.1 Task Using Seen Data

We perform tertiary sentiment classification (positive, neutral, or negative) on ZuCo-1 data set, using the same network architecture as Hollenstein et al. [8]. The network is composed of a GloVe [18] word embedding layer, a bidirectional LSTM with 150 units, two attention layers, and a linear layer to output the logits for classification. We, however, do not expect to replicate their results because of the following reasons: first, we could not use one of the subject's eye tracking data as previously mentioned; second, we construct the vocabulary with the same method used for the gaze predictor model; and third, we optimize the model with a different method. We use Stochastic Gradient Descent (SGD) with a learning rate of 0.01, and Nesterov momentum of 0.95. We train for a maximum of 85 epochs and perform 10-fold cross validation. Similar to Sect. 4, these hyperparameters are chosen based on experimentation.

We repeat this four times, one trial each for the following source of gaze data: None, ZuCo-1's actual collected gaze features, a model trained on ZuCo-1 sentences, and a model trained on all the data sets.

6.2 Task Using Unseen Data

We perform Named Entity Recognition (NER) task on the CoNLL 2003 data set [22]. CoNLL 2003 consists of text data from Reuters news articles. It contains 14,987 sentences in the training set, 3,466 in the development set, and 3,684 in the test set.

To train the model for NER, we utilize Flair [1,2], a framework for NLP. This framework includes the researchers' code to replicate their results on various NLP tasks, and we follow their instructions for the NER task. However, to test only on baseline models, we do not use their FlairEmbeddings and instead use only GloVe [18] word embedding. The model consists of an embedding layer, a Dropout layer with $p = 0.5$, a Locked Dropout layer also with $p = 0.5$, a linear layer of the same dimension as the embedding, a 256-unit bidirectional LSTM, and finally, a linear layer that maps to the classification. We train the model using a mini-batch size of 64, and an initial learning rate of 0.1 which is decayed by a factor of 0.5 with a patience of 3 epochs. The training stops at either a learning rate of 1e−4, or at a max number of epochs of 100.

6.3   Results

Table 3. F1 Scores achieved on the ZuCo sentiment task (ZuCo-1) and on the NER task on CoNLL 2003.

Gaze features	ZuCo-1 sentiment	CoNLL 2003 NER
None	53.96	87.16
Actual	54.98	-
ZuCo-1 Model	55.66	-
Full Model	56.63	87.53

Table 3 summarizes the results evaluated by F1 Score, given as $F1 = 2TP/(2TP + FP + FN)$ (TP: True Positive, FP: False Positive, FN: False Negative). For the sentiment classification task on ZuCo-1, it is interesting to note that using gaze features predicted by a model trained on the same data set yields a better F1 Score than using the actual gaze feature values. This may be caused by the smoothing effect of regression, where the predicted values take on a less noisy distribution.

Gaze features predicted by the ZuCo-1 model increased performance by 1.7, and the Full model increased performance by 2.67. Though the sentences in ZuCo-1 are used in the Full model, they count for only 400 out of 6,730, or 5.9%, of all the sentences used. This result is encouraging, as it indicates that the model has indeed learned from the other sentences and that learning from as many sentences as possible may be a simple yet effective method to take to improve prediction performance.

For the NER task, we see an increase of 0.37, which is too small to be conclusive. Note, however, that CoNLL 2003 consists of 22,137 sentences, while the Full model is trained on only 6,730 sentences. The model had to predict gaze features for triple the number of sentences that it has seen. This result further highlights the need to train the predictor model on more sentences.

7   Conclusion

Reading time measurements can be used to improve language understanding of machines. However, there should be a way to do this without repeatedly collecting data for each new data set. This paper presents a novel attempt to directly predict gaze features for each word given its sentence. We use a 2-layer bidirectional LSTM, and six data sets with different reading tasks, materials, and experiment design.

Our model can predict the words' gaze features up to an average R^2 score of 91.02. Our results offer observations and insights should this work be done in a larger-scale setting. We find that the early gaze features, FFD and GD, are easiest to predict, and this finding coincides with that of Singh et al.'s work [20]. We also observe that gaze features from ZuCo-3 are hardest to predict, indicating that task-specific reading may elicit different gaze patterns across readers. This may introduce noise to the model.

Furthermore, we use trained models to predict gaze features to augment word embeddings for a seen and an unseen data set. Our results on the tertiary sentiment classification task using ZuCo-1, a seen data set, further support its originating work [8], while also showing the promise of increased performance by learning gaze features from more sentences. On the other hand, our result on NER task of CoNLL 2003 is considered inconclusive but encourages further experimentation on unseen data sets and using more training data.

8   Recommendations

To improve prediction, a more rigorous preprocessing step may be done. Outliers in terms of sentence length and gaze feature values may be filtered out. Additionally, factors that affect reading should be investigated. This includes the type of reading material (e.g. novels, news), and the presentation of the material to the subject (e.g. one sentence at a time vs. a paragraph) may have subtle but important effects on the cognitive information that are being extracted.

References

1. Akbik, A., Bergmann, T., Blythe, D., Rasul, K., Schweter, S., Vollgraf, R.: FLAIR: an easy-to-use framework for state-of-the-art NLP. In: Proceedings of the 2019 Conference of the North American Chapter of the Association for Computational Linguistics (Demonstrations), pp. 54–59. Association for Computational Linguistics, Minneapolis, Minnesota, June 2019

2. Akbik, A., Blythe, D., Vollgraf, R.: Contextual string embeddings for sequence labeling. In: COLING 2018, 27th International Conference on Computational Linguistics, pp. 1638–1649 (2018)

3. Barrett, M., Bingel, J., Hollenstein, N., Rei, M., Søgaard, A.: Sequence classification with human attention. In: Proceedings of the 22nd Conference on Computational Natural Language Learning, pp. 302–312. Association for Computational Linguistics, Brussels, Belgium, October 2018

4. Cop, U., Dirix, N., Drieghe, D., Duyck, W.: Presenting geco: an eyetracking corpus of monolingual and bilingual sentence reading. Behav. Res. Methods 49(2), 602–615 (2017)

5. Frank, S.L., Fernandez Monsalve, I., Thompson, R.L., Vigliocco, G.: Reading time data for evaluating broad-coverage models of english sentence processing. Behav. Res. Methods 45(4), 1182–1190 (2013)

6. González-Garduño, A., Søgaard, A.: Learning to predict readability using eye-movement data from natives and learners (2018)

7. Hochreiter, S., Schmidhuber, J.: Long short-term memory. Neural Comput. 9(8), 1735–1780 (1997)

8. Hollenstein, N., Barrett, M., Troendle, M., Bigiolli, F., Langer, N., Zhang, C.: Advancing NLP with cognitive language processing signals http://arxiv.org/abs/1904.02682
9. Hollenstein, N., Rotsztejn, J., Troendle, M., Pedroni, A., Zhang, C., Langer, N.: ZUCO, a simultaneous EEG and eye-tracking resource for natural sentence reading. Scientific Data 5, 180291 EP - (12 2018)
10. Hollenstein, N., Zhang, C.: Entity recognition at first sight: Improving NER with eye movement information. In: Proceedings of the 2019 Conference of the North American Chapter of the Association for Computational Linguistics: Human Language Technologies, Volume 1 (Long and Short Papers), pp. 1–10. Association for Computational Linguistics, Minneapolis, Minnesota, June 2019
11. Kingma, D.P., Ba, J.: Adam: a method for stochastic optimization. arXiv preprint arXiv:1412.6980 (2014)
12. Luke, S.G., Christianson, K.: The provo corpus: a large eye-tracking corpus with predictability norms. Behav. Res. Methods 50(2), 826–833 (2018)
13. Mikolov, T., Sutskever, I., Chen, K., Corrado, G., Dean, J.: Distributed representations of words and phrases and their compositionality. In: Proceedings of the 26th International Conference on Neural Information Processing Systems, NIPS 2013, vol. 2, pp. 3111–3119. Curran Associates Inc., USA (2013)
14. Mishra, A., Dey, K., Bhattacharyya, P.: Learning cognitive features from gaze data for sentiment and sarcasm classification using convolutional neural network. In: Proceedings of the 55th Annual Meeting of the Association for Computational Linguistics (Volume 1: Long Papers), pp. 377–387. Association for Computational Linguistics, Vancouver, Canada, July 2017
15. Mishra, A., Kanojia, D., Nagar, S., Dey, K., Bhattacharyya, P.: Harnessing cognitive features for sarcasm detection. In: Proceedings of the 54th Annual Meeting of the Association for Computational Linguistics (Volume 1: Long Papers), pp. 1095–1104. Association for Computational Linguistics, Berlin, Germany, August 2016
16. Mishra, A., Kanojia, D., Nagar, S., Dey, K., Bhattacharyya, P.: Leveraging cognitive features for sentiment analysis. In: Proceedings of The 20th SIGNLL Conference on Computational Natural Language Learning, pp. 156–166. Association for Computational Linguistics, Berlin, Germany, August 2016
17. Mishra, A., Tamilselvam, S., Dasgupta, R., Nagar, S., Dey, K.: Cognition-cognizant sentiment analysis with multitask subjectivity summarization based on annotators' gaze behavior (2018)
18. Pennington, J., Socher, R., Manning, C.: Glove: global vectors for word representation. In: Proceedings of the 2014 Conference on Empirical Methods in Natural Language Processing (EMNLP), pp. 1532–1543. Association for Computational Linguistics, Doha, Qatar, October 2014
19. Rayner, K.: Eye movements in reading and information processing: 20 years of research. Psychol. Bull. 124(3), 372 (1998)
20. Singh, A.D., Mehta, P., Husain, S., Rajakrishnan, R.: Quantifying sentence complexity based on eye-tracking measures. In: Proceedings of the Workshop on Computational Linguistics for Linguistic Complexity (CL4LC), pp. 202–212. The COLING 2016 Organizing Committee, Osaka, Japan, December 2016

21. Srivastava, N., Hinton, G., Krizhevsky, A., Sutskever, I., Salakhutdinov, R.: Dropout: a simple way to prevent neural networks from overfitting. J. Mach. Learn. Res. **15**(1), 1929–1958 (2014)
22. Tjong Kim Sang, E.F., De Meulder, F.: Introduction to the CONLL-2003 shared task: Language-independent named entity recognition. In: Proceedings of the Seventh Conference on Natural Language Learning at HLT-NAACL 2003 - Volume 4, CONLL 2003, pp. 142–147. Association for Computational Linguistics, Stroudsburg (2003)

Chaining Polysemous Senses
for Evocation Recognition

Arkadiusz Janz(iD) and Marek Maziarz(✉)(iD)

Wroclaw University of Science and Technology, 50-370 Wrocław, Poland
{arkadiusz.janz,marek.maziarz}@pwr.edu.pl

Abstract. In this paper we present a new individual measure for the task of evocation strength prediction. The proposed solution is based on Dijkstra's distances calculated on the WordNet graph expanded with polysemy relations. The polysemy network was constructed using chaining procedure executed on individual word senses of polysemous lemmas. We show that the shape of polysemy associations between WordNet senses has a positive impact on evocation strength prediction and the measure itself could be successfully reused in more complex ML frameworks.

Keywords: Evocation strength · Graph-based similarity · WordNet · Semantic similarity · NLP

1 Introduction

A computational linguist looking for a good description of lexico-semantic subsystem will reach out to electronic dictionaries and thesauri. Princeton WordNet is a prominent example of such a computational model of mental lexicon [7]. Unfortunately, the knowledge obtainable from a dictionary is not sufficient to predict all possible sense relations, especially the associations useful in evocation recognition. Evocations are simply associations of meanings [3]. These semantic couplings go across different parts of speech and jump from one semantic category to another [15].

The fact that probably affects evocation recognition is the absence of lexico-semantic resources other than the ones built up mainly from taxonomic relations (hyponymy, meronymy etc.). Polysemy is yet another type of semantic relatedness that could facilitate noticing some hidden associations. It links distant parts of our lexicon through lexicalised metaphor or metonymy.

Lexical polysemy is a linguistic phenomenon characterised by the coexistence of two or more semantically related senses tied to the same lemma [14]. Some words are monosemous and they have only one meaning, e.g. *smartphone* or *lexical*. Polysemous words can express multiple meanings, e.g. *castle* ('fortified building', 'imposing old mansion', 'rock in chess') or *line* (with dozens of meanings). In the actual usage, words may slightly change their (basic) meanings adjusting to a particular sentence context. This introduces a myriad of contextually motivated meaning shades.

© Springer Nature Switzerland AG 2020
N. T. Nguyen et al. (Eds.): ICCCI 2020, LNAI 12496, pp. 792–804, 2020.
https://doi.org/10.1007/978-3-030-63007-2_62

In many theories semantic nets are used as models of polysemy. Especially, relational semantics treats related polysemy senses as a kind of semantic net [10] often called *polysemy net* (cf. [19]). One particular kind of lexical net is of great importance to linguists: wordnets. Wordnets have been widely used in experiments regarding polysemy, e.g. [1,9]. In this paper we focus on constructing a high-quality lexical resource for English based on Princeton WordNet and polysemy links, for the needs of recognizing evocation strength. As far as we know, earlier studies ignored the properties of polysemy nets that could be a source of useful semantic knowledge.

2 Related Work

Evocation Data Sets. In this paper we use a gold standard evocation data set [3] that contains a list of paired senses with manually assigned scores representing association (evocation) strength. Around 120,000 concept pairs were randomly selected from the set of 1,000 WordNet core synsets. As the data was annotated by multiple annotators, we averaged the scores assigned to evocation pairs, which is a standard procedure in the treatment of this resource (cf. [11]).

Wordnets lack the full description of polysemy. Senses are simply enlisted within different synsets and then integrated with the whole net of paradigmatic relations (like hyponymy or antonymy), and they remain unrelated, unless they are linked via taxonomic relations (like auto-hyponymy). On the other hand, wordnets do contain derivational relations. Why do they then omit polysemy links representing *semantic* derivation? If one considers this problem, they immediately discover that this asymmetry is unjustified [13, p. 120, 183].

This weakness of wordnets cannot be easily resolved, since it is not obvious which senses should be linked together, mainly because of the difficulty in distinguishing between homonymous and polysemous pairs. Undoubtedly, this situation affects evocation recognition. If we want to efficiently match associated senses, we should have as accurate model of mental lexicon as possible.

Evocation Recognition. Evocation recognition is considered a difficult task for NLP. It is said to be more difficult than similarity/relatedness recognition, since something more than bare taxonomy structure is needed to sufficiently predict the evocation strength [6]. Simple WordNet-based similarity measures are very inefficient in recognizing the strength of evocation [3].

The recent progress in distributional modelling and knowledge-based embeddings allowed to design more effective approaches for many different NLP tasks, and some of them were directly applied to the task of evocation recognition. The model proposed by Hayashi [11] combined many different features, e.g. wordnet-based similarity and relatedness features, lexical resource features, and distributional features. Surprisingly, most of them were of the same significance. He argued that progress in this area could be obtained only by introducing to a computational model a new high-quality individual measure.

Researchers working on similar tasks, i.e., *word* associations [4,12], reported the same conclusions. Knowledge-based similarity measures were performing slightly worse, and the best way to achieve higher correlations in the task was to combine many different individual measures [4].

Polysemy Chains. Polysemy topologies were studied by Ramiro et al. [17] in the context of English language evolution. Starting from the etymologically first sense, the authors were able to successfully reproduce the order in which senses appeared during the millennia of history of the English language. They studied several net construction algorithms: inter alia – random, prototype, progenitor and nearest-neighbor ones. In their experiments the latter one achieved the best results.

3   Polysemy Nets in Evocation Recognition

In our approach a graph for evocation recognition combines Princeton WordNet with polysemous links extracted from WordNet glosses (sense definitions).[1] We decided to expand the base graph with three different polysemy networks, each of which might have been treated as a graph model of real lexical polysemy. We tested the following structures:

- A complete polysemy graph which – for a given lemma – linked all its senses together ("WN-g-co"). The graph was built for each polysemous lemma existing in the graph.
- An incomplete graph built by extracting polysemy links from SemCor [5]. We constructed the second graph out of those sense pairs that closely co-occurred in the same text (symbol "WN-g-sc").
- The last model was more sophisticated, as we tried to predict contemporary semantic relations between senses of all polysemous words/lemmas on the basis of WordNet structure. We used here the nearest-neighbor chaining algorithm ("WN-g-ch", Sect. 3.1).

With the graphs we proceeded in the following way:

- We optimised edge weights for each polysemy network type and chose the best polysemy model (Sect. 3.1).
- We tested the impact of a selected model on the evocation strength recognition within a ML framework (Random Forest and Multi-layer Perception, Sect. 3.2).

To avoid overfitting the evocation data set was divided into three parts. A subset of 2,000 evocation pairs was devoted to setting optimal weights in each polysemy graph (*evo2k* set). The next subset of 10,000 evocation instances was used to evaluate the performance of each model in predicting evocation strength, as well as to perform attribute selection for the Random Forest framework and for setting the best Neural Network topology (*evo10k* set). The remaining 108,000 synset pairs (*evo108k* set) were used as a test set to evaluate our model and compare the results with [11].

---

[1] WordNet glosses were semi-automatically interlinked with contextually appropriate synsets, https://wordnetcode.princeton.edu/glosstag.shtml.

The Complete Polysemy Graph was constructed out of the list of all WordNet senses for each polysemous lemma. For a given m-sense lemma l we linked all its senses, obtaining $\frac{m \cdot (m-1)}{2}$ bidirectional sense relations.

The SemCor Polysemy Graph. SemCor is a sense annotated sub-part of the Brown Corpus [5]. The annotations were based on WordNet. We decided to use this language resource assuming that senses occurring in the same context must be semantically related. This assumption allowed us to retrieve distributional properties of word meanings and map them onto WordNet graph. As a dominant direction of each link, we chose the one from the consecutive meaning to the preceding one, hence in the sequence of sense occurrences $(s_{l,1}^t, s_{l,2}^t, s_{l,3}^t, ...)$ of the same lemma l taken from the text t we established a polysemy relation $s_{l,i}^t \rightarrow s_{l,(i-1)}^t$ between neighbouring word occurrences, with an additional constraint that inequality $s_{l,i}^t \neq s_{l,(i-1)}^t$ was fulfilled (i.e., only different senses of the same lemma were linked).

3.1   Nearest-Neighbor Chaining Algorithm

To evaluate the impact of polysemy nets on evocation strength recognition we decided to introduce polysemy links between WordNet senses. This task is not trivial, since the actual shape of polysemy associations still remains mysterious for the present day linguistics.

Let us consider three different polysemy net topologies tested in this paper. Figure 1 presents polysemy nets for the word *slaughter*. A complete graph simply links all senses together. SemCor-based polysemy net just groups such sense pairs that co-occur in the corpus, giving rather poor completeness but probably good precision. The chaining algorithm tries to connect senses that are the closest in the WordNet graph. The difficulty of the task is demonstrated by a polysemy net constructed manually on the basis of dictionary descriptions (based on three contemporary English dictionaries, namely – Oxford Lexico[2], Merriam-Webster[3] and Cambridge Dictionary[4], and on the etymological English dictionary[5]).

In this paper we adopted the nearest-neighbor approach as presented in [17] to construct polysemy nets. Ramiro et al. [17] tried to predict the order of appearance of different word senses in the history of English starting with one sense given by an oracle (from a historical English dictionary). They found that the best results were obtained with the use of the chaining algorithm. We applied their algorithm with two main modifications:

- Since we are not aware which sense should be fixed as the first one, we try to deduce it from vertex degrees.
- We apply an asymmetric measure of distance in the directed Word-Net+glosses graph (*WN-g*).

---

[2] https://www.lexico.com/.
[3] https://www.merriam-webster.com/.
[4] https://dictionary.cambridge.org/.
[5] https://www.etymonline.com/.

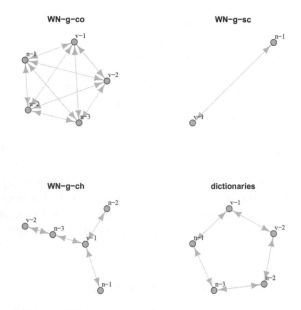

Fig. 1. Three polysemy net topologies for the word *slaughter*: complete graph *WN-g-co* on the topmost left, SemCor-based *WN-g-sc*, and the network built with nearest neighbor chaining algorithm *WN-g-ch*. In the bottom-right corner we present a polysemy net extracted manually from four English dictionaries (three contemporary and an etymological one), taking into account direct proximity of senses in *slaughter* entries of the dictionaries. WordNet definitions are as follows: n-1 – '*the killing of animals (as for food)*', n-2 – '*a sound defeat*', n-3 – '*the savage and excessive killing of many people*', v-1 – '*to kill (animals) usually for food consumption*', v-2 – '*to kill a large number of people indiscriminately*'.

The First Sense Choice. We start with computing the importance scores for each node (synset) based on a vertex degree measure. To be more specific, we calculate the vertex degree $deg(v)$ being the harmonic mean of two different vertex degree measures – the square root of the number of edge instances $\sqrt{deg_i(v)}$ and the number of edge types $deg_t(v)$:

$$deg(v) = \frac{2 \times \sqrt{deg_i(v)} \times deg_t(v)}{\sqrt{deg_i(v)} + deg_t(v)}. \tag{1}$$

The chaining algorithm starts from the node with the highest $deg(v)$ measure.

Geodesics in Polysemy Nets. For each lemma we compute the shortest paths in the directed WordNet graph (*WN-g*) between its senses (synsets). We treat the length of the shortest path as an asymmetric measure of a distance between graph vertices (synsets). We denoted this with $Dist(v_1, v_2)$.

The Chaining Algorithm. Let us assume that we have an m-sense lemma. The chaining algorithm proceeds in the following way:

– Step 1: We start with establishing the first sense that has the highest vertex degree value $deg(v)$. We call such a vertex *fixed*, i.e., $v_j = v_j^{fix}$ iff $deg(v_j) = \max[deg(v_i)]$, where $i \in I$, I being the set of non-fixed vertices, $j \in F$, F being the set of fixed vertices.

– Step 2: For each remaining vertex $v_i, i \in I$, we check the distances $Dist(v_i, v_j^{fix})$ to all fixed vertices $v_j^{fix}, j \in F$, and establish the edge $v_l \rightarrow v_k^{fix}$, iff $Dist(v_l, v_k^{fix}) = \min[Dist(v_i, v_j^{fix})]$, $i, l \in I, j, k \in F$. Again, we call the newly attached l^{th} vertex *fixed*, i.e., $v_l = v_l^{fix}, l \in F$.

– We repeat Step 2 in a loop until all vertices are fixed. We call the set of edges $\{v_i^{fix} \rightarrow v_j^{fix}\}_{i \neq j}$ the *polysemy net*, where $i, j \in F = \{1, 2, ..., m\}$. At the end $I = \emptyset$.

Dijkstra's Distance in Modified Nets. We use the polysemy nets to expand Word-Net graph. On such modified graph we compute the semantic distance between concepts (with all edge weights set as 1) using Dijkstra's shortest path algorithm. Out of the new distance measure $dist_{Dijkstra}$ we construct the final evocation measure $DSch$:

$$DSch = \begin{cases} \frac{1}{dist_{Dijkstra}} & , when \quad dist_{Dijkstra} \geq 1 \\ 1 & , when \quad dist_{Dijkstra} < 1 \end{cases} \tag{2}$$

For each synset in the evocation set we calculated the $dist_{Dijkstra}$ measure and compared $DSch$ to the evocation strength. The performance of a proposed similarity measure was evaluated with the use of Spearman's correlation ρ.

Optimisation. We tested the impact of different cost values of newly introduced polysemy links on evocation strength prediction. The cost values were used as weights for Dijkstra's shortest path algorithm. For *WN-g-co* and *WN-g-sc* models the weights in the graphs were equal to 1.0, then they were multiplied by optimisation parameters (marked with capital letters A or B). In the case of *WN-g-ch* graph, we took the shortest path length (the geodesic) in *WN-g* as a base cost (as described above), the basic cost was then multiplied by optimisation parameters. For *WN-g-sc* and *WN-g-ch* one link direction was preferred. The chaining algorithm set the direction from the newly attached vertex to its fixed predecessor in a polysemy chain. SemCor links were directed also in a reversed order, i.e., from the consecutive sense to the preceding one. These link costs were marked with As. We also inserted the oppositely directed semantic links, marking them with Bs. All links other than polysemy relations (i.e., taxonomic and gloss links) were equipped with the cost of 1. The baseline model *WN-g* achieved in such a setting is $\rho = 0.218$ (see Table 1).

For the complete graph (*WN-g-co*), we applied only one cost parameter A, because the graph edges were bidirectional ($B = A$). The $\rho = \rho(A)$ curve turned to be discontinuous, which is clearly visible in Fig. 2. When the cost of polysemy links was lower than 1 (i.e., the constant cost of WordNet taxonomic and gloss relations), the merged network seemed to perform worse than the *WN-g* baseline. Having passed the threshold of 1, the $\rho(A)$ curve suddenly rose, and reached the maximum value of Spearman's correlation $\rho = 0.226$ for $A \in [1.525, \ 1.650]$, then slowly descended to get to the baseline value 0.218 at the end of inspected area (at $A = 4$). The optimum was obtained in two steps: first, we checked $\rho(A)$ values for $A = 0, 0.25, 0.5, ..., 3.75, 4$, second, we concentrated on the range $A \in [1, 2]$ having thickened the mesh five times ($A = 1, 1.05, 1.1, ..., 2$). Finally, we took the point $A_{opt} = 1.6$ located in the middle of the maximum region as the approximation of the optimal point.

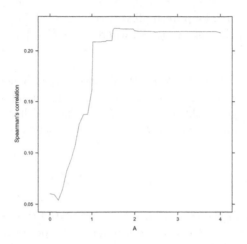

Fig. 2. Spearman's correlation ρ in the function of the cost parameter A for WordNet-gloss graph expanded with complete lemma polysemy nets. Please note that in the case of the *WN-g-co* model $B = A$, due to the impossibility of distinguishing the preferred directions in such a graph.

We tested *WN-g-sc* and *WN-g-ch* models on the mesh of 11×11 points, magnifying interesting regions with the denser mesh of 9×9 points, checking altogether roughly 200 combinations of parameters A and B. Each net model was optimised with a visual inspection of level plots (Figs. 3 and 4). We tested different values of costs in Dijkstra's algorithm, $\rho = \rho(A, B)$.

For the SemCor-based polysemy graph (*WN-g-sc*), the maximum point was thus identified to be near the point $A = 0.75$, $B = 1$. The chaining-algorithm-based polysemy net (*WN-g-ch*) optimum seemed to be located close to the $(0.425, 0.425)$ point.

Table 1 presents polysemy network sizes together with the estimations of optimal points and maximum Spearman's ρ values. The *WN-g-co* is the biggest one, but the quality of links is not so high ($A = 1.6$, which is greater than the basic cost of 1 for WordNet taxonomic relations and glosses). SemCor-based optimal graph (*WN-g-sc*) received lower cost for A ($A = 0.875$, $B = 1$), which is not surprising since the net, though relatively small, is possibly almost completely error-free. Taking into account that the discovered optimal costs for the *WN-g-ch* graph were the lowest, one might argue that the relation set was the best

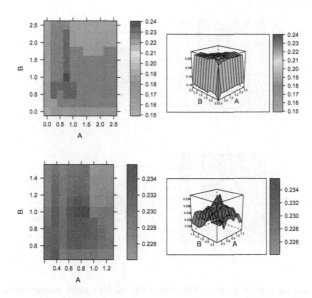

Fig. 3. Spearman's correlation ρ in the function of the cost parameters A and B for WordNet-gloss graph expanded with polysemy links between word senses co-occurring in the very same text in SemCor. Top: Correlations for the square $[0, 2.5] \times [0, 2.5]$. Bottom: 2-times magnification of the optimum area.

model. The graph complements the links for all WordNet senses, while *WN-g-sc* only for those that co-occurred in the corpus.

Choosing the Best Model. We optimised the parameters of the chaining algorithm and two other models. The next step was to evaluate these findings on a larger independent subset of the evocation data set, counting 10,000 evocation pairs, with the optimal parameter settings (Table 1, *evo10k* columns). As a baseline, we have chosen the *WN-g* (the gloss-expanded WordNet graph).

Table 1. Different variants of polysemy nets: *WN-g-co* - the complete graph of inter-sense links, WN-g-sc – the SemCor-based graph of polysemy senses co-occurring in the same text, *WN-g-ch* – the chaining algorithm model with a fixed starting point. Results were obtained on the *evo2k* tuning data set and evaluated on the *evo10k* data set.

Polysemy network	Size [10^3]	Vector of costs (w_{WN}, w_g, A, B)	ρ evo2k	ρ evo10k	r evo10k
WN	0.0	(1,1,-,-)	0.138	.149	.215
WN-g	0.0	(1,1,-,-)	0.218	.183	.237
WN-g-co	377.7	(1,1,1.6,1.6)	0.226	.181	.239
WN-g-sc	28.6	(1,1,0.875,1)	0.235	.195	.251
WN-g-ch	110.0	(1,1,0.425,0.425)	0.242	.198	.263

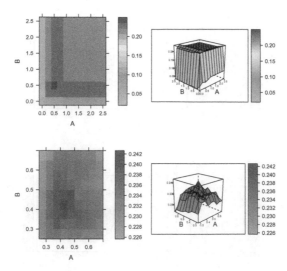

Fig. 4. Spearman's correlation in the function of the cost parameters A and B for WordNet-gloss graph expanded with polysemy links between word senses obtained through the chaining algorithm. Top: Correlations on the square $[0, 2.5] \times [0, 2.5]$. Bottom: 5-times magnification.

The comparison was performed with the use of a bootstrap percentile method ($B = 1,000$ repetitions). The evaluation setting is presented in Table 2 ($m = 7$ is a number of comparisons). Both the chaining algorithm (*WN-g-ch*) and the SemCor-based model (*WN-g-sc*) turned out sufficient in beating the baseline model *WN-g* and a large complete graph (*WN-g-co* model). Polysemy chains were not significantly better than a smaller SemCor co-occurrence model. The semantic network built from SemCor seemed to be incomplete, though. The corpus itself missed many valuable sense associations. Having taken into account the advantages of our chaining procedure which produced at least as good polysemy model and yet a more-complete polysemy network, we decided to choose the *WN-g-ch* model for further experiments.

3.2 Chaining Algorithm in Evocation Recognition

The modified graph *WN-g-ch* contains semantic links introduced by applying the chaining procedure to polysemous words. We use the new resource and our new similarity metric to compute additional feature set for evocation strength prediction. The additional features (mainly the *DSch* feature, but also few frequency-based features) were used as an expansion for the feature set proposed by [11]. We mark the additional features by a cross symbol in Table 3.

The features proposed by Hayashi [11] were based on different language resources. We implemented some of the similarity measures as described in the original work (e.g. the cosine similarity of *AutoExtend* sense representations using the same pre-trained model, symbol: *cosAE*), or replaced the remaining

Table 2. P-values of the one-sided paired bootstrap test for the difference between ρ values (*DSch* measure, $B = 1,000$ repetitions). Alternative hypotheses are formulated in the following manner: 'a row is greater than a column', with an exception of the *WN/WN-g* comparison which has the hypothesis reversed. Statistical significance was calculated through Benjamini-Hochberg procedure at the confidence level of 95% ($m = 7$ comparisons). We mark statistically significant results with asterisks.

Graph		WN-g	WN-g-co	WN-g-sc
Type	ρ	.183	.181	.195
WN	.149	0.000*	—	—
WN-g-co	.181	0.647	—	—
WN-g-sc	.195	0.014*	0.016*	—
WN-g-ch	.198	0.01*	0.005*	0.354

functions with equivalent measures (e.g., *Wu-Palmer* similarity of lexicalised concepts was replaced by the Jaccard similarity measure, also calculated on WordNet). To predict evocation strength we followed the same approach and we treated the task as a regression problem. We used two different regression models: i) a regressor based on Random Forest framework, and ii) a regressor based on Feed-Forward Neural Network.[6] The final feature set that was used to train our models is presented in Table 3.

- Frequency index $FREQsc(s)$ represents the frequency of a given lemma sense s computed on the basis of the SemCor corpus.
- Frequency-based score $FRANic(s)$ represents a fraction of the overall frequency $FREQic$ of lemma l computed for each of its senses s, where the final score is inversely proportional to sense variant (as they were ordered in WordNet). The lower sense variant number $VAR(s)$ was (e.g. $1^{st}, 2^{nd}, 3^{rd}, ...$), the bigger fraction of the frequency $FREQic(l)$ it received:

$$FRANic(s) = \frac{FREQic(l)}{(VAR(s) + 1)}. \tag{3}$$

We used the frequencies provided by an internet corpus of English[7].
- The Jaccard Index $JaccSim(s, t)$ is the number of common neighbors divided by the number of nodes that are the neighbors of at least one of input senses (source or target) being considered.
- $Dist(s, t)$ is the length of the shortest path between source and target synset (cf. the description in the previous section).
- $GlossDice(s, t)$ represents Dice similarity measure based on glosses. The measure is computed using all the neighbours in the vicinity of $k = 3$ steps from source and target concepts. We take all of the senses appearing in the glosses

---

[6] The experimental part was conducted in WEKA framework [8].
[7] Published by Centre for Translation Studies, University of Leeds: http://corpus. leeds.ac.uk/list.html, CC-BY licence.

Table 3. Prediction of evocation strength (individual features): 5-fold cross-validation on the set of 108,000 evocation pairs. Symbols: DV - corpus-based distributional vectors, KB - knowledge-based measures, KV - WordNet-based vector spaces. All numbers represent Pearson's r correlations. Hayashi's data are given for the whole 120,000 pair evocation set. The features marked with an asterisk sign were implemented after [11].

	NN	RF
DV features:		
$cosFT$	0.1980	0.1247
$cosGV$	0.2487	0.1547
$FRANic$	0.0663	0.0626
$FREQsc$	0.0510	0.0420
KB features:		
$Dist$	0.1823	0.2476
$GlossDice$	0.1288	0.0403
$JaccSim$	0.1131	0.1178
$DSch$	**0.2596**	**0.2688**
KV measures:		
$cosAE^*$	0.2122	0.1239
$relVecAE^*$	0.0341	—
$posSem^*$	0.1428	0.1731
All features	**0.4415**	0.4363
Hayashi (2016)	**0.4391**	0.3695

of source and target entities as well as the senses from glosses of their neighbours.

- The $posSem(s,t)$ feature is inspired by the work of [11], with a minor alteration – instead of 5 PoS we have 4 PoS.
- $cosFT(s,t)$, $cosGV(s,t)$, and $cosAE(s,t)$ represent the cosine similarity of vector space representations of source and target concepts s and t computed using $fastText$ [2], $GloVe$ [16], and $AutoExtend$ [18] embeddings.
- $relVecAE$ - a 300D vector of differences between two AutoExtend vector embeddings (each for one sense in an evocation pair).

The last feature was removed from the RF feature set after preliminary experiments on the $evo10k$ data set, since using word (or sense) embeddings directly as feature vector did not improve the quality of the model. In the NN framework the impact of AutoExtend vector differences was positive, though small.

Final Results. In all paired t-tests our $DSch$ measure proved to behave better in predicting the evocation strength than any other individual measure at 5% significance level (with Benjamini-Hochberg correction, Table 3). Without Hayashi's original validation folds we were unable to compare the final performance in a direct way – for our NN model we have obtained the absolute mean value of Pearson's r correlation slightly higher than that of Hayashi's NN [11] (see Table 3), but the one-sided one-sample t-test was inconclusive (p-value above 0.05). We were able to prove better performance of both our NN i RF models over Hayashi's RF model at the significance level of 0.001.[8]

4   Conclusions and Further Work

In this paper we presented a novel method of expanding WordNet with polysemy links based on the nearest-neighbor chaining algorithm. We have proven that the new lexical resource facilitates evocation recognition, compared to competitive WordNet-based graphs. We also re-used it successfully within the Neural Network and Random Forest frameworks. We proved that the polysemy-based Dijkstra's distance measure was quite efficient in recognizing evocation, especially when compared to efficiencies of other knowledge-based measures.

Hayashi [11] believed that the real progress in evocation strength recognition could be obtained through merging diverse language resources representing different aspects of human linguistic competence. In this work we focused on a small piece of the puzzle, namely lexical polysemy links. Since we did not utilize *all* Hayashi's features (e.g., the LDA topic modelling measure), there is still space for further improvements.

Applications of the polysemy expanded WordNet go beyond detecting evocation strength. We plan to verify its usefulness in similarity recognition tasks as well as Word Sense Disambiguation.

Acknowledgments. This research was financed by the National Science Centre, Poland, grant number 2018/29/B/HS2/02919, and supported by the Polish Ministry of Education and Science, Project CLARIN-PL.

References

1. Barque, L., Chaumartin, F.R.: Regular polysemy in WordNet. J. Lang. Technol. Comput. Linguist. **24**(2), 5–18 (2009)
2. Bojanowski, P., Grave, E., Joulin, A., Mikolov, T.: Enriching word vectors with subword information. arXiv preprint arXiv:1607.04606 (2016)
3. Boyd-Graber, J., Fellbaum, C., Osherson, D., Schapire, R.: Adding dense, weighted, connections to WordNet. In: Proceedings of the Global WordNet Conference (2006). docs/jbg-jeju.pdf
4. Cattle, A., Ma, X.: Predicting word association strengths. In: Proceedings of the 2017 Conference on Empirical Methods in Natural Language Processing, pp. 1283–1288 (2017)
5. Chklovski, T., Mihalcea, R.: Building a sense tagged corpus with open mind word expert. In: Proceedings of the ACL-02 Workshop on Word Sense Disambiguation: Recent Successes and Future Directions, vol. 8, pp. 116–122. Association for Computational Linguistics (2002)

---

[8] Shapiro-Wilk tests gave p-values equal to 0.4804 (NN) and 0.4923 (RF).

6. Cramer, I.: How well do semantic relatedness measures perform?: A meta-study. In: Proceedings of the 2008 Conference on Semantics in Text Processing, pp. 59–70. Association for Computational Linguistics (2008)
7. Fellbaum, C.: WordNet: An Electronic Lexical Database. The MIT Press, Cambridge (1998)
8. Frank, E., Hall, M., Witten, I.: The WEKA Workbench. Online Appendix for "Data Mining: Practical machine Learning Tools and Techniques". Morgan Kaufmann, Cambridge (2016)
9. Freihat, A.A., Giunchiglia, F., Dutta, B.: A taxonomic classification of WordNet polysemy types. In: Proceedings of the 8th GWC Global WordNet Conference (2016)
10. Geeraerts, D.: Theories of Lexical Semantics. Oxford University Press, New York (2010)
11. Hayashi, Y.: Predicting the evocation relation between lexicalized concepts. In: Proceedings of COLING 2016, the 26th International Conference on Computational Linguistics: Technical Papers, pp. 1657–1668 (2016)
12. Kacmajor, M., Kelleher, J.D.: Capturing and measuring thematic relatedness. Lang. Resour. Eval. **54**(3), 645–682 (2019). https://doi.org/10.1007/s10579-019-09452-w
13. Lipka, L.: An Outline of English Lexicology: Lexical Structure, Word Semantics, and Word-formation, vol. 3. Walter de Gruyter, Berlin (2010)
14. Lyons, J.: Semantics, vol. 2. Cambridge University Press, Cambridge (1977)
15. Nikolova, S.S., Boyd-Graber, J., Fellbaum, C., Cook, P.: Better vocabularies for assistive communication aids: connecting terms using semantic networks and untrained annotators. In: ACM Conference on Computers and Accessibility (2009). docs/evocation-viva.pdf
16. Pennington, J., Socher, R., Manning, C.D.: GloVe: global vectors for word representation. In: EMNLP (2014)
17. Ramiro, C., Srinivasan, M., Malt, B.C., Xu, Y.: Algorithms in the historicalemergence of word senses. Proc. Natl. Acad. Sci. **115**(10), 2323–2328 (2018). https://doi.org/10.1073/pnas.1714730115, https://www.pnas.org/content/115/10/2323
18. Rothe, S., Schütze, H.: Autoextend: extending word embeddings to embeddings for synsets and lexemes. arXiv preprint arXiv:1507.01127 (2015)
19. Youn, H., et al.: On the universal structure of human lexical semantics. Proc. Natl. Acad. Sci. **113**(7), 1766–1771 (2016)

Computational Intelligence for Multimedia Understanding

Deep Convolutional Generative Adversarial Networks for Flame Detection in Video

Süleyman Aslan[1] , Uğur Güdükbay[1] , B. Uğur Töreyin[2]([⊠]) ,
and A. Enis Çetin[3]

[1] Department of Computer Engineering, Bilkent University, Ankara, Turkey
suleyman.aslan@bilkent.edu.tr, gudukbay@cs.bilkent.edu.tr
[2] Informatics Institute, Istanbul Technical University, Istanbul, Turkey
toreyin@itu.edu.tr
[3] Department of Electrical and Computer Engineering,
University of Illinois at Chicago, Chicago, IL, USA
aecyy@uic.edu
http://cs.bilkent.edu.tr/~gudukbay, https://spacing.itu.edu.tr/,
https://ece.uic.edu/profiles/ahmet-enis-cetin-phd/

Abstract. Real-time flame detection is crucial in video-based surveillance systems. We propose a vision-based method to detect flames using Deep Convolutional Generative Adversarial Neural Networks (DCGANs). Many existing supervised learning approaches using convolutional neural networks do not take temporal information into account and require a substantial amount of labeled data. To have a robust representation of sequences with and without flame, we propose a two-stage training of a DCGAN exploiting spatio-temporal flame evolution. Our training framework includes the regular training of a DCGAN with real spatio-temporal images, namely, temporal slice images, and noise vectors, and training the discriminator separately using the temporal flame images without the generator. Experimental results show that the proposed method effectively detects flame in video with negligible false-positive rates in real-time.

Keywords: Fire detection · Flame detection · Deep Convolutional Generative Adversarial Neural Network

1 Introduction

Fires pose a great danger in open and large spaces. Flames may spread fast and cause substantial damages to properties and human life. Hence, immediate and accurate flame detection plays an instrumental role in fighting fires.

A. Enis Çetin's research is partially funded by NSF with grant number 1739396 and NVIDIA Corporation. B. Uğur Töreyin's research is partially funded by TÜBİTAK 114E426, İTÜ BAP MGA-2017-40964 and MOA-2019-42321.

© Springer Nature Switzerland AG 2020
N. T. Nguyen et al. (Eds.): ICCCI 2020, LNAI 12496, pp. 807–815, 2020.
https://doi.org/10.1007/978-3-030-63007-2_63

Among different approaches, the use of the visible-range video captured by surveillance cameras is particularly convenient for fire detection, as they can be deployed and operated in a cost-effective manner [3]. One of the main challenges is to provide a robust vision-based detection system with negligible false positive rates while securing rapid response. If the flames are visible, this may be achieved by analyzing the motion and color clues of a video in the wavelet domain [5, 21]. Similarly, wavelet-based contour analysis [20] can be used for the detection of possible smoke regions. Modeling various spatio-temporal features such as color and flickering, and dynamic texture analysis [6] can detect fire, as well. In the literature, there are several computer vision algorithms for smoke and flame detection using wavelets, support vector machines, Markov models, region covariance, and co-difference matrices [4]. An important number of fire detection algorithms in the literature not only employ spatial information, but also use the temporal information [4,11,19].

Deep convolutional neural networks (DCNN) achieve successful recognition results on a wide range of computer vision problems [8,15]. Deep neural network-based fire detection algorithms using regular cameras have been developed by many researchers in recent years [9,10,22]. As opposed to earlier computer vision-based fire detection algorithms, in all of the existing DCNN-based methods, the temporal nature of flames is not utilized. Instead, flames are recognized from image frames. In this paper, we utilize the temporal behavior of flames to recognize uncontrolled fires. Uncontrolled flames flicker randomly. The bandwidth of the spectrum of flame flicker can be as high as 10 Hz [7]. To detect such behavior, we group the video frames and obtain temporal slice images. We process the temporal slices using deep convolutional networks.

Radford et al. [17] demonstrate that a class of convolutional neural networks, namely, Deep Convolutional Generative Adversarial Networks (DCGANs), can learn general image representations on various image datasets. In our earlier work, we utilize DCGANs for detecting wildfire smoke based on motion-based geometric image transformation [2]. We utilize a two-stage training approach to have a robust representation of sequences with and without smoke. We first train the network with real images and noise vectors and then train the discriminator using the smoke images without the generator. In a pre-processing stage before training, we integrate the temporal evolution of smoke with a motion-based transformation of images.

We propose utilizing the discriminator of a DCGAN to effectively distinguish ordinary image sequences without flame from those with flame. Additionally, we define a two-stage training approach for the DCGAN such that the discriminator is trained adversarially and to detect flame at the same time. Our main contribution is training the discriminator in such a way that the discriminator acts as a classifier that identifies the images with flame. We develop a DCGAN to utilize adversarial learning in a classification task.

The rest of the paper is organized as follows. Section 2 describes the proposed method that effectively detects flame. Section 3 presents the experimental results of the approach. Finally, Sect. 4 concludes the paper.

2   Method

We describe the proposed flame detection method in this section. In our method, we group the video frames in order to obtain temporal slice images. Then, we process the temporal slices using a DCGAN structure accepting input with size $64 \times 128 \times 384$ pixels. The generator network consists of a fully-connected layer followed by five transposed convolutional layers and the discriminator network consists of five convolutional layers with a fully-connected layer. Figure 1 depicts the neural network architectures and the training framework of the DCGAN.

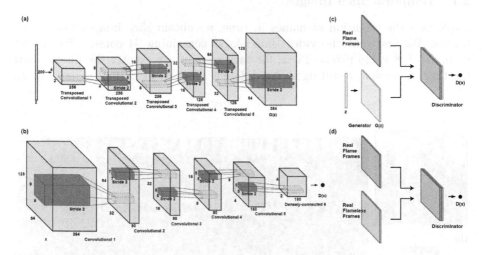

Fig. 1. The block diagram of the DCGAN: (a) the generator of DCGAN, (b) the discriminator of DCGAN, (c) the adversarial learning stage of training, and (d) the second stage of training

We first train the neural networks using a noise distribution z and images that contain flame. The discriminator of the DCGAN is trained to learn a representation of the temporal nature of flames and distinguishes non-flame videos because of the adversarial training. Then, we improve the classification performance by refining and retraining the discriminator network without a generator, where actual non-flame video images constitute the "generated" training data and regular flame images correspond to "real" data as usual. Compared to a generic CNN structure, adversarial training of the DCGAN using the noise vector z and flame data, in addition to the training with the actual non-flame data makes the recognition system more robust.

In our model, we use batch normalization [13] layers and Rectified Linear Unit (ReLU) activation function [16] after each transposed convolutional layer in the generator network, except the last layer, which has a hyperbolic tangent (tanh) activation. Similarly, for the discriminator network, we use batch normalization layers and Leaky ReLU activation function after each convolutional layer, except the last layer, which has a sigmoid activation. During training, we randomly drop out [18] the outputs of the layers in the discriminator network to prevent overfitting and add Gaussian noise to the inputs to increase the generalization capabilities of the network. We initialize the weights of the convolutional and transposed convolutional layers according to the "MSRA" initialization [12]. Finally, we use Adam optimizer for the stochastic optimization [14]. We use the TensorFlow machine learning framework to train the discriminator and generator networks [1].

2.1   Temporal Slice Images

Exploiting the evolution of flames in time, we obtain slice images from video frames. We first split the videos into blocks containing 64 consecutive frames with size 128 × 128 pixels. Then, for each column, we extract the pixels along the time dimension, resulting in 128 different 128 × 64 pixel images (see Fig. 2).

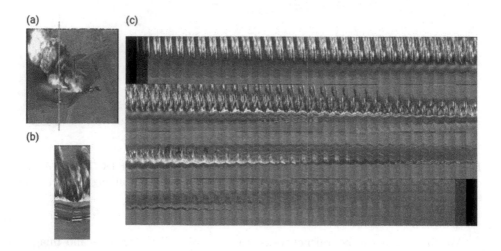

Fig. 2. (a) An example frame from the input video. (b) Temporal slice image of column corresponding to the green line in (a), where the leftmost column contains pixels from the initial frame, namely, the frame at time index $t = 1$, and the rightmost column contains pixels from the final frame, namely, the frame at time index $t = 64$ of the block. (c) Visualization of all 128 slice images. (Color figure online)

To feed the slice image data to the DCGAN model, we stack all 128 slices on top of each other. Thus, we obtain an RGB image cube of size $64 \times 128 \times 384$ pixels because the slice images have three channels each. Figure 3 shows an example of an image cube.

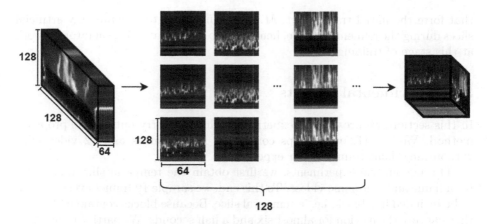

Fig. 3. An example image cube obtained from the input video.

2.2 Proposed GAN-type Discriminator Network

Flame, by its nature, have no particular shape or specific feature as some other objects such as faces, buildings, or cars. Hence, we focus on the temporal behavior of flame instead of spatial information. We utilize the discriminator network of the GAN to distinguish regular camera views from flame videos. This DCGAN structure produces above 0.5 probability value for real temporal flame slices and below 0.5 for slices that do not contain flame, because non-flame slices are not in the initial training set.

In the standard GAN training, the discriminator network that outputs a probability value, D, is updated using the stochastic gradient (Eq. 1)

$$SG_1 = \nabla_{\theta_d} \frac{1}{M} \sum_{i=1}^{M} (\log D(x_i) + \log(1 - D(G(z_i)))), \tag{1}$$

where z_i and x_i are the input noise vector and i^{th} temporal slice, respectively, and G represents the generator network of the GAN which outputs a "fake slice" based on the noise vector z_i; the vector θ_d includes the parameters of D. In this stage, we train the generator network adversarially as in [8]. During this first stage of training, we do not take slices from flame-less videos into account. This GAN can detect flame because discriminator is trained to distinguish flame from any other input. To improve the detection performance, we perform a second stage of training by fine-tuning the discriminator using the stochastic gradient given in Eq. 2.

$$SG_2 = \nabla_{\theta_d} \frac{1}{L} \sum_{i=1}^{L} (\log D(x_i) + \log(1 - D(y_i)), \tag{2}$$

y_i represents the ith slice obtained from regular camera views. The number of non-flame slices, L, is smaller than the size of the slice samples of flame videos that form the initial training set, M. We do not need to generate any artificial slices during the refinement stage, hence, we do not update the generator network at this stage of training.

3 Experimental Results

In this section, we present the experiments that we carry out for the proposed method. We use 112 video clips containing flame frames and 72 video clips without any flame frames in our experiments.

Throughout the experiments, we first obtain the temporal slice images for both flame and non-flame videos. To this end, we sample 10 frames every second, to be included in a block, i.e., a temporal slice. Because blocks contain 64 frames, they capture the motion for almost six and a half seconds. We partition the video clips into non-overlapping temporal slices. Each video clip has a duration of one minute. Consequently, the dataset is composed of over 210 thousand slices from over 1600 blocks in total.

After this procedure, we split the data into training, validation, and test sets. The training set consists of 60% of the videos and the validation and test sets consist of 20% of videos each. We fine-tune the hyperparameters of the neural networks based on the classification performance on the validation set, then report the final results achieved on the test set.

We evaluate the proposed method, namely, DCGAN with Temporal Slices, in terms of frame-based results. Because all the other deep learning methods are essentially based on CNNs, we compare CNN with Temporal Slices, DCGAN with Video Frames (no temporal information), and DCGAN without refinement stage-based approaches to our CNN implementation. It should be also noted that researchers use different fire datasets, therefore the recognition results are not comparable.

In our approach, we aim to reduce the false positive rate while keeping the hit-rate as high as possible. Experimental results show that the proposed method achieves the best results on the test set (cf. Table 1), where a false-positive rate of 3.91% is obtained corresponding to a hit-rate of 92.19%. We show that the adversarial training in DCGAN structure yields more robust results when compared to a CNN (same architecture as the discriminator). As for the utilization of temporal slices to exploit flame evolution, it can be seen that utilizing the temporal information of flames results in much lower false-positive rates. Figure 4 shows some examples of false negative and false positive temporal slices.

Table 1. The true negative rate (TNR) and true positive rate (TPR) values obtained on the test set for frame-based evaluation.

Method	TNR (%)	TPR (%)
DCGAN with Temporal Slices (Our method)	**96.09**	92.19
CNN with Temporal Slices	87.39	93.23
DCGAN with Video Frames (no temporal information)	92.55	92.39
DCGAN without refinement stage	86.61	90.10

Fig. 4. Examples of false negative temporal slices on the left and false positive temporal slices on the right.

4   Conclusion

We propose a DCGAN-based flame detection method in video exploiting the spatio-temporal evolution of fires and employing an unsupervised pre-training stage. We develop a two-stage DCGAN training approach to represent and classify image sequences with and without flames. To reveal the spatio-temporal dynamics of flame regions, we acquire temporal slice images obtained from consecutive frames.

The main contribution of the proposed method is to utilize not only spatial information but also temporal characteristics of flame regions and the unsupervised representation learning capabilities of the DCGAN-based approach. The results indicate that the proposed method achieves significantly lower false alarm rates, compared to CNNs with temporal slices, while keeping the detection rates high.

References

1. Abadi, M., et al.: TensorFlow: a system for large-scale machine learning. In: Proceedings of the 12th USENIX Conference on Operating Systems Design and Implementation, OSDI 2016, pp. 265–283 (2016)

2. Aslan, S., Güdükbay, U., Töreyin, B.U., Çetin, A.E.: Early wildfire smoke detection based on motion-based geometric image transformation and deep convolutional generative adversarial networks. In: Proceedings of the International Conference on Acoustics, Speech, and Signal Processing, ICASSP 2019, pp. 8315–8319. IEEE, Brighton (2019)
3. Çetin, A.E., et al.: Video fire detection-review. Digit. Signal Proc. **23**(6), 1827–1843 (2013)
4. Çetin, A.E., Merci, B., Günay, O., Töreyin, B.U., Verstockt, S.: Methods and Techniques for Fire Detection. Academic Press, Oxford (2016)
5. Dedeoğlu, Y., Toreyin, B.U., Güdükbay, U., Cetin, A.E.: Real-time fire and flame detection in video. In: Proceedings of the International Conference on Acoustics, Speech, and Signal Processing. ICASSO 2005, vol. 2, pp. ii–669. IEEE (2005)
6. Dimitropoulos, K., Barmpoutis, P., Grammalidis, N.: Spatio-temporal flame modeling and dynamic texture analysis for automatic video-based fire detection. IEEE Trans. Circuits Syst. Video Technol. **25**(2), 339–351 (2015)
7. Erden, F., et al.: Wavelet based flickering flame detector using differential PIR sensors. Fire Saf. J. **53**, 13–18 (2012)
8. Goodfellow, I., et al.: Generative adversarial nets. In: Advances in Neural Information Processing Systems, pp. 2672–2680 (2014)
9. Günay, O., Töreyin, B.U., Köse, K., Çetin, A.E.: Entropy-functional-based online adaptive decision fusion framework with application to wildfire detection in video. IEEE Trans. Image Process. **21**(5), 2853–2865 (2012)
10. Günay, O., Çetin, A.E.: Real-time dynamic texture recognition using random sampling and dimension reduction. In: Proceedings of the International Conference on Image Processing, ICIP 2015, pp. 3087–3091. IEEE (2015)
11. Habiboğlu, Y.H., Günay, O., Çetin, A.E.: Covariance matrix-based fire and flame detection method in video. Mach. Vis. Appl. **23**(6), 1103–1113 (2012)
12. He, K., Zhang, X., Ren, S., Sun, J.: Delving deep into rectifiers: surpassing human-level performance on ImageNet classification. In: Proceedings of the International Conference on Computer Vision, ICCV 2015, pp. 1026–1034. IEEE (2015)
13. Ioffe, S., Szegedy, C.: Batch normalization: accelerating deep network training by reducing internal covariate shift. CoRR abs/1502.03167 (2015). http://arxiv.org/abs/1502.03167
14. Kingma, D.P., Ba, J.: Adam: a method for stochastic optimization. CoRR abs/1412.6980 (2014). http://arxiv.org/abs/1412.6980
15. LeCun, Y., Bengio, Y., Hinton, G.: Deep learning. Nature **521**(1), 436–444 (2015)
16. Nair, V., Hinton, G.E.: Rectified linear units improve restricted Boltzmann machines. In: Proceedings of the 27th International Conference on Machine Learning, ICML 2010, pp. 807–814. Omnipress, Madison (2010)
17. Radford, A., Metz, L., Chintala, S.: Unsupervised representation learning with deep convolutional generative adversarial networks. CoRR abs/1511.06434 (2015). http://arxiv.org/abs/1511.06434
18. Srivastava, N., Hinton, G., Krizhevsky, A., Sutskever, I., Salakhutdinov, R.: Dropout: a simple way to prevent neural networks from overfitting. J. Mach. Learn. Res. **15**(1), 1929–1958 (2014)
19. Toreyin, B.U., Cetin, A.E.: Online detection of fire in video. In: Proceedings of the Conference on Computer Vision and Pattern Recognition, CVPR 2007, pp. 1–5. IEEE (2007)
20. Toreyin, B.U., Dedeoğlu, Y., Cetin, A.E.: Contour based smoke detection in video using wavelets. In: Proceedings of the European Signal Processing Conference, EUSIPCO 2006 (2006)

21. Töreyin, B.U., Dedeoğlu, Y., Güdükbay, U., Cetin, A.E.: Computer vision based method for real-time fire and flame detection. Pattern Recogn. Lett. **27**(1), 49–58 (2006)
22. Zhao, Y., Ma, J., Li, X., Zhang, J.: Saliency detection and deep learning-based wildfire identification in UAV imagery. Sensors **18**(3), 712 (2012)

Melanoma Detection Using Deep Learning

Florent Favole[1(✉)], Maria Trocan[1], and Ercüment Yilmaz[2]

[1] Institut Supérieur d'Électronique de Paris, Paris, France
{florent.favole,maria.trocan}@isep.fr
[2] Karadeniz Technical University, Trabzon, Turkey
ercument@ktu.edu.tr

Abstract. In this paper, we describe a region of interest-based app-roach for the classification of dermoscopic images of skin lesions, which nowadays contributes to early identification of skin melanoma. Once the region of interest detected, it will be further processed in order to be used for training and hence classification using deep learning methods. The main goal is to compare three different convolutional neural net-works (CNNs) models and determine the one which provides the best accuracy, knowing that only salient parts of the skin lesions images have been used for training.

Keywords: Image classification · Melanoma detection · Convolutional neural network

1 Introduction

Early detection of skin cancer is vital for patients. Differential diagnosis of skin lesions, especially malignant and benign melanoma is a challenging task even for specialist dermatologists. The diagnostic performance of melanoma has signifi-cantly improved with the use of images obtained via dermoscopy devices. With the recent advances in medical image processing field, it is possible to improve the dermatological diagnostic performance by using computer-assisted diagnos-tic systems. For this purpose, various machine learning algorithms are designed and tested to be used in the diagnosis of melanoma [7]. Deep learning models, which have gained popularity in recent years, have been effective in solving image recognition and classification problems. Concurrently with these developments, studies on the classification of dermoscopic images using CNN models are being performed.

In this study, the performance of AlexNet, Inception-V1 (a.k.a. GoogLeNet) and Resnet50 CNNs will be examined for the classification problem of skin lesions, especially benign, malignant and unknown melanoma cancers on dermo-scopic images. Dermoscopic images of 23 906 lesions obtained from ISIC database

Dr. E. Yilmaz's contribution was supported by The Scientific and Technological Research Council of Turkey (TUBITAK) under Grant 1059B191802000.

© Springer Nature Switzerland AG 2020
N. T. Nguyen et al. (Eds.): ICCCI 2020, LNAI 12496, pp. 816–824, 2020.
https://doi.org/10.1007/978-3-030-63007-2_64

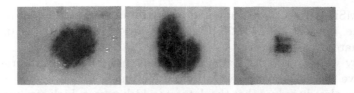

Fig. 1. Benign (left), malignant (center), unknown (right) melanoma

will be used in the experiments. After comparison of these 3 methods the one which will achieve the best accuracy will be determined. The main goal of this paper is to determine the most successful architecture having the best accuracy, to classify the images in three classes : benign, malignant and unknown.

2   Proposed Method

In the sequel, prior of introducing our images pre-processing and data augmentation methods, we describe the complexity of the dermoscopic database and introduce the deep-learning architectures used within this paper.

2.1   Datasets

Table 1. Datasets used in our approach

Dataset name	Number of images	Resolution of images
HAM10000	10015	600 × 450 pixels
SONIC	9251	3024 × 2016 pixels
MSK	3918	Varying
UDA	617	Varying
2018 JID Editorial	100	Varying

The main datasets used in our classification are provided by the ISIC archive database[1], composed by these datasets : HAM10000, SONIC, MSK, UDA and 2018 JID Editorial Images.

The HAM10000 dataset [5] is made up of 10 015 images, each one have a size of 600 × 450 pixels.

The SONIC dataset is made up of 9251 images, each one have a size of 3024 × 2016 pixels.

---

[1] ISIC Archive: ISIC Archive Database, https://www.isic-archive.com/#!/topWith Header/onlyHeaderTop/gallery.

The MSK dataset [6] is composed of subdatasets with different image resolution size, in range 1024 × 720 pixels to 6600 × 4400 pixels. The dataset has approximately 3900 images.

Finally we have two others datasets (UDA and 2018 JID Editorial images) which have 700 images with several resolution image sizes.

We can already induce that the datasets which possess high resolution images will not be fed directly to the CNN models without apply a pre-processing on these images.

2.2 Considered Deep Learning Models

With 60 million parameters, AlexNet has 8 layers — 5 convolutional and 3 fully-connected. At the point of publication, the authors pointed out that their architecture was "one of the largest convolutional neural networks to date on the subsets of ImageNet". They were the first to implement Rectified Linear Units (ReLUs) as activation functions [2].

Inception-V1 (a.k.a. GoogLeNet) has 22 layers architecture with 5 million parameters. The Network In Network approach is heavily used, as mentioned in the paper [3]. This is done by means of 'Inception modules'. The design of an architecture with Inception modules is a product of research on approximating sparse structures. This design was novel by his building networks, using dense modules/blocks, instead of stacking convolutional layers, stacking modules or blocks which are convolutional layers.

ResNet50 with his 26 million parameters and 50 layers was consequently design for this problem, using skip connections (a.k.a. shortcut connections, residuals), while building deeper models. ResNet50 is one of the first adopters of batch normalisation [4].

Table 2. CNN models used in our approach

Model	Parameters	Layers	Year of publication
AlexNet	60 M	8	2012
Inception-V1	5 M	22	2014
RestNet50	26 M	50	2015

2.3 Dermoscopic Image Pre-processing

Each image undergoes the following pre-processing [1] before being fed into the classification models. Indeed the datasets MSK, SONIC and UDA, have images with several high resolutions (for example MSK-1 has 1000 images with 6400 × 4400 pixels resolution). Furthermore the models need images with the same resolutions. Therefore at the end of the pre-processing the images will be all to the resolution 256 × 256 pixels.

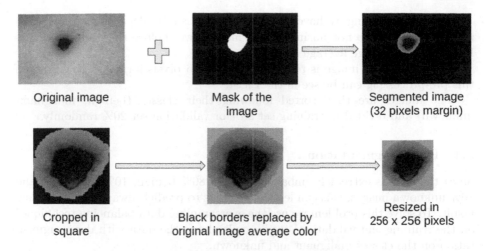

Original image

Mask of the
image

Segmented image
(32 pixels margin)

Cropped in
square

Black borders replaced by
original image average color

Resized in
256 x 256 pixels

Fig. 2. The pre-processing procedure.

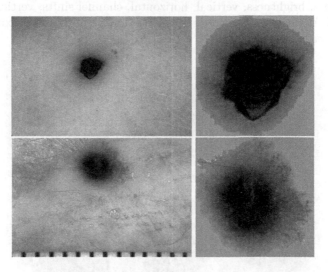

Fig. 3. Before (left) and after (right) pre-processing

Since the main ISIC archive database provides segmentation for these datasets, we started firstly by apply a skin lesion segmentation with a margin of 32 pixels.

The dataset HAM10000 will not have segmentation application, in place just a resizing to 256 × 256 pixels, because the images are already enough usable for classification.

Based on the segmentation image we remove, in rectangular format, the black borders until the remaining colored pixels. Then we keep the highest dimension to be able to crop in square format. Using this format allows to keep the original ratio of the image and consequently to loss the less information possible.

After the cropping we have an image which has still black pixels which originally has not, so to not misinform the models, we replace these black borders by the original image average color.

At the end, the image is resized to 256 × 256 pixels format. The results of this pre-processing can be see in the Fig. 4.

The images are then sorted following their classes (benign, malignant, unknown) and divided in training set 80% or validation set 20% randomly.

2.4   Data Augmentation

Since the data is extremely unbalanced, with 80% benign, 10% malignant and 10% unknown images, this can lead the models to predict always the same class result. To solve this problem we use the oversampling data balancing technique[2] on the training and validation sets by multiplying the data with data augmentation on the classes malignant and unknown.

The standard data augmentations used, as you can see in the Fig. 4, are: random zoom, brightness, vertical, horizontal, channel shifts, vertical and horizontal flips. At the end of the data augmentation we obtain approximately 33% division for each class.

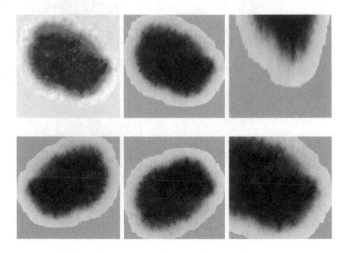

Fig. 4. Data augmentation examples.

---

[2] S. Chatterjee: Deep learning unbalanced training data? solve it like this. https://towardsdatascience.com/deep-learning-unbalanced-training-data-solve-it-like-this-6c528e9efea6.

3   Classification Performance Evaluation

Training a model simply means learning (determining) good values for all the weights and the bias from labeled examples. In supervised learning, a machine learning algorithm builds a model by examining many examples and attempting to find a model that minimizes loss; this process is called empirical risk minimization. Loss is the penalty for a bad prediction, namely loss is a number indicating how bad the model's prediction was on a single example. If the model's prediction is perfect, the loss is zero; otherwise, the loss is greater. The goal of training a model is to find a set of weights and biases that have low loss, on average, across all the training set[3].

In our case the models were train on 10 000 steps. Contrary to the approach in [7], and above mentioned, we consider only the saliency generated region of interest for training our data.

The value global step present on the x axis of the Fig. 5 and 6 is the actualization of the weights of the model after computed the batch size (of 32 images in our case). The loss graph of the three models is showed in the Fig. 5.

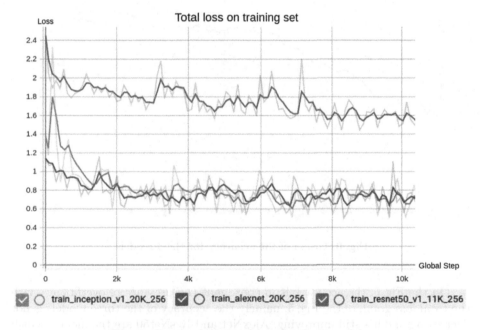

Fig. 5. Graph of the total loss for the 3 models.

On the Fig. 5, the total loss of ResNet50 model is superior by 0.9 points than Inception-V1 and AlexNet models. These differences are due to its architecture,

---

[3] Google: Descending into machine learning:Training and loss, https://developers. google.com/machine-learning/crash-course/descending-into-ml/training-and-loss.

containing two times more layers than the two others models. Moreover we can notice than the loss of the three models are still decreasing, consequently the models are still currently learning, and they are not overfitting, so we could have done the training on more steps. However for time issues the training was done only on 10 000 steps.

Accuracy is one metric for evaluating classification models. Informally, accuracy is the fraction of predictions our models got right. Formally for binary classification, accuracy has the following definition[4]:

$$Accuracy = \frac{TP + TN}{TP + TN + FP + FN} \tag{1}$$

where: TP = True Positives, TN = True Negatives, FP = False Positives, and FN = False Negatives.

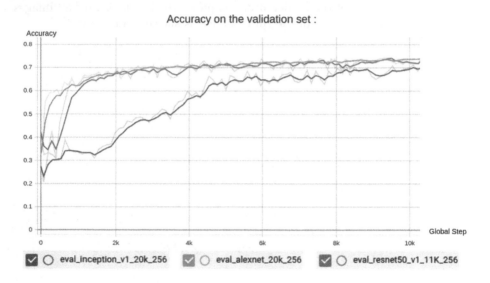

Fig. 6. Graph of the accuracy for the 3 models.

On the Fig. 6, the accuracy is in consonant (no presence of overfitting) with the total loss graph of the Fig. 5, namely the accuracy of the three models is not decreasing and it's still improving. AlexNet and ResNet50 are the models which gets the best final accuracy (0.74), Inception-V1 has the worst accuracy (0.70) but it's the fastest (in term of seconds) model to train and evaluate.

---

[4] Google: Classification: Accuracy, https://developers.google.com/machine-learning/crash-course/classification/accuracy.

Table 3. Final accuracy - no overfitting

Model	Accuracy	Training Time
AlexNet	0.74	55 min 36 s
Inception-V1	0.70	46 min 40 s
RestNet50	0.74	72 min 12 s

4   Conclusion

In this paper, an image region of interest based approach has been used on three deep learning architectures - both for training and validation- in order to evaluate their accuracy in melanoma detection. The networks ResNet50 and AlexNet have a similar and superior accuracy than Inception-V1. Nevertheless RestNet50 takes approximately double time of training than AlexNet. Therefore AlexNet seems to be the best CNN model for this skin lesion classification problem. However, some further improvements are possible, given the reported results. One can be the use of higher resolution for the images. We resized the images to (256, 256, 3). Using a higher resolution like (512, 512, 3) would improve the accuracy of the model.The different datasets have plenty of corrupted images therefore before to apply the pre-processing, cleaning the datasets by removing these might improve the training phase. Moreover, for the use architectures, the most sensitive layers are the last ones, so in freezing the first layers we can gain time in training. This will significantly decrease the computational load. For ISIC database, a model prediction for the metadata can be concatenated with the CNN models, resulting theoretically in higher accuracy.

References

1. Dat, T., et al.: Ensembled skin cancer classification (ISIC 2019 challenge submission)(2019)
2. Krizhevsky, A., Sutskever, I., Hinton, G.E.: Imagenet classification with deep convolutional neural networks. In: Advances in Neural Information Processing Systems, pp. 1097–1105 (2012)
3. Szegedy, C., et al.: Going deeper with convolutions. In: Proceedings of the IEEE Conference on Computer Vision and Pattern Recognition, pp. 1–9 (2015)
4. He, K., Zhang, X., Ren, S., Sun, J.: Deep residual learning for image recognition. In: Proceedings of the IEEE Conference on Computer Vision and Pattern Recognition, pp. 770–778 (2016)
5. Tschandl, P., Rosendahl, C., Kittler, H.: The ham10000 dataset, a large collection of multi-source dermatoscopic images of common pigmented skin lesions. Sci. Data 5, 180161 (2018)

6. Codella, N.C., et al.: Skin lesion analysis toward melanoma detection: a challenge at the 2017 international symposium on biomedical imaging (ISBI), hosted by the international skin imaging collaboration (ISIC). In: 2018 IEEE 15th International Symposium on Biomedical Imaging (ISBI 2018), pp. 168–172. IEEE (2018)
7. Yilmaz, E., Trocan, M.: Benign and malignant skin lesion classification comparison for three deep-learning architectures. In: Nguyen, N.T., Jearanaitanakij, K., Selamat, A., Trawiński, B., Chittayasothorn, S. (eds.) ACIIDS 2020. LNCS (LNAI), vol. 12033, pp. 514–524. Springer, Cham (2020). https://doi.org/10.1007/978-3-030-41964-6_44

Transfer Learning of Mixture Texture Models

Michal Haindl[1,2]([✉]) [iD] and Vojtěch Havlíček[1]

[1] The Institute of Information Theory and Automation of the Czech
Academy of Sciences, Prague, Czechia
{haindl,havlicek}@utia.cz
[2] Faculty of Management, University of Economics, Jindřichův Hradec, Czechia

Abstract. A transfer learning approach for multidimensional parametric mixture random field-based textural representation is introduced. The proposed transfer learning approach allows alleviating the multidimensional mixture models requirement for sufficiently large, but not always available, learning data sets. These compound random field models consist of an underlying structure model that controls transitions between several sub-models, each of them has different characteristics. The structure model proposed is a two-dimensional probabilistic mixture model, either of the Bernoulli or Gaussian mixture type. Local textures are modeled using the fully multispectral three-dimensional Gaussian mixture sub-models. Both presented compound random field models allow the reproduction of, compresses, edits, and enlarges a given measured color, multispectral, or bidirectional texture function (BTF) texture so that ideally, both measured and synthetic textures are visually indiscernible.

Keywords: Texture · Texture modeling · Transfer learning ·
Three-dimensional Gaussian mixture · Compound random field model ·
Bidirectional texture function

1 Introduction

Realistic, visually convincing, and physically correct virtual models require precise object shapes and their surfaces covered with nature-like surface material textures to present realism in virtual scenes. The principal objective of any modeling texture approach is to reproduce and enlarge a given measured material texture so that ideally, both measured natural and modeled synthetic texture will be mutually visually indiscernible. This aim is not easy to reach due to the enormous variability of the natural material's appearance. The surface material semblance dramatically changes with illumination and viewing variations, among others, and we cannot even measure them in their full complexity. The most advanced current texture representation is the seven-dimensional Bidirectional Texture Function (BTF) [11]. Although BTF texture data can be measured, this task is expensive and requires a very demanding measurement setup. Additionally, measured BTF data are nearly always too limited to estimate reliably

© Springer Nature Switzerland AG 2020
N. T. Nguyen et al. (Eds.): ICCCI 2020, LNAI 12496, pp. 825–837, 2020.
https://doi.org/10.1007/978-3-030-63007-2_65

complex seven-dimensional BTF models, inevitably leading to some simplifying factorization [11], such as the presented compound random field models which use a set of three-dimensional factor models for the estimation of the complex overall BTF material model [11]. Very often not enough data is available such that the multidimensional mixture model can be trained [4–6,16,17]. Transfer learning (or domain adaptation) [21–24] partially alleviates the problem of lack of learning data by transferring knowledge learned from other similar learning tasks. Compound random field models (CRF) consist of several sub-models with different characteristics along with an underlying structure model that controls transitions between these sub-models [19]. Several image restoration [2,3,19,20], segmentation [25], or modeling [8,9,12] applications already benefitted of the compound Markov field models. However, these models always require demanding numerical solutions with all their well-known drawbacks. Our exceptional CMRF [8] model allows analytical synthesis at the cost of a slightly compromised compression rate. The transfer learning is illustrated on the three-dimensional Gaussian mixture model (3DGMM) but the same conclusion also holds for other atypical multidimensional mixture models such as 3D Bernoulli distribution mixture model [17] or 3D discrete distribution mixture model [17].

We propose two textural models - $\mathrm{CRF}^{BM-3DGMM}$, $\mathrm{CRF}^{GM-3DGMM}$, based on complex spatial probabilistic mixture models. These models have both the two-dimensional control field model and the three-dimensional local, regional models, either Gaussian mixture or probabilistic Bernoulli models. They differ only in dimensionality. While the principal control field is a simpler two-dimensional field, the local, regional models are much more demanding than three-dimensional. The three-dimensional random fields require much larger learning set to reliable estimate or their parameters, but unfortunately, their learning sets are also much smaller than the learning control fields. Thus we often face the situation when there are not enough data to use such models.

2   Compound Random Field Texture Models

Let us denote a multiindex $r = (r_1, r_2)$, $r \in I$, where I is a discrete two-dimensional rectangular lattice and r_1 is the row and r_2 the column index, respectively. $X_r \in \mathcal{K} = \{1, 2, \ldots, K\}$ is a random variable with natural number value (a positive integer), Y_r is multispectral pixel at location r and $Y_{r,j} \in \mathcal{R}$ is its j-th spectral plane component. Both random fields (X, Y) are indexed on the same lattice I. Let us assume that each multispectral or BTF observed texture $\tilde{Y}$ (composed of d spectral planes) can be modelled by a compound random field model, where the principal random field X controls switching to a regional local model $Y = \bigcup_{i=1}^{K} {}^{i}Y$. Single K regional sub-models ${}^{i}Y$ are defined on their corresponding lattice subsets ${}^{i}I$, ${}^{i}I \cap {}^{j}I = \emptyset$ $\forall i \neq j$ and they are of the same random field (RF) type. The sub-models differ only in their contextual support sets ${}^{i}I_r$ and the corresponding parameters sets ${}^{i}\theta$. The CRF model has posterior probability $P(X, Y \mid \tilde{Y}) = P(Y \mid X, \tilde{Y}) P(X \mid \tilde{Y})$ and the corresponding optimal MAP solution is:

$$(\hat{X}, \hat{Y}) = \arg \max_{X \in \Omega_X, Y \in \Omega_Y} P(Y \mid X, \tilde{Y}) \, P(X \mid \tilde{Y}) \ ,$$

where Ω_X, Ω_Y are corresponding configuration spaces for random fields (X, Y). To avoid an iterative MCMC MAP solution, we propose the following two step approximation [8]:

$$(\check{X}) = \arg \max_{X \in \Omega_X} P(X \mid \tilde{Y}) \ , \tag{1}$$

$$(\check{Y}) = \arg \max_{Y \in \Omega_Y} P(Y \mid \check{X}, \tilde{Y}) \ . \tag{2}$$

This simplifying approximation significantly reduces the BTF-CRF$^{BM-3DGMM}$, BTF-CRF$^{GM-3DGMM}$ learning set requirements because it allows to estimate the principal switching random field X (1) and regional sub-models ^iY (2) independently.

3 Principal Switching Model

The principal part (X) of the BTF compound random models (BTF-CMRF) is assumed to to be independent on illumination and observation angles, i.e., it is identical for all possible combinations $\phi_i, \phi_v, \theta_i, \theta_v$ azimuthal and elevation illumination/viewing angles, respectively. This assumption does not compromise the resulting BTF space quality, because it influences only a material texture macro-structure, which is independent of these angles for static BTF textures.

The control RF $(P(X \mid \tilde{Y}))$ is supposed to be represented by a two-dimensional random filed model. Such model can be a non-parametric random field [8, 14, 15] or some parametric random field hierarchical two-scale Potts model [9], Potts-Voronoi Markov random field model [18], and Gaussian or Bernoulli distribution mixture model [13], respectively. Mixture models are appropriate for regular or near-regular textures such as textile materials presented in this article. The mixture distribution $P(X_{\{r\}})$ has the form:

$$P(X_{\{r\}}) = \sum_{m \in \mathcal{M}} P(X_{\{r\}} \mid m) \, p(m) = \sum_{m \in \mathcal{M}} \prod_{s \in I_r} p_s(X_s \mid m) p(m) \tag{3}$$

where $X_{\{r\}} \in \mathcal{K}^\eta$, $\mathcal{M} = \{1, 2, \dots, M\}$, $I_r \subset I$ is an index set, $\eta = cardinality\{I_r\}$, and $p(m)$ are probability weights $\sum_{m \in \mathcal{M}} p(m) = 1$. The maximum-likelihood parameter estimates $p(m)$ (probability weights), μ_{ms}, σ_{ms} (Gaussian mixture component means and standard deviation), $\theta_{m,s}$ (Bernoulli mixture component parameters) are computed using the EM algorithm [1,5] $p_s^{(t+1)}(. \mid m)$ and

$$q^{(t)}(m \mid X_{\{r\}}) = \frac{p^{(t)}(m) \, P^{(t)}(X_{\{r\}} \mid m)}{\sum_{j \in \mathcal{M}} p^{(t)}(j) P^{(t)}(X_{\{r\}} \mid j)} \ , \tag{4}$$

$$p^{(t+1)}(m) = \frac{1}{|\mathcal{S}|} \sum_{X_{\{r\}} \in \mathcal{S}} q^{(t)}(m \mid X_{\{r\}}) \ . \tag{5}$$

3.1   Principal Field Synthesis

We can assume without loss of generality at a given position r of the contextual neighborhood I_r to have some part of the pixel-wise synthesized control field $X_{\{r\}}$ already specified. If $X_{\{\rho\}}$ is a sub-vector of all of $X_{\{r\}}$ pixels previously specified within this window and $I_\rho \subset I_r$ the corresponding index subset, then the statistical properties of the remaining unspecified variables are fully described by the corresponding conditional distribution:

$$p_{n\,|\,\rho}(X_n\,|\,X_{\{\rho\}}) = \sum_{m=1}^{M} W_m(X_{\{\rho\}})\,p_n(X_n\,|\,m) \ , \qquad (6)$$

where $W_m(X_{\{\{\rho\}\}})$ are the a posteriori component weights corresponding to the given sub-vector $X_{\{\rho\}}$:

$$W_m(X_{\{\rho\}}) = \frac{p(m)P_\rho(X_{\{\rho\}}\,|\,m)}{\sum_{j=1}^{M} p(j)P_\rho(X_{\{\rho\}}\,|\,j)} \ , \qquad (7)$$

$$P_\rho(X_{\{\rho\}}\,|\,m) = \prod_{n\in\rho} p_n(X_n\,|\,m) \ .$$

X_n can be randomly generated by the conditional distribution $p_{n\,|\,\rho}(X_n\,|\,X_{\{\rho\}})$ whereby Eq. (6) can be applied to all the unspecified variables $n = \eta - \mathrm{card}\{\rho\}$ given a fixed position of the control field. Each newly generated X_n is used to upgrade the conditional weights $W_m(X_{\{\rho\}})$.

3.2   Bernoulli Distribution Mixture Model

We assume that the control field distinguishes between K sub-models and the distribution $P(X_{\{r\}})$ to be a multivariable Bernoulli mixture (BM), The control field is further decomposed into separate binary bit planes of binary variables $\xi \in \mathcal{B}, \mathcal{B} = \{0, 1\}$ and these planes are separately modeled and can be estimated from a much smaller learning texture than a multi-level discrete mixture model. We further suppose that a bit factor of a control field can be fully characterised by a marginal probability distribution of binary levels on pixels within the scope of a window centered around the location r and specified by the index set $I_r \subset I$, i.e., $X_{\{r\}} \in \mathcal{B}^\eta$ and $P(X_{\{r\}})$ is the corresponding marginal distribution of $P(X\,|\,\tilde{Y})$. The component distributions $P(\cdot\,|\,m)$ are factorisable, and multivariable Bernoulli:

$$P(X_{\{r\}}\,|\,m) = \prod_{s\in I_r} \theta_{m,s}^{X_s}(1 - \theta_{m,s})^{1-X_s} \qquad X_s \in X_{\{r\}} \ . \qquad (8)$$

The mixture model parameters (8) include component weights $p(m)$ and the univariate discrete distributions of binary levels. They are defined by one parameter $\theta_{m,s}$ as a vector of probabilities:

$$p_s(\cdot\,|\,m) = (\theta_{m,s}, 1 - \theta_{m,s}) \ . \qquad (9)$$

The EM solution is (4), (5) and

$$p_s^{(t+1)}(\xi \mid m) = \frac{1}{|\mathcal{S}| \, p^{(t+1)}(m)} \sum_{X_{\{r\}} \in \mathcal{S}} \delta(\xi, X_s) \, q^{(t)}(m \mid X_{\{r\}}), \quad \xi \in \mathcal{B} . \tag{10}$$

The total number of mixture $(3), (9)$ parameters is thus $M(1 + \eta)$ – confined to the appropriate norming conditions. The advantage of the multivariable Bernoulli model (9) is a simple switch-over to any marginal distribution by deleting superfluous terms in the products $P(X_{\{r\}} \mid m)$.

3.3 Gaussian Mixture Model

The principal (control) random field is discrete, but a continuous RF can alternatively model it if we map single indices into continuous random variables with uniformly separated mean values and small variance. The continuous synthetic results are subsequently inversely mapped back into a corresponding synthetic discrete control field. We assume the joint probability distribution $P(X_{\{r\}})$, $X_{\{r\}} \in \mathcal{K}^\eta$ in the form of a two-dimensional normal mixture and the mixture components are defined as products of univariate Gaussian densities

$$P(X_{\{r\}} \mid \mu_m, \sigma_m) = \prod_{s \in I_{\{r\}}} p_s(X_s \mid \mu_{ms}, \sigma_{ms}) , \tag{11}$$

$$p_s(X_s \mid \mu_{ms}, \sigma_{ms}) = \frac{1}{\sqrt{2\pi}\sigma_{ms}} \exp\left\{ -\frac{(X_s - \mu_{ms})^2}{2\sigma_{ms}^2} \right\} ,$$

i.e., the components are multivariate Gaussian densities with diagonal covariance matrices. The maximum-likelihood estimates of the parameters $p(m), \mu_{ms}, \sigma_{ms}$ can be computed by EM algorithm [1,5]. Anew we use a data set $\mathcal{S}$ obtained by pixel-wise shifting the observation window within the original texture image $\mathcal{S} = \{X_{\{r\}}^{(1)}, \ldots, X_{\{r\}}^{(K)}\}$, $X_{\{r\}}^{(k)} \subset X$. The corresponding log-likelihood function is maximized by the EM algorithm $(m \in \mathcal{M}, n \in \mathcal{N}, X_{\{r\}} \in \mathcal{S})$ and the iterations are (4), (5) and

$$\mu_{m,n}^{(t+1)} = \frac{1}{\sum_{X_{\{r\}} \in \mathcal{S}} q^{(t)}(m \mid X_{\{r\}})} \sum_{X_{\{r\}} \in \mathcal{S}} X_n \, q(m \mid X_{\{r\}}) , \tag{12}$$

$$(\sigma_{m,n}^{(t+1)})^2 = -(\mu_{m,n}^{(t+1)})^2 + \frac{\sum_{X_{\{r\}} \in \mathcal{S}} X_n^2 \, q^{(t)}(m \mid X_{\{r\}})}{\sum_{X_{\{r\}} \in \mathcal{S}} q(m \mid X_{\{r\}})} . \tag{13}$$

Details and examples about both principal random field models are illustrated in [13]. These BTF principal models usually do not suffer from lack of learning data, because there is one common principal field for thousands of measured combinations of illumination and observation angles. However, in the rare case of insufficient data, the transfer learning from the subsequent section can be applied without any change.

3.4   Constant Principal Model

The simplest principal model is a constant field which contains only one model BTF-CMRF$^{c \cdots}$ $P(X \mid \tilde{Y}) = 1$. Then there is no need to use the MAP approximation (1), (2), and the compound Markov model simplifies into a single random field BTF-MRF model, and this model can be any of the local MRF or mixture models. To simplify further exposition and better illustrate the achieved results (Fig. 2) on larger images, we will further assume the constant principal field.

4   Local Spatial 3D Gaussian Mixture Model

A homogeneous static texture image Y is assumed to be defined on a finite rectangular $N_1 \times N_2 \times d$ lattice I, $r = (r_1, r_2, r_3) \in I$ denotes a pixel multiindex with the row, columns and spectral indices, respectively. Let us suppose that Y represents a realization of a random vector with a probability distribution $P(Y)$. The statistical properties of interior pixels of the moving window on Y are translation invariant due to assumed textural homogeneity. They can be represented by a joint probability distribution and the properties of the texture can be fully characterized by statistical dependencies on a sub-field, i. e., by a marginal probability distribution of spectral levels on pixels within the scope of a window centered around the location r and specified by the index set:

$$I_r = \{r + s : |r_1 - s_1| \le \alpha \wedge |r_2 - s_2| \le \beta\} \subset I \ .$$

The index set I_r depends on modeled visual data and can have any other than this rectangular shape. $Y_{\{r\}}$ denotes the corresponding matrix containing all Y_s in some fixed order arrangement such that $s \in I_r$, $Y_{\{r\}} = [Y_s \ \forall s \in I_r]$, $Y_{\{r\}} \subset Y$, $\eta =$ cardinality$\{I_r\}$ and $P(Y_{\{r\}})$ is the corresponding marginal distribution of $P(Y)$. If we assume the joint probability distribution $P(Y_{\{r\}})$, in the form of a normal mixture

$$P(Y_{\{r\}}) = \sum_{m \in \mathcal{M}} p(m) \, P(Y_{\{r\}} \mid \mu_m, \Sigma_m) \qquad Y_{\{r\}} \subset Y \ ,$$

$$= \sum_{m \in \mathcal{M}} p(m) \prod_{s \in I_r} p_s(Y_s \mid \mu_{m,s}, \Sigma_{m,s}) \tag{14}$$

where $Y_{\{r\}} \in \Re^{d \times \eta}$ is $d \times \eta$ matrix, μ_m is $d \times \eta$ mean matrix, Σ_m is $d \times d \times \eta$ a covariance tensor, and $p(m)$ are probability weights and the mixture components are defined as products of multivariate Gaussian densities

$$P(Y_{\{r\}} \mid \mu_m, \Sigma_m) = \prod_{s \in I_{\{r\}}} p_s(Y_s \mid \mu_{ms}, \Sigma_{ms}) \ , \tag{15}$$

$$p_s(Y_s \mid \mu_{ms}, \Sigma_{ms}) = \frac{|\Sigma_{m,s}|^{-\frac{1}{2}}}{(2\pi)^{\frac{d}{2}}} \exp\left\{-\frac{1}{2}(Y_r - \mu_{m,s})^T \Sigma_{m,s}^{-1}(Y_r - \mu_{m,s})\right\} \tag{16}$$

i. e., the components are multivariate Gaussian densities with covariance matrices (23). The underlying structural model of conditional independence is estimated from a data set $\mathcal{S}$ obtained by the step-wise shifting of the contextual window I_r within the original texture image, i. e., for each location r one realization of $Y_{\{r\}}$.

$$\mathcal{S} = \{Y_{\{r\}} \ \forall r \in I, I_r \subset I\} \qquad Y_{\{r\}} \in \Re^{d \times \eta} \ . \tag{17}$$

4.1 Parameter Estimation Using Transfer Learning

Local i-th texture region (not necessarily continuous) is represented by the 3D Gaussian mixture random (3DGMM) field model [7,10]. This model can be analytically estimated as well as synthetically enlarged to any required size if there is enough learning data, what is its typical application problem. The unknown parameters of the approximating the mixture can be estimated using the iterative EM algorithm [1]. To obtain robust parameter estimates for the unusually large 3DGMM models, we need an extensive learning set. The lower frequencies are in the BTF texture the larger cardinality η of $Y_{\{r\}} \in \mathcal{K}^\eta$, is needed. The lack of learning data is bypassed other similar texture ^1Y with approximately similar frequencies as the target texture ^2Y. We assume the same GMM model structure for both textures, i.e., $^1m = {}^2m$. However, both textures can differ in their spectral information. The similar first texture ^1Y is used to learn the initial estimates for the target texture ^2Y with the exception of the component mean vectors:

$$^2p^{(0)}(m) = {}^1p^{(t+1)}(m) \qquad \forall m \ , \tag{18}$$

$$^2\Sigma_{m,s}^{(0)} = {}^1\Sigma_{m,s}^{(t+1)} \qquad \forall m, s \ . \tag{19}$$

The parameter transfer learning algorithm can be summarized:

1. EM estimation (20)–(23) of GMM parameters from ^1Y,
2. EM estimation (20)–(23) of GMM parameters from ^2Y using the EM initialization (18),(19).

In order to estimate the unknown distributions $p_s(\cdot \, | \, m)$ and the component weights $p(m)$ we maximize the likelihood function corresponding to the training set (17):

$$L = \frac{1}{|\mathcal{S}|} \sum_{{}^iY_{\{r\}} \in \mathcal{S}} \log \left[\sum_{m \in \mathcal{M}} P({}^iY_{\{r\}} \, | \, \mu_m, \Sigma_m) \, p(m) \right] \ .$$

The likelihood is maximized using the iterative EM algorithm (with non-diagonal covariance matrices):
E:

$$q^{(t)}(m | \, {}^iY_{\{r\}}) = \frac{P^{(t)}({}^iY_{\{r\}} \, | \, \mu_m, \Sigma_m) \, p^{(t)}(m)}{\sum_{j \in \mathcal{M}} P^{(t)}({}^iY_{\{r\}} \, | \, \mu_j, \Sigma_j) \, p^{(t)}(j)} \ , \tag{20}$$

M:

$$p^{(t+1)}(m) = \frac{1}{|\mathcal{S}|} \sum_{^iY_{\{r\}} \in \mathcal{S}} q^{(t)}(m \,|\, {}^iY_{\{r\}}) \;, \tag{21}$$

$$\mu_{m,s}^{(t+1)} = \frac{1}{\sum_{^iY_{\{r\}} \in \mathcal{S}} q^{(t)}(m \,|\, {}^iY_{\{r\}})} \sum_{^iY_{\{r\}} \in \mathcal{S}} {}^iY_s \, q^{(t)}(m \,|\, {}^iY_{\{r\}}) \;. \tag{22}$$

The $M\eta$ covariance matrices are:

$$\begin{aligned}
\Sigma_{m,s}^{(t+1)} &= \frac{\sum_{^iY_{\{r\}} \in \mathcal{S}, {}^IY_s \in {}^IY_{\{r\}}} q^{(t)}(m \,|\, {}^iY_{\{r\}})}{\sum_{^iY_r \in \mathcal{S}} q^{(t)}(m \,|\, {}^iY_{\{r\}})} ({}^iY_s - \mu_{m,s}^{(t+1)})({}^iY_s - \mu_{m,s}^{(t+1)})^T \\
&= \frac{\sum_{^iY_{\{r\}} \in \mathcal{S}, {}^iY_s \in {}^iY_{\{r\}}} q^{(t)}(m \,|\, {}^iY_{\{r\}}) \, {}^iY_s^i Y_s^T}{\sum_{^iY_r \in \mathcal{S}} q^{(t)}(m \,|\, {}^iY_{\{r\}})} \\
&\quad - \frac{p^{(t+1)}(m) \,|\mathcal{S}|\, \mu_{m,s}^{(t+1)} \left(\mu_{m,s}^{(t+1)}\right)^T}{\sum_{^iY_r \in \mathcal{S}} q^{(t)}(m \,|\, {}^iY_{\{r\}})} \;.
\end{aligned} \tag{23}$$

The iteration process is stopped when the criterion increments are sufficiently small. The EM algorithm iteration scheme has the monotonic property: $L^{(t+1)} \geq L^{(t)}$, $t = 0, 1, 2, \ldots$ which implies the convergence of the sequence $\{L^{(t)}\}_0^\infty$ to a stationary point of the EM algorithm (local maximum or a saddle point of L).

4.2   Texture Synthesis

The advantage of a mixture model is its simple synthesis based on the marginals:

$$p_{n\,|\,\rho}(Y_n \,|\, Y_{\{\rho\}}) = \sum_{m=1}^{M} W_m(Y_{\{\rho\}}) \, p_n(Y_n \,|\, m) \;, \tag{24}$$

where $W_m(Y_{\{\{\rho\}\}})$ are the a posteriori component weights corresponding to the given submatrix $Y_{\{\rho\}} \subset Y_{\{r\}}$:

$$W_m(Y_{\{\rho\}}) = \frac{p(m) P_\rho(Y_{\{\rho\}} \,|\, m)}{\sum_{j=1}^{M} p(j) P_\rho(Y_{\{\rho\}} \,|\, j)} \;, \tag{25}$$

$$P_\rho(Y_{\{\rho\}} \,|\, m) = \prod_{n \in \rho} p_n(Y_n \,|\, m) \;. \tag{26}$$

The unknown multivariate vector-levels Y_n can be synthesized by random sampling from the conditional density (24) or the mixture RF can be approximated using the GMM mixture prediction [17].

5   Experiments

The proposed compound random field models ($BTF - CRF^{BM-3GMM}$, $BTF - CRF^{GM-3GMM}$) are well convenient for near-regular textures such as textile materials. Textures with the near-regular structure are difficult for Markov random field type of textural models [8,11], which are better suited for the random type of materials. The dimension of the estimated control field model distribution is not too high ($\eta \approx 10^1 - 10^2$) and the number of the training data vectors is relatively large ($|\mathcal{S}| \approx 10^4 - 10^5$). However, the window size should always be kept reasonably small and the sample size as large as possible. We have used a regular left-to-right and top-to-down shifting of the generating window in our experiments. Figure 1 illustrates the synthesis of Cloth35 texture control field using the two-dimensional Bernoulli mixture model ($BTF - CRF^{BM-3DGMM}$). Figure 2 shows four textile BTF material measurements (only one measurement with perpendicular viewing and illumination angle from the whole sets of 6561 measurements per material). These samples were synthesized using the $BTF - CRF^{c-3DGMM}$ models either with the transfer learning from similar textile textures or without. If we are comparing both synthesis variants, the usefulness of the additional information obtained from the transfer learning is pronounced. The transfer learning cost doubles the learning time because, in our experiments, we double (2×512^2) the overall learning set. Experiments with a chain of two similar textures suggest no further noticeable improvement. Significantly different textures might even decrease the performance (negative transfer).

| Cloth35 | BM X | Fabric024 |

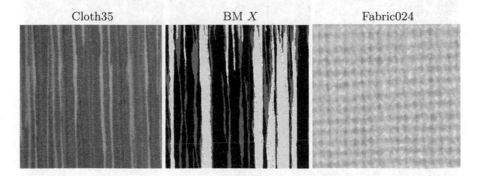

Fig. 1. Cloth measurements (left), its synthesized control field using the BM model with $K = 4$ (middle), and Fabric024 texture used in the transfer learning (Fig. 2 first row).

Fabric028   TL from Fabric024

Fabric119   TL from Fabric120

Fabric120   TL from Fabric119

Fabric122   TL from Fabric120

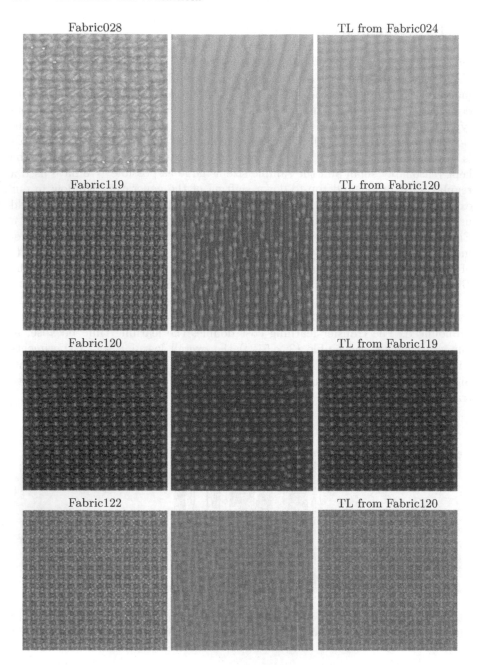

Fig. 2. Fabric measurements (left column), synthesis without transfer learning (TL, middle column), and with the transfer learning (right column) using the $3DGMM$ model.

6 Conclusion

Both presented BTF-CRF ($BTF - CRF^{GM-3DGMM}$, $CRF^{BM-3DGMM}$ methods with the local random field models learned using the supported information from similar textures through transfer learning suggest improved visual achievement on selected real-world measured textile materials. The models do not compromise spectral correlation; thus, they reliably model and enlarge motley textures. Both methods can be smoothly generalized for color, hyperspectral or BTF texture editing by learning some local models from alternative target materials. The proposed transfer learning approach allows alleviating typical multidimensional mixture models drawback - their requirement of sufficiently large learning data that are not always available.

Acknowledgements. The Czech Science Foundation project GAČR 19-12340S supported this research.

References

1. Dempster, A., Laird, N., Rubin, D.: Maximum likelihood from incomplete data via the em algorithm. J. Roy. Stat. Soc. B **39**(1), 1–38 (1977)
2. Figueiredo, M., Leitao, J.: Unsupervised image restoration and edge location using compound Gauss - Markov random fields and the mdl principle. IEEE Trans. Image Process. **6**(8), 1089–1102 (1997)
3. Geman, S., Geman, D.: Stochastic relaxation, gibbs distributions and Bayesian restoration of images. IEEE Trans. Pattern Anal. Mach. Intell. **6**(11), 721–741 (1984)
4. Grim, J., Haindl, M.: A discrete mixtures colour texture model. In: Chantler, M. (ed.) Texture 2002, The 2nd International Workshop on Texture Analysis and Synthesis, pp. 59–62. Heriot-Watt University, Glasgow (2002). http://citeseer.ist.psu.edu/533346.html
5. Grim, J., Haindl, M.: Texture modelling by discrete distribution mixtures. Comput. Stat. Data Anal. **41**(3–4), 603–615 (2003)
6. Haindl, M., Grim, J., Somol, P., Pudil, P., Kudo, M.: A Gaussian mixture-based colour texture model. In: Kittler, J., Petrou, M., Nixon, M. (eds.) Proceedings of the 17th IAPR International Conference on Pattern Recognition, vol. III, pp. 177–180. IEEE Press, Los Alamitos (2004). http://dx.doi.org/10.1109/ICPR.2004.1334497
7. Haindl, M., Havlíček, V.: A multiscale colour texture model. In: Kasturi, R., Laurendeau, D., Suen, C. (eds.) Proceedings of the 16th International Conference on Pattern Recognition, pp. 255–258. IEEE Computer Society, Los Alamitos (2002). http://dx.doi.org/10.1109/ICPR.2002.1044676
8. Haindl, M., Havlíček, V.: A compound MRF texture model. In: Proceedings of the 20th International Conference on Pattern Recognition, ICPR 2010, pp. 1792–1795. IEEE Computer Society CPS, Los Alamitos (2010).https://doi.org/10.1109/ICPR.2010.442, http://doi.ieeecomputersociety.org/10.1109/ICPR.2010.442
9. Haindl, M., Remeš, V., Havlíček, V.: Potts compound markovian texture model. In: Proceedings of the 21st International Conference on Pattern Recognition, ICPR 2012, pp. 29–32. IEEE Computer Society CPS, Los Alamitos (2012)

10. Haindl, M.: Visual data recognition and modeling based on local Markovian models. In: Florack, L., Duits, R., Jongbloed, G., van Lieshout, M.-C., Davies, L. (eds.) Mathematical Methods for Signal and Image Analysis and Representation. CIV, vol. 41, pp. 241–259. Springer, London (2012). https://doi.org/10.1007/978-1-4471-2353-8_14

11. Haindl, M., Filip, J.: Visual Texture. Advances in Computer Vision and Pattern Recognition. Springer-Verlag, London (2013). https://doi.org/10.1007/978-1-4471-4902-6

12. Haindl, M., Havlíček, V.: A plausible texture enlargement and editing compound markovian model. In: Salerno, E., Cetin, A., Salvetti, O. (eds.) Computational Intelligence for Multimedia Understanding, Lecture Notes in Computer Science, vol. 7252, pp. 138–148. Springer, Heidelberg (2012). https://doi.org/10.1007/978-3-642-32436-9_12, http://www.springerlink.com/content/047124j43073m202/

13. Haindl, M., Havlíček, V.: Two compound random field texture models. In: Beltrán-Castañón, C., Nyström, I., Famili, F. (eds.) CIARP 2016. LNCS, vol. 10125, pp. 44–51. Springer, Cham (2017). https://doi.org/10.1007/978-3-319-52277-7_6

14. Haindl, M., Havlíček, V.: BTF compound texture model with fast iterative non-parametric control field synthesis. In: di Baja, G.S., Gallo, L., Yetongnon, K., Dipanda, A., Castrillon-Santana, M., Chbeir, R. (eds.) Proceedings of the 14th International Conference on Signal-Image Technology & Internet-Based Systems (SITIS 2018), pp. 98–105. IEEE Computer Society CPS, Los Alamitos (2018). https://doi.org/10.1109/SITIS.2018.00025

15. Haindl, M., Havlíček, V.: BTF compound texture model with non-parametric control field. In: The 24th International Conference on Pattern Recognition (ICPR 2018), pp. 1151–1156. IEEE (2018). http://www.icpr2018.org/

16. Haindl, M., Havlíček, V., Grim, J.: Probabilistic discrete mixtures colour texture models. In: Ruiz-Shulcloper, J., Kropatsch, W.G. (eds.) CIARP 2008. LNCS, vol. 5197, pp. 675–682. Springer, Heidelberg (2008). https://doi.org/10.1007/978-3-540-85920-8_82

17. Haindl, M., Havlíček, V., Grim, J.: Probabilistic mixture-based image modelling. Kybernetika 46(3), 482–500 (2011). http://www.kybernetika.cz/content/2011/3/482/paper.pdf

18. Haindl, M., Remeš, V., Havlíček, V.: BTF potts compound texture model, vol. 9398, pp. 939807-1–939807-11. SPIE, Bellingham (2015). https://doi.org/10.1117/12.2077481

19. Jeng, F.C., Woods, J.W.: Compound Gauss-Markov random fields for image estimation. IEEE Trans. Signal Process. 39(3), 683–697 (1991)

20. Molina, R., Mateos, J., Katsaggelos, A., Vega, M.: Bayesian multichannel image restoration using compound Gauss-Markov random fields. IEEE Trans. Image Process. 12(12), 1642–1654 (2003)

21. Pan, S.J., Yang, Q.: A survey on transfer learning. IEEE Trans. Knowl. Data Eng. 22(10), 1345–1359 (2017). https://doi.org/10.1109/TKDE.2009.191

22. Singh, R., Vatsa, M., Patel, V.M., Ratha, N.: Domain Adaptation for Visual Understanding. Springer, Heidelberg (2020). https://doi.org/10.1007/978-3-030-30671-7

23. Torrey, L., Shavlik, J.: Transfer learning. In: Handbook of Research on Machine Learning Applications and Trends: Algorithms, Methods, and Techniques, pp. 242–264. IGI Global (2010)

24. Weiss, K., Khoshgoftaar, T.M., Wang, D.D.: A survey of transfer learning. J. Big Data **3**(1), 1–40 (2016). https://doi.org/10.1186/s40537-016-0043-6

25. Wu, J., Chung, A.C.S.: A segmentation model using compound Markov random fields based on a boundary model. IEEE Trans. Image Process. **16**(1), 241–252 (2007)

A Procedure for the Routinary Correction of Back-to-Front Degradations in Archival Manuscripts

Pasquale Savino$^{(\boxtimes)}$ ⓘ and Anna Tonazzini ⓘ

Istituto di Scienza e Tecnologie dell'Informazione, Consiglio Nazionale delle Ricerche,
Via G. Moruzzi 1, 56124 Pisa, Italy
{pasquale.savino,anna.tonazzini}@isti.cnr.it

Abstract. Virtual restoration of the nowadays frequently available digital copies of the human documental heritage is crucial for facilitating both the traditional work of philologists and paleographers and the automatic analysis of the contents. Here we propose a fast procedure for the correction of the typically complex background of recto-verso historical manuscripts, which does not need for a preliminary registration of the images of the two page sides. The simplicity of the procedure makes it suitable for the routinary use in the archives. The method consists of two stages, degradation identification and degradation cancellation. The first step performs the detection of both the primary text and the spurious strokes via soft segmentation based on the statistical decorrelation of the two recto and verso images. In the second step, the noisy pattern in the background is substituted with pixels that simulate the texture of the clean surrounding background, through an efficient technique of image inpainting. As shown in the experimental results, the proposed procedure is able to perform a fine and selective removal of the degradation, while preserving the original appearance of the manuscript.

1 Introduction

The virtual restoration of historical, archival manuscripts entails the correction of a complex, noisy background, where spurious strokes or other patterns interfere with the primary foreground text. Often, text binarization is proposed as a way to remove degradations from documents, especially when some enhancement is required prior tasks such as word spotting or character recognition. Binarization is thus performed to extract a mask of the interesting foreground text against all other features, considered noise as a whole. In the context of this approach, a large variety of methods have been developed for degraded document binarization [1,2]. Among the most recent, recurrent, convolutional or deep neural networks have been shown to cope, to some extent, with degradations such as uneven illumination, image contrast variation, changes in stroke width and connection, faded ink of faint characters [3–6].

However, strong degradations due to interferences, especially occurring in ancient, historical manuscripts, cannot be normally removed by binarization

© Springer Nature Switzerland AG 2020
N. T. Nguyen et al. (Eds.): ICCCI 2020, LNAI 12496, pp. 838–849, 2020.
https://doi.org/10.1007/978-3-030-63007-2_66

alone, due to the significant overlap of the interfering patterns with the foreground text and the wide variation of their extent and intensity. Furthermore, binarization produces a boolean result, whereas the added value of virtual restoration is instead its capability to free the original contents from extra, foreign elements that have been added due to the ravages of time. In other words, virtual restoration should simulate on the digital images the process of physical and/or chemical restoration to be performed on the original, tangible manuscript. In fact, virtual restoration can represent the only viable way to restore the original appearance of precious and fragile historical manuscripts, when physical restoration is not practicable for safeguard reasons.

From the image processing perspective, virtual restoration should consist in substituting the noisy pixels with simulations of plausible background pixels, in such a way that the restored manuscript appears as much natural as possible. In most methods, this is accomplished in two steps: a first step where the unwanted motif is detected, and a second step where the detected motif is inpainted with proper values. The detection step is usually a three-classes segmentation problem, where the three classes are the background, the foreground text and the interferences. For instance, in [7], a recursive unsupervised segmentation is suggested to detect the manuscript components, and the interfering one is then replaced by the average of the detected background pixels. In [8] the distortion pattern, segmented through a conditional random field (CRF), is replaced with background pixels randomly selected from the neighbourhood. These kinds of generic fill-in usually create visible artifacts when the background is textured.

In the case of the so called bleed-through effect, caused by the porosity of the paper that makes the ink penetrate the fiber and appear, more or less attenuated and smeared, also in the opposite side of the sheet, the availability of the extra information provided by the back page allows improvements in the segmentation step. Examples in this respect can be found in [9], where a classification is performed by segmenting the recto-verso joint histogram with the aid of ground truths, in [10], where a dual-layer Markov Random Field (MRF) prior is combined with a data term derived from user-labeled pixels, and in [11], where also the inpainting of the bleed-through pixels detected by the model-based method in [12] has been improved through sparse image representation and dictionary learning. The performance of the recto-verso based methods depends however on the alignment of the two images, which should ensure an accurate matching between the information carried on by corresponding pixels. In other words, the values of two opposite pixels must be the spectral signatures in the two sides of the same geometrical point. Accurate registration is difficult to achieve in this specific case, due to document skews, different image resolutions, or wrapped pages when scanning books. Furthermore, the intensity of corresponding foreground and bleed-through areas are usually very different, bleed-through might only occur sparsely across the page, and the binding of the page in case of books may have different degrees of curvature in the two sides. Thus, dedicated recto-verso registration algorithms have to be designed [13–15], and joint registration and restoration has also been proposed [16].

Single step enhancement methods have been proposed as well, under the requirement of multiple acquisitions of the same manuscript. These methods are based, for instance, on disentangling patterns that appear superposed in the degraded manuscript, according to a principle of mixing of source images. Thus, in [17] and [18] independent component analysis and correlated component analysis, respectively, are experimented to separate the overlapped information layers from spectrally diverse acquisitions. Similarly, in [19] the information of the recto and verso images is exploited to uncouple the front and back texts via specular modelling and symmetric whitening decorrelation of the two images. Other variants of source separation techniques have been proposed in [20] and [21]. With these techniques, it may happen that in some of the output images the foreground text dominates the grayscale whereas the interfering patterns tend to merge with the background, thus vanishing. However, often, some unpleasant imprints of the removed patterns remain in the enhanced, separated images, or discoloration of the inks can be observed in correspondence of the crossings between the foreground text and the spurious patterns.

The different approaches surveyed above have all merits and disadvantages. In this work we tried to catch their positive features to build an automatic procedure for the virtual restoration of RGB manuscripts degraded by back-to-front ink seeping. Our procedure does not aim at providing results that can be evaluated quantitatively, our scope is instead to define a simple and fast processing pipeline that can facilitate the legibility of the intricate content of very damaged manuscripts, and consent a plainer readability of the main text, without destroying the peculiar features of the manuscript, related to its origin and history.

The procedure is basically constituted of three main computational blocks: image enhancement and soft segmentation based on statistical decorrelation, detection and classification of the components based on binarization, and cancellation of the degradation class based on inpainting. The peculiar feature of the procedure, which significantly streamlines it, is that it does not require prior registration of the two sides. Indeed, we assume that, at local level, the misalignment between the recto-verso pair always reduces to a translation only, and hence, for each pair of image patches located at the same position in the two images, we compute their mutual shift to correct it. We then perform binarization of the two aligned recto-verso patches, after having decorrelated them through symmetric whitening. This specific type of source separation is particularly suited to reduce back-to-front interferences in either manuscripts or scanned printed documents [19], while preserving all other marks genuinely belonging to each side. In practice, it performs a very fast and parameter-free soft segmentation that can significantly improve the results of a subsequent binarization. Through binarization of both the decorrelated sides we obtain, for each side, the three-class segmentation of each patch into foreground text, ink-bleed degradation, plus a background class that includes all other interesting patterns in the scene. The union of the detected foreground text and degradation pattern is inpainted in each side with the texture of the surrounding background, and then the pertinent, detected foreground text is replaced in the corrected background map. In this way, we obtain the selective removal of the unwanted interference alone, leaving unaltered the rest of the content.

The paper is organized as follows. In Sect. 2 we describe the procedure through the aid of a block diagram, and the salient mathematical details of the processing blocks are given. Section 3 is devoted to the description and the analysis of some preliminary results obtained by applying the procedure to letters from the correspondence of Christoforus Clavius, conserved at the Historical Archive of the Pontificia Università Gregoriana in Rome. Section 4 concludes the paper.

2   The Virtual Restoration Procedure

The virtual restoration procedure that we propose is illustrated in Figs. 1 and 2. Figure 1 summarizes the local mechanism by which the procedure operates. The two images in input are subdivided into subsequent patches, each pair of homologous recto and verso patches are processed together in order to obtain the restored version of the recto patch. After the elaboration of the whole recto image, the two inputs are inverted, and the procedure is repeated again to obtain the restored verso image. The two output images maintain the geometry of the corresponding input ones, in that no registration between the recto and the verso is performed. Hence, as a consequence, the resolution of the images is not reduced by any interpolation process.

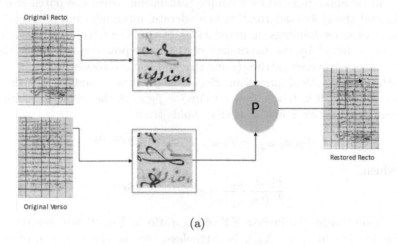

Fig. 1. Image-level procedure: patch-by-patch processing.

Figure 2 illustrates the procedure at the level of each pair of patches. This is constituted of three main steps: pre-processing, segmentation, and degradation removal, which, in turn, are subdivided into a number of consecutive phases,

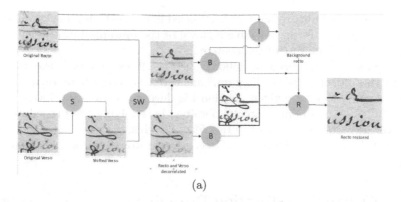

(a)

Fig. 2. Patch-level procedure: elaboration of each pair of opposite patches.

namely patch alignment (A - alignment), patch decorrelation (SW - symmetric whitening), patch binarization (B - binarization), background map estimation (I - inpainting), and foreground text repositioning (R - restoration).

2.1   Phase A - Alignment

In Phase A, given a recto patch, the corresponding patch in the mirrored verso that best matches it is searched for. We observed that, at the local level, the geometric transformation between a recto patch and its corresponding verso patch can be approximated by a simple translation, when the patch size is not too big and the global deformation is moderate, although even non-rigid, as in the cases of book bindings or undulations of the sheet [16]. The value of the shift can be found by the maximizer of the cross-power spectrum of the two homologous recto-verso patches (same size and same position in the two sides).

In the mathematical formalism, given two patches f_1 and f_2 such that, in a common support, it is $f_1(x + \Delta x_0, y + \Delta y_0) = f_2(x, y)$, the following relationship between their Fourier Transforms (FT) holds true:

$$F_2(\omega_x, \omega_y) = F_1(\omega_x, \omega_y)e^{j(\omega_x \Delta x_0 + \omega_y \Delta y_0)} \tag{1}$$

from which:

$$\frac{F_2(\omega_x, \omega_y)}{F_1(\omega_x, \omega_y)} = e^{j(\omega_x \Delta x_0 + \omega_y \Delta y_0)} \tag{2}$$

Then, theoretically, the inverse FT of the ratio in Eq. (2) will return a Dirac impulse located in $(\Delta x_0, \Delta y_0)$. Nevertheless, due to the presence of random noise, dissimilar parts and gain changes, inverse filtering produces a very noisy map, where a trustable peak cannot be located. A more robust estimate of the cross correlation between f_1 and f_2 is given by the inverse FT of the cross power spectrum:

$$\frac{F_2(\omega_x, \omega_y) \cdot F_1^*(\omega_x, \omega_y)}{|F_2(\omega_x, \omega_y)| \cdot |F_1^*(\omega_x, \omega_y)|} = e^{j(\omega_x \Delta x_0 + \omega_y \Delta y_0)} \tag{3}$$

where $*$ denotes the complex conjugate. The location of the well emerging peak of the cross-correlation function computed using Eq. (3) defines the relative translation between the two patches. Using FFT, this computation is very fast.

2.2   Phase SW - Symmetric Whitening

Back-to-front degradations have the peculiarity that, when the images of the two opposite sides are perfectly registered, the location of the main text in one side corresponds to that of the degradation in the other, and the background is given by the area outside the union of the two texts. Thus, if satisfactory text binarization can be achieved in each side, the two binarized front and back images automatically provide the three classes that constitute each side, i.e. pure background, foreground and interfering pattern.

To improve binarization, noise filtering and contrast enhancement are often applied as a pre-processing [22]. In our procedure, image enhancement is performed in Phase SW, where the two aligned recto-verso patches are first decorrelated via symmetric whitening, in order to reduce the degradation coming from the opposite side.

The rationale for using decorrelation lies in considering the recto and verso images, in presence of ink seeping, as different observations of a same scene, where the different texts and, possibly, other features (paper texture and watermarking, stains, stamps, pencil annotations, etc.) appear as overlapped layers of information. Diversity of the acquisition modality is constituted by the different intensities of a same text pattern in the two observations. To describe this fact, a linear, instantaneous overlapping model has been proposed in [19]. This is a 2×2 model, whose mixing matrix is related to the percentage of ink seeping from one side to the other. Since it is reasonable to assume that the ink penetrates the paper in the same way from recto to verso and from verso to recto, the mixing matrix can be assumed symmetric. In the mathematical formalism, let $r(t)$ and $v(t)$, $t = 1, 2, ..., T$, be the pair of the acquired (mirrored and registered) images, with t the pixel index. We consider $r(t)$ and $v(t)$ as a linear combination of the two images $s_1(t)$ and $s_2(t)$, $t = 1, 2, ..., T$, representing the clean main texts in the recto and the verso, respectively. We can write:

$$r(t) = A_{11}s_1(t) + A_{12}s_2(t)$$
$$v(t) = A_{21}s_1(t) + A_{22}s_2(t) \tag{4}$$

where $A_{12} = A_{21}$. Viewing s_1 and s_2 as the sources, and A as the unknown mixing matrix, Eq. (4) turns out to define a 2×2 blind source separation (BSS) problem [23,24]. In the assumption of mutually independent sources, both the sources and the mixing coefficients can be estimated from the data alone, through techniques such as independent component analysis (ICA) [24]. In our case, as the mixing matrix is expected to be symmetric, decorrelating the data through symmetric whitening is equivalent to ICA [23], and much faster and simpler.

2.3   Phase B - Binarization

In most cases, after decorrelation a more effective binarization of the pertinent foreground text can be performed in each side.

As an example, Figs. 3(a) and (b) show the results of the binarization of the recto side of a manuscript, obtained with the Sauvola algorithm [25] before and after decorrelation of the two sides.

(a)   (b)

Fig. 3. Application of Sauvola binarization before and after symmetric whitening: (a) binarized original recto; (b) binarized recto after decorrelation of the recto-verso pair.

In our procedure, the individual binarization of the decorrelated recto and verso patches is performed in Phase B, with the aim, as said, to segment the foreground text of each side. The procedure can use any of the many degraded document binarization algorithms proposed in the literature. At present, we have included the Sauvola algorithm [25].

Binarization of the two sides detects also a safe background area in the recto, from which to drawn samples for filling in the complementary area, i.e. the area of the union of the two texts. This is highlighted in the map shown in the diagram of Figure 2, where the blue mask corresponds to foreground, the red mask to bleed-through, and the green pixels are the crossings between the two texts. Since the bleed-through text of the recto is estimated from the corresponding foreground text of the verso, it is likely that the former is underestimated, because of the effect of diffusion of the penetrating ink. We then dilate its mask to account for this fact.

2.4   Phase I - Inpainting

In Phase I, the white pixels of the map are replaced with the values of the corresponding pixels of the safe background of the original recto, and the masks in color are inpainted with samples drawn from the closest safe background region itself. In this way, a full-image background map is generated, which simulates the empty page, that is the texture of the paper prior the writing. To do that, we tested various state-of-the art still image inpainting techniques, and selected as the best one for our purposes the exemplar-based image inpainting technique described in [26].

2.5   Phase R - Restoration

Finally, Phase R produces the final restored recto, by placing the original foreground text in the simulated background map. At present, we use the binarized recto to locate the pixels to be replaced with the proper values. However, the technique proposed in [12] could give a finer estimation of the foreground map, to be used at this stage.

3   Experimental Results

We show here the results of the procedure on pairs of recto-verso letters from the correspondence of Christoforus Clavius, conserved at the Historical Archive of the Pontificia Università Gregoriana in Rome (APUG 529/530 - Fondo Clavius).

Figure 4 shows a details of a very damaged manuscript letter. Comparing recto and verso, it is possible to appreciate the significant misalignment introduced during the acquisition. This misalignment appears also in the restored images, since the procedure does not require image registration. Although the results are not quantitatively perfect, from a qualitative point of view they are correct, in that the two completely overlapped texts, almost indistinguishable in the originals, have been fully separated. We expect that better results can be obtained by refining binarization through performing state-of-the-art algorithms specifically designed for degraded documents.

Figures 5 and 6 show the full page and a detail, respectively, of the verso side of another letter.

Note that the non-periodic texture of the paper and other local marks on the support have been preserved, and now they appear even enhanced, whereas only the seepage has been exclusively removed.

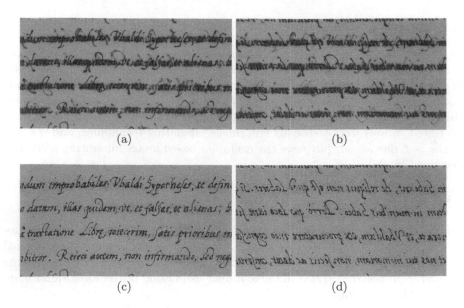

Fig. 4. Application of the whole procedure, a detail of the results: (a) original recto; (b) original verso; (c) recto restored; (d) verso restored. Original images (a) and (b): reproduction by courtesy of The Historical Archive of the Pontificia Università Gregoriana, APUG 529/530, c. 131r/v (Fondo Clavius).

4   Conclusions

As opposite to the popular approach of completely removing the complex background, e.g. through binarization, we proposed to virtually restore degraded, archival manuscripts by removing the unwanted interference alone, while preserving the fine details related to the original appearance. To this aim, exploiting the information contained in the verso side is crucial, in that it allows a very fine discrimination among features due to ink seepage or originally present in the side at hand. In this paper, we proposed a procedure that does not require prior registration of the two sides, and exploits joint binarization of only mutually translated opposite patches to perform a three-classes segmentation of the manuscript contents into main foreground text, pattern interfering from the back side, and pure background. Restoration is then obtained by inpainting the region containing the union of foreground and interference with the texture of the surrounding background, and repositioning the original foreground text in the so estimated background map. Experimental results obtained on historical manuscripts demonstrate the potentiality of the procedure for a significant improvement of the quality of even highly degraded manuscripts, and its large scale usage in historical archives. From a quantitative point of view, the performance of the procedure can be boosted by the choice of more effective degraded

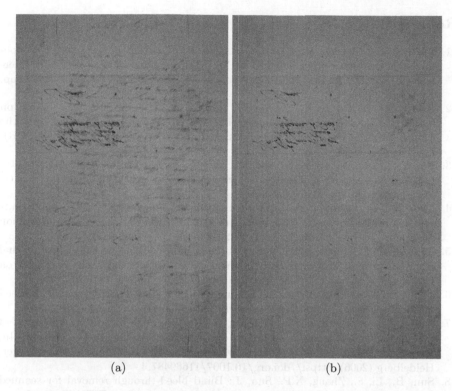

(a)   (b)

Fig. 5. Application of the whole procedure: (a) original verso; (b) verso restored. Original image (a): reproduction by courtesy of The Historical Archive of the Pontificia Università Gregoriana, APUG 529/530, c. 071r/v (Fondo Clavius).

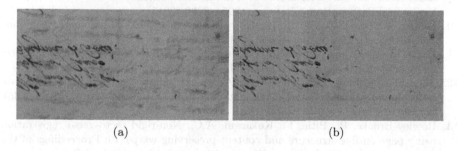

(a)   (b)

Fig. 6. A detail of the images shown in Fig. 5: (a) original verso; (b) verso restored.

document binarization and inpainting algorithms. As both fields of research are very active, with specialized contest being held annually, we plan to carry on a large comparative experimentation.

References

1. Pratikakis, I., Zagoris, K., Barlas, G., Gatos, B.: ICDAR2017 competition on document image binarization (DIBCO 2017). In: Proceedings of the 14th IAPR International Conference on Document Analysis and Recognition (ICDAR 2017), pp. 1396–1403 (2017)
2. Pratikakis, I., Zagori, K., Kaddas, P., Gatos, B.: ICFHR 2018 competition on handwritten document image binarization (H-DIBCO 2018). In: Proceedings of the 16th International Conference on Frontiers in Handwriting Recognition (ICFHR), pp. 489–493 (2018)
3. Pai, Y., Chang, Y., Ruan, S.: Adaptive thresholding algorithm: efficient computation technique based on intelligent block detection for degraded document images. Pattern Recogn. **43**, 3177–3187 (2010)
4. Westphal, F., Lavesson, N., Grahn, H.: Document image binarization using recurrent neural networks. In: Proceedings of the 13th IAPR International Workshop on Document Analysis Systems (DAS 2018), pp. 263–268 (2018)
5. Tensmeyer, R., Martinez, T.: Document image binarization with fully convolutional neural networks. In: Proceedings of the 14th IAPR International Conference on Document Analysis and Recognition (ICDAR 2017), pp. 99–104 (2017)
6. Vo, Q., Kim, S., Yang, H., Lee, G.: Binarization of degraded document images based on hierarchical deep supervised network. Pattern Recogn. **74**, 568–586 (2018)
7. Fadoua, D., Le Bourgeois, F., Emptoz, H.: Restoring ink bleed-through degraded document images using a recursive unsupervised classification technique. In: Bunke, H., Spitz, A.L. (eds.) DAS 2006. LNCS, vol. 3872, pp. 38–49. Springer, Heidelberg (2006). https://doi.org/10.1007/11669487_4
8. Sun, B., Li, S., Zhang, X.P., Sun, J.: Blind bleed-through removal for scanned historical document image with conditional random fields. IEEE Trans. Image Process. **25**(12), 5702–5712 (2016)
9. Rowley-Brooke, R., Pitié, F., Kokaram, A.: A non-parametric framework for document bleed-through removal. In: Proceedings of the IEEE Conference on Computer Vision and Pattern Recognition, pp. 2954–2960 (2013)
10. Huang, Y., Brown, M.S., Xu, D.: User assisted ink-bleed reduction. IEEE Trans. Image Process. **19**(10), 2646–2658 (2010)
11. Hanif, M., Tonazzini, A., Savino, P., Salerno, E.: Non-local sparse image inpaintig for document bleed-through removal. J. Imaging **4**, 68 (2018)
12. Tonazzini, A., Savino, P., Salerno, E.: A non-stationary density model to separate overlapped texts in degraded documents. SIViP **9**(1), 155–164 (2014). https://doi.org/10.1007/s11760-014-0735-3
13. Rowley-Brooke, R., Pitié, F., Kokaram, A.C.: Non-rigid recto-verso registration using page outline structure and content preserving warps. In: Proceedings of the 2nd International Workshop on Historical Document Imaging and Processing, pp. 8–13 (2013)
14. Wang, J., Tan, C.L.: Non-rigid registration and restoration of double-sided historical manuscripts. In: Proceedings of the International Conference on Document Analysis and Recognition (ICDAR), pp. 1374–1378 (2011)
15. Savino, P., Tonazzini, A.: Digital restoration of ancient color manuscripts from geometrically misaligned recto-verso pairs. J. Cult. Herit. **19**, 511–521 (2016)
16. Savino, P., Tonazzini, A., Bedini, L.: Bleed-through cancellation in non-rigidly misaligned recto–verso archival manuscripts based on local registration. Int. J. Doc. Anal. Recogn. **22**(2), 163–176 (2019). https://doi.org/10.1007/s10032-019-00323-2

17. Tonazzini, A., Bedini, L., Salerno, E.: Independent component analysis for document restoration. Int. J. Doc. Anal. Recogn. **7**, 17–27 (2004). https://doi.org/10. 1007/s10032-004-0121-8

18. Tonazzini, A., Bedini, L.: Restoration of recto–verso colour documents using correlated component analysis. EURASIP J. Adv. Signal Process. **2013**(1), 1–10 (2013). https://doi.org/10.1186/1687-6180-2013-58. Article no. 58

19. Tonazzini, A., Salerno, E., Bedini, L.: Fast correction of bleed-through distortion in grayscale documents by a blind source separation technique. Int. J. Doc. Anal. Recogn. **10**, 17–25 (2007). https://doi.org/10.1007/s10032-006-0015-z

20. Merrikh-Bayat, F., Babaie-Zadeh, M., Jutten, C.: Using non-negative matrix factorization for removing show-through. In: Vigneron, V., Zarzoso, V., Moreau, E., Gribonval, R., Vincent, E. (eds.) LVA/ICA 2010. LNCS, vol. 6365, pp. 482–489. Springer, Heidelberg (2010). https://doi.org/10.1007/978-3-642-15995-4_60

21. Ophir, B., Malah, D.: Show-through cancellation in scanned images using blind source separation techniques. In: Proceedings of the International Conference on Image Processing ICIP, vol. III, pp. 233–236 (2007)

22. Lu, D., Huang, X., Sui, L.X.: Binarization of degraded document images based on contrast enhancement. Int. J. Doc. Anal. Recogn. **21**(1), 123–135 (2018). https:// doi.org/10.1007/s10032-018-0299-9

23. Cichocki, A., Amari, S.: Adaptive Blind Signal and Image Processing. Wiley, New York (2002)

24. Hyvärinen, A., Karhunen, J., Oja, E.: Independent Component Analysis. Wiley, New York (2001)

25. Sauvola, J., Pietikäinen, M.: Adaptive document image binarization. Pattern Recogn. **33**, 225–236 (2000)

26. Criminisi, A., Pérez, P., Toyama, K.: Region filling and object removal by exemplar-based image inpainting. IEEE Trans. Image Processing **13**, 1200–1212 (2004)

Intelligent Processing of Multimedia in Web Systems

Activity-selection Behavior and Optimal User-distribution in Q&A Websites

Anamika Chhabra[1]([✉]), S. R. S. Iyengar[1], Jaspal Singh Saini[2], and Vaibhav Malik[3]

[1] Indian Institute of Technology Ropar, Rupnagar, India
{anamika.chhabra,sudarshan}@iitrpr.ac.in
[2] Oregon State University, Corvallis, USA
singjasp@oregonstate.edu
[3] Synaptic Ltd., Gurgaon, India
vaibhav@synaptic.com

Abstract. Based on various factors such as experience, interest, and motivation, users in any system choose to perform certain activities more than the others. In this study, we investigate a similar behavior and its dynamics in the websites of StackExchange. We find that most of the users in these websites tend to contribute predominantly to one of the activities available on these websites. Such a behavior yields a high-level distribution of users across the activities, referred to as *User-distribution*. We find that this distribution varies for different websites of StackExchange. We also observe that the users contributing to different activities trigger each other to provide more contribution. Using these insights, we build a model that explains the effect of change in user-distribution on the amount of knowledge produced on these websites. The model shows that one can formulate an optimal ecosystem by motivating the right kind of users, which leads to the maximum fostering of knowledge on these websites.

Keywords: Activity-selection · Q&A · Role-playing · Triggering · StackExchange

1 Introduction

The users in crowdsourced websites such as StackExchange, Wikipedia, Github etc. exhibit diverse behavior due to their disparate levels of motivation, expertise and interests [5,15]. This behavior shows up in the form of different activities that they choose to perform on these websites which is sometimes termed as *role-playing* behavior [9]. Here, role refers to an activity or a set of activities that users

---

A preliminary version of this work reporting the activity-selection behavior of users is published here [7].

J. S. Saini—The author contributed while he was a student at Indian Institute of Technology Ropar, India.

© Springer Nature Switzerland AG 2020
N. T. Nguyen et al. (Eds.): ICCCI 2020, LNAI 12496, pp. 853–865, 2020.
https://doi.org/10.1007/978-3-030-63007-2_67

typically choose to perform on a website throughout their interaction with the website. There is a large body of research in the direction of examining the kind of roles that users play in different websites such as Usenet [17], Wikipedia [12], StackExchange [8,18], Yahoo Answers [1] and annotation systems [6]. However, there are still several aspects of this behavior that merit further investigation. Particularly, questions related to the distribution of users across these roles are still unexplored. For instance, how does this distribution vary when observed across different websites. Further, how do the users performing a role affect those performing other roles? Finally, do the changes in users' distribution across the roles affect the amount of knowledge produced? As an example, if there are very few users performing a given role, does it affect the overall productivity of the website? These research questions are interesting as well as important as they have several practical implications. Most of the existing studies identify roles of users while hardly examining the ramifications of such a behavior. This prevents putting these findings in actual practice towards the betterment of collaborative systems.

In this work, we analyze 156 websites of StackExchange and find that in Q&A websites, users not only play roles, but also exhibit inclination towards performing mainly one of the primary activities such as questioning, answering or voting. We term this behavior as *Activity-selection Behavior*. Based on this observation, we compute a high-level distribution of users across the activities of the websites, which we call *User-distribution*. This distribution provides an estimate of the kind of users present on these websites. We also make observations indicating that the users performing different activities trigger each other. Based on these findings, we build a model that demonstrates the effect of change in user-distribution on the amount of knowledge produced on these websites. It also shows that in any website, there is an optimal user-distribution that leads to the maximum knowledge generation. Finally, we apply this model on a few SE websites and gain insights on the under-represented activities of these websites. The results highlight the need to build incentivization policies that encourage users towards performing such activities.

2   Related Work

There is a decent amount of work pursued in the direction of identifying the roles played by users in online communities. These roles have been examined considering different perspectives. For example, in Wikipedia, roles have been studied based on whether users revert, add, delete or update the text, links or references [3]. On Usenet, roles have been studied based on the kind of users' contribution [17] or the network structure of users' interaction [2]. Considering the quantity and quality of users' contribution, Furtado et al. [8] determined ten behavioral profiles on a few Stackexchange websites where the roles contained overlapping activities. A few related studies have been conducted on other Q&A websites such as Yahoo Answers [1].

Although past work has observed disparity in the way different users interact with collaborative portals, very limited attention has been given towards investigating the effect of such a behavior towards the amount of knowledge produced on these portals.

3   Analysis

StackExchange (SE) is a collection of more than 150 Q&A websites on topics ranging from programming to operating systems to cooking. The data set for the current study was downloaded from the publicly available archive[1]. It consists of the temporal data of SE websites in XML format storing the details of the question threads, users, tags, links, votes, badges, suggest-edits, deleted posts etc. In this Section, we report the analysis conducted on SE, where we observe the presence of activity-selection behavior of users as well as triggering among the users performing different activities.

3.1   Activity-Selection Behavior of Users

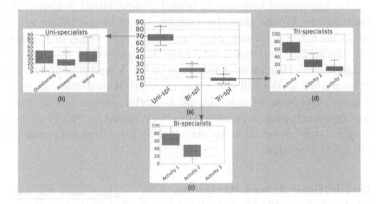

Fig. 1. (a) Fraction of uni/bi/tri-specialists observed across the websites. (b) Uni-specialists: Proportion across the activities. (c) Bi-specialists: Relative contribution across the two activities (Sorted). (d) Tri-specialists: Relative contribution across the three activities (Sorted).

The primary activities performed by users on a Q&A website are questioning, answering and voting. We processed the SE data set to extract the number of questions, answers and votes added by each user for a given website. From this data, we created a *Task Vector* for each user where Task Vector V_i^w for a user i on website w is a vector that contains the percentage contribution of user i in

---

[1] https://archive.org/download/stackexchange.

the activities questioning, answering and voting with respect to their total contribution on w. As an example, if a user 'XYZ' posts 150 questions, 50 answers and no votes on a website, then the task vector of 'XYZ' will be [75, 25, 0]. We explicitly considered the percentage contribution since for this study, we intend to find the basic traits of users. We further define *uni-specialists*, *bi-specialists* and *tri-specialists* as the users who contribute in only one, two or all three activities respectively. For each website, out of all task vectors, we computed the proportion of them belonging to uni/bi/tri-specialists. It was interesting to note that despite the rigid definition of uni-specialists, i.e., the users contributing in *precisely* one activity, there was a very high proportion of users exhibiting such a behavior in all the websites (See Fig. 1(a)). The average proportion of uni, bi, and tri-specialists in the websites was 68.51% ($\sigma = 6.01$), 22.19% ($\sigma = 4.14$) and 9.29% ($\sigma = 3.54$) respectively. Figure 1(b) further shows the proportion of uni-specialists across questioning, answering and voting. We observed a high SD in the proportion of uni-specialists across the activities in the websites. This is an important observation and points towards variability in the user-distribution of different websites as discussed in detail later. We also examined the task vectors of bi-specialists and tri-specialists to see how their contribution was spread across the two and three activities respectively. That is, whether it was evenly spread across the activities or were they inclined towards one or a subset of these activities. The aggregated behavior of bi and tri-specialists is shown in Fig. 1(c) and (d) respectively. We see that the contribution of bi-specialists is not equally spread out in both the activities. Similarly, the contribution of tri-specialists is very less in the second and third activities. Together with the observations in Fig. 1(a), this depicts that most of the users in Q&A websites mainly contribute in one of the activities. We call this behavior 'Activity-selection Behavior'. This is indeed a stronger case of role-playing behavior, where a role may contain a collection of overlapping activities. Observed across a variety of websites on different topics, this observation points towards a general prevalence of such a behavior in Q&A websites.

'User-Distribution' Across Activities. The uni-specialists analysis allows us to label users based on the activity they are mostly performing. We, therefore, use K-means clustering to group users into clusters where the users in each cluster behave similarly. Knowing that the users are performing in mainly one of the three activities, it is justified to take the value of k as three. Nevertheless, to confirm this, we followed the method given by He et al. [10] for finding ideal k. We varied the value of k from 2 to 10 in k-means and then applied their method on the obtained clusters. The best value of k was found to be 3 in more than 72% of the websites thus

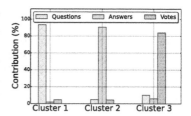

Fig. 2. Average of centroids of the clusters obtained. The main contribution of users falling in the three clusters is questioning, answering and voting respectively.

substantiating the uni-specialism behavior as well as the choice of k to be 3 for further analysis. Figure 2 shows the mean of the centroids of the three clusters obtained across all SE websites. The centroids depict a clean division of users with each cluster grouping users specializing in either questioning, answering or voting with very less contribution in the rest of the activities. We, therefore, call the corresponding clusters as *Questioners, Answerers* and *Voters* accordingly. Of primary importance for this analysis are the relative sizes of the three clusters obtained for each website which gives us the user-distribution for a given website. This distribution provides insights into the website's user base composition. For instance, it may tell whether a website has more users inclined towards questioning as compared to answering or vice-versa. We observe that all the SE websites do not exhibit a similar distribution of users, rather it widely varies across the websites. The percentage of questioners varies from 6.13% to 64.73%, the percentage of answerers varies from 4.64% to 43.16% and the percentage of voters varies from 11.47% to 82.55%. This leads to a few websites exhibiting a peculiar distribution where some of the activities are under-represented.

3.2   Triggering Among Users Performing Different Activities

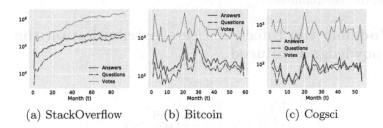

(a) StackOverflow   (b) Bitcoin   (c) Cogsci

Fig. 3. Number of questions, answers and votes produced in each month. (Y-axis is log-scaled.)

The phenomenon of triggering among users has been observed to be prevalent in collaborative settings [11,13], under which, the contribution by one user affects or prompts the contribution by other users. While a few studies have been performed to examine this phenomenon in Wikipedia [4,14], Q&A portals in this direction have hardly been explored. In this Section, we examine growth of questions, answers and votes over time in SE websites that substantiates the prevalence of triggering in Q&A settings. We computed the growth rate of questions, answers and votes produced in each month for each of the SE websites. In some websites, it was found to be increasing with time, while in the others, it was either reducing or kept fluctuating. However, the notable observation was that in all the websites, the questions, answers and votes showed patterns of growth that were highly correlated. For instance, Fig. 3 shows the number of questions, answers and votes produced in each month for three of the websites.

As can be seen, any change in the contribution in one activity seemed to quickly affect the rest two, making them move in a similar fashion. Overall, the average Pearson Correlation between the growth of questions and answers per month across the websites was found to be 0.886 ($\sigma = 0.138$), between answers and votes it was 0.844 ($\sigma = 0.161$) and between questions and votes it was 0.778 ($\sigma = 0.199$). The reason is that the knowledge units of different types in a collaborative environment are not independent contributions. Rather, they are highly dependent pieces of knowledge such that the production of one directly affects the production of the other. It should be noted that although the triggering of answers due to questions, and the triggering of votes due to questions and answers is direct, it takes place in the opposite direction as well. That is, receiving answers to the questions asked by themselves or others motivates users to ask more questions. Similarly, votes obtained on the questions and answers instigate users to post more questions and answers. Figure 3 also shows a small ratio between the number of answers and questions produced in each month, while a large ratio between the votes and questions; and votes and answers respectively. This shows that the knowledge units of different types are dependent on each other with varying degrees. This variability in triggering among knowledge units of different kinds is captured by the triggering matrix, as defined in the next Section, where we mathematically model the growth of knowledge in a collaborative environment.

4   Modeling the Effect of User-Distribution on the Knowledge Produced

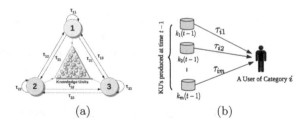

(a)   (b)

Fig. 4. (a) A three-category system. τ_{ij} is the number of KU's of the category i that get triggered *per user* of the category i due to one KU of the category j. (b) KU's generated by one user of category i at time t. Here categories refer to the activities. (KU: Knowledge Units)

Taking insights from the empirical investigations made in the Subsects. 3.1 and 3.2, we now build a generalized model of a knowledge building system where users are categorized based on the kind of activities they mainly perform. These users then trigger each other over time through their different kinds of contributions and lead to knowledge production in the system, which is systematically tracked by the model. In order to particularly focus on the effect of user-distribution on the amount of knowledge produced, we assume that the number of users remains fixed over time.

We consider a knowledge building system having n users who contribute mainly in one of the m activities. These users, therefore, may be divided into m categories based on whichever activity they mostly perform. Further, due to the effect of triggering, the users in each category trigger the users in other categories with varying degrees given by the following triggering matrix (T):

$$T = \begin{bmatrix} \tau_{11} & \tau_{12} & \cdots & \tau_{1m} \\ \tau_{21} & \tau_{22} & \cdots & \tau_{2m} \\ \vdots & & & \vdots \\ \tau_{m1} & \tau_{m2} & \cdots & \tau_{mm} \end{bmatrix} \tag{1}$$

where τ_{ij} represents the number of knowledge units (KUs) of category i that will be triggered *per user* of the category i due to one KU of the category j. The values in this matrix are variable depending on how much triggering the KUs of one kind produce for the other kind. For example, in a Q&A website, the triggering from a question to an answer will be different from triggering from an answer to a question. Figure 4(a) shows the triggering phenomenon occurring in a three-category system. Given this setting, the objectives of the model are to (i) delineate the effect of changing the user-distribution on the amount of knowledge produced, and (ii) investigate whether or not there is a particular distribution of n users across m categories that leads to the maximum knowledge.

4.1   Total Knowledge Produced in the System

We track the knowledge produced in the system by using one simplifying assumption that the knowledge produced in the system at time t is triggered by the knowledge produced at time $t - 1$ only. This is not an extreme assumption as we observe in SE websites that when a question is asked, most of the answers are received in the first month. In particular, in StackOverflow, on an average, 91% of the answers are received in the first month, only 6% are received in the 2nd to 12th month, and only 3% are received after one year. Similar values are observed for the rest of the SE websites as well. We, therefore, consider t to be a period of one month and define $k_i(t)$ to be the number of KUs of category i produced at time t. We see that $k_i(t)$ depends on (a) The number of KUs of all the categories that get added to the system at time $t - 1$, i.e., $k_j(t - 1)$, $\forall 1 \leq j \leq m$. (b) The triggering factors from all other categories to the category i, i.e. τ_{ij}, $\forall j, 1 \leq j \leq m$. (See Fig. 4(b)) and (c) The number of users in category i, i.e. n_i.

Therefore, $\forall i, 1 \leq i \leq m$, $k_i(t)$ can be computed as:

$$k_i(t) = n_i(\tau_{i1}k_1(t - 1) + \tau_{i2}k_2(t - 1) + \cdots + \tau_{im}k_m(t - 1))$$

Alternatively, we can write,

$$k_i(t) = n_i \left(\sum_{j=1}^{m} \tau_{ij} k_j(t-1) \right) \tag{2}$$

To start the system, let r_i be the average initial knowledge entered into the system by each user of category i. Therefore, the amount of initial knowledge of category i into the system, i.e., $k_i(0)$ will be:

$$k_i(0) = n_i r_i \tag{3}$$

Let $K(t)$ be the column vector consisting of the knowledge generated by different categories at time t as its elements, N be a diagonal matrix storing the number of users n_i in each category i, and R be a column vector storing the average internal knowledge of each category *per user* as shown below:

$$K(t) = \begin{bmatrix} k_1(t) \\ k_2(t) \\ \vdots \\ k_m(t) \end{bmatrix} \quad N = \begin{bmatrix} n_1 & & \\ & \ddots & \\ & & n_m \end{bmatrix} \quad R = \begin{bmatrix} r_1 \\ r_2 \\ \vdots \\ r_m \end{bmatrix}$$

Using these definitions of $K(t)$, N, R and T, the Eqs. (3) and (2) respectively can be written as,

$$K(0) = NR \tag{4} \qquad\qquad K(t) = NTK(t-1) \tag{5}$$

Equation (5) gives a recursive formula for computing the total number of KUs produced in the system at time t. The following theorem provides a closed form of the formula for the knowledge built in the system at time t.

Theorem 1. *The vector representing the knowledge generated in various categories at time t, i.e $K(t)$ is given by:*

$$K(t) = (NT)^t NR \tag{6}$$

Proof. Substituting the value of $K(t-1)$ in Eq. (5),

$$K(t) = NT(NTK(t-2)) = (NT)^2 K(t-2)$$

Continuing like this, we get, $K(t) = (NT)^t K(0)$
Substituting the value of $K(0)$ from Eq. (4), we get, $K(t) = (NT)^t NR$ □

Equation (6) gives the amount of knowledge generated in the system at time t. To get the total knowledge generated *upto* time t, which we call $K_c(t)$, we have the following theorem:

Theorem 2. *The vector representing the total knowledge generated in each category 'upto' time t is given by:*

$$K_c(t) = ((NT)^t - I)((NT) - I)^{-1}NR \tag{7}$$

Proof.

$$\text{We know that, } K_c(t) = \sum_{j=0}^{t} K(j) \tag{8}$$

Therefore, from Theorem 1,

$$K_c(t) = \sum_{j=0}^{t}(NT)^j NR = ((NT)^0 + (NT)^1 + (NT)^2 + \cdots + (NT)^t)NR$$

$$K_c(t) = ((NT)^t - I)((NT) - I)^{-1}NR$$

where I is an $m \times m$ identity matrix.   □

From Eq. (8), we can also compute the total knowledge that ever gets generated in the system, i.e. $K_c(\infty)$, as given by the following corollary:

Corollary 1. *The vector representing the total knowledge ever produced in each category in the system is given by:*

$$K_c(\infty) = \sum_{t=0}^{\infty} K(t) = \sum_{t=0}^{\infty}(NT)^t NR \tag{9}$$

$$K_c(\infty) = ((NT)^0 + (NT)^1 + (NT)^2 + \cdots + \infty)NR \tag{10}$$

There can be two cases depending on the value of the spectral radius of NT, i.e. $\rho(NT)$ which is equal to $max\{|\Lambda_1|, \ldots, |\Lambda_e|\}$ where Λ_i's are the eigenvalues of the matrix NT. As per the Eq. (10), if $\rho(NT) \geq 1$, the knowledge keeps on increasing exponentially with time and reaches infinity (See Fig. 5(b)). In this case, a bound on the total knowledge produced in the system can not be computed. However, if

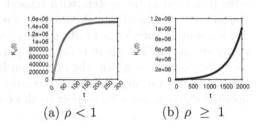

(a) $\rho < 1$ (b) $\rho \geq 1$

Fig. 5. Total knowledge produced upto time t for (a) $\rho < 1$ and (b) $\rho \geq 1$ respectively.

$\rho(NT) < 1$, then initially the knowledge production rate is high, which keeps decreasing with time and eventually converges (See Fig. 5(a)). In this case, the total knowledge produced in the system is bounded. This is because $(NT)^0 + (NT)^1 + (NT)^2 + \cdots + \infty$ converges to $(I - NT)^{-1}$. Therefore, we get the following closed form for the total knowledge produced in the system.

$$K_c(\infty) = (I - NT)^{-1}NR \tag{11}$$

Equation (10) shows that whether a system keeps growing its knowledge base or stops after a while, largely depends on the division of users in the diagonal matrix (N) as well as the amount of triggering among them (T).

4.2   Optimal User-Distribution

The optimal user-distribution is the distribution of users across the activities of the system such that it leads to the maximum knowledge generation. The values in the diagonal matrix N, i.e., $\{n_1, n_2, ... n_m\}$ represent the number of users in the categories 1, 2, ... m. Therefore, from the matrix N corresponding to the maximum $K_c(\infty)$, one can find the distribution of users $\mathcal{D} = \{d_{n_1}, d_{n_1}, ..., d_{n_m}\}$, where, $d_{n_i} = \frac{n_i}{\sum_{j=1}^{m} n_j}$. To examine

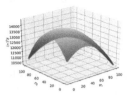

Fig. 6. Total knowledge produced $(K_c(\infty))$ with respect to all possible distributions (n_1, n_2, n_3) in 3-category systems. (*Note:* Here $n_3 = 100 - n_1 - n_2$).eps

how $K_c(\infty)$ varies as we change the distribution in three categories' case, we simulated the model while taking random values for the triggering matrix such that $\rho(NT)$ is less than 1. This is because when $\rho(NT)$ is greater than 1, the knowledge in the system becomes unbounded. Moreover, as per many existing studies [16], the knowledge growth in practical settings follows *Heap's law* [11] which follows a sub-linear power law growth rather than exponential, suggesting that given sufficient time in a closed system, the rate of knowledge growth decreases with time. For simplicity, we kept the initial knowledge in the system to be [100, 100, 100]. We then varied the value of N by checking all possible distributions of users across the three categories and computed the total knowledge produced in the system with respect to each distribution. Figure 6 shows the amount of knowledge produced in one such system. The plot shows that the amount of knowledge produced keeps varying with the change in the users' distribution. Further, there is always a particular distribution, viz., the optimal user-distribution at which, the maximum knowledge is produced. We simulated the model by varying its parameters and observed a similar plot yielding the optimal distribution with respect to those parameters.

5   Examining Optimal User-Distribution for StackExchange Websites

Examining the optimal user-distribution for SE websites first requires identifying the values of triggering across the three primary activities. It is possible to get an estimate of the relative triggering among the knowledge produced across the activities by examining their growth pattern over time. In Figure 3, we observed that triggering from questions to answers is higher than from answers to questions. Similarly, the triggering from questions to votes as well as answers to votes is very high as compared to that in the reverse direction. To know the relationship among them, we computed the average association among the values of questions, answers and votes produced in each month by the websites and thus estimated the values of the triggering matrix for SE websites with a given 'n'. For instance, we have the following triggering matrix for SE websites with $n = 1000$.

$$\begin{bmatrix} 0 & 0.00189 & 0.01326 \\ 0.000529 & 0 & 0.00709 \\ 0.0000754 & 0.000141 & 0 \end{bmatrix}\begin{matrix} q \\ a \\ v \end{matrix}$$

q   a   v

Using this, we compute the amount of knowledge produced for all possible distributions as per Eq. 11. The surface plot obtained for these parameters is shown in Fig. 7 (a).

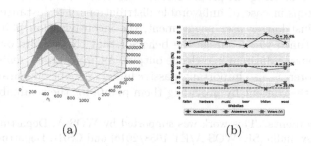

(a)   (b)

Fig. 7. (a) Surface plot obtained for StackExchange websites(n = 1000) leading to an optimal distribution of (35.4, 25.2, 39.4) (b) Distribution of StackExchange websites with around 1000 users as compared to the reference distribution.

The plot shows $\mathcal{D}_{1000} = (35.4, 25.2, 39.4)$ to be the distribution that may lead to the maximum knowledge in SE websites with $n = 1000$. We now examine the websites having the number of users close to 1000 and compare their user-distributions with respect to $\mathcal{D}_{1000}$. Figure 7 (b) compares their distributions with respect to the reference line of $\mathcal{D}_{1000}$. We see that many of these websites have a smaller proportion of users inclined towards asking questions (the top plot), while the proportion of users who are only voting (the bottom plot) is higher compared to the reference line. In particular, the website 'beer' was found to be having only 8.38% of users engaged in asking questions as opposed to a suggested value of 35.4%. The administrators of these websites may therefore take measures to motivate users to ask questions and thus improve the knowledge-building on these websites. The way we computed $\mathcal{D}_{1000}$ for $n = 1000$, we can similarly compute optimal $\mathcal{D}_n$ corresponding to other SE websites as per the number of users present in them and find which of the activities are under-represented.

6   Conclusion

This work examines the tendency of users of a Q&A website to exhibit inclination towards contribution in mainly one of the activities and the effect of this behavior on the amount of knowledge produced. Based on this behavior, we examine the distribution of users across the activities, that may affect the functioning of a Q&A website. An extreme example to understand the importance of the right user-distribution may be a hypothetical Q&A based portal where all the users only ask questions and none of them is interested in or capable of providing answers. Another similar case would be that of a portal where nobody asks questions. We obviously can not expect such portals to be doing even a mediocre job of building knowledge. Combining the empirical insights gained from a comprehensive data set of SE websites with a theoretical model, the study shows that for a given Q&A website, there is an optimal distribution of users performing different activities that leads to the maximum knowledge. The study suggests periodically monitoring the proportion of users across the activities of the portal and taking steps in case of unfavorable distributions. For instance, rather than focusing on just longer user engagement, the incentivization policies could be dynamically tuned to encourage the behavior that the website owners want in order to encourage optimal knowledge output. As an instance, realizing that the presence of voters is also important, passive lurkers may be encouraged to upvote or downvote the content by providing them points for their valuable judgment.

Acknowledgements. This work was supported by WOS-A, Department of Science and Technology, India [SR/WOS-A/ET-1058/2014] and CSRI, Department of Science and Technology, India [SR/CSRI/344/2016].

References

1. Adamic, L.A., Zhang, J., Bakshy, E., Ackerman, M.S.: Knowledge sharing and yahoo answers: everyone knows something. In: Proceedings of the 17th International Conference on World Wide Web, pp. 665–674. ACM (2008)
2. Agrawal, R., Rajagopalan, S., Srikant, R., Xu, Y.: Mining newsgroups using networks arising from social behavior. In: Proceedings of the 12th International Conference on World Wide Web, pp. 529–535. ACM (2003)
3. Arazy, O., Lifshitz-Assaf, H., Nov, O., Daxenberger, J., Balestra, M., Cheshire, C.: On the 'how' and 'why' of emergent role behaviors in Wikipedia. In: Conference on Computer-Supported Cooperative Work and Social Computing, vol. 35 (2017)
4. Chhabra, A., Iyengar, S.S.: Characterizing the triggering phenomenon in Wikipedia. In: Proceedings of the 14th International Symposium on Open Collaboration, p. 11. ACM (2018)
5. Chhabra, A., Iyengar, S.: How does knowledge come by? arXiv preprint arXiv:1705.06946 (2017)
6. Chhabra, A., Iyengar, S., Saini, P., Bhat, R.S.: Presence of an ecosystem: a catalyst in the knowledge building process in crowdsourced annotation environments. In: Proceedings of the 2015 International Conference on Advances in Social Networks Analysis and Mining (ASONAM 2015) (2015)
7. Chhabra, A., RS Iyengar, S.: Activity-selection behavior of users in StackExchange websites. In: Companion Proceedings of the Web Conference 2020, pp. 105–106 (2020)
8. Furtado, A., Andrade, N., Oliveira, N., Brasileiro, F.: Contributor profiles, their dynamics, and their importance in five q&a sites. In: Proceedings of the 2013 Conference on Computer Supported Cooperative Work, pp. 1237–1252. ACM (2013)

9. Golder, S.A., Donath, J.: Social roles in electronic communities. Internet Res. **5**, 19–22 (2004)
10. He, J., Tan, A.H., Tan, C.L., Sung, S.Y.: On quantitative evaluation of clustering systems. In: Wu, W., Xiong, H., Shekhar, S. (eds.) Clustering and Information Retrieval. Network Theory and Applications, vol. 11, pp. 105–133. Springer, Boston (2004). https://doi.org/10.1007/978-1-4613-0227-8_4
11. Iacopini, I., Milojević, S., Latora, V.: Network dynamics of innovation processes. Phys. Rev. Lett. **120**(4), 048301 (2018)
12. Liu, J., Ram, S.: Who does what: collaboration patterns in the Wikipedia and their impact on article quality. ACM Trans. Manag. Inf. Syst. (TMIS) **2**(2), 11 (2011)
13. Marengo, L., Zeppini, P.: The arrival of the new. J. Evol. Econ. **26**(1), 171–194 (2016). https://doi.org/10.1007/s00191-015-0438-0
14. Rezgui, A., Crowston, K.: Stigmergic coordination in Wikipedia. In: Proceedings of the 14th International Symposium on Open Collaboration, p. 19. ACM (2018)
15. Tausczik, Y.R., Pennebaker, J.W.: Participation in an online mathematics community: differentiating motivations to add. In: Proceedings of the ACM 2012 Conference on Computer Supported Cooperative Work, pp. 207–216. ACM (2012)
16. Tria, F., Loreto, V., Servedio, V.D.P., Strogatz, S.H.: The dynamics of correlated novelties. Sci. Rep. **4**, 5890 (2014)
17. Welser, H.T., Gleave, E., Fisher, D., Smith, M.: Visualizing the signatures of social roles in online discussion groups. J. Soc. Struct. **8**(2), 1–32 (2007)
18. Yang, J., Tao, K., Bozzon, A., Houben, G.-J.: Sparrows and owls: characterisation of expert behaviour in StackOverflow. In: Dimitrova, V., Kuflik, T., Chin, D., Ricci, F., Dolog, P., Houben, G.-J. (eds.) UMAP 2014. LNCS, vol. 8538, pp. 266–277. Springer, Cham (2014). https://doi.org/10.1007/978-3-319-08786-3_23

Reliability of Video Conferencing Applications Based on the WebRTC Standard Used on Different Web Platforms

Kazimierz Choroś$^{(\boxtimes)}$ ⓘ and Michał Hiterski ⓘ

Department of Applied Informatics, Wrocław University of Science and Technology,
Wyb. Wyspiańskiego 27, 50-370 Wrocław, Poland
`kazimierz.choros@pwr.edu.pl, michal.hiterski@gmail.com`

Abstract. Video conferencing applications allow two or more people to connect and conduct video calls. During the call, people can see and hear each other. Therefore, to make a video call we need a device equipped with a camera and a microphone. One of the technologies that permits us to send video and audio stream is WebRTC (Web Real-Time Communication). In the paper, the applications using the WebRTC technology were tested for performance and reliability. Application performance refers to image quality, delay, number of frames depending on the speed of the Internet connection, and its type. The reliability was checked for establishing a connection in various environments (Web browser or mobile device) and maintaining the established connection during changing conditions (accidental interruption, interruption due to external circumstances or errors). The purpose of the experimental research was to examine the WebRTC technology in the context of using it to conduct video conferences on desktop and mobile platforms. The performance of this technology was tested on the native as well as developed implementations available by the most popular browsers.

Keywords: Video conferencing applications · Video conferencing reliability · WebRTC standard · Desktop and mobile platforms · Web browsers · Network interruptions · Real-time media transfers · Peer-to-peer connections

1 Introduction

Video conferencing applications allow two or more people to connect and conduct video calls. During the call, people can see and hear each other. Therefore, to make a video call we need a device equipped with a camera and a microphone. One of the technologies that permits us to send video and audio stream is WebRTC (Web Real-Time Communication). WebRTC is a free open-source project. It is standardized by the World Wide Web Consortium (W3C) and the Internet Engineering Task Force (IETF). This standard enables browsers and mobile applications to communicate in real-time (RTC) via a programming interface (API). WebRTC ensures direct video and peer-to-peer audio communication. WebRTC is a component of HTML5, it means that this standard is

© Springer Nature Switzerland AG 2020
N. T. Nguyen et al. (Eds.): ICCCI 2020, LNAI 12496, pp. 866–877, 2020.
https://doi.org/10.1007/978-3-030-63007-2_68

implemented in all HTML5 compatible browsers. This eliminates the need to install additional native plugins or applications.

In the paper, the applications using the WebRTC technology will be tested for performance and reliability. The application performance refers to image quality, delay, number of frames depending on the speed of the Internet connection and its type. The reliability of the application will be checked by establishing a connection in various environments (Web browser or mobile device) and maintaining the established connection during changing conditions (accidental interruption, interruption due to external circumstances, interruption due to errors). The purpose of the research is to examine the properties of the WebRTC technology in the context of using it to conduct video conferences on desktop and mobile platforms. Important issues to examine are the correlation of user locations in the case of peer-to-peer connections for delays in sending data packets, and to check whether the servers that mediate data exchange affect the performance and reliability of the WebRTC connection. Nowadays, mobile devices are gaining great popularity and with the increase in their popularity the performance of devices on all platforms is also increasing. One of the goals is to examine the performance of WebRTC-based video conferencing applications on smartphones, both one-to-one and also one-to-many connections. The performance of this technology will be tested on the native implementations on the iOS and Android systems. It is also planned to compare the video compression capacity of available codecs and their impact on the efficiency of media transmission during a connection.

The paper is structured as follows. In Sect. 2 the standard WebRTC will be briefly characterized. Then Sect. 3 discusses related work on the analysis of videoconferencing applications based on WebRTC standard. The next Section presents the measures which can be used to evaluate the efficiency of video conferencing applications. The Sect. 5 describes the tests performed to estimate the efficiency of video conferencing applications. Next the improvements and recommendations as well as the final conclusions are presented in two last sections: Sect. 6 and Sect. 7.

2 WebRTC Standard

Nowadays the very common architecture used to transfer data in real-time is WebRTC – Website Real-time Communication. It ensures network connections and information transfer between clients without involvement of any server. In practice, a server is required to help start and connect peer-to-peer connection. WebRTC is a standard which can have multiple implementations and today we can distinguish two most common: WebRTC (https://webrtc.org/) and OpenWebRTC (http://www.openwebrtc.org).

The history of WebRTC was started in February 2010, when Google acquired On2 – a video codec company that was developing the VP codecs series. The main goal of On2 was to replace well-known H.26x codecs to new VP. In May 2010 another acquisition has taken place when Google bought Global IP Solutions (GIPS). GIPS was designed to simplify the development of VoIP and video calling applications. In fact, Google was not the only one company which was working on video streaming solutions. The Ericsson Labs also provided parallel research. In October 2010 the first meetings hosted by main contributors (W3C and IETF) took place to asses interest in implementing and standardizing whole infrastructure like protocols and APIs in Web browsers. Later on, in May 2011 Google released an early version of WebRTC as an open source project for Web browsers. In October 2011 W3C released first drafts of specification, known today as WebRTC 1.0 along with Media Capture and Streams specification.

One month later the first version of WebRTC standard was implemented for Google Chrome browser, but partially – there was lack of some capabilities like peer connection data channels. Then in January 2013 Firefox applied WebRTC to its own Web browser. Finally, in February 2011 the first cross-browser connection was conducted. For this day, the standard is still improved and a whole new bunch of features are introduced.

WebRTC is a client-side technology which means that it is used on browsers or native apps run on user device. The client-side technologies that are currently covered by WebRTC Working Group are:

- getting and investigating capabilities of devices (microphones, speakers, cameras),
- capturing local streams – media,
- processing media streams (encoding, compressing, decoding),
- establishing and providing P2P connections,
- handling and delivering streams to other peers.

The first three points are Stream API related. Stream API allows us to read, transfer, and write readable chunks of data (blob) from static files. Stream API similarly to WebRTC uses the MediaStream interface to get devices and streams. Such stream of media consists of audio and video tracks (left and right channels).

To get local media stream from a Web browser we have to refer to a global object in a given browser API called window. A window object consists of all main data and configuration of a Web page. One of them is the *mediaDevices* property which offers the *getUserMedia* method. The *getUserMedia* function allows interacting with Stream API when it is called by asking the client for permission and returning a *promise*.

At the beginning Web browsers were only capable to make a http requests for resources like html pages and display response like Web pages. Over the years the new features were introduced like Web sockets, JavaScript languages, new version of API, etc. Then there was an opportunity to transfer data between browsers with any encourage of intermediate servers. This feature allowed the developers to make a new kind of applications due to peer-to-peer connections.

The number of all devices connected to the global Internet is enormous. A very popular address reservation tool is Network Address Translation (NAT) which hides a specific address space under one IP address. This is achieved by modifying the header in IP packets as the routing device sends data. The routing device translates returned packets. Thanks to the NAT mechanism, one IPv4 address can be shared by many devices when connected to a global network. However, this solution has its drawbacks creating a difficult barrier to make new incoming connections. In peer-to-peer connections devices should be able to connect directly to each other. When using NAT, there is no guarantee that a P2P connection will be established. To deal with this problem, several techniques have been introduced that helped to repeatedly and securely establish a connection under the NAT shield – it was called NAT Traversal.

NAT Traversal introduces the new path necessary to establish a connection. Instead of trying to make a direct connection, the real-time application makes the connection using the server. Both peers transmit to the server their data such as IP address, information about the Internet connection, resolution, equipment, type of browser. Then this information is exchanged between peers via the server. The entire information exchange process is called negotiation and allows re-establishing a connection. In this case the server is called *signaling*. The information exchange process must be carried out in the correct order. In order to establish a WebRTC connection, a connection initiator is required, it sends an information packet called *offer* to *signaling* which then forwards this *offer* to the second participant. The other peer receives *offer* and generates *answer* – that is an information packet. When *signaling* passes *answer* to the peer who generated *offer*, the connection will be established.

In some situations, when two peers are behind NAT, the establishing of connection is more complex. In this case, NAT traversal mechanisms must be used before attempting to establish a direct connection. Another such mechanism is Session Traversal Utilities for NAT in short STUN. The STUN protocol is a set of methods used in both real-time video and audio applications. It allows clients to get a public IP address and a port number that is reserved in NAT. This operation requires a connection to an external server (STUN server). The whole mechanism works as follows. A client who is in a private network sends a query to the STUN server. The STUN server returns a response that contains the IP address and the port number. Once the customer obtains his public IP address, it can be used to communicate with other clients via *signaling*. In this case, the client only sends its public IP address instead of the private one which is not available to other users outside the network. The STUN mechanism may to establish a connection not correctly because of network or firewall configurations. Then relay servers – Traversal Using Relays around NAT (TURN) can be used. Both clients connect to TURN servers that exchange data with each other. Unfortunately, it is the most expensive way because it uses large network and hardware resources of servers.

3 Related Work

The Internet network is more and more widely used not only to exchange data such as e-mails or files but also voice, animation, video, so different kinds of media. Internet telephony, Internet TV, and video conferencing used in distance learning and in different distributed group work required the development of new Internet architectures and new Internet protocols such as RTP (Real-Time Transmission Protocol), RTCP (Real-Time Transmission Control Protocol), or RTSP (Real-Time Streaming Protocol) [1].

Mobile technologies and real-time communication between browsers using the WebRTC standard are recently a very popular object of experiments and academic research. The methodology of determining the minimum hardware requirements in mobile devices for conducting a three-way video conference is described in [2]. The QoE (Quality of Experience) for mobile applications has been studied as well as the impact of various smartphone specifications. Mobile phones may vary in processor, display size, resolution, and RAM. The test results clearly showed the impact of device specifications on the user's QoE. Based on empirical research into the subjective opinions of users, the minimum requirements were set.

Performance statistics research related to video conferencing in an application using WebRTC were reported in [3]. The characteristics and their relationship with the quality and experience of users were examined. The transmission of video media was examined in good as well as poor network conditions. Although the application offered the option of video, audio, and screen sharing, only video was the subject of the study, audio was not included. The connection was made only between two users connected to each other in a WLAN. It was noted that in the tests with good network conditions, QoE was sufficient for video conferencing despite the fact that during the conversation some deviations occurred. However, a very weak connection video transmission was unacceptable and it manifested itself as a slide show. The final conclusion was that the packet loss and bucket delay parameters were good candidates for QoE assessment and may be the basis for further research on the reliability of WebRTC transmissions.

The black-box technique was used in [4] to assess the audio quality. Research has been carried out with various network delays and jitter. Audio recorded from the peer listener website was compared with the original using the PESQ algorithm. Research showed that changing base delay and jitter had a big impact on PESQ results.

The concept of a new system for video conferencing is discussed in [5]. The system is multiplatform, capable to operate on many types of devices, and is multifunctional. It offers good quality in poor network conditions. Subjective and objective tests for frame rate, delay assessment, and bandwidth consumption results were carried out. The goal was to prove that at low bitrates, good video streaming quality can be preserved.

An example architecture of video conferencing application using the WebRTC standard was presented in [6] as well as in [7] and many others. It was concluded that this technology allows secure data transmitting via a peer-to-peer and peer-to-group connection in real-time. In order to evaluate QoE analyses of survey data were conducted in [8]. It was necessary to collect survey data such as physiological data and subjective feelings. Then it was possible to determine performance statistics. The changing quality conditions were well reflected by users in the questionnaires. Irritation occurred in the case of the lowest picture and sound quality. This paper focuses only on the evaluation of survey data, because the authors stated that the analysis of physiological data requires deeper and detailed analysis.

The methodology of conducting compliance tests on various browsers and various operating systems has been described in [9]. The authors also took into account mobile platforms. When testing browsers on different operating systems, this is not enough, because some Web browsers are dedicated only to corresponding operating systems. Then it is not possible to test all possible browser-operating system pairs on one machine. The authors proposed an open source, generic, reusable, and easy to maintain automated testing environment for testing WebRTC P2P interoperability across all types of WebRTC-compliant clients.

A testing framework developed within the open source project Kurento and aimed to simplify the testing process of WebRTC services was presented in [10]. This framework is called Kurento Testing Framework (KTF).

4 WebRTC Statistics

The W3C organization has specified a set of methods and APIs for calculating statistics of video, audio, and packets that are sent through the *PeerConnection* channel in the WebRTC standard. The W3C consortium defines appropriate JavaScript objects for WebRTC that will give access to statistics for peer-to-peer connections. The content of uploaded media is represented in the WebRTC API in the MediaStream interface. Applications using WebRTC extract statistics from a real-time peer-to-peer connection using the provided API. During the connection, each MediaStream instance contains several (depending on the number of connections) tracks for audio and video streams.

4.1 WebRTC-Internals

The Google Chrome Web browser provides a built-in metric tool called webrtc-internals. Other browsers such as Mozilla Firefox, Microsoft Edge, Safari require external tools for such purposes. Webrtc-internals allows us to download connection measures in real-time [11]. Due to such data it is possible to represent them on charts and compare them with each other. During the WebRTC connection session the user can download browser data also from API method *getStats()* on the *PeerConnection* object. However, in both cases access to this data is only allowed during the active session of connection. After its completion, these data will be deleted from the memory of a browser. The data should be gathered in real-time and merged with previous. If the event of a failure occurs, the unsaved data with measures will also be deleted. The webrtc-internals does not allow data collection on the browser side at a larger time interval, this should be done manually by the *getStats()* operation.

Through the *getStats()* query and webrtc-internals on the *PeerConnection* object we get access to a number of connection measures that change over time. The Web browser sends values of local variables such as statistics on outgoing and incoming RTP streams. Unlike in webrtc-internals in the *getStats()* method the time interval between consecutive local measurements can be specified. However, it should be considered that the metrics contain both local and remote data. In this case, if the local sampling frequency is higher than the remote one, remote measurements will be duplicated until the next data packets are received. For example, if the time interval locally is set to 0.5 s and the remote data will be coming in one second, it will be visible on the characteristics as a duplicate remote measurement.

The statistics downloaded by webrtc-internals tool is limited to a maximum of 1000 measurement points, which means that these are only the last statistical data – the earlier ones will be deleted. Statistical data in the WebRTC API are very poorly documented. The analysis of downloaded data and parameters is very difficult due to missing measure descriptions in the official documentation.

Data on WebRTC statistics are collected by individual browsers, which means that in order to evaluate the statistics during a multi-video conference connection, it is necessary to collect data from all browsers participating in the conversation. Then these data should be combined and synchronized. This means that data should be recorded and downloaded manually at equal times. Devices should use equal sampling time and have synchronized clocks. At the moment, Google Chrome webrtc-internals tool does not provide the ability to change the sampling times of measurements. What's more, sampling times may vary depending on the operating system.

4.2 Performance and Reliability Measures

The metrics provided by the WebRTC API can be divided into two categories: network and application impact metrics. Network impact metrics are measurements only for data transmission. This can be very useful in diagnosing the network problems. Packet loss is a measurement that determines the number of packets lost in the context of currently sent packets – it is usually represented as a percentage of lost packets. Packet loss refers to errors during data transmission which results in the loss of a certain amount of data [12]. Rejected packets occur when the latency in the network was so large that they were interpreted by the reception as not suitable for further conversion. Another component of network usability measurement is Round Trip Time (RTT) which is defined as the transmission time of the data packet from source to destination and back.

The application impact metrics focus on data in the application itself and media processing. One of these types is a bit rate which describes the number of bits that can be sent or received in a certain period of time. The maximum bit rate is determined by bandwidth, whose value may change during a peer-to-peer connection. It measures the amount of data transferred in a given time unit. Another metric of application impact is frame rate, which can be defined as the number of frames per second (fps). The value of fps may decrease depending on network conditions, bandwidth, endpoints, computer computing power (video processing). Jitter is also encountered as an application impact measure. Jitter is associated with delay and RTT and is defined as the variation between delay and successive packages. These statistics are helpful in determining whether subsequent packages arrive in the correct order.

In the case of the performance examination, measures are strictly related to operation platform (desktop, mobile) and hardware specification. Hardware usage unlike the application and network impact metrics is strictly defined for one user and does not depend on the type of network. In video conferencing applications, the key components used for media processing are CPU load, memory usage, and energy impact in the case of mobile devices [13–15].

5   Tests and Results

To perform performance and reliability measures a test platform has been developed. The video conference WebRTC-based application has been deployed on a public server in order to make it available for testing. In the case of applications that allow clients to connect directly and the communication takes place in real-time, the location of users may play a very important role. The connection delay will directly depend on the location. In order to investigate this case, the application has been tested in different locations: Asia, Europe, East US, West US. To run applications in different locations PaaS (Platform as a Service) were used, i.e. servers with the Linux operating system physically located in those places to which it is possible to connect via the SSH (Secure Shell Protocol). Thanks to this type of connection, it was possible to install appropriate software such as a Web browser allowing us to run video conferencing applications on a given computer.

5.1 RTT Measures

TURN servers are used as proxies to establish the connection when clients using WebRTC-based application are not able to establish a direct connection because devices are behind NAT, i.e. are using private addresses in subnets or another network restriction are imposed. In conducted tests two types of such servers were used: with fixed location in Europe and with variable location – provided by SaaS. To investigate the impact of TURN on RTT metric the test with clients in Asia with TURN server and without TURN was provided.

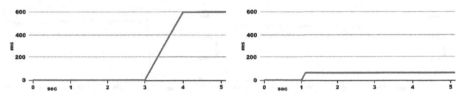

Fig. 1. Average RRT during connection, both peers in Asia, with relay.

Fig. 2. Average RRT during connection, both peers in Asia, without relay.

Figure 1 presents the case in which users located in one geographical place (Asia) are trying to connect, however, due to network conditions they are not able to connect directly. In this case, a TURN server located in Europe is used to establish the connection. It is presented on Fig. 1 that RTT oscillates around 600 ms (Y axis). This delay is too high to allow free real-time communication. A connection test was also carried out for direct P2P communication without using any TURN servers (Fig. 2). For comparison, using TURN provided by SaaS servers in which the service provides a server located in Asia, RTT is about 70 ms. This result is similar to RTT in direct peer-to-peer connection, and it is an acceptable delay for providing real-time videoconferences.

5.2 Impact of Different Types of Codecs on Bit Rate

Browser applications based on the WebRTC standard are very flexible, no additional external software is needed to participate in P2P video conferences because WebRTC is one of the HTML5 standards. However, this flexibility means that the application can be opened in different browsers in which the WebRTC standard is implemented differently, even versions and varieties of the same browser are of great importance. At this point, the topic of choosing the most appropriate codecs for a browser type will be examined. The WebRTC standard offers following three types of video encoding H.264, VP8, VP9. The test environment has been examined using different versions of browsers and codecs.

On the Chrome browser (Fig. 3), bit rate video using H.264 was stable during the connection and establishing and negotiating the best image quality took about 10 s. In the case of Firefox (Fig. 4), the graph shows periodic decreases in bit rate over time,

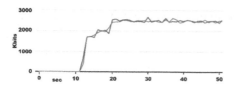
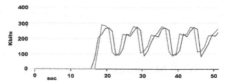

Fig. 3. Incoming (blue line) and outgoing (red line) bit rate in Chrome with H.264 codec during connection. (Color figure online)

Fig. 4. Incoming (blue line) and outgoing (red line) bit rate in Firefox with H.264 codec during connection. (Color figure online)

the maximum obtained bit rate fluctuated within 300 Kbits, this value does not allow free real-time communication, for comparison on the Chrome browser bitrate fluctuated within 2600 Kbits which is sufficient to provide good image quality.

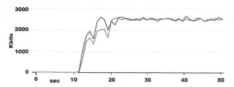
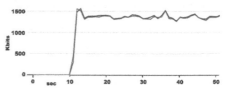

Fig. 5. Incoming (blue line) and outgoing (red line) bit rate in Chrome with VP8 codec during connection. (Color figure online)

Fig. 6. Incoming (blue line) and outgoing (red line) bit rate in Firefox with VP8 codec during connection. (Color figure online)

The next test was a one-to-one video conversation using VP8 codecs. Figure 5 shows that it took less than five seconds to obtain max bit rate, which is two times less than in the case of H.264, and in bit rate during the connection it fluctuated within 2500 Kbits, which is sufficient to exchange video in high quality. In the case of Firefox – Fig. 6, the bit rate was about 1400 Kbits, however, compared to the Chrome browser, the bitrate obtained the maximum value in two seconds after the connection started.

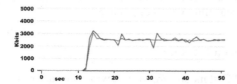
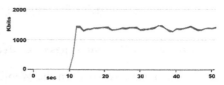

Fig. 7. Incoming (blue line) and outgoing (red line) bit rate in Chrome with VP9 codec during connection. (Color figure online)

Fig. 8. Incoming (blue line) and outgoing (red line) bit rate in Firefox with VP9 codec during connection. (Color figure online)

The aim of the last test was to examine a video conferencing call using VP9 codecs. Figures 7 and 8 show that the bit rate on the Chrome browser is not as stable as using VP8 but the increase took about five seconds which is a much better result. Random fluctuations in the waveform may cause temporary decreases in video quality, but they are not associated with other parameters such as RTT, FPS, Jitter. For Firefox the bit rate was 1500 Kbits and the graph does not contain any deviations.

5.3 WebRTC on Mobile Platforms

To check the efficiency of providing mobile video conferences, tests were carried out on smartphones with iOS and Android systems. During the tests, parameters were collected that described the hardware load during the WebRTC connection. A dedicated application using the native implementation of the WebRTC standard has been prepared for testing.

Table 1. Comparison of WebRTC performance on mobile platforms.

	Android	iOS
Energy impact	Heavy	Very heavy
Memory usage per WebRTC instance	~150 MB	~200 MB
CPU usage	~50%	~62%

Performance tests on mobile devices have shown that WebRTC is better optimized for the Android platform than for iOS. With a one-to-one connection, the native WebRTC instance consumed about 50 Mb less of memory (Table 1). The battery load indicator was also lower. Subjectively it was stated that the Android phone during the WebRTC connection got less warm. Tests have shown that it is possible to run one-to-one video conferences without any problems, but with more participants (more than three) there were problems with image smoothness. The WebRTC multi-conference in the mesh topology requires a WebRTC instance for each connected user. Power consumption in this situation increases proportionally with the number of participants. The tests revealed that the mobile video conferencing application in the browser on mobile platforms consume an average of 50 Mb of memory more in comparison to native implementation.

6 Improvements and Recommendations

The tests performed have shown that the use of TURN servers located relatively close to the client does not significantly affect RTT statistics and the measurements using proxy servers do not differ from those with a direct peer-to-peer connection. However, if as a result of the NAT mechanism clients in Asia were not able to connect directly, TURN servers located in Europe were used. RTT statistics increased to 600 ms and the quality of video transmission was not able to provide an adequate degree of usability. It shows that the location of TURN servers has a direct impact on the delay during media transmission. It is recommended to use TURN infrastructure depending strictly on user locations.

A video conference connection works best when it is implemented via the UDP protocol. In corporate networks, a very common feature is security based on blocking traffic with this protocol. WebRTC also allows us to make calls via the TCP, however such a connection may be unstable, lost data packets will cause increasing delay and in turn it may lead to loss of video fluidity, lowering the fps. Therefore, it is recommended to test network conditions before allowing users to use video conferencing. The best choice will be a test program that will make the test connection to the specified address, save and send the parameters of such connection to the server. This would allow choosing the right configuration for WebRTC before making a video conferencing call. It is recommended that the program using the WebRTC standard enables remote configuration, so that this configuration is sent by the server to the client before each video call.

The video quality during the WebRTC connection depends on the type of codec used. The tests have shown that VP8 is currently the best choice. The bit rate index was the most stable for this traffic. The connections using the latest available version of VP9 were also checked, however, although the time to obtain the maximum bit rate was the shortest, fluctuations were visible in the course which resulted in periodic deterioration of video quality. In the case of VP9 codecs, artefacts were visible on a dedicated mobile application using the native implementations of the WebRTC standard. This proves that not all platforms currently support this type of codec. Provided tests with H.264 codecs were also carried out, but in this case the bit rate fluctuations were the highest in the described ones which resulted in the worst video quality.

Comparing the mobile implementation of the native WebRTC with that available in mobile browsers, we can notice that native WebRTC is much more efficient and on average use 50 Mb less memory. This is due to the fact that during the video conferencing on the mobile browser there is an additional overhead of hardware usage for peripheral tasks such as rendering of DOM of HTML elements, processing of TCP queries, WebSocket, Javascript engine, and browser add-ons. It is recommended to use native implementation of a WebRTC application instead of implemented by the Web browsers to achieve the best performance results.

7 Conclusions

The WebRTC technology is becoming very popular and is regarded as a very efficient real-time communication technology. However, developing video conferencing applications using the WebRTC standard requires the infrastructure of the TURN proxy servers that should be selected in a dynamic way. This will result in limiting the RTT quality index to a minimum and thus improving the experience of application users. The location of such servers plays a key role in the case of a relay connection. By using an additional middleware, it is possible to ensure a stable connection even when users are on private subnets where the IP address is not public. Access to the computer from outside the network is provided by a network address translation. It is necessary to provide clients with addresses for specific TURN servers when a new connection is establishing. It will be used in case of problems with a direct peer-to-peer connection. This can be a big challenge for own infrastructure. That is why specialized services providing such servers can be used for a fee. But in the case of a video conferencing call, data consumption will procure a significant cost. Therefore, creating own TURN server infrastructure has some advantages when the application's purpose has a local dimension, e.g. in schools, hospitals, offices, universities, where users are relatively in the same geographical regions.

References

1. Durresi, A., Jain, R.: RTP, RTCP, and RTSP – Internet protocols for real-time multimedia communication. In: Żurawski, R. (ed.) The Industrial Information Technology Handbook, pp. 28.1–28.11. CRC Press LLC (2005)
2. Vucic, D., Skorin-Kapov, L.: The impact of mobile device factors on QoE for multi-party video conferencing via WebRTC. In: 13th International Conference on Telecommunications (ConTEL), pp. 1–8. IEEE (2015)
3. Ammar, D., De Moor, K., Xie, M., Fiedler, M., Heegaard, P.: Video QoE killer and performance statistics in WebRTC-based video communication. In: IEEE Sixth International Conference on Communications and Electronics (ICCE), pp. 429–436. IEEE (2016)
4. Cinar, Y., Melvin, H.: WebRTC quality assessment: dangers of black-box testing. In: The 10th International Conference on Digital Technologies, pp. 31–35. IEEE (2014)
5. Xue, H., Zhang, Y.: A WebRTC-based video conferencing system with screen sharing. In: 2nd IEEE International Conference on Computer and Communications (ICCC), pp. 485–489. IEEE (2016)
6. Wang, W., Mei, L.: A design of multimedia conferencing system based on WebRTC Technology. In: 8th IEEE Annual Information Technology, Electronics and Mobile Communication Conference (IEMCON), pp. 148–153. IEEE (2017)
7. Nayyef, Z.T., Amer, S.F., Hussain, Z.: Peer to peer multimedia real-time communication system based on WebRTC technology. Int. J. Eng. Technol. 7(29), 125–130 (2018)
8. De Moor, K., Arndt, S., Ammar, D., Voigt-Antons, J.N., Perkis, A., Heegaard, P.E.: Exploring diverse measures for evaluating QoE in the context of WebRTC. In: 2017 Ninth International Conference on Quality of Multimedia Experience (QoMEX), pp. 1–3. IEEE (2017)
9. Gouaillard, A., Roux, L.: Real-time communication testing evolution with WebRTC 1.0. In: Principles, Systems and Applications of IP Telecommunications (IPTComm), pp. 1–8. IEEE (2017)
10. García, B., López-Fernández, L., Gallego, M., Gortázar, F.: Testing framework for WebRTC services. In: Proceedings of the 9th EAI International Conference on Mobile Multimedia Communications, pp. 40–47 (2016)
11. Ammar, D., De Moor, K., Heegaard, P.E., Fiedler, M., Xie, M.: Revealing the dark side of WebRTC statistics collected by Google Chrome. In: Proceedings from Eighth International Conference on Quality of Multimedia Experience (QoMEX). IEEE (2016)
12. Bondal, K.V.D., Castellano, J.F.S., Esteban, L.A.F., Teodoro, C.K.V., dela Cruz, A.R.: Video packet loss rate prediction over delay-prone packet-based networks. In: International Conference on Humanoid, Nanotechnology, Information Technology, Communication and Control, Environment and Management (HNICEM), pp. 1–6. IEEE (2015)
13. Franklin, G.F., Powell, J.D., Emami-Naeini, A., Sanjay, H.S.: Feedback Control of Dynamic Systems, 8th edn. Pearson, London (2015)
14. Husić, J.B., Baraković, S., Veispahić, A.: What factors influence the quality of experience for WebRTC video calls?. In: 40th International Convention on Information and Communication Technology, Electronics and Microelectronics (MIPRO), pp. 428–433. IEEE (2017)
15. Parmar, N., Ranga, V.: Performance analysis of WebRTC and SIP for video conferencing. Int. J. Innov. Technol. Explor. Eng. (IJITEE) 8(9S), 679–686 (2019)

Comparison of Procedural Noise-Based Environment Generation Methods

Marek Kopel$^{(\boxtimes)}$ (ID) and Grzegorz Maciejewski

Faculty of Computer Science and Management, Wroclaw University of Science
and Technology, Wybrzeze Wyspiańskiego 27, 50-370 Wroclaw, Poland
marek.kopel@pwr.edu.pl

Abstract. In this paper a comparison of selected algorithms used to
procedurally generate terrain for video games is presented. The algorithms' performance is tested with two implementation environments:
Unity and Godot. Results are aggregated and discussed. Conclusions
drawn are of two types: intuitive and counter-intuitive.

Keywords: Procedural generation · Terrain · Video game ·
Environment · Game world

1 Introduction

With rapid development of video games in the last thirty years the need for
more and more realistic, photo-like looking imagery is constantly growing. On
the other hand there is also a demand for always new, always fresh content. One
of the solutions are procedural generation algorithm. When applied to generating
terrain and landscape as the environment in which a video game is set, the state-
of-the-art algorithms tend to fulfill the demand in more and more precise way.

One common trend in procedural generation of terrain are algorithms based
on noise. The most common algorithms of the class are described below.

Perlin noise is the most basic and popular noise used for procedural generation. It was initially developed by Ken Perlin in 1983 and published in [9].
The purpose of it was initially to procedurally generate 3D textures to look
more natural. Most common implementation includes 3 steps: grid definition,
dot product, interpolation.

Simplex noise algorithm is comparable to Perlin noise algorithm, but it can
be used for n-dimensions. It is also designed by Perlin and published in [8].
The difference is its computational complexity. Simplex noise is less complicated
and requires less computational power to reach the same goal. It's complexity
is: $O(N^2)$, where N is the number of dimensions. Perlin noise complexity is:
$O(2^N)$. Another difference between simplex and Perlin noise is that simplex
noise operates on the grid on n-dimensional triangles instead of hypercubes as
it is in Perlin's case [1].

Simplex noise is also very often compared to others. It is expected that it
will work faster than Perlin noise in large number of dimensions. References

© Springer Nature Switzerland AG 2020
N. T. Nguyen et al. (Eds.): ICCCI 2020, LNAI 12496, pp. 878–887, 2020.
https://doi.org/10.1007/978-3-030-63007-2_69

to Simplex noise in comparison with other noise algorithms can be found in number of publications. E.g. in [10], where authors investigate different methods of procedural generation focused on Two-Dimensional terrain. They also point at the problem that there doesn't exist any proper survey or comparison of procedural terrain generation methods.

Voronoi diagram is another terrain generation algorithm. It initially randomly chooses n points, called seeds, localized on some surface. Next the surface is divided into n areas so that each seed point lays on only one area, called cell. The important thing in this division is that all the points in a cell are closer to the seed of this cell, than to any other seed. Voronoi diagrams can be used to generate map division, or to generate some sharp-edge shapes, sea or land. In video games Voronoi diagrams can be used for example to properly displace resources for players, it is not limited only to terrain issues.

Ridged multifractal noise is very similar to previous with one exception, all output values that are less than zero are taken as absolute value. As a result of that ridge formations are created therefore this particular noise of often used to generate mountain terrain areas.

References to multi-fractal noise can be found in many publications often compared with Perlin and simplex noise. E.g. in [7], where simple fractal noise is used to generate terrain along with erosion algorithms. Fractal noise is also a part of survey [11], where it is mentioned as a way to generate heightmap for mountain areas.

There are multiple types of algorithms that can be used to generate terrain, which will lead to choose specific implementations.

Procedural generation algorithms can be divided into:

- Teleological
- Ontogenetical

Teleological algorithms are used to simulate real world processes in order to accomplish desired goal – which is to create world as closest to reality, these algorithms are simulating natural processes they are a kind of nature-reproducing machines.

Opposite to teleological algorithms are ontogenetical algorithms, these one are not simulating physical or natural processes as teleological. Ontogenetical algorithms are in simple words "goal based" which means that it is trying to reach the end result without intermediate steps.

There are number of publications about procedural terrain generation. Some of them involves noise functions as the main part of the research. Hyttinen [3] work mentions multiple noise algorithms such as Perlin, Simplex, Gabor, and few more. In chapter 3.6 entitled "Comparison of the noise functions", author does not mention any numeric results about actual performance of different noise algorithms while generating terrain. Mostly publication if focused around usability of particular noises, it is mentioned that noise functions are widely used in game industry to generate large areas, and realistic worlds when properly combined with other procedures and algorithms. Hyttinen points that procedural noises are very important and base element of procedural techniques, and generating complex terrain, and it thanks to noise algorithm it is possible to generate infinite worlds. Good example of such usage is well known game entitled "No Man's Sky". The game was released in 2016, and it is a world which is build from almost 18 Q planets with procedurally generated terrain [3].

Publication does not provide proper comparison of mentioned noise algorithms, therefore it is direction worth of exploring, as noises are the very base of procedural terrain generation in many approaches. Based on the criteria accepted in this chapter publication can deliver useful information about noises and different techniques of terrain generation, which can be helpful to extend the view at the noise algorithms and provides information about how important noise algorithms are. Based on this research it is possible to say that noises are the fundamental element for terrain generation in.

Thorimbert and Chopard in their work [13] are testing specific noise algorithms, Perlin noise is one of them. Study is focused around texture generation methods which allow to generate 3D terrain which is close to research that will be carried out in this study. Authors are stating that their new method is significantly faster than other methods based on fractal Brownian [13] approach. Mentioned work is relatively close to performance study, however it is based on other terms and it does not show the results in the way in which it will be easy to understand, this work is a valuable source of information about Perlin noise and because simplex noise and ridged – fractal noise are pretty close to Perlin noise it can deliver important information for analysis of the conclusions after the experiment. By looking at the result of the tests that were run by Thorimbert and Chopard we can distinguish two compared methods one using Perlin and second approach called D2M1N3. This research however does not give us the results in a straight way, and work is mainly focused on showing differences between this new approach and others. Therefore there is an existing gap that could be filled with proper research comparing not only noises between each other but also looking at the performance and time indicators from perspective of two different engines. Spiridis master thesis [12] treats about procedural generation with special care to heightmap generation which means indirectly that attention of this work is can be gathered around noise algorithms. Thesis contains a number of benchmarks, in chapter 10.1 entitled heightmap generation benchmark and in another chapter 10.2 Real-time heightmap generation benchmark. Both are more based on heightmap size and are using only one noise implementation as mentioned 4D Perlin noise, by Ian McEwan, therefore we do not have clear vision of noise algorithm performance itself as I would like to show it in current work. Authors of [4] are introducing a research about multiple noise functions, among all listed are gradient noises, Gabor noise, spot noise, Perlin noise, and many more. Authors are discussing variety of important noise-algorithm related topics such as studying noises functioning on surfaces, filtering. The survey presents the analysis results, however the comparison does not cover performance testing, mean time needed to generate simple part of terrain, CPU usage as well as memory consumption, in terrain generation using chosen noises.

2   Experiment

In this paper we focus on the four first algorithm from previous section called for short: Perlin, Simplex, Voronoi, Fractal. We compare their performance using 2 implementation environments: Godot and Unity.

Godot Engine, is an open source project, it can work as engine for 2D and 3D games [5]. Godot implementation comes with a lot of tools and modules with access to engine code accessible via GitHub and it is possible to implement custom modules. The engine supports all major platforms: Linux, Windows, MacOS, Android, iOS, HTML5 and four ways of development: GDScript, Visual Script, C# and C++.

Unity is most popular multi-platform game development system [2]. It has very extensive asset store with payed content, but also free to use packages for beginning developers. In Unity it is possible to develop software for almost any platforms. It supports implementations for virtual reality. The primary development language is C# and Visual Studio support. The IDE is very intuitive and simple - many elements work on the basis of drag and drop.

2.1   Gathering Data

There are two aspects used for the purpose of measuring algorithms performance. First aspect is time measured directly from the code. In implementation there is a part of code responsible for generating one chunk, based on a plane mesh with fixed amount of vertices. Each period of time needed for rendering each chunk based on noise is measured.

The second measured aspect are readings of CPU and RAM usage from process monitor software [6]. Within the tool, it is possible to register process and thread activity and using process monitor view CPU and memory usage in each second of monitoring time.

2.2   Algorithms Implementations Library

For most of chosen algorithms: Perlin, Voronoi and Fractal, free online implementation libraries were used. For Godot Fast noise library is used. It is available on GitHub[1]. Corresponding library for Unity is taken from GitHub[2].

For simplex noise the implementation is based on implementation used in another work on procedural terrain generation.

For the comparison sake, basic versions of the algorithms are used. This means only the height map generation is used. Any other elements, like plants, stones, trees, water, water movement, grass, any kind of surface graphics are omitted not to influence result of the experiment. Therefore terrain generated in experiment is expected to be "raw". Tested implementation works based on the player position. Chunks are generated around the player while he moves.

---

[1] https://github.com/Zylann/godot_fastnoise.
[2] https://github.com/ricardojmendez/LibNoise.Unity.

Initially there is a fixed number of chunks generated. With the movement of the player, chunks that are getting too far from the player are deleted and new chunks are generated in the direction of player movement.

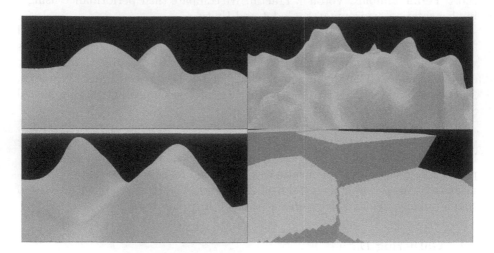

Fig. 1. Screenshots showing the "raw" results of 4 tested algorithms: (clockwise from top-left) Perlin, Simplex, Voronoi, Fractal.

The screenshots in Fig. 1 show the "raw" terrain generated with 4 algorithms: Perlin, Simplex, Voronoi, Fractal.

2.3   Environment Setup and Measures

Research platform used in experiment includes following components: CPU - Intel I5-7400, GPU - NVIDIA GeForce GTX 1060, RAM - 8 GB 2400 MHz. The values measured in during the experiment for each tested algorithm are:

– chunk generation time in microseconds,
– CPU usage in each second of the test,
– memory (RAM) usage in each second of the test.

It is noticeable that FPS (frames per seconds) is not measured. This is because noise algorithm works before rendering phase, which uses GPU. Therefore FPS would not show the algorithm impact on generation time.

It is evident that most meaningful indicator in the experiment is the time. After all eventually it is the final and most direct indicator of performance. If algorithm consumes more CPU power it is fine as long as there is more power available. The same thing applies to memory usage. Plus there are optimization techniques, e.g. do not store in RAM the terrain that is too far away from the player. Time is most valuable aspect for real time work, because CPU power and RAM availability can always be extended.

Single test run includes the following steps:

- check if initial conditions are met,
- run the test program with desired noise algorithm,
- move player with constant speed for 30 s in order to generate new chunks,
- store measured values for time, CPU and RAM usage,
- reset test platform to initial conditions.

Initial conditions include neutral CPU usage, and neutral RAM usage in state of inactivity, which means that programming environment (Unity or Godot) do not use any additional CPU or RAM above that used in idle state.

For the test cases, chunk is an object, a plane mesh with 120 vertexes. For each vertex a noise value is calculated. Each single run is performed three times for each tested noise algorithm.

3   Results

All tested noise algorithm implementations show common trend to work stable. Simplex, Voronoi and Fractal noise implementations work in similar time.

It is expected that different engines – in this case Godot and Unity will show differences. It is expected that implementation used in Godot engine - fast noise library (C++) - will be noticeably faster that noise library imported to unity (C#). Most significant determinant is time, because when generating terrain, it is better if algorithm use more available computing power and finish faster, than compute less and finish late. In worst case scenario finishing late may prevent the algorithm from using it in real time generation. So, it is expected that more power-consuming noise algorithms will generate chunks faster.

3.1   Godot

First the results for the faster, Godot implementations. As Fig. 2 shows the fastest is Perlin creating chunks in less than 300 µs. In second place comes Fractal with times just below 400 µs. Then there is Voronoi and Simplex with additional 50 µs.

Perlin, as expected, uses the most RAM - always above 100MB (see Fig. 4), but apparently is not the most CPU consuming (see Fig. 3).

Voronoi's time may be explained with lowest CPU usage most of the time (see Fig. 3) and significantly lower than others RAM usage (see Fig. 4).

Simplex, being less computationally complex than Perlin, is disappointing with worst (highest) time while CPU and RAM usage similar to others.

3.2   Unity

Unity implementations, expected to be slower, also show less stability than Godot's. At least in case of Voronoi and Fractal, which have correspondingly, the worst, and second the worst (highest) times raising up to 2200 µs and 1600 µs (see Fig. 5).

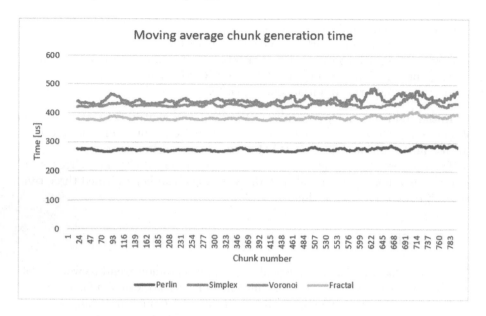

Fig. 2. Moving average chunk generation time - Godot

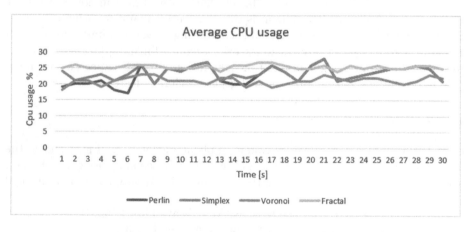

Fig. 3. Average CPU usage - Godot

On the other hand Perlin and Simplex have very stable and similar times, but still about 3 times higher that its corresponding Godot implementations.

In case of CPU usage it is hard to tell the winner (see Fig. 6). All algorithms at different times get lowest and highest usage percentage ranging from 10 to almost 30.

But as Fig. 7 shows the RAM usage is stable, for all between 300 MB and 400 MB. This time lowest usage is by Perlin and highest by Simplex, with Fractal and Voronoi in between.

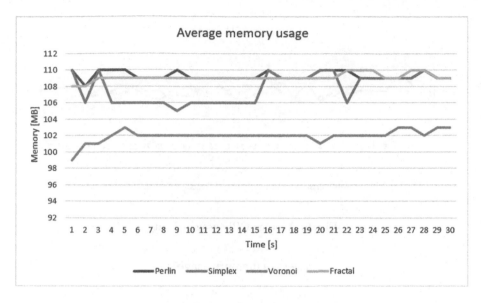

Fig. 4. Average memory usage - Godot

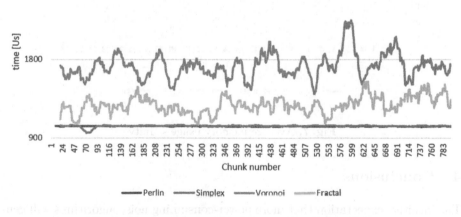

Fig. 5. Moving average chunk generation time - Unity

So Perlin gets the best times and in Unity even lowest RAM usage. Voronoi having close to worst times in Godot, but with significantly lower RAM usage in Godot, in Unity gets significantly worst times with common CPU and RAM usage.

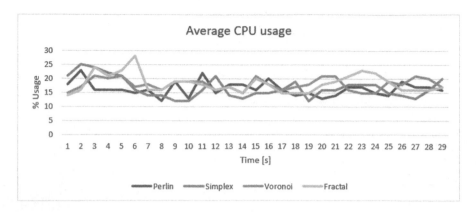

Fig. 6. Average CPU usage - Unity

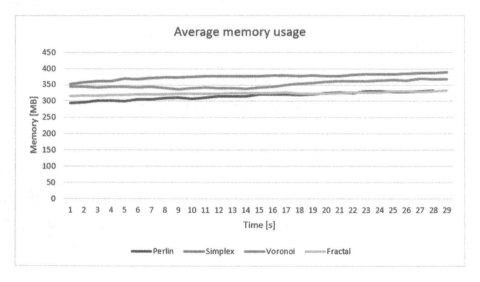

Fig. 7. Average memory usage - Unity

4   Conclusions

The intuitive expectation that more power-consuming noise algorithms will generate chunks faster was mostly confirmed with the results. Perlin being the quickest in both implementations is one of the most power consuming algorithms in the experiment.

The higher computational complexity of Perlin over its younger brother - Simplex could not be intuitively confirmed with the results. In Unity implementation, Simplex having similar times to Perlin uses the most of RAM among all algorithms. And in Godot implementation, while not being the most CPU and RAM consuming, still generates the chunks in the worst (longest) times.

It is not confirmed if used implementations are optimal. It is possible that some of the algorithms could be rewritten with positive impact on performance. However we accept that fact as a part of certain error threshold. It would be a good direction for further research, to try and improve performance of some chosen algorithms and confirm them being optimal in order to run some more specific and detailed tests in more narrowed area.

References

1. Gustavson, S.: Simplex noise demystified. Research report, Linköping University, Linköping, Sweden (2005)
2. Haas, J.K.: A history of the unity game engine (2014)
3. Hyttinen, T.: Terrain synthesis using noise. Master's thesis (2017)
4. Lagae, A., et al.: A survey of procedural noise functions. In: Computer Graphics Forum, vol. 29, pp. 2579–2600. Wiley Online Library (2010)
5. Linietsky, J., Manzur, A.: Godot engine (2019)
6. Margosis, A., Russinovich, M.E.: Windows Sysinternals Administrator's Reference. Pearson Education, UK (2011). https://www.pearson.com/uk/educators/higher-education-educators/program/Margosis-Windows-Sysinternals-Administrator-s-Reference/PGM1079784.html?tab=overview
7. Olsen, J.: Realtime procedural terrain generation (2004)
8. Perlin, K.: Noise hardware. In real-time shading'. In: SIGGRAPH Course Notes (2001)
9. Perlin, K.: An image synthesizer. ACM Siggraph Comput. Graph. **19**(3), 287–296 (1985)
10. Rose, T.J., Bakaoukas, A.G.: Algorithms and approaches for procedural terrain generation-a brief review of current techniques. In: 2016 8th International Conference on Games and Virtual Worlds for Serious Applications (VS-GAMES), pp. 1–2. IEEE (2016)
11. Smelik, R.M., De Kraker, K.J., Tutenel, T., Bidarra, R., Groenewegen, S.A.: A survey of procedural methods for terrain modelling. In: Proceedings of the CASA Workshop on 3D Advanced Media In Gaming And Simulation (3AMIGAS), pp. 25–34 (2009)
12. Spiridis: Procedural heightmap generation for level of detail purposes. Master's thesis (2018)
13. Thorimbert, Y., Chopard, B.: Polynomial methods for fast procedural terrain generation. arXiv preprint arXiv:1610.03525 (2016)

Usability Study of Data Entry Design Patterns for Mobile Applications

Sebastian Waloszek[1], Patient Zihisire Muke[1] (iD), Mateusz Piwowarczyk[1] (iD),
Zbigniew Telec[1] (iD), Bogdan Trawiński[1]([✉]) (iD), and Loan Thi Thuy Nguyen[2] (iD)

[1] Department of Applied Informatics, Wrocław University of Science and Technology,
Wrocław, Poland
walloschek.sebastian@gmail.com,
{patient.zihisire,mateusz.piwowarczyk,zbigniew.telec,
bogdan.trawinski}@pwr.edu.pl
[2] School of Computer Science and Engineering, International University, Ho Chi Minh City,
Vietnam
nttloan@hcmiu.edu.vn

Abstract. A study of usability testing of data entry methods in mobile applications was conducted. The motivation for this work was to find alternative ways of entering data that are characterized by high usability and to identify problems of currently used methods along with the proposals how to solve them. The following types of inputted data were chosen credit card details, date, time, small numbers and longer texts. In order to conduct the experiments a mobile application was implemented. It was divided into different versions depending on the input methods used. Each user tested one version of the application by executing predefined usage scenarios. The obtained results confirmed the great potential of data input methods that use voice recognition and text scanning. According to the conducted research, these methods achieve both good performance and satisfaction with users.

Keywords: Usability testing · Data entry · Design patterns · Mobile applications

1 Introduction

Mobile devices have become an inseparable element in everyone's everyday life. Many people perceive them as the preferred ways of fast communication with others and, thanks to broad access to the Internet, are the most commonly used information search tool. In addition, the diverse number of mobile applications that are available on the market allows you to take advantage of many amenities and services provided from the device level. With the development of these applications, the key concept is primarily the way in which data entry is carried out, which is further limited by the characteristics of the devices used.

The main feature of mobile devices is their portability, which determines, among others about restrictions on the amount of available screen space that can be used to

N. T. Nguyen et al. (Eds.): ICCCI 2020, LNAI 12496, pp. 888–901, 2020.
https://doi.org/10.1007/978-3-030-63007-2_70

display information. In addition, touch screens of mobile devices act as an interface through which users interact with the system used, which determines the form and type of data entry methods that can be used. Another challenge is the very variable context of the use of these devices, which has a significant impact on the ability to concentrate people, because the small size and mobility of these devices usually allow you to perform many activities simultaneously in different environmental conditions.

In the light of the challenges set by mobile devices, an important concept is becoming usability, which determines the degree to which a given system can be used by users so that they can achieve specific goals with appropriate efficiency, efficiency and satisfaction. The methods of data entry used largely contribute to the usability of the entire application, and their incorrect selection may result in the construction of an inappropriate system that will not meet the requirements set by users and expose its creators to high costs.

Carrying out usability tests on mobile devices is primarily motivated by the constant search for alternative ways of entering data and finding improvements to current methods. Together with the selection of specific methods of data entry, the creators of mobile applications shape the habits of users, which then become universally recognized and accepted standards, which is why their proper selection is important.

The main purpose of this work is to make a comparative analysis on issues of the level of usability both classic and potentially new methods of data entry in mobile applications. In addition, the usability tests carried out are aimed at: checking the level of user performance when using each method, determining the level of susceptibility to errors of each method, formulating recommendations for the use of methods, verify the adequacy of classic methods on the latest generation of devices, identify problems associated with alternative methods for data input.

2 Related Works

Several research works describe mobile applications usability evaluation with numerous usability metrics, measurements and methods. Harrison et al. [1] stated that mobile devices require special usability models. For this reason, by extending the well-known Nielsen's as well as the ISO usability models [2, 3] in the context of mobile applications, they devised the PACMAD (People at the Centre of Mobile Application Development) usability model. The PACMAD model presents seven attributes including cognitive load, satisfaction, errors, efficiency, effectiveness, memorability and learnability. The authors describe cognitive load as the main innovation of PACMAD model. Saleh et al. [4] expanded the PACMAD usability model into 21 low level metrics for usability attributes.

The GQM usability model core values are: task list and user satisfaction questionnaire for gathering subjective and objective data of usability evaluation. In turn, Hussain et al. [5] introduced the mGQM model relying on the ISO 9241-11 standard usability measurements such as satisfaction, efficiency and effectiveness. The mGQM model is quite comprehensive and was designed to evaluate the usability of mobile applications.

Shitkova et al. [6] and Coursaris et al. [7] assembled 39 usability guide-lines for websites and mobile applications. Ammar [8] reviewed existing studies on the usability of mobile applications and developed a usability model for early usability evaluation of mobile applications created using a model-driven approach.

Several studies regarding interactive and mobile applications usability testing with experts and users have been published recently by Bernacki et al. [9], Blazejczyk et al. [10], Krzewińska et al. [11], and Myka et al. [12]. In turn, Arain et al. [13] and Moumane et al. [14] conducted usability evaluations of mobile applications by combining questionnaires, observations and video analyses. They utilized usability evaluation criteria defined by the ISO 9241, 9126, and 25062 standards. Silvennoinen et al. [15] analysed user preferences and experiences in connection with the visual elements of colour and perceived dimensionality by examining in details two distinct mobile application contexts.

3   Setup of Usability Tests

The challenge in performing usability tests of data input methods is the need of keeping them inside of the same usage scenario which in this case constitutes the context of a mobile application. The context should be easily recognizable by the user and preferably constitute daily usage scenarios as to test the user's long-term habits and usage tendencies. While one can conduct tests of each input method by creating a mobile application which would present each method of data input in a sequence, doing so could lead to results that do not fully represent the user's daily usage patterns.

An alternative method of performing such usability tests and the one that was chosen for this study is the creation of a dedicated application in different versions each of which contains different input methods for the same tested data type and realized scenario. Furthermore, the application should simulate an intuitive use case that is be familiar to most users.

The benchmark application simulated a mobile hotel booking system with the main functionality consisting of creating a personal account, looking though room offers and performing a booking using a credit card. The data types tested are shown in Table 1. They include entering credit card details, dates, times, small numbers, and longer text. As the matter of fact, two more data types were examined during our study, namely email addresses and postal addresses. However, the results obtained for them are not presented in this paper due to the limited space.

The study was carried out with 23 users in laboratory conditions with the participation of the moderator. Before the experiments the participants completed a personal questionnaire. The most numerous age group were young people under 30 years who constituted 61% of the participants, 22% were between 30 and 40, only 17% were over 40. The gender was evenly distributed between men and women. Regarding education, 48% of the participants had a master's degree, 17% had a bachelor's degree and 35% completed high school. The activities most frequently used by the participants were: browsing the Internet (100%), sending messages (87%), calling (78%), social networking (78%), and taking pictures (70%).

During research, each participant performed a set of eight tasks grouped in three scenarios. These tasks were performed on one of four versions of the application, which was randomly assigned to the respondents. While performing tasks, the measures of effectiveness and efficiency were collected by appropriate components implemented in the application. Additionally the entire testing session was recorded using screen

Table 1. Tested input methods divided into different app versions

Data type	A	B	C	D
Credit card details	Onscreen keyboard	Onscreen keyboard	Camera scanning	Camera scanning
Date	Numeric keyboard	Spinner	Numeric keyboard	Voice typing
Time	Numeric keyboard	Spinner	Numeric keyboard	Voice typing
Small number	Numeric keyboard	Slider	−/+ buttons	Voice typing
Longer text	Onscreen keyboard	Gestures	Camera scanning	Voice typing

recording software (AZ Screen Recorder). These recordings were later used to count and analyse user taps and errors. After accomplishing each task, the user was given three questionnaires to complete. The first one was the single ease question (SEQ) with a 7-point rating scale from 1 to 7, where the higher number the lower perceived task difficulty. The second one measured how the user assessed that the chosen method was adequate for a given type of data. A 5-point rating scale from 1 to 5 was used, where the bigger numbers the higher perceived adequacy. The last questionnaire was based on the NASA's Task load Index tool used for measuring the subjective perceived workload of the realized task [16]. The user was asked to evaluate the mental, physical, temporal demands, his/her performance, level of effort needed to complete the task and the level of experienced frustration from a scale of 1–20 where lower numbers amounted to a lower task load for a given dimension. User ratings have been remapped on a scale of 5–100 to facilitate interpretation of results.

Two usability testing scenarios, the second one, i.e. Credit card details, and the third one, i.e. Room reservation, are presented in Table 2. Due to the limited space in the paper this table does not contain the first scenario, i.e. Registration, which included two tasks of inputting an email address and entering a postal address.

4   Results of Usability Tests

After finishing usability testing with all the participants each tested data input method was analysed in terms of task completion time, tap count, percentage of error-free sessions, task difficulty using SEQ scores, method adequacy and the perceived task load using NASA-TLX.

4.1   Entering Credit Card Details

Two methods of entering credit card details were compared in the context of a mobile application. The first method (CR1) consisted in manual input of all the credit card details

Table 2. Usability testing scenarios with task description

Scenario	Task	Description
Credit card	Input credit card details	User is asked to input credit card details (number, expiry date, CCV)
Room reservation	Enter date	User is asked to input predefined dates of the reservation
	Enter time	User is asked to input the preferred time of checking in to the hotel
	Select option	User is asked to customize his room using predefined options
	Enter small number	User is asked to input the number of products he/she is willing to order as room service
	Input larger text	User is asked to input additional information about his room in the form of a large text

into the required text fields utilizing the onscreen keyboard. The second method (CR2) used camera scanning with text capturing capabilities for automated filling in the credit card number and expiration date. The method was based on the use of a smartphone camera to obtain an image containing the front side of the credit card on which its data appeared. Using the appropriate machine models, it was possible to recognize the text in the image and extract the card number and expiry date from it. The security code placed of the other side of the card was entered manually by the user.

The average results for entering credit card details are depicted in Fig. 1.

Neither of the tested method turned out to be much faster in terms of the average time required to complete the task with a slight gap of 6% in favour of scanning (CR2). In turn the method leveraging scanning (CR2) outperformed keyboard typing (CR1), requiring on average 85% less onscreen taps. No errors were committed by the users while using both tested methods. Based on SEQ scores one can state that both tasks had a similar level of difficulty. Only a small difference of about 5% in favour of typing all details (CR1). Similarly, the difference in adequacy of each of the methods turn out to be negligible. Both methods are perceived to be adequate for entering credit card data. Additionally, the results from the NASA-TLX questionnaire reveal that using credit card scanning (CR2) results in a perceived workload bigger than 10% only in terms of physical demands and the level of frustration experienced by the user.

4.2 Entering Dates

The following four ways of entering a date were tested to assess the advantages and disadvantages of each of them: DT1 – entering date using a numeric keyboard, DT2 – using a spinner for entering each of date component, DT3 – entering dates using the calendar picker, DT4 – entering dates using voice typing. The average results for entering dates are shown in Fig. 2.

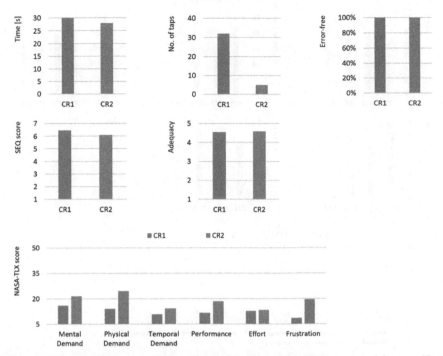

Fig. 1. Average results for entering credit card details, where CR1 – manual input with the onscreen keyboard, CR2 – camera scanning with automatic filling in the card number and expiration date.

The resulting average times indicate that the fastest way of entering a date is using a numeric keyboard (DT1). The second place is taken by the calendar picker (DT3) with a time slower on average by 20% compared to the numeric keyboard (DT1). Both date input using the spinner (DT2) and voice typing (DT4) were on average slower by about 20% compared to the calendar picker (DT3). In terms of the average number of onscreen taps shows that the fewest taps are required by the voice typing (DT4) whereas the largest number of taps by input with the numeric keyboard (DT1). The spinner (DT2) and calendar picker (DT3) methods require on average about 35–40% fewer onscreen taps to accomplish the given task than with the numeric keyboard (DT1).

The obtained data indicate that no errors were made when entering the date using both the calendar picker (DT3) and voice typing (DT4). The percentage of error-free attempts drops to around 80% for the methods using the numeric keyboard (DT1) and spinner (DT2). Entering date with the numeric keyboard (DT1) was assessed as the easiest, whereas using the spinner (DT2) turned out to be about 25% more difficult. Selecting a date using the calendar (DT3) was perceived as easier by about 7% than entering the date by voice (DT4). The results of the NASA-TLX survey suggest that voice typing (DT4) has a substantial 30% increase in mental demand when compared to the other methods. Moreover using the spinner (DT2) and voice typing (DT4) have approximately 15–20% higher physical demand in comparison with the other methods.

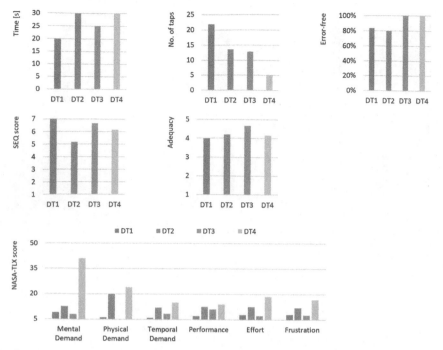

Fig. 2. Average results for entering dates, where DT1 – using a numeric keyboard, DT2 – using a spinner, DT3 – using the calendar picker, DT4 – using voice typing.

4.3 Entering Time

Four following methods for entering time were tested: TM1 – entering a time using the onscreen numeric keyboard, TM2 – entering time using a spinner for each time component, TM3 – entering time using a clock widget, TM4 – entering time using voice typing. The average results for entering time are illustrated in Fig. 3.

Comparison of average times of task completion reveals that the fastest method of entering time is using the numeric keyboard (TM1). Slightly behind are using the spinner (TM2) and voice typing (TM4) with an average time higher by about 40%. The slowest method turned out to be using the clock widget (TM3) which was slower by about 75% when compared to the best result. Voice typing outperforms the other tested methods by about 50–60% in respect to average onscreen taps.

The obtained results show that none of the users made a mistake when entering time using the numeric keyboard (TM1) and the spinner (TM2). For voice typing (TM4) the percentage of error-free tasks is around 80%. Using the clock widget (TM3) each user made on average two errors which was resulted in the lowest error-free rate of 20%. The maximum level of ease of completing the given task was achieved by the numeric keyboard (TM1) and the lowest by selecting the time using the clock widget (TM3). Choosing time by voice (TM4) turned out to be of similar difficulty as selecting with the spinner (TM2). According to the respondent's opinions, the spinner (TM2) was the most adequate method for entering time whereas using the clock widget (TM3) was assessed to be the least adequate method with the score less by 17–26% than the other methods The NASA-TLX survey score suggests that the voice typing (TM4) has a 10–15% increase in mental demand compared to the numeric keyboard (TM1) and the spinner (TM2). Using the clock widget (TM3) turned out to have perceived lower performance and higher temporal demand than other methods by approximately 10%.

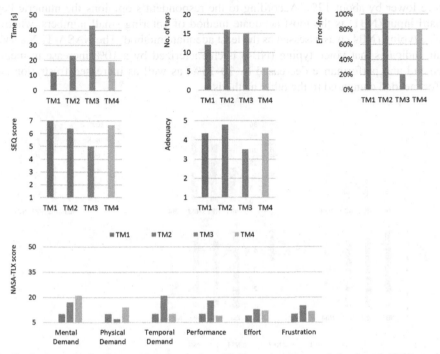

Fig. 3. Average results for entering time, where TM1 – using a numeric keyboard, TM2 – using a spinner, TM3 – using a clock widget, TM4 – using voice typing.

4.4 Entering Small Numbers

Four following methods of entering small numbers have been tested: NB1 – entering a small number using the numeric keyboard, NB2 – using dedicated increment and decrement buttons, NB3 – using a slider for selecting the desired value, NB4 – entering small numbers using voice typing. The average results for entering small numbers are presented in Fig. 4. The obtained graphs with average times show that the fastest method of entering small numbers was the numeric keyboard (NB1). The slowest method turned out to be voice input (NB4), which achieved an average time almost 3 times slower than the keyboard typing (NB1). The largest number of taps is required by using dedicated buttons (NB2) and the slider (NB3). Almost 2 times fewer taps is required when using the numeric keyboard (NB1). The fewest number of taps was achieved by means of voice input (NB4).

The obtained results reveal that users did not make any errors when using the numeric keyboard (NB1) and dedicated buttons (NB2). Using the slider (NB3) reduced the percentage of error-free attempts to 83%. On average, each user made two mistakes using voice input method (NB4), which resulted in the error-free rate of 60%. The maximum level of ease of completing the task was achieved by entering a number with the numeric keyboard (NB1) and the lowest was by means of voice input, which achieved the SEQ score lower by about 12%. According to the respondent's opinions the numeric keyboard input (NB1) is the most adequate method of entering small numbers, whereas voice typing (NB4) was assessed as the least adequate method. The NASA-TLX survey data indicates that voice typing (NB4) is characterized by a 10% increase in mental demand and performance decreased by 20–25%, as well as increased frustration and effort needed compared to the other methods.

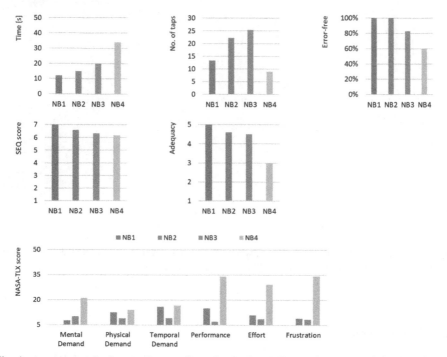

Fig. 4. Average results for entering small numbers, where NB1 – using a numeric keyboard, NB2 – using increment and decrement buttons, NB3 – using a slider, NB4 – using voice typing.

4.5 Entering Longer Texts

Four following methods of entering longer texts were tested: TX1 – manual keyboard typing, TX2 – entering text using gestures on onscreen keyboard, TX3 – text scanning with the device's camera and applying text recognition algorithms, TX4 – entering text using voice input. The average results for entering longer texts are depicted in Fig. 5. The obtained graphs with average times show that the fastest way to enter longer texts was to use the text scanning method (TX3). Similar results provided voice typing (TX4) which was 22% slower than text scanning (TX3). Manual text input using the keyboard (TX1) took 50% longer than applying scanning (TX3) and voice input (TX4) techniques. The least efficient method in terms of time was entering text using gestures (TX2), which turned out to be slower than the other methods by about 50–80%. The bar chart with the average number of taps shows that the largest number of taps clicks are required by keyboard typing (TX1). Using gestures (TX2) can reduce the number of taps by 35%. The fewest number of taps were required by both text scanning (TX3) and voice typing (TX4), where the number of taps was reduced by 93–96% compared to keyboard typing (TX1). It is shown that text scanning (TX3) is characterized by the lowest average number of errors and the highest percentage of error-free tasks. Input of text using gestures (TX2) was the most susceptible to user errors. Keyboard typing (TX1) was perceived as the easiest method for entering longer texts. In turn the lowest SEQ score obtained entering text using gestures on onscreen keyboard (TX2), which is 33% lower than the score of the best technique. According to the users' opinions keyboard typing (TX1) is the most adequate method for longer text input, followed by text scanning (TX3) and voice typing (TX4) while the least adequate proved to be using gestures (TX2). The NASA-TLX scores suggest that the gesture input method (TX2) has the highest perceived task load in all dimensions.

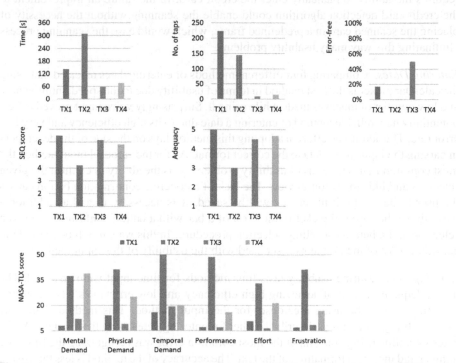

Fig. 5. Average results for entering longer texts, where TX1 – keyboard typing, TX2 – using gestures, TX3 – text scanning, TX4 – voice typing.

5   Recommendations

After completing all usability tests and conducting the required data analysis the following conclusions and recommendation for improvement and best usage cases of each of the tested methods were devised.

Entering Credit Card Details. Comparing both manual and camera scanning methods of entering credit card details in a mobile application revealed that although the average speeds of data input between both methods are similar, in ideal cases scanning the card with the device's camera can be faster than entering its number, expiry date and security code manually. Additionally, this gap can be widened with the usage of more sophisticated text recognition methods which would enable the recognition of additional data that could be stored on credit cards. To ensure a greater level of usability of the credit card scanning method for people who use this method for the first time, it is crucial to improve the scanning process by informing the user when the credit card is placed in an incorrect position inside the predefined card frame visible in the camera view. This can be achieved by means of simple instructions with suggestions appearing in the camera view to which actions should be performed or by manipulating the card frame look. The efficiency of credit card scanning is highly dependent on the lighting conditions which sometimes could prevent the card from being scanned which always requires the ability to manually enter the credit card. In the future an improvement to the credit card detection algorithm could enable the scanning without the necessity of placing the scanned card in a predefined frame, which would ease the scanning process eliminating this way many usability problems.

Entering Dates. Comparing four different methods of entering dates revealed that using the calendar picker is the best method in terms of usability due to the speed, intuitiveness and low number of mistakes made while using it. Surprisingly voice input proved to be a potentially new reliable method of entering a date due to its high efficiency and very low error rate. The additional effort in adopting this method lays on the side of the developers in parsing the input voice data to the correct format. As for the carousel input method the most common issues in terms of usability problems was the ability to confirm the given selection and hide the carousel view. The lack of a concrete confirmation button causes the user to be unsure if his choice will be saved. It is necessary to add an additional view above the carousel picker in the form of a bar with a button confirming the given selection and a button cancelling selection procedure. In this way, it will be possible to get rid of most of the problems associated with the usability of this input method.

Entering Time. During usability tests four methods for time input were analysed. The most adequate method of achieving high efficiency and low error rates when entering time turns out to be using a carousel for the input method. This method shares the same usability problems as described earlier for entering dates using this method. As for entering a time using voice input the most common error was recognizing the time as a number and incorrect formatting of the text. The accuracy of the method is less than using it for entering dates, because the context of the spoken words is smaller, which makes the voice algorithm more likely to make a mistake. An improvement in the voice recognition algorithms is necessary to be able to enter time with greater accuracy. The clock widget in a variant where after selecting the hour the widget does not change the selection automatically to minutes turns out to have serious usability problems. After selecting the desired hour the participants had trouble finding a way to change the selection mode. It is therefore required that the view should change itself after selecting the hours part of the time variable or one should provide a visible and intuitive button for switching between the modes.

Entering Small Numbers. Based on the conducted usability studies of four types of methods for entering small numbers the fastest and most accurate method was using a numeric keypad on a text field. Entering a small number using voice input turned out to be the most error-prone method, because the entered data is represented by short words with little context, that reduces the accuracy of the voice algorithm. To be able to take full advantage of voice typing as a method for entering such data, it is necessary to firstly improve its accuracy so that it would be possible to identify the underlying context of the spoken words.

Entering Long Texts. Comparing all four ways of entering long text that were tested during the usability study shows that entering text by means of gestures is the least efficient and most error-prone method of data entry even while reducing the number of onscreen taps. Both text scanning and voice input provided better results than classical text input via the onscreen keyboard. Additionally, both methods were characterized by low error rates with text scanning having the lowest one of all the tested methods. The only mistakes commonly made by this method of input and the potential areas of improvement were: trimming and moving individual words to other lines and incorrect recognition of similar letters (e.g. 'e' instead of 'a'). In the case of voice input the most common mistakes were: incorrect punctuation and wrong verb conjugation. It is advisable therefor to provide users with the option to enter longer texts using scanning if such use case is possible and to enter data which structure is known beforehand enabling the extraction of useful data from the scanned text.

6 Conclusions

Our study confirms the credibility of tests with users as an effective method of conducting usability tests. Thanks to the obtained conclusions, it is possible to make a decision as to the choice of methods of data entry used in own applications, taking into account the requirements set by the context of use.

The obtained results also confirmed the large potential of data entry methods in mobile applications that use voice recognition and text scanning. According to research, these methods achieve both good performance and great satisfaction among users. Since machine learning technologies on which these methods are based are constantly evolving in terms of correctness and speed of operation, their predicted utility should also increase with time. First of all, voice input, which is a natural way of communication between people, will gain great support in the future by using it in digital voice assistants, which will be integrated with any mobile system and with which it will be possible to perform tasks inside the application without much involvement on the part of the user. The text scanning process also offers great possibilities to quickly transfer data from the real world to digital form, which can then be processed depending on the needs.

The open problems of these methods include, above all, restrictions related to the impact of environmental conditions and the context of use on their speed and accuracy. For voice input, a key element affecting the usability of this method will be the ability to quickly recognize the context of the speech and the accuracy of the voice model, which may also vary depending on the input language used. In the case of image scanning, the key problem is how to present the method using it so that the context of using the system is not lost.

It is therefore advisable to include these technologies in future mobile application projects and to conduct further usability research in order to detect their potential applications and identify related problems.

References

1. Harrison, R., Flood, D., Duce, D.: Usability of mobile applications: literature review and rationale for a new usability model. J. Interact. Sci. **1**, 1 (2013). https://doi.org/10.1186/2194-0827-1-1
2. Nielsen, J.: Usability Engineering. Morgan Kaufman, Burlington (1993)
3. ISO 9241-11:2018. Ergonomics of human-system interaction - Part 11: Usability: Definitions and concepts (2018)
4. Saleh, A., Isamil, R.B., Fabil, N.B.: Extension of PACMAD model for usability evaluation metrics using Goal Question Metrics (GQM) Approach. J. Theor. Appl. Inf. Technol. **79**(1), 90–100 (2015)
5. Hussain, A., Hashim, N.L., Nordin, N.: mGQM: evaluation metric for mobile and human interaction. Commun. Comput. Inf. Sci. **434**, 42–47 (2014)
6. Shitkova, M., Holler, J., Heide, T., Clever, N., Becker, J.: Towards usability guidelines for mobile websites and applications. In: Thomas, O., Teuteberg, F. (eds.) Proceedings of the 12th International Conference on Wirtschaftsinformatik (WI 2015), pp. 1603–1617 (2015)
7. Coursaris, C.K., Kim, D.J.: A meta-analytical review of empirical mobile usability studies. J. Usability Stud. **6**(3), 117–171 (2011)
8. Ammar, L.B.: A usability model for mobile applications generated with a model-driven approach. Int. J. Adv. Comput. Sci. Appl. **10**(2), 140–146 (2019). https://doi.org/10.14569/IJACSA.2019.0100218
9. Bernacki, J., Błażejczyk, I., Indyka-Piasecka, A., Kopel, M., Kukla, E., Trawiński, B.: Responsive web design: testing usability of mobile web applications. In: Nguyen, N.T., Trawiński, B., Fujita, H., Hong, T.-P. (eds.) ACIIDS 2016. LNCS (LNAI), vol. 9621, pp. 257–269. Springer, Heidelberg (2016). https://doi.org/10.1007/978-3-662-49381-6_25
10. Błażejczyk, I., Trawiński, B., Indyka-Piasecka, A., Kopel, M., Kukla, E., Bernacki, J.: Usability testing of a mobile friendly web conference service. In: Nguyen, N.-T., Manolopoulos, Y., Iliadis, L., Trawiński, B. (eds.) ICCCI 2016. LNCS (LNAI), vol. 9875, pp. 565–579. Springer, Cham (2016). https://doi.org/10.1007/978-3-319-45243-2_52
11. Krzewińska, J., Indyka-Piasecka, A., Kopel, M., Kukla, E., Telec, Z., Trawiński, B.: Usability testing of a responsive web system for a school for disabled children. In: Nguyen, N.T., Hoang, D.H., Hong, T.-P., Pham, H., Trawiński, B. (eds.) ACIIDS 2018. LNCS (LNAI), vol. 10751, pp. 705–716. Springer, Cham (2018). https://doi.org/10.1007/978-3-319-75417-8_66
12. Myka, J., Indyka-Piasecka, A., Telec, Z., Trawiński, B., Dac, H.C.: Comparative analysis of usability of data entry design patterns for mobile applications. In: Nguyen, N.T., Gaol, F.L.,

Hong, T.-P., Trawiński, B. (eds.) ACIIDS 2019. LNCS (LNAI), vol. 11431, pp. 737–750. Springer, Cham (2019). https://doi.org/10.1007/978-3-030-14799-0_63

13. Arain, A.A., Hussain, Z., Rizvi, W.H., Vighio, M.S.: Evaluating usability of M-learning application in the context of higher education institute. In: Zaphiris, P., Ioannou, A. (eds.) LCT 2016. LNCS, vol. 9753, pp. 259–268. Springer, Cham (2016). https://doi.org/10.1007/978-3-319-39483-1_24

14. Moumane, K., Idri, A., Abran, A.: Usability evaluation of mobile applications using ISO 9241 and ISO 25062 standards. SpringerPlus 5(1), 1–15 (2016). https://doi.org/10.1186/s40064-016-2171-z

15. Silvennoinen, J., Vogel, M., Kujala, S.: Experiencing visual usability and aesthetics in two mobile application contexts. J. Usability Stud. 10(1), 46–62 (2014)

16. Hart, S.G., Staveland, L.E.: Development of NASA-TLX (Task Load Index): results of empirical and theoretical research. In: Hancock, A., Meshkati, N. (eds.) Human Mental Workload. North Holland Press, Amsterdam (1988)

Author Index